ATHLE

'89/9

THE INTERNA

TRACK AND FIELD ANNUAL

ATHLETICS

'89/90

THE INTERNATIONAL TRACK AND FIELD ANNUAL

ASSOCIATION OF
TRACK & FIELD STATISTICIANS

EDITED BY PETER MATTHEWS

Published by Sports World Ltd, a division of London and International Publishers 1989

London & International Publishers Ltd, 49 St. James's Street, London SW1A 1JT

This publication incorporates the ATFS Annual.

Photographs provided by Mark Shearman, 22 Grovelands Road, Purley, Surrey CR2 4LA. Tel: 01-660 0156, George P. Herringshaw, Associated Sports Photography, 21/23 Green Walk, Leicester LE3 6SE. Tel: 0533-879666 and Mobil Oil Inc.

British Library Cataloguing in Publication Data

Athletics: the international track and
field annual. —89-90
1. Athletics. Track & field events—
Serials
I. International athletics annual *(London)*
796.4'2'05

ISBN 0-948209-33-X

Design by Sandie Boccacci
Cover photograph: Allsport

Typesetting by Florencetype Ltd., Kewstoke, Avon
Printed by Van Boekhoven-Bosch bv,
Utrecht, The Netherlands

CONTENTS

Special Features

Biographies

World and Continental Records

Men's Lists

Women's Lists

Index

Indoor Championships

Final Thoughts

INTRODUCTION

The aim of the ATFS is to present in this Annual a detailed review of the past season, with the most comprehensive listings possible for world athletics. The chief compilers put in extraordinary amounts of time in compiling and checking the data contained in the lists. They are aided in their endeavours by scores of enthusiasts worldwide who submit information from their countries or areas of interest. We strive for completeness, yet know that in the infinite field of athletic endeavour such is well-nigh impossible. Multi-page letters cross national boundaries as the compilers check their listings with one another—and the lists in this Annual are the results of those labours.

Undoubtedly the lists provide vital information for everybody interested in athletics, but purists may sometimes quibble over some points therein. The least reliable statistics are those for height and weight of athletes. Weight will often vary during a season, and data on entry forms may well vary wildly. We have tried to assess the most likely figures, but we must do no more than trust that the vast majority give at least a good guide to the physique of the athletes concerned.

Names might seem to be the easiest part of international listings, but even for some of the world's top athletes it is hard to be exact! Firstly we try to adopt a consistent approach to translations from other alphabets, but an athlete may for instance have a different name in Ukranian to that shown in Soviet lists. Then there are sometimes variations even amongst those close to the athletes concerned. Should the marathon men be Saleh or Salah, Dinsamo or Densimo? We try to find out from the athletes themselves if there are difficulties. A fascinating example of the problems we have encountered is that of the Olympic pole vault silver medallist. For several years we have shown him as Rodion Gataullin. But we see that he is included in Soviet documents as Radion, and further checking determined that that was given in his passport. So we changed, but ATFS member Ed Gordon asked him for confirmation, and Gataullin himself said that his passport was wrong and he spells his name Rodion, so back we go!

Dates of birth can vary—those given for leading Soviet athletes on entry forms for major championships have done so, and it is practically impossible to be sure for athletes from nations, without comprehensive birth certification. Some Ethiopians and Kenyans come into this category. We show the year of birth for Olympic steeplechase champion Julius Kariuki as 1961, but, when asked, he thought he might have been born in 1965. As he ran the steeplechase in 1981 and was entered for the 1984 Olympics as being born in 1961, we have stayed with that, but cannot be sure. However we have now determined that Said Aouita was born in 1959 not 1960.

Times and distances are measured meticulously (usually!), but we must always take care on the interpretation of such data. Extremes of temperature, humidity, wind and altitude make material differences. Times must only be reported to hundredths of a second if fully automatic timing was in use, but there are sometimes doubts as to whether this was the case or whether the equipment was properly operated. This year there have, for instance, been questions over the times reported for the Ibero-American Cahmpionships in Mexico City, and doubts persist on some at least of the races. While much attention is paid to the timing systems, wind gauges are infrequently checked, and may not be properly operated, so one must be wary of over precise interpretation in every individual case.

I am particularly grateful this year for the considerable help and advice that I have received over computerisation from my colleague Rob Whittingham. With his help I have been able to take in lists produced by other compilers, notably Richard Hymans and Jiří Havlín, into my Apple® Macintosh™ II. I have been able to format, check and ultimately produce the lists as camera-ready copy to a higher quality and consistency than in previous years.

The annual review takes the same shape as in previous editions, but I have expanded the

Championships section this year to include records for major world and continental events as well as just the results of those staged last year.

Some enthusiasts complained when we cut back the men's all-time lists last year—and trying to satisfy the wants of all readers is impossible without exceeding the publishers' limit on the number of pages—but those enthusiasts will be pleased to see that men's and women's all-time lists this year include the top 30 performances and the top 50 performers. I have also introduced shorter lists for some of the non-standard events, such as the 300 metres or 2000 metres steeplechase, which are run occasionally at major meetings.

Once again I would like to express my most sincere thanks to everybody who has contributed in major or minor ways to this Annual, and to the IAAF and national federations for their continuing support. As always I would be pleased to receive amendments, but trust that they will be few compared to the mass of data contained in this, the definitive compendium of our sport. Now we look forward to another thrilling season of competition.

Peter Matthews
March 1989.

Peter Matthews has been an ATFS member for nearly 20 years. He is a member of the ITV television commentary team, covering all major athletics events, since 1985, having for the previous ten years broadcast on athletics for BBC Radio. He is also a sports consultant for the *Guinness Book of Records,* following several years as editorial director of Guinness Books. He is a regular contributor to leading athletics magazines. His *Track & Field Athletics – The Records* was published by Guinness in 1986, and his *Guinness Encyclopaedia of Sports Records & Results,* with Ian Morrison, was published in October 1987.

ABBREVIATIONS

Championships and Governing Bodies

AAA	Amateur Athletic Association (UK)
AfCh	African Championships
AfG	African Games
AsCh	Asian Championships
AsG	Asian Games
CAC	Central American and Caribbean Championships
CAmG	Central American and Caribbean Games
CG	Commonwealth Games
ECh	European Championships
ECp	European Cup
EI	European Indoor Championships
EJ	European Junior Championships
IAAF	International Amateur Athletic Federation
LT	Lugano Trophy/ World Race Walking Cup
NCAA	National Collegiate Athletic Association (USA)
OG	Olympic Games
PAm	Pan American Games
SACh	South American Championships
TAC	The Athletics Congress (USA)
WAAA	Women's Amateur Athletic Association (UK)
WCh	World Championships
WCp	World Cup
WI	World Indoor Championships
WJ	World Junior Championships
WSG	World Student Games

EVENTS

CC	Cross-country
Dec	Decathlon
DT	Discus
h	Hurdles
Hep	Heptathlon
HJ	High jump
HT	Hammer
JT	Javelin
LJ	Long jump
Mar	Marathon
PV	Pole vault
R	Relay
SP	Shot
St	Steeplechase
TJ	Triple Jump
W	Walk

MISCELLANEOUS

b.	date of birth
dnf	did not finish
dnq	did not qualify
dns	did not start
exh	exhibition
h	heat
hr	hour
i	indoor
kg	kilograms
km	kilometres
m	metres
M	miles
pb	personal best
qf	quarter final
sf	semi final
w	wind assisted
y	yards

ABBREVATIONS USED FOR NATIONS

ALB	Albania
ALG	Algeria
ANG	Angola
ANT	Antigua
ARG	Argentina
AUS	Australia
AUT	Austria
BAH	Bahamas
BAR	Barbados
BEL	Belgium
BER	Bermuda
BHN	Bahrain * (BHR)
BIR	Burma
BRA	Brazil
BUL	Bulgaria
BUR	Burundi
CAM	Cameroon * (CMR)
CAN	Canada
CHL	Chile * (CHI)
CHN	P.R.China
COL	Colombia
CON	Congo * (CG0)
CRC	Costa Rica
CS	Czechoslovakia * (TCH)
CUB	Cuba
CYP	Cyprus
DEN	Denmark
DJI	Djibouti
DOM	Dominican Republic
ECU	Ecuador
EGY	Egypt
ENG	England
ETH	Ethiopia
FIN	Finland
FRA	France
FRG	Federal Republic of Germany
GAB	Gabon
GAM	The Gambia
GDR	German Democratic Republic
GHA	Ghana
GRE	Greece
GUA	Guatemala
GUY	Guyana
HOL	Holland (Netherlands)
HUN	Hungary
ICE	Iceland * (ISL)
INA	Indonesia
IND	India
IRL	Ireland * (IRE)
IRN	Iran
IRQ	Iraq
ISR	Israel
ITA	Italy
IVC	Ivory Coast * (CIV)
JAM	Jamaica
JAP	Japan
KEN	Kenya
KOR	South Korea (or SKO)
KUW	Kuwait
LES	Lesotho
LUX	Luxembourg
MAD	Madagascar
MAL	Malaysia
MEX	Mexico
MOR	Morocco * (MAR)
MOZ	Mozambique
NIG	Nigeria * (NGR)
NKO	Korea PDR * (PRK)
NOR	Norway
NZ	New Zealand * (NZL)
OMA	Oman
PAK	Pakistan
PAN	Panama
PER	Peru
PHI	Philippines
POL	Poland
POR	Portugal
PR	Puerto Rico * (PUR)
QAT	Qatar
RSA	South Africa
RUM	Romania * (ROM)
RWA	Rwanda
SCO	Scotland
SEN	Sénégal
SOM	Somalia
SPA	Spain * (ESP)
SU	Soviet Union * (URS)
SUD	Sudan
SWE	Sweden
SWZ	Switzerland * (SUI)
TAI	Taiwan * (TPE)
TAN	Tanzania
THA	Thailand
TRI	Trinidad & Tobago
TUN	Tunisia
TUR	Turkey
UGA	Uganda
UK	United Kingdom * (GBR)
URU	Uruguay
USA	United States of America
UVI	US Virgin Islands * (ISV)
VEN	Venezuela
WAL	Wales
YUG	Yugoslavia
ZAM	Zambia
ZIM	Zimbabwe

** These ATFS abbreviations differ from those used by the IAAF (which are shown in brackets).*

ACKNOWLEDGEMENTS

Once again the compilation of the statistics for the Annual has been very much as a team effort by ATFS members, with a large number of experts contributing valuable assistance.

The principal lists and index compilers were Richard Hymans, Jiří Havlín and the CS group (see below), with Nejat Kök. Roberto Quercetani and fellow Italians Silvio Caravaglia, Pino Mappa and Luigi Mengoni (Ita) gave their usual great assistance. David Martin compiled the marathon lists, Palle Lassen and Egon Rasmussen the walks lists. Milan Skočovský and Ian Hodge the junior lists, with help from Lionel Peters and the records section was prepared by ATFS president Bob Sparks.

CS group: men's events: *sprints:* Alfons Juck, *400m:* Robert Blaho, *middle distance* Jiří Stola, *3000m-10000m:* Jiří Ranný, *Marathon & steeple:* Jiří Stavjar, *hurdles:* Svatopluk Dubský, *HJ:* Marián Malek, *PV:* Vladimír Braun, *LJ, TJ:* Peter Horváth, *SP, DT:* Josef Potuček, *HT, JT:* Pavel Formánek, *Decathlon:* Vaclav Klvaňa, *relays:* Miloš Alter, *walks:* Dr Zdeněk Jebavý; women's events: *sprints:* Zdeněk Kašlík, *middle distance* Ludvík Novak, *2000m-Mar:* Pavel Tucka, *100mh & relays:* Josef Ríha, *400mh:* Lubomír Slavíček, *HJ, LJ:* Miroslav Ondruška, *SP, DT:* Jiří Kanský, *JT:* Přemysl Hartman, *Heptathlon:* Milan Urban.

The ATFS are indebted to the following experts for vital assistance on specific sections:

Marathon: Antonin Hejda (Swz), *Indoor marks:* Ed Gordon (USA, *Decathlon:* Leo Heinla, *Middle and long distance events:* Ian Smith (UK), *Relays:* Emmerich Götze (GDR), *Cross-country:* Ernesto Díaz (Spa).

The following specialists supplied information for their respective areas and countries:

Africa: Yves Pinaud (Fra); *Algeria:* Kamel Bensemmane; *Asia:*T.C.Ong (Sin) & Balwant Singh Kler (Mal); *Australia:* Paul Jenes; *Austria:* Erich Kamper and Karl Graf; *Belgium:* André de Hooghe; *Bulgaria:* Grigor Khristov and Alexander Vangelov; *Canada:* Cecil Smith; *Central America:* Bernard Linley; *China:* Gao Dianmin; *Cuba* Basilio Fuentes; *Cyprus:* Antonios Dracos; *Czechoslovakia:* Čeněk Kohlman and Milan Skočovský; *Denmark:* Erik Laursen; *Finland:* Juhani Jalava and Matti Hannus; *France:* Jean Gilbert-Touzeau and Jean Moreau; *GDR:* Dieter Huhn, Werner Kunze and *Der Leichtathlet*; *FRG:* Klaus Amrhein, Sven Kuus, Heinrich Hubbeling and Heinz Vogel; *Greece:* Karolos Sargologos and John Theodorakopoulos; *Hungary:* Gabriel Szabó, Zoltan Subert and Gabor Kobzos (Swz); *Ibero-America:* Francisco Baraona; *Iceland:* Gunnar Pall Joakimsson; *India:* Ranjit Bhatia; *Ireland:* Liam Hennessy; *Israel:* David Eiger; *Italy:* Silvio Caravaglia, Gianfranco Colasante and Raul Leoni; *Jamaica:* Richard Ashenheim; *Japan:* Tatsumi Senda; *Mexico:* Cesar Moreno; *Netherlands:* Jacobus Koumans; *New Zealand:* Barry Hunt; *Norway:* Tore Johansen, Hans Halvorsen, Jo Nesse, Ole Petter Sandvig, Jan Jorgen Møe and Bernd Solaas; *Philippines:* Col. Romulo A. Constantino; *Poland:* Tadeusz Wolejko, Wojciech Gaczkowski, Tadeusz Dziekonski and Edward Szatkowski; *Portugal:* Luis Lopes; *Romania:* Alexandru Ardeleanu and Al Paraschivescu; *South Africa:* Gert Le Roux; *South America:* Luis Vinker (Arg); *Soviet Union:* Ants Teder with Leonid Epstein, Nikolay Ivanov, Vladimir Spichkov and Andris Stagis; *Spain:* José Maria Garcia, Ignacio Romo, Manuel Villuendas, Andres de Acuña Lopez and Josep Corominas; *Sweden:* Lennart Julin and Owe Fröberg; *Switzerland:* Fulvio Regli and Alberto Bordoli; *UK:* Peter Matthews and Ian Hodge; *USA:* Scott Davis, Jeff Hollobaugh, Jack Pfeiffer, Howard Willman and Hal Bateman; *Yugoslavia:* Ozren Karamata.

Special features were written and compiled by Roger Gynn, Heinz Klatt, Lennart Julin, Ladislav Krnáč, David Martin, Andy Milroy, Roberto Quercetani, Andrew Huxtable and David Eveleigh.

The compilers wish to thank all the above and others that they have contacted during the past year, also many national federations and athletics magazines.

Finally we would like to thank the IAAF for its continuing cooperation and assistance.

ASSOCIATION OF TRACK & FIELD STATISTICIANS (ATFS) MEMBERS

Executive Committee (1988–91)

President: R. Sparks (UK)
Secretary General: D. Martin (UK)
Treasurer: P. Lassen (DEN)

S.S. Davis (USA)
J. Havlín (CS)
A. Huxtable (UK)
R. Hymans (UK)
N. Kök (TUR)
R. Magnusson (SWE)
P.J. Matthews (UK)
Y. Pinaud (FRA)
D.H. Potts (USA)
R.L. Quercetani (ITA)
H. Vogel (FRG)

Members

As at 1 January 1989

ALGERIA
Kamel Bensemmane
ARGENTINA
Gerardo Bönnhoff
Luis R. Vinker
AUSTRALIA
Ron Casey
Paul Jenes
Fletcher McEwen
Michael J. McLaughlin
AUSTRIA
Karl Graf
Erich Kamper (HM)
BAHAMAS
Gerald L. Wisdom
BELGIUM
Willy Bouvier
André de Hooghe
Bienvenu Lams
BOLIVIA
Juan Coronel Quiroga
BRAZIL
José C. Gonçalves
Ulf Lagerström
BRITISH VIRGIN IS
Reynold O'Neal
BULGARIA
Grigor Christov
Georgi Kaburov
Alexander Vangelov
CANADA
Paul F. Houde
Dave Lach
Tom MacWilliam
Ted Radcliffe
Cecil Smith
CHILE
J. Francisco Baraona Urzúa
COLOMBIA
Jaime Ortiz Alvear
CUBA
Prof Jesus Arguëlles
Basilio Fuentes
Severo Nieto Fernández
CYPRUS
Antonios Dracos
CZECHOSLOVAKIA
Miloš Alter
Vladimír Braun
Svatopluk Dubský
Luděk Follprecht
Přemysl Hartman
Jiří Havlín
Jiří Hetfleiš
Milan Hlaváček
Peter Horváth
Stanislav Hrnčíř
Zdeněk Jebavý
Vladimír Jorda
Alfons Juck
Jiří Kánský
Zdeněk Kašlík
Václav Klvaňa
Čeněk Kohlmann
Ladislav Krnáč
Otto Kudelka
Marián Malek
Karel Míšek
Miroslav Ondruška
Josef Potůček
Josef Ríha
Milan Skočovský
Lubomír Slavíček
Jiří Stavjař
Jiří Štola
Milan Sýkora
Milan Urban
Vladimír Višek
Josef Zdychynec
DENMARK
Hans A. Larsen
Palle Lassen
Valborg Lassen
Egon Rasmussen
Emanuel Rose
ECUADOR
Ramiro Almeida Rothenbach
FINLAND
Kaj Böstrom
Matti Hannus
Juhani Jalava
Erkki Kiilunen
Esa Laitinen
Torsten Lindqvist
Kauko Niemelä
Björn-Johan Weckman (HM)
FRANCE
André Alberty
Alain Bouillé
Jacques Carmelli
Jean-Louis Absin de Cassière
Jean Creuzé
Jean Gilbert-Touzeau
Vincenzo Guglielmelli
André Halphen
Guy Kerfant
Michel Nazé
Robert Parienté
Jean Claude Patinaud
Yves Pinaud
Daniel Urien
GERMAN DEM. REPUBLIC
Werner Gessner
Emmerich Götze
Dieter Huhn

Werner Kurtze
FEDERAL REP. GERMANY
Walter Abmayr
Klaus Amrhein
Hans-Peter Car
Max Heilrath
Raymund Herdt
Heinrich Hubbeling
Heinz Klatt
Winfried Kramer
Rolf von der Laage
Jürgen Martin
Ekkehard zur Megede
Reinhard Müller
Axel Schäfer
Fritz Steinmetz (HM)
Otto Verhoeven
Heinz Vogel
GIBRALTAR
Mark Sanchez
GREECE
Akis Andrikopulos
Angelos Cocconis
Yorgos Konstantopoulos
John A. Kyriacos
Karolos Sargologos
Leandros J. Slavis
John Theodorakopoulos
HUNGARY
Endre Kahlich
György Lévai
Zoltán Subert
Gabriel Szabó
Dr István Zahumenszky
ICELAND
Ørn Eidsson
Brynjolfur Ingolfsson
INDIA
Ranjit Bhatia
Inder Khanna
Rameshchandra G. Kharkar
R. Murali Krishnan
Jal D. Pardivala
Norris Pritam
Lokesh Sharma
IRAN
Fred Sahebjam
IRELAND
Fionnbar Callanan
Liam Hennessy
John Murray
Tony O'Donoghue
ISRAEL
Elchanan Bar-Lev
David Eiger
Dr Uri Goldbourt
ITALY
Marco Buccellato
Ottavio Castellini
Gastone Dannecker
Gianni Galeotti
Tiziano Gambalonga
Silvio Garavaglia
Michelangelo Granata
Raul Leoni
Giorgio Malisani
Gabriele Manfredini
Giuseppe Mappa
Salvatore Massara
Luigi Mengoni (HM)
Gianni Menicatti
Pino Montagna
Matteo Piombo
Dr Roberto L. Quercetani (HM)
Mauro Rossi
Carlo Santi
Raffaele Tummolo
Edoardo Zorzetti
JAMAICA
Richard G. Ashenheim
JAPAN
Atsushi Hoshino
Naoshi Ito
Wakaki Maeda
Yashimasa Noguchi
Tatsumi Senda
LIECHTENSTEIN
Robert Schumacher
LUXEMBOURG
Gérard Rasquin
MALAYSIA
Balwant Singh Kler
Gurbaksh Singh Kler
Loong Teck Chew
MEXICO
Jorge Molina Celis
NETHERLANDS
Jacobus Koumans
Nic Lemmens
NEW ZEALAND
Dr Brian Dawkins
Barry S. Hunt
NORWAY
Hans T. Halvorsen
Tore Johansen
Jan-Jørgen Moe
Ingmund Ofstad
Einar Otto Øren
Ole Petter Sandvig
Bernt A. Solaas
Magne Teigen
PHILIPPINES
Col Romulo A. Constantino
Sy Yinchow
POLAND
Zbigniew Dobrowolny
Marek Drzewowski
Wojciech Gaczkowski
Zygmunt Głuszek
Daniel Grinberg
Henryk Kurzyński
Zbigniew Łojewski
Adam Parczewski
Henryk Paskal
Stefan J.K. Pietkiewicz
Josef Pliszkiewicz
Janusz Rozum
Maciej Rychwalski
Lesław Skinder
Włodzimierz Szymański
Jerzy Szymonek
Janusz Waśko
Edward Więcek
Tadeusz Wołejko
PORTUGAL
Luis O.H. Lopes
PUERTO RICO
Fernando Rodil-Vivas
ROMANIA
Adrian Ionescu
Nicolae Marasescu
Romeo Vilara
Tudor Vornicu
SINGAPORE
Ong Teong Cheng
SOUTH AFRICA
Harry N. Beinart (HM)
Mrs Naomi Beinart
Hennie A.J. Ferreira
Colin E. Hasses
Riël Hauman
Harry Lombaard
Allister Matthews
Hans Prinsloo
Gert J.J. le Roux
Joe Stutzen
SPAIN
Andres de Acuña Lopez
José Corominas
Pedro Escamilla
José Maria Garcia
Pedro Molero Ortega
Ignacio Romo
Alberto Sanchez Traver
Manuel Villuendas Zarza
SWEDEN
Mats Åkesson

Owe Fröberg
Jöran Hedberg
A. Lennart Julin
Ove Karlsson
Rooney Magnusson (HM)
Stig L. Nilsson (HM)
Reino Sepp
Ture Widlund

SWITZERLAND
Alberto Bordoli
Antonin Hejda
Gabor Kobzos
Fulvio Regli (HM)

SYRIA
Fouad Habash

TAIWAN
Liao Han-shui

TRINIDAD & TOBAGO
Bernard A. Linley

TURKEY
Turhan Göker
Nejat Kök
Cüneyt E. Koryürek
I. Süreyya Yigit

USSR
Leonid Epstein
Leo Heinla
Nikolay Ivanov
Anatoliy K. Kashcheyev
Boris Y. Kozvintsev
Ilya M. Lokshin
Andrey B. Mikhailov
Rostislav V. Orlov
Vladimir A. Otkalenko
Jaan Otsason
Eugen Piisang
Andris Stagis
Ants Teder
Erlend Teemägi

UNITED KINGDOM
John W. Brant
John Bromhead
Ian Buchanan
Mark Butler
Eric L. Cowe
Leslie J. Crouch
Dr David P. Dallman
Charles Elliott
Peter Graham
Stan Greenberg
Roger W.H. Gynn
Ian M.M. Hodge
John B. Holt (HM)
Andrew Huxtable
Richard Hymans
Tony Isaacs
Alan Lindop
Peter H. Lovesey
Tim Lynch-Staunton
Norris D. McWhirter (HM)
David Martin
Peter V. Martin
Peter J. Matthews
Ted O'Neill
Lionel Peters
Ian R. Smith
Bob Sparks
Dr Richard Szreter
M. David Terry
Melvyn F. Watman
Rob Whittingham
Mark A.A. Woodlands

USA
Jon W. Alquist
David A. Batchelor
Hal Bateman
Kirk Blackerby
Jed Brickner
Frank Candida
Dave Carey
Tom Casacky
Pete Cava
Scott S. Davis
Wally Donovan
James O. Dunaway
Tom Feuer
Edward C. Gordon
Robert Hersh
Dr Istvan Hidvegi
E. Garry Hill
David Johnson
Michael Kennedy
Frank Litsky
Steven McPeek
Dr Bill Mallon MD
Dr David E. Martin
Alan Mazursky
Walt Murphy
Albert D. Nelson
Cordner B. Nelson
Rich Perelman
Jack Pfeifer
Martin A. Post
Dr Donald H. Potts
S.F. Vince Reel
Mike Renfro
Stan Saplin
Alan Sigmon
James L. Spier
J. Larry Story
Carol R. Swenson
Michael Takaha
Bruce Tenen
H.D. Thoreau
Howard Willman
Frank Zarnowski

URUGUAY
Eduardo Gonzalez Gomez
Henryk Taskal

YUGOSLAVIA
Olga Acić
Mladen Delić
Ozren Karamata

ZAMBIA
Matthew Mulwanda

(HM = Honorary Member)

REVIEW OF 1988

BY PETER MATTHEWS

Chronological survey of major events in the world of track and field athletics during the year.

JANUARY

10 **Sydney**, Australia. The first world record of the year was set by Kerry Saxby, 20:55.76 for 5000m walk, an improvement of nearly 25 seconds.

15 **Hamilton,** Canada. Ben Johnson started his indoor campaign by improving the world record for 50 yards from 5.22 to 5.20. Second was Brian Cooper in 5.25.

29 **Toronto.** Over 50 yards Ben Johnson further improved the world indoor best to 5.15 and Angella Issajenko equalled Evelyn Ashford's 1983 women's time of 5.74.

31 **Osaka Marathon**, Japan. Lisa Martin won this women's only race in 2:23:51, a Commmonwealth record and the fastest ever run on a loop course. She passed 10km in 33:59, 20km 1:07:42, halfway in 1:11:24, 30km 1:24:40 and 40km 2:16:18.

FEBRUARY

5 **Millrose Games**, New York. There was an attendance of 18,126 for the 81st running of this famous meeting at the Madison Square Garden. Doina Melinte ran the second fastest ever indoor mile, 4:21.45. Gwen Torrence beat Evelyn Ashford 6.64 to 6.71 at 55m.

5 **Sindelfingen**, FRG. Thomas Schönlebe improved his world indoor 400m record from 45.41 to 45.05. Ben Johnson won his 60m heat in 6.45, but although he won the final in 6.50, a pulled muscle just before the finish ended his indoor season, in which he had won all seven finals.

6 **Red Lobster 10km**, Orlando, Florida, USA. Just as in 1987 Liz McColgan ran the fastest ever women's time, 30:59 (31:07 before), on a certified loop course.

10 **Turin**, Italy. Christine Wachtel set a world indoor 800m record with 1:57.64 with Sigrun Wodars, 1:58.22, also under her old record.

13 **Vienna**, Austria. There were three world indoor records by GDR athletes: Ronald Weigel 5000m walk 18:11.41, Christine Wachtel 800m 1:56.40 and Heike Drechsler long jump 7.37. The latter was the final jump of a series which started 4.51, N, 6.71, 6.97, N.

13 **Vitalis/Olympic Invitational**, East Rutherford, New Jersey. Doina Melinte set a women's indoor mile record in 4:18.86 and Marcus O'Sullivan won the men's race in 3:50.94, passing 1500m in 3:35.4, the fastest ever run indoors, but not eligible for a record as timed on only one watch. Tim Lewis set a world indoor record for 1500m walk with 5:13.53.

14 **Tokyo Marathon**. Four men broke 2:09, just as they had in this race in 1986. Abebe Mekonnen won in 2:08:33 from Juma Ikangaa 2:08:42, Jörg Peter 2:08:47 and Rob de Castella 2:08:49. World champion Douglas Wakiihuri was seventh in 2:11:57.

19/20 **East Berlin**, GDR. The world record for women's 60m hurdlkes went four times. In the heats Gloria Siebert ran 6.69, Cornelia Oschkenat 6.68, and then in the semis Siebert 6.67 and Oschkenat 6.58. Meeting in the final the latter won in 6.60 with Siebert second in 6.65.

20 **The Hague**, Netherlands. Rob Druppers improved the world indoor record for 1000m to 2:16.62. Some fault on the photo-finish later resulted in this being recognised by the IAAF on the hand timing of 2:16.4.

20 **Piraeus**, Greece. Stefka Kostadinova cleared a third indoor record height, this time 2.06.

24 **Auckland**, New Zealand. One hour multi-events records were set by Simon Poelman, decathlon 7647, and Chantal Beaugeant, pentathlon 6241.

25/26 **GDR v USSR multi-events** at Senftenberg. World indoor records were set by Ivan Babiy, 6821 in the octathlon, and Anke Behmer, 4995 in the pentathlon. The latter (8.27, 1.83, 14.95, 6.66, 2:08.03) equalled her mark at the same venue on 2 Feb 1988 (8.21, 1.78, 14.94, 6.80, 2:07.72).

26 **West Berlin**. Carlo Thränhardt won the annual high jump with music event with 2.42m, equalling the outdoor best. It later became the first indoor mark to be accepted as a world record, as being set under identical conditions to outdoors. Two previous record holders followed: Dietmar Mögenburg 2.36 and Patrik Sjöberg 2.34.

26 **TAC Indoor Championships** at New York. Victories at 400m by Antonio McKay and 3000m walk by Maryanne Torrellas sealed their overall Mobil Grand Prix victories for the indoor season. McKay's 46.55 was the fastest ever run on an 11-lap track. Gwen Torrence increased her indoor sprint unbeaten run to 20 finals 1986–8, but she only just managed it as she tied with Evelyn Ashford in 6.66 for 55m. *See the 1988 Annual for TAC winners.*

28 **Women's Ekiden Relay**, Yokohama, Japan. The women's international road relay race over the marathon distance was won by the USSR: Yelena Romanova, Zoya Ivanova, Natalya Artyomova, Yekaterina Khramenkova and Olga Bondarenko in 2:15:41. Second were China 2:17:36 and third Japan 2:17:40.

MARCH

5/6 **European Indoor Championships**, Budapest, Hungary. Nelli Cooman won her fourth successive 60m title. High jumpers Patrik Sjöberg and Stefka Kostadinova each won their third title in four years, with 2.39 and 2.04 respectively, and Heike Drechsler won her third successive long jump title with 7.30. *Medallists were listed in the 1988 Annual.*

Stefka Kostadinova – again European Indoor champion (Mark Shearman)

11/12 **NCAA Indoor Championships**, Oklahoma City, USA. Arkansas, with a 1M/3000m double by Joe Falcon, won their fifth successive men's title with 34 points from Illinois 30 and Florida 26, and women's champions were Texas, for whom Carlette Guidry won 55m and LJ, 71 from Villanova, with Vicki Huber winning 1M and 3000m, 52 and Alabama 33.

20 **World Women's 15km Road race**, Adelaide, Australia. Ingrid Kristiansen outclassed the rest of the field to win in 48:24, despite very hot weather. She passed 5km in 15:41 and 10km in 31:59. Second was Wang Xiuting 50:18 for the second team China, and third Zoya Ivanova who led home the victorious Soviet team in 50:26. There were 83 runners, with 77 finishing, from 26 teams.

26 **World Cross-country Championships**, Auckland, New Zealand. John Ngugi won his third successive title and, as in 1987, Paul Kipkoech was second. They led the greatest ever domination as the Kenyan senior team placed eight men in the top nine with a record low score of 23 (six to score), and packed all six of their juniors in the first seven for another record low of 11 (four to score). However the second placed junior Cosmas Ndeti was later disqualified following a positive dope test for pseudoephedrine. Abebe Mekonnen, for the second placed senior team Ethiopia, was fifth to split the Kenyans, and third were France, for whom Paul Arpin, at 11th, was the top European. Wilfred Oanda Kirochi became the first junior runner ever to retain his title. Ingrid Kristiansen completed a road and cross-country double within a week as she won the women's race from Angela Tooby and Annette Sergent. The team winners were the USSR from Great Britain and France. For the first time in the history of the event the four British countries combined to form a UK team. *See the 1988 Annual for further details.*

27 **Australian Championships**, Perth. Kerry Saxby further improved her world 5000m walk record to 20:45.32.

APRIL

2 **Bali**, Indonesia. Despite hot weather and near 100% humidity John Ngugi won the 10km road race in 27:29, equal to the second fastest ever run on the roads, to beat Paul Kipkoech 27:31 and win $30,000. John

Treacy was third in 28:34. The women's winner, with a $25,000 prize, was Nancy Tinari in 32:14.

9 **Ekiden Relay, New York**. Five-men teams ran 50km with legs of 5, 8, 12, 15 and 10 kilometres. Ireland (Marcus O'Sullivan, Frank O'Mara, Ray Dooney, John Treacy and John Doherty) won in 2:25:12 from USA 2:26:02 and Great Britain 2:27:32.

15/16 **IAAF Council Meeting**, London. There was considerable debate concerning the eligibility of Zola Budd and the Council asked the BAAB to further consider the matter and to take appropriate action. The Council felt that Budd had 'at the very least been in breach of the spirit of the rules of the IAAF' in being present, other than as a mere spectator at a cross-country meeting in South Africa in June 1987. The Council also decided to adjust the long jump result from the 1987 World Championships by ignoring the sixth round long jump of Giovanni Evangelisti. The latter had been clearly demonstrated to have been wrongly recorded, although such evidence had previously been disallowed by the IAAF. The result was that Larry Myricks moved up to third with Evangelisti fourth. A week earlier the Italian chief national coach and five long jump judges had their resignations accepted by the Italian Federation.

17 **Rotterdam Marathon**, Netherlands. Belayneh Dinsamo ran the world's fastest ever, 2:06:50. He ran amazingly consistently in the windless conditions, with each 5km split between 14:58 and 15:09, as follows: 15:05, 30:05, 45:06, 1:00:12. 1:15:12, 1:30:13, 1:45:22, 2:00:20. Until 35km he was behind the schedule of Carlos Lopes in the previous world best. Ahmed Salah, 2:07:07, also broke the old record.

17 **London Marathon**. There were 20889 finishers from 22469 starters, just under the 1987 New York figures. Winners were men: Henrik Jørgensen 2:10:20; women: Ingrid Kristiansen, a record fourth win, 2:25:41; wheelchair: Ted Vince (Can) 2:01:37, a course record.

18 **Boston Marathon**. There was $80,000 for the winners of this, the 92nd race in the series. Ibrahim Hussein set a Kenyan record 2:08:43 in winning by a second from Juma Ikangaa, followed by national records by John Treacy (Ire) 2:09:15 and Gelindo Bordin (Ita) 2:09:27. Rosa Mota, 2:24:30, was again a clear women's winner. Mustapha Badid (Fra) set a world wheelchair record with 1:43:19.

Henrik Jørgensen after his win in the 1988 London marathon (George Herringshaw/ASP)

MAY

1 **European Marathon Cup**, Huy, Belgium. The USSR were first and France second in both men's and women's team competitions. *See Championships section for leading results.*

7 **Softeland Grand Prix**, Norway. Yelena Nikolayeva won the women's 10,000m in a world record 43:36.5 (although Kerry Saxby had recorded 42:14.2 in a mixed rcae in Canberra in January). Aleksey Pershin set a European 20,000m track record of 1:19:22.5.

15 **Bay To Breakers**, San Francisco, USA. Run over 7.5 miles, the world's largest race again had 100,000 runners, a figure actually estimated at c.110,000 including unregistered runners. Winners were Arturo Barrios 34:57.6 and Lisa Martin 39:16.4.

22 **Khania**, Greece. Ulf Timmermann regained the world shot record with the second throw of this series: 22.20, 23.06, N, N, 22.35, 22.45. It was the first ever over 23m.

22 **Pac-10**, Westwood, Cal., USA. Danny Everett achieved the best ever 200m/400m double with 20.23 (second to Atlee Mahorn

20.21) and 44.34. Second at 400m was Steve Lewis in his first world junior record of 44.65.

28 **Bruce Jenner's Bud Light Classic**, San Jose, USA. This again started the IAAF/Mobil Grand Prix season. Jackie Joyner-Kersee ran her second US 100mh record of the season, 12.61. Mary Slaney ran, and won in 8:49.43, her first 3000m race for three years.

JUNE

1–4 **NCAA Championships** at Eugene, Oregon, USA. The men's team title was won easily by UCLA, their seventh win, with 82 points; followed by Texas 41 and Arkansas 32. UCLA's 4x400m relay team ran 2:59.91, the first collegiate time under 3 minutes. Their team included the 400m 1–2 Danny Everett (in 44.52) and Steve Lewis, the 400mh (47.85) winner Kevin Young, and Henry Thomas. Other outstanding winners included Joe DeLoach 100m 10.03, Lorenzo Daniel 200m 19.87, and Paul Ereng 800m 1:46.76. Women's champions were Louisiana State 61 from UCLA 58 and Oregon 45. Gail Devers won the 100m in 10.86w and Vicki Huber the 3000m in 8:47.35 for the outstanding individual performances. *See US section for winners.*

4/5 **European Men's Club Cup**, Venice, Italy, First three teams: 1. Racing Club de France (third successive win) 118, 2. TV Wattenscheid 116, 3. Pro Patria Osama (Ita) 112.5.

5 **European Women's Club Cup** at Lisbon, Portugal. Bayer Leverkusen (FRG) won their eighth win in the eight editions of this competition with 211.5 points from Snia Milano (Ita) 199 and Roter Stern Beograd (Yug) 185.

8/9 **PTS, Bratislava**, Czechoslovakia. At 7.27pm on the second day Sergey Bubka cleared 6.05m on his first attempt for his eighth outdoor pole vault world record. It was his third jump of the competition, following clearances at 5.70 and 5.90. Three other world leading marks were a 2.36 high jump by Rudolf Povarnitsyn, 17.55 triple jump of Oleg Protsenko and 12.47 100mh by Yordanka Donkova, who just beat her compatriot Ginka Zagorcheva 12.50.

11/12 **Znamenskiy Memorial**, Leningrad, USSR. Galina Chistyakova first tied the world long jump record in the fourth round and then improved it in the last. Her series: 7.21, 7.38w, 7.21, 7.45 (+1.0), N, 7.52 (+1.4). Yelena Byelevskaya was over 7m five times and achieved the best ever second place mark of 7.36. The European 110mh record of 13.20 was equalled by Aleksandr Markin. Petra Felke won the javelin with 74.02 as Fatima Whitbread was only fourth with 66.44.

13 **Tokyo**, Japan. The 100m was run in 10.32 by Marty Krulee, as the big news was caused by Ben Johnson pulling up at halfway with a slight tear of his left hamstring in his opening race of the outdoor season.

15 **London**. The appeal by Sandra Gasser against her 2 year ban imposed after a positive drugs test at the 1987 World Championships was disallowed in the High Court.

16–18 **TAC/Mobil Championships** at Tampa, Florida. With separate US Olympic Trials to follow, this meeting had somewhat less significance than usual. Eric Metcalf won the long jump with 8.44 to complete the NCAA/TAC double and there was a great triple jump competition, won on his last jump by Mike Conley 17.35 to Willie Banks 17.16. Mac Wilkins won his seventh title in the discus, and there were meeting records by Roger Kingdom (tied) 13.15 for 110mh and Doug Nordquist 2.34 HJ, and in women's events by Brenda Webb 15:18.71 5000m and Jan Wohlschlag 1.97 HJ. Larry Myricks won the 200m, having earlier been awarded his bronze medal from the 1987 World Championships long jump, after the cheating by officials over the distance given to Giovanni Evangelisti had at last been recognised. *See US section for winners.*

18/19 **Gotzis,** Austria. The decathlon winner was Uwe Freimuth 8381, and the heptathlon Anke Behmer 6805.

19 **UK v USSR and France**, Portsmouth. The UK 155 beat USSR 149, with France third at 137, for the first men in a full men's international. Women's score: USSR 143, UK 112, France 77. Yelena Nikolayeva set a European 5000m walk record of 21:08.65.

19/20 **FRG v GDR**, Düsseldorf. Both men's and women's matches in this, the first ever international between the two Germanies, were won easily by the GDR, 131–92 and 119.5–59.5.

24 **Athletissima 88**, Lausanne, Switzerland. This meeting was added to the Grand Prix circuit for the first time. Carl Lewis won his 54th successive long jump with 8.43, and in the 400m, won by Danny Everett in 44.40 from Roberto Hernandez 44.57, Steve Lewis equalled his own world junior record of

44.65. At 800m Abdi Bile 1:45.25 beat Seb Coe 1:45.50.

24–26 **GDR Championships**, Rostock. Marlies Göhr won her tenth GDR title at 100m and Heike Drechsler won the 200m and LJ to take her total of GDR outdoor titles to nine. Jürgen Schult won his sixth at discus and there were fifth wins for Thomas Schönlebe at 400m and Petra Felke JT. *See GDR section for winners.*

29 **Olympischer Tag**, Berlin, GDR. Delayed by heavy rain, the most notable mark was perhaps by Petra Felke JT 74.92.

30 **World Games**, Helsinki. The lead in the Grand Prix standings was taken by shot winner Remigius Machura and by Petra Felke, with her third GP javelin win of the year, at 73.86.

Shot putter Remigius Machura was an early leader in the 1988 Mobil Grand Prix (George Herringshaw/ASP)

JULY

2 **Bislett Games**, Oslo. Two British athletes set national records at 10000m. Liz McColgan's 31:06.99 was especially notable for the fact that she handed Ingrid Kristiansen her first ever track defeat at the distance. Finishing in pain, clutching her side, Kristiansen was second in 31:31.37, having been with McColgan until 1500m to go. Eamonn Martin made a marvellous debut as he beat a great field in 27:23.06, with a last lap in 56.4. There were four men at 27:26.00 or better, and 14 under 28 minutes. Steve Cram retained his Dream Mile title, winning in 3:48.85 from Peter Elliott, Jens-Peter Herold and Abdi Bile, who were all under 3:50. Nine men under 3:52.5 (ninth was John Walker 3:52.48) was a new record. Both Grand Prix leaders had further wins, Javier Sotomayor the high jump 2.33 and Petra Felke the javelin 75.16.

4–7 **USSR Championships**, Tallinn. The top mark was the third best ever women's shot, 22.55 by Natalya Lisovskaya , and there was a 1988 year best at 800m, 1:56.03 by Nadezhda Olizarenko. The closest event was probably the hammer in which both Juri Tamm and Yuriy Nikulin threw 82.34, the former winning on next best, 82.30 to 82.18. Lyudmila Kondratyeva returned to win, at 200m, her first Soviet title for six years. *See USSR section for winners.*

5 **DN Galan**, Stockholm. Said Aouita made his first Grand Prix appearance of 1988 and won the 1500m in 3:35.70. World bests for the year came in the steeplechase from Peter Koech 8:15.72 and 5000m from John Doherty 13:17.14. Petra Felke achieved maximum Grand Prix points with her fifth javelin win, 71.60.

8 **Peugeot Games**, London. The most exciting race was at 1000m in which Abdi Bile 2:17.75 beat Steve Cram 2:17.80 and Peter Elliott 2:17.90. Julius Kariuki edged the year's best steeplechase time to 8:15.71 as he beat Peter Koech.

9 **Neubrandenberg**, GDR. Gabrielle Reinsch added over two metres to the world discus record with her opening throw of 76.80. She followed with 73.10, N, 70.56, 70.06, 71.98. Her pre-season best was 67.18 and she had improved to 69.86 in May, then 71.64 and 73.42 in June.

10 **Nikaia**, Nice, France. Sergey Bubka as usual entered the pole vault at 5.70m, cleared that and 5.85 first time, and then smoothly succeeded at 6.06m for his ninth outdoor world record. He failed three times at 6.10m. Grace Jackson doubled successfully, improving by over a second to 49.57 at 400m and then winning the 200m in 22.27. World bests for the year were set by Said Aouita 1500m 3:32.69, Peter Koech 3000mSt 8:11.61, Paula Ivan 1500m 4:00.14, and Yvonne Murray 3000m 8:37.22.

15–23 **US Olympic Trials**, Indianapolis. Exceptionally hot weather, over 100 degrees

F, on the first three days brought with it amazing sprinting. Florence Griffith-Joyner won both 100m and 200m, and in the former ran 10.49, which took 0.27 off the world record. Great depth was shown with six women under 11 seconds for 100m, and eleven men broke 45 seconds just in the quarter-finals of the 400m, in the finals of which Butch Reynolds and Danny Everett broke 44.00, the fastest ever at low altitude. Reynolds was timed at 21.2 at 200m and 32.0 at 300m during his 43.93. Carl Lewis ran the fastest ever 100m, 9.78 with the wind well over the legal limit at 5.2 m/s, and also won the long jump, but was second at 200m, his first loss at the event for two years. Willie Banks became the first man to triple jump over 18m, albeit wind aided at 18.06 in the first round and then bounded 18.20 in the sixth, leading seven men over 17.50, and Jackie Joyner-Kersee broke the world heptathlon record. In the men's 400m hurdles Danny Harris ran 47.76 but was only fifth, and was but one who had to face the unrelenting fact that only the first three at each event could go to the Olympics. The winner of the event, Edwin Moses, became the first athlete ever to win an event four times in a row. He was one of five athletes to make their fourth US Olympic team, joining Henry Marsh, Larry Myricks, Mac Wilkins and Karen Smith. Amongst those who qualified for their third team was Francie Larrieu-Smith, who had first competed in 1972.

16–17 **Talence**, France. Many of the world's best multi-eventers took part as Christian Plaziat 8512 won the decathlon and Anke Behmer 6733 the heptathlon.

22–24 **Ibero-American Championships**, Mexico City. Aided by the high altitude the best marks came in the sprints, with Robson Caetano da Silva winning 100m and 200m in 10.08 and 20.05. *See Championships section for winners.*

27 **Golden Gala**, Verona, Italy. Paula Ivan continued to get better, running 1500m in 3:58.80, while Said Aouita showed that he was serious about running 800m, beating Peter Elliott 1:44.64 to 1:44.75. The meeting was moved from its usual home as the Olympic Stadium in Rome was being renovated for the 1990 World Cup at soccer.

27–31 **World Junior Championships**, Sudbury, Canada. *See results section for report and details of all medallists.*

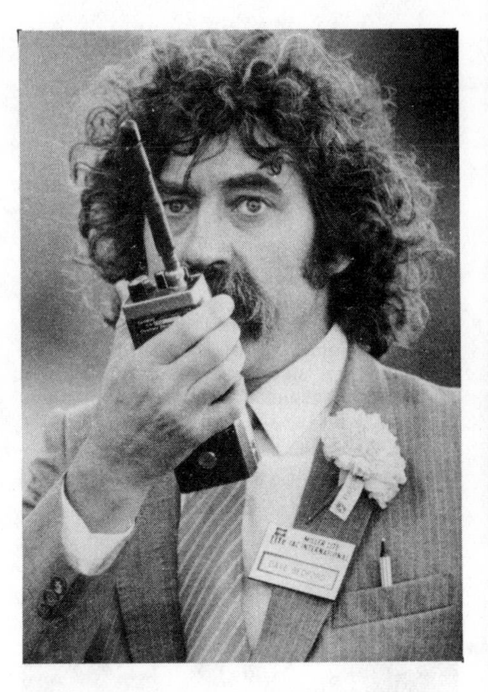

Dave Bedford set a world record 27:30.80 for 10000 metres in 1973. Fifteen years later he is a picture of sartorial elegence in his role as meeting director of the IAC International (George Herringshaw/ASP)

29 **Miller Lite IAC International**, Edinburgh. There was a sign of changing times as Britain had the 1–2-3 in the 110mh won by Colin Jackson 13.21w from Anthony Jarrett and Jon Ridgeon, over the Americans Renaldo Nehemiah and Arthur Blake.

30–2 Aug **USSR Championships**, Kiev; at distance and combined events. Mikhail Shchennikov set a world road best for 20km walk; his times at each kilometre: 19:59, 39:48, 59:30, 1:19:08. Yevgeniy Misyulya and Viktor Mostovik also broke 1:20, there were eight men under 1:21 and 14 under 1:22. Yelena Nikolayeva set a world record for the 10000m track walk, 43:36.41.

AUGUST

5–7 **AAA/WAAA Championships**, Birmingham. It was the first ever joint staging of these championships, which were also the British Olympic Trials. These were conducted for the first time on the basis that the first two at each event were assured of

Olympic selection, providing the athletes had met the qualifying standards. Then a third athlete was a matter for selection. Headlines were generated by Seb Coe's elimination in his 1500m heat, fourth in 3:45.01, and his form was not enough to gain the extra place at either 800m or 1500m. These went to Peter Elliott and Steve Cram, who at this meeting won at 1500m and 800m respectively. Steve Ovett was fourth in the 1500m, so it seemed to be the end of an era.

11 **Sestriere**, Italy. A new track was opened at this 2065m high altitude venue. Roger Kingdom won the 110mh in 12.97, the second best of all-time, from Colin Jackson's European record 13.11. Other fast sprint winners were Ben Johnson 9.98 and Carl Lewis 19.82.

11–13 **Kenyan Olympic Trials**, Nairobi. Three great champions failed to make the Kenyan Olympic team, as through illness and injury Billy Konchellah, Paul Kipkoech and Julius Korir were unable to run. Nonetheless, as was later to be proven in Seoul, Kenyan running standards are the best in the world, In the 800m Paul Ereng set off at an amazing pace (400m 49, 600m 1:14), but just held on to third place behind the fast winning time at the 1675m altitude of 1:44.5 by Nixon Kiprotich. The other Olympic Champions to be Peter Rono, John Ngugi and Julius Kariuki all won their events.

12 **Budapest Grand Prix**, Hungary. The best marks were at the long jumps, won by Larry Myricks 8.61 and Galina Chistyakova 7.45 (with an average of 7.23 for her six jumps). Stefka Kostadinova high jumped 2.05, the best of the year to that date.

17 **Weltklasse, Zürich**, Switzerland. The highlight of a very great meeting was the world record of 43.29 for 400m run by Butch Reynolds. Innocent Egbunike went out fast and reached 200m in 20.9. Inside him Reynolds was pulled along to reach 200m in 21.4 and then 300m in 32.2, before powering home in the finishing straight to win clearly from Danny Everett 44.20 and Steve Lewis 44.26, with Egbunike fading to sixth 44.97. Hugely anticipated was the 100m clash between Carl Lewis and Ben Johnson over 100m, with the pair reportedly sharing $250,000 in TV fees. Lewis rocketted past at the close to win in 9.93, equalling his US record, as Johnson virtually gave up to come third in 10.00, beaten also by Calvin Smith 9.97. It was Lewis's ninth win in 15 clashes with Johnson. There was, as always, great depth of top-class competition and a magnificent atmosphere. Paula Ivan improved her Romanian record for 1500m to 3:56.22, another world best of 1988, as was Johnny Gray's 800m of 1:42.65.

19 **Van Damme Memorial**, Brussels, Belgium. Steve Cram ran 1988's fastest 1500m and the third best ever for him at 3:30.95 from Peter Elliott's pb 3:32.94. Their great rival Said Aouita won the 800m in a Moroccan record 1:44.36, beating Johnny Gray by 0.07. José Regalo's 13:15.62 at 5000m was another year's best.

20 **Stara Zagora**, Bulgaria. Yordanka Donkova regained the world record for 100m hurdles with 12.21, with wind of 0.63 m/s. Second was Karamfilka Petrova in 14.63.

21 **Weltklasse, Köln**, FRG. Said Aouita continued to go faster at 800m, with 1:43.86, well clear of Joaquim Cruz and José-Luiz Barbosa. Ben Johnson again showed that he was far from his best, as he ran the 100m in 10.29 behind Calvin Smith 10.16 and Dennis Mitchell 10.27.

26 **IAAF/Mobil Grand Prix Final**, ISTAF, West Berlin. Said Aouita ensured a win in the overall men's Grand Prix with a win in the mile, and the women's title went to Paula Ivan, who maintained her unbeaten record in the 1988 series with a 4:00.24 win at 1500m. She had the same points as Grace Jackson, winner here at 200m, but had the best single performance as scored on IAAF tables. The best performance at the meeting was Roger Kingdom's 13.04 for 110mh, the fifth fastest ever run. Rodion Gataullin scored a notable victory in the pole vault with 5.95 to Sergey Bubka's 5.80. He even had the temerity to attack the world record, long Bubka's preserve, but failed at 6.08. Liz McColgan scored another victory over Ingrid Kristiansen, this time at 5000m 15:03.29 to 15:10.89. *See Mobil Grand Prix section for winners and report.*

27 **Canberra**, Australia. Kerry Saxby smashed the world record for women's road 10km with 41:29.71.

28 **Koblenz**, FRG. José-Luiz Barbosa won the 800m in 1:43.34, with Seb Coe showing what might have been in Seoul with his best run of the year, second in 1:43.93. Jim Spivey, also missing the Olympics, ran 1500m in 3:31.01.

28 **Stockholm**. There was the largest entry ever for a women's only race: about 23,000 for a

10km race won by Evy Palm in 34:09.

30–2 Sep **African Championships**, Annaba, Algeria *See results section.*

SEPTEMBER

2/3 **Finland v Sweden**, Helsinki. Finland won both matches: men 229.5–180.5, women 170–150.

8 **Salamanca**, Spain. Javier Sotomayor added a centimetre to the world high jump record with his second attempt clearance at 2.43m.

The first 80m javelin throw by a woman was Petra Felke's fourth world record in four years (George Herringshaw/ASP)

9 **Potsdam**, GDR. At this pre-Olympic meeting Petra Felke became the first women's 80m javelin thrower, with the final throw of this series: 77.16, N, N, 73.92, 77.62, 80.00. Her throw was actually measured at 80.011m.

8/11 **Asian Junior Championships**, Singapore. Contested by 350 athletes from 25 nations, of whom the most successful were China with 14 gold medals, Japan 13 and Taiwan 6.

11 **Race Against Time**. An estimated 50 million people in 1289 countries took part in this international fund-raising venture organised by Sport Aid.

23–2 Oct **Olympic Games**, Seoul. *See Championships section for report and first eight at each event.*

OCTOBER

16 **Mercedes Mile**, Fifth Avenue, New York. Men's and women's winners were Steve Scott 3:53.43 and Mary Slaney 4:20.03.

16 **Beijing Marathon**, China. Unable to compete in Seoul, Abebe Mekonnen won in 2:07:35.

30 **Chicago Marathon**, USA. Back after missing a year, with a new sponsor, Heileman's Old Style Beer, the winners were Alejandro Cruz 2:08:57 and Lisa Weidenbach 2:29:17.

NOVEMBER

6 **New York Marathon**, USA. Steve Jones returned to form to win by more than three minutes in 2:08:20, and Grete Waitz won the women's race for the ninth time, in 2:28:07. There were records for 23,463 starters and 22,244 finishers, 889 under 3 hours.

DECEMBER

5 **Fukuoka Marathon**, Japan. Toshihiro Shibutani won in 2:11:04, and Belayneh Dinsamo was only second in 2:11:09, but he had been misdirected when leading on approaching the stadium.

THE ATHLETES OF 1988 – MEN

BY PETER MATTHEWS

The Olympic Games in Seoul provided the vast majority of the world's best athletes with their ultimate goal for the season. Seven nations declined to take part: The North Koreans, due to their inabiltity to accept the award of the Games to Seoul, and five other nations in sympathy with them: Cuba, Ethiopia, Madagascar, Nicaragua and the Seychelles. Albania were also, as usual, absent. The athletes of all these nations were the losers, and in particular the Ethiopian distance runners and the strong Cuban team. However the best Cubans competed extensively in Europe and elsewhere.

Several women athletes stood out as outstanding athletes in 1988. There were great world records, such as the first 80m javelin throw by Petra Felke and two in the heptathlon by Jackie Joyner-Kersee, at 100mh by Yordanka Donkova, and above all those of Florence Griffith-Joyner, who took women's sprinting into a new era. All these women were Olympic champions and were undefeated at their specialities, as were Paula Ivan at 1500m, Rosa Mota at the marathon and Natalya Lisovskaya at the shot.

It was harder to find similar dominaton of men's events. Sergey Bubka added two more world pole vault records to his collection, but did lose once. Ulf Timmermann, however, was undefeated in the shot and achieved the first ever 23m put. His countryman Jürgen Schult won everything at the discus, although he did not approach the world mark, and Carl Lewis was again supreme at the long jump, at which he has not lost since 1981, and also at 100m, bar his "loss" to Ben Johnson in the Olympic final. The most complete supremacy at one event was, however, surely that of Roger Kingdom at the high hurdles, 25 wins in 25 races, competing regularly against the world's best and usually winning clearly.

The single best individual performance of the year by a man was surely the magnificent 400m world record by Butch Reynolds in Zürich. His 43.29 was an amazing improvement, even if there had been keen anticipation of his ability to take the record. After all, the 43.86 run by Lee Evans, set at the high altitude of Mexico City, had stood inviolate for nearly twenty years. Reynolds, however, was beaten in the Olympic final by the Junior Athlete of the Year, Steve Lewis, and in a close call my vote for Male Athlete of the Year goes to Carl Lewis.

Carl Lewis
Male Athlete of the Year – 1988

Carl Lewis had the goal for the year of repeating his 1984 feat of winning four Olympic gold medals. It was not to be, but two golds and a silver was nonetheless a brilliant achievement,

Olympic long jump gold again for Carl Lewis – the male athlete of 1988 (George Herringshaw/ASP)

and at major championships Lewis now has the remarkable medal collection of 13 gold, 2 silver and 1 bronze.

Lewis started 1988 in low gear, competing just once indoors, when he ran 20.83 for 200m in Stuttgart, losing to James Butler but beating his great rival Calvin Smith. Outdoors he made his debut at Walnut on 24 April at 100m, but he managed only 10.29 for 5th behind Ray Stewart, 10.13, his Santa Monica teammates Mark Witherspoon and Joe DeLoach, and Brian Cooper. However Lewis explained that his blocks had slipped, and thereafter his preparations for the Olympics went smoothly as prior to Seoul he won six finals at 100m, three long jump competitions and four out of five at 200m. That one loss was to Joe DeLoach at the US Olympic Trials, when even Lewis had to give best, understandably a little tired after victories at 100m and long jump already earned in that cauldron of intensive competition. Indeed he had given one of his greatest performances in the long jump, when he responded to the 8.74 by Larry Myricks in the third round with 8.76 just two minutes later, and he had run man's fastest ever 100 metres, 9.78 albeit aided by a strong breeze. So on to Seoul, where he looked at his majestic, flowing best in the heats of the 100 metres to confirm his status as favourite over Ben Johnson. But the latter produced the greatest ever sprint performance in the final, with a staggering 9.79. Lewis couldn't match that, but took 1/100th second off his US record and then was rewarded with the gold medal when Johnson was disqualified. He went on to a clear win at the long jump, but once again, just as in the US Trials such intensity of top-class competition was just too much to sustain, and he again had to yield to DeLoach at 200m. Then there was the anticlimax of not even getting to run in the relay due to the disqualification of the US team in the heats, when Lewis had been critical of the composition of that team. All in all, however, another great year for perhaps the most graceful sprinter we have ever seen. We are in grave danger of taking him for granted.

sub 10.00 times at 100m with legal wind

12 Carl Lewis 1983- 1, 84- 3, 85- 1, 87- 1, 88- 6.
6 Ben Johnson 1986- 1, 87- 4, 88- 1 (and 9.79 dq)
4 Calvin Smith 1983- 2, 88- 2
1 five other athletes

sub 20.00 times at 200m with legal wind

8 Carl Lewis 1983- 1, 84- 3, 87- 1, 88- 3
3 Pietro Mennea 1979- 2, 80- 1
3 Joe DeLoach 1988- 3
2 Lorenzo Daniel 1988- 2
1 six other athletes

Long jumps over 8.53m/28ft

All jumps in series included: legal/windy (w)
50 Carl Lewis 1981- 1/2, 82- 7, 83- 5/1, 84- 7/1, 85- 2/2, 86- 1w, 87- 10/6, 88- 3/2
14 Larry Myricks 1982- 1, 83- 1w, 84- 1, 86- 1w, 87- 2/2, 88- 6
5 Robert Emmiyan 1986- 1, 87- 4
3 Mike Conley 1985- 1w, 86- 1w, 87- 1w
1 Lutz Dombrowski 1980- 1
1 Jason Grimes 1982- 1w

EVENT BY EVENT SURVEY

SPRINTS

The sensational disqualification of **Ben Johnson** after his Olympic 100 metres victory is dealt with elsewhere in the Annual. He had been injured in his season's debut at 100m in Tokyo in May, so did not return to the track until the Canadian Championships which he won in 9.90w. He showed, with third places in Zürich and Köln, that he was not back to peak form. However his 9.79 in the Olympic final was amazing; sadly he was found to have cheated.

Carl Lewis (see above) is thus clearly number one at 100m. Arguably the world's best eight 100m specialists contested that important race in Zürich. Lewis won in 9.93 from **Calvin Smith** 9.97 and Johnson 10.00. The followed Chidi Imoh 10.04, Linford Christie 10.07, Dennis Mitchell 10.08, Ray Stewart 10.09 and Desai Williams 10.19. Chidi Imoh, who beat Stewart 4–1 and Mitchell 3–1 in 1988, was injured and went out in the Olympic quarter-finals but otherwise those same runners contested the Olympic final with the addition of Robson da Silva, who had won the Ibero-American title at altitude in 9.99. Ray Stewart was injured in Seoul, and this time **Linford Christie** got a good start to gain the silver medal behind Lewis in a European record 9.97, with Smith also under 10 seconds getting the bronze.

Joe DeLoach concentrated on the 200m, at which he had a few early season losses, and he went out in the heats at the NCAA, but from July he was unbeaten, winning the US Trials, in Zürich and Brussels, and at the Olympics. He showed his class at 100m too, as he beat Stewart and Mitchell to take the NCAA title, but was fifth in the Trials, that amazing race at which seven men ran sub-10.00 times with the hot wind behind them. **Robson Da Silva** got the Olympic 200m bronze ahead of Christie,

Ben Johnson shows he is number one as he crosses the line to short-lived victory in the Olympic 100 metres. He was followed by Carl Lewis (lane 3), Linford Christie (lane 4) and Calvin Smith (lane 5). Robson da Silva, sixth, is in lane 1 (George Herringshaw/ASP)

and he also had a 3–2 advantage over Calvin Smith, who as usual raced hard and often, but who had surprisingly been only fifth at 200m in the US Trials. NCAA 200m champion Lorenzo Daniel had twice broken 20 seconds and was unbeaten until he was injured in Indianapolis; he beat Olympic fifth placer Atlee Mahorn to take the NCAA title.

400 METRES

Only Lee Evans and Larry James had run under 44 seconds for 400m, both in that epic Olympic final at the high altitude of Mexico City in 1968, but in 1988 three brilliant Americans also broke through that barrier, and all at sea-level. **Butch Reynolds** and **Danny Everett** both did so in the US Trials at Indianapolis, and then Reynolds achieved the 20-year-dream of 400m runners in breaking the 43.86 world record. Not only that but he smashed it in his epic run in Zürich. **Steve Lewis** set his fourth world junior record of the year in Indianapolis with 44.11 and came through brilliantly to take the Olympic title from Reynolds, who had left his charge too late, and Everett. Both Lewis and Reynolds were under 44.00. This trio set new standards

The greatest single run by a male athlete in 1988 was achieved by Butch Reynolds (George Herringshaw/ASP)

Paul Ereng, Olympic champion in his first year of 800m running (George Herringshaw/ASP)

in the quality in depth of their running during the year. Reynolds raced sparingly, winning 6/7 finals, Everett 9/12 and Lewis just 3/12, losing 9–1 to his UCLA teammate Everett!

Darren Clark had been troubled by injury and had a year's best of only 45.93 prior to the Olympics, but he ran 44.38 in the semis before fourth place in the final in 44.55 ahead of **Innocent Egbunike**, who won the African title, but didn't match his brilliance of the previous year, and the 1983 world champion **Bert Cameron**, who improved his Jamaican record in Seoul. Two other prominent 400m runners in 1988 did not compete in Seoul. The Cuban **Roberto Hernandez** ran often, winning 17/24, but lost 2–1 to **Andrew Valmon** who, although only sixth in the US Trials, was the best of the other Americans on the European circuit. 1987 had been a brilliant year for 400m running, with 17 men breaking 45 seconds, but 27 did so in 1988.

Most times under 44.50 in career (no. in 1988)
13 Butch Reynolds (5), 7 Danny Everett (6), 6 Steve Lewis (6), 5 Innocent Egbunike, 3 Gabriel Tiacoh

Most times under 45.00 in one year
14 Danny Everett 1988
13 Steve Lewis 1988
12 Butch Reynolds 1987
12 Innocent Egbunike 1987
9 Gabriel Tiacoh 1986
8 Butch Reynolds 1988
8 Roberto Hernández 1988

800 METRES

Paul Ereng had never raced at 800m prior to 1988, and yet he ended the year with a brilliant Olympic victory. After a successful US campaign capped by the NCAA title, he came to Europe, where he only won once in seven races. Then he just made the Kenyan team in third place to Nixon Kiprotich and Juma Ndiwa, holding off Sammy Koskei by inches. He had set an extravagant pace (49 and 1:14!). His full racing programme is shown in the table.

Paul Ereng at 800m in 1988

Date	*Time*	*Place*	*Venue*
7.2	1:49.31i	1	Fairfax
11.3	1:50.64i	1h	Oklahoma City
12.3	1:52.18i	6	" NCAA
26.3	1:48.08	1	Raleigh
2.4	1:47.95	1	Chapel Hill
9.4	1:46.74	1	Baton Rouge
22.4	1:46.66	1h	Durham, NC
23.4	1:50.27	1	"
20.5	1:46.92	1h	Knoxville
21.5	1:46.61	1	Knoxville
1.6	1:46.24	2h	Eugene
3.6	1:46.76	1	" NCAA
9.6	1:44.82	2	Kvarnsveden
24.6	1:46.56	7	Lausanne
27.6	1:48.37	3	Villeneuve d'Ascq
30.6	1:47.17	1	Västerås
5.7	1:46.66	3	Stockholm
8.7	1:47.14	4	Crystal Palace
13.7	1:46.08	2	Barcelona
17.7	1:47.77	2	Gateshead
12.8	1:47.6	3h	Nairobi
13.8	1:45.1	3	" Kenyan Trials
23.9	1:46.14	1h	Seoul
24.9	1:46.38	2q	"
25.9	1:44.55	1s	"
26.9	1:43.45	1	" Olympics

The Olympic final was keenly anticipated. **Said Aouita** had looked as if he might achieve the 'impossible', a 5000m champion stepping down so far. He won all four 800m races prior to the Games, with national records of 1:44.36 in Brussels, when he beat **Johnny Gray**, who in the previous week had run the two fastest times of the year to win in Zürich and Hengelo, and then 1:43.86 in Köln ahead of **Joaquim Cruz** and **José-Luiz Barbosa**, who during 1988 ran the next two fastest times after Gray. In Seoul Barbosa tried to take the sting out of Aouita's finish, and paid the penalty by fading to sixth, a long way behind Gray, who in turn was well out of medal contention. Ereng's supreme drive carried him to a five metre win as Cruz took silver and Aouita held off **Peter Elliott** for the bronze. **Abdi Bile** missed the Olympics through injury, but won his two 800m races in June, beating Ereng at Kvarnsveden, and Seb Coe, also to miss the Games, in Lausanne.

1500 METRES AND 1 MILE

Peter Rono had started his year wih five mediocre losses in the indoor season, but made a breakthrough with 3:35.59 in Canada. He then had a busy three weeks in Europe before returning to Kenya, and he was a fine winner of the Olympic final from Elliott, Herold, Cram and Scott. Yet that race seemed unsatisfactory as a world championship due to the fact that some of the world's élite were not there and others not at their best (see Olympic Games section). **Said Aouita** won all nine races at 1500m or 1 mile prior to Seoul, at which he was fourth in his heat and then did not run the semis through injury. **Jim Spivey**, who had amazingly not made the US Olympic team, ran 3:31.01 at Koblenz two days after placing second to Aouita in the Grand Prix final. However the year's fastest times at both 1500m and 1 mile were run by **Steve Cram**, with 3:30.95 at Brussels, when **Peter Elliott** was second in 3:32.94, and 3:48.95 in the Dream Mile in Oslo. In that, perhaps the year's most important clash between the world's best, he won from Elliott 3:49.20, **Jens-Peter Herold** 3:49.22, **Abdi Bile**, 3:49.40 in his only major race of the year at 1500m or 1M, **Steve Scott** 3:50.09 and Spivey 3:50.57. On that day Rono had to run in the B event, which he won at 1500m.

5000 METRES

John Ngugi, after winning his third world cross-country title and beating Paul Kipkoech 27:29 to 27:31 in the Bali 10km road race, ran one track 10000m race, beating Panetta, but otherwise concentrated on 5000m. He won the three major Kenyan races and ran consistently in Europe, but did not win any of his five races. However he was undoubtedly the master in Seoul, and ran the year's only sub 13:15 time. **José Regalo** had been the king of the Grand Prix circuit, and won all six of his 5000m races including two wins over Ngugi, including the Grand Prix final, at which Eamonn Martin was second, **Domingos Castro** third and Ngugi fourth. Regalo, however, had to drop out of the Olympic final in which Castro tried so hard to win, only to be pipped for a medal by **Dieter Baumann**, who had been third to John Doherty and Arturo Barrios, but ahead of Brahim Boutayeb and Dom. Castro in Stockholm, and **Hansjörg Kunze**, whose only other 5000m had been a win against FRG. At Stockholm seven men bettered 13:20, and at the Bislett Games, won by Pascal Thiébaut from Ngugi, three were under 13:20 and ten under 13:24.

10000 METRES
As with the Kenyan Olympic champions **Brahim Boutayeb** had a hectic racing season, but at all events won only half his 18 races. He missed his pb by less than a second in his first 10000m of the year, a winning 28:41.15 in Lisbon, and then improved by over a minute, running 27:39.12 for fifth at the Bislett Games in Oslo. He won both 5000m and 10000m at the African Championships, and then won a classic Olympic final. In Oslo **Eamonn Martin** made a marvellous 10000m debut to smash the 10-year-old British record with 27:23.06. Behind him came **Salvatore Antibo**, **Arturo Barrios** and **Hansjörg Kunze**, who were to finish 2–5-6 in Seoul. The next most important 10000m race of the year was in Brussels, won by **Francesco Panetta** from Paul Arpin and Addis Abebe, who added a world junior record to his world junior gold. **Jean-Louis Prianon** was only 7th in Oslo and 6th in Brussels but moved up to fourth in Seoul behind the other medallist **Kipkemboi Kimeli**. Eamonn Martin also beat Boutayeb at 3000m and twice at 5000m during 1988, but dropped out of the Olympic final.

MARATHON
The Olympic marathon was surely affected by the boycott of the Ethiopians. **Belayneh Dinsamo** set a world best of 2:06:50 to win in Rotterdam from **Ahmed Salah**, and two more Ethiopians Wodajo Bulti and **Abebe Mekonnen**. The latter also had big race wins in February at Tokyo, from **Juma Ikangaa**, Jörg Peter and Rob de Castella, and in October at Beijing over Hiromi Taniguchi. **Douglas Wakiihuri** had only been seventh in Tokyo, but as in 1987 showed himself ready for the big race, when he got the Olympic silver, ahead of Salah and **Takeyuki Nakayama**, but all had to yield to **Gelindo Bordin**, who added Olympic gold to the European he had won two years earlier. Due to the hot weather times in Seoul were much slower than in the big Spring and Autumn races, but Bordin's winning 2:10:32 was certainly worth a lot more than the 2:09:27 he had run in his other 1988 marathon, fourth at Boston, won by Ibrahim Hussein with Ikangaa second. The big end of year races in the US were won by Alejandro Cruz, Chicago 2:08:57, and Steve Jones, New York 2:08:20.

STEEPLECHASE
Julius Kariuki came to Seoul as the favourite, and won six of eight steeplechases during the year. He was beaten by **Alessandro Lambruschini** in Verona, but his fourth place in Nice was due to a fall as his teammates **Peter Koech** and **Patrick Sang** ran the year's fastest times prior to Seoul. Those two were also first and second in Stockholm ahead of **Mark Rowland**, but in the Grand Prix final the order was 1. Kariuki, 2. Sang, 3. Koech, 4. Lambruschini. **Francesco Panetta** won all his five pre-Olympic steeplechases, but did not meet the Kenyans. He set his usual pace in Seoul, but faded to ninth as Kariuki missed the hand-timed world record by just 0.11 to win from Koech and Rowland as these three ran the secnd, third and fifth fastest times ever. Lambruschini, William van Dijck, Henry Marsh, Sang and Boguslaw Maminski were also under 8:16 to beat the previous best of five in one race.

110M HURDLES
Roger Kingdom had a perfect season, as he won all his 25 races, including 17 finals from April to October. He ran history's second and third sub 13.00 times with legal wind: 12.97 at high altitude in Sestriere and then 12.98 to take the Olympic gold. His great strength enabled him to beat all the world's best, usually by a clear margin, and he ran the year's four fastest times and 10 of the 14 times under 13.20. The second quickest was the European record of 13.11 by **Colin Jackson** in Sestriere. Jackson took the Olympic silver and **Tonie Campbell** the bronze. In all Jackson beat Campbell 4–2. Only seventh in Seoul was **Mark McKoy**, but he had been runner-up to Kingdom in Zürich, ahead of Campbell and Jackson, was 2–2 v Jackson and beat Campbell 3–1. **Greg Foster** lost twice to Kingdom, but then suffered a compound fracture of the left forearm. He bravely tried to run with this in the US Trials but had to drop out in the semis.

400M HURDLES
Andre Phillips took the gold and **Amadou Dia Bâ** the silver in Seoul ahead of the great **Ed Moses**, and they ran the fifth and sixth fastest times ever, leaving Moses still with the top four. Kevin Young also broke 48 seconds in the Olympic final but five men had run 47.76 or better in the US Trials. Moses won in his season's best 47.37 from Phillips and Young, with **Danny Harris** and **Dave Patrick** the unlucky ones to miss Seoul. Harris in particular would have been a medal threat and indeed he beat Dia Bâ 5–0 during the year including their 1–2, with Patrick third in the Grand Prix Final. Young had the greatest depth of times with 15

The Kenyans have built up a formidable record at the steeplechase. Here at 2000m in Gateshead Julius Kariuki (6) leads from teammates (l-r) Kip Rono (12), Patrick Sang (3), Micah Boinett (5) and Boniface Merande (George Herringshaw/ASP)

sub 49.00 to 11 by Harris and 9 by Dia Bâ. The top two Americans raced sparingly: Moses with 8 sub 49.00 times won 6/7 finals, and Phillips with 7, won 4/5. **Winston Graham** was fifth in Seoul, having beaten Patrick 2–1.

deserves to be ranked first. Presumably on the basis of his past record, Igor Paklin was preferred to **Sergey Malchenko** for Seoul, but the latter was second in the Soviet championships, won by Avdeyenko, and might well have done

On the way to Olympic victory, Andre Phillips in lane 6, from Amadou Dia Ba (898), Ed Moses (1114) and Kevin Young (1137) (George Herringshaw/ASP)

HIGH JUMP

Gennadiy Avdeyenko again showed his big meet temperament to jump 2.38 to win in Seoul. Although he had won the Soviet title, his season's record was otherwise only fair, and he lost three times to one win over **Javier Sotomayor**. The Cuban won 17/26 with 24 competitions at 2.30 or more, to 21 by **Patrik Sjöberg,** and improved the world record to 2.43m, just half an inch short of eight feet. Sjöberg also won the European Indoor title and tied for third at the Olympics with **Rudolf Povarnitsyn**; he lost 4–5 to Sotomayor, but beat Avdeyenko 3–2. The top men were thus closely matched but Sotomayor probably beter than Paklin's seventh equal. **Hollis Conway** jumped consistently, but his Olympic silver was a surprise as his 2.36 was a 3cm improvement on his previous yearly best and he had only won three major competitions.

POLE VAULT

Sergey Bubka set his eighth and ninth world records outdoors, and was world number one for the sixth successive year. He had six of the nine competitions at 5.90 or above and won 11 of his 12 competitions, losing to **Rodion Gataullin** at the ISTAF meeting. The latter was clearly the world's number two, and **Grigoriy Yegorov**, second to Gataullin at the Znamenskiy, but Soviet champion in the absence of the big two, completed a USSR clean sweep of the Olympic medals. In the clashes between the top Americans **Kory Tarpenning** beat **Earl Bell** 8–7, but at the Olympics they were fourth and tenth respectively. Both had a 3–2 edge on Philippe Collet who tied for fifth in Seoul with Thierry Vigneron. **Miroslaw Chmara** was the third man to clear 5.90 and beat the Frenchmen in the three big vault competitions in France.

World pole vault world records and bests*

Most	*Name*	*out*	*in*
18	Sergey Bubka (SU)	9	9
16	Charles Hoff (Nor)	5	11
13	Cornelius Warmerdam (USA)	7	6
14	Bob Seagren (USA)	6	8
11	John Pennel (USA)	9	2
11	Billy Olson (USA)	–	11
8	Thierry Vigneron (Fra)	5	3

* *whether officially ratified or not*

LONG JUMP

As usual **Carl Lewis** competed rarely at this event, but he extended his win streak to over seven years with another four victories. **Larry Myricks** jumped better than ever, with five of the seven best winning jumps of the year. He pressed Lewis hard, particularly at the US Trials, but couldn't end the latter's supremacy. Myricks won 22 competitions and lost six, once to Bruno Surin, and three each to Lewis and **Mike Powell**, including at Seoul when he was beaten by both his US teammates. Overall Myricks beat Powell 6–3, having won their first five clashes. Of 8.50m jumps Lewis had 7 in 2 competitions, Myricks 9 in 5. The Cuban Jaime Jefferson was the best in the world after the three Americans, but then few jumpers displayed much consistency. **Eric Metcalf** won the NCAA/TAC double, but was only eighth in the US Trials.

TRIPLE JUMP

Khristo Markov lost four times, but completed his major championship portfolio with the Olympic gold. The USSR filled the next three places in Seoul and had 9 of the top 14 jumpers in the world. The newcomer **Igor Lapshin** took silver from **Aleksandr Kovalenko** and **Oleg Protsenko**, while in the Soviet championships the order had been Kovalanko, Lapshin, Oleg Sakirkin, Vladimir Chernikov and Protsenko. Although Willie Banks produced the longest triple jump ever, a wind-aided 18.20m to win

Khristo Markov, ever the winner of the big events (George Herringshaw/ASP)

the US Trials, leading seven men over 17.50m, **Mike Conley**, only fourth that day, was again the best American, beating Banks 4–1, and ending a good season in Europe with a win in the Grand Prix final over Protsenko.

SHOT

Ulf Timmermann had a marvellous year winning 12/12 and upping the world record to 23.06m. He had to display great competitive ability, as after setting three Olympic records he was passed by **Randy Barnes** in the last round in Seoul. He responded to take the gold by an 8cm margin. Barnes lost only twice in ten competitions, the other being to the Olympic bronze medallist **Werner Günthör** in Bern, but he had a 2–1 advantage over the Swiss with a win in Zürich. **Udo Beyer** lost only to the

An early season world record and the end of season Olympic title for Ulf Timmermann (George Herringshaw/ASP)

big three and he was followed in Seoul by the European Indoor winner **Remigius Machura**, who was well over 21m five times indoors but had an outdoor best of only 20.94. Sergey Gavrushin did not appear in Seoul but won the Soviet title from Sergey Smirnov who was 1.5m down on his season's best when eighth at the Olympics.

DISCUS

Jürgen Schult was again well short of his world record, but won all 11 competitions. Two more highly consistent throwers earned silver and bronze medals behind him at the Olympics: **Romas Ubartas** and **Ralf Danneberg**, who lost just thrice and twice respectively. The Soviet champion **Yuriy Dumchev** confirmed that form with fourth in Seoul, but his teammate Vaclavas Kidikas faded after good early season form to fail to qualify for the Olympic final, having only been 7th in the SU Champs. Second in that event and with a better overall record was **Vladimir Zinchenko**. The 1976 champion **Mac Wilkins** returned for the Olympic challenge, and although he had to settle for fifth was always in medal contention. The runner-up in 1976 also returned – Wolfgang Schmidt. Although he was not able to compete in Seoul, it was good to see him back, this time in West German colours, having eventually been allowed to leave the East after missing six years of competition. He was consistently over 65 metres and beat Wilkins 3–1. Also missing from the Games were the Cubans, of whom **Juan Martinez** was the best, beating Luis Delis 10–4.

HAMMER

Sergey Litvinov beat his great rival **Yuriy Sedykh** 3–2, losing to him at the Znamenskiy meet and in Vladivostok just prior to the Olympics, but comforatbly handled everybody else. In Seoul Litvinov threw all six throws beyond Sedykh's best to take the gold. Just as in Moscow in 1980 **Juri Tamm** completed the Soviet clean sweep of medals. Tamm had won the Soviet title from **Igor Nikulin** and **Igor Astapkovich**. Although Nikulin had the next best throw in 1988, his overall record was not as good as Astapkovich, who had the consolation of winning the Grand Prix final from Tibor Gécsek, with Nikulin fifth. **Ralf Haber** was the best non-Soviet and was fourth in Seoul ahead of Heinz Weis, again the best from the West, and Gécsek.

JAVELIN

The Finnish javelin tradition was maintained as **Tapio Korjus** took the Olympic gold with his last throw and **Seppo Räty** the bronze. The favourite **Jan Zelezný** won the silver and led Korjus on the list of best throws for the year from **Klaus Tafelmeier**, who was fourth in Seoul, just ahead of the consistent **Viktor Yevsyukov**. Korjus lost just once in 15 meets, and Zelezny also only one other time; both in the World Games at Helsinki, an event in which most of the world's best met, but in which the order was rather in contrast to the rest of the year's form. Then it was 1. Einar Vilhjalmsson, 2. Räty, 3. Yevsyukov, 4. David Ottley, 5. Korjus, 6. Zelezný, 7. Tafelmeier. In Seoul Vilhjalmsson missed the final by one place, and Ottley, although fourth best in qualifying, in which incidentally Zelezny's 85.90 was not matched in the final, was 11th.

DECATHLON

Christian Schenk was an inspired Olympic champion from his teammate **Torsten Voss**. Voss had won his other decathlon of 1988, but Schenk had been beaten in his three previous decathlons. At Götzis **Uwe Freimuth** won with 8381 from Dave Steen, Thomas Fahner, Christian Plaziat and Schenk; while at Talence

Christian Plaziat won with 8512, the year's best total, from Schenk, Steen, Alain Blondel, Robert de Wit and Fahner. Freimuth headed Fahner and Schenk in the GDR champs, but then faded to eighth in Talence and 18th in Seoul. The second and third best scores of the year were by Siggy Wentz, who did not finish his other two decathlons and through injury could not compete in Seoul, and by Valter Külvet, who failed to finish there.

In a fascinating Olympic contest Daley Thompson battled hard throughout but was just pipped by Steen for the bronze medal, with Plaziat fifth.

WALKS

At 20km walk **Jozef Pribilinec** (see Ladislav Krnáč's article) was a popular winner following his two World silver medals. He had been disqualified at Hospitalet in April, but had won his other race at the distance, at the CS championships. He had also won the European Indoor title at 3000m. He won the Olympic gold by only three seconds, the second narrowest margin in Olympic walking history. **Ronald Weigel** took the silver which he matched a week later at 50km. In the latter he beat his great rival **Hartwig Gauder**, and had won GDR titles at both distances, having started the year with a world best at 3000m indoors. Both the East Germans had to give best in Seoul to **Vyacheslav Ivanenko**, the USSR champion. Each of these medallists had won their other races at 50km.

Mikhail Shchennikov, just 20 years old, set a world best at 20km, when he won the USSR championships, in which three men broke 1hr 20, but he was sixth in Seoul. **José Marin** continued his great big race consistency with fourth and fifth places in Seoul; which made five Olympic placings from 4th to 6th since 1980! Add to those three top six placings at both Europeans and Worlds.

The male all-rounder of 1988 – Christian Schenk (George Herringshaw/ASP)

Gold for Vyacheslav Ivanenko in the longest Olympic athletics event (George Herringshaw/ASP)

THE ATHLETES OF 1988 – WOMEN

BY PETER MATTHEWS

Florence Griffith-Joyner

Florence Griffith-Joyner after her world record 21.34 at 200 metres and her second Olympic gold medal (George Herringshaw/ASP)

My choice for the title of woman athlete of the year is Florence Griffith-Joyner, ahead of her sister-in-law Jackie Joyner-Kersee.

Before her marriage to Al Joyner in October 1987 Florence Griffith had compiled a good record in the sprints, particularly at the 200 metres, at which she had won silver medals in the 1984 Olympics and 1987 Worlds, after fourth place in the 1983 World Championships. While at UCLA she had won NCAA titles at 200m in 1982 and 400m in 1983, but to the world at large she was known as much for her beauty and fashion sense, with fingernails up to six inches long, and those stunning outfits in Rome in 1987, as for her sprinting ability.

Always a talented sprinter, Florence went to Cal State-Northridge for a year after graduating from Jordan High in Los Angeles. But, due to lack of finance, she dropped out after a year and began work as a bank teller. However the young Northridge sprint coach Bobby Kersee helped her apply for assistance, and when he went to UCLA she followed him. That led to NCAA titles and the Olympic silver, and it was Kersee who stirred her into action when she had drifted away from running in 1986.

During the winter prior to the Olympics she worked with a new intensity, with lots of heavy weightlifting and endurance runs to build up the strength which was so evident during the track season. She made a late season's debut at Santa Monica on 12 June, when she won the 100m in 10.99 and the 200m in 22.15. Then she smashed her 100m pb with 10.89 at San Diego on 25 June. That was all prior to the US Trials in Indianapolis, when she burst into the headlines with a fabulous series of runs and a no less fabulous collection of one-legged running outfits. She had just two easy 100m races in Europe between the Trials and the Games, and then once again there was the stunning series of races at the Olympics.

The world 100m record of 10.76 was set by Evelyn Ashford in 1984, and still nobody has matched that figure apart from 'FloJo', as she does not like to be known. She bettered that in seven races of the eight she ran in Indianapolis

(10.60w, 10.49, 10.70, 10.61) and Seoul (10.88, 10.62, 10.70w, 10.54w). And in the matching four races at 200m, she was under 22 seconds seven times, with US records at 21.77 and 21.76, then those two world records in semi-final and final at the Olympics, 21.56 and 21.34. As if that was not enough she produced an anchor 400m relay leg of 48.1 for the USA.

Truly she has taken women's sprinting into a new era. Nobody has ever burst through sprint world records by such margins, and the smile of triumph as she powered through the finish line to take her second Olympic gold told its own story of hard work fulfilled.

EVENT BY EVENT REVIEW

SPRINTS

Florence Griffith-Joyner beat some of the greatest women sprinters in history by huge margins. Her 10.49 at Indianapolis was greeted with incredulity, but she had optimum conditions for a world record, with exceptionally hot weather and freak wind conditions. However, doubters were converted to believers by her marvellous running in Seoul. In the 1988 season she won all her races, 13 at 100m and 9 at 200m including heats. In the 100m **Evelyn Ashford** and **Heike Drechsler** followed in that order in Seoul. Ashford lost three minor races, to Issajenko and Cooman in June and to Onyali in July, but otherwise won nine finals and followed FloJo home three times. Drechsler lost only once, to Marlies Göhr at 100m, outside her two Olympic bronze medals. In seven of her nine 100m races she was under 11.00 and was under 22.00 four times at 200m.

Grace Jackson was a superb second in the Olympic 200m as well as fourth at 100m. She had a very hectic racing schedule on the Grand Prix circuit, especially at 200m at which she won 9/13 races, but she also won 5/6 at 400m. At 200m she beat **Dannette Young**, who was only sixth in the US Trials, 4–3. In contrast her Jamaican teammate **Merlene Ottey** raced very sparingly, winning all eight events, four each at 100m and 200m prior to Seoul, but for once she missed out on the medals, with fourth at 200m, but she was suffering from recurring leg cramps.

After maintaining her long winning streak indoors **Gwen Torrence** made the US team at both sprints and was a solid 5th and 6th in the Olympic finals. As usual **Anelia Nuneva** ran a lot of fast times, but she was most unlucky to pull a muscle when heading for a medal in the Olympic 100m final. **Silke Möller** was unable to capture her sparkle of 1987, and like Marlies Göhr went out in the 100m semis, but was fifth at 200m in the Olympics.

No. of sub-11.00 times at 100m on automatic timing

Number each year, with athletes achieving most (+w wind assisted)

1977	1+1w	Göhr 1, Lannaman 1w
1978	1–	Göhr 1
1979	2+1w	Göhr 1, Ashford 1
1980	3+4w	Göhr 2+1w
1981	3+2w	Ashford 3+1w, Ottey 1w
1982	8+2w	Göhr 3, Ashford 3
1983	9+7w	Göhr 4, Ashford 2+2
1984	15+2w	Göhr 9, Ashford 5+2
1985	14+1w	Göhr 5+1, Ottey 5
1986	13+11w	Ashford 4+2, Drechsler 4+1
1987	26+10w	Nuneva 7, Ottey 7+1, Gladisch 3+1
1988	35+20w	Griffith-Joyner 8+3, Ashford 5+2, Drechsler 5+2, Nuneva 5+1, Torrence 2+4, Göhr 3+1

Most overall: Göhr 33+3, Ashford 23+9, Ottey 12+5, Nuneva 12+1, Drechsler 11+3, Griffith-Joyner 10+4.
33 athletes in all, with or without wind-assistance, have broken this barrier.

400 METRES

Olga Bryzgina, just as in 1987, had a relatively quiet season prior to the big event, losing three and winning three of her major races before Seoul. But there she was supreme, and won the gold medal by 0.8 from **Petra Müller**, who had won all five races indoors and for whom this was her only loss in nine finals outdoors. The Soviet champion **Olga Nazarova** couldn't match her 49.11 semi-final time in the final, but took the bronze medal ahead of **Valerie Brisco**. Actually only the first two did better their semi-final times in the Olympic final, and Jillian Richardson ran 49.91, the first ever non-qualifying sub-50 second mark.

The Cuban **Ana Quirot** won the Grand Prix and beat Olympic fifth placer **Diane Dixon** 2–1, and Grace Jackson had run the world's fastest time of the year when she beat Quirot in Nice.

800 METRES

Just as in 1987 **Christine Wachtel** was beaten for the gold medal by her teammate **Sigrun Wodars** after building up supremacy over her. Wachtel was particularly strong indoors, with three world indoor records, and she beat Wodars 3–0 indoors and then 5–1 outdoors. In Seoul, however, it was Wodars from Wachtel and the American **Kim Gallagher**. Another favourite was **Nadezhda Olizarenko**, who had run the two fastest times of the year and won all four of her major races, including the Soviet title, but she trailed off in the semis through injury. However **Ana Quirot** has a very strong claim to be the world number one. She won 12/12, including wins over Wodars in Oslo, Wachtel twice, and Gallagher in the Grand Prix final.

1500 AND 3000 METRES

Paula Ivan and **Tatyana Samolenko** won Olympic medals in both these events. First Samolenko won a thrilling 3000 metres, in which all the leaders smashed their personal bests by huge margins, with Ivan taking silver and **Yvonne Murray** the bronze. All these three had been unbeaten at 3000m prior to Seoul; Samolenko in one indoor and two outdoor races, and both Ivan and Murray had just two races at the distance, both winning their national titles. However while Murray had had a very light racing programme, with just one winning race at each of 800m and 1500m races in addition to those at 3000m, Ivan had raced hard. She had won the Balkan title and placed second to Tudorita Ghidu at 800m, and had won ten major races at 1500m or 1 mile. With determined front-running she dominated the Grand Prix season. She used just the same tactics, only with even more force, in the Olympic final and ran away from the field to win in a time bettered only by Tatyana Kazankina back in 1980. Far behind **Laima Baikauskaite**, who had won Soviet 1500m titles both indoors and out, finished with a devastating late burst to pick off the silver from Samolenko and Chris Cahill. Samolenko was only sixth in the Soviet 1500m race, but did win her other five major races at 1500m.

Paula Ivan was the top middle distance woman runner in 1988 (George Herringshaw/ASP)

Mary Slaney made an encouraging return with wins at both 1500m and 3000m at the US Trials, and was the only woman apart from Ivan to break 4 minutes for 1500m, but she was beaten by Elly van Hulst over 3000m at Zürich, and could manage only eighth and tenth places in Seoul, but at least she at last finished an Olympic final. Also disappointing in Seoul was **Doina Melinte**, ninth at 1500m. She had won 7/7 indoors at 1500m including the European title, and had a series of second places outdoors. At 3000m the fourth and fifth places in Seoul went to the Soviets Yelena Romanova and Natalya Artyomova, who had been 1–2 in the reverse order in the Soviet Championships.

10000 METRES

Liz McColgan scored an important win at the Bislett Games, when she handed **Ingrid Kristiansen** her first ever track defeat at 10000m. McColgan won by nearly 25 seconds, but Kristiansen was troubled by injury, and remained the one to beat in Seoul. However there she stepped off the track with a foot injury, and McColgan, who had shown good speed with three wins in four races at 3000m, was left to try to take the sting out of the finish of **Olga Bondarenko**. She shook off the rest of the field, but Bondarenko's kick is devastating and it brought her the gold medal. Bondarenko went on to win in Tokyo, but had settled for second in the Soviet Championships behind Lyudmila Matveyeva, who was to place 12th in Seoul. Both beat **Yelena Zhupiyeva**, who was third at the Olympics ahead of the GDR champion **Kathrin Ullrich**.

MARATHON

Rosa Mota continued her run of success in major events. In the spring she won the Boston Marathon in 2:24:30 and then triumphed in Seoul in 2:25:40. Those finishing in the next four places behind her had each won their only previous marathon of the year. **Lisa Martin** had run the year's fastest time, 2:23:51, at Osaka in January, **Kathrin Dörre** had won the European Cup from the Soviets Raissa Smekhnova and Zoya Ivanova, **Tatyana Polovinskaya** had won the Soviet title, and **Zhao Youfeng** improved the Asian record she had set in Nagoya.

Ingrid Kristiansen won London in 2:25:41 to rank third fastest, and her compatriot **Grete Waitz** had to drop out in Seoul, but earlier had won the Stockholm marathon and later won her ninth New York race.

100 METRES HURDLES

Yordanka Donkova returned to the top, with a stellar year, winning all 15 finals and setting her fifth world record. At the Olympics **Gloria Siebert** made it four medals in four major championships, but all silver, and was clearly ahead of the surprising bronze medallist **Claudia Zaczkiewicz**. The latter had showed she was moving into top form with a win in the Grand Prix final.

Cornelia Oschkenat had an unbeaten season indoors, with the European title at 60mh and two world records at 50mh. Outdoors she won 6/8, including the GDR title, losing once each to her GDR colleagues Siebert and Kerstin Knabe, but she was last in the Olympic final through injury. Also missing out at the Olympics were the Soviet number two Lyudmila Narozhilenko, who fell in the semis, and the world champion **Ginka Zagorcheva**, who ran four fast times in June behind Donkova, but then was injured, and trying to return in Seoul was unable to finish her heat.

Times for 100m hurdles under 12.50

Legal + wind aided

27+1	Yordanka Donkova 1982- 1, 86- 11, 87- 4, 88- 11+1
12	Ginka Zagorcheva 1983- 1, 85- 1, 86- 3, 87- 5, 88- 1
6	Lucyna Kalek 1980- 2, 82- 2, 84- 2
4+1	Cornelia Oschkenat 1987- 4+1
3+2	Grazyna Rabsztyn 1978- 1, 79- 1+1, 80- 1+1
2+1	Bettina Jahn 1983- 2+1
2+1	Gloria Uibel 1987- 1+1, 88- 1
1	Vera Komissova 1980- 1
1	Natalya Grigoryeva 1988- 1
1w	Kerstin Knabe 1983- 1w

400 METRES HURDLES

The Olympic final could hardly have been closer as **Debbie Flintoff-King** beat **Tatyana Ledovskaya** by 0.01 sec. They ran the second and third fastest times in history. Ledovskaya's time represented nearly four seconds improvement in the year. She had won the Soviet title from Tatyana Kurochkina, who also improved

Ingrid Kristiansen leads but lost to Liz McColgan here in Oslo (Mark Shearman)

substantially. **Sabine Busch** won the GDR title from **Ellen Fiedler** and was unbeaten in five finals prior to the Olympics, beating Fiedler four times, but in the faster race in Seoul, Fiedler came third and Busch fourth. Flintoff-King had been third to Busch and Susanne Losch, but ahead of Fiedler, at the Olympic Day meeting at the end of June and also lost to **Sandra Farmer-Patrick** at Hengelo. The latter switched nationality but lost her Olympic chance when she was harshly disqualified in the semis of the US Trials for running out of her lane. This, however, was only in the home straight and came after a last minute switch from lane 4 to lane 5. Magnificent improvement was registered by **Sally Gunnell**, who prior to 1988 had just one 400mh race, 59.5 in 1987. After a UK indoor record at 400m, she turned to the 400m hurdles with immediate success, and, improving with nearly every race, broke the UK record four times, culminating in 54.03 for fifth in Seoul. For good measure she added the UK record at 100mh too.

HIGH JUMP

Stefka Kostadinova added another 17 competitions at 2 metres or higher, 7 indoors and 10 out, to her career total, so she was again well ahead of the field. She won all nine indoor events, including the European title, and a further ten outdoors, but she also lost four times, including at the Olympics in a jump-off at 2.03 to **Louise Ritter**. The latter had some early season losses, but set a US record of 2.03 in July and then competed only at the US Trials, which she won with 1.99, before her Olympic triumph.

Tamara Bykova again showed big meet expertise to take the Olympic bronze from **Olga Turchak**. However **Silvia Costa** of Cuba had a better record overall than these two, with a best of 2.02 in Nice. **Galina Astafei** won the world junior title with her first 2m jump and was also fifth equal in Seoul with Lyudmila Andonova, who had returned from a drugs ban.

LONG JUMP

Jackie Joyner-Kersee achieved double gold at this event and heptathlon, just as she had in 1987. She was unbeaten in four indoor and five outdoor competitions and was the only jumper to defeat **Heike Drechsler**, Olympic silver medallist. Indoors Dreschler won 6/6, including the European Indoors and set a new world record at 7.37. Outdoors she won 7/8, including 7.48 for the GDR record. The world record outdoors however went to **Galina Chistyakova**, 7.52 at Leningrad. Chistyakova lost just twice, second in the European Indoors and third in Seoul. Completing a quartet of Olympians over 7m, well ahead of the rest of the field was **Yelena Byelevskaya**. Five other Soviet jumpers cleared 7m during 1988, including their champion Inessa Kravets, and also Vali Ionescu of Romania, who did not appear in Seoul, but won all six of her outdoor competitions between 7.00 and 7.08.

SHOT

Natalya Lisovskaya was by far the best woman's shot putter, and she capped a fine season with her 13th win of the year and 23rd in succession to take the Olympic gold with all six puts ahead of the runner-up's best. **Kathrin Neimke** was that silver medallist and also won the GDR title, and **Li Meisu** took the bronze, the first athletics medal won by a Chinese woman. She had earlier improved her Asian record to 21.76. Following at Seoul were the GDR 2–3 **Ines Müller** and **Heike Hartwig**, split by the European Indoor champion **Claudia Losch**, who was as usual the top Western shot putter.

DISCUS

The GDR had the problem of whom to select for Seoul. **Martina Hellmann**, already with two world titles to her credit, duly took the gold and **Diana Gansky** the silver, but **Gabrielle Reinsch**, who had upped the world record to 76.80 in July, failed to make it a clean sweep and placed seventh. Missing out on selection was **Ilke Wyludda**, once again the World Junior athlete of the year. Hellmann only won one of her other five competitions, Gansky won 3/10, and Reinsch who had the best win-loss record, won 8/12, headed Hellmann 3–1, Wyludda 4–1 and Gansky 5–3, but the latter also won the GDR title with Reinsch second.

Daniela Costian was regularly over 70m in the first half of the season, winning 10/11, but having won the Balkan title from **Tsvetanka Khristova**, later the Olympic bronze medallist, she sought political asylum in Turkey, and this was granted two months later.

JAVELIN

Petra Felke was out on her own in 1988. She won all 17 competitions, with an average winning throw of 75.06. In eight competitions she threw over 75m, and ducked below 71.60 just once, with 69.00 at the Peugeot Games. **Tiina**

Lillak threw 73.30, but that was her only time over 69m, and she failed to qualify for the Olympic final, as did the woman with the next best throw, **Tessa Sanderson**. The latter was most unfortunate to be injured then, for she had started the year with two wins over **Fatima Whitbread** and then threw her year's best of 71.70. Her first injury problem then struck and she only managed 60.98 for third at the IAC meet, but it looked as if she was ready for Seoul with 69.06 behind Whitbread at the end of August. However a foot injury ended her hopes, while Whitbread, who had two months away from competition in mid-season due to a back operation and glandular fever, worked her way back to an overall record of 7/11 and the Olympic silver. There were two others over 70m: the Cuban Ivonne Leal tailed off towards the end of a long season, but **Silke Renk** threw 71.00m at the GDR Champs behind Felke and ahead of **Beate Koch**. However the latter took the Olympic bronze, with Soviet champion Irina Kostyuchenkova, Renk and Natalya Yermolovich following.

The barrier breakers at women's javelin – the first to reach:

40m: Mildred Didrikson (USA) 40.62m Dallas 4 Jul 1930
50m: Klavdiya Mayuchaya (USSR) 50.32m Moscow 23 Sep 1947
60m: Elvira Ozolina (USSR) 61.38m Kiev 27 Aug 1964
70m: Tatyana Biryulina (USSR) 70.08m Moscow 12 Jul 1980
80m: Petra Felke (GDR) 80.00m Potsdam 9 Sep 1988

HEPTATHLON

Two competitions and two world records for **Jackie Joyner-Kersee**, who was once again was a class apart. At Indianapolis she totalled 7215 and at Seoul 7291, as during the year she also set two US records at 100m hurdles, was unbeaten and Olympic champion at long jump, was 11th fastest in the world at 200m and set new pbs at high jump and 800 metres, the latter to seal her Olympic gold.

Sabine John (formerly Paetz) returned to take the Olympic silver from her GDR teammate **Anke Behmer** with 6897 and 6858 points respectively, more than 150 points more anyone else achieved during the year. Paetz won her other heptathlon with 6659 points and Behmer won the two big international events, at Götzis and at Talence. On both occasions **Chantal Beaugeant** was second, but she fell in the hurdles at the Olympics to stagger home in 16.76. So her chance was gone and she gave up after three events. Following at Götzis were Iris Schulz and Heike Tischler, who in reverse order were 1–2 in the GDR Champs, with Jane Flemming fifth. The latter was again fifth at Talence as third went to Sibylle Thiele and fourth Natalya Shubenkova. At Seoul Shubenkova was fourth, Remigia Sablovskaite, who had beaten Shubenkova for the USSR title, fifth, Schulz sixth and Flemming seventh.

WALKS

There was little international focus for women's walking in 1988, as they had neither an Olympic event nor a world-wide championship, except at junior level as **Maria Cruz Diaz**, already well established in world class, won the world junior 5000m title. Her compatriot **Maria Reyes Sobrino** won the European Indoor 3000m title from Dana Vavřačová and Cruz Diaz, but all were beaten outdoors at both 5km and 10km on the road by the top woman walker of 1988, **Kerry Saxby**. In Australia Saxby improved the world track record twice for 5000m and once for 3000m, and at 10km clocked astonishing times, 42:14.2 on the track, but that was in a mixed race and therefore ineligible for world record ratification, and later 41:30 on the road. At Varnamo she walked 20km in 1:29:40, three minutes faster than her previous women's word best. Claiming the world track record was **Yelena Nikolayeva** with 43:36.5 to win the Softeland Grand Prix from Natalya Spirodonova, and 43:36.41 for the Soviet title from Nadezhda Ryashkina as Spiridonova was disqualified. Spiridonova and Ryashkina had been 1–2 at the Znamenskiy meeting. Nikolayeva also set two European track records at 5000m.

JUNIOR ATHLETES OF 1988

BY PETER MATTHEWS

There can be little doubt as to the identity of the junior athlete of the year for 1988. For most of the world's juniors the major target for the year was the World Junior Championships in Sudbury. One man, however, gave that event a miss, and his confidence was well justified as he ended a great season with two Olympic gold medals.

Steve Lewis

Born in Los Angeles on 16 May 1969, Steve Lewis first came to national prominence in 1986, when at American HS, Fremont, California he ran the 400m in 46.50. That ranked him second in the US High School lists, but way behind the prodigious William Reed who ran 45.4. In 1987 Lewis won the California HS title in 46.7, and then improved his best to 45.76 in the TAC junior championships, but that was behind Reed's 45.17. With those times Reed and Lewis ranked first and second amongst world juniors, and Reed in particular, with two years left of junior eligibility, seemed poised for greatness. However while he dropped out of sight in 1988, Lewis stormed through.

Steve Lewis, two Olympic gold medals and the title of world junior athlete of 1988 (George Herringshaw/ASP)

He joined the highly talented squad at UCLA under coach John Smith, who had run 440y in 44.5 to take the 1971 AAU title. With teammates such as Danny Everett, Henry Thomas and Kevin Young, Lewis had to excel just to make the team, and together these men became, at the NCAAs, the first collegiate squad to break 3 minutes for the 4 x 400m relay.

Lewis made his outdoor debut in 1988 for UCLA v California in Los Angeles on 26 March. He ran the 400m in 45.68, a personal best, and he pressed Danny Everett hard, the latter winning in 45.65. Everett went on to beat him in eight successive encounters during the year, including their 1-2 at the NCAA Championships, but Lewis improved fast, and right at the end of the year beat both his teammate and Butch Reynolds for the first time – and what a time to emerge from their shadow, in the Olympic final!

After that early start Lewis did not run another individual 400m until May, but then he ran 44.96 in the heats and 44.65 in the final of the Pac-10, behind Everett's 44.34. The final time was the first of five world junior records that he was to run during the year, as he equalled that mark in his first European race at Lausanne, then ran 44.61 in the heats and 44.11 in the semis of the US Trials, when he qualified with third place in the final at 44.37. Finally he broke through to 43.87 to take the gold medal in Seoul. By the end of the year he had run the nine fastest 400m times ever by juniors.

By winning that gold medal Lewis joined a small élite, for only seven men have won an individual Olympic gold medal while still a junior:

Year	*Name, event, age (years-days)*
1904	Ralph Rose (USA), shot, 19-168
1908	Reggie Walker (RSA), 100m, 19-129
1920	Ugo Frigerio (Ita), 10km walk, 18-337
1924	Lee Barnes (USA), pole vault, 17-360
1948	Bob Mathias (USA), decathlon, 17-263
1972	Randy Williams (USA), long jump, 19-18
1988	Steve Lewis (USA), 400m, 19-135

The best junior men in 1988

At the 100 metres two outstanding juniors took gold and silver in the World Junior Championships. The winner in 10.22 was **Andre Cason**, who ran the year's fastest time of 10.08, just 0.01 off the WJR, to win the TAC junior title by three metres. **Sven Matthes** shone indoors at 60 metres with a GDR record 6.53 and won his national title, before fourth in the European Indoors. Outdoors at 100 metres he set European Junior records at 10.18 and 10.14, but was beaten by Cason as he ran 10.28 in Sudbury.

The world junior 400m champion was **Tomasz Jedrusik**, and while overshadowed by Lewis, he ran 45.27, the second best ever by a European junior, won the Polish title and was a quarter-finalist in Seoul. Fourth behind him in Sudbury was Mark Richardson, just three days after his 16th birthday, so with three more years of junior eligibility.

The outstanding feat of being the first junior ever to retain the world junior cross-country title by **Wilfred Oanda Kirochi** was matched when he retained his track title at 1500 metres. He headed the world junior lists at 800m and 1500m, and with fourth place in both the Kenyan championships and trials at 1500m was close to making their Olympic team.

Although we do not know their exact dates of birth three men bettered the previous world junior record of 28:29.32 for 10000 metres in 1988. Having taken gold at 10000m and bronze

Vladimir Ovchinnikov (Mark Shearman)

at 5000m in Sudbury, **Addis Abebe** smashed the record with 27:50.24 in Brussels, just five days after improving that for 5000m to 13:23.27 in Hengelo. Runner-up to Abebe in Sudbury was his Ethiopian compatriot **Bedelu Kibret**, who ran 28:12.78 in Brussels. The record had been broken earlier in the year by the Moroccan **Mohamed Choumassi** at 28:25.77; he took the silver in Sudbury behind Henry Kirui, who maintained the Kenyan tradition.

In the field the world junior record was improved three times in the javelin and equalled at the pole vault. In the former event **Steve Backley** achieved 79.50 when he won the UK title in June, but he had to settle for silver in Sudbury behind **Vladimir Ovchinnikov**, who improved to 80.18 in Vilnius and 80.26 in the qualifying round in Seoul, where he finished a creditable seventh in the final as a late addition to the Soviet Olympic team. The world junior pole vault champion was Istvan Bagyula, as his 5.65 matched the record. He needed that height as Maxim Tarasov cleared 5.60 in Sudbury, a height also achieved earlier in the year by the bronze medallist Andrey Grudinin.

The man with the greatest margin of superiority in the field over his contemporaries was long jumper Luis Bueno. He won the world title with 7.99 and had bests of 8.28 and 8.25 for second on the all-time list at the event.

The best junior women athletes of 1988

Once again, as in 1986 and 1987 it is **Ilke Wyludda** who is my nomination as junior woman athlete of the year. Just as in 1987 she was in titanic form, and unapproachable by other juniors. She took her tally of world junior records to 14, adding 20.23 for the shot in her only competition of the year at that event, when she won the GDR junior title, and the following at the discus: 71.88 (unofficial), 70.80, 71.54, 71.98, 72.24, 72.70 and 74.40. She would surely have been a contender for an Olympic medal, but she did not quite make the GDR team. Hellmann and Gansky, who took gold and silver, just as they had in the World Championships, were the two selections, and Wyludda contested the third spot with the world record holder, Gabriele Reinsch. The latter got the verdict but apparently both threw over the world record in a test competition.

The regulations changed in 1988 and junior women were those 19 and under in the year rather than 18 and under. So there was an extra year for the top stars of 1987. The IAAF determined not to make the ruling retrospective, so world junior records could be set which were not as good as those recorded in the past by women in this new age range. Thus for instance in the high jump there were new WJRs by **Yelena Yeleshina** at 1.97 and by **Galina Astafei** at 1.97, 1.98 and 2.00, but the all-time list is headed by Olga Turchak at 2.01 and Stefka Kostadinova jumped 2.00 in 1984 at age 19. Astafei's 2.00 came in Sudbury, with Yelesina second at 1.96, and she was later fifth equal in Seoul.

The one junior woman to share in Olympic glory was **Grit Breuer**, for she ran the first leg for the GDR team in the heats of the 4 x 400m relay in Seoul. The GDR went on to get the silver medal. Breuer won three gold medals in Sudbury, at 400 metres and with both relay teams, making her the first triple world junior gold medallist. Both those relay squads set new official world junior records. Breuer (born 16 Feb 1972) will be eligible for the next World Juniors and the next two European Juniors! She ranked second at both 400m, behind Sudbury silver medallist Maicel Malone, and at 200m amongst world juniors in 1988.

Leading both sprints, and in record times, was **Kathrin Krabbe**. She won golds at 200m and sprint relay in Sudbury, and her 100m best of 10.89 was only 0.01 off the 11-year-old age best of Marlies Oelsner, now Göhr. However she was beaten at 100m in Sudbury by teammate **Diana Dietz**, who also took silver at 200m, but thus missed repeating her triple gold of the European Juniors of 1987.

The best of the distance runners was **Birte Bruhns**, who won the world junior 800m title at the age of 17, and was the one junior to better two minutes.

Other notable champions in Sudbury included **Aliuska Lopez**, who did not match her 12.84 WJR of 1987 but took the Cuban title and was a clear winner at 100mh, **Fiona May** at long jump, who went on to sixth place in Seoul, and **Svetla Dimitrova**, 187 points clear in the heptathlon and Olympics 12th placer. **Maria Cruz Diaz** became world junior champion at 5km walk to seal her junior career. She had been a European junior gold medallist back in 1985, and of course European senior champion in 1986.

WJR = World Junior Record

CROSS-COUNTRY – NATIONAL CHAMPIONS 1988

Country	Men	Women
Algeria	Abbès Tehami	Mébarka Hadj Abdellah
Australia	Rob de Castella	Jenny Lund
Austria	Gerhard Hartmann	Marion Feigl
Belgium	Vincent Rousseau	Veronique Collard
Bulgaria	Evgenie Ignatov	Radka Naplatanova
Canada (trials)	Paul McCloy	Brenda Shackleton
Czechoslovakia	Luboš Gaisl	Mária Starovská
Denmark	Henrik Jørgensen	Gitte Karlshøj
England	David Clarke	Helen Titterington
Ethiopia	Abebe Mekonnen	Tigest Morada
Finland	Matti Valkonen	Tuija Jousimaa
France	Paul Arpin	Annette Sergent
GDR	Rainer Wachenbrunner	Kristina Garlipp
F.R.Germany	Christoph Herle	Antje Winkelmann
Hungary	Zoltán Kadlót	Helén Barocsi
Iceland	Már Hermansson	Rosa Vesteinsdóttir
Ireland	David Taylor	Catherine Rooney
Italy	Francesco Panetta	Maria Curatolo
Japan	Andrew Lloyd (Aus)	Caroline Schuwalow (Aus)
Kenya	Paul Kipkoech	Jane Ngotho
Netherlands	Tonny Dirks	Christien Toonstra
New Zealand	John Campbell	Lesley Morton
Northern Ireland	Deon McNeilly	Dawn Hargan
Norway	Geir Kvernmo	Grete Kirkeberg
Poland	Boguslaw Psujek	Malgorzata Birbach
Portugal	Ezequiel Canario	Albertina Machado
Romania	Ilie Elena	Iulia Negura
Scotland	Neil Tennant	Sandra Branney
South Africa	Matthews Temane	Elana Van Zyl
Spain	Constantino Esparcia	Ana Alonso
Switzerland	Arnold Mächler	Cornelia Bürki
UK Trials	Eamonn Martin	Angela Tooby
USA (Nov)	Pat Porter	Lynn Jennings
USSR	Yevgeniy Sherebin	Marina Rodchenkova
Wales	Neil Adams	Melissa Watson
Yugoslavia	Mladen Krsek	Silva Rozic
World Students	José Serrano (Spa)	Viorica Ghican (Rom)
European Clubs Cup	Francesco Panetta (Ita)	Angela Tooby (Wal)
–Team	Pro Patria Freedent (Ita)	Sporting Braga (Por)
NCAA (Nov)	Robert Kennedy (USA)	Michelle Dekkers (RSA)

Where countries have national championships over more than one distance the winners of the event over c.10–12 km for men, or 5–8km for women are listed.

Classic races:

Five Mills, Milan	Paul Kipkoech (Ken)	Annette Sergent (Fra)
San Sebastian	John Ngugi (Ken)	Angelina Rodriguez (Spa)
Hannut	Vincent Rousseau (Bel)	
L'Equipe, Paris	José Regalo (Pol)	Ingrid Kristiansen (Nor)
Lidingö Loppet	30km: Tommy Ekblom (Fin)	15km: Grete Waitz (Nor)
EEC Cup	Roger Hackney (UK)	Nicola Morris (UK)
Bolbec	José Regalo (Por)	Albertina Dias (Por)
Vanves	Tim Hutchings (UK)	Jill Hunter (UK)
Figaro (Dec)	Tim Hutchings (UK)	Ann Mwangi (Ken)
IAC, Cardiff (Dec)	Steve Tunstall (UK)	Jull Hunter (UK)

WORLD CROSS-COUNTRY CHAMPIONSHIPS 1989

See Athletics '88/9 page 567 for the first 20 places in senior men's and women's events. In the junior men's race the second finisher Cosmas Ndeti was subsequently disqualified as his use of the drug pseudoephedrine was traced, thus Alfonce Muindi moved up to second and Bedelu Kibret (Eth) to third.

Steve Tunstall (2) won three major cross-country races in December 1988 – January 1989. He was third European at 14th in the 1988 World Championships when he ran for France at the end of a five-year spell in the French Foreign Legion. He has now returned to British citizenship. Number 3 is David Lewis (Mark Shearman)

1988 MARATHON REVIEW

BY DAVID MARTIN

As with other track and field events, top-level marathon runners worldwide placed a primary emphasis on the best possible preparation scenario for earning a berth on their nation's Olympic team. In some nations, such as the USA and the Soviet Union, a specific closed trials race was held, at Tallinn for Soviet men and women in June, and at Jersey City (April – men) and Pittsburgh (May – women) for the Americans. For other nations, athlete pre-selection by committee, on the basis of past performances, allowed them the freedom to plan their training and racing for a peak performance in Seoul without the interference of a trials race. Still other nations used either major open races, such as Houston and London, or regional championships such as the European Cup at Huy (BEL), for athlete selection. Discussion continues to reign among coaches, athletes, and race directors as to the best format for Olympic marathon team selection. So often, nuances of past fitness, recovery from injury, present training effectiveness (often determined by weather), and mental preparation add an important element of individuality to such selection.

Some of the early marathons of 1988 gave indication of the quality that could be expected at the Olympic Games. Lisa Martin's 2:23:51 at Osaka in January was a world best for a women-only, out-and-back race, with Japan's Misako Miyahara setting a national record 5:46 behind in second place (2:29:37). Four men under 2:09:00 – and within 16 sec of each other – at Tokyo in February – gave a clear signal that competitive tension could be electric when a sizable number of top-level runners found themselves in one race. And these at Tokyo were well-established experts: Mekonnen of Ethiopia (2:08:33), Ikangaa of Tanzania (2:08:43), the GDR's Jörg Peter with a national record 2:08:47, and Australian Rob de Castella's 2:08:49.

The weekend of 16–18 April was most significant during the pre-Olympic months of 1988, with major races at London, Boston, and Rotterdam. London was an important selection race for the British team, but perhaps best known for the last marathon race of Ingrid Kristiansen before she focused her training upon the inaugural women's Olympic 10,000 metre event. Her 2:25:41 victory, 4:57 ahead of a fine field, gave her 6 of the fastest 18 women's performances in history. The next day in Boston, Rosa Mota's 4:56 victory (2:24:30) over another excellent field left no doubt that she would challenge seriously in Seoul. Also at Boston, an interesting match-up between Kenyan and Tanzanian distance runners for Olympic team selection gave them a one-two finish in the race, Kenyan Ibrahim Hussein darting in front of Tanzanian Juma Ikangaa in the final few metres for a one second victory with 2:08:43. Hussein's race was a national record for Kenya; similar new marks were recorded by third place John Treacy (IRL) with 2:09:15 and Italian Gelindo Bordin in fourth 2:09:27).

Ethiopia was one of only a handful of NOCs who opted not to permit their athletes the privilege of an Olympic experience, and stayed home. At Rotterdam, their male marathoners had their spot in the sun, with Belayneh Dinsamo, Wodajo Bulti, and Abebe Mekonnen finishing 1, 3 and 4, respectively. Only Djiboutian Ahmed Salah split the group, showing his Olympic readiness. Densimo's 2:06:50 was a new world best, achieved with 5km splits of 15:05, 30:05, 45:06, 1:00:12, 1:15:12, 1:30:13, 1:45:22, and 2:00:19. The half-way split was 1:03:22, showing his remarkably steady pace, which physiologically is the most efficient strategy for optimum performance. Bulti's 2:08:44 was a new debut best effort.

As in Los Angeles, the Seoul Olympic marathons bracketed the time frame designated for athletics. On the first day, the women ran under a morning sun with mild temperatures, but the men were relegated on the final day to a considerably warmer sunny afternoon. Both races were wonderfully competitive throughout. Rosa Mota added an Olympic gold to her similar Rome World Championships victory, with Lisa Martin only 15 sec behind. European

Cup champion Katrin Dörre captured the bronze. Gelindo Bordin ran a strong second half, passing Rome World Champion Douglas Wakiihuri (KEN) in the closing stages to take the gold medal. Djiboutian Ahmed Salah earned the bronze, holding his lead over Japanese stars Takeyuki Nakayama and Toshihiko Seko who, unaccustomed to the warm-weather racing, were relegated to 4th and 9th, respectively.

Following the Games, top-level marathon racing continued to make headlines. Grete Waitz, sidelined by injury after an outstanding 2:28:24 on a hilly course in a chilly rain at Stockholm in June, won her ninth New York City marathon (2:28:07) – her 13th victory in 14 completed events. In that race, Los Angeles gold medallist Joan Benoit-Samuelson placed a creditable third in her return to top-level competition after an extended break that included starting a family. At Chicago the week prior, the Mexican national record fell as unheralded Alejandro Cruz stunned his adversaries with 2:08:57, 23 sec ahead of a new Soviet record 2:09:20 by Yakov Tolstikov.

Just as road-racing at the shorter distances continues to gain in popularity, so also is this true for the marathon. During 1988 140 marathons world-wide had performances by men faster than 2:20:00 (nearly 950 total performances). Among the women, 185 marathons had performances faster than 2:55:00 (1150 performances in all). The big races continue to grow, and although some races cease operation (primarily due to insufficient sponsorship funds), others start up or begin again, revitalized with an infusion of financial support. The sheer delight of intense competition at the top is now accompanied by ever greater prize money purses and merchandise as an enhancement toward entry. This increases the quality of performance at the highest levels. For the men, 75 nations now have national records faster than 2:20:00; 61 nations have women running faster than 2:55:00.

There still is an increasing interest among health and fitness devotees who love the challenge of endurance running. The New York City marathon achieved a new record of 22,405 finishers (95% of its 23,463 starters). At London, 20,889 completed the race, the fourth such year of 20,000+ finishers. At West Berlin, another record – 13,156 finishers – put it very near the top in total participants. The combination of large population center, flat course, cool weather, good organization, and aggressive sponsorship marketing are essential for the long-term success of such races. The successful co-existence of both aspects of the sport – élite-level and participant-oriented – if carefully nutured by race directors worldwide, will ensure the popularity of this event in years to come.

IMPORTANT WORLD MARATHONS - RESULTS DIARY 1988

DATE	*VENUE*	*MEN'S WINNER*	*TIME*	*WOMEN'S WINNER*	*TIME*
17 Jan	Houston	Geir Kvernmo (NOR)	2:11:44	Linda Zeman (USA)	2:34:52
17 Jan	Marrakesh	Thomas Hughes (IRL)	2:15:48	Carolyn Naisby (UK)	2:41:35
31 Jan	Osaka	Women only		Lisa Martin (AUS)	2:23:51
6 Feb	Las Vegas	Brad Ingram (USA)	2:16:55	Maire Rollins (IRL)	2:37:55
7 Feb	Beppu	Bruno Lafranchi (SWZ)	2:11:58	Men only	
7 Feb	Hamilton NZL	Peter Lyrenmann (SWZ)	2:19:30	Cathy Schiro (USA)	2:40:18
7 Feb	Valencia	Alfonso Abellan (SPA)	2:14:42	Maria Luisa Irizar (SPA)	2:41:03
14 Feb	Manila	Johan Geirnaert (BEL)	2:25:22	Maria Alda Manzone (ITA)	2:48:49
4 Feb	Tokyo	Abebe Mekonnen (ETH)	2:08:33	Men only	
20 Feb	Miami	Dennis Rinde (USA)	2:23:19	Maureen Hurst (UK)	2:50:32
27 Feb	Kaapstad	Thompson Magawana (RSA)	2:14:45	Monica Drogemoller (RSA)	2:45:14
6 Mar	Los Angeles	Martin Mondragon (MEX)	2:10:19	Jaime Blanca (MEX)	2:36:11
6 Mar	Nagoya	Women only		Zhao Youfeng (CHN)	2:27:56
6 Mar	Sevilla	Pavel Klimes (UK)	2:12:59		
6 Mar	Taipei	Akio Tokoro (JPN)	2:18:03	Kathy Matson (USA)	2:49:25
10 Mar	Tel Aviv	Jean-Claude Louison (FRA)	2:22:21	Adriana Andreescu (RUM)	2:44:03
12 Mar	Arusha	John Burra (TAN)	2:09:30	Susana Mkuki (TAN)	3:15:32
13 Mar	Barcelona	Fernando Diaz Perez (SPA)	2:19:58	Deborah Heath (UK)	2:45:35
13 Mar	Otsu	Toshihiko Seko (JAP)	2:12:41	Men only	
19 Mar	Agrinio	Georgios Afordakos (GRE)	2:17:08	Maria Polunou (GRE)	2:44:49
20 Mar	Seoul	Kim Won-tak (KOR)	2:12:41	Lee Mi-ok (SKO)	2:33:14
26 Mar	Szeged	Karel David (CS)	2:15:26	Karolina Szabó (HUN)	2:30:57
27 Mar	Debno	Wiktor Sawicki (POL)	2:12:26	Wanda Panfil (POL)	2:32:23
9 Apr	Maassluis	Cornelius Saelmans (BEL)	2:13:12	Ilona Janko (HUN)	2:42:16
10 Apr	Canberra	Gerard Barrett (AUS)	2:15:07	Annette McNeill (AUS)	2:48:18
10 Apr	Wien	Miroslav Vindis (YUG)	2:17:45	Glynis Penny (UK)	2:36:49
17 Apr	London	Henrik Jørgensen (DEN)	2:10:20	Ingrid Kristiansen (NOR)	2:25:41
17 Apr	Marseille	Patrick Clabaut (FRA)	2:14:32	Enikö Fehér (HUN)	2:45:38
17 Apr	Rotterdam	Belayneh Dinsamo (ETH)	2:06:50	Hong-Yan Xiao (CHN)	2:37:46
17 Apr	Uzhgorod	Igor Braslavskiy (SU)	2:13:31	Alevtina Chasova	2:29:49
18 Apr	Boston	Ibrahim Hussein (KEN)	2:08:43	Rosa Mota (POR)	2:24:30
24 Apr	Budapest	Radames Tamayo (CUB)	2:15:28	Agota Farkas (HUN)	2:42:56
24 Apr	Hamburg	Martin Vrabel (CS)	2:14:55	Charlotte Teske (FRG)	2:30:23
24 Apr	Jersey City	Mark Conover (USA)	2:12:26	USA Olympic Trial for Men	
24 Apr	Madrid	Juan Garcia (SPA)	2:14:32	Czeslawa Mentlewicz (POL)	2:37:19
24 Apr	Wexford	John Woods (IRL)	2:11:28	Maire Murphy-Rollins (IRL)	2:40:48
24 Apr	Zürich	Manuel de Oliveira (POR)	2:15:34	Luzia Sahli (SWZ)	2:34:36
25 Apr	Roma	Sam Ngatia (KEN)	2:16:46	Fabiola Paolette (ITA)	2:48:45
30 Apr	Huy	Ravil Kashapov (SU)	2:11:30	Katrin Dörre (GDR)	2:28:28
1 May	Kaapstad	Willie Mtolo (RSA)	2:11:18	Annette Falkson (RSA)	2:33:39
1 May	Long Beach	Noek Sagala (INA)	2:21:37	Dianne Ridger (NZ)	2:44:52
1 May	Pittsburgh	USA Olympic Trial for men		Margaret Groos (USA)	2:29:50
8 May	Amsterdam	Gerard Nijboer (HOL)	2:12:38	Elena Murgoci (RUM)	2:41:56
8 May	Bologna	Giuseppe Denti (ITA)	2:17:55	Maria Curatolo (ITA)	2:33:48
8 May	München	Ernest Tjela (LES)	2:12:55	Janette Mayal (BRA)	2:42:34
15 May	Paris	Manuel Matias (POR)	2:13:53	Aurora Cunha (POR)	2:34:55
15 May	Wroclaw	Henryk Wiesik (POL)	2:33:51	Anna Krol (POL)	2:52:29
4 Jun	Stockholm	Suleiman Nyambui (TAN)	2:14:26	Grete Waitz (NOR)	2:28:24
5 Jun	Kotka	Vesa Kahkola (FIN)	2:18:58	Sirpa Kytölä (FIN)	2:48:08
11 Jun	Duluth	Armando Azocar (VEN)	2:20:07	Jacqueline Gareau (CAN)	2:43:27
12 Jun	Koge	Jens Woerzner (DEN)	2:21:04	Joan Carstensen (DEN)	2:53:33
26 Jun	Rio de Janeiro	Valmir Carvalho (BRA)	2:17:10	Angelica de Almeida (BRA)	2:37:38
26 Jun	Tallinn	Yakov Tolstikov (SU)	2:14:29	Tatyana Polovinskaya (SU)	2:28:02
9 Jul	Nove Mesto	Michael Heilmann (GDR)	2:11:34	Uta Pippig (GDR)	2:36:58
24 Jul	Surfers Paradise	Patrick Carroll (AUS)	2:10:44	Ngaire Drake (AUS)	2:39:25
7 Aug	Jakarta	Naek Nagala (INA)	2:26:01	Maria Lawalata (INA)	2:57:12
13 Aug	Helsinki	Douglas Orr (CAN)	2:16:43	Ritva Lemettinen (FIN)	2:42:35
14 Aug	Adelaide	John Duck (AUS)	2:27:42	Mollie Whitehorn (AUS)	2:59:14
21 Aug	Reykjavík	Borut Podgornik (YUG)	2:27:27	Connie Eriksen (DEN)	3:00:54
31 Aug	Annaba	Dereje Nedi (ETH)	2:27:51	Men only	
3 Sep	Lille	Helmuth Stuhlpfarrer (AUT)	2:13:08	Fabiola Rueda (COL)	2:42:25
3 Sep	Oslo	Øyvind Trongmo (NOR)	2:22:30	Cassandra Mihailovic (FRA)	2:42:39

4 Sep	Berlin (East)	Heiko Klimmer (GDR)	2:18:46	Marya Lantsova (SU)	2:43:29
4 Sep	Sapporo	Masayuki Nishi (JAP)	2:17:11	Jane Welzel (USA)	2:40:53
4 Sep	Montreal	Richard Sayre (USA)	2:18:07	Cindy New (CAN)	2:44:37
11 Sep	Bremen	Agapius Masong (TAN)	2:17:18	Angelika Dunke (FRG)	2:39:48
23 Sep	Seoul	Olympic Marathon for women		Rosa Mota (POR)	2:25:40
25 Sep	Portland OR	Yoshihiro Nishimura (JAP)	2:22:43	Elizabeth Brim (USA)	2:47:27
25 Sep	Toronto	Isamu Sennai (JAP)	2:16:05	Susan Stone (CAN)	2:40:39
25 Sep	Warszawa	Pawel Tarasiuk (POL)	2:17:37	Stefania Kozik (POL)	2:55:34
2 Oct	St. Paul	Daniel Boltz (AUS)	2:14:10	Ria van Landeghem (BEL)	2:28:11
2 Oct	Seoul	Gelindo Bordin (ITA)	2:10:32	Olympic Marathon for men	
7 Oct	Belaja Cerkov	Sergey Yanenko (SU)	2:15:13	Vera Sukhova (SU)	2:30:09
9 Oct	Berlin (West)	Suleiman Nyambui (TAN)	2:11:45	Renata Kokowska (POL)	2:29:16
9 Oct	Penang	Douglas Kurtis (USA)	2:29:40	Satsuko Hanafusa (JAP)	3:10:24
9 Oct	Melbourne	Thomas Hughes (IRL)	2:18:44	Coral Farr (AUS)	2:47:38
16 Oct	Basel	Jakob Marti (SWZ)	2:19:50	Helen Comsa (SWZ)	2:39:20
16 Oct	Beijing	Abebe Mekonnen (ETH)	2:07:35	Men only	
16 Oct	Eisenhüttenstadt	Rainer Wachenbrunner (GDR)	2:17:19	Andrea Fleischer (GDR)	2:49:51
16 Oct	Venezia	Orlando Pizzolato (ITA)	2:15:24	Graziella Striuli (ITA)	2:39:04
30 Oct	Chicago	Alejandro Cruz (MEX)	2:08:57	Lisa Weidenbach (USA)	2:29:17
30 Oct	Frankfurt	Jos Sasse (HOL)	2:13:16	Grete Kirkeberg (NOR)	2:35:44
31 Oct	Dublin	John Griffin (IRL)	2:16:02	Moira O'Neill (UK)	2:37:06
6 Nov	New York	Stephen Jones (UK)	2:08:20	Grete Waitz (NOR)	2:28:07
6 Nov	Washington	James Hage (USA)	2:21:58	Lori Lawson (USA)	2:51:26
13 Nov	Columbus	Mark Plaatjes (RSA)	2:12:17	Julie Isphording (USA)	2:31:09
20 Nov	Tokyo	Women only		Aurora Cunha (POR)	2:31:26
30 Nov	Tiberias	Patrick Joannes (FRA)	2:18:08	Maija Vuorinen (FIN)	2:40:01
3 Dec	Fukuoka	Toshihiro Shibutani (JAP)	2:11:04	Men only	
4 Dec	Sacramento	Richard McCandless (USA)	2:12:45	Janis Klecker (USA)	2:34:18
6 Dec	Bridgetown	Reuben McCollin (BAR)	2:29:40	Laura Konantz (CAN)	2:44:40
11 Dec	Honolulu	Gianni Poli (ITA)	2:12:47	Cyndie Welte (USA)	2:41:52
11 Dec	Singapore	Hans Pfisterer (FRG)	2:22:49	Li Yemei (CHN)	2:46:04

1988 Road Race Review
Events to Half-Marathon

BY ROGER GYNN

The Mexican men were not as dominant as in 1987, even though Arturo Barrios achieved another five wins, including the Gold Coast (Aus) 15k (44:31) and the Nara (Jap) half-marathon (62:03). He lost once (to Matthews Motshawaretu in New Orleans) and his road record for the three years since 1986 now reads 19 wins to three defeats. Colleagues Marcus Barreto, Mauricio Gonzalez and Alejandro Cruz each had a major win. Apart from Motshawaretu, the only other athletes under 28:00 for 10km were John Ngugi and Paul Kipkoech, who finished 1–2 at Bali, thus duplicating their positions at the previous week's World cross country race.

After being runner-up to Barrios in Nara, John Treacy finished a distant third in Bali, but then won the Portland 15k, the Newcastle (Great North Run) half-marathon and Baltimore 10k to offset early season losses. Steve Jones returned to form later in the year after finishing second to Treacy in Newcastle, winning the Providence and Bowling Green 10k races plus the Philadelphia half-marathon. Probably the most consistent American was Jon Sinclair, who, after a slow start, began to roll in the autumn, winning the Fair Lakes 10k, Lynchburg 10M and Tulsa 15k, before losing to John Gregorek at Raleigh. Gregorek had earlier won the New York City 10M and was one of several runners who picked up at least a pair of good wins, another being Mark Curp who also had no less than six second places to his credit.

The women were again outstanding in 1988. Liz McColgan took eight seconds off her own World 10k standard and became the first to officially better 31:00 over a certified course (30:59 at Orlando). She set a second record at the infrequently run 5k with 15:29.7 at Carlsbad, CA (27 Mar) and also won the Tampa 15k and Miami 10k before Nancy Tinari and Jill Hunter (UK) got the better of her in Bali.

Ingrid Kristiansen successfully defended her World 15k title (just *when* are the IAAF going to sanction a similar event for the men?) and on

Arturo Barrios again fared well on the roads as well as having a successful track campaign in 1988 (Mark Shearman)

her extensive travels picked up the Gold Coast 15k (50:21), Ohme (Jap) 10k (31:38) and L'Eggs (New York) 10k. Selecting her races carefully, Anne Audain scored four wins on the circuit, including taking the Washington 10M ahead of Lisa Martin (Aus), but she lost to McColgan (at Torrance) and was fifth in L'Eggs.

Although Kellie Cathey had six wins in at least 17 races, and Betty Geiger three wins, the best of the Americans was Lynn Jennings, who won at Albany, Charlotte and Jacksonville, prior to winning the Raleigh 10k in US record time (31:34). Her one defeat came at the hands of the year's outstanding road runner, newcomer Anne Hannam.

The 27 year-old Hannam (née Ross) finished third in her American debut at the Alaska 10k (June 11) but then proceeded to win nine straight races, of which seven were in course record time. In so doing she amassed some $24,000 from just five of those wins, and duly returned home to continue her winning streak, which included running the fastest third leg (32:01 for 10k) in New Zealand's winning Ekiden relay team.

Anne Hannam's road race wins 1988

Date	Venue	Event	Time	Place	Course Record
31 Jul	Anchorage	10k	32:40	(1)	CR
13 Aug	Asbury Park	10k	32:37	(1)	
21 Aug	Falmouth	7M	36:36	(1)	
4 Sep	Fort Collins	10k (A)	33:08	(1)	CR
18 Sep	Fair Lakes	10k	32:14	(1)	CR
24 Sep	Lynchburg	10M	54:40	(1)	CR
10 Oct	Boston	10k	31:38	(1)	CR
22 Oct	Bowling Green	10k	31:33	(1)	CR / NZ NR
29 Oct	Tulsa	15k	48:14	(1)	CR / NZ NR (31:47 at 10k)
13 Nov	Auckland (NZ)	10k	32:09	(1)	

CR – *Course record,* NR – *National record,* A – *Altitude*

All Time Top Ten Lists – 10,000 Metres Road

Following the 15k and Half-marathon lists which appeared in the previous two editions of this annual, there now follows a similar list for the 10k. This is one of the most popular distances run on the road, yet outside the United States and Great Britain one which is often subject to incorrect or uncertified measurement.

Time	Name	Nation	Place	Venue	Date	
27:22	Mark Nenow	USA	(1)	New Orleans	1 Apr	1984
27:29	Mike Musyoki	KEN	(2)	New Orleans	1 Apr	1984
27:29	John Ngugi	KEN	(1)	Bali	2 Apr	1988
27:31	Paul Kipkoech	KEN	(2)	Bali	2 Apr	1988
27:34	Nick Rose	UK	(3)	New Orleans	1 Apr	1984
27:41	Arturo Barrios	MEX	(1)	Phoenix	1 Mar	1986
27:43	Zacharia Barie	TAN	(1)	Phoenix	5 Mar	1984
27:46	John Treacy	IRE	(1)	Phoenix	2 Mar	1985
27:47	Peter Koech	KEN	(2)	Phoenix	1 Mar	1986
27:47	Paul McCloy	CAN	(1)	Ukiah	19 Oct	1986
WOMEN						
30:59	Liz McColgan	UK	(1)	Orlando	6 Feb	1988
31:29	Wendy Sly	UK	(1)	New Orleans	27 Mar	1983
31:31	Ingrid Kristiansen	NOR	(1)	New York	4 Jun	1988
31:33	Grete Waitz	NOR	(1)	Miami	15 Jan	1983
31:33	Anna Hannam	NZ	(1)	Bowling Green	22 Oct	1988
31:34	Lynn Jennings	USA	(1)	Raleigh	13 Nov	1988
31:35	Rosa Mota	POR	(1)	Ohme	21 Feb	1987
31:37	Joan Samuelson	USA	(1)	Boston	10 Oct	1983
31:38	Mary Decker	USA	(1)	Eugene	6 May	1984
31:38	Brenda Webb	USA	(1)	Ukiah	19 Oct	1986
Uncertified course						
30:46	Ingrid Kristiansen	NOR	(1)	København	21 Sep	1988

1988 World Lists – certified courses

Time	Name	Nation	Place	Venue	Date
MEN					
10km					
27:29	John Ngugi	KEN	(1)	Bali	2 Apr
27:31	Paul Kipkoech	KEN	(2)	Bali	2 Apr
27:54	Matthews Motshwaretu	BOT	(1)	New Orleans	16 Apr
28:04	Mauricio Gonzalez	MEX	(1)	Mobile	12 Mar
28:04	Steve Jones	UK	(1)	Bowling Green	22 Oct
28:17	Arturo Barrios	MEX	(1)	Torrance	13 Mar
28:17	Jean-Pierre N'dayisenga	BEL	(1)	Atlanta	4 Jul
28:18	Paul Davies-Hale	UK	(1)	Orlando	6 Feb
28:19	Steve Moneghetti	AUS	(1)	Sydney	28 May
28:20	Mark Curp	USA	(2)	Atlanta	4 Jul
15km					
42:37	Marcus Barreto	MEX	(1)	Tampa	13 Feb
42:47	John Treacy	IRE	(1)	Portland	26 Jun
42:56	Mauricio Gonzalez	MEX	(2)	Tampa	13 Feb
43:02	Mark Curp	USA	(2)	Portland	26 Jun
43:04	Markus Ryffel	SWZ	(3)	Tampa	13 Feb
43:06	Ed Eyestone	USA	(4)	Tampa	13 Feb
43:06	Steve Spence	USA	(3)	Portland	26 Jun
43:10	Carlos Retiz	MEX	(5)	Tampa	13 Feb
43:13	Geir Kvernmo	NOR	(4)	Portland	26 Jun
43:20	Steve Jones	UK	(5)	Portland	26 Jun
43:20	Jon Sinclair	USA	(1)	Tulsa	29 Oct
10 Miles					
46:44	Ed Eyestone	USA	(1)	Flint	27 Aug
46:50	Mark Curp	USA	(2)	Flint	27 Aug
47:20	Steve Taylor	USA	(1)	Raleigh	8 Oct
47:22	Bill Reifsnyder	USA	(2)	Raleigh	8 Oct
47:33	Jean-Pierre N'dayisenga	BEL	(1)	Washington	27 Mar
47:33	George Nicholas	USA	(3)	Raleigh	8 Oct
47:35	Martyn Brewer	UK	(2)	Washington	27 Mar
Uncertified courses					
46:49	Kazuya Wakakura	JAP	(1)	Karatsu	14 Feb
46:55	Domingos Castros	POR	(1)	Amsterdam	9 Oct
46:57	Kenji Ide	JAP	(2)	Karatsa	14 Feb
46:57	William Musyoki	KEN	(2)	Amsterdam	9 Oct
47:00	Peter Koech	KEN	(1)	Antwerp	22 May
47:00	Joaquim Pinheiro	POR	(3)	Amsterdam	9 Oct
47:00	Henrik Jørgensen	DEN	(1)	Den Haag	6 Nov
47:05	Suleiman Nyambui	TAN	(2)	Antwerp	22 May
47:09	Yobes Ondieki	KEN	(3)	Antwerp	22 May
47:09	Tonnie Dirks	UK	(2)	Den Haag	6 Nov
47:10	Colin Moore	UK	(3)	Den Haag	6 Nov
Half Marathon					
61:00	John Treacy	IRE	(1)	Newcastle	24 Jul
61:58	Steve Jones	UK	(2)	Newcastle	24 Jul
62:03	Arturo Barrios	MEX	(1)	Nara	24 Jan
62:20	Gabriel Kamau	KEN	(1)	New Bedford	20 Mar
62:20	Alejandro Cruz	MEX	(1)	Orlando	10 Dec
62:24	Mark Curp	USA	(2)	New Bedford	20 Mar
62:25	Kozo Akutsu	JAP	(3)	Nara	24 Jan
62:30	Dionisio Ceron	MEX	(2)	Philadelphia	18 Sep

The Great North Run 1988, when John Treacy (7) and Steve Jones (25) ran the two fastest half marathon times of 1988. Sharing the lead is No.4 Tony Milovsorov (Mark Shearman)

Half Marathon (continued)

62:42	Mike O'Reilly	IRE	(3)	Newcastle	24 Jul
62:42	Mark Stickley	USA	(2)	Orlando	10 Dec
Uncertified courses					
61:14	Matthews Temane	RSA	(1)	Cape Town	23 Jan
61:16	Zithulele Singe	RSA	(2)	Cape Town	23 Jan
61:20	Xolile Yawa	RSA	(3)	Cape Town	23 Jan
61:27	Simon Malibeng	RSA	(4)	Cape Town	23 Jan
62:13	Geir Kvernmo	NOR	(1)	Stockholm	27 Aug
62:13	Suleiman Nyambui	TAN	(2)	Stockholm	27 Aug
62:19	Willie Mtolo	RSA	(5)	Cape Town	23 Jan
62:20	Marti ten Kate	HOL	(1)	Den Haag	26 Mar
62:28	John Burra	TAN	(3)	Stockholm	27 Aug
62:39	Neil Tennant	UK	(1)	Lincoln	8 May
62:41	Kevin McCluskey	UK	(1)	Middlesbrough	11 Sep

Time	Name	Nation	Place	Venue	Date
WOMEN					
10km					
30:59	Liz McColgan	UK	(1)	Orlando	6 Feb
31:31	Ingrid Kristiansen	NOR	(1)	New York	4 Jun
31:33	Anne Hannam	NZ	(1)	Bowling Green	22 Oct
31:34	Lynn Jennings	USA	(1)	Raleigh	13 Nov
31:41	Sabrina Dornhoefer	USA	(2)	Bowling Green	22 Oct
32:04	Lisa Martin	AUS	(2)	New York	4 Jun
32:07	Lorraine Moller	NZ	(1)	Boston	10 Apr
32:09	Grete Waitz	NOR	(1)	Atlanta	4 Jul
32:10	Francie Larrieu-Smith	USA	(3)	New York	4 Jun
32:13	Betty Geiger	USA	(3)	Raleigh	13 Nov
32:14	Nancy Tinari	CAN	(1)	Bali	3 Apr
32:14	Lynn Nelson	USA	(1)	New Orleans	16 Apr
15km					
47:43	Liz McColgan	UK	(1)	Tampa	13 Feb
48:14	Anne Hannam	NZ	(1)	Tulsa	29 Oct
48:24	Ingrid Kristiansen	NOR	(1)	Adelaide	20 Mar
49:01	Anne Audain	NZ	(1)	Portland	26 Jun
49:06	Nancy Tinari	CAN	(2)	Tulsa	29 Oct
49:24	Wendy Sly	UK	(3)	Tampa	13 Feb
49:34	Diane Brewer	USA	(3)	Tulsa	29 Oct
49:37	Lisa Weidenbach	USA	(4)	Tampa	13 Feb
49:39	Carla Beurskens	HOL	(5)	Tampa	13 Feb
49:41	Teresa Ornduff	USA	(6)	Tampa	13 Feb
Uncertified course					
49:29	Grete Waitz	NOR	(1)	Stockholm	10 Sep
10 Miles					
53:10	Lisa Weidenbach	USA	(1)	Flint	27 Aug
53:26	Anne Audain	NZ	(1)	Washington	27 Mar
53:48	Grete Waitz	NOR	(1)	New York	16 Apr
53:54	Diane Brewer	USA	(2)	Flint	27 Aug
54:06	Lisa Martin	AUS	(2)	Washington	27 Mar
54:08	Patty Murray	USA	(1)	Park Forest	5 Sep
54:19	Nancy Ditz	USA	(3)	Washington	27 Mar
54:40	Anne Hannam	NZ	(1)	Lynchburg	24 Sep
54:44	Kim Jones	USA	(4)	Washington	27 Mar
54:45	Betty Geiger	USA	(1)	Raleigh	8 Oct
Uncertified courses					
52:32	Grete Waitz	NOR	(1)	Bern	14 May
52:52	Carla Beurskens	HOL	(1)	Den Haag	6 Nov
53:25	Susan Tooby	UK	(1)	Aylesbury	29 Aug
Half Marathon					
68:49	Grete Waitz	NOR	(1)	Newcastle	24 Jul
69:43	Lisa Martin	AUS	(1)	Brisbane	24 Jul
69:56	Susan Tooby	UK	(2)	Newcastle	24 Jul
70:40	Veronique Marot	UK	(1)	Oslo	3 Sep
70:47	Lesley Lehane	USA	(1)	Philadelphia	18 Sep
71:24	Grete Kirkeberg	NOR	(2)	Oslo	3 Sep
71:34	Kim Jones	USA	(2)	Philadelphia	18 Sep
71:37	Paula Fudge	UK	(3)	Newcastle	24 Jul
71:44	Sissel Grottenberg	NOR	(4)	Newcastle	24 Jul
71:52	Bente Moe	NOR	(5)	Newcastle	24 Jul
Uncertified course					
71:18	Evy Palm	SWE	(1)		16 Jul
71:31	Carla Beurskens	HOL	(1)	Deurne	11 Sep

United States Road Race Circuit: Major Race Winners 1988

Date	Venue	Event	Winners	Nation	Time
6 Feb	Orlando	Red Lobster 10k	Paul Davies-Hale	UK	28:18
			Liz McColgan	UK	30:59
7 Feb	Phoenix	Runners Den 10k	Bo Reed	USA	28:56
			Monica Joyce	IRE	34:03
13 Feb	Tampa	Gasparilla 15k	Marcus Barreto	MEX	42:37
			Liz McColgan	UK	47:43
21 Feb	Miami	Orange Bowl 10k	Mark Rowland	UK	28:54
			Liz McColgan	UK	32:22
5 Mar	Jacksonville	River Run 15k	Steve Spence	USA	43:20
			Lynn Jennings	USA	50:02
12 Mar	Mobile	Azalea 10k	Mauricio Gonzalez	MEX	28:04
			Teresa Ornduff	USA	32:27
13 Mar	Torrance	Tom Sullivan 10k	Arturo Barrios	MEX	28:17
			Liz McColgan	UK	31:43
20 Mar	New Bedford	NB Half marathon	Gabriel Kamau	KEN	62:20
			Cathy O'Brien	USA	72:20
27 Mar	Washington	Cherry Blossom 10M	Jean-Pierre N'dayisenga	BEL	47:33
			Anne Audain	NZ	53:26
10 Apr	Boston	Milk Run 10k	Jim Cooper	USA	28:24
			Lorraine Moller	NZ	32:07
16 Apr	New Orleans	Crescent City 10k	Matthews Motshwaratu	BOT	27:54
			Lynn Nelson	USA	32:14
16 Apr	New York	Trevira 10M	John Gregorek	USA	48:31
			Grete Waitz	NOR	53:48
1 May	Spokane	Bloomsday 12k	Peter Koech	KEN	34:22
			Anne Audaun	NZ	39:35
15 May	Cleveland	Revco 10k	Sam Ngatia	KEN	28:53
			Anne Audain	NZ	33:05
15 May	San Francisco	Bay to Breakers 12k	Arturo Barrios	MEX	34:58
			Lisa Martin	AUS	39:17
28 May	Wheeling	Elbys 20k	Rob de Castella	AUS	61:08
			Kellie Cathey	USA	72:26
29 May	Albany, NY	Freihofers 10k	women only		
			Lynn Jennings	USA	32:39
30 May	Boulder	Bolder 10k	Rolando Vera	ECU	29:53
			Rosa Mota	POR	34:41
4 Jun	New York	L'Eggs 10k	women only		
			Ingrid Kristiansen	NOR	31:31
12 Jun	Middletown, NY	Orange Classic 10k	Ibrahim Hussein	KEN	29:07
			Susan Tooby	UK	33:27
26 Jun	Portland	Cascade 15k	John Treacy	IRE	42:47
			Anne Audain	NZ	49:01
4 Jul	Atlanta	Peachtree 10k	Jean-Pierre N'dayisenga	BEL	28:17
			Grete Waitz	NOR	32:09
10 Jul	Utica	Boilermakers 15k	Joseph Kipsang	KEN	44:55
			Ria van Landeghem	BEL	52:45
30 Jul	Davenport	Bix 7M	Mark Curp	USA	33:22
			Joan Samuelson	USA	37:59
13 Aug	Asbury Park	Classic 10k	Keith Brantly	USA	29:35
			Anne Hannam	NZ	32:37
21 Aug	Falmouth	Falmouth 7M	Mark Curp	USA	32:22
			Anne Hannam	NZ	36:36
27 Aug	Waynesville	Maggie Valley 8k	Arega Abraha	ETH	23:00
			Margaret Groos	USA	26:48
27 Aug	Flint	Bobby Crim 10M	Ed Eyestone	USA	46:44
			Lisa Weidenbach	USA	53:10
5 Sep	New Haven	National Bank 20k	Bill Reifsnyder	USA	60:57
			Diane Brewer	USA	69:33

18 Sep	Philadelphia	Philly Half Marathon	Steve Jones	UK	62:17
			Lesley Lehane	USA	70:47
24 Sep	Lynchburg	Virginia 10M	Jon Sinclair	USA	48:09
			Anne Hannam	NZ	54:40
1 Oct	Davenport	Heartland 10k	Bill Rodgers	USA	29:48
			Priscilla Welch	UK	34:28
8 Oct	Raleigh	Capital Trail 10M	Steve Taylor	USA	47:20
			Betty Geiger	USA	54:45
10 Oct	Boston	Tufts 10k	women only		
			Anne Hannam	NZ	31:38
22 Oct	Bowling Green	Classic 10k	Steve Jones	UK	28:04
			Anne Hannam	NZ	31:33
23 Oct	Baltimore	Festival 10k	John Treacy	IRE	28:29
			Betty Geiger	USA	32:48
29 Oct	Tulsa	Tulsa Run 15k	Jon Sinclair	USA	43:20
			Anna Hannam	NZ	48:14
30 Oct	South End	Sportsmed 10k	Arturo Barrios	MEX	28:18
			Sabrina Dornhoefer	USA	32:03
13 Nov	Raleigh	Old Reliable 10k	John Gregorek	USA	28:23
			Lynn Jennings	USA	31:34
10 Dec	Orlando	Citrus Half Marathon	Alejandro Cruz	MEX	62:20
			Kellie Cathey	USA	72:54

Ultrarunning Review 1988

BY ANDY MILROY

1988 was a momentous year for ultrarunning, both in terms of performances, and in terms of its development as a world sport.

Notable performances came thick and fast, but perhaps the most startling mark of the year came in April in South Africa. The shorter ultra records are always vulnerable to fast marathon runners, and Thompson Magawana, a 2:10 man, emphasised this with a stunning 2:43:38 for 50km over the undulating Two Oceans course to win a R38,000 Jetta car. His time broke his previous world road best for the event by 3½ minutes!

Almost equally startling was the result of a race at the other extreme of the ultra spectrum. In May, in the International Association of Ultrarunners' 1000 mile World Championships in New York, the remarkable Greek runner, Yiannis Kouros, knocked a day off the previous best, with 10d 10h 30:35, to average over 153km a day! En route he also surpassed his 6 Day track best with 1028.37km. In the same race, Sandra Barwick of New Zealand became the first woman to run 1000 miles in under 15 days, a performance that less than a dozen men have bettered.

Barwick's performance was just one of a series of remarkable runs by women ultrarunners in 1988. In the vanguard of this upsurge in feminine standards was Hilary Walker of the UK. On a road circuit at Preston in late August she broke both the 100 miles and 200km world road bests (14:49:34 & 20:05:50) before increasing the women's absolute 24 hour best to 236.453km. Then in November at Blackpool on the track she added the world 100 mile track best to her collection with another sub-15 hour mark, en route to 366.521km in 48 hours, adding nearly 20km to the previous best! She won both the Preston and Blackpool races *outright* leaving a number of top British male ultraperformers struggling behind her! In the Blackpool race women showed just how strong they can be in a race of such length, taking first, third, fourth, sixth and seventh places. Hilary has not been alone in setting excellent 24 hour marks this year; Marianne Savage (UK) and Angela Mertens and Monika Kuno (FRG) have joined with her to produce six of the top nine marks of all time.

Eleanor Adams, the other major figure in such races, has not had a quiet year. Amid races in Australia, Trinidad and Spain she found time to fit in a new 12 hour best at Harrogate in Yorkshire.

At the 100km the situation has been similar. In two major races on successive weekends two women went under 8 hours in the same event. The first race was the toughest competition of the year, the IAAF World Cup/IAU World Championships 100km at Santander in Spain in October. Runners from over 20 countries took part, including most of the élite performers from Europe. The tough, hilly course didn't suit some runners, but Domingo Catalan, the current World Champion, revelled in the home conditions, and handled a strong challenge from Italian Normano Di Gennaro to emerge a clear winner. But, as I have said, it was the women who stole the show. American trail runner Ann Trason, ran a free, relaxed race to win, and set a new world 100km best on a course measured by calibrated bicycle of 7.30.49, with the Hungarian woman Marta Vass less than half an hour behind her.

A week later in the FRG Championships Birgit Lennartz recorded the second fastest time on such a course, and her compatriot, Iris Reuter, emphasised this new upsurge in standards with the fourth sub-8 hour clocking in a week.

Moving away from the standard events for the moment, it was very much business as usual. Kouros again won the 1000km Sydney to Melbourne race. To make the event more interesting he gave the rest of the field 12 hours start, but he was still able to cope with such a disadvantage. The Comrades was won for the *eighth* successive time by Bruce Fordyce, 5.27:42, and Frith van der Merwe set a new women's course record, 6:32:55. Rune Larsson again won the 254km Spartathlon from Athens to Sparta (24:42:05), and the former child prodigy, Mark Pickard, came back after several seasons of illness, injuries and indifferent form to win the London to Brighton.

Over the past few seasons there has been a gradual movement by National Federations towards recognising 100km national championships. In 1988 this development really began to become general with such races being a feature in the calendar of most of the leading ultra-running countries, with the likelihood that many others will follow suit in 1989. In parallel with this national recognition of ultrarunning has come developing links with the IAAF, with fruitful discussions underway with its Road Running and Cross Country Committee about the future of ultrarunning, and the place of the IAU within the IAAF structure. After the successful Santander race it was decided that the next World Cup/World Championships 100km would be held at Paris on June 18th. With the added impetus of the bicentennial celebration of the French Revolution, and the 45th anniversary of the Liberation of Paris, there should be a very memorable event!

This development in standards and official recognition of ultrarunning has been more than matched by increasing interest in the sport around the world. Japanese competitors and television crews have been a notable presence at such events as the Spartathlon and Sydney to Melbourne, and over 400 runners contested a 100km race at Hokkaido in July. There have been similar developments in places as wide-spread as Australia and New Zealand (where there are thriving ultra organisations), the Soviet Union (1300 runners in the Odessa 100km) and California in the United States, where one 100 miles trail race is so popular they have to have a lottery to decide who will run. Competition is fiercest in the heartland of the sport in Europe, where the Europa Cup now embraces most countries, enabling runners to earn points towards a yearly classification while tasting different ultrarunning cultures. If this year is anything to go by, 1989 should be quite something in the world of ultrarunning!

1988 Men's 100km Lists

hr:min:sec	Name	Nation	Born	Place	Venue	Date
A. On road courses measured by calibrated bicycle:						
6:30:41	Jean-Paul Praet	BEL	56	1	Amiens	10 Sep
6:33:40	Jan Szumiec	POL	54	1	Rodenbach	23 Apr
6:34:18	Jean-Marc Bellocq	FRA	57	2	Amiens	10 Sep
6:34:41	Domingo Catalan	SPA	48	1	Santander	1 Oct
6:38:37	Bruno Joppen	HOL	52	2	Rodenbach	23 Apr
6:39:12	Bruno Scelsi	FRA	54	3	Amiens	10 Sep
6:41:41	Heinz Hüglin	FRG	50	1	Hamm	8 Oct
6:41:50	Bellocq			2	Santander	1 Oct
6:48:18	Scelsi			3	Santander	1 Oct
6:48:46	Tomas Rusek	CS	48	4	Amiens	10 Sep
6:49:25	Christian Roig	FRA	52	5	Amiens	10 Sep
6:53:40	Herbert Cuntz	FRG	48	2	Hamm	8 Oct
6:55:56	Noel Mailly	FRA	52	6	Amiens	10 Oct
6:56:43	Rae Clark	USA	53	1	Duluth	22 Oct
6:59:15	Hans Schnyder	SWZ	51	4	Santander	1 Oct
6:59:30	Manfred Trager	FRG	49	3	Hamm	8 Oct
B. On certified road course – uncertain method						
6:53:49	Wim Akkermans	HOL	57	1	Winschoten	10 Sep
6:59:30	Szumiec			2	Winschoten	10 Sep
C. Uncertified road courses						
6:25:06	Jean-Paul Praet	BEL	56	1	St. Amand	2 Apr
6:26:46	Praet			1	Torhout	17 Jun
6:31:40	Jean-Marc Bellocq	FRA	57	1	Belves	30 Apr
6:36:02	Andrzej Lisowski	POL	61	1	Kalisz	15 Oct
6:37:10	Normano Di Gennaro	ITA	50	1	Faenza	29 May
6:40:36	Domingo Catalan	SPA	48	1	Madrid	13 Mar

6:41:09	Bellocq			2	Faenza	29 May
6:42:57	Bruno Scelsi	FRA	54	2	Torhout	17 Jun
6:45:08	Catalan			3	Torhout	17 Jun
6:48:28	Bellocq			1	Millau	24 Sep
6:50:28	Martin Daykin	UK	47	1	Chavagnes	14 Apr
6:51:29	Stefan Fekner	CAN	52	4	Torhout	17 Jun
6:52:03	Jan Szumiec	POL	54	2	Kalisz	15 Oct
6:53:29	Attila Kovacs	HUN	63	3	Faenza	29 May
6:55:37	Christian Roig	FRA	52	2	Madrid	13 Mar
6:56:03	Don Ritchie	UK	44	4	Faenza	29 May
6:57:12	Hans Schnyder	SWZ	51	1	Biel	4 Jun
6:57:42	Dutov Hribenicki	YUG		5	Faenza	29 May
6:58:37	Roland Vuillemenont	FRA	46	6	Faenza	29 May

1988 Women's 100km Lists

hr:min:sec	Name	Nation	Born	Place	Venue	Date
A. On road courses measured by calibrated bicycle:						
7:30:49	Ann Trason	USA	60	1	Santander	1 Oct
7:42:00	Birgit Lennartz	FRG	65	1	Hamm	8 Oct
7:56:07	Marta Vass	HUN	62	2	Santander	1 Oct
7:56:20	Iris Reuter	FRG	61	2	Hamm	8 Oct
8:07:38	Eleanor Adams	UK	47	3	Santander	1 Oct
8:12:32	Katharina Janicke	FRG	42	4	Santander	1 Oct
8:13:20	Sigrid Lomsky	FRG	42	3	Hamm	8 Oct
8:20:45	Marie France Plas	FRA	58	1	Amiens	10 Sep
8:27:50	Hilary Walker	UK	53	1	Preston	27 Aug
8:33:33	Anne Marie Deguilhem	FRA	43	2	Amiens	10 Sep
8:34:00	Eniko Feher	HUN	62	5	Santander	1 Oct
8:37:17	Angela Mertens	BEL	41	3	Amiens	10 Sep
8:38:00	Joaquima Casas	SPA	51	6	Santander	1 Oct
8:40:40	Liane Winter	FRG	42	4	Hamm	8 Oct
8:40:42	Mertens			6	Santander	1 Oct
8:41:21	Mausi Gantenbein	LUX	39	1	Rodenbach	23 Apr
8:43:36	Casas			1	Costa Brava	22 May
8:45:39	Walker			1	Solihull	24 Apr
8:46:05	Walker			1	Lincoln	19 Jun
8:46:20	Gisela Schneider-Endrowait	FRG	52	5	Hamm	8 Oct
8:48:56	Monika Juno	FRG	43	6	Hamm	8 Oct
B. Uncertified road courses						
8:02:50	Marta Vass	HUN	62	1	Hirtenberg	24 Jun
8:06:35	Katharina Janicke	FRG	42	1	Torhout	17 Jun
8:27:10	Angela Mertens	BEL	41	2	Torhout	17 Jun
8:30:05	Birgit Lennartz	FRG	65	1	Biel	6 Jun
8:32:11	Monique Exbrayat	FRA	45	1	Rognonas	31 Jan
8:32:28	Monika Kuno	FRG	43	1	Faenza	29 May
8:34:19	Rösli Brechbuhl	SWZ	52	2	Biel	4 Jun
8:39:18	Mertens			1	St Amand	2 Apr
8:40:07	Takao Suzuki	JAP		1	Lake Saroma	3 Jul
8:43:03	Silvia Andonie	MEX	56	1	Lake Marced	23 Jan
8:45:47	Mertens			1	Stabroeck	26 Mar
C. Track						
8:28:20	Hilary Walker	UK	53	1	Blackpool	5 Nov
8:38:43	Sue Andrews	NZ		1		Sep
8:42:22	Sandra Barwick	NZ	49	1	Canberra	1 Oct

1988 24 Hours Lists

km	Name	Nation	Born	Place	Venue	Date
A. Track – MEN						
256.513	Paul Bream	UK	44	1	Frechen	25/26 Jun
250.512	Hans-Martin Erdmann	FRG	44	2	Frechen	25/26 Jun
244.393	Terry Edmondson	UK	45	1	Doncaster	28/29 May
244.000	Milan Furin	CS	50	1	Kosice	21/22 May
243.719	Anthoine Melchior	FRA		1	Arcueil	8/ 9 Oct
243.413	Tony Lenagan	UK	44	1	Solihull	2/ 3 Jul
239.200	Harry Arndt	FRG	36	1	Elze	17/18 Jun
235.949	Dave Cooper	UK	34	2	Solihull	2/ 3 Jul
233.755	Cooper			1	Chevilly	4/ 5 Jun
B. Road – MEN						
249.881	Jacky Frick	FRA	42	1	Basle	7/ 8 May
248.247	Karl-Heinz Springer	FRG	47	1	Mörlenbach	10/11 Sep
245.786	Lászó Simon	HUN	58	1	Apeldoorn	13/14 May
244.380	Patrick Ligerot	FRA	52	1	Niort	12/13 Nov
244.326	Waldemar Rettig	FRG	38	2	Mörlenbach	10/11 Sep
239.400	Gilbert Mainix	FRA	35	1	Le Puy	25/26 Jun
239.020	Joseph Tudo	FRA	34	1	d'Eppeville	4/ 5 Jun
238.969	Helmut Schieke	FRG	39	2	Apeldoorn	13/14 May
237.040	Bernard Goudeau	FRA		2	Niort	12/13 Nov
236.106	Aribert Hannappel	SWZ		2	Basle	7/ 8 May
234.693	Roy Pirrung	USA		1	Atlanta	17/18 Sep
233.492	William Verdonck	BEL	44	1	Heusden	15/16 Oct
232.812	Gerd Kurschuss	FRG	48	3	Apeldoorn	13/14 May
232.318	Richard Brown	UK	46	2	Preston	27/28 Aug
231.745	Yiannis Kouros	GRE	56	1	Queens	20/21 May
231.650	Max Courtillon	FRA	27	3	Niort	12/13 Nov
C. Indoor track – MEN						
232.668	Don Ritchie	UK	44	1	Glasgow	19/20 Nov
Track mark omitted from last year's men's list						
255.680	Vladimir Kubecek	CS		1	Zilina 1987	12/13 Sep

km	Name	Nation	Born	Place	Venue	Date
A. Track – WOMEN						
230.013*	Marianna Savage	UK	49	1	Solihull	2/ 3 Jul
226.237*	Angela Mortens	BEL	41	1	Izegem	2/ 3 Jul
225.312	Hilary Walker	UK	53	1	Blackpool	5/ 6 Nov
218.150	Monika Kuno	FRG	43	1	Frechen	25/26 Jun
208.840	Helen Grant	NZ	49	1	Christchurch	7/ 8 May
205.599	Sandra Barwick	NZ	49	2	Blackpool	5/ 6 Nov
202.890	Sue Andrews	NZ		1	Coburg	13/14 Feb

* *Not ratifiable as world bests for technical reasons*

km	Name	Nation	Born	Place	Venue	Date
B. Road – WOMEN						
236.453	Hilary Walker	UK	53	1	Preston	27/28 Aug
232.107	Angela Mertens	BEL	41	1	Heusden	15/16 Oct
209.795	Walker			1	Apeldoorn	13/14 May
203.480	Marie Bertrand	FRA		1	Niort	12/13 Nov

World Records and Bests – Long Distance Track Events

Event	hr:min:sec	Name	Nation	Venue	Date	
15 km	0:42:54.8	Jos Hermens	HOL	Papendal	14 Sep	1985
10 miles	0:45:57.6	Jos Hermens	HOL	Papendal	14 Sep	1975
20 km	0:57:24.2	Jos Hermens	HOL	Papendal	1 May	1976
15 miles	1:11:43.1	Bill Rodgers	USA	Saratoga, Cal.	21 Feb	1979
25 km	1:13:55.8	Toshihiko Seko	JAP	Christchurch, NZ	22 Mar	1981
30 km	1:29:18.8	Toshihiko Seko	JAP	Christchurch, NZ	22 Mar	1981
20 miles	1:39:14.4	Jack Foster	NZ	Hamilton, NZ	15 Aug	1971
30 miles	2:42:00	Jeff Norman	UK	Timperley	7 Jun	1980
50 km	2:48:06	Jeff Norman	UK	Timperley	7 Jun	1980
40 miles	3:48:35	Don Ritchie	UK	Hendon, London	16 Oct	1982
50 miles	4:51:49	Don Ritchie	UK	Hendon, London	12 Mar	1983
100 km	6:10:20	Don Ritchie	UK	Crystal Palace	28 Oct	1978
150 km	10:36:42	Don Ritchie	UK	Crystal Palace	15 Oct	1977
100 miles	11:30:51	Don Ritchie	UK	Crystal Palace	15 Oct	1977
200 km	15:11:10#	Yiannis Kouros	GRE	Montauban, FRA	15–16 Mar	1985
200 miles	27:48:35	Yiannis Kouros	GRE	Montauban, FRA	15–16 Mar	1985
500 km	60:23.00	Yiannis Kouros	GRE	Colac, AUS	26–29 Nov	1984
500 miles	105:42:09	Yiannis Kouros	GRE	Colac, AUS	26–30 Nov	1984
1000 km	136:17:00	Yiannis Kouros	GRE	Colac, AUS	26–31 Nov	1984
1500 km	14d 20:10:13	Malcolm Campbell	UK	Gateshead	11–26 Nov	1985
1000 miles	15d 21:07:43	Malcolm Campbell	UK	Gateshead	11–27 Nov	1985
	km					
1 hour	20.944	Jos Hermens	HOL	Papendal	1 May	1976
2 hrs	37.944	Jim Alder	UK	Walton-on-Thames	17 Oct	1964
24 hrs	283.600	Yiannis Kouros	GRE	Montauban, FRA	15–16 Mar	1985
48 hrs	452.270	Yiannis Kouros	GRE	Montauban, FRA	15–17 Mar	1985
6 days	1023.200	Yiannis Kouros	GRE	Colac, AUS	26 Nov–1 Dec	1984

 # Running watch time, no stopped times taken

Long Distance Road Bests

Where superior to track bests and run on properly measured road courses

Event	hr:min:sec	Name	Nation	Venue	Date	
15 km	0:42:27.6	Mike Musyoki	KEN	Portland, Oregon	26 Jun	1983
10 miles	0:45:13	Ian Stewart	UK	Stoke-on-Trent	8 May	1977
Half mar	1:00:43	Mike Musyoki	KEN	Newcastle, UK	8 Jun	1986
30 km	1:28:40	Steve Jones	UK	Chicago	10 Oct	1985
20 miles	1:35:22	Steve Jones	UK	Chicago	10 Oct	1985
50 km	2:43:38	Thompson Magawana	SAf	Claremont-Kirstenbosch	12 Apr	1988
40 miles	3:46:31	Barney Klecker	USA	Chicago	5 Oct	1980
50 miles	4:50:21	Bruce Fordyce	SAf	London–Brighton	25 Sep	1983
1000 miles	10d:10:30:35	Yiannis Kouros	GRE	New York	21–30 May	1988
	km					
24 hours	286.463	Yiannis Kouros	GRE	New York	28–29 Sep	1985
6 days	1028.370	Yiannis Kouros	GRE	New York	21–26 May	1988

It should be noted that road times must be assessed with care as course conditions can vary considerably

p = pending confirmation

Women's World Bests

World Records – Long Distance Track Events

Event	Time *hr:min:sec*	Name	Venue	Date
15 km	0:49:44.0	Silvana Cruciata (ITA)	Rome	4 May 1981
20 km	1:06:55.5	Rosa Mota (POR)	Lisbon	14 May 1983
25 km	1:29:30	Karolina Szabó (HUN)	Budapest	23 Apr 1988
30 km	1:47:06	Karolina Szabó (HUN)	Budapest	23 Apr 1988
30 miles	3:28:12	Ann Franklin (UK)	Barry, Wales	4 Mar 1986
50 km	3:36:58	Ann Franklin (UK)	Barry, Wales	9 Mar 1986
40 miles	4:47:27	Ann Franklin (UK)	Barry, Wales	9 Mar 1986
50 miles	6:17:30 †	Monika Kuno (FRG)	Vogt	8–9 Jul 1983
100 km	8:01:01	Monika Kuno (FRG)	Vogt	8–9 Jul 1983
100 miles	14:56:20	Hilary Walker (UK)	Blackpool	5–6 Nov 1988
200 km	20:09:28 †	Eleanor Adams (UK)	Honefoss, Nor	12–13 Jul 1986
200 miles	39:09.03	Hilary Walker (UK)	Blackpool	5–6 Nov 1986
500 km	86:26.02	Eleanor Adams (UK)	Colac, Aus.	24–28 Feb 1986
500 miles	143:49:00	Eleanor Adams (UK)	Colac, Aus.	26 Nov-1 Dec 1984
	kilometres			
24 hrs	229.459*	Marianne Savage (UK)	Birmingham	2–3 Jul 1988
	225.312	Hilary Walker (UK)	Blackpool	5–6 Nov 1988
48 hrs	366.521	Hilary Walker (UK)	Blackpool	5–7 Nov 1988
6 days	838.800	Eleanor Adams (UK)	Colac, Aus.	16–22 Nov 1987

** Paced for part of race, † Timed on one running watch only*

Long Distance Road Bests

Run on properly measured road courses

Event	Time	Name	Venue	Date
10 km	0:30:59	Liz McColgan (UK)	Orlando	9 Feb 1988
	0:30:46u	Ingrid Kristiansen (NOR)	København	21 Sep 1986
15 km	0:47:17	Ingrid Kristiansen (NOR)	Monte Carlo	21 Nov 1987
10 miles	0:52:07	Ingrid Kristiansen (NOR)	London	10 May 1987
	0:50:31u	Ingrid Kristiansen (NOR)	Amsterdam	11 Oct 1987
20 km	1:04:59	Ingrid Kristiansen (NOR)	London	10 May 1987
Half mar	1:06:40	Ingrid Kristiansen (NOR)	London	10 May 1987
25 km	1:21:21	Ingrid Kristiansen (NOR)	London	10 May 1987
30 km	1:38:27	Ingrid Kristiansen (Nor)	London	10 May 1987
20 miles	1:46:04	Ingrid Kristiansen (Nor)	London	10 May 1987
50 km	3:13:51	Janis Klecker (USA)	Tallahassee	17 Dec 1983
40 miles	4:43:22	Marcy Schwam (USA)	Chicago	3 Oct 1982
50 miles	5:59:26	Marcy Schwam (USA)	Chicago	3 Oct 1982
100 km	7:26:01 ‡	Chantal Langlacé (Fra)	Migennes	17 Jun 1984
	7:30:49	Ann Trason (USA)	Santander	1 Oct 1988
100 miles	14:49.34	Hilary Walker (UK)	Preston	27–28 Aug 1988
200 km	20:05:50	Hilary Walker (UK)	Preston	27–28 Aug 1988
500 km	82:10 #	Annie van der Meer (Hol)	Paris-Colmar	8–11 Jun 1983
1000 miles	14d 20:45:16	Sandra Barwick (NZ)	New York	21 May–3 Jun 1988
	kilometres			
24 hrs	236.453	Hilary Walker (UK)	Blackpool	5–6 Nov 1988

‡ Uncertain course measurement, # 518 km

OBITUARIES 1988

BY PETER MATTHEWS

Jim BALL (CAN) (b.7 May 1903) on 2 July. At 400m he won a silver medal in the 1928 Olympics, in pb 47.9, and a bronze on Canada's 4x400m relay team in both 1928 and 1932. At the 1930 Empire Games he was fifth at both 220y and 440y and was also a silver medallist at the 4x400y relay.

Ray BARBUTI (USA) (b.12 Jun 1905) on 8 July. Gold medallist at 400m (in pb 47.8) and 4x400m relay (world record 3:14.2) at 1928 Olympics. Also in 1928 was AAU 400m champion and ran on the US team that set a world record for 4x440 yards, 3:13.4 against the British Empire. Played fullback for Syracuse University and became a leading official in Eastern college football.

Ursula BIRKHOLZ (FRG) on 26 Oct aged 78. German 80mh champion 1930, ran national records 12.4 '30 and 12.3 '31.

Craig CALK (USA) (b.31 Jan 1965) on 5 August when he fell seven floors at an hotel in Texas. 400mh pb 49.05 '87. At Texas A&M University, sixth NCAA 1986.

Rosetta CATTANEO (ITA) (b.14 Feb 1919) on 15 July. Bronze medal at 4x100m relay in 1938 Europeans. Italian 200m champion 1939–40, 1942–3. Italian 200m record 25.3 '40.

Glenn CUNNINGHAM (USA) (b.4 Aug 1909) on 10 March. Silver medal at 1500m in the 1936 Olympics. World records for 800m 1:49.7 '36 and 880y 1:50.9 '33. Also US records at 1500m: 3:53.1 '32, 3:52.3 '33, 3:48.4 '36 (pb 3:48.0 '40) and 1 mile: 4:11.1 '32, 4:09.8 '33, 4:06.7 '34. Fastest ever mile was 4:04.4 in a handicap race on the 6 2/3 laps to the mile indoor board track at Hanover, NH in 1938. On smaller indoor tracks set world indoor bests at 1000y 2:10.1 '35, 3 at 1500m, best 3:48.4 '38, 3 at 1M to 4:07.4 '38. Won AAU 800m 1933, 1500m 1933, 1935–38, indoor 1500m 1934–5, 1938–9. Severely injured in a fire as a child he became America's greatest miler. Sullivan Award winner 1933.

Jasmin FEIGE (FRG) (b.20 Jun 1959) on 19 June in a motorcycle accident. FRG indoor LJ champion 1983 & 1985. pb LJ 6.71i '85.

Jack HASLAM (UK) (b.26 Jul 1929) in March. Ran his best marathon time of 2:24:00 when third in the AAAs 1957. He was second in the 1964 AAA marathon.

Gerd HORNBERGER (FRG) (b.17 Feb 1910) in September. European gold medallist at 4x100mR in 1934 and 1938; 6th 100m 1934. Bronze at 4x100m in 1936 Olympics. German champion 100m 1936, 1938; 200m 1937. pbs: 100m 10.4 '34, 200m 21.3 '35.

Karl HORNBERGER (FRG) (b.30 Mar 1900) on 29 May. German long jump champion 1920 and national records of 7.19 '20 and 7.33 '21.

Nell JACKSON (USA) (b.1 Jul 1929) on 1 Apr 1988. Ran for the USA at the 1948 Olympics (did not qualify at 200m and 4x100mR), and at the Pan-American Games 1951, when she was 2nd at 200m and gold medallist in the sprint relay. AAU 200m champion 1949–50, pb 24.2 '49. Women's head coach at 1952 and 1972 Olympics.

Fred KUDU (USSR) in October in Tartu, Estonia. Soviet decathlon coach.

Gladys LUNN (UK) (b.1 Jun 1908) on 3 January. World records at 880y 2:18.2 '30, 1000m: 3:04.4 '31, 3:00.6 '34; 1M: 5:23.0 '36, 5:20.8 & 5:17.0 '37. Won World Games 800m 1930 and her best 800m (generously estimated at 2:14.2) was when third in the 1934 World Games. Won seven WAAA titles, five at 800m/880y, two at 1 mile. At the Empire Games won 880y and javelin 1934, third javelin 1938.

Rudolf MATZ (YUG) (b.19 Sep 1901) on 22 March. Set Yugoslav records at 100m (11.0) and 200m (22.6) in 1921. Later he became a renowned composer and conductor.

Vilim MESSNER (YUG) (b.11 Apr 1904) on 5 June. Yugoslav javelin record 58.43m in 1928.

Paula MOLLENHAUER (FRG) (b.22 Dec 1908) on 7 July. Bronze medallist at discus in 1936 Olympics (also 12th 1928) and 1938 Europeans. Set German records 39.61 '31 and 42.57 '34; pb 43.58 '39. German discus champion 1929, 1931 and 1943, and three 2nds, four 3rds.

Roy MOOR (UK) (b. 9 Sep 1910) on 14 June. As a much respected journalist covered all Olympic Games 1936–84. British 400m international 1933.

Fritz SCHAUMBURG (GER) (b.30 Dec 1905) on 19 December. German champion at 1500m 1934–7, 5000m 1931. German records at 2000m, 5:27.4'36 and 3000m, 8:17.2'36; pbs: 1500m: 3:53.2'37, 5000m: 14:28.4'39. At 1500m fourth 1934 Europeans, tenth 1936 Olympics.

Jock SEMPLE (USA) on 9 March in his 80s. Originally from Scotland, he ran pb 2:45:06 when he won the New England marathon in 1932. For years he was associated with the Boston marathon, eventually as organiser. In 1967 he vainly tried to prevent Kathrine Switzer running in the race, but he was happy to allow women runners from 1972.

George SHAW (USA) (b.12 Aug 1931) on 6 December. At the triple jump was 19th in 1952 and 12th in 1956 at the Olympics; was AAU champion in 1953 and NCAA in 1952. pbs: LJ: 7.54'56, TJ: 15.38'52.

Paul SIEVERT (FRG) (b. 7 Aug 1895) on 18 December. Set a world record 4:34:03 for 50 km walk in 1924, although this was actually a road performance. German champion at 50 km 1924–5 and 1933, and sixth at 1932 Olympics.

Freddie WOLFF (UK) (b.13 Oct 1910) on 26 January. Ran first leg on gold medal winning 4 x 400m relay team at 1936 Olympics. AAA 440 yards champion 1933. pb 400m 48.6 '32.

Jon YOUNG (USA) (b.22 Apr 1948) on 3 August from lung cancer. Seventh 1972 US Olympic Trials 100m in pb 10.1.

OLYMPIC GAMES 1988

Seoul 23 September – 2 October

BY PETER MATTHEWS

They were a Games full of controversies, incidents, upsets, but above all much splendid competition. That Ben Johnson was caught for drug abuse cast a long shadow on the integrity of the sport, but it should not be forgotten that he was the only athlete caught for steroids use. A record 161 nations participated in the Games, of which 145 had competitors in athletics, with a total of over 2000 taking part.

Carl Lewis and Roger Kingdom were the only champions to successfully defend their titles. Results of many events certainly upset the form book, especially in the men's middle and long distance events. It often seemed like the end of an era and the opening of a new one. Who could have believed that none of these group, many of the greatest names of recent years: Aouita, Cram, Göhr, Kostadinova, Kristiansen, and the double Olympic champions Moses, Sedykh and Thompson would win a gold medal? Instead there were new names, Brahim Boutayeb, Steve Lewis, Tapio

Analysis of Places 1–8 by Nation

With points from 8 for 1st to 1 for 8th (splitting points for ties)

Nation	1st	2nd	3rd	4th	5th	6th	7th	8th	Points	Rank
USA	13	7	6	4	9	6	2	4	271	2
USSR	10	6	10	11	4	4	5†	3	275	1
GDR	6	11	10	6	2	5	1	3	243	3
Kenya	4	2	1	–	–	–	2	3	59	6
Bulgaria	2	1	1	1	2*	–	–	3	44.5	8
Italy	1	1	1	2	1	1	3	2	46	7
Australia	1	1	–	1	2	2	2	2	40	11
Czechoslovakia	1	1	–	–	2	2	1	–	31	12
Romania	1	1	–	–	1*	–	–	–	18.5	15
Finland	1	–	1	–	–	–	–	–	14	17=
Morocco	1	–	1	–	–	–	–	–	14	17=
Portugal	1	–	–	1	–	–	–	–	13	20
United Kingdom	–	6	2	5	3	6	4†	2*	117.5	4
Jamaica	–	2	–	3	2	1	2	–	44	9=
F.R.Germany	–	1	3	3	2	3	3†	3	65	5
Brazil	–	1	1	–	1	1	–	–	20	14
France	–	–	1	1	3	3	5	2	44	9=
Canada	–	–	1	–	2	2	2	2	26	13
China	–	–	1	–	1	–	1	2	14	17=
Spain	–	–	–	1	2	–	1	–	15	16
Hungary	–	–	–	–	–	2	2	1	11	21

*† includes a three-way tie, * includes a two-way tie*

Further points scores – Sweden 9; Poland, Senegal 7; Mexico, Djibouti, Nigeria, Switzerland 6; Japan, Yugoslavia 5; Belgium, Bermuda, Netherlands 4; Chile 3; Luxembourg, Norway, Tanzania, Trinidad & Tobago 2; Ireland, Oman 1; Korea 0.5.

Korjus maintaining the Finnish javelin tradition, Paula Ivan and the extraordinary running of the Kenyan distance men. There was sizzling sprinting, especially by the most successful athlete of the Games, Florence Griffith-Joyner. She set two world records (at 200m) and won three gold medals and a silver. World records were also set by both 4 x 400m relay winners and by Jackie Joyner-Kersee at heptathlon. Two individual events were won by Carl Lewis and the sisters-in-law FGJ and JJK.

Events Survey – Men

Listed are the first eight in each event together with brief comments.

Ben Johnson wears the gold medal, but he kept it for only three days, as Carl Lewis (l) got that and Linford Christie (r) the silver. Calvin Smith thus missed the opportunity of standing on the rostrum (George Herringshaw/ASP)

100 METRES

The greatest sensation in Olympic history came with Ben Johnson's disqualification for a positive test for the anabolic steroid Stenozolol, just three days after his victory in 9.79, which would have smashed the amazing 9.83 world record that he had run in Rome in 1987. In the final he was off evenly with Carl Lewis and Linford Christie, reaction times .132, .136 and .138 respectively, but picked up .05 on Lewis between 10m and 20m and steadily forged ahead to a peak lead of .17 (8.06 to 8.23) over Lewis at 80m to win by over a metre. Johnson passed 60m in a record 6.37, compared to 6.38 in Rome. Then came Lewis 6.53, Williams 6.54, Christie 6.55, Smith 6.56, Mitchell and da Silva 6.58. Both Johnson (40m-50m) and Lewis (80m-90m) had a peak 10m split of .83s, a speed of 43.37 km/h (26.95 mph).

So Lewis got the gold medal, to become the first man, apart from Archie Hahn in 1904 and 1906, to retain an Olympic 100m title. Christie's 9.97 was a European record, and for the first time with legal wind three (four!) men beat 10.00. Lewis had been the most impressive in the heats, 10.14 and 9.99 (+1.4) on the first day and 9.97 (+0.6) to win the first semi, with Johnson winning the second in 10.03 (–1.2). Two of the medal favourites pulled muscles: Ray Stewart in the final and Chidi Imoh in the second round.

1. Carl Lewis (USA) 9.92 OR
2. Linford Christie (UK) 9.97
3. Calvin Smith (USA) 9.99
4. Dennis Mitchell (USA) 10.04
5. Robson da Silva (Bra) 10.11
6. Desai Williams (Can) 10.11
7. Ray Stewart (Jam) 12.26

dq Ben Johnson (Can) 9.79
(wind in final +1.1m/s)

200 METRES

Joe DeLoach ended the ambitions of his training companion Carl Lewis of replicating his four gold medals feat from LA with a time that equalled the world best at low altitude. Da Silva set a South American record to take the bronze ahead of the UK record by Linford Christie, whose teammate Rosswess was a surprise finalist in his first serious year of competition. However John Regis, world bronze medallist, was only seventh in his semi. Times at 100m: Lewis 10.24, DeLoach 10.27, Christie 10.34, da Silva 10.35. Pietro Mennea ran at his fifth Olympics but scratched from the second round with a groin injury.

1. Joe DeLoach (USA) 19.75 OR
2. Carl Lewis (Bra) 19.79
3. Robson da Silva (Bra) 20.04
4. Linford Christie (UK) 20.09
5. Atlee Mahorn (Can) 20.39
6. Gilles Quénehérvé (Fra) 20.40
7. Michael Rosswess (UK) 20.51
8. Bruno Marie-Rose (Fra) 20.58

(wind +1.7)

400 METRES

Butch Reynolds was the clear favourite to win but he left his charge too late, and Steve Lewis became the first teenager ever to win the Olympic 400m gold, running his fifth world junior record of the year. He started fast and was nearly level with Danny Everett, who led at 200m in 21.37. Times at 300m: Lewis 32.08, Everett 32.13, Al Malky 32.43, Reynolds 32.53.

Expected to contest the major medals, Said Aouita (l) and Steve Cram (r), had disappointing Games (George Herringshaw/ASP)

The US clean sweep emulated those of 1904 and 1968. Three men under 44.10 and seven under 45.00 were new records for any race. Eliminated in the semis with fifth places in 44.90 were the world champion Thomas Schönlebe (GDR) and Susumu Takano (Jap).

1. Steve Lewis (USA) 43.87
2. Butch Reynolds (USA) 43.93
3. Danny Everett (USA) 44.09
4. Darren Clark (Aus) 44.55
5. Innocent Egbunike (Nig) 44.72
6. Bert Cameron (Jam) 44.94
7. Ian Morris (Tri) 44.95
8. Mohamed Al Malky (Oman) 45.03

800 METRES

Indication was given that the big favourites would be challenged by the Kenyans, as Paul Ereng, who was in his first year at the event, and Nixon Kiprotich won the semis in 1:44.55 and 1:44.71 respectively. In the final Ereng became the first Kenyan 800m champion and strode majestically to victory after he passed his teammate Kiprotich with 200m to go. To try to take the sting out of Aouita's finish a very fast pace was set by Kiprotich and the Brazilians: 23.6 at 200m, and Barbosa passed 400m in 49.54 from Kiprotich, Cruz and Elliott, with Aouita and Ereng back at c.50.8. Kiprotich then took the lead to 600m in 1:16.6 before Cruz charged for home, only to be passed by Ereng with some 30m left. Aouita became the first man in Olympic history to win medals at 5000m and 800m. Out in the second round went two UK favourites: Steve Cram, sixth in 1:46.47, and Tom McKean, who was disqualified after barging his way into a qualifying spot.

1. Paul Ereng (Ken) 1:43.45
2. Joaquim Cruz (Bra) 1:43.90
3. Said Aouita (Mor) 1:44.06
4. Peter Elliott (UK) 1:44.12
5. Johnny Gray (USA) 1:44.80
6. José Luiz Barbosa (Bra) 1:46.39
7. Donato Sabia (Ita) 1:48.03
8. Nixon Kiprotich (Ken) 1:49.55

1500 METRES

Another Kenyan win, and in fine style by Peter Rono, but the world's best were either absent or not at their best. Said Aouita (hamstring injury) and Joaquim Cruz withdrew from the semis, Abdi Bile and José Luis Gonzalez were absent injured, Jim Spivey had not made the US team or Seb Coe the British. Steve Cram was below par, and Peter Elliott had been receiving injections for a groin strain before each race in the 800m and 1500m. Nonetheless the latter battled his way to a silver medal. In the final O'Sullivan led at 400m 59.65, with Rono taking over from 500m to lead at 800m 2:00.31 and 1200m 2:56.69, with that lead conclusive as his chasers could not narrow the gap.

1. Peter Rono (Ken) 3:35.96
2. Peter Elliott (UK) 3:36.15
3. Jens-Peter Herold (GDR) 3:36.21
4. Steve Cram (UK) 3:36.24
5. Steve Scott (USA) 3:36.99
6. Han Kulker (Hol) 3:37.08
7. Kip Cheruiyot (Ken) 3:37.94
8. Marcus O'Sullivan (Ire) 3:38.39

5000 METRES

John Ngugi kicked in a 58.2 400m from the 1000m point, reached in 2:42.75 and a 2:32.19 second km to reach 2000m in 5:14.96. No one went with that but Domingos Castro made a brave attempt to narrow the gap, reducing Ngugi's lead from 6.24 at 3000m, 7:56.12, to 3.69 at 4000m, 10:36.20. But sadly Castro, five seconds up on the pack at that point, was passed just before the finish by Baumann and Kunze, who each kicked in a 55.0 last lap to leave the unlucky Portugese distraught. José Regalo, perhaps the favourite, dropped out after 3000m. Kunze and Paul Arpin (14th) were the only men to make both 5000m and 10000m finals, with Salvatore Antibo and Eamonn Martin the fastest in the semis to miss the final at 13:25.64 and 13:26.26.

1. John Ngugi (Ken) 13:11.70
2. Dieter Baumann (FRG) 13:15.52
3. Hansjörg Kunze (GDR) 13:15.73
4. Domingos Castro (Por) 13:16.09
5. Sydney Maree (USA) 13:23.69
6. Jack Buckner (UK) 13:23.85
7. Stefano Mei (Ita) 13:26.17
8. Evgeni Ignatov (Bul) 13:26.41

10,000 METRES

The Africans, with Salvatore Antibo of Italy, dominated this race. Antibo set a fast pace with an opening km of 2:41.74. At 2km Tanui led in 5:28.50 and after a 62.7 lap the leading group was down to four: 3000m: Kimeli 8:07.78, Boutayeb, Antibo and Tanui. The 4km time was 10:50.05 and at 5000m it was Kimeli 13:35.32, Boutayeb 13:35.52, Tanui 13:36.74, Antibo 13:37.71, then the pack led by Barrios 13:45.37. Boutayeb then steadily gained ground and settled into a rhythm, his km splits: 16:20.07, 19:04.56, 21:50.17, 24:35.79 before easing down through the line in a new African record to become, at 21, the youngest ever Olympic 10,000m champion. European record holder Eamonn Martin dropped out, to save himself for the 5000m, a little after halfway (13:46.66). The 1984 1–2 Alberto Cova (Ita) and Mike McLeod (UK) failed to make the final.

1. Brahim Boutayeb (Mor) 27:21.46 OR
2. Salvatore Antibo (Ita) 27:23.55
3. Kipkemboi Kimeli (Ken) 27:35.16
4. Jean-Louis Prianon (Fra) 27:36.43
5. Arturo Barrios (Mex) 27:39.32
6. Hansjörg Kunze (GDR) 27:39.35
7. Paul Arpin (Fra) 27:39.36
8. Moses Tanui (Ken) 27:47.23

John Ngugi is away from the pack after only three and a half laps of the 5000 metres (George Herringshaw/ASP)

MARATHON

A marvellous race, run in warm weather up to 26°C, in which a leading group of some 25 runners formed very early. This contained all the top men, all experienced marathoner runners, with no newcomers. The leaders passed 5km in 15:29, before speeding up to 10km in 30:32; then 15km in 45:57, 20km in 1:01:21 and 25km 1:16:57. As the relentless pace continued, with the Africans, including Kenyans Ibrahim Hussein and Joseph Kipsang, who both dropped out, prominent, the big names gradually peeled off the back of the pack. By soon after 30km reached in 1:32:49 there were just six left in the first group who were timed at 35km in 1:48:25. First Spedding and Ikangaa gave way, then Nakayama. At 38km Salah burst away to pass 40km in 2:03:39 with Wakiihuri second and Bordin third, the same three medallists as in Rome last year. But as the leaders tired Bordin strode through to take the lead at 40.6km and to become the first ever Italian to take the Olympic marathon title, which Dorando Pietri got so close to in 1908. Moneghetti, fourth in Rome, picked up three places in the closing miles. From the 118 starters there were 20 non-finishers including 1984 silver medallist John Treacy.

1. Gelindo Bordin (Ita) 2:10:32
2. Douglas Wakiihuru (Ken) 2:10:47
3. Ahmed Salah (Dji) 2:10:59
4. Takeyuki Nakayama (Jap) 2:11:05
5. Steve Moneghetti (Aus) 2:11:49
6. Charlie Spedding (UK) 2:12:19
7. Juma Ikangaa (Tan) 2:13:06
8. Rod de Castella (Aus) 2:13:07

3000M STEEPLECHASE

Francesco Panetta, as usual, set the pace in the final, through 1km in 2:42.93 and 2km in 5:28.29, but he was unable to dominate, and when Peter Koech kicked with just under two laps to go he could not respond and finished ninth in 8:17.79. Kariuki swept past his team-mate and finished, with a last 400m in 63.83, just outside Henry Rono's ten-year-old hand timed world record of 8:05.4. Kenyans have contested four of the last six Olympics, winning the steeplechase gold each time, and the silver three times. In third place Mark Rowland took 8.38 off his best to smash the British record. There were a record ten men under 8:20 and best ever marks for places 2–8.

1. Julius Kariuki (Ken) 8:05.51 OR
2. Peter Koech (Ken) 8:06.79
3. Mark Rowland (UK) 8:07.96
4. Alessandro Lambruschini (Ita) 8:12.17
5. William van Dijck (Bel) 8:13.99
6. Henry Marsh (USA) 8:14.39
7. Peter Sang (Ken) 8:15.22
8. Boguslaw Maminski (Pol) 8:15.97

110 METRES HURDLES

Roger Kingdom won clearly, the second man to retain an Olympic high hurdles title. He was the fastest in each round, 13.40, 13.17 OR, 13.37 and 12.98 in the final, the third fastest of all-time, his 24th win in 24 110mh races in 1988. The USA had three men in the final, as usual, but so too did Britain, all the more remarkable as there had been no British 110mh finallist since 1936, when Don Finlay had won the silver medal.

1. Roger Kingdom (USA) 12.98 OR
2. Colin Jackson (UK) 13.28
3. Tonie Campbell (USA) 13.38
4. Vladimir Shishkin (SU) 13.51
5. Jonathan Ridgeon (UK) 13.52
6. Tony Jarrett (UK) 13.54
7. Mark McKoy (Can) 13.61
8. Arthur Blake (USA) 13.96

(wind +1.5)

400 METRES HURDLES

Edwin Moses lost for the first time in a major championship. The man to end his era of success was Andre Phillips, who ran in lane six in the final. Moses in lane three was always behind, and was overtaken off the last hurdle by Dia Bâ, who finished exceptionally quickly to nearly catch Phillips, as the two of them ran times bettered only by Moses. Moses and Phillips had won the semis in 47.89 and 48.19 respectively. For the first time ever all eight men were under 49 sec.

1. Andre Phillips (USA) 47.19
2. Amadou Dia Bâ (Sen) 47.23
3. Ed Moses (USA) 47.56
4. Kevin Young (USA) 47.94
5. Winthrop Graham (Jam) 48.04
6. Kriss Akabusi (UK) 48.69
7. Harald Schmid (FRG) 48.76
8. Edgar Itt (FRG) 48.78

HIGH JUMP

Gennadiy Avdeyenko, who has won world gold and silver medals and world indoor silver, showed that he is a man for the big event by clearing 2.38m on his second attempt, as six other men failed that height. Avdeyenko was never headed as he had cleared 2.20, 2.25, 2.31, 2.34 and 2.36 on his first attempts. He failed once at 2.40m and twice at 2.44m. The previous Olympic record height of 2.36m was cleared by Conway on his first attempt and by the bronze medallists, both clear to that height, on their second.

1. Gennadiy Avdeyenko (SU) 2.38 OR
2. Hollis Conway (USA) 2.36
3= Rudolf Povarnitsyn (SU) 2.36
3= Patrik Sjöberg (Swe) 2.36
5. Clarence Saunders (Ber) 2.34
6. Dietmar Mögenburg (FRG) 2.34
7= Dalton Grant (UK) 2.31
7= Igor Paklin (SU) 2.31
7= Carlo Thränhardt (FRG) 2.31

POLE VAULT

Sergey Bubka has proved many times that he is the greatest ever pole vaulter, but he faced a real challenge here as, after 5.70 on his second attempt, he passed the next heights and then failed twice at 5.90. Needing a clearance or he would be fourth equal, he soared over. That was enough to secure the gold as Yegorov failed this height and Gataullin, who had a third attempt clearance at 5.85, went out at 5.95. The clean sweep by the Soviets, who all set new Olympic records, meant that for the first time, apart from their boycott in 1980, an American did not win an Olympic pole vault medal.

1. Sergey Bubka (SU) 5.90 OR
2. Rodion Gataullin (SU) 5.85
3. Grigoriy Yegorov (SU) 5.80
4. Earl Bell (USA) 5.70
5= Thierry Vigneron (Fra) 5.70
5= Philippe Collet (Fra) 5.70
7. István Bagyula (Hun) 5.60
8. Philippe D'Encausse (Fra) 5.60

LONG JUMP

Carl Lewis became the first to retain an Olympic long jump title. Unlike LA he took all his jumps (8.41, 8.56w, 8.52, 8.72, 8.52m, N), for although he finished well clear there was always a threat from his teammates, who ensured a US clean sweep, emulating those of 1896 and 1904. Powell's best jump came in the third round and Myricks's in the second, but the latter had a huge no jump in the fifth round. The overall depth was disappointing.

1. Carl Lewis (USA) 8.72
2. Mike Powell (USA) 8.49
3. Larry Myricks (USA) 8.27
4. Giovanni Evangelisti (Ita) 8.08w
5. Antonio Corgos (Spa) 8.03
6. László Szalma (Hun) 8.00
7. Norbert Brige (Fra) 7.97
8. Leonid Voloshin (SU) 7.89

TRIPLE JUMP

Khristo Markov proved to be the supreme champion in the triple jump, at which he has now won all the major titles. The three Soviets headed by Lapshin's 17.37 were the only men over 17m in qualifying. In the final after Kovalenko had jumped 17.42 OR and Protsenko 17.38, Markov produced 17.61 in the first round. This remained the best as the Bulgarian followed with N, 15.71, 17.54, N, 17.10. Lapshin, lying fifth with 17.09, produced 17.52 in the last round to take the silver.

1. Khristo Markov (Bul) 17.61 OR
2. Igor Lapshin (SU) 17.52
3. Aleksandr Kovalenko (SU) 17.42
4. Oleg Protsenko (SU) 17.38
5. Charlie Simpkins (USA) 17.29
6. Willie Banks (USA) 17.03
7. Ivan Slanař (Cs) 16.75
8. Jacek Pastusiński (Pol) 16.72

SHOT

This was one of the greatest ever shot battles. The Olympic record was broken six times. Werner Günthör started with 21.45 only for Ulf Timmermann, who had led the qualifiers with 21.27, to push out to 22.02m. Timmermann progressed with new records in the third and fifth rounds as his series followed at 21.31, 22.16, 21.90 and 22.29. Meanwhile Günthör followed with 21.59, 21.70, 20.98, 21.99 and 21.61 and Udo Beyer was third with his second round 21.40. In the final round Randy Barnes, then lying fourth with 21.31, at last got everything into his rotational effort and took the Olympic record with 22.39. Günthör managed 21.61, and then Timmermann proved the master of the moment with his fourth Olympic record 22.47 to take his first major championships gold medal outdoors.

1. Ulf Timmermann (GDR) 22.47 OR
2. Randy Barnes (USA) 22.39
3. Werner Günthör (Swi) 21.99
4. Udo Beyer (GDR) 21.40
5. Remigius Machura (Cs) 20.57
6. Gert Weil (Chl) 20.38
7. Alessandro Andrei (Ita) 20.36
8. Sergey Smirnov (SU) 20.36

DISCUS

Jürgen Schult won with his first throw of the final and a series which included four throws better than the runner-up: 68.82, 67.92, 65.76,

68.18, 65.70, 68.26. After the first round Ubartas was second with 66.86 and Danneberg third 65.58. In the fifth round Mac Wilkins moved into a medal spot with 65.90, only for Danneberg to respond with 67.38. Ubartas passed him in the sixth round, when Dumchev and Valent also produced their best throws. A surprise non-qualifier was Vaclavas Kidikas (SU), 13th with 60.88, and Imrich Bugár (Cs) was only 12th with 60.88.

1. Jürgen Schult (GDR) 68.82 OR
2. Romas Ubartas (SU) 67.48
3. Ralf Danneberg (FRG) 67.38
4. Yuriy Dumchev (SU) 66.42
5. Mac Wilkins (USA) 65.90
6. Gejza Valent (Cs) 65.80
7. Knut Hjeltnes (Nor) 64.94
8. Alois Hannecker (FRG) 63.28

HAMMER

The medallists were the same as in Moscow 1980, but this time Litvinov was too good for Sedykh. Litvinov led the qualifiers with 81.24, and then smashed Sedykh's old Olympic record of 81.80, with his opening throw of the final, 84.76. His fine series was 84.76, 83.82, 83.86, 83.98, 84.80, 83.80, all better than Sedykh's 80.96, 83.62, 83.44, 83.44, N, 83.76. The Soviet clean sweep, their third in succession, apart from their boycott year of 1984, was never threatened, although Haber went over 80m in the final round. Defending champion Juha Tiainen failed to qualify with 73.74.

1. Sergey Litvinov (SU) 84.80 OR
2. Yuriy Sedykh (SU) 83.76
3. Juri Tamm (SU) 81.16
4. Ralf Haber (GDR) 80.44
5. Heinz Weis (FRG) 79.16
6. Tibor Gécsek (Hun) 78.36
7. Imre Szitás (Hun) 77.04
8. Ivan Tanev (Bul) 76.08

JAVELIN

Jan Zelezný set the Olympic record with the new javelin with his one throw of the qualifying round, 85.90. That was over four metres better than the next qualifiers, the two Finns Räty and Korjus. In the final Korjus led with 82.74 in the first round after 81.42 by Yevsyukov, who improved to 82.32 in the second round, a distance matched by Zelezný. Then the lead was taken by Räty, a third round 83.26, and Zelezný 83.46 in the fourth. Zelezný seemed to have sealed it with his 84.12 in the last round, but with the last throw Korjus, who had passed twice with leg cramps and had a no throw in the fifth, fulfilled the hopes of Finland, winning their seventh gold medal at the event, with 84.28 in his first major championships.

1. Tapio Korjus (Fin) 84.28
2. Jan Zelezný (Cs) 84.12
3. Seppo Räty (Fin) 83.26
4. Klaus Tafelmeier (FRG) 82.72
5. Viktor Yevsyukov (SU) 82.32
6. Gerald Weiss (GDR) 81.30
7. Vladimir Ovchinnikov (SU) 79.12
8. Dag Wennlund (Swe) 78.30

DECATHLON

Jürgen Hingsen created a sensation when he false started three times in the opening event, the 100m. So his challenge did not even start, nor did the injured Siegfried Wentz, and Daley Thompson was clearly lacking the sharpness which has brought him so many gold medals. Nonetheless he stayed in contention for a medal throughout and only just missed, despite his pole breaking at his opening height (4.70) in the vault. This exacerbated a thigh injury, but he jumped 4.90 and then threw a pb 64.04 javelin. He battled in the 1500m with six men able to pass his points total and take bronze. Just one did, Dave Steen. Overall most men were below their best, the one exception being the deserved gold medallist Christian Schenk, who achieved five pbs, most notably in his beautiful demonstration of straddle high jumping, topped by 2.27. At the end of the first day the order had been: Schenk 4470, Plaziat 4375, Thompson 4332, Voss 4299. The latter came through well on the second day, but Plaziat's chances went with a javelin throw of only 52.18. A very big field (39 started, 34 finished), meant that the competitors were in action for over 13 hours on the second day, when Tim Bright soared to a world decathlon best 5.70 in the vault.

1. Christian Schenk (GDR) 8488
2. Torsten Voss (GDR) 8399
3. Dave Steen (Can) 8328
4. Daley Thompson (UK) 8306
5. Christian Plaziat (Fra) 8272
6. Alain Blondel (Fra) 8268
7. Tim Bright (USA) 8216
8. Robert De Wit (Hol) 8189

20KM WALK

There was a leading group of 18 at 5km in 20:08 and seven at 10km in 40:37. At 15km three men were together in 1:00:39: Pribilinec, Weigel and defending champion Ernesto Canto (Mex), who was to be disqualified. They led by 8 sec from Damilano and Shchennikov. Pribilinec won, but the closeness was emphasised by the fact that the first seven were on on the track together for the final 400m in the stadium. Twenty men beat the old Olympic record of 1:23:13.

1. Jozef Pribilinec (Cs) 1:19:57 OR
2. Ronald Weigel 1:20:00
3. Maurizio Damilano (Ita) 1:20:14
4. José Marin (Spa) 1:20:34
5. Roman Mrázek (Cs) 1:20:43
6. Mikhail Shchennikov (SU) 1:20:47
7. Carlos Mercenario (Mex) 1:20:53
8. Axel Noack (GDR) 1:21:14

The GDR duo of Hartwig Gauder (l) and Ronald Weigel (r) raise their conqueror Vyacheslav Ivanenko (George Herringshaw/ASP)

50KM WALK

Vyacheslav Ivanenko, a medallist in Stuttgart and Rome, won his first gold and his revenge over the two East Germans. The early pace was set by the Mexicans Herman Andrade, disqualified after 20km, and Martin Bermudez, who finished 15th in 3:49:22. They passed 5km in 22:37 and 10km 45:23, before Andrade broke away through 15km 1:07:35 and 20km 1:29:47 to Bermudez 1:30:01 and a large pack 1:30:33. Bermudez led, but was caught just after 30km (2:14:25). He, with the men who eventually placed 1–5 and Sandor Urbanik (Hun) were together at 35km 2:35:50. Thereafter Ivanenko forged ahead, was 3 sec up at 40km in 2:56:29 and 18 sec up at 45km in 3:17:22. His final time was just 12 sec off the world best. Urbanik dropped out after 40km. The overall standard was exceptional with the best ever times from 2nd place downwards and a record 15 men under 3:50 and 27 under 4 hours.

1. Vyacheslav Ivanchenko (SU) 3:38:29 OR
2. Ronald Weigel (GDR) 3:38:56
3. Hartwig Gauder (GDR) 3:39:45
4. Aleksandr Potashov (SU) 3:41:00
5. José Marin (Spa) 3:43:03
6. Simon Baker (Aus) 3:44:07
7. Bo Gustafsson (Swe) 3:44:49
8. Raffaello Ducceschi (Ita) 3:45:43

4 x 100 METRES RELAY

The USA were clear favourites but their final change from Calvin Smith to reserve Lee McNeill in the heat was effected out of the zone, and they were disqualified. So Carl Lewis did not even get a run. In the final the smooth baton changing of the Soviet quartet: Viktor Bryzgin, Vladimir Krylov, Vladimir Muravyov and Vitaliy Savin, took them to victory. Linford Christie ran fine anchor legs to take the British team to new national records of 38.52 in the semis and 38.28 in the final.

1. USSR 38.19
2. United Kingdom 38.28
3. France 38.40
4. Jamaica 38.47
5. Italy 38.54
6. FR Germany 38.55
7. Canada 38.93
8. Hungary 39.19

4 x 400 METRES RELAY

The brilliant US team equalled the world record which had been set 20 years ago at the high altitude of Mexico City. They were given a marvellous start by the fastest ever lead off leg: 43.79 by Danny Everett, followed by Steve Lewis 43.69, Kevin Robinzine 44.74 and Butch Reynolds 43.94. Other fast anchor legs included a 44.4 by Darren Clark (Aus), and running 44.6–44.7 to bring home the teams in places 2–4 were Bert Cameron, Ralf Lübke and Thomas Schönlebe.

1. USA 2:56.16 =WR
2. Jamaica 3:00.30
3. FRG 3:00.56
4. GDR 3:01.13
5. UK 3:02.00
6. Australia 3:02.49
7. Nigeria 3:02.50
8. Kenya 3:04.69

EVENTS SURVEY – WOMEN

100 METRES

After the sensations of the US Olympic Trials the sprinting of Florence Griffith-Joyner was keenly anticipated. She quickly demonstrated how she is in a different league to any woman sprinter in history. Prior to her 1988 Olympic debut in heat 7, the only sub-11.00 time in Olympic history had been the 10.97 that Evelyn Ashford ran to win the 1984 final. But 'Flo-Jo' ran 10.88 (+1.0), followed by 10.62 OR (+1.0) in the second round heat two and 10.70w (+2.6) in the semis. Evelyn Ashford had equalled that 10.88 OR in the second round, when a total of seven women broke 11 sec. But Griffith-Joyner's margin of superiority was clearly shown in the final with another sensational run, albeit wind aided, her smile widening to sheer joy as she finished. Anelia Nuneva was in second place when she pulled a muscle with some 30m to go. The great GDR sprinters Silke Möller and Marlies Göhr were fifth and sixth in the first semi, running 11.12 and 11.13.

1. Florence Griffith-Joyner (USA) 10.54w
2. Evelyn Ashford (USA) 10.83
3. Heike Drechsler (GDR) 10.85
4. Grace Jackson (Jam) 10.97
5. Gwen Torrence (USA) 10.97
6. Natalya Pomoshnikova (SU) 11.00
7. Juliet Cuthbert (Jam) 11.26
8. Anelia Nuneva (Bul) 11.49

(wind +3.0)

200 METRES

Griffith-Joyner completed the sprint double and took two huge bites off the world record of 21.71. After an easy 22.51, she took the Olympic record with 21.76 (+0.7) in the second round, and then opened up in the semi when she passed 100m in 11.24 to finish in 21.56 (+1.7). In the final she ran the first 100m in 11.18 to which she added a second 100m in 10.16 for 21.34. Behind her Grace Jackson (11.32/10.40) sparkled with her first sub-22 run and Heike Drechsler (11.36/10.59) collected her third medal of the Games. For the first time in a major championship 200m Merlene Ottey (11.19/10.80) missed a medal, but a record four women broke 22 sec, and there were best ever times for each place.

1. Florence Griffith-Joyner (USA) 21.34 WR
2. Grace Jackson (Jam) 21.72
3. Heike Drechsler (GDR) 21.95
4. Merlene Ottey (Jam) 21.99
5. Silke Möller (GDR) 22.09
6. Gwen Torrence (USA) 22.17
7. Maya Azarashvili (SU) 22.33
8. Galina Malchugina (SU) 22.42

(wind +1.3m/s)

400 METRES

The two Soviets Olga Nazarova and Olga Bryzgina won the semis clearly in 49.11 and 49.33 respectively. In the final Bryzgina won easily after Brisco was well clear at 200m, 22.94 to Bryzgina 23.41 and Nazarova 23.59, and led until the final bend. Seven women broke 50 sec

Al Joyner had much to celebrate in Seoul. He had won gold in 1984 but watched with joy as his wife added three golds and a silver to the family collection, and celebrated with her afterwards (George Herringshaw/ASP)

in the semis, including Jillian Richardson (Can), who ran 49.91 yet did not qualify her for the final; it was the fastest ever fifth place.
1. Olga Bryzgina (SU) 48.65 OR
2. Petra Müller (GDR) 49.45
3. Olga Nazarova (SU) 49.90
4. Valerie Brisco (SU) 50.16
5. Diane Dixon (USA) 50.72
6. Denean Howard (USA) 51.12
7. Helga Arendt (FRG) 51.17
8. Maree Holland (Aus) 51.25

800 METRES
Just as in Rome Sigrun Wodars beat her more-fancied teammate Christine Wachtel. Wodars led through 200m in 27.0, 400m 56.43 and 600m 1:25.6. Wachtel then took over but Wodars came back to pass her 40m from the line. Nadezhda Olizarenko was last in her semi in 2:05.27, having led at 400m in 57.46, but then succumbing to a leg injury.
1. Sigrun Wodars (GDR) 1:56.10
2. Christine Wachtel (GDR) 1:56.64
3. Kim Gallagher (USA) 1:56.91
4. Slobodanka Čolović (Yug) 1:57.50
5. Delisa Walton-Floyd (USA) 1:57.80
6. Inna Yevseyeva (SU) 1:59.37
7. Teresa Zuñiga (Spa) 1:59.82
8. Diane Edwards (UK) 2:00.77

Paula Ivan had a huge margin of victory in the 1500 metres (George Herringshaw/ASP)

1500 METRES
Paula Ivan gave a magnificent front-running display to clock the second fastest of all-time. With her opening 400m of 62.52 she had three metres over Mary Slaney with Doina Melinte third. By 800m in 2:05.76 she was 6m up on Melinte (who finished ninth in 4:02.89) and Samolenko. The race was over as she passed 1200m in 3:08.25 to Melinte's 3:12.07. Ivan's last lap was 61.3. Far behind the two Soviets took silver and bronze with Baikauskaite, who had been eighth, 8m behind the pack, with 300m to go, making a very late charge.
1. Paula Ivan (Rom) 3:53.96 OR
2. Laima Baikauskaite (SU) 4:00.24
3. Tatyana Samolenko (SU) 4:00.30
4. Christina Cahill (UK) 4:00.64
5. Lynn Williams (Can) 4:00.86
6. Andrea Hahmann (GDR) 4:00.96
7. Shireen Bailey (UK) 4:02.32
8. Mary Slaney (USA) 4:02.49

3000 METRES
A great race, in which the first six took huge chunks off their previous pbs: Samolenko 9.47 sec, Ivan 12.13, Murray 8.09, Romanova 10.70, Artyomova 7.17, Huber 10.10. As expected Mary Slaney took the early lead, with a very fast 64.4 first lap to pass 1000m in 2:46.68. A big group stayed together and at 2000m, reached in 5:44.08, Huber led. Murray then made a long bid for home, but Ivan passed her with 300m to go, and neither could resist the finishing kick of Samolenko, a 59.95 last lap. Slaney came in tenth in 8:47.13 with another favourite Elly van Hulst ninth in 8:43.92. Defending champion Maricica Puica pulled out of her heat with a calf muscle injury with just 200m to go.
1. Tatyana Samolenko (SU) 8:26.53 OR
2. Paula Ivan (Rom) 8:27.15
3. Yvonne Murray (UK) 8:29.02
4. Yelena Romanova (SU) 8:30.45
5. Natalya Artyomova (SU) 8:31.67
6. Vicki Huber (USA) 8:37.25
7. Wendy Sly (UK) 8:37.70
8. Lynn Williams (Can) 8:38.43

10000 METRES
After a careful start with Lyudmila Matveyeva leading at 1km in 3:09.79 and Lynn Nelson at 2km in 6:23.23, Ingrid Kristiansen took up the pace. She broke the field apart, with only those who had placed 2–5 behind her in Rome in contention. But at 2800m she stepped off the track in agony from a foot injury. Only Kathrin Ullrich was with her at the time, so she was left to pass 3km in 9:19.64, two seconds ahead of Zhupiyeva, McColgan and Bondarenko, with the rest of the field well back. Ullrich led by three seconds at 4km 12:24.13 but was then caught and McColgan led for the rest of the race, until Bondarenko kicked past, running

Mary Slaney leads Yvonne Murray and Paula Ivan in the heats of the 3000 metres (George Herringshaw/ASP)

30.9 for the last 200m. At 5000m the leaders were McColgan 15:37.89, Ullrich 15:37.99, Zhupiyeva 15:38.17, Bondarenko 15:38.28 then Albertina Machado 15:49.22. McColgan's further km splits were 18:48.21, 21:57.70, 25:04.27 and 28:09.26. In fifth place 35-year-old Larrieu-Smith set a world veteran's record.

1. Olga Bondarenko (SU) 31:05.21 OR
2. Liz McColgan (UK) 31:08.44
3. Yelena Zhupiyeva (SU) 31:19.82
4. Kathrin Ullrich (GDR) 31:29.27
5. Francie Larrieu-Smith (USA) 31:35.52
6. Lynn Jennings (USA) 31:39.93
7. Wang Xiuting (Chn) 31:40.23
8. Susan Lee (Can) 31:50.51

MARATHON

Rosa Mota is the woman marathon racer par excellance. A quartet of Mota, Martin, Dörre and Raisa Smekhnova (SU) broke away early, passing 5km in 17:10, but were joined by others through 10km in 34:13, 15km in 51:30 and 20km in 1:08:46. Smekhnova lost contact after 25km 1:25:55 and eventually finished 16th in 2:33:19. 30km was reached in 1:43:13 and 35km in 2:01:09. Mota left her pursuers at 38km, and her 2:18:10 at 40km was 14 sec clear. There were 69 starters, of whom five did not finish, the most notable being Grete Waitz (Nor). Evy Palm (Swe), at 46, the oldest competitor in the athletics events, was 24th in 2:34:41.

1. Rosa Mota (Por) 2:25:40
2. Lisa Martin (Aus) 2:25:53
3. Katrin Dörre (GDR) 2:26:21
4. Tatyana Polovinskaya (SU) 2:27:05
5. Zhao Youfeng (Chn) 2:27:06
6. Laura Fogli (Ita) 2:27:49
7. Danièle Kaber (Lux) 2:29:23
8. Maria Curatolo (Ita) 2:30:14

100 METRES HURDLES
Yordanka Donkova twice improved the Olympic record, running 12.47 (+1.3) in the second round before her 12.38 in the final. Oschkenat was in medal contention before hit by an injury in the final. The world champion Ginka Zagorcheva, injured in June, was unable to finish her first round race.
1. Yordanka Donkova (Bul) 12.38 OR
2. Gloria Siebert (GDR) 12.61
3. Claudia Zaczkiewicz (FRG) 12.75
4. Natalya Grigoryeva (SU) 12.79
5. Florence Colle (Fra) 12.98
6. Julie Rocheleau (Can) 12.99
7. Monique Ewanje-Epeé (Fra) 13.14
8. Cornelia Oschkenat (GDR) 13.73
(wind +0.2)

400 METRES HURDLES
The Olympic record first went to Ellen Fiedler in the heats at 54.58. Then in the semis Debbie Flintoff-King ran 54.00 to beat Ledovskaya by just 0.01. There was the same differential between them in the final when Ledovskaya led from the gun but was caught by the Australian just before the finish. They moved to 2nd and 3rd on the all-time list. The times for second to eighth were records for all those places.
1. Debbie Flintoff-King (Aus) 53.17 OR
2. Tatyana Ledovskaya (SU) 53.18
3. Ellen Fiedler (GDR) 53.63
4. Sabine Busch (GDR) 53.69
5. Sally Gunnell (UK) 54.03
6. Gudrun Abt (FRG) 54.04
7. Tatyana Kurochkina (SU) 54.39
8. LaTanya Sheffield (USA) 55.32

HIGH JUMP
Stefka Kostadinova was the odds-on favourite, but after failing three times at 2.03m, lost the gold when Louise Ritter went over that height on the first attempt of the jump-off. Both had seven successive first-time clearances at all heights from 1.80 to 2.01. Bykova secured the bronze with a third attempt 1.99. Astafei was the highest placed of the World Junior champions who competed in Seoul.
1. Louise Ritter (USA) 2.03 OR
2. Stefka Kostadinova (Bul) 2.01
3. Tamara Bykova (SU) 1.99
4. Olga Turchak (SU) 1.96
5= Galina Astafei (Rom) 1.93
5= Lyudmila Andonova (Bul) 1.93
7. Christine Stanton (Aus) 1.93
8. Diana Davies (UK) 1.90

During and after Louise Ritter's gold medal clearance in Seoul (George Herringshaw/ASP)

LONG JUMP
Jackie Joyner-Kersee had improved the Olympic record to 7.27 in the heptathlon and improved it again to 7.40 in the fifth round in the individual event to secure her second gold and repeat her World Championships double. The lead changed hands as follows: first round: Drechsler 6.92, JJK 7.00, Chistyakova 7.11; then Drechsler took over with 7.18 in the third and 7.22 in the fourth, at which stage JJK was second with 7.16 and Chistyakova third. Then came the winning effort. Drechsler, who had a 7.06 in the second round, ended with 7.16 and 7.17. The first four were way ahead of the rest. Byelevskaya, 7.06, had the only 7m plus qualifying jump.
1. Jackie Joyner-Kersee (USA) 7.40 OR
2. Heike Drechsler (GDR) 7.22
3. Galina Chistyakova (SU) 7.11
4. Yelena Byelevskaya (SU) 7.04
5. Nicole Boegman (Aus) 6.73
6. Fiona May (UK) 6.62
7. Agata Karczmarek (Pol) 6.60
8. Sabine John (GDR) 6.55

SHOT
Natalya Lisovskaya had all six puts in the final ahead of the silver medal throw. Her series: 21.69, 21.49, 21.24, 21.74, 21.11, 22.24. Li Meisu's bronze was the first medal ever won by a Chinese woman athlete. Neimke moved from third to second in the last round. Although in a slightly different order the first seven were the same as in Rome 1987.
1. Natalya Lisovskaya (SU) 22.24
2. Kathrin Neimke (GDR) 21.07
3. Li Meisu (Chn) 21.06
4. Ines Müller (GDR) 20.37
5. Claudia Losch (FRG) 20.27
6. Heike Hartwig (GDR) 20.20
7. Natalya Akhrimenko (SU) 20.13
8. Huang Zhihong (Chn) 19.82

DISCUS
Martina Hellmann led the qualifiers with 67.12 and set new Olympic records with her first and fourth throws of this final series: 71.84, 64.80, 68.70, 72.30, 69.66, 67.50. Gansky, seventh after four rounds, produced 71.88 and 68.08 in the last two rounds, Khristova's best was in the fifth round, and Mitkova and Zvereva both had their best throws in the final round. The order of the first three were the same as in Rome.
1. Martina Hellmann (GDR) 72.30 OR
2. Diana Gansky (GDR) 71.88
3. Tsvetanka Khristova (Bul) 69.74

A second gold medal for Jackie Joyner-Kersee (George Herringshaw/ASP)

4. Svetla Mitkova (Bul) 69.14
5. Ellina Zvereva (SU) 68.94
6. Zdenka Šilhavá (Cs) 67.84
7. Gabrielle Reinsch (GDR) 67.26
8. Hou Xuemei (Chn) 65.94

JAVELIN
Petra Felke gained her revenge for major wins in recent years by Fatima Whitbread with a series of: 72.62 OR, 74.68 OR, 66.12, 66.76, 71.12, 68.38. Whitbread, with a season of illness and injury behind her, needed three throws to qualify, but then produced 68.44 to Felke's 67.06. In the final Koch was second in the first round with 67.30 before Whitbread moved into

the silver spot in the second round, with a series of 61.98, 67.46, 66.58, 64.86, 67.82, 70.32, the latter a season's best. Defending champion Tessa Sanderson had a leg injury and struggled to throw merely 56.70 in the qualifying round. Others to fail to qualify included Beate Peters 60.20 and Tiina Lillak 60.06.

1. Petra Felke (GDR) 74.68
2. Fatima Whitbread (UK) 70.32
3. Beate Koch (GDR) 67.30
4. Irina Kostyuchenkova (SU) 67.00
5. Silke Renk (GDR) 66.38
6. Natalya Yermolovich (SU) 64.84
7. Donna Mayhew (USA) 61.78
8. Ingrid Thyssen (FRG) 60.76

HEPTATHLON

Jackie Joyner-Kersee led from the opening event, 12.69 for 100mh. A little down on expectations in HJ 186m and SP 15.80m, she ran a blistering 22.56 for 200m to end the first day with 4264 points, leading from John 4083 and Behmer 3986. That medal order stayed throughout the second day, which JJK opened with an Olympic record long jump of 7.27 (+0.7). After a 45.66 JT she needed 2:13.6, and ran a pb 800m of 2:08.51, for her fourth world record. The two East Germans produced the best ever marks for second and third places. Chantal Beaugeant (Fra) crashed in the 100mh, running 16.76, and withdrew after three events.

1. Jackie Joyner-Kersee (USA) 7291 WR
2. Sabine John (GDR) 6897
3. Anke Behmer (GDR) 6858
4. Natalya Shubenkova (SU) 6540
5. Remigia Sablovskaite (SU) 6456
6. Ines Schulz (GDR) 6411
7. Jane Flemming (Aus) 6351
8. Cindy Greiner (USA) 6297

4 x 100 METRES RELAY

Alice Brown, Sheila Echols and Florence Griffith-Joyner got the baton, just, to Evelyn Ashford to take the US team to victory over her old rival Marlies Göhr, anchoring the GDR team.

1. USA 41.98
2. GDR 42.09
3. USSR 42.75
4. FR Germany 42.76
5. Bulgaria 43.02
6. Poland 43.93
7. France 44.02

dns Jamaica

4 x 400 METRES RELAY

The splits for the USSR team were: Tatyana Ledovskaya 50.12, Olga Nazarova 47.82, Maria Pinigina 49.43 and Olga Bryzgina 47.80. Denean Howard had led for the USA with 49.82, then Diane Dixon ran 49.17 behind Nazarova's brilliant run, Valerie Brisco closed the gap to just 0.06 with a 48.44 and the stage was set for the final Olympic run in 1988 of Florence Griffith-Joyner. She ran marvellously for a 48.08 leg but couldn't match her Soviet rival, so ended the Games with three golds and a silver. Both teams bettered the old world record of 3:15.92 set by the GDR in 1984.

1. USSR 3:15.17 WR
2. USA 3:15.51
3. GDR 3:18.29
4. FR Germany 3:22.49
5. Jamaica 3:23.13
6. United Kingdom 3:26.89
7. France 3:29.37

dnf Canada

WR – *world record*, OR – *Olympic record*

OLYMPIC GAMES – RECORDS

The first Olympic Games of the modern era were staged in Athens, Greece from the 6th to 15th April 1896. Those in Seoul, the Games of the XXIVth Olympiad, were the 21st to be staged, including the intercalated Games of 1906.

Just 59 athletes from ten nations contested the athletics events in 1896.

Olympic Games records after 1988

MEN

Event	Performance	Holder
100m	9.92	Carl Lewis (USA) 1988
200m	19.75	Joe DeLoach (USA) 1988
400m	43.86A	Lee Evans (USA) 1968
800m	1:43.00	Joaquim Cruz (Bra) 1984
1500m	3:32.53	Sebastian Coe (UK) 1984
5000m	13:05.59	Said Aouita (Mor) 1984
10000m	27:21.46	Brahim Boutayeb (Mor) 1988
Marathon	2hr 09:21	Carlos Lopes (Por) 1984
3000mSt	8:05.51	Julius Kariuki (Ken) 1988
110mh	12.98	Roger Kingdom (USA) 1988
400mh	47.19	Andre Phillips (USA) 1988
4x100mR	37.83	USA 1984
4x400mR	2:56.16	USA 1968 (A) & 1988
20km walk	1hr 19:57	Jozef Pribilinec (Cs) 1988
50km walk	3hr 38:29	Vyacheslav Ivanenko (SU) 1988
High jump	2.38	Gennadiy Avdeyenko (SU) 1988
Pole vault	5.90	Sergey Bubka (SU) 1988
Long jump	8.90A	Bob Beamon (USA) 1968
Triple jmp	17.61	Khristo Markov (Bul) 1988
Shot	22.47	Ulf Timmermann (GDR) 1988
Discus	68.82	Jürgen Schult (GDR) 1988
Hammer	84.80	Sergey Litvinov (SU) 1988
Javelin	85.90	Jan Zelezný (Cs) *1988
old	94.58	Miklos Nemeth (Hun) 1976
Decathlon	8847	Daley Thompson (UK) 1984

WOMEN

Event	Performance	Holder
100m	10.54	Florence Griffith-Joyner (USA) 1988
200m	21.34	Florence Griffith-Joyner (USA) 1988
400m	48.65	Olga Bryzgina (SU) 1988
800m	1:53.43	Nadezhda Olizarenko (SU) 1980
1500m	3:53.96	Paula Ivan (ROM) 1988
3000m	8:26.53	Tatyana Samolenko (SU) 1988
10000m	31:05.21	Olga Bondarenko (SU) 1988
Marathon	2hr 24:52	Joan Benoit (USA) 1984
100mh	12.38	Yordanka Donkova (Bul) 1988
400mh	53.17	Debbie Flintoff-King (Aus) 1988
4x100mR	41.60	GDR 1980
4x400mR	3:15.17	USSR 1988
High jump	2.03	Louise Ritter (USA) 1988
Long jump	7.40	Jackie Joyner-Kersee (USA) 1988
Shot	22.41	Ilona Slupianek (GDR) 1980
Discus	72.30	Martina Hellmann (GDR) 1988
Javelin	74.68	Petra Felke (GDR) 1988
Heptathlon	7291	Jackie Joyner-Kersee (USA) 1988

** performance made in qualifying round, A at high altitude, Mexico City 2240m*

Most gold medals – all events

MEN

- 10 Raymond Ewry (USA) StHJ and StLJ 1900–04–06–08, StTJ 1900–04
- 9 Paavo Nurmi (Fin) 1500m 1924, 5000m 1924, 10000m 1920–28, 3000mSt 1924, CC 1920–24, CC team 1920–24
- 6 Carl Lewis (USA) 100m, 200m, LJ & 4x100mR 1984; 100m, LJ 1988
- 5 Martin Sheridan (USA) DT 1904–06–08, SP 1906, DT (Greek style) 1908
- 5 Ville Ritola (Fin) 10000m, 3000mSt, CC team & 3000m team 1924, 5000m 1928
- 4 twelve men

WOMEN

- 4 Fanny Blankers-Koen (Hol) 100m, 200m, 80mh & 4x100mR 1948
- 4 Betty Cuthbert (Aus) 100m, 200m, 4x100mR 1956, 400m 1964
- 4 Bärbel Wöckel (GDR) 200m & 4x100mR 1976–80

Most medals – all events
(G gold, S silver, B bronze)
MEN
12 Paavo Nurmi (Fin) 9G as above; 3S 5000m 1920–28, 3000mSt 1928
10 Raymond Ewry (USA) 10G as above
9 Martin Sheridan (USA) 5G as above; 3S StHJ, StLJ & Stone 1906; 1B StLJ 1908
8 Ville Ritola (Fin) 5G as above; 3S 5000m & CC 1924, 10000m 1928
7 Carl Lewis (USA) 6G as above; 1S 200m 1988
WOMEN
7 Shirley de la Hunty (Aus) 3G as above; 1S 4x100mR 1948; 3B 100m 1948–52, 80mh 1948
7 Irena Szewinska (Pol) 3G as above; 2S 200m & LJ 1964, 2B 100m 1968, 200m 1972

Most gold medals at one Games:
5 Paavo Nurmi (Fin) 1924

Most medals at one Games:
6 (4 gold, 2 silver) Ville Ritola (Fin) 1924

The most Games contested:
Lia Manoliu (Rom) 1952–72 at discus

The most finals (or first eight) at the same event:
5 Vladimir Golubnichiy (SU) 20kmW 1960–76 (1–3-1–2-7)

Oldests
(y – years, d – days)
MEN
Winner
42y 24d Pat McDonald (USA) 56lb Wt 1920
Medallist
48y 115d Tebbs Lloyd Johnson (UK) 3rd 50kmW 1948
Competitor
52y 199d Percy Wyer (Can) Mar 1936
WOMEN
Winner
36y 176d Lia Manoliu (Rom) DT 1968
Medallist
37y 348d Dana Zatopkova (Cs) 2nd JT 1960
Competitor
46y 282d Joyce Smith (UK) 11th Mar 1984

Youngests
MEN
Winner
17y 263d Bob Mathias (USA) Dec 1948
Medallist
17y 169d Frank Castleman (USA) 2nd 200mh 1904
17y 206d Pal Simon (Hun) 3rd Medley relay 1908
(born 1891, but exact date unknown, 17–206 is oldest possible)
Ind. medal
17y 263d Bob Mathias (as above)

WOMEN
Winner
15y 123d Barbara Pearl Jones (USA) 4x100mR 1952
Ind. winner
16y 123d Ulrike Meyfarth (GFR) HJ 1972
Medallist
15y 123d Barbara Pearl Jones (as above)
Ind. medal
16y 115d Dorothy Odam (UK) 2nd HJ 1936

Medal table of leading nations (including 1906 Games)

Nation	Men			Women			Total
	Gold	Silver	Bronze	Gold	Silver	Bronze	Medals
USA	241	178	152	32	21	11	635
USSR	34	35	40	30	20	34	193
UK	41	54	38	4	20	12	169
GDR	14	19	14	25	28	24	124
Finland	47	32	29	–	2	–	110
F.R.Germany *	11	24	34	11	13	12	105
Sweden	17	24	41	–	–	3	85
Australia	6	9	11	11	8	11	56
France	7	19	17	3	1	2	49
Canada	9	9	16	2	5	6	47
Italy	13	7	18	3	4	2	47
Poland	9	7	4	6	8	7	41
Hungary	6	13	16	3	1	2	41

In all 62 nations have won medals at track and field sports, with Djibouti and Senegal added to the list in 1988.

* *Germany 1896–1952, since then the Federal Republic of Germany. Medals won by the combined German teams of 1956, 1960 and 1964 have been allocated to FRG or GDR according to the athlete's origin.*

WORLD CHAMPIONSHIPS

Athletics events at the Olympic Games have had world championship status, but the first championships for athletics alone were staged in the Olympic Stadium, Helsinki, Finland in 1983. The second world championships were held in Rome in September 1987. Champions:

MEN	1983			1987		
100m	Carl Lewis	USA	10.07	Ben Johnson	Can	9.83
200m	Calvin Smith	USA	20.14	Calvin Smith	USA	20.16
400m	Bert Cameron	Jam	45.05	Thomas Schönlebe	GDR	44.33
800m	Willi Wülbeck	FRG	1:43.65	Billy Konchellah	Ken	1:43.06
1500m	Steve Cram	UK	3:41.59	Abdi Bile	Som	3:36.80
5000m	Eamonn Coghlan	Ire	13:28.53	Said Aouita	Mor	13:26.44
10000m	Alberto Cova	Ita	28:01.04	Paul Kipkoech	Ken	27:38.63
Marathon	Rob de Castella	Aus	2:10:03	Douglas Wakiihuri	Ken	2:11:48
3000m St:	Patriz Ilg	FRG	8:15.06	Francesco Panetta	Ita	8:08.57
110mh	Greg Foster	USA	13.42	Greg Foster	USA	13.21
400mh	Edwin Moses	USA	47.50	Edwin Moses	USA	47.46
High jump	Gennadiy Avdeyenko	SU	2.32	Patrik Sjöberg	Swe	2.38
Pole vault	Sergey Bubka	SU	5.70	Sergey Bubka	SU	5.85
Long jump	Carl Lewis	USA	8.55	Carl Lewis	USA	8.67
Triple jump	Zdzislaw Hoffmann	Pol	17.42	Khristo Markov	Bul	17.92
Shot	Edward Sarul	Pol	21.39	Werner Günthör	Swi	22.23
Discus	Imrich Bugár	Cs	67.72	Jürgen Schult	GDR	68.74
Hammer	Sergey Litvinov	SU	82.68	Sergey Litvinov	SU	83.06
Javelin	Detlef Michel	GDR	89.48*	Seppo Räty	Fin	83.54
Decathlon	Daley Thompson	UK	8714	Torsten Voss	GDR	8680
4x100mR	USA		37.86	USA		37.90
4x400mR	USSR		3:00.79	USA		2:57.29
20km walk	Ernesto Canto	Mex	1:20:49	Maurizio Damilano	Ita	1:20:45
50km walk	Ronald Weigel	GDR	3:43:08	Hartwig Gauder	GDR	3:40:53
WOMEN						
100m	Marlies Göhr	GDR	10.97	Silke Gladisch	GDR	10.90
200m	Marita Koch	GDR	22.13	Silke Gladisch	GDR	21.74
400m	Jarmila Kratochvílová	Cs	47.99	Olga Bryzgina	SU	49.38
800m	Jarmila Kratochvílová	Cs	1:54.68	Sigrun Wodars	GD	1:55.26
1500m	Mary Decker	USA	4:00.90	Tatyana Samolenko	SU	3:58.56
3000m	Mary Decker	USA	8:34.62	Tatyana Samolenko	SU	8:38.73
10000m	not held			Ingrid Kristiansen	Nor	31:05.85
Marathon	Grete Waitz	Nor	2:28:09	Rosa Mota	Por	2:25:17
100mh	Bettina Jahn	GDR	12.35	Ginka Zagorcheva	Bul	12.34
400mh	Yekaterina Fesenko	SU	54.14	Sabine Busch	GDR	53.62
High jump	Tamara Bykova	SU	2.01	Stefka Kostadinova	Bul	2.09
Long jump	Heike Daute	GDR	7.27w	Jackie Joyner-Kersee	USA	7.36
Shot	Helena Fibingerova	Cs	21.05	Natalya Lisovskaya	SU	21.24
Discus	Martina Opitz	GDR	68.94	Martina Hellmann (née Opitz)	GDR	71.62
Javelin	Tiina Lillak	Fin	70.82	Fatima Whitbread	UK	76.64
Heptathlon	Ramona Neubert	GDR	6770	Jackie Joyner-Kersee	USA	7128
10km walk	not held			Irina Strakhova	SU	44:12
4x100mR	GDR		41.76	USA		41.58
4x400mR	GDR		3:19.73	GDR		3:18.63

Championship bests not included above:

MEN:

1500m	3:35.67	Abdi Bile	Som	1987 sf
5000m:	13:22.68	John Ngugi	Ken	1987 ht
110mh:	13.20	Greg Foster	USA	1987 ht
High jump:	2.38	Gennadiy Avdeyenko	USSR	& Igor Paklin USSR 2nd equal

WORLD JUNIOR CHAMPIONSHIPS

First held at Athens, Greece 16–20 July 1986, the second edition was held at Sudbury, Canada 27–31 July 1988, contested by 1052 athletes from 122 countries, with medals being won by athletes from 31 countries.

Conditions were dry throughout, often very hot (up to 40°C), but breezy. The heat adversely affected the distance events but was conducive to fast sprinting. There was a high standard of competition and the meeting was staged with wholehearted and friendly support from the people of Sudbury in Northern Ontario.

Overall the GDR women and the Kenyan distance runners made the greatest impact. The highest class performance was, as in 1986, probably by the great Ilke Wyludda who retained her title in the women's discus. She was also European junior champion in 1985 and 1987. Also retaining their titles were Svetla Dimitrova in the heptathlon and Wilfred Oanda Kirochi, who produced a 53 second last lap in the 1500m. The Kenyan has certainly dominated junior running as he has also twice won the World Junior cross-country title. Galina Astafei first equalled her world junior record in the high jump at 1.98m and then improved to 2.00m, and István Bagyula equalled the WJR pole vault with 5.65m. Sharing a new WJR in the 4x400m relay was 16-year-old Grit Breuer, who thus won the most medals as she had won the 400m and also ran on the GDR 4x100m relay team. That team also set an official WJR, although they had run a faster 43.33 eleven days earlier in a warm-up meeting. Breuer's teammates on the latter, Diana Dietz and Kathrin Krabbe, both won two golds and a silver.

Medallists in 1988

MEN

100m: (–2.7) 1. Andre Cason (USA) 10.22 (10.17 =CBP qf), 2. Sven Matthes (GDR) 10.28, 3. Aleksandr Shlychkov (SU) 10.37

200m: (+4.2) 1. Kevin Braunskill (USA) 20.87, 2. Oladape Adeniken (Nig) 20.88, 3. Dimitriy Bartenyev (SU) 20.92

400m: 1. Tomasz Jedrusik (Pol) 46.19, 2. Stephen Perry (Aus) 46.74, 3. Anthony Eziuka (Nig) 46.81

800m: 1. Jonah Birir (Ken) 1:50.03, 2. Kevin McKay (GB) 1:50.79, 3. Melfort Homela (Zim) 1:51.34

1500m: 1. Wilfred Oanda Kirochi (Ken) 3:46.52 (3:43.51 CBP h), 2. Nourredine Morceli (Alg) 4:46.93, 3. Fermin Cacho (Spa) 3:47.31

5000m: 1. Henry Kirui (Ken) 13:54.29 CBP, 2. Mohamed Choumassi (Mor) 13:54.36 Addis Abede (Eth) 13:58.08

10000m: 1. Addis Abebe (Eth) 28:42.13 CBP, 2. Bedelu Kibret (Ken) 28:48.55, 3. James Songok (Ken) 28:50.42

20km Road: 1. Zeleke Metaferia (Eth) 59:27 CBP, 2. Thomas Osano (Ken) 1:00:14, 3. Abel Gisemba (Ken) 1:00.36

3000mSt: 1. William Chemitei (Ken) 8:41.61 CBP, 2. Mathew Birir (Ken) 8:44.54, 3. Arto Kuusisto (Fin) 8:46.42

110mh: (+3.1) 1. Reynaldo Quintero (Cub) 13.71, 2. Stephen Brown (USA) 13.73, 3. Elbert Ellis (USA) 13.78

400mh: 1. Kelly Carter (USA) 49.50 CBP, 2. Musur Matescu (Rom) 50.70, 3. Vadim Zadoynov (SU) 50.88

HJ: 1. Artur Partyka (Pol) 2.28 CBP, 2. Lambros Papacostas (Gre) 2.25, 3= Park Jae-hong (Kor) & Jaroslaw Kotewicz (Pol) 2.22

PV: 1. István Bagyula (Hun) 5.65 =WJR, 2. Maxim Tarasov (SU) 5.60, 3. Andrey Grudinin (SU) 5.30

LJ: 1. Luis Bueno (Cub) 7.99 (-1.0) CBP, 2. Saul Isalgue (Cub) 7.78, 3. Nai Hui-fang (Tai) 7.77w

TJ: 1. Vladimir Melikhov (SU) 16.69 (+1.6), 2. Galin Georgiev (Bul) 16.18, 3. Eugene Greene (Bah) 16.16

SP: 1. Aleksandr Klimenko (SU) 18.92 CBP, 2. Michael Stulce (USA) 18.47, 3. Aleksandr Klimov (SU) 18.06

DT: 1. Andreas Seelig (GDR) 58.60, 2. Kami Keshmiri (USA) 54.68, 3. Yuriy Nesterets (SU) 53.70

HT: 1. Vadim Kolsenik 69.52, 2. Oleg Palushik (SU) 69.00, 3. Thomas Hommel (GDR) 66.06

JT: 1. Vladimir Ovchinnikov (SU) 77.08, 2. Steve Backley (UK) 75.40, 3. Jens Reimann (GDR) 71.64

Dec: 1. Michael Kohnle (FRG) 7729 CBP, 2. Robert Zmelik (CS) 7659, 3. Eduard Hamalyainen (SU) 7596

10kmW: 1. Alberto Cruz (Mex) 41:16.11, 2. Valentin Massana (Esp) 41:33.95, 3. Mikhail Khmelnitskiy (SU) 41:38.36

4x100mR: 1. USA (Kevin Braunskill, Quincy Watts, Andre Cason, Terrance Warren) 39.27 CBP, 2. Nigeria 39.66, 3. United Kingdom 40.06

4x400mR: 1. USA (Jesse Carr, Christopher Nelloms, Jerome Williams, Ralph Carrington) 3:05.09, 2. Australia 3:07.60, 3. Jamaica 3:08.00

WOMEN

100m: (-0.4) 1. Diana Dietz (GDR) 11.18 CBP, 2. Kathrin Krabbe (GDR) 11.23, 3. Liliana Allen (Cub) 11.36

200m: (+2.3) 1. Kathrin Krabbe (GDR) 22.34 CBP(w), 2. Diana Dietz (GDR) 22.88, 3. Liliana Allen (Cub) 22.97

400m: 1. Grit Breuer (GDR) 51.24 CBP, 2. Maicel Malone (USA) 52.23, 3. Olga Moroz (SU) 53.20

800m: 1. Birte Bruhns (GDR) 2:00.67 CBP, 2. Catalina Gheorghiu (Rom) 2:01.96, 3. Dorota Buczkowska (Pol) 2:02.94

1500m: 1. Doina Homneac (Rom) 4:12.94 CBP, 2. Snežana Pajkić (Yug) 4:16.19, 3. Yvonne van der Kolk (Hol) 4:16.35

3000m: 1. Ann Mwangi (Ken) 9:13.99, 2. Fernanda Ribeiro (Por) 9:15.33, 3. Yvonne Lichtenfeld (GDR) 9:16.02

10000m: 1. Jane Ngotho (Ken) 33:49.45, 2. Olga Nazarkina (SU) 33:50.03, 3. Monica Gama (Por) 34:16.13

100mh: (-2.6) 1. Aliuska Lopez (Cub) 13.23 (12.96 +1.6 CBP sf), 2. Birgit Wolf (FRG) 13.51, 3. Zhanna Gurbanova (SU) 13.64

400mh: 1. Antje Axmann (GDR) 57.47, 2. Ann Maenhout (Bel) 57.58, 3. Silvia Rieger (FRG) 57.88

HJ: 1. Galina Astafei (Rom) 2.00 WJR, 2. Yelena Yeleshina (SU) 1.96, 3. Karen Scholz (GDR) 1.92

LJ: 1. Fiona May (UK) 6.88w +2.1/6.82 +1.8 CBP, 2. Anu Kaljurand (SU) 6.78w, 3. Joanne Wise (UK) 6.69w

SP: 1. Ines Wittich (GDR) 18.54 CBP, 2. Heike Rohrmann (GDR) 17.84, 3. Elvira Polyakova (SU) 17.10

DT: 1. Ilke Wyludda (GDR) 68.24 CBP, 2. Astrid Kumbernuss (GDR) 64.08, 3. Proletka Voycheva (Bul) 58.94

JT: 1. Karen Forkel (GDR) 61.44, 2. Isel López (Cub) 57.86, 3. Malgorzata Kielczewska (Pol) 57.04

Hep: 1. Svetla Dimitrova (Bul) 6289 CBP, 2. Yelena Petushkova (SU) 6102, 3. Peggy Beer (GDR) 6067

5kmW: 1. Maria Cruz Diaz (Spa) 21:51.31 CBP, 2. Olga Sanchez (Spa) 21:58.17, 3. Maria Grazia Orsani (Ita) 22:04.74

4x100mR: 1. GDR (Grit Breuer, Kathrin Krabbe, Diana Dietz, Katrin Henke) 43.48 CBP, 2. Cuba 44.04, 3. USA 44.27

4x400mR: 1. GDR (Manuela Deer, Stefanie Fabert, Anke Wöhlk, Grit Breuer) 3:28.39 WJR, 2. USA 3:31.48, 3. USSR 3:31.89

Medal table for leading nations

Nation	1st	2nd	3rd
GDR	11	5	5
Kenya	6	2	2
USA	5	5	2
USSR	4	6	12
Cuba	3	3	2
Romania	2	2	–
Ethiopia	2	1	1
Poland	2	–	3
UK	1	2	2
Spain	1	2	1

The top four nations were the same in 1986 when their tallies were:

GDR 8–4-7,
USSR 6–6-7,
USA 5–4-2,
Kenya 4–4-0

Championship bests

Those set in 1988 are indicated above by CBP. Those still standing from 1986 are:

MEN

100m:	Derrick Florence (USA) 10.17 (=1988)
200m:	Stanley Kerr (USA) 20.74
400m:	Roberto Hernández (Cub) 45.53 sf
800m:	Pedrag Melnjak (Yug) 1:48.25 sf
2000mSt:	(1986 only) Juan Azkueta (Spa) 5:28.56
110mh:	Colin Jackson (UK) 13.44
TJ:	Igor Parigin (USSR) 16.97
DT:	Vasil Baklarov (Bul) 60.60
HT:	Vitaliy Alissevich (SU) 72.00

JT: Vladimir Zasimovich (SU) 78.84
10kmW: Mikhail Shchennikov (SU) 40:38.01
4x400mR: USA (Clifton Campbell, Chip Rish, Percy Waddle, William Reed) 3:01.90

WOMEN
200m: Falilat Ogunkoya (Nig) 23.11 (legal best)
3000m: Cleopatra Palacian (Rom) 9:02.91
10000m: Katrin Kley (GDR) 33:19.67
400mh: Claudia Bartl (GDR) 56.76
JT: Xiomara Rivero (Cub) 62.86

Most World Championships gold medals

MEN
2 Peter Chumba (Ken) 5000m & 10000m 1986
2 W. Oanda Kirochi (Ken) 1500m 1986 & 1988
2 Andre Cason (USA) 100m & 4x100mR 1988
2 Kevin Braunskill (USA) 200m & 4x100mR 1988

WOMEN
3 Grit Breuer (GDR) 400m, 4x100mR, 4x400mR 1988
2 Ilke Wyludda (GDR) DT 1986 & 1988
2 Svetla Dimitrova (Bul) Hep 1986 & 1988
2 Diana Dietz (GDR) 100m & 4x100mR 1988
2 Kathrin Krabbe (GDR) 200m & 4x100mR 1988

Most medals
5 Kathrin Krabbe (GDR) 3rd 200m, 2nd 4x100mR 1986; 1st 200m & 4x100mR, 2nd 100m 1988

Most championship bests
7 Ilke Wyludda (GDR) DT 61.58, 62.26, 62.30, 64.02 1986; 65.78, 67.00, 68.24 1988

Youngest champions

MEN
16yr 221d W. Oanda Kirochi (Ken) 1500m 1986
16yr 215d Jonah Birir (Ken) 800m 1988

WOMEN
15yr 102d Wang Yan (Chn) 5000m walk 1986
15yr 169d Ann Mwangi (Ken) 3000m 1988

THE I.A.A.F. WORLD CUP

BY PETER MATTHEWS

The fifth IAAF World Cup in Athletics will be staged in Barcelona, the Catalonian capital in north-east Spain on 8–10 September 1989. The venue will be the Olympic Stadium of Montjuich, which will be the main Olympic competition venue in 1992. Its original 500m track was been relaid, eleven metres lower to conform with IAAF regulations as a 400m oval.

The idea of having a competition between teams representing the continents and top athletics nations was conceived in 1975 and the first World Cup was staged in Düsseldorf (FRG) on 2–4 Sep 1977. Subsequent World Cups have been held: 1979 Montreal, 1981 Rome, 1985 Canberra. The aims of the IAAF for these events have been to provide a great athletics meeting, to offer additional world-class competition for the sport's elite, to stimulate the continental areas not only in the World Cup competition itself but also by the staging of trial meetings to determine the teams, and not least to provide additional revenue for the development of athletics throughout the world.

The competing teams represent each of the five continents, with national teams from the USA and the top two men's and women's teams from the European Cup. In 1989 host nation Spain competes as a ninth team as did Italy in 1981.

Yifter the Shifter, who used his devastating kick to doubles in two World Cups (Mark Shearman)

Team Positions

	MEN				WOMEN			
Team	**1977**	**1979**	**1981**	**1985**	**1977**	**1979**	**1981**	**1985**
Africa	6	6	7	5	7	7	9	8
Americas	5	5	5	6	5	5	5	4
Asia	8	8	9	8	8	8	8	7
Europe	4	2	1	4	1	3	2	3
GDR	1	3	2	3	2	1	1	1
FRG	3	–	–	–	–	–	–	–
Italy	–	–	6	–	–	–	6	–
Oceania	7	7	8	7	6	6	7	6
USA	2	1	3	1	4	4	4	5
USSR	–	4	4	2	3	2	3	2

Best Performances

MEN

100m	10.00	Ben Johnson (Can) 1985
200m	20.17	Clancy Edwards (USA) 1977
400m	44.47	Mike Franks (USA) 1985
800m	1:44.04	Alberto Juantorena (Cub) 1977
1500m	3:34.45	Steve Ovett (UK) 1977
5000m	13:13.82	Miruts Yifter (Eth) 1977
10000m	27:38.43	Werner Schildhauer (GDR) 1981
3000mSt	8:19.89	Boguslaw Maminski (Pol) 1981
110mh	13.32	Greg Foster (USA) 1981
400mh	47.31	Edwin Moses (USA) 1981
HJ	2.31	Patrik Sjöberg (Swe) 1985
PV	5.85	Sergey Bubka (SU) 1985
LJ	8.52	Larry Myricks (USA) 1979
TJ	17.58	Willie Banks (USA) 1985
Shot	22.00	Ulf Timmermann (GDR) 1985
Discus	69.08	Gennadiy Kolnootchenko (SU) 1985
Hammer	82.12	Juri Tamm (SU) 1985
JT (old)	96.96	Uwe Hohn (GDR) 1985
4x100mR	38.03	USA 1977
4x400mR	2:59.12	USA 1981

WOMEN

100m	11.02	Evelyn Ashford (USA) 1981
200m	21.83	Evelyn Ashford (USA) 1979
400m	47.60	Marita Koch (GDR) 1985
800m	1:57.48	Lyudmila Veselkova (SU) 1981
1500m	4:03.33	Tamara Sorokina (SU) 1981
3000m	8:36.32	Svyetlana Ulmasova (SU) 1979
10000m	32:07.50	Aurora Cunha (Por) 1985
100mh	12.67	Grazyna Rabsztyn (Pol) 1979
400mh	54.45	Sabine Busch (GDR) 1985
HJ	2.00	Stefka Kostadinova (Bul) 1985
LJ	7.27	Heike Drechsler (GDR) 1985
Shot	20.98	Ilona Slupianek (GDR) 1979
Discus	69.78	Martina Opitz (GDR) 1985
Javelin	70.08	Antoaneta Todorova (Bul) 1981
4x100mR	41.37	GDR 1985
4x400mR	3:19.50	GDR 1985

Grete Waitz won the 3000 metres in the first World Cup in Düsseldorf in 1977 (George Herringshaw/ASP)

Three world records have been set in World Cup competition:

MEN:
4x100mR USA (Bill Collins, Steve Riddick, Cliff Wiley and Steve Williams) 38.03 1977

WOMEN:
400m Marita Koch (GDR) 47.60 1985; 4x100mR GDR (Silke Gladisch, Sabine Rieger, Ingrid Auerswald, Marlies Göhr) 41.37 1985.

Most individual event wins

MEN
4 Miruts Yifter (Afr/Eth) 5000m & 10000m 1977–79
3 Ed Moses (USA) 400mh 1977–79–81
3 João de Oliveira (Ame/Bra) TJ 1977–79–81
3 Udo Beyer (GDR) SP 1977–79–81

WOMEN
4 Evelyn Ashford (USA) 100m & 200m 1981–83
3 Marita Koch (GDR) 400m 1979–85, 200m 1985

WORLD CROSS-COUNTRY CHAMPIONSHIPS

BY PETER MATTHEWS

Two stalwarts of the International Cross-Country Championships: Gaston Roelants (98) and Mariano Haro (40), the former had four wins, the latter four successive second places (Mark Shearman)

The IAAF World Cross-Country Championships were first held on 17 Mar 1973 at the Hippodrome de Waregem, Belgium. This series was preceded by the International Cross-Country Championships, which were first held at Hamilton Park Racecourse, Glasgow on 28 Mar 1903. Then a race over 8 miles (12.87km) was contested by the four countries from the British Isles, so it was international in name only. From then the race was held annually, with France entering in 1907, Belgium in 1923 and thereafter the event steadily gained in international prestige.

The first non-European nation to enter a team was Tunisia in 1958, the first Oceanic team was New Zealand in 1965 and the USA competed for the first time in 1966. A junior race was first added in 1961, although there had been an international race for juniors between England, France and Belgium in 1940, and the first women's race was at Barry, Wales in 1967. There were two women's races in 1970. A junior women's race was introduced in 1989.

The distances raced now are: Men – 12km, Women – 6km (5km to 1987), Junior Men – 8km. Teams are: Men – maximum of nine runners, six to score; Women and Junior Men – maximum of six runners, four to score.

Records were set for the numbers of competitors (and teams) in 1986 at Neuchatel, Switzerland when the finishers were: 328 men (39 teams), 171 junior men (29), and 161 women (28).

Winning teams – World and International Cross-Country

MEN

England	1903–14, 1920–1, 1924–5, 1930–8, 1951, 1953–5, 1958–60, 1962, 1964–72, 1976, 1979–80
France	1922–3, 1926–9, 1939, 1946–7, 1949–50, 1952, 1956, 1978
Belgium	1948, 1957, 1961, 1963, 1973–4, 1977
Ethiopia	1981–5
Kenya	1986–8
New Zealand	1975

WOMEN

USA	1968–9, 1975, 1979, 1983–5, 1987
England	1967, 1970–74, 1986
USSR	1976–7, 1980–2, 1988
Romania	1978

JUNIOR MEN

England	1961–2, 1964–71, 1978
USA	1974–7, 1981
Ethiopia	1982–7
Spain	1973, 1979
Belgium	1965
Italy	1972
USSR	1980
Kenya	1988

England, Northern Ireland, Scotland and Wales competed separately prior to 1988 when a combined UK team competed for the first time.

IAAF World Cross-country Champions 1973–88

Year	Men	Women	Junior Men
1973	Pekka Paivarinta (Fin)	Paola Cacchi (Ita)	Jim Brown (Sco)
1974	Eric De Beck (Bel)	Paola Cacchi (Ita)	Richard Kimball (USA)
1975	Ian Stewart (Sco)	Julie Brown (USA)	Robert Thomas (USA)
1976	Carlos Lopes (Por)	Carmen Valero (Spa)	Eric Hulst (USA)
1977	Leon Schots (Bel)	Carmen Valero (Spa)	Thom Hunt (USA)
1978	John Treacy (Ire)	Grete Waitz (Nor)	Mick Morton (Eng)
1979	John Treacy (Ire)	Grete Waitz (Nor)	Eddy de Paauw (Bel)
1980	Craig Virgin (USA)	Grete Waitz (Nor)	Jorge Garcia (Spa)
1981	Craig Virgin (USA)	Grete Waitz (Nor)	Mohammed Chouri (Tun)
1982	Mohamed Kedir (Eth)	Maricica Puica (Rom)	Zurubachev Gelaw (Eth)
1983	Bekele Debele (Eth)	Grete Waitz (Nor)	Fesseha Abede (Eth)
1984	Carlos Lopes (Por)	Maricica Puica (Rom)	Pedro Casacuberta (Spa)
1985	Carlos Lopes (Por)	Zola Budd (Eng)	Kimeli Kipkemboi (Ken)
1986	John Ngugi (Ken)	Zola Budd (Eng)	Melese Feyisa (Eth)
1987	John Ngugi (Ken)	Annette Sergent (Fra)	W.Oanda Kirochi (Ken)
1988	John Ngugi (Ken)	Ingrid Kristiansen (Nor)	W.Oanda Kirochi (Ken)

Most successful individuals

MEN

Most wins: 4 Jack Holden (Eng) 1933–5, 1939; Alain Mimoun (Fra) 1949, 1952, 1954, 1956; Gaston Roelants (Bel) 1962, 1967, 1969, 1972

Most placings in first three: 7 Gaston Roelants (4 wins, 3 seconds)

Most placings in first ten (years): 10 Jack Holden (1930–46)

Most appearances: 20 Marcel van de Wattyne (1946–65)

WOMEN

Most wins: 5 Doris Brown (USA) 1967–71, 5 Grete Waitz (Nor) 1978–81, 1984.

Most placings in first three: 7 Grete Waitz (5 wins, 2 thirds)

Most placings in first ten: 7 Grete Waitz (1978–84)

Most appearances: 16 Jean Lochhead (Wal) (1967–84)

Athletes to have won Junior and Senior race: Mike Tagg (Eng) Jnr 1966, Snr 1970; Dave Bedford (Eng) Jnr 1969, Snr 1971.

Greatest winning margins:

Men	Women	Junior
56 sec Jack Holden (Eng) 1934	40 sec Grete Waitz (Nor) 1980	25 sec Ian McCafferty (Sco) 1964

IAAF WORLD MARATHON CUP

The third edition of this event will be at Milan, Italy on 15/16 May 1989. The course through the city centre will comprise three loops.

This event was first staged at Hiroshima, Japan on 13/14 April 1985. With three team members to score, 41 men's teams and 17 women's teams completed the course. The men's race was of exceptionally high standard, with the first three running times in the world's fastest six of all time.

The second World Marathon Cup was held in Seoul on a course, parallel to the Han river, later used for the Olympics in 1988. 28 men's and 14 women's teams finishing three athletes.

Previous champions

Men's team:
1985 Djibouti, 1987 Italy
Women's team:
1985 Italy, 1987 USSR
Men's individual:
1985 Ahmed Salah (Dji) 2:08:09
1987 Ahmed Salah (Dji) 2:10:55
Women's individual:
1985 Katrin Dörre (GDR) 2:33:30
1987 Zoya Ivanova (SU) 2:30:39

Ingrid Kristiansen conquers the heat in Adelaide to complete the world cross-country and road double in 1988 (Mark Shearman)

IAAF WORLD ROAD RACE CHAMPIONSHIP FOR WOMEN

This annual event was first held at 10km at San Diego, California on 4 Dec 1983. It was also contested at 10km in 1984, but from 1985 the distance has been 15km.

1988 result
– at Adelaide, Australia 20 March

Individual:
1. Ingrid Kristiansen (Nor) 48:24
2. Wang Xiuting (Chn) 50:18
3. Zoya Ivanova (SU) 50:28
4. Zhong Huandi (Chn) 50:29
5. Malin Wästlund (Swe) 50:42
6. Yekaterina Khramenkova (SU) 50:43
7. Lizianne Bussières (Can) 50:46
8. Conçeicao Ferreira (Por) 50:51
9. Tani Ruckle (Aus) 50:59
10. Jocelyne Villeton (Fra) 51:00
11. Marty Cooksey (USA) 51:07
12. Lyudmila Matveyeva (SU) 51:30
13. Albertina Dias (Por) 51:38
14. Maria Curatolo (Ita) 51:46
15. Kerstin Pressler (FRG) 51:49

Team:
1. USSR 21, 2. CHN 31, 3. POR 37, 4. NOR 50, 5. USA 52, 6. FIN 79, 7. FRG 86, 8. FRA 99, 9. ITA 105, 10. KEN 116. 16 teams completed.

Previous winners

	Team	*Individual*	
1983	USA	Wendy Sly (UK)	32.23
1984	UK	Aurora Cunha (Por)	33:04
1985	UK	Aurora Cunha (Por)	49:17
1986	USSR	Aurora Cunha (Por)	48:31
1987	Por	Ingrid Kristansen (Nor)	47:17

IAAF WORLD RACE WALKING CUP

This competition is held biennially for the Lugano Trophy (men) and the Eschborn Cup (women). Lugano, Switzerland was the first venue for this competition, which was then for men's European teams; the first team from the rest of the world to take part was the USA in 1967. From 1977 the event has been officially recognised by the IAAF with the above name.

Until 1985 there was a final contested by nations from each continent, with additional European nations qualifying for the final from three qualifying matches, but in 1987 in New York competitors from 35 nations took part in one event. L'Hospitalet, Barcelona, Spain will host the 1989 races on 27–28 May.

Lugano Cup

Winning teams
5 GDR 1965, 1967, 1970, 1973, 1985
3 USSR 1975, 1983, 1987
2 United Kingdom 1961, 1963
2 Mexico 1977, 1979
1 Italy 1981

Best performances
20km: 1:19:24 Carlos Mercenario (Mex) 1987
1:18:49 (short) Daniel Bautista (Mex) 1979
50km: 3:42:26 Ronald Weigel (GDR) 1987

Most individual wins
3 Christoph Höhne (GDR) 50km 1965, 1967, 1970
3 Raúl González (Mex) 50km 1977, 1981, 1983
2 Ken Matthews (UK) 20km 1961, 1963
2 Hans-Georg Reimann (GDR) 20km 1970, 1973
2 Daniel Bautista (Mex) 20km 1977, 1979

Most finals:
7 Gerhard Weidner (GFR) 50km 1965–77 (best 2nd 1975)

Eschborn Cup

In 1975 a women's race over 5km was held in conjunction with the Lugano Trophy races. This event was maintained and when held at Eschborn in 1979 a Cup was introduced for the team competition. The distance was increased to 10km from 1983. 23 nations contested the 1987 competition.

Winning teams
China 1983, 1985
USSR 1981, 1987
United Kingdom 1979

Most individual wins:
2 Siw Gustavsson (Swe) 5km 1977, 1981

Best 10km time:
44:12 Irina Strakhova (SU) 1987

WORLD STUDENT GAMES

BY PETER MATTHEWS

The 'Universiade' or World Student Games, organised by the Féderation Internationale du Sport Universitaire (FISU), is well established as one of the world's most important meetings.

The first 'International Universities' Games was held in 1924 in Warsaw, organised by the Conféderation Internationale des Étudiants (CIE). From 1951 to 1962 rival Games were staged by FISU and the UIE. The latter, Communist inspired, were known as the World Youth Games from 1954 and these had the higher standards. From 1963, however, the Games merged and are now held bienially. Having originally been scheduled for São Paulo, Brazil the venue for the 1989 Games was undetermined at the time of going to press.

Championship Best Performances prior to 1989

Event		Name	Nation	Year
MEN				
100m	10.07	Lee McRae	USA	1985
	9.97w	Andrés Simon	Cub (heat)	1985
200m	19.72	Pietro Mennea	Ita	1979
400m	44.98	Harald Schmid	GFR	1979
800m	1:43.44	Alberto Juantorena	Cub	1977
1500m	3:38.43	Said Aouita	Mor	1981
5000m	13:41.25	Mikhail Zhelobovskiy	SU	1973
10000m	28:48.90	Dane Korica	Yug	1973
Marathon	2hr 17:10	Osvaldo Faustini	Ita	1983
3000mSt	8:21.26	John Gregorek	USA	1981
110mh	13.21	Alejandro Casanas	Cub	1977
400mh	48.44	Harry Schulting	Hol	1979
4x100mR	38.42	Italy		1979
4x400mR	3:00.98	USA		1979
20kmW	1:24:03	Guillaume LeBlanc	Can	1983
High jmp	2.41	Igor Paklin	SU	1985
Pole vault	5.75	Konstantin Volkov	SU	1981
	5.75	Rodion Gataullin	SU	1985
Long jmp	8.21	Yusuf Alli	Nig	1983
	8.23w	Laszlo Szalma	Hun	1981
Triple	17.86	Charlie Simpkins	USA	1985
Shot	21.13	Remigius Machura	Cs*	1985
	20.85	Alessandro Andrei	Ita	1985
Discus	69.46	Luis M. Delis	Cub	1983
Hammer	77.74	Klaus Ploghaus	GFR	1981
Javelin	81.42	Marek Kaleta	SU	1987
(old)	89.52	Dainis Kula	SU	1981
Dec	8348	Siegfried Wentz	FRG	1987
WOMEN				
100m	11.00	Marlies Göhr	GDR	1979
200m	21.91	Marita Koch	GDR	1979
400m	50.35	Maria Pinigina	SU	1979
800m	1:56.88	Slobodanka Čolović	Yug	1987
1500m	4:01.32	Paula Ivan	Rom	1987
3000m	8:53.61	Paula Ivan	Rom	1987
10000m	32:58.45	Marina Rodchenkova	SU	1985

Marathon	2:44:54	Mami Fukao	Jap	1985
100mh	12.62	Lucyna Langer	Pol	1979
400mh	54.97	Yekaterina Fesenko	SU	1983
4x100mR	42.82	USA		1983
4x400mR	3:24.97	USSR		1983
5km walk	21:51.50	Li Sujie	Chn	1987
High jmp	2.01	Silvia Costa	Cub	1985
Long jmp	7.04	Irina Valyukevich	SU	1985
	7.06w	Anisoara Cusmir	Rom	1983
Shot	20.82	Nadyezhda Chizhova	SU	1973
Discus	67.96	Tsvetanka Khristova	Bul	1987
Javelin	71.82	Leal Bravo	Cub	1985
Hep	6616	Malgorzata Nowak	Pol	1985

** Later found to have had a positive drugs test at the preceding European Cup Final*

17 world records have been set in these meetings from 1933: 3:49.2 at 1500m by Luigi Beccali (Ita) and 14.4 at 110mh by John Morriss (USA), to 1985: 2.41m high jump by Igor Paklin.

Most gold medals – individual events
With the confused state of this meeting in the 1950s and early 1960s it was possible to gain many more medals at that time than from 1963, with the present stricter rules on participation. The best during this period:

MEN
5 Janusz Sidlo (Pol) JT 1951–54–55–57–59
5 Igor Ter-Ovanesyan (SU) LJ 1959–61–62–63–65

WOMEN
10 Aleksandra Chudina (SU) HJ 1949–51–53, 80mh 1951, LJ & Pen 1951–53, JT 1953–55
8 Iolanda Balas (Rom) HJ UIE 1954–55–57–59–62, FISU 1957–59–61
8 Tamara Press (SU) SP 1959–61–62–63–65, DT 1959–61–63

The highest totals in pre-war or post-1963 days:

MEN:
4 Pietro Mennea (Ita) 200m 1973–75–79, 100m 1975 (and 4x100mR 1979)

WOMEN:
5 Gisela Mauermeyer (Ger) HJ & DT 1935–37, SP 1937

Most individual wins at one Games:
4 Aleksandra Chudina (SU) 1951 and 1953 (UIE) as above
Claudia Testoni (Ita) won five medals in 1933: gold LJ & 4x100mR, silver 80mh & HJ, bronze 100m.

Iolanda Balas won eight World Student titles and set 14 world records from 1.75m in 1956 to 1.91m in 1961 (Mark Shearman)

Three wins at one event since 1963

MEN
200m: Pietro Mennea (Ita) 1973–75–79

WOMEN
Shot: Natalya Lisovskaya (SU) 1983–85–87

COMMONWEALTH GAMES

The 14th Commonwealth Games will be staged in Auckland, New Zealand in January-February 1990. These multi-sport competitions are held every four years, and contested by athletes representing the nations of the British Commonwealth. They were first staged as the British Empire Games at Hamilton, Canada in 1930. The Games became the British Empire and Commonwealth Games in 1954, and simply the British Commonwealth Games in 1970, in which year the Games went metric, rather than the yards and miles Imperial distances raced hitherto.

Commonwealth Games Best Performances prior to 1990

Event		Name	Nation	Year
MEN				
100m	10.02w	Allan Wells	Sco	1982
	10.07	Ben Johnson	Can	1986
200m	20.12w	Allan Wells	Sco	1978
	20.43	Allan Wells & Mike McFarlane	Eng	1982
400m	45.01	Charles Asati	Ken	1970
800m	1:43.22	Steve Cram	Eng	1986
1500m	3:32.16	Filbert Bayi	Tan	1974
5000m	13:14.4	Ben Jipcho	Ken	1974
10000m	27:46.4	Richard Tayler	NZ	1974
Marathon	2:09:12	Ian Thompson	Eng	1974
3000mSt	8:20.8	Ben Jipcho	Ken	1974
110mh	13.31w	Mark McKoy (& 13.37 1982)	Can	1986
400mh	48.83	Alan Pascoe	Eng	1974
4x100mR	39.15	Nigeria		1982
		Canada		1986
4x400mR	3:02.8y	Trinidad & Tobago		1966
30km walk	2:07:47	Simon Baker	Aus	1986
High jump	2.31	Milt Ottey	Can	1982
	2.31	Stephen Wray	Bah	1982
Pole vault	5.30	Andrew Ashurst	Eng	1986
Long jump	8.13	Gary Honey	Aus	1982
Triple jump	17.81w	Keith Connor	Eng	1982
	16.87	Mike Makin 2nd	Eng	1986
Shot	20.74	Geoff Capes	Eng	1978
Discus	64.04	Brad Cooper	Bah	1982
Hammer	75.08	Robert Weir	Eng	1982
Javelin	80.62	David Ottley	Eng	1986
(old)	89.48	Michael O'Rourke	NZ	1982
Decathlon	8663	Daley Thompson	Eng	1986
WOMEN				
100m	10.92w	Angella Taylor (& 11.00*)	Can	1982
200m	22.19w	Merlene Ottey	Jam	1982
	22.50	Raelene Boyle	Aus	1974
400m	51.02	Marilyn Neufville	Jam	1970
800m	2:00.94	Kirsty Wade	Wal	1986
1500m	4:06.34	Mary Stewart	Eng	1978
3000m	8:45.53	Anne Audain	NZ	1982
10000m	31:41.42	Elizabeth Lynch	Sco	1986
Marathon	2:26:07	Lisa Martin	Aus	1986
100mh	12.78w	Shirley Strong	Eng	1982
	13.07*	Lorna Boothe	Eng	1982
400mh	54.94	Debbie Flintoff	Aus	1986

4x100mR	43.15	England		1982
4x400mR	3:27.19	England		1978
High jump	1.93	Katrina Gibbs	Aus	1978
Long jump	6.91w	Shonel Ferguson	Bah	1982
	6.73	Sheila Sherwood	Eng	1970
Shot	19.00	Gael Martin	Aus	1986
Discus	62.98	Margaret Ritchie	Sco	1982
Javelin	69.80	Tessa Sanderson	Eng	1986
Heptathlon	6282w	Judy Simpson	Eng	1986

** performance made in heat or qualifying round*

Most gold medals – all events

MEN
6 Don Quarrie (Jam)
100m 1970–74, 200m 1970–74–78, 4x100mR 1970
4 Harry Hart (SAf)
SP and DT 1930–34
4 Charles Asati (Ken)
400m and 4x400mR 1970–74
4 Allan Wells (Sco)
100m 1982, 200m 1978–82, 4x100mR 1978

WOMEN
7 Marjorie Jackson (Aus)
100y 1950–54, 220y 1950–54, 4x110yR 1954, 440yR and 660yR 1950
7 Raelene Boyle (Aus)
100m 1970–74, 200m 1970–74, 400m 1982, 4x100mR 1970–74
6 Pam Kilborn/Ryan (Aus)
80mh 1962–66–70, LJ 1962, 4x100mR 1966–70
5 Decima Norman (Aus)
100y, 220y, LJ, 440yR, 660yR 1938
5 Valerie Sloper/Young
(NZ) SP 1962–66–70, DT 1962–66
4 Yvette Williams (NZ)
LJ 1950–54, SP and DT 1954

Most medals – all events

MEN

6	Don Quarrie	1970–78
6	Harry Hart	1930–34
6	Allan Wells	1978–82

WOMEN

9	Raelene Boyle	1970–82
8	Denise Robertson/ Boyd (Aus)	1974–82
7	Marjorie Jackson	1950–54
7	Valerie Young	195?–72
7	Kathy Cook (Eng)	1978–86
7	Angella Issajenko (Can)	1982–86
6	Pam Ryan	1962–70
6	Gael Martin (Aus)	1978–86

The most medals at one Games:

MEN
4 Keith Gardner 1958 2G, 1S, 1B

WOMEN
5 Decima Norman 1938 5G
5 Shirley Strickland 1950 3G, 2S

The most Games contested:
6 Robin Tait (NZ)
1962–82, successively 4–3–6–1-4–8 at discus

Oldests (y years, d days)

MEN
Winner
42y 335d Jack Holden (Eng) marathon 1950
Medallist
42y 335d Jack Holden

WOMEN
Winner
37y 60d Rosemary Payne (Sco) DT 1970
Medallist
40y 252d Rosemary Payne (Sco) 2nd DT 1974

Youngests

MEN
Winner
16y 263d Sam Richardson (Can) LJ 1934
Medallist
16y 260d Sam Richardson (Can) 2nd TJ 1934

WOMEN
Winner
17y 137d Debbie Brill (Can) HJ 1970
Medallist
c15y Sabine Chebichi (Ken) 3rd 800m 1974

AFRICAN CHAMPIONSHIPS

The first African Games, at ten sports, were contested in Brazzaville, Congo on 18–25 July 1965. Subsequent Games were staged at Lagos, Nigeria in 1973, at Algiers in 1978 and Nairobi, Kenya in 1988.

African Championships, for athletics only, were first held at Dakar, Senegal in 1979, and have subsequently been held at Cairo, Egypt in 1982, Rabat, Morocco in 1984, and Cairo 1985, before Annaba, Algeria in 1988.

African Championships 1988

At Annaba, Algeria 29 August – 2 September. First three at each event:

MEN

100m: 1. John Myles-Mills (Gha) 10.25
2. Charles-Louis Seck (Sen) 10.29
3. Iziaq Adeyanju (Nig) 10.34

200m: 1. Davidson Ezinwa (Nig) 20.97w
2. Emmanuel Tuffour (Gha) 21.00
3. Mustapha Kamel Selmi (Alg) 21.21

400m: 1. Innocent Egbunike (Nig) 45.43
2. Gabriel Tiacoh (IvC) 45.86
3. Moses Ugbisie (Nig) 46.04

800m: 1. Babacar Niang (Sen) 1:46.99
2. Getahun Ayana (Eth) 1:47.46
3. Ahmed Belkessam (Alg) 1:47.49

1500m: 1. Getahun Ayana (Eth) 3:42.77
2. Mahmoud Kalboussi (Tun) 3:43.44
3. Mustapha Lachaal (Mor) 3:43.48

5000m: 1. Brahim Boutayeb (Mor) 13:49.69
2. Haji Bulbula (Eth) 13:50.08
3. Mohamed Issengar (Mor) 14:02.25

10000m: 1. Brahim Boutayeb 28:55.28
2. Haji Bulbula 29:04.65
3. Mohammed Choumassi (Mor) 29:30.59

Mar: 1. Dereje Nedi (Eth) 2:27:51
2. Allaoua Khéllil (Alg) 2:28:11
3. Kebede Balcha (Eth) 2:29:04

3000mSt: 1. Azzedine Brahmi (Alg) 8:26.56
2. Abdelaziz Sahere (Mor) 8:27.30
3. Kamel Benlakhlef (Alg) 8:38.21

110mh: 1. Nourreddine Tadjine (Alg) 14.33
2. Marcellin Dally (IvC) 14.35
3. Zouhair Khazine (Mor) 14.46

400mh: 1. Amadou Dia Bâ (Sen) 48.81
2. Henry Amike (Nig) 49.36
3. Hamidou Mbaye (Sen) 50.27

HJ: 1. Boubacar Guèye (Sen) 2.16
2. Paul Ngadjadoum (Chad) 2.16
3. Fred Ebong Salle (Cam) 2.13

PV: 1. Choukri Abahnini (Tun) 4.90
2. Mejdi Drine (Tun) 4.80
3. Samir Agsous (Tun) 4.80

LJ: 1. Yusuf Alli (Nig) 7.78
2. Fred Ebong Salle 7.53
3. Lotfi Kaida (Alg) 7.51

TJ: 1. António Santos (Ang) 16.43
2. Lotfi Kaida 16.22w
3. Fethi Aboud (Libya) 16.00

SP: 1. Mohamed Achouche (Egy) 19.40
2. Ahmed Kamel Shatta (Egy) 19.00
3. Adewale Olokoju (Nig) 17.70

DT: 1. Adewale Olokoju (Nig) 62.12
2. Hassan Hamad (Egy) 55.94
3. Yacine Louail (Alg) 47.72

HT: 1. Hakim Toumi (Alg) 69.06
2. Djamel Zouiche (Alg) 63.92
3. Cherif El Hennawi (Egy) 59.28

JT: 1. Justin Arop (Uga) 74.52
2. Tarek Chaabani (Tun) 67.50
3. Samir Ménouar (Alg) 64.62

Dec: 1. Mahmoud Aît Ouhamou (Alg) 7160
2. Mourad Mahour Bacha (Alg) 7128
3. Abdennacer Moumen (Mor) 7051

20kmW: 1. Mohamed Bouhalla (Alg) 1:27:43,
2. Abdelwahab Ferguène (Alg) 1:34:07
3. Rezki Boumrar (Alg) 1:41:46

4x100mR: 1. Nigeria 39.27
2. Ghana 39.44
3. Senegal 39.66

4x400mR: 1. Ethiopia 3:07.11
2. Ivory Coast 3:08.45
3. Burundi 3:09.11

WOMEN

100m: 1. Mary Onyali (Nig) 11.25
2. Falilat Ogunkoya (Nig) 11.51
3. Lalao Ravaonirina (Mad) 11.54

200m: 1. Falilat Ogunkoya 23.33w
2. Martha Appiah (Gha) 23.72
3. Veronica Bawuah (Gha) 24.35

400m: 1. Airat Bakare (Nig) 52.15
2. Célestine N'Drin (IvC) 52.77
3. Mercy Addy (Gha) 52.88

800m: 1. Hassiba Boulmerka (Alg) 2:06.16
2. Lourdes Mutola (Moz) 2:06.55
3. Sheila Seeballuck (Maur) 2:08.26

1500m: 1. Hassiba Boulmerka (Alg) 4:12.14
2. Fatima Aouam (Mor) 4:12.57
3. Getenesh Urge (Eth) 4:17.61

3000m: 1. Fatima Aouam (Mor) 8:59.19
2. Josiane Nairac-Boullé (Maur) 9:14.37
3. Tigist Moreda (Eth) 9:15.92

10000m: 1. Marcianne Mukamurenzi (Rwa) 33:03.98
2. Hassania Darami (Mor) 33:41.75
3. Malika Benhabylès (Alg) 35:41.80

100mh: 1. Maria Usifo (Nig) 13.71
2. Dinah Yankey (Gha) 13.94
3. Yasmina Azzizi (Alg) 14.08

400mh: 1. Maria Usifo (Nig) 56.74
2. Ruth Kyalisima (Uga) 57.32
3. Marie Womplou (IvC) 57.60

HJ: 1. Lucienne N'Da (IvC) 1.80
2. Constance Senghor (Sen) 1.68
3. Salamata Coulibaly (IvC) 1.68

LJ: 1. Juliana Yendork (Gha) 5.70
2. Néné Sangharé (Sen) 5.68w
3. Fatou Tambédou (Sen) 5.56w

SP: 1. Hanane Khaled (Egy) 15.02
2. Souad Malloussi (Mor) 14.85
3. Jeanne Ngo Minyemeck (Cam) 13.92

DT: 1. Grace Apiafi (Nig) 50.60
2. Hanane Khaled 47.58
3. Zoubida Laayouni (Mor) 47.50

JT: 1. Yasmina Azzizi (Alg) 48.82
2. Samia Djémaa (Alg) 45.74
3. Schola Mujjawamaria (Uga) 44.86

Hep: 1. Yasmina Azzizi (Alg) 5740
2. Marie-Lourdes Ally Samba (Maur) 4821
3. Houida Hachem Ismail (Egy) 4289

5000mW: 1. Sabiha Mansouri (Alg) 25:51.7
2. Dalila Frihi (Alg) 27:06.2
3. Kheira Sadat (Alg) 29:19.3

4x100mR: 1. Ghana 44.68
2. Ivory Coast 45.59
3. Senegal 46.45

4x400mR: 1. Uganda 3:37.74
2. Ivory Coast 3:38.30
3. Morocco 3:50.25

Most gold medals at African Championships & Games – individual events

MEN

6 Amadou Dia Bâ (Sen)
400mh 1982–84–85–87–88, 400m 1982

4 Nagui Assad (Egy)
SP 1973–78–79–82

4 Paul Emordi (Nig)
LJ 1984–85–87, TJ 1985

4 Hakim Toumi (Alg)
HT 1984–85–87–88

WOMEN

6 Maria Usifo (Nig)
100mh 1984–85–87–88, 400mh 1987–88

5 Modupe Oshikoya (Nig)
100mh 1973, HJ 1973–78, LJ 1973–78

5 Nawal el Moutawakil (Mor)
100mh 1982, 400mh 1982–84–85, 200m 1984

4 Justina Chepchirchir (Ken)
800m 1984, 1500m 1982–84, 3000m 1982

4 Zoubida Laayouni (Mor)
DT 1979–82–84–85

Eastern African Championships 1988

At Kasarani Stadium, Nairobi, Kenya
29 June – 2 July

Winners (all from Kenya unless stated):

MEN

100m: Kennedy Ondieki 10.5, 200m: Joseph Gikonyo 21.1, 400m: Luka Sang 46.1, 800m: Nixon Kiprotich 1:46.8, 1500m: Charles Cheruiyot 3:42.8, 5000m: Jackson Ruto 13:54.3, 10000m: Gidamis Shahanga (Tan) 29:17.3, 3000mSt: Boniface Merande 8:37.0, 400mh: Joseph Maritim 49.9, LJ: David Lamai 7.39, SP: Joshua Pondo 13.99, JT: Zakayo Malekwa 70.07 (Tan), 4x100mR/4x400mR: Kenya 40.0/3:07.3.

WOMEN

100m: Joyce Odhiambo 11.6, 200m: Pharis Wanja 24.4, 400m: Esther Kavaya 53.8, 800m: Francisca Chepkurui 2:01.2, 1500m: Susan Sirma 4:13.4, 3000m: Anne Wangari 9:30.2, LJ: Ruth Onsarigo 5.84, SP: Elizabeth Olaba 14.45, JT: Mathilda Kisava (Tan) 49.82.

ASIAN GAMES

The first Asian Games were held at New Delhi, India on 8–11 Mar 1951, when ten nations took part. These multi-sport Games have since 1954 been held at four-yearly intervals, and a record 29 nations competed in 1982.

Asian Games Best Performances prior to 1989

Event		Name	Nation	Year
MEN				
100m	10.30	Talal Mansoor	Qatar	1986
200m	20.71	Chang Jae-keun	SKo	1986
400m	45.00	Susumu Takano	Jap	1986
800m	1:46.81	Charles Boromeo	Ind	1982
1500m	3:43.49	Faleh Naji Jarallah	Iraq	1982
5000m	13:50.63	Masanari Shintaku	Jap	1986
10000m	28:26.74	Masanari Shintaku	Jap	1986
Mar	2hr 08:21	Takeyuki Nakayama	Jap	1986
3000mSt	8:36.98	Shigeyuki Aikyo	Jap	1986
110mh	14.07	Yu Zhicheng	Chn	1986
400mh	49.31	Ahmed Hamada	Bah	1986
4x100mR	39.17	China 1986		
4x400mR	3:02.33	Japan 1986		
20kmW	1hr 25:46	Sun Xiaoguang	Chn	1986
HJ	2.33	Zhu Jianhua	Chn	1982
PV	5.40	Ji Zebiao	Chn	1986
LJ	8.07	T.C.Yohanan	Ind	1974
TJ	17.01	Norifumi Yamashita	Jap	1986
Shot	18.53	Bahadur Singh	Ind	1982
Discus	58.50	Li Weinan	Chn	1982
Hammer	71.14	Shigenobu Morofushi	Jap	1982
Javelin	76.60	Kazuhiro Mizoguchi	Jap	1986
(old)	79.24	Shen Mao Mao	Chn	1978
Dec	7417	Wang Kangqiang	Chn	1982
WOMEN				
100m	11.53	Lydia de Vega	Phi	1986
200m	23.44	P.T.Usha	Ind	1986
400m	52.16	P.T.Usha	Ind	1986
800m	2:05.69	Chang Jong-ae	NKo	1982
1500m	4:18.40	Chang Jong-ae	NKo	1982
3000m	9:11.92	Lim Chun-ae	SKo	1986
10000m	32:47.77	Wang Xiuting	Chn	1986
Mar	2hr 41:03	Eriko Asai	Jap	1986
100mh	13.31	Esther Rot	Isr	1974
400mh	56.08	P.T.Usha	Ind	1986
4x100mR	44.78	China 1986		
4x400mR	3:34.58	India 1986		
10kmW	48:40	Guan Ping	Chn	1986
HJ	1.89	Zheng Dazhen	Chn	1982
		Zheng Dazhen		1986
		Megumi Satoh	Jap	1986
		Kim Hee-sun	SKo	1986
LJ	6.41	Liao Wenfeng	Chn	1982
Shot	17.77	Li Meisu	Chn	1982
Discus	59.28	Hou Xuemei	Chn	1986
Javelin	60.52	Emi Matsui	Jap	1982
Hep	5580	Zhu Yuqing	Chn	1986

Most gold medals – individual events

MEN
5 Shigenobu Murofushi (Jap)
HT 1970–74–78–82–86

WOMEN
5 Toyoko Yoshino (Jap)
SP & DT 1951–54, JT 1951
5 Esther Rot (Isr)
100mh 1970–74, Pen 1970, 100m & 200m 1974

Three individual event gold medals at one Games were won by Toyoko Yoshino in 1951, Esther Rot in 1974, P.T.Usha and Lim Chun Ae 1986.

Asian Track and Field Championship

The first Asian Championships, as opposed to the multi-sport Games, were held at Marakina, near Manila, Philippines in 1973. They are now entitled Asian Track & Field meetings, rather than Championships due to the exclusion of Israel.

The most individual gold medals is four by Anat Ratanapol (Tha) 100m & 200m 1973–75. Athletes to have won their event three times:

MEN:
Suchart Chairsuvaparb (Tha) 1979–81–83, Mohamed Zinkhawi (Kuwait) SP 1979–81–83, Liu Yuhuang (Chn) LJ 1981–83–85, Li Weinan (Chn) DT 1981–83–85.

WOMEN:
Li Xiaohui (Chn) DT 1979–81–85. Lee Chiuhsia (Tai) won at 800m, 1500m and 3000m in 1975, but this was surpassed by P.T.Usha (Ind) in 1985, when she won at 100m, 200m, 400m and 400mh, a fifth gold at 4x400mR and a bronze at 4x100mR. She also won at 400m in 1983.

BALKAN GAMES

The first official Balkan Games were contested in 1930.

The 46th Games were held in Ankara, Turkey 16–17 August 1988.

Winners:

MEN:
100m: Anri Grigorov (Bul) 10.37, 200m: Bogomil Karadimov (Bul) 21.02, 400m: Ismael Macev (Yug) 46.06, 800m: Miroslaw Chochkov (Bul) 1:47.80, 1500m: Constantin Gavrila (Rom) 3:40.47, 5000m: Dragan Sekulic (Yug) 14:31.83, 10000m: Manolis Chantzos (Gre) 30:00.55, Mar: Mehmet Terzi (Tur) 2:23:00, 3000mSt: Panayot Kashanov (Bul) 8:40.69, 110mh: George Boroi (Rom) 13.74, 400mh: Athanassios Kalogiannis (Gre) 49.36, HJ: Sorin Matei (Rom) 2.31, PV: Atanas Tarev (Bul) 5.50, LJ: Vladimir Amidzhinov (Bul) 7.85, TJ: Djordje Kožul (Yug) 16.96, SP: Georgi Todorov (Bul) 19.87, DT: Kamen Dimitrov (Bul) 60.96, HT: Ivan Tanev (Bul) 76.76, JT: Milan Stjepovic (Yug) 79.32, Dec: Saša Karan (Yug) 7784, 20kmW: Dimitris Orfanopoulos (Gre) 1:32:39, 4x100mR: Bulgaria 39.84, 4x400mR: Yugoslavia 3:03.94.
Team: 1. Bulgaria 212, 2. Greece 191.5, 3. Yugoslavia 191

WOMEN:
100m/200m: Nadezhda Georgieva (Bul) 11.11/22.66, 400m: Rositsa Stamenova (Bul) 52.22, 800m/1500m: Paula Ivan (Rom) 1:56.42/4:05.32, 3000m: Viorica Ghican (Rom) 9:07.99, Mar: Donika Hanxhara (Alb) 36:02.00, 100mh: Mihaela Pogacian (Rom) 12.84, 400mh: Nicolata Carutasu (Rom) 55.85, HJ: Biljana Petrović (Yug) 1.96, LJ: Vali Ionescu (Rom) 7.00, SP: Svetla Mitkova (Bul) 18.60, DT: Daniela Costian (Rom) 70.20, JT: Anna Verouli (Gre) 68.76, Hep: Petra Vaidean (Rom) 6241, 4x100mR/4x400mR: Bulgaria 42.89/3:31.04.
Team: 1. Bulgaria 172, 2. Romania 119, 3. Yugoslavia 112

EUROPEAN CHAMPIONSHIPS

The first European Championships were staged at the Stadio Communale, Turin in 1934 for men only. Women's championships were held separately in 1938, but men's and women's events were combined at one venue from 1946. The championships are held at four-yearly intervals, although there was a break in that pattern when they were held in 1969 and 1971. The 1990 Championships are due to be held at Split in Yugoslavia.

1986 Champions

Event	Name	Nation	
MEN			
100m	Linford Christie	UK	10.15
200m	Vladimir Krylov	SU	20.52
400m	Roger Black	UK	44.59
800m	Sebastian Coe	UK	1:44.50
1500m	Steve Cram	UK	3:41.09
5000m	Jack Buckner	UK	13:10.15
10000m	Stefano Mei	Ita	27:56.79
Marathon	Gelindo Bordin	Ita	2:10:54
3000mSt	Hagen Melzer	GDR	8:16.65
110mh	Stéphane Caristan	Fra	13.20
400mh	Harald Schmid	FRG	48.65
4x100mR		USSR	38.29
4x400mR		United Kingdom	2:59.84
20 km walk	Jozef Pribilinec	Cs	1:21:15
50 km walk	Hartwig Gauder	GDR	3:40:55
High jump	Igor Paklin	SU	2.34
Pole vault	Sergey Bubka	SU	5.85
Long jump	Robert Emmiyan	SU	8.41
Triple jump	Khristo Markov	Bul	17.66
Shot	Werner Günthör	Swi	22.22
Discus	Romas Ubartas	SU	67.08
Hammer	Yuriy Sedykh	SU	86.74
Javelin	Klaus Tafelmeier	FRG	84.76
Decathlon	Daley Thompson	UK	8811
WOMEN			
100m	Marlies Göhr	GDR	10.91
200m	Heike Drechsler	GDR	21.71
400m	Marita Koch	GDR	48.22
800m	Nadezhda Olizarenko	SU	1:57.15
1500m	Ravilya Agletdinova	SU	4:01.19
3000m	Olga Bondarenko	SU	8:33.99
10000m	Ingrid Kristiansen	Nor	30:23.25
Marathon	Rosa Mota	Por	2:28:38
100mh	Yordanka Donkova	Bul	12.38
400mh	Marina Styepanova	SU	53.32
4x100mR		GDR	41.84
4x400mR		GDR	3:16.87
10km walk	Maria Cruz Diaz	Spa	46:09
High jump	Stefka Kostadinova	Bul	2.00
Long jump	Heike Drechsler	GDR	7.27
Shot	Heidi Krieger	GDR	21.10
Discus	Diane Sachse	GDR	71.36
Javelin	Fatima Whitbread	UK	76.32
Heptathlon	Anke Behmer	GDR	6717

Championship Bests other than by 1986 winners

Event	Name	Nation		Year
MEN				
200m	Pietro Mennea	Ita	20.16	1978
800m	Olaf Beyer	GDR	1:43.84	1978
1500m	Steve Ovett	UK3:35.59	1978	
10000m	Martti Vainio	Fin	27:30.99	1978
3000mSt	Bronislaw Malinowski	Pol	8:15.04	1974
400mh	Harald Schmid	FRG	47.48	1982
Discus	Wolfgang Schmidt	GDR	67.20	1978 (q)
WOMEN				
400m	Marita Koch	GDR	48.15	1982
800m	Olga Minayeva	SU	1:55.41	1982
1500m	Olga Dvirna	SU	3:57.80	1982
3000m	Svetlana Ulmasova	SU	8:30.28	1982
High jump	Ulrike Meyfarth	FRG	1.82	1982
Shot	Ilona Slupianek	GDR	21.59	1982
Javelin	Fatima Whitbread	UK	77.44	1986 (q)

Most gold medals at all events:

MEN
5 Harald Schmid (FRG) 1978–86

WOMEN
6 Marita Koch (GDR) 1978–86
5 Fanny Blankers-Koen (Hol) 1946–50
5 Irena Szewinska (Pol) 1966–74
5 Marlies Göhr (GDR) 1978–86

Most medals:

MEN
6 Harald Schmid (FRG) 5/1/0 1978–86
6 Pietro Mennea (Ita) 3/2/1 1971–74

WOMEN
10 Irena Szewinska (Pol) 5/1/4 1966–78
8 Fanny Blankers-Koen (Hol) 5/1/2 1938–50
8 Renate Stecher (GDR) 4/4/0 1969–74
7 Marlies Göhr (GDR) 5/1/1 1978–86
6 Yevgeniya Sechenova (SU) 2/2/2 1946–50
6 Marita Koch (GDR) 6/0/0 1978–86

Most medals at one event:
5 Igor Ter-Ovanesyan (SU) long jump 3/2/0 1966–71

Most medals at one Championship:
4 Fanny Blankers-Koen (Hol) 3/1/0 1950
4 Irena Kirszenstein/Szewinska (Pol) 3/1/0 1966
4 Stanislawa Walasiewicz (Pol) 2/2/0 1938

EUROPEAN JUNIOR CHAMPIONSHIPS

Most gold medals
4 Thomas Schröder (GDR) 100m 1979; 100m, 200m, 4x100mR 1981
3 four men and eleven women, including one at three individual events:
Ilke Wyludda (GDR) SP 1987; DT 1985, 1987

Athletes who have won their event at two Championships

MEN
Yevgeniy Gavrilenko (SU) 4x400mR 1968, 1970
Sergey Korovin (SU) 4x100mR 1968, 1970
Ari Paunonen (Fin) 1500m 1975, 1977
Thomas Schröder (GDR) 100m 1979, 1981
Jens Carlowitz (GDR) 4x400mR 1981, 1983
Nikolay Matyushenko (SU) 2000mSt 1983, 1985

WOMEN
Ilke Wyludda (GDR) DT 1985, 1987

Most medals
5 Thomas Schröder (GDR) 4 gold as above, 1 silver 200m 1979
4 Jens Carlowitz (GDR) 2 gold as above, 2 silver 400m 1981 & 1983
4 Ilke Wyludda (GDR) 3 gold as above, 1 silver SP 1985

The GDR have by far the best record of any nation, with a total of 155 gold medals to 94 by the USSR, 36 UK and 33 FRG. The greatest GDR domination was in 1981 when from the 38 events their athletes won 22 gold, 13 silver and 7 bronze medals.

The first European Junior Championships were held at Colombes Stadium, Paris on 11–13 September 1970. Before then, however, European Junior Games had been held in 1964, 1966 and 1968. From 1973 the European Junior Championships have been held at two-yearly intervals and the 1989 event is due to be staged at Varazdin, Yugoslavia on 24–27 August.

There was a record entry of 966 athletes from 30 nations for the 1987 championships at Birmingham.

Championship Best Performances prior to 1989

Event		Name	Nation	Year
MEN				
100m	10.21	Jamie Henderson	UK	1987
200m	20.37	Jürgen Evers	FRG	1983
400m	45.36	Roger Black	UK	1985
800m	1:46.17	József Bereczky	Hun	1981
1500m	3:38.96	Graham Williamson	UK	1979
3000m	7:57.18	Rainer Wachenbrunner	GDR	1981
5000m	13:44.37	Steve Binns	UK	1979
10000m	29:19.38	Jens Karrass	GDR	1987
2000mSt	5:27.44	Gaetano Erba	Ita	1979
3000mSt	8:54.83	Andreas Fischer	FRG	1987
110mh	13.46	Jonathan Ridgeon	UK	1985
400mh	49.71	Ruslan Mishchenko	SU	1983
4x100mR	39.25		FRG	1983
4x400mR	3:04.58		GDR	1981
10km walk	39:44.71	Giovanni Di Benedictis	Ita	1987
High jump	2.30	Vladimir Yashchenko	SU	1977
Pole vault	5.55	Radion Gataulin	SU	1983
Long jump	8.17	Vladimir Ochkan	SU	1987
Triple jump	16.93	Volker Mai	GDR	1985
Shot	19.65	Udo Beyer	GDR	1973
Discus	60.02	Attila Horváth	Hun	1985
Hammer	74.28	Sergey Dorozhon	SU	1983
Javelin	75.14	Steven Backley	UK	1987
(old	86.56	Uwe Hohn	GDR	1981
Decathlon	7906	Mikhail Romanyuk	SU	1981
WOMEN				
100m	11.21	Kerstin Behrend	GDR	1985
200m	22.85	Bärbel Eckert	GDR	1983
400m	51.25	Christine Brehmer	GDR	1975
800m	2:00.25	Katrin Wühn	GDR	1983
1500m	4:07.47	Inger Knutsson	Swe	1973
3000m	8:56.33	Fernanda Ribeiro	Por	1987
10000m	33:44.37	Birgit Jerschabek	GDR	1987
100mh	13.10	Monique Ewanje-Epée	Fra	1985
400mh	56.01	Radostina Shtereva	Bul	1983
4x100mR	43.77		GDR	1981
4x400mR	3:30.39		GDR	1981
5km walk	21:30.92	Oksana Shchastnaya	SU	1987
High Jump	1.94	Yelena Topchina	SU	1983
	1.94	Natalya Golodnova	SU	1985
Long jump	6.68	Sofia Bozhanova	Bul	1985
	7.02w	Heike Daute	GDR	1981
Shot	19.45	Ilke Wyludda	GDR	1987
Discus	70.58	Ilke Wyludda	GDR	1987
Javelin	64.88	Anja Reiter	GDR	1987
Heptathlon	6465	Sybille Thiele	GDR	1983

EUROPEAN CUP

BY PETER MATTHEWS

The European Cup is contested biennially by European nations, with each team entering one athlete per event and one team in each relay. The Cup is dedicated to the memory of Dr Bruno Zauli, the former President of the European Committee of the IAAF, who died suddenly in 1963 soon after the decision had been made to start this competition.

From 1965 until 1981 the competition was staged with a qualifying round, semi-finals and final, but from 1983 the nations have been arranged into groups according to strength, with eight men's and eight women's teams in A and B groups, with additional nations in C1 and C2 groups. There is one up and one down promotion and relegation between A and B, and two up and two down between B and C.

The 1989 Finals will be contested on 5–6 August as follows:

A final at Gateshead:

Men USSR, GDR, UK, FRG, ITA, CS, SPA, FRA

Women GDR, USSR, BUL, FRG, UK, CS, POL, ROM

Placings in the Final (or A Final)

MEN	1965	1967	1970	1973	1975	1977	1979	1981	1983	1985	1987
GDR	4	2	1	2	1	1	1	1	1	2	2
USSR	1	1	2	1	2	3	2	2	2	1	1
FRG	2	3	3	3	5	2	3	4	3	3	4
UK	6	–	–	4	4	4	5	3	4	4	3
Poland	3	4	4	–	3	5	4	6	5	5	8
France	5	5	5	6	7	6	7	7	7	8	–
Italy	–	–	7	–	8	8	6	5	6	6	5
Finland	–	–	–	5	6	7	–	–	–	–	–

Three finals: Finland 5th 1973, 6th 1975, 7th 1977.
Two finals: Hungary 6th 1967, 8th 1983; Czechoslovakia 1985 7th, 1987 6th; Yugoslavia 8th 1979 and 1981.
One final: Sweden 6th 1970, Spain 7th 1987.

B Final winners: 1977 France, 1979 Yugoslavia, 1981 France, 1983 Czechoslovakia, 1985 Spain, 1987 France

WOMEN	1965	1967	1970	1973	1975	1977	1979	1981	1983	1985	1987
GDR	2	2	1	1	1	1	1	1	1	2	1
USSR	1	1	3	2	2	2	2	2	2	1	2
FRG	4	3	2	4	3	3	6	3	5	6	4
UK	–	5	5	5	7	4	4	4	4	3	5
Poland	3	4	4	–	4	5	7	6	7	5	7
Bulgaria	–	–	–	3	6	7	3	5	6	4	3
Romania	–	–	–	6	5	6	5	–	–	–	–
Hungary	5	6	6	–	–	–	–	7	8	–	–

Three finals: Czechoslovakia 3rd 1983, 7th 1985, 6th 1987.
Two finals: Italy 8th 1975 and 1981; France; 8th 1975 and 1987.
One final: Netherlands 6th 1965, Finland 8th 1977; Yugoslavia 8th 1981.

B Final winners: 1977 Bulgaria, 1979 Romania, 1981 Poland, 1983 Italy, 1985 France, 1987 Romania

B final at Brussels

Men POL, BUL, SWE, HUN, AUT, SWZ, GRE, BEL
Women FRA, HUN, ITA, SWZ, FIN, SWE, YUG, SPA

CI final at Copenhagen

Men DEN, FIN, NOR, CYP, TUR
Women DEN, NOR, BEL, CYP, AUT, TUR

C2 final at Dublin

Men IRE, ICE, POR, HOL, YUG
Women IRE, ICE, POR, HOL, GRE

European Cup Best Performances

(Achieved in final, or A final, unless specified on right); SF in semi-final

Event		Name	Nation	Year
MEN				
100m	10.12	Eugen Ray	GDR	1977
200m	20.15	Pietro Mennea	Italy	1977 SF
400m	44.96	Thomas Schönlebe	GDR	1985 & 1987
800m	1:45.70	Dieter Fromm	GDR	1973 SF
1500m	3:33.63	José Manuel Abascal	Spa	1983 B
5000m	13:25.2	Emiel Puttemans	Bel	1973 SF
10000m	27:32.85	Fernando Mamede	Por	1983 C
3000mSt	8:13.32	Mariano Scartezzini	Ita	1981
110mh	13.37	Thomas Munkelt	GDR	1977
400mh	47.85	Harald Schmid	FRG	1979 & 1985
High jump	2.39	Patrik Sjöberg	Swe	1987 B
Pole vault	5.80	Sergey Bubka	SU	1985
Long jump	8.38	Robert Emmiyan	SU	1987
Triple	17.77	Khristo Markov	Bul	1985 B
Shot	22.05	Sergey Smirnov	SU	1985
Discus	68.64	Wolfgang Schmidt	GDR	1981 SF
Hammer	82.90	Juri Tamm	SU	1985
Javelin	84.86	Viktor Yevsyukov	SU	1987
(old	92.88	Uwe Hohn	GDR	1985
4x100mR	38.28		USSR	1985
4x400mR	3:00.33		FRG	1985
WOMEN				
100m	10.93w	Sonia Lannaman	UK	1977 SF
	10.95	Marlies Göhr	GDR	1985 & 1987
200m	21.99	Silke Gladisch	GDR	1987
400m	48.60	Marita Koch	GDR	1979
	48.60	Olga Vladykina	SU	1985
800m	1:55.91	Jarmila Kratochvilová	Cs	1985
1500m	3:58.40	Ravilya Agletdinova	SU	1985
3000m	8:35.32	Zola Budd	UK	1985
10000m	31:47.38	Olga Bondarenko	SU	1985
100mh	12.47	Cornelia Oschkenat	GDR	1987
400mh	54.13	Sabine Busch	GDR	1985
High Jump	2.06	Stefka Kostadinova	Bul	1985
Long jump	7.28	Galina Chistyakova	SU	1985
Shot	21.56	Natalya Lisovskaya	SU	1987
Discus	73.90	Diana Gansky	GDR	1987
Javelin	73.20	Petra Felke	GDR	1985
4x100mR	41.65		GDR	1985
4x400mR	3:18.58		USSR	1985

Most individual event wins in finals

MEN
5 Harald Schmid (FRG) 400m 1979, 400mh 1979–83–85–87
3 by twelve men

WOMEN
6 Marlies Göhr (GDR) 100m 1977–79–81–83–85–87
5 Renate Stecher (GDR) 100m 1973–75, 200m 1970–73–75
4 Irena Szewinska (Pol) 100m 1967, 200m 1967–77, 400m 1975
4 Ruth Fuchs (GDR) JT 1970–73–75–77
4 Marita Koch (GDR) 200m 1985, 400m 1977–79–81

Most wins in finals including relays

MEN
8 Harald Schmid (FRG) 5 as above, 4x400mR 1977–79–85
4 Thomas Munkelt (GDR) 3 110mh 1977–79–83, 4x100mR 1975

WOMEN
11 Marlies Göhr (GDR) 6 as above, 4x100mR 1977–79–81–83–85–87
9 Marita Koch (GDR) 4 as above, 4x100mR 1983–85, 4x400mR 1977–79–81
7 Renate Stecher (GDR) 5 as above, 4x100mR 1973–75
5 Irena Szewinska (Pol) 4 as above, 4x100mR 1965
5 Ingrid Auerswald (GDR) 4x100mR 1977–79–83–85–87

The most wins in one final is three (two individual and one relay) by:

MEN:
Eugen Ray (GDR) 100m, 200m, 4x100mR 1977; Harald Schmid (FRG) 400m, 400mh, 4x400mR 1979.

WOMEN:
Renate Stecher (GDR) 100m, 200m, 4x100mR 1973 and 1975; Jarmila Kratochvilova (Cs) 200m, 800m, 4x400mR 1983.

Highest points scorers in finals
Eight points have been scored for 1st, seven for 2nd, down to 1 for 8th. The 6/7 team finals from 1965 to 1973 have been rescored. Relay points have been divided by four.

MEN
61.5 Harald Schmid (FRG) 1977–87
48.75 Pietro Mennea (Ita) 1975–83
46 Allan Wells (UK) 1977–83
42.5 Frank Emmelmann (GDR) 1981–7
42.25 Marian Woronin (Pol) 1977–85

WOMEN
77.5 Irena Szewinska (Pol) 1965–79
67 Marlies Göhr (GDR) 1977–87
52.75 Renate Stecher (GDR) 1970–5
49 Marita Koch (GDR) 1977–85
45 Ruth Fuchs (GDR) 1967–79

The most individual points scored in a final is 21 by Irena Szewinska in 1975: 1st 400m, 2nd 200m, 6th 100m, and she also ran on the 4th-placed 4x100mR team.

Irena Szewinska (POL), Thomas Wessinghage (FRG) and Brigitte Kraus (FRG) competed in a record six European Cup Finals.

Eleven world records have been set in European Cup Finals, all by women:

1965 Irina Press (SU) 80mh 10.4, Tamara Press (SU) SP 18.59; 1973 Faina Melnik (SU) DT 69.48, Ruth Fuchs (GDR) 66.10; 1977 Karin Rossley (GDR) 400mh 55.63, Rosemarie Ackermann (GDR) HJ 1.97; 1979 Marita Koch (GDR) 400m 48.60, GDR 4x100mR 42.09; 1981 Antoaneta Todorova (Bul) JT 71.88; 1983 Ulrike Meyfarth (SU) and Tamara Bykova (SU) HJ 2.03m.

The powerful Renate Stecher leads Mona-Lisa Pursiainen of Finland (Mark Shearman)

European Combined Events Cup

This competition has been held bienially since 1973. As with the European Cup nations are now divided into A, B, C1 and C2 groups.

The 1989 events will be held on 15–16 July as follows:

A Finals	Men at Tönsberg, Norway, women at Helmond, Netherlands
Men	FRA, FRG, GDR, NOR, POL, SWZ, UK, USSR
Women	BUL, CS, FIN, FRA, FRG, HOL, UK, USSR
B Finals	Men at Helmond, women at Tönsberg
Men	BUL, CS, FIN, HOL, HUN, IRE, ITA, SWE
Women	GDR, HUN, ITA, NOR, POL, SPA, SWE, SWZ
C Finals	in Vienna, Austria
Men	AUT, BEL, CYP, DEN, GRE, ICE, SPA, YUG
Women	AUT, BEL, CYP, DEN, GRE, ICE, IRE, YUG

Previous winners

Men's decathlon:
1973 Poland, 1975 USSR, 1977 USSR, 1979 GDR, 1981 FRG, 1983 FRG, 1985 USSR, 1987 GDR

Women's pentathlon:
1973 GDR, 1975 GDR, 1977 USSR, 1979 GDR; **heptathlon** 1981 GDR, 1983 GDR, 1985 GDR, 1987 USSR

Individual records

Athletes to have won two finals: Burglinde Pollak (GDR) women's pentathlon 1973 and 1975, Ramona Neubert (GDR) women's heptathlon 1981 and 1983.

Most finals: 7 Guido Kratschmer (FRG), decathlon each year from 1975 to 1985, with a best placing of second in 1979.

Cup records: Decathlon: 8551 Uwe Freimuth (GDR) 1983; **Heptathlon:** 6772 Ramona Neubert (GDR) 1983.

Ulrike Meyfarth (l) and Tamara Bykova (r) both set a world high jump record of 2.03m in the 1983 European Cup Final, with Meyfarth winning on countback (Mark Shearman)

European Marathon Cup

This event was first held in 1981. Men's and women's races have been held each year, but the latter did not incorporate a team competition until 1985.

1988 results at Huy, Belgium 30 April

MEN
Individual: 1. Ravil Kashapov (SU) 2:11:30, 2. Alessio Faustini 2:11:52, 3. Alain Lazare (Fra) 2:12:24, 4. Nikolay Tabak (SU) 2:12:33, 5. Alex Gonzales (Fra) 2:12:52, 6. Honorato Hernandez (Spa) 2:13:17.
Team: 1. USSR 31, 2. FRA 54, 3. BEL 66, 4. ITA 75, 5. POL 77, 6. GDR 88, 7. UK 118, 8. FRG 133, 9. TUR 196, 10. IRE 206

WOMEN
Individual: 1. Kathrin Dörre (GDR) 2:28:28, 2. Raisa Smekhnova (SU) 2:28:40, 3. Zoya Ivanova (SU) 2:29:37, 4. Yekaterina Khramenkova (SU) 2:29:37, 5. Yelena Tsukhlo (SU) 2:32:48, 6. Maria Lelut (Fra) 2:33:16.
Team: 1. USSR 14, 2. France 52, 3. GDR 54, 4. POL 62, 5. ITA 69, 6. BEL 86, 7. SPA 109, 8. UK 128

Previous winners

MEN
Individual: 1981 Massimo Magnani (Ita) 2:13:29, 1983 Waldemar Cierpinski (GDR) 2:12:26, 1985 Michael Heilmann (GDR) 2:11:28
Team: 1981 Italy, 1983 GDR, 1985 GDR

WOMEN
Individual: 1981 Zoya Ivanova (SU) 2:38:58, 1983 Nadezhda Gumerova (SU) 2:38:36, 1985 Katrin Dörre (GDR) 2:30:11
Team: 1985 GDR

3rd Ibero-American Championships

Mexico City 22–24 July 1988

Winners:
MEN
100m/200m: Robson Caetano da Silva (Bra) 10.08/20.05, 400m: Roberto Hernández (Cub) 44.44, 800m: Colomán Trabado (Spa) 1:47.16, 1500m: Manuel Pancorbo (Spa) 3:52.11, 5000m: Arturo Barrios (Mex) 14:10.72, 10000m: Jesus Herrera (Mex) 29:51.09, Mar: Filemon Lopez (Mex) 2:23:59, 3000mSt: Martin Fiz (Spa) 9:05.21, 110mh: Emilio Valle (Cub) 13.71, 400mh: José Alonso (Spa) 49.20, HJ: Javier Sotomayor (Cub) 2.35, PV: Alberto Ruiz (Spa) 5.30, LJ: Jaime Jefferson (Cub) 8.37, TJ: Juan-Miguel Lopez (Cub) 16.98, SP: Paul Ruiz (Cub) 19.18, DT: Luis M.Delis (Cub) 65.20, HT: Andrés Charadia (Arg) 68.46, JT: Ramón González (Cub) 75.56, 20kmW: Carlos Mercenario (Mex) 1:21:47, 4x100mR/4x400mR: Cuba 38.86/2:59.71.

WOMEN
100m: Sandra Myers (Spa) 11.47, 200m: Blanca Lacambra (Spa) 23.04, 400m/800m: Ana Quirot (Cub) 50.54/2:01.52, 1500m: Soraya Vieira Telles (Bra) 4:28.91, 3000m: Estela Esteves (Spa) 9:46.35, 10000m: Marta Tenorio (Ecu) 35:33.67, Mar: Zoila Munoz (Ecu) 3:00:42, 100mh: Odalys Adams (Cub) 13.28, 400mh: Tania Fernández (Cub) 56.73, HJ: Silvia Costa (Cub) 1.97, LJ: Madeline de Jesus (PR) 6.96, SP: Belsis Laza (Cub) 17.23, DT: Bárbara Echevarria (Cub) 56.34, JT: Herminia Bouza (Cub) 62.48, 10kmW: Maria Colin (Mex) 51:08.1, 4x100mR: Spain 44.47, 4x400mR: Brazil 3:29.22.

IAAF/MOBIL GRAND PRIX

Half the standard events are held each year. There is an Individual Event Grand Prix for each event and an Overall Grand Prix for men and women.

Qualified athletes for the Grand Prix are basically those who, in the current or preceding year have achieved a performance equal to or better than the 50th best in the world in the past year.

For all events prior to the Grand Prix Final: 9 points for 1st, then 7–6–5–4–3–2-1 for 2nd to 8th. At the final double points are awarded. In assessing the event totals, although an athlete may compete at any of the meetings, only his or her best five points scores count.

The 1988 award structure was as follows: For each event: first $10,000, second $8000, third $6000, fourth $5000, fifth $4000, sixth $3000, seventh $2000, eight $1000.

Men's and women's overall Grand Prix awards (all events): first $25,000, second $15,000, third $10,000.

Schedule of Events

	1988	1989
Bruce Jenner's Bud Lite Classic, San Jose (USA)	28 May	27 May
Pravda Televizia Slovnaft, Bratislava (Cs)	9 Jun	Not GP
Znamenskiy Memorial, Leningrad (1988), Volgograd (1989) (SU)	12 Jun	11 Jun
Athletissima, Lausanne (Swi)	24 Jun	27 Jun
Olympischer Tag, East Berlin (GDR)	29 Jun	5 Jul
Maailmankisat (World Games), Helsinki (Fin)	30 Jun	29 Jun
Bislett Games, Oslo (Nor)	2 Jul	1 Jul
DN Galan, Stockholm (Swe)	5 Jul	3 Jul
Peugeot Games, London (UK)	8 Jul	14 Jul
Nikaia, Nice (Fra)	10 Jul	10 Jul
Golden Gala, Verona (1988), Rome (1989) (Ita)	27 Jul	19 Jul
Miller Lite IAC International, Edinburgh (UK)	29 Jul	7 Jul
Hungalu Budapest Grand Prix (Hun)	12 Aug	8 Aug
Weltklasse, Zürich (Swi)	17 Aug	16 Aug
Ivo van Damme Memorial, Brussels (Bel)	19 Aug	25 Aug
ASV Sportfest der Weltklasse, Köln (FRG)	21 Aug	20 Aug
ISTAF, West Berlin (FRG) (Final in 1988)	26 Aug	18 Aug
Grand Prix Final, Monte Carlo, Monaco		1 Sep

IAAF/MOBIL Overall Grand Prix winners

Year	Men	Women
1985	Doug Padilla (USA)	Mary Slaney (USA)
1986	Said Aouita (Mor)	Yordanka Donkova (Bul)
1987	Tonie Campbell (USA)	Merlene Ottey (Jam)
1988	Said Aouita (Mor)	Paula Ivan (Rom)

Most points scored 1985–8

MEN		WOMEN	
223	Said Aouita (Mor)	183	Doina Melinte (Rom)
209	Mike Conley (USA)	163	Maricica Puica (Rom)
188	Calvin Smith (USA)	161	Mary Slaney (USA)
176	Sydney Maree (USA)	142	Ana Quirot (Cub)
169	Steve Scott (USA)	132	Merlene Ottey (Jam)
117	Sergey Bubka (SU)	126	Genowefa Blaszak (Pol)
115	Danny Harris (USA)	124	Stefka Kostadinova (Bul)
112	Chidi Imoh (Nig)	119	Elly Van Hulst (Hol)
110	Jim Spivey (USA)	114	Yordanka Donkova (Bul)
106	Tom Petranoff (USA)	108	Petra Felke (GDR)

IAAF/MOBIL Individual Grand Prix Event winners

Event	1985	1987
MEN		
200m	Calvin Smith (USA)	Thomas Jefferson (USA)
400m	Mike Franks (USA)	Innocent Egbunike (Nig)
1500m	Steve Scott (USA)	Abdi Bile (Som)
5000m	Doug Padilla (USA)	Arturo Barrios (Mex)
110mh	Mark McKoy (Can)	Tonie Campbell (USA)
Pole vault	Sergey Bubka (SU)	Sergey Bubka (SU)
Long jump	Mike Conley (USA)	Larry Myricks (USA)
Discus	Imrich Bugár (Cs)	Romas Ubartas (SU)
Javelin	Tom Petranoff (USA)	Tom Petranoff (USA)
WOMEN		
100m	Alice Brown (USA)	Merlene Ottey (Jam)
800m	Jarmila Kratochvilova (Cs)	Ana Quirot (Cub)
1 mile	not held	Elly Van Hulst (Hol)
3000m	Mary Slaney (USA)	Maricica Puica (Rom)
400mh	Judi Brown King (USA)	Debbie Flintoff-King (AUS)
High jump	Stefka Kostadinova (Bul)	Stefka Kostadinova (Bul)
Long jump	Galina Chistyakova (SU)	Vali Ionescu (Rom)
Shot	Helena Fibingerová (Cs)	Helena Fibingerová (Cs)

Event	1986	1988
MEN		
100m	Chidi Imoh (Nig)	Chidi Imoh (Nig)
800m	José Luiz Barbosa (Bra)	Tom McKean (UK)
1 mile	Steve Scott (USA)	Said Aouita (Mor)
5000m	Said Aouita (Mor)	Eamonn Martin (UK)
3000mSt	William van Dijck (Bel)	Julius Kariuki (Ken)
400mh	Andre Phillips (USA)	Danny Harris (USA)
High jump	Jim Howard (USA)	Javier Sotomayor (Cub)
Triple jump	Mike Conley (USA)	Mike Conley (USA)
Shot	Werner Günthör (Swi)	Remigius Machura (Cs)
Hammer	Yuriy Sedykh (SU)	Tibor Gécsek (Hun)
WOMEN		
200m	Evelyn Ashford (USA)	Grace Jackson (Jam)
400m	Diane Dixon (USA)	Ana Quirot (Cub)
1500m	Maricica Puica (Rom)	Paula Ivan (Rom)
5000m	Svetlana Guskova (SU)	Liz McColgan (UK)
100mh	Yordanka Donkova (Bul)	Claudia Zaczkiewicz (FRG)
Discus	Tsvetanka Khristova (Bul)	Hilda Ramos (Cub)
Javelin	Petra Felke (GDR)	Manuela Alizadeh (FRG)

Leading scorers 1988 – Men

Overall
63 Said Aouita (Mor)
61 Mike Conley (USA)
58 Danny Harris (USA)
57 Javier Sotomayor (Cub)
55 Oleg Protsenko (SU)
55 Chidi Imoh (Nig)

100 Metres
55 Chidi Imoh (Nig)
46 Brian Cooper (USA)
43 Calvin Smith (USA)

800 Metres
48 Tom McKean (UK)
45 Said Aouita (Mor)
45 Moussa Fall (Sen)

1 Mile
54 Said Aouita (Mor)
39 Jim Spivey (USA)
36 Sydney Maree (USA)

5000 Metres
39 Eamonn Martin (UK)
37 Brahim Boutayeb (Mor)
36 José Regalo (Por)

3000m Steeplechase
48 Julius Kariuki (Ken)
46 Peter Koech (Ken)
43 Patrick Sang (Ken)

400 Metres Hurdles
58 Danny Harris (USA)
51 Amadou Dia Bâ (Sen)
37 Nat Page (USA)

High Jump
57 Javier Sotomayor (Cub)
44 Patrik Sjöberg (Swe)
36.5 Sorin Matei (Rom)

Triple Jump
61 Mike Conley (USA)
55 Oleg Protsenko (Su)
46 Juan Miguel Lopez (Cub)

Shot
51 Remigius Machura (Cs)
50 Ron Backes (USA)
46 Georg Andersen (Nor)

Hammer
48 Tibor Gécsek (Hun)
31 Igor Astapkovich (SU)
29 Igor Nikulin (SU)

Leading scorers – Women

Overall
63 Paula Ivan (Rom)
63 Grace Jackson (Jam)
57 Ana Quirot (Cub)
55 Liz McColgan (UK)
50 Claudia Zaczkiewicz (FRG)
49 Dannette Young (USA)

200 Metres
63 Grace Jackson (Jam)
49 Dannette Young (USA)
48 Mary Onyali (Nig)

400 Metres
57 Ana Quirot (Cub)
48 Grace Jackson (Jam)
44 Jillian Richardson (Can)

1500 Metres
63 Paula Ivan (Rom)
47 Mitica Constantin (Rom)
41 Elly Van Hulst (Hol)

5000 Metres
51 Liz McColgan (UK)
32 Annette Sergent (Fra)
28 Julia Besliu (Rom)

100 Metres Hurdles
50 Claudia Zaczkiewicz (FRG)
45 Yordanka Donkova (Bul)
42.5 Laurence Elloy (Fra)
42.5 Ulrike Denk (FRG)

Discus
42 Hilda Ramos (Cub)
38 Maritza Marten (Cub)
23 Tsvetanka Khristova (Bul)

Javelin
46 Manuela Alizadeh (FRG)
45 Petra Felke (GDR)
41 Ivonne Leal (Cub)

1988 Final 1st 3

MEN

100m: 1. Calvin Smith 10.12
2. Chidi Imoh (Nig) 10.16
3. Brian Cooper (USA) 10.16

800m: 1. Tom McKean (UK) 1:47.60
2. Sebastian Coe (UK) 1:47.87
3. Dieudonné Kwizéra (Bur) 1:48.25

1 mile: 1. Said Aouita (Mor) 3:56.21
2. Jim Spivey (USA) 3:56.55
3. José Luis Gonzalez (Spa) 3:56.67

5000m: 1. José Regalo (Por) 13:22.20
2. Eamonn Martin (UK) 13:22.88
3. Domingos Castro (Por) 13:24.03

3000mSt: 1. Julius Kariuki (Ken) 8:24.52
2. Patrick Sang (Ken) 8:25.27
3. Peter Koech (Ken) 8:27.09

400mh: 1. Danny Harris (USA) 49.29
2. Amadou Dia Bâ (Sen) 49.50
3. David Patrick (USA) 49.54

HJ: 1. Patrik Sjöberg (Swe) 2.33
2. Javier Sotomayor (Cub) 2.30
3. Rudolf Povarnitsyn (SU) 2.27

TJ: 1. Mike Conley (USA) 17.59
2. Oleg Protsenko (SU) 17.39
3. Robert Cannon (USA) 16.87

SP: 1. Helmut Krieger (Pol) 20.79
2. Ron Backes (USA) 19.96
3. Georg Andersen (Nor) 19.70

HT: 1. Igor Astapkovich (SU) 81.26
2. Tibor Gécsek (Hun) 79.72
3. Christoph Sahner FRG) 77.96

WOMEN

200m: 1. Grace Jackson (Jam) 22.70
2. Mary Onyali (Nig) 22.80
3. Pauline Davis (Bah) 23.12

400m: 1. Ana Quirot (Cub) 50.27
2. Jillian Richardson (Can) 50.52
3. Grace Jackson (Jam) 51.11

1500m: 1. Paula Ivan (Rom) 4:00.24
2. Mitica Constantin (Rom) 4:04.97
3. Elly van Hulst (Hol) 4:06.52

5000m: 1. Liz McColgan (UK) 15:03.29
2. Ingrid Kristiansen (Nor) 15:10.89
3. Jill Hunter (UK) 15:17.77

100mh: 1. Claudia Zaczkiewicz (FRG) 12.93
2. Ulrike Denk (FRG) 12.96
3. Marjan Olyslager (Hol) 13.05

DT: 1. Hilda Ramos (Cub) 66.58
2. Dagmar Galler (FRG) 61.72
3. Maritza Marten (Cub) 60.88

JT: 1. Manuela Alizadeh (FRG) 62.52
2. Beate Peters (FRG) 62.14
3. Ingrid Thyssen (FRG) 61.70

MAJOR INTERNATIONAL EVENTS 1989–92

1989 (from May)

World Race Walking Cup – L'Hospitalet, Spain (27–28 May)
European Cup for Combined Events – Tönsberg (Nor), Helmond (Hol), Vienna (Aut) (15–16 Jul)
Pan-American Junior Championships – Santa Fe, Argentina (22–25 June)
European Cup – A final at Gateshead, UK and other venues (5–6 Aug)
World Veterans (Masters) Championships – Eugene, Oregon, USA (Aug)
World University Games (17–27 Aug)
European Junior Championships – Varazdin, Yugoslavia (24–27 Aug)
IAAF/Mobil Grand Prix Final – Monte Carlo, Monaco (1 Sep)
World Cup – Barcelona, Spain (8–10 Sep)
World 15km Road Race Championship for Women – Rio de Janeiro, Brazil

1990

Commonwealth Games – Auckland, New Zealand (Jan – Feb)
European Indoor Championships – Glasgow, UK (3–4 Mar)
World Cross-Country Championships – Aix-Les-Bains, France (25 Mar)
World Junior Championships – Plovdiv, Bulgaria
Goodwill Games – Seattle, USA (20 Jul – 5 Aug)
European Championships – Split, Yugoslavia (27 Aug – 1 Sep)
Asian Games

1991

World Indoor Championships – Seville, Spain
World Marathon Cup
African Games – Cairo, Egypt
World Student Games – Sheffield, UK
Pan-American Games – Havana, Cuba (3–18 Aug)
World Championships – Tokyo, Japan (24 Aug – 1 Sep)
World Race Walking Cup
Mediterranean Games – Athens, Greece

1992

Olympic Games – Barcelona, Spain (26 Jul – 10 Aug)

NOTES FROM THE EDITOR

BY PETER MATTHEWS

Olympic years are always those in which there is the greatest public interest in track and field athletics. That was certainly so in 1988, amplified by a seemingly endless flow of controversies, which hit the headlines far more than just for sport. We had cheating at the 1987 World Championships, the Zola Budd affair and participation by some Americans in South Africa, selection arguments, wrangles between athletes and their managers and coaches, and of course above all the sensation of the disqualification at the Olympic Games of Ben Johnson following his positive drugs test.

Many of these controversies attracted adverse publicity, but we also had a fascinating year of sport. A new era of women's sprinting was ushered in by Florence Griffith-Joyner, Butch Reynolds smashed the 20-year-old world record for 400 metres, there was the first 80m javelin throw by a woman, and much more, to push back the barriers of achievement. Above all we had a great Olympic Games, at which

The chief judge has a quiet word with Ben Johnson in Seoul (George Herringshaw/ASP)

nearly all the world's best competed, and which were staged with great dedication and enthusiasm by the South Koreans, to whom the honour of staging the Games was a recognition of their important place in the world and hard work in rebuilding their great capital city of Seoul after the devastation of the Korean War some 35 years ago.

Ben Johnson

Ben Johnson ran magnificently in the 1988 Olympic 100 metres. His 9.83 to win the world title the previous year had been acclaimed as one of the greatest performances in the history of running. So his 9.79 in Seoul when he again beat the great Carl Lewis by a clear metre had to be even more so. Then we learnt that he had been caught with a positive drugs test. He vociferously protested his innocence and continued to do so months after the event. It seemed that the testing procedures were ahead of those who would get round them.

Despite the proof positive of cheating Johnson has run the 100 metres far faster than any human being in history. Artificially aided it may have been, but he still did it, and it was not drugs alone that got him into the condition to be able to do so, but enormous quanties of hard work. The problem is that athletes might only contemplate such prodigious work loads with the aid of drugs. Cecil Smith, publisher of *Athletics Canada* and chairman of the Ottawa Track & Field Association takes an informed look at the affair elsewhere in this annual.

The one positive test

The first four in every event at the Olympics were tested, with other random controls and Johnson's was the one confirmed case of abuse. There was however a scare when word leaked out that one of the British team had been found positive. It turned out to be Linford Christie, not after his 100m silver medal, but following the 200 metres a few days later. Christie had long been a vociferous opponent of drug taking, so this caused much amazement. It transpired that a small amount (6–8.4 parts per million) of ephedrine was found in his urine sample; and this was considered to be in the normal therapeutic range. Christie's statement that he had inadvertently taken this in a ginseng tea preparation was accepted by the IOC Medical Committee and subsequently by the full International Committee. He was also given full support by the BAAB, who deplored the leak of information in this case.

Further action needed

Because of the difficulty in where to draw the line between natural and unnatural aids, stimulants and diet, there are many who still adopt an equivocal attitude to the problem. Nonetheless the medical evidence of the damage done by steroids, let alone the ethics of the problem shows that this scourge of our sport has to be fiercely contested. Fair-minded sportsmen and women will otherwise shun athletics. While the Johnson disqualification brought the sport into disrepute, it at least showed that action could and would be taken against anyone who transgressed, no matter how mighty. And there was considerable activity after the Games to do more; that might not have happened without the extra impetus given by the Johnson affair. Particularly important was the accord reached between the USSR and the USA on testing.

Vital too was the support declared by top athletes for the IAAF anti-doping campaign and to eradicate totally the use of forbidden drugs in the sport. That came in a statement signed by Rosa Mota, Sergey Bubka, Edwin Moses and Alberto Juantorena on behalf of top athletes and issued in Seoul on 29 September, just after the test result on Johnson.

More good news came from the end of year TAC convention in Phoenix, Arizona, for there a random drugs testing programme involving the top 25 performers in each event was unanimously approved. That programme awaited the approval of TAC directors in March 1989, but it must be hoped that it will be operated effectively. This will be partiularly important in the USA where there has been much muddled thinking about the so-called freedom of the individual. It should be realised that freedom to indulge in drug use is at the expense of the rights and freedoms of others.

Once again I urge worldwide random testing throughout the year, not just in competition but perhaps especially in training. I would also like to see those most responsible – the people who administer the drugs, maybe to unwitting athletes - removed from influence and active participation in the sport. But how to test them and prove their guilt?

Climate of suspicion

The Johnson affair served to exacerbate the climate of suspicion surrounding athletes.

Whispered allegations continue to be made concerning this or that athlete, and the result is that few, especially those who have made especial improvement, escape the doubters. It just may be that some we might suspect most highly are clean, and some whom we could not believe to have trangressed the rules might have been drug abusers. It is so sad that this is currently the case.

South Africa

The South African AAU was expelled from the IAAF in 1976 (227 votes to 145). This meant that their athletes have since been barred from international competition, and no athletes from IAAF member nations have been able to compete in South Africa. The abhorrent regime of apartheid, which has had a stranglehold on the country, gave rise to this decision, and the principle of no normal sporting contacts with an unnatural society has been effective in athletics, as in other international sports. This is in contrast to sports with a more limited base, but important in South Africa, such as rugby and cricket, where less clear-cut breaks have been established, and where the problems, with their effects on other sports, continue. While sporting links with South Africa would be seen as supporting the regime, the lack of international competition has sadly marred the careers of their native athletes, even though at the top level the sport is now multi-racial in South Africa.

Until the visit by a group of 14 American athletes led by Dick Tomlinson in late 1988 no organised effort had been made to break the ban on athletes from other nations competing in South Africa. The inevitable result was that those athletes were suspended by the TAC. All had perhaps passed their peak, and were willing to cash in. Top names were the former world record holders John Powell and Tom Petranoff, the others: Kevin Akins, Joel Andrews, Carol Cady, Tom Hintnaus, Tyrus Jefferson, Dave Laut, James Robinson, Cedric Silder, Milan Stewart, Keith Thibodeaux, Ray Wicksell and Ruth Wysocki. No doubt all felt that they should be free to compete as they wished and that they were in no way supporting apartheid, and it is hard to disagree with the principle, but that is to ignore the feelings of others, and above all the democratic decision of the world's representatives against such contacts.

Zola Budd

A limited number of South Africans have been able to escape the effects of the international ban. Sydney Maree was the most notable of those who left their native country. He established himself in the USA, went through the due processes, and in due course established his US citizenship. The marathon runner Mark Plaatjes in now doing the same. Others, such as the 1988 NCAA women's cross-country champion Michelle Dekkers, have been able to go to American Universities, although still not able to compete outside collegiate events.

Maree and Plaatjes emigrated, but the position has not been so clear cut in the case of Zola Budd, which has become a real cause célèbre.

Zola Budd gained her British passport in the spring of 1984, and since then has rarely seemed far from the headlines in the newspapers. She gained that passport through the fortune of her grandfather's birthplace; the processes being rushed through just a few days prior to her 18th birthday, after which she would not have been eligible to establish such a claim. That year she disappointed the ridiculous hopes that were placed on her at the Los Angeles Olympics, although her clash with Mary Slaney ensured her notoriety. However in 1985 she had a fine season, winning the European Cup 3000m race in Moscow for Britain, taking the world record for 5000m, and challenging the world's best Mary Slaney and Maricica Puica.

Still, however, she returned regularly to South Africa and the lack of continuous residence in Britain led to her not being allowed to run in the Commonwealth Games, which were nonetheless marred by the withdrawal of some 32 nations over the refusal of the British government to impose economic sanctions on South Africa. Budd did however compete in the 1986 European Championships before losing nearly all the 1987 season through injury.

Given the circumstances of South Africa's ostracism from world sport, the fact that Budd continued to live and train in South Africa for most of the time meant that she could be accused of blatent abuse of her ability to compete internationally by a passport of convenience. Nonetheless the sport's administrators threatened to venture into unreality with debates over whether her warming up and jogging outside of a cross-country race in South Africa constituted participation. If of course she had actually competed, then she would have been banned from international competition. After the buck had been passed back and forth, Budd temporarily at least resolved the issue by returning to South Africa, without seeking to run in Britain or at the Olympic Games. If she had determined to make her home in Britain and shown continuing evidence of that, she ought by now to have been accepted as British, but sadly she did not. However much sympathy one may have with her for seeking the comfort of her homeland and family it is hard to imagine how she could possibly again be accepted on the world stage.

In interviews at the end of the year she showed that she was keeping her options open, but, on principle, she refused to denounce Apartheid. That will hardly win her any friends and later she changed her stance. The reality of world politics is such that she surely cannot both run for Britain and live in South Africa.

Selection

I wrote last year about the problems of selection. In 1988 these problems came to the surface. The British authorities determined on a policy which gave automatic places to the first two athletes at a trials meeting, with no preselection. This gave rise to the likelihood that the best possible team would not be in Seoul as, even with the third place open for selection, two places would be fixed for athletes who were not necessarily those most likely to perform with distinction at the Games. All sorts of possibilities could be contemplated, and Britain would not have the depth of, say, the USA to cover for catastrophies, such as several potential medallists falling over each other and letting in fringe candidates. Another problem was that the trials meeting was held over 2/3 days and athletes found it difficult to double as they might at the big event. On the other hand there was the major benefit to athletes of knowing exactly what was required for selection.

Seb Coe not picked for Seoul

As it transpired the meeting was held in perfect weather and to a considerable extent the best athletes came through on the day to take their places.

With such a policy the press were bound to find fault whatever happened, and they made hay when a superstar fell foul of the system. Seb Coe, who had been a severe critic of the policy in advance, failed to advance from the heats of the 1500 metres final. It was then too late for him the try the 800m, at which he had some good form in the preceding few weeks. However with Cram and McKean at 800m and Elliott and Crabb at 1500m he could hardly have been preferred either to Elliott at the former or Cram at the latter. The team was chosen on 8th August, selectors were split, but the deciding vote went against him, as surely it should have done on the evidence shown to that date. Ironically by the end of August he had shown Olympic-class form at 800m and might well have been at Seoul if the team had been chosen later and on a true selection basis.

Intervention of IOC President

The real problem was not just the selection method but the restriction for each event to three athletes per event. In my notes last year I advocated the opening of major Games and championships to all in the world élite for each event. That thought may have gained credence from the publicity attendant upon the intervention in the controversy by the President of the International Olympic Committee, Juan Antonio Samaranch. Amazingly he asked the British Board to reconsider their selection; that of course could not be done, but he then suggested a possible 'wild card' entry for Coe, as a distinguished Olympian. Fine in principle, but as was pointed out by other athletes, rules cannot be ignored even when the idea came from such a distinguished source. If Coe, then surely also at least other defending champions, and there were several who were still active, who had not made their national teams: French pole vaulter Pierre Quinon, Kenyan steeplechaser Julius Korir, and the Americans Alonzo Babers, Benita Fitzgerald-Brown, Al Joyner and Joan Samuelson.

I hope that the idea may lead to a change in regulations to allow perhaps defending medallists to compete, as long as they have reached a certain standard in the past year, as well as anybody who has attained a super high standard, perhaps of world top ten level.

Potential medallists only?

Great Britain's team had arguably a few too many members in Seoul, although I see nothing wrong in a policy which gives the opportunity of Olympic competition to those who have proved themselves the best in their countries and who have met the qualifying conditions. Many nations, however, set very much higher standards for selection, to my mind sometimes absurdly high. That may not have affected the medals but I would like to see all potential finalists competing at major Games. An over élitist attitude does not seem to give adequate encouragement to a nation's athletes.

Romania

The worst case of élitism that I have noticed is that of Romania, whose teams for major Games are getting smaller. They sent no men and nine women to the 1984 Olympics, and their 1988 team was one man, Sorin Matei, and four women: Paula Ivan, Doina Melinte, Maricica Puica and Galina Astafei. A talented bunch for sure, and two other middle distance runners, Tudorita Ghidu and Mitica Constantin, were entered but did not compete. Perhaps injury struck them and Vali Ionescu, undoubtedly a medal contender at the long jump, but they had many other athletes who bettered the Olympic standards. They also lost one of their top stars Daniela Costian, who applied for political asylum in Turkey at the Balkan Games, and later went to Australia. Matei had also been their only male competitor at the 1987 World Championships, but they did then have 13 women. There is something wrong here.

World records indoors

From the start of 1987 the IAAF has maintained a separate list of world indoor records. From 1988 they also amended their rules to allow world records to be set with a roof over the athletes' heads provided that conditions were otherwise the same as outdoors. So marks on 200m tracks or board surfaces would not be accepted. The first beneficiary of this ruling was high jumper Carlo Thränhardt, who cleared 2.42m in West Berlin on 26 Feb 1988. This equalled the outdoor best of Patrik Sjöberg.

Money, money, money

The ability of athletes to earn money, albeit for their trust funds, has been of great benefit to the sport. It has considerably extended the careers of many great athletes and played its part in improving standards. It is only fair that athletes who help to fill stadiums or ensure high viewing figures for television should be rewarded for their endeavours. Of course it is only the few who earn more than enough to cover their basic needs. Nonetheless one of the major tasks facing governing bodies is to control the excesses brought about by blatantly commercial forces. These have to be harnessed to the overall good of the sport, with at least a reasonable level of compromise.

Meeting promotors, even those with large budgets, have realised that there had to be a halt to the escalation in fees paid to the superstars, and there is evidence that this is being done. However their careful planning can be severely affected by the sort of money (around $200,000 apiece) that was reportedly paid, particularly by Japanese television, for the Carl Lewis–Ben Johnson clash at Zürich in 1988. Just as with the Mary Slaney–Zola Budd rematch in 1985, when there was a similar severe distortion in market rates, the two highly paid protagonists did not finish first and second. The 'lesser fry' could thus have every reason to be aggrieved at the imbalance in their rewards, but most worrying of all is that such one-off payments might escalate demands out of all proportion to economic reality. And that could be catastrophic for the sport.

Accuracy and honesty

The very nature of athletics is that performances are measurable and comparable whether by stopwatch or measure. As a body the ATFS strives to the highest degree for accuracy and completeness of information, and athletes need to know exactly what they have achieved. It was thus with concern that I received a detailed review of the timing of the first semi-final at the 1988 Olympic Games in Seoul from our Swedish expert, A. Lennart Julin. In his research he offers apparently irrefutable proof that the timings in this race were about 0.6 sec. too fast. Now this in itself is fairly trivial, and fortunately did not affect the qualifying conditions for the final, although it very nearly did, with fastest loser places in contention. However what is of deep concern is the fact that such incorrect times, which must have been known to some officials, were released without comment. The most likely explanation of the inaccuracy was that the timing systems did not receive the automatic starting impulse. In which case hand times could have been used, but instead apparently automatic, but faulty timings became official.

No harm was done here, and few bar very diligent observers would have noticed, but that was not the case with Giovanni Evangelisti's long jump measurement at the 1987 World Championships, where there appears to have been a conspiracy to produce a fraudulent result. Even then, the evidence, so blatant to observers, was resisted at first by the authorities. We must have accuracy and commitment from those governing our sport to such accuracy. If mistakes are made, and of course they will be from time to time, then they must be honestly admitted.

The post-Olympic season

Once upon a time the season after an Olympic Games was a quiet one. Many athletes retired after each Olympiad, and there was little top-class international competition to aim at. Now, however, athletes stay in competition much longer, and even without the major championships there is a plethora of activity. It may be that the middle and long distance stars will aim their sights at world records, and their attempts could be most exciting. It could hardly be expected, however, that we could be in line for a rerun of the amazing breakthroughs that happened in another post-Olympic season, 24 years ago in 1965; in his article Lennart Julin looks at that year when Ron Clarke inspired a generation of athletes.

Meanwhile we bid farewell to men and women who have been at the forefront of our sport for more than a decade. It is sometimes difficult to know how serious are retirement claims; a few months away can reawake competitive urges. But we may have seen the last on the track or road of such stars as Marlies Göhr, Udo Beyer, Eamonn Coghlan, Toshihiko Seko and Henry Marsh, so our good wishes go to them and others who have withdrawn for the competitive arena, and our thanks for the pleasure they have brought.

Peter Matthews

Seb Coe leaves the track after his failure to qualify for the 1500 metres final at the 1988 Olympic Trials (Mark Shearman)

Udo Beyer has retired after 14 successive years in the world top ten shot putters with seven years ranked as number one (George Herringshaw/ASP)

SUSPENDED AFTER FAILING DRUGS TEST

A complete list of those suspended for failing drugs tests from 1974 to 1986 was given in Athletics '87. Those suspended in 1986 and 1987 were listed in Athletics '88/9 (page 94).

Those suspended prior to 1987 who have returned and are currently active in competition at top level include:

MEN
Duncan Attwood (USA) 1985
Lazaro Betancourt (Cub) 1986
Ronald Desruelles (Bel) 1980
Versteinn Hafsteinsson (Ice) 1984
Knut Hjeltnes (Nor) 1977
Dariusz Juzyszyn (Pol) 1983
Juan-Miguel Lopez (Cub) 1986
Remigius Machura (Cs) 1985
Gary McSeveney (USA) 1986
Antoni Niemczak (Pol) 1986
Juan Nuñez (Dom) 1983
Ben Plucknett (USA) 1981
Elisio Rios (Por) 1983
Ahmed Kamel Shatta (Egy) 1985
Lars Sundin (Swe) 1985
Göran Svensson (Swe) 1985
Art Swarts (USA) 1986
László Szabo (Hun) 1981
Martti Vainio (Fin) 1984
August Wolf (USA) 1985 *

WOMEN
Lyudmila Andonova (Bul) 1985
Ilona Briesenick (GDR) 1977
Daniela Costian (Rom) 1986
Emilia Dimitrova (Bul) 1986
Agnes Herczeg (Hun) 1983
Gael Martin (Aus) 1981
Zdenka Silhava (Cs) 1985
Anna Verouli (Gre) 1984

** Suspended for refusing test*
 # 3 month suspension (ephedrine)

Suspended in 1987

MEN
Chris de Beer (RSA)
Eric de Smedt (Fra)
Louis Demarne (Fra)
Temel Erbek (Tur) #
Bill Green (USA)
Nikolay Kolev (Bul)
Thomas Menne (FRG) #
Lars Arvid Nilsen (Nor)
Paul Quirke (Ire) *
Leon Rheeder (RSA)
Antoine Richard (Fra)
Lynn Valley (USA)

WOMEN
Doina Calenic (Rom)
Mihaela Chindae (Rom)
Sandra Gasser (Swi)
Sue Howland (Aus)
Hye-Young Jung (SKo)
Gabriela Mihalcea (Rom)

Suspended by the Norwegian federation for bringing the sport into disrepute:

Jan Sagedål (Nor)
Kare Sagedål (Nor)
Trond Ulleberg (Nor)
Arne Pedersen (Nor) (also in 1982)

Suspended in 1988

MEN
Jeff Gutteridge (UK)
Ben Johnson (Can)
Dmitriy Kovtsun (SU)
Robert Kurnicki (Pol)
Aleksandr Leonov (SU)
Luis Morales (PR)
Cosmas Ndeti (Ken) #
Andrea Pantani (Ita)
Luis Rodriguez (Bra)
Jean-Pol Schlatter (Bel)
Sasa Stojilovic (Yug)

WOMEN
Sabine Dewachter (Bel)
Inna Ivanova (SU)
Satomi Kawazu (Jap)
Linda McCurdy-Cameron (Can) #
Suzanne Matz (USA)

1965 – THE MAGICAL YEAR OF DISTANCE RUNNING

BY A. LENNART JULIN

To a large extent the 'historical' years of our sport coincide with the years of the Olympic Games. This is a logical situation as the Olympic cycle has governed the world of organized sport right from the start with the Olympic gold medal as the ultimate sign of outstanding ability. Therefore Olympic years have traditionally brought about a noticeable rise of standards.

Although the long historical tradition still makes Olympic years special, the situation has changed somewhat in the 1980s as new attractive high-status competitions outdoors and indoors have been added to the programme, making every year 'important'. So the 'Post-Olympic Blues' will probably not be as noticeable this time as it usually was previously.

I say 'usually' because there was one very strange anomaly in the traditional patterns almost a quarter of a century ago. In fact the post-Olympic year of 1965 will for future athletics historians stand out as perhaps the most exciting revolutionary year ever! Because in 1965 the official world records in all but one of the seventeen individual men's running events from 1000m upwards were improved upon at least once! Only Herb Elliott's 3:35.6 survived – by a scant 8/10s of a second.

The adjoining tables show: (a) that the total number of individual world records was 25! (b) that several of the records were truly obliterated – e.g. the 3000m and the 5000m by some 10 seconds and the 10000m by 36 seconds! (c) that 11 different runners from 8 different countries in 4 different continents got entries in the world record lists!

That it was a true avalanche and not something concerning just a couple of outstanding athletes at the top is also proven by the fact that the No. 10 in the yearly lists of 1965 was at approximately the same level as the No. 10 of all-time pre-1965 for events like the 3000m (7:56.2/7:55.6), the 5000m (13:41.4/13:42.4) and the 10000m (28:46.0/28:39.6)!

The 5000m contributed the most extreme case of 'The ketchup bottle effect'. At 1 Jan 1965 the world record was 13:35.0, run by Vladimir Kuts in 1957. One year later that mark had been surpassed no less than 20 times by 6 different runners! (One way to understand the magnitude of this revolution is to try to think of 6 runners dippling below 12:58.39 some 20 times this year!)

But what was the reason for the running revolution of 1965? Was it some kind of breakthrough in equipment like the fibre-glass pole a few years earlier? No, the tracks used by the runners in 1965 were of the same cinders type as in previous years. The modern type of synthetic all-weather surfaces didn't come into use until a few years later.

Was it some kind of technical advancement like the flop technique in the high jump a couple of years later? No, the runners in 1965 used the same method (left foot – right foot – left foot – right foot – . . .) of moving forward as previously.

Was it a revolution in training methods like the modern strength training brought into the throwing events ten years earlier? No, the vastly improved runners coming from all parts of the world were following all kinds of different training philosophies. Some were Lydiard-inspired while some were still doing the type of heavy intervals that dominated in Europe during the 1950s.

Was there something 'wrong' with 1964 as with 1968 when the high altitude of Mexico City made record times impossible for distance events, although the physical capacity was there? No, the year 1964 – with the OG at sea level in the autumn – had presented a sufficient number of great opportunities of running fast in middle and long distance races.

But if there wasn't any 'logical' reason for the 'explosion' of 1965, what then provided the ignition? The answer is one name – RON CLARKE!

The middle and long distance running events are characterized by the facts that you can't run all out from the start and that you, through intermediate times, have a continuous feedback telling you what you are doing. It is inevitable that these circumstances create mental barriers

Ron Clarke leads Gerry Lindgren in the 1965 AAA 3 Miles, when he became the first man to run the distance in less than 13 minutes (Mark Shearman)

Kip Keino set world records at 3000m and 5000m in 1965 (Mark Shearman)

that are very hard to get out of your mind. However a few times in the history of our sport there have been athletes with the exquisite ability of forgetting what is possible and reasonable, and who instead, without hesitation, try to break into unknown territory. Ron Clarke is perhaps the most brilliant example of this, and it is beyond all doubt that it was Clarke who in 1965 opened wide the doors into the future.

The single most important race was the 5000m at the Compton Invitational in Los Angeles on June 4 where he took 8 seconds away from his own – just four months old – world record by running 13:25.8. One week later Michel Jazy did 13:29.0 and another 19 days later the two met in Helsinki. The results were truly sensational. Not just Jazy (13:27.6) and Clarke (13:29.4) but also Kipchoge Keino (13:28.2 – pb by 25.4) and Mike Wiggs (13:33.0 – pb by 12.6) surpassed Kuts 13:35.0. A time that was almost reached also by Thor Helland (13:37.4 – pb by 15.0) and Bengt Nåjde (13:37.8 – pb by 15.4). Half a year earlier nobody would have dreamt of Helland and Nåjde as runners capable of threatening Kuts' WR but now that Ron Clarke had showed that it was possible to run 13:25 there was no reason to be afraid of trying to run 10–12 seconds slower. The doors were open!

As a 5000m-runner Ron Clarke was not the undisputed No. 1 as both Jazy and Keno proved to be able to beat him and to run similar times, but at the 10000m Clarke ruled supreme. The greatest of all great world records run in 1965 was his 27:39.4 for 10000m on July 14 in Oslo. In that race he lowered his own four weeks old WR by almost 35 seconds. On average he ran each of the 25 laps 1.4 seconds faster than ever before! How could anyone dare trying something like that – especially when it wasn't at all 'necessary' as he already had the record himself? That almost unique asset did not just make Ron Clarke one of the most fascinating athletes of all time, it also made 1965 one of the magical years in the history of athletics!

The Distance Running World Records of 1965

	Time	Name	Nation	Venue	Date
1000m					
Pre-1965	*2:16.6*	*Peter Snell*	*NZ*		*1964*
1965	2:16.2	Jürgen May	GDR	Erfurt	20 Jul
1 mile					
Pre-1965	*3:54.1*	*Peter Snell*	*NZ*		*1964*
1965	3:53.6	Michel Jazy	FRA	Rennes	9 Jun
2000m					
Pre-1965	*5:01.6*	*Michel Jazy*	*FRA*		*1962*
1965	5:01.2	Josef Odlozil	CS	Stará Boleslav	8 Sep
3000m					
Pre-1965	*7:49.2*	*Michael Jazy*	*FRA*		*1962*
1965	7:49.0	Michael Jazy	FRA	Melun	23 Jun
	7:46.0	Siegfried Herrmann	GDR	Erfurt	5 Aug
	7:39.5	Kipchoge Keino	KEN	Helsingborg	27 Aug
2 miles					
Pre-1965	*8:26.4*	*Bob Schul*	*USA*		*1964*
1965	8:22.6	Michael Jazy	FRA	Melun	23 Jun
3 miles					
Pre-1965	*13:07.6*	*Ron Clarke*	*AUS*		*1964*
1965	13:00.4	Ron Clarke	AUS	Los Angeles	4 Jun
	12:52.4	Ron Clarke	AUS	London	10 Jul
5000m					
Pre-1965	*13:35.0*	*Vladimir Kuts*	*SU*		*1957*
1965	13:34.8	Ron Clarke	AUS	Hobart	16 Jan
	13:33.6	Ron Clarke	AUS	Auckland	1 Feb
	13:25.8	Ron Clarke	AUS	Los Angeles	4 Jun
	13:24.2	Kipchoge Keino	KEN	Auckland	30 Nov
6 miles					
Pre-1965	*27:17.8*	*Ron Clarke*	*AUS*		*1963*
1965	27:11.6	Billy Mills	USA	San Diego	27 Jun
	27:11.6	Gerry Lindgren	USA	San Diego	27 Jun
	26:47.0	Ron Clarke	AUS	Oslo	14 Jul
10000m					
Pre-1965	*28:15.6*	*Ron Clarke*	*AUS*		*1963*
1965	28:14.0	Ron Clarke	AUS	Turku	16 Jun
	27:39.4	Ron Clarke	AUS	Oslo	14 Jul
10 miles					
Pre-1965	*47:26.8*	*Mel Batty*	*UK*		*1964*
1965	47:12.8	Ron Clarke	AUS	Melbourne	3 Mar
20000m					
Pre-1965	*59.28.6*	*Bill Baillie*	*NZ*		*1963*
1965	59:22.8	Ron Clarke	AUS	Geelong	27 Oct
1 hour					
Pre-1965	*20,190m*	*Bill Baillie*	*NZ*		*1963*
1965	20,232m	Ron Clarke	AUS	Geelong	27 Oct
15 miles					
Pre-1965	*1:14:01.0*	*Emil Zatopek*	*CS*		*1955*
1965	1:12:48.2	Ron Hill	UK	Bolton	21 Jul
25000m					
Pre-1965	*1:16:36.4*	*Emil Zatopek*	*CS*		*1955*
1965	1:15:22.6	Ron Hill	UK	Bolton	21 Jul
30000m					
Pre-1965	*1:34:01.8*	*Jim Alder*	*UK*	*Walton*	*1964*
1965	1:32:34.6	Tim Johnston	UK	Walton	16 Oct
3000m Steeplechase					
Pre-1965	*8:29.6*	*Gaston Roelants*	*BEL*		*1963*
1965	8:26.4	Gaston Roelants	BEL	Brussels	7 Aug
4×1500m Relay					
Pre-1965	*14:58.0*	*GDR*			*1963*
1965	14:49.0	FRANCE		Saint-Maur	25 Jun

LOOKING BACK TO 1939, THE GREATEST OF PRE-WAR YEARS

BY R.L. QUERCETANI

Trackwise 1939 can be remembered as a great prelude to a supposedly greater symphony that never followed. As destiny and rueful men would have it, a tragic World War broke out before the end of that year and eventually caused the cancellation of the 1940 Olympic Games (first assigned to Tokyo, then transferred to Helsinki), and those of 1944 (London) as well.

As it was, only one of the top ranking men of 1939 was to last long enough and well enough to be crowned Olympic champion in London *nine* years later, when the quadrennial event was finally resumed: That man was the 20-year-old Roy Cochran of Indiana University and USA. In the 1939 World List for the 400m hurdles he was actually second to Friedrich-Wilhelm Hölling of Germany, who could point to a new European record of 51.6. But under the criteria we usually follow in ranking athletes (honours won, win–loss record, sequence of marks) Cochran definitely excelled Hölling: he beat the German over 440y hurdles in London, 52.7 to 53.1, and amassed six performances in the range 51.9/52.9.

Similarly, only one of the top ranking women of 1939 was to reappear at the top in 1948. She was Dorothy Odam, a British high jumper. As early as 1936, at the unripe age of 16, she had unofficially tied the world record, 1.65. She broke it in a meeting at Brentwood in 1939, clearing 1.66. Under her married name of Tyler she showed up again at the 1948 Olympics, aged 28, and won a silver medal with 1.68. This durable performer had the unhappy privilege of clearing the same height as the winner in two Olympics (1936 and 1948) only to take second place both times, in accordance with the rules then in force for breaking ties.

1939 excelled all previous years in quality and quantity of class performances. Counting Olympic events only, it offered four world records in the men's ranks and three for the distaff side. I have chosen to review that memorable season by groups of events. En passant I will briefly discuss prospects for the 1940 Games that never materialized.

Sprints – The great Jesse Owens had left the scene in August 1936, but the inexhaustible reservoir of US sprint power offered a lot of promising prospects. At the AAU Championships in Lincoln, Nebraska, the 100m final was contested by four blacks and two whites. It fell to a paleface hailing from North Daokta, the powerful Clyde Jeffrey, to win the day with a wind-aided 10.2. Third was a young black by the name of Norwood 'Barney' Ewell, who turned the tables on Jeffrey in the 200m, winning in 21.0. Ewell, always a great competitor, was again near the top in the 1948 Olympics, placing a close second in both 100m and 200m and finally hitting gold as a member of the US 4×100m relay team.

In all probability, Americans would have had the upper hand in the 1940 Olympics as Europe had no sprinters of comparable calibre. Maybe some attention would have been due to a couple of sprinters from the Caribbean area, Jennings Blackett of Panama and Jacinto Ortiz of Cuba, who had turned in some fast times in 1938.

The 400m was the 'lower half' of the Harbig-Lanzi epic of 1939. The ascetic looking German and the heavily muscled Italian had two tussles at this distance. In the first (Milan, 16 July) they finished virtually abreast. Harbig got the verdict, as both equalled Godfrey Brown's European record, 46.7. The second round took place at Frankfurt/M. on 12 August, again on a 500m track. As was his custom, Lanzi shot the fireworks and was timed in 21.7 at the halfway mark, with Harbig in attendance at 22.0. In the second half the well-trained German easily outshone his rival and went home in 46.0 for a new world record, as Lanzi eased up in 47.2.

By comparison, American quartermilers were a bit less impressive in 1939. 'Long John' Woodruff suffered one of his rare defeats at the hands of Erwin Miller in a curiously slow (48.3) 400m title race at Lincoln, a few weeks after accomplishing his third straight 440/880y one-day double at the IC4A Championships with times of 47.0 and 1:51.2. Had the 1940 Games materialized, I suspect that he and Harbig would have preferred the 800m for their eagerly awaited clash. Yet each had the stamina to become a Juantorena 'ante litteram' . . . (In 1976 the Cuban was the first man to achieve the 400/800m double in the Olympics.) It should be added, however, that by 1940 USA had an even greater 400m prospect in the 19-year-old Grover Klemmer (who was to match Harbig's world record in 1941).

Middle Distances – The 800m was the main bone of contention between Rudolf Harbig and Mario Lanzi. Their most celebrated duel took place on Saturday, 15 July, at the Milan Arena. Both had posted times just under 1:50 in previous weeks and thus looked capable of threatening Sydney Wooderson's world record (1:48.4 in 1938). Yet hardly anybody would have expected a time of 1:46.6 . . . That was what Harbig achieved, after wresting the lead from Lanzi as they entered the homestretch. The Italian set the stage for this (then) phenomenal performance, passing the 400m in 52.5, while Harbig was content to follow (52.8) a long stride behind. The 26-year-old man from Dresden had the benefit of advanced training methods thanks to his coach Woldemar Gerschler and proved his stamina with a second 400m in 53.8. Even after Lanzi ceased to offer strong opposition, Rudi punished himself to the utmost and was finally rewarded with a world record that was to remain unsurpassed for 16 years. Lanzi went home in 1:49.0. A rematch took place at Berlin's Olympiastadion on 29 July and this time Harbig was content with a decision 'on points', edging his rival 1:48.7 to 1:49.2.

As previously hinted, I think the greatest threat to Harbig and Lanzi in the 1940 Games would have come from Woodruff, who withdrew from the 1939 US title race 'in order to let Curtis Giddings, his friend, have an unobstructed shot at the title and a trip to Europe'. Giddings was beaten anyway and the title went to a 'big kicker' named Charles Beetham in 1:51.7.

1939 was also the ante-chamber of the 'Swedish Revolution' in middle distance running. In the traditional Sverige vs. Suomi match in Stockholm, 22-year-old named Arne Andersson won the 1500m in 3:48.8. That was the fastest time of the year, but a mark of comparable value was credited over a mile to Sydney Wooderson of Britain: 4:07.4. Shortly after that, Sydney went to America – a nice trip on the Normandi – to meet the best Americans in the famed Princeton Invitational mile, a race which unfortunately ended in controversy. The Briton was arguably hampered by Blaine Rideout, who cut across in front of him in the crucial stage of the race. The race was won by Charles Fenske in 4:11.0 as Wooderson wound up fifth in 4:13.0. The 'bumping' incident, some 175 yards from the finish, gave rise to controversial opinions on the two sides of the Atlantic.

Bearing in mind what Wooderson showed to the track world as late as 1946 – when at 32 he won the European 5000m title in 14:08.6 – there can be little doubt that he would have been a prime contender for the Olympic 1500m title in 1940. But the Americans and budding Swedes such as Andersson and a certain Gunder Hägg (who rose to international class in 1940) would have made things difficult for him.

Long Distances – Finnish domination in this department reached spectacular heights in 1939. When the season was over (the bitter end being provided by the Soviet invasion of Finland), Finnish distance men took positions 1, 2, 4, and 5 in the 5,000m World List and positions 1, 2, 3, 4, 5 and 10 in the 10,000m! Hero of the play was Taisto Mäki, 29, who set new world records for 2 Miles (8:53.2), 3 Miles (13:42.4), 5000m (14:08.8), 6 Miles (28:55.6) and 10,000m (29:52.6). In his record attempts he usually had the cooperation of his fellow Finns, particularly Kauko Pekuri, but the end would invariably find Taisto on top. His 5000m record was set in the new Olympic Stadium in Helsinki on 16 June and he shaved 8.2 seconds off the mark set by his countryman Lauri Lehtinen in 1932. At the same site on 17 September he became the first man to beat the half hour in the 10 kilometres, with halves in 14:58.2 and 14:54.4. This record effort was curiously preceded, about two hours earlier, in a smaller stadium of the capital, by a 'warm-up' race over 1500m, which Mäki won in a leisurely 4:23.0, outsprinting Volmari Iso-Hollo, the Olympic steeplechase champion of 1932 and 1936.

Mäki lost only one major race, a 3000m at Helsinki on 2 August, when he was nosed out by Henry Jonsson of Sweden, 8:15.4 to 8:15.6. I suspect that the latter – who later changed his name to Kälarne – could have been a thorn in the flesh of Finnish runners even in the 1940 Games.

Hurdles – No. 1 performer of 1939 in the

'highs' was a blond Texan endowed with great speed, Fred Wolcott. His winning streak was broken at the AAU Championships when he hit the last three hurdles and barely lost to a 20-year-old high school boy, Joe Batiste (14.1). Wolcott had won his heat in a wind-aided 13.8. In the 1939 World List he also tied for first in the 100y with an impressive 9.5. With such men, plus Edward Dugger who came on in fine style a year later, USA would have been hard to beat in the Helsinki Games, even though Europe had two fine hurdlers in Don Finlay of Britain and Håkan Lidman of Sweden. The former was hampered by an injury in 1939, while Lidman tied for third in the World List with 14.2.

The above-mentioned Roy Cochran was a novice in the 400m hurdles and his performances both in USA and Europe make me wonder what he could have done in subsequent years . . . if he had lived in a better world. As it was, he was clever enough to lower his lifetime best to 51.1 the day he won the Olympic title in 1948. From the looks of things, his strongest rivals in the 1940 Games could have been Hölling and British Commonwealth champion John Loaring of Canada.

Scandinavian steeplechasers found a serious rival in 1939 in Ludwig Kaindl of Germany, who in addition to posting the year's fastest time, 9:06.8, also ran a significant 3:50.2 in winning the 1500m in the Germany vs. Britain match at Köln, the last major dual meet before the outbreak of the war.

Jumps – Les Steers won the AAU high jump title at 2.035, beating Bill Stewart, David Albritton and world record holder Melvin Walker. Steers was the most consistent of them all and in 1941 he went on to conquer the world record with 2.108, a mark that was to remain unsurpassed for 12 years. European and Japanese jumpers were a good shade under such standards.

Cornelius Warmerdam, who in the early Forties was to become the undisputed king of pole vaulters, was only second in the 1939 US title meet at 4.34 as victory went to George Varoff with 4.37. The best non-American vaulters of those days were Erling Kaas of Norway, Nikolay Ozolin of USSR and Sueo Oe of Japan. This last was to be among the victims of the global conflict.

No one dominated the long jump picture in 1939. European record holder Luz Long of Germany (7.90 in 1937) was excelled by Arturo Maffei of Italy but neither produced marks reminiscent of the great 1936 Olympic final. Americans too failed to better 26 feet (7.92): one of the best was Bill Watson, whose potential as a decathlon man was never fully revealed. In the World Year List he tied for first in the long jump with AAU champion Bill Lacefield with 7.76, was second in the shot put with 16.62 and thirteenth in the discus with 49.84.

The cream of the triple jump was mostly located in Japan and Australia, but Europe had a good and consistent competitor in Onni Rajasaari of Finland.

Throws – An eventful shot put battle took place in the NCAA Championships at Los Angeles, when a toss of 16.20 – equal to the Olympic record – only sufficed for fourth place. The winner was Elmer Hackney, whose 17.02 (preceded a few weeks earlier by a 17.04 in a duel meet in Kansas) finally convinced experts that the 'unbelievable' world record set by Jack Torrance in Oslo five years earlier (17.40) was not unassailable after all. Hackney, who had shown consistency in the 16.50-plus area throughout the season, was the victim of his own self-confidence at the AAU Meet in Lincoln. He refused to let a valid toss of 16.43 be measured and that toss was called a foul. At the end of the battle the winner had done no better than 16.33 – and it wasn't Hackney, who wound up a disappointing fourth with 16.02.

The 1940 Games would have seen a major battle here too as Europe had four strong contenders in Aleksander Kreek of Estonia, Hans Woellke, Heinrich Trippe and Gerhard Stöck of Germany. By 1940, however, a new great prospect appeared in the person of Alfred Blozis, a 1.98m, 109 kg giant from Georgetown University. He was to tower above all iron ball men for three years, with several marks in the 17m range. He met an untimely death on the Western front in 1945. Along with Rudolf Harbig – who died on the Eastern front in 1944 – he was among the most famous track casualties of WW2.

1939 seasonal leader in the discus was Phil Fox (formerly Levy), who won the AAU title with 52.54, almost three meters ahead of his nearest rival. In Europe the good discus men had ups and downs but a young stalwart from Verona, Adolfo Consolini, was by then beginning to scale the heights. Whether the 1940 Games would have come too early for him or not we will never know. But fortunately we do know that he topped the élite of the world in the London Games of 1948.

The hammer was in German hands as Karl Storch, Erwin Blask and Karl Hein amassed a fine series of superlative performances in the 57–58m range. Strangely enough, however, position no. 1 in the year list went to Uuno Veirilä of Finland, who in a meeting in Sweden got one off to 58.67, pretty close to the world record but nearly 4 metres over his second best for the season.

The indestructible Matti Järvinen turned the tables on his younger countryman Yrjö Nikkanen, who had taken the world's javelin record away from him in a late season meet the year before. The year list showed Finnish names in positions 1, 2, 3, 5, 7 and 10. Trying to figure out who could have beaten the Finns at the 1940 Games in Helsinki is beyond my imagination.

Decathlon – As it usually happened in those days, international competition in the 10-event grind was virtually nil outside of Olympic Games years. Surely, the perspective of an Olympic battle in 1940 would have brought to light new figures, just as it happened in 1932 and 1936.

Women's Events – Women's athletics was still in the infant stage, witness the fact that in the last pre-war Olympics (Berlin 1936) there was only one individual race on the programme (the 100m) and six events altogether, which were to be increased to nine in the London Games of 1948.

There was virtually no major international championship in 1939, save perhaps for the Student Games in Vienna, in which the Germans ruled the roost, just as they had done at the first European Championships the year before.

Apart from the above-mentioned Dorothy Odam, the only non-German girl to shine in international competition in 1939 was Claudia Testoni of Italy, who brought the world's 80m hurdles record to 11.3, a time she returned on two occasions, both times beating the redoubtable German hurdlers.

1939 was a historic year in the sense that it saw the first world record performance by a Russian athlete. The girl in question was a gorgeous 20-year-old from Georgia, Nina Dumbadze, and the occasion was Moscow, 18 September, when she threw the discus 49.11, 80 centimetres beyond Gisela Mauermayer's official world record. Dumbadze eventually improved to 49.54 in her hometown of Tbilisi on 29 October. Since USSR was not yet a member of the IAAF, her marks were to remain confined to statistical books. Nine years later that formal obstacle had been removed and Dumbadze entered the official IAAF book with a throw of 53.25. Being almost as durable as was Adolfo Consolini in the men's ranks, she hit a lifetime best of 57.04, still at Tbilisi, in 1952.

A world record was bettered also in the long jump as Christel Schulz of Germany, 18, sailed to 6.12 in a big international meet in Berlin. It is interesting to note that the same distance, albeit unofficially, was reached a few weeks earlier by Stanislawa Walasiewicz of Poland, whose gender status was said to be questionable. By the way, one of our longtime friends, Erich Kamper of Austria, recently made a unique discovery. He secured a copy of Walasiewicz's birth certificate, in which she appears as *Stefania* Walasiewicz and born on 3 April (not 11 April as given by most sources) 1911.

Those we have mentioned were just a few of the girls who could have made history in 1940, if . . .

1939 world lists will be included in Volume 2 of Track & Field Performances through the Years, to be published in 1989. See BOOKS section.

THE PARADOX OF BEN JOHNSON

BY CECIL SMITH
PUBLISHER OF *ATHLETICS* (CANADA)

At the time of writing, nothing, other than the gathering of information, has happened regarding the Ben Johnson drug scandal.

In an attempt to unmask this deceit the Canadian Government has ordered a judicial inquiry into the use of drugs in sport, not only in Canada but around the world.

Chief Justice Charles Dubin began his examination of that perilous game, that first made Johnson a hero and then swallowed him whole, on 11 January 1989. It has now become a game of duplicity, drugs and money, a game dominated by those who cheat and those who turn a blind eye to the cheating.

Dubin's task is to unmask the players of deceit, a daunting challenge to say the least, and one that could drag into 1990 and cause great embarrassment for the sport from top to bottom. Many rumours abound about cover-ups, bought lanes (i.e. paying an athlete to withdraw in order to get another athlete in the competition), suppression of information, deliberate planning to ensure certain athletes are not tested; high ranking officials 'fixing' who will be tested and who won't; athletes turning up for competition, then finding out that there is drug testing and withdrawing from the meet. All this is not new of course. What however will make it new is the fact that for the first time a neutral body, and not a sports governing body, is intervening. One cannot compare the Dubin inquiry to that of the 1988 British inquiry into the Matt Girvin allegations. The Dubin inquiry has the power of subpoena and is neutral. The British inquiry was not. Also, because this is a judicial inquiry, third party information and 'what I've heard' types of information can be attested to. Again the British inquiry would not allow this type of information, consequently reaching the facts there was very difficult. In Canada Dubin wishes to receive this information in order that the investigators (RCMP) can flush out more information which ultimately may force someone to tell the truth.

To date literally dozens upon dozens of athletes, coaches and administrators have been interviewed privately, not only Canadians, but Americans and Europeans as well. Of the 'gang of four' only Larry Heidebrecht and Dr M. Astaphan have not been interviewed and neither of these can be sunpoenaed because they are living outside Canada. However, they may 'volunteer' to be interviewed. Time will tell. Both Francis and Johnson have been extensively interviewed by counsel of inquiry. The world will have to wait and see the outcome of these interviews when they take the stand.

Johnson is still saying that he has never 'knowingly' taken drugs. No doubt his lawyer will hammer this point when he has the opportunity to cross examine. Francis on the other hand has behaved like a recluse, surfacing only periodically. Rumours abound that he will 'tell all' and give evidence of cover-ups. I give you these tid-bits simply to show you why everyone cannot wait for Francis to be placed under the microscope (so to speak) by the inquiry's counsel. It is only then that the world will know the real truth. The track and field portion of the inquiry commences February 20 and will last until at least March 20.

When the inquiry finishes, hopefully sport will be the benefactor, because after all, most people are fed up of listening to rumours, innuendos and speculation. Justice Charles Dubin will be doing the world of sports a huge favour by finding that although drugs may not be endemic they are most certainly prevalent. Following this, it will then be up to international federations and governments to come down hard on all offenders to once more make sport enjoyable.

What is Johnson doing now? All sponsorships have been cut off. Diadora is supplying him with clothes, shoes and so on. Work has ceased on his Toronto 'mansion' that he was having built. However he still drives his Porsche and Testerosa and is still seen quite regularly at night clubs and holiday resorts such as Hawaii. There is talk about a film on Johnson, maybe this will depend on the outcome of the inquiry. On April 24 this year he will appear in court to give his explanation as to why he aimed a gun (starter's pistol) at another motorist on an expressway in Toronto. The maximum jail sentence for this apparently is 15 years! The motorist took his licence number and reported the incident and the Police later found the gun in his Porsche. When he appeared in court last December, it was only to set a trial date.

Ben JOHNSON b.30 Dec 1961 Falmouth, Jamaica 1.78m 77kg. Mazda TC. Came to Canada in 1976.
At 100m/R- 4x100m relay: OG: '84- 3/3R; WCh: '83- sf, '87- 1; CG: '82- 2/2R, '86- 1/1R (3 200m); PAm: '83- 6; WSG: '83- 5/2R; WCp: '85- 1/2R. 2nd GP 1986. Member 1980 Olympic team. At 60m: WI: '85- 1, '87- 1. Canadian champion 100m 1984–8, 200m 1985, 1987.
Records at 100m: world 1987, three world low altitude 1986–7, five Commonwealth 1985–7, eight Canadian 1984–7. WIB: 50y: 5.20 & 5.15 '88, 60m: 6.50, 6.50 '86; 6.44, 6.44, 6.41 '87; 50m: 5.55 '87.
Progression at 100m: 1978- 10.79/10.4, 1979- 10.66, 1980- 10.62/10.38w/10.2, 1981- 10.25, 1982- 10.30/10.05w, 1983- 10.19, 1984- 10.12/10.01w, 1985- 10.00, 1986- 9.95, 1987- 9.83/9.7w, 1988- 9.98/9.90w/9.79dq. pb 200m: 20.41 '85, 20.37w '82.
The first Canadian to win an Olympic medal since 1964, he became the world's fastest man. Lost just once in 1986, when he had ten sub 10.10 times, the most ever run in a season. In 1987 he smashed world indoor sprint records and outdoors won all 21 finals at 100m, with the highlight his 9.83 world record in Rome. He passed the 60m point in 6.38, easily a world's best. He won the 1988 Olympic 100m in a sensational 9.79 but was disqualified on a positive drugs test for steroids.

UNPRONOUNCEABLE NAMES, UNKNOWN COUNTRIES AND UNBELIEVABLE PERFORMANCES

BY DAVID EVELEIGH

When I produced a book with the unlikely title of 'Papua New Guinea Athletics 1985' I felt it was purely a self-indulgent exercise. However within a few months I was proven wrong as a modest print-run sold out to readers within and outside of that country. Its purchase within the country indicates that there is enthusiasm for the sport there, and the other sales that there is a fascination at the sometimes unexpectedly wide spread of such enthusiasm throughout the world. However why is it that, without doubt, the title must be described as obscure, to say the least? Consideration of the question may lead us to think a little more deeply about athletics in the Third World.

We can begin by examining something as simple as the list of abbreviations in my book! There are only ten locations within the country listed, and of these only four or five have seen regular athletics competition in the last few years, and this in a nation with a population of three million. Here is the nub of the problem, and I suspect it is the same in most Third World countries: there just is not a strong base to the sport.

In 1966 two very competent coaches toured the South Pacific at IAAF expense, giving advice on cross country. In 1987 ten senior men and two senior women competed in the Papua New Guinea Championships. It does not seem that the IAAF's money was well spent, does it? What should the IAAF be doing to help then? Increased and underwritten opportunities for international competition would certainly encourage participation by some of the more talented, but how to draw in a much larger *number* of particpants within the country? That is a tough question but if it were answered successfully, higher levels of performance by international competitors from Third World nations like Papua New Guinea might be a spin-off. It is less likely that increased participation would be a spin-off of international success. When perusing an African Athletics Annual recently, for example, I could find no record of any Djiboutian National Championships even, despite the phenomenal success of some of its athletes internationally.

The IAAF needs to recognise that competition and not coaching is the basic stimulus for improving athletic performance. I suggest, without reserve, that the IAAF sending coaches to the least athletically developed Third World countries is a mistake. Their first aim should be to establish national championships for senior men and women in track and field, cross country, and at selected distances on the road. This might require administrative advice or help, provision of courses for officials or even financial help (in Papua New Guinea, where road links do not always exist, it can cost hundreds of pounds to fly a handful of athletes to National Championships held in the capital, Port Moresby). After this the aim should be to establish local championships in significant centres around the country, as a basis for providing opportunities for competition nationwide. It is important though that the sport is not organised from outside the country, but that local enthusiasts are identified, encouraged and help to run it themselves in the long term. In Papua New Guinea, Australian Tom Brandt introduced a system of camps, sponsored by Colgate Palmolive and attended by talented schoolchildren, in a series of centres around the country, but now largely staffed by local teacher–coaches, a useful prototype for the IAAF to consider. The situation within athletically successful Third World countries such as Kenya, should also be considered, although it should be remembered that the foreign development of locally discovered talent is not part of the answer to the question of how to increase mass participation. Coaching and coach education should follow the establishment of competition, and this may then help to prevent the 'legs drain' just referred to.

To return to Third World athletes competing at international level, how could the IAAF help here? Consider for example the Papua New Guinean Takale Tuna, a name hidden amongst the results of the 400 metres second round heats at Seoul where he achieved a National Record of 47.48. How could he achieve the one second or so improvement needed to place him in the annual world lists of this very publication? Coaching would certainly be useful but I tend to believe in the stimulus of competition. Another Papua New Guinean running 47.48 would mean that Takale would have to run faster before he could even reach the Olympics, hence my claim that a broader base would lead to better international performances. International competiton, *at an appropriate level*, might also be useful and the PNGAAU has worked hard to provide this in countries such as Australia, New Zealand and Singapore. The IAAF could help by establishing a South Pacific Championships in the even numbered years when there are neither South Pacific Games or mini-Games, and they might establish similar events in other areas around the world. The IAAF and IOC already help Third World athletes attend major championships, but this is a somewhat pointless exercise when, as in Rome in 1987, each athlete only participates in one event. Its value is also limited because seeding means that athletes without qualifying performances are often left alone at the back of fields, making motivation to achieve targets such as national records difficult. My suggestion here is that such athletes should take part in a qualifying competition from which leading performers, including anybody who achieves a qualifying performance, could proceed to the competition proper. This would have the added advantage of reducing the rounds contested by more established athletes, as well as providing good international competition for competitors from all *athletically* undeveloped nations. If this competition was held just prior to the main event, and at the same venue, the athletes would still have the experience of being part of a major international festival. Finally the IAAF needs to consider locating international events within the Third World, for at the moment the movement of athletic talent is rather one way, and the foreign earnings of a handful of athletes is not as significant as the potential earnings from staging a major international event, even if this was initially a relatively small one, such as the Grand Prix Final, or World Cup.

So, when you next look at the first round results of an international championships, and notice unpronouncable names from unknown countries with unbelievable performances please don't grin and pass on, but consider how this most simple, and therefore most accessible of sports might become truly international.

THE COUNTRY BOY – JOZEF PRIBILINEC

BY LADISLAW KRNÁČ

Three months before the Olympic Games in Seoul, Jozef Pribilinec, one of the most successful walkers of the eighties, the only gold medal hope of Czechoslovak track and field, made a surprising move. He wanted, and got, the green light from the leadership of the Army sport centre in Banská Bystrica to practice alone, without his long time coach Kuraj Benčík. After eleven years the athlete usually knows better than anyone else what helps his body and mind and what does harm. He needs a consultant and not a teacher with a cane in his hand. At the age of 28, Pribilinec mastered the risk of his decision and made it his way, preferring more speed work than endurance. Today he is the first Slovak Olympic champion in track and field, and the first walker to better a time of 1:20 for twenty kilometres at the Olympics. Afterwards he gave no interview without praising the share of his coach, but everytime added – I fought on my own . . .

Maurizio Damilano told me during the 1986 European Championships that Pribilinec is the man with the most devastating kick of all contemporary walkers. The duel between Ronald Weigel and Priblinec in Seoul proved that the successor to Frigerio, Dordoni and Pamich was right with his statement.

Jozef Pribilinec on his way to gold in Seoul (Mark Shearman)

Pribilinec has one sister and four brothers, but only he chose sport as the mainstay of his life. As a boy he loved to ski around his native village of Kopernice in the mountains of middle Slovakia. He came to walking by chance. With entries full for every event of a youth meet except for the ten kilometres walk, he learnt in just one day the rules and technique, and won in about 62 minutes. Winning ever the motivation, Pribilinec said goodbye to skiing. That happened back in 1977 when he was seventeen; eleven years later he was an Olympic champion.

What was the price? Earlier, knees not protesting, he managed 10,000 kilometres in a year, later reduced to around 7,500. He wrecked a pair of shoes after every 750–900 kilometres. During a race he usually loses about three kilograms. He married in 1978 and his wife well understands solitude!

Hobbies sometimes tell much about the man, and what Pribilinec likes most is hunting. In his fourth season his trophies are interesting – a big brown bear and a boar weighing, without entrails, about 170 kilograms. That is why he chose to fly home the day after his victory in Seoul .

The question after the Olympics was quite clear: should he call it a day or have one or two more seasons? As usual it was a compromise. He is taking a year's rest and will start training again in 1990. His plans? First of all to cure his knees, especially the right one which he can feel even when driving his Lada. Then to spend more time with his family, including his two daughters. As I know him, only serious health problems can stop him going for the only title still missing – to be world champion – in Tokyo in 1991. After all compared to Vladimir Golubnichiy, Pribilinec will still be a young walker when competing in Japan.

PROUD WOMAN – MARLIES GÖHR

BY LADISLAW KRNÁČ

There is a proverb well known in Eastern Europe – an apple does not fall far away from the tree. This was the case with Marlies Göhr, besides Irena Szewinska surely the woman with the longest career in post-war sprinting. Her mother and one of her aunts sprinted fairly well too. Göhr was at the top from 1976 until 1988.

It was not so easy to talk with her in these years. She was not very communicative to reporters, a rather introverted person and a proud one, afraid to show weaknesses. Nobody likes to lose and Göhr was highly sensitive in this area, thinking for a long time about those rare failures. Every time she used them to motivate herself and find new ways to new victories. Psychology student or not, she too had a talisman – a striped T-shirt from Mexico. Rarely did she talk about her private life.

Her hobbies were decorating and completing her Jena flat. Gardening belongs to her husband Ulli, formerly a mediocre soccer player, nowadays a coach of a district team called Chemie Kahla. Göhr's father is a joiner and she often helped him in his workshop. Once with a rare broad smile in public, she joked: 'I can fix every nail into the wall . . .' A budgie's cage has a prominent place in their living room, between an old wall-clock and the window. How about fashion? There are problems for her only in connection with long travels. At any other time she wears short but not miniskirts, and she likes fancy clothes for various occasions, not mentioning jeans. In all those years she had no problem with her weight – or her waist. The more you eat the more movement you need was her credo. She weighed around 58.5 kilograms at the start of the season, about 56–57 later, with no special diet.

A trademark of Göhr was her outspokenness. Many of us still remember her harsh comment on Evelyn Ashford's fall during the final in first World Championships at Helsinki. Five years later she had not changed a bit. About Florence Griffith-Joyner's 10.49 for 100 metres her comment was acid: 'To run this time you need jets in your feet, because it is reserved to men . . .'

Her idol for years was Renate Stecher, the first woman to run the hundred, hand timed, under eleven seconds. Her goal was to run faster, and Marlies did it 36 times. It is interesting that during her career Göhr never ran more than five kilometres uninterruptedly, maybe because she likes to drive fast cars and for 100 metres she needed only 54 steps. The happiest moment for Marlies was her first world record, back in 1977 in Dresden – 10.88.

Marlies Göhr bows out after 14 years of world-class sprinting (George Herringshaw/ASP)

The 1986 season, full of health problems, long inactivity periods and only four outdoor starts was a classic example of what it means when the years go by. Knowing that she had no chance to better her first thirty and last twenty metres she has now reached the end of a glorious career. Before the Seoul Olympics she mentioned that she had three wishes for her last season: to win two more medals, for 100m and a gold one in 4 x 100m, that GDR, as in 1976, would show the whole world what her country could achieve in the field of sports, . . . and finally she would like to have a baby who would grow up in a peaceful world.

MARLIES GÖHR

Born 21 Mar 1958 Gera 1.65m 55kg. née Oelsner. SC Motor Jena. Psychology student. Coached by Horst-Dieter Hille.

Performances in major championships

	100 metres	4x100m relay
OLYMPIC GAMES		
1976	8th 11.34	1st 42.55 (first leg)
1980	2nd 11.07	1st 41.60
1988	6sf 11.13	2nd 42.09
WORLD CHAMPIONSHIPS		
1983	1st 10.97	1st 41.76
1987	7sf 11.33	2nd 41.95
EUROPEAN CHAMPIONSHIPS		
1978	1st 11.13	3rd 43.07
	2nd 200m 22.53	
1982	1st 11.01	1st 42.19
1986	1st 10.91	1st 41.84
EUROPEAN JUNIOR CHAMPIONSHIPS		
1975	2nd 11.43	1st 44.05 (third leg)
WORLD STUDENT GAMES		
1979	1st 11.00	
WORLD CUP		
1977	1st 11.16	
1979	2nd 11.17	2nd 42.32
1981	3rd 11.13	1st 42.22
1985	1st 11.10	1st 41.37
EUROPEAN CUP		
1977	1st 11.07	1st 42.62
1979	1st 11.03	1st 42.09
1981	1st 11.17	1st 42.53
1983	1st 11.28	1st 42.63
1985	1st 10.95	1st 41.65
1987	1st 10.95	1st 41.94

EUROPEAN INDOORS	60 metres
1977	1st 7.17
1978	1st 7.12
1979	1st 7.16
1982	1st 7.11
1983	1st 7.09
1985	2nd 7.13
1986	2nd 7.08
1987	3rd 7.12
1988	3rd 7.07

GDR Championships

100 METRES:	1st 1977–85, 1988; 3rd 1976, 1987
200 METRES:	1st 1978, 1981, 1984; 4th 1976
Indoors	
60 METRES:	1st 1977–8, 1980, 1982–3, 1986–7; 2nd 1979, 1984–5, 1988
100 YARDS:	1st 1977, 1980, 1982; 2nd 1979, 1985, 1987–8
GDR Spartakiad:	2nd 100m and 200m 1972, won 100m 1975.

World records

100 METRES		
10.88	Dresden	1 Jul 1977
10.88	Karl-Marx-Stadt	9 Jul 1982
10.81	Berlin	8 Jun 1983
4 x 100 METRES RELAY		
42.50	Karl-Marx-Stadt	29 May 1976 (first leg)
42.27	Potsdam	19 Aug 1978
42.10	Karl-Marx-Stadt	10 Jun 1979
42.09	Torino	4 Aug 1979
42.09	Berlin	9 Jul 1980
41.85	Potsdam	13 Jul 1980
41.60	Moskva	1 Aug 1980
41.53	Berlin	31 Jul 1983
41.37	Canberra	6 Oct 1985
4 x 200 METRES RELAY		
1:32.4	Karl-Marx-Stadt	13 Aug 1976 (second leg)
1:28.15	Jena	9 Aug 1980

World Indoor Bests

60 METRES		
6.9	(hand) Cottbus	10 Feb 1979
7.12	Milano	12 Mar 1978
7.12	Berlin	12 Jan 1980
7.10	Senftenberg	26 Jan 1980
100 YARDS		
10.41	Senftenberg	17 Feb 1978
10.29	Senftenberg	27 Jan 1980
10.29	Senftenberg	20 Feb 1883
100 METRES		
11.37	Berlin	16 Feb 1977
11.29	Berlin	7 Feb 1979

World Junior Records

100 METRES		
11.17	Karl-Marx-Stadt	29 May 1976
4 x 100 METRES RELAY		
44.3	Kharkov	16 Jun 1975 (first leg)
44.05	Athinai	24 Aug 1975

Annual progression

100 METRES

1971- 12.8, 1972- 12.1, 1973- 11.8, 1974- 11.6/11.81, 1975- 11.54/11.42w

Year	TFN Rank	Best time	No. times under 11.00*	No. times under 11.20*	Outdoor Finals
1976	10th	11.17	-	1	won 0/6
1977	1st	10.88	1	3	won 11/12
1978	1st	10.94	1	8	won 12/12
1979	2nd	10.97	1	9	won 10/12
1980	1st	10.93/10.79w	2/1	12/2	won 9/10
1981	2nd	11.09	-	6	won 8/11
1982	1st	10.88	3	6/1	won 8/10
1983	1st	10.81	4	5/1	won 9/9
1984	2nd	10.84	9	3	won 9/10
1985	1st	10.86	5/1	7	won 11/13
1986	3rd	10.91	2	5	won 2/4
1987	10th	10.93	2	2/1	won 3/8
1988		10.89	3/1	6	won 7/11

* *first figure is 'legal' times, and after the / are wind assisted marks*

200 METRES

1972- 24.8, 1973- 24.5, 1974- 24.3, 1975- 23.8, 1976- 23.26, 1977- 23.23

Year	TFN Rank	Best	Sub 23.00
1978	2nd	22.38	5
1979	4th	22.36	5
1980	10th	22.45	1
1982		22.78	1
1984	3rd	21.74	4
1988		22.28	1

Her outstanding sprinting career includes a record number of European Cup Final victories, and five European outdoor gold medals, including a hat trick of 100m titles. The first woman to run a sub 11 second 100 metres, to the end of 1988 she had run a record 36 such times, including 3 with excess wind assistance.
Except where specified all her relay runs in these tables were on the anchor leg.

INDOOR SPRINTS

Best times each year and place in world list

Year	50 metres	60 metres
1976	6.32 2=	7.37 15=
1977	6.24 1	7.17 1
1978		7.12 1
1979		7.16 1=
1980	6.12 2	7.10 1
1982		7.11 1
1983		7.09 2
1984		7.12 1=
1985	6.21 1=	7.13 3
1986	6.16 2	7.07 2
1987	6.13 2	7.07 3
1988	—	7.07 3

Best at other events

Event	Time	Year
60 yards:	6.61	1986
100 yards:	10.28	1987
100 metres:	11.16	1980

THE MEN'S PENTATHLON – A FORGOTTEN EVENT?

BY ANDREW HUXTABLE

Although the event is referred to in IAAF Rule 195.1 and was included in the programme of the 1912, 1920 and 1924 Olympic Games, the Men's Pentathlon has been largely ignored by statisticians.

However, a small nucleus of ATFS members has been working (in some cases, for many years) on collating data, and this short feature attempts merely to present the main historical developments.

The composition of the Men's Pentathlon, since its introduction in 1912, has been in competition order: long jump, javelin throw, 200m, discus throw, 1500m. Scoring was originally by position in each of the five events, although the decathlon tables were to be used to split ties.

The progression of the world best is shown below, using up to five sets of IAAF scoring tables (the 1964 Tables were supplemented later to cater for fully-automatic timing).

Perhaps we shall see this long-standing world best improved upon before the start of the next decade?

With acknowledgements to Hal Bateman, Alain Bouillé, Dr Hans-Peter Car, Tore Johansen, Erkki Kiilunen, Rooney Magnusson, Gabriele Manfredini, Fulvio Regli, Bob Sparks and Dr Frank Zarnowski.

World record progression since the advent of fully-automatic timing

1964/77 Tables	1985 Tables						
3787	3948	Sepp Zeilbauer		AUT	Südstadt		8 May 78
		695	6184	22.58		4612	4:27.05
3807	3974	Hans-Joachim Häberle		FRG	Ludwigshafen		13 Jul 80
		680	6634	22.40		4464	4:26.03
3864	4026	Häberle			Sindelfingen		12 Jul 81
		719	6288	22.22		4320	4:22.47
3931	4079	Herbert Peter		FRG	Lahr		11 Jul 82
		713	6236	22.26		4200	4:07.50
4032	4222	Guido Kratschmer		FRG	Salzburg		5 May 84
		748	6586	21.58		4872	4:37.29

Bill Toomey's pentathlons prior to his world record

1964	1985						
3275	3384	1		Stanford			4Jul 59
			696	4926	22.6	3196	4:37.2
3302	3402	1		Kansas City			16 Jul 60
			675	4868	22.4	3246	4:29.9
3599	3703	1		Boulder			8 Jul 61
			711	5416	21.3	3392	4:30.4
3335	3475	2		Boulder			7 Jul 62
			710	5510	21.7	2533	4:35.1
3517	3659	1		Seattle			4 Jul 63
			739	5998	22.2	3270	4:43.8
3766	3890	1		Westbrook			25 Jul 64
			726	5894	22.0	3836	4:21.4

Pentathlon World Records

1920	1934	1952	1964	1985						
3320.325	2901	2575	3003	3098	Jim Thorpe		USA	New York		18 May 12
					661	4153		23.4	3506	4:49.8
3679.855	3216	2930	3264	3370	Jim Thorpe		USA	Stockholm		7 Jul 12
					707	4671		22.9	3557	4:44.8
3761.880	3214	2881	3241	3346	Helge Løvland		NOR	Oslo*		18 Jun 19
					693	5070		23.4	3907	4:56.7
3808.900	3221	2881	3239	3346	Helge Løvland		NOR	Oslo*		13 Jul 19
					660	5512		23.5	3891	4:52.8
3762.6455	3234	2915	3267	3374	Evert Nilsson		SWE	–		18 Jul 20
					665	5253		23.7	3695	4:34.6
3773.440	3242	2943	3275	3383	Eero Lehtonen		FIN	Antwerpen		16 Aug 20
					663	5467		23.03	464	4:40.2
3794.467	3317	3038	3326	3428	Robert LeGendre		USA	Philadelphia		29 Apr 22
					692	5214		22.2	3423	4:48.8
3861.215	3302	2981	3313	3415	Eero Lehtonen		FIN	Paris (Colombes)		7 Jul 24
					668	5093		23.0	4044	4:47.0
3874.125	3405	3183	3387	3525	Robert LeGendre		USA	Paris (Colombes)		7 Jul 24
					7765	4804		23.0	3676	4:52.6
3929.540	3381	3058	3358	3464	Bertil Fastén		SWE	Uppsala		2Oct 27
					637	5474		24.2	4099	4:21.9
3979.490	3429	3150	3415	3542	Martti Tolamo		FIN	Darmstadt		10 Aug 30
					709	5754		23.0	3511	4:40.6
4005.370	3454	3182	3436	3558	Martti Tolamo		FIN	Tampere		17 Aug 30
					715	5664		22.7	3625	4:46.3
4078.830	3465	3147	3410	3545	Matti Sippala		FIN	Helsinki		16 Aug 31
					678	6238		24.2	3872	4:34.4
4067.745	3472	3151	3426	3542	Paavo Yrjölä		FIN	Helsinki		16 Aug 31
					653	5789		23.8	4120	4:28.5
4163.535	3534	3223	3448	3565	Hans-Heinrich Sievert		GER	Torino		9 Sep 33
					699	5755		22.6	4408	5:10.0
	3546	3189	3400	3543	Gerhard Stöck		GER	Jena		30 Jun 35
					683	6395		24.2	4675	5:08.0
	3669	3359	3483	3639	Gerhard Stöck		GER	Budapest		17 Aug 35
					730	6666		23.5	4508	5:24.0
	3596	3337	3534	3673	Robert Clark		USA	Eureka		6 Jun 36
					746	5758		23.1	3860	4:43.6
	3824	3621	3711	3841	Fritz Müller		GER	Paris		28 Aug 37
					711	6238		21.8	3808	4:33.4
	3867	3667	3757	3863	Fritz Müller		GER	Wien		24 Aug 39
					687	5847		21.7	4032	4:20.9
		3668	3714	3860	Yuriy Kutyenko		SU	Lvov		14 May 55
					680	6825		22.0	4282	4:45.0
		3736	3762	3913	Vasiliy Kuznyetsov		SU	Kiev		21 May 56
					703	6535		22.1	4718	4:51.0
		3901	3857	4010	Vasiliy Kuznyetsov		SU	Nalchik		22 Apr 58
					701	6453		21.9	5035	4:46.2
		4007	3864	4051	Vasiliy Kuznyetsov		SU	Torino		3 Sep 59
					718	7279		22.2	4951	4:59.5
			4016	4223	Kurt Bendlin		FRG	Krefeld		31 Jul 65
					747	7742		21.8	4453	4:43.7
			4079	4272	Rein Aun		SU	Tartu		17 Jul 68
					733	7226		21.9	5005	4:34.5
			4123	4282	Bill Toomey		USA	London		16 Aug 69
					758	6618		21.3	4453	4:20.3

** Christiania until 1925*

The world all-time list at the end of 1988 is given below (hand and fully-automatic timing combined):

4282	1	Bill Toomey	USA	39	London			16 Aug 69
				758	6618	21.3	4453	4:20.3
4272	1	Rein Aun	SU	40	Tartu			17 Jul 68
				733	7226	21.9	5005	4:34.5
4230	1	Kurt Bendlin	FRG	43	Bonn			31 Oct 70
				731	7210	21.3w	4516	4:33.4
4222	1	Guido Kratschmer	FRG	53	Salzburg			5 May 84
				748	6586	21.58	4872	4:37.29
4172	1	Raimo Pihl	SWE	48	Göteborg			13 Jul 74
				718	7650	22.1	4486	4:34.9
4144	1	Hans-Joachim Häberle	FRG	59	Leverkusen			6 Jul 84
				716	6574	21.6	4708	4:28.0
4108	1	Lennart Hedmark	SWE	44	Karlskrona			7 Jun 75
				718	7334	22.2	4476	4:35.4
4083	1	Heinz-Dieter Antretter	FRG	55	Voerde			29 Sep 79
				756	6204	22.0	4294	4:24.6
4079	1	Herbert Peter	FRG	57	Lahr			11 Jul 82
				713	6236	22.26	4200	4:07.50
4051	1	Vasiliy Kuznyetsov	SU	32	Torino			3 Sep 59
				718	7279	22.2	4951	4:59.5
4049	2	Siegfried Wentz	FRG	60	Salzburg			15 Jun 85
				724	6200	22.02	4822	4:37.54
4028	1	Bruce Jenner	USA	49	San Jose			3 May 75
				700	6378	22.3	4632	4:22.3
4023	1	Georg Werthner	AUT	56	Krems			18 May 83
				709	7158	22.84	4110	4:23.6
4018	2	Fred Samara	USA	50	San José			3 May 75
				743	6330	21.7	4160	4:32.8
4017	1	Fred Dixon	USA	49	Santa Barbara			13 Jul 74
				720	6422	21.6	4586	4:41.8
4007	2	Kenneth Riggberger	SWE	49	Karlskrona			7 Jun 75
				672	6292	21.8	4488	4:16.7
3983	1	Rainer Sonnenburg	FRG	60	Hamburg			5 May 84
				754	6050	21.7	4242	4:38.4
3976	1	Karl-Heinz Fichtner	FRG	62	Unterhaching			25 Apr 87
				744	5746	22.37	4580	4:32.70
3975	4	Fritz Mehl	FRG	55	Salzburg			5 May 84
				711	6162	22.07	4404	4:29.20
3970	1	Hans-Joachim Walde	FRG	42	Bonn			16 May 71
				737	6308	22.1	4422	4:39.6

The world best by William Anthony Toomey (b. Philadelphia, 10 Jan 39), was set nearly 20 years ago at Crystal Palace, London, 'in almost perfect conditions', to quote from the present author's contemporary report in *Athletics Weekly*. Toomey opened by long-jumping: 751 (+0.1), 758 (+1.1), 753 (+1.0). This was followed by a javelin series of 6618, F, 6466. In the 200m his time was recorded on three watches as: 21.2, 21.32,21.4 (+1.4). He threw the discus successively: 4388,4382, 4453 (rounded to 4452, in accordance with IAAF Rule 145.2, although the 1964 Tables made provision for a performance of 4453). The two official watches on his 1500m read: 4:20.2 and 4:20.3. This world best came 10 months after Toomey had won the 1968 OG decathlon title with 8181/8144. Some four months later, he was to improve the world decathlon record in Los Angeles to 8417/8309.

ATHLETICS REFERENCE BOOKS 1988

BY PETER MATTHEWS

ATFS statistical publictions can be ordered from Palle Lassen, Bülowsvej 40/3, 1870 Fredriksberg C, Denmark.

IAAF/ATFS 1988 Seoul Olympic Games Statistics Handbook, published by the IAAF and compiled by ATFS members. A5 400pp. £6.50 from the IAAF. The IAAF maintains its most valuable practice of bringing out such statistical handbooks. Included in this one were 150 pages of national records for all IAAF member nations by Winfried Kramer, progressive world records lists, biographies of leading Olympic contenders, and a valuable Olympic section by Bill Mallon, including progressive Olympic records and best marks in Olympic competition (about 20 performances and performers per event).

IAAF/ATFS Statistics Handbook for the 2nd World Junior Championships 1988, A5 188 pp. A team of ATFS members produced this book for Sudbury. £6.50 from the IAAF. This is planned as an annual series. The largest section, compiled by Milan Skočovský comprises junior lists for the previous year, in this case for 1987 30-deep, and 50-deep all-time lists, although those for women were disappointingly for the old age group, rather than under 19 in the year of competition as introduced for 1988. There were also Continental junior records and championships medallists, brief profiles on 1986 champions and contenders for 1988, and progressive world junior best performance lists by Alain Bouillé and Jacques Carmelli.

USSR Athletics Statistics by Richard Hymans. A5 353pp. $22 US from the author, 37 Colehill Lane, London SW6 5EF, England or from Palle Lassen. This is the second edition of this invaluable and fact-packed handbook. Many additions have been made to the 1985 first edition. All-time lists 100 deep are given for all standard events, togther with comprehensive details of Soviet championships, an index of all athletes taking part in the major international championships, yearly trends, and statistical profiles of leading performers.

ATFS National Statistics - Poland by Tadeusz Wołejko, Zbigniew Lojewski & Wojciech Gaczkowski. A5 292pp. $17 US from Palle Lassen. This follows similar lines to the USSR book above. In addition to the all-time lists and indexes there are complete lists of all Polish international matches and yearly event leaders.

America's Best by Hal Bateman. 275 x 215mm 132pp. Listed are the 1576 men and 469 women who represented the USA in Olympic, World, World Indoor, Pan-American and World University Games competition from 1896 to 1987. Details are given of their performances in those meetings, national titles won, personal bests, height, weight and date of birth. Available from TAC.

The Sackville Illustrated Dictionary of Athletics by Tom Knight and Nick Troop. 263 x 183mm. 170pp. £14.95. A slightly misleading title as the book contains mostly biographies of 250 all-time greats.

The Long Distance Record Book by Andy Milroy, A5, 98pp. £4 in UK, £5.50 in Europe, $9 USA from Don Bonser, 76 Benhill Wood Road, Sutton, Surrey. The second edition, and much expanded from the first which came out in 1981. The booklet starts with a thorough history of distance running and of the ultra-marathon events, and then there are comprehensive progressive records lists for all distances from 15km to 1000 miles as well as for well-established races. Plentiful footnotes, miscellany and an index of athletes.

The Olympic Games Complete Track and Field Results 1896–1988 by Barry J. Hugman and Peter Arnold published by The Arena Press, Russell Chambers, The Piazza, Covent Garden, London WC2E 8AA, England. A5 384pp. An attractively produced volume, which gives brief descriptions of every Olympic athletics event, plenty of photographs and a directory of all performances Games by Games. This is an important work and the editors have been helped by Dave Terry and ATFS secretary Andrew Huxtable, and it was good to see the inclusion of auto-times for 1952–68, researched especially by Bob Sparks. The publishers did very well to include details of the 1988 Games, but it was irritating to see several typographical errors and the inaccurate use of the word Russia instead of the USSR. The complete absence of accents also gave rise to numerous inconsistencies - Marlies Göhr was variously Goehr or Gohr. Then for the Järvinen family: Jaervinen for four of them in 1932, but in 1936 Matti appears as Jarvinen separate in the directory from brother Akilles Jaervinen. In his preface Barry Hugman says that the reader can analyse the complete careers of athletes, but that is made harder by considerable inconsistencies in names, for instance Kouznetsov in 1956 changing to Kuznyetsov 1960 and Kuznetsov 1964. Not everyone would be sure that they were the same man. While all heats results are given where known, qualifying performances by finalists are lacking in field events, so while a worthy effort this is not yet the definitive volume for all Olympic athletic results.

The Fastest Men on Earth by Neil Duncanson. 265 x 194mm 192pp. Collins Willow, 8 Grafton St, London W1. £7.95. Tying in with a splendid six-part television series this book tells the history of the Olympic champions of the men's 100 metres. Meticulously researched, this book presents fascinating accounts of the careers of these men, and importantly what happened to them after their Olympic triumphs. Highly recommended.

Track's Greatest Women by Jon Hendershott. A5 246pp. $12 including postage from Track & Field News, Box 296, Los Altos, CA 94023, USA. Published 1987. An admirable collection of in-depth biographies of 15 of the all-time greats, with further profiles on more than 100 women, varying from a few lines to more than a page.

Birchfield Harriers 1877–1988 by Prof. W.O. Alexander and Wilfred Morgan. A4 124pp. £9.95 (add postage outside UK) from V. Stokes, 80 Craythorne Ave., Handsworth Wood, Birmingham B20 1LN. A fascinating story of a club which has by far the best record over the years of any in Britain, with scores of international athletes, both men and women. Indeed their ladies section was formed in 1922, one of the first three in the country.

Temps Automatiques – 100 Metres by Jean-Claude Patinaud. A4 33pp packed with data on automatic timings for the men's 100 metres: all marks to 10.50 for the years 1983 to 1987, together with progressive records for all nations, continental all-time lists, world junior lists etc.. This updates his comprehensive 100m survey to 1982. These and works on the 200m, 400m, 110mh and 400mh from the compiler at Sainte-Marie, 87130 Chateauneuf-la-Foret, France.

Annuals

Annuals in varying sizes are produced for most major athletics nations. The following, containing year lists for 1987, records and in some cases results for the previous season, are amongst the most notable ones seen by this reviewer, and all give comprehensive details for their respective countries. Most should be obtainable from their national federations, whose addresses are given elsewhere in this Annual. It is anticipated that new editions of these annuals covering 1988 will be published in 1989, mostly coincident with this Annual.

Svetove Tabulky World Lists 1987. Edited by Jiří Havlin, Svatopluk Dubský amd Milan Urban and the Czechoslovak statistical group. A4, 156pp. As in previous years a most useful adjunct to the International Athletics Annual, with 200 deep performance lists, national bests for each event and the best marks by the 15 top athletes at each event in 1987.

TAFWA All-Time Indoor List 1989 by Ed Gordon. A5 120pp. This annual compilation has been reformated this year so that its all-time indoor lists of performers and performances for all events, men and women, are to standard ATFS specifications. From Ed Gordon, 180 Ardmore Road, Berkeley, CA 94707, USA.

The Race Walking World Statistics 1988 by Egon Rasmussen and Palle Lassen. Year and all-time lists for the walks. Two volumes, A5 size – men's 54pp and women's 36pp, each US $6 from Palle Lassen.

Marathon Handbook 1988 compiled by Ottavio Castellini. 48pp, from the compiler Via Bonatelli 3, 25123, Brescia, Italy. The booklet includes 1987 world and Italian lists, Olympic marathon race results, and career surveys of Rosa Mota, Kee Chung-Sohn and the top current Italian marathoners.

L'Athlétisme Africain/African Athletics 1988 by Yves Pinaud and Walter Abmayr A5, 144p. 100 deep men's and women's lists for Africa for 1987, with 10 deep junior and all-time lists, and national championships results. FF 69 from Yves Pinaud, 66 rue Labrouste, 75015 Paris, France or for £8 from Tony Isaacs, see Pacific Islands below.

Athlerama 87–88. The 26th edition of the French Annual, edited by Jean Gilbert-Touzeau. A5, 408pp. FF 100 from the Fédération Française d'Athlétisme. As usual this contains most comprehensive lists covering all age groups of French athletes, with championships and internationals, all-time lists etc.

Atletismo 88 by Luis R. Vinker. A5, 236p. Very thorough coverage of results, records, and year lists for the whole of South America as well as for Argentina. From the Confederacion Argentina de Atletismo, Bvd. Irigoyen 396, 3260 Concepcion del Uruguay, Entre Rios, Argentina.

British Athletics 1988, compiled by the National Union of Track Statisticians. A5, 368p. The biggest and most comprehensive yet, the 30th NUTS annual gives detailed results and statistics on 1987 for the UK. £6.95 plus postage from BAAB Sales Office, 5 Church Road, Great Bookham, Surrey, KT23 3PW, England.

Canadian Athletics Annual 1987. A5, 166p. Compiled for the CTFA by the Canadian Association of Track Statisticians, chairman Cecil Smith. From the Canadian T&F Association, 333 River Road, Ottawa, Ontario, K1L 8H9.

DLV-Jahrbuch 1987/88 and **DLV-Bestenliste 1987**, published by the DLV, Julius-Reiber-Strasse 19, 6100 Darmstadt, FRG. A5, 386 and 500pp respectively. Comprehensive coverage of West German athletics. The former (DM 20), edited by Lutz Nebenthal, includes articles, detailed results of 1987 meetings, records and top ten lists as well as illustrations, some in colour. The latter, edited by Eberhard Vollmer, gives 50-deep lists for senior and various junior age groups for all men's and women's events.

Kenya Track & Field Best Performances 1987 by Walter Abmayr. A5 56pp. DM 15 from the compiler, Diamantweg 16, 6906 Leimen 2, FRG.

De Beste Nederlandse Atlekiekprestaties 1988, edited by Jacobus Koumans. A5, 168pp. 18 florins from the editor, Postbus 19127, 2500 CC Den Haag, the Netherlands. Always one of the earliest of national annuals to appear annually.

Friidretts-kalenderen 1988, editor Jo Nesse. A5, 320pp. Meticulously compiled year lists for Norway. 80 kroner from Jo Nesse, Gjønnesskogen 2, 1340 Bekkestua, Norway.

Pacific Islands Athletics Annual 1988 by Tony Isaacs. A5, 100pp. £4 or $7 from Tony Isaacs, 11 Manton Close, Trowbridge, Wiltshire BA14 0RZ, England.

Polish all-time and year lists. The Polish group of statisticians, especially Wojciech Gaczkowski and Tadeusz Wołejko, compile most useful booklets on Polish athletics. They would be most interested in exchanging these for books from other countries, Contact Tadeusz Wołejko, Sikorskiego 17, 62 020 Swarzedz, Poland. During 1988 they produced several statistical booklets.

SA Athletics '88. A5, 168p. The 36th edition of the South African Annual. Rand 5.00 from Harry Beinart, PO Box 1566, Cape Town 8000, Republic of South Africa.

Sverige Bästa 1987, edited by A.Lennart Julin. A5 260pp. From SFIF Statistik, Sofiatornet, Stadion, 114 33, Stockholm, Sweden. As always a most meticulously and attractively compiled annual, with very detailed lists for Sweden.

United States Annual 1988, general editors Scott Davis and Dave Johnson for FAST, Federation of American Statisticians of Track. A5 size, 448p. #14 (USA) or $18 (elsewhere) from Scott Davis, 4432 Snowbird Circle, Cerritos, CA 90701, USA. This tenth anniversary issue is the biggest yet with all the usual US lists and biographical details.

American Athletics Annual 1988, general editor Hal Bateman. A5 316pp. Published by TAC, PO Box 120, Indianapolis, IN 46206. $8 in

US and Canada, $12 elsewhere. Whereas the US Annual concentrates on all-time and year lists, this annual has detailed results of US and international meetings for the past year and lists of winners of AAU/TAC and NCAA championships, although again there is some duplication, with the index of athletes.

Australian Athletic Union Handbook of Records and Results 1988–89. Covering the Australian season to the end of April 1988. From the AAU, A5 100p.

Los Mejores de Ibero-America. Annual A5 booklets of 80 pages giving lists for Ibero-America are available at DM 20 from Francisco Baraona, Im Tannenwinkel 16, D-5330 Konigswinter 41, Federal Republic of Germany.

General

Idrottsboken 1988. 640 pp, A4. 631 Swedish kroner from Strömbergs/Brunnhages, Box 65, S-162 11 Vällingby, Sweden. The 44th edition of this magnificently produced and illustrated compendium gives results for 1987 on a very large number of sports. Coverage is both international as well as Swedish.

World Indoor Lists

The industrious CS statistical group have produced a 142 page booklet with world indoor lists for 1986 and for 1987. They intend to produce such booklets on an annual basis, which should prove a most useful complement to this yearbook, as our deadlines prevent completion of full indoor lists. Contact the booklet's editor Alfons Juck, Ciernovodska 7, 821 07 Bratislava, Czechoslovakia.

World indoor lists for 1986/7 and 1987/8 were also published by the recently formed Asociacion de Estadisticos Españoles de Atletismo in bumper editions of their bulletin (Nos.4 & 7). Contact Manuel Villuendas, Canario 10, 3'-C, 28904 Getafe – Madrid, Spain.

1989 Publications

Books to be published during 1989 include new editions of the annuals above and:

Track & Field Performances through the Years 1937/44 by Roberto Quercetani and Rooney Magnusson. The second volume in this invaluable series, price c.$15. Volume I covering 1929–36 is available from Palle Lassen at $14.

National Records of all Countries by Winfried Kramer, Kohlrodweg 12, 6680 Neunkirchen-Kohlhof, FR Germany.

Previous editions of the International Athletics Annual

Those for 1985–1988 from: London & International Publishers, 49 St James St, London SW1A 1JT, England.

Available from Palle Lassen, Bülowsvej 40/3, 1870 Fredriksberg C, Denmark are the following:
1975 and 1979 – $7.50; 1982, 1983, 1984 – $8.00; 1985 – $12; 1986, 1987 – $17, 1988 – $19.

Payments for these Annuals, or for other ATFS publications to Palle Lassen in cash, cheque or to Danish Postal account no.2 21 51 52.

Some editions of the Annual may also be available from Scott Davis, 4432 Snowbird Circle, Cerritos, California 90701, USA.

Books for review would be welcomed by the editor: **Peter Matthews, 10 Madgeways Close, Great Amwell, Ware, Herts SG12 9RU, England.**

AMENDMENTS TO ATHLETICS'88

Not including those shown on pages 561, 567 and 569 of Athletics '88.

P.45 World Championships 1987: LJ: 2.Byelevskaya, 3.Drechsler

Men's Lists 1987

100m 10.22 Robson Caetano da Silva 1 Cayenne 25 Apr (delete 10.20); irregular performances (wrong positioning of timer): 10.35A Fuentes, 10.39A Rojas, 10.42A Widoycovich CHL 69; add 10.40 Cai Jianming CHN 63 23 Nov, 10.41 Florencio Aguilar PAN 59 18 Jul; amend 10.19w Tomohiro Osawa

200m add 20.88 Chang Jae-keun SKO 62 2 Oct, 20.67w +2.2 Daniel Sangouma FRA 65 2 Walnut 31 May

400m 46.00 Gerson Andrade Souza BRA 1 Warendorf 25 Jun (from 46.26)

800m 1:46.29 Balamceda 1 Jul, 1:46.7m Mauricio Hernandez and Luis K.Toledo (not 1:46.64); add 1:47.2 m Eduardo Cabrera MEX 67 all at Guadalajara 5 Jul

1500m 3:40.86 Ameur ALG

2000m indoor marks at Inglewood on 21 Feb

5000m add 13:41.8 m Omar Aguilar CHL 19 Jul

10000m 28:18.23 Aguilar, 28:18.6 Temane 12 Oct, 28:30.00 Zhang at Roma; delete 28:40.65 Llorente

Mar 2:10:34 Shintaku 6 Dec

3000mSt 8:25.09 Gurny; add 8:41.56 George Bradley RSA 61 10 Apr

20km walk track - add 1:27:16.1 Chen Helin CHN 64 (1) - 12 Jun
road - add 1:24:18 Liu Lifeng CHN 65 (2) Zhengzhou 23 Nov; delete 1:24:00 Ivanov

50km walk add 4:02:28 Andrey Popov SU 62 5 Sep

4x100mR add 38.80 USA (McRae, McNeill, Glance, Mitchell) (1)h1 WC Roma 5 Sep

4x400mR 2:59.86, 3:00.91 and 3:00.92 all at Durham; 3:04.22 Australia 5 Sep; 3:04.92 Brazil's team: Dias Ferreira, A.Oliveira, Cherpe De Silva, Franco Menezes

110mh 13.72 Yu 1s2, 13.76 Valle b.67; delete 13.78i Ustinov & 13.98i Makhombetov - not auto, 14.01 Vallaeys; add 13.99 +1.7 Anatoliy Titov SU 56 23 Aug, 14.00 +1.7 Aleksey Anikeyev SU 66 23 Aug hand times: add 13.4i Vyacheslav Ustinov SU 57 1 Moskva 21 Feb (from 13.5), 13.7 Wu Jiang CHN 63 Beijing 18 Apr, 13.8 +1.3 Oleg Moszhukhin SU 65 12 Jun. Amend 13.7w Randy Cox USA.
Note pages 290 and 291 reversed.

400mh 49.41 Scholz at Stuttgart, 50.73 Huang 24 Nov (from 51.03), 50.80 Song 24 Nov (from 50.92), add 50.92 Li Kunjun CHN 66 23 Nov, 51.03 Yao Yongzhi CHN 62 24 Nov, 51.04 Efrain Williams PR 65 6 Jun. Hand times: 49.4 Kitur 12 Jun and not NC, 50.5 Huang 22 Mar, add 50.7 Li Kumjun CHN 66 15 Apr

HJ 2.28i Grebenstein 1 Bautzen 18 Feb, 2.26 Ni 10 Nov, 2.23 Koji Ono, 2.22 Cho Hyon-uk SKO 70 delete best outdoor 2.22 Pagani (see 2.24)

PV 5.50 Mike Shafe, 5.40i Jie 28 Feb, also 5.40 on 28 Nov, 5.40i Sivillon (from 5.30), 5.30 Qing Chang 6 Jun. add 5.30 Yuan Shunen CHN 66 (3) and 5.30 Chen Guoming CHN 59 (4) both on 28 Nov. Series: Vigneron 8 Mar also 5.50/3

LJ 8.14 Harrison 17 Apr, 8.05 Wolf 20 Aug, 8.04 Hydel Warszawa 31 May, 7.89 Pang Yan 3 Guangzhou 25 Nov (delete 7.94 mark); add 7.89 Li Lianghua CHN 63 5 Jun, 7.88 Lin Rongmin CHN 64 5 Jun, 7.87A Ricardo Valiente PER 68 Huancayo 15 Nov, 7.82A Carlos Casar MEX 60 9 May, 7.79 Zhang Zhuliang CHN 63 30 Oct, 7.77 Liang Fang CHN 64 25 Jul. Delete best outdoor 7.87 Chantzopoulos

TJ add 16.79 Ernesto Torres PR 59 Salinas 6 Jun, 16.72A Ricardo Valiente PER 68 Huancayo 14 Nov, 16.29 Chen Yanping CHN 66 29 Nov

SP 20.68 Gert Weil 1 Runkel 2 Aug (from 20.41), 20.35 Kobza. delete 18.88 Minns

DT 67.12 Fernholm 21 May, 64.80 Brenner at San Diego, 61.52 Scott Lofquist (1) 25 May Winfield (from 59.10); add 59.20 Wu Wenge CHN 66 8 Nov

HT add 70.24 Luo Jun CHN 64 24 Nov

JT 79.48 Ji and 76.98 Zhang on 14 Apr, 78.48 de la Garza 3 Jul; delete 75.80 Kim Jae-sang

Dec 7986 Halamoda b.66, 7967 Robinson b.64, 7883 Kryuchkov, 7475h Leeson

Men's Junior Lists 1987

100m delete three Mexico City times, by Fuentes, Rojas and Wydoycovich - irregular position of auto-timer; add 10.2 Luis Smith PAN 3.01.68 Texas 11 Apr; 10.36w Holmes 4.1.69

200m add 20.3 Alvin Daniel USA 30.5.68 1 Port of Spain 13 Jun

400m delete 46.54 Cadogan - irregular (wrong position of auto-timer)

800m add 1:48.5 Wilson Kipketer KEN .68 Nakuru 27 Jun; amend 1:48.8 Azarov 2 on 14 Jun

1500m add 3:44.51 Mohammed Sulaiman QAT .69 7r2 Köln 16 Aug

3000m add 8:04.3 Gennaro Di Napoli ITA 5.3.68 2 San Donato Milano 20 May, 8:14.33 Enrico Vivian ITA 22.7.68 9 Padova 13 Sep; amend 8:09.1 Kaldy - no details; 8:08.28 Karrass 7 Leipzig 24 Jul, 8:09.35 Baccani 1 Torino 29 May

5000m add 13:51.85 Guo Yijiang CHN .68 2 NC Guangzhou 29 Nov, 13:53.9 Ryu Ok-hyon NKO .68 1 Pyongyang 13 May, 13:54.69 Zhang Yuejin CHN .68 3 Nanjing 20 Sep, 14:07.1 David Lord AUS .68 13 Melbourne 26 Nov, 14:11.6 Heydar Dogan TUR 3.3.69 Izmir 6 Jun (marks to 14:12.2)

10000m add 29:27.6 Ryu Ok-hyon NKo .68 1 Pyongyang 11 May, 29:31.32 Raymond Kunzwayo RSA 24.6.68 10 Stellenbosch 10 Apr, 29:38.5 Shuji Yamaguchi JAP 26.9.68 Hachioji 29 Nov, 29:41.47 Guo Yijiang CHN .68 (5) Guangzhou 25 Nov, 29:42.4 Pan Shao.. CHN .68 Jinan 15 Apr, 29:54.8 Hirokazu Tatsumi JAP 23.4.69 Omiya 18 Oct (to 29:55.83)

110mh add 14.12 Wen Jun CHN .68 5s2 NC Guangzhou 29 Nov, also 13.9 hand timed on 14 Apr; delete 14.12 Carmona 17.09.69, 14.14 Qunitero & 14.17 Guevara - to 14.2 hand times.

400mh 50.97 Carrington 30.6.69, 51.4 Rondon 17.01.70

2000mSt add 5:33.9 Anton Nicolaisen RSA 25.1.68 1 Bloemfontein 16 Feb

3000mSt add 8:42.34 Wang Shubo (1), 8:45.03 Zou Jinguo (3), 8:47.48 Gao Shuhai (5) all CHN 68 Guangzhou 24 Nov; 8:51.3 William Kosgei KEN 29.12.70, 8:56.8 Mathew Birir KEN .59 both Nairobi 15 Jul, 8:52.02 Ali Ahmed Salah QAT .68 (7) and 8:54.15 Abdullah Dosari BAH .68 (8) both Warendorf 25 Jun, 8:54.68 Alemayehu Semretu ETH .70 9 Saint Denis 11 Jun, 8:57.9 Pasquale Rega ITA .68 2 Colleferro 11 Jul

HJ 2.22 Cho Hyun-ok (not 2.20), 2.18 Martinez 1 Ft.Lupton 11 Apr; add 2.19 Mark Cannon USA 10.2.69 1 Columbus 6 Jun, 2.18 Xu Yang CHN .70 2 Anshan 27 Jun, 2.18i Andras Tresch HUN 12.4.68 6 Budapest 14 Feb; delete 2.18 Stanton

PV 5.40 Tarasov 2.12.70, 5.22 Holloway 12.7.69 1 Winter Park 10 Apr, 5.22 Henderson 1 Ingleside 28 Mar; add 5.25 Huang Guopin CHN 68 Guangzhou 14 Feb

LJ add 7.87A Ricardo Valiente PER 22.08.68 1 Huancayo 15 Nov. 7.81 Yemi Alade NIG Benin City 12 Mar

TJ add 16.72A Ricardo Valiente PER 22.08.68 1 Huancayo 15 Nov; 16.18 Saúl Isalgué 3.11.69

SP 18.90 Pogorelyi 1 and 18.63 Palchikov 2 both Moskva 25 Jul, 17.56 Klimov 25.6.69; add 17.15 Cui Guangyuan CHN 69 (6) NC Guangzhou 29 Nov

DT 55.72 Nesterets 26.2.69, 55.44 Zulic

HT 70.58 Palyushchik 23.4.69, 70.12 Yeroshin 12.4.69, 68.16 Sundas at Cagliari; add 68.06 Argiris Klapanaras GRE 17.9.68 1 Saloniki 2 Aug, 68.00 Bi Zhong CHN .68 2 Guangzhou 7 Jun

JT 73.34 Kim Jae-sang Seoul 19 Apr (not 75.80), 73.14 Palyunin 6.4.69, 72.70 Yamada 1 Yokohama 24 May, 72.58 Filippov 29.11.69; add 73.18 Geng Shengli CHN 68 Beijing 9 Oct, 72.96 Park Yong-young SKO 30.12.69 Seoul 16 May

Dec 8037 Steen 59, 7936 Gellens 43.46, 7884 Günther 11.47w, 7.21w, 7669 Eseimokumoh 2 14.57w, 7661h Golub 4:48.8, 7651 Valle, 7617 Trefny, 7381 Ramil Ganeyev, 7369 Hämäläinen 21.1.69

10kmW add 42:13.7 Karoly Kirszt HUN 23.7.69 no details, 42:41.8 Cruz 6.6.72

4x100mR note 40.97 BUL (Danailov, Stoianov, Pinter, Sotzenier)

4x400mR note 3:12.17 CUB (Rondon, Ramos, Canete, Cadogan)

Women's Lists 1987

Note that in women's lists up to 400mh Chinese names were shown reversed, i.e. with the family name second

100m add all CHN on 23 Nov: 11.55 Zhang Xiaoqiong 66, 11.56 Tian Yumei (from 11.60), 11.57 Pan Weixin 63, 11.59 Lu Zongying 68, 11.60 Liu Shaomei 63, 11.64 Xu Yaqin 63, 11.65 Cao Liling 65; add 11.61 Amparo Caicedo COL 65 11 Apr; delete 11.62A Rosado - irregular (wrong position of auto-timer)
add hand-timed 11.3i Madezhda Rashchupkina SU 64 20 Feb, 11.3 Tian Yumei CHN 65 21 Mar

200m 23.43i Zolotaryova; 23.0 +1.7 Kleyankina. add hand-timed: 23.4 Xie Zhiling CHN 63 31 Oct; wa: all +2.1: 22.3A Maya Azarashvili SU 64, 22.5A +2.1 Olga Nazarova both -h Tsakhkadzor 23 May

400m 52.79 Keough; add 52.88 Leng Guoming CHN 61 & 52.98 Gao Yanqing CHN 58 both 25 Nov, 53.26 Shiny Abraham IND 60 28 Dec

800m 1:55.86 Wachtel 21 Aug, 2:03.52 Chalmers

1500m 4:12.8 Zheng 10 Sep; add all CHN on 25 Nov: 4:13.58 Liu Aicun 63, 4:13.91 Wang Yanling 64, 4:14.12 Geng Xiujan 64, 4:14.55 Wang Yuelan 66, 4:14.90 Feng Yanbo 65, 4:15.07 Chen Lijun 68

3000m 8:57.57 Wang 1, 8:59.09 Wang Yuelan 3, 9:01.52 Li 5; add 9:09.54 Liu Aicun CHN 62 & 9:10.12 Gao Suju CHN 62 both 28 Nov; note Sue Bruce 9:00.3# and 9:06.70

5000m 15:35.82 Zhao 6, 15:43.43 Liu 7, 15:52.27 Wang 8, 15:52.28 Li 9; add 16:06.83 Xiao Hongyan CHN 65 25 Nov, 16:08.66 Xie Lihua CHN 66 25 Nov

10000m 32:53.68 Zhong 2, 33:59.1 Lasaga USA; add all CHN at Guangzhou on 29 Nov: 33:32.36 Yang Xiufeng 65, 33:38.38 Chen Qingmei 63, 33:43.85 Li Juan 66, 33:49.99 Chen Zhanxiu 65, 33:52.44 Bai Chunyan 66, 33:53.25 Zhao Yueyuan 66, 34:13.05 Sung Guoxiu 64

100mh 13.09 Feng Yinghau 2, 13.17 Du 2s2 24 Nov, 13.23 Xiao 3, 13.29 Zheng 4, 13.36 Zhu 1h3 24 Nov, 13.39 Yu 3s1 24 Nov, 13.39 Yin 1B; add: 13.30 Pang Diewen CHN 67 5 Guangzhou 25 Nov, 13.56 Elisavet Pandazi GRE 56 22 Aug, delete 13.63 Tavares
hand-timed: add 13.0 Feng Yinghua CHN 66 Beijing 8 Apr, 13.1i Marina Sukhareva SU 61 1 Moskva 21 Feb, 13.1 Zhu Yuqing CHN 63 & 13.1 Xiao Zifang CHN 64 both Beijing 11 Apr, 13.1 Xu Rongxiu CHN 66 & 13.2 Chen Kemei CHN 63 both Beijing 8 May, 13.3 Yin Shujin CHN 64 27 Aug; amend 13.1 -0.5 Filatova, 13.2 Smirnova 0.2, 13.3 Yermilova 0.0

400mh add 54.19 Flintoff-King 2 WC Roma 3 Sep; amend 57.40 Zhang 2h2, 57.83 Chen 2h1, 58.50 Zhang Linuo; all CHN at Guangzhou 27 Nov: 57.93 Zhang Fengqin (from 58.60), 58.07 Zhou Qing (from 58.68), 58.15 Song Meiyu (from 58.20), 58.16 Yuan Haiying (from 58.60), add 58.30 Liang Li 70, 58.43 Tai Hong 67. 58.78 Zhao Qianqian CHN 61 7 Jun. Hand timed: add 58.8 Guo Yue CHN 69 9 Oct; 56.7 mixed race Jenny Laurendet AUS 14 Mar Sydney

HJ 1.97 Albina Kazakova H Moskva 26 Jul (from 1.96), 1.93 Ni at Nanning, 1.92 Ye 1, 1.90 Jin 1, 1.89 Ye 4, 1.86 Gisladóttir 16 May; add at 1.86, all CHN on 25 Nov: Wu Jiefang 61, Du Wenjie 63, Huang Caixia 67

LJ 6.69 Zhuang at Nanning, 6.59 Xiong 1, 6.57 Huang 3, 6.53 Li 5, 6.51 Ma 6, 6.51 Liu 3, 6.48 Deng 8, 6.42 Wei 4 Sep; add 6.46 Chen Zhaojing CHN 69 4 Zhengzhou 6 Jun, 6.45 Madeline de Jesus PR 57 San German 14 Mar, 6.43 Wang Chunfang CHN 70 27 Nov, 6.40 Ou Yanghong CHN 66 29 Sep, 6.37 Fu Han CHN 68 31 Oct

SP all on 25 Nov: 20.95 Li, 19.86 Cong 2, 18.87 Sui 4, 18.55 Zhou 5, 18.40 Zhang 6, 18.38 Peng 7, 17.61 Zhen 8, 17.56 Kuang (not 7 Jun); 18.42 Leng 4, 18.17 Li 5, 17.80 Wang 7, 16.81 Wang b.67, 16.76 Min 20 Jun (from 16.45), 16.56 Wang 27 Jun (from 16.45), 16.56i Runne SU; add, all CHN, 16.78 Wu Xiaofeng 67 7 Jun, 16.76 He Xiuqin 67 18 Apr, 16.74 Zhang Liuhong 69 27 Jun, 16.60 Hou Xuemei 62 28 Mar, 16.59 Ma ...... 66 7 Jun.

DT 62.50 Min 3, 58.88 Xie 6, 58.08 Li 3, 56.90 Zhang Hui 67 5 Jun (from 54.80), 56.86 Xiao 10 Sep (from 55.76), 56.22 Chen 28 Nov (from 55.82); add 58.24 Lyudmila Fyodorova SU 66 1 Novopolotsk 26 Sep, 55.64 Nadezhda Frantseva SU 61 26 Jul; all CHN: 56.50 Li Hongmei 68 7 Jun, 56.04 Yan Yingxia 62 7 Jun, 55.66 Deng Hua .. 18 Apr, 55.48 Deng Zhifeng 67 31 Mar, 55.46 Deng Yanyi 67 27 Jún

JT 64.14 Zhang 3, 63.96 Xin 2, 63.72 Liu 3, 61.06 Wang 1 Shijiazhuang 20 Sep, 60.72 Ding 7, 60.54 Song 3, 60.42 Zheng 8, 56.56 Wang 63 14 Apr (from 55.50); add 58.62 Zhu Hongyang CHN 64 6 Zhengzhou 6 Jun, 57.96 Yu Xueqing CHN 63 Hangzhou 28 Apr, 57.84 Gong Jin... CHN 67 6 Jun, 57.64 Bai Liyun CHN 69 18 Apr, 56.90 Zhu Yu CHN 66 29 Nov, 56.86 Sung Xiurong CHN 69 27 Mar, 56.54 Iris Grönfeldt ICE 63 25 Jul; delete 56.68 Maria Djaleva

Hep 6692 Behmer 61, 6585 Buraga SU, 6190h Romanchenkova 1.76, 6131 Cornateanu (14.16, 1.80, 15.05, 24.56...2:09.94),6001h Beinhauer 2:22.3, 5999 Gautzsch 1.72, 2:17.31, 5961w Petushkova - 6.16W LJ, 5896 Wu 2, 5869 Petrashkevich 62 7 Leningrad 10 Aug, 5852 Pfeil 2:19.23, 5812h Polyakova 14.0, 5769h Hochrein 2:19.4, 5764 Vanyek 6.31, 39.50, 5625 Geremias 12 Jul (from 5591); add all CHN: 5826 Ye Lianying 60 4 Guangzhou 28 Nov (14.00 1.86 12.42 25.20 6.13 35.10 2:23.81), 5683 Shi Guiqing 68 28 Nov, 5678 (5680?) 64 28 Nov, 5530 (5633?) Qian Xiaohong 68 28 Nov

Junior Women's Lists 1987

100m 11.61w Fields; delete 11.62A Rosado. Hand: add 11.4 Ge Weidong CHN 4.1.69 Shijiazhuang 10 Sep

400m add 53.94 Larisa Oganesyan SU .69 Leningrad 19 Aug, 53.98A Grace Ofori GHA .69 Nairobi 2 Aug, 54.05 Zhou Qing CHN .69 4h2 Guangzhou 25 Nov; 53.9A Ximena Restrepo COL 10.03.69 1 Medellin 10 Sep

800m 2:04.35 Bortoi Bucaresti 14 Jun

1500m 4:06.85 Misaros, add 4:17.09 Liu Shixiang CHN 13.1.71 Guangzhou 25 Nov, 4:18.10 Wang Renmei CHN 70 Guangzhou 25 Nov, 4:18.18 Lihuan Zhang CHN 70 Zhengzhou 7 Jun; delete 4:12.86 Parkhuta, 4:20.01 Holmes

3000m add 9:13.0 Linah Yator KEN .71 Nakuru 28 Jun, 9:14.6 Nina Glotova SU .69 I-F 19 Sep, 9:18.37 Liu Shiyuan CHN 13.1.71 9 Guangzhou 28 Nov

10000m delete 32:59.21 Wang probably born 1968; add 34:26.2 Alice Chemtai KEN .72, 34:50.6 Delilah Asiogo KEN .72 & 35:20.7 Norah Maraga KEN .71, all Nairobi 10 Jul, 35:38.66 Susanne Nedergård DEN .69 1 Tarnby 13 Jun

100mh 13.68 Luo Bin .69 (1), 13.71 Yu Wenhui 2, 13.78 +0.5 Bokovec 1; add 13.76 Zhang Aimei CHN 69 3 Hangzhou 23 Sep; delete 13.67A Valiente. Hand: 13.3 Vasilkina 10.6.69, Antipova

400mh all CHN at Guangzhou 27 Nov: amend 58.07 Zhou Qing 3h1, 58.16 Yuan Haiying 2h3, add 58.30 Liang Li 29.9..70 3h3; add 58.50 Zhang Linuo CHN .70 2 Anshan 21 Jun, 59.20 Guo Yue CHN .69 (2) Hangzhou 25 Sep (also 58.8 Beijing 9 Oct); amend 58.9 Voloboyeva 12.2.70

LJ 6.51 Ma 6, 6.29i Hübel 6.4.69; add 6.46 Chen Zhaojing CHN 69 4 Zhengzhou 6 Jun, 6.43 Wang Chunfang CHN 70 9 Guangzhou 27 Nov

SP 16.76 Min 1 Anshan 20 Jun (from 16.45), 16.09 Polyakova; add 16.74 Zhang Liuhong CHN 69 7 Anshan 27 Jun

DT 62.50 Min Chunfeng, 55.88 Tirneci 2 Poiana Brasov, 54.28 Li Qing .69 8 Zhengzhou 7 Jun; add 53.22 Ines Wittich GDR 14.11.69 1 Karl-Marx-Stadt 22 Jul; delete 52.84 Akimoto

JT add 57.64 Bai Liyun CHN .69 Zhengzhou 18 Apr, 56.86 Sung Xiurong CHN 27.3.69 Jinan 27 Mar

Hep add 5344 Monika Steigauf FRG 17.1.70 3 5336 Seel Dagmar FRG 1.5.69 both Salzgitter 30 Aug

4x400mR note 3:40.54 BUL (Taneva, Slavcheda, Kondova, Gzudeva)

Acknowledgements to Milan Skocovsky, Francisco Baraona, Jiri Havlín, Heinrich Hubbeling, Winfried Kramer, Lionel Peters, Leandros Slavis, Ari Nurkkala, José Maria Garcia - and Chinese lists

NATIONAL CHAMPIONS 1988 AND BIOGRAPHIES OF LEADING ATHLETES

BY PETER MATTHEWS

This section incorporates biographies of 633 of the world's top athletes, listed by nation, with national champions at standard events for the leading countries prominent in athletics.

Once again the biographies have changed materially from the previous year's Annual, not only that all entries have been updated, but also that many newcomers have been introduced to replace those who have retired or faded a little from the spotlight.

Since this section was introduced in the 1985 Annual, biographies have been given for a total of 1130 athletes. This year there are 108 newcomers, with 20 reinstated from previous Annuals. The latter category includes former Olympic champions Mac Wilkins and Lyudmila Kondratyeva, who made notable returns to top-class competition in 1988, having missed three Annuals. Two athletes who make their first appearance are Wolfgang Schmidt and Francie Larrieu-Smith, who would have been included in years prior to the introduction of this section in 1985. There are 222 athletes who have been featured in each of the five editions of this Annual.

Once again no doubt some of those dropped from this compilation will also again make their presence felt; the keen reader can look up their credentials in previous Annuals, and, of course, basic details may be in the athletes' index at the end of this book.

The biographical information includes:

a) Name; date and place of birth; height (in metres); weight (in kilograms).

b) Previous name(s) for married women; club or university; occupation.

c) Major championships record - all placings in such events as the Olympic Games, World Championships, European Championships, Commonwealth Games, World Cup and European Cup Final; leading placings in the European or World Junior Championships, and other Continental Championships; and first three in European Indoors or World Student Games.

d) National titles won or successes in other major events.

e) Records set: world, continental and national; indoor world bests (WIB).

f) Progression of best marks over the years at major event(s).

g) Personal best performances at other events.

h) Other comments.

Details are to the end of 1988.

See Introduction to this Annual for lists of abbreviations used for events and championships.

Note that for comparison purposes decathlons and heptathlons have been rescored using the 1984 IAAF Tables, except those marked *, for which event breakdowns were unavailable. Women's pentathlons (p) have not been rescored.

I am most grateful to various ATFS members who have helped check these details. Additional information or corrections would be welcomed for next year's Annual.

Peter Matthews, 10 Madgeways Close, Great Amwell, Ware, Herts SG12 9RU, England

ALBANIA

Governing body: Albanian Athletic Federation, Rruga Kongresi 1 Permetit 41, Tirana.

National Championships first held in 1945 (women 1946).

1988 Champions: MEN

100m: Niko Laro 10.9, 200m/400m: Mehmet Bozgo 21.9/49.2, 800m: Nikolin Dionizi 1:52.9, 1500m: Jonel Ndoci 3:51.2, 5000m: Skender Ruci 14:42.6, 10000m: Isuf Curri 31:05.0, Mar: Vasil Myrto 2:40:00, 3000mSt: Krenar Meçani 9:06.0, 110mh: Artan Spahiu 14.3, 400mh: Artur Dibra 55.3, HJ: Muhamet Abazi 2.10, PV: Sazan Fisheku 5.00, LJ: Arben Mlloja 7.34, TJ: Azgan Damnori 15.49, SP: Emil Kosta 16.14, DT: Andrea Pali 47.64, HT: Ajet Toska 72.54, JT: (old) Arben Bulku 61.74, Dec: Franc Zojzi 6042, 20kmW: Enver Dollani 1:38:17.

WOMEN

100m/200m: Arbana Xhani 12.2/25.1, 400m/400mh: Valbona Sina 56.0/60.1, 800m: Adriana Vejkollari 2:05.6, 1500m/ Pavlina Evro 4:27.4, 3000m: Donika Hanxhara 9:34.8, 100mh/Hep: Alma Qeramizhi 14.3/5341, HJ: Klodeta Gjini 1.91, LJ: Vera Bregu 6.08, SP: Besa Ciurçiali 13.27, DT: Anila Jatru 48.68, JT: Vergjinush Limani 53.46.

ALGERIA

Governing body: Fédération Algerienne d'Athlétisme, Maison des Fédérations, BP 88, El Biar, Alger. Founded 1963.

National Champions 1988: MEN

100m/200m: Mustapha Kamel Selmi 10.43/21.17w, 400m: Filali Mohamed 47.38, 800m: Réda Abdenouz 1:47.53, 1500m: Abbès Téhami 3:45.54, 5000m/10000m: Miloud Djellal 13:46.15/29:34.11, 3000m St: Azzedine Brahmi 8:29.43, 110mh: Nourredine Tadjine 14.02, 400mh: Lyès Bernaoui 53.05, HJ: Othmane Belfaa 2.20, PV: Samir Agsous 4.80, LJ/TJ: Lotfi Kaida 7.50/15.77, SP: Mohamed Talaboulma 14.33, DT: Yacine Louail 48.66, HT: Hakim Toumi 68.94, JT: Ahmed Mahour Bacha 61.88, 20kmW: Abdelwahab Ferguène 1:24:37.6 short.

WOMEN

100m/200m: Rachida Ferdjauoi 12.32/25.89, 400m: Dalila Harek 58.25, 800m/1500m: Hassiba Boulmerka 2:04.46/4:13.47, 3000m: Mébarka Hadj Abdellah 9:19.81, 10000m: Malika Benhabylès, 100mh: Fazia Gaouaoui 15.36w, 400mh: Nacèra Chetibi 64.08, HJ: Zahira Attar 1.55, LJ: Nadia Abdou 5.30, SP: Fatiha Larab 14.59, DT: Aicha Dahmous 47.44, JT: Samia Djémaa 53.98, 5kmW: Sabiha Mansouri 25:24.77.

Azzedine BRAHMI b.13 Sep 1966 Setif 1.78m 64kg. C.M. Belcourd.

At 3000m St: OG: '88- 13; AfCh: '88- 1. Algerian Champion 1986, 1988.

Algerian 3000m steeplechase record 1988.

Progression at 3000m St: 1985- 9:01.3, 1986- 8:40.80, 1987- 8:36.52, 1988- 8:16.54. pbs: 1500m 3:47.4'86, 3000m: 8:01.1'88, 5000m: 13:56.9'88.

ARGENTINA

Governing body: Confederacion Argentina de Atletismo, Bvd.Irigoyen 396, 3260 Concepcion del Uruguay, Entre Rios.

National Championships first held in 1920 (men), 1939 (women)

1988 Champions: MEN

100m/200m: Claudio Arcas 10.81/21.38, 400m: José Beduino 48.49, 800m: Luis Migueles 1:50.78, 1500m/3000mSt Marcelo Cascabelo 3:49.07/ 8:37.60, 5000m/10000m: Antonio Silio 14:18.6/ 30:12.7, Mar: Toribio Gutierrez 2:19:26, 110mh: Carlos MacGarry 14.77, 400mh: Fernando Marzano 52.39, HJ: Fernando Moreno 2.14, PV: Oscar Veit 4.80, LJ/TJ: Alejandro Gats 7.13/15.44, SP: Gerardo Carucci 15.57, DT: Marcelo Pugliese 50.66, HT: Andrés Charadia 67.28, JT: Juan Garmendia 60.84, Dec: Martin Badano 6990.

WOMEN

100m: Laura de Falco 12.52, 200m/400m: Olga Conte 24.03/54.72, 800m/1500m: Mabel Arrua 2:12.61/4:33.91, 3000m/10000m: Stella Maris Selles 9:42.8/36:30.5, Mar: Susana Etchegoin 3:35:50, 100mh/HJ: Liliana Derfler 14.62/1.74, 400mh: Paula Val 61.4, LJ: Ana Vizioli 5.93, SP: Berenica da Silva (URU) 15.36, DT: Daphne Birnios 47.24, JT: Sonia Favre 50.14, Hep: Ana Maria Comaschi 5454.

AUSTRALIA

Governing body: Australian Athletic Union, P.O.Box 254, Moonee Ponds, Victoria 3039. Founded 1897.

National Championships first held in 1893 (men), 1930 (women)

1988 Champions: MEN

100m: Shane Naylor 10.61, 200m: Kieran Finn (Ire) 21.16, 400m: Miles Murphy 44.71, 800m: Ian Gaudry 1:47.67, 1500m: Mike Hillardt 3:47.62, 5000m: Andrew Lloyd 13:36.15, 10000m: Steve Moneghetti 28:18.98, Mar: Pat Carroll 2:10:44, 3000mSt: Brendan Hewitt 8:45.91, 110mh: Don Wright 14.04, 400mh: Leigh Miller 49.85, HJ: David Anderson 2.26, PV: Neil Honey 5.15, LJ: Gary Honey 8.30w, TJ: Peter Beames 16.55w, SP: John Minns 18.91, DT: Werner Reiterer 62.48, HT: Sean Carlin 72.90, JT: Ben Hodgson 68.28, Dec: Simon Shirley 7814, 5kmWt/20kmW: Simon Baker 19:40.76/1:21:19.

WOMEN
100m/100mh/Hep: Jane Flemming 11.90/13.96/6166, 200m: Kerry Johnson 23.73, 400m: Maree Holland 52.04, 800m: Sharon Stewart 2:02.36, 1500m: Margaret Leaney 4:32.14, 3000m: Jackie Perkins 9:11.63, 10000m: Carolyn Schuwalow 32:38.46, Mar: Ngaire Drake (NZ) 2:39:25, 400mh: Debbie Flintoff-King 56.27, HJ: Vanessa Browne 1.96, LJ: Nicole Boegman 6.44w, TJ: Lynette Smith 12.09, SP/DT: Astra Etienne 17.27/54.44, HT: Bernadette Serone 45.74, JT: Kate Farrow 54.74, 5kmW/10kmW: Kerry Saxby 20:45.32/41:30R.

Simon BAKER b.6 Feb 1958 Oakleigh, Vic. 1.86m 70kg. Club: Oakleigh. Qualified mechanical engineer, now at Australian Institute of Sport.
At 50kmW: OG: '88- 6. At 30kmW: CG: '86- 1. At 20kmW: OG: '84- 14, '88- 11; WCh: '83- 29, '87- 24; LT: '83- 14, '85- 12, '87- 11. Australian champion 5kmW 1988, 20kmW 1985, 1988.
Commonwealth 50km road walk best 1988.
Progression at 20kmW/50kmW: 1983- 1:24:43, 1984- 1:24:29, 1985- 1:25:22, 1986- 1:23:13, 1987- 1:21:57/3:58:51, 1988- 1:21:19/3:44:07. Track pbs: 3kmW: 11:42.4 '88, 5kmW: 19:32.15 '88, 10kmW: 41:06.0 '85, 1HrW: 14609m '86. Road 30kmW: 2:07:47 '86.

Darren CLARK b.6 Sep 1965 Sydney 1.78m 76kg. Randwick Botany (NSW).
At 400m: OG: '84- 4, '88- 4; WCh: '83 & '87- sf; CG: '86- 2 (2 4x400mR); WCp: '85- 4 (3 at 200m). Australian champion 1986, AAA champion 1983–6.
Four Australian 400m records 1984–8. Two Commonwealth 300m bests 1985–6.
Progression at 400m: 1982- 46.62, 1983- 45.05, 1984- 44.75, 1985- 44.80, 1986- 44.72, 1987- 44.97, 1988- 44.38. pbs: 100m: 10.47/10.3 '83, 10.36w '87, 200m: 20.49 '83, 300m: 31.88 '86, 600m: 1:16.91 '88.
Set world age-17 best to win AAA title in 1983. Ran a 43.86 relay leg in 1984 Olympics.

Robert de CASTELLA b.27 Feb 1957 Melbourne 1.80m 71kg. Mazda TC. Athletics consultant, trained as a biophysicist. Married to Gayelene Clews (10000m: 33:53.1 '85 and cross-country international).
At Mar: OG: '80- 10, '84- 5, '88- 8; WCh: '83- 1, '87- dnf; CG: '82- 1, '86- 1. Australian champion 1979. World CC: '81- 6, '83- 6. Won Pacific Conference 10000m 1977.
Commonwealth records: 20km (58:37.2) and 1 hour (20516m) 1982. Marathon world best 1981, Australian record 1986.
Progression at Mar: 1979- 2:13:23, 1980- 2:10:44, 1981- 2:08:18, 1982- 2:09:18, 1983- 2:08:37, 1984- 2:09:09, 1985- 2:08:48, 1986- 2:07:50, 1987- 2:14:24, 1988- 2:08:49. pbs: 1500m: 3:48.0 '86, 3000m: 8:00.01 '87, 5000m: 13:34.28 '81, 10000m: 28:02.73 '83.
Has run 19 marathons, winning eight of them, seven sub 2:10 and all sub 2:15 except for his failure to finish in Rome 1987; fourth at Tokyo 1988. Very strong runner, who has stayed clear of injuries. His younger brother Nick ran 2:15:04 in 1983.

Michael HILLARDT b.22 Jan 1961 Brisbane 1.80m 72kg. St.Stephens Harriers (Vic).
At 1500m: OG: '84- sf; WCh: '87- 7; CG: '82- 5, '86- 8; WCp: '85- 5; WI: '85- 1, '87- 5. At 800m: WCh: '83- sf, WCp: '81- 4. Australian champion 800m 1981, 1983; 1500m 1980, 1982–8. Austrian champion 800m 1979–80, 1500m 1980. 3rd GP 1500m 1987.
Australian records at 1000m (3), 1500m (3), 1 mile (5) 1982–5.
Progression at 1500m/1M: 1978- 3:46.0, 1979- 4:01.6M, 1980- 3:39.67, 1981- 3:41.74/3:56.6, 1982- 3:38.04/3:53.33, 1983- 3:41.51/3:57.09, 1984- 3:34.20/3:52.34, 1985- 3:33.39/3:51.82. 1986- 3:34.51/3:56.6i, 1987- 3:34.7/3:53.30, 1988- 3:34.06. pbs: 400m: 47.8 '80, 800m: 1:45.74 '83, 1000m: 2:17.49 '84, 2000m: 5:06.0 '85, 3000m: 7:52.17 '84, 5000m: 13:38.31 '86, 400mh: 52.44 '79.
Missed 1988 Olympics due to Achilles injury.

Gary HONEY b.26 Jul 1959 Thomastown, Melbourne 1.83m 70kg. Ivanhoe (Vic). Insurance agent.
At LJ: OG: '80- dnq, '84- 2; WCh: '83- 6; CG: '82- 1, '86- 1 (4 TJ); WCp: '79- 5, '81- 2, '85- 4. Australian champion 1979, 1981–8.
Five Australian long jump records 1981–4, including two Commonwealth records 1984.
Progression at LJ: 1977- 7.32, 1978- 7.64, 1979- 7.97/8.09w, 1980- 7.98/8.10w, 1981- 8.11/8.13w, 1982- 8.13, 1983- 8.12, 1984- 8.27/8.39w, 1985- 8.05/8.08w, 1986- 8.08/8.12w, 1987- 8.16/8.28w, 1988- 8.04/8.30w. pbs 100m: 10.4 '85, 400m: 46.9, TJ: 16.16 '86.
Unable to compete in 1988 Olympics through injury.

Stephen MONEGHETTI b.26 Sep 1962 Ballarat 1.76m 60kg. Ballarat YCW Harriers (Vic). Teacher.
At Mar: OG: '88- 5; WCh: '87- 4; CG: '86- 3 (5 at 10000m). World CC: '87- 11. Won World Students CC 1986. Australian 10000m champion 1988.
Progression at 10000m/Mar: 1982- 30:41.7, 1983- 29:00.0, 1984- 28:56.50, 1985- 28:49.37, 1986- 28:20.95/2:11:18, 1987- 28:07.37/2:12:49, 1988- 28:18.98/2:11:49. pbs: 3000m: 8:01.53 '86, 5000m: 13:31.55 '88.
His only marathons have been the three major championships above.

Miles MURPHY b.19 May 1967 Blacktown 1.85m 75kg. Eastern Suburbs (NSW). Student.
At 400m/R- 4x400m relay: OG: '88- qf; CG: '86- sf/

2R; WJ: '86- 1. Australian champion 1985, 1987–8.
Progression at 400m: 1982- 49.73, 1983- 47.13, 1984- 46.5, 1985- 46.20, 1986- 45.64, 1987- 45.42, 1988- 44.71. pb 200m: 20.59 '88.

Miles Murphy (Mark Shearman)

Nicole Boegman (George Herringshaw/ASP)

Women

Nicole BOEGMAN b.5 Mar 1967 Sydney 1.74m 62kg. Revesby Workers, NSW and Hounslow, UK. Receptionist/typist.
At LJ: OG: '88- 5; WCh: '87- 8. Australian champion 1987–8. Won WAAA 1988.
Australian long jump record 1988.
Progression at LJ: 1981- 5.72w, 1982- 6.45, 1983- 6.55/6.71w, 1984- 6.43, 1985- 6.50/6.67w, 1986- 6.55/6.63w, 1987- 6.67, 1988- 6.87. pbs: 100m: 11.86 '88. 200m: 24.56 '82, 100mh: 15.15 '81.
Engaged to Gary Staines, UK 5000m Olympian.

Jane FLEMMING b.14 Apr 1965 Melbourne 1.68m 56kg. Knox-Sherbrooke. Student at Australian Institute of Sport.
At Hep: OG: '88- 7; WCh: '87- 10, CG: '86- 2 (6 at 100mh). Australian champion 1985–8 (and 100m & 100mh 1988).
Three Australian heptathlon records 1987–8.
Progression at Hep: 1982- 5232, 1983- 5472*, 1985- 5901, 1986- 6278w, 1987- 6390, 1988- 6492. pbs: 100m: 11.50 '88, 200m: 23.59 '88, 23.37w '88; 800m: 2:11.75 '88, 100mh: 13.17 '88, 13.32w '87; HJ: 1.87 '87, LJ: 6.46 '87, SP: 14.01 '88, JT: 44.46 '88.

Debbie FLINTOFF-KING b.20 Apr 1960 Melbourne 1.71m 57kg. Glenhuntly. Sports promotion officer.
At 400mh/R- 4x100m relay: OG: '84- 6, '88- 1; WCh: '83- sf, '87- 2; CG: '82- 1/2R, '86- 1/3R (1 at 400m); WCp: '85- 3. Australian champion 400m 1985–6, 400mh 1982–6, 1988. GP 3rd 1985, 1st 1987.
Ten Australian, including eight Commonwealth, 400mh records 1982–8; two Australian 400m records 1985–6.
Progression at 400mh: 1980- 59.34, 1981- 57.94, 1982- 55.89, 1983- 56.22, 1984- 56.02, 1985- 54.80, 1986- 53.76, 1987- 53.95, 1988- 53.17. pbs: 100m: 11.5 '86, 200m: 23.71 '86, 400m: 50.78 '86, 800m: 2:04.0 '88, 100mh: 14.2w '79, HJ: 1.69 '79.
Married her coach Phil King in 1986.

Maree HOLLAND b.25 Jul 1963 Parramatta 1.72m 55kg. Former married name Chapman. Secretary.
At 400m: OG: '88- 8; CG: '86- 6 (5 200m, 3 4x400mR). At 200m: WCp: '85- 6. Australian champion 200m 1985, 400m 1984, 1988. Won WAAA 1985.
Australian record 1988.
Progression at 400m: 1979- 55.0, 1980- 53.74, 1981- 55.84, 1984- 52.99, 1985- 51.51, 1986- 51.66, 1988- 50.24. pbs: 100m: 11.69/11.48w '88, 11.4 '85; 200m: 22.83 '88.

Lisa MARTIN b.12 May 1960 Gawler, SA 1.66m 47kg. née O'Dea, was married to Kenny Martin (US steeplechaser/marathoner). Nike TC, USA; was at University of Oregon.
At Mar: OG: '84- 7, '88- 2; WCh: '87- dnf; CG: '86- 1. TAC champion 1985. At 10km: WCp: '85- dnf.
Commonwealth marathon bests 1986 and 1988, four Australian records at marathon and 10000m 1983–6. World 10 miles road best 52:23 '87.
Progression at Mar: 1983- 2:32:22, 1984- 2:27:40, 1985- 2:29:48, 1986- 2:26:07, 1987- 2:30:59, 1988- 2:23:51. pbs: 1500m: 4:21.2 '83, 3000m: 9:09.67 '85, 5000m: 15:34.7 '85, 10000m: 32:17.86 '85, 400mh: 60.5 '79.
Started as a hurdler, switching to distance running in 1981. Has won six out of 13 marathons to Olympic silver medal 1988. Won at Osaka 1988, when she ran the world's fastest for a loop course; 2nd New York 1985–6. Ran Commonwealth half marathon best of 1:09:45 to win Great North Run 1986.

Kerry SAXBY b.2 Jun 1961 Ballina, NSW. Clerk/typist. Australian Institute of Sport.
At 10kmW: WCh: '87- 2; WCp: '85- 10, '87- 4. Australian champion 5kmW, 10kmW 1986–8, 3kmW 1987, 20kmW 1986–7.
World road walking bests: four at 5km 1987, best 20:34; two at 10km 1987–8, 15km: 1:09:33 '85, 20km: 1:33:30 '85, 1:32:52 '87, 1:29:40 '88; world track bests: 1500mW: 6:03.3 '85, 3km: 12:20.07 '87 (mixed), 12:14.48 '88; 5km: 21:16.4 '87 (mx), 20:55.76 & 20:45.32 '88; 10km 42:14.2 '88 (mx).
Commonwealth 10kmW track best: 45:08.13 '86.
Progression at 10kmW: 1983- 50:52, 1984- 48:22, 1985- 46:13, 1986- 44:53, 1987- 42:52, 1988- 41:30/42:14.2t.

Christine STANTON b.12 Dec 1959 Cottesloe, WA 1.83m 67kg. née Annison. Karrinyup (WA). TV journalist.
At HJ: OG: '80- 6=, '84- 11=, '88- 7; WCh: '83 & '87- dnq; CG: '82- 2, '86- 1; WCp: '77- 6, '81- 4, '85- 5. Australian champion HJ 1976–7, 1980–1, 1983, 1985–7; LJ 1981.
Four Australian high jump records 1984–5, Commonwealth heptathlon record 1981.
Progression at HJ: 1974- 1.69, 1975- 1.79, 1976- 1.83, 1977- 1.88, 1978- 1.88, 1980- 1.91, 1981- 1.92, 1982- 1.88, 1983- 1.92, 1984- 1.95, 1985- 1.96, 1986- 1.94, 1987- 1.88, 1988- 1.93. pbs: 200m: 24.6 '85, 100mh: 13.82 '85, 13.7 '84; LJ: 6.40/6.45w '81, SP: 13.25 '85, Hep: 5938 '85.

AUSTRIA

Governing body: Osterreichischer Leichtathletik Verband, A - 1040 Vienna, Prinz Eugenstrasse 12. Founded 1900.
National Championships first held in 1911 (men), 1918 (women)
1988 Champions: MEN
100m/200m: Andreas Berger 10.55/21.33, 400m: Alfred Hugl 47.31, 800m/1500m: Karl Blaha 1:50.19/3:49.53, 5000m: Dietmar Millonig 14:12.49, 10000m: Gerhard Hartmann 28:58.31, Mar: Horst Röthel 2:26:09, 3000mSt: Wolfgang Fritz 8:53.54, 110mh: Thomas Weimann 14.09, 400mh: Klaus Ehrle 50.62, HJ: Markus Einberger 2.20, PV: Gerald Kager 5.10, LJ: Andreas Steiner 7.83, TJ: Alfred Stummer 16.46, SP/DT: Erwin Weitzl 16.70/63.22, HT: Johann Lindner 72.80, JT/Dec: Georg Werthner 68.32/7916,, 20kmW/50kmW: Stefan Wögerbauer 1:36:13/4:28.18.
WOMEN
100m/100mh: Sabine Seitl 12.28/13.70, 200m/400m/400mh: Gerda Haas 24.45/53.09/59.19, 800m: Ernestine Waldhör 2:07.42, 1500m: Erika Zenz 4:39.24, 3000m/10000m: Anni Müller 9:59.48/35:18.39, Mar: Carina Quintero 2:55:31, HJ: Sigrid Kirchmann 1.77, LJ: Ulrike Kleindl 6.37, SP: Veronika Längle 15.59, DT: Ursula Weber 54.28, JT: Lisbeth Mischkounig 52.64, Hep: Beate Krawcewicz 5367.

BELGIUM

Governing bodies: Ligue Royale Belge d'Athlétisme, Rue St.Laurent 14–26 (Bte 6), 1000 Bruxlles (KBAB). Vlaamse Atletiek Liga (VAL); Ligue Belge Francophone d'Athlétisme (LBFA). Original governing body founded 1889.
National Championships first held in 1889 (men), 1921 (women)
1988 Champions: MEN
100m/200m: Patrick Stevens 10.44/20.72, 400m: Jeroen Fischer 46.24, 800m: Marniz Mabbe 1:48.47, 1500m: Vincent Rousseau 3:40.84, 5000m: Jean-Pierre N'Dayisenga 13:56.55, 10000m: Jean-Pierre Paumen 28:53.58, Mar: Dirk Vanderherten 2:13:33, 3000mSt: William van Dijck 8:27.19, 110mh: Hubert Grossard 14.07, 400mh: Alain Cuypers 50.03, HJ: Dimitri Maenhout 2.08, PV: Marc Maes 5.00, LJ: Eric Van de Vijver 7.78, TJ: Didier Falise 16.25, SP: Noel Legros 16.19, DT: Jordy Beernaert 50.06, HT: Marnix Verhegghe 66.06, JT: Jean-Paul Schlatter 70.92, Dec: Roland Marloye 7498, 20kmW/50kmW: Godfried de Jonckheere 1:26:24/3:51:55.
WOMEN
100m/200m: Ingrid Verbruggen 11.51/23.24, 400m: Sonja Van Renterghem 53.54, 800m: Regine Berg 2:09.10, 1500m/3000m: Corine Debaets 4:15.83/9:04.46, 10000m: Marleen Renders 33:00.6, Mar: Magda Ilands 2:35:36, 100mh: Sylvia Dethier 13.31, 400mh: Ann Maenhout 57.72, HJ: Natalja Jonckheere 1.87, LJ: Jacqueline Hautenauve 6.05, SP/

DT: Marie-Paule Geldhof 15.83/54.90, JT: Martine Florent 52.66, Hep: Jacqueline Hautenauve 5928, 10kmW: Christa Ceulemans 53:27.3.

Vincent ROUSSEAU b.29 Jul 1962 Mons 1.76m 60kg. MOHA. Soldier.
At 5000m: OG: '88- sf; WCh: '87- 5; ECh: '86- 13. 2nd GP 1986. At 10000m: WCp: '85- 5. Belgian champion 5000m 1984, 1500m 1985–6, 1988.
Progression at 5000m: 1980- 14:30.5, 1981- 14:08.32, 1982- 13:40.21, 1983- 13:33.2, 1984- 13:24.81, 1985- 13:18.94, 1986- 13:15.01, 1987- 13:28.56, 1988- 13:19.16. pbs: 1500m: 3:36.38 '85, 1M: 3:54.69 '85, 2000m: 4:58.97 '87, 3000m: 7:42.15 '86, 10000m: 28:40.63 '85.
An inconsistent runner, who had many wins at cross-country and on the track over the past couple of years, but also bad losses in several important races.

Vincent Rousseau (George Herringshaw/ASP)

William VAN DIJCK b.24 Jan 1961 Leuven 1.85m 65kg. Looise AV. Teacher.
At 3km St: OG: '84- sf, '88- 5; WCh: '83- sf, '87- 3; ECh: '86- 5. Belgian champion 1983, 1985–8. Won GP 1986.
Eight Belgian 3kmSt records 1983–6.
Progression at 3kmSt: 1981- 8:44.92, 1982- 8:36.40, 1983- 8:21.73, 1984- 8:18.75, 1985- 8:13.77, 1986- 8:10.01, 1987- 8:12.18, 1988- 8:13.99. pbs: 800m: 1:51.8 '83, 1500m: 3:41.2 '85, 1M: 3:57.59 '85, 3000m: 7:45.40 '88, 5000m: 13:23.40 '85, 10000m: 30:25.4 '80, 2000mSt: 5:22.24 '87.

BERMUDA

Governing body: Bermuda Track and Field Association, P.O.Box DV 397, Devonshire.

Clarence 'Nick' SAUNDERS b.14 Sep 1963 1.90m 72kg. Was at Boston University, USA.
At HJ: OG: '84- dnq, '88- 5; WCh: '83- dnq, '87- 5; CG: '82- 3; PAm: '87- 5; CAmG: '82- 3.
Progression at HJ: 1980- 2.05, 1981- 2.22, 1982- 2.19, 1983- 2.30i/2.27, 1984- 2.28, 1985- 2.26, 1986- 2.26, 1987- 2.32, 1988- 2.34.
Has a fine record of setting personal bests at major meetings as at 1982 Commonwealth and his fifth places in Rome and Seoul.

BRAZIL

Governing body: Confederaçao Brasileira de Atletismo (CBAT), Avenida Graça Aranha, 81-Conj 808/811, 20030 Rio de Janeiro. Founded 1914.
National Championships are held bienially (not in 1988).

José Luiz BARBOSA b.27 May 1961 Tres Lagoas 1.84m 68kg. Student in the USA.
At 800m: OG: '84- sf, '88- 6 (h 1500m); WCh: '83- sf, '87- 3; WI: '87- 1; PAm: '83- 2 (2 4x400mR), '87- 2; SACh: '83- 1. AAA champion 1985.
Progression at 800m: 1979- 1:53.0, 1980- 1:50.0, 1981- 1:48.3, 1982- 1:47.4, 1983- 1:44.3, 1984- 1:44.98, 1985- 1:44.79, 1986- 1:44.10, 1987- 1:43.76, 1988- 1:43.20. pbs: 400m: 45.9 '83, 1000m: 2:17.36 '85, 1500m: 3:38.84 '88.
A very consistent 800m runner, he has 20 sub-1:45 times.

Robson CAETANO da SILVA b.4 Sep 1964 Rio de Janeiro 1.87m 74kg.
At 200m (100m, R- 4x100m relay): OG: '84- sf, '88- 3 (5); WCh: '83- (qf), '87- 4 (qf); WI: '87- 3; WCp: '85- 1/2R; PAm: '83- sf/3R, '87- 2; SACh: '85- 1 (2/1R), '87- 1 (1/1R). 3rd GP 1987. Won PAm-J 100m 1982, SA-J LJ 1981, 100m & 200m 1983.
South American records: two at 100m, four at 200m 1985–8.
Progression at 100m/200m: 1982- 10.34w/10.54/10.2/21.46, 1983- 10.40/10.3/20.95, 1984- 10.50/10.3/20.71, 1985- 10.22/10.1/20.44, 1986- 10.02/0.28, 1987- 10.20/10.0/20.20, 1988- 10.00/20.04. pbs: 400m: 46.5 '85, LJ: 7.40 '81.

Joaquim CRUZ b.12 Mar 1963 Taguatinga, Brasilia 1.87m 73kg. Team Nike. Student at Oregon University.
At 800m (1500m): OG: '84- 1 (sf), '88- 2 (sf); WCh: '83- 3; WCp: '81- 6. At 1500m: PAm: '87- 1. Won PAm-J 800m & 1500m 1980; NCAA 800m 1983–4, 1500m 1984.

South American records: 6 800m 1981–4, 3 1000m 1983–4, 6 1500m 1983–8, 1 1M 1984. World junior 800m record 1981.
Progression at 800m: 1978- 1:51.4, 1979- 1:49.8, 1980- 1:47.85, 1981- 1:44.3, 1982- 1:46.95, 1983- 1:44.04, 1984- 1:41.77, 1985- 1:42.49, 1987- 1:45.74, 1988- 1:43.90. pbs: 400m: 47.17 '80, 1000m: 2:14.09 '84, 1500m: 3:34.63 '88, 1M: 3:53.00 '84.
Has six of the twelve sub 1:43 800m times ever run. Missed 1986 season due to Achilles tendinitis and had surgery; although he came back in 1987, also had to miss World Championships.

BULGARIA

Governing body: Bulgarian Athletics Federation, 18 Tolboukhin Bd, Sofia. Founded 1924
National Championships first held in 1926 (men), 1938 (women)
1988 Champions: MEN
100m: Valentin Atanassov 10.22, 200m: Bogomil Karadimov 21.53, 400m: Dimitar Rangelov 46.40, 800m/1500m: Miroslaw Chochkov 1:52.52/3:50.34, 5000m/10000m: Evgeni Ignatov 13:53.64/28:18.20, Mar: Stanimir Nenov 2:22:27, 3000mSt: Panayot Kashanov 8:46.31, 110mh: Plamen Krastev 13.99, 400mh: Toma Tomov 49.30, HJ: Georgi Dakov 2.25, PV: Atanas Tarev 5.60, LJ: Vladimir Amidjinov 7.91, TJ: Khristo Markov 17.77, SP: Georgi Todorov 21.01, DT: Georgi Georgiev 65.18, HT: Ivan Tanev 82.08, JT: Emil Tzvetanov 79.90, Dec: Borislav Kolov 7542, 10kmW/20kmW: Ljubomir Ivanov 39:49.56/1:22.38, 50kmW: Mario Marinov 4:19:32.
WOMEN
100m: Anelia Nuneva 10.87, 200m: Nadezhda Georgieva 22.57, 400m: Rositsa Stamenova 51.45, 800m: Nikolina Shtereva 2:04.15, 1500m/3000m/10000m: Radka Naplatanova 4:17.37/9:00.88/33:10.82, Mar: Rumiana Ruseva 2:59:04, 100mh: Svetla Dimitrova 13.49, 400mh: Bonka Peneva 58.25, HJ: Stefka Kostadinova 2.07, LJ: Tsetza Kancheva 6.60, SP: Verzhinia Vesselinova 19.23 (guest Svetla Mitkova 20.58), DT: Tsvetanka Khristova 69.46, JT: Antoaneta Selenska 62.38, Hep: Emilia Dimitrova 5990, 10kmW: Atanasska Dzivkova 49:32.41.

Evgeniy IGNATOV b.25 Jun 1959 Nikolaevo, Ruse 1.83m 65kg. Lokomotiv, Ruse. Financier.
At 5000m: OG: '88- 8 (12 10000m); WCh: '87- 6; ECh: '82- 4, '86- 4. At 3000m: EI: '81- 2. Balkan champion 1985. Bulgarian champion at 1500m 1986–7, 5000m 1985–8, 10000m 1987–8.
Bulgarian records 1980–6: 4 at 5000m, 3 2000m & 3000m, 2 10000m, 1 1500m.
Progression at 5000m: 1977- 15:08.5, 1978- 14:18.4, 1979- 13:58.9, 1980- 13:48.4, 1981- 13:30.82, 1982- 13:27.78, 1983- 14:03.9, 1984- 13:26.35, 1985- 13:30.09, 1986- 13:13.15, 1987- 13:24.42, 1988- 13:24.76. pbs: 800m: 1:51.6 '80, 1500m: 3:39.53 '82, 2000m: 4:59.02 '85, 3000m: 7:46.34 '87, 10000m: 27:56.26 '88.
Has placed consistently highly in major championships.

Khristo MARKOV b.27 Jan 1965 Dimitrovgrad 1.84m 78kg. CSKA Septemvrisko Zname. Sports student.
At TJ: OG: '88- 1; WCh: '83- dnq, '87- 1; WI: '85- 1, '87- 4; ECh: '86- 1; EJ: '83–1; EI: '85- 1, '87- 2. Balkan champion 1985, Bulgarian 1984–8. 2nd GP 1986.
World Junior record 1984 and five European Junior records in 1983–4. Ten Bulgarian TJ records 1983–7, the last four also European records. Equalled European indoor LJ best 1985.
Progression at TJ: 1982- 15.72, 1983- 16.88, 1984- 17.42, 1985- 17.77, 1986- 17.80, 1987- 17.92, 1988- 17.77. pb LJ: 8.23i '85, 8.16w/8.04 '86.
Only athlete ever to be champion at all six of: European Juniors, European and World Championships indoors and out, and Olympics. The latter, in Seoul, was the first ever by a Bulgarian man in athletics.

Plamen MINEV b.28 Apr 1965 Sofia 1.92m 110kg. CSKA Septemvrisko Zname. Sports student.
At HT: OG: dnq 14; WCh: '87- 8.
Bulgarian hammer record 1988. Balkan champion 1985, Bulgarian 1985.
Progression at HT: 1982- 58.22, 1983- 65.40, 1984- 73.08, 1985- 78.46, 1986- 70.06, 1987- 79.58, 1988- 81.70.

Nikolay NIKOLOV b.15 Oct 1964 Beloslav 1.82m 82kg. Akademik Sofia. Student.
At PV: WCh: '87- 5=; ECh: '86- 9=; EI: '88- 2; EJ: '83- 5. Bulgarian champion 1987.
Progression at PV: 1980- 4.30, 1981- 4.60, 1982- 5.10, 1983- 5.00, 1984- 5.20, 1985- 5.50, 1986- 5.65, 1987- 5.70, 1988- 5.70i.

Ivan TANEV b.1 May 1957 1.90m 112kg. Akademik Sofia. Student.
At HT: OG: '88- 8; WCh: '87- 10; ECh: '86- dnq. Balkan champion 1988, Bulgarian 1984, 1988.
Bulgarian hammer record 1988.
Progression at HT: 1975- 58.08, 1976- 60.52, 1977- 64.08, 1978- 65.86, 1979- 69.28, 1980- 62.90, 1981- 64.44, 1982- 69.72, 1983- 72.14, 1984- 76.50, 1985- 77.40, 1986- 79.70, 1987- 79.32, 1988- 82.08.

Atanas TAREV b.31 Jan 1958 Bolyarzi, Plovdiv 1.80m 78kg. Trakia, Plovdiv. Physical education student.
At PV: OG: '80 & '88- dnq; WCh: '83- 3, '87- 8;

WI: '87- 6; ECh: '82- 3, '86- 4; EJ: '77- 3; EI: '85- 3, '86- 1, '88- 3. Balkan champion 1979–80, 1985, 1988; Bulgarian 1976–86.
18 Bulgarian pole vault records from 5.07m in 1977.
Progression at PV: 1974- 4.00, 1975- 4.50, 1976- 4.90, 1977- 5.15, 1978- 5.22, 1979- 5.40, 1980- 5.44, 1981- 5.51, 1982- 5.70, 1983- 5.71, 1984- 5.72, 1985- 5.75, 1986- 5.80, 1987- 5.70i/5.60, 1988- 5.71.

Toma TOMOV b.21 May 1958 Inzovo, Yambol 1.79m 68kg. Levski Spartak. Graduate.
At 400mh: OG: '88- sf; WCh: '83- sf, '87- sf; ECh: '82- 8, '86- 4. Balkan champion 1984–7, Bulgarian 1982–8.
Bulgarian records at 400mh (7) and 400m (1) 1982–6.
Progression at 400mh: 1981- 51.81, 1982- 49.74, 1983- 49.24, 1984- 48.99, 1985- 49.49, 1986- 48.48, 1987- 48.59, 1988- 48.90. pb 400m: 45.86 '84, 800m: 1:50.68i '87.

Women

Lyudmila ANDONOVA b.6 May 1960 Novocherkassk, USSR 1.77m 58kg. née Zhecheva. Married to Atanas Andonov (Bulgarian decathlon record 8199 '81). CSKA Septemvrisko Zname.
At HJ: OG: '88- 5=; WCh: '87- 12; ECh: '82- 6=; WSG: '81- 2; ECp: '81- 2. Balkan champion 1981, 1984; Bulgarian 1981–2, 1984.
World high jump record 1984. Seven Bulgarian records 1981–4.
Progression at HJ: 1977- 1.70, 1978- 1.73, 1979- 1.70, 1980- 1.84, 1981- 1.95, 1982- 1.94, 1983- 1.85i, 1984- 2.07, 1985- 1.96, 1987- 1.95, 1988- 1.95.
Two children. Has a Bulgarian father and Soviet mother. Soared 30cm above her own height to a new world record in 1984. Suspended following a positive drug test, a pain-killer she had taken contained an amphetamine, in 1985.

Svetla DIMITROVA b.27 Jan 1970 1.70m 57kg.
At Hep: OG: '88- 12; WJ: '86- 1, '88- 1.
Progression at Hep: 1986- 6041, 1988- 6289. pbs: 200m: 23.31 '88, 800m: 2:12.29 '86, 100mh: 13.24 '88, HJ: 1.88 '86, LJ: 6.45 '88, 6.48w '86, SP: 13.83 '88, JT: 39.88 '88.

Yordanka DONKOVA b.28 Sep 1961 Gozni Bogorov, Sofia 1.77m 67kg. Levski Spartak, Sofia. PE student.
At 100mh: OG: '80- sf, '88- 1; WCh: '87- 4; ECh: '82- 2, '86- 1/2R; EJ: '79- 8; ECp: '81- 5, '87- 2/2R. At Hep: ECp: '83- 7. At 60mh: WI: '87- 2; EI: '82- 3, '84- 3, '87- 2. Balkan champion 1980, 1984, 1986; Bulgarian 1984, 1986. Won GP 100mh and overall 1986, 2nd 1988.
Eleven Bulgarian 100mh records 1982–8, including five world records: four 1986, one 1988. WIB 60mh 7.74 '86.
Progression at 100mh: 1977- 14.84, 1978- 13.91, 1979- 13.57, 1980- 13.24, 1981- 13.39/12.9, 1982- 12.44, 1983- 12.65, 1984- 12.50, 1985- 13.24, 1986- 12.26/12.0w, 1987- 12.33, 1988- 12.21. pbs: 100m: 11.27 '82, 200m: 22.95 '82, HJ: 1.78 '82, LJ: 6.39 '82, Hep: 6187 '83.
Displayed the finest ever sprint hurdling by a woman in 1986, with very sharp speed and technique, running ten sub-12.50 times. She ran a further four such times in 1987, and a record 12 in 1988 when she was unbeaten. She lost three fingers on her right hand in an accident on her fifth birthday.

Nadezhda GEORGIEVA b.2 Sep 1961 Gabrovo 1.58m 48kg. CSKA Septemvrisko Zname. Physical education student.
At 100m/200m/R- 4x100m relay: OG: '88- -/sf; WCh: '83- sf/sf/4R, '87- sf/8/4R; ECh 100m: '82- 7/4R, '86- h/2R; ECp: '87- 2 200m/2R. Bulgarian champion 100m 1983–4, 200m 1983–4, 1988; Balkan 100m 1988, 200m 1984 & 1988.
Bulgarian records at 100m and 200m in 1983.
Progression at 100m/200m: 1977- -/25.99, 1978- 12.20/25.02, 1979- 12.37/24.91, 1980- 11.97/24.21, 1981- 11.52/23.51/23.40w, 1982- 11.33/22.90, 1983- 11.09/22.42, 1984- 11.21/22.51, 1986- 11.27/23.21, 1987- 11.09/22.44, 1988- 11.11/11.08w/22.53. Married with one child.

Svetlana ISAEVA b.18 Mar 1967 Mikhaylovograd 1.78m 63kg. Spartak, Pleven. PE student.
At HJ: WCh: '87- 7; ECh: '86- 2; WSG: '87- 1; EJ: '83- 4=, '85- 3. 3rd GP 1987.
Progression at HJ: 1981- 1.80, 1982- 1.79, 1983- 1.87, 1984- 1.84, 1985- 1.93, 1986- 1.97, 1987- 2.00, 1988- 1.93.

Tsvetanka KHRISTOVA b.14 Mar 1962 Kazanluk 1.75m 85kg. Rozova Dolina, Kazanluk. Graduate.
At DT: OG: '88- 3; WCh: '83- 4, '87- 3; ECh: '82- 1, '86- 2; EJ: '79- 3; WSG: '85- 2, '87- 1; ECp: '85- 3, '87- 2. Balkan champion 1984, 1986. Bulgarian champion 1985–8. Won GP 1986, 3rd 1988.
Four Bulgarian discus records 1986–7.
Progression at DT: 1977- 46.90, 1978- 48.84, 1979- 54.76, 1980- 58.44, 1981- 64.38, 1982- 70.64, 1983- 66.88, 1984- 68.34, 1985- 68.68, 1986- 72.52, 1987- 73.22, 1988- 71.06.

Stefka KOSTADINOVA b.25 Mar 1965 Plovdiv 1.80m 60kg. Trakia Plovdiv. PE student.
At HJ: OG: '88- 2; WCh: '87- 1; WI: '85- 1, '87- 1; ECh: '86- 1; EJ: '81- 10; EI: '85- 1, '87- 1, '88- 1; WCp: '85- 1; ECp: '85- 1, '87- 1. Balkan and Bulgarian champion 1985–6, 1988. Won GP 1985, 1987 (3rd overall).

Three world records 1986–7. WIB: 2.04 & 2.05 '87, 2.06 '88.
Progression at HJ: 1977- 1.45, 1978- 1.66, 1979- 1.75, 1980- 1.84, 1981- 1.86, 1982- 1.90, 1983- 1.83i, 1984- 2.00, 1985- 2.06, 1986- 2.08, 1987- 2.09, 1988- 2.07.
Won 34 successive high jump competitions 1984–6, her one loss (to Heike Redetzky) in the latter year was then followed by 19 further wins 1986–7. Lost three times in 1987, but showed brilliant form to set world record in Rome. Won 20/24 in 1988. Has jumped 2 metres in 62 competitions, with 11 of the best 12 of all-time.

Svetla MITKOVA b.17 Jun 1964 Medovo 1.78m 96kg. Rozova Dolina, Kazanluk. PE student.
At SP/DT: OG: '88- 10/4; WCh: '83- -/10, '87- 9/5; ECh: '86- 12/5; EJ: '81: 3/2; ECp: SP '83- 5, '85- 5, '87- 4. Bulgarian champion shot 1984–7, discus 1983; Balkan shot 1988. 2nd GP DT 1986.
Progression at SP/DT: 1979- 13.80/44.30, 1980- 14.10/50.70, 1981- 17.16/59.84, 1982- 18.03/60.58, 1983- 18.83/66.80, 1984- 19.11/64.84, 1985- 18.87/54.34, 1986- 20.05/68.90, 1987- 20.91/69.72, 1988- 20.58/69.14.

Anelia NUNEVA b.30 Jun 1962 Byala, Ruse 1.69m 62kg. Levski Spartak, Sofia. PE student. Married name VECHERNIKOVA.
At 100m/R- 4x100m relay (200m): OG: '88- 8; WCh: '83- sf (6), '87- 6/4R; ECh: '82- 4 (6), '86- 2/2R; WCp: '85- 4; ECp: '83- 2 (4), '85- 3, '87- 2/2R; WSG: '85- 2/3R. At 60m: WI: '87- 3; EI: '84- 2, '87- 2. Balkan champion 100m 1984–6, 200m 1986. 2nd GP 100m 1987.
Bulgarian records 1982–8: six 100m, two 200m.
Progression at 100m/200m: 1978- 12.23/25.60, 1979- 12.10/25.90, 1980- 12.50, 1981- 11.34/11.31w/23.58, 1982- 11.14/22.93, 1983- 11.07/22.58, 1984- 11.10/22.67, 1985- 11.14/22.73, 1986- 11.04/10.9/22.58, 1987- 10.86/22.01, 1988- 10.85/22.88.
Ran seven sub-11.00 100m races in 1987 and five in 1988. She was heading for a medal in the Olympic final when she pulled a hamstring.

Ginka ZAGORCHEVA b.12 Apr 1958 Rakovski, Plovdiv 1.75m 67kg. Levski Spartak. PE student. Now BOYCHEVA.
At 100mh/R- 4x100m relay: OG: '88- h; WCh: '83- 3, '87- 1/4R; ECh: '82- 8, '86- 3/2R; WSG: '85- 1/3R; WCp: '85- 2/3R; ECp: '83- 3, '85- 1, '87- 2R. Balkan champion 1985, Bulgarian 1983, 1985. 3rd GP 1986. At 60mh: WI: '87- 3; EI: '85- 2, '87- 3.
World 100mh record 1987, Bulgarian record 1985.
Progression at 100mh: 1974- 14.4, 1975- 13.9, 1976- 14.01, 1977- 13.90, 1978- 13.39, 1979- 13.22, 1981- 13.74, 1982- 12.73, 1983- 12.49, 1984- 12.62, 1985- 12.42, 1986- 12.39/12.1w, 1987- 12.25, 1988- 12.48. pbs: 100m: 11.38 '83, 200m: 24.13 '85.
Married with one child. Injured in June 1988 and crashed out in Olympic heats.

BURUNDI

Dieudonné KWIZÉRA b.6 Jun 1967 1.84m 60kg. Tutsi tribe. University of Chicago.
At 800m: WCh: '87- sf (h 1500m); AfG: '87- 3 (3 4x400mR).
Progression at 800m: 1985- 1:49.2, 1986- 1:48.23, 1987- 1:45.06, 1988- 1:44.82. pbs: 400m: 46.49 '87, 1000m: 2:20.12 '87, 1500m: 3:38.13 '88 (all national records).
Unable to run at the Olympics as Burundi does not have a National Olympic Committee.

CANADA

Governing body: Canadian Track and Field Association, 1600 James Naismith Drive, Gloucester, Ontario K1B 5NA. Formed as the Canadian AAU in 1884.
National Championship first held in 1884 (men), 1925 (women).
1988 champions: MEN
100m: Ben Johnson 9.90w, 200m: Cyprian Enweani 20.70, 400m: Carl Folkes 46.47, 800m: Simon Hoogewerf 1:46.99, 1500m: Dave Campbell 3:42.64, 5000m: Paul Williams 14:00.83, 10000m: Art Boileau 29:07.77, Mar: Gordon Christie 2:18:40, 3000mSt: Graeme Fell 8:38.20, 110mh: Mark McKoy 13.25, 400mh: John Graham 50.41, HJ: Milt Ottey 2.25, PV: Paul Just 5.40, LJ: Glenroy Gilbert 8.10w, TJ: Edrick Floreal 16.50, SP: Rob Venier 18.41, DT: Ray Lazdins 58.46, HT: Darren McFee 62.28, JT: Mike Mahovlich 76.38, Dec: Richard Hesketh 7311w/7287, 20kmW: Guillaume Leblanc 1:29:39.19.
WOMEN
100m: Angella Issajenko 11.01, 200m: Jillian Richardson 23.28, 400m: Charmaine Crooks 51.33, 800m: Renée Bélanger 2:02.94, 1500m: Lynn Williams 4:05.54, 3000m: Alison Wiley 9:00.81, 10000m: Carole Rouillard 32:52.63, Mar: Jean Payette 2:54:27, 100mh: Karen Nelson 13.39, 400mh: Rosey Edeh 56.26, HJ: Linda McCurdy-Cameron 1.84, LJ: Tracy Smith 6.64w, TJ: Lavern Clark 12.89, SP: Shannon Kekula 15.28, DT: Gale Dolegiewicz 55.04, HT: Theresa Brick 51.70, JT: Isabelle Surprenant 52.72, Hep: Donna Smellie 5637, 10kmW: Ann Peel 49:52.07t/Alison Baker 49:46R.

Graeme FELL b.19 Mar 1959 Romford, England 1.84m 73kg. Richmond Kajaks. UK international,

married Canadian runner Debbie Campbell (800m: 2:02.8 '79) in 1982, Canadian citizenship 1986–7. Nottingham University graduate.
At 3kmSt: OG: '88- 11; WCh: '83- 6, '87- 5; ECh: '82- 10; CG: '82- 2, '86- 1; WCp: '85- 3. Canadian champion 1985–8. 3rd GP 1986.
Records at 3kmSt: UK 1983, Canadian (twice) 1985.
Progression at 3kmSt: 1975- 9:57.2, 1976- 9:32.4, 1977- 8:56.6, 1978- 8:48.43, 1979- 8:36.94, 1980- 8:49.92, 1981- 8:31.80, 1982- 8:19.72, 1983- 8:15.16, 1984- 8:17.71, 1985- 8:12.58, 1986- 8:14.57, 1987- 8:16.46, 1988- 8:19.99. pbs: 1500m: 3:39.3 '85, 1M: 3:57.5 '83, 2000m: 5:07.54 '82, 3000m: 7:42.26 '83, 2M: 8:22.7i '82, 5000m: 13:33.57 '88.

Guillaume LEBLANC b.14 Apr 1962 Sept-Iles 1.84m 75kg. Club Athlétique Imaculée Conception.
At 20kmW: OG: '84- 4 (dnf 50kmW), '88- 10; WCh: '83- 8; WSG: '83- 1, '85- 3; LT: '83- 11, '85- 5; Won America's Cup 1986. CG 30kmW: '82- 3, '86- 2. On 1980 Olympic team. Canadian champion 20kmW 1982, 1985–6, 1988; 50kmW 1983.
Commonwealth 20kmW track record 1:23:17 '86.
Progression at 20kmW: 1979- 1:33:35, 1981- 1:26:32, 1982- 1:24:28, 1983- 1:22.04, 1984- 1:24:29, 1985- 1:23:51, 1986- 1:21:13, 1988- 1:21:29. pbs: 5kmWt: 18:53.25i '88, 10kmWt: 40:32.4 '82, 30kmW: 2:08:38 '86, 50kmW: 3:58:33 '83.
Arthroscopic surgery on right knee in Feb 1987.

Mark McKOY b.10 Dec 1961 Georgetown, Guyana 1.81m 70kg. Mazda Optimists. PE graduate from Louisiana State University, USA.
At 110mh/R- 4x100m relay: OG: '84- 4, '88- 7; WCh: '83- 4, '87- 7; CG: '82- 1/2R, '86- 1/1R; WSG: '83- 3; PAm: '83- 6. Won GP 1985, 3rd 1987. At 60mh: WI: '87- fell. Member 1980 Olympic team. Canadian champion 1981–8.
Ten Canadian, including six Commonwealth 110mh records 1982–8. WIB: 50mh: 6.25 '86, 60mh: 7.47 '86. Commonwealth indoor record 50yh: 5.95 '85.
Progression at 110mh: 1979- 14.19, 1980- 14.02, 1981- 13.97, 1982- 13.37, 1983- 13.53/13.51w, 1984- 13.27/13.16w, 1985- 13.27, 1986- 13.35/ 13.31w, 1987- 13.23, 1988- 13.17. pbs: 100m: 10.21 '86, 200m: 20.96 '85, 400mh: 53.75 '79.
Lived in England 1962–74. Suspended for two years from representing Canadian team after leaving Seoul prior to the sprint relay following the Johnson disqualification.

Atlee MAHORN b.27 Oct 1965 Clarendon, Jamaica 1.87m 77kg. Mazda Optimists. Political science student at University of California, Berkeley, USA.
At 200m/R- 4x100m relay: OG: '84- sf, '88- 5; WCh: '83- qf, '87- 8; CG: '86- 1/1R (3 4x400mR); WSG: '85- 2/2R. Canadian champion 1986.
Canadian records: 200m (2) 1988, 400m 1986.
Progression at 200m: 1982- 21.63/21.3, 1983- 20.65, 1984- 20.69, 1985- 20.65, 1986- 20.34/ 20.31w, 1987- 20.62, 1988- 20.20. pbs: 100m: 10.26 '86, 10.19w '85; 400m: 45.62 '86.

Milt OTTEY b.29 Dec 1959 May Pen, Jamaica 1.78m 66kg. Transamerica Life TC. Moved to Canada at age of ten. Was at University of Texas at El Paso.
At HJ: OG: '84- 6, '88- dnq 17; WCh: '83- 9; WI: '87- 7; CG: '82- 1, '86- 1; PAm: '79- 3; WCp: '79- 5, '81- 5. Won TAC and NCAA 1982. Member 1980 Olympic team. Canadian champion 1981–4, 1986–8.
Three Commonwealth high jump records 1982–6.
Progression at HJ: 1977- 1.95, 1978- 2.11, 1979- 2.19, 1980- 2.20i, 1981- 2.24, 1982- 2.32, 1983- 2.30, 1984- 2.29, 1985- 2.31, 1986- 2.33, 1987- 2.28i/2.25, 1988- 2.31i/2.28.

Michael SMITH b.14 Sep 1967 Kenora, Ontario 1.95m 98kg. Student at University of Toronto.
At Dec: OG: '88- 14; WCh: '87- dnf; CG: '86- 7; WJ: '86- 2.
Progression at Dec: 1986- 7523, 1987- 8126, 1988- 8039. pbs: 100m: 10.93 '85, 400m: 47.63 '87, 1500m: 4:20.04 '87, 110mh: 14.47 '88, HJ: 2.08 '87, PV: 4.40 '87, LJ: 7.70 '87, SP: 15.30i '87, DT: 43.88 '88, JT: 66.54 '88.

Dave STEEN b.14 Nov 1959 New Westminster, BC 1.85m 80kg. University of Toronto TC. Student at the Univerity of Toronto.
At Dec: OG: '84- 8, '88- 3; WCh: '87- dnf; CG: '82- 2, '86- 2 (4 PV); WSG: '81- 5, '83- 1; PAm: '83- 1. Member 1980 Olympic team. Canadian champion Dec 1982, 1986; PV 1987; LJ 1977.
Eight Canadian records at decathlon 1981–8.
Progression at Dec: 1977- 6829, 1978- 6860*, 1979- 7543, 1980- 7654, 1981- 7923, 1982- 8003, 1983- 8213, 1984- 8248, 1985- 8316w, 1986- 8254w, 1987- 8037, 1988- 8415. pbs: 100m: 10.91 '86, 10.8 '85, 10.7w '84; 400m: 47.58 '85, 1500m: 4:14.10 '83, 110mh: 14.60 '88; HJ: 2.15i '83, PV: 5.30 '85, LJ: 7.78 '88, SP: 14.36 '84, DT: 51.58 '83, JT: 67.20 '82, new- 65.36 '88.
Uncle Dave won Commonwealth shot title in 1966 and 1970, father Don was Canadian decathlon champion in 1956. Married to Andrea Page (400mh 57.19 '83).

Desai WILLIAMS b.12 Jun 1959 Basseterre, St.Kitts 1.75m 72kg. York U. Optimists. Was at York University, now store owner.
At 100m/200m/R- 4x100m relay: OG: '84- sf/sf/3R, '88- 6/-; WCh: '83- 8/sf, '87- qf/-/4R; CG: '78- 4R, '82- 8/8/2R, '86- 4/-/1R; PAm: '79- 8/6; WSG: '83- 2

100m/2R; WCp: '85- 2R. On 1980 Olympic team. Canadian champion at 100m 1979–81, 1983 and 200m 1977, 1979–83. 3rd GP 200m 1986.
Canadian records: three at 200m 1978–81 and one at 100m 1983; Commonwealth indoor 200m best 21.14 '82.
Progression at 100m, 200m: 1976- 10.7; 1977- 10.55/10.54w, 21.2; 1978- 10.31, 20.68; 1979- 10.43, 20.70; 1980- 10.26/10.12w, 20.71/20.35w; 1981- 10.32, 20.60; 1982- 10.30/10.17w, 20.54; 1983- 10.17, 20.29; 1984- 10.27/10.19w, 20.45/20.40w; 1985- 10.21, 20.46; 1986- 10.21, 20.70; 1987- 10.21, 20.44; 1988- 10.11/10.00w. pb 400m: 45.92 '84.

Women

Debbie BOWKER b.16 Dec 1958 Victoria, BC 1.63m 52kg. née Scott. Vikes, BC. Education student.
At 3000m (1500m): OG: '84- (10), '88- 15 (12); WCh: '87- 13 (11); CG: '78- 9, '82- 12 (sf), '86- 2 (2); WCp: '77- 6; WI: '85- 1; PAm: '87- (2). Canadian champion 1500m 1982–5, 1987; 3000m 1982.
Canadian records at 1M, 3000m, 5000m 1982; 2000m 1986.
Progression at 3000m: 1976- 9:41.8, 1977- 9:18.7, 1978- 9:18.3, 1979- 9:16.6, 1980- 9:03.9, 1981- 8:58.30, 1982- 8:48.85, 1984- 8:58.5, 1985- 8:49.80, 1986- 8:53.28, 1987- 8:46.88, 1988- 8:43.81. pbs: 800m: 2:03.1 '85, 1000m: 2:39.76 '84, 1500m: 4:05.63 '87, 1M: 4:29.67 '82, 2000m: 5:39.96 '86, 5000m: 15:48.99 '82.
Married to coach Ron Bowker.

Angella ISSAJENKO b.28 Sep 1958 Jamaica 1.65m 61kg. née Taylor. Mazda Optimists.
At 100m/200m/R- 4x100m relay: OG: '84- -/8/2R, '88- qf/-; WCh 100m: '83- 7, '87- 5; CG: '78- -/h, '82- 1/3/2R (1 4x400mR), '86- 3/1/2R; PAm: '79- 3/2; WCp: '79- 5/5, '81- 4/4; WSG: '83- 3/4/2R. At 60m: WI: '87- 2. Member 1980 Olympic team. Canadian champion 100m/200m 1979–84, 1986–7; 100m 1988.
Commonwealth 100m record 1982. Canadian records: 100m (5), 200m (7) 1979–87. WIB: 50y: 5.74 '88, 50m: 6.06 '87, 200m 23.15 '80, 300m 36.91 '80.
Progression at 100m, 200m: 1977- 12.4; 1978- 12.07, 23.87; 1979- 11.20, 22.80/22.74w; 1980- 11.23/11.03w, 22.61; 1981- 11.12, 22.55/22.46w; 1982- 11.00/10.92w, 22.25/22.19w; 1983- 11.22/11.17w, 22.81; 1984- 11.16/11.09w, 22.61/22.44w, 1986- 11.24/11.08w/11.0A, 22.80; 1987- 10.97/10.8w, 22.55; 1988- 11.01, 23.18/22.87w. pb 400m: 51.81 '81.
Gave birth to daughter, Sasha, September 1985.

Marita PAYNE-WIGGINS b.7 Oct 1960 Barbados 1.72m 57kg. Came to Canada as 9-year-old. Was at Florida State University.
At 400m/R- 4x400m relay: OG: '84- 4/2R (2 at 4x100mR), '88- sf; WCh: '83- 5, '87- sf/4R; CG: '82- sf (2 at 4x100mR), '86- 4/1R; PAm: '79- 7, '87- 7/2R; WCp: '79- 4, '81- 3R. WSG: '83- 2 at 200m, 4x100mR and 4x400mR. Won NCAA 1984. On 1980 Olympic team. Canadian champion 1981. Commonwealth 400m record 1983.
Progression at 400m: 1979- 53.01, 1981- 52.01, 1982- 51.99, 1983- 50.06, 1984- 49.91, 1986- 51.77, 1987- 51.75, 1988- 50.29. pbs: 100m: 11.43, 11.34w '83; 200m: 22.62 '83, 300m: 37.20 '86.
Coaches sprints at Rice University, Houston, Texas. Married Houston Rockets basketball player Mitchell Wiggins 7 Sep 1985.

Ann PEEL b.27 Feb 1961 Ottawa 1.68m 54kg. East Ottawa Lions. Articled with law firm.
At 10kmW: WCh: '87- 8; PAm: '87- 2; WSG: '87- 3; WCp: '85- 7, '87- 7. Won Pan Am Cup 1988. At 3kmW: WI: '85- 3, '87- 3; won PAm-J 1980.
Progression at 10kmW: 1981- 50:42, 1982- 48:04, 1983- 47:02, 1984- 47:11, 1985- 46:46, 1986- 45:26, 1987- 45:06, 1988- 46:33. track pbs: 1500mW: 6:02.14i '87, 3kmW: 12:38.97i '87, 5kmW: 22:01.09 '87, 10kmW: 46:12.79 '86.

Jillian RICHARDSON b.10 Mar 1965 Trinidad 1.72m 59kg. Calgary Spartans. Physical education student.

Jillian Richardson (George Herringshaw/ASP)

At 400m/R- 4x400m relay: OG: '84- 2R, '88- sf; WCh: '83- 4R, '87- 6/4R; CG: '82- 1R, '86- 2/1R; PAm: '83- 2R (3 4x100mR), '87- 2/2R; WSG: '83- 2R. 3rd GP 1988. Won PAm-J 1982, Canadian champion 400m 1987, 200m 1988.
Equalled Canadian record 1988.
Progression at 400m: 1980- 53.70, 1981- 52.95, 1982- 52.70, 1983- 51.91, 1984- 51.58, 1985- 53.19, 1986- 51.55, 1987- 50.35, 1988- 49.91. pbs: 100m: 11.60 '87, 200m: 23.08 '88.

Julie ROCHELEAU b.17 June 1964 St.Jerome, Québec. Psycholgy student at Concordia University.
At 100mh: OG: '88- 6 (qf 100m); CG: '86- 4.
Commonwealth 100mh record 1988.
Progression at 100mh: 1981- 14.32, 1982- 14.19, 1983- 13.93, 1984- 13.81, 1985- 13.8, 1986- 13.46/13.32w, 1987- 13.38, 1988- 12.78. pb 100m: 11.13 '88.
Won the Mobil Grand Prix series at sprint hurdles, and was third overall, in 1988 when she set seven Canadian indoor records.

Nancy TINARI b.13 Jun 1959 Toronto 1.55m 40kg. née Rooks. New Balance Optimists. Psycholgy student.
At 10000m: OG: '88- 13; WCh: '87- 16; CG: '86- 4; PAm: '87- 2. At 3000m: CG: '78- 5. World road 10km: '83- 4, 15km: '86- 8, '87- 2. Canadian champion 10000m 1987, CC 1978, 1982, 1984, 1986.
Two Canadian 10000m records 1983.
Progression at 10000m: 1983- 32:23.04, 1986- 32:30.71, 1987- 32:15.82, 1988- 32:14.05. pbs: 800m: 2:10.0 '78, 1500m: 4:17.0 '83, 3000m: 9:02.08 '86, Mar: 2:40:50 '83.
Won Bali road 10km race in April 1988 in 32:14.

Lynn WILLIAMS b.11 Jul 1960 Regina, Saskatoon 1.55m 49kg. Valley Royals. née Kanuka, married to Paul Williams (Canadian 10km record holder). Graduate of San Diego State University, USA.
At 3000m: OG: '84- 3, '88- 8 (5 1500m); WCh: '83- 10, '87- 9; WI: '87- 6; CG: '86- 1 (3 1500m); WSG: '83- 3. Canadian champion 3000m 1983–4, 1986–7; 1500m 1988. 3rd GP 1985.
Commonwealth 5000m record 1985. Canadian records: 3000m (4), 5000m (2), 1000m, 1500m, 1M, 2000m (1 each) 1983–5.
Progression at 1500m/3000m: 1979- 4:29.3/9:47.0, 1980- 4:23.9/9:21.1, 1981- 9:13.13, 1982- 4:17.28/9:13.1, 1983- 4:08.64/8:50.20, 1984- 4:06.09/8:42.14, 1985- 4:00.27/8:37.38, 1986- 4:07.71/8:52.91, 1987- 4:06.41/8:45.14, 1988- 4:00.86/8:37.30. pbs: 800m: 2:01.72 '88, 1000m: 2:39.23 '84, 1M: 4:27.61i '87, 4:28.03 '85, 2000m: 5:43.8 '88, 5000m: 15:07.71 '85.

CHILE

Governing body: Federacion Atlética de Chile, Calle Santo Toribio No 660 - Castilla 820, Santiago de Chile. Founded 1917.

Gert WEIL b.3 Jan 1960 Puerto Montt 1.97m 124kg. Administrator.
At SP: OG: '84- 10, '88- 6; WCh: '87- 10; PAm: '83- 2, '87- 1; WCp: '85- 5. SACh 1st 1979–81–83–85–87.
Nine S.American shot records 1984–6.
Progression at SP: 1978- 14.88, 1979- 16.42, 1980- 16.77, 1981- 17.48, 1982- 17.54, 1983- 18.29, 1984- 19.94, 1985- 20.47, 1986- 20.90, 1987- 20.68, 1988- 20.74. pb DT: 55.98 '87.

Gert Weil (George Herringshaw/ASP)

CHINA

Governing body: Athletic Association of the People's Republic of China, 9 Tiyuguan Road, Beijing.
National Championships first held in 1910 (men), 1959 (women).
1988 Champions MEN: 100m: Li Tao 10.65, 200m: Cai Jianming 21.26, 400m: Wang Jianming 47.85, 800m: Lou Shaolong 1:51.01, 1500m: Zhang Yuejin 3:47.26, 5000m: Wang Helin 14:15.15, 10000m: Zhang Gouwei 28:39.17, 3000mSt: Gao Shuhai 8:51.08, 110mh: Yu Zicheng 13.97, 400mh: Song Xinliang 50.99, HJ: Zhu Jianhua 2.21, PV: Qin Cheng 5.40, LJ: Pang Yan 7.91, TJ: Chen Yanping 17.01, SP: Ma Yongfen 18.07, DT: Zhang Jinglong

60.40, JT: Ji Zhanzheng 73.38, Dec: Wang Yan 7018.
WOMEN
100m: Tian Yumei 11.90, 200m: Xie Zhiling 23.42, 400m: Su Sumei 54.40, 800m: Mao Yuiie 2:07.69. 1500m: Liu Aicun 4:20.84, 3000m: Wang Yanling 9:06.24, 5000m: Wang Huabi 15:56.86, 10000m: Li Xiuxen 33:43.10, 100mh: Liu Huayin 13.06, 400mh: Chen Dongmei 57.50, HJ: Jin Ling 1.93, LJ: Xiong Qiying 6.74, SP: Huang Zhihong 20.61, DT: Hou Xuemei 68.62, JT: Zhang Li 62.10, Hep: Dong Yuping 6018.

WOMEN

GUAN PING b.1 Feb 1966 1.69m 50kg.
At 10kmW: WCh: '87- dq; AsG: '86- 1; WCp: '83- 6, '85- 2, '87- dq.
World 5000m and 10000m walk records 1986. World junior best for 10kmW road 1983.
Progression at 10kmW: 1983- 46:39, 1984- 47:40, 1985- 44:28, 1986- 44:44.2t, 1988- 44:38.9t. pb track 5kmW: 21:26.5 '86.

HOU XUEMEI b.17 Feb 1962 1.77m 85kg.
At DT: OG '88- 8; WCh: '87- dnq 14; AsG: '86- 1; WSG: '87- 3.
Two Asian discus records 1986–8.
Progression at DT: 1985- 56.70, 1986- 63.48, 1987- 66.12, 1988- 68.40. pb SP: 16.60 '88.

HUANG ZHIHONG b.7 May 1965 1.74m 100kg.
At SP: OG: '88- 8; WCh: '87- 11; AsG: '86- 1.
Progression at SP: 1983- 16.12, 1984- 17.04, 1985- 18.01, 1986- 18.89, 1987- 20.22, 1988- 21.28.
Has shown a regular metre per year improvement.

JIN BINGJIE b.1 Apr 1971 1.66m 50kg.
At 10kmW: WCh: '87- 7; WCp: '87- 3.
Progression at 10kmW: 1985- 45:59, 1987- 43:45. Track pbs: 5kmW: 22:02.75 '86, 10kmW: 44:26.7 '87; Road: 5kmW: 21:53 '87.

LI MEISU b.17 Apr 1959 Hebei Prov. 1.76m 92kg.
At SP: OG: '84- 5, '88- 3; WCh: '83- dnq, '87- 7; AsG: '82- 1.
Eleven Asian shot records 1984–8.
Progression at SP: 1979- 16.33, 1980- 16.33, 1981- 16.95, 1982- 17.88, 1983- 17.97, 1984- 18.47, 1985- 18.07, 1986- 18.61, 1987- 20.95, 1988- 21.76. Her bronze in Seoul was the first ever Olympic medal won by a Chinese woman athlete.

WANG XIUTING b.11 May 1965 Shandong Prov. 1.64m 48kg. PE student.
At 10000m (3000m): OG: '88- 7 (h); WCh: '87- 8 (h); AsG: '86- 1. World 15km Rd: '88- 2. Three Asian 10000m records, one at 3000m & 5000m 1987.
Progression at 10000m: 1986- 32:47.77, 1987- 31:27.00, 1988- 31:40.23. pbs: 3000m: 8:50.68 '87, 5000m: 15:27.44 '87.

YAN HONG b.23 Oct 1966 Liaoning 1.54m 44kg.
At 10kmW: WCh: '87- 3; WCp: '85- 1. At 3kmW: WI '85- 2.
World walk records: 5km (21:40.3) and 10km in 1984. Three world junior 5km walk records 1983–4. World 10km road best 1985.
Progression at 10kmW: 1983- 49:09, 1984- 45:39.5t, 1985- 44:14, 1986- 45:32.4t, 1987- 44:42. Track pbs: 3kmW: 13:05.56i '85, 5kmW: 21:20.2 '87.
Amazingly has three times crossed the finish line first in the World Cup, but was disqualified in both 1983 and 1987.

YU HOURUN b.10 Nov 1963 1.80m 95kg.
At DT: OG: '88- 9.
Three Asian discus records 1987–8.
Progression at DT: 1985- 57.14, 1986- 62.08, 1987- 66.76, 1988- 68.62/68.92u.

ZHAO YOUFENG b.5 May 1965 1.68m 49kg.
At Mar: OG: '88- 5.
Two Asian marathon records in 1988, with her 2:27:56 win at Nagoya and at the Olympics.
Progression at Mar: 1988- 2:27:06. pbs: 5000m: 15:35.82 '87, 10000m: 32:46.14 '87.

CUBA

Governing body: Federacion Cubana de Atletismo, Calle 13 No.601, Zona Postal 4, Vedado, Ciudad de La Habana. Founded 1922
National Champions 1988: MEN
100m: Andrés Simon 10.34, 200m/400m: Roberto Hernández 20.98/45.90, 800m: Raúl Mesa 1:48.36, 1500m: Amado Ramos 3:43.95, 5000m/3kmSt: Juan Conde 14:05.17/8:46.69, 10000m: Alberto Cuba 29:26.24, Mar: Dimas Alvarez 2:18:34, 110mh: Emilio Valle 13.81, 400mh: Francisco Velazco 50.94, HJ: Javier Sotomayor 2.25, PV: Angel Garcia 4.90, LJ: Jaime Jefferson 7.91, TJ: Juan M.Lopez 16.83, SP: Paul Ruiz 19.05, DT: Juan Martinez 63.52, HT: Eladio Hernádez 68.40, JT: Ramon Gonzalez 76.28, Dec: Luis Milanes 7670, 20kmW: Daniel Vargas 1:30:09, 50kmW: Edel Oliva 4:05:30.
WOMEN
100m/200m: Liliana Allen 11.84/24.01, 400m: Ana Fidelia Quirot 53.83, 800m: Maura Savon 2:10.06, 1500m/3000m: Milagros Rodriguez 4:29.63/ 9:59.93, 5000m/10000m: Maribel Durruthy 17:00.42/35:44.02, Mar: Emperatriz Wilson 2:52:44, 100mh: Aliuska Lopez 13.43, 400mh: Tania Fernandez 57.5, HJ: Silvia Costa 1.87, LJ: Niurka Montalvo 6.62, SP: Belsis Laza 18.39, DT: Hilda Ramos 62.50, JT: Ivonne Leal 70.48, Hep: Yolaida Pompa 5004, 5kmW/10kmW: Margarita Morales 25:17/51:28.

Men

Luis Alberto BUENO b.22 May 1969 1.74m 67kg.
At LJ: WJ: '88- 1. Ibero-American champion 1986
Progression at LJ: 1985- 7.62, 1986- 8.25, 1987- 8.01, 1988- 8.28. pb 100m: 10.47/10.4 '88.

Luis Mariano DELIS b.6 Dec 1957 Guantanamo 1.85m 106kg.
At DT: OG: '80- 3; WCh: '83- 2, '87- 3; PAm: '79- 3, '83- 1 (1 at SP), '87- 1; WCp: '79- 3, '81- 2, '85- 3; WSG: '83- 1, '85- 1; CAmG: '78- 1, '82- 1 (1 at SP), '86- 1. Woin US title 1982. CAC champion 1985.
Six Cuban discus records 1979–83.
Progression at DT: 1973- 43.54, 1974- 49.02, 1975- 50.70, 1976- 56.82, 1977- 61.02, 1978- 62.14, 1979- 66.52, 1980- 68.04, 1981- 67.28, 1982- 70.58, 1983- 71.06, 1984- 69.74, 1985- 70.00, 1986- 68.00, 1987- 67.92, 1988- 65.80. pb SP: 19.89 '82.
Has a marvellous big meeting record, always winning a medal.

Roberto HERNANDEZ b.6 Mar 1967 Matanzas 1.79m 74kg. Student.
At 400m/R- 4x400m relay: WCh: '87- 4/3R; PAm: '87- 3/2R; WJ: '86- 2/1R; WSG: '85- 2/1R; WI: '87- 2. CAC champion 1985; won PAm-J 200m & 400m 1986.
Cuban 400m record 1988.
Progression at 400m: 1983- 48.0, 1984- 46.44, 1985- 45.14, 1986- 45.05, 1987- 44.61, 1988- 44.22. pbs: 200m: 20.24 '88, 300m: 32.34 '85.

Jaime JEFFERSON b.17 Jan 1962 Guantanamo 1.89m 78kg.
At LJ: WCh: '87- 6; PAm: '83- 1, '87- 3; CAmG: '86- 1; WSG: '85- 1. CAC champion 1985.
Six Cuban long jump records 1984–7.
Progression at LJ: 1981- 7.25, 1982- 7.50, 1983- 8.05, 1984- 8.37, 1985- 8.24/8.28w, 1986- 8.47, 1987- 8.51, 1988- 8.37. pbs: 100m: 10.2/10.35/10.33w '85, TJ: 16.28 '85.

Juan MARTINEZ b.17 May 1958 Habana 1.86m 122kg.
At DT: WCh: '83- 7; WSG: '85- 3; PAm: '79- 4, '83- 3, '87- 4; CAmG: '86- 2. Won AAA 1985.
Progression at DT: 1975- 47.90, 1976- 53.98, 1977- 57.24, 1978- 60.34, 1979- 64.88, 1980- 66.46, 1982- 63.70, 1983- 70.00, 1984- 67.32, 1985- 69.32, 1986- 68.40, 1987- 66.60, 1988- 66.24. pb SP: 15.98 '76.

Andrés SIMON b.15 Sep 1961 Guantanamo 1.60m 67kg. Student.
At 100m/R- 4x100mR: WCh: '87- sf; PAm: '87- 5/2R; CAmG: '86- 1/1R; WSG: '85- 2/1R. CAC champion 1985.
Progression at 100m: 1983- 10.60, 1984- 10.25, 1985- 10.10/9.97w, 1986- 10.18, 1987- 10.06/10.04w, 1988- 10.13.

Javier SOTOMAYOR b.13 Oct 1967 Limonar, Matanzas 1.95m 82kg.
At HJ: WCh: '87- 9; PAm: '87- 1; WJ: '86- 1; WCp: '85- 3; WI: '85- 2, '87- 4. Cuban champion 1984, CAC 1985, PAm-J 1986. Won GP 1988 (third overall).
World high jump record 1988, World junior record 1986, seven Cuban records 1984–8.
Progression at HJ: 1980- 1.65, 1981- 1.84, 1982- 2.00, 1983- 2.17, 1984- 2.33, 1985- 2.34, 1986- 2.36, 1987- 2.37, 1988- 2.43.

Women

Maria Caridad COLON b.25 Mar 1958 Baracoa, Guantanano 1.70m 70kg.
At JT: OG: '80- 1; WCh: '83- 8, '87- dnq; PAm: '79- 1, '83- 1, '87- 2; WSG: '85- 3; CAmG: '78- 1, '82- 1, '86- 1; WCp: '79- 3, '85- 7.
12 Cuban javelin records 1978–84.
Progression at JT: 1974- 42.24, 1975- 43.62, 1976- 49.74, 1977- 54.32, 1978- 63.50, 1979- 64.38, 1980- 68.40, 1982- 62.80, 1983- 65.70, 1984- 69.96, 1985- 68.20, 1986- 70.14, 1987- 67.42, 1988- 67.44.
Formerly married to her coach Angel Salcedo; had a baby in 1981.

Maria Colon (George Herringshaw/ASP)

Silvia COSTA b.4 May 1964 Pinar del Rio 1.79m 60kg.
At HJ: WCh: '83- 10=, '87- 4; PAm '79-8, '83- 2, '87- 2; WSG: '83- 2, '85- 1; WCp: '85- 4; CAmG: '82- 1, '86- 1; WIG: '85- 3=. CAC champion 1985.
Two world junior high jump records 1982. 13 Cuban records 1980–8.
Progression at HJ: 1977- 1.57, 1978- 1.64, 1979- 1.82, 1980- 1.90, 1981- 1.88, 1982- 1.95, 1983- 1.98, 1984- 1.99, 1985- 2.01, 1986- 1.99, 1987- 1.96, 1988- 2.02. pb 100mh: 13.73 '88.

Ivonne LEAL b.27 Feb 1966 San Nicolas de Bari, Habana 1.64m 64kg.
At JT: WCh: '87- 8; PAm: '87- 1; CAmG: '86- 2; WSG: '85- 1. 3rd GP 1988.
Cuban javelin record 1985.
Progression at JT: 1980- 40.20, 1981- 47.00, 1982- 55.00, 1983- 56.82, 1984- 58.54, 1985- 71.82, 1986- 69.82, 1987- 67.18, 1988- 70.48.

Aliuska LOPEZ b.29 Aug 1969 Habana 1.69m 53kg.
At 100mh: WCh: '87- sf; PAm: '87- 3 (2R); WJ: '86- 2, '88- 1; WSG: '87- 2.
Two world junior 100mh records 1987; four Cuban records 1986–7.
Progression at 100mh: 1984- 14.4, 1985- 13.5/ 13.97, 1986- 13.14, 1987- 12.84, 1988- 12.96. pbs: 100m: 11.53 '87, 200m: 24.22 '87, 400mh: 64.32 '86.

Maritza MARTEN b.17 Aug 1963 Habana 1.77m 83kg.
At DT: WCh: '87- 9; PAm: '83- 2, '87- 1; CAmG: '86- 2; WCp: '85- 3; WSG: '85- 1. Won PAm-J 1982, CAC 1985, Cuban champion 1984–5. 2nd GP 1988.
Cuban discus record 1985.
Progression at DT: 1977- 41.34, 1978- 47.46, 1979- 53.30, 1980- 54.94, 1981- 53.70, 1982- 59.54, 1983- 63.94, 1984- 67.76, 1985- 70.50, 1986- 66.86, 1987- 66.98, 1988- 67.02. pb SP: 15.52 '85.

Ana Fidelia QUIROT b.23 Mar 1963 Santiago de Cuba 1.65m 59kg.
At 400m/800m/R- 4x400m relay: WCh: '87- -/4; PAm: '79- 2R, '83- 2/3R, '87- 1/1; WSG: '85- 2/3; WCp: '85- 4/4; CAmG: '78- 1R, '82- 4/-/1R, '86- 1/1/ 1R. Double CAC champion 1985. 1st GP 800m 1987, 400m 1988, 3rd overall 1988.
Cuban records: four 400m, six 800m 1985–8.

Progression at 400m/800m: 1977- 57.0, 1978- 53.74, 1979- 55.24, 1980- 55.0, 1981- 54.2, 1982- 52.61, 1983- 51.83, 1984- 50.87, 1985- 50.86/ 1:59.45, 1986- 50.41/1:58.80, 1987- 50.12/1:55.84, 1988- 49.62/1:56.36. pb 200m: 23.07 '88, 22.9 '84.

Hilda Elisa RAMOS b.1 Sep 1964 Matanzas 1.76m 80kg.
At DT: PAm: '87- 2; CAmG: '86- 1. Won GP 1988.
Progression at DT: 1980- 45.32, 1981- 50.04, 1982- 52.62, 1983- 63.60, 1984- 67.56, 1985- 67.52, 1986- 67.92, 1987- 67.90, 1988- 66.58. pb SP: 16.36 '85.

CZECHOSLOVAKIA

Governing body: Ceskoslovensky atléticky svaz, Na Porici 12, 115 30 Praha 1. Founded 1897 (AAU of Bohemia).
National Championships first held in 1907 (Bohemia), 1919 (CS)
1988 Champions: MEN
100m/200m: Jiri Valik 10.38/20.81, 400m: Lubos Balasak 46.55, 800m: Milan Drahanovsky 1:48.08, 1500m: Radim Kuncicky 3:48.87, 5000m: Jozef Vybostok 13:58.70, 10000m: Martin Vrabel 28:45.79, Mar: Vlastimil Bukovjan 2:19:15, 3000mSt: Lubos Gaisl 8:37.61, 110mh: Pavel Sada 14.13, 400mh: Stanislav Navesnak 49.64, HJ: Robert Ruffini 2.26, PV: Zdenek Lubensky 5.50, LJ/TJ: Milan Mikulas 8.25/17.53, SP: Remigius Machura 19.91, DT: Imrich Bugar 65.36, HT: Frantisek Vrbka 69.06, JT: Zdenek Nenadal 77.26, Dec: Petr Horn 6870, 20kmW: Jozef Pribilinec 1:21:34, 50kmW: Pavol Szikora 3:46:52.
WOMEN
100m: Renata Cernochova 11.66, 200m: Jana Nikova 23.98, 400m: Alena Parikova 52.66, 800m: Gabriela Sedlakova 2:04.90, 1500m: Vera Nozickova 4:13.99, 3000m: Alena Mocariova 9:05.37, 10000m: Maria Starovska 33:22.19, Mar: Dana Kelnarova 2:54:12, 100mh: Jana Petrikova 13.80, 400mh: Zuzana Machotka 56.56, HJ: Sarka Kasparkova 1.83, LJ/Hep: Vanda Novakova 6.18/5706, SP: Sona Vasickova 20.42, DT: Martina Polisenska 60.32, JT: Elena Revayova 58.56, 10kmW: Jana Zarubova 48:57.

Pavol BLAZEK b.9 Jul 1958 Trnava 1.68m 58kg. Dukla B.Bystrica. Soldier.
At 20kmW (50kmW): OG: '80- 14 (10), '88- 15 (12); WCh: '83- 6 (17), '87- 11 (18); ECh: '78- 14, '82- 3 (dnf), '86- 6; LT: '79- 18, '81- 11, '83- 9, '85- 10. CS 20kmW champion 1981.
Progression at 20kmW: 1977- 1:33:34, 1978- 1:27:50, 1979- 1:25:14, 1980- 1:25:00t, 1981- 1:24:07, 1982- 1:23:59, 1983- 1:21:37, 1984- 1:21:24t, 1985- 1:22:30, 1986- 1:21:21, 1987- 1:21:36, 1988- 1:20:17. Track pbs: 3kmW: 11:36.7i '85, 5kmW: 18:58.1i '86, 10kmW: 39:31.83i '86; Road pb 50kmW: 3:47:31 '88.

Imrich BUGAR b.14 Apr 1955 Dunajska Streda 1.90m 120kg. Dukla Praha. Civil servant.

At DT: OG: '80- 2, '88- 12; WCh: '83- 1, '87- 7; ECh: '78- 3, '82- 1, '86- 8; WCp: '81- 3, '85- 4; ECp: '85- 1, '87- 4. CS champion 1978–86, 1988. Won GP 1985, 2nd 1987.
Six CS discus records 1981–5.
Progression at DT: 1972- 44.42, 1973- 48.22, 1974- 51.38, 1975- 53.88, 1976- 57.52, 1977- 62.54, 1978- 65.96, 1979- 64.88, 1980- 66.38, 1981- 67.48, 1982- 68.60, 1983- 70.72, 1984- 70.26, 1985- 71.26, 1986- 67.38, 1987- 67.22, 1988- 66.42. pb SP: 15.46 '86.
World and European discus champion who competes often and throws consistently well. He was a handball prospect at school, but learned to throw the discus in a few weeks at the age of 17 in 1972.

Zdenek LUBENSKY b.3 Dec 1962 Kutna Hora 1.85m 75kg. VS Praha. Student.
At PV: OG: '88- 11; WCh: '87- dns; ECh: '86- 6; ECp: '85- 4, '87- 2. CS champion 1985–8.
Three CS pole vault records 1985–7.
Progression at PV: 1980- 4.30, 1981- 4.90, 1982- 5.05/5.10i, 1983- 5.20, 1984- 5.30, 1985- 5.66, 1986- 5.72, 1987- 5.73, 1988- 5.65.

Remigius MACHURA b.3 Jul 1960 Rychnov n. Kneznou 1.87m 118kg. VS Praha. Student.
At SP: OG: '88- 5; WCh: '83- 3, '87- 4; ECh: '82- 3; EI: '82- 2, '85- 1, '88- 1; EJ: '79- 1 (5 at DT); WSG: '85- 1dq; ECp: '85- 2dq, '87- 3; WI: '85- 1. Won GP 1988. CS champion 1983–5, 1987–8.
Two CS shot records 1982–7.
Progression at SP: 1976- 14.50, 1977- 16.61, 1978- 17.46, 1979- 18.64, 1980- 19.23, 1981- 19.22i, 1982- 21.74, 1983- 21.41, 1984- 21.52, 1985- 21.79i/21.88dq, 1987- 21.93, 1988- 21.71i/20.94. pb DT: 60.30 '82.
Disqualified for 18 months on a positive drugs test when second at the 1985 European Cup final. His brother Martin was the CS decathlon record holder (7941 '83).

Roman MRAZEK b.21.1.62 Sokolov 1.68m 55kg. Dukla B.Bystrica. Soldier.
At 20kmW (50kmW): OG: '88- 5 (17); WCh: '83- 27, '87- 6; ECh: '86- dq (20). CS champion 1987. At 5kmW: WI: '85- 4, '87- 4; EI: '87- 3, '88- 2.
Progression at 20kmW: 1980- 1:40:19, 1981- 1:36:56, 1982- 1:29:08, 1983- 1:24:30, 1984- 1:24:19, 1985- 1:22:18, 1986- 1:21:41, 1987- 1:21:17, 1988- 1:20:43. Track pbs: 3kmW: 11:14.95 '87, 5kmW: 18:42.55i '88, 10kmW: 38:47.84 '87. 50kmW road: 3:50:46 '87.

Jozef PRIBILINEC b.6 Jul 1960 Kremnica 1.68m 66kg. Dukla B.Bystrica. Sports instructor.
At 20kmW: OG: '80- 20, '88- 1; WCh: '83- 2, '87- 2; ECh: '82- 2, '86- 1; LT: '79- 10, '83- 1, '85- dq. At 10kmW: EJ: '79- 1. At 5kmW: WI: '87- 2; EI: '88- 1. CS 20kmW champion 1979, 1982–6, 1988.
World track bests: 3kmW: 11:00.2 '85, 5kmW: 18:51.2 '81 & 18:42.0 '85, 10kmW: 38:02.60 '85, 15kmW: 58:22.4 '86, 1 hour: 15447m '86. World junior records: 3kmW: 11:13.2, 10kmW: 40:55.4 in 1979. World road best 20kmW 1983.
Progression at 20kmW: 1978- 1:33:07, 1979- 1:22:44, 1980- 1:21:39.2t, 1981- 1:21:56, 1982- 1:22:27, 1983- 1:19:30, 1984- 1:25:07, 1985- 1:20:40, 1986- 1:21:15, 1987- 1:21:07, 1988- 1:19:57. pbs: 5kmW: 18:37.54i '88, 50kmW: 4:16:41 '84.
Disqualified after finishing first in the 1985 Lugano Cup race, otherwise has a magnificent record in major races.

Ivan SLANAR b.11 Jan 1961 Kolin 1.91m 84kg. Dukla Praha. Sports instructor.
At TJ: OG: '88- 7; WCh: '87- 10; ECh: '86- dnq 15; ECp: '87- 4. CS champion 1987.
Progression at TJ: 1978- 13.30, 1980- 14.22, 1981- 15.14, 1982- 15.76, 1983- 16.28, 1986- 16.83, 1985- 16.98, 1986- 16.94, 1987- 17.25, 1988- 17.19. pbs: HJ: 2 01 '79, LJ: 7.78 '87.

Pavol SZIKORA b.26 Mar 1952 Lucenec 1.76m 65kg. Dukla Banska Bystrica. Technician.
At 50kmW: OG: '88- 10; WCh: '83- 11, '87- 7; ECh: '86- 8. CS champion 1983, 1985–6, 1988.
Progression at 50kmW: 1980- 4:01:03, 1981- 4:19:46, 1982- 4:02:42, 1983- 3:56:14, 1984- 3:45:53, 1985- 3:54:58, 1986- 3:49:00, 1987- 3:42:20, 1988- 3:46:52. pb 20kmW: 1:23:20 '87.

Gejza VALENT b.3 Oct 1953 Praha 1.96m 120kg. Vitkovice. Technician.
At DT: OG: '88- 6; WCh: '83- 3, '87- 9; ECh: '82- 6, '86- 5. 3rd GP 1985. CS champion 1987.
Progression at DT: 1970- 44.76, 1971- 46.38, 1972- 49.44, 1973- 49.94, 1974- 54.00, 1975- 54.96, 1976- 56.64, 1977- 56.10, 1978- 53.04, 1979- 55.56, 1980- 58.64, 1981- 65.42, 1982- 67.56, 1983- 67.26, 1984- 69.70, 1985- 68.40, 1986- 65.58, 1987- 65.72, 1988- 66.42. pb SP: 16.80 '84.
Leapt into world class in the 1980s after a decade of little progress. His father, Gejza, had a personal best discus mark of 53.84m in 1956, which ranked him 16th in the world.

Jan ZELEZNY b.16 Jun 1966 Mlada Boleslav 1.86m 77kg. Dukla B.Bystrica. Soldier.
At JT: OG: '88- 2; WCh: '87- 3; ECh: '86- dnq 18; EJ: '83- 6, '85- 4; ECp: '87- 3. CS champion 1986.
World javelin record 1987; three CS records 1986–7.
Progression at JT: 1982- 57.22, 1983- 74.34, 1984- 80.32, 1985- 84.68, new: 1986- 82.48, 1987- 87.66, 1988- 86.88.

Jan ZVARA b.12 Feb 1963 Banska Bystrica 1.92m 85kg. Sparta Praha. Sports instructor.
At HJ: WCh: '87- 7; ECh: '86- 9=; WI: '87- 3; ECp: '85- 1, '87- 2. CS champion 1985–6.
Seven CS high jump records 1985–7.
Progression at HJ: 1979- 1.85, 1980- 1.95, 1981- 2.01, 1983- 2.12, 1984- 2.20, 1985- 2.35, 1986- 2.34, 1987- 2.36, 1988- 2.26. pb TJ: 15.21 '84.

Women

Gabriela SEDLAKOVA b.2 Mar 1968 Topolcany 1.69m 51kg. Slavia UK Bratislava. Student.
At 800m: WCh: '87- sf; ECh: '86- sf; WI: '87- 2; WJ: '86- 2; EJ: '85- 1=. CS champion 1987.
Progression at 800m: 1983- 2:15.03i, 1984- 2:04.01, 1985- 2:03.22, 1986- 2:00.61, 1987- 1:58.37, 1988- 2:00.35. pbs: 400m: 53.60 '86, 1500m: 4:29.62 '86.

Zdenka SILHAVA b.15 Jun 1954 Krnov 1.78m 85kg. Formerly Kusa and Bartonova, now married to Josef Silhavy (discus 64.90 '75). RH Praha. Civil Servant.
At SP/DT: OG: '80- 10/11, '88- 11/6; WCh: '83- 9/6, '87- -/6; ECh: '78- 9/-, '82- 9/13; ECp DT: '83- 4, '85- 3dq. CS champion SP 1980, DT 1981–5, 1987. World discus record 1984. Ten CS discus records 1980–4.
Progression at SP/DT: 1970- 11.96, 1971- 12.30, 1972- 12.51, 1973- 13.07/39.84, 1974- 14.28/42.88, 1975- 16.82/49.08, 1976- 17.40/49.02, 1977- 18.42i/53.22, 1978- 19.42/56.70, 1979- 18.70/56.30, 1980- 20.00/64.50, 1981- 19.54/65.74, 1982- 20.55/68.66, 1983- 21.05/70.00, 1984- 20.12/74.56, 1985- 20.13dq/70.70, 1987- 19.43/69.52, 1988- 19.78/71.68.
Suspended for drugs abuse after placing third in 1985 European Cup discus.

DENMARK

Governing body: Dansk Athletik Forbund, Idraettens Hus, Brondby Stadion 20, DK-2605 Brondby.
National Championships first held in 1894
1988 Champions: MEN
100m/200m: Lars Pedersen 10.47/21.29, 400m: Niels Ole Lindberg 47.71, 800m: Mogens Guldberg 1:48.68, 1500m: Lars Bøgh 3:50.82, 5000m: Allan Zachariasen 14:01.06, 10000m: Henrik Jørgensen 29:05.90, Mar: Jens Wørzner 2:21:04, 3000mSt: Peter Troldborg 8:53.72, 110mh: Erik S.Jensen 13.83, 400mh: Kristian Strømgård 53.07, HJ: Michael Mikkelsen 2.16, PV/TJ: Kenneth Kapsch 5.00/14.92, LJ: Finn Nielsen 7.22, SP: Klaus Jacob Jensen 16.32, DT: Allan Laursen 50.44, HT: Torben S.Hansen 59.34, JT: Kenneth Petersen 77.14, Dec: Lars Warming 7441, 20kmW: Peer Jensen 1:42:07, 50kmW: Mogens Corfitz 4:32:36.
WOMEN
100m: Trine Bogner 12.29w, 200m: Charlotte Petersen 25.42, 400m: Ane Skak 56.58, 800m/1500m: Tina Krebs 2:08.15/4:21.21, 3000m: Gitte Karlshøj 9:25.1, 10000m: Dorthe Rasmussen 34:55.49, Mar: Joan Carstensen 2:53:33, 100mh/SP: Lisbeth Pedersen 14.30/13.32, HJ/TJ Dorthe Wolfsberg 1.80/12.19, 400mh: Pia Vanggård 62.27, LJ: Lene Demsitz 6.27, DT: Vivian Krafft 50.22, HT: Gitte Gregersen 41.72, JT: Jette Jeppesen 53.20, Hep: Dorte Klein 5266, 5kmW/10kmW: Karin Jensen 25:08.0/50:27.2.

Mogens GULDBERG b.2 Aug 1963 Kalundborg 1.84m 65kg. Sparta. Law student.
At 1500m: OG: '88- sf; WCh: '87- sf; ECh: '86- h. Danish champion 800m 1986, 1988; 1500m 1984–5.
Danish records 1500m (2) 1988, 2000m 1987.
Progression at 1500m: 1981- 4:01.7, 1982- 3:45.51, 1983- 3:45.43, 1984- 3:42.15, 1985- 3:42.95, 1986- 3:37.95, 1987- 3:37.75, 1988- 3:35.32. pbs: 800m: 1:48.68 '88, 1000m: 2:20.2 '84, 1M: 3:57.18 '88, 2000m: 4:59.56 '87, 3000m: 7:52.47i '87, 5000m: 13:45.47 '87.

Henrik JØRGENSEN b.10 Oct 1961 København 1.78m 59kg. KIF. Economics student.
At Mar: OG: '84- 19, '88- 22; WCh: '83- 19 (h 10km), '87- 9. At 5000m: ECh: '82- h. Danish champion 5000m 1985, 10000m 1980, 1982–3, 1988.
Danish records 1980–8: 5 10000m, 2 5000m, 2 Mar.
Progression at Mar: 1979- 2:26:15, 1981- 2:18:45, 1982- 2:19:50, 1983- 2:10:47, 1984- 2:11:31, 1985- 2:09:43, 1986- 2:11:49, 1987- 2:14:58, 1988- 2:10:20. pbs: 1500m: 3:46.2 '82, 3000m: 7:55.92 '82, 5000m: 13:27.76 '85, 10000m: 27:57.98 '85.
Won London marathon 1988.

DJIBOUTI

Governing body: Fédération Djiboutienne d'Athlétisme, BP 16, Djibouti.

Ahmed SALAH Houssain b.1956 Ali Sabieh 1.80m 60kg. Army lieutenant.
At Mar: OG: '84- 20, '88- 3; WCh: '83- dnf, '87- 2; WCp: '85- 1, '87- 1; AfCh: '85- 1. At 10km: AfCh: '82- 6, '84- 2. Won Paris marathon 1984, 1986. 2nd New York 1985, Chicago 1986, Rotterdam 1988.
African marathon record 1985.
Progression at Mar: 1983- 2:17:29, 1984- 2:11:58, 1985- 2:08:09, 1986- 2:09:57, 1987- 2:10:55, 1988- 2:07:07. pbs: 3000m: 8:08.62 '84, 5000m: 13:51.5 '85, 10km: 28:17.40 '84.

Has won five of his 17 marathons. In Seoul won the first Olympic medal for Djibouti at any sport.

ETHIOPIA

Governing body: National Ethiopian Athletic Federation, Addis Ababa Stadium, PO Box 3241, Addis Ababa.

Addis ABEBE b.1970. Menelik High Schol, Addis Abada.
At 10000m: WJ: '88- 1 (3 5000m).
World junior records in 1988 at 5000m: 13:23.27 and 10000m: 27:50.24. No previously known form.

Wodajo BULTI b.11 Mar 1957 Gione 1.85m 60kg. Soldier.
At 5000m/10000m: WCh: '83- 7 5000m, '87- 24 10000m; WCp: '85- 3/1; AfG: '87- 4/4; AfCh: '82- 1/- (3 1500m), '85- 1/1. World CC: '85- 3.
Progression at 5000m/10000m: 1981- 13:40.20, 1982- 13:07.29, 1983- 13:22.32, 1984- 13:10.08/27:58.24, 1985- 13:31.02/28:22.43, 1986- 28:33.90, 1987- 13:24.64/27:29.41, 1988- 13:33.68/27:56.35. pbs: 1500m: 3:40.08 '82, 3000m: 7:40.64 '83.
Marathon debut in 1988: 2:08:44 for third at Rotterdam, then 12th at New York.

Belayneh DINSAMO b.1965. 1.67m 60kg. Policeman.
At Mar: AfG: '87- 1.
Ethiopian record 1986 in first major marathon race. World best 1988.
Progression at Mar: 1985- 2:28:26, 1986- 2:08:29, 1987- 2:11:59, 1988- 2:06:50.
Second in 1986 Tokyo and Rotterdam marathons, and won at the Goodwill Games. Won at Rotterdam 1987–8 and second at Fukuoka 1988.

Abebe MEKONNEN b.9 Jan 1964 1.58m 59kg. Army.
At Mar: WCh: '87- dnf; WCp: '85–5; AfCh: '85- 5. At 10000m: AfG: '87- 2. World CC: '86- 2, '87- 4, '88- 5.
Progression at Mar: 1984- 2:11:30, 1985- 2:09:05, 1986- 2:08:39, 1987- 2:11:10, 1988- 2:07:35. pb 10000m: 28:58.70 '87.
Of his 19 marathons has won 6: Rotterdam, Addis Abada and Montreal 1986, Paris 1987, Tokyo and Beijing 1988.

Dereje NEDI b.10 Oct 1955 1.75m 55kg. Soldier.
At Mar: OG: '80- 7; WCh: '83- dnf; WCp: '85- 16; AfG: '78- 2, '87- 2; AfCh: '79- dnf, '82- dnf, '85- 3, '88- 1.
Ethiopian marathon records in 1983 and 1984.
Progression at Mar: 1976- 2:17:07, 1977- 2:14:49, 1978- 2:23:08, 1979- 2:22:13, 1980- 2:12:44, 1981- 2:12:14, 1982- 2:13:25, 1983- 2:10:39, 1984- 2:10:32, 1985- 2:12:22, 1986- 2:16:20, 1987- 2:15:27, 1988- 2:14:27.
Started athletics in 1974. Won Frankfurt and Moscow marathons in 1984, Abebe Bikila marathon 1984–5.

FINLAND

Governing body: Suomen Urheiluliitto, Radiokatu, SF-00240 Helsinki. Founded 1906.
National Championships first held in 1907 (men), 1913 (women)
1988 Champions: MEN
100m: Jarkko Toivonen 10.64, 200m: Sakari Syväoja 21.15, 400m: Mika Hänninen 47.38, 800m/1500m: Ari Suhonen 1:47.24/3:41.76, 5000m: Matti Valkonen 13:36.25, 10000m: Martti Vainio 28:30.06, Mar: Vesa Kähkölä 2:18:58, 3000mSt: Jörgen Salo 8:36.27, 110mh: Mikael Ylöstalo 13.53w, 400mh: Markku Karvonen 51.13, HJ: Veli-Pekka Kokkonen 2.22, PV: Asko Peltoniemi 5.45, LJ: Jarmo Kärnä 7.77, TJ: Esa Viitasalo 16.62, SP: Jari Kuoppa 19.07, DT: Mika Muukka 59.36, HT: Harri Huhtala 75.90, JT: Tapio Korjus 84.38, Dec: Kaj Ekman 7482, 20kmW: Reima Salonen 1:24:28, 50kmW: Veijo Savikko 4:02:45.
WOMEN
100m/200m: Sisko Hanhijoki 11.51/23.50, 400m: Sonja Finell 53.17, 800m: Tiina Pakkala 2:06.74, 1500m: Kaisa Siitonen 4:14.46, 3000m: Päivi Tikkanen 9:14.28, 10000m: Tuija Jousimaa 32:55.16, Mar: Sirpa Kytölä 2:48:08, 100mh: Satu Ruotsalainen 13.75, 400mh: Laila Andersson 59.32, HJ: Marita Pakarinen 1.85, LJ: Ringa Ropa 6.52, SP: Asta Hovi 17.96, DT: Anne Känsäkangas 58.12, JT: Tuula Laaksalo 63.12, Hep: Tina Rättyä 5531, 5kmW/10kmW: Sari Essayah 22:14.85/44:26.0t.

Arto BRYGGARE b.26 May 1958 Kouvola 1.94m 88kg. Lappeenrannan Urheilu-Miehet. Economics student.
At 110mh: OG: '80- 6, '84- 3; WCh: '83- 2, '87- dns; ECh: '78- 3, '82- 3, '86- 2; EJ: '75- 7, '77- 1; ECp: '77- 4. At 50mh/60mh: WI: '87- 5; EI: '77- 3, '79- 2, '81- 1, '83- 2, '87- 1. Finnish 110mh champion 1977–87.
Eleven Finnish 110mh records 1976–84. Two European junior records 1977, WIB 13.58'82.
Progression at 110mh: 1975- 14.46, 1976- 14.04, 1977- 13.66/13.55w, 1978- 13.56, 1979- 13.81, 1980- 13.76, 1981- 13.77, 1982- 13.57, 1983- 13.44, 1984- 13.35, 1985- 13.63/13.61w, 1986- 13.42, 1987- 13.51, 1988- 13.85. pbs: 100m: 10.5, 10.60 '77, 200m: 21.3 '77, 200mh: 23.1 '78.
Very consistent hurdler in the major events, with eleven successive Finnish 110mh titles, but torn Achilles ended that run in 1988. Father Unto put the shot 15.77 in 1959.

Tapio KORJUS b.10 Feb 1961 Vehkalahti 1.96m 105kg. Physical education teacher.
At JT: OG: '88- 1. Finnish champion 1987–8.
Two Finnish javelin records 1988.

Tapio Korjus (George Herringshaw/ASP)

Progression at JT: 1978- 67.50, 1979- 70.12, 1980- 71.52, 1981- 78.00, 1982- 74.50, 1983- 81.16, 1984- 87.24, 1985- 89.30, new: 1986- 74.92, 1987- 79.52, 1988- 86.50.
Started javelin training in 1980, having been a most promising cross-country skier. His Olympic gold was Finland's 100th at all sports at the summer Games.

Seppo RÄTY b.27 Apr 1962 Helsinki 1.88m 105kg. Tohmajärven Urheilijat. Railwayman.
At JT: OG: '88- 3; WCh: '87- 1; ECh: '86- 17. Finnish champion 1985–6.
Three Finnish javelin records 1986–7. Unofficial world best 1986.
Progression at JT: 1978- 59.04, 1979- 63.20, 1980- 71.14, 1981- 75.44, 1982- 72.74, 1983- 74.38, 1984- 82.60, 1985- 85.72, new: 1986- 81.72, 1987- 83.54, 1988- 83.26.
One of the most surprising world champions of 1987; he twice improved his national record in Rome.

Ari SUHONEN b.19 Dec 1965 Porvoo 1.84m 67kg. Porvoo Urheilijat. Student.
At 1500m (800m): OG: '88- h (qf); ECh: '86: h (sf); EI: '87- (3), '88- 1. Finnish champion at 800m 1985–8, 1500m 1986–8.
Two Finnish 1000m records 1986–7.
Progression at 1500m: 1982- 4:04.5, 1983- 3:53.8, 1984- 3:50.1, 1985- 3:49.83, 1986- 3:39.82, 1987- 3:36.89, 1988- 3:37.31. pbs: 400m: 48.15 '85, 800m: 1:45.14 '88, 1000m: 2:16.88 '87.

Ari Suhonen wins the 1,500m. at the European Indoor Championships, Budapest 1988 (Mark Shearman)

Juha TIAINEN b.5 Dec 1955 Uukuniemi 1.83m 108kg. Lappeenrannan Urheilu-Miehet. Policeman.
At HT: OG: '80- 10, '84- 1, '88- dnq 16; WCh: '83- 9, '87- 13; ECh: '82- 12, '86- 18; ECp: '77- 6. Finnish hammer champion 1977, 1979, 1981, 1984, 1987.
Eight Finnish records 1976–84.
Progression at HT: 1972- 40.94, 1973- 49.62, 1974- 51.64, 1975- 65.12, 1976- 71.80, 1977- 72.62, 1978- 71.08, 1979- 74.42, 1980- 75.88, 1981- 76.64, 1982- 78.34, 1983- 81.02, 1984- 81.52, 1985- 78.10, 1986- 79.32, 1987- 77.94, 1988- 78.46. pb SP: 15.14 '76.
Finland's first ever Olympic champion at the hammer and best ever non-Eastern bloc thrower in 1984.

Women

Tuija HELANDER-KUUSISTO b.23 May 1961 Eura 1.72m 63kg. Euran Raiku. Economics student.
At 400mh: OG: '84- 7; WCh: '83- ht, '87- 5; ECh: '86- sf. Finnish champion 400mh 1977, 1980, 1982–7; 400m 1985, 1987.
Fourteen Finnish 400mh records 1980–7.
Progression at 400mh: 1977- 60.29, 1978- 59.78,

1979- 59.81, 1980- 57.84, 1981- 60.11, 1982- 59.17, 1983- 58.81, 1984- 56.55, 1985- 55.21, 1986- 56.17, 1987- 54.62, 1988- 55.90. pbs: 100m: 12.10/11.96w '85, 200m: 24.30 '87, 23.9 '85, 400m: 52.32 '85, 800m: 2:10.84 '87, 100mh: 13.87 '84, 300mh: 40.68 '87, HJ: 1.65 '78, LJ: 5.69 '77, Pen: 3729* '78.
A collapsed lung ended her 1988 season.

Tiina LILLAK b.15 Apr 1961 Helsinki 1.81m 74kg. Esbo IF. PR consultant.
At JT: OG: '80- dnq, '84- 2, '88- dnq 15; WCh: '83- 1, '87- 6; ECh: '82- 4, '86- 4; EJ: '79- 14. Finnish champion 1980–1, 1983, 1985–7.
Eleven Finnish records 1980–3, including two world records 1982–3, the first ever set by a Finnish woman thrower.
Progression at JT: 1976- 44.94, 1977- 47.92, 1978- 51.60, 1979- 56.36, 1980- 61.02, 1981- 66.34, 1982- 72.40, 1983- 74.76, 1984- 74.24, 1985- 70.62, 1986- 72.42, 1987- 67.64, 1988- 73.30. pb SP: 14.31 '83.
Full name Ilse Kristiina Lillak. Her win on the final throw in Helsinki in 1983, and the attendant roar of the crowd will long be remembered as one of the great moments in athletics history. In 1984 she was held back by a broken bone in her foot, but still managed to gain the Olympic silver medal, and has had further injury problems ever since.

FRANCE

Governing body: Fédération Française d'Athlétisme, 10 rue du Faubourg Poissonnière, 75480 Paris Cedex 10. Founded 1920.
National Championships first held in 1888 (men), 1918 (women)
1988 Champions: MEN
100m: Max Morinière 10.32, 200m: Jean-Charles Trouabal 20.64, 400m: Patrick Barré 45.72, 800m: Claude Diomar 1:47.74, 1500m: Hervé Phelippeau 3:41.47, 5000m: Paul Arpin 13:42.73, 10000m: Thierry Pantel 28:47.23, Mar: Alexandre Rachide 2:17:29, 3kmSt: Raymond Pannier 8:17.49, 110mh: Philippe Tourret 13.62, 400mh: Olivier Gui 50.44, HJ: Dominique Hernandez 2.25, PV: Philippe Collet 5.70, LJ: Norbert Brige 7.99, TJ: Pierre Camara 16.79, SP: Luc Viudes 19.20, DT: Patrick Journoud 59.04, HT: Frédéric Kuhn 73.24, JT: Pascal Lefèvre 81.48, Dec: Christian Plaziat 8441, 20kmW: Martial Fesselier 1:23:55.5, 50kW: Thierry Toutain 4:02:08.
WOMEN
100m: Laurence Bily 11.24, 200m: Marie-Christine Cazier 23.12, 400m: Marie-Josée Pérec 51.35, 800m: Barbara Gourdet 2:01.72, 1500m: Patricia Demilly 4:14.56, 3000m: Marie-Pierre Duros 8:59.31, 10000m: Maria Lelut 32:38.88, Mar: Odile Poirot 2:49:00, 100mh: Anne Piquereau 12.83, 400mh: Hélène Huart 55.72, HJ: Maryse Éwanje-Épée 1.95, LJ: Nadine Fourcade 6.42, SP/DT: Valérie Hanicque 15.84/55.22, JT: Nadine Auzeil 59.54, Hep: Chantal Beaugeant 6312, 5kmW: Suzanne Griesbach 23:38.06, 10kW: Anne Catherine Berthonnaud 49:51.9.

Paul ARPIN b.20 Feb 1960 Bourg-Saint-Maurice 1.70m 56kg. AS Aix-Les-Bains. Ski instructor/shepherd.
At 10000m: OG: '88- 7 (14 5000m); WCh: '87- 13; ECh: '86- dnf. World CC: '87- 3, '88- 11. French champion 5000m and CC 1986–8.
Progression at 5000m/10000m: 1980- 14:30.75, 1983- 14:17.4, 1985- 13:52.36, 1986- 13:31.2/28:07.29, 1987- 13:27.64/27:47.05, 1988- 13:22.03/27:39.36. pbs: 1500m: 3:40.5 '85, 3000m: 7:43.58 '88.
French cadet cross-country champion 1977.

Alain BLONDEL b.7 Dec 1962 Petit-Quevilly 1.85m 76kg. Stade Sotteville CC. Computer scientist.
At Dec: OG: '88- 6; WCh: '87- 7; ECh: '86- 8. French champion 1986.
Progression at Dec: 1981- 5873, 1982- 6494*, 1983- 6959, 1984- 7668, 1985- 7763, 1986- 8185, 1987- 8228, 1988- 8387. pbs: 100m: 10.74w '86, 200m: 21.78 '88, 400m: 47.44 '88, 1500m: 4:15.67 '88, 110mh: 14.07 '86, 400mh: 51.16 '87, HJ: 2.04 '84, PV: 5.20 '87, LJ: 7.50/7.56i '87, 7.59w '86, SP 13.99 '87, DT: 45.28 '88, JT: 62.32 '86.

Norbert BRIGE b.9 Jan 1964 Angres 1.84m 77kg Nancy AEC. PE instructor.
At LJ: OG: '88- 7; WCh: '87- 15; ECh: '86- 6; EJ: '81- 14, '83- 4. French champion 1985–8.
Progression at LJ: 1979- 6.38, 1980- 7.00, 1981- 7.54, 1982- 7.68, 1983- 7.86i/7.83, 1984- 7.97, 1985- 8.08, 1986- 8.09, 1987- 8.14, 1988- 8.22. pb 100m: 10.65 '83, 10.5 '88.

Stéphane CARISTAN b.31 May 1964 Créteil 1.87m 75kg. US Créteil. Bank employee.
At 110mh: OG: '84- 6, '88- sf; WCh: '83- h, '87- sf; ECh: '86- 1; EJ: '82- dnf. French champion 1983–6.
At 60mh: WI: '85- 1, '87- 2.
Two European 110mh records 1986.
Progression at 110mh: 1981- 14.95, 1982- 14.35, 1983- 13.86, 1984- 13.43, 1985- 13.47/13.4, 1986- 13.20/13.0, 1987- 13.44, 1988- 13.47. pbs: 100m: 10.51 '84, 200mh: 23.17 '87, PV: 5.00 '83, LJ: 7.79 '84, JT: 62.38 '83.
Brother Alain has PV best 5.30 '81, sister Chantal 100mh 14.10/14.01w '80. Operation on right knee in March 1987.

Philippe COLLET b.13 Dec 1963 Nancy 1.76m 71kg. ASPTT Grenoble. Student.
At PV: OG: '88- 5=; WCh: '87- dnq; ECh: '86- 3; E

'86- 3; WCp: '85- 2; EJ: '81- 11; ECp: '85- 2; WSG: '85- 2. French champion 1985, 1988.
Progression at PV: 1978- 3.30, 1979- 4.10, 1980- 4.90, 1981- 5.10, 1982- 5.20, 1983- 5.60, 1984- 5.60, 1985- 5.80, 1986- 5.85, 1987- 5.80i/5.75, 1988- 5.80. pbs: 100m: 10.81 '85, Dec: 7011 '86.

Bruno MARIE-ROSE b.20 May 1965 Bordeaux 1.93m 83kg. CA Ouest (St Germain). Engineer.
At 100m/R- 4x100m relay: OG: '84- qf/6R; ECh: '86- 3/4R (sf 200m); EJ: '83- dnf; WSG: '87- 3. At 60m: EI: '86- 3; WI: '87- 8. At 200m: OG: '88- 8/3R; WCh: '87- qf; WI: '87- 2, EI: '87- 1. French champion 100m 1984, 200m 1986–7.
WIB 200m 20.36 '87.
Progression at 100m/200m: 1981- 10.78/10.62w, 1982- 10.88/10.4w/22.01, 1983- 10.43/10.33w/ 21.65, 1984- 10.29/21.26, 1985- 10.38/20.94/20.8, 1986- 10.18/20.53, 1987- 10.21/20.36i/20.50, 1988- 10.25/10.11w/10.1/20.45.
In the French junior basketball squad in 1983. Of Martinique descent.

Raymond PANNIER b.12 Feb 1961 Saint-Quentin-en-Yvelines 1.74m 63kg. Marignane SA. Civil servant.
At 3000mSt: OG: '88- 12; WCh: '87- 10; ECh: '82 & '86- h. French champion 1987–8.
Progression at 3km St: 1980- 9:28.8, 1981- 8:34.22, 1982- 8:28.61, 1983- 8:40.70, 1984- 8:34.47, 1985- 8:22.36, 1986- 8:18.82, 1987- 8:13.88, 1988- 8:16.01. pbs: 1000m: 2:22.77 '85, 1500m: 3:40.5 '82, 2000m: 5:12.84 '85, 3000m: 7:45.82 '88, 5000m: 13:35.71 '88, 2kmSt: 5:34.3 '80.

Christian PLAZIAT b.28 Oct 1963 Lyon 1.90m 83kg. PL Pierre Bénite de Lyon. Postal worker.

Christian Plaziat (George Herringshaw/ASP)

At Dec: OG: '88- 5; WCh: '87- 4; ECh: '86- 7. French champion 1987–8. AT HJ: EJ: '81- 12.
Four French decathlon records 1987–8.
Progression at Dec: 1981- 6489, 1982- 7221, 1983- 7770, 1985- 8211w, 1986- 8196, 1987- 8315, 1988- 8512. pbs: 100m: 10.69/10.59w/10.3w '88, 10.4 '86; 200m: 21.84/21.6 '88, 400m: 47.73 '88, 1500m: 4:23.59 '87, 110mh: 14.10 '88, HJ: 2.20 '83, PV: 5.10 '88, LJ: 7.83 '86, SP: 15.86 '86, DT: 49.08 '86, JT: 63.02 '85, new: 58.22 '87.

Jean-Louis PRIANON b.22 Feb 1960 Saint-Joseph, Réunion 1.76m 58kg. ASPP Paris. Policeman.
At 10000m: OG: '88- 4; WCh: '87- 9; ECh: '86- 8. At 5000m: ECp: '85- 7. French champion 5000m 1985, 10000m 1985–6.
French 10000m record 1987.
Progression at 10000m: 1985- 28:06.02, 1986- 27:52.48, 1987- 27:34.38, 1988- 27:36.43. pbs: 1500m: 3:46.6 '84, 3000m: 7:48.9 '85, 5000m: 13:28.7 '86.
Best French junior at 5000m in 1979.

Gilles QUÉNÉHERVÉ b.17 May 1966 Paris 1.83m 74kg. Racing Club de France. Student of marketing.
At 200m/R- 4x100m relay: OG: '88- 6/3R; WCh: '87- 2; EJ: '85- 4 (5 100m). At 100m: ECh: '86- h/4R.
Three French 200m records 1987.
Progression at 200m: 1985- 21.11/21.0, 1986- 20.87/20.7, 1987- 20.16, 1988- 20.20. pb 100m: 10.31 '87, 10.3 '86.
Made sensational progress from taking up athletics in 1984 to his silver medal in Rome. Was fourth at 200m in both European and World Indoors 1987.

Pierre QUINON b.20 Feb 1962 Lyon 1.80m 74kg. Racing Club de France. Business student.
At PV: OG: '84- 1; WCh: '83- nh; ECh: '82- 12=; EI: '84- 2; EJ: '81- 2. French champion 1982–4. 2nd GP 1985.
World pole vault record 1983.
Progression at PV: 1976- 3.40, 1977- 3.90, 1978- 4.50, 1979- 5.00, 1980- 5.10i, 1981- 5.50, 1982- 5.70, 1983- 5.82, 1984- 5.80, 1985- 5.90, 1986- 5.72i/5.70, 1987- 5.60, 1988- 5.70.

Pascal THIÉBAUT b.6 Jun 1959 Nancy 1.75m 61kg. ASPTT Nancy. Postal worker.
At 5000m: OG: '88- 11; WCh: '87- h. At 3000m: WI: '87- 7; EI: '87- 3. At 1500m: OG: '84- sf; WCh: '83- h; ECh: '86- h; ECp: '83- 4, '85- 7. French champion 1984–6.
French 5000m record 1987.
Progression at 5000m: 1986- 13:37.05, 1987- 13:14.60, 1988- 13:17.48. pbs: 800m: 1:47.1 '84, 1000m: 2:17.71 '85, 1500m: 3:34.91 '87, 1M: 3:52.02 '84, 2000m: 4:56.70 '87, 3000m: 7:45.02 '87.

After several seasons as a useful 1500m runner, broke through quickly to the ranks of the top 5000m men in 1987, breaking the French record at the Bislett Games.

Thierry VIGNERON b.9 Mar 1960 Gennevilliers, Paris 1.81m 73kg. Racing Club de France. Physical education instructor.
At PV: OG: '80- 7, '84- 3=, '88- 5=; WCh: '83- 8=, '87- 2; ECh: '82- 5=, '86- nh; WI: '85- 2, '87- 3; EI: '81- 1, '84- 1, '87- 1; EJ: '77- 9, '79- 3; WSG: '81- 4, '83- 2. French champion 1980, 1986. GP: 3rd 1985, 2nd 1987.
Five world pole vault records: 5.75 twice '80, 5.80 '81 (world's first 19ft vault), 5.83 '83, 5.91 '84. Three WIB: 5.70 twice '81, 5.85 '84, and four world junior records from 5.45m to 5.61m in 1979.
Progression at PV: 1974- 3.70, 1975- 4.20, 1976- 4.95i, 1977- 5.10, 1978- 5.30, 1979- 5.61, 1980- 5.75, 1981- 5.80, 1982- 5.71, 1983- 5.83, 1984- 5.91, 1985- 5.80, 1986- 5.90, 1987- 5.85, 1988- 5.81i/5.70. pbs: 110mh: 15.06 '87, LJ: 6.99 '78, Dec: 7035 '87.
A prolific vaulter, who has set many records, and who in recent years also has the championship results to match. His last world record lasted just ten minutes for it came in his epic duel with Sergey Bubka in Rome in 1984.

Women

Chantal BEAUGEANT b.16 Feb 1961 Saint Etienne 1.70m 63kg. CSM Clamart. Office worker.
At Hep: OG: '84- dnf, '88- dnf (sf 400mh); WCh: '87- dnf; ECh: '86- 8. French champion 400mh 1986, Hep 1984–5, 1988.
Six French heptathlon records 1984–8.
Progression at Hep: 1980- 5188, 1981- 4989, 1982- 5240, 1983- 5693w/5594, 1984- 5993, 1985- 6305, 1986- 6242, 1987- 6410, 1988- 6702. pbs: 200m: 23.96w '88, 24.16 '87; 800m: 2:05.44 '88, 100mh: 13.10 '88, 400mh: 56.86 '87, 56.7 '85, HJ: 1.84 '88, LJ: 6.45 '88, SP: 14.01 '88, JT: 50.96 '88.
World 1 hour heptahlon best of 6241 at Auckland 24 Feb 1988.

Marie-Christine CAZIER b.23 Aug 1963 Paris 1.78m 59kg. Nancy AEC. Sports instructor. Married to Jean-Marie Ballo, Mali discus thrower pb 55.54 '85.
At 200m/R- 4x100m relay: OG: '88- qf; WCh: '83- qf, '87- sf; ECh: '82- 8/3R, '86- 2/4R; EI: '84- 2, '87- 3; EJ: '81- 5/2R; WI: '85- 2. French champion 100m 1985, 200m 1985–8.
Three French 200m records 1986.
Progression at 100m, 200m: 1978- 25.51, 1979- 24.96/24.7, 1980- 24.97, 1981- 23.76/23.53w, 1982- 22.94, 1983- 23.21, 1984- 23.48i/23.4, 1985- 22.75/22.7, 1986- 22.32, 1987- 22.79, 1988- 22.78. pbs: 100m: 11.23 '86, 11.12w '85, 11.1 '83; 400m: 54.18i '86, 55.5 '83; 400mh: 57.2/57.71 '85.

Florence COLLE b.4 Dec 1965 Annecy 1.69m 55kg. CAP Saumur. Medical student.
At 100mh: OG: '88- 5; WCh: '87- sf; WSG: '87- 3; EJ: '83- 5. French champion 1987.
Progression at 100mh: 1981- 14.7, 1983- 13.66, 1984- 13.52/13.51w/13.2w, 1985- 13.60, 1986- 13.11/13.1, 1987- 12.84, 1988- 12.84/12.78w. pbs: 100m: 11.84/11.7 '87, 200m: 24.36 '87, HJ: 1.72 '83, LJ: 6.58 '86, Hep: 5570 '87.

Laurence ELLOY b.3 Dec 1959 Rouen 1.68m 57kg. Previous married name Machabey. Stade Français. Secretary.
At 100mh: OG: '80- sf, '84- h; WCh: '83- sf, '87- 6; ECh: '78- h, '82- sf, '86- 6; EJ: '77- 4. 3rd GP 1988. French champion 1979, 1982, 1984–6. At 60mh: WI: '85- 2.
Four French 100mh records 1982–6.
Progression at 100mh: 1976- 14.9, 1977- 13.82, 1978- 13.47, 1979- 13.33, 1980- 13.13, 1981- 13.19, 1982- 12.90/12.81w, 1983- 12.95, 1984- 12.94/12.72w, 1985- 12.79/12.72w, 1986- 12.69, 1987- 12.83, 1988- 12.91/12.83w. pb 100m: 11.94 '82, 11.93w/11.8 '76.
Her father Georges Elloy was at 400mh: sixth European 1950, French champion 1950–1; he won the World University Games title in 1949 in his pb 53.0, the third world junior record he set that year.

Maryse EWANJE-EPÉE b.4 Sep 1964 Poitiers 1.77m 62kg. US Créteil. Student of literature and drama.
At HJ: OG: '84- 4, '88- 10; WCh: '83- 12=; ECh: '82- 10, '86- dnq; EI: '83- 3, '84- 2; WSG: '83- 3. French champion 1982–5, 1988. At Hep: EJ: '81- 6.
Four French high jump records 1983–5.
Progression at HJ: 1977- 1.52, 1978- 1.61, 1979- 1.69, 1980- 1.76, 1981- 1.87, 1982- 1.89, 1983- 1.95, 1984- 1.95i/1.94, 1985- 1.96, 1986- 1.94i/1.92, 1987- 1.91, 1988- 1.95. pbs: 100m: 12.1 '84, 200m: 24.83 '88, 100mh: 13.49 '88, LJ: 6.26 '85; Hep: 5867 '85.
Her younger sister Monique (b.11 Jul 1967) at 100mh: pb 12.87/12.86w '88, won the 1985 European Junior 100mh title in a European Junior record 13.10, and was 7th in the 1988 Olympics.

Anne PIQUEREAU b.15 Jun 1964 Poitiers 1.70m 67kg. Stade Clermontois. Student.
At 100mh: OG: '88- qf; WCh: '87- 5; ECh: '86- sf; EJ: '81- 3; ECp: '87- 5; WSG: '85- 3. French champion 1988. At 60mh: EI: '85- 3, '86- 2; WIG: '85- 3.
Progression at 100mh: 1980- 14.3/13.86w, 1981- 13.76/13.67w, 1982- 13.64/13.5w, 1983- 13.22/13.0, 1984- 13.39/13.30w, 1985- 12.89, 1986-

12.95, 1987- 12.82, 1988- 12.94/12.83w. pbs: 100m: 11.87/11.5 '87, LJ: 6.40 '85.

Annette SERGENT b.17 Nov 1962 Chambéry 1.57m 47kg. ASU Lyon. Student of psychology.
At 3000m: OG: '84- h, '88- 12 (19 10000m); WCh: '87- h; ECh: '86- 8 (8 1500m); ECp: '87- 4. 2nd GP 5000m 1988. French champion 1500m 1984–5 3000m 1983–5, CC 1985–8. World CC: '86- 3, '87- 1, '88- 3.
French records 1985–8: 5 at 3000m, 2 at 5000m, 1 2000m & 10000m.
Progression at 3000m: 1979- 11:19.7, 1980- 10:14.9, 1981- 9:48.16, 1982- 9:19.76, 1983- 9:12.74, 1984- 9:02.05, 1985- 8:50.56, 1986- 8:46.94, 1987- 8:46.12, 1988- 8:44.19. pbs: 800m: 2:06.4 '86, 1000m: 2:41.5 '85, 1500m: 4:10.14 '85, 2000m: 5:39.00 '86, 5000m: 15:18.24 '88, 10000m: 32:04.78 '88.
Her sister Agnès had pbs of 2:09.9, 4:17.3 and

Jocelyne VILLETON b.17 Sep 1954 Vals-les-Bains 1.70m 55kg. Saint-Etienne. Office worker.
At Mar: OG: '88- 19; WCh: '87- 3; ECh: '86- 5; WCp: '87- 19. French champion 10000m 1986–7. World road 15km: '88- 10.
French 10000m record 1986.
Progression at Mar: 1982- 3:00:46, 1983- 2:50:09, 1984- 2:47:09, 1985- 2:35:50, 1986- 2:32:23, 1987- 2:32:03, 1988- 2:34:02. pbs: 1500m: 4:28.2 '85, 3000m: 9:23.0 '88, 5000m: 16:19.83 '86, 10000m: 32:51.37 '88.
Surprised with high placings in both European and World Championships. Ran short course 2:28:02, and third New York in 1987. Has two children.

GERMAN DEMOCRATIC REPUBLIC

Governing body: Deutscher Verband für Leichtathletik der DDR, Storkower Strasse 118, Berlin 1055. Founded 1950.
National Championships first held in 1950.
1988 Champions: MEN
100m: Sven Matthes 10.19, 200m: Frank Emmelmann 20.37, 400m: Thomas Schönlebe 45.56, 800m: Ralph Schumann 1:47.38, 1500m: Jens-Peter Herold 3:46.62, 5000m: Axel Krippschock 13:48.63, 10000m: Hansjörg Kunze 27:55.85, Mar: Rainer Wachenbrunner 2:17:20, 3kmSt: Hagen Melzer 8:19.22, 110mh: Holger Polger 13.67, 400mh: Uwe Ackermann 50.15, HJ: Gerd Wessig 2.26, PV: Uwe Langhammer 5.60, LJ: Ron Beer 7.92, TJ: Volker Mai 16.80, SP: Ulf Timmermann 21.88, DT: Jürgen Schult 66.92, HT: Ralf Haber 80.30, JT: Silvio Warsönke 82.64, Dec: Uwe Freimuth, 20kmW/50kmW: Ronald Weigel 1:20:57/ 3:42:33.
WOMEN
100m: Marlies Göhr 11.07, 200m/LJ: Heike Drechsler 21.84/7.20, 400m: Petra Müller 50.26, 800m: Christine Wachtel 1:58.29, 1500m: Birgit Barth 4:09.33, 3000m/10000m: Kathrin Ullrich 8:48.80/ 31:26.79, Mar: Andrea Fleischer 2:49:51, 100mh: Cornelia Oschkenat 12.52, 400mh: Sabine Busch 54.11, HJ: Gabriele Günz 1.91, SP: Kathrin Neimke 21.06, DT: Diana Gansky 72.54, JT: Petra Felke 73.86, Hep: Heike Tischler 6404, 5kmW/10kmW: Beate Anders 21:36/46:28.

Udo BEYER b.9 Aug 1955 Eisenhüttenstadt 1.95m 130kg. ASK Potsdam. PE student, captain in the National People's Army.
At SP: OG: '76- 1, '80- 3, '88- 4; WCh: '83- 6, '87- 6; ECh: '74- 8, '78- 1, '82- 1, '86- 3; EJ: '73- 1; WSG: '79- 1; WCp and ECp: '77- 1, '79- 1, '81- 1, ECp: '85- 3; WI: '85- 2. GDR champion 1977–87.
Six GDR shot records 1977–86, inc. three world records 1978, 1983, and 1986; five European junior records 1973–4.
Progression at SP: 1971- 15.71, 1972- 17.08, 1973- 19.65, 1974- 20.20, 1975- 20.97, 1976- 21.12, 1977- 21.74, 1978- 22.15, 1979- 21.74, 1980- 21.98, 1981- 21.69, 1982- 21.94, 1983- 22.22, 1984- 22.04, 1985- 21.88, 1986- 22.64, 1987- 22.31, 1988- 22.10. pbs: DT: 56.42 '74, HT: 66.84 '73.
Ranked as the world's number one shot putter seven times 1977–82 and 1984 after winning the 1976 Olympic title at the age of 20, losing only a handful of times in this period. A pulled back muscle cost him the chance of winning the 1980 Olympic title. Although he has won a record number of GDR titles, he has fared less well recently in major championships.

Steffen BRINGMANN b.11 Mar 1964 Leipzig 1.83m 78kg. SC DHfK Leipzig. Gastronomic student.
At 100m (R- 4x100m relay): ECh: '86- 2 (2R); EJ: '81- sf (1R); WCp: '85- 4R; ECp: '85- 2R, '87- 2 (2 200m/2R). GDR champion 1987. At 60m: EI: '86- 2. European indoor best 6.54 for 60m and WIB 9.50 for 100y 1986.
Progression at 100m: 1976- 13.0, 1977- 12.5, 1978- 11.63, 1979- 11.52, 1980- 10.86/10.7, 1981- 10.60/ 10.53w, 1982- 10.83, 1983- 10.27/10.25w, 1984- 10.43/10.30w, 1985- 10.22/10.17w, 1986- 10.13, 1987- 10.19, 1988- 10.21. pb 200m: 20.77 '87, 20.72w '88.

Jens CARLOWITZ b.8 Aug 1964 Karl-Marx-Stadt 1.85m 76kg. SC Karl-Marx-Stadt. Electrician.
At 400m/4x400m relay: OG: '88- sf/4R; WCh: '87- sf; EI: '88- 1; EJ: '81- 2/1R, '83- 2/1R; ECp: '83- 2R, '85- 2R, '87- 1R.
Progression at 400m: 1978- 55.9, 1979- 51.81, 1980- 48.5, 1981- 46.58, 1982- 47.13, 1983- 45.72,

1984- 44.95, 1985- 44.95, 1986- 46.71, 1987- 44.92, 1988- 45.08. pbs: 200m: 20.94 '87, 800m: 1:54.6 '80.

Marco DELONGE b.16 Jun 1966 Magdeburg 1.94m 81kg. SC Dynamo Berlin. Mechanical engineering student.
At LJ: EJ: '85- 2; ECp: '87- 2. GDR champion 1987.
Progression at LJ: 1983- 7.16, 1984- 7.87/7.96w, 1985- 7.92, 1986- 8.16, 1987- 8.27, 1988- 8.23.

Frank EMMELMANN b.15 Sep 1961 Schneidlingen 1.85m 78kg. SC Magdeburg. Fitter. Married Kirsten Siemon (qv) in 1984.
At 100m/200m/R- 4x100m relay: WCh: '83- sf/5/4R; ECh: '82- 1/3/2R, '86- -/8/2R; WCp: '81- 3/3/2R, '85- 3/2; ECp: '81- 2/1, '83- 1/-, '85- 3/1/2R, '87- 2R. GDR champion: 100m 1981–2, 1985; 200m 1981, 1984–5, 1987–8.
Two GDR records each at 100m 1984–5, 200m 1981–5.
Progression at 100m, 200m: 1977- 10.9; 1978- 10.70, 22.00; 1979- 10.42/10.2, 20.90; 1980- 10.39; 1981- 10.19/10.15w, 20.33/20.23w; 1982- 10.20/ 10.11w, 20.47; 1983- 10.18, 20.55; 1984- 10.11, 20.46; 1985- 10.06, 20.23, 1986- 10.32, 20.62; 1987- 10.21, 20.65; 1988- 10.26, 20.37. pb 400m: 47.16 '87.

Thomas FAHNER b.18 Jul 1966 Fürstenberg 1.86m 85kg. ASK Potsdam. PE student.
At Dec: EJ: '85- 1; ECp: '87- 3.
Progression at Dec: 1983- 6764, 1984- 7358, 1985- 7815, 1986- 8170, 1987- 8187, 1988- 8362. pbs: 100m: 10.82 '86, 400m: 47.90 '86, 1500m: 4:27.53 '87, 110mh: 14.54 '88, HJ: 2.00 '85, PV: 5.10 '86, LJ: 7.35 '86, 7.55w '88; SP: 15.17 '88; DT: 47.14 '87, JT: 68.40 '88.

Uwe FREIMUTH b.10 Sep 1961 Rathenow 1.91m 92kg. ASK Potsdam. Sports instructor.
At Dec: OG: '88- 18; WCh: '83- 4; ECh: '86- 6; ECp: '81- 3, '83- 1, '85- 7, '87- 2. GDR champion 1985–6, 1988.
Four GDR decathlon records 1983–4.
Progression at Dec: 1978- 7221, 1979- 7449, 1980- 7733, 1981- 8221, 1982- 8026, 1983- 8551, 1984- 8792, 1985- 8504, 1986- 8322, 1987- 8220, 1988- 8381. pbs: 100m: 10.82 '86, 10.98w '85, 400m: 47.90 '86, 1500m: 4:23.25 '83, 110mh: 14.54 '83, HJ: 2.15 '81, PV: 5.15 '84, LJ: 7.79 '83, SP: 16.42 '84, DT: 51.54 '84, JT: 73.02 '84, new: 64.78 '86.

Hartwig GAUDER b.10 Nov 1954 Vaihingen, FRG 1.86m 70kg. SC Turbine Erfurt. Architectural student.
At 50kmW: OG: '80- 1, '88- 3; WCh: '87- 1; ECh: '82- 4, '86- 1; LT: '81- 2, '85- 1, '87- 2. At 20kmW: ECh: '78- 7; LT: '79- 7. At 10kmW: EJ: '73- 1. GDR champion: 20kmW 1975–6, 1985–6; 50kmW 1979, 1982, 1986.
WIB 1 hour walk 14906m 1986.
Progression at 20kmW/50kmW: 1972- 1:34:19, 1973- 1:32:55, 1974- 1:28:47, 1975- 1:26:29, 1976- 1:26:25, 1977- 1:27:07, 1978- 1:24:22.7t, 1979- 1:21:39/4:01:20, 1980- 1:23:36.6i/3:48:15, 1981- 3:46:57, 1982- 1:29:29/3:49:44, 1983- 1:21:33/ 3:43:23, 1984- 1:22:53/3:41:24, 1985- 1:23:03/ 3:43:33, 1986- 1:21:15/3:40:55, 1987- 1:20.51/ 3:40:53, 1988- 1:23:15/3:39:45. Track pbs: 3kmW: 11:20.0 '84, 5kmW: 18:59.67i '88, 10kmW: 39:13.15i '88.
Family moved from West Germany when he was aged five. Completed his set of major event gold medals in 1987. The feat of winning European junior and senior, Olympic and World titles is matched only by Daley Thompson and Khristo Markov.

Ralf HABER b.18 Aug 1962 Altenburg 1.90m 118kg. SC Karl-Marx-Stadt. PE student.

Ralf Haber (George Herringshaw/ASP)

At HT: WCh: '87- 3, '88- 4; ECh: '86- 6; EJ: '81- 4; ECp: '87- 2. GDR champion 1984, 1987–8.
Two GDR hammer records 1983 & 1988.
Progression at HT: 1979- 52.18, 1980- 66.44, 1981- 70.88, 1982- 76.42, 1983- 79.02, 1984- 79.38, 1985- 78.68, 1986- 80.60, 1987- 81.84, 1988- 83.40.

Jens-Peter HEROLD b.25 Oct 1965 Neuruppin 1.76m 68kg. ASK Potsdam. Mechanic, staff sergeant in the People's Army.
At 1500m: OG: (88- 3; WCh: '87- 6; EI: '87- 2; ECp: '87- 3. GDR champion 800m 1987, 1500m 1987–8.
GDR records 1500m 1987, 1 mile 1988.
Progression at 1500m: 1983- 3:48.87, 1984- 3:49.67, 1985- 3:43.9, 1986- 3:37.92, 1987- 3:33.28, 1988- 3:33.33. pbs: 400m: 49.5 '85, 800m: 1:46.44 '87, 1000m: 2:18.61 '88, 1M: 3:49.22 '88, 3000m: 8:03.88i '88, 5000m: 14:14.5 '86.

Hansjörg KUNZE b.28 Dec 1959 Rostock 1.79m 63kg. SC Empor Rostock. Medical student.
At 10000m: '88- 6; WCh: '83- 3, '87- 3. At 5000m: OG: '80- sf, '88- 3; ECh: '82- 9, '86- dnf; WCp: '79- 4, '81- 2; ECp: '79- 1, '81- 3, '83- 4. At 3000m: EJ: '73- 3. World CC: '82- 4. GDR champion 5000m 1981, 1983–4, 1986–7; 10000m 1984, 1986–8.
At 5000m: European record 1981, WIB 13:13.3 '83; world junior 3000m record 7:56.4 '76. GDR 3000m record 1983.
Progression at 5000m/10000m: 1974- 15:14.6, 1975- 14:20.4, 1978- 13:42.2/29:57.9, 1979- 13:27.7, 1980- 13:26.4/28:00.73, 1981- 13:10.40/ 28:12.25, 1982- 13:12.53, 1983- 13:13.3i/27:30.69, 1984- 13:33.90i/27:33.10, 1986- 13:31.05/27:34.68, 1987- 13:24.00/27:39.60, 1988- 13:15.73/27:26.00. pbs: 1500m: 3:40.04 '79, 2000m: 5:10.0i '84, 3000m: 7:44.05 '83.

Volker MAI b.3 May 1966 Templin 1.94m 75kg. SC Neubrandenburg. Medical student.
At TJ: ECh: '86- 7, EI: '85- 3; EJ: '83- 5, '85- 1 (1 LJ); WCp: '85- 4; ECp: '85- 2. GDR champion 1988.
World junior and GDR TJ record in 1985.
Progression at TJ: 1981- 14.72, 1982- 15.90, 1983- 16.20/16.22w, 1984- 17.12, 1985- 17.50, 1986- 17.02, 1987- 17.24, 1988- 17.23. pbs: 100m: 10.9 '86, 200m: 21.91 '85, LJ: 8.04 '85.

Sven MATTHES b.23 Aug 1969 Berlin 1.86m 77kg. SC Dynamo Berlin. Student.
At 100m (200m, R- 4x100m relay): OG: '88- qf; WJ: '88- 2 (5); EJ: '87- 3 (4, 3R). GDR champion 1988.
Two European Junior 100m records 1988.
Progression at 100m: 1984- 11.41, 1985- 11.14, 1986- 10.69, 1987- 10.35, 1988- 10.14. pb 200m: 20.99 '87.
Showed sharp sprinting indoors in 1988 with 5.72 for 50m and 6.53 for 60m, at which he was fourth at the European Indoors.

Dietmar MEISCH b.10 Feb 1959 Weida 1.78m 65kg. TSC Berlin. Electronics student.
At 50kmW: OG: '80- dq, '88- 9; WCh: '83 &'87- dq; ECh: '82- dnf, '86- 6; LT: '79- 8, '81- 4, '85- 6, '87- 3. GDR champion 1987.
Progression at 50kmW: 1979- 3:50:02, 1980- 3:47:38, 1981- 3:48:57, 1982- 3:48:01, 1983- 3:46.12, 1984- 3:43:33, 1985- 3:49:44, 1986- 3:48:01, 1987- 3:43:14, 1987- 3:46:50, 1988- 3:46:31. pbs: 10kmW: 40:29.10i '88, 20kmW: 1:22:15 '88.

Hagen MELZER b.16 Jun 1959 Bautzen 1.78m 63kg. SC Einheit Dresden. Engine fitter.
At 3000mSt: OG: '88- 10; WCh: '83- 11, '87- 2; ECh: '82- 4, '86- 1; WCp: '85- 5; ECp: '79- 5, '83- 4, '85- 6, '87- 3. GDR champion 1980, 1983, 1985–8. At 2000mSt: EJ: '77- 6.
GDR 3000m steeplechase record 1987.
Progression at 3000mSt: 1978- 8:38.66, 1979- 8:31.7, 1980- 8:27.7, 1981- 8:27.68, 1982- 8:21.27, 1983- 8:20.28, 1984- 8:21.32, 1985- 8:28.56, 1986- 8:16.65, 1987- 8:10.32, 1988- 8:16.27. pbs: 1500m: 3:40.68 '84, 3000m: 7:51.43 '82.

Detlef MICHEL b.13 Oct 1955 Berlin 1.85m 95kg. TSC Berlin. Plumber.
At JT: OG: '80- dnq, '88- dnq 17; WCh: '83- 1; ECh: '78- 4, '82- 3, '86- 2; WCp: '81- 2; ECp: '75- 4, '81- 1, '83- 1. GDR champion 1975, 1979–80, 1982–3, 1986–7.
Five GDR javelin records 1981–3, the last equalled the European record.
Progression at JT: 1970- 64.08, 1971- 67.96, 1972- 75.80, 1973- 72.48, 1974- 76.70, 1975- 84.58, 1976- 84.72, 1977- 82.44, 1978- 86.12, 1979- 89.74, 1980- 90.98, 1981- 92.48, 1982- 94.52, 1983- 96.72, 1984- 93.68, 1985- 84.74, new: 1986- 83.52, 1987- 81.86, 1988- 84.06. pb LJ: 7.20 '77.

Axel NOACK b.23 Sep 1961 Görlitz 1.82m 74kg. TSC Berlin. building worker/PE student.
At 20kmW: OG: '88- 8; WCh: '87- dnf; ECh: '86- dq; LT: '87- 6. At 50kmW: LT: '85- 3. GDR champion 20kmW 1987, 50kmW 1984.
World 20km road walk best 1987.
Progression at 20kmW/50kmW: 1981- 1:35:23, 1982- 1:33:23, 1983- 1:24:19/4:22:41, 1984- 1:26:20/4:00.41, 1985- 1:26:54/3:56.22, 1986- 1:21:55, 1987- 1:19:12, 1988- 1:20:39. pbs: 3kmW: 11:36.11 '87, 5kmW: 19:28.09 '87, 10kmW: 39:29.72 '87.

Jörg PETER b.23 Oct 1955 Dresden 1.73m 63kg. Club: SC Einheit Dresden. Vehical technician.
At Mar: OG: '88- dnf; ECp: '85- 3, '88- 15; 10km: OG: '80- 6; WCp: '77- 2; ECp: '77- 1. At 5000m: ECh: '78- 12. At 3000m: '78- 3. GDR champion at 5000m 1976–8 & 1980, 10000m 1977, marathon 1982, 1985.
GDR marathon records 1984 and 1988.
Progression at Mar: 1980- 2:12:56, 1983- 2:15:34, 1984- 2:09:14, 1985- 2:12:16, 1986- 2:16:05, 1987- 2:11:22, 1988- 2:08:46. pbs: 800m: 1:49.86 '76, 1500m: 3:39.2 '76, 3000m: 7:50.1i '78, 5000m:

13:23.5 '79, 10000m: 27:55.50 '77.
Has won four of his 15 marathons 1980–8, including at Kosice 1987. Third at Tokyo 1988 in national record.

Gunther RODEHAU b.6 Jul 1959 Meissen 1.79m 114kg. SC Einheit Dresden. Vehicle mechanic.
At HT: OG: '88- 12; WCh: '83- 5, '87- 9; ECh: '86- 4; WCp: '85- 2; ECp: '83- 3. GDR champion 1986.
Two GDR hammer records 1984–5.
Progression at HT: 1977- 49.94, 1978- 60.84, 1979- 68.90, 1980- 74.02, 1981- 74.42, 1982- 72.18, 1983- 78.14, 1984- 80.20, 1985- 82.64, 1986- 81.70, 1987- 81.58, 1988- 81.82.

Christian SCHENK b.9 Feb 1965 Rostock 2.00m 93kg. SC Empor Rostock. Medical student.
At Dec: OG: '88- 1; WCh: '87- 5; EJ: '83–2; ECp: '85- 4.
Progression at Dec: 1983- 7558, 1984- 8036, 1985- 8163, 1987- 8304, 1988- 8488. pbs: 100m: 11.10 '88, 400m: 48.90 '88, 1500m: 4:16.02 '88, 110mh: 14.91 '87, HJ: 2.27 '88, PV: 4.70 '88, LJ: 7.69 '87, 7.71w '88, SP: 15.48 '88, DT: 49.28 '88, JT: 67.14 '85, new: 64.04 '87.
A rare straddle high jumper, who excelled at the 1988 Olympics with pbs at five of the ten events. His father Eberhard was GDR 110mh champion 1955, with pb 14.8 '54.

Mathias SCHERSING b.7 Oct 1964 Halle 1.82m 67kg. SC Chemie Halle. Computer operator/ electronics student.
At 400m (R- 4x400m relay): OG: '88- 4R; WCh: '87- sf; ECh: '86- 3; EJ: '83- 1R; EI: '86- 3; WCp: '85- 2R; ECp: '85- 2R, '87- 1R. GDR champion 1986.
Progression at 400m: 1982- 47.91, 1983- 47.06, 1984- 44.86, 1985- 45.12, 1986- 44.85, 1987- 45.03, 1988- 45.20. pbs: 100m: 10.5 '82, 200m: 20.80 '86.

Thomas SCHÖNLEBE b.6 Aug 1965 Frauenstein 1.85m 76kg. SC Karl-Marx-Stadt. Physics student.
At 400m/4x400m relay: OG: '88- sf/4R; WCh: '83- 6, '87- 1; ECh: '86- 2; EJ: '83- 1/1R; WCp: '85- 2; ECp: '83- 2/2R, '85- 1/2R, '87- 1/1R; EI: '86- 1; WI: '85- 1. GDR champion 1983–5, 1987–8.
At 400m: two European records 1987, two GDR records 1985, three European Junior records 1983–4, three WIB: 45.60 '85, 45.41 '86, 45.05 '88.
Progression at 400m: 1981- 47.50, 1982- 46.71, 1983- 45.29, 1984- 45.01, 1985- 44.62, 1986- 44.63, 1987- 44.33, 1988- 44.62. pbs: 100m: 10.98 '82, 200m: 20.48 '87, 800m: 1:57.7 '81, LJ: 6.83 '81.

Jürgen SCHULT b.11 May 1960 Neuhaus, Kr. Hagenow 1.93m 110kg. SC Traktor Schwerin. Machine fitter.
At DT: OG: '88- 1; WCh: '83- 5, '87- 1; ECh: '86- 7; EJ: '79- 1; WCp: '85- 2; ECp: '83- 1, '85- 4, '87- 2. GDR champion 1983–8.
World discus record 1986.
Progression at DT: 1978- 51.82, 1979- 57.22, 1980- 61.26, 1981- 61.56, 1982- 63.18, 1983- 66.78, 1984- 68.82, 1985- 69.74, 1986- 74.08, 1987- 69.52, 1988- 70.46. pb SP: 18.59 '84.
Although he has not matched his world record distance he has been most consistent, never placing lower than second and winning the world title in 1987, and remaining undefeated in 1988 when he won Olympic gold.

Ulf TIMMERMANN b.1 Nov 1962 Berlin 1.94m 120kg. TSC Berlin. Joiner, economics student.
At SP: OG: '88- 1; WCh: '83- 2, '87- 5; WI: '87- 1; ECh: '86- 2; EI: '85- 2, '87- 1; EJ: '81- 2 (9 at DT); WCp: '85- 1; ECp: '83- 2, '87- 1. GDR champion 1988.
World shot records 1985 & 1988, WIB: 22.15 '85.
Progression at SP: 1979- 16.23, 1981- 19.00, 1982- 20.22, 1983- 21.36, 1984- 21.75, 1985- 22.62, 1986- 22.60, 1987- 22.24i/22.01, 1988- 23.06. pb DT: 52.68 '81.
At last won a major outdoor gold medal at the Olympics, when he four times improved the Olympic record.

Torsten VOSS b.24 Mar 1963 Güstrow 1.86m 88kg. SC Traktor Schwerin. Mechanic/student teacher.
At Dec: OG: '88- 2; WCh: '83- 7, '87- 1; ECh: '82- dnf, '86- 4; EJ: '81- 2, ECp: '85- 1. GDR champion 1982–3, 1987.
World junior decathlon record 1982.
Progression at Dec: 1977- 5083*, 1978- 6325*, 1979- 7160, 1980- 7518, 1981- 8003, 1982- 8397, 1983- 8335, 1984- 8543, 1985- 8559, 1986- 8450, 1987- 8680, 1988- 8399. pbs: 100m: 10.54 '84, 10.53w '86; 200m: 21.45 '87, 400m: 47.51 '87, 1500m: 4:17.00 '81, 110mh: 13.94 '85, HJ: 2.11 '81, PV: 5.15i '86, LJ: 8.02 '84, SP: 15.61 '88, DT: 46.52 '88, JT: 62.90 '82, new: 61.76 '88.
Added 121 points to his pb to win the 1987 world title, when he set no individual event pbs, but performed consistently close to them.

Silvio WARSÖNKE b.2 Aug 1967 Finsterwalde 1.97m 105kg. SC Cottbus. Electrician.
At JT: OG: '88- dnq 15. GDR champion 1988.
GDR javelin record 1988,
Progression at JT: 1984- 64.70, 1985- 69.44, new: 1986- 72.78, 1987- 70.02, 1988- 84.14.
Made a huge improvement to throw a GDR record 84.14m in his first meeting of 1988.

Ronald WEIGEL b.8 Aug 1959 Hildburghausen 1.76m 63kg. ASK Potsdam. Student of journalism.
At 50kmW: OG: '88- 2 (2 20kmW); WCh: '83- 1,

'87- 2; ECh: '86- dq; LT: '87- 1. At 10kmW: EJ: '77- 2. At 5kmW: EI: '87- 2. GDR champion 20kmW 1984, 1988; 50kmW 1983, 1985, 1988.
At 20km walk: European track record 1:20:54.9 1983. WIB: 5kmW: 18:44.97 '87 & 18:11.41 '88, 20kmW: 1:20:40 '80. World fastest 50km road walk 1984 and 1986; GDR road bests at 30km (2:12:41) and 35km (2:34:40) 1984.
Progression at 20kmW/50kmw: 1975- 1:40:56, 1976- 1:30:49, 1977- 1:27:51, 1978- 1:27:00, 1979- 1:25:00, 1980- 1:20:40i/1:22:50, 1981- 1:22:40/ 3:49:53, 1982- 1:25:12t/3:44:20, 1983- 1:20:55/ 3:41:31, 1984- 1:19:56/3:38:31, 1985- 1:22:12/ 3:47.15, 1986- 1:20:39/3:38:17, 1987- 1:20:40/ 3:41:30, 1988- 1:20:00/3:38:56. Track pbs: 3kmW: 11:18.0 '84, 5kmW: 18:53.38 '84, 18:11.41i '88; 10kmW: 38:35.5i '80, 1hrW: 14750mi '84.

Gerald WEISS b.8 Jan 1960 Lübz 1.93m 105kg. SC Traktor Schwerin. Mechanic.
At JT: OG: '88- 6; ECh: '86- 11; EJ: '79- nt; WSG: '81- 2; ECp: '87- 5. GDR champion 1981.
Progression at JT: 1974- 49.82, 1975- 58.12, 1976- 70.80, 1977- 71.82, 1978- 73.42, 1979- 82.02, 1980- 85.92, 1981- 89.56, 1982- 83.26, 1983- 86.28, 1984- 90.06, 1985- 82.84, new: 1986- 81.40, 1987- 81.76, 1988- 83.30.

Women

Anke BEHMER b.5 Jun 1961 Stavenhagen 1.74m 62kg. née Vater. SC Neubrandenburg. Medical student.
At Hep: OG: '88- 3; WCh: '83- 3, '87- 4; ECh: '82- 4, '86- 1; ECp: '81- 5; EJ: '79- 3 (Pen). GDR champion 1983, 1986.
Progression at Pen (p)/Hep: 1977- 3648p, 1978- 4114p, 1979- 4321p, 1980- 5792, 1981- 6251, 1982- 6371, 1983- 6531, 1984- 6775, 1986- 6717, 1987- 6692, 1988- 6858. pbs: 200m: 23.10/22.73w '88; 800m: 2:03.76 '84, 100mh: 13.11 '88, HJ: 1.87 '86, LJ: 6.84 '84, 6.89w '88; SP: 15.26 '82, JT: 44.54 '88.
Missed 1985 season due to pregnancy. Broke her collar-bone in the 1987 European Cup heptathlon.

Kerstin BEHRENDT b.2 Sep 1967 Leisnig/Kreis Döbeln 1.77m 64kg. DHfK Leipzig. Medical student.
At 100m/200m/R- 4x100m relay: OG: '88- 2R; WCh: '87- 2R; EJ: '85- 1/1/1R.
Progression at 100m/200m: 1981- 12.36, 1982- 11.9, 1983- 12.04/24.8, 1984- 11.86/24.44, 1985- 11.21/23.21, 1986- 11.62/23.89, 1987- 11.09/ 11.05w/22.76, 1988- 11.05/10.89w/22.36, 11.0/22.3
Set a national age-10 record of 8.2 for 60m in 1978.

Susanne BEYER b.24 Jun 1961 Suhl 1.76m 58kg. née Helm. SC Dynamo Berlin. Physiotherapy student.
At HJ: WCh: '83- 7, '87- 3; WI: '87- 2; ECh: '86- 4=; EI: '85- 2, '87- 3=; WCp: '85- 3; ECp: '85- 3, '87- 4. GDR champion 1983, 1985, 1987.
Progression at HJ: 1977- 1.55, 1978- 1.77, 1979- 1.83, 1980- 1.88, 1981- 1.88, 1982- 1.91, 1983- 1.97, 1984- 1.96, 1985- 1.97, 1986- 1.96, 1987- 2.02i/1.99, 1988- 1.97i/1.94.

Grit BREUER b.16 Feb 1972 Röbel 1.65m 59kg. SC Neubrandenburg. Schoolgirl.
At 400m (R- 4x400m relay): OG: '88- resR; WJ: '88- 1 (1R & 1 4x100mR).
World junior records 4x100mR and 4x400mR 1988.
Progression at 400m: 1985- 56.21, 1986- 55.7, 1987- 52.59, 1988- 51.14. pbs: 100m: 11.53 '88, 200m: 23.04 '88.
Bronze medal as ran in heats of Olympic 4x400m relay.

Ilona BRIESENICK b.24 Sep 1956 Demmin 1.80m 95kg. née Schoknecht, formerly Slupianek. Married to Hartmut Briesenick, European shot champion 1971 and 1974. SC Dynamo Berlin.
At SP: OG: '76- 5, '80- 1; WCh: '83- 3; ECh: '78- 1, '82- 1; WI: '87- 2; EI: '76- 3, '77- 2, '79- 1, '81- 1; WCp: '77- 1, '79- 1, '81- 1; ECp: '77- dq (1), '79- 1, '81- 1; EJ: '73- 1 (2 at DT). GDR shot champion 1977, 1979–84.
Seven GDR shot records 1977–80, inc. two world records, 22.36m & 22.45m in 1980. Eleven world junior records 1973–4.
Progression at SP: 1970- 12.50, 1971- 13.32, 1972- 14.40, 1973- 17.05, 1974- 19.23, 1975- 20.12, 1976- 21.30, 1977- 21.79, 1978- 22.06, 1979- 22.04, 1980- 22.45, 1981- 21.61, 1982- 21.80, 1983- 22.40, 1984- 21.85, 1986- 19.48, 1987- 20.71i/20.52, 1988- 20.81. pb DT: 64.40 '77.

Sabine BUSCH b.21 Nov 1962 Erfurt 1.77m 66kg. SC Turbine Erfurt. Sports student.
At 400mh/R- 4x400m relay: OG: '88- 4/3R; WCh: '87- 1/1R; ECh: '86- 2/1R; WCp: '85- 1/1R; ECp: '85- 1/2R, '87- 1/2R. At 400m: WCh: '83- sf/1R; WI: '87- 1; ECh: '82- 4/1R; EI: '85- 1, '86- 1; ECp: '83- 4/3R. GDR champion 400m 1983, 400mh 1985–8.
Ran on 4x400m world record team 1984. Three GDR 400mh records: 53.83 on her debut and a world record of 53.55 in 1985, 53.24 in 1987.
Progression at 400m: 1978- 62.4, 1979- 53.97, 1980- 51.41/51.0, 1981- 52.03, 1982- 50.57, 1983- 50.26, 1984- 49.24, 1985- 51.07, 1986- 50.43, 1987- 51.10i. At 400mh: 1985- 53.55, 1986- 53.60, 1987- 53.24, 1988- 53.69. pbs: 100m: 11.80 '82, 200m: 22.83 '83.
Has run 15 sub-54.00 times for 400mh, 1985–8.

Diane DIETZ b.30 Aug 1969 Magdeburg 1.62m 48kg. SC Magdeburg.
At 100m/200m (R- 4x100m relay): WJ: '88- 1/2/1R; EJ: '87- 1/1/1R.

World junior record 4x100mR 1988.
At 100m, 200m: 1983- 12.61/12.5, 1984- 12.09, 25.08; 1985- 11.92, 24.63; 1986- 12.40; 1987- 11.38/11.24w, 23.18/23.10w; 1988- 11.18, 23.40/ 22.88w.

Katrin DÖRRE b.6 Oct 1961 Leipzig 1.70m 56kg. SC DHfK Leipzig. Medical student.
At Mar: OG: '88- 3; ECh: '86- dnf; WCp: '85- 1, '87- 3; ECp: '85- 1, '88- 1. GDR champion 3000m 1980, Mar 1982.
Seven GDR marathon records 1982–7.
Progression at Mar: 1982- 2:43:19, 1983- 2:37:41, 1984- 2:26:52, 1985- 2:30:11, 1986- 2:29:33, 1987- 2:25:24, 1988- 2:26:21. pbs: 800m: 2:05.4 '80, 1000m: 2:44.8 '80, 1500m: 4:18.7 '79, 3000m: 9:04.01 '84, 10000m: 33:00.0 '84.
Has won 13 of her 17 marathons, including Osaka 1984, Tokyo 1984–5, 1987, Nagoya and Karl-Marx-Stadt 1986.

Heike DRECHSLER b.16 Dec 1964 Gera 1.80m 70kg. née Daute. SC Motor Jena. Optical instrument maker.
At LJ: OG: '88- 2 (3 100m & 200m); WCh: '83- 1, '87- 3 (2 100m); WI: '87- 1 (1 200m); ECh: '82- 4, '86- 1 (1 200m); EI: '83- 3, '85- 3, '86- 1, '87- 1, '88- 1; EJ: '81- 1; WCp: '85- 1; ECp: '83- 1, '85- 2, '87- 1 (1 4x100mR, 2 4x400mR). GDR champion LJ 1981, 1983–8; 200m 1986, 1988.
Eight GDR long jump records 1983–8, inc. three world 1983–6. Two world records at 200m 1986. WIB: LJ (6): 6.88 '83, 6.99 '84 & '85, 7.25 & 7.29 '86, 7.37 '88; 100y: 10.24 '86, 10.24 & 10.15 '87; 200m: 22.27 '87. World junior LJ records 1981 and 1982, heptathlon 1981.
Progression at LJ, 100m/200m: 1977- 4.46; 1978- 5.69; 1979- 5.90; 1980- 6.64/6.70w; 1981- 6.91/ 7.01w, 11.75/24.16; 1982- 6.98; 1983- 7.14/7.27w; 1984- 7.40; 1985- 7.44, -/23.19; 1986- 7.45, 10.91/ 10.80w/21.71; 1987- 7.40, 10.95/22.18; 1988- 7.48, 10.91/10.85w//21.84. pbs: 800m: 2:17.07 '81, 100mh: 14.12 '80, HJ: 1.84i '87, 1.81 '80, SP: 13.31 '81, Hep: 5812 '81.
The youngest gold medallist of the 1983 world championships, she has jumped consistently over 7 metres ever since. She made a sensational breakthrough in 1986 into a great sprinter, starting with the GDR indoor 100 yards title in 10.24; she set world records at long jump and equalled Marita Koch over 200 metres. Showed further evidence of her versatility with 50.0 400m relay leg in European Cup 1987. Injured during long jump at world championships, ending a run of 27 successive LJ wins, and had to withdraw from relay. Three Olympic medals, but no gold.

Kirsten EMMELMANN b.19 Apr 1961 Warnemünde 1.73m 63kg. née Siemon. Married to Frank Emmelmann (qv). SC Magdeburg. Economics student.
At 400m/R- 4x400m relay: OG: '88- sf/3R; WCh: '87- 3/1R; ECh: '82- 1R, '86- 4/1R; EI: '83- 2, '85- 2; ECp: '85- 2/2R, '87- 2R. WCp '85- 1R, '81- 1 4x100mR. GDR champion 1985. At 200m: EI: '86- 3, '87- 1; EJ: '79- 5 (2 at 100m, 1 4x100mR).
World junior record 4x100mR 1979.
Progression at 400m: 1981- 52.03, 1982- 51.14, 1983- 51.32, 1984- 50.62, 1985- 50.07, 1986- 50.43, 1987- 50.20, 1988- 50.39. pbs: 100m: 11.23 '82, 11.2 '79; 200m: 22.50 '81.

Petra FELKE b.30 Jul 1959 Saalfeld 1.72m 64kg. SC Motor Jena. PE student.
At JT: OG: '88- 1; WCh: '83- 9, '87- 2; ECh: '82- 7, '86- 2; EJ: '77- 2; WSG: '81- 1; WCp: '81- 2, '85- 2; ECp: '85- 1, '87- 1. GDR champion 1984–8. Won GP 1986, 2nd 1988.
Four world javelin records 1985–8, including the first 80m throw, also GDR record 1984.
Progression at JT: 1973- 36.07, 1974- 42.10, 1975- 50.40, 1976- 49.32, 1977- 61.24, 1978- 61.90, 1979- 61.38, 1980- 62.10, 1981- 66.60, 1982- 65.56, 1983- 69.02, 1984- 74.72, 1985- 75.40, 1986- 75.04, 1987- 78.90, 1988- 80.00.
In 1984–8 won 71 out of 78 competitions, including 26 in succession from May 1984 to September 1985, and all 17 in 1988 when her average winning throw was 75.06!. Lost just once in 1986 and twice in 1987, on all three occasions to Fatima Whitbread.

Ellen FIEDLER b.26 Nov 1958 Demmin 1.74m 66kg. née Neumann. SC Dynamo Berlin. Clerk, sergeant in People's Police.
At 400mh: OG: '88- 3; WCh: '80- 2, '83- 3; ECh: '86- 6; WCp: '81- 1; ECp: '81- 1, '83- 1. GDR 400mh champion 1981–3.
GDR 400mh record 1983.
Progression at 400mh: 1978- 58.12, 1980- 54.56, 1981- 54.79, 1982- 54.96, 1983- 54.20, 1984- 55.40, 1985- 55.20, 1986- 54.76, 1988- 53.63. pbs: 200m: 23.58/23.44w '81, 400m: 52.13 '83, 100mh: 13.4 '75.

Diana GANSKY b.14 Dec 1963 Bergen 1.84m 92kg. née Sachse. ASK Potsdam. PE student, lieutenant in National People's Army.
At DT: OG: '88- 2; WCh: '87- 2; ECh: '86- 1; EJ: '83- 1; ECp: '87- 1. GDR champion 1988.
GDR discus record 1987.
Progression at DT: 1977- 36.36, 1979- 44.46, 1980- 57.36, 1981- 59.00, 1982- 60.80, 1983- 61.88, 1984- 66.36, 1985- 69.14, 1986- 73.26, 1987- 74.08, 1988- 72.94.
A record 24 discus competitions over 70m in 1986–8 in 30 competitions.

Gabriele GÜNZ b.8 Sep 1961 Eisenach 1.82m

63kg. SC DHfK Leipzig. née Niebling. Student.
At HJ: EI: '86- 2. GDR champion 1988.
Progression at HJ: 1977- 1.73, 1978- 1.78, 1979- 1.80, 1980- 1.88, 1981- 1.84, 1982- 1.90, 1983- 1.92, 1984- 1.80, 1985- 1.95, 1986- 1.90, 1987- 1.97, 1988- 2.01i/1.94.

Andrea HAHMANN b.3 Jun 1966 Ludwigsfelde 1.77m 59kg. née Lange. ASK Potsdam. PE student, sergeant in National People's Army.
At 1500m: OG: '88- 6; WCh: '87- 5; ECp: '87- 3.
Progression at 1500m: 1981- 4:58.2, 1984- 4:27.08, 1985- 4:21.67, 1986- 4:08.50, 1987- 4:00.07, 1988- 4:00.96. pbs: 400m: 56.44 '84, 800m: 1:57.31 '87, 1000m: 2:33.4 '87, 3000m: 8:45.00i/8:50.94 '88.

Andrea Hahmann (George Herringshaw/ASP)

Grit HAMMER b.4 Jun 1966 1.80m 93kg. née Haupt. SC Motor Jena. Child care student.
World junior records at shot (two) and discus in 1984.
Progression at SP: 1980- 14.32, 1981- 13.23, 1982- 14.56, 1983- 16.68, 1984- 19.57, 1986- 19.22, 1987- 20.72, 1988- 20.50. pb DT: 65.96 '84.

Heike HARTWIG b.30 Dec 1962 Bernburg 1.80m 95kg. née Dittrich. SC Dynamo Berlin. Clerk, staff sergeant in People's Police.
At SP: OG: '88- 6; WCh: '87- 6; ECh: '86- 5; EI: '87- 3; WCp: '85- 2. GDR champion 1987.
Progression at SP: 1978- 13.38, 1979- 14.06, 1980- 15.76, 1981- 17.60, 1982- 19.48, 1983- 19.50, 1984- 20.28, 1985- 20.65, 1986- 20.72, 1987- 21.11, 1988- 21.31. pb DT: 63.12 '86.

Martina HELLMANN b.12 Dec 1960 Leipzig 1.78m 81kg. née Opitz. SC DHfK Leipzig. Sociology student.
At DT: OG: '88- 1; WCh: '83- 1, '87- 1; ECh: '86- 3; WCp: '85- 1; ECp: '83- 1, '85- 2. GDR champion 1985–7.
Held GDR discus record for a week in 1984.
Progression at DT: 1974- 34.67, 1975- 41.42, 1976- 44.92, 1977- 55.00, 1978- 57.82, 1979- 64.50, 1980- 64.32, 1981- 52.12, 1982- 64.32, 1983- 70.26, 1984- 72.32, 1985- 69.78, 1986- 72.52, 1987- 72.92, 1988- 72.30. pb SP: 17.10 '78.
18 competitions over 70m 1983- 8.

Sabine JOHN b.16 Oct 1957 Döbeln 1.78m 66kg. née Möbius, formerly Paetz. SC DHfK Leipzig. PE teacher.
At Pen/Hep: OG: '88- 2 (8 LJ); WCh: '83- 2; ECh: '82- 2; ECp: '79- 4, '81- 4, '85- 1, '87- dnf.
GDR pentathlon record 1979, world heptathlon record 1984. World indoor pentathlon best, 4862* points in 1984.
Progression at 100mh/Pen (p) or Hep: 1972- 14.8, 1973- 14.5, 1974- 14.1, 1975- 14.4, 1976- 13.9, 1977- 13.50, 1978- 13.40/4154p, 1979- 13.41/4619p, 1980- 13.21/4627p, 1981- 13.36/6200, 1982- 12.83/6629, 1983- 13.06/6713, 1984- 12.54/6946, 1985- 12.97/12.78w/6595, 1986- 12.89/6456, 1987- 13.67, 1988- 12.85/12.71w/6897. pbs: 100m: 11.46 '84, 200m: 23.23w/23.37 '84, 800m: 2:06.14 '88, HJ: 1.83 '82, LJ: 7.12 '84, SP: 16.23 '88, JT: 44.62 '84.

Susanne JUNG b.17 May 1963 1.78m 74kg. SC Turbine Erfurt.
At JT: WCh: '87- 5; WSG: '87- 2.
Progression at JT: 1979- 43.60, 1980- 45.14, 1981- 54.92, 1982- 59.40, 1983- 63.14, 1985- 66.08, 1986- 61.78, 1987- 69.60, 1988- 67.74.

Kerstin KNABE b.7 Jul 1959 Oschatz 1.80m 70kg. née Claus. SC DHfK Leipzig. Cosmetician.
At 100mh: OG: '80- 4, '88- sf; WCh: '83- 2; ECh: '82- 3, '86- 5; EJ: '77- 1/1R; WCp: '79- 3, '81- 2; ECp: '81- 2. GDR champion 1979, 1981. At 60mh: EI: '82- 1, '83- 2, '86- 3.
Progression at 100mh: 1974- 14.0, 1975- 13.7, 1976- 14.25, 1977- 13.32, 1978- 13.28, 1979- 12.87, 1980- 12.60, 1981- 12.85, 1982- 12.54, 1983- 12.62, 1984- 12.98, 1985- 12.98, 1986- 12.64, 1987- 12.76, 1988- 12.70. pbs: 100m: 11.51/11.44w '82, 200m: 23.29 '85.

Beate KOCH b.18 Aug 1967 Jena 1.81m 75kg. SC Motor Jena. Precision mechanic.

At JT: OG: '88- 3.
Progression at JT: 1985- 49.38, 1986- 58.88, 1987- 57.78, 1988- 68.80.

Hildegard KÖRNER b.20 Dec 1959 Urnshausen 1.70m 56kg. née Ulrich. SC Turbine Erfurt. PE teacher.
At 800m: OG: '80- 5; ECh: '78- 5, '82- 5; EJ: '75- 4 (1 at 4x400mR), '77- 2; EI: '81- 1. GDR champion 1980 & 1984. At 1500m: WCh: '87- 2; WCp: '85- 1; ECp: '85- 3.
World junior records: 4x400mR 1975, 1000m 2:36.8 in 1977.
Progression at 800m/1500m: 1972- 2:26.4, 1973- 2:16.3, 1974- 2:09.4, 1975- 2:04.3, 1976- 2:04.7/4:20.7, 1977- 2:01.9/4:25.7, 1978- 1:57.45/4:11.97, 1979- 1:58.8/4:07.1, 1980- 1:57.20/4:06.5, 1981- 1:57.56/4:06.96, 1982- 1:58.19/4:14.05, 1984- 1:57.77/4:06.65, 1985- 1:57.53/4:03.55, 1987- 1:59.70/3:58.67, 1988- 2:01.06/4:03.74. pbs: 400m: 54.15 '79, 1000m: 2:34.8 '84, 3000m: 9:32.4 '87, 400mh: 56.47 '78.
Daughter Stefanie born 1986.

Katrin KRABBE b.22 Nov 1969 Neubrandenburg 1.81m 63kg. SC Neubrandenberg. Student kindergarten teacher.
At 100m/200m (R- 4x100m relay): OG: '88- -/sf; WJ: '86- 4/3/2R, '88- 2/1/1R; EJ: '87- 1R.
World junior records 100m and 4x100mR 1988.
Progression at 100m/200m: 1983- 12.69/12.5, 1984- 12.2/24.88/24.7, 1985- 11.7/24.63, 1986- 11.49/23.31/23.25w, 1987- 11.81, 1988- 10.89/22.51/22.34w.

Heidi KRIEGER b.20 Jul 1965 1.87m 95kg. SC Dynamo Berlin.
At SP: WI: '87- 4; ECh: '86- 1; EI: '84- 3, '86- 2, '87- 2; EJ: '83- 1 (1 at DT).
Progression at SP: 1980- 11.93, 1981- 14.05, 1982- 16.82, 1983- 19.03i, 1984- 20.51i/20.24, 1985- 20.39i/19.82, 1986- 21.10, 1987- 20.85i/19.72, 1988- 19.65. pb DT: 61.98 '83.

Ingrid LANGE b.2 Sep 1957 Jena 1.68m 59kg. née Brestrich, then Auerswald. SC Motor Jena. PE teacher.
At 100m (R- 4x100m relay): OG: '80- 3/1R, '88- 2R; WCh: '83- 1R; ECh: '86- 5/1R; WCp: '85- 1R; ECp: 1R '77, '79, '83, '85, '87.
Ran on seven world record 4x100m teams 1979–85.
Progression at 100m: 1975- 11.9, 1976- 11.71, 1977- 11.29, 1978- 11.36, 1979- 11.28, 1980- 11.08/10.93w, 1981- 11.34, 1982- 11.77, 1983- 11.17, 1984- 11.04, 1985- 11.12, 1986- 11.11, 1987- 11.34/11.27w, 1988- 11.17/11.04w. pb 200m: 22.60 '80.
Has been a vital part of the GDR sprint relay teams, running the third leg, for more than a decade.

Susanne LOSCH b.12 Feb 1966 Erfurt 1.78m 60kg. SC Turbine Erfurt. Architectural student.
At 400mh: OG: '88- sf. At 100mh: EJ: '83- 1.
Progression at 400mh: 1985- 56.62, 1986- 56.89, 1987- 56.09, 1988- 54.24. pbs: 100m: 11.86 '83, 400m: 52.96 '87, 100mh: 13.22 '83.

Silvia MADETZKY b.24 Jun 1962 Schkopau 1.86m 92kg. SC Chemie Halle. Student.
At DT: ECh: '82- 5; EJ: '79- 2.
Progression at DT: 1976- 39.04, 1977- 45.10, 1978- 51.74, 1979- 59.26, 1981- 59.04, 1982- 68.24, 1983- 62.46, 1984- 65.20, 1985- 66.52, 1986- 67.08, 1987- 69.34, 1988- 70.22. pb SP: 18.28 '80.

Irina MESZYNSKI b.24 Mar 1962 Berlin 1.76m 98kg. TSC Berlin. Law student.
At DT: ECh: '82- 8, '86- 4; EJ: '79- 1. GDR champion 1982.
World discus record 1984 and two world junior records 1980.
Progression at DT: 1974- 36.26, 1975- 44.12, 1976- 45.00, 1977- 48.48, 1978- 50.54, 1979- 62.42, 1980- 64.86, 1981- 67.38, 1982- 71.40, 1984- 73.36, 1985- 68.18, 1986- 68.74, 1987- 68.98, 1988- 69.14. pb SP: 17.33 '81.
Her world discus record at the Friendship Games in 1984 followed a year out of competition when she had a knée operation.

Silke MÖLLER b.20 Jun 1964 Stralsund 1.68m 59kg. née Gladisch, married Dietmar Möller October 1987. SC Empor Rostock. Student teacher.
At 100m/200m/R- 4x100m relay: OG: '88- sf/5/2R; WCh: '83- sf/-/1R, '87- 1/1/2R; ECh: '86- 4/3/1R; WCp: '85- 1R; EJ: '81- 1R. At 200m: ECp: '83- 1R, '85- 1R, '87- 1/1R. GDR champion 100m 1986–7, 200m 1987. At 60m: EI: '83- 2, '86- 3, '88- 2; WI: '85- 1.
At 4x100mR: world junior record 1981, two world records 1983–5.
Progression at 100m/200m: 1978- 12.6, 1979- 12.39/25.51, 1980- 11.8/24.6, 1981- 11.63/23.69, 1982- 11.54/11.33w/23.30, 1983- 11.03/22.72, 1984- 11.10/22.70, 1985- 10.99/22.12, 1986- 10.96/22.07, 1987- 10.86/10.82w/21.74, 1988- 11.06/22.09.
For long regarded as the successor to Marlies Göhr, she came into her own in 1987 with her brilliant double in Rome.

Ines MÜLLER b.2 Jan 1959 Grimmen 1.82m 90kg. née Reichenbach. SC Empor Rostock. PE student.
At SP: OG: '80- 8, '88- 4; WCh: '87- 3; ECh: '86- 2; ECp: '85- 3, '87- 2; WI: '85- 2. GDR champion 1985–6. At DT: EJ: '77- 1.
Progression at SP: 1975- 13.03, 1976- 13.07, 1977-

17.30, 1978- 18.24, 1979- 20.81, 1980- 21.00, 1981- 21.14, 1982- 20.93, 1983- 20.54, 1984- 21.32, 1985- 21.26i/20.68, 1986- 21.45, 1987- 21.20, 1988- 21.57. pb DT: 66.40 '85.

Petra MÜLLER b.18 Jul 1965 Quedlinburg 1.80m 65kg. SC Chemie Halle. Student of botany.
At 400m/R- 4x400mR: OG: '88- 2/3R; WCh: '87- 2/1R; ECh: '86- 3/1R; EJ: '83- 1/1R; EI: '86- 2, '88- 1; ECp: '85- 2R, '87- 1/2R. GDR champion 1986–8.
Progression at 400m: 1983- 51.79, 1984- 51.38, 1985- 50.14, 1986- 49.79, 1987- 49.64, 1988- 49.30. pbs: 100m: 11.91 '83, 200m: 22.61 '87.

Katrin NEIMKE b.18 Jul 1966 Magdeburg 1.80m 95kg. SC Magdeburg. Clerk.
At SP: OG: '88- 2; WCh: '87- 2; EI: '88- 3; WSG: '87- 2. GDR champion 1988.
Progression at SP: 1983- 15.76, 1984- 16.09, 1985- 18.09, 1986- 19.68, 1987- 21.21, 1988- 21.11. pb DT: 58.82 '86.

Dagmar NEUBAUER b.3 Jun 1962 Suhl 1.70m 58kg. née Rübsam. SC Turbine Erfurt. PE student.
At 400m (R- 4x400m relay): OG: '88- sf/3R; WCh: '83- 7/1R, '87- sf/1R; ECh: '82- 6/1R; EI: '82- 2, '85- 2, '88- 3; EJ: '79- 1/1R; WCp: '81- 1R, '85- 1R; ECp: '81- 1R, '83- 3R, '85- 2R. GDR champion 1982.
At 4x400mR: world junior record 1979, two world records 1982–4.
Progression at 400m: 1977- 58.6, 1979- 51.55, 1980- 51.01, 1981- 50.98, 1982- 50.52, 1983- 50.48, 1984- 49.58, 1985- 50.38, 1986- 50.92, 1987- 50.55, 1988- 50.45. pbs: 100m: 11.73 '80, 200m: 22.87 '84, 800m: 1:58.36 '84.

Cornelia OSCHKENAT b.29 Oct 1961 Neubrandenburg 1.78m 68kg. née Riefstahl. Married Andreas Oschkenat (2nd EJ 1981, 5th ECh 1986 at 110mh, pb 13.50 '83) in 1984. SC Dynamo Berlin. Economics student.
At 100mh: OG: '88- 8; WCh: '83- 7, '87- 3/2R; ECh: '82- h, '86- 2; WCp: '85- 1; ECp: '85- 3, '87- 1. GDR champion 1984–6, 1988. 2nd GP 1986. At 60mh: WI: '87- 1; EI: '85- 1, '86- 1, '88- 1.
WIB: 50mh (6) 6.73–6.58 '86–8; 55mh: 7.37 '87.
Progression at 100mh: 1978- 14.36, 1979- 14.36, 1980- 13.78/13.73w, 1981- 13.25/13.09w, 1982- 12.90, 1983- 12.72, 1984- 12.57, 1985- 12.70/12.56w, 1986- 12.50, 1987- 12.45/12.28w, 1988- 12.52/12.50w. pbs: 100m: 11.32/11.21w '87, 11.1w '84; 200m: 23.15 '84.

Helga RADTKE b.16 May 1962 Sanitz 1.71m 64kg. SC Empor Rostock. Sports student.
At LJ: WCh: '83- 12, '87- 4; WI: '85- 1, '87- 2; ECh: '86- 3; EI: '83- 2, '86- 2; EJ: '79- 1.
Progression at LJ: 1977- 5.68, 1978- 5.74, 1979- 6.63, 1980- 6.71, 1982- 6.83, 1983- 6.83, 1984- 7.21, 1985- 7.19, 1986- 7.17, 1987- 7.16/7.17w, 1988- 6.76i/6.73. pbs: 100m: 11.6 '85, 100mh: 14.67 '79, HJ: 1.75 '82.

Gabriele REINSCH b.23 Sep 1963 Cottbus 1.88m 89kg. SC Cottbus. PE student.
At DT: OG: '88- 7; WSG: '87- 2; EJ: '81- 6 (2 SP).
World discus record 1988.
Progression at DT: 1980- 45.74, 1981- 53.84, 1982- 58.46, 1983- 60.02, 1984- 61.68, 1985- 65.78, 1986- 65.44, 1987- 67.18, 1988- 76.80. pb SP: 17.45 '86.

Silke RENK b.30 Jun 1967 Querfurt 1.73m 72kg. SC Chemie Halle. PE student.
At JT: OG: '88- 5.
Progression at JT: 1981- 42.62, 1982- 45.28, 1983- 51.16, 1984- 51.36, 1985- 59.08, 1986- 62.06, 1987- 64.74, 1988- 71.00.

Sylke Renk (George Herringshaw/ASP)

Ines SCHULZ b.10 Jul 1965 Karl-Marx-Stadt 1.77m 64kg. SC Karl-Marx-Stadt. Hairdresser.
At Hep: OG: '88- 6.
Progression at Hep: 1982- 5120, 1984- 5830, 1985- 6011, 1986- 6250, 1988- 6660. pbs: 200m: 24.29/23.93w '88, 800m: 2:05.79 '88, 100mh: 13.56 '88, HJ: 1.84 '88, LJ: 6.70 '88, SP: 13.95 '88, JT: 42.94 '87.

Gloria SIEBERT b.13 Jan 1964 Ortrand 1.72m 59kg. née Kovarik, then Uibel, married Carsten Siebert (HJ 2.25 '87) in 1987. SC Cottbus. Sports student.
At 100mh: OG: '88- 2; WCh: '87- 2; EJ: '81- 2. GDR champion 1987. At 60mh: EI: '87- 2.
WIB 50mh: 6.69 & 6.67 '88.
Progression at 100mh: 1979- 14.29, 1981- 13.26, 1983- 13.00, 1984- 12.79, 1985- 13.12, 1986- 12.91, 1987- 12.44/12.37w, 1988- 12.48/12.47w. pbs: 100m: 11.46w/11.60 '84, 200m: 24.34 '81.
Four major championship silver medals.

Heike THEELE b.4 Oct 1964 Magdeburg 1.72m 63kg. née Terpe. SC Magdeburg. Physiotherapy student.
At 100mh: ECh: '86- 4; WSG: '87- 1.
European junior 100mh record 1982.
Progression at 100mh: 1981- 13.69, 1982- 13.17, 1983- 13.05, 1984- 13.02/12.99w, 1985- 13.03, 1986- 12.63, 1987- 12.84/12.81w, 1988- 13.01. pbs: 100m: 11.53 '86, 200m: 23.70 '86, 400mh: 62.42 '81

Sybille THIELE b.6 Mar 1965 Meiningen 1.79m 74kg. SC Dynamo Berlin. Student.
At Hep: EJ: '83- 1; ECp: '83- 9, '85- 3.
Three world junior heptathlon records 1982–3. GDR champion 1985.
Progression at Hep: 1980- 5304, 1981- 5705, 1982- 6046, 1983- 6465, 1984- 6387, 1985- 6487, 1986- 6635, 1988- 6526. pbs: 200m: 24.07 '83, 800m: 2:11.13 '88, 100mh: 13.14 '86, HJ: 1.90 '83, LJ: 6.77 '85, SP: 16.00 '86, 16.08i '87; JT: 48.68 '86.

Heike TISCHLER b.4 Feb 1964 Saalfeld 1.76m 61kg. SC Motor Jena. Instrument maker.
At heptathlon: GDR champion 1988.
Progression at Hep: 1980- 5156, 1981- 5539, 1982- 5916, 1983- 6057, 1984- 6366, 1985- 6272, 1987- 6329, 1988- 6569. pbs: 200m: 23.62w/24.23 '88; 800m: 2:07.62 '84, 100mh: 14.26/13.99w '87, HJ: 1.81 '83, 1.83i '88; LJ: 6.68 '88, SP: 14.27 '85, JT: 52.52 '88.

Cornelia ULLRICH b.26 Apr 1963 Halberstadt 1.72m 59kg. née Feuerbach. SC Magdeburg. Sports student.
At 400mh: WCh: '87- 3; ECh: '86- 3. At 4x400mR: EJ: '81- 1.
Progression at 400mh: 1985- 54.64, 1986- 54.13, 1987- 53.58, 1988- 54.81. pbs: 100m: 11.48/11.31w '84, 200m: 23.50 '82, 400m: 53.21i '85, 100mh: 12.86 '83.
Moved up from 100mh to 400mh with immediate success in 1985.

Kathrin ULLRICH b.14 Aug 1967 Annaberg 1.72m 52kg. SC Dynamo Berlin. Student teacher.
At 10000m: OG: '88- 4; WCh: '87- 3; ECp: '87- 1.

Katrin Ullrich (George Herringshaw/ASP)

At 3000m: EJ: '85- 8. GDR champion 3000m and 10000m 1987–8.
GDR records 10000m 1987, 5000m 1988.
Progression at 3000m/10000m: 1982- 9:36.37, 1983- 9:23.78, 1984- 9:17.04, 1985- 9:14.47, 1986- 9:09.92, 1987- 8:50.51/31:11.34, 1988- 8:41.79i/ 8:44.81/31:26.79. pbs: 1000m: 2:44.1 '86, 1500m: 4:06.91i '88, 5000m: 15:20.23 '88.
In her first year at 10000m improved with each of her four races: firstly winning the GDR title, then the European Cup race, then 32:01.05 for second at the Bislett Games and finally nearly 50 seconds improvement for her World bronze medal.

Christine WACHTEL b.6 Jan 1965 Altentreptow 1.66m 56kg. SC Neubrandenburg. Clerk.
At 800m: OG: '88- 2; WCh: '87- 2; ECh: '86- 8; WI: '87- 1; EI: '87- 1; EJ: '83- 2 (1 4x400mR); WCp: '85- 1; ECp: '85- 3, '87- 3. GDR champion 1983, 1985, 1987–8.
World junior 800m record 1983. WIB 800m 1:57.64 & 1:56.40 '88.
Progression at 800m: 1976- 2:29.5, 1977- 2:19.8, 1978- 2:16.4, 1979- 2:09.1, 1980- 2:04.7, 1981- 2:03.35, 1982- 2:01.16, 1983- 1:59.40, 1984- 1:58.24, 1985- 1:56.71, 1986- 1:58:59, 1987- 1:55.32, 1988- 1:56.40i/1:56.64. pbs: 400m: 51.86 '87, 1500m: 4:18.03 '82, 400mh: 58.08 '82.

Sigrun WODARS b.7 Nov 1965 Neu-Kaliss 1.66m 54kg. née Ludwigs. SC Neubrandenburg. PE student.

At 800m: OG: '88- 1; WCh: '87- 1; ECh: '86- 2; EI: '86- 1, '87- 2; EJ: '81- 4 400mh, '83- 5 400m, 1 4x400mR. GDR 800m champion 1986.
GDR 800m record 1987.
Progression at 800m: 1982- 2:05.09, 1983- 2:03.40, 1984- 1:59.53, 1985- 1:58.32, 1986- 1:57.05, 1987- 1:55.26, 1988- 1:56.10. pbs: 200m: 24.36 '83, 400m: 51.80 '87, 1000m: 2:40.42 '85, 400mh: 56.18 '85.
Although runner-up to Wachtel in the GDR championships in 1987 and 1988 went on to win the major gold medals.

Katrin WÜHN b.19 Nov 1965 Berlin 1.74m 58kg. SC Chemie Halle.
At 800m: EJ: '83- 1.
Progression at 800m: 1982- 2:08.4, 1983- 2:00.18, 1984- 1:57.86, 1985- 2:00.56i, 1986- 1:58.80, 1987- 1:57.90, 1988- 2:00.62i. pbs: 400m: 54.24 '83, 1000m: 2:35.4 '84, 1500m: 4:03.77 '87, 3000m: 9:09.70i '88.

Ilke WYLUDDA b.28 Mar 1969 Leipzig 1.84m 92kg. SC Chemie Halle. Schoolgirl.
At DT: WCh: '87- 4; WJ: '86- 1; EJ: '85- 1 (2 SP), '87- 1 (1 SP).
Eleven world junior records at discus 1986–8 and two at shot 1987–8.
Progression at SP/DT: 1982- 13.72/46.54, 1983- 15.18/51.12, 1984- 16.42/57.74, 1985- 18.27/62.36, 1986- 19.08/65.86, 1987- 20.11/71.64, 1988- 20.23/74.40.

FEDERAL REPUBLIC OF GERMANY

Governing body: Deutscher Leichtathletik Verband (DLV), Julius-Reiber-Strasse 19, 6100 Darmstadt. Founded in 1898.
National Championships first held in 1891.
1988 champions: MEN
100m: Andreas Maul 10.50, 200m/400m: Ralf Lübke 20.76/45.89, 800m: Thomas Giessing 1:47.52, 1500m/5000m: Dieter Baumann 3:45.60/13:38.31, 10000m: Ralf Salzmann 29:01.53, Mar: Udo Reeh 2:14:56, 3000mSt: Patriz Ilg 8:23.19, 110mh: Florian Schwarthoff 13.50, 400mh: Harald Schmid 48.23, HJ: Dietmar Mögenburg 2.25, PV: Wladyslaw Kozakiewicz 5.40, LJ: Dietmar Haaf 7.83, TJ: Wolfgang Knabe 17.31w, SP: Karsten Stolz 20.18, DT: Ralf Danneberg 67.20, HT: Heinz Weis 79.58, JT: Peter Blank 80.84, Dec: Rainer Sonnenburg 8025, 20kmW: Torsten Zervas 1:30:01, 50kmW: Alfons Schwarz 3:56:14.
WOMEN
100m: Ulrike Sarvari 11.28, 200m: Andrea Thomas 22.82, 400m: Helga Arendt 50.77, 800m: Gabriele Lesch 2:02.07, 1500m/3000m: Vera Michallek 4:12.41/9:05.77, 10000m: Kerstin Pressler 33:31.37, Mar: Charlotte Teske 2:30:23, 100mh: Claudia Zaczkiewicz 12.87, 400mh: Gudrun Abt 55.16, HJ: Heike Redetzky 1.97, LJ: Andrea Hannemann 6.55, SP: Claudia Losch 19.84, DT: Dagmar Galler 62.60, JT: Ingrid Thyssen 66.00, Hep: Sabine Everts 6306, 10kmW: Barbara Kollorz 49:24.

Dieter BAUMANN b.9 Feb 1965 Blaustein 1.78m 62kg. VfL Waiblingen. Photographic worker, now in the army.
At 5000m: OG: '88- 2; ECh: '86- h. At 1500m: WCh: '87- sf; ECp: '87- 5. At 3000m: EI: '87- 2. At 1500m: ECp: '87- 5. FRG champion 1500m 1987–8, 5000m 1986, 1988.

Dieter Baumann (George Herringshaw/ASP)

Progression at 1500m/5000m: 1982- 4:03.75, 1983- 3:52.99, 1984- 3:50.37/14:21.59, 1985- 3:40.48/13:48.0, 1986- 3:36.40/13:35.04, 1987- 3:33.54/13:30.85, 1988- 3:34.82/13:15.52. pbs: 800m: 1:49.49 '87, 1000m: 2:22.4 '86, 1M: 3:58.37 '85, 2000m: 4:59.88 '87, 3000m: 7:40.25 '87.
Improved his 5000m best to 13:18.43 in July 1988, and produced a 55.0 last lap to take the Olympic silver.

Peter BOUSCHEN b.16 May 1960 Düsseldorf 1.80m 78kg. DJK Agon Düsseldorf. Student.
At TJ: OG: '84- 5; WCh: '83- 9, '87- 7; ECh: '86- dnq;

EJ: '79- 5; ECp: '81- 6, '83- 1, '87- 3. FRG champion 1981, 1983, 1986–7.
FRG triple jump records 1983 and 1988.
Progression at TJ: 1976- 12.67, 1977- 14.20, 1978- 14.97, 1979- 16.06, 1980- 15.99, 1981- 16.97i, 1982- 16.69, 1983- 17.33, 1984- 17.20, 1986- 16.78, 1987- 17.20/17.26w, 1988- 17.43. pb LJ: 7.43 '84.

Peter BRAUN b.1 Aug 1962 Tuttlingen 1.83m 64kg. LG Tuttlingen-Fridingen. Toolmaker.
At 800m: OG: '88- sf; WCh: '87- qf; ECh: '86- 6; EI: '86- 1; ECp: '85- 3, '87- 3. FRG champion 1987.
Progression at 800m: 1982- 1:52.24, 1983- 1:47.10, 1984- 1:45.62, 1985- 1:44.15, 1986- 1:44.03, 1987- 1:45.17, 1988- 1:44.21. pb 400m: 47.19 '86.

Rolf DANNEBERG b.1 Mar 1953 Hamburg 1.98m 125kg. LG Wedel/Pinneberg. Teacher.
At DT: OG: '84- 1, '88- 3; WCh: '87- 4; ECh: '82- dnq, '86- 11; ECp: '87- 3. FRG champion 1980, 1988.
Progression at DT: 1974- 50.56, 1975- 55.30, 1976- 55.96, 1977- 56.02, 1978- 61.12, 1979- 61.02, 1980- 62.86, 1981- 62.50, 1982- 63.74, 1983- 62.84, 1984- 67.40, 1985- 64.94, 1986- 66.16, 1987- 67.60, 1988- 67.38. pb SP: 17.80 '86.
Caused major upset to win Olympic discus title, but has subsequently become one of the world's most consistent throwers.

Alois HANNECKER b.10 Jul 1961 München 1.94m 118kg. MTV Ingolstadt.
At DT: OG: '88- 8; WCh: '87- 11; ECh: '86- 12; EJ: '79- 11. FRG champion 1986–7.
Progression at DT: 1978- 50.20, 1979- 54.16, 1980- 55.38, 1981- 58.28, 1982- 59.28, 1983- 63.86, 1984- 64.82, 1985- 62.10, 1986- 65.28, 1987- 65.32, 1988- 65.90. pb SP: 18.44 '87.

Jürgen HINGSEN b.25 Jan 1958 Duisburg 2.00m 102kg. LAV Bayer Uerdingen/Dormagen.
At Dec: OG: '84- 2, '88- dnf; WCh: '83- 2, '87- dnf; ECh: '78- 13, '82- 2, '86- 2; EJ: '77- 3; WSG: '79- 2; ECp: '79- 10, '81- 2. FRG champion decathlon 1982, long jump 1983.
Three decathlon world records: one each year 1982–4.
Progression at Dec: 1977- 7483, 1978- 7944, 1979- 8218, 1980- 8409, 1981- 8146, 1982- 8741, 1983- 8825, 1984- 8832, 1985- dnf, 1986- 8730, 1987- dnf, 1988- 8360. pbs: 100m: 10.70w '84, 10.74 '82, 200m: 21.66 '82, 400m: 47.65 '82, 1500m: 4:12.3 '79, 110mh: 14.07/13.84w '84, 13.8w '83, HJ: 2.18 '78, PV: 5.10 '84, LJ: 8.04 '82, SP: 16.57 '86, DT: 50.82 '84, JT: 67.42 '83, new: 64.38 '86.
Great decathlete who ranked as world number two five times, 1981–6. Had three false starts in the 100m, the opening event of the 1988 Olympic decathlon.

Patriz ILG b.5 Dec 1957 Aalen-Oberalfingen 1.73m 63kg. LAC Quelle Fürth. Physical education and crafts teacher.
At 3kmSt: WCh: '83- 1, 1987- 12; ECh: '78- 2, '82- 1, '86- 3; ECp: '81- 3, '85- 1. FRG champion 1978, 1980–2, 1985–8. At 3000m: EI: '82- 1; EJ: '75- 2.
Progression at 3kmSt: 1977- 8:40.4, 1978- 8:16.92, 1980- 8:25.89, 1981- 8:21.13, 1982- 8:17.04, 1983- 8:15.06, 1984- 8:40.53, 1985- 8:16.14, 1986- 8:16.92, 1987- 8:18.73, 1988- 8:23.19. pbs: 1500m: 3:40.54 '83, 2000m: 5:05.84i '84 3000m: 7:45.06 '78, 5000m: 13:24.4 '83, 10000m: 28:47.6 '78.
The former World and European steeplechase champion missed most of the 1979, 1984 and 1988 seasons through injuries. A great finisher who did not run all out for fast times. He is the only steeplechaser to win medals at three European Championships.

Edgar ITT b.8 Jun 1967 Gedern 1.86m 75kg. TV Gelnhausen. Student.
At 400mh/R- 4x400m relay: OG: '88- 8/3R; WCh: '87- h/4R. At 400m: ECh: '86- 2R; WJ: '86- 3; EJ: '85- 2R; ECp: '87- 3/3R.
Progression at 400m/400mh: 1983- -/58.1, 1984- 47.49/54.3, 1985- 47.20/55.1, 1986- 45.72/49.68, 1987- 45.38/49.14, 1988- 45.43/48.65. pbs: 200m: 20.95 '87, 800m: 1:45.70 '88, 110mh: 14.3 '85.
On 19 June 1988 became the first FRG athlete to defeat Harald Schmid at 400mh for eight years.

Edgar Itt (George Herringshaw/ASP)

Dietmar MÖGENBURG b.15 Aug 1961 Leverkusen 2.01m 78kg. OSC Berlin. Architectural student.
At HJ: OG: '84- 1, '88- 6; WCh: '83- 4, '87- 4; ECh: '82- 1, '86- 4; EI: '80- 1, '81- 2=, '82- 1, '84- 1, '86- 1, '88- 2; EJ: '79- 1; ECp: '79- 1, '83- 3. FRG champion 1980–5, 1987–8.
Six FRG high jump records, including a world, and world junior, record 2.35m in 1980 and two European records at 2.36m 1984. WIB 2.39 '85.
Progression at HJ: 1972- 1.41, 1973- 1.67, 1974- 1.74, 1975- 1.90, 1976- 2.05, 1977- 2.10, 1978- 2.23, 1979- 2.32, 1980- 2.35, 1981- 2.30, 1982- 2.34i/2.30, 1983- 2.32, 1984- 2.36, 1985- 2.39i/2.31, 1986- 2.34i/2.30, 1987- 2.35, 1988- 2.37i/2.34. pb LJ: 7.76 '80.
A supreme competitor, who has made a habit of winning important competitions, since his first major success when he won the 1979 European Cup Final high jump at the age of 17. 68 competitions at 2.30m or over to end 1988.

Christoph SAHNER b.23 Sep 1963 Illingen 1.80m 103kg. TV Wattenscheid. Mining mechanic.
At HT: OG: '84- nt, '88- dnq 13; WCh: '83- 11, '87- 4; ECh: '82- dnq, '86- 8; EJ: '81- 1; ECp: '85- 4, '87- 3. FRG champion 1985–6.
Progression at HT: 1980- 61.34, 1981- 72.06, 1982- 75.24, 1983- 77.88, 1984- 78.04, 1985- 81.56, 1986- 80.38, 1987- 80.74, 1988- 81.78.

Harald SCHMID b.29 Sep 1957 Hanau 1.87m 82kg. TV Gelnhausen. Physical education student. Married to Elzbieta Rabsztyn (7th European 100mh 1978 for Poland).
At 400mh/R- 4x400m relay: OG: '76- sf/3R, '84- 3, '88- 7; WCh: '83- 2/2R, '87- 3/4R; ECh: '78- 1/1R, '82- 1/1R, '86- 1/2R; WCp: '77- 3/1R, '79- 2, '85- 3; ECp: '77- 2, '79- 1/1R, '81- 2, '83- 1, '85- 1/1R, '87- 1/3R. At 400m: EJ: '75- 7/2R; ECp: '79- 1/1R. FRG champion 400mh 1977–8, 1980–8 (FRG record 11 titles at one event) and 400m 1979.
Five FRG 400mh records 1977–87, including three European records 1979–87. World junior record 1976.
Progression at 400mh: 1974- 54.9, 1975- 51.8, 1976- 49.61, 1977- 48.85, 1978- 48.43, 1979- 47.85, 1980- 48.05, 1981- 48.64, 1982- 47.48, 1983- 48.49, 1984- 47.69, 1985- 47.85, 1986- 47.89, 1987- 47.48, 1988- 48.23. pbs: 100m: 10.3 '78, 200m: 20.68 '87, 3000m: 33.0 '78, 400m: 44.92 '79, 500m: 1:01.22 '78, 800m: 1:44.83 '87, 110mh: 14.7 '78.
He was the last man to beat Edwin Moses at 400mh (at the 1977 ISTAF meeting) before his long win streak, and was consistently in the world's top three 1977–87, when he never failed to gain a medal at a major championships. He has a men's record of five European gold medals. Equalled his European record in that memorable final in Rome in 1987. FRG sportsman of the year 1979 and 1987. In his career has run 119 sub 50.00 400mh times, including 63 sub 49.00, 7 sub 48.00.

Wolfgang SCHMIDT b.16 Jan 1954 Berlin 1.98m 110kg. Stuttgarter Kickers.
At DT: OG: '76- 2, '80- 4; ECh: '74- 8, '78- 1 (3 SP); EJ: '73- 1 (2 SP) WSG: '79- 1; WCp: '77- 1, '79- 1; ECp: '75- 1, '77- 1, '79- 1. GDR champion 1975–80. World record 1978. Five GDR records 1975–8; FRG record 1988.

Wolfgang Schmidt (George Herringshaw/ASP)

Progression at DT: 1970- 48.52, 1971- 54.40, 1972- 57.90, 1973- 61.30, 1974- 64.10, 1975- 66.80, 1976- 68.60, 1977- 68.26, 1978- 71.16, 1979- 69.08, 1980- 68.48, 1981- 69.60, 1982- 62.70, 1988- 68.22. pb SP: 20.76 '78.
The great discus thrower, after imprisonment in the GDR, was eventually allowed to go to the West, and made a fine return to top-class competition in 1988 after missing five seasons. His father, Ernst Schmidt, won ten GDR titles (5 shot, 4 discus, 1 decathlon) 1950–4 and set 12 GDR shot records to 15.85m '52, 8 discus to 46.24m '54 and two decathlon.

Klaus TAFELMEIER b.12 Apr 1958 Singen 1.90m 94kg. Bayer Leverkusen. Physical education student.
At JT: OG: '84- dnq, '88- 4; WCh: '83- 8, '87- dnq; ECh: '82- 13, '86- 1; EJ: '75- 6, '77- 1; ECp: '81- 4, '83- 3, '85- 7, '87- 2. FRG champion 1982–5, 1987.
World best, two European records for new javelin 1986; five FRG records 1986–7.
Progression at JT: 1974- 62.46, 1975- 77.82, 1976- 82.12, 1977- 84.14, 1978- 86.00, 1979- 89.78, 1980- 88.34, 1981- 88.48, 1982- 87.30, 1983- 91.44, 1984- 91.04, 1985- 89.38, new: 1986- 85.74, 1987- 86.64, 1988- 85.96.
Many long throws, but he failed to place well in major events from his European Junior win in 1977 until he triumphed in Stuttgart with the gold medal and European record.

Carlo THRÄNHARDT b.5 Jul 1957 Bad Lauchstädt 1.99m 85kg. LG Bayer Leverkusen. Student of journalism.
At HJ: OG: '84- 10, '88- 7=; WCh: '83- 7, '87- 8; ECh: '78- 5, '86- 3; EI: '81- 2=, '83- 1, '84- 2=, '86- 2, '87- 2; WCp: '77- 4; ECp: '77- 5, '85- 4. FRG champion 1986. Won AAA title 1980.
Eight FRG high jump records 1977–88, including European records 2.36 & 2.37 in 1984. WIB: 2.37 '84, 2.40 '87, 2.42 '88 (also world record as set under outdoor conditions).
Progression at HJ: 1975- 2.09, 1976- 2.15, 1977- 2.25, 1978- 2.26i, 1979- 2.30, 1980- 2.31, 1981- 2.28i, 1982- 2.30, 1983- 2.34, 1984- 2.37, 1985- 2.30, 1986- 2.36i/2.32, 1987- 2.40i/2.31, 1988- 2.42i/2.34/2.35u.
Jumped 2.30m or more in 66 competitions 1979–88.

Heinz WEIS b.14 Jul 1963 Trier 1.93m 110kg. Bayer Leverkusen. Clerk.
At HT: OG: '88- 5; WCh: '87- 6; WSG: '85- 1, '87- 2. FRG champion 1988.
FRG hammer record 1988.
Progression at HT: 1980- 53.34, 1981- 60.86, 1982- 61.56, 1983- 65.30, 1984- 68.98, 1985- 78.18, 1986- 76.08, 1987- 80.18, 1988- 82.52. pb SP: 14.30 '87.
Threw brilliantly in the World Championships, being in a medal place up to his pb in the fifth round, only to end up sixth.

Siegfried WENTZ b.7 Mar 1960 Röthenbach 1.93m 93kg. Bayer Leverkusen. Medical student.
At Dec: OG: '84- 3; WCh: '83- 3, '87- 2; ECh: '82- 20, '86- 3; EJ: '79- 1; WSG: '87- 1; ECp: '81- 4, '83- 3, '85- 5. FRG champion 1985 (and 110mh 1986).
Progression at Dec: 1977- 6907, 1978- 7391, 1979- 7775, 1980- 7876, 1981- 8178, 1982- 8301, 1983- 8762, 1984- 8497, 1985- 8440, 1986- 8676, 1987- 8645, 1988- 8403. pbs: 100m: 10.60 '87, 200m: 21.66 '84, 400m: 47.38 '83, 1500m: 4:19.78 '82, 110mh: 13.76 '86, HJ: 2.12 '86, PV: 4.90 '86, LJ: 7.63 '85, TJ: 14.86 '78, SP: 16.80 '87, DT: 51.90 '87, JT: 75.08 '83, new: 67.42 '86.
Unable to compete in Seoul through an ankle injury.

WOMEN

Gudrun ABT b.3 Aug 1962 Riedlingen 1.80m 59kg. TSV Genkingen. Teacher.
At 400mh/R- 4x400m relay: OG: '88- 6/4R; WCh: '87- sf/5R; ECh: '86- sf; ECp: '87- 4. FRG champion 1986–8.
Three FRG 400mh records 1988.
Progression at 400mh: 1980- 66.8, 1981- 61.8, 1982- 59.01, 1983- 57.93, 1984- 57.85, 1985- 57.48, 1986- 56.36, 1987- 55.56, 1988- 54.04. pbs: 100m: 11.3 '88, 200m: 23.37/23.35w '88, 400m: 52.22 '88, 800m: 2:08.15 '86, 100mh: 13.61 '87, Hep: 4973 '82.

Manuela ALIZADEH b.20 Jan 1963 Feuerbach 1.72m 75kg. LAV Bayer Uerdingen-Dormagen.
At JT: WCh: '87- 10; ECh: '86- 11. Won GP 1988.
Progression at JT: 1978- 44.76, 1979- 48.48, 1980- 54.20, 1981- 53.60, 1982- 56.54, 1983- 58.26, 1984- 60.50, 1985- 61.20, 1986- 62.50, 1987- 63.40, 1988- 65.34. pb SP: 13.69 '87.

Helga ARENDT b.24 Apr 1964 Köln 1.78m 64kg. Eintracht Hamm. Law student.
At 400m: OG: '88- 7/4R; WCh: '87- sf/5R; EI: '88- 2; ECp: '87- 3R. FRG champion 1988.
Progression at 400m: 1979- 58.0, 1980- 56.99, 1981- 55.29, 1982- 53.85, 1983- 53.57, 1984- 54.35, 1985- 54.36, 1986- 52.22, 1987- 51.70, 1988- 50.36. pbs: 100m: 11.82/11.3 '88, 200m: 23.13 '88, 300m: 36.49i '88, 400mh: 60.33 '84.

Sabine EVERTS b.4 Mar 1961 Düsseldorf 1.69m 55kg. Bayer Uerdingen/Dormagen. Student of physical education and philology.
At Pen/Hep: OG: '84- 3, '88- dnf; WCh: '83- 4; ECh: '82- 3; EJ: '79- 1; ECp: '79- 7, '81- 3, '83- 6, '85- 6. At LJ: WCh: '83- dnq; ECh: '82- 6; EJ: '77- 6, '79- 2; EI:

'80- 3, '82- 1; ECp: '83- 5. At 400mh: ECp: '83- 5, '85- 4. FRG titles at Pen/Hep 1980–3, 1985, 1988; LJ 1979–80, 1982; 400mh 1985.
World junior pentathlon record 1979. Five FRG heptathlon records 1981–2.
Progression at Pen (p) or Hep: 1977- 4225p, 1978- 4366p, 1979- 4627p, 1980- 4657p, 1981- 6363, 1982- 6523, 1983- 6388, 1984- 6388, 1985- 6368, 1987- 5879, 1988- 6306. pbs: 100m: 11.81/11.72w '82, 11.5 '80; 200m: 23.43 '82, 400m: 52.35i '81, 800m: 2:06.17 '83, 100mh: 13.17 '82, 400mh: 55.48 '85, HJ: 1.89 '82. LJ: 6.77 '82, SP: 13.09 '88, JT: 38.70.

Brigitte KRAUS b.12 Aug 1956 Bensberg 1.80m 58kg. ASV Köln. Draughtswoman.
At 3000m: OG: '84- dnf; WCh: '83- 2; ECh: '82- 7, '86- h; EI '84- 1, '86- 3, '87- 3; ECp: '77- 5. At 1500m: OG: '76- sf; WCh: '87- h; ECh: '78- sf; EI: '76- 1, '78- 3, '82- 2, '83- 1, '85- 3, '88- 3; ECp: '79- 6, '81- 4, '85- 6, '87- 4. At 800m: ECp '75- 7. 60 FRG internationals and a record 61 FRG junior and senior titles indoors and out. Senior outdoor titles: 800m 1976; 1500m 1976, 1978–9, 1981, 1983, 1985–7; 3000m 1976–7, 1979, 1983–7.
FRG records at 1000m (3), 1500m (3), 1M (1) and 3000m (5) 1976–85. WIB 1000m 2:34.8 '78. Women's record 60 internationals for FRG 1973–88.
Progression at 1500m/3000m: 1971- 4:38.4, 1972- 4:22.97, 1973- 4:24.0, 1974- 4:17.4, 1975- 4:13.91, 1976- 4:04.21/9:05.6, 1977- 4:08.7/9:01.29, 1978- 4:01.54/9:10.4i, 1979- 4:04.8/8:54.4, 1980- 4:06.62/ 9:26.2, 1981- 4:05.47/9:16.6, 1982- 4:04.22i/ 8:44.43, 1983- 4:02.42/8:35.11, 1984- 4:06.00/ 8:40.90, 1985- 4:03.64i/8:58.55, 1986- 4:04.65/ 8:47.83, 1987- 4:05.23/8:53.01i, 1988- 4:07.51/ 4:07.06i. pbs: 400m: 55.6 '78, 800m: 1:59.28 '83, 1000m: 2:33.44 '79, 1M: 4:25.03 '85.

Claudia LOSCH b.10 Jan 1960 Wanne-Eickel 1.81m 84kg. LCO München. Optician.
At SP: OG: '84- 1, '88- 5; WCh: '83- 7, '87- 4; WI: '87- 3; ECh: '86- 4 (9 DT); EI: '84- 2, '85- 2, '86- 1, '88- 1; WSG: '83- 2; ECp: '87- 5. FRG champion SP 1982–8, DT 1986.
FRG shot record 1987.
Progression at SP: 1975- 12.58, 1976- 13.14, 1977- 13.71, 1978- 14.14, 1979- 15.00, 1980- 15.85, 1981- 15.50, 1982- 18.51, 1983- 20.08, 1984- 20.55, 1985- 20.59i/19.96, 1986- 21.46i/20.92, 1987- 22.19, 1988- 20.57. pb DT: 63.12 '85.
Has been the top Western shot-putter for several years.

Vera MICHALLEK b.6 Nov 1958 Lindau 1.68m 53kg. LG Frankfurt. née Steiert.
At 3000m (1500m): OG: '88- h (h); WCh: '83- h, '87- 11 (h); ECh: '86- 10 (h); EI: '88- 2; ECp: '83- 5. FRG champion 1500m & 3000m 1988.
Progression at 3000m: 1975- 9:46.1, 1976- 10:00.0, 1978- 10:05.4, 1980- 9:16.0, 1981- 8:52.57, 1982- 9:14.94/9:03.27i, 1983- 8:52.67, 1984- 8:54.62, 1986- 8:50.99, 1987- 8:49.61, 1988- 8:46.97i/ 8:47.62. pbs: 800m: 2:02.9 '84, 1000m: 2:42.63 '81, 1500m: 4:04.29 '86, 1M: 4:28.29i '88, 5000m: 15:41.68 '86, 10000m: 34:08.0 '86.

Beate PETERS b.12 Oct 1959 Marl 1.78m 80kg. TV Wattenscheid. Student of PE and biology.
At JT: OG: '84- 7, '88- dnq 14; WCh: '83- 7, '87- 3; ECh: '86- 3; WSG: '81- 2, '83- 1, '85- 2; ECp: '83- 4, '85- 4, '87- 3. FRG champion 1985–6.
FRG javelin record 1986.
Progression at JT: 1976- 40.18, 1977- 46.84, 1978- 56.64, 1979- 57.16, 1980- 50.50, 1981- 56.98, 1982- 60.24, 1983- 66.86, 1984- 63.02, 1985- 64.40, 1986- 69.56, 1987- 68.84, 1988- 62.14. pb SP: 14.63 '78.

Iris PLOTZITZKA b.7 Jan 1966 Memmingen 1.81m 80kg. LCO München.
At SP: OG: '88- dnq 14; WCh: '87- 12; ECh: '86- 7; WI: '87- 8.
Progression at SP: 1981- 11.38, 1982- 12.72, 1983- 14.15, 1984- 17.67, 1985- 17.82, 1986- 19.76, 1987- 20.18, 1988- 20.53. pb DT: 56.06 '86.

Kerstin PRESSLER b.2 Feb 1962 Augsburg 1.60m 50kg. NSF Berlin. Medical student.
At Mar: OG: '88- 21. At 10000m: WCh: '87- 10; ECh: '86- 20; ECp: '87- 6. FRG champion 1986–8.
Progression at 10000m/Mar: 1983- 36:40.8, 1984- 34:32.54, 1985- 33:58.88/2:52:35, 1986- 32:46.24/ 2:36:33, 1987- 31:56.80/2:31:22, 1988- 32:35.33/ 2:30:37. pbs: 800m: 2:07.75 '86, 1500m: 4:17.91 '86, 3000m: 8:58.26 '87, 5000m: 15:38.81 '88.
Won Berlin marathon 1987.

Heike REDETZKY b.5 May 1964 Kiel 1.81m 64kg. LG Bayer Leverkusen. Student.
At HJ: OG: '84- 11=, '88- dnq 13; WCh: '87- 6; ECh: '86- 6; EJ: '81- 5; ECp: '85- 6, '87- 3; WI: '87- 6; EI: '88- 2=. FRG champion 1984–8.
Progression at HJ: 1979- 1.69, 1980- 1.85, 1981- 1.87i, 1982- 1.89, 1983- 1.87i, 1984- 1.91, 1985- 1.92, 1986- 1.93, 1987- 1.96, 1988- 1.98. pbs: 100mh: 14.04/14.0 '81, LJ: 6.13 '81.

Ulrike SARVARI b.22 Jun 1964 Heidelberg 1.62m 50kg. VfL Sindelfingen. Arts student.
At 100m (200m): OG: '88- sf/4R; WCh: '87- sf/5R (sf); ECh: '86- sf; ECp: '87- 3/3R. FRG champion 100m 1987–8, 200m 1987.
Progression at 100m: 1982- 12.16, 1983- 11.97, 1984- 11.82, 1985- 11.46/11.28w, 1986- 11.53, 1987- 11.23/11.15w, 1988- 11.16/11.05w. pb 200m: 22.88 '87.

Three FRG indoor 60m records to 7.13 in 1988 and fourth at European Indoors.

Ute THIMM b.10 Jul 1958 Bochum 1.68m 54kg. née Finger. TV Wattenscheid. Sociology student.
At 400m/R- 4x400m relay: OG: '84- 6/5 4x100mR/3R, '88- sf/4R/4R; WCh: '83- 6R (qf 200m), '87- sf; ECh: '82- 4R, '86- 5/2R; ECp: '87- 4 200m/3R/3R). FRG champion 200m 1987, 400m 1981, 1984, 1987.
Progression at 400m: 1977- 55.4, 1980- 54.6, 1981- 52.32, 1982- 51.47, 1983- 50.78, 1984- 50.37, 1985- 53.53, 1986- 51.15, 1987- 50.82, 1988- 50.28. pbs: 100m: 11.31 '85, 200m: 22.87 '87.

Ingrid THYSSEN b.9 Jan 1956 Aachen. 1.71m 72kg. LG Bayer Leverkusen. Physical education teacher.
At JT: OG: '84- 6, '88- 8; WCh: '83- 14, '87- 9; ECh: '78- 7, '82- 9, '86- 7; WSG: '81- 4; ECp: '81- 3. FRG champion 1978–84, 1987–8.
Three FRG javelin records 1982–7.
Progression at JT: 1970- 35.50, 1971- 39.66, 1972- 46.08, 1973- 49.38, 1974- 51.90, 1975- 55.72, 1976- 60.00, 1977- 57.14, 1978- 60.42, 1979- 60.40, 1980- 64.04, 1981- 65.56, 1982- 68.10, 1983- 65.80, 1984- 66.12, 1985- 68.84, 1986- 67.34, 1987- 69.68, 1988- 66.00. pb HJ: 1.76 '71.
German schools four-event (75m, LJ, SP, HJ) champion 1970.

Claudia ZACZKIEWICZ b.4 Jul 1962 Oberhausen 1.70m 57kg. née Reidick. MTG Mannheim. Works in husband's medical practice, qualified teacher.
At 100mh: OG: '88- 3; WCh: '87- 7; ECh: '86- h; ECp: '87- 3. FRG champion 1987–8. Won GP 1988.
Four FRG 100mh records 1987–8.
Progression at 100mh: 1978- 14.7, 1979- 14.0, 1980- 13.8, 1981- 13.85, 1982- 14.07, 1983- 13.67/13.52w, 1984- 13.45, 1985- 13.24, 1986- 13.24, 1987- 12.80, 1988- 12.75. pbs: 100m: 11.61 '88, 200m: 24.28 '84.

GREECE

Governing body: Hellenic Amateur Athletic Association (SEGAS), 137 Syngrou Avenue, Athens 171 21. Founded 1896.
National Championships first held in 1896 (men), 1930 (women).
1988 Champions: MEN
100m: Kosmas Stratos 10.61, 200m: Vasilis Kaliposis 21.46, 400m: Georgios Panagiotopoulos 46.88, 800m/1500m: Nikos Vouzis 1:50.37/3:46.63,5000m: Panagiotis Fotiou 14:14.46, 10000m: Savas Kouburas 29:26.40, Mar: Georgios Afordakos 2:17:08, 3000mSt: Kiriakos Moutesidis 8:45.65, 110mh: Stelios Bisbas 14.27, 400mh: Thanasis Kalogiannis 50.39, HJ: Labros Papakostas 2.26, PV: Andreas Tsonis 5.31, LJ: Dimitris Delifotis 7.63, TJ: Marios Haziadreou (Cyp) 16.80, SP: Dimitrios Koutsoukis 18.38, DT: Kostas Georgakopoulos 58.52, HT: Triandafilos Apostolidis 67.24, JT: Giannis Peristeris 66.74, Dec: Thanasis Pampaliaris 7119, 20kmW: Hristos Karagiorgos 1:34:02.2.
WOMEN
100m: Parasveki Patoulidou 11.73, 200m: Georgia Zouganeli 24.72, 400m: Natasa Bardopoulou 54.38, 800m: Georgia Troubouki 2:10.13, 1500m/3000m: Dimitra Anagnostou 4:27.93/9:35.44, Dimitra Papaspirou 34:36.26, Mar: Maria Polizou 2:44:49, 100mh: Angeliki Stogianoudi 14.38, 400mh: Anna Rodakou 60.43, HJ: Niki Bakogianni 1.83, LJ: Silvia Kanakari 6.02, SP/JT: Anna Verouli 14.38/58.94, DT: Magda Karava 50.06, Hep: Alexandra Kourli 5152, 10kmW: Popi Gavalaki 53:40.8.

Women

Anna VEROULI b.13 Nov 1956 Kavala 1.66m 75kg. Physical education teacher.
At JT: OG: '84- dnq 13, '88- dnq 19; WCh: '83- 3, '87- 13; ECh: '82- 1, '86- 10. Balkan champion 1988.
Five Greek javelin records 1973–82.
Progression at JT: 1971- 34.90, 1972- 40.96, 1973- 45.50, 1974- 48.94, 1975- 50.22, 1976- 54.24, 1977- 49.94, 1978- 48.42, 1979- 53.62, 1980- 57.70, 1981- 62.28, 1982- 70.02, 1983- 70.90, 1984- 72.70, 1986- 64.30, 1987- 68.52, 1988- 68.76. pb SP: 15.24 '82.
There were emotional scenes in 1982 in her hometown of Athens, where she won the first European Championships gold medal by a Greek woman. She was disqualified at the 1984 Olympics for illegal drug use.

HUNGARY

Governing body: Magyar Atlétikai Szövetség, 1143 Budapest, Dozsa György utca 1–3. Founded 1897.
National Championships first held in 1896 (men), 1932 (women)
1988 Champions: MEN
100m/200m: Attila Kovacs 10.28/20.96, 400m: Tamas Molnar 45.8, 800m: Istvan Szalai 1:49.22, 1500m: Robert Banai 3:43.48, 5000m: Tibor Velczenbach 13:50.73, 10000m: Zoltan Kadlot 29:00.15, Mar: Gabor Szabo 2:17:06, 3000mSt: Bela Vago 8:29.91, 110mh: György Bakos 13.78, 400mh: Istvan Simon-Balla 50.48, HJ: Beno Bese 2.18, PV: Istvan Bagyula 5.40, LJ: Laszlo Szalma 7.78, TJ: Gyula Paloczi 16.14, SP: Laszlo Szabo 19.54, DT: Jozsef Ficsor 61.60, HT: Tibor Gecsek

79.76, JT: Laszlo Stefan 74.82, Dec: Dezsö Szabo 8209, 20kmW: Sandor Urbanik 1:25:43, 50kmW: Laszlo Sator 3:59:40.
WOMEN
100m/200m: Irma Könye 11.86/23.98, 400m Erzsebet Szabo 52.3, 800m: Erzsebet Todoran 2:03.37, 1500m: Katalin Racz 4:12.24, 3000m: Zita Agoston 8:58.1, 5000m/10000m: Erika Vereb 15:41.36/32:37.87, Mar: Karolina Szabo 2:30:57, 100mh: Xenia Siska 13.2, 400mh: Zsofia Antok 59.0, HJ: Katalin Sterk 1.87, LJ: Zsuzsa Vanyek 6.38, SP: Viktoria Szelinger 17.90, DT: Marta Bacskai 60.24, JT: Katalin Hartai 62.74, Hep: Margit Palombi 5636, 10kmW: Aniko Szebenszki 46:00.

Istvan BAGYULA b.2 Jan 1969 Budapest 1.84m 75kg. Csepel SC. Student.
At PV: OG: '88- 7; WJ: '86- dnq, '88- 1; EJ: '87- 3. Hungarian champion 1988.
World junior pole vault record and two Hungarian records 1988
Progression at PV: 1982- 4.30, 1983- 4.63, 1984- 4.90, 1985- 5.10, 1986- 5.50, 1987- 5.50, 1988- 5.65.

György BAKOS b.6 Jul 1960 Zalaegerszeg 1.87m 82kg. Ujpesti Dozsa. Economics graduate from Budapest University.
At 110mh: OG: '88- qf; WCh: '83- 6, '87- sf; ECh: '82- sf, '86- 8; EJ: '79- 2; WSG: '85- 2; WCp: '85- 5= Hungarian champion 1980–8. At 60mh: EI: '84- 2, '85- 1.
Eight Hungarian 110mh records 1981–5.
Progression at 110mh: 1979- 14.21, 1980- 14.12, 1981- 13.77/13.5w, 1982- 13.80, 1983- 13.49, 1984- 13.45, 1985- 13.45, 1986- 13.60, 1987- 13.56, 1988- 13.61/13.58w. pbs: 100m: 10.44/ 10.39w '88, 200m: 21.21 '83, 300m: 33.03 '81, 400m: 48.11 '78, 400mh: 52.25 '79.

Tibor GECSEK b.22 Sep 1964 Szentgotthard 1.83m 104kg. Haladas VSE. Diesel engine mechanic.
At HT: OG: '88- 6; WCh: '87- 7; EJ: '83- 6. Hungarian champion 1986–8. Won GP 1988.
Four Hungarian hammer records 1987–8.
Progression at HT: 1980- 34.26, 1981- 50.62, 1982- 60.60, 1983- 67.90, 1984- 73.66, 1985- 77.62, 1986- 77.66, 1987- 79.14, 1988- 81.68. pbs: SP: 14.65 '85, DT: 48.72 '85.

Attila KOVACS b.2 Sep 1960 Szekszard 1.82m 80kg. Ujpesti Dozsa.
At 100m (200m): OG: '88- sf (qf); WCh: '87- 5 (sf); ECh: '82- h, '86- 7. Hungarian champion 100m 1981, 1984–8; 200m 1984, 1987–8.
Hungarian records: 100m (2), 200m (2) 1984–7.
Progression at 100m/200m: 1979- 10.7, 22.24; 1980- 10.58, 21.30; 1981- 10.41, 20.86; 1982- 10.42, 20.81; 1983- 10.45, 21.22; 1984- 10.18, 20.60/20.51w; 1985- 10.27, 20.98; 1986- 10.29/ 10.26w, 20.50; 1987- 10.09/20.11, 1988- 10.26/ 10.17w/20.96.

László SZALMA b.21 Oct 1957 Nagymaros 1.91m 78kg. Vasas. Sales representative
At LJ: OG: '80- 4, '88- 6; WCh: '83- 4; WI: '87- 6; ECh: '78- dnq, '82- 11; EI: '78- 1, '83- 1, '85- 2, '86- 2, '88- 2; WSG: '81- 1; WCp: '81- 7, '85- 3. Hungarian champion 1978, 1980–3, 1985, 1988.
Eight Hungarian long jump records 1977–85.
Progression at LJ: 1974- 6.91, 1975- 7.50, 1976- 7.81, 1977- 7.97, 1978- 8.00i, 1979- 7.82i, 1980- 8.13/8.25w, 1981- 8.12/8.23w, 1982- 8.20, 1983- 8.24, 1984- 8.27, 1985- 8.30, 1986- 8.24i/8.03/ 8.07w, 1987- 8.16i, 1988- 8.03i/8.02. pb 100m: 10.4 '80, 10.54 '85, 10.44w '87.

Imre SZITAS b.4 Sep 1961 Mosonmagyarovar 1.85m 82kg. Haladas VSE.
At HT: OG: '88- 7; EJ: '79- 12. Hungarian champion 1984–5.
Four Hungarian records 1984–8.
Progression at HT: 1979- 61.66, 1980- 66.74, 1981- 69.42, 1982- 74.08, 1984- 78.84, 1985- 78.50, 1986- 77.28, 1987- 78.24, 1988- 80.60. pb DT: 51.38 '85.

Women

Karolina SZABÓ b.17 Nov 1961 Dunaföldvár 1.49m 36kg. Budapesti Honved.
At Mar: OG: '88- 13; WCh: '83- 18, '87- 9; ECh: '82- 6; WCp: '85- 3. At 10000m: ECh: '86- 8. Hungarian champion 3000m 1982, 1986; 10000m 1984–7, marathon 1982, 1986, 1988.
World record 30000m: 1:47:06 '88. Hungarian records: 5000m, 10000m (2), marathon (5) 1982–6.
Progression at Mar: 1981- 2:54:55, 1982- 2:38:03, 1983- 2:36:22, 1984- 2:33:43, 1985- 2:34:57, 1986- 2:30:31, 1987- 2:32:48, 1988- 2:30:57. pbs: 1500m: 4:17.75 '86, 3000m: 8:57.97i '85, 9:01.78 '84; 5000m: 15:32.49 '85, 10000m: 31:55.93 '86, 1Hr: 16620m '88, 20000m: 1:11:48.9 '88.

ICELAND

Governing body: Frjalsiprottasamband Islands, P.O.Box 1099, Iprottamidstodinni Laugardal, Reykjavik. Founded in 1947.
National Championships first held in 1927.
1988 Champions: MEN
100m: Jon A.Magnusson 10.81, 200m/400m Oddur Sigurdsson 22.09/51.62, 800m: Steinn Johansson 2:10.4, 1500m: Gudmundor Sigurdsson 4:03.5, 5000m/10000m: Mar Hermansson 15:03.5/31:41.1,

Mar: Sighvatur Gudmundsson 2:42:44, 3000mSt: Johann Ingibergsson 9:34.6, 110mh: Thorvaldur Thorsson 15.0w, 400mh: Gudmundor Skulason 57.59, HJ: Gunnlaugur Grettisson 2.08, PV: Sigurdur Sigurdsson 4.70, LJ: Olafur Gudmundsson 7.11, TJ: Olafur Thorarinsson 14.13, SP: Petur Gudmundsson 18.83, DT: Vesteinn Hafsteinsson 62.28, HT: Gudmundur Karlsson 58.00, JT: Einar Vilhjalmsson 84.66, Dec: Unnar Vilhjalmsson 6549.
WOMEN
100m/200m/100mh/400mh: Helga Halldorsdottir 11.81w/24.44w/14.3/60.92, 400m: Oddny Arnadottir 59.60, 800m/1500m: Frida Thordardottir 2:23.81/ 4:52.0, 3000m/5000m: Martha Ernstdottir 9:55.4/ 16:54.3, HJ: Thordis Gisladottir 1.75, LJ: Susanna Helgadottir 5.97w, SP: Gudbjörg Gylfadottir 14.03, DT: Margrét Oskarsdottir 39.14, JT/Hep: Bryndis Holm 41.42/45.62.

Einar VILHJALMSSON b.1.6.60 Reykjavik 1.88m 97kg. Graduate of University of Texas, USA.
At JT: OG: '84- 6, '88- dnq 13; WCh: '83, '87- dnq 13; ECh: '82- dnq, '86- 13; WSG: '83- 4. NCAA champion 1983–4. 3rd GP 1985.
Icelandic javelin record holder since 1980. US collegiate record 1984.
Progression at JT: 1980- 76.76, 1981- 81.22, 1982- 80.74, 1983- 90.66, 1984- 92.42, 1985- 91.84, new: 1986- 80.28, 1987- 82.96, 1988- 84.66.
Missed final in both Rome and Seoul by one place. His father, Vilhjalmur Einarsson, won Iceland's only Olympic medal when second in the 1956 triple jump.

INDIA

Governing body: Amatuer Althletic Federation of India, Room No. 1148A, Gate No 28, East Block, Jawaharlal Nehru Stadium, Lodi Road, New Delhi 110003. Founded 1946.
National Championships first held as Indian Games in 1924.
1988 Open National Champions: MEN
100m: Canute Meghales 10.4, 200m: Anand Shetty 21.6, 400m: Vijay Kumaran 48.7, 800m: Budhwa Oraon 1:51.8, 1500m/3000mSt: P. Sholamuthu 3:50.9/9:20.3, 5000m: K.M. Suresh 14:25.8, 10000m: E. Rajendra 30:56.2, 110mh: Vijay Kumar 14.7, 400mh: Surinder Singh 52.7, HJ: N. Ammavi 2.10, PV: Pal Singh 4.50, LJ: Shyam Kumar 7.45, TJ: S. Murali 15.68, SP: Balwinder Singh 18.19, DT: Sarjit Singh 52.92, HT: Piarey Lal 58.50, JT: S.B. Mishra 69.24, Dec: Satyadeo Singh 6541.
WOMEN
100m: Zenia Ayrton 12.2, 200m: Ashwini Nachappa 24.4, 400m: Mercy Kuttan 54.0, 800m: Rosa Kutty 2:11.8, 1500m/3000m: Vijay Neelmani Khalko 4:38.8/9:58.4, 10000m: Nanda Jadhav 36:38.0, 100mh/400mh: Kum Kum Mondal 14.4/61.5, HJ: Angela Lincy 1.68, LJ: Rekha Lal 5.84, SP: Rajender Kaur 13.78, DT: Germeet Kaur 45.26, JT: Shiny Verghese 50.12, Hep: Jolly Joseph 4022.

IRELAND

Governing Body: Bord Luthchleas na h'Eireann (BLE), 11 Prospect Road, Glasnevin, Dublin 9. Founded in 1967. Original Irish AAA founded in 1885.
National Championships first held in 1873.
1988 champions: MEN
100m/200m: Philip Snoddy 10.55w/20.50w, 400m: Gerry Delaney 46.85, 800m: Mark Kirk (NI) 1:50.82, 1500m: Frank O'Mara 3:47.27, 5000m: John Doherty 13:43.29, 10000m: Gerry Curtis 28:49.26, Mar: John Woods 2:11:30, 3kmSt: Brendan Quinn 8:42.83, 110mh: T.J.Kearns 14.41, 400mh: J.J. Barry 52.82, HJ: Peter Minogue 2.07, PV: Alan Burke 4.50, LJ/TJ: Billy Oakes 6.91/14.68w, SP: Victor Costelloe 16.49, DT: John Farrelly 46.96, HT: Conor McCullouch 74.16, JT: Terry McHugh 69.20, Dec: Ian Condron 6092, 3kmW: Pat Murphy 12:43.42, 20kmWt: Jimmy McDonald 1:27:29.67.
WOMEN
100m: Michelle Carroll 11.86w, 200m: Patricia Amond 23.47w, 400m: Patricia Walsh 54.39, 800m: Aisling Molloy 2:05.48, 1500m: Monica Joyce 4:20.43, 3000m/10000m: Rose Lambe 9:22.77/ 33:45.0, Mar: Marie Murphy-Rollins 2:40:48, 100mh: Olive Burke 14.00, 400mh: Barbara Johnson 57.93, HJ: Liz Comerford 1.74, LJ: Terri Horgan 6.27, SP/DT: Marita Walton 14.89/47.64, HT: Breda Wall 39.78, JT: Dara Shakespeare 43.76, Hep: Brid Hallisey 4775, 3kmW/10kmW: Perry Williams 14:21.72/51:52.2.

John DOHERTY b.22 Jul 1961 Leeds 1.75m 60kg. Leeds City.
At 5000m: OG: '88- 9. Irish champion 1988. At 3000m: EJ: '79- 4.
Progression at 5000m: 1978- 14:24.2, 1979- 13:50.5, 1980- 13:48.84, 1981- 13:47.52, 1984- 13:26.33, 1985- 13:23.48, 1987- 13:42.23, 1988- 13:17.14. pbs: 800m: 1:54.0 '80, 1500m: 3:46.0 '80, 1M: 4:01.5 '82, 2000m: 5:09.53 '82, 3000m: 7:44.85 '88, 2M: 8:19.45 '88, 3000mSt: 9:14.4 '79.
Took up Irish nationality in 1987, having previously run for Britain.

Frank O'MARA b.17 Jul 1961 Limerick City 1.76m 61kg. Limerick and Reebok TC, USA. Post graduate student at University of Arkansas.
At 5000m: WCh: '87- 9, '88- h. At 1500m: OG: '84- ht; ECh: '86- 8. Irish champion 1983, 1986, 1988; NCAA champion 1983. At 3000m: WI: '87- 1.
Irish 5000m record 1987. Ran on Ireland's 4x1M world best 1985.

Progression at 1500m/1M, 5000m: 1979- 3:45.0, 1980- 3:40.36/3:59.19, 1981- 3:39.85/3:58.86, 1983- 3:37.7/3:52.50, 1984- 3:37.91, 1985- 3:34.02/ 3:55.92, 14:04.02; 1986- 3:35.04/3:51.06, 13:24.70; 1987- 3:36.23/3:53.58, 13:13.02; 1988- 3:38.44, 13:26.75. pbs: 800m: 1:47.72 '84, 2000m: 4:59.00 '87, 3000m: 7:42.99 '87, 2M: 8:17.78 '88.

Marcus O'SULLIVAN b.22 Dec 1961 Cork City 1.75m 60kg. Leevale and New Balance TC, USA. Degree in accountancy from Villanova University.
At 1500m: OG: '84- sf, '88- 8; WCh: '87- sf; WI: '87- 1; ECh: '86- 6; EI: '85- 2. AAA champion 1985, Irish champion 1500m 1984, 800m 1986.
Ran on Ireland's 4x1M world best 1985. Three Irish 800m records 1984–5.
Progression at 1500m/1M: 1980- 3:47.7, 1981- 3:48.5/4:03.0i, 1982- 3:42.7/4:00.1, 1983- 3:43.2/ 3:56.65, 1984- 3:37.40/3:55.82, 1985- 3:37.20/ 3:52.64, 1986- 3:35.76/3:53.55, 1987- 3:36.7/ 3:52.76, 1988- 3:35.4i/3:36.04/3:50.94i. pbs: 800m: 1:45.87 '85, 1000m: 2:19.15 '87, 3000m: 7:50.09 '86, 5000m: 13:29.21 '86.

John TREACY b.4.6.57 Villierstown, Waterford 1.75m 59kg. Deise & New Balance TC, USA. MBA from Providence University, USA.
At 5000m: OG: '80- 7; WCh: '87- 13; ECh: '78- 4; EJ: '75- 2. At 10000m: OG: '80- ht, '84- 9; WCh: '83- h, '87- 26; ECh: '78- 11, '86- 6. Irish champion 5000m 1978, 1980–1, 1983–4; 10000m 1978, 1985, 1987. Won AAA 10000m 1979. At marathon: OG: '84- 2, '88- dnf. World CC: 78- 1, '79- 1, '85- 5 (3rd Junior 1974–5).
Irish records: 5000m (3), 10000m (2), marathon (2), 3000m, 1 hour.
Progression at 5000m/10000m: 1975- 14:04.6, 1976- 28:04.8 (6 miles), 1977- 13:39.8/28:41.37, 1978- 13:26.5/27:55.2, 1979- 13:32.1/28:12.10, 1980- 13:21.93/27:48.7, 1981- 13:28.45/28:41.65, 1982- 13:34.96i, 1983- 13:35.02/28:35.58, 1984- 13:16.81/28:01.3, 1985- 13:19.11/28:04.92, 1986- 13:22.11/28:04.10, 1987- 13:20.98/28:12.79, 1988- 13:32.34/28:16.37. At marathon: 1984- 2:09:56, 1987- 2:17:50, 1988- 2:09:15. pbs: 1500m: 3:44.2 '79, 1M: 4:02.3 '86, 3000m: 7:45.22 '80, 20km: 61:10.1 '87, 1Hr: 19625m '87.
Had run five marathons, including in 1988 third at Boston and New York.

ISRAEL

Governing body: Israeli Athletic Association, 4 Marmorek Street, PO Box 4575, Tel Aviv 61044. Founded as Federation for Amateur Sport in Palestine 1931.
National Championships first held in 1935.
1988 Champions: MEN
100m/200m: David Kirton (UK) 10.65/21.63, 400m: Pascal Chichignoud (Fra) 47.71, 800m: Thierry Caquelard (Fra) 1:51.09, 1500m: José Moreira (Por) 3:46.03, 5000m: Jeremy Barton (UK) 13:58.90, 10000m: Arie Gamliel 30:07.70, Mar: Patrick Joannes (Fra) 2:18:08, 3000mSt: Gai Ben-Ephraim 9:43.51, 110mh: Tzafrir Mintzer 15.23, 400mh: Martin Briggs (UK) 50.04, HJ: Eric Monnerais (Fra) 2.16, LJ: Mark Forsythe (UK) 7.95, TJ: Rogel Nachum 16.11, SP: Yoav Sharf 15.29, DT: Offer Gershon 45.18, HT: Danny Nemeth 47.10, JT: Michael Cohen 51.10.
WOMEN
100m: Maria Gomes (Por) 11.58, 200m: Ina Cordes (FRG) 23.31, 400m: Karin Janke (FRG) 53.42, 800m: Edna Lankri 2:12.79, 1500m/3000m: Zehava Shmueli 4:35.59/9:54.2, 10000m: Amal Abdullah 41:20.56, Mar: Maija Vuorinen (Fin) 2:40:01, 100mh: Christine Hurtlin (Fra) 13.55, 400mh: Maria Lopes (Por) 59.02, HJ: Janet Boyle (UK) 1.88, LJ: Maria Teloni (Cyp) 6.32, SP: Tzila Asher 12.99, DT: Ilana Goldberg 38.06, JT: Chrysoula Georgiou (Cyp) 46.46, Hep: Michal Weiler 3430.

ITALY

Governing Body: Federazione Italiana di Atletica Leggera (FIDAL), via Tevere 1/A, Roma. Constituted 1926. First governing body formed 1896.
National Championships first held in 1906 (men), 1927 (women). **1988 champions:** MEN
100m: Antonio Ullo 10.48, 200m: Stefano Tilli 20.85, 400m: not contested, the athletes refusing to run due to the non-selection of a 4x400m relay team for the Olympics, 800m: Donato Sabia 1:51.90, 1500m: Davide Tirelli 3:46.03, 5000m/3000mSt: Francesco Panetta 13:37.43/8:21.45, 10000m: Giuseppe Miccoli 28:30.81, Mar: Carlo Terzer 2:18:09, 110mh: Gianni Tozzi 14.21, 400mh: Luca Cosi 51.47, HJ: Luca Toso 2.24, PV: Marco Andreini 5.40, LJ: Milko Campus 7.53, TJ: Dario Badinelli 16.29, SP: Marco Montelatici 18.15, DT: Marco Martino 60.10, HT: Lucio Serrano 78.02, JT: Fabio De Gaspari 71.90, Dec: Marco Rossi 7673, 10kmW: Giovanni De Benedictis 40:33.00, 20kmW: Maurizio Damilano 1:20:26, 50kmW: Raffaelo Duccheschi 3:44:27.
WOMEN
100m/200m: Marisa Masullo 11.60/23.70, 400m: Rosanna Morabito 53.83, 800m: Nicoletta Tozzi 2:07.50, 1500m/3000m: Roberta Brunet 4:16.79/ 8:58.97, 10000m: Maria Curatolo 33:35.07, Mar: Graziella Striuli 2:36:02, 100mh: Carla Tuzzi 13.73, 400mh: Irmgard Trojer 56.44, HJ: Barbara Fiammengo 1.87, LJ: Antonella Capriotti 6.50, SP: Concetta Milanese 15.81, DT: Mario Marello 55.24, JT: Stefania Galbiati 52.02, Hep: Herta Steiner 5570, 5kmW: P.Carola Pagani 22:33.82, 10kmW: Erika Alfridi 52:27.

Alessandro ANDREI b.3 Jan 1959 Firenze 1.91m 118kg. Fiamme Oro Padova. Policeman.
At SP: OG: '84- 1, '88- 7; WCh: '83- 7, '87- 2; ECh: '82- 10, '86- 4; EI: '84- 3; EJ: '77- 9; WSG: '85- 1; WCp: '81- 7, '85- 3; ECp: '83- 4, '85- 2, '87- 2. Italian champion 1983–6.
21 Italian shot records 1982–7, inc. three world records 1987.
Progression: 1976- 15.32, 1977- 17.46, 1978- 17.38i, 1979- 18.41, 1980- 19.58, 1981- 19.92, 1982- 20.35, 1983- 20.19, 1984- 21.50, 1985- 21.95, 1986- 22.06, 1987- 22.91, 1988- 20.61. pb DT: 47.54 '79.
Improved the world record three times at Viareggio on 12 Aug 1987, with 22.72, 22.84 and 22.91 and all six puts over 22m, although there were reports that a raised circle may have been used.

Salvatore ANTIBO b.7 Feb 1962 Altofonte, Palermo 1.70m 52kg. CUS Roma. Accountancy student.
At 5000m/10000m: OG: '84- sf/4, '88- sf/2; WCh: '87- 16; ECh: '82- h/6, '86- 10/3; ECp: '87- 3/2. At 5000m: WCh: '83- 13; EJ: '81- 2.
Italian records: two 10000m, one 2M 1988.
Progression at 10000m: 1981- 30:16.4, 1982- 28:16.25, 1983- 29:32.47, 1984- 27:48.02, 1985- 28:27.49, 1986- 27:39.52, 1987- 28:33.77, 1988- 27:23.55. pbs: 1500m: 3:43.1 '86, 2000m: 5:05.92 '86, 3000m: 7:49.4 '85, 2M: 8:20.79 '87, 5000m: 13:16.1 '88.

Alessandro BELLUCCI b.21 Feb 1955 Lanuvio, Roma 1.70m 55kg. Fiamme Gialle Ostia. Accountant.
At 50kmW: OG: '84- 3, '88- 32; WCh: '83- 7, '87- 6; ECh: '78- 7, '82- dq, '86- 11; LT: '79- 11, '81- 3, '85- 4, '87- 9. At 20kmW: ECh: '74- 7; LT: '77- 11.
Progression at 50kmW: 1976- 4:21:02, 1977- 4:15:53, 1978- 3:58:26, 1979- 3:51:20, 1980- 3:56:48, 1981- 3:54:57, 1982- 3:54:52, 1983- 3:55:38, 1984- 3:53:45, 1985- 3:58:22, 1986- 3:54:10, 1987- 3:48:52, 1988- 3:48:08. pbs: track 10kmW: 41:01.4 '87, road 20kmW: 1:23:16 '82.

Gelindo BORDIN b.2 Apr 1959 Longare, Vicenza 1.80m 68kg. Alitans Verona. Surveyor.
At Mar: OG: '88- 1; ECh: '86- 1; WCp: '85- 12; ECp: '85- 7.
Italian marathon record when fourth at Boston 1988.
Progression at Mar: 1984- 2:13:20, 1985- 2:11:29, 1986- 2:10:54, 1987- 2:12:40, 1988- 2:09:27. pbs: 5000m: 14:06.6 '79, 10000m: 29:00.65 '83, 3kmSt: 8:49.2 '83.
His Olympic victory was his fifth marathon win in ten races from his first at Milan in 1984.

Alberto COVA b.1 Dec 1958 Inverigo, Como 1.76m 58kg. Pro Patria Freedent.
At 10km: OG: '84- 1, '88- h; WCh: '83- 1; ECh: '82- 1, '86- 2; ECp: '83- 2, '85- 1. At 5km: ECh: '82- dq, '86- 8; ECp: '81- 6, '83- 3, '85- 1; EJ: '77- 5. At 3km: EI: '82- 2. World CC: '82- 7, '83- 10, '84- 13, '86- 9. Italian champion 5000m 1980, 1982–3, 1985; 10000m 1981–2, CC 1982–6.
Italian records: 5000m 1982, 1985; 2M 1981, 1982.
Progression at 5km/10km: 1976- 14:38.4, 1977- 14:04.0, 1978- 14:07.4, 1979- 13:58.2, 1980- 13:40.4/29:20.5, 1981- 13:27.20/28:29.12, 1982- 13:13.71/27:41.03, 1983- 13:38.13/27:37.59, 1984- 13:18.24/27:47.54, 1985- 13:10.06/27:49.36, 1986- 13:15.86/27:57.93, 1987- 13:40.14/28:44.00, 1988- 13:33.85/27:52.80. pbs: 800m: 1:53.2 '78, 1500m: 3:40.6 '85, 2000m: 5:09.0 '86, 3000m: 7:46.40 '83, 3000mSt: 8:37.2 '80.
Famed for the blistering finish that has brought him great success at 10000 metres.

Maurizio DAMILANO b.6 Apr 1957 Scarnafigi 1.83m 70kg. Sisport Torino.
At 20kmW (50kmW): OG: '80- 1, '84- 3 (dnf), '88- 3; WCh: '83- 7, '87- 1; ECh: '78- 6, '82- dq (dq), '86- 2 (dnf); WSG: '81- 1, '83- 2; LT: '77- 4, '81- 6, '83- 4, '85- 2, '87- 7. At 10kmW: EJ: '75- 4. At 5kmW: WI: '85- 2. 17 Italian championships (6 at 10kmW, 1 15kmW, 8 20kmW, 2 50kmW) 1978–88.
Three Italian 20kmW records. World records at 25km, 30km and 2 hours walk 1985, world best 3kmW 1980.
Progression at 20kmW: 1975- 1:41:46, 1976- 1:29:15, 1977- 1:25:33, 1978- 1:24:58, 1979- 1:22:59.1t, 1980- 1:21:47.8t, 1981- 1:22:26, 1982- 1:22:06, 1983- 1:20:10, 1984- 1:20:09, 1985- 1:21:43, 1986- 1:21:17, 1987- 1:20:45, 1988- 1:20:14. pb 50kmW: 3:51:50 '86. Track pbs: 3kmW: 11:07.75 '81, 5kmW: 19:07.96i '84, 10kmW: 39:05.8 '88, 25kmW: 1:44:54.0 '85, 30kmW: 2:06:07.3 '85, 1hr: 14932m '84, 2hr: 28565m '85.
When he won the 1980 Olympic 20km walk title, his twin brother Giorgio was 11th. Started walking career in 1972.

Giovanni DE BENEDICTIS b.8 Jan 1968 Pescara 1.78m 51kg. Carabinieri.
At 20kmW: '88- 9. At 10kmW: WJ: '86- 4; EJ: '85- 3, '87- 1. Italian 10km walk champion 1988.
Progression at 20kmW: 1988- 1:21:18. pbs: 5kmW: 18:58.40i '88, 19:31.04 '87; 10kmW: 39:44.71 '87.

Raffaello DUCCESCHI b.25 Feb 1962 Sesto San Giovanni 1.83m 65kg. Fiamme Oro Padova. Policeman.
At 50kmW: OG: '84- 5, '88- 8; WCh: '87- 4; ECh: '86- 13; LT: '85- 5, '87- 10. At 20kmW: WSG: '87- 1. Italian champion 1983, 1984 (short course 3:43:02), 1988.
Progression at 50kmW: 1983- 3:58:28, 1984- 3:59:26, 1985- 3:56:18, 1986- 3:56:42, 1987-

3:47:49, 1988- 3:44:27. pbs: 10kmW (track): 40:56.0 '87, 20kmW: 1:25:02 '87.

Giovanni EVANGELISTI b.11 Sep 1961 Rimini 1.79m 71kg. PP Osama Milano. Architectural student.
At LJ: OG: '84- 3, '88- 4; WCh: '83- dnq, '87- 4; WI: '85- 3, '87- 3; ECh: '82- 6, '86- 3; EI: '82- 3, '87- 2, '88- 3; WCp: '81- 6; ECp: '81- 8, '83- 6, '85- 8, '87- 4. Italian champion 1981–2, 1986.
Seven Italian long jump records 1982–7.
Progression at LJ: 1976- 5.40, 1977- 6.10, 1978- 6.68, 1979- 7.30, 1980- 7.84, 1981- 7.94, 1982- 8.10i/8.07/8.21w, 1983- 8.09/8.11w, 1984- 8.24, 1985- 8.14i/8.01, 1986- 8.24, 1987- 8.43, 1988- 8.07/8.37w. pbs: 100m: 10.4 '81, 10.73 '84; TJ: 16.30 '80.
Has won several major championship bronze medals, but his one at the 1987 World Championships was a judging error (eventually accepted by IAAF). His 8.38m was probably some 50cm less, and his earlier 8.19m placed him fourth.

Alessandro LAMBRUSCHINI b.7 Jan 1965 Fucecchio, Firenze 1.78m 63kg. Fiamme Oro Padova. Policeman.
At 3000mSt: OG: '88- 4; WCh: '87- 9; ECh: '86- h. At 2000mSt: EJ: '83- 4. Italian champion 1500m 1986, 3000mSt 1986–7.
Progression at 3000mSt: 1983- 9:06.0, 1984- 8:55.43, 1985- 8:36.09, 1986- 8:18.39, 1987- 8:19.17, 1988- 8:12.17. pbs: 800m: 1:47.81 '86, 1500m: 3:35.27 '87, 1M: 4:00.17 '87, 2000m: 5:05.85 '86, 3000m: 8:07.84 '87, 400mh: 55.7.
Beat Said Aouita to win Mediterranean Games steeplechase 1987.

Stefano MEI b.3 Feb 1963 La Spezia 1.82m 66kg. ASSI Banca Toscana Firenze.
At 1500m: OG: '84- sf; WCh: '83- sf; ECh: '82- h; ECp: '85- 3, '87- 6. At 3000m: EI: '86- 2; EJ: '79- 8, '81- 4. At 5000m: OG: '88- 7; ECh: '86- 2; WSG: '85- 1; WCp: '85- 2. 3rd GP 1986. At 10000m: ECh: '86- 1. Italian champion 5000m 1984, 1986; 1500m 1985. 3rd World Junior CC 1982.
Italian records: 2000m 1984; 1500m, 3000m and 2 miles 1986.
Progression at 5000m/10000m: 1979- 14:36.7, 1980- 13:55.91/31:04.7, 1981- 13:52.51, 1982- 13:45.48, 1983- 13:32.06, 1984- 13:29.61, 1985- 13:21.05, 1986- 13:11.57/27:43.97, 1987- 13:42.52, 1988- 13:24.20/27:57.06. pbs: 800m: 1:48.1 '85, 1000m: 2:20.04 '84, 1500m: 3:34.57 '86, 1M: 3:58.65 '86, 2000m: 4:58.65 '84, 3000m: 7:42.85 '86, 2M: 8:28.49 '86.

Francesco PANETTA b.10 Jan 1963 Siderno 1.75m 64kg. PP Osama. Student.
At 3000mSt: OG: '84- sf (h 10000m), '88- 9; WCh: '87- 1 (2 10000m); ECh: '86- 2; ECp: '85- 7, '87- 1. At 2kmSt: EJ: '81- 7. World CC: '84- 10. Italian champion 3kmSt 1985, 1988; 5000m 1988, 10000m 1986, CC 1987.
Italian 3000m, 10000m and 3000mSt records 1987.

Progression at 3000mSt/10000m: 1981- 9:09.3, 1982- 8:33.24/29:31.6, 1983- 8:35.39/28:41.2, 1984- 8:26.90/28:03.99, 1985- 8:21.60/27:44.65, 1986- 8:16.85/27:51.05, 1987- 8:08.57/27:26.95, 1988- 8:16.04/27:33.14. pbs: 1500m: 3:39.88 '87, 2000m: 5:05.50 '87, 3000m: 7:42.73 '87, 2M: 8:30.7 '86, 5000m: 13:20.93 '85.
Followed his valiant silver in the 1986 European steeplechase with gold and silver in Rome 1987.

Orlando PIZZOLATO b.30 Jul 1958 Thiene, Vicenza 1.79m 62kg. CUS Universo Ferrera. Physiotherapy student.
At Mar: OG: '88- 16; WCh: '87- 7; ECh: '86- 2; WSG: '85- 1; WCp: '85- 6.
Progression at Mar: 1978- 2:22:20, 1979- 2:17:28, 1980- 2:15:07, 1982- 2:14:42, 1983- 2:15:28, 1984- 2:14:53, 1985- 2:10:23, 1986- 2:10:57, 1987- 2:12:50, 1988- 2:12:32. pbs: 1500m: 3:48.3 '82, 3000m: 8:01.42 '84, 5000m: 13:45.0 '83, 10000m: 28:22.9 '83.
The surprise winner of the 1984 New York marathon confirmed his status in 1985, when he triumphed in hot conditions to win the World Student Games title before again winning in New York; these three are his only wins in 28 marathons.

Gianni POLI b.5 Nov 1957 Lumezzane 1.80m 61kg. S.Rocchino BS.
At Mar: OG: '88- 19; WCh: '83- 7; ECh: '82- 13, '86- 13; ECp: '81- 9; '83- 3. Italian champion 1984.
Four Italian marathon records 1981–5.
Progression at Mar: 1979- 2:20:10, 1980- 2:14:12, 1981- 2:11:19, 1982- 2:15:38, 1983- 2:11:05, 1984- 2:11:05, 1985- 2:09:57, 1986- 2:11:06, 1987- 2:10:15, 1988- 2:09:33. pbs: 5000m: 14:05.1 '79, 10000m: 28:58.5 '86.
Has won two of his 22 marathons 1979–88, at Milan in 1984 and New York 1986.

Donato SABIA b.11 Sep 1963 Potenza 1.80m 70kg. PP Osama Milano.
At 800m: OG: '84- 5, '88- 7; WCh: '83- h; ECh: '82- h; EI: '84- 1; ECp: '83- 4, '87- 2 (8 400m). Italian champion 400m 1984, 800m 1983–4, 1988.
World best 500m 1:00.08 and WIB 600m 1:15.77 in 1984.
Progression at 800m: 1979- 1:58.0, 1980- 1:50.6, 1981- 1:49.19, 1982- 1:47.29, 1983- 1:46.62, 1984- 1:43.88, 1985- 1:50.03, 1987- 1:46.38, 1988- 1:44.90. pbs: 400m: 45.73 '84, 600m: 1:15.33 '84.
Achilles tendon operation in 1985 and came back slowly to his second Olympic final.

Women

Maria CURATOLO b.10 Oct 1963 Torino 1.47m 39kg. Fiat Sud Formia.
At Mar: OG: '88- 8. At 10000m: WCh: '87- dnf h; ECh: '86- 10. World 15km road: '86- 7, '87- 3. Italian 10000m champion 1985, 1987.
Italian 10000m record 1986.
Prgression at Mar: 1984- 2:36:05, 1985- 2:40:10, 1987- 2:38:30/2:30:15sh, 1988- 2:30:14. pbs: 1500m: 4:18.56 '87, 3000m: 8:53.55 '87, 5000m: 15:45.54 '87, 10000m: 32:06.38 '86.
Must be the world's smallest top-class athlete. Has won four of her eight marathons.

Laura FOGLI b.5 Oct 1959 Comacchio 1.68m 50kg. Snia Milano. Housewife.
At Mar: OG: '84- 9, '88- 6; WCh: '83- 6; ECh: '82- 2, '86- 2; WCp: '85- 4; ECp: '81- 5, '85- 6. Italian champion 1980. At 10km: ECp: '85- 6.
Three Italian marathon bests 1983–8.
Progression at Mar: 1981- 2:45:41/2:34:48sh, 1982- 2:33:01/2:31:08 short, 1983- 2:31:49, 1984- 2:29:28, 1985- 2:31:36, 1986- 2:29:44, 1988- 2:27:49. pbs: 800m: 2:11.4 '79, 1500m: 4:19.8 '80, 3000m: 9:17.3 '78, 5000m: 16:06.19 '85, 10000m: 33:39.04 '84.
Her New York marathon positions (4th 1981–2, 3rd 1983–6, 2nd 1988) and two European silver medals point to her consistency, but of her 19 marathons, she has only won two, Rome 1982 and Pittsburgh 1986.

IVORY COAST

Governing body: Fédération Ivoirienne d'Athlétisme, Boulevard Lagunaire, BP 2844, Abidjan 01. Founded 1960.

Gabriel TIACOH b.10 Sep 1963 1.80m 75kg. Club: Larios, Italy. Business student, was at Washington State University, USA.
At 400m: OG: '84- 2, '88- qf; WCh: '83- qf, '87- 7; AfCh: '84- 1, '85- 2, '88- 2 (4 at 200m). Won French 400m 1984, AAA 1987.
Seven Ivory Coast inc. three African 400m records 1983–6. African 300m best 1986.
Progression at 400m: 1980- 51.5, 1981- 48.79, 1982- 46.94, 1983- 45.86, 1984- 44.54, 1985- 44.87, 1986- 44.30, 1987- 44.69, 1988- 45.49. pbs: 100m: 10.7 '82, 200m: 20.71 '84, 300m: 31.74 '86.
Won first ever Olympic medal for the Ivory Coast. Was the world's best 400m runner in 1986, when he lost just once. He has run 15 sub-45 second times, including nine in 1986.

JAMAICA

Governing body: Jamaica Amateur Athletic Association, PO Box 272, Kingston 5. Founded 1932.

1988 Champions MEN
100m: Ray Stewart 10.08, 200m: Clive Wright 20.75, 400m: Bert Cameron 45.67, 1500m: Gawain Guy 3:40.0, 110mh: Richard Bucknor 13.69, 400mh: Winthrop Graham 50.09.
WOMEN
100m: Merlene Ottey 11.03, 200m: Grace Jackson 22.5, 400m: Sandie Richards 51.98, 800m: Sharon Powell 2:01.99.

Bert CAMERON b.16 Nov 1959 Spanish Town 1.88m 79kg. Converse TC, USA. Graduate of University of Texas at El Paso.
At 400m/R- 4x400m relay: OG: '80- qf, '84- dns, '88- 6/2R; WCh: '83- 1, '87- sf; CG: '78- qf/2R, '82- 1/2R; PAm: '79- 4/2R, '87- 2; WCp: '81- 3/3R; CAmG: '78- 1R, '82- 1. NCAA champion 1980–1, 1983 (also indoors 1980–1).
Six Jamaican 400m records 1980–8, one Commonwealth 1981.
Progression at 400m: 1978- 47.20, 1979- 45.97, 1980- 45.23, 1981- 44.58, 1982- 44.69, 1983- 44.62, 1984- 45.07, 1985- 44.94, 1986- 44.66, 1987- 44.72, 1988- 44.50. pbs: 200m: 20.74 '83, 800m: 1:49.57 '82.
Ran his first national record for seven years in the 1988 Olympic semis. Gave amazing performance to qualify at the 1984 Olympics after stopping in the semis, but unable to take part in the final through injury. Married to Linda McCurdy, Canadian HJ champion indoors and out 1988 (pb 1.88i).

Winthrop GRAHAM b.17 Nov 1965 St.Elizabeth 1.75m 71kg. University of Texas.
At 400mh/R- 4x400m relay: OG: '88- 5/2R; WCh: '87- sf; PAm: '87- 1/3R.
Two Jamaican 400mh records 1987.
Progression at 400mh: 1986- 50.03, 1987- 48.49, 1988- 48.04. pb 400m: 45.59 '88.

Ray STEWART b.18 Mar 1965 1.78m 73kg. Student at Texas Christian University, USA.
At 100m/R- 4x100m relay: OG: '84- 6/2R, '88- 7; WCh: '83- sf, '87- 3/3R; PAm: '83- 5, '87- 2/3R; CAm: '86- 3. Jamaican 100m champion 1984, 1986. Won NCAA 1987.
Progression at 100m: 1982- 10.73, 1983- 10.22, 1984- 10.19, 1986- 10.29/10.21w, 1987- 10.08/9.89w/9.8w, 1988- 10.08/10.01w. pb 200m: 20.41 '88, 20.31w '87.
Showed his promise when he was the youngest man in the 1984 Olympic 100m final. Missed 1985 season, but reached top form in 1987 with two bronze medals in Rome

Women

Juliet CUTHBERT b.4 Sep 1964 1.60m 52kg. Was at University of Texas.
At 100m: OG: '84- sf; '88- 7; WCh: '83- qf/3R. Won NCAA 100m 1986, 200m 1985–6.
Progression at 100m: 1979- 11.6w, 1980- 12.25/12.0, 1983- 11.39w/11.63, 1984- 11.42, 1985- 11.18, 1986- 11.24/10.97w, 1987- 11.07/10.95w, 1988- 11.03/10.96w. pbs: 200m: 22.59 '87, 22.25w/21.8w '87, 400m: 53.1 '86.

Grace JACKSON b.14 Jun 1961 St.Ann 1.78m 59kg. Atoms TC, USA.
At 100m/200m/R- 4x100m relay: OG: '84- 5/5, '88- 4/2; WCh: '83: -/5; WI: '87- -/3; CG: '82- sf/7/3R; WSG: '83- 6/3, '85- 3/1; WCp: '85- 2=/2. At HJ: CAmG: '78- 2.
Commonwealth 200m record 1988; three Jamaican 400m records 1986–8.

Grace Jackson (George Herringshaw/ASP)

Progression at 100m, 200m/400m: 1981- 11.86/11.7/11.81w; 1982- 11.68/11.45w, 22.92; 1983- 11.27/11.22w, 22.46/51.69; 1984- 11.24, 22.20; 1985- 11.24w/11.26/11.0, 22.57/22.48w; 1986- 11.31/11.2, 22.39/50.94; 1987- 11.22, 22.34/21.8w/51.28; 1988- 11.08/10.97w, 21.72/49.57. pbs: 100mh: 14.06 '81, 400mh: 59.49 '84, HJ: 1.75 '81.
Achieved her greatest success to date in 1988, when she set national records at 400m, was second overall in the Mobil Grand Prix (won 200m, 2nd 400m), and then took the Olympic silver at 200m after fourth at 100m.

Merlene OTTEY b.10 May 1960 Jamaica 1.74m 57kg. Mazda TC, USA. Graduate of Nebraska University. Formerly married to Nat Page (USA).
At 100m/200m/R- 4x100m relay: OG: '80- -/3, '84- 3/3, '88- sf/4; WCh: '83- 4/2/3R, '87- 3/3; WI: '87- 5(60m)/2; CG: '82: 2/1/3R; PAm: '79- -/3. Won NCAA 100m 1982–3, 200m 1983; TAC 100m 1984–5, 200m 1982 and 1984–5; CAC 100m & 200m 1985. Won overall GP 1987, 100m 2nd 1985, 1st 1987.
Five Commonwealth records at 200m and four at 100m, 1980–7. WIB 1980–2: 300y (8), best 32.63 '82, 300m (3), best 35.83 '81.
Progression at 100m, 200m: 1975- ,25.9; 1976- 12.0, 24.7; 1977- 12.2, 25.1; 1978- 12.6, 24.5; 1979- 11.59/11.4, 23.10/22.79w, 1980- 11.36/11.0, 22.20; 1981- 11.07/10.97w, 22.35; 1982- 11.03/10.97w, 22.17; 1983- 11.07/10.98w, 22.19/22.11w, 1984- 11.01, 22.09, 1985- 10.92/21.93, 1986- 11.06/10.7w/22.43, 1987- 10.87/10.8/22.06, 1988- 11.00/10.7, 21.99. pb 400m: 51.12 '83.
Graceful sprinter, who has been consistently in the medals in major championships prior to Seoul.

JAPAN

Governing body: Nippon Rikujo-Kyogi Renmei, 1-1-1 Jinnan, Shibuya-Ku, Tokyo 150. Founded 1911.
National Championships first held in 1914 (men), 1925 (women)
1988 Champions: MEN
100m: Takahiro Kasahara 10.60, 200m: Kenji Yamauchi 21.13, 400m: Susumu Takano 45.78, 800m: Yasushi Kano 1:50.07, 1500m: Shigeki Nakayama 3:42.99, 5000m/10000m: Haruo Urata 13:39.29/28:42:43, Mar: Toshihiko Seko 2:12:41, 3kmSt: Kazuhito Yamada 8:33.97, 110mh: Hiroki Tebira 14.35, 400mh: Ryōichi Yoshida 50.99, HJ: Takao Sakamoto 2.22, PV: Toshiyuki Hashioka 5.30, LJ: Hiroyuki Shibata 8.06w, TJ: Norifumi Yamashita 16.46, SP: Toshiyuki Yamato 16.56, DT: Hiroshi Ikeda 53.30, HT: Hisakazu Shiono 67.48, JT: Kazuhiro Mizoguchi 76.36, Dec: Katsuhiko Matsuda 7446, 20kmW: Atsumi Tanoue 1:31:25, 50kmW: Tadahiro Kosaka 4:03:14.

WOMEN
100m: Etsuko Hara 12.13, 200m Hiromi Isozaki 24.48, 400m: Kasumi Yamaji 54.97, 800m: Ayako Arai 2:05.03, 1500m: Masako Matsumoto 4:23.64, 3000m: Chen Qingmei (Chn) 9:12.85, 10000m: Akemi Matsuno 32:53.75, 100mh: Chizuko Akimoto 14.05, 400mh: Hitomi Koshimoto 59.03, HJ: Megumi Satoh 1.94, LJ/Hep: Minako Isogai 6.33/5333, TJ: Yumiko Tsuchiya 12.44, SP: Aya Suzuki 15.58, DT: Ikuko Kitamori 55.16, JT: Emi Matsui 57.76, 10kmW: Hideko Hirayama 48:49.

Kazuhiro MIZOGUCHI b.18 Mar 1962 Shirama 1.81m 87kg. Graduate of Kyoto Sangyo University. With Goldwin sporting goods company.
At JT: OG: '84- dnq 20, '88- dnq 19; WCh: '87- 6; AsG: '86- 1; AsCh: '83- 2, '85- 3. Japan champion 1985, 1987–8.
Two Asian javelin records 1986–7.
Progression at JT: 1977- 49.86, 1978- 59.56, 1979- 60.72, 1980- 72.86, 1981- 75.10, 1982- 73.42, 1983- 82.70, 1984- 82.78, 1985- 85.56, new: 1986- 78.80, 1987- 84.16, 1988- 82.34. pbs: SP: 13.94 '86, DT: 48.58 '86.

Takeyuki NAKAYAMA b.20 Dec 1959 Ikeda 1.80m 58kg. Employee, Daiei Store.
At Mar: OG: '88- 4; AsG: '86- 1; WCp: '85- 2. Japan champion 1987.
Asian 10000m record 1987, Japan marathon record 1985.
Progression at 10000m/Mar: 1983- 2:14:15, 1984- 2:10:00, 1985- 28:26.9/2:08:15, 1986- 28:07.0/ 2:08:21, 1987- 27:35.33/2:08:18, 1988- 28:01.74/ 2:11:05. pbs: 5000m: 13:43.80 '85, 30km: 1:31:50 '83.
Has won four of his ten marathons: Fukuoka 1984 and 1987, Seoul 1985 and the 1986 Asian Games. 2nd Tokyo 1987.

Susumu TAKANO b.21 May 1961 Fujinomiya 1.78m 70kg. Graduate student at Tokai University.
At 400m (R- 4x400mR): OG: '84- sf, '88- sf; WCh: '83 & '87- qf; AsG: '82- 1 (1R, 6 200m), '86- 1 (1R); WSG: '83- 5. Japan champion 1982, 1985–8.
Japanese records: 200m 1986, ten 400m, inc. four Asian, 1985–8.
Progression at 400m: 1979- 48.6, 1980- 48.02, 1981- 47.01, 1982- 46.51, 1983- 45.86, 1984- 45.69, 1985- 45.30, 1986- 45.00, 1987- 45.68, 1988- 44.90. pbs: 100m: 10.53 '88, 200m: 20.74 '86, 300m: 32.97 '88.

Hiromi TANIGUCHI b.4 Apr 1960 Miyazaki Pre. 1.71m 56kg. Graduate of Nihon College of Physical Education, employee of Asahi Kasei Chemical.
At Mar: AsG: '86- 2.
Progression at Mar: 1985- 2:10:01, 1986- 2:10:08, 1987- 2:09:50, 1988- 2:07:40. pbs: 1500m: 3:54.0 '82, 5000m: 13:56.08 '85, 10000m: 28:37.68 '88.
Has won three of nine marathons: Beppu 1985, Tokyo and London 1987. Ran best time when second in Beijing 1988.

Women

Megumi SATOH b.13 Sep 1966 Niigata 1.78m 54kg. Student at Fukuoka University.
At HJ: OG: '84- dnq, '88- 11; WCh: '83, '87- dnq; WSG: '87- 3=; AsG: '82- 4, '86- 1; AsCh: '81- 3. Japan champion 1981, 1983, 1985, 1987–8.
Japan high jump record 1987.
Progression at HJ: 1979- 1.60, 1980- 1.79, 1981- 1.87, 1982- 1.83, 1983- 1.90, 1984- 1.87, 1985- 1.92, 1986- 1.91i/1.89, 1987- 1.95, 1988- 1.94. pb LJ: 6.03/6.11w '87.

KENYA

Governing body: Kenya Amateur Athletic Association, Nyayo National Stadium, PO Box 46722, Uhuru-High-Way, Nairobi. Founded 1951.
National Championships
1988 Champions: MEN
100m: Elkana Nyangau 10.3, 200m/400m: Simon Kipkemboi 20.7/45.4, 800m: Juma Ndiwa 1:46.3, 1500m: Joseph Chesire 3:37.3, 5000m: John Ngugi 13:54.0, 10000m: Moses Tanui 28:45.8, 3000mSt: Boniface Merande 8:29.6, 110mh: Gideon Yego 14.1, 400mh: Shem Ochako 49.3, HJ: Samson Kebenei 2.10, PV: Gilbert Sanga 4.10, LJ: David Lamai 7.92, TJ: Benson Mugun 16.59, SP: Ronald Welikhe 16.60, DT: James Nyamburuti 49.46, HT: Cornelius Kemboi 49.24, JT: George Odera 71.12, Dec: James Tarus 6769, 10kmW: Philip Kipkemboi 42:39.6.
WOMEN
100m/200m: Joyce Odhiambo 11.5/23.7, 400m/ 800m: Francisca Chepkirui 52.7/2:01.8, 1500m/ 3000m: Susan Sirma 4:17.6/9:06.7, 10000m: Jane Ngotho 34:32.5, 100mh: Ruth Onsarigo 14.6, 400mh: Rose Tata-Muya 57.2, HJ: Lenah Serem 1.64, LJ: Jacinta Serete 5.61, SP/DT: Elizabeth Olaba 13.53/43.21, JT: Esther Chepkemboi 44.41, 5kmW: Agneta Chelimo 26:16.6.

Kipkoech CHERUIYOT b.2 Dec 1964 1.65m 54kg. Was at Mount St.Mary's University, USA. Elgeyo.
At 1500m: OG: '84- h, '88- 7; WCh: '83- h, '87- 11; AfCh: '82- 1.
World junior 1500m record and African junior mile record 1983. Kenyan 1500m record 1983.
Progression at 1500m: 1981- 3:40.73, 1982- 3:42.0, 1983- 3:34.92, 1984- 3:37.0, 1985- 3:40.48, 1986- 3:33.07, 1987- 3:38.91, 1988- 3:36.2. pbs: 800m: 1:46.48 '86, 1M: 3:52.39 '88, 5000m: 14:21.63 '85.
His twin brother Charles, world junior record holder for 5000m 1983, was 6th in the 1984 Olympic 5000m in 13:18.41 and semi-finalist in 1988.

Joseph CHESIRE b.12 Nov 1957 1.67m 57kg. Army sergeant. Nandi.
At 1500m: OG: '84- 4, '88- 11; WCh: '87- 4; WI: '85- 3; AfG: '87- 3; AfCh: '85- 3. Kenyan champion 800m 1986, 1500m 1985–8.
Progression at 1500m: 1984- 3:34.52, 1985- 3:37.67, 1986- 3:34.32, 1987- 3:35.82, 1988- 3:36.2. pbs: 800m: 1:44.38 '88, 1000m: 2:18.34 '88, 1M: 3:53.09 '88, 3000m: 7:49.4 '84.

Paul ERENG b.22 Aug 1967 Trans-Nzoia 1.86m 72kg. Univerity of Virginia, USA.
At 800m: OG: '88- 1. Won NCAA 1988.
Progression at 400m/800m: 1984- 49.6, 1985- 47.6, 1986- 47.0, 1987- 45.6, 1988- 46.3/1:43.45.
A Turkana, he made amazing progress in 1988, his first year of 800m running, to end the year with a brilliant victory at the Olympics.

Ibrahim Kipkemboi HUSSEIN b.3 Jun 1958 1.70m 57kg. Economics student. Was at University of New Mexico.
At Mar: OG: '88- dnf.
Kenyan marathon record 1988.
Progression at Mar: 1985- 2:12:08, 1986- 2:11:44, 1987- 2:11:01, 1988- 2:08:43. pbs: 1500m: 3:42.9 '83, 1M: 4:00.2 '83, 3000m: 7:51.19 '84, 5000m: 13:50.65 '84, 3000mSt: 8:35.4 '84.
Has won four of his seven marathons: Honolulu 1985–6, New York 1987, Boston 1988.

32:04.78 '88. Her sister Agnès had pbs of 2:09.9, 4:17.3 and 9:03.10 in 1988.

At 3000mSt: OG: '84- 7, '88- 1; AfCh: '85- 1; WCp: '85- 1. Won GP 1988. At 3000m: WI: '87- 6.

Julius Kariuki (George Herringshaw/ASP)

Progression at 3000mSt: 1981- 9:34.5, 1984- 8:17.47, 1985- 8:20.74, 1986- 8:15.92, 1988- 8:05.51. pbs: 1500m: 3:37.79 '86, 1M: 4:00.43 '86, 2000m: 5:04.71 '86, 3000m: 7:47.35 '86, 5000m: 13:41.4 '88, 10000m: 30:19.87 '88.
In his brilliant Olympic win he ran the second fastest time ever, and the fastest on auto timing. Kikuyu tribe.

Kipkemboi KIMELI b.30 Nov 1966 1.73m 64kg. USC Heidelberg, FRG. Nandi.
At 10000m: OG: '88- 3. World junior CC champion 1985.
Progression at 10000m: 1981- 31:59.4, 1982- 29:19.1, 1983- 31:05.7, 1984- 29:49.5, 1985- 28:55.2, 1986- 30:41.5, 1987- 28:17.20, 1988- 27:25.16. pbs: 3000m: 8:00.38 '87, 5000m: 13:31.21 '87.

Joshua KIPKEMBOI b.22 Feb 1959 1.70m 56kg. Army corporal.
At 3000mSt: WCh: '87- dnq; AfG: '87- 2; AfCh: '82- 3, '84- 1, '85- 2.
Progression at 3000mSt: 1981- 9:08.8, 1982- 8:31.0, 1983- 8:28.41, 1984- 8:27.88, 1985- 8:21.70, 1986- 8:14.13, 1987- 8:20.75, 1988- 8:18.02. pbs: 1500m: 3:41.02 '83, 3000m: 7:58.19 '83, 5000m: 13:39.8 '83.
Highly touted for the 3000m steeplechase in Rome, he was unfortunate to fall at the halfway stage.

Paul KIPKOECH b.6 Jan 1963 Kapsabet 1.73m 58kg. Army sergeant. Nandi.
At 10000m: WCh: '87- 1; AfG: '87- 1; AfCh: '82- 5, '85- 3. At 5000m: OG: '84- 5; WCh: '83- 9; AfG: '87- 2; AfCh: '82- 4, '85- 2. World CC: 2nd 1985 & 1987–8, 5th 1986. Kenyan champion 10000m 1983 and 1985; 5000m 1984, 1986.
Progression at 5000m/10000m: 1982- 13:51.03/ 29:35.56, 1983- 13:25.08/28:36.05, 1984- 13:14.40/ 28:05.4, 1985- 13:17.64/27:58.26, 1986- 13:18.91/ 27:43.31, 1987- 13:35.0/27:38.63, 1988- 28:57.4. pbs: 1500m: 3:41.41 '86, 2000m: 5:05.0 '86, 3000m: 7:39.38 '86, 2M: 8:26.30 '86, 3000mSt: 8:56.4 '83.
He dominated the 10000m World Championships in Rome, when after throwing in a 60 second lap early on, he ran the second 5000m in 13:25. Second in the Bali 10km road race in April 1988 in 27:31, but illness through malaria caused win to drop out of the Kenyan 10000m trials in 1988.

Nixon KIPROTICH b.4 Dec 1962 1.85m 68kg. Soldier (private). Nandi.
At 800m: OG: '88- 8. East African champion 1988.
Progression at 800m: 1986- 1:47.58, 1987- 1:46.8, 1988- 1:44.5. pb 400m: 45.9 '88.

Wilfred Oanda KIROCHI b.12 Dec 1969 1.67m 62kg. Railway Club, Nairobi. Kisii.
At 1500m: WJ: '86- 1, '88- 1; AfG: '87- 2. World junior CC champion 1987–8.
Progression at 1500m: 1986- 3:40.8, 1987- 3:39.01, 1988- 3:36.07. pbs: 800m: 1:46.8 '88, 1000m: 2:18.94 '88, 1M: 3:58.59 '88, 3000m: 7:57.49 '88, 5000m: 14:15.8 '87.

Had unparalleled success as a junior, with four world titles.

Peter KOECH b.18 Feb 1958 Kiliburani, Nandi district 1.80m 67kg. Was at Washington State University, USA.
At 3000mSt: OG: '88- 2; WCh: '87- 7; NCAA champion 1985, 2nd GP 1988. At 5000m: CG: '82- 3 (15 10km), AfG: '87- 3.
Kenyan 2000m record 1987.
Progression at 5000m/3000mSt: 1981- 13:57.23, 1982- 13:09.50, 1983- 13:44.0, 1984- 13:30.59/ 8:29.09, 1985- 13:24.5/8:19.84, 1986- 13:34.2/ 8:13.33, 1987- 13:20.85/8:15.77, 1988- 8:06.79. pbs: 1500m: 3:35.67 '86, 1M: 4:04.21 '87, 2000m: 4:58.51 '87, 3000m: 7:39.09 '82, 2M: 8:17.05 '82, 10000m: 28:07.28 '82, Mar: 2:18:57 '86.

Billy KONCHELLAH b.20 Oct 1961 Kilgoris 1.88m 74kg. Mazda TC, USA. Masai.
At 800m: OG: '84- 4; WCh: '87- 1; AfG: '87- 1.
African junior 800m record 1979.
Progression at 800m: 1980- 1:46.79, 1981- 1:49.79, 1982- 1:51.3, 1984- 1:44.03, 1985- 1:43.72, 1986- 1:50.6i, 1987- 1:43.06. pbs: 200m: 21.2/21.20w '80, 400m: 45.38 '79, 600m: 1:17.4 '82, 1000m: 2:16.71 '85, 1500m: 3:44.5 '85.
He made a great impact as a junior in 1979–80, then little until his Olympic fourth place in 1984. In 1985 he contracted tuberculosis, but came back as the world's no. one 800m runner in 1987. Ill again in 1988.

Julius KORIR b.21 Apr 1960 Nandi district 1.72m 64kg. Student at Washington State University, USA.
At 3000mSt: OG: '84- 1; WCh: '83- 7; CG: '82- 1; AfCh: '82- 2. Kenyan champion 1982. Won NCAA 5000m 1984, 3kmSt 1986.
Progression at 3000mSt: 1981- 8:44.0, 1982- 8:23.94, 1983- 8:20.02, 1984- 8:11.80, 1986- 8:12.74, 1987- 8:12.80, 1988- 8:26.76. pbs: 800m: 1:48.42 '84, 1500m: 3:39.8 '86, 1M: 4:04.4i '84, 2000m: 5:08.27 '87, 3000m: 7:48.90 '86, 5000m: 13:38.7 '82.
While his Commonwealth victory was a surprise, he confirmed his status with a clear Olympic win. Missed 1985 outdoor season through injury, and was passed over for the World Championships, but showed what might have been with a storming win in the Grand Prix Final.

Sammy KOSKEI b.14 May 1961 Nandi district 1.83m 68kg. Club: Mazda TC, USA. Was at Southern Methodist University, now at North Texas State University, USA studying for a business degree.
At 800m: WCh: '83- sf; CG: '82- 9; AfCh: '84- 1, '85- 1; WCp: '85- 1. Won NCAA 1981.
African records: two 800m 1984, one 1000m 1985.
Progression at 800m: 1980- 1:46.90, 1981- 1:45.32, 1982- 1:44.93, 1983- 1:46.40, 1984- 1:42.28, 1985- 1:43.78, 1986- 1:45.89, 1987- 1:44.87, 1988- 1:44.06. pbs: 1000m: 2:14.95 '85, 1500m: 3:40.14 '85, 1M: 3:56.79 '82.

Stephen Ole MARAI b.11 Nov 1962 Kilgoris 1.84m 65kg. Army corporal. Masai.
At 800m: WCh: '87- 6; AfG: '87- 2.
Progression at 800m: 1985- 1:48.0, 1986- 1:49.7, 1987- 1:44.84, 1988- 1:46.0. pb 1500m: 3:44.9 '88.

John NGUGI b.10 May 1962 Nyahururu 1.78m 62kg. Army sergeant.
At 5000m: OG: '88- 1; WCh: '87- 12; AfG: '87- 1; AfCh: '85- 3 (4 at 1500m). Won East & Central African 1500m 1985, 5000m 1986; Kenyan 5000m 1987–8. Won World CC 1986–8.
Progression at 5000m/10000m: 1985- 13:18.99, 1986- 13:29.0/28:37.38, 1987- 13:22.68, 1988- 13:11.70/27:51.35. pbs: 1500m: 3:37.02 '85, 2000m: 5:06.50 '86, 3000m: 7:49.35 '86.
A Kikuyu, he looked to be ready to make a major impact on the track, but faded in the final of the 1987 World Championships 5000m through injury, which subsequently meant the removal of a cyst behind his knee. A week after his third world cross-country title he won the Bali road 10km race in 27:29 in April 1988. Burst away with a 58.2 400m after 1000m at the Olympics.

Peter RONO b.31 Jul 1967 Kapsabet 1.67m 53kg. Nandi. Economics student at Mount St. Mary College, USA
At 1500m: OG: '88- 1; WCh: '87- sf; WJ: '86- 2 (14 5000m).
Progression at 1500m: 1983- 3:48.0, 1984- 3:43.86, 1985- 3:39.2, 1986- 3:42.2, 1987- 3:39.52, 1988- 3:35.59. pbs: 800m: 1:46.66 '88, 1M: 3:56.91 '88, 5000m: 14:01.4 '86.
A junior prodigy, he won Kenyan Trials before his 1988 Olympic triumph.

Patrick SANG b.11 Apr 1964 1.80m 65kg. Was at the University of Texas 1983–6.
At 3000mSt: OG: '88- 7; WCh: '87- 8; AfG: '87- 1. 3rd GP 1988.
Progression at 3000mSt: 1982- 9:13.2, 1983- 8:41.00, 1984- 8:22.45, 1985- 8:23.68, 1986- 8:31.1, 1987- 8:14.75, 1988- 8:12.00. pbs: 1500m: 3:44.17 '86, 3000m: 7:49.25 '87, 5000m: 13:41.82 '87.

Moses TANUI b.20 Aug 1965/68? 1.65m 65kg. Soldier (SPTE). Nandi.
At 10000m: OG: '88- 8. World CC: '88- 6.
Progression at 10000m: 1987- 28:53.1, 1988- 27:40.59. pbs: 2M: 8:33.47 '88, 5000m: 13:36.74 '88.

Won Kenyan services, championships and trial 10000m races in 1988.

Douglas WAKIIHURI b.26 Sep 1963 Mombasa 1.86m 65kg. Works for SB Foods, Japan.
At Mar: OG: '88- 2; WCh: '87- 1. Japanese 5000m champion 1987.
Progression at Mar: 1986- 2:16:26, 1987- 2:11:48, 1988- 2:10:47. pbs: 1500m: 3:50.22 '83, 3000m: 8:03.24 '86, 5000m: 13:24.01 '88, 10000m: 27:59.60 '88.
A Kikuyu, he went to Japan in 1983 to train under the late Kiyoshi Nakamura. Made his marathon debut in 1986, improving to 2:13:34 for sixth in Beppu marathon on 1 Feb 1987 and then to win the world title in 2:11:48. Seventh Tokyo 1988 before second in Seoul.

MEXICO

Governing body: Federacion Mexicana de Atletismo, Anillo Periférico y Av. del Conscripto, 11200 M. Hidalgo D.F. Founded 1933.

Arturo BARRIOS b.12 Dec 1963 Mexico City 1.74m 60kg. Mechanical engineering graduate of Texas A&M University, USA.
At 10000m: OG: '88- 5 (h 5000m); WCh: '87- 4. At 5000m: PAm: '87- 1; Won PAm-J 1980, GP 1987. CAC 3000m and 5000m records 1987.
Progression at 5000m/10000m: 1985- 13:46.37/ 28:42.77, 1986- 13.25.83/27:50.28, 1987- 13:13.52/ 27:56.1, 1988- 13:17.82/27:25.07. pbs: 1500m: 3:39.38 '87, 3000m: 7:44.63 '87, 2M: 8:24.99 '86, Mar: 2:14:09 '86, 2kmSt: 5:46.0 '80, 3kmSt: 8:47.8 '84.
Had an outstanding season on the 1986 US road running circuit, when he set a world 10km road best for a loop course of 27:41 at Phoenix and also had important 15km wins at Jacksonville and Portland. Concentrated on track racing with much success in 1987. First major win was in 1980 Pan-American Junior 5000m.

Martin BERMUDEZ b.19 Jul 1958 1.75m 70kg.
At 50kmW: OG: '80- dnf, '84- dq, '88- 15; WCh: '83- dq, '87- 5; PAm: '79- 2, '83- 2, '87- 1; LT: '79- 1, '81- 6, '87- 8; CAmG: '86- 1. Won CAC 1985, Pan Am Cup 1986 and 1988.
Progression at 50kmW: 1977- 4:19:07, 1978- 3:58:48, 1979- 3:43:36, 1980- 3:48:22, 1981- 3:53:10, 1982- 3:53:00, 1983- 3:50:43, 1984- 3:48:03, 1985- 4:22:33, 1986- 3:56:21, 1987- 3:48:27, 1988- 3:49:22. pbs: Track: 3kmW: 11:51.0 '83, 5kmW: 19:34.0 '86, 10kmW: 39:49.0 '86, 20kmW: 1:23:44 '86, 1hrW: 14742m '86. Road: 10kmW: 39:29 '86, 20kmW: 1:22:22 '80.

Ernesto CANTO b.18 Oct 1959 1.70m 60kg.
At 20kmW: OG: '84- 1 (10 at 50kmW), '88- dq; WCh: '83- 1, '87- dq; PAm: '83- 2, '87- dnf; LT: '79- 6, '81- 1, '83- 2, '87- 5; CAmG: '82- 1, '86- 1. CAC champion 1985. At 5kmW: WI: '87- 3.
World walking records at 20km, 1:18:40.0 and 1 hour, 15253m in 1984.
Progression at 20kmW: 1979- 1:21:12, 1980- 1:19:02, 1981- 1:23:08, 1982- 1:23:13, 1983- 1:19:41, 1984- 1:18:40t, 1985- 1:28:26, 1986- 1:22:58, 1987- 1:19:37, 1988- 1:21:18. pbs: Track: 3kmW: 11:50.0 '83, 5kmW: 18:38.71i '87, 10kmW: 39:29.2 '84. Road 50kmW: 3:51:10 '82.

Carlos MERCENARIO b.3 May 1967 1.75m 63kg.
At 20kmW: OG: '88- 7; WCh: '87- dq; LT: '87- 1; PAm: '87- 1. Won Pan Am Cup 1988, PAm-J 10kmW 1984 & 1986.
At 20km road walk: world junior best when second Pan Am Cup 1986, world best 1987.
Progression at 20kmW: 1985- 1:24:07, 1986- 1:21:33, 1987- 1:19:24, 1988- 1:20:53.

MOROCCO

Governing Body: Fédération Royale Marocaine d'Athlétisme, Centre National des Sports Bellevue, Avenue Ibn sina, Rabat. Founded 1957.

Said AOUITA b.2 Nov 1959 Kenitra 1.75m 58kg. Club: Larios, Spain.
At 5000m: OG: '84- 1; WCh: '87- 1. At 1500m: OG: '88- sf; WCh: '83- 3; WSG: '83- 1; AfCh: '79- 9, '82- 2; '84- 1. At 800m: OG: '88- 3; AfCh: '82- 3. Pan-Arab 1500m champion 1985. Won GP 5000m 1986, 1M 1988, overall 1986 & 1988.
African records: 1500m- 3, 1M- 2, 2000m- 4, 5000m- 4 in 1984–7, including world records at 1500m and 5000m in 1985; 2000m and 5000m (and 2 miles world best) in 1987
Progression at 800m, 1500m/5000m: 1978- -/14:10.0; 1979- 3:42.3/13:48.5; 1980- 1:47.8, 3:37.08; 1981- 1:48.26, 3:37.69/13:39.0?; 1982- 1:47.4, 3:37.37/14:05.7; 1983- 1:44.83, 3:32.54; 1984- 1:46.81, 3:31.54/13:04.78; 1985- 1:45.81, 3:29.46/13:00.40; 1986- 3:36.1/13:00.86; 1987- 1:44.74, 3:30.69/12:58.39; 1988- 1:43.86, 3:32.69. pbs: 1000m: 2:15.16 '88, 1M: 3:46.76 '87, 2000m: 4:50.81 '87, 3000m: 7:32.23 '86, 2M: 8:13.45 '87, 10000m: 27:26.11 '86, 3000mSt: 8:21.92 '87.
First notable performance was 37th in world junior cross-country 1978. Trained in France and Italy in the early 1980s. Unbeaten at 5000m since 1979. He lost to Steve Cram in his world record 1500m at Nice in 1985, but from then won 44 consecutive races until beaten by Alessandro Lambruschini in the 1987 Mediterranean Games 3000m steeplechase; it was Aouita's first run at that event since he set an

African junior record 8:40.2 in 1979. He had an amazing sequence of near misses at world records in 1986. Of the fastest ever times has 2/3 at 1500m and 1M, 4/6 at 3000m, 6/8 at 5000m (end '87). In 1988 he stepped down to 800m and won the Olympic bronze medal after four big race wins, but had to withdraw from the 1500m through injury.

Moulay Brahim BOUTAYEB b.15 Aug 1967 Khemisset 1.78m 61kg. Larios, Italy.
At 10000m: OG: '88- 1, AfCh: '88- 1. At 5000m: WCh: '87- h; WJ: '86- 4; AfCh: '88- 1. 2nd GP 1988. African 10000m record 1988.
Progression at 5000m/10000m: 1985- 14:22.4, 1986- 13:52.49/29:29.43, 1987- 13:17.47/28:40.34, 1988- 13:18.68/27:21.46. pbs: 1000m: 2:24.57 '87, 1500m: 3:38.75 '88, 1M: 3:54.86 '87, 2000m: 5:07.74 '87, 3000m: 7:43.22 '88, 2M: 8:24.86 '88.

Moulay Brahim Boutayeb (Kamel Bensemmane)

Faouzi LAHBI b.2 Mar 1960 1.74m 63kg. Racing Club de France. Student.
At 800m: OG: '84- qf (h 1500m), '88- qf; WCh: '83- h, '87- 5; WI: '87- 3.
Progression at 800m: 1980- 1:52.6, 1981- 1:47.07, 1982- 1:46.78, 1983- 1:45.82, 1984- 1:45.67, 1985- 1:46.58, 1986- 1:44.66, 1987- 1:44.72, 1988- 1:45.11. pbs: 400m: 47.7 '84, 1000m: 2:17.90 '82, 1500m: 3:42.67 '85, 2000m: 5:10.4 '87.

NETHERLANDS

Governing body: Koninklijke Nederlandse Atletiek-Unie (KNAU), Nachtegaalstraat 67, P.O.Box 14444, 3508 SM Utrecht. Founded 1901.
National Championships first held in 1910 (men), 1921 (women)
1988 Champions: MEN
100m/200m: Ahmed de Kom 10.49/21.08, 400m: Arjen Visserman 46.45, 800m: Robin van Helden 1:47.55, 1500m: Bob Dielis 3:54.92, 5000m: Martin ten Kate 13:44.09, 10000m Tony Dirks 28:51.0, Mar: Gerd Nijboer 2:12:38, 3000mSt: Hans Koeleman 8:26.37, 110mh: Ysbrand Visser 14.43w, 400mh: Pel v.d.Kerkhof 51.34, HJ: Ruud Wielart 2.14, PV: Mark Kok 4.80, LJ: Emiel Mellaard 8.19, TJ: Paul Lucassen 15.53, SP/DT: Erik de Bruin 18.79/61.88, HT: Peter van Noort 67.98, JT: Jeroen v.d.Meer 74.66, Dec: Robert de Wit 8447, 20kmW(t): Jan Cortenbach 1:33:52.08, 50kmW: Godfried de Jonckheere (Bel) 3:57:58.
WOMEN
100m: Nelli Fiere 11.38, 200m: Els Scharn 23.18, 400m: Yvonne van Dorp 54.31, 800m/1500m/3000m: Elly van Hulst 2:03.774:20.18/9:07.92, 10000m: Carlien Harmsd 35:20.9, Mar: Jolanda Homminga 2:46:41, 100mh/400mh: Grethe Tromp 13.33/56.17, HJ: Monique v.d.Weide 1.79, LJ: Mieke v.d.Kolk 6.44, SP/DT: Deborah Dunant 16.28/47.20, JT: Gerda Vetter 55.82, Hep: Marjan Wijnsma 6213.

Erik DE BRUIN b.25 May 1963 Hardinxveld 1.86m 110kg. VLTC'86. Student.
At DT (SP): OG: '84- 9 (8), '88- 9; ECh: '86- 6; EJ: '81- 3 (8).
Dutch records: 16 shot, 6 discus 1982–6.
Progression at SP/DT: 1979- 14.71/48.04, 1980- 16.22/55.76, 1981- 17.36/55.94, 1982- 17.99/57.88, 1983- 19.49i/18.95/56.70, 1984- 20.58i/20.20/63.66, 1985- 20.60i/20.24/66.38, 1986- 20.95/66.78, 1987- 20.49i/65.84, 1988- 20.30i/66.08. pb HT: 60.24 '87.

Robert DE WIT b.7 Aug 1962 Eindhoven 1.86m 88kg. Unitas. Student of physics.
At Dec: OG: '88- 8; WCh: '83- 12, '87- dnf; ECh: '82- dnf, '86- 9; EJ: '81- 4. Dutch champion 110mh 1982, 1986, PV 1987, Dec 1982, 1984, 1988.
Dutch records: six decathlon 1981–8, one 110mh 1988.
Progression at Dec: 1980- 7183*, 1981- 7561, 1982- 7742, 1983- 7875, 1984- 7381, 1986- 7962, 1987- 8039w/7987, 1988- 8447. pbs: 100m: 11.05 '88, 400m: 48.21 '88, 1500m: 4:16.45 '82, 110mh: 14.05/14.01w '88, HJ: 2.05 '83, PV: 5.10 '87, LJ: 7.14 '88, SP: 16.62 '88, DT: 46.20 '88, JT: 63.94 '88.

Rob DRUPPERS b.29 Apr 1962 1.86m 70kg. Hellas.
At 800m: OG: '88- qf; WCh: '83- 2, '87- h; ECh: '82- 5, '86- 4; EI: '87- 1, '88- 2; EJ: '81- h; WCp: '85- 5.
WIB 1000m 2:16.62 '88. Dutch records 1982–5: 800m (4), 1000m (4), 1500m (2).
Progression at 800m: 1976- 2:10.5, 1977- 2:03.9, 1978- 1:59.1, 1979- 1:52.6, 1980- 1:48.8, 1981- 1:46.88, 1982- 1:44.54, 1983- 1:44.20, 1984- 1.44.60, 1985- 1:43.56, 1986- 1:45.29, 1987- 1:45.49, 1988- 1:44.98. pbs: 400m: 47.1 '83, 1000m: 2:15.23 '85, 1500m: 3:35.07 '85, 1M: 3:57.22 '85.

Han KULKER b.15 Aug 1959 Den Haag 1.83m 64kg. Bataven.
At 1500m: OG: '88- 6; WCh: '87- 9; WI: '87- 3; ECh: '86- 3; EI: '86- 3, '87- 1.
Dutch 1 mile record 1986.
Progression at 1500m: 1982- 3:52.0, 1984- 3:42.98, 1985- 3:39.3, 1986- 3:36.54, 1987- 3:36.08, 1988- 3:36.99. pbs: 400m: 48.8 '85, 800m: 1:46.85 '83, 1000m: 2:18.07 '86, 1M: 3:53.93 '86, 3000m: 8:10.31 '85.
A surprise European 1500m bronze medallist both indoors and out in 1986, he has continued to place well in major races.

Frans MAAS b.13 Jul 1964 1.96m 89kg. Sprint. Student at University of Texas at El Paso, USA.
AT LJ: WCh: '88- dnq; EI: '88- 1. Dutch champion TJ 1987.
Progression at LJ: 1982- 7.02/7.13w, 1983- 7.63/7.65w, 1984- 7.70, 1985- 7.60, 1986- 7.91, 1987- 7.96/8.02w, 1988- 8.06i/8.27w. pbs: 100m: 10.63w '85, 200m: 21.56 '85, TJ: 16.12/16.36w '87, 16.24i '88.

Emiel MELLAARD b.21 Mar 1966 Spijkenisse 1.89m 74kg. Amsterdamse AC. Student.
At LJ: OG: '88- 11; WCh: '87- dnq; ECh: '86- 4; EJ: '85- 3. Dutch champion 1984–8.
Five Dutch long jump records 1986–8.
Progression at LJ: 1981- 6.55, 1982- 7.01/7.05w, 1983- 7.48/7.67w, 1984- 7.84, 1985- 7.99i/7.97, 1986- 7.98, 1987- 8.02/8.19w, 1988- 8.19/8.21w. pbs: 100m: 10.57 '88, 10.5 '87, 200m: 21.59 '87, 60mh: 7.87i '87, 110mh: 14.34/14.31w '87.

Women

Carla BEURSKENS b.15 Feb 1952 Tegelen 1.65m 45kg. now Roemerman. Festina.
At Mar: OG: '84- 22, '88- 34; WCh: '83- 17; ECh: '82- 5, '86- 7. At 3000m: ECh: '78- 21. World road 15km: '86- 3.
Dutch records 1981–7: 5 marathon, 3 10000m, 2 5000m, 1 half-marathon (70:44 '85).
Progression at Mar: 1981- 2:42:56, 1982- 2:34:14, 1983- 2:39:25, 1984- 2:32:53, 1985- 2:27:50, 1986- 2:27:35, 1987- 2:26:34, 1988- 2:28:58. pbs: 800m: 2:14.5 '79, 1000m: 2:54.2 '81, 1500m: 4:23.9i '81, 4:24.1 '79; 3000m: 9:08.32 '81, 5000m: 15:46.20 '85, 10000m: 32:28.28 '85.
Major marathon wins: Rotterdam 1984, Frankfurt 1985, Honolulu 1986, Nagoya 1987. 2nd Boston 1986, Tokyo 1987, Nagoya 1988.

Nellie FIERE-COOMAN b.6 Jun 1964 Paramaribo, Surinam 1.57m 60kg. née Cooman. AV Rotterdam.
At 100m: OG: '88- sf; WCh: '87- sf; ECh: '86- 3; EJ: '81- 7. At 60m: WI: '87- 1; EI: '84- 3, '85- 1, '86- 1, '87- 1, '88- 1. Dutch champion 1985–6, 1988.
WIB 60m 7.00 in 1986. Four Dutch 100m records 1986–8.
Progression at 100m: 1981- 11.74/11.52w, 1982- 11.54/11.48w, 1983- 11.58, 1984- 11.39/11.26w, 1985- 11.46/11.39w/11.2, 1986- 11.08, 1987- 11.14, 1988- 11.08. pbs: 200m: 23.79/23.03w '86, LJ: 6.12 '83.
After making her name as a 60m sprinter indoors, reached top class outdoors at 100m in 1986. Equalled record with four successive European Indoor titles, at 60m 1985–8.

Marjan OLYSLAGER b.8 Mar 1962 Den Haag 1.72m 58kg. Sprint. Teacher.
At 100mh: OG: '88- sf; WCh: '83- sf; ECh: '86- sf; EJ: '79- h. Dutch champion 1982, 1985, 1987. At 60mh: WI: '87- 5; EI: '88- 2.
Eleven Dutch 100mh records 1983–8.
Progression at 100mh: 1979- 14.00, 1980- 13.9, 1981- 13.52, 1982- 13.56/13.52w/13.2, 1983- 13.0/13.26, 1984- 13.20, 1985- 13.01/12.96w, 1986- 13.07, 1987- 13.19/13.18w, 1988- 12.83. pbs: 100m: 11.77 '87, 11.56w '85; 200m: 23.93 '83, 23.53w '85; LJ: 6.29 '83

Elly VAN HULST b.9 Jun 1959 Culemborg 1.78m 58kg. PAC.
At 3000m: OG: '88- 9; WCh: '87- 6; ECh: '86- 9; EI: '86- 2, '88- 1; WI: '87- 8. At 1500m (800m): OG: '84- 12 (sf), '88- h; WCh: '87- 8; ECh: '82- 8 (sf), '86- 11; EI: '84- 2; WIG: '85- 1. At 800m: EJ: '77- 4. 53 Dutch titles, including senior at 800m 1978–9, 1981–6, 1988; 1500m 1981–8, 3000m 1982–8, 5000m 1983–4, 10000m 1984. Won GP mile 1987, 3rd 1500m 1988.
Dutch records 1981–8: 7 at 3000m; 2 each 800m, 1000m, 1500m, 1M, 2000m; 1 5000m (and 16 more indoors).
Progression at 1500m/3000m: 1976- 4:45.5, 1977- 4:34.1, 1978- 4:20.8, 1979- 4:21.6, 1980- 4:21.6/9:50.7, 1981- 4:08.86/9:10.3, 1982- 4:03.78/9:06.15, 1983- 4:10.50/9:00.61, 1984- 4:05.44/9:11.13, 1985- 4:08.30i/8:58.28, 1986- 4:04.32/8:48.25, 1987- 4:03.63/8:42.57, 1988- 4:04.88/

Elly Van Hulst wins the 3,000m final, European Indoor Champs, Budapest 1988. (Mark Shearman)

8:33.97. pbs: 400m: 54.66 '77, 800m: 1:59.62 '81, 1000m: 2:36.70 '81, 1M: 4:22.40 '86, 2000m: 5:39.52 '86, 5000m: 15:42.5 '85, 10000m: 32:48.15 '88.

NEW ZEALAND

Governing body: New Zealand Amateur Athletic Association, PO Box 741, Wellington.
National Championships first held in 1888 (men), 1926 (women)
1988 Champions: MEN
100m/110mh/PV/LJ: Simon Poelman 10.66/14.16/ 4.75/7.51, 200m: Dale McClunie 21.19, 400m: Craig Purdy 47.40, 800m: John Walker 1:51.01, 1500m: Andrew Campbell 3:47.35, 5000m: Phillip Clode 14:09.64, 10000m: Tom Birnie 29:29.15, Mar: Paul Ballinger 2:16:05, 3000mSt: Gregor Cameron 8:57.25, 400mh: Wayne Paul 52.15, HJ: Steven Hollings 2.13, TJ: Alan Whitton 15.39, SP/DT: Henry Smith 15.74/53.36, HT: Phillip Jensen 64.02, JT: Mike O'Rourke 76.30, Dec: Terry Lomax 6770, 20kmW: Derek Beaven 1:35:43, 50kmW: Paul McElwee 4:39:49.
WOMEN
100m: Bev Peterson 11.66, 200m: Andrea Wade 23.90, 400m/800m: Carlene Dillimore 53.22/ 2:04.41, 1500m: Wendy Breed 4:26.87, 3000m: Chrissy Pfitzinger 9:09.72, 5000m: Sonia Barry 16:06.47, 10000m: Barbara Moore 33:11.31, Mar: Jillian Costley 2:39:20, 100mh: Vanessa Jack 14.35, 400mh: Karen Green 60.27, HJ: Tania Murray 1.82, LJ/TJ: Jayne Mitchell 6.04/11.96, SP: Christine Davis 14.28, DT: Elizabeth Ryan 49.96, JT: Kaye Nordstrom 49.74, 5kmW:Jane Jackson 25:52.03.

Simon POELMAN b.27 May 1963 1.87m 91kg. North Shore-Bays, Auckland.
At decathlon: OG: '88- 16, WCh: '87- 6; CG: '86- 3. NZ champion 1984, 1986–7; 110mh & PV 1986–8; LJ 1987–8, 100m 1988.
Five NZ decathlon records 1985–7.
Progression at Dec: 1984- 7417, 1985- 7854, 1986- 8158, 1987- 8366, 1988- 7792. pbs: 100m: 10.66 '88, 400m: 49.4 '87, 1500m: 4:24.35 '84, 110mh: 14.10 '87, HJ: 2.06 '87, PV: 5.10 '87, LJ: 7.56 '87, SP: 16.23 '88, DT: 47.62 '87, JT: 58.90 '87, 59.68 (old) '85.
World best for one hour decathlon with 7647 points at Auckland on 24 Feb 1988.

John WALKER b.12 Jan 1952 Papakura 1.83m 74kg. Manurewa, Auckland. Sports co-ordinator.
At 1500m: OG: '76- 1 (h 800m); WCh: '83- 9; CG: '74- 2 (3 at 800m), '82- 2 (4 800m); WCp: '77- dnf, '81- 2. At 5000m: OG: '84- 8; CG: '86- 5. World CC: '75- 4. NZ champion 800m 1972–3, 1977, 1980–2, 1988; 1500m 1974, 1979–83, 1986.
World records: 1M 1975, 2000m 1976. WIB 1500m 3:37.4 '79.
Progression at 1500m/1M: 1970- 3:52.4, 1972- 3:46.4, 1973- 3:38.0/3:58.8, 1974- 3:32.52/3:54.9, 1975- 3:32.4/3:49.4, 1976- 3:34.19/3:53.07, 1977- 3:32.72/3:52.0, 1978- 3:40.3/3:56.4, 1979- 3:37.0/ 3:52.85, 1980- 3:33.31/3:52.7, 1981- 3:34.5/ 3:50.12, 1982- 3:33.7/3:49.08, 1983- 3:33.84/ 3:49.73, 1984- 3:35.93/3:49.73, 1985- 3:34.97/ 3:53.20, 1986- 3:35.74/3:53.72, 1987- 3:34.79/ 3:55.07, 1988- 3:36.3/3:52.48. At 5000m: 1981- 13:20.89, 1984- 13:24.46, 1985- 13:47.87, 1986- 13:19.28, 1987- 13:30.51. pbs: 400m: 48.9 '73, 800m: 1:44.92 '74, 1000m: 2:16.57 '80, 2000m: 4:51.52 '76, 3000m: 7:37.49 '82, 2M: 8:20.57 '75.
The first sub 3:50 miler ran his 100th sub four-minute mile on 17 Feb 1985. Has retained top-class form for the longest ever period for a middle-distance runner, but sadly injury cut short his season in 1988 and prevented his competing at the Olympics.

Women

Anne AUDAIN b.1 Nov 1955 Auckland 1.68m 53kg. née Garrett. Otahuhu and Team Nike, USA. Qualified as teacher.
At Mar: OG: '84- dnf. At 10000m: OG: '88- 11; CG:

'86- 2. At 3000m: CG: '82- 1. At 1500m: OG: '76- h (h 800m); CG: '74- 6; WCp: '77- 8. NZ champion 800m 1979; 1500m 1976, 1979–80; 3000m 1982, 1986. World CC best 9th 1973 & 1977.
Commonwealth records: 3000m 1982, 10000m 1983 and 1986, 5000m 1982, the latter also a world record. Has set NZ records from 1500m to 10000m 1976–86.
Progression at 3000m/Mar: 1975- 9:14.9, 1980- 8:59.2, 1982- 8:45.53, 1983- 2:32:14, 1984- 2:32:07, 1986- 9:03.32. At 10000m: 1983- 32:21.47, 1985- 32:57.40, 1986- 31:53.31, 1987- 31:57.56, 1988- 32:05.8. pbs: 800m: 2:04.1 '80, 1500m: 4:10.68 '76, 1M: 4:33.93 '83, 2000m: 5:53.86 '86, 5000m: 15:13.22 '82.
Now lives in Boise, Idaho, USA and has had considerable success for many years on the US road running circuit. Ran the then fastest debut marathon for fourth at Chicago in 1983.

Lorraine MOLLER b.1 Jun 1955 Putaruru 1.74m 58kg. Housewife, former school teacher. PE diploma from University of Otago. Married marathoner Ron Daws in 1981.
At Mar: OG: '84- 5, '88- 33; CG: '86- 2. At 10000m: WCh: '87- 21. At 3000m: WCh: '83- 14; CG: '82- 3 (3 at 1500m), '86- 5. At 800m: CG: '74- 5. World CC: '75- 5.
Two Commonwealth marathon bests 1979–80, further NZ best 1986.
Progression at Mar: 1979- 2:37:37, 1980- 2:31:42, 1981- 2:29:36, 1982- 2:36:13, 1984- 2:28:34, 1985- 2:34:55, 1986- 2:28:17, 1987- 2:30:40, 1988- 2:37:52. pbs: 800m: 2:03.6 '74, 1500m: 4:10.35 '85, 1M: 4:32.97 '85, 2000m: 5:47.97 '85, 3000m: 8:51.78 '83, 5000m: 15:32.90 '86, 10000m: 32:40.61 (mx) '86.
Won her first eight marathons, before second to Joyce Smith at London in 1982. Of 20 marathons she has won 12, including Avon 1980, 1982 and 1984; Boston 1982, 1984; Osaka 1986–7.

NIGERIA

Governing body: Amateur Athletic Association of Nigeria, P.O.Box 211, Lagos. Founded 1944.
National Championships
1988 Champions: MEN
100m/200m: Iziak Adeyanju 9.9/20.73, 400m: Sunday Uti 46.43, 800m: Ado Maude 1:46.97, 1500m: Ibrahim Saidu 4:02.0, 5000m: Mohammed Abbas 15:02.84, 10000m: Yohanna Waziri 31:50.0, 3000mSt: Zacharia Fwangfur 9:10.0, 110mh: Emeka Osaji 14.1, 400mh: Henry Amike 50.51, HJ: Obiora Oranu 2.10, PV: William Kaduna 4.20, LJ: Yusuf Alli 8.00, TJ: Joseph Taiwo 17.22, SP/DT: Adewale Olokoju 18.42/51.68, JT: Samuel Lakudos 64.00.

WOMEN
100m/200m: Mary Onyali 11.09/22.69, 400m: Airat Bakare 53.07, 800m/1500m: Ngozi Ohaechesi 2:19.93/4:58.85, 3000m: Grace Isiaku 10:28.28, 100mh: Maria Usifo 13.51, HJ: Stella Agbaegbu 1.70, SP: Cecilia Eziefula 12.66, JT: Chinweoke Chikwelu 47.94.

Henry AMIKE b.4 Oct 1961 1.85m 71kg. All Star International, USA. Was at University of Missouri.
At 400mh: OG: '84- 8; WCh: '87- 6; WSG: '85- 2; AfG: '87- 3 (1 4x400mR); AfCh: '84- 2, '85- 2, '88- 2. Five Nigerian 400mh records 1984–7.
Progression at 400mh: 1981- 50.9, 1982- 52.07, 1983- 51.34, 1984- 49.33, 1985- 48.88, 1986- 49.13, 1987- 48.50, 1988- 49.36. pbs: 200m: 21.55 '84, 21.5 '81, 400m: 46.29 '84, 800m: 1:51.89 '85.

Innocent EGBUNIKE b.30 Nov 1961 1.74m 68kg. Puma TC, USA. Was at Azusa Pacific College.
At 400m/R- 4x400m relay: OG: '84- 7/3R, '88- 5; WCh: '87- 2; WSG: '85- 1; WCp: '85- 3; AfG: '87- 1/1R; AfCh: '85- 1, '88- 1. At 200m: WCh: '83- 7 (qf 100m); WSG: '83- 1; AfCh: '84- 1, '85- 2. 1st GP 400m 1987.
Four Commonwealth 400m records 1986–7, African records: 200m 1983, 100m 1984, 400m (2) 1987. Commonwealth indoor 300m best 33.35 '83, and Nigerian records: 100m (1), 200m (2), 400m (6) 1983–7.
Progression at 400m: 1982- 47.99, 1984- 44.81, 1985- 44.66, 1986- 44.50, 1987- 44.17, 1988- 44.72. pbs: 100m: 10.15/10.12w '84; 200m: 20.42/20.4 '83, 20.23w '84; 300m: 32.05 '87; 800m: 1:52.67 '87.
Most unluckily had the baton knocked out of his hand at the end of the 1985 World Cup 4x400m relay in Canberra. Ran 12 sub 45.00 times in 1987, then a season's record.

Chidi IMOH b.27 Aug 1963 1.88m 77kg. University of Missouri, USA.
At 100m: OG: '84- qf, '88- qf; WCh: '83- qf, '87- sf; WSG: '83- 1, '85- 1; AfCh: '84- 1, '85- 1, '88- 1R; WCp: '85- 2. Won GP 100m 1986 & 1988.
African records: three 100m 1985–6, 200m 1988.
Progression at 100m: 1981- 10.6, 1982- 10.2, 1983- 10.23, 1984- 10.30/10.25w, 1985- 10.11/10.04w, 1986- 10.00, 1987- 10.17/9.92w, 1988- 10.04. pb 200m: 20.31 '88, 19.9w '85.

Joseph TAIWO b.24 Aug 1959 1.83m 74kg. Was at Washington State University, USA.
At TJ: OG: '84- 9, '88- 9; WCh: '87- 6; WI: '87- 6; AfG: '87- 2; AfCh: '84- 1. AAA champion 1986. 2nd NCAA 1981 & 1984. 3rd GP 1986.
Progression at TJ: 1979- 15.77, 1980- 16.13w/15.72, 1981- 16.68, 1982- 16.91, 1983- 16.42, 1984- 17.19, 1985- 16.80, 1986- 17.18/17.26w,

1987- 17.09/17.29w, 1988- 17.22. pb LJ: 7.50i '82.

Women

Mary ONYALI b.3 Feb 1968 1.65m 52kg. Student at Texas Southern University, USA,
At 200m/R- 4x100m relay (100m): OG: '88- sf; WCh: '87- 6; AfG: '87- 1/1R (3, 1 4x400mR); AfCh: '85- 2; WSG: '87- 2/3R; WI: '87- 5; WJ: '86- 2/3R (dq). Won NCAA 1988. 3rd GP 1988. At 100m: AfCh: '88- 1.
African records: 100m 1986, six 200m 1986–8.
Progression at 200m: 1984- 25.3, 1985- 23.85, 1986- 22.90/22.77w, 1987- 22.52, 1988- 22.43. pbs: 100m: 11.09 '88, 11.2/11.24w '87, 400m: 52.50 '87.

NORWAY

Governing body: Norges Fri-Idrettsforbund, Tollbugt.11, 0152 Oslo 1. Founded 1896.
National Championships first held in 1897 (men), 1947 (women).
1988 Champions: MEN
100m/LJ: Einar Sagli 10.58/7.40, 200m: Geir Moen 21.50, 400m: Richard Sandberg Hansen 47.84, 800m: Atle Douglas (UK) 1:49.43, 1500m: Espen Borge 3:47.59, 5000m: Are Nakkim 13:32.66, 10000m: Bjørn Nordheggen 28:54.87, Mar: Kjetil Berg 2:20:50, 3000mSt: Roger Gjøvåg 8:40.65, 110mh/400mh: Per Nicolaisen 14.20/51.47, HJ: Håkon Särnblom 2.19, PV: Alex Grelland 4.85, TJ: Roar Haugland 15.57, SP: Georg Andersen 20.63, DT: Knut Hjeltnes 61.24, HT: Richard Olsen 61.14, JT: Reidar Lorentzen 80.06, Dec: Knut Gundersen 7307.
WOMEN
100m: Sølvi Olsen 11.75, 200m: Mona Karin Riisnes 24.25, 400m: Lisbeth Andersen 53.51, 800m: Toril Hatling 2:03.07, 1500m: Sissel Grottenberg 4:15.08, 3000m: Grethe Fosse 9:10.32/15:54.10, Mar: Oddrun Hovsengen 2:49:25, 100mh: Anne Brit Skjaeveland 13.97, 400mh: Monica Grefstad 59.55, HJ: Tove Svendby 1.81, LJ: Rita Rosseland 6.07, SP: Grete Gjermshus 15.04, DT: Mette Bergmann 59.46, JT: Trine Solberg 61.94, Hep: Kristin Skjaerpe 4552.

Erling ANDERSEN b.22 Sep 1960 Bergen 1.82m 66kg. Søfteland IL.
At 20kmW (50kmW): OG: '84- 8 (dq), '88- 22 (dnf); WCh: '83- 21 (dq), '87- 15 (12); ECh: '78- 23. At 50kmW: ECh: '82- dnf, '86- 10. At 10kmW: EJ: '75- 10, '77- 11, '79- 2; EI: '88- 4.
European 20km walk records 1980 and 1984. World junior records at 5kmW, 19:56.9 and 10kmW, 40:50.0 in 1979.
Progression at 20kmW/50kmW: 1978- 1:27:47, 1979- 1:23:59, 1980- 1:20:57t, 1981- 1:23:47/3:58:19, 1982- 1:23:54/4:03:40, 1983- 1:23:50t/3:54:00, 1984- 1:20:36.7t/3:53:16, 1985- 1:22:26/3:44:24, 1986- 1:21:08t/3:49:49, 1987- 1:22:15/3:55:52, 1988- 1:23:30/3:49:10. pbs: track: 3kmW: 11:11.2 '81, 5kmW: 18:49.10i '88, 19:09.92 '87; 10kmW: 39:31.9 '87, 1 hrW: 14957m '84; road: 30kmW: 2:13:36 '85.

Knut HJELTNES b.8 Dec 1951 Ulvik 1.92m 120kg. IL Gular. Was at Western Maryland and Penn State Universities, USA.
At DT: OG: '76- 7, '84- 4, '88- 7; WCh: '83- 9, '87- 13; ECh: '78- 5, '82- 12, '86- 4; WCp: '79- 4. Norwegian champion DT: 1975–6, 1979–84, 1986, 1988; SP 1975–6, 1978–84. 2nd GP DT 1985.
Norwegian records: 9 DT 1975–85, 4 SP 1975–80.
Progression at DT: 1968- 41.90, 1969- 49.00, 1970- 51.52, 1971- 50.68, 1972- 58.96, 1973- 58.92, 1974- 56.70, 1975- 61.52, 1976- 64.64, 1977- 65.66, 1978- 65.44, 1979- 69.50, 1980- 67.66, 1981- 67.64, 1982- 64.24, 1983- 66.74, 1984- 67.30, 1985- 69.62, 1986- 68.50, 1987- 65.86, 1988- 65.40. pb SP: 20.55 '80, JT: 77.86 '76.
Suspended for drugs abuse in 1977.

Women

Ingrid KRISTIANSEN b.21 Mar 1956 Trondheim 1.69m 50kg. née Christensen. IL i BUL, Oslo.
At Mar: OG: '84- 4; ECh: '82- 3. At 10000m: OG: '88- dnf; WCh: '87- 1; ECh: '86- 1. At 3000m: WCh: '80- 3; ECh: '78- 10, '82- 8. At 1500m: ECh: '71- h. Won world road 15km 1987–8. World CC: '82- 6, '84- 4, '85- 3, '87- 3, '88- 1. Major marathon wins: Stockholm 1980–2, Houston 1983–4, London 1984 (in European best time), 1985 (world best time), 1987–8; Boston and Chicago 1986.
World records: 5000m (3) 1981, 1984 and 1986; 10000m (2) 1985–6. World road bests: 10km: 30:45.7 '86, 10M: 50:37 '87, 15km: 47:16 '87, half marathon 1:07:59 '86, 1:06:40 '87.
Progression at Mar: 1977- 2:45:15, 1980- 2:34:25, 1981- 2:30:09sh/2:41:34, 1982- 2:33:36, 1983- 2:33:27, 1984- 2:24:26, 1985- 2:21:06, 1986- 2:24:55, 1987- 2:22:48, 1988- 2:25:41. At 5000m/10000m: 1981- 15:28.43, 1982- 15:21.81, 1984- 14:58.89, 1985- 14:57.43/30:59.42, 1986- 14:37.33/30:13.74, 1987- 15:19.76/31:05.85, 1988- 15:10.89/31:31.37. pbs: 800m: 2:09.7 '81, 1500m: 4:05.97 '86, 3000m: 8:34.10 '86.
She is the only athlete to hold world records at 5000m, 10000m and marathon, and the only world champion at track, road and cross-country. Won Houston marathon just five months after giving birth to son, Gaute in August 1983. Has won 12/21 marathons and her first five track 10km races (not including heat in 1987 Worlds) before defeat by Liz McColgan in 1988. At cross-country skiing was 21st in the 1978 world championships, and had won gold, silver and bronze medals as a member of the

Norwegian team in the European Junior Champs 1973–5. Ran 10km on the road in 30:39 in the 1986 Ekiden Relay, the fastest ever by a woman, then took 45.68 sec off the world track 10000m record. Bone fracture on arch of right foot caused her to drop out while leading the Olympic 10000m in 1988.

Trine SOLBERG b.18 Apr 1966 Lorenskog 1.72m 65kg. IF Minerva. Bank clerk.
At JT: OG: '84- 5, '88- dnq 18; WCh: '87- dnq 24; ECh: '82- dnq, '86- 9; EJ: '81- 5, '83- 2. Norwegian champion 1983–6, 1988. 3rd GP 1986.
Seven Norwegian javelin records 1981–5.
Progression at JT: 1978- 31.04, 1979- 44.08, 1980- 49.54, 1981- 56.06, 1982- 58.02, 1983- 61.58, 1984- 65.02, 1985- 68.94, 1986- 67.80, 1987- 68.20, 1988- 67.50.
Full name Else Katrine Solberg. She was the top goalscorer in Norwegian second division handball in 1984, and but for her interest in the javelin would have been a candidate for the national team.

Grete WAITZ b.1 Oct 1953 Oslo 1.72m 52kg. née Andersen, married Jack Waitz (né Nilsen), who is now her coach, in 1975. SK Vidar.
At marathon: OG: '84- 2, '88- dnf; WCh: '83- 1. At 3000m: ECh: '78- 3; WCp: '77- 1, '79- 2. At 1500m: OG: '72- h, '76- sf; ECh: '71- h (h 800m), '74- 3, '78- 5. World CC: record five wins 1978–81 and 1983, third 1982 & 1984.
Two world records at 3000m: 8:46.6 '75 and 8:45.4 '76, European 5000m record 15:08.80 '82, and European junior 1500m record 4:17.0 '71. Four world marathon bests 1978–83.
World road bests for 15km: 47:53 '84, 10M: 53:05 '79, 20M: 1:51:23 '80. 24 Norwegian records from 800m to marathon 1971–83.
Progression at marathon: 1978- 2:32:30, 1979- 2:27:33, 1980- 2:25:41, 1982- 2:27:14, 1983- 2:25:29, 1984- 2:26:18, 1985- 2:28:34, 1986- 2:24:54, 1988- 2:28:06. pbs: 400m: 57.6 '72, 800m: 2:03.1 '75, 1500m: 4:00.55 '78, 1M: 4:26.90 '79, 3000m: 8:31.75 '79, 5000m: 15:08.80 '82, HJ: 1.61 '71.
Unbeaten for twelve years in cross-country races, and her first ever loss on the road was to Maricica Puica in 1981. A statue of her was erected outside the Bislett Stadium in Oslo in 1984. Of her 18 marathons she has won 13: nine New York marathons 1978–80, 1982–6, 1988; London 1983 and 1986; Stockholm 1988 and the 1983 world title. She was second in Los Angeles 1984 and did not finish four times. Unable to defend her world title in 1987 through injury.

OMAN

Governing body: Oman Athletic Association, PO Box 6990, Ruwi. Founded 1982.

Mohammed Amer AL MALKI b.1 Dec 1962 1.76m 62kg.
At 400mh: OG: '88- 8; WCh: '87- qf; AsG: '86- 3; AsCh: '85- 2, '87- 1. Arab champion 1987.
Asian 400m record 1988
Progression at 400m: 1985- 46.45, 1986- 46.42, 1987- 45.56, 1988- 44.56. pb 300m: 32.38 '88.
Formerly a football fanatic.

POLAND

Governing body: Polski Zwiazek Lekkiej Atletyki (PZLA), 00–372 Warszawa, ul.Foksal 19. Founded 1919.
National Championships first held in 1920 (men), 1922 (women)
1988 Champions: MEN
100m: Marian Woronin 10.34, 200m: Czeslaw Pradzynski 21.14, 400m: Tomasz Jedrusik 46.34, 800m: Piotr Piekarski 1:47.14, 1500: Waldemar Lisicki 3:41.01, 5000m: Czeslaw Mojzysz 13:51.58, 10000m: Jan Marchewka 29:02.75, Mar: Wiktor Sawicki 2:12:26, 3kmSt: Miroslaw Zerkowski 8:24.31, 110mh: Krzysztof Platek 13.88, 400mh: Robert Zajkowski 50.92, HJ: Jacek Wszola 2.29, PV: Ryszard Kolosa 5.30, LJ: Miroslaw Hydel 7.90, TJ: Andrzej Grabarczyk 17.08w, SP: Helmut Krieger 20.61, DT: Dariusz Juzyszyn 61.86, HT: Mariusz Tomaszewski 71.48, JT: Miroslaw Witek 75.44, Dec: Dariusz Grad 8050, 20kmW: Zdzislaw Szlapkin 1:25:12, 50kmW: Jerzy Wroblewicz 4:03:13.
WOMEN
100m: Ewa Pisiewicz 11.33, 200m: Agnieszka Siwek 22.92, 400m/400mh: Genowefa Blaszak 52.62/56.49, 800m/1500m: Malgorzata Rydz 2:03.05/4:14.00, 3000m: Grazyna Kowina 9:10.89, 5000m/Mar: Wanda Panfil 15:42.67/2:32:23, 10000m: Renata Kokowska 33:07.08, 100mh: Grazyna Tadrzak 13.53, HJ: Danuta Bulkowska 1.86, LJ: Agata Karczmarek 6.55, SP: Malgorzata Wolska 17.07, DT: Renata Katewicz 62.96, JT: Genowefa Patla 59.42, Hep: Urszula Wlodarczyk 5775, 5kmW: Kazimiera Mosio 23:25.94, 10kmW: Ewa Musur 47:21

Miroslaw CHMARA b.9 May 1964 Tczew 2.01m 86kg. Zawisza Bydgoszcz. Soldier.
At PV: OG: '88- nh; WCh: '87- dnq 17; EI: '86 & '88- 4. Two Polish pole vault records 1988.
Progression at PV: 1981- 4.90, 1982- 5.00, 1983- 5.25, 1984- 5.30, 1985- 5.40, 1986- 5.67i, 1987- 5.65, 1988- 5.90.
Won Masters pole vault at Grenoble in March 1988.

Marian KOLASA b.12 Aug 1959 Gdansk 1.97m 90kg. Baltyk Gdynia. Political economist.
At PV: OG: '88- nh; WCh: '87- 4; WI: '87- 5; EI: '86- 2, '87- 3; ECp: '85- 3, '87- nh. Polish champion 1985, 1987.
Polish PV record 1985 & 1987.
Progression at PV: 1972- 3.00, 1973- 3.50, 1974- 4.00, 1975- 4.40, 1976- 4.95, 1977- 5.13, 1978- 5.20i, 1979- 5.10, 1980- 5.40, 1981- 5.50, 1982- 5.30, 1983- 5.50, 1984- 5.60, 1985- 5.80, 1986- 5.50/5.71exh/5.81i, 1987- 5.80, 1988- 5.70.
His brother Ryszard has a PV best of 5.60 '85 and 5.71exh '86.

Krzysztof KRAWCZYK b.28 Jan 1962 Walbrzych 1.86m 74kg. AZS Wroclaw. Student.
At HJ: OG: '88- 12; WCh: '87- 10=; ECh: '86- 5; EJ: '81- 1; ECp: '87- 3=. Polish champion 1987.
Progression at HJ: 1976- 1.55, 1977- 1.70, 1978- 1.90, 1979- 2.06, 1980- 2.21, 1981- 2.26, 1983- 2.20, 1984- 2.27i, 1985- 2.26, 1986- 2.31, 1987- 2.30i/2.29, 1988- 2.32.

Helmut KRIEGER b.17 Jul 1958 Slawecice/Opole 1.96m 137kg. Chemik Kedzierzyn. Lathe operator.
At SP: OG: '88- 12; WCh: '87- 12; ECh: '86- 9; ECp: '85- 4, '87- 4. Polish champion 1986–7.
Progression at SP: 1978- 17.45, 1979- 17.18, 1980- 17.81, 1981- 18.23, 1982- 18.85, 1983- 20.28, 1984- 21.03, 1985- 21.07, 1986- 21.30, 1987- 20.82, 1988- 21.03.

Boguslaw MAMINSKI b.18 Dec 1955 Kamien Pomorski 1.81m 68kg. Legia Warszawa. Mechanic.
At 3kmSt: OG: '80- 7, '88- 8; WCh: '83- 2, '87- h; ECh: '82- 2, '86- dnf; WCp: '81- 1; ECp: '81- 2, '83- 1, '85- 2, '87- 4 ('79- 6 at 1500m). Polish champion 3kmSt 1979, 1985; 5000m 1983, 1987.
Polish 2000m record 1982.
Progression at 3kmSt: 1978- 8:34.8, 1979- 8:23.0, 1980- 8:18.78, 1981- 8:16.66, 1982- 8:17.41, 1983- 8:12.62, 1984- 8:09.18, 1985- 8:15.70, 1986- 8:20.56, 1987- 8:20.74, 1988- 8:15.97. pbs: 1000m: 2:20.8 '78, 1500m: 3:38.93 '80, 2000m: 5:02.12 '82, 3000m: 7:45.12 '85, 5000m: 13:26.09 '80.

Ryszard OSTROWSKI b.6 Feb 1961 Poznan 1.76m 62kg. Olimpia Poznan. Student.
At 800m: OG: '88- qf; WCh: '87- 4; ECh: '86- 5; WSG: '83- 1, '85- 1. Polish champion 1982–4, 1987. At 1500m: ECp: '85- 5.
Polish records: 800m (2) 1985, 1000m 1982..
Progression at 800m: 1978- 1:54.3, 1979- 1:51.1, 1980- 1:48.5, 1981- 1:47.44, 1982- 1:47.06, 1983- 1:45.90, 1984- 1:45.68, 1985- 1:44.38, 1986- 1:45.14, 1987- 1:44.59, 1988- 1:46.08. pbs: 400m: 46.73 '84, 1000m: 2:18.56 '82, 1500m: 3:40.69 '85.

Artur PARTYKA b.25 Jul 1969 1.91m 69kg. LKS Lodz. Student.
At HJ: OG: '88- dnq 20; WJ: '88- 1; EJ: '87- 1.
Progression at HJ: 1984- 1.94, 1985- 2.04, 1986- 2.18, 1987- 2.23, 1988- 2.28.

Jacek PASTUSINSKI b.8 Sep 1964 Nowa Deba 2.00m 90kg. Legia Warszawa. Metalwork technician.
At TJ: OG: '88- 8; WCh: '87- 5; ECh: '86- dnq. Polish champion 1985–7.
Progression at TJ: 1980- 14.12, 1981- 14.77, 1982- 15.97, 1983- 16.48/16.49w, 1984- 16.36, 1985- 17.09, 1986- 17.11, 1987- 17.35, 1988- 16.72/ 16.93w.

Women

Genowefa BLASZAK b.22 Aug 1957 Ksiaz Wielkopolski 1.68m 57kg. née Nowaczyk. Chemik Kedzierzyn. Shop assistant.
At 400mh/R- 4x400m relay: OG: '88- sf; WCh: '87- dq h; ECh: '74- 4R (h 400m),'78- 8/3R, '82- 8, '86- 5/ 3R; EJ: '73- 3R; WCp: '81- 2, '85- 7; ECp: '81- 3, '83- 8, '85- 3, '87- 2. 2nd GP 1985. Polish champion 400m 1976, 1982, 1984, 1987–8; 400mh 1976, 1981, 1983, 1985–6, 1988.
Four Polish 400mh records 1984–5.
Progression at 400mh: 1975- 58.8, 1976- 59.59, 1978- 56.67, 1981- 55.78, 1982- 55.76, 1983- 55.97, 1984- 54.78, 1985- 54.27, 1986- 54.47, 1987- 54.96, 1988- 55.14. pbs: 100m: 11.64 '84, 200m: 22.90 '85, 400m: 50.70 '86.

Ewa KASPRZYK b.7 Sep 1957 Poznan 1.64m 56kg. née Witkowska. Olimpia Poznan. Trainee teacher.
At 200m: WCh: '83- 8, '87- 7; ECh: '86- 5 (3 at 4x400mR); EI: '86- 2, '88- 1; EJ: '75- 2R; WCp: '85- 4 (3 4x100mR); ECp: '83- 8 (6 100m), '85- 3, '87- 3 (7 100m). 2nd GP 1986. Polish champion 100m 1986, 200m 1983–7.
Polish records: 100m, 200m (2) 1986.
Progression at 100m, 200m: 1972- 25.5; 1973- 24.2; 1974- 23.7; 1975- 11.90/11.3, 24.05/23.5; 1976- 11.77, 23.85; 1977- 12.09, 23.79; 1979- 24.32; 1980- 11.97, 24.01; 1981- 24.85; 1982- 11.65/11.4, 23.59; 1983- 11.53, 22.79; 1984- 11.22, 22.42; 1985- 11.32, 22.61/22.60w; 1986- 10.93, 22.13; 1987- 11.22, 22.52, 1988- 22.69i/23.61. pb 400m: 51.30 '86.

PORTUGAL

Governing body: Federaçao Portuguesa de Atletismo, Av.Infante Santo, 68-E-F, 1300 Lisboa. Founded 1921.
National Championships first held in 1910 (men), 1937 (women)

1988 Champions: MEN
100m: Pedro Agostinho 10.50, 200m: Luis Barroso 20.66w, 400m: Filipe Lombà 47.32, 800m: António Abrantes 1:52.10, 1500m: José Moreira 3:51.60, 5000m/10000m: José Regalo 13:29.56/28:02.4, Mar: Telmo Fernandes 2:25.03, 3000mSt: José Carlos Pereira 8:36.74, 110mh: Joao Lima 14.39w, 400mh: Antonio Perpétuo 53.26, HJ: Fernando Costa 2.09, PV: Pedro Palma 4.90, LJ: Antonio Veiga 7.23, TJ: José Leitão 16.22, SP: Fernando Alves 15.25, DT: Paulo Santos 54.04, HT: Antonio Peixoto 54.76, JT: Carlos Cunha 67.24, Dec: José Durao 6194, 50kw: José Magalhães 4:43.59.
WOMEN
100m/200m: Virginia Gomes 11.73/23.88w, 400m/800m: Elsa Amaral 54.66/2:08.61, 1500m: Fernanda Marques 4:25.58, 3000m: Albertina Machado 9:03.31, 10000m: Conçeicao Ferreira 32:28.6, Mar: Fátima Pereira 3:30.51, 100mh: Emilia Tavares 14.86, 400mh: Maria João Lopes 59.59, HJ: Graça Borges 1.72, LJ: Ana Oliveira 6.17w, SP/DT: Teresa Machado 14.68/50.16, JT: Helena Gouveia 41.66, Hep: Nora Araújo 4431, 10kmW: Ana Bela Aires 55:05.1.

Domingos CASTRO b.22 Nov 1963 Guimaraes 1.67m 56kg. Sporting Club de Portugal.
At 5000m: OG: '88- 4; WCh: '87- 2. At 10000m: ECh: '86- 5. Portugese champion 5000m, 10000m 1986–7.
Progression at 5000m/10000m: 1982- 14:59.3, 1983- 13:48.52/30:29.1, 1984- 13:52.54/30:39.6, 1985- 13:38.60, 1986- 13:19.03/28:01.62, 1987- 13:18.59/28:09.54, 1988- 13:16.09/27:43.30. pbs: 1500m: 3:39.2 '86, 3000m: 7:50.11 '88.
Broke into top class in 1986, and continued his progress in 1987 when he was a surprise silver medallist at 5000m in Rome. Desperately unlucky to miss a medal at 5000m in Seoul. His twin brother Dionisio has pbs: 5000m: 13:18.69 '88, 10000m: 27:42.84 '88; he was 8th in 1987 World 5000m and 11th in 1986 European 10000m.

José REGALO b.22 Nov 1963 Vila Real 1.80m 60kg. S.L. Benfica.
At 5000m: OG: '88- dnf. 3rd GP 1988. At 3000mSt: WCh: '87- 11; ECh: '86- 9. Portugese champion 3000mSt 1984–6, 5000m & 10000m 1988.
Three Portugese 3000mSt records 1986–7.
Progression at 5000m/3000mSt: 1981- 9:34.8, 1982- 9:31.9, 1983- 14:15.24/8:51.06, 1984- 14:09.0/8:44.90, 1985- 13:37.53/8:32.10, 1986- 13:28.91/8:21.41, 1987- 13:23.24/8:20.70, 1988- 13:15.62/8:21.64. pbs: 800m: 1:52.8 '88, 1500m: 3:40.1 '88, 2000m: 5:06.7 '87, 3000m: 7:59.7 '88, 10000m: 28:02.4 '88.
Won six major races in Europe in 1988 to become Olympic favourite, but he dropped out of the final through injury.

Women

Aurora CUNHA b.31 May 1959 Ronfe, near Guimaraes 1.55m 48kg. FC do Porto. Textiles worker.
At 10000m: WCh: '87- 17; ECh: '86- 4. At 3000m: OG: '84- 6; WCh: '83- 9; ECh: '82- 10 (10 at 1500m). At 10000m: WCp: '85- 1. World road: 10km '84–1, 15km '85- 1, '86- 1. Won 20 Portugese titles: 7 3000m, 6 1500m, 5 5000m, 4 CC.
42 Portugese records (1976–86): 15 at 3000m, 12 1500m, 6 5000m, 3 each 2000m and 10000m, 2 1000m, 1 800m.
Progression at 3000m/5000m: 1976- 9:54.0, 1977- 9:42.35, 1978- 9:28.4, 1979- 9:16.7, 1980- 9:04.7/16:41.6, 1981- 9:30.2, 1982- 8:54.5/15:35.2, 1983- 8:50.20/15:31.7, 1984- 8:46.37/15:09.07, 1985- 8:48.10/15:06.96, 1986- 8:57.31/15:25.59, 1987- 9:01.04/15:24.41, 1988- 9:04.1. At 10000m: 1983- 31:52.85, 1984- 32:30.91, 1985- 31:35.45, 1986- 31:29.41, 1987- 32:26.81, 1988- 32:33.9. pbs: 800m: 2:05.4 '82, 1000m: 2:45.8 '82, 1500m: 4:09.31 '83, 2000m: 5:54.0 '82, Mar: 2:31:26 '88.
Won first two marathons: Paris and Tokyo 1988.

Maria Albertina MACHADO b.25 Dec 1961 Sabrosa 1.68m 56kg. Sporting Club de Braga.
At 10000m: OG: '88- 9; WCh: '87- 7. At 3000m: OG: '84- h. World road 15km: '87- 6. World CC: '86- 8, '88- 5. Portugese champion 800m & 1500m 1985, 3000m 1988, 10000m 1987, CC 1987–8.
Portugese records 800m and 1M 1985.
Progression at 10000m: 1987- 31:46.61, 1988- 31:52.04. pbs: 400m: 58.2 '84, 800m: 2:04.1 '85, 1500m: 4:13.35 '87, 1M: 4:38.83 '85, 3000m: 8:52.02 '87, 5000m: 16:05.00 '88.

Rosa MOTA b.29 Jun 1958 Foz do Douro 1.57m 45kg. CA do Porto.
At Mar: OG: '84- 3, '88- 1; WCh: '83- 4, '87- 1; ECh: '82- 1 (12 at 3000m), '86- 1. World road: 10km '84- 2, 15km '86- 2; World CC: '86- 5. Portugese titles: 1 800m, 3 1500m, 2 3000m, 1 5000m, 7 CC.
Portugese records (1974–87): 6 at 1500m, 5 3000m, 2 5000m, 1 each 1000m, 15km, 20km, 1 hour; also seven marathon bests.
Progression at Mar: 1982- 2:36:04, 1983- 2:31:12, 1984- 2:26:01, 1985- 2:23:29, 1986- 2:27:15, 1987- 2:25:17, 1988- 2:24:30. pbs: 800m: 2:10.76 '85, 1500m: 4:19.53 '83, 3000m: 8:53.84 '84, 5000m: 15:22.97 '85, 10000m: 32:33.51 '85, 20km: 1:06:55.5 '83 (world best), 1 hour: 18027m '83.
Has won 10 of her 13 marathons, including the European gold in her first marathon in 1982, and again in 1986, before completing the triple with World and Olympic titles. She improved her best in each of her first seven marathons and won the first ever Olympic medal by a Portugese woman. Her other marathon wins: Rotterdam 1983, Chicago

1983–4, Tokyo 1986, Boston 1987–8. In 1985 she won the Great North Run half marathon in 1:09:54. Her sister Ana Paula Mota was Portugese 400mh champion 1987.

Rosa Mota (George Herringshaw/ASP)

ROMANIA

Governing body: Federation Romana de Atletism, Str. Vasile Conta 16, 70139 Bucaresti. Founded 1912.
National Championships first held in 1921 (men), 1925 (women)
1988 Champions: MEN
100m/200m: Valentin Chiriac 10.73/21.24, 400m: Daniel Cojocaru 47.10, 800m: Petre Dragoescu 1:51.12, 1500m/5000m: Valentin Coruja 3:45.16/ 14:05.66, 10000m: Eugen Enachioiu 30:45.54, Mar: Alexandru Chiran 2:20:44, 3000mSt: Marcel Martinas 8:48.70, 110mh: Liviu Giurgean 13.92, 400mh: Mugur Mateescu 51.43, HJ: Eugen Popescu 2.32, PV: Ravzan Enescu 5.00, LJ: Bogdan Tudor 7.56, TJ: Mihai Bran 16.67, SP/DT: Costel Grasu 18.97/60.82, HT: Nicolae Bindar 71.36, JT: Dumitru Negoita 78.76, Dec: Ion Buliga 6911, 20kmW: Gheorghe Frecateanu 1:26:17, 50kmW: Constantin Ispas 4:20:28.
WOMEN
100m: Marieta Ilcu 11.45, 200m/400m: Iolanda Oanta 22.82/50.55, 800m: Tudorita Ghidu 1:57.80, 1500m: Elena Fidatov 4:16.88, 3000m: Paula Ivan 8:50.82, 8:55.95, 10000m: Elena Murgoci 33:19.98, Mar: Elena Murgoci 2:33:03, 100mh: Mihaela Pogacian 13.05, 400mh: Nicoleta Carutasu 55.88, HJ: Galina Astafei 1.92, LJ: Vali Ionescu 7.04, SP: Mihaela Loghin 19.79, DT: Mariana Lengyel 63.82, JT: Aurica Bujnita 63.22, Hep: Liliana Nastase 6344, 10kmW: Victoria Oprea 44:59.

Sorin MATEI b.6 Jul 1963 Bucaresti 1.84m 71kg. Student.
At HJ: OG: '88- dnq 20=; WCh: '83- 17, '87- 6; WI: '87- 5=; ECh: '82- dnq, '86- 14; EI: '88- 3; EJ: '81- 5; WSG: '87- 3. 3rd GP 1988.
Nine Romanian high jump records 1980–8.
Progression at HJ: 1977- 1.88, 1978- 2.03, 1979- 2.12i, 1980- 2.27, 1981- 2.22, 1982- 2.28, 1983- 2.30, 1984- 2.34, 1985- 2.35, 1986- 2.32, 1987- 2.32, 1988- 2.37.
One of the smallest top-class high jumpers.

Women

Galina ASTAFEI b.7 Jun 1969 Bucaresti 1.81m 60kg.
At HJ: OG: '88- 5; WCh: '87- dnq 17=; WJ: '86- 2, '88- 1; EJ: '87- 2. Romanian champion 1986, 1988.
Three world junior and three Romanian high jump records 1988.
Progression at HJ: 1984- 1.80, 1985- 1.89, 1986- 1.93, 1987- 1.93i/1.88, 1988- 2.00.

Tudorita CHIDU b.17 Oct 1967 1.70m 57kg.
Romanian 800m champion 1988.
Progression at 800m: 1984- 2:07.8, 1986- 2:00.62, 1987- 1:59.96, 1988- 1:57.64. pb 400m: 52.18 '88, 1500m: 4:24.10 '88.

Mitica CONSTANTIN b.18 Aug 1962 Silistea 1.73m 55kg. née Junghiatu. Student.
At 800m: WCh: '87- 6 (12 at 1500m); ECh: '86- 6; WSG: '87- 2. At 1500m: WSG: '87- 3; WI: '87- 4; EI: '86- 3, '88- 2; 2nd GP 1988 Balkan champion 1985–6.
Progression at 800m/1500m: 1978- 2:07.7, 1979- 2:05.9, 1980- 2:04.52, 1982- 2:02.39/4:14.61, 1983- 2:01.99/4:14.32, 1984- 2:03.52, 1985- 1:59.20, 1986- 1:57.87/4:06.61, 1987- 1:58.52/4:03.04, 1988- 1:58.72/4:03.49. pbs: 1000m: 2:38.04 '87, 1M: 4:31.55i '88, 3000m: 9:12.70 '88.

Daniela COSTIAN b.30 Apr 1965 Braila 1.83m 92kg. Dinamo Bucaresti.
At DT: ECh: '86- 7dq; EJ: '83- 5; WSG:'85- 3. Balkan champion 1988.
Three Romanian discus records 1986–8.
Progression at DT: 1979- 32.30, 1980- 40.16, 1981- 40.60, 1982- 55.08, 1983- 60.50, 1984- 65.22, 1985- 67.54, 1986- 69.66, 1988- 73.84.
Suspended for contravening IAAF doping rules

when placing 7th at the 1986 European Championships. Political asylum in Turkey after winning 1988 Balkan title and then went to Australia.

Valeria 'Vali' IONESCU b.31 Aug 1960 Turnu Magurele 1.72m 64kg.
At LJ: OG: '84- 2; WCh: '83- 9, '87- dnq; WI: '87- 5; ECh: '82- 1, '86- 4; EI: '82- 3; WSG: '81- 3, '83- 3. Romanian champion 1980–3, 1986–8. Balkan champion 1984, 1988. Won GP 1987.
World record long jump 1982. WIB 6.92 '83.
Progression at LJ: 1976- 5.52, 1977- 5.49, 1978- 5.58, 1979- 6.07, 1980- 6.54, 1981- 6.75, 1982- 7.20, 1983- 6.92, 1984- 7.11, 1985- 6.97, 1986- 7.10, 1987- 7.04, 1988- 7.08.

Paula IVAN b.20 Jul 1963 Heresti 1.70m 55kg. née Ilie.
At 1500m/3000m: OG: '88- 1/2; WCh: '87- h/h; ECh: '86- h/- WSG: '87- 1/1. GP: 2nd 1M 1987, 1st 1500m 1988. Romanian champion 1500m 1987, 3000m 1988; Balkan 800m 1988.
Romanian records: 1500m (2), 3000m 1988.
Progression at 800m/1500m/3000m: 1981- 2:17.1, 1982- 2:12.4/4:31.3, 1983- 2:02.31/4:13.92/9:27.6, 1984- 2:00.63/4:14.37/9:14.37, 1985- 2:02.8/4:10.84/8:47.62, 1986- 4:05.19/8:55.50, 1987- 1:57.2/4:01.03/8:39.28, 1988- 1:56.42/3:53.96/8:27.15. pb 1M: 4:25.80 '88.
Trained since her emergence in 1983 by Ion Puica. Had a marvellous season in 1988, when she won the overall Mobil Grand Prix and then, after her silver medal for 3000m, ran away with the 1500m in the fastest time since 1980 for her eleventh major win in eleven races at 1500m/1M.

Ella KOVACS b.11 Dec 1964 1.70m 53kg.
At 800m: EI: '85- 1.
Progression at 800m: 1982- 2:04.55, 1984- 1:58.42, 1985- 1:55.68, 1986- 1:59.91, 1987- 1:56.76, 1988- 1:58.10. pbs: 400m: 53.30 '87, 1500m: 4:06.38 '84.

Mariana LENGYEL b.14 Apr 1953 1.74m 86kg. née Ionescu.
At DT: WCh: '87- 8; WSG: '81- 3. Romanian champion 1987–8.
Progression at DT: 1976- 45.54, 1977- 50.86, 1978- 50.94, 1979- 58.70, 1980- 62.14, 1981- 63.52, 1982- 64.92, 1983- 59.90, 1984- 61.70, 1985- 66.34, 1986- 69.08, 1987- 67.28, 1988- 67.62. pb SP: 19.00 '87.

Doina MELINTE b.27 Dec 1956 Hudesti 1.73m 59kg. née Besliu.
At 800m/1500m: OG: '80- sf/-, '84- 1/2, '88- -/9; WCh: '83- 6/6, '87- -/3; WI: '87- -/1; ECh: '82- 6/9, '86- -/3 (dnf h 3000m); WSG: '81- 1/2, '83- 3/2; EI: 800m: '82- 1, '84- 2; 1500m: '85- 1, '88- 1. Balkan champion 1500m 1982, 1984. 2nd GP 800m 1985, 1987; 1500m 1986; 3rd 1M 1987; 2nd overall 1987.
Romanian 800m record 1982. WIB 1M 1988.
Progression at 800m/1500m: 1976- 2:13.4/4:43.4, 1977- 2:11.8/4:38.4, 1978- 2:06.1, 1979- 2:04.4/4:18.6, 1980- 2:00.5/4:00.68, 1981- 1:57.81/4:03.70, 1982- 1:55.05/4:01.40, 1983- 1:57.06/4:01.49, 1984- 1:56.53/3:58.1, 1985- 1:56.81/3:59.88, 1986- 1:56.2/3:56.7, 1987- 1:57.46/3:59.27, 1988- 2:00.7i/4:00.85. pbs: 400m: 52.5 '85, 600m: 1:23.5 '86 (world best), 1000m: 2:36.94 '87, 1M: 4:18.86i '88, 3000m: 8:37.11 '86.
Gained the World bronze medal at 1500m after Gasser's disqualification.

Liliana NASTASE b.1 Aug 1962 1.69m 62kg. née Alexandru.
At Hep: WCh: '87- 5; WSG: '85- 2, '87- 1. Balkan champion 1985 (and 100mh 1983). Romanian champion 100mh 1984, Hep 1984–8.
Five Romanian heptathlon records 1984–7.
Progression at Hep: 1980- 4652*, 1982- 5378*, 1983- 5753, 1984- 6086, 1985- 6313, 1986- 6172, 1987- 6364, 1988- 6352. pbs: 100m: 12.16 '83, 200m: 23.50 '84, 800m: 2:10.88 '85, 100mh: 12.85 '86, 12.8w '84, 400mh: 59.41 '83, HJ: 1.77 '87, LJ: 6.68 '87, 6.78w '85; SP: 13.90 '87, JT: 43.54 '88.

Mihaela POGACIAN b.27 Jan 1958 Bucharest 1.65m 60kg. née Stoica, formerly Dumitrescu.
At 100mh: WCh: '83- qf; ECh: '86- 5; EJ: '77- 5. Romanian champion 1981–3, 1985–8, Balkan 1988. At 60mh: EI: '88- 3.
Three Romanian 100mh records 1985–7.
Progression at 100mh: 1973- 14.6, 1974- 13.8, 1975- 13.6, 1976- 13.6, 1977- 14.4, 1978- 13.29, 1979- 13.27, 1980- 13.21/12.9w, 1981- 13.42, 1982- 13.15, 1983- 12.92, 1985- 12.79, 1986- 12.75, 1987- 12.70, 1988- 12.79. pb LJ: 6.23 '83.

Maricica PUICA b.29 Jul 1950 Iasi 1.68m 54kg. née Luca, married to trainer Ion Puica.
At 3000m (1500m): OG: '76- (h), '80- (7), '84- 1 (3), '88- h; WCh: '87- 2; ECh: '78- 4 (11), '82- 2 (4), '86- 2 (5); WI: '87- 3; EI: '82- 2; WSG: '77- (3); WCp: '81- 2; ECp: '77- 2, '79- 2. Balkan champion 1500m 1978, 3000m 1978, 1981–2, 1984. Romanian champion 1500m 1982, 3000m 1977, 1980–1, 1984–5; 10000m 1987. World CC: '78- 3, 82- 1, '84- 1. GP: 3000m 2nd 1985, 1st 1987; won 1500m and 2nd overall 1986.
World records: 1 mile 1982, 2000m 1986; European 1M record 1981. Romanian records: 1500m 1984; 1M, 2000m, 3000m (2) and 5000m 1985; 1000m and 2000m 1986.
Progression at 1500m/3000m: 1969- 4:35.8, 1970- 4:34.1, 1971- 4:28.8, 1972- 4:28.7, 1973- 4:22.6/9:33.0, 1974- 4:18.2/9:19.0, 1975- 4:12.8, 1976- 4:06.1/9:18.4, 1977- 4:05.1/8:46.44, 1978- 4:05.13/8:40.94, 1979- 3:59.8/8:49.1, 1980- 3:59.3/9:00.2,

1981- 3:58.29/8:34.30, 1982- 3:57.48/8:31.67, 1983- 4:10.91/9:04.20, 1984- 3:57.22/8:33.57, 1985- 3:57.73/8:27.83, 1986- 3:59.62/8:35.92, 1987- 4:05.90/8:39.45, 1988- 8:53.85. pbs: 800m: 1:57.8 '79, 1000m: 2:31.5 '86, 1M: 4:17.33 '85, 2000m: 5:28.69 '86, 5000m: 15:06.04 '85, 10000m: 33:32.97 '87.
Dropped out of her heat in the Olympic 3000m in 1988 with just 200m to go.

SENEGAL

Governing body: Fédération Sénégalaise d'Athlétisme, B.P.1737, Dakar.

El Hadji Amadou Dia BA b.22 Aug 1958 Dakar 1.90m 82kg. Racing Club de France.
At 400mh: OG: '84- 5, '88- 2; WCh: '83- 7, '87- 5; WSG: '83- 2; AfG: '87- 1; AfCh: '82- 1 (1 at 400m), '84- 1, '88- 1; WCp: '85- 4. 2nd GP 1988. At HJ: AfG: '78- 3; WCp: '81- 7.
14 Senegal records 400mh 1982–8, African record 1988.
Progression at 400mh: 1982- 49.5/49.71, 1983- 49.03, 1984- 48.73, 1985- 48.29, 1986- 48.07, 1987- 48.03, 1988- 47.23. pbs: 100m: 10.7 '84, 200m: 21.51/21.3w '85, 400m: 45.78 '86, 100mh: 14.6 '86, HJ: 2.18 '81.
After a knee operation switched from high jump with immediate success in 1982, now one of the world's most consistent men at 400mh, with 39 sub-49.00 times. Greatest success in 1988 Olympics when he took 0.8 off his best and nearly won. His silver was the first Olympic medal at any sport for Sénégal, although Abdou Seye, a Sénégalese, won the 200m bronze in 1960 for France.

Moussa FALL b.28 Aug 1963 St.Louis du Sénégal 1.78m 67kg. Club: Assi B.Toscana, Firenze, Italy.
At 800m: OG: '84- sf, '88- h; WCh: '87- sf; WSG: '87- 2; AfCh: '84- 2, '85- 2. At 400m: WCh: '83- h.
Progression at 800m: 1982- 1:51.7, 1983- 1:49.0, 1984- 1:45.03, 1985- 1:44.68, 1986- 1:44.86, 1987- 1:44.74, 1988- 1:44.06. pbs: 400m: 47.3 '83, 1000m: 2:18.1 '85, 1500m: 3:44.86 '86, 1M: 3:59.44 '86.

SOMALIA

Governing body: Somali Amateur Athletic Association, P.O.Box 523, Mogadiscio. Founded 1959.

Abdi BILE Abdi b. 28 Dec 1962 Las Anod 1.85m 75kg. Student of marketing at George Mason University, USA.
At 1500m: OG: '84- sf (qf 800m); WCh: '87- 1; AfCh: '85- 2. NCAA champion 1985, 1987. 1st GP 1987.
Progression at 800m/1500m: 1981- 1:50.0, 1982- 3:51.6, 1984- 1:46.1/3:39.86/3:35.89dq, 1985- 1:47.24/3:34.24, 1986- 3:34.01, 1987- 1:44.47/3:31.71, 1988- 1:44.42/3:33.6. pbs: 800m: 1000m: 2:17.15 '85, 1M: 3:49.40 '88, 2000m: 4:59.77 '87.
Previously concentrating on soccer, he took up running as an 18-year-old. Was disqualified in semi-final of Olympic 1500m in 1984; three years later won the world title in majestic style, for the first ever world championships medal at any sport by a Somali. A stress fracture caused him to miss the 1988 Olympics.

SOUTH AFRICA

Governing body: South African Amateur Athletic Union, P.O. Box 1261, Pretoria 0001. Founded 1894. Membership of the IAAF terminated in 1976.
National Championships first held in 1894 (men), 1929 (women)
1988 Champions: MEN
100m/200m: Johan Rossouw 10.25/20.51, 400m: Henry Mohoanyane 45.50, 800m: David Hlabahlaba 1:48.54, 1500m: Deon Brummer 3:40.06, 5000m: Matthews Temane 14:05.31, 10000m: Xolile Yawa 28:44.3, Mar: Willie Mtolo 2:10:18, 3000mSt: Anton Nicolaisen 8:41.6, 110mh: Kobus Schoeman 13.68, 400mh: Dries Vorster 49.74, HJ: Gert Pieterse 2.18, PV: Corne van As 5.05, LJ: Francois Fouché 8.04, TJ: Vincent McBride 15.80, SP: Eugene Nysschen 18.68, DT/HT: George Tossel 57.24/63.76, JT: Herman Potgieter 71.10, Dec: Bertus de Klerk 7072, 20kmW: Chris Britz 1:29:26.
WOMEN
100m/200m: Evette de Klerk 11.51/23.71, 400m/400mh: Myrtle Bothma 51.29/55.47, 800m: Zelda Botes 2:03.03, 1500m: Ciska Swart 4:21.04, 3000m: Elana van Zyl 9:13.50, Mar: Annette Falkson 2:33:39, 100mh: Ina van Rensburg 13.17, HJ: Charmaine Gale 1.95, LJ: Sanet Fouché 6.40, SP: Luzanda Swanepoel 14.23, DT: Sandra Willms 54.14, JT: Ansie Rogers 57.28, Hep: Adri Henningse 5078.

Matthews TEMANE b.14 Dec 1960 Hammanskraal 1.71m 54kg.
SA champion 5000m 1982–3, 1985–8, CC 1984, 1986–8.
World best for half marathon: 60:11 '87. SA record 5000m 1986. pbs: 1500m: 3:38.3 '84, 1M: 3:55.4 '83, 3000m: 7:47.5 '85, 5000m: 13:25.15 '86, 10000m: 28:16.28 '88.
SA road champion at 10km 1985–7, 15km 1985, 1987, half marathon 1985–7.

Xolile YAWA b.29 Sep 1962 Lady Frere 1.71m 50kg.
SA champion 10000m 1985–8.

Two SA 10000m records 1987.
Progression at 10000m: 1984- 28:54.32, 1985- 28:13.64, 1986- 28:02.13, 1987- 27:39.65, 1988- 28:10.49. pbs: 1500m: 3:51.9 '84, 3000m: 7:57.01 '88, 5000m: 13:40.86 '86.

Women

Myrtle BOTHMA b.18 Feb 1964 East London 1.74m 57kg. née Simpson.
SA champion 400m and 400mh 1984–6, 1988.
SA records 1986: 1 at 400m, 4 at 400mh.
Progression at 400mh: 1983- 55.74, 1984- 56.25, 1985- 56.10, 1986- 53.74, 1987- 58.46, 1988- 55.13. pbs: 200m: 22.83 '88, 400m: 50.12 '86.
Had a baby in early 1987.

Charmaine GALE b.27 Feb 1964 Estcourt 1.78m 65kg. Policewoman.
SA HJ champion 1980, 1988.
Two world junior high jump bests 1981; seven SA records 1980–5.
Progression at HJ: 1977- 1.72, 1978- 1.77, 1979- 1.83, 1980- 1.92, 1981- 1.96, 1982- 1.90, 1983- 1.90, 1984- 1.88, 1985- 2.00, 1986- 1.99, 1987- 1.96, 1988- 1.97.

SPAIN

Governing body: Real Federacion Española de Atletismo, Calle Miguel Angel 16, Madrid 28010. Founded 1920.
National Championships first held in 1917 (men), 1931 (women)
1988 Champions: MEN
100m: José J.Arques 10.25w, 200m: Cayetano Cornet 20.87w, 400m: Angel Heras 46.50, 800m: Coloman Trabado 1:49.73, 1500m: Jaume Villalonga 3:55.48, 5000m: Juan-Carlos Paul 13:53.44, 10000m: Juan Rosario 28:44.40, Mar: Alfonso Abellán 2:14.42, 3000mSt: Juan Azkueta 8:31.88 110mh: Carlos Sala 13.67w, 400mh: José Alonso 50.25, HJ: Arturo Ortiz 2.25, PV: Alberto Ruiz 5.25, LJ: Antonio Corgos 8.15w, TJ: Santiago Moreno 16.46, SP: Matias Jiménez 16.82, DT: David Martinez 56.70, HT: Francisco Fuentes 68.60, JT: Julian Sotelo 69.60, Dec: Carlos Azulay 7197, 20kmW/50kmW: José Marin 1:23:05/3:50:30.
WOMEN
100m/200m: Sandra Myers 11.42w/23.47, 400m: Teresa Züiga 53.98, 800m: Rosa Colorado 2:02.68, 1500m: Lourdes Miquel 4:21.25, 3000m: Dolores Rizo 9:20.47, 10000m: Ana Isabel Alonso 32:41.27, Mar: María Luisa Irizar 2:41:03, 100mh: M.José Mardomingo 13.81w, 400mh: Cristina Pérez 57.27, HJ: Monica Calvo 1.77, LJ: Isabel Lopez 6.28w, SP: Margarita Ramos 15.31, DT: Angeles Barreiro 54.26, JT: Natividad Vizcaino 48.04, Hep: Maria Diez 5323, 5kmW/10kmW Rd: Reyes Sobrino 22:41.22/47:48.

José Manuel ABASCAL b.17 Mar 1958 Alceda, Santander 1.82m 67kg. Nike. Physical education teacher.
At 1500m: OG: '80- h, '84- 3; WCh: '83- 5; WI: '87- 2; ECh: '78- h, '82- 3, '86- h; WCp: '85- 4; EI: '82- 2, '83- 2; EJ: '75- 8, '77- 1 at 3000m. At 5000m: WCh: '87- h; ECp: '87- 1. Spanish 1500m champion 1978, 1981–2, 1984–5. 3rd GP 1985.
Eight Spanish records 1977–86: 5 2000m, 3 1500m.
Progression at 1500m/1M, 5000m: 1974- 4:02.2/ 15:50.4, 1975- 3:48.8, 1976- 3:47.7, 1977- 3:38.2/ 14:02.4, 1978- 3:40.0/14:13.0, 1979- 3:37.93, 1980- 3:37.4/13:56.7, 1981- 3:36.6, 1982- 3:33.12/ 13:52.1, 1983- 3:33.18/13:53.7, 1984- 3:33.69/ 13:39.27, 1985- 3:31:69, 1986- 3:31.13/13:17.71, 1987- 3:33.66/13:12.49, 1988- 3:39.39/13:48.4. pbs: 800m: 1:49.5 '80, 1000m: 2:19.57 '81, 1M: 3:50.54 '86, 2000m: 4:52.40 '86, 3000m: 7:54.56 '84, 3000mSt: 8:38.8 '81.

Abel ANTON b.24 Oct 1962 Ojoel, Soria 1.79m 63kg. Kelme.
At 5000m: OG: '88- sf; WCh: '87- 14; ECh: '86- h; EJ: '81- 5. At 10000m: ECp: '87- 1.
Progression at 5000m: 1981- 14:18.29, 1982- 14:13.94, 1983- 14:06.04, 1984- 13:27.95, 1985- 13:25.81, 1986- 13:32.61, 1987- 13:21.44, 1988- 13:20.67. pbs: 1000m: 2:20.44 '86, 1500m: 3:37.5 '85, 2000m: 5:01.35 '87, 3000m: 7:46.08 '87, 10000m: 28:46.65 '87.

Antonio CORGOS b.10 Mar 1960 Barcelona 1.83m 78kg. Club: Larios. Student.
At LJ: OG: '80- 7, '84- 10, '88- 5; WCh: '83- 7, '87- dnq; ECh: '82- 2, '86- dnq; EI: '81- 2. Spanish champion 1980, 1982–8. At TJ: EJ: '77- 9; ECp: '87- 8.
Four Spanish long jump records 1978–80 and European junior records in 1978 and 1979.
Progression at LJ: 1975- 6.03, 1976- 6.87, 1977- 7.30/7.35w, 1978- 8.05, 1979- 8.09, 1980- 8.23, 1981- 7.97i, 1982- 8.19, 1983- 8.06, 1984- 8.02, 1985- 8.20, 1986- 8.08/8.12i, 1987- 7.97, 1988- 8.16. pbs: 100m: 10.62/10.57w '83, 10.4/10.2w '84; HJ: 2.08 '78; TJ: 16.33i '80, 16.28 '87.

José Luis GONZALEZ b.8 Dec 1957 Villaluenga de la Sagra, Toledo 1.80m 63kg. Kelme.
At 1500m: OG: '80- sf, '84- h; WCh: '83- sf, '87- 2; ECh: '86- 4; EI: '82- 1, '85- 1 '86- 1; WI: '85- 2; ECp: '87- 1. At 3000m: EI: '87- 1, '88- 1; EJ: '75- 3. 2nd World Jnr CC 1975. Spanish champion 1500m 1976, 1979–80, 1986 and CC 1980–1. 2nd GP 1M 1986.
WIB 1500m 3:36.04 '86. 14 Spanish records 1979–87: 4 1500m & 1M, 4 3000m, 2 5000m.
Progression at 1500m/1M, 5000m: 1974- 3:51.3; 1975- 3:46.1, 14:00.8; 1976- 3:45.8, 14:20.6; 1977-

3:49.1, 14:14.4; 1978- 3:43.4, 14:05.9; 1979- 3:36.32/3:55.47, 13:48.6; 1980- 3:35.1/3:57.82, 13:38.0; 1981- 3:34.41/3:49.67; 1982- 3:38.70i/ 3:56.12i; 1983- 3:33.44/3:50.76, 14:03.56; 1984- 3:34.61/3:56.41; 1985- 3:30.92/3:47.79, 13:15.90; 1986- 3:32.90/3:50.59, 13:25.90; 1987- 3:33.01/ 3:51.75, 13:12.34; 1988- 3:36.41/3:55.00i, 13:27.30. pbs: 800m: 1:46.6 '83, 2000m: 5:02.25 '85, 3000m: 7:42.93 '87, 10000m: 29:03.5 '80.

Jorge LLOPART b.5 May 1952 El Prat de Llobregat, Barcelona 1.69m 59kg. CGR La Seda. Textile factory worker.
At 50kmW: OG: '80- 2, '84- 7, '88- 13; WCh: '83- dnf (28 at 20kmW), '87- dq; ECh: '78- 1, '82- 6, '86- 9; LT: '83- 4, '85- 8. Spanish champion 1978–9, 1981, 1985–6.
Progression at 50kmW: 1975- 4:30:11, 1976- 4:22:43, 1978- 3:53:30, 1979- 3:44:33, 1980- 3:45:55, 1981- 3:48:17, 1982- 3:51:12, 1983- 3:47:48, 1984- 4:03:09, 1985- 3:52:28, 1986- 3:50:26, 1987- 3:55:35, 1988- 3:48:09. pb 20kmW: 1:25:20 '80; track pbs: 5kmW: 19:51.1 '85, 10kmW: 41:17.8 '85, 30kmW: 2:08:39 '79, 1hrW: 14285m '86, 2hrW: 27986m '79.

José MARIN b.21 Jan 1950 El Prat de Llobregat, Barcelona 1.64m 60kg. CN Barcelona. Electrician.
At 20kmW/50kmW: OG: '80- 5/6, '84- 6/-, '88- 4/5; WCh: '83- 4/2, '87- 3/-; ECh: '78- 5/dnf, '82- 1/2, '86- dq/-; LT: 50kmW: '79- 7; 20kmW: '81- 5, '85- 1. Spanish champion 20kmW: 1974–5, 1977, 1979, 1981, 1985, 1987–8; 50kmW: 1980, 1982–4, 1988. World records for 2 hours (28165m) and 30km (2:07:59.8) in 1979.
Progression at 20kmW/50kmW: 1973- 1:35:12t, 1974- 1:33:27t, 1975- 1:31:17t/4:23:30, 1976- 1:29:16t/4:13:43, 1977- 1:33:24t, 1978- 1:24:39/ 4:10:48, 1979- 1:24:18/3:49:46, 1980- 1:23:52/ 3:43:35, 1981- 1:23:54/3:55:37, 1982- 1:23:43/ 3:49:08, 1983- 1:20:00/3:40:46, 1984- 1:25:17/ 3:50:12, 1985- 1:21:42, 1986- 1:29:00, 1987- 1:21:24, 1988- 1:20:34/3:43:03. Track pbs: 3kmW: 11:40.1i '79, 5kmW: 19:24.5 '80, 10kmW: 40:18.7 '81, 1hrW: 14420m '83.

Carlos SALA b.20 Mar 1960 Barcelona 1.86m 75kg. Larios. Student.
At 110mh: OG: '80- sf, '84- 7, '88- sf; WCh: '87- 6; ECh: '86- 3; EJ: '79- 5. Spanish champion 1986, 1988. At 60mh: EI: '88- 3.
Progression at 110mh: 1978- 14.7, 1979- 14.23/ 13.8w, 1980- 13.84, 1981- 13.90, 1982- 13.93, 1983- 13.64/13.55w, 1984- 13.56, 1985- 13.62/ 13.4, 1986- 13.50, 1987- 13.44, 1988- 13.67w/ 13.69. pb 200mh: 22.96 '87.

Women

Maria Cruz DIAZ b.24 Oct 1969 Barcelona 1.60m 46kg. CN Barcelona. Public relations student.
At 10kmW: WCh: '87- 4; ECh: '86- 1; WCp: '83- 29, '85- 22, '87- 10. At 5kmW: WJ: '86- 4, '88- 1; EJ: '85- 1=, '87- 2. At 3kmW: EI: '88- 2. Spanish champion 5kmW 1984–6, 10kmW 1985–6.
European junior 5km walk record 1985, and road best for 10kmW 1986.
Progression at 10kmW: 1983- 50:18.2, 1984- 48:51, 1985- 47:26, 1986- 46:09, 1987- 44:48, 1988- 46:34. Track pbs: 3kmW: 12:48.82i '88, 13:32.4 '86; 5kmW: 21:36.92 '87.
Was the youngest ever Spanish international at age 13 in the 1983 World Race Walking Cup and the youngest ever individual European champion in 1986.

Maria Reyes SOBRINO b.6 Jan 1967 1.62m 52kg. CN Barcelona.
At 10kmW: WCh: '87- 9; ECh: '86- 5; WCp: '87- 15. At 5kmW: EJ: '85- 1=. At 3kmW: EI: '88- 1. Spanish champion 5kmW 1987–8, 10kmW 1988

Reyes Sobrino (Spain) wins the 3,000m. walk at the European Indoor Championships, Budapest 1988. (Mark Shearman)

Progression at 10kmW: 1984- 48:55, 1985- 48:32, 1986- 46:35, 1987- 45:37, 1988- 45:52. 5kmW road pb: 21:25 '87; track pbs: 3kmW: 12:48.99i '88; 5kmW: 22:09.21 '87.

Maria Teresa ZUÑIGA b.28 Dec 1964 Eibar, Guipuzcoa 1.67m 55kg.
At 800m: OG: '88- 7. Spanish champion 400m 1988. Spanish records: two 800m, one 1500m 1988

Progression at 800m: 1980- 2:11.5, 1981- 2:10.4, 1982- 2:07.38, 1983- 2:05.36, 1984- 2:06.59, 1985- 2:08.54, 1986- 2:06.83, 1987- 2:02.61, 1988- 1:57.45. pbs: 400m: 52.71 '88, 1500m: 4:06.44 '88.

SWEDEN

Governing body: Svenska Fri-Idrottsförbundet, Sofiatornet, Stadion, S-114 33 Stockholm. Founded 1895.

National Championships first held in 1896 (men), 1927 (women)

1988 Champions: MEN

100m: Thomas Leandersson 10.73, 200m: Eric Josjö 21.05, 400m: Moses Kyeswa (Uga) 46.26, 800m: Martin Enholm 1:49.98, 1500m: Östen Buskas 3:46.11, 5000m: Mats Erixon 13:47.68, 10000m: Lars-Erik Nilsson 28:58.70, Mar: Sören Hellmark 2:16:41, 3000mSt: Patric Nilsson 8:37.00, 110mh: Ulf Söderman 13.88, 400mh: Thomas Nyberg 50.08, HJ: Mats Kollbrink 2.17, PV: Miro Zalar 5.40, LJ: Peter Widén 7.39, TJ: Håkan Malmberg 15.50, SP/DT: Lars Sundin 18.66/62.58, HT: Tore Gustafsson 75.52, JT: Peter Borglund 78.78, Dec: Bengt Järlsjö 7422.

WOMEN

100m: Maria Fernström 11.68, 200m: Gunilla Ascard 23.81, 400m: Ewa Johannson 53.74, 800m: Maria Akraka 2:02.84, 1500m: Malin Ewerlöf 4:12.44, 3000m: Anette Westerberg 9:25.89, 10000m: Midde Hamrin 32:47.52, Mar: Jutta Pedersen 2:42:11, 100mh/HJ/Hep: Monica Westén 13.76/1.83/5663, 400mh: Christina Wennberg 56.74, LJ: Lena Wallin 6.46, SP: Caroline Isgren 15.12, DT: Karin Colberg 48.22, JT: Elisabet Nagy 59.10.

Peter BORGLUND b.29 Jan 1964 Söderhamn 1.83m 85kg. Gefle IF. Was at Texas University.
At JT: OG: '88- 9; WCh: '87- 11; ECh: '86- dnq; EJ: '81- dnq, '83- 4. Swedish champion 1987–8.
Progression at JT: 1978- 55.40, 1979- 67.60, 1980- 71.12, 1981- 73.78, 1982- 76.96, 1983- 82.26, 1984- 81.34, 1985- 79.80; new: 1986- 80.74, 1987- 80.86, 1988- 81.38.

Stefan FERNHOLM b.2 Jul 1959 Norrköping 1.86m 120kg. IK Tiwaz. Student. Was at Brigham Young University, USA.
At DT: OG: '84- 8; WCh: '87- dnq; ECh: '86- 10. Swedish champion 1984.
Progression at DT: 1979- 44.82, 1980- 57.08, 1981- 41.18, 1982- 50.66, 1983- 62.08, 1984- 67.00, 1985- 67.72, 1986- 65.08, 1987- 69.80dh/68.30, 1988- 68.26. pbs: SP: 19.99 '81, HT: 54.42 '84.
Switched main event from shot to discus from 1983.

Bo GUSTAFSSON b.29 Sep 1954 Strömstad 1.75m 68kg. IK Vikingen. Economist.
At 50kmW: OG: '80- dnf (dq 20kmW), '84- 2, '88- 7; WCh: '83- dnf, '87- dq; ECh: '78- 10 at 20kmW, '82- 3 (dq 20kmW), '86- 7. Swedish champion 10kmW 1975–7, 1980–4; 20kmW 1980–5; 50kmW 1983, 1985, 1987.
Progression at 50kmW: 1979- 4:14:57, 1981- 4:03:55, 1982- 3:53:22, 1983- 3:51:49, 1984- 3:53:19, 1985- 3:48:35, 1986- 3:50:13, 1987- 3:56:41, 1988- 3:44:49. pbs: 3kmW: 11:29.91 '83, 5kmW: 19:32.5 '83, 10kmW: 40:05.21 '83, road: 20kmW: 1:21:38 '83, Mar: 2:30:38 '83.
Disqualified at 1987 World Championships, although completed course in fourth place.

Sven NYLANDER b.1 Jan 1962 Varberg 1.93m 85kg. IF Göta. Student. Was at Southern Methodist University, USA.
At 400mh: OG: '84- 4; WCh: '83- 4, '87- 4; ECh: '82- 7, '86- 3; Won NCAA 1983. At 110mh: EJ: 79- 6. Swedish champion at 400mh 1982 and 1987, 110mh 1979 and 1983.
Five Swedish 400mh records 1982–7.
Progression at 400mh: 1978- 54.8, 1979- 52.62, 1981- 51.58, 1982- 49.64, 1983- 48.88, 1984- 48.97, 1985- 50.39, 1986- 48.83, 1987- 48.37, 1988- 49.35. pbs: 100m: 10.63 '87, 200m: 21.18 '86, 400m: 47.8i '81, 48.10 '82; 110mh: 13.98/13.73w/ 13.7 '86, LJ: 6.82i '79.
Has a remarkable record of making all major championships finals 1982–7, setting national records in 1982, 1986 and 1987 in these races.

Patrik SJÖBERG b.5 Jan 1965 Göteborg 2.00m 82kg. Örgryte IS.
At HJ: OG: '84- 2, '88- 3=; WCh: '83- 11, '87- 1; ECh: '82- 10=, '86- 6; EI: 1st 1985, 1987–8; EJ: '81- 8, '83- 3; WCp: '85- 1; WIG: '85- 1. 2nd GP 1988. Swedish champion 1981–6.
Twelve Swedish high jump records 1982–7, European record 1985, World record 1987. WIB: 2.38 '85, 2.41 '87.
Progression at HJ: 1975- 1.30, 1976- 1.40, 1977- 1.59, 1978- 1.80, 1979- 1.91, 1980- 2.07, 1981- 2.21, 1982- 2.26, 1983- 2.33, 1984- 2.33, 1985- 2.38, 1986- 2.34, 1987- 2.42, 1988- 2.39i/2.37. pbs: LJ: 7.72 '87, TJ: 15.87 '83.

Dag WENNLUND b.9 Oct 1963 Mariestad 1.88m 94kg. Mariestads AIF. Was at Texas University, USA.
At JT: OG: '88- 8; WCh: '87- 8; ECh: '86- 15; EJ: '81- 12. Swedish champion 1985–6. Won NCAA 1986–7.
Three Swedish javelin records 1985–7.
Progression at JT: 1980- 65.06, 1981- 70.50, 1982- 78.20, 1983- 81.06, 1984- 82.34, 1985- 92.20. new: 1986- 81.86, 1987- 82.64, 1988- 81.30. pbs: SP: 13.09 '82, DT: 40.74 '84, HT: 41.70 '84.

Women

Monica GUNNARSSON b.22 Apr 1965 Borås 1.63m 44 kg. SK Svången.
At 10kmW: WCh: '87- 6; ECh: '86- 8. At 3kmW: EI: '87- 3.
Progression at 10kmW: 1982- 52:18.0t, 1983- 49:49.6t, 1984- 47:40, 1985- 46:45.6t, 1986- 46:05, 1987- 45:09, 1988- 46:07. Track pbs: 3kmW: 13:06.46i '87, 10kmW: 46:42.0 '87, road: 5kmW: 22:18 '86, 20kmW: 1:38:38 '87.

Ann-Louise SKOGLUND b.28 Jun 1962 Karlstad 1.74m 58kg. IF Göta. Clerk.
At 400mh: OG: '84- 5; WCh: '83- 6; ECh: '82- 1. At 400m: OG: '80- ht, EI: '86- 3; EJ: '79- 6. Swedish champion 100m 1980, 200m 1982–5, 400m 1980–1, 100mh 1981 and 1984–5, 400mh 1978 and 1980.
Three world junior 400mh records 1978–80. Swedish records (1978–86): 400m (5), 100mh (2), 400mh (10).
Progression at 400mh: 1977- 62.6, 1978- 57.58, 1979- 57.87, 1980- 56.68, 1981- 56.00, 1982- 54.57, 1983- 54.80, 1984- 55.17, 1985- 55.44, 1986- 54.15, 1988- 57.05. pbs: 100m: 11.70/11.57w '85, 11.5w '77; 200m: 23.27 '85, 400m: 51.69 '86, 100mh: 13.25 '85, 13.23w '86; LJ: 5.59 '82.
Has met peak form at the European Championships. She won in 1982 with a Swedish record which she improved in 1986 when she was fourth.

SWITZERLAND

Governing body: Schweizerischer Leichtathletikverband (SLV), Case Postale 2233, CH 3001, Berne. Formed in 1905 as the Athletischer Ausschuss des Schweizerischen Fussball-Verbandes.
National Championships first held in 1906 (men), 1934 (women).
1988 Champions: MEN
100m: Stefan Burkart & René Mangold 10.58, 200m: René Mangold 21.46, 400m: Bernhard Notz 46.74, 800m: Markus Trinkler 1:47.04, 1500m: Markus Hacksteiner 3:48.09, 5000m: Kai Jenkel 14:13.96, 10000m: Daniel Boltz 29:22.11, Mar: Jakob Marti 2:19:50, 3kmSt: Roland Hertner 8:43.60, 110mh: Fabien Niederhäuser 13.93, 400mh: Massimo Balestra 51.20, HJ: Roland Dalhäuser 2.14, PV: Severin Moser 5.00, LJ: René Gloor 7.69, TJ: Fritz Berger 15.82, SP: Werner Günthör 21.71, DT: Christian Erb 57.38, HT: Oliver Sack 62.94, JT: Rudolf Steiner 74.66, Dec: Beat Gähwiler 8112, 10kmW: René Haarpaintner 44:33.20, 20kmW/50kmW: Aldo Bertoldi 1:29:18/ 4:14:59.
WOMEN
100m: Jacqueline Häuselmann 11.88, 200m: Regula Aebi 22.88, 400m: Anita Protti 52.40, 800m: Simone Meier 2:06.79, 1500m/3000m: Cornelia Bürki 4:12.62/9:08.98, 10000m: Rosmarie Müller 36:45.96, Mar: Helen Comsa 2:39:20, 100mh/LJ: Rita Heggli 13.27/6.30, 400mh: Monika Schediwy 58.13, HJ: Anja Barelkowski 1.85, SP: Ursula Stäheli 18.02, DT: Nathalie Ganguillet 47.64, JT: Denise Thièmard 63.08, Hep: Corinne Schneider 6072, 5kmW/10kmW: Margot Vetterli 26:01.78/ 54:23.4.

Pierre DÉLÈZE b.25 Sep 1958 Nendaz 1.75m 62kg. LC Zürich. Arts graduate.
At 1500m: OG: '80- h, '84- h; WCh: '83- 6; ECh: '78- h, '82- 7; EI: '80- 3; EJ: '77- 3; WSG: '79- 2. 2nd GP 1985. At 5000m: OG: '88- h; WCh: '87- 4; ECh: '86- 7. Swiss champion 1500m 1978–81, 5000m 1985. Ten Swiss records 1979–87: 4 1500m, 3 1M, 2 2000m, 1 1000m.
Progression at 1500m/5000m: 1974- 4:01.82, 1975- 3:49.84, 1976- 3:49.8, 1977- 3:41.8, 1978- 3:39.82, 1979- 3:36.7, 1980- 3:33.80, 1981- 3:36.90, 1982- 3:34.40/13:28.27, 1983- 3:32.97, 1984- 3:33.64, 1985- 3:31.75/13:53.97, 1986- 3:38.38/13:15.31, 1987- 3:34.85/13:24.07, 1988- 3:39.46/13:32.64. pbs: 800m: 1:48.92 '82, 1000m: 2:16.87 '83, 1M: 3:50.38 '82, 2000m: 4:54.46 '87, 3000m: 7:43.46 '88.
Moved up to 5000 metres in 1986, and ran fast times, although only seventh in Stuttgart. Progressed to fourth in Rome 1987. Fast finisher.

Werner GÜNTHÖR b.1 Jun 1961 2.00m 126kg. LC Zürich. Sports student.
At SP: OG: '84- 5, '88- 3; WCh: '83- dnq, '87- 1; WI: '87- 2; ECh: '86- 1; EI: '84- 2, '85- 3, '86- 1, '87- 2. Swiss champion 1981–8. Won GP 1986.
Thirteen Swiss shot records 1984–8. WIB 22.26 '87.
Progression at SP: 1977- 12.12, 1978- 13.60, 1979- 15.08, 1980- 16.42, 1981- 16.65, 1982- 17.51i, 1983- 20.01, 1984- 20.80, 1985- 21.55i/21.26, 1986- 22.22, 1987- 22.47, 1988- 22.75. pbs: HJ: 2.00 '85; DT: 54.48 '85, JT: 74.88 '81.
Had a brilliant season in 1986, with European titles both indoors and out. In the latter he added 56cm to his Swiss record. Carried this form over to 1987, when he lost only once outdoors, and improved further in 1988.

Markus HACKSTEINER b.18 Nov 1964 Appenzell 1.86m 74kg. TV Windisch. Electrician.
At 1500m: OG: '88- sf; WCh: '87- h; ECh: '86- h, EJ: '83- 6. Swiss champion 1983, 1985, 1987–8. At 3000m: EI: '88- 2.
Progression at 1500m: 1982- 3:52.18, 1983- 3:43.80, 1984- 3:46.38, 1985- 3:42.52, 1986- 3:38.44, 1987- 3:34.11, 1988- 3:37.07. pbs: 800m: 1:46.26 '87, 1000m: 2:19.70 '86, 1M: 3:55.67 '87,

Markus Hacksteiner (Switzerland). (Mark Shearman)

3000m: 7:50.57i '88, 7:51.49 '86, 5000m: 13:46.94 '87.
His brother Daniel ran 3:44.02 for 1500m in 1988.

Markus RYFFEL b.5 Feb 1955 Stäfa 1.67m 57kg. STV Bern. Businessman, formerly a typographer.
At 5000m (10000m): OG: '76- h, '80- 5 (dnf), '84- 2; WCh: '83- 12 (dnf), '87- h (17); ECh: '78- 2=, '82- 10, '86- dnf; EJ: '73- 7. At 3000m: EI: '77- 3, '78- 1, '79- 1, '84- 2. Swiss champion: 1500m 1974; 5000m 1976–79, 1981–83, 1986; 10000m 1976, 1985, 1987.
17 Swiss records 1976–85: 7 5000m, 4 3000m & 10000m, 2 2000m.
Progression at 5000m/10000m: 1972- 15:15.8, 1973- 14:03.1, 1974- 14:08.8/30:21.8, 1975- 13:50.8/28:54.04, 1976- 13:32.65/28:05.37, 1977- 13:23.93/28:36.0, 1978- 13:19.97/28:21.55, 1979- 13:13.32/28:41.7, 1980- 13:23.03/28:47.8, 1981- 13:19.74/27:54.99, 1982- 13:17.80/28:19.9, 1983- 13:19.38/27:54.88, 1984- 13:07.54/29:05.89, 1985- 13:17.27/27:54.29, 1986- 13:16.28, 1987- 13:33.07/ 28:08.44, 1988- 13:30.03/28:13.32. pbs: 1500m: 3:38.57 '79, 1M: 3:58.05 '84, 2000m: 4:59.54 '78, 3000m: 7:41.00 '79, Mar: 2:16:40 '83.

Women

Cornelia BÜRKI b.3 Oct 1953 Humansdorp, South Africa 1.60m 53kg. née de Vos. Swiss national by marriage. LC Zürich.
At 1500m(/3000m): OG: '80- h, '84- (5), '88- h/11; WCh: '83- 10/11, '87- 4/4; ECh: '78- 8/6, '82- (11), '86- 8/7. 3rd GP 1500m 1986. World CC: '78- 5, '85- 5, '87- 7. 43 Swiss titles: 1500m 1975–88, CC 1976–88, 3000m 1975–8, 1980–5, 1988; 800m 1976–7, 1979, 1984.
25 Swiss records 1976–86: 8 3000m, 7 1500m, 6 800m, 3 1M, 1 1000m & 2000m.
Progression at 1500m/3000m: 1974: 4:32.20/-, 1975- 4:14.5/9:15.4, 1976- 4:09.9/9:33.8, 1977- 4:12.14/9:07.56, 1978- 4:04.60/8:46.13, 1979- 4:06.3/-, 1980- 4:04.39/8:53.76, 1981- 4:09.65/ 9:16.02, 1982- 4:07.88/8:55.67, 1983- 4:07.85/ 8:46.94, 1984- 4:05.67/8:45.20, 1985- 4:02.05/ 8:38.71, 1986- 4:03.38/8:44.44, 1987- 3:59.90/ 8:40.31, 1988- 4:08.08/8:45.81. pbs: 800m: 2:00.99 '86, 1000m: 2:39.67 '77, 1M: 4:24.85 '86, 2000m: 5:35.59 '86, Mar: 2:42:33 '84.
Her two daughters, Sorita and Esther, were born in 1972, before she began her running career. Very consistent in major events, she achieved her best ever placings in Rome in 1987.

Anita PROTTI b.4 Aug 1964 Lausanne 1.70m 61kg. Lausanne-Sports. Clerk.
At 400mh: OG: '88- sf. Swiss 400m champion 1988. Swiss records 1987–8: five 400mh, one 400m.
Progression at 400mh: 1980- 67.28, 1981- 62.75, 1982- 62.06, 1983- 61.34, 1984- 59.98, 1985- 58.72, 1986- 59.58, 1987- 56.69, 1988- 54.56. pbs: 400m: 52.12 '88, 800m: 2:02.20 '87.

Denise THIÉMARD b.24 Mar 1960 Orsonnens 1.69m 66kg. LC Zürich. Clerk.
At JT: OG: '88- 9; WCh: '87- dnq 21; ECh: '86- 12. Swiss champion 1983, 1985–8.
Three Swiss javelin records 1983–7.
Progression at JT: 1977- 42.12, 1978- 43.52, 1979- 45.84, 1980- 52.44, 1981- 52.84, 1982- 52.96, 1983- 61.34, 1984- 57.10, 1985- 63.96, 1986- 62.30, 1987- 64.04, 1988- 63.62. pb SP: 13.28 '84.

TANZANIA

Governing body: Tanzania Amateur Athletic Association, PO Box 2172, Dar es Salaam. Founded 1954.

Juma IKANGAA b.19 Jul 1957 Dodoma 1.63m 58kg.
At Mar: OG: '84- 6, '88- 7; WCh: '83- 15, '87- 6; CG: '82- 2; AfCh: '82- 1; WCp: '85- 10.
Progression at Mar: 1982- 2:09:30, 1983- 2:08:55,

1984- 2:10:49, 1985- 2:11:06, 1986- 2:08:10, 1987- 2:12:19, 1988- 2:08:42. pbs: 5000m: 13:41.0 '86, 10000m: 28:15.13 '86.
First African to better 2hrs 10min for marathon, when second to de Castella in epic Commonwealth duel in 1982. Improved his African best when second at Fukuoka in 1983. Has won 7 of his 21 marathons including Melbourne 1983–4, Tokyo 1984 and 1986, Fukuoka 1986, Beijing 1987. Second Boston 1988.

TRINIDAD & TOBAGO

Governing body: National Amateur Athletic Association of Trinidad & Tobago, 9 King Street, Arima, Trinidad. Founded 1945, reformed 1971.

Ian MORRIS b.30 Nov 1961 Siparia 1.75m 65kg. Karamu Flyers. Student at Abilene Christian University, USA.
At 400m: OG: '88- 7; WCh: '87- h (h 200m); PAm: '87- 4; WCp: '85- 6R, CAmG: '86–2 (2R).
Two national 400m records 1988.
Progression at 400m: 1985- 45.38/45.1, 1986- 45.02, 1987- 45.03, 1988- 44.60. pb 200m: 20.71 '88, 20.4/20.45w '87.
Started track in 1985, having previously played soccer.

TUNISIA

Governing body: Fédération Tunisienne d'Athlétisme, 13 rue de Cologne, 1002 Tunis Belvédère.

Féthi BACCOUCHE b.16 Nov 1960 1.71m 59kg. Club: ASM Tunis & Larios, Italy.
At 5000m: WCh: '83- sf; WSG: '83- 2 (3 10000m). At 3000mSt: OG: '84- 12, '88- sf; WCh: '87- h; AfCh: '85- 3. Arab champion 5000m, 10000, 3kmSt 1983; Pan-Arab champion 5000m 1985, 3000mSt 1987.
Progression at 5000m/3000mSt: 1978- 14:02.7, 1980- 13:59.5, 1981- 13:57.70/8:32.34, 1982- 13:48.8/8:45.99, 1983- 13:38.04/8:34.1, 1984- 13:27.1/8:18.70, 1985- 13:29.83/8:34.80, 1986- 13:55.78/8:23.69, 1987- 13:13.94/8:15.07, 1988- 13:36.31/8:18.12. pbs: 800m: 1:51.5 '85, 1500m: 3:37.98 '87, 1M: 3:57.90 '87, 2000m: 4:59.89 '86, 3000m: 7:46.17 '86, 2M: 8:32.34 '86, 10000m: 28:39.66 '87.

UNITED KINGDOM

Governing body: British Amateur Athletic Board, Francis House, Francis Street, London SW1P 1DL. Founded 1932. The Amateur Athletic Association was founded in 1880 and the Women's Amateur Athletic Association in 1922.
National Championships (first were English Championships 1863–79):
UK National Championships first held in 1977.
1988 Champions: MEN
100m: John Regis 10.65, 200m: Linford Christie 20.75, 400m: Brian Whittle 46.08, 800m: Paul Herbert 1:45.64, 1500m: Richard McDonnell 3:48.02, 5000m: Mark Harris 13:50.63, 10000m: David Lewis 28:08.44, 3000mSt: Neil Smart 8:37.37, 110mh: Anthony Jarrett 13.97, 400mh: Philip Harries 50.01, HJ: Geoff Parsons 2.25, PV: Andrew Ashurst 5.10, LJ: Derrick Brown 7.91w, TJ: Rezlimond Cameron 16.20, SP: Graham Savory 17.95, DT: Paul Mardle 59.42, HT: David Smith 70.66, JT: Steve Backley 79.50, 10kmW: Ian McCombie 40:39.77.
WOMEN
100m/200m: Paula Dunn 11.49/23.46, 400m: Linda Keough 52.25, 800m: Christina Cahill 2:02.71, 1500m: Beverley Nicholson 4:15.13, 3000m: Melissa Watson 9:04.85, 5000m: Elizabeth McColgan 15:10.17, 100mh: Lynn Green 13.71, 400mh: Elaine McLaughlin 56.22, HJ: Diana Davies 1.88, LJ: Mary Berkeley 6.53, SP: Judy Oakes 18.76, DT: Venissa Head 53.66, JT: Fatima Whitbread 70.10, 5kmW: Betty Sworowski 24:03.38.
National Road Walk Champions: MEN 20kmW: Ian McCombie 1:23:31, 50kmW: Les Morton 4:17:05. WOMEN 5kmW: Betty Sworowski 23:43, 10kmW: Julie Drake 49:26.

AAA Championships first held in 1880. 1988 Champions:
100m/200m: Linford Christie 10.15/20.46, 400m: Kriss Akabusi 44.93, 800m: Steve Cram 1:44.16, 1500m: Peter Elliott 3:44:48, 5000m: Eamonn Martin 13:50.03, 10000m: Steve Binns 28:40.14, 3000mSt: Mark Rowland 8:32.60, 110mh: Colin Jackson 13.29, 400mh: Max Robertson 50.23, HJ: Geoff Parsons 2.28, PV: Simon Arkell (Aus) 5.10, LJ: Stewart Faulkner 7.98, TJ: John Herbert 17.12, SP: Simon Williams 17.78, DT: Paul Mardle 58.06, HT: David Smith 72.08, JT: David Ottley 80.34, Dec: Eugene Gilkes 7529, 10kmW: Ian McCombie 41:36.51.

WAAA Championships first held in 1922. 1988 Champions:
100m: Paula Dunn 11.26, 200m: Simmone Jacobs 23.37, 400m: Linda Keough 51.65, 800m: Kirsty Wade 2:01.52, 1500m: Christina Cahill 4:08.26, 3000m: Yvonne Murray 8:47.34, 10000m: Angela Tooby 33:13.95, 100mh/400mh: Sally Gunnell 13.02/55.40, HJ: Janet Boyle 1.91, LJ: Nicole Boegman (Aus) 6.82, SP: Judy Oakes 18.76, DT: Jackie McKernan 51.80, JT: Sharon Gibson 57.32, Hep: Joanne Mulliner 5728, 5kmW: Betty Sworowski 24:24.32.

Kriss Akabusi (Stuart D. Franklin/ASP)

Kriss AKABUSI b.28 Nov 1958 Paddington. 1.85m 79kg. Team Solent. Army sergeant, PT instructor.
At 400m/R- 4x400m relay: OG: '84- sf/2R, '88- 6; ECh: '86- 3R; CG: '86- 4/1R; ECp: '83- 1R, '85- 3R. At 400mh: WCh: '87- 7/2R. Won UK 400m 1984, 400mh 1987 (tie); AAA 400m 1988.
European 4x400m relay records 1984 and 1987
Progression at 400m: 1980- 48.0, 1981- 48.0/48.13, 1982- 48.0/48.18, 1983- 46.10, 1984- 45.43, 1985- 45.55, 1986- 45.65, 1987- 45.99, 1988- 44.93. At 400mh: 1983- 55.0, 1987- 48.64, 1988- 48.67. pbs: 100m: 10.7 '83, 200m: 21.46 '84, 21.2w '88; 300m: 32.76 '88, 800m: 1:48.2 '85.
Has been an invaluable member of 4x400m relay teams, and consistently sub-46 seconds. Turned to 400m hurdling in 1987, and improved in his first three meetings: 51.7 to 50.16 to 49.56. Made a great breakthrough with 48.64 and 48.74 at the World Championships. Full name: Kriss Kezie Uche Chukwu Duru-Akabusi!

Roger BLACK b.31 Mar 1966 Portsmouth 1.90m 83kg. Team Solent.
At 400m/R- 4x400m relay: WCh: '87- 2R; ECh: '86- 1/1R; CG: '86- 1/1R; EJ: '85- 1/1R; ECp: '87- 2/2R. UK 200m champion 1987.
UK 400m record and European 300m best 1986, European 4x400m relay record 1987.
Progression at 400m: 1984- 47.7, 1985- 45.36, 1986- 44.59, 1987- 44.99. pbs: 100m: 10.65 '86, 10.4 '87; 200m: 20.63 '86, 300m: 32.08 '86.
Made a brilliant start to his international career with six gold medals, both 400m and 4 x 400m relay, in three international championships in 1985–6. His first notable performance had been third in the 1983 English Schools 200m. In 1987 had to miss the individual 400m in Rome through injury, but ran in the relay final. Operation on stress fracture in left ankle August 1988.

Jack BUCKNER b.22 Sep 1961 Wells, Somerset 1.73m 59kg. Charnwood. Geography graduate of Loughborough University.
At 5000m: OG: '88- 6; WCh: '87- 3; ECh: '86- 1; CG: '86- 2. UK champion 1986. Won AAA 10km road 1985.
Progression at 5000m: 1984- 13:45.57, 1985- 13:21.06, 1986- 13:10.15, 1987- 13:10.48, 1988- 13:23.8e. pbs: 800m: 1:49.8 '81, 1000m: 2:18.88 '82, 1500m: 3:35.28 '86, 1M: 3:51.57 '84, 2000m: 4:53.06 '87, 3000m: 7:40.43 '86, 2M: 8:17.12 '86.
Stepped up to 5000m in 1986 and now has gold, silver and bronze medals. Has 10km road best of 28:03.

Linford CHRISTIE b.2 Apr 1960 St.Andrews, Jamaica 1.89m 77kg. Thames Valley Harriers. Youth worker.
At 100m/R- 4x100m relay (200m): OG: '88- 2/2R (4); WCh: '87- 4; ECh: '86- 1/3R (sf); CG: '86- 2/2R; ECp: '87- 1 (1). At 200m: EI: '86- 1, '88- 3. At 60m: EI: '88- 1. Won UK 100m 1985, 1987; 200m 1985 (tie), 1988; AAA 100m 1986, 1988; 200m 1988.
European 100m record 1988. UK records: three 100m 1986–8, one 200m 1988.
Progression at 100m, 200m: 1977- 10.9, 23.2; 1978- 22.5; 1979- 10.7/10.6w, 21.89/21.8; 1980- 10.73/10.6/10.5w, 22.0/21.4w; 1981- 10.85/10.7, 21.6/21.70i; 1982- 10.50, 21.38/21.2; 1983- 10.46/10.4, 21.71i/21.31w; 1984- 10.44/10.31w, 21.0/21.44; 1985- 10.42/10.20w, 21.37i; 1986- 10.04, 20.51; 1987- 10.03, 20.48; 1988- 9.97, 20.09. pb 300m: 33.80 '88.

Sebastian COE b.29 Sep 1956 Chiswick, London 1.77m 54kg. Haringey. Graduate of Loughborough University.
At 800m: OG: '80- 2, '84- 2; ECh: '78- 3, '82- 2, '86- 1; EI: '77- 1; WCp: '81- 1; ECp: '77- 4, '79- 1, '81- 1. At 1500m: OG: '80- 1, '84- 1; ECh: '86- 2; EJ: '75- 3. Won UK 800m 1978, AAA 800m 1981.
Britain's most prolific world record setter: 800m (2), 1000m (2), 1500m (1), 1M (3), 4x800mR (1) 1979–82. WIB: 800m: 1:46.0 '81, 1:44.91 '83; 1000m: 2:18.58 '83. UK records: 800m (5), 1000m (2), 1500m (2), 1M (3) 1977–81.
Progression at 800m, 1500m/1M: 1970- 4:31.8;

1971- 2:08.4, 4:18.0; 1972- 1:59.9, 4:05.9; 1973- 1:56.0, 3:55.0; 1975- 1:53.8, 3:45.2; 1976- 1:47.7, 3:42.67/3:58.35; 1977- 1:44.95, 3:57.67M; 1978- 1:43.97, 4:02.17M; 1979- 1:42.33, 3:32.03/3:48.95; 1980- 1:44.7, 3:32.19; 1981- 1:41.73, 3:31.95/ 3:47.33; 1982- 1:44.48, 3:39.1/3:59.5; 1983- 1:43.80, 3:35.17/3:52.93; 1984- 1:43.64, 3:32.39/ 3:54.6; 1985- 1:43.07, 3:32.13/3:49.22; 1986- 1:44.10, 3:29.77; 1987- 1:46.18, 1988- 1:43.93, 3:35.72. pbs: 400m: 46.87 '79, 600m: 1:16.2 '78, 1000m: 2:12.18 '81, 2000m: 4:58.84 '82, 3000m: 7:54.32i '86, 5000m: 14:06.2 '80.
Made wonderful recovery from serious illness in 1983 to retain Olympic 1500m title. Was undefeated in a 1500m or 1 mile final from 14 Sep 1976 to 24 Jun 1983. Missed 1986 Commonwealth 800m final and 1500m through virus illness, but came back to share titles with Steve Cram at the Europeans and then narrowly missed the 1500m world record at Rieti. Appointed vice-chairman of the Sports Council 1986. Controversialy omitted from 1988 Olympic team after failing in the trials through illness.

Steve CRABB b.30 Nov 1963 Edmonton, London 1.88m 70kg. Borough of Enfield H. Gas service engineer.
At 1500m: OG: '88- sf; WCh: '87- sf. AAA champion 1987.
Progression at 1500m: 1981- 3:55.7, 1982- 3:48.6, 1983- 3:49.7, 1984- 3:35.16, 1986- 3:35.50, 1987- 3:33.34, 1988- 3:33.95. pbs: 400m: 48.2 '84, 800m: 1:45.69 '88, 1000m: 2:17.75 '87, 1M: 3:51.76 '87.
Won his first national medals in 1980 at 800m, with second indoors and third out in the AAA youths 800m.

Steve CRAM b.14 Oct 1960 Gateshead 1.86m 69kg. Jarrow & Hebburn.
At 1500m (800m): OG: '80- 8, '84- 2, '88- 4 (qf); WCh: '83- 1, '87- 8; CG: '78- h, '82- 1, '86- 1 (1); ECh: '82- 1, '86- 1 (3); ECp: '81- 3, '83- 1, '85- 1, '87- 2. At 3000m: EJ: '79- 1. AAA champion 1500m 1981–3; 800m 1984, 1986, 1988.
World records at 1500m, 1M and 2000m 1985, and on 4 x 800m relay team 1982.
Progression at 800m, 1500m/1M: 1973- 4:31.5; 1974- 2:11.0, 4:22.3; 1975- 2:07.1, 4:13.9; 1976- 1:59.7, 4:07.1; 1977- 1:56.3, 3:47.7; 1978- 1:53.5, 3:40.09/3:57.43; 1979- 1:48.5, 3:42.5/3:57.03; 1980- 1:48.41, 3:34.74/3:53.8; 1981- 1:46.29, 3:34.81/3:49.95; 1982- 1:44.45, 3:33.66/3:49.90; 1983- 1:43.61, 3:31.66/3:52.56; 1984- 1:46.0, 3:33.13/3:49.65; 1985- 1:42.88, 3:29.67/3:46.32; 1986- 1:43.22, 3:30.15/3:48.31; 1987- 1:45.31, 3:31.43/3:50.08, 1988- 1:43.42, 3:30.95/3:48.85. pbs: 400m: 49.1 '82, 600m: 1:16.79 '83, 1000m: 2:12.88 '85, 2000m: 4:51.39 '85, 3000m: 7:43.1 '83, 2M: 8:14.93 '83, 5000m: 13:48.0 '84.
Set world age 17 mile best in 1978. Completed a major championship treble in 1983 and went on to gain Olympic silver before his wonderful 1985 season. In 1986 became third man to win Commonwealth 800m/1500m double and then won gold and bronze at the Europeans. Has suffered from calf injuries.

Peter ELLIOTT b.9 Oct 1962 Rawmarsh, Rotherham 1.81m 67kg. Rotherham. Joiner with British Steel.
At 800m: OG: '84- sf, '88- 4 (2 1500m); WCh: '83- 4, '87- 2; CG: '86- 3; EI: '83- 2; EJ: '81- 4; ECp: '83- 3. UK 800m champion 1983–4, 1986. Won AAA 800m 1982, 1987; 1500m 1984, 1988.
Ran on world record 4 x 800m team 1982.
Progression at 800m/1500m: 1975- 2:20.8, 1976- 2:05.9, 1977- 2:01.9, 1978- 1:52.05, 1979- 1:50.7, 1980- 1:51.3, 1981- 1:47.35/3:53.3, 1982- 1:45.61/ 3:49.1, 1983- 1:43.98, 1984- 1:45.49/3:36.97, 1985- 1:49.4/3:39.79, 1986- 1:44.06/3:35.62, 1987- 1:43.41/3:33.23, 1988- 1:44.12/3:32.94. pbs: 400m: 48.2 '84, 600m: 1:16.6 '83, 1000m: 2:16.47 '88, 1M: 3:49.20 '88, 2000m: 4:52.82 '87.
In 1984 became the first British runner to beat Seb Coe at 1500m since 1976. Missed most of 1985 season through injury. Finished 1987 with the World silver medal and pbs at 1500m and 2000m as well as three major road mile wins. Had a magnificent Olympic Games in 1988 despite a groin injury.

Michael HILL b.22 Oct 1964 Leeds 1.90m 100kg. Leeds City. Student.
At JT: OG: '88- dnq 20; WCh: '87- 7; ECh: '86- 8; CG: '86- 2; EJ: '83- 11; ECp: '87- 4. UK champion 1985–7, AAA 1987. 2nd GP 1987.
UK and Commonwealth javelin record 1987.
Progression at JT: 1980- 56.32, 1981- 59.14, 1982- 64.72, 1983- 74.36, 1984- 71.08, 1985- 82.30, 1986- 82.04; new: 1986- 78.56, 1987- 85.24, 1988- 81.30.

Tim HUTCHINGS b.4 Dec 1958 London 1.83m 71kg. Crawley. Graduate of Loughborough University.
At 5000m: OG: '84- 4; WCh: '87- 7; ECh: '82- 7, '86- 3; CG: '82- 14, '86- 3; ECp: '87- 2. At 1500m: CG: '78- 10. UK champion 1982, AAA 1986.
World CC: '84- 2. English National CC champion 1983, 1986.
Progression at 5000m: 1979- 14:06.76, 1981- 14:18.4, 1982- 13:25.08, 1983- 13:24.10, 1984- 13:11.50, 1985- 13:33.24, 1986- 13:12.88, 1987- 13:24.77, 1988- 13:23.24. pbs: 800m: 1:51.8 '77, 1000m: 2:22.6 '82, 1500m: 3:38.06 '84, 1M: 3:54.53 '82, 2000m: 5:00.37 '83, 3000m: 7:44.55 '84, 2M: 8:15.53 '86.

Colin JACKSON b.18 Feb 1967 Cardiff 1.82m 73kg. Cardiff AAC. Student.

At 110mh: OG: '88- 2; WCh: '87- 3; CG: '86- 2; WJ: '86- 1; EJ: '85- 2; ECp: '87- 2. Won UK 1986, AAA 1986, 1988. At 60mh: WI: '87- 4, EI: '87- 2.
European junior 110mh record 1986. Two UK and one Commonwealth and European 110mh records 1988.
Progression at 110mh: 1984- 13.92, 1985- 13.69, 1986- 13.44/13.42w, 1987- 13.37, 1988- 13.11. pbs: 100m: 10.49 '86, 10.4w '88; 200m: 21.19 '88, HJ: 1.81 '82, LJ: 7.96w '86, 7.56 '85; JT: 52.86 '84.
Injury cost him the chance of medal at the 1986 European Championships.

Anthony JARRETT b.13 Aug 1968 1.88m 82kg. Part-time community worker.
At 110mh: OG: '88- 6; EJ: '87- 1/1 4x100mR. UK champion 1987–8.
Progression at 110mh: 1985- 15.1, 1986- 14.14/14.06w, 1987- 13.72, 1988- 13.45/13.35w. pbs: 100m: 10.83/10.6/10.42w '87, 200m: 21.02/20.9 '88.

Anthony Jarrett (George Herringshaw/ASP)

Hugh JONES b.1 Nov 1955 North London 1.79m 62kg. Ranelagh H. Graduate of Liverpool University.
At Mar: OG: '84- 12; WCh: '83- 8, '87- 5; ECh: '86- 5; ECp: '81- 5.
Progression at Mar: 1978- 2:25:13, 1979- 2:20:28, 1980- 2:18:56, 1981- 2:11:00, 1982- 2:09:24, 1983- 2:09:45, 1984- 2:11:54, 1985- 2:10:36, 1986- 2:11:42, 1987- 2:10:11, 1988- 2:11:08. pbs: 5000m: 14:04.2 '78, 10000m: 28:49.51 '78.
Has run 23 marathons, winning six including AAA 1981 and London 1982. Much troubled by Achilles tendon injuries, and had to miss the 1988 Olympics, but a consistently top-class runner.

Steve JONES b.4 Aug 1955 Tredegar, Gwent 1.78m 62kg. Newport H.
At marathon: ECh: '86- 20. At 10000m: OG: '84- 8; WCh: '83- 12; ECh: '82- 7; CG: '82- 11, '86- 3; ECp: '83- 5. At 5000m: CG: '78- 11. World CC: '79- 7, '80- 9, '84- 3. AAA 10000m champion on track and road 1984, half marathon 1985.
World marathon best 1984 and Commonwealth record 1985. UK half marathon best (1:00:59) 1986.
Progression at 10000m: 1980- 28:13.25, 1981- 28:00.58, 1982- 28:05.74, 1983- 27:39.14, 1984- 27:58.64, 1985- 27:53.91, 1986- 28:02.48, 1988- 29:05.11. At Mar: 1984- 2:08:05, 1985- 2:07:13, 1986- 2:22:12, 1987- 2:12:37, 1988- 2:08:20. pbs: 1500m: 3:42.3 '82, 1M: 4:00.6* '80, 3000m: 7:49.80 '84, 2M: 8:26.71 '80, 5000m: 13:18.6 '82, 3000mSt: 8:32.00 '80.
Won the 1984 Chicago marathon in the world's best time. He had dropped out in only previous marathon, at Chicago in 1983. In 1985 he won at London (2:08:16) and at Chicago, when just a second outside the world best. In 1986 won his first major championships medal at 10000m at the Commonwealth Games, but after leading by two minutes before halfway fell back sharply in the European marathon. Left his job as an air frame technician in the Royal Air Force in 1988 and returned to form to win the New York marathon, his fourth win in eight marathons.

Tom McKEAN b.27 Oct 1963 1.83m 71kg. Bellshill YMCA.
At 800m: OG: '88- qf; WCh: '87- 8; ECh: '86- 2; CG: '86- 2; ECp: '85- 1, '87- 1; UK champion 1985. Won GP 1988.
Progression at 800m: 1977- 2:05.0, 1978- 1:58.6, 1979- 1:55.3, 1980- 1:56.15, 1981- 1:53.2, 1982- 1:49.01, 1983- 1:49.48, 1984- 1:48.40, 1985- 1:46.05, 1986- 1:44.80, 1987- 1:44.45, 1988- 1:45.05. pbs: 200m: 22.3 '82, 400m: 47.60 '86, 1000m: 2:18.91 '85.
Had string of successes in his debut season in international athletics in 1985, culminating in his win in the European Cup Final. He earlier completed a remarkable 34 successive wins at 800m. Won medals in both his major races in 1986. Undefeated at 800m in 1987 except for his eighth place in Rome. Disqualified in the 1988 Olympic quarter-finals.

Eamonn MARTIN b. 9 Oct 1958 Basildon 1.82m 68kg. Basildon. Components testing engineer at Ford Motors.

At 5000m: OG: '84- 13, '88- sf (dnf 10000m); WCh: '83- sf. Won GP 1988. Won National CC 1984, AAA 5000m 1988.
Progression at 5000m/10000m: 1979- 14:47.8, 1983- 13:20.94, 1984- 13:23.33, 1985- 13:44.07, 1987- 13:39.12, 1988- 13:22.88/27:23.06. pbs: 800m: 1:52.00 '84, 1500m: 3:40.54 '83, 1M: 3:59.30 '83, 2000m: 5:01.09 '84, 3000m: 7:40.94 '83, 2M: 8:18.98 '88.
Won English Schools junior cross-country title 1973, and intermediate 1500m 1975. Had operations on both Achilles and missed most of 1985 and 1986 seasons. Had run some good 10km road races in 1985 and won the AAA road title in 1988, then on the track ran the fastest ever debut at 10000m to win at the Bislett Games and smash the ten-year-old British record.

Derek REDMOND b.3 Sep 1965 Bletchley 1.83m 67kg. Birchfield H.
At 400m/R- 4x400m relay: WCh: '87- 5/2R; ECh: '86- 4/1R; EJ: '83- sf/4R; ECp: '85- 3/3R. 3rd GP 1987.
Two UK 400m records 1985–7.
Progression at 400m: 1980- 53.6, 1981- 52.8, 1982- 49.5, 1983- 47.55, 1984- 46.32, 1985- 44.82, 1986- 45.25, 1987- 44.50, 1988- 44.67. pbs: 100m: 10.2 '87, 200m: 21.36 '87, 21.0w '85, 300m: 32.32 '88, 800m: 1:55.3 '84.
At the age of 19 in 1985 broke David Jenkins' ten-year-old British record. Missed 1986 Commonwealth Games due to a serious hamstring injury, but returned in fine style for the Europeans, and improved further in 1987, breaking the UK record in the semi-finals in Rome. Missed 1988 Olympics through injury.

John REGIS b.13 Oct 1966 Lewisham 1.81m 86kg. Belgrave H.
At 200m/R- 4x100m relay: OG: '88- sf/2R (h 100m); WCh: '87- 3; CG: '86- 8; EI: '87- 3. Won UK 200m 1985 (tie), 1986, 100m 1988; AAA 200m 1986–7. At 100m: EJ: '85- 2/1R.
UK 200m record 1987.
Progression at 200m: 1982- 22.6, 1983- 22.0, 1984- 21.31, 1985- 20.78, 1986- 20.41, 1987- 20.18, 1988- 20.32. pbs: 100m: 10.31 '88, 300m: 32.53 '87, 400m: 46.57 '88, 200mh: 24.0 '87, TJ: 14.28 '82.
So nearly won the World 200m title, as he led at 195m, and was rewarded with the UK record. Showed much promise at 400m with a 45.56 relay leg indoors for England v USA at Cosford. Cousin of soccer international Cyrille Regis.

Jonathan RIDGEON b.14 Feb 1967 Bury St Edmunds 1.83m 75kg. Haringey. Student at Cambridge University.
At 110mh: OG: '88- 5; WCh: '87- 2; ECh: '86- 6; CG: '86- 5; WSG: '87- 1; WJ: '86- 2 (1 at 4x100mR); EJ: '85- 1. AAA champion 1987. At 60mh: WI: '85- 2; EI: '88- 2.
Three UK 110mh records 1987. European junior record 1985.
Progression at 110mh: 1984- 13.92, 1985- 13.46, 1986- 13.66, 1987- 13.29, 1988- 13.52/13.45w. pbs: 100m: 10.49 '86, 10.3w '85; 200m: 21.08 '87, 200mh: 22.9w '87, 23.00w/23.2 '87, LJ: 7.35 '87.
Following his European Junior title in 1985, was overtaken by arch-rival Colin Jackson in 1986, but was the UK male athlete of the year in 1987. Olympic finalist despite virus infection 1988.

Michael ROSSWESS b.11 Jun 1965 Dudley 1.87m 75kg. Birchfield H.
At 200m: OG: '88- 7.
Progression at 100m, 200m: 1987- 10.85/10.7, 21.89/21.6; 1988- 10.40, 20.51.
Only started in athletics in 1987 and 18 months later reached the Olympic final!

Mark ROWLAND b.7 Mar 1963 Watersfield, W. Sussex. 1.83m 68kg. Phoenix.
At 3000mSt: OG: '88- 3. At 3000m: EI: '87- 4; WI: '87- 4. Won UK 1500m 1985, AAA 3000mSt 1988.
European best 2km steeple 8:19.86 in 1988. UK 3000mSt record 1988.
Progression at 1500m/3000mSt: 1980- 3:57.5, 1983- 3:47.9, 1984- 3:42.6, 1985- 3:42.6, 1986- 3:37.2, 1987- 3:39.24/8:21.03, 1988- 3:34.53/ 8:07.96. pbs: 800m: 1:49.8 '84, 1500m: 3:34.53 '88, 1M: 3:52.99 '86, 2000m: 5:08.07 '85, 3000m: 7:50.63i '87, 7:53.05 '88, 2M: 8:26.19 '87, 5000m: 13:21.83 '88.
Second in English Schools 800m 1979, but gave up athletics for soccer 1981–2. Took up the steeplechase in 1987, running 8:26.76 on his debut. Took 8.38 sec off his best in the 1988 Olympic final.

Charlie SPEDDING b.19 May 1952 Bishop Auckland, Co.Durham 1.74m 63kg. Club: Gateshead H. Product services manager for Nike. Qualified as pharmacist.
At Mar: OG: '84- 3, '88- 6; CG: '86- dnf. At 10000m: ECh: '82- 8; CG: '82- 4. AAA champion at 10000m 1983, marathon 1984.
Progression at Mar: 1984- 2:09:57, 1985- 2:08:33, 1986- 2:10:13, 1987- 2:10:32, 1988- 2:12:19. pbs: 1500m: 3:45.36 '73, 1M: 4:03.5 '76, 2000m: 5:12.02 '82, 3000m: 7:54.0 '75, 2M: 8:26.87 '76, 5000m: 13:28.7 '78, 10000m: 28:08.12 '83.
Major success since the age of 30, but he has had a long career, placing second in the 1971 English Schools 1500m, but had many injuries in the 1970s. Won his first two marathons, Houston and London, in 1984. Second at London 1985, third Chicago 1986. When an Achilles operation went wrong in 1987 it was feared that he would never run again, but he made a wondrous recovery in 1988.

Daley THOMPSON b.30 Jul 1958 Notting Hill, London 1.84m 88kg. Newham & Essex Beagles.
At Dec: OG: '76- 18, '80- 1, '84- 1, '88- 4; WCh: '83- 1, '87- 9; ECh: '78- 2, '82- 1, '86- 1; CG: '78- 1, '82- 1, '86- 1; EJ: '77–1 (5 at LJ). UK long jump champion 1979. Won AAA decathlon 1976 and LJ 1977.
Four world decathlon records (8648 in 1980, 8730 and 8774 in 1982, 8847 in 1984), three world junior records 1976–7, ten UK and Commonwealth records 1976–84.
Progression at Dec: 1975- 6941, 1976- 7748, 1977- 8082, 1978- 8470w, 1979- 6949dnf, 1980- 8648, 1981- 7797, 1982- 8774, 1983- 8714, 1984- 8847, 1986- 8811, 1987- 8124, 1988- 8306. pbs: 100m: 10.26 '86, 200m: 20.88 '79, 300m: 33.94 '81, 400m: 46.86 '82, 1500m: 4:20.3 '76, 110mh: 14.04 '86, 400mh: 52.14 '86, HJ: 2.14i '82, 2.11 '80; PV: 5.25 '86, LJ: 8.01 '84, 8.11w '78, SP: 16.10 '84, DT: 49.10 '86, JT: 65.38 '80, new: 64.04 '88.
His supreme competitive ability has brought him unparallelled decathlon success. In his career, from 1975 to 1988, he has won 19 of the 30 decathlons that he has contested. He did not finish two decathlons, one in 1979 and one in 1984, but otherwise won ten in succession from his European second place in 1978 until his ninth in Rome in 1987, when his preparations had been interrupted by a groin injury. Has never contested a decathlon in England!

Women

Shireen BAILEY b.27 Sep 1959 Kensington, London 1.73m 66kg. née Hassan. Bromley Ladies. Part-time dental assistant.
At 1500m: OG: '88- 7. At 800m: OG: '88- sf; ECh: '86- sf; CG: '82- 5. UK and WAAA champion 1983.
Progression at 1500m: 1983- 4:18.9, 1984- 4:16.6, 1985- 4:18.4, 1986- 4:10.78, 1987- 4:05.32, 1988- 4:02.32. pbs: 400m: 54.6 '83, 600m: 1:26.8 '85, 800m: 1:59.36 '85, 1000m: 2:35.32 '86, 1M: 4:46.6 '86.
Britain's second sub-2 minute 800m lady. Selected for the 1983 European Cup final, but couldn't find her femininity certificate in time!

Zola BUDD b. Bloemfontein, South Africa 26 May 1966 1.61m 43kg. British citizenship by parentage obtained 6 April 1984. Aldershot, Farnham & District.
At 3000m: OG: '84- 7; ECh: '86- 4 (9 at 1500m); ECp: '85- 1. World CC: '85- 1, '86- 1. South African champion 1500m and 3000m 1982–3. Won UK 1500m 1984, WAAA 3000m 1985, 1500m 1986.
While in South Africa ran world 5000m best: 15:01.83 '84 and world junior bests at 1500m (2), 1M (1), 2000m (2), 3000m (3) and 5000m (4). Since taking up British citizenship: world record 5000m 1985, and in 1984: world best 2000m, world junior best 1M, European junior records 1500m (4:04.39) and 3000m (8:40.22). WIB 3000m 8:39.79 '86. Commonwealth indoor records: 3000m 1985–6; 1500m 1986. UK & Commonwealth records at 1500m, 1M, 3000m (2) and 5000m 1985.
Progression at 1500m/3000m/5000m: 1980- 4:24.3/10:06.5, 1981- 4:19.0, 1982- 4:09.1/8:59.2, 1983- 4:06.87/8:39.00/15:10.65, 1984- 4:01.81/8:37.5/15:01.83, 1985- 3:59.96/8:28.83/14:48.07, 1986- 4:01.93/8:34.43. pbs: 800m: 2:00.9 '84, 1000m: 2:37.9 '83, 1M: 4:17.57 '85, 2000m: 5:30.19 '86.
Not permitted to run in the 1986 Commonwealth Games. Returned after a year off through injury to run a road 10km in 32:22 in September 1987.

Christina CAHILL b.25 Mar 1957 Northolt, Middlesex 1.63m 51kg. née Boxer. Club: Gateshead H. Student adviser at Sunderland Polytechnic. Formerly at Loughborough. Married to Sean Cahill (3:56.95 mile in 1979).
At 1500m: OG: '84- 6, '88- 4; WCh: '83- 9; ECh: '86- ht, CG: '78- 11, '82- 1, '86- 4; ECp: '85- 2. At 800m: OG: '80- sf; ECp: '79- 6, '81- 5. Won UK 800m 1979–80, 1984, 1988; 1500m 1986; WAAA 800m 1977–8, 1985; 1500m 1982 & 1988.

Christina Cahill (George Herringshaw/ASP)

UK and Commonwealth 1500m and 1M records 1984; UK 800m and 1M records 1979.
Progression at 1500m: 1970- 4:44.1, 1971- 4:39.1, 1972- 4:29.0, 1977- 4:20.7, 1978- 4:10.0, 1979- 4:07.06, 1980- 4:09.15, 1981- 4:10.22, 1982- 4:04.48, 1983- 4:06.74, 1984- 4:00.57, 1985- 4:02.58, 1986- 4:07.74, 1987- 4:07.13, 1988-

4:00.64. pbs: 400m: 55.14 '79, 800m: 1:59.05 '79, 1000m: 2:34.92 '82, 1M: 4:22.64 '84, 2000m: 5:33.85 '84, 3000m: 8:49.89 '85.
Has had a long and distinguished career, since winning National junior cross-country title in 1971. After two moderate years ran marvellously to place fourth in Olympic 1500m.

Sally GUNNELL b.29 Jul 1966 Chigwell 1.67m 56kg. Essex Ladies. Accounts clerk.
At 400mh: OG: '88- 5. At 100mh: OG: '88- sf; WCh: '87- sf; ECh: '86- ht; CG: '86- 1; EJ: '83- sf (13 Hep). At 400m: EI: '88- 4. Won UK 100mh 1986, WAAA 100mh 1986–8, 400mh 1988.
UK records: four at 400mh, one 100mh 1988.
Progression at 100mh/400mh: 1982- 15.0, 1983- 13.71, 1984- 13.30, 1985- 13.48/13.46w, 1986- 13.11, 1987- 13.01/59.9, 1988- 12.82/12.80w/ 54.03. pbs: 100m: 12.00/11.8 '87, 11.79w '86; 200m: 23.69/23.4 '88, 23.38w '86; 400m: 51.77i '88, 800m: 2:13.22 '84, HJ: 1.67 '83, LJ: 6.08 '83, SP: 11.18 '84, Hep: 5493 '84.
First national titles were at long jump: WAAA junior 1980, intermediate 1981. After reaching international class at 100mh, showed her 400mh potential with a UK indoor record at 400m in 1988. After a 59.9 for 400mh in 1987, she ran 57.5 and 56.47 in her first two 400mh races in 1988, and improved rapidly, with UK records at 55.40 and 55.00 in August, then 54.48 and 54.03 in Seoul.

Elizabeth McCOLGAN b.24 May 1964 Dundee 1.68m 45kg. née Lynch. Dundee Hawkhill H. Married steeplechaser Peter McColgan (pb 8:29.35 and 7 CG 1986 for 3000mSt) in 1987.
At 10000m: OG: '88- 2; WCh: '87- 5; CG: '86- 1; ECh: '86- 7 (12 at 3000m); WSG: '86- 3. Won UK 5000m, 10000m 1986. World CC: '87- 2. GP: 3rd 3000m 1987, won 5000m 1988.
Three Commonwealth 10000m records 1986–8.
Progression at 3000m/10000m: 1979- 11:15.1, 1980- 10:41.8, 1982- 9:42.3, 1983- 9:34.5, 1984- 9:49.2, 1985- 9:03.80/33:19.14, 1986- 8:46.53/ 31:41.42, 1987- 8:39.85/31:19.82, 1988- 8:42.50/

Sally Gunnell (George Herringshaw/ASP)

31:06.99. pbs: 800m: 2:05.9 '87, 1000m: 2:41.8 '87, 1500m: 4:01.38 '87, 1M: 4:26.11 '87, 2000m: 5:40.24 '87, 5000m: 15:01.08 '87.
NCAA indoor mile champion 1986, while at University of Alabama. World road bests 10km on a loop course 31:07 '87 and 30:59 '88.

Fiona MAY b.12 Dec 1969 Slough 1.81m 60kg. Club: Derby. Student at South East Derbyshire College.
At LJ: OG: '88- 6; WJ: '86- 8, '88- 1; EJ: '87- 1.
Progression at LJ: 1982- 5.34, 1983- 5.91, 1984- 6.30, 1985- 6.22/6.23w, 1986- 6.27/6.47w, 1987- 6.53/6.64w, 1988- 6.82/6.88w. pbs: 100m: 12.16 '88, HJ: 1.72 '83.
Won WAAA junior long jump 1984, intermediate 1986.

Yvonne MURRAY b.4 Oct 1964 Musselburgh. 1.70m 50kg. Edinburgh AC. Clerk.
At 3000m (1500m): OG: '88- 3; WCh: '87- 7 (h); ECh: '86- 3; CG: '82- 10 (10), '86- 3 (5); EJ: '81- 6; EI: '85- 3, '86- 2, '87- 1; ECp: '87- 2. Won UK 3000m 1985, 1987; 5000m 1983; WAAA 3000m 1988.
Commonwealth 2000m record 1986. UK junior 3000m record 1982.
Progression at 3000m: 1980- 10:11.8, 1981- 9:30.0, 1982- 9:07.77, 1983- 9:04.14, 1984- 8:58.54, 1985- 9:00.97/9:00.94i, 1986- 8:37.15, 1987- 8:42.07, 1988- 8:29.02. pbs: 800m: 2:00.80 '87, 1000m: 2:37.75 '86, 1500m: 4:01.20 '87, 1M: 4:23.08 '86, 2000m: 5:29.58 '86, 5000m: 15:50.54 '84, 10000m: 33:43.80 '85.
Surged into the lead with two and a half laps to go in the Commonwealth 3000m, and had enormous home crowd support but had to settle for the bronze medal. In the European Championships she improved her 3000m pb by 5.76 sec. in the heat and a further 12.41 sec. in the final. Improved by 8.13 in the 1988 Olympic final.

Judy OAKES b.14 Feb 1958 Lewisham, London 1.63m 81kg. Croydon H. Gymnasium assistant.
At SP: OG: 84- 4, '88- dnq 16; WCh: '83- 12, '87- 15; ECh: '86- 14; CG: '78- 3, '82- 1, '86- 2; EI: '79- 3; ECp: '77- 7, '85- 4, '87- 6. UK champion 1978, 1982, 1984–5, 1988. Won record number of WAAA titles: nine outdoor 1979–80, 1982–8 and ten indoors.
Seven UK shot records 1979–88.

Progression at SP: 1973- 11.73, 1974- 12.50, 1975- 14.22, 1976- 15.94, 1977- 16.24i, 1978- 16.74i, 1979- 16.72, 1980- 17.20, 1981- 16.88, 1982- 17.92, 1983- 18.28, 1984- 18.35i/18.28, 1985- 18.10i/18.02, 1986- 19.00, 1987- 18.73, 1988- 19.36. pbs: DT: 53.44 '88, JT: 46.66 '86.
Won world powerlifting titles at 75kg in 1981 and 82kg in 1982 and set world records at these weights.

Tessa SANDERSON b.St.Elizabeth, Jamaica 14 Mar 1956 1.68m 72kg. Wolverhampton & Bilston. Television presenter.
At JT: OG: '76- 9, '80- dnq, '84- 1, '88- dnq 21; WCh: '83- 4, '87- 4; ECh: '74- 13, '78- 2; CG: '74- 5, '78- 1, '86- 1; EJ: '73- 12; WCp: '77- 2; ECp: '75- 7, '77- 2, '79- 3, '81- 2. UK champion 1977–78 and won WAAA 1975–7, 1979–80, 1985.
Ten UK, including five Commonwealth javelin records 1976–83; also two UK & Commonwealth heptathlon records 1981.
Progression at JT: 1970- 31.86, 1971- 42.02, 1972- 43.06, 1973- 51.34, 1974- 55.04, 1975- 54.40, 1976- 57.20, 1977- 67.20, 1978- 64.00, 1979- 65.34, 1980- 69.70, 1981- 68.86, 1982- 66.00, 1983- 73.58, 1984- 69.56, 1985- 71.18, 1986- 69.80, 1987- 67.86, 1988- 71.70. pbs: 200m: 24.89 '81, 400m: 57.3 '72, 800m: 2:26.20 '81, 100mh: 13.46 '81, 400mh: 60.46 '77, HJ: 1.69 '73, LJ: 5.97 '81, SP: 13.27 '81, Hep: 6125 '81.
Injury reduced her ability in Seoul when her season's form indicated a strong medal chance.

Judy SIMPSON b.Kingston, Jamaica 14 Nov 1960 1.82m 72kg. née Livermore, married to Robin Simpson (4.60m PV). Birchfield H.
At Pen/Hep: OG: '80- 13, '84- 5 (dnq HJ), '88- dnf; WCh: '83- dnf (sf 100mh); ECh: '82- 7, '86- 3; CG: '82- 2 (5 at 100mh), '86- 1; WSG: '81- 4, '83- 3, '85- 3; ECp: '83- 5, '85- 9. WAAA champion 1982–3.
Four Commonwealth heptathlon records 1981–6.
Progression at Hep (p Pen): 1977- 3870p, 1978- 4028wp, 1979- 4908/4090p, 1980- 4357p, 1981- 5844, 1982- 6259, 1983- 6347, 1984- 6264, 1985- 6082, 1986- 6623, 1987- dnf, 1988- 5905. pbs: 200m: 24.75 '83, 400m: 53.76 '81, 800m: 2:11.49 '82, 100mh: 13.05 '86, HJ: 1.92 '83, LJ: 6.40 '84, 6.56w '86; SP: 15.14 '88, JT: 40.92 '86.
Had a marvellous European Championships in 1986 with five pbs in seven events. Former UK champion at Tae Kwan Do. Bursitis in knee caused her to miss the 1987 World Championships, and she withdrew after two events in Seoul.

Wendy SLY b.5 Nov 1959 Hampton, Middlesex 1.66m 51kg. née Smith, married to Chris Sly (2nd European Junior 1500m 1977). Hounslow and Brooks Racing Team, USA.
At 3000m: OG: '84- 2, '88- 7; WCh: '80- dnf, '83- 5, '87- 8; CG: '82- 2, '86- 8; EI: '88- 3. At 1500m: WCh: '83- 5; ECp: '83- 4; EJ: '77- 11; WSG: '81- 6. Won IAAF world road 10km 1983, UK 3000m 1983, WAAA 3000m 1987, English national CC 1981.
UK & Commonwealth records: 3000m 1982 and 1983, 1M 1984.
Progression at 3000m: 1977- 9:32.0, 1978- 9:21.8, 1980- 8:53.78, 1981- 8:56.7i, 1982- 8:46.01, 1983- 8:37.06, 1984- 8:39.47, 1986- 8:47.00, 1987- 8:43.82, 1988- 8:37.70. pbs: 400m: 57.9 '78, 800m:

2:02.89 '83, 1000m: 2:39.94 '80, 1500m: 4:04.14 '83, 1M: 4:28.07 '84, 2000m: 5:42.15 '82, 5000m: 15:21.45 '87, 10000m: 31:53.36 '88. UK road bests: 10km: 31:29 '83, 15km: 48:17 '85.
Has fared most successfully at road running in the USA. Had a knée operation in 1985.

Angela TOOBY b.24 Oct 1960 Woolhope, Hereford 1.66m 51kg. Cardiff. Teacher.
At 10000m: OG: '88- h; WCh: '87- 9; CG: '86- 3; ECh: '86- 9; ECp: '85- 3. Won UK 5000m 1984, WAAA 10000m 1988. World CC: '84- 8, '85- 6, '88- 2.
Progression at 10000m: 1984- 32:58.07, 1985- 33:04.66, 1986- 31:56.59, 1987- 31:55.30, 1988- 33:13.95. pbs: 1500m: 4:14.3 '85, 1M: 4:38.39 '87, 2000m: 5:51.2 '87, 3000m: 8:47.86 '87, 5000m: 15:13.22 '87, Mar: 3:29 '81.
Won fifth successive European Club's CC 1988. Twin sister Susan has pbs of 3000m: 8:57.17 '84, 5000m: 15:32.19 '85, 10000m: 32:49.30 '87 and was 12th in the 1988 Olympic marathon in 2:31:33.

Kirsty WADE b. 6 Aug 1962 Girvan, Scotland 1.69m 56kg. née McDermott. Blaydon H. Was at Loughborough University. Runs a fitness centre at Rowlands Gill, Tyne & Wear.
At 800m: OG: '88- h; CG: '82- 1, '86- 1; EJ: '79- 6; ECp: '85- 4; WSG: '83- 8. At 1500m: OG: '88- h; WCh: '87- 6; WI: '87- 5; ECh: '86- 7; CG: '86- 1; ECp: '87- 1. 3rd GP 800m 1987. Won WAAA 800m 1988.
UK & Commonwealth records at 800m, 1000m and 1M 1985.
Progression at 800m/1500m: 1975- 2:16.2, 1976- 2:11.1, 1977- 2:11.20, 1978- 2:07.74, 1979- 2:04.8/4:34.9, 1980- 2:05.42/4:58.49M, 1981- 2:02.88i/2:04.01/4:21.3, 1982- 2:00.56/4:22.9, 1983- 2:01.88, 1984- 2:02.34/4:14.81, 1985- 1:57.42/4:02.83, 1986- 2:00.01/4:03.74, 1987- 1:58.45/4:00.73, 1988- 2:00.61/4:05.33. pbs: 100m: 12.2 '78, 200m: 25.1 '78, 400m: 54.46 '87, 600m: 1:26.5 '85, 1000m: 2:33.70 '85, 1M: 4:19.41 '85, 2000m: 5:45.81i '87, 3000m: 8:47.7 '87.
In 1986 became the first woman ever to win the Commonwealth 800m/1500m double. Operations on both Achilles tendons January 1989.

Fatima WHITBREAD b.Hackney, London 3 Mar 1961 1.67m 77kg. Thurrock H. Born of Cypriot parents, former name Vedad, and adopted by Margaret Whitbread, UK javelin coach and ex-international (45.18m in 1959).
At JT: OG: '80- dnq, '84- 3, '88- 2; WCh: '83- 2, '87- 1; ECh: '82- 8, '86- 1; CG: '78- 6, '82- 3; EJ: '79- 1; WCp: '85- 3; ECp: '83- 1, '85- 2. WAAA champion 1981–4, 1986–7; UK champion 1981–5, 1987–8. 2nd GP 1986.
World javelin record 1986.
Progression at JT: 1975- 34.94, 1976- 41.20, 1977- 48.34, 1978- 53.88, 1979- 58.20, 1980- 60.14, 1981- 65.82, 1982- 66.98, 1983- 69.54, 1984- 71.86, 1985- 72.98, 1986- 77.44, 1987- 76.64, 1988- 70.32. pbs: 200m: 24.38 '84, SP: 15.41 '84.
Has 52 javelin throws over 70m. Produced a staggering world record at 9.18am at the 1986 European Championships. Having defeated Petra Felke in the final she then threw the world's second best ever to seal that victory. Although she suffered a shoulder injury in 1987, she won 16/17 competitions, beating Felke twice, including by a huge margin in Rome; her one loss was to Tessa Sanderson. In 1988 she had a back operation and suffered from glandular fever.

USA

Governing body: TAC- The Athletics Congress of the USA, P.O.Box 120, Indianapolis, Indiana 46206. Founded 1979, when it replaced the AAU (founded 1888) as the governing body.
National Championships first held in 1876 (men), 1923 (women)
1988 Champions: MEN
100m: Emmitt King 10.04, 200m: Larry Myricks 20.50, 400m: Tim Simon 44.92, 800m: Mark Everett 1:45.05, 1500m: Mark Deady 3:39.41, 5000m: Doug Padilla 13:42.69, 10000m: Steve Taylor 30:08.64, Mar: *, 3000mSt: Brian Diemer 8:25.69, 110mh: Roger Kingdom 13.15, 400mh: Kevin Henderson 48.68, HJ: Doug Nordquist 2.34, PV: Kory Tarpenning 5.65, LJ: Eric Metcalf 8.44, TJ: Mike Conley 17.35, SP: Ed Wade 19.41, DT: Mac Wilkins 65.28, HT: Ken Flax 78.10, JT: Dave Stephens 79.70, Dec:*, 20kmW: Tim Lewis 1:29:34, 50kmW: Carl Schueler 4:02:55.
WOMEN
100m/LJ: Sheila Echols 11.04/6.44, 200m: Gwen Torrence 22.71, 400m: Lillie Leatherwood 50.70, 800m: Joetta Clark 1:59.79, 1500m: Vicki Huber 4:07.40, 3000m: Lynn Jennings 8:55.42, 5000m: Brenda Webb 15:18.71, 10000m: Carol Urish-McClatchie 34:25.33, Mar: *, 100mh: Kim McKenzie 12.84, 400mh: Schowonda Williams 55.24, HJ: Jan Wohlschlag 1.97, TJ: Wendy Brown 13.82, SP: Connie Price 19.15, DT: Lacy Barnes 62.10, JT: Donna Mayhew 59.38, Hep: Sheila Tarr 5881w, 10kmW: Maryanne Torrellas 48:25.3.
* combined with Olympic Trials

US Olympic Trials 1988 Winners: MEN
100m/LJ: Carl Lewis 9.78w/8.76, 200m: Joe DeLoach 19.96, 400m: Butch Reynolds 43.93, 800m: Johnny Gray 1:43.96, 1500m: Jeff Atkinson 3:40.94, 5000m: Doug Padilla 13:37.86, 10000m: Bruce Bickford 29:07.35, Mar: Mark Conover 2:12:26, 3000mSt: Brian Abshire 8:23.64, 110mh:

Roger Kingdom 13.21w, 400mh: Ed Moses 47.37, HJ: Jim Howard 2.34, PV: Kory Tarpenning 5.89, TJ: Willie Banks 18.20w, SP: Randy Barnes 21.88, DT: Mac Wilkins 66.00, HT: Ken Flax 77.28, JT: Dave Stephens 79.66, Dec: Gary Kinder 8293.
WOMEN
100m/200m: Florence Griffith-Joyner 10.61/21.85, 400m: Diane Dixon 50.38, 800m: Kim Gallagher 1:58.01, 1500m/3000m: Mary Slaney 3:58.92/ 8:42.53, 10000m: Lynn Nelson 31:51.27, Mar: Margaret Groos 2:29:50, 100mh: Jackie Humphrey 12.88, 400mh: Schowanda Williams 54.93, HJ: Louise Ritter 1.99, LJ/Hep: Jackie Joyner-Kersee 7.45w/7215, SP: Ramona Pagel 18.94, DT: Connie Price 61.28, JT: Donna Mayhew 63.66.

NCAA Championships first held in 1921 (men), 1982 (women)
1988 champions: MEN
100m: Joe DeLoach 10.03, 200m: Lorenzo Daniel 19.87, 400m: Danny Everett 44.52, 800m: Paul Ereng 1:46.76, 1500m: Joe Falcon 3:38.91, 5000m: Matt Giusto 13:55.94, 10000m: John Scherer 28:50.39, 3000mSt: Karl Van Calcar 8:32.35, 110mh: James Purvis 13.58, 400mh: Kevin Young 47.85, HJ: Tom Smith 2.33, PV: Kelly Riley 5.57, LJ: Eric Metcalf 8.28w, TJ: Edrick Floreal (Can) 17.19w, SP: Mike Stulce 18.99, DT: Kari Nisula (Fin) 58.08, HT: Stefan Jonsson (Swe) 71.08, JT: Kenneth Pedersen (Den) 76.56, Dec: Mikael Olander (Swe) 8021.
WOMEN
100m: Gail Devers 10.86w, 200m: Mary Onyali (Nig) 22.70, 400m: Rochelle Stevens 51.23, 800m: Sharron Powell (Jam) 2:03.35, 1500m: Suzy Favor 4:13.91, 3000m: Vicki Huber 8:47.35, 5000m: Annette Hand 15:38.47, 10000m: Sylvia Mosqueda 32:28.57, 100mh: Lynda Tolbert 12.82, 400mh: Schowonda Williams 55.53, HJ: Amber Welty 1.92, LJ: Nena Gage 6.62w, TJ: Sheila Hudson 13.92w, SP: Jennifer Ponath 16.57, DT: Laura Levine 57.34, JT: Jill Smith 55.08, Hep: Wendy Brown 5701w.

Brian ABSHIRE b.14 Nov 1963 El Sobrante, Cal. 1.80m 57kg. Athletics West. Was at Auburn University.
At 3kmSt: OG: '88- sf; WCh: '83- h; PAm: '87- 3. Won US Olympic Trials 1988.
Progression at 3000mSt: 1985- 8:34.0, 1986- 8:26.46, 1987- 8:20.83, 1988- 8:23.64. pbs: 800m: 1:50.52 '87, 1500m: 3:42.97 '86, 1M: 3:58.62i '88, 2000m: 5:07.54i '87, 3000m: 7:41.57i '88 (US indoor record), 5000m: 13:38.8 '86.

Willie BANKS b.11 Mar 1956 Travis Air Force Base, California 1.90m 77kg. Mazda TC. Graduate of UCLA. Sports consultant.
At TJ: OG: '84- 6, '88- 6; WCh: '83- 2, '87- dnq; PAm: '79- 2, '87- 2; WCp: '79- 5, '81- 3, '85- 1; WSG: '77- 3, '79- 1. Won US Olympic Trials 1980 & 1988, TAC 1980–1, 1983, 1985.
Five US records 1981–5, including world low-altitude bests of 17.56 '81, 17.67 '85, and world record 1985. WIB 17.41 '82.
Progression at TJ: 1973- 15.02, 1974- 15.62, 1975- 16.79, 1976- 16.66/16.88w, 1977- 16.88, 1978- 17.05, 1979- 17.23/17.43w, 1980- 17.13/17.36w, 1981- 17.56, 1982- 17.41i, 1983- 17.26/17.32w, 1984- 17.39, 1985- 17.97, 1986- 17.58/17.82w, 1987- 17.49/17.60w, 1988- 17.19/18.20w. pbs: HJ: 2.08 '77, LJ: 8.11 '81.
The ebullient Banks has made the triple jump into a star event by the force of his own personality, encouraging crowds to clap him down the runway to an accelerating tempo. Married Louise Romo (pbs 800m 1:59.63 '85, 1500m 4:09.29 '84) in 1986.

Randy Barnes (George Herringshaw/ASP)

Randy BARNES b.16 Jun 1966 Charleston, W. Virginia 1.94m 132kg. New York AC. Student at Texas A&M University.
At SP: OG: '88- 2. Won US Olympic Trials 1988.
Progression at SP: 1984- 15.77, 1985- 18.56, 1986- 21.88, 1987- 20.94, 1988- 22.42. pb DT: 61.18 '86.
A spinner, from a 1985 best of 20.36m with the 12lb shot, he made a sensational start to his senior career, from 19.83 indoors to 21.08 and 21.88 in April 1986, the latter improving Randy Matson's university record (the world record 21.78 '67).

Earl BELL b.25 Aug 1955 Ancon, Panama Canal Zone 1.91m 75kg. Pacific Coast Club. Graduate of Arkansas State University.

At PV: OG: '76- 6, '84–3=, '88- 4; WCh: '87- 5=; WI: '87- 2; PAm: '75- 1. US champion 1976 and 1984. Won NCAA 1975–7, AAA 1981. 3rd GP 1987.
World record 1976 and US record 1984.
Progression at PV: 1968- 3.22, 1969- 3.50, 1970- 3.85, 1971- 4.11, 1972- 4.40, 1973- 4.72, 1974- 5.09, 1975- 5.51, 1976- 5.67, 1977- 5.60, 1978- 5.50, 1979- 5.48i, 1980- 5.60, 1981- 5.65, 1982- 5.65i, 1983- 5.65, 1984- 5.80, 1985- 5.60/5.61i, 1986- 5.81, 1987- 5.86i/5.75, 1988- 5.87.

Arthur BLAKE b.19 Aug 1966 Haines City, Florida 1.83m 75kg. Mazda TC. Student at Florida State University.
At 110mh: OG: '88- 8; WSG: '87- 2. Won PAm-J 1984.
Progression at 110mh: 1984- 13.84, 1985- 13.87/ 13.86w, 1986- 13.57/13.39w, 1987- 13.29, 1988- 13.24. pbs: 100m: 10.64 '85, 200m: 20.63 '87, 400mh: 50.66 '84.
Was fourth at TAC 1987 so missed Rome, but was consistently amongst the world's best. Was TAC and Pan-American junior champion in 1984.

John BRENNER b.4 Jan 1961 Long Beach 1.92m 127kg. Mazda TC. Was at UCLA.
At SP: WCh: '87- 3 (dnq DT). Won NCAA shot and discus 1984, TAC shot 1986–7. 3rd GP 1986.
Two US shot records 1987.
Progression at SP: 1979- 16.75, 1980- 17.10, 1981- 18.08, 1982- 19.71, 1983- 20.80, 1984- 21.92, 1985- 21.05, 1986- 21.78, 1987- 22.52, 1988- 20.52. pbs: DT: 66.62 '86, HT: 64.34 '84, JT (old): 69.86 '84.
A smashed left kneecap while weight-training curtailed his 1988 season.

Tim BRIGHT b.28 Jul 1960 Taft, Cal. 1.88m 79kg. Athletics West. Was at Abilene Christian University.
At Dec: OG: '84- 12, '88- 7; WCh: '87- dnf. At PV: WCp: '85- 3.
Progression at PV/Dec: 1978- 4.37, 1979- 4.90, 1980- 5.08i, 1981- 5.33, 1982- 5.51/7569*, 1983- 5.35i/7737, 1984- 5.50i/5.40/8106, 1985- 5.52/ 8221, 1986- 5.70/8302, 1987- 5.75/8340, 1988- 5.75/8287. pbs: 100m: 10.90 '87, 10.73w/10.7 '85, 400m: 48.72 '86, 1500m: 4:39.35 '86, 110mh: 14.16 '87, 14.09w '85, 13.9 '83; HJ: 2.11 '86, PV: 5.75 '87, LJ: 7.38 '88, 7.49w '85, SP: 14.41 '.., DT: 44.80 '84, JT: 61.60 '88.
His 5.70 pole vault at the 1988 Olympics is the best ever in decathlon competition. Was fourth in the 1988 US Trials at pole vault on the same day that he was second in the decathlon.

Mike BUNCIC b.25 Jul 1962 Fair Lawn, NJ 1.93m 115kg. New York AC. Was at University of Kentucky.
At DT: OG: '88- 10; WSG: '85- 5, '87- 5.
Progression at DT: 1981- 53.04, 1982- 58.78, 1983- 59.68, 1984- 64.74, 1985- 66.42, 1986- 65.10, 1987- 68.98, 1988- 68.92. pb SP: 19.50i '84.

James BUTLER b.21 Jun 1960 Broken Bow, Oklahoma 1.75m 66kg. Mazda TC. Graduate of Oklahoma State University. Recreation director.
At 200m: WI: '87- 5. Won US Olympic Trials 1980, NCAA 1982.
Progression at 200m: 1979- 20.96, 1980- 20.36/ 20.22w, 1981- 20.93/20.64w/20.2w, 1982- 20.23/ 20.07w, 1983- 20.32, 1984- 20.31, 1985- 20.51, 1986- 20.58, 1987- 20.36/20.35w, 1988- 20.36. pbs: 100m: 10.14/10.13w '82, 400m: 46.62 '86.

Tonie CAMPBELL b.14 Jun 1960 Los Angeles 1.88m 77kg. Bee-Fit TC. Graduate of University of Southern California.
At 110mh: OG: '84- 5, '88- 3; PAm: '83- 2; WSG: '81- 4; WCp: '85- 1. Won TAC 1984. US Olympic Trials: 3rd 1980, 2nd 1984. GP 110mh: 3rd 1985, 1st and won overall 1987. At 60mh: WI: '87- 1.
US indoor 60mh record 7.58 '84.
Progression at 110mh: 1979- 14.31, 1980- 13.44, 1981- 13.44, 1982- 13.48/13.46w, 1983- 13.32/ 13.1, 1984- 13.23/13.1, 1985- 13.27, 1986- 13.39/ 13.0/13.29w, 1987- 13.19, 1988- 13.17. pbs: 100m: 10.79 '83, 200m: 21.02 '87, 400mh: 50.28 '81.
Made great recovery after surgery to repair snapped ligaments and torn cartilege in right knee in April 1985. Missed the World Championships in 1987, through stumbling at the TAC, but gained some recompense by beating Greg Foster in Brussels to win the overall Grand Prix title.

Jerome CARTER b.25 Mar 1963 Augsburg, FRG 1.86m 74kg.
At HJ: WCh: '87- dnq; PAm: '87- 3. Won TAC 1987.
US high jump record 1988.
Progression at HJ: 1980- 2.03, 1981- 2.11i, 1983- 2.31i/2.27, 1984- 2.30, 1985- 2.30, 1986- 2.33, 1987- 2.34, 1988- 2.37.

Cletus CLARK b.20 Jan 1962 Austin, Texas 1.93m 88kg. Santa Monica TC. Graduated from University of Houston. Health club coordinator.
At 110mh: WCh: '87- h; PAm: '87- dnf; WSG: '85- 1. 2nd TAC 1985 & 1987.
Progression at 110mh: 1980- 14.13, 1981- 13.81/ 13.79w, 1982- 13.68, 1983- 13.56, 1984- 13.41/ 13.39w, 1985- 13.38, 1986- 13.57, 1987- 13.39, 1988- 13.30.

Mike CONLEY b.5 Oct 1962 Chicago 1.85m 78kg. Tyson International. University of Arkansas. Coach.
At TJ: OG: '84- 2; WCh: '83- 4, '87- 2; PAm: '87- 1; WI: '87- 1; WSG: '83- 2. At LJ: WCh: '83- 3, '87- 8; WCp: '85- 1. Won US Trials TJ 1984, NCAA LJ/TJ

1984–5 (2nd 200m 1985). Won TAC LJ 1985, TJ 1987–8; AAA TJ 1983. Won GP LJ 1985, TJ 1986 & 1988.
WIB triple jump 17.76 '87.
Progression at LJ, TJ: 1978- 5.84, 13.00; 1979- 7.14, 13.99; 1980- 6.84, 15.13; 1981- 7.46/7.56w, 15.80/15.83w; 1982- 8.19, 17.01; 1983- 8.38w/8.28, 17.23i/17.37w; 1984- 8.21/8.23w, 17.50; 1985- 8.43/8.53w, 17.71/17.72w; 1986- 8.33/8.63w, 17.69/17.84w; 1987- 8.32/8.55w, 17.87; 1988- 8.23, 17.59/17.62w. pbs: 100m: 10.36 '86, 200m: 20.21/20.12w '85, 20.0 '84.
The greatest ever LJ/TJ combined exponent. Won the NCAA double indoors and out 1984–5. In 1988 only fourth at the US Trials but won the Grand Prix TJ and was second overall.

Hollis CONWAY b.8 Jan 1967 Chicago 1.83m 66kg. Atlantic Coast Club. Student at Southwestern Louisiana University.
At HJ: OG: '88- 2; WJ: '86- 2.
Progression at TJ: 1985- 2.18, 1986- 2.29, 1987- 2.34, 1988- 2.36. pb TJ: 16.17 '87.

Hollis Conway (George Herringshaw/ASP)

Brian COOPER b.21 Aug 1965 Portsmouth, Va. 1.83m 89kg. McNeese State University.
AT LJ: WI: '87- 5; Won TAC indoor 1987. At 100m: WSG: '87- 2; 2nd GP 1988.
Progression at 100m, LJ: 1984- 7.97, 1985- 10.45, 7.95i/7.94, 1986- 10.40/10.22w, 7.90i, 1987- 10.21/10.1/10.05w, 8.22i/8.21, 1988- 10.07. pb 200m: 20.63w/20.85 '86.
Excelled indoors in 1988 with sprint pbs of 50y: 5.25, 55m: 6.05 and 60m: 6.55

Lorenzo DANIEL b.23 Mar 1966 Louisville, Georgia 1.83m 77kg. Mississippi State University.
WSG '87: 1 at 4x100mR and 4x400mR. NCAA 200m champion 1988.
World junior 200m record 1985.
Progression at 200m: 1984- 21.3, 1985- 20.07, 1986- 20.17/20.11w, 1987- 20.39/19.88w, 1988- 19.87. pbs: 100m: 10.08/10.00w '86, LJ: 7.25 '84.
Two US collegiate 200m records 1988.

Joe DELOACH b.5 Jun 1967 Bay City, Texas 1.84m 75kg. Santa Monica TC. Student at University of Houston.
At 200m: OG: '88- 1. Won US Olympic Trials 1988. Won PAm-J 100m & 200m 1984, NCAA 100m 1987.
US and world low altitude 200m record 1988.
Progression at 100m, 200m: 1983- 10.5, 21.33; 1984- 10.38/10.34w/10.0w, 20.91/20.79w; 1985- 10.21, 20.24; 1986- 10.39, 10.24; 1987- 10.21/10.10w/9.9w, 20.63; 1988- 10.03/9.90w, 19.75.
His 19.75 to win the 1988 Olympic title equalled the world low-altitude best of his training companion Carl Lewis.

Joe de Loach (George Herringshaw/ASP)

Joe DIAL b.26 Oct 1962 Marlow, Oklahoma 1.75m 68kg. Athletics West. Graduate of Oklahoma State University.
At PV: WCh: '87- dnq. Won NCAA 1984–5, TAC 1985, 1987.
Eight US pole vault records 1985–7. WIB 5.91 '86.
Progression at PV: 1976- 2.77, 1977- 3.83, 1978- 4.47, 1979- 4.94, 1980- 5.31, 1981- 5.52, 1982- 5.60, 1983- 5.62i/5.60, 1984- 5.66, 1985- 5.85, 1986- 5.90/5.91i, 1987- 5.96, 1988- 5.70.

US high school record in 1981. One of the smallest ever top-class vaulters.

Brian DIEMER b.10 Oct 1961 Grand Rapids, Michigan 1.78m 64kg. Athletics West. Graduate of University of Michigan. Landscape designer.
At 3000mSt: OG: '84- 3, '88- h; WCh: '83- sf, '87- 4. Won NCAA 1983, TAC 1988.
Progression at 3000mSt: 1981- 8:45.48, 1982- 8:37.96, 1983- 8:22.13, 1984- 8:13.16, 1985- 8:20.64, 1986- 9:09.4, 1987- 8:14.46, 1988- 8:20.44. pbs: 1500m: 3:48.05 '87, 1M: 3:59.93i '83, 2000m: 5:07.89i '87, 3000m: 7:51.95 '85, 2M: 8:30.49i '83, 3M: 13:14.60i '84, 5000m: 13:47.15 '82, 10000m: 30:08.8 '81.

Danny EVERETT b.1 Nov 1966 Van Alystine, Texas 1.86m 71kg. Santa Monica TC. Economics student at UCLA.
At 400m/R- 4x400m relay: OG: '88- 3/1R; WCh: '87- 1R. 2nd GP 1987. Won NCAA 1988.
World record 4x400m relay 1988.
Progression at 400m: 1984- 48.65, 1985- 45.76, 1986- 45.10, 1987- 44.47, 1988- 43.98. pbs: 200m: 20.23 '88, 800m: 1:49.55 '88.
Became fourth sub-44 sec. 400m runner when second at the 1988 US Olympic Trials.

Joe FALCON b.23 Jun 1966 Grand Forks, ND 1.68m 52kg. Lives in Belton, Missouri. Student at University of Arkansas.
Seven NCAA titles: 10000m and CC 1987, 1500m 1988; indoor 1500m 1988, 3000m 1987–8.
Progression at 1500m/1M: 1984- 3:52.8/4:08.24, 1985- 3:46.95, 1986- 3:45.2/4:03.19i, 1987- 3:40.81/3:56.77Mi, 1988- 3:35.84/3:52.14. pbs: 800m: 1:52.5 '84, 3000m: 7:46.57 '88, 2M: 8:35.4i '86, 5000m: 13:45.91 '87, 10000m: 28:34.3 '87/

Greg FOSTER b.4 Aug 1958 Maywood, Illinois 1.90m 84kg. World Class AC. Graduate of UCLA.
At 110mh: OG: '84- 2; WCh: '83- 1, '87- 1; PAm: '87- dnf; WCp: '81- 1. Won TAC 110mh 1981, 1983, 1986–7; NCAA 110mh 1978, 1981 and 200m 1979; US Olympic Trials 1984. 2nd GP 110mh and overall 1987. At 60mh: WI: '87- dq. Won overall Mobil indoor Grand Prix 1987.
US 110mh record 1978; WIB: 50yh: 5.88 '86; 50mh: 6.35 '85; 60mh: 7.36 '87.
Progression at 110mh: 1977- 13.54 (120yh), 1978- 13.22, 1979- 13.28/13.0, 1980- 13.27, 1981- 13.03, 1982- 13.22, 1983- 13.11, 1984- 13.15, 1985- 13.24, 1986- 13.25, 1987- 13.17/13.15w, 1988- 13.39. pbs: 100m: 10.28 '79, 200m: 20.20 '79.
Eleven successive years in the world top ten 1977–87, nine of them in the top two. Has run a record 41 (and 4 wa) sub 13.30 times, including 11 sub 13.20. His 7.36 for 60mh indoors in January 1987 was ruled to have been with a flying start. Did not make the 1988 US Olympic team, but competed at the 1988 Olympic Trials wearing a plaster cast for a compound fracture of his left forearm three weeks earlier.

Michael FRANKS b.23 Sep 1963 St Louis, Missouri 1.80m 73kg. Vaxa TC. Was at Southern Illinois University.
At 400m/R- 4x400m relay: WCh: '83- 2, '87- res1R; WSG: '87- 1; WI: '87- 3; WCp: '85- 1/1R. Won GP 400m and second overall 1985.
Progression at 400m: 1981- 48.74, 1983- 44.96, 1984- 45.20, 1985- 44.47, 1986- 45.33, 1987- 44.81, 1988- 44.82. pbs: 100m: 10.25 '84, 10.2 '87; 200m: 20.62/20.58w '84, 20.5 '87; 300m: 32.26 '85, 800m: 1:52.25 '85.
Sixth in 1987 TAC 400m, so ran only as a relay reserve at the World Championships. 19 races sub 45.50 in 1987.

Johnny GRAY b.19 Jun 1960 Los Angeles 1.93m 76kg. Santa Monica TC. Majoring in civil engineering at Cal State, Los Angeles.
At 800m: OG: '84- 7, '88- 5; WCh: '87- qf; PAm: '87- 1. Won US Olympic Trials 1988, TAC 1985, 1987.
Five US 800m records 1984–5. Two 600m world bests 1984–6. WIB 1000y 2:04.39 '86.
Progression at 800m: 1977- 2:06.0y, 1978- 1:51.8, 1979- 1:49.39, 1980- 1:47.06, 1982- 1:45.41, 1983- 1:45.50, 1984- 1:42.96, 1985- 1:42.60, 1986- 1:43.46, 1987- 1:44.09, 1988- 1:42.65. pbs: 400m: 46.3 '83, 600m: 1:12.81 '86, 1000m: 2:17.27 '84, 1500m: 3:43.98 '84, 1M: 4:07.64 '84.
Ran fastest ever 800m relay leg, 1:43.3, on 6 Apr 1985 at Tempe. Has run 11 sub 1:44 times for 800m.

Roddie HALEY b.6 Dec 1965 Texarkana, Texas 1.78m 64kg. Team Adidas. University of Arkansas.
At 400m/R- 4x400m relay: WCh: '87- 8/1R; PAm: '87- 1R. Won NCAA 1985.
WIB 500m: 61.18 (and short course 60.69 & 59.82) '86, 59.90 '87.
Progression at 400m: 1983- 48.3, 1984- 45.66, 1985- 44.67, 1986- 44.48, 1987- 44.76, 1988- 44.76. pb 200m: 20.99 '86.

Danny HARRIS b.7 Sep 1965 Torrance, Cal. 1.83m 77kg. Athletics West. Was at Iowa State University.
At 400mh: OG: '84- 2; WCh: '87- 2. Won NCAA 1984–6, TAC 1986. 2nd GP 1986.
Progression at 400mh: 1984- 48.02, 1985- 47.63, 1986- 47.82, 1987- 47.48, 1988- 47.74. pbs: 100m: 10.5 '84, 9.9w '85; 200m: 20.91 '84; 400m: 45.19 '86, 110mh: 14.00 '86.
US high school record at 35.52 for 300mh in 1983. Made his debut at 400mh on 24 Mar 1984, set world junior records in his 3rd, 4th, 6th, 9th and 11th races at the event, taking the record from 49.55 to 48.02!

Good footballer, but concentrating on track. On 4 Jun 1987 ran a pb 47.56 to end the long win streak of Edwin Moses, but as in Los Angeles had to settle for silver in Rome when he again ran a pb.

Tranel HAWKINS b.17 Sep 1962 Dayton, Ohio 1.96m 80kg. Accusplit SC. Angelo State University, Texas.
At 400mh: OG: '84- 6.
Progression at 400mh: 1983- 50.35, 1984- 48.28, 1985- 49.03, 1986- 49.56, 1987- 48.89, 1988- 48.65. pb 400m: 45.94 '87.
Recruited to Angelo State as basketball player, made remarkable progress at 400mh in 1984.

Floyd HEARD b.24 Mar 1966 West Point, Miss. 1.78m 71kg. Student at Texas A&M University.
At 200m/R- 4x100m relay: WCh: '87- 6; PAm: '87- 1; WSG: '87- 2/1R. Won TAC 1986, NCAA 1986–7.
Progression at 200m: 1983- 21.43, 1984- 21.00/20.7w, 1985- 20.61, 1986- 20.12/20.03w, 1987- 19.95, 1988- 20.50. pb 100m: 10.17 '86, 10.09w '86.
Shot to the fore in 1986 with a championship double and victory at the Goodwill Games over 200m. Was only fourth in the TAC 1987, but gained a place in Rome due to the withdrawal of Carl Lewis from the 200m.

Jim HOWARD b.11 Sep 1959 Texas City 1.96m 80kg. Mazda TC. Graduate of Texas A&M University. Chemical engineer.
At HJ: OG: '88- 10; WCp: '85- 2. Won TAC 1984. US Olympic Trials '80- 3, '88- 1. Won GP 1986.
Two US high jump records 1985–7. Three US indoor records: 2.34 '85 to 2.36 '86.
Progression at HJ: 1978- 2.11, 1979- 2.21i, 1980- 2.23, 1981- 2.26, 1982- 2.19i, 1983- 2.30, 1984- 2.33, 1985- 2.35, 1986- 2.36i/2.34, 1987- 2.36, 1988- 2.34.
Won USA/Mobil Indoor Grand Prix overall title 1985 and 1986.

Thomas JEFFERSON b.6 Aug 1962 Cleveland 1.83m 75kg. Mazda TC. Kent State University.
At 200m: OG: '84- 3. Won GP 1987. WSG: '85- 3 4x100mR.
Progression at 200m: 1980- 21.4, 1981- 21.2, 1982- 21.11, 1983- 20.90, 1984- 20.26/20.21w, 1985- 20.45, 1986- 20.36, 1987- 20.30/20.25w, 1988- 20.52/20.1. pb 100m: 10.17 '86, 10.08w '85, 10.1 '88, 9.9w '84; 300m: 31.73 '87.

Michael JOHNSON b.13 Sep 1967 1.83m 77kg. Baylor University.
Progression at 200m: 1986- 21.30, 1987- 20.41, 1988- 20.07. pbs: 100m: 10.19w '88, 400m: 45.23 '88.
Ran a 43.5 400m relay split in April 1988 before broken leg curtailed his season.

Al JOYNER b.19 Jan 1960 East St.Louis, Illinois 1.86m 77kg. World Class AC. Graduate of Arkansas State University.
At TJ: OG: '84- 1; WCh: '83- 8; WI: '85- 5. Won TAC 1984.
Progression at TJ: 1978- 15.30, 1979- 15.76/16.05w, 1980- 15.80, 1981- 16.27, 1982- 16.78i, 1983- 17.12/17.14w, 1984- 17.19/17.26w, 1985- 17.46, 1986- 16.97/17.11w, 1987- 17.53, 1988- 16.79/17.58w. pbs: 200m: 21.9 '80, 400m: 48.7 '79, 110mh: 13.41 '88, 400mh: 52.43 '83, HJ: 1.95 '78, LJ: 7.79 '87.
Won Olympic gold while sister Jackie (qv) won silver. His three best jumps have been while not qualifying for US teams! 17.50 and 17.53 qualifying for fourth at the 1987 TAC, and 17.58w for fifth at 1988 US Trials. Married Florence Griffith (qv) in October 1987.

Emmit KING b.24 Mar 1959 Hueytown, Alabama 1.75m 78kg. New Balance TC. Was at University of Alabama.
At 100m: WCh: '83- 3 (1 4x100mR), PAm: '79- 3. Won NCAA 1983, TAC 1988.
World record 4x100m relay 1983.
Progression at 100m (y 100 yards): 1977- 9.5y, 1978- 9.5y, 1979- 10.16/10.0, 1980- 10.30, 1981- 10.18/10.14w, 1982- 10.13, 1983- 10.06/10.05w, 1984- 10.18/10.17w, 1985- 10.32, 1986- 10.07/10.0, 1987- 10.38/10.19w, 1988- 10.04/9.98w. pb 200m: 20.86 '82.
Won TAC indoor 60y 1984, when he was the overall USA/Mobil Indoor Grand Prix winner, and returned to his best in 1988 when he won at 55m.

Roger KINGDOM b.26 Aug 1962 Vienna, Georgia 1.85m 91kg. Was at University of Pittsburgh.
At 110mh: OG: '84- 1, '88- 1; PAm: '83- 1. Won NCAA 1983, US Olympic Trials 1988, TAC 1985, 1988.
Progression at 110mh: 1982- 14.07, 1983- 13.44, 1984- 13.16/13.1/13.00w, 1985- 13.14, 1986- 13.40/13.39w, 1987- 13.51/13.3/13.44w, 1988- 12.97. pbs: 200m: 21.08w '84, HJ: 2.14i '84.
Became the second man to run 110m hurdles in sub-13.00, at high altitude in 1988, when he won all 25 races at 110mh. Ran the third fastest ever time, 12.98, to take the Olympic title.

Carl LEWIS b.1 Jul 1961 Birmingham, Alabama 1.88m 80kg. Santa Monica TC. Was at Houston University.
At 100m/LJ/R- 4 x100m relay: OG: '84- 1/1/1R (1 200m), '88- 1/1 (2 200m); WCh: '83- 1/1/1R, '87- 2/1/1R; PAm: LJ '79- 3, '87- 1/1R; WCp: '81- 9/1. Won TAC 100m 1981–3, 1986; 200m 1983, 1987; LJ 1981–3, 1986–7. Won PAm-J 100m & 200m 1980; NCAA 100m 1980–1, LJ 1981; 100m/200m/LJ at US Olympic Trials 1984, 100m/LJ (2nd 200m) 1988.

Two world records at 4x100mR 1983–4. Low altitude world bests at 100m (3), 200m, LJ (4). WIB: 60y: 6.02 '83, LJ: 8.49 '81, 8.56 '81, 8.79 '84. US records 100m 1987 and 1988, 200m 1983.
Progression at 100m, 200m, LJ: 1974- 5.77 LJ; 1975- 6.01 LJ; 1976- 11.1y, -, 6.93; 1977- 10.6y, -, 7.26; 1978- 10.5/9.3yw, -, 7.57/7.85w; 1979- 10.3, 20.9, 8.13; 1980- 10.21/10.16w, 20.66, 8.11/8.35w; 1981- 10.00/9.99w, 20.73, 8.62/8.73w; 1982- 10.00, 20.27, 8.76; 1983- 9.97/9.93w, 19.75, 8.79; 1984- 9.99, 19.80, 8.79i/8.71; 1985- 9.98/9.90w, 20.69/20.3w, 8.62/8.77w; 1986- 10.06/9.91w, 20.41/20.23w/20.1, 8.67w/8.37i/8.35; 1987- 10.05, 19.92, 8.66/8.76w; 1988- 9.92/9.78w, 19.79, 8.76. pb 300m: 32.18 '84.
Has won 56 successive long jump competitions 1981–8, and has 50 of the 74 long jumps in history over 28ft (8.53m). Also the most legal times: 11 sub-10.00 100m and 8 sub-20.00 200m. Emulated Jesse Owens in winning four Olympic gold medals and added two more in 1988. Sullivan Award winner 1981. Numerous awards as best athlete of the year 1982–3-4. Sister Carol was World long jump bronze medallist in 1983 and made the US Olympic teams of 1980, 1984 and 1988.

Steve LEWIS b.16 May 1969 Los Angeles 1.88m 84kg. Santa Monica TC. Student at UCLA.
At 400m/R- 4x400m relay: OG: '88- 1/1R.
Five world junior 400m records 1988. World 4x400m relay record 1988.
Progression at 400m: 1982- 54.2, 1983- 51.9, 1984- 50.8, 1985- 48.65, 1986- 46.50, 1987- 45.76, 1988- 43.87. pbs: 100m: 10.68 '88, 200m: 20.96 '88.
His sensational 1988 season, when he passed the World Junior Championships, but ran the nine fastest ever 400m times by a junior, was climaxed by his Olympic gold medals.

Jud LOGAN b.19 Jul 1959 Canton, Ohio 1.93m 125kg. Athletics West. Was at Kent State University. Fitness instructor.
At HT: OG: '84- dnq 14, '88- dnq 19; WCh: '87- 14; PAm: '87- 1; WCp: '85–3. TAC champion 1984–5, 1987.
Ten US hammer records 1984–8. Six US indoor 35lb weight records.
Progression at HT: 1979- c48.50, 1980- c56.10, 1981- 59.64, 1982- 64.06, 1983- 67.66, 1984- 74.56, 1985- 77.24, 1986- 80.88, 1987- 79.36, 1988- 81.88. pbs: SP: 16.18 '82, DT: 51.10 '81, 35lb Wt: 23.71 '86.

Walter McCOY b.15 Nov 1958 Daytona Beach, Florida 1.78m 75kg. Mazda TC. Graduate of Florida State University.
At 400m/R- 4x400m relay: WSG: '79- 3/1R, '81- 2/2R; WCp: '81- 1R, '85- 1R. 3rd US Olympic Trials 1980.
Progression at 400m: 1976- 47.8y, 1977- 46.52, 1978- 45.56, 1979- 45.16, 1980- 45.49, 1981- 44.99, 1982- 44.97, 1983- 44.97, 1984- 44.76, 1985- 45.12, 1986- 45.07, 1987- 45.16, 1988- 44.84. pbs: 200m: 20.86 '84, 20.7w '83; 300m: 32.16 '84, 800m: 1:49.80 '87.
Prodigiously consistent 400m runner, who has run 150 sub-46 sec. races 1978–88.

Antonio McKAY b.9 Feb 1964 Atlanta 1.83m 75kg. Was at Georgia Tech University.
At 400m/R- 4x400m relay: OG: '84- 3/1R, '88- resR; WCh: '87- qf/1R; WI: '87- 1. Won NCAA (indoors and out) and US Trials in 1984.
WIB: 300m: 32.52 '87, 400m: 45.79 '84, 440y: 45.45 '86 (oversized track).
Progression at 400m: 1981- 47.84y, 1982- 45.9, 1984- 44.71, 1985- 46.47i, 1986- 44.69, 1987- 44.69, 1988- 44.79. pb 200m: 20.97 '87.
Underwent surgery on a torn cartilage in his right knee in 1982, and missed the 1983 season, but stormed through first indoors and then out in 1984. Passed 1985 outdoor season. Won overall USA/Mobil indoor Grand Prix 1988. Olympic gold medal as he ran in the preliminary rounds of the 4x400m relay 1988.

Lee McNEILL b.2 Dec 1964 Lumberton, NC 1.65m 65kg. Student at East Carolina University.
At 100m/R- 4x100mR: WCh: '87- 1R; PAm: '87- 1R; WSG: '85- 3/3R.
Progression at 100m: 1983- 10.56, 1984- 10.45, 1985- 10.17/10.11w, 1986- 10.14, 1987- 10.14, 1988- 10.09/10.08w/10.0w. pb 200m: 20.60 '86.
Ran the anchor leg for the US sprint relay team which was disqualified for his faulty take-over from Calvin Smith in the heats at the 1988 Olympics.

Lee McRAE b.23 Jan 1966 Pembroke, NC 1.76m 71kg. Team Adidas. Student at University of Pittsburgh.
At 100m/R- 4x100m relay: WCh: '87- 7/1R; PAm: '87- 1/1R; WSG '87- 1/1R. Won NCAA 1986. At 60m: WI: '87- 2; won TAC indoor 60y/55m 1986–7, NCAA 55m 1986–8.
WIB 55m 6.00 '86.
Progression at 100m: 1982- 10.63, 1983- 10.53, 1984- 10.45, 1985- 10.27/10.07w, 1986- 10.11/10.02w, 1987- 10.07/10.05w, 1988- 10.11/10.05w. pb 200m: 20.50/20.44w '87.
Very fast starter, who came to the fore in the 1986 indoor season, when he won the TAC 60y in 6.06, won that title again in 1987 and NCAA 55m indoors 1986–8. Playing college football.

Sydney MAREE b.9 Sep 1956 Atteridgeville, Pretoria, S.Africa 1.80m 66kg. Puma TC. Graduate of Villanova University. Left South Africa for the USA in 1978, permanent resident from 1981 and granted

full US citizenship on 1 May 1984.
At 1500m: WCh:'83- sf; WCp: '81- 5. At 5000m: OG: '88- 5; WCh: '87- 11; 2nd GP 1985, 1987. US champion 1500m 1981, 5000m 1984, 1987. Won NCAA 1500m 1980–1, 5000m 1979. 3rd GP 1M 1988.
World 1500m record 1983. US records at 1500m, 2000m and 5000m 1985.
Progression at 1500m/1 mile, 5000m: 1976- 3:42.0/3:57.9; 1977- 3:41.2/3:57.2; 1978- 3:38.87/3:56.0, 13:50.2; 1979- 3:38.2i/3:53.7, 13:20.63; 1980- 3:38.64/3:55.9; 1981- 3:32.30/3:48.83, 13:38.3i; 1982- 3:32.12/3:48.85, 13:32.40; 1983- 3:31.24/3:50.30; 1984- 3:37.02, 13:51.31; 1985- 3:29.77/3:50.34, 13:01.15; 1986- 3:32.56/3:53.29, 13:14.62; 1987- 3:33.28/3:54.26, 13:15.07; 1988- 3:36.47/3:52.85, 13:15.85. pbs: 800m: 1:48.11 '82, 1000m: 2:19.2 '85, 2000m: 4:54.20 '85, 3000m: 7:33.37 '82, 2M: 8:24.32 '87, 10000m: 28:21.46 '80.
Third in US Olympic 1500m Trials 1984 but had to withdraw from the Olympics due to injury.

Roy MARTIN b.25 Dec 1966 Dallas 1.85m 79kg. Student at Southern Methodist University.
At 200m: OG: '88- sf. Olympic Trials '84- 4, '88- 3. World junior 200m record 1985.
Progression at 200m: 1981- 21.9, 1982- 21.69/21.33w, 1983- 21.00/20.28w, 1984- 20.28, 1985- 20.13, 1986- 20.16/19.86w, 1987- 20.45/20.0w, 1988- 20.05. pbs: 100m: 10.12/9.97w '86, 10.0 '85; 400m: 46.42 '88.

Eric METCALF b.23 Jan 1968 Seattle 1.75m 81kg. Texas University.
Won NCAA long jump 1986 in a world age 18 best. Won NCAA & TAC 1988.
Progression at LJ: 1984- 7.50, 1985- 7.75i, 1986- 8.24, 1987- 8.07/8.13w, 1988- 8.44. pbs: 100m: 10.3 '85, 200m: 21.68 '87.
Star American footballer. His father Terry Metcalf had a LJ pb of 7.87 in 1971, and became an All-Pro NFL footballer.

Dennis MITCHELL b.20 Feb 1966 Cherry Point, NC 1.75m 70kg. Team Elite. Student at University of Florida.
At 100m: OG: '88- 4. Won PAm Jnr 400m 1984.
World junior 4x100m relay record 1983.
Progression at 100m: 1982- 10.50w, 1983- 10.47/10.2, 1984- 10.47, 1985- 10.21, 1986- 10.33/10.23w, 1987- 10.12/10.11w, 1988- 10.03/9.86w. pbs: 200m: 20.29 '88, 300m: 32.22 '88, 400m: 45.26 '86.
Sister Denise was 3rd NCAA and 6th TAC in pb 51.72 at 400m in 1987.

Edwin MOSES b.31 Aug 1955 Dayton, Ohio 1.87m 77kg. Team Adidas. Graduate of Morehouse College, Atlanta, Georgia; now lives at Laguna Hills, California.
At 400mh: OG: '76- 1, '84- 1, '88- 3; WCh: '83- 1, '87- 1; WCp: '77- 1, '79- 1, '81- 1. US champion 1977, 1979, 1981, 1983, 1987; AAA champion 1979. Won US Trials 1976, 1980, 1984 and 1988.
Four world 400mh records 1976–83.
Progression at 400mh: 1975- 52.0 (440y), 1976- 47.63, 1977- 47.45, 1978- 47.94, 1979- 47.53, 1980- 47.13, 1981- 47.14, 1983- 47.02, 1984- 47.32, 1986- 47.38, 1987- 47.46, 1988- 47.37. pbs: 200m: 21.43 '77, 400m: 45.60 '77, 800m: 1:48.98 '83, 110mh: 13.64/13.5 '78.
Dominated his event for nearly a decade, and set up the greatest ever winning streak by a track athlete, 122 successive 400mh races (107 finals) between defeats by Harald Schmid in Berlin on 26 Aug 1977 and Danny Harris in Madrid on 4 Jun 1987. His loss in the 1988 Olympic final was his first ever in a championship race. Total career record at 400mh, 1975–88, is 178 wins in 187 races. 13 of the 18 times under 47.50, 45 of the 79 under 48.00. Sullivan Award winner 1983. Missed 1982 and 1985 seasons through injury.

Larry MYRICKS b.10 Mar 1956 Clinton, Mississippi 1.86m 79kg. Mazda TC. Was at Mississippi College. Company personnel recruiter.
At LJ: OG: '76- nj, '84- 4, '88- 3; WCh: '87- 3; WI: '87- 1; WCp: '79- 1. US champion 1979–80, won NCAA 1976 and 1979, AAA 1981. Won US Olympic Trials 1980, 2nd 1976 and 1984. GP: 2nd 1985, 1st 1987. At 200m: WCh: '83- h; TAC champion 1988.
WIB long jump 8.38 (twice) '80.
Progression at LJ: 1974- 7.17i, 1975- 7.83, 1976- 8.09i/8.26w, 1978- 8.05, 1979- 8.52, 1980- 8.38i, 1981- 8.45, 1982- 8.56, 1983- 8.23/8.64w, 1984- 8.59, 1985- 8.44, 1986- 8.50/8.55w, 1987- 8.66, 1988- 8.74. pbs: 100m: 10.31 '83, 200m: 20.03 '83, 400m: 46.74 '84.
Broke his leg warming up for the 1976 Olympic long jump final, but returned to Montreal to win at the 1979 World Cup with world low altitude best. Awarded 1987 World bronze medal in April 1988. Has 14 long jumps at 28ft (8.53m) or better.

Renaldo NEHEMIAH b.24 Mar 1959 Newark, NJ 1.85m 78kg. Mazda TC. Was at University of Maryland.
At 110mh: WCp: '79- 1; PAm: '79- 1. Won AAU 1978–80, NCAA 1979, AAA 1981, Olympic Trials 1980.
Three world 110m hurdles records 1979–81 and the fastest ever hand timed 110mh 1979. World junior records: 4x100mR 1977, five 110mh 1978. WIB: 1979–82 with best times: 50yh (4) 5.92 '82, 50mh (1) 6.36 '79, 60yh (5) 6.82 '82, 60mh (1) 7.62 '79.
Progression at 110mh: 1976- 14.2, 1977- 13.89/13.5, 1978- 13.23, 1979- 13.00/12.91w/12.8, 1980- 13.21, 1981- 12.93, 1986- 13.48, 1987- 13.71,

1988- 13.43. pbs: 100m: 10.24/10.1 '79, 10.18w '78; 200m: 20.37 '79, 400m: 47.5 '79, LJ: 7.61 '77.
'Skeets' Nehemiah, arguably the finest high hurdler ever, achieved his long-sought wish in 1986, when he was readmitted to international competition by the IAAF. He had turned professional footballer with the San Francisco 49ers in 1982. He had ranked number one in the world each year 1978–81.

Mark NENOW b.16 Nov 1957 Fargo, N.Dakota 1.72m 59kg. Puma TC. Accountancy degree from University of Kentucky.
At 10000m: WCh: '83- 12; PAm: '83- 3.
US 10000m record 1986. World road 10km best (point-to-point) 27:22 in 1984.
Progression at 10000m: 1978- 28:46.5, 1979- 30:55.9, 1980- 28:32.7, 1981- 28:45.86, 1982- 27:36.7, 1983- 27:52.41, 1984- 27:40.56, 1985- 27:40.85, 1986- 27:20.56, 1987- 27:48.94, 1988- 29:11.74. pbs: 3000m: 7:45.37 '87, 5000m: 13:18.54 '84, Mar: 2:14:21 '88.

Billy OLSON b.19 Jul 1958 Abilene, Texas 1.88m 73kg. Mazda TC. Graduate of Abilene Christian University.
At PV: OG: '88- 12; WCh: '83 & '87- nh; WCp: '81- 3. US champion 1981 and 1982 (tie).
US pole vault record 1982 and eleven WIB from 5.71m in 1982 to 5.93m 1986.
Progression at PV: 1975- 4.49, 1976- 4.82, 1977- 5.18, 1978- 5.45, 1979- 5.50, 1980- 5.67, 1981- 5.60, 1982- 5.74i/5.72, 1983- 5.80i/5.70, 1984- 5.80i/5.54, 1985- 5.86i/5.70, 1986- 5.93i/5.50, 1987- 5.80, 1988- 5.72.
USA/Mobil Indoor Grand Prix overall winner 1982 and 1983.

Doug PADILLA b.4 Oct 1956 Oakland, California 1.76m 60kg. Athletics West. Graduate of Brigham Young University, studying for Masters degree in electrical engineering.
At 5000m: OG: '84- 7, '88- sf; WCh: '83- 5, '87- h; WSG: '81- 1; WCp: '85- 1. US champion 1983, 1985, 1988; won US Olympic Trials 1984 & 1988. Won 5000m and overall Grand Prix 1985, 3rd 5000m 1987. At 3000m: WI: '87- 5.
US 3000m record 1983.
Progression at 5000m: 1975- 15:14.0, 1979- 13:43.0, 1980- 13:36.50, 1981- 13:33.5, 1982- 13:20.55i, 1983- 13:17.69, 1984- 13:23.56, 1985- 13:15.44, 1986- 13:42.45/13:32.64i, 1987- 13:22.34, 1988- 13:32.81. pbs: 800m: 1:48.30 '85, 1500m: 3:37.95 '83, 1M: 3:56.3i '82, 3:56.66 '83; 2000m: 4:59.78i '87, 5:03.84 '83, 3000m: 7:35.84 '83, 2M: 8:15.3i '85.
Went on Mormon mission to El Salvador 1976–8.

David PATRICK b.12 Jun 1960 Centralia, Illinois 1.83m 72kg. Stars & Stripes. Graduate of University of Tennessee. Married Sandra Farmer (JAM 400mh) 2 Jan 1988. Twin brother Mark 49.88 for 400mh in 1983.
At 800m: WCh: '83- 8. At 400mh: WCh: '87-sf; PAm: '87- 3; WSG: '81- 5 (2R), '87- 1/1R. Won TAC 400mh 1982 and 1984, 800m 1983; NCAA 400mh 1982.
Progression at 400mh: 1979- 54.26, 1980- 50.90, 1981- 49.25, 1982- 48.44, 1983- 48.05, 1984- 48.80, 1985- 49.01, 1986- 48.59, 1987- 48.56, 1988- 47.75. pbs: 400m: 47.06 '83, 800m: 1:44.70 '83.
Fourth US Trials 1988 in 47.75.

Andre PHILLIPS b.5 Sep 1959 Milwaukee 1.88m 84kg. World Class AC. Graduate of UCLA.
At 400mh: OG: '88- 1; WCh: '83- 5; WCp: '85- 1 (1 at 4x400mR). Won NCAA 1981, TAC 1985. 2nd GP 1985.

Andre Phillips (George Herringshaw/ASP)

Progression at 110mh/400mh: 1977- 53.41 (440yh), 1978- 50.67, 1979- 14.32/49.47, 1980- 14.01/49.30, 1981- 13.95/48.10, 1982- 48.45, 1983- 47.78, 1984- 48.42, 1985- 13.25/47.67, 1986- 47.51, 1987- 49.02, 1988- 13.36/13.33w/47.19. pbs: 100m: 10.4 '86, 200m: 20.51 '88, 400m: 44.71 '86.
For many years was the closest American challenger to Ed Moses and finally succeeded him as Olympic champion in 1988. Also developed into a world class high hurdler in 1985.

Jack PIERCE b.23 Sep 1962 Cherry Hill, NJ 1.85m 75kg. Karamu Flyers. Was at Morgan State University.
At 110mh: WCh: '87- 4.

Progression at 110mh: 1981- 14.18/14.09w, 1982- 13.77/13.7w, 1983- 13.61/13.6/13.44w, 1984- 13.60, 1985- 13.36, 1986- 13.55/13.4/13.53w, 1987- 13.41, 1988- 13.41. pb 200m: 20.90 '84.

Raymond PIERRE b.19 Sep 1967 Washington DC 1.80m 73kg. Student at Baylor University.
At 400m/R- 4x400m relay: WCh: '87- resR; PAm: '87- 1/1R; WSG: '87- 3/1R.
Progression at 400m: 1985- 46.7, 1986- 46.12, 1987- 44.60, 1988- 45.49. pb 200m: 21.12 '86.

Pat PORTER b.31 May 1959 Wadena, Minn. 1.83m 60kg. Athletics West. Graduate of Adams State College. Lives in Alamosa, Colorado. Disc jockey.
At 10000m: OG: '84- 15, '88- h; WSG: '87- 3; WCp: '85- 2. World CC: '83- 9, '84- 4, '86- 6, '87- 7. US CC champion 1982–8 (seven wins equals record).
Progression at 10000m: 1982- 28:26.27, 1983- 28:04.31, 1984- 27:49.5, 1985- 28:12.46, 1986- 27:57.3, 1987- 28:07.9, 1988- 27:46.80. pbs: 3000m: 7:51.0 '88, 2M: 8:43.2i '83, 5000m: 13:33.91 '88, 3000mSt: 8:58.81 '81.

Mike POWELL b.10 Nov 1963 Philadelphia 1.90m 77kg. Was at UC/Irvine then UCLA.
At LJ: OG: '88- 2; WSG: '87- 1. 3rd GP 1987.
Progression at LJ: 1982- 7.48, 1983- 8.06, 1984- 7.98/8.14w, 1985- 8.17/8.28w, 1986- 8.04/8.22w, 1987- 8.27, 1988- 8.49. pbs: 100m: 10.45 '85, 200m: 20.99 '85, HJ: 2.18 '82, TJ: 15.71 '84.
After eight successive competitions at 8.32m or more, took the Olympic silver with a pb in 1988.

Butch REYNOLDS b.8 Jun 1964 Akron, Ohio 1.93m 84kg. Athletics West. Ohio State University.
At 400m/R- 4x400m relay: OG: '88- 2/1R; WCh: '87- 3/1R. Won NCAA and TAC 1987, Olympic Trials 1988.
World records 400m and 4x400m relay 1988. WIB 500m 1:00.86 '86, 600y 1:06.87 '87 (oversized track).
Progression at 400m: 1983- 48.1, 1984- 45.47, 1986- 45.36, 1987- 44.10, 1988- 43.29. pbs 200m: 20.46 '87, 300m: 32.05 '87.
Actual name is Harry Reynolds Jr. In 1987 ran the three fastest ever low-altitude times, 44.10, 44.13 and 44.15, and in all ran 12 sub 45.00 times. In 1988 after another low-altitude record of 43.93 to win the US Trials, smashed Lee Evans's 20-year-old world record in Zürich, but was surprisingly defeated at the Olympics. Brother Jeff has 400m pb 44.98 '88.

Albert ROBINSON b.28 Nov 1964 Chicago 1.87m 84kg. Indiana TC, was at University of Indiana. Chauffeur.
Progression at 100, 200: 1982- 10.3/10.39w, 21.26; 1983- 10.57, 20.78; 1984- 10.24/10.23w, 20.07; 1985- 10.40, 20.53/20.5/20.40w; 1986- 10.22, 20.53; 1987- 10.35, 20.63/20.55w; 1988- 10.11/9.88w, 20.05.
Fourth at both 100m and 200m in 1988 US Olympic Trials. Ran on the disqualified US sprint relay team in the 1988 Olympic heats.

Darrell ROBINSON b.23 Dec 1963 Chinon, France 1.86m 66kg. Mazda TC. Dancer.
2nd TAC 400m 1982 and 1985.
World junior 400m record 1982.
Progression at 400m: 1980- 47.26, 1981- 46.8, 1982- 44.69, 1983- 45.29, 1984- 45.40, 1985- 44.71, 1986- 44.45, 1987- 45.34, 1988- 44.99. pbs: 200m: 20.48/20.41w '86, 300m: 32.17 '86.
Ran six sub-45 sec 400m races 1986.

Kevin ROBINZINE b.12 Apr 1966 Fort Worth 1.78m 64kg. Accusplit SC. Student at Southern Methodist University.
At 4x400mR: OG: '88- 1; PAm: '87- 1; WSG: '87- 1.
World record 4x400m relay 1988.
Progression at 400m: 1983- 47.4, 1984- 45.8, 1985- 45.09, 1986- 45.25, 1987- 45.04, 1988- 44.61. pb 200m: 20.85w '87.
Has three relay gold medals at major championships.

Steve SCOTT b.5 May 1956 Upland, California 1.86m 73kg. Tiger TC. Graduate of University of California at Irvine.
At 1500m: OG: '84- 10, '88- 5; WCh: '83- 2, '87- 12; PAm: '87- 3; WCp: '77- 2, '79- 4. US champion 1977–9, 1982–3, 1986. Won US Trials 1980, NCAA 1978 at 1500m and AAA 800m 1979.
US records at 1500m (2), 1 mile (4), 2000m (2), 3000m (1). WIB 2000m 4:58.6 '81. Won GP 1500m 1985, 1 mile 1986.
Progression at 1500m/1 mile: 1973- 4:25.0M, 1974- 3:56.8/4:15.0, 1975- 3:47.5/4:08.0, 1976- 3:40.43/4:05.5, 1977- 3:36.13/3:55.21, 1978- 3:36.0/3:52.93, 1979- 3:34.6/3:51.11, 1980- 3:33.33/3:52.7, 1981- 3:31.96/3:49.68, 1982- 3:32.33/3:47.69, 1983- 3:32.71/3:49.21, 1984- 3:33.46/3:52.99, 1985- 3:31.76/3:49.93, 1986- 3:33.71/3:48.73, 1987- 3:35.91/3:52.36, 1988- 3:34.9/3:50.09. pbs: 800m: 1:45.05 '82, 1000m: 2:16.40 '81, 2000m: 4:54.71 '82, 3000m: 7:36.69 '81, 5000m: 13:30.39 '87, Mar: 2:32:32 '77.
America's top miler of past decade, with prolific fast times, ran his 100th sub-four-minute mile in May 1985 and has a record eight sub 3:50 miles.

Charlie SIMPKINS b.19 Oct 1963 Aiken, S.Carolina 1.85m 70kg. Athletics West. Student at Baptist College.
At TJ: OG: '88- 5; WCh: '87- dnq; WSG: '85- 1, '87- 1. Won TAC 1986.
WIB triple jump 17.50 '86.
Progression at TJ: 1982- 15.23, 1983- 16.64, 1984-

16.76/17.18w, 1985- 17.86, 1986- 17.50i/17.42/17.91w, 1987- 17.32/17.59w, 1988- 17.29/17.93w. pbs: HJ: 2.18 '85, LJ: 7.35 '85.

Calvin SMITH b.8 Jan 1961 Bolton, Mississippi 1.78m 64kg. Vaxa TC. Was at University of Alabama.
At 200m/R- 4x100m relay: WCh: '83- 1/1R (2 at 100m), '87- 1. At 100m: OG: '84- 1R, '88- 3; WSG: '81: 2/1R; WCp: '85- 1R. Won TAC 200m 1982. Won GP 200m 1985, 2nd 1987 3rd 100m 1988
World records: 100m 1983 and twice at 4x100m relay 1983–4; low-altitude 100m best 1983.
Progression at 100m, 200m: (y 100y/220y): 1978- 9.6y, 21.5y; 1979- 10.36/10.30w, 20.7; 1980- 10.17/10.12w, 20.64; 1981- 10.21, 21.00; 1982- 10.05/9.91w, 20.31/20.20w; 1983- 9.93, 19.99; 1984- 10.11/9.94w, 20.33; 1985- 10.10, 20.14; 1986- 10.14, 20.29; 1987- 10.07, 20.10; 1988- 9.97/9.87w, 20.08. pb 400m: 46.43 '82.
Thrives off hard racing, his repeat world championships gold in 1987 was his 22nd sub 20.70 race of the year (14th sub 20.50).

Jim SPIVEY b.7 Mar 1960 Schiller Park, Illinois 1.78m 61kg. Athletics West. Graduate of Indiana University.
At 1500m: OG: '84- 5; WCh: '87- 3; PAm: '87- 2; WI: '87- 4; WSG: '81- 4. Won NCAA 1982, TAC 1984–5, 1987. GP 1M/1500m: 3rd 1986, 2nd 1987–8. At 5000m: WCh: '83- sf.
US 2000m record 1987.
Progression at 1500m/1M: 1976- 4:35.5M, 1977- 4:18.3M, 1978- 4:08.0*M, 1979- 3:44.66, 1980- 3:38.56/3:58.9i, 1981- 3:37.24/3:57.0, 1982- 3:37.34/3:55.56, 1983- 3:36.4/3:50.59, 1984- 3:34.19/3:53.88, 1985- 3:35.15/3:52.95, 1986- 3:34.4/3:49.80, 1987- 3:34.37/3:51.91, 1988- 3:31.01/3:50.57. pbs: 800m: 1:46.5 '82, 1000m: 2:16.54 '84, 2000m: 4:52.44 '87, 3000m: 7:48.61 '88, 2M: 8:24.14 '86, 5000m: 13:19.24 '83.
Has a renowned finishing kick. Enjoyed his most successful season in 1987, when he followed his world championships bronze with his first national record. Missed Olympic selection as he was fourth in the US Trials, but showed that he would have been a prime contender with his 3:31.01 in Koblenz.

Gregg TAFRALIS b.9 Apr 1958 San Francisco 1.83m 127kg. Stars & Stripes TC. Health instructor.
At SP: OG: '88- 9; WCh: '87- 13; PAm: '87- 2; WI: '87- 4.
Progression at SP: 1979- 17.63, 1980- 17.91, 1981- 18.24, 1982- 20.12, 1983- 20.20, 1984- 21.25, 1985- 21.32, 1986- 21.45, 1987- 21.32, 1988- 21.36/21.45u. pb DT: 62.38 '86.

Keith TALLEY b.28 Jan 1964 Indianapolis 1.93m 88kg. Karamu Flyers. University of Alabama.
At 110mh: WSG: '85- 3 (3 4x100mR), '87- 3. NCAA champion 1986.
Progression at 110mh: 1983- 14.1, 1984- 13.69/13.50w, 1985- 13.59/13.33w, 1986- 13.31, 1987- 13.40/13.33w, 1988- 13.50/13.36w/13.0w. pbs: 100m: 10.28/10.24w '86, 200m: 21.08 '86, LJ: 8.05 '86, 8.44w '85.

Kory TARPENNING b.27 Feb 1962 Portland 1.80m 75kg. Pacific Coast Club. PE graduate of University of Oregon.
At PV: OG: '88- 10. Won Olympic Trials and TAC 1988.
Progression at PV: 1980- 4.52, 1981- 5.03, 1982- 5.10, 1983- 5.28, 1984- 5.50, 1985- 5.65, 1986- 5.70, 1987- 5.80, 1988- 5.89.

Henry THOMAS b.10 Jul 1967 Torrance, Cal. 1.88m 77kg. Student at UCLA.
Progression at 200m, 400m: 1982- 48.57; 1983- 21.02, 48.5; 1984- 20.73, 45.82; 1985- 20.69/20.4, 45.09; 1986- 20.49, 45.42, 1987- 20.24/20.22w, 45.05; 1988- 20.18. pbs: 100m: 10.15 '87, 10.0w '85; 300m: 32.49 '85.
Brilliant high school career at Hawthorne, California.

Mike TULLY b.21 Oct 1956 Long Beach, Cal. 1.90m 86kg. Mazda TC. Graduate of UCLA.
At PV: OG: '84- 2; PAm: '83- 1, '87- 1; WCp: '77–1, '79- 1. US champion 1977, 1979, 1986; won NCAA 1978, AAA 1976 and 1979. Won US Olympic Trials 1984 (2nd= 1980).
Two world junior records 1975, unratified world pole vault best 1978; WIB: 5.59 & 5.62 '78. Three US records 1984.
Progression at PV: 1972- 3.50, 1973- 4.31, 1974- 5.10, 1975- 5.43, 1976- 5.44, 1977- 5.60, 1978- 5.71, 1979- 5.56, 1980- 5.65, 1982- 5.60, 1983- 5.49, 1984- 5.82, 1985- 5.80, 1986- 5.80, 1987- 5.83, 1988- 5.84. pb HJ: 1.93 '77.

Andrew VALMON b.1 Jan 1965 Brooklyn, NY 1.85m 76kg. Team Elite. Was at Seton Hall University.
At 4x400mR: OG: '88- resR. 2nd PAm Jnr 400m 1984.
Progression at 400m: 1983- 46.81, 1984- 45.92, 1985- 45.13, 1986- 45.61, 1987- 44.89, 1988- 44.55.
Gold medal as he ran in preliminary rounds for the US 4x400m relay team at the 1988 Olympics.

Mac WILKINS b.15 Nov 1950 Eugene, Oregon 1.93m 110kg. Reebok RC. Graduate of University of Oregon.
At DT: OG: '76- 1, '84- 2, '88- 5; WCh: '83- 10; PAm: '79- 1; WCp: '77- 2, '79- 2. US champion 1973, 1976–80, 1988. NCAA champion 1973. Won US Olympic Trials 1976, 1980, 1988.

Four world records in 1976, three in one competition at San Jose. Also US record in 1980.
Progression at DT: 1968- 44.00, 1969- 47.24, 1970- 49.84, 1971- 53.64, 1972- 59.72, 1973- 64.77, 1974- 65.14, 1975- 66.79, 1976- 70.86, 1977- 69.18, 1978- 70.48, 1979- 70.66, 1980- 70.98, 1981- 62.88, 1982- 68.20, 1983- 70.36, 1984- 70.44, 1985- 57.98, 1986- 60.36, 1987- 60.90, 1988- 67.96. pbs: SP: 21.06i '77, HT: 63.66 '77, JT: 78.44 '70.
After three years in semi-retirement came back to make his fourth Olympic team in 1988.

Kevin YOUNG b.16 Sep 1966 Los Angeles 1.93m 80kg. Santa Monica TC. Sociology student at UCLA.
At 400mh: OG: '88- 4; PAm: '87- 2. Won NCAA 1987–8.
Progression at 400mh: 1985- 51.09, 1986- 48.77, 1987- 48.15, 1988- 47.72. pbs: 400m: 45.67 '88, 800m: 1:51.42 '88, 110mh: 13.84 '86, LJ: 7.73 '86, TJ: 14.91 '85.
Uses 12 strides for first four to five hurdles and then switches to 13 strides.

Women

Evelyn ASHFORD b.15 Apr 1957 Shreveport, Louisiana 1.65m 54kg. Mazda TC. Was at UCLA. Married to basketball player Ray Washington.
At 100m/R- 4x100m relay (200m): OG: '76- 5, '84- 1/1R, '88- 2/1R; WCh: '83- dnf; PAm: '79- 1 (1); WCp: '77- 5 (4), '79- 1 (1), '81- 1 (1). US champion 100m 1977, 1979, 1981–3; 200m 1977–9, 1981, 1983. Won GP 100m 1986.
Two 100m world records 1983–4. US records at 100m (5) and 200m (4) 1977–84. WIB: 50y: 5.77 & 5.74 '83; 60y: 6.54 '82.
Progression at 100m, 200m: 1975- 11.5, 24.2; 1976- 11.21, 23.9w; 1977- 11.25, 22.62; 1978- 11.16, 22.66; 1979- 10.97, 21.83; 1980- 11.33; 1981- 10.90, 21.84; 1982- 10.93, 22.10; 1983- 10.79, 21.88; 1984- 10.76, 22.75; 1986- 10.88/10.85w, 21.97; 1987- 11.13/10.8, 22.55/21.9w; 1988- 10.81, 23.09/22.69w. pbs: 400m: 51.08 '84, 800m: 2:13.07 '84.
Her daughter, Raina Ashley Washington, was born on 30 May 1985. Has mostly concentrated on the 100m, at which with automatic timing she has run 32 sub-11 second times (including 9 wa). From 1978 to 1986 she had 27 successive finals wins at 200m. Had to withdraw from 1987 world championships through injury, having qualified at 200m, but was back at her best in 1988.

Valerie BRISCO b.6 Jul 1960 Greenwood, Miss. 1.70m 63kg. World Class AC. Formerly married to Alvin Hooks (10.36 for 100m '80), with one child (Alvin Jr.).
At 400m/R- 4x400m relay: OG: '84- 1/1R (1 at 200m), '88- 4/2R; WCh: '87- 3R. At 200m: PAm: '79- 4 (1 at 4x100mR), '87- 1R. US 400m champion 1984. 2nd GP 400m, 3rd 200m 1986.
US 200m and 400m (2) records 1984. WIB 1982–5: 220y (2), 440y, 500y 1:03.3 '85.
Progression at 200m/400m: 1977- 24.4/54.19; 1978- 23.77/53.70; 1979- 23.16/22.53w/52.08; 1980- 56.56i; 1981- 23.49/52.62; 1983- 23.10/53.61; 1984- 21.81/48.83; 1985- 21.98/49.56; 1986- 22.24/50.21, 1987- 22.28/50.00, 1988- 22.11/49.90. pb 100m: 10.99 '86.
Won three Olympic gold medals in 1984, a feat previously achieved by only three other women. Her victory celebration with coach Bob Kersee will long be remembered! USA/Mobil Indoor Grand Prix overall winner 1985.

Alice BROWN b.20 Sep 1960 Jackson, Mississippi 1.59m 59kg. Was at Cal State Northridge.
At 100m/R- 4x100m relay: OG: '84- 2/1R, '88- 1R; WCh: '83- sf, '87- sf/1R; WCp: '81- 2R. Won TAC and US Trials in 1980. Won GP 100m 1985.
WIB 60y 6.62 '81.
Progression at 100m: 1976- 12.20, 1977- 11.86, 1978- 11.64, 1979- 11.73/11.65w, 1980- 11.21/11.17w, 1981- 11.28/11.13w, 1982- 11.37, 1983- 11.08, 1984- 11.13/11.07w, 1985- 11.02, 1986- 11.06/10.84w, 1987- 11.01/10.93w, 1988- 10.92/10.88w. pbs: 200m: 22.41 '83, 400m: 53.42 '87.

Judi BROWN KING b.14 Jul 1961 Milwaukee 1.80m 66kg. Athletics West. Michigan State University.
At 400mh: OG: '84- 2; WCh: '83- sf, '87- 8; PAm: '83- 1 (1 at 4x400mR), '87- 1; WCp: '85- 2. Won NCAA 1983, TAC 1984–7 and US Trials 1984. Won GP 1985, 3rd 1987.
Five US 400mh records 1984–7.
Progression at 400mh: 1980- 59.95, 1981- 59.49, 1982- 57.80, 1983- 56.03, 1984- 54.93, 1985- 54.38, 1986- 55.20, 1987- 54.23, 1988- 55.30. pbs: 100m: 11.3 '86; 200m: 23.53 '84, 23.2 '86; 400m: 51.88 '87, 800m: 2:06.6 '85, 100mh: 13.60 '85, 13.43w '87.
Her uncle, Bill Brown won a silver medal at 800m and gold at 4x400m relay in the 1951 Pan-American Games. Married Garland King in 1984.

Gail DEVERS-ROBERTS b.19 Nov 1956 Seattle 1.62m 52kg. World Class AC. Studying sociology at UCLA.
At 100m/R- 4x100m relay: PAm: '87- 1/1R. At 100mh: OG: '88- sf. Won NCAA 100m 1988.
Two US 100mh records 1988.
Progression at 100m, 100mh: 1983- 11.69; 1984- 11.51/11.34w, 14.32; 1985- 11.19, 13.16/13.15w; 1986- 11.12/10.96w, 13.08; 1987- 10.98/10.85w, 13.28/13.1w; 1988- 10.97/10.86w, 12.61. pbs:

200m: 22.71/22.55w '87, 400m: 52.66 '87, 800m: 2:11.07 '82, 400mh: 59.26 '85, LJ: 6.77 '88, TJ: 12.97/13.31w '86.
Married Ron Roberts in June 1988.

Diane DIXON b.23 Sep 1964 Brooklyn, NY 1.65m 57kg. Was at Ohio State University. Student at Baruch College.
At 400m: OG: '84- resR, '88- 5/2R; WCh: '87- 7/3R; PAm: '87- 4/1R; WI: '85- 1. Won GP 1986, US Olympic Trials 1988.
WIB 500y 1:02.29 '86.
Progression at 400m: 1979- 56.1, 1980- 55.34, 1981- 53.91, 1982- 51.75, 1983- 51.60, 1984- 51.19, 1985- 50.29, 1986- 50.24, 1987- 50.41, 1988- 49.84. pbs: 100m: 11.27 '86, 200m: 22.53 '86, 800m: 2:09.61i '84.
USA/Mobil Indoor Grand Prix overall winner 1986. Gold medal at 1984 Olympics on 4x400m relay team, when she ran in the heats, although not the final.

Sheila ECHOLS b.2 Oct 1964 Memphis 1.63m 50kg. Athletics West. Was at Louisiana State University.
At LJ/R- 4x100m relay: OG: '88- dnq 16/1R; WCh: '87- 11; PAm: '87- 1R. Won NCAA LJ 1987, TAC 100m & LJ 1988.
Progression at 100m/LJ: 1982- 6.09w; 1983- 12.14, 5.79; 1985- 11.43/11.41w, 6.57; 1986- 11.15/10.9w, 6.69/6.89w; 1987- 11.09, 6.94; 1988- 10.83, 6.88. pb 200m: 22.90 '86.
Olympic sprint relay gold in 1988, having been fourth at 100m in the US Trials, as well as second at long jump.

Sandra FARMER-PATRICK b.18 Aug 1962 1.73m 63kg. Puma TC. Was at Cal.State University, Los Angeles.
At 400mh: OG: '84- 8; WCh: '83- h, '87- 4; CG: '82- 9; PAm: '83- 4, '87- 2; CAmG: '82- 1/3R. 2nd GP 1987. Jamaican 400mh record holder from 1977.
Progression at 400mh: 1977- 58.90, 1978- 59.8, 1979- 58.31, 1980- 58.62, 1981- 57.54, 1982- 57.4, 1983- 56.43, 1984- 56.05, 1985- 55.75, 1986- 55.89, 1987- 54.38, 1988- 54.49. pbs: 200m: 23.62 '88, 400m: 51.88 '88, 100mh: 13.75 '88.
Made great progress in 1987 with six Jamaican records. Married Dave Patrick (400mh) 2 Jan 1988 and changed nationality to US, but disqualified after winning semi at US Trials 1988.

Kim GALLAGHER b.11 Jun 1964 Philadelphia 1.65m 49kg. Los Angeles TC.
At 800m: OG: '84- 2, '88- 3 (11 1500m). Won TAC 800m and 1500m and US Trials 800m in 1984, US Trials 800m 1988.
Progression at 800m (y- 880y): 1973- 2:33.2y, 1974- 2:32.9y, 1975- 2:30.7y, 1976- 2:26.6, 1977- 2:15.9, 1978- 2:11.7, 1979- 2:07.6, 1980- 2:04.75, 1981- 2:01.82, 1982- 2:00.07, 1983- 2:05.39, 1984- 1:58.50, 1985- 2:00.85, 1986- 2:01.34, 1987- 2:00.72, 1988- 1:56.91. pbs: 400m: 52.44 '85, 1000m: 2:44.2 '84, 1500m: 4:03.29 '88, 1M: 4:36.94 '82, 3000m: 9:19.67 '81, 5000m: 16:34.7 '79.
Was just 0.01 off Mary Slaney's US 800m record when she took her second Olympic medal in 1988, and is the only double Olympic medallist at the women's 800m. Ran a 5:34.7 mile at age 9 in 1974.

Florence GRIFFITH-JOYNER b.21 Dec 1959 Los Angeles 1.70m 59kg. World Class AC. Graduate of UCLA. Married Al Joyner (qv) in October 1987. Beauty consultant.
At 200m/R- 4x100m relay: OG: '84- 2, '88- 1/1R (1 100m, 2 4x400mR); WCh: '83- 4, '87- 2/1R. WCp: '81- 2R. 3rd GP 1985. Won Olympic Trials 100m & 200m 1988, NCAA 200m 1982, 400m 1983.
World record 100m and two at 200m, four US 200m records in 1988.
Progression at 100m, 200m: 1978- 10.85yw, 24.4y; 1980- 11.51, 23.55/23.02w; 1981- 11.23, 22.81/22.61w; 1982- 11.12, 22.39/22.23w; 1983- 11.06/10.96w, 22.23; 1984- 10.99, 22.04; 1985- 11.00, 22.46; 1986- 11.42, 23.51/23.57yi; 1987- 10.96, 21.96/21.7w; 1988- 10.49, 21.34. pb 400m: 50.89 '85.
The athlete of 1988 as she produced astonishing sprinting. First captured the headlines with her amazing series of runs at the 1988 US Trials, especially her 10.49 quarter-final 100m, and then showed brilliant form at the Olympics, where she followed her sprint treble (and two world records at 200m) with a 48.07 400m relay leg. Her four medals equals the women's Olympic record. Her attire in 1988 was equally impressive. Formerly had six-inch fingernails on her left hand!

Denean HOWARD b.5 Oct 1964 Sherman, Texas 1.68m 56kg. Tyson International. Was at UCLA. Married Virgil Hill, WBA light-heavyweight boxing champion, on 10 May 1988. Word processor operator.
At 400m/R- 4x400m relay: OG: '84- resR, '88- 6/2R; WCh: '83- sf/5R, '87- sf/3R; PAm: '87- 3/1R; WSG: '87- 1/1R; WCp: '81- 4. Won TAC 1981–3.
Progression at 400m: 1978- 61.0, 1979- 53.82, 1980- 51.70, 1981- 51.65, 1982- 50.87, 1983- 50.99, 1984- 51.05, 1985- 52.19, 1986- 51.55, 1987- 50.72, 1988- 49.87. pbs: 100m: 11.70 '82, 200m: 23.25 '82, 800m: 2:07.9 '84.
With her three sisters Artra, Tina and Sherri set a US high school 4x440y relay record of 3:44.1 in 1979 for San Gorgonio HS. Denean and Sherri became, in 1980, the first sisters ever to qualify for the US team, when they were 3rd and 1st respectively at 400m; at 15 Denean was the youngest member of the team, which then boy-

cotted the Olympics. In 1984 both sisters won 4x400m relay golds, although Denean ran only in the heats. Her husband had won an Olympic silver medal in 1984, she achieved this on the relay in 1988, as did sister Sherri who ran in the heats.

Vicki HUBER b.29 May 1967 Wilmington, Delaware 1.68m 51kg. Reebok TC, student at Villanova University.
At 3000m: OG: '88- 6. NCAA champion indoors and out 1987–8 also 1M indoor 1988.
Progression at 3000m: 1986- 9:28.7, 1987- 8:54.41, 1988- 8:37.25. pbs: 800m: 2:03.89 '88, 1500m: 4:07.40 '88, 1M: 4:28.31i/4:28.77 '88, 2000m: 5:44.08 '88.

Lynn JENNINGS b.1 Jul 1960 Princeton, NJ 1.65m 50kg. Athletics West. History graduate of Princeton University. Freelance writer.
At 10000m: OG: '88- 6; WCh: '87- 6. Won TAC 3000m 1988, 10000m 1987, CC 1985, 1987–8. World CC: '86- 2, '87- 4, '88- 4.
WIB 2 miles 9:28.15 to win 1986 TAC title.
Progression at 3000m/10000m: 1979- 9:51.2, 1982- 9:35.6, 1983- 9:01.44, 1984- 9:45.4, 1985- 8:49.86/ 32:03.37, 1986- 8:53.19i, 1987- 8:49.23/31:45.43, 1988- 8:48.19/31:39.93. pbs: 800m: 2:06.54 '86, 1500m: 4:10.87 '86, 1M: 4:31.86 '85, 2000m: 5:52.62 '86, 2M: 9:28.15i '86, 5000m: 15:08.36 '86.
TAC junior 1500m champion 1977.

Jackie JOYNER-KERSEE b.3 Mar 1962 East St. Louis, Illinois 1.78m 70kg. World Class AC. UCLA, where she is now assistant basketball coach. Sister of triple jumper Al Joyner. Married coach Bobby Kersee on 11 Jan 1986.
At Hep (LJ): OG: '84- 2 (5), '88- 1 (1); WCh: '83- dnf, '87- 1 (1). Won TAC 1982, 1987; NCAA 1982–3. At LJ: Won PAm-J 1980, TAC 1987; 3rd GP 1985. Won overall Mobil Indoor GP 1987.
Four world heptathlon records 1986–8, world long jump record 1987. US records: 100mh (2) 1988, LJ (3) 1985–7, heptathlon (5) 1986–8.
Progression at LJ, Hep: 1974- 5.10, 1975- 5.22, 1976- 5.31, 1977- 5.69, 1978- 5.55/6.06w; 1979- 6.28/6.30w; 1980- 6.34/6.42w; 1981- 6.39/6.47w, 5754w; 1982- 6.44/6.61w, 6066; 1983- 6.74/6.77w, 6390; 1984- 6.81, 6579; 1985- 7.24, 6718; 1986- 7.12/7.15w, 7158; 1987- 7.45, 7128, 1988- 7.40/ 7.45w, 7291. pbs: 100m: 11.71 '86, 200m: 22.30 '87, 400m: 54.0 '83, 800m: 2:08.51 '88, 100mh: 12.61 '88; 400mh: 55.05 '85, HJ: 1.93 '88, TJ: 13.20 '85, SP: 16.84 '88, JT: 50.12 '86.
Sullivan Award winner 1986. Won both long jump and heptathlon by huge margins at the 1987 World Championships and went on to the Olympic double in 1988. Has won nine successive heptathlons 1985–8; in her career has won 17/27, with the six highest ever scores, including all five over 7000.

Francie LARRIEU-SMITH b.23 Nov 1952 Palo Alto 1.65m 48kg. Team New Balance.Was at UCLA and Cal State Long Beach.
At 10000m: OG: '88- 5: WCh: '87- 15. At 1500m: OG: '72- sf, '76- sf; WCp: '77- 2, '79- 4 (3 3000m). US champion 1500m 1970, 1972–3, 1976–7, 1979–80; 3000m 1979, 1982; 10000m 1985. French 1500m champion 1974.
US records 1971–7: 1000m (1), 1500m (6), 1M (5), 3000m (5). WIB 1973–5: 1500m (3), 1M (4), 2000m & 3000m (1), 2M (2).
Progression at 10000m: 1985- 32:18.29, 1987- 32:30.00, 1988- 31:35.52. pbs: 800m: 2:00.22 '76, 1000m: 2:38.2 '76, 1500m: 4:05.09 '76, 1M: 4:27.52 '79, 2000m: 5:47.5 '76, 3000m: 8:50.54 '85, 2M: 9:38.1i '81, 5000m: 15:15.2 '88, Mar: 2:32:31 '88.
After a 20-year top-level career she set two world veteran's records at 10000m in 1988; the latter, just .22 off Mary Slaney's US record, was her finest international performance at her fourth Olympics. Formerly married to Mark Lutz, 1976 US 200m Olympian. Her brother Ron Larrieu was a leading distance runner in the 1960s.

Lillie LEATHERWOOD b.6 Jul 1964 Tuscaloosa, Alabama 1.68m 57kg. Reebok TC. University of Alabama. Married sprinter Emmit King (WCh '83: 3rd 100m, 1st 4x100mR) 1986.
At 400m/R- 4x400m relay: OG: '84- 5/1R, '88- resR; WCh: 5/3R; WI: '87- 2; WCp: '85- 3. Won TAC 1985, 1987–8; NCAA 1986–7. 3rd GP 1986.
Progression at 400m: 1983- 53.2, 1984- 50.19, 1985- 50.43, 1986- 50.18, 1987- 49.95, 1988- 50.68. pbs: 100m: 11.74/11.42w '84, 200m: 22.38 '87, 300m: 36.15 '85.
Gold medal as a reserve in the 1988 Olympic 4x400m relay.

Lillie Leatherwood (George Herringshaw/ASP)

Pam MARSHALL b.16 Aug 1960 Hazelhurst, Michigan 1.78m 63kg. World Class AC.
At 200m: OG: '88- h; WCh: '87- 4 (8 100m, 1R); WCp: '85- 5. Won TAC 100m 1986, 200m 1986–7.
Progression at 100m, 200m: 1978- 11.78, 23.82; 1980- 11.6, 23.56/23.31w; 1981- 11.69, 23.66; 1982- 11.44, 23.34; 1984- 11.43, 22.67/22.59w; 1985- 11.15, 22.39; 1986- 11.21/10.80w/10.9, 22.12; 1987- 11.01/10.95w, 22.06/21.6w; 1988- 11.18, 21.93. pb 400m: 49.99 '86.
Pulled a muscle in heats of 1988 Olympic 200m.

LaVonna MARTIN b.18 Nov 1966 Dayton, Ohio 1.70m 66kg. Reebok TC. Student at University of Tennessee.
At 100mh: OG: '88- sf; WCh: '87- 8; PAm: '87- 1. Won PAm-J 1984, TAC and NCAA 1987.
Progression at 100mh: 1983- 13.63, 1984- 13.55, 1985- 13.10/13.02w, 1986- 12.95, 1987- 12.80, 1988- 12.85. pbs: 100m: 11.46 '86, 11.44w '88; 200m: 23.24 '87, 22.94w '85; 400m: 52.6 '85, 400mh: 57.84 '85.

Ramona PAGEL b.10 Nov 1961 Los Angeles 1.81m 86kg. née Ebert. Mazda TC. Was at Long Beach State. Fitness instructor.
At SP: OG: '84- 11, '88- dnq 15 (15 DT); WCh: '87- dnq; PAm: '87- 1; WI: '87- 6; WCp: '85- 6; WSG: '85- 3. Won TAC 1985–7, NCAA 1984, Olympic Trials 1988. 3rd GP 1987. Eight US shot records 1986–8.
Progression at SP: 1980- 14.94, 1981- 15.90, 1982- 16.25, 1983- 16.72, 1984- 17.89, 1985- 19.13, 1986- 19.03, 1987- 19.83i/19.22, 1988- 20.18. pbs: DT: 61.92 '87, JT: 45.78 '84.

Louise RITTER b.18 Feb 1958 Dallas, Texas 1.78m 60kg. Mazda TC. Graduate of Texas Woman's University. Assistant coach at SMU.
At HJ: OG: '84- 8, '88- 1; WCh: '83- 3, '87- 8=; PAm: '79- 1; WCp: '77- 4, '79- 5. US champion 1978, 1983, 1985–6, won US Olympic Trials 1980, 1984 and 1988. Won AIAW 1977–9. 2nd GP 1985, 1987. Ten US high jump records 1978–88.
Progression at HJ: 1973- 1.74, 1974- 1.78, 1975- 1.80, 1976- 1.82, 1977- 1.86, 1978- 1.90, 1979- 1.93, 1980- 1.95, 1981- 1.94, 1982- 1.93i, 1983- 2.01, 1984- 1.96i, 1985- 2.00, 1986- 1.93, 1987- 2.01, 1988- 2.03.
Switched to 'flop' in 1977, straddle best 1.82m. Equalled four-year old US record at 2.01m in Zurich, and then 'cleared' 2.04m, but bar fell off while she was celebrating on the landing pit. Won the 1988 Olympic title on a jump-off.

Joan SAMUELSON b.16 May 1957 Cape Elizabeth, Maine 1.60m 47kg. née Benoit. Athletics West. Graduate of Bowdoin College.
At Mar: OG: '84- 1. At 3000m: PAm: '83- 1. World CC: '83- 4.
Five US marathon records 1979–85, including world best in 1983. US road bests: 10M: 53:18 '86, half marathon: 1:08:34 '84.
Progression at Mar: 1979- 2:35:15, 1980- 2:31:23, 1981- 2:30:16, 1982- 2:26:11, 1983- 2:22:43, 1984- 2:24:52, 1985- 2:21:21, 1988- 2:32:40. pbs: 1500m: 4:24.0i '83, 1M: 4:36.48i '83, 3000m: 8:53.49 '83, 5000m: 15:40.42 '82, 10000m: 32:07.41 '84.
Has won eight of her thirteen marathons, climaxed by her sensational Olympic victory, made possible by winning the US Trials race just 17 days after undergoing arthroscopic surgery on her right knee. She won the 1985 Chicago marathon in a time just 15 seconds outside the world best, but did not run another marathon until third in New York 1988. Sullivan Award winner 1985. Gave birth to daughter, Abigail, 24 Oct 1987.

LaTanya SHEFFIELD b.11 Oct 1963 Los Angeles 1.65m 55kg. San Diego TC. Was at San Diego State University.
At 400mh: OG: '88- 8; WCh: '87- sf; PAm: '87- 3. Won NCAA 1985.
US 400mh record 1985.
Progression at 400mh: 1983- 59.68, 1984- 56.02, 1985- 54.66, 1986- 55.74, 1987- 55.05, 1988- 54.36. pbs: 100m: 11.76 '83, 200m: 23.88 '84, 400m: 52.64 '87, 100mh: 13.46 '86.

Mary SLANEY b.4 Aug 1958 Flemington, New Jersey 1.68m 49kg. née Decker. Athletics West. Was at University of Colorado. Married British discus thrower Richard Slaney (pb 64.66m in 1984, CG: 4th at SP and DT 1982, 6th DT 1986) on 1 Jan 1985. Formerly married to 2:09:32 marathon runner Ron Tabb.
At 3000m: OG: '84- dnf, '88- 10; WCh: '83- 1. At 1500m: OG: '88- 8; WCh: '83- 1; PAm: '79- 1. US champion at 800m 1974, 1500m 1982–3, 3000m 1983. Won US Olympic Trials at 1500m 1980, 3000m 1984, 1500m & 3000m 1988. Won GP 3000m 1985.
World records: 3 at 1M 1980–5, 1 each at 5000m and 10000m 1982. 21 US records at eight distances from 800m to 10000m. World junior records at 800m: 2:02.43 '74 and 2:02.29 '74, 1M: 4:37.4 '73. 16 WIB 1974–85, with best times: 800m (1) 2:01.8 '74, 880y (3) 1:59.7 '80, 1000y (2) 2:23.8 '78, 1500m (2) 4:00.2 '80 (oversized track), 1M (4) 4:17.55 '80 (oversized), 2000m (2) 5:34.52 '85, 3000m (1) 8:47.3 '82, 2M (1) 9:31.7 '83.
Progression at 1500m (M 1 mile)/3000m: 1971- 5:04.8M, 1972- 4:35.9, 1973- 4:37.4M, 1974- 5:00.8M, 1978- 4:08.9, 1979- 4:05.0, 1980- 3:59.43/ 8:38.73, 1982- 4:01.7/8:29.71, 1983- 3:57.12/ 8:34.62, 1984- 3:59.19/8:34.91, 1985- 3:57.24/ 8:25.83, 1986- 4:42.64M, 1988- 3:58.92/8:34.69. pbs: 400m: 53.84 '73, 800m: 1:56.90 '85, 1000m: 2:34.8 '85, 1M: 4:16.71 '85, 2000m: 5:32.7 '84,

5000m: 15:06.53 '85, 10000m: 31:35.3 '82.
USA/Mobil Indoor Grand Prix overall winner 1982. Decker became the youngest ever US international at 14 years 224 days when she ran 1M indoors against the USSR in 1973. Later that year she won at 800m v USSR, and she set a world indoor best for 880y in 1974. For the next four years she competed rarely due to a series of injuries, but overcame these to dominate US distance running, and score double success at the 1983 world championships. Seeking to add Olympic success, she fell in the 3000m final in Los Angeles. Came back in invincible form in 1985 and won the women's overall Grand Prix title. Gave birth to a daughter, Ashley Lynn, on 30 May 1986.

Gwen Torrence (George Gerringshaw/ASP)

Gwen TORRENCE b.12 Jun 1965 Atlanta 1.70m 57kg. Athletics West. University of Georgia, taking degree in family and child development.
At 100m/200m/R- 4x100m relay: OG: '88- 5/6, WCh: '87- 5; PAm: '87- 1/1R; WSG: '85- 1R, '87- 1/1/1R. Won TAC 200m 1988, NCAA 100m and 200m 1987. NCAA indoor 55m champion 1986–7 (6.56 WIB '87).
Progression at 100m, 200m: 1982- 24.2; 1983- 11.92, 24.34/23.9y; 1984- 11.41/11.37w, 23.54; 1985- 11.40/11.11w, 22.96; 1986- 11.30/11.01w, 22.53; 1987- 11.09/11.08w, 22.40/22.33w/22.2w, 1988- 10.91/10.78w/22.02. pb 400m: 51.1 '88, 51.60 '87.
Unbeaten in 20 finals and 20 heats at indoor short sprints from 31 Jan 1986 to her tie with Evelyn Ashford in the TAC 55m on 26 Feb 1988.

Delisa WALTON-FLOYD b.28 Jul 1961 Chicago 1.73m 58kg. Houston TC. Was at University of Tennessee. Nurse.
At 800m: OG: '88- 5; WCh: '87- sf; PAm: '87- 2. Won TAC and NCAA 1982. At 400m: WSG: '81- 5/2R.
Progression at 800m: 1978- 2:08.22, 1979- 2:10.7y, 1980- 2:01.93, 1981- 2:01.37, 1982- 2:00.67, 1983- 2:03.10yi, 1984- 2:00.94, 1985- 2:00.17, 1986- 2:00.00, 1987- 1:58.70, 1988- 1:57.80. pbs: 400m: 51.21 '87, 600m: 1:25.90 '88.
Married to Stanley Floyd (100m 10.03 '82, AAU champion 1980, NCAA 1980 and 1982), with daughter Ebony, born 1983.

Diane WILLIAMS b.14 Dec 1961 Chicago 1.63m 54kg. Puma TC. Was at Cal State University, Los Angeles and Michigan State University.
At 100m/R- 4x100m relay: WCh: '83- 3, '87- 4/1R; PAm: '87- 2. Won TAC 1987.
Progression at 100m: 1980- 11.37/11.32w, 1982- 11.14/11.13w, 1983- 10.94, 1984- 11.04, 1985- 11.23, 1986- 11.18/10.92w, 1987- 11.07/10.90w, 1988- 10.86. pbs: 200m: 22.60 '86, 400m: 55.00 '86.

Schowanda WILLIAMS b.3 Dec 1966 Winter Haven, Florida. 1.63m 50kg. Louisiana State University.
At 400mh: OG: '88- sf; WCh: '87- 7. Won NCAA, TAC and Olympic Trials 1988, only the third women ever to do this triple.
Progression at 400mh: 1982- 61.7y, 1983- 61.50, 1984- 59.2, 1985- 55.65, 1986- 55.38, 1987- 54.82, 1988- 54.93. pbs: 400m: 52.71 '86, 100mh: 13.32/13.25w '88, 13.1 '86.

Dannette YOUNG b.6 Oct 1964 Jacksonville 1.68m 55kg. Reebok TC. Was at Alabama A&M. Sales clerk.
At 200m/R- 4x100m relay: OG: '88- resR; WSG: '87- 3/1R. 2nd GP 1988.
Progression at 200m: 1982- 24.0y, 1983- 23.76, 1984- 23.38/23.32w, 1985- 22.92/22.85w, 1986- 23.12/22.84w, 1987- 22.72, 1988- 22.23/22.21w. pbs: 100m: 11.10 '88, 400m: 52.46 '88.
Gold medal at 4x100m relay at 1988 Olympics as she ran in the heats.

USSR

Governing body: Light Athletic Federation of the USSR, Luzhnetskaya Naberezhnaya 8, 119270 Moscow.
National Championships first held in 1920 (men), 1922 (women)
1988 Champions: MEN
100m: Andrey Razin 10.27, 200m: Vladimir Krylov 20.62, 400m: Aleksandr Kurochkin 46.00, 800m: Andrey Sudnik 1:46.02, 1500m: Sergey Afanasyev

3:37.39, 5000m: Vitaliy Tishchenko 13:41.42, 10000m: Sergey Smirnov 28:27.20, Mar: Yakov Tolstikov 2:14:29, 3000mSt: Gatis Deksnis 8:33.42, 110mh: Vladimir Shishkin 13.42, 400mh: Aleksandr Vasilyev 49.00, HJ: Gennadiy Avdeyenko 2.36, PV: Grigoriy Yegorov 5.85, LJ: Leonid Voloshin 8.46, TJ: Aleksandr Kovalenko 17.47, SP: Sergey Gavryushin 21.39, DT: Yuriy Dumchev 66.04, HT: Juri Tamm 82.34, JT: Viktor Yevsyukov 79.80, Dec: Aleksandr Apaychev 8424, 20kmW: Mikhail Shchennikov 1:19:08, 50kmW: Vyacheslav Ivanenko 3:44:01.

WOMEN

100m: Marina Zhirova 11.14, 200m: Lyudmila Kondratyeva 22.65, 400m: Olga Nazarova 50.09, 800m: Nadezhda Olizarenko 1:56.03, 1500m: Laima Baikauskaite 4:00.66, 3000m: Natalya Artyomova 8:42.19, 10000m: Lyudmila Matveyeva 31:38.02, Mar: Tatyana Polovinskaya 2:28:02, 100mh: Natalya Grigoryeva 12.46w, 400mh: Tatyana Ledovskaya 55.10, HJ: Yelena Rodina 1.94, LJ: Inessa Kravets 7.23, SP: Natalya Lisovskaya 22.55, DT: Galina Murashova 67.72, JT: Irina Kostyuchenkova 66.82, Hep: Remigia Zablovskaite 6566, 10kmW: Yelena Nikolayeva 43:36.41.

Note: USSR clubs are shown in the biographies after height and weight. Based on the major cities, they have affiliations, abbreviated as follows: Dyn – Dynamo, SA – Soviet Army, Sp – Spartak, TR – Trudovye Reservye.

Vitaliy ALISEVICH b.15 Jun 1967 1.86m 112kg. Minsk SA.
At HT: WJ: '86- 1.
Progression at HT: 1983- 61.46, 1984- 62.94, 1985- 70.20, 1986- 73.22, 1987- 78.60, 1988- 82.16.

Aleksandr APAYCHEV b.6 May 1961 Kirov 1.87m 92kg. Kirov TR. Sports student.
At Dec: OG: '88- dnf; ECh: '86- 5; ECp: '85- 6. USSR champion 1988.
Two USSR decathlon records 1984.
Progression at Dec: 1978- 7028*, 1979- 7387, 1980- 7576, 1981- 7962, 1982- 8104, 1983- 8270, 1984- 8709, 1985- 8112, 1986- 8244, 1988- 8424.
pbs: 100m: 10.87 '84, 400m: 48.40 '84, 1500m: 4:18.78 '84, 110mh: 13.93 '84, HJ: 2.00 '84, PV: 5.00i '84, LJ: 7.61 '83, SP: 16.30i '86, 16.20 '84, DT: 48.72 '84, JT: 76.52 '81, new: 68.62 '86.

Igor ASTAPKOVICH b.4 Jan 1963 Minsk 1.91m 118kg.
At HT: WSG: '87- 1. 2nd GP 1988.
Progression at HT: 1982- 68.08, 1983- 75.02, 1984- 79.98, 1985- 80.16, 1986- 80.68, 1987- 82.96, 1988- 83.44.

Gennadiy AVDEYENKO b.4 Nov 1963 Odessa 2.02m 82kg. Odessa SA. Refrigeration mechanic.
At HJ: OG: '88- 1; WCh: '83- 1, '87- 2=; WI: '87- 2; EI: '87- 3. USSR champion 1987.
Progression at HJ: 1980- 2.06, 1981- 2.21, 1982-

Gennadiy Avdeyenko (George Herringshaw/ASP)

2.22, 1983- 2.32, 1984- 2.31, 1985- 2.35, 1986- 2.35, 1987- 2.38, 1988- 2.38. pb TJ: 15.57 '80.
Perhaps the most surprising world champion of 1983, he was a double world silver medallist in 1987 and became Olympic champion in 1988. Married to Lyudmila Avdeyenko (qv).

Maris BRUZIKS b.25 Aug 1962 Stuchka, Latvia 1.86m 70kg. SKA Riga. Sports student.
At TJ: ECh: '86- 2; EI: '86- 1; WI: '87- 7; WSG: '87- 3. WIB triple jump 17.54 '86.
Progression at TJ: 1977- 11.60, 1978- 13.57, 1979- 14.60, 1980- 15.43, 1981- 15.48i, 1982- 15.55, 1983- 16.47, 1984- 17.15, 1985- 17.38, 1986- 17.54i/17.33, 1987- 16.97i/16.90, 1988- 17.56. pbs: HJ: 2.15, LJ: 7.91 '84.

Viktor BRYZGIN b.22 Aug 1962 Voroshilovgrad 1.80m 78kg. Voroshilovgard Dyn. Student.
At 100m/R- 4x100m relay: OG: '88- 1R; WCh: '83- qf/3R, '87- 6/2R; ECh: '86- 9/1R; ECp: '83- 4, '87- 4/1R. USSR champion 1986.
Progression at 100m: 1978- 10.6, 1979- 10.6, 1980- 11.04, 1981- 10.64, 1982- 10.54/10.2, 1983- 10.20, 1984- 10.18/10.0, 1985- 10.24/10.0, 1986- 10.03?w/10.11, 1987- 10.12, 1988- 10.20.
Has looked very good at times, less so at others, as in the contrast between heats and final of the 1986 European 100m. Married to Olga Bryzgina (qv); they were the only husband and wife gold medallists of the 1988 Olympic athletics events.

Sergey BUBKA b.4 Dec 1963 Voroshilovgrad, Ukraine 1.83m 80kg. Donyetsk Sp. Student.
At PV: OG: '88- 1; WCh: '83- 1, '87- 1; WI: '85- 1, '87- 1; ECh: '86- 1; EJ: '81- 7=; EI: '85- 1; WCp: '85- 1; ECp: '85- 1. USSR champion 1984. Won GP 1985, 1987 (3rd overall).
Nine world pole vault records 1984–8, including the world's first six-metre jump. Nine WIB from 5.81 '84 to 5.97 '87.
Progression at PV: 1975- 2.70, 1976- 3.50, 1977- 3.60, 1978- 4.40, 1979- 4.80, 1980- 5.10, 1981- 5.40, 1982- 5.55, 1983- 5.72, 1984- 5.94, 1985- 6.00, 1986- 6.01, 1987- 6.03, 1988- 6.06.
The surprise world champion in 1983 has gone on to dominate the world of pole vaulting, and has not been beaten in a championships since then. Has the speed and strength to manage a very high hold on the pole. By the end of 1988 had jumped 5.90m or higher in 20 competitions.

Vasiliy BUBKA b.26 Nov 1960 Voroshilovgrad, Ukraine 1.84m 76kg. Donyetsk Sp. Teacher. Elder brother of Sergey.
At PV: ECh: '86- 2; WI: '85- 3. USSR champion 1985.
Progression at PV: 1975- 3.25, 1976- 4.20, 1977- 4.90, 1978- 5.05, 1979- 5.20i, 1980- 5.20, 1981- 5.30, 1982- 5.50, 1983- 5.60i, 1984- 5.70i, 1985- 5.85, 1986- 5.80, 1987- 5.75, 1988- 5.86.

Yuriy DUMCHEV b.5 Aug 1958 Rossosh, Voronezh 2.00m 128kg. Moskva SA.
At DT: OG: '80- 5, '88- 4; WCh: '83- 17; EJ: '77- 1. USSR champion 1980–1.
World discus record 1983. Three USSR records 1980–3.
Progression at DT: 1976- 53.57, 1977- 58.32, 1978- 59.28, 1979- 61.64, 1980- 68.16, 1981- 66.42, 1982- 69.16, 1983- 71.86, 1984- 67.42, 1985- 66.18, 1986- 63.14, 1987- 64.42, 1988- 70.30. pb SP: 18.40 '82.

Robert EMMIYAN b.16 Feb 1965 Leninakan, Armenia 1.78m 69kg. Leninaken Sp. Soviet army instructor.
At LJ: WCh: '87- 2; WI: '87- 4; ECh: '86- 1; EJ: '83- 3; EI: '84- 3, '86- 1, '87- 1; WSG: '85- 2; WCp: '85- 2; ECp: '87- 1. 2nd GP 1987.
Two European long jump records 1986–7, European junior record 1984, European indoor records 8.34 '86, 8.49 '87.
Progression at LJ: 1980- 7.70, 1981- 7.77, 1982- 7.91, 1983- 8.01, 1984- 8.13, 1985- 8.30/8.38w, 1986- 8.61, 1987- 8.86, 1988- 8.00i/7.96. pb TJ: 14.71i '87.
Has come through as a major talent. Following his high altitude 8.86m, fared well with his silver medal in Rome at his first meeting with Carl Lewis.

Rodion GATAULLIN b.23 Nov 1965 Tashkent 1.89m 78kg. Tashkent Sp. Medical student.
At PV: OG: '88- 2; WCh: '87- 3; ECh: '86- nh; EI: '88- 1; EJ: '83- 1; WSG: '85- 1, '87- 2. USSR champion 1985.
World junior pole vault record 1984.
Progression at PV: 1978 - 3.10, 1979- 3.80, 1980- 4.20, 1981- 4.80, 1982- 5.20, 1983- 5.55, 1984- 5.65, 1985- 5.75, 1986- 5.85, 1987- 5.90, 1988- 5.95. pb 110mh: 14.4.

Sergey GAVRYUSHIN b.27 Jun 1959 Karaganda 1.92m 125kg. Moskva TR. Teacher.
At SP: WCh: '87- 8; ECh: '82- 8; WSG: '85- 3. USSR champion 1988.
Progression at SP: 1975- 15.20, 1976- 16.97, 1977- 17.52, 1978- 17.97, 1980- 18.89, 1981- 19.99, 1982- 21.03, 1983- 20.97, 1984- 21.60, 1985- 20.96, 1986- 22.10, 1987- 21.85, 1988- 21.39.

Vladimir GRAUDYN b.26 Aug 1963 1.82m 70kg. Minsk Sp. Mechanic.
At 800m: WCh: '87- sf; WI: '87- 2; ECh: '86- sf; EI: '87- 2. At 1500m: ECp: '87- 4.
Progression at 800m: 1984- 1:48.26, 1986- 1:45.80, 1987- 1:45.19, 1988- 1:44.10. pbs: 1000m: 2:17.66 '86, 1500m: 3:42.64 '88.

Vyacheslav IVANENKO b.3 Mar 1961 Kemerovo 1.64m 56kg. Kemerovo Sp. Teacher.
At 50kmW: OG: '88- 1; WCh: '87- 3; ECh: '86- 2; LT: '87- 4. USSR champion 20kmW 1987, 50kmW 1988.
USSR 50km walk record 1988.
Progression at 20kmW/50kmW: 1985- 1:22:36, 1986- 1:22:18/3:41:54, 1987- 1:21:28/3:44:02, 1988- 3:38:29. pb 10kmW: 40:57.0 '87.
After following home GDR walkers at the major events of 1986–7, he won the Olympic title in the second fastest ever time.

Ravil KASHAPOV b.15 Nov 1956 1.72m 61kg. Naberezhyne Chelny Dyn.
At Mar: OG: '88- 10; WCh: '87- 8; ECp: '88- 1. USSR champion 1987.
Progression at Mar: 1986- 2:17:10, 1987- 2:12:43, 1988- 2:11:19. pbs: 1500m: 3:46.0, 5000m: 13:46.13 '88, 10000m: 27:56.75 '88.
Ran marathon best when third at Fukuoka 1988.

Igor KAZANOV b.24 Sep 1963 1.86m 81kg. Dnepropetroksk Dyn.
At 110mh: WCh: '87- 5; ECh: '86- sf; ECp: '87- 1. USSR champion 1987.
Progression at 110mh: 1980- 14.2, 1981- 14.38, 1982- 14.1/14.53, 1983- 14.08/13.7, 1984- 13.59, 1985- 13.3/13.62, 1986- 13.42/13.14w, 1987- 13.38/13.3, 1988- 13.38/13.1.

Vaclavas KIDIKAS b.17 Oct 1961 Klaipeda, Lithuania 1.97m 110kg. Kaunas Dyn. Vetinary student.
At DT: OG: '88- dnq 13; WCh: '87- 8; ECh: '86- 3; WSG: '85- 2, '87- 2; ECp: '87- 1.
Progression at DT: 1978- 33.24, 1979- 41.42, 1980- 47.86, 1981- 55.42, 1982- 59.80, 1983- 61.42, 1984- 62.60, 1985- 67.34, 1986- 67.00, 1987- 66.80, 1988- 68.44.

Aleksandr KOVALENKO b.8 May 1963 Bobruysk 1.79m 76kg. Minsk SA.
At TJ: OG: '88- 3; WCh: '87- 4. USSR champion 1987–8.
Progression at TJ: 1979- 12.80, 1980- 13.99, 1981- 15.05, 1982- 15.40, 1983- 15.67, 1984- 16.40, 1985- 16.58, 1986- 17.25, 1987- 17.77, 1988- 17.47. pbs: 100m: 10.4, LJ: 8.06 '87.

Vladimir KRYLOV b.26 Feb 1964 Sengiley 1.84m 73kg. Ulyanovsk Dyn. Student at Ulyanovsk Institute of Electromechanics.
At 200m/R- 4x100mR: WCh: '87- 5/2R; ECh: '86- 1 (3 4x400mR); EI: '87- 2. At 400m: WCp: '85- 5; ECp: '85- 2. At 100m: OG: '88- sf/1R; ECp: '87- 1R. USSR champion 400m 1984–5, 200m 1988.
Progression at 200m/400m: 1982- 20.9, 1983- 21.76/48.52, 1984- 46.05, 1985- 20.61/45.22, 1986- 20.50/45.20, 1987- 20.23/45.3, 1988- 20.62. pb 100m: 10.13 '88, 9.9 '85.
Best ever all-round Soviet sprinter. After achieving prominence at 400m in 1985 has concentrated on 100m/200m.

Igor LAPSHIN b.8 Aug 1963 1.88m 71kg. Minsk Sp.
At TJ: OG: '88- 2.
Progression at TJ: 1981- 15.68, 1984- 16.56, 1985- 17.17, 1986- 17.20, 1987- 17.11, 1988- 17.69. pb LJ: 7.98 '88.

Sergey LAYEVSKIY b.3 Mar 1959 Dnepropetrovsk 1.84m 72kg. Dnepropetrovsk Sp. Metallurgy engineer.
At LJ: WCh: '87- 9; ECh: '86- 2; EI: '85- 3; ECp: '85- 1. USSR champion 1984–7. 3rd GP 1985.
Progression at LJ: 1977- 7.18, 1978- 7.22, 1979- 7.55, 1980- 7.59, 1981- 7.91, 1982- 8.13, 1983- 7.87, 1984- 8.32, 1985- 8.20, 1986- 8.20, 1987- 8.32, 1988- 8.35. pbs: 100m: 10.56 '86, 400m: 47.8.

Sergey LITVINOV b.23 Jan 1958 Tsukarov, Krasnodar 1.80m 106kg. Rostov-on-Don SA. Teacher.
At HT: OG: '80- 2, '88- 1; WCh: '83- 1, '87- 1; ECh: '82- 3, '86- 2; EJ: '75- 3, '77- 2; WCp: '79- 1; ECp: '79- 2, '83- 1, '87- 1. USSR champion 1979 and 1983. 2nd GP 1986.
Three world hammer records, in 1980, 1982 and 1983; two world junior records 1976–7.
Progression at HT: 1974- 60.68, 1975- 65.32, 1976- 72.38, 1977- 74.32, 1978- 76.22, 1979- 79.82, 1980- 81.66, 1981- 79.60, 1982- 83.98, 1983- 84.14, 1984- 85.20, 1985- 76.94, 1986- 86.04, 1987- 83.48, 1988- 84.80.
Only two men have thrown the hammer more than 85m, yet Litvinov has twice thrown over this distance and lost to Yuriy Sedykh: at Cork in 1984 and at the 1986 European Championships, when he opened with 85.74. Beat his great rival to gain the Olympic title.

Vyacheslav LYKHO b.16 Jan 1967 1.96m 120kg. Moskva SA.
At SP: WCh: '87- 9; WJ: '86- 2.
Progression at SP: 1985- 16.40i/15.83, 1986- 19.53i/19.34, 1987- 21.20, 1988- 20.96.

Sergey MALCHENKO b.2 Nov 1963 Tula 1.91m 74kg. Moskva SA. Sports instructor.
At HJ: WCh: '87- nh; ECh: '86- 2.
Progression at HJ: 1979- 1.95, 1980- 2.06, 1981- 2.12, 1982- 2.15, 1983- 2.29, 1984- 2.25, 1985- 2.31, 1986- 2.33, 1987- 2.30, 1988- 2.38.

Viktor MOSTOVIK b.7 Jan 1963 Moldavia 1.79m 58kg. Student. Tiraspol Dyn.
At 20kmW: WCh: '87- 4; ECh: '86- 4; LT: '85- 3,

'87- 2; WSG: '85- 1. EJ: '81- 3 at 10kmW. USSR champion 1985.
Progression at 20kmW: 1982- 1:26:04, 1983- 1:23:57, 1984- 1:22:57, 1985- 1:21:33, 1986- 1:21:52, 1987- 1:19:32, 1988- 1:19:47. pb 10kmW: 39:56.0 '85.

Vladimir MURAVYOV b.30 Sep 1959 Karaganda 1.78m 74kg. Karaganda TR. Serviceman.
At 200m/R- 4x100mR: OG: '88- 1R; WCh: '83- sf/3R; ECh: '82- 7; WSG: '81- 5/2R, '83- 4; WCp: '81- 4R, '85- 6/3R; ECp: '83- 6. At 100m: OG: 6/1R; WCh: '87- qf/2R; ECh: '82- sf, '86- sf/1R; ECp: '81- 5/2R, '85- 2, '87- 1R. At 50m: EI: '81- 2. USSR champion 100m 1985 and 1987, 200m 1983.
Progression at 100m: 1984- 12.3, 1975- 11.1, 1976- 10.6, 1977- 10.64/10.4, 1978- 10.4, 1979- 10.44/10.3, 1980- 10.34, 1981- 10.36, 1982- 10.48, 1983- 10.36, 1984- 10.23, 1985- 10.22, 1986- 10.19?w/10.20, 1987- 10.26, 1988- 10.29. pb 200m: 20.34 '84.
A great third leg sprint relay runner. The only man apart from Frank Wykoff (1928–36) to win two Olympic sprint relay gold medals.

Igor NIKULIN b.14 Aug 1960 Moscow 1.91m 106kg. Leningrad SA. Teacher.
At HT: WCh: '83- 4, '87- 5; ECh: '82- 2, '86- 3; EJ: '79- 1; WSG: '81- 3, '85- 3. USSR champion 1981 and 1984. 3rd GP 1988.
Progression at HT: 1975- 48.50, 1976- 58.14, 1977- 63.40, 1978- 71.60, 1979- 75.20, 1980- 80.34, 1981- 77.50, 1982- 83.54, 1983- 82.92, 1984- 82.56, 1985- 78.88, 1986- 82.34, 1987- 82.00, 1988- 83.78.
He became the youngest ever 80m hammer thrower in 1980. His father Yuriy was fourth in the 1964 Olympic hammer.

Vladimir OCHKAN b.13 Jan 1968 Poltava 1.81m 70kg. Poltava SA. Economics student.
At LJ: EJ: '87–1. European junior LJ record 1987.
Progression at LJ: 1980- 5.10, 1981- 5.81, 1982- 6.04, 1983- 6.64, 1984- 7.18, 1985- 7.67, 1986- 7.72, 1987- 8.24, 1988- 8.34.

Vladimir OVCHINNIKOV b.2 Aug 1970 1.90m 86kg. Volgograd TR.
At JT: OG: '88- 7; WJ: '88- EJ: '87- 7.
Two world junior javelin records 1988.
Progression at JT: 1987- 72.80, 1988- 80.26.

Igor PAKLIN b.15 Jun 1963 Frunze, Kirghizia 1.93m 71kg. Frunze Sp. Student at Polytechnic Institute, Frunze.
At HJ: OG: '88- 7=, WCh: '83- 4=, '87- 2=; WI: '87- 1; ECh: '86- 1; EJ: '81- 4; WCp: '85- 4; ECp: '85- 3, '87- 1; WSG: '83- 1, '85- 1. USSR champion 1985. 3rd GP 1986.
World high jump record 1985; WIB 2.36 '84.
Progression at HJ: 1978- 1.85, 1979- 2.06, 1980- 2.18, 1981- 2.21, 1982- 2.24, 1983- 2.33, 1984- 2.36i/2.30, 1985- 2.41, 1986- 2.38, 1987- 2.38, 1988- 2.36.
Following his world record at the end of the 1985 season, has become the world's most consistent jumper in the major events.

Aleksey PERSHIN b.20 Feb 1962 Kzyl-Orda 1.73m 67kg. Kuibyshev Sp.
At 20kmW: OG: '88- 14; ECh: '86- 7.
European 20km walk record 1988.
Progression at 20kmW: 1982- 1:27:12, 1984- 1:24:04, 1985- 1:22:54, 1986- 1:23:29, 1987- 1:21:50, 1988- 1:19:22.5t.

Aleksandr POTASHOV b.12 Mar 1962 1.87m 80kg. Vitebsk SA.
At 50kmW: OG: '88- 4; LT: '87- 7. At 10kmW: '81- 2.
Progression at 50kmW: 1983- 3:56:54, 1984- 4:00:46, 1985- 3:54:40, 1986- 3:51:17, 1987- 3:46:28, 1988- 3:41:00. pbs: 10kmWt: 40:02.0 '85, 20kmW: 1:21:21 '80.

Rudolf POVARNITSYN b.13 Jun 1962 Votkinsk, Udmurt ASR 2.01m 75kg. Kiev TR.
At HJ: OG: '88- 3=.

Oleg Protsenko (George Herringshaw/ASP)

World record high jump 1985 with 14cm improvement in personal best.
Progression at HJ: 1980- 2.02, 1981- 2.15, 1982- 2.18, 1983- 2.22, 1984- 2.21, 1985- 2.40, 1986- 2.30, 1987- 2.29, 1988- 2.36.

Oleg PROTSENKO b.11 Aug 1963 Soltsy, Novgorod 1.91m 82kg. Moskva Dyn. Sports student.
At TJ: OG: '88- 4; WCh: '87- 8; WI: '87- 2; ECh: '86- 3; WCp: '85- 2; ECp: '85- 3, '87- 1. 2nd GP 1988. USSR champion 1985–6.
European TJ record 1985, WIB 17.67m 1987.
Progression at TJ: 1979- 15.05i, 1980- 15.94, 1981- 16.68, 1982- 16.59, 1983- 17.27, 1984- 17.52, 1985- 17.69, 1986- 17.59, 1987- 17.67i/17.61, 1988- 17.68. pb LJ: 8.00i '86, 8.18w '87.

Oleg SAKIRKIN b.23 Jan 1966 1.82m 72kg. Chimkent TR, Kazakh SSR.
At TJ: WCh: '87- 3; EI: '88- 1.
Progression at TJ: 1984- 15.93, 1985- 16.39, 1986- 17.12, 1987- 17.43, 1988- 17.50. pb LJ: 7.76 '87.

Vitaliy SAVIN b.23 Jan 1966 1.78m 84kg. Alma-Ata Sp.
At 100m/R: 4x100mR: OG: '88- qf/1R; EJ: '85- 4/3R.
Progression at 100m: 1983- 10.73/10.5, 1984- 10.51, 1985- 10.43, 1987- 10.39/10.1, 1988- 10.15/9.9. pb 200m: 20.90 '87.

Mikhail SHCHENNIKOV b.24 Dec 1967 Moskva 1.83m 71kg. Moskva SA. Serviceman.
At 20kmW: OG: '88- 6. USSR champion 1988. At 10kmW: WJ: '86- 1; EJ: '85- 1. At 5kmW: WI: '87- 1.
World road best 20km walk 1988. At 5kmW WJR 19:19.3 '86, WIB 18:27.79 '87.
Progression at 20kmW: 1987- 1:23:08, 1988- 1:19:08. pbs: 3kmW: 11:05.14i '87, 10kmW: 39:27.59 '88.

Yuriy SEDYKH b.11 Jun 1955 Novocherkassk 1.86m 106kg. Moskva SA. Graduate of the Kiev Institute of Physical Culture.
At HT: OG: '76- 1, '80- 1, '88- 2; WCh: '83- 2; ECh: '78- 1, '82- 1, '86- 1; EJ: '73–1; WSG: '75- 3, '77- 2, '79- 3; WCp: '77- 4, '81- 1; ECp: '77- 3, '81- 1. USSR hammer champion 1976, 1978, 1980.
World junior records 1973 and 1974, and eight Soviet records, including six world records: 80.38, 80.64 and 81.80 in 1980, 86.34 in 1984, 86.66 and 86.74 in 1986.
Progression at HT: 1971- 57.02, 1972- 62.96, 1973- 69.04, 1974- 70.86, 1975- 75.00, 1976- 78.86, 1977- 76.60, 1978- 79.76, 1979- 77.58, 1980- 81.80, 1981- 80.18, 1982- 81.66, 1983- 80.94, 1984- 86.34, 1985- 82.70, 1986- 86.74, 1987- 80.34, 1988- 85.14. pb 35lb Wt: 23.46 '79 (three WIB).
The greatest hammer thrower of all-time, who reached new peaks in 1984, throwing consistently over 85 metres, and even better in 1986. At the European Championships he responded to Litvinov's opening 85.74 with five throws averaging 86.16 following the world record of 86.74 with 86.68 and 86.62! Coached by his predecessor as Olympic champion, Anatoliy Bondarchuk. Won the 1980 Olympic title by setting a new world record with the first throw of the competition. Has treated odd years as low-key, peaking for the Europeans and Olympics.

Lev SHATILO b.21 Oct 1962 1.91m 98kg. Moskva Sp. Student.
At JT: WCh: '87- 5.
USSR javelin record 1987.
Progression at JT: 1983- 80.60, 1985- 83.04, 1986- 80.60, new: 1987- 84.30, 1988- 82.22.

Vladimir SHISHKIN b.16 Jan 1964 1.93m 80kg. Gorkiy Dyn..
At 110mh: OG: '88- 4. USSR champion 1988.
Progression at 110mh: 1981- 14.7, 1982- 14.0, 1983- 14.15, 1984- 13.94, 1985- 13.6, 1986- 13.50/13.36w, 1987- 13.55/13.4, 1988- 13.21/13.0.

Vasiliy SIDORENKO b.1 May 1961 1.86m 100kg. Volgograd Dyn.
Progression at HT: 1979- 59.98, 1980- 68.78, 1981- 69.30, 1983- 74.10, 1984- 76.80, 1985- 80.40, 1986- 80.70, 1987- 80.02, 1988- 80.52.

Sergey SMIRNOV b.17 Sep 1960 Leningrad 1.92m 126kg. Leningrad SA. Engineer.
At SP: OG: '88- 8; WCh: '83- dnq; WI: '87- 3; ECh: '86- dnc; EI: '86- 2, '87- 3; WSG: '83- 3; WCp: '85- 2; ECp: '85- 1, '87- 5. USSR champion 1985–7.
Two USSR shot records 1985–6.
Progression at SP: 1980- 16.31, 1981- 18.86, 1982- 20.42, 1983- 21.00, 1984- 21.63, 1985- 22.05, 1986- 22.24, 1987- 21.74, 1988- 21.88.
Although he qualified, did not take part in the European shot final in 1986.

Juri TAMM b.5 Feb 1957 Parnu, Estonia 1.93m 120kg. Kiev SA. Teacher.
At HT: OG: '80- 3, '88- 3; WCh: '87- 2; WCp: '85- 1; ECp: '85- 1; WSG: '81- 2, '83- 1. USSR champion 1987–8.
World hammer record in 1980, only to be overtaken by Yuriy Sedykh in same competition.
Progression at HT: 1974- 49.16, 1975- 54.76, 1976- 66.86, 1977- 72.44, 1978- 74.58, 1979- 75.18, 1980- 80.46, 1981- 77.26, 1982- 74.82, 1983- 79.18, 1984- 84.40, 1985- 84.08, 1986- 80.88, 1987- 82.02, 1988- 84.16.

Pavel TARNOVETSKIY b.22 Feb 1961 1.83m 83kg. Lipetsk SA.
At Dec: OG: '88- 10; WCh: '87- 3; ECp: '87- 4.
Progression at Dec: 1979- 6693, 1980- 7242, 1982- 7593, 1983- 7957, 1984- 8207, 1985- 7809, 1986- 8214, 1987- 8375, 1988- 8299. pbs: 100m: 11.01 '87, 400m: 48.19 '88, 1500m: 4:19.00 '84, 110mh: 14.60 '84, 14.2 '82, HJ: 2.09 '83, PV: 5.20 '88, LJ: 7.53 '88, SP: 15.32 '87, DT: 48.52 '87, JT: 60.24 '83, new: 59.48 '88. Surprise medallist in Rome, when he improved his pb by 161 points.

Romas UBARTAS b.26 May 1960 Lithuania 2.02m 123kg. Vilnius Dyn. Teacher.
At DT: OG: '88- 2; WCh: '87- 6; ECh: '86- 1. USSR champion 1986. Won GP 1987.
Progression at DT: 1977- 44.32, 1978- 49.34, 1979- 53.08, 1980- 57.52, 1981- 65.62, 1982- 59.80, 1983- 66.64, 1984- 66.92, 1985- 63.86, 1986- 67.88, 1987- 66.10, 1988- 70.06. pb SP: 18.52.

Gennadiy VALYUKEVICH b.1 Jun 1958 Brest Litovsk 1.82m 74kg. Minsk SA.
At TJ: WCh: '83- 10; ECh: '78- 5, '82- 4; EI: '79- 1, '82- 2, '83- 2; EJ: '77- 1; WCp: '79- 2. USSR champion 1979 and 1984.
WIB triple jump 17.18 & 17.29 '79.
Progression at TJ: 1974- 13.65, 1975- 14.71, 1976- 15.68, 1977- 16.60, 1978- 17.02, 1979- 17.29i, 1980- 16.61, 1981- 17.18, 1982- 17.42, 1983- 17.23, 1984- 17.47, 1985- 17.48, 1986- 17.53/ 17.75w, 1987- 17.32i/17.10, 1988- 17.44. pbs: 100m: 10.4, LJ: 7.41.
Married to Irina Valyukevich (6 WCh LJ and 7.17 '87). His 17.75m in 1986 exceeded the then European record, but there was no wind gauge.

Aleksandr VASILYEV b.26 Jul 1961 Shostka, Ukraine 1.91m 83kg. Kiev SA. Teacher.
At 400mh: WCh: '87- sf; ECh: '86- 2; WCp: '85- 2; ECp: '85- 2. USSR champion 1985–8.
Three USSR 400mh records 1985.
Progression at 400mh: 1977- 55.6, 1978- 53.69, 1979- 52.06, 1980- 51.51, 1981- 49.84, 1982- 49.64/49.4, 1983- 49.07, 1984- 48.45, 1985- 47.92, 1986- 48.24, 1987- 48.85, 1988- 49.00. pbs: 400m: 46.76 '85, 110mh: 14.31.

Grigoriy YEGOROV b.12 Jan 1967 1.85m 75kg. Alma-Ata Dyn.
At PV: OG: '88- 3; ECp: '87- 1; WJ: '86- 5; EJ: '85- 2.
Progression at PV: 1983- 5.00, 1984- 5.45, 1985- 5.55, 1986- 5.61i/5.50, 1987- 5.70, 1988- 5.85.

Viktor YEVSYUKOV b.6 Oct 1956 Donetsk 1.90m 100kg. Alma-Ata Dyn. Teacher.
At JT: OG: '88- 5; WCh: '87- 2; ECh: '86- 3; ECp: '85–2, '87- 1. USSR champion 1984, 1987–8. 3rd GP 1987.
World new javelin best 1986. Two USSR records 1986–7.
Progression at JT: 1977- 79.32, 1978- 76.76, 1979- 84.48, 1980- 85.20, 1981- 84.42, 1982- 87.50, 1983- 88.10, 1984- 90.94, 1985- 93.70, new: 1986- 83.68, 1987- 85.16, 1988- 82.76.

Vladimir ZINCHENKO b.25 Jul 1959 1.92m 115kg. Zaporozhye Sp.
At DT: WCh: '87- 5. USSR champion 1987.
Progression at DT: 1977- 60.60, 1978- 59.96, 1979- 62.02, 1980- 66.14, 1981- 60.74, 1983- 66.70, 1984- 66.16, 1985- 66.46, 1986- 63.26, 1987- 67.58, 1988- 68.88. pb SP: 19.37i '83.

Women

Natalya AKHRIMENKO b.12 May 1955 Novokuybyshevsk 1.84m 90kg. née Petrova. Leningrad Dyn. Teacher.
At SP: OG: '80- 7, '88- 7; WCh: '87- 5; WI: '87- 5; ECh: '86- 3; EI: '87- 1; WSG: '83- 3 (2 DT).
Progression at SP: 1972- 15.25, 1973- 14.34, 1974- 16.13, 1977- 18.18, 1978- 19.09, 1979- 18.24, 1980- 20.44, 1981- 17.44, 1982- 20.34, 1983- 20.25, 1984- 20.10, 1985- 21.08, 1986- 21.39, 1987- 21.34, 1988- 21.73. pb DT: 64.60 '80.

Natalya ARTYOMOVA b.5 Jan 1963 Rostov-on-Don 1.67m 54kg. Leningrad Dyn. Student.
At 3000m: OG: '88- 5; WCh: '83- 8; WSG: '87- 3. USSR champion 1983, 1988.
Unratified world 1 mile record 4:15.8 in 1984, USSR 5000m record 1985.
Progression at 1500m/3000m: 1979- 5:00.6, 1980- 4:36.0, 1981- 4:32.2, 1982- 4:10.6/9:15.0, 1983- 4:02.63/8:47.98, 1984- 4:00.68/8:38.84, 1985- 3:59.28/8:46.1, 1987- 4:11.4/8:58.29, 1988- 4:04.03/8:31.67. pbs: 400m: 53.5 '84, 800m: 1:58.05 '85, 1000m: 2:37.45i '84, 1M: 4:15.8 '84, 5000m: 14:54.80 '85, 10000m: 31:56.33 '88.

Lyudmila AVDEYENKO b.14 Nov 1963 Minsk 1.80m 62kg. née Petrus. Odessa SA. Student.
At HJ: OG: '88- dnq 17=; WCh: '87- 8=; WSG: '85- 2. USSR champion 1987.
Progression at HJ: 1977- 1.75, 1978- 1.81, 1979- 1.80, 1981- 1.84, 1982- 1.83, 1983- 1.88, 1984- 1.95, 1985- 1.94, 1986- 1.90i, 1987- 2.00, 1988- 2.00i/1.98.
Married to Gennadiy Avdeyenko (qv), with daughter Alissa born 1986.

Maya AZARASHVILI b.6 Apr 1964 Tbilisi 1.70m 60kg. Tbilisi Sp. Student.
At 200m: OG: '88- 7; WCh: '87- sf; ECp: '87- 5.
Progression at 200m: 1978- 25.25, 1979- 24.7, 1980- 24.88, 1981- 24.48, 1982- 24.42, 1983- 23.67, 1984- 22.63, 1985- 23.25, 1986- 22.51,

1987- 22.52/22.3w, 1988- 22.24. pbs: 100m: 11.08/10.9 '88, 400m: 52.13 '88.

Laima BAIKAUSKAITE b.10 Jun 1956 Lithuania 1.62m 58kg. Vilnius SA.
At 1500m: OG: '88- 2. USSR champion 1988.
Progression at 1500m: 1978- 4:14.3, 1979- 4:09.1, 1980- 4:03.6, 1981- 4:03.71, 1983- 4:12.19, 1984- 4:08.4, 1985- 4:03.5, 1986- 4:02.92, 1987- 4:07.3, 1988- 4:00.24. pbs: 800m: 1:58.3 '85, 1000m: 2:35.5i '87, 2:36.9 '85; 2000m: 5:50.7i '87, 3000m: 9:00.4 '80.

Olga BONDARENKO b.2 Jun 1960 Slavgorod, Altayskiy Kray 1.54m 41kg. née Krentser. Volgograd SA. Teacher.
At 3000m: WCh: '87- dns; WI: '87- 2; ECh: '86- 1; EI: '85- 2; ECp: '87- 3. At 10000m: OG: '88- 1; WCh: '87- 4; ECh: '86- 2; WCp: '85- 3; ECp: '85- 1. USSR champion 3000m 1985, 1987; 5000m 1985; 10000m 1984–5, 1987. World CC '85- 7.
World 10000m 1981 and 1984, USSR records: 5000m 1985, 10000m (3) 1981–6. WIB: 3000m 8:42.3 '86.
Progression at 3000m/10000m: 1977- 9:41.2, 1978- 9:24.8, 1979- 9:08.2, 1980- 8:52.5, 1981- 8:51.5/32:30.80, 1982- 8:57.73i/35:08.0, 1983- 8:47.02/31:35.61, 1984- 8:36.20/31:13.78, 1985- 8:42.19/31:25.18, 1986- 8:33.99/30:57.21, 1987- 8:45.81/31:18.38, 1988- 8:43.95/31:05.21. pbs: 1500m: 4:06.2 '84, 1M: 4:27.48 '87, 2000m: 5:40.15 '86, 5000m: 14:55.76 '85, Mar: 2:43:24 '84.
Misjudged the finish of the 1985 World Cup 10000m to mar a great season, but returned to another fine year in 1986 with gold and silver at the Europeans. Fast finisher, as she showed to run away from Liz McColgan to win the Olympic 10000m title.

Olga BRYZGINA b.30 Jun 1963 Krasnokamsk, Perm 1.73m 68kg. née Vladykina. Married to Viktor Bryzgin (qv). Voroshilovgrad Dyn. Economics student.
At 400m/4x400m relay: OG: '88- 1/1R; WCh: '87- 1/2R; ECh: '86- 2; WCp: '85- 2/2R; ECp: '85- 1/1R. USSR champion 1984–5.
Four USSR 400m records 1984–5. World record 4x400m relay 1988.
Progression at 400m: 1977- 63.0, 1978- 59.8, 1979- 57.8, 1980- 55.49, 1981- 54.23, 1982- 51.89, 1983- 50.48, 1984- 48.98, 1985- 48.27, 1986- 49.67, 1987- 49.38, 1988- 48.65. pbs: 100m: 11.2 '86, 200m: 22.44 '85.
Has become the worthy successor to Marita Koch, after being world number two to her in 1985–6. Ran a 47.7 final leg in the Soviet WR Olympic victory.

Svetlana BURAGA b.4 Sep 1965 1.68m 56kg. née Besprozvannaya. Minsk TR. Instructor.
At Hep: OG: '88- 10; WCh: '87- 14; ECp: '87- 1.

Olga Bryzguina (George Herringshaw/ASP)

Progression at Hep: 1983- 5352, 1985- 5743, 1986- 6073, 1987- 6585, 1988- 6597. pbs: 200m: 23.18 '87, 800m: 2:08.45 '88, 100mh: 12.83/12.8 '88, HJ: 1.82 '88, LJ: 6.79i/6.63 '87, SP: 13.78 '88; JT: 42.80 '87.

Yelena BYELEVSKAYA b.11 Oct 1963 Evpatoria 1.77m 57kg. née Mityayeva, married to Sergey Byelevskiy (17.03 '84 TJ). Minsk TR. Teacher.
At LJ: OG: '88- 4; WCh: '87- 2; WI: '87- 3; ECh: '86- 7; EI: '87- 3. USSR champion 1986–7.
USSR long jump record 1987.
Progression at LJ: 1976- 5.21, 1977- 5.56, 1978- 5.96, 1979- 5.95, 1980- 6.23, 1981- 6.41, 1982- 6.61, 1983- 6.76, 1984- 6.88, 1985- 7.00, 1986- 7.31, 1987- 7.39, 1988- 7.36.

Tamara BYKOVA b.21 Dec 1958 Azov, near Rostov-on-Don 1.80m 60kg. Moskva SA. Student of education.
At HJ: OG: '80- 9, '88- 3; WCh: '83- 1, '87- 2; WI: '87- 4; ECh: '82- 2, '86- dnq; EI: '83- 1; WSG: '81- 3, '83- 1; WCp: '81- 2, '85- 2; ECp: '83- 2, '85- 2, '87- 2. USSR champion 1980, 1982–3, 1985. 3rd GP 1985.
World records: 2.03m and 2.04m 1983, 2.05m 1984. Eight USSR records. WIB: 2.00, 2.02 & 2.03 '83.
Progression at HJ: 1974- 1.50, 1975- 1.72, 1976- 1.70, 1977- 1.70, 1978- 1.85, 1979- 1.88, 1980- 1.97, 1981- 1.96, 1982- 1.98, 1983- 2.04, 1984- 2.05, 1985- 2.02, 1986- 1.96, 1987- 2.04, 1988- 1.99.

Returned to her best in 1987 to so nearly retain her world title.

Yolanda CHEN b.26 Jul 61 1.69m 52kg. Moskva Sp.
Progression at LJ: 1980- 6.44, 1981- 6.60, 1982- 6.75, 1983- 6.77, 1984- 6.83, 1985- 6.51i, 1986- 6.80, 1987- 6.50, 1988- 7.16.

Galina CHISTYAKOVA b.26 Jul 1962 Izmail, Ukraine 1.69m 54kg. Moskva Sp. Teacher. Married to Aleksandr Beskrovniy (TJ: 17.53m '84, 1 EJ '79, 5 ECh '82).
At LJ: OG: '88- 3; WCh: '87- 5; WI: '87- 4; ECh: '86- 2; EI: '85- 1, '87- 2, '88- 2; WCp: '85- 2; ECp: '85- 1, '87- 2. Won GP 1985.
World long jump record 1988, four USSR records 1984–8. WIB: long jump 7.25 '85, four triple jump 13.58 '86; 13.86, 13.96, 13.98 '87.
Progression at LJ: 1973- 3.75, 1974- 4.20, 1975- 4.96, 1976- 5.25, 1977- 5.80, 1978- 6.04, 1979- 6.43, 1980- 6.43, 1981- 6.36/6.54w, 1982- 6.43, 1984- 7.29, 1985- 7.28, 1986- 7.34, 1987- 7.27, 1988- 7.52. pb 100m: 11.6 '84, TJ: 13.98i '87.
Gave birth to a daughter in 1983.

Natalya GRIGORYEVA b.3 Dec 1962 Ishimbay 1.71m 62kg. Kharkov Sp. née Dorofeyeva. Student.
At 100mh: OG: '88- 4; ECh: '86- 7; ECp: '87- 4. USSR champion 1988.
Progression at 100mh: 1982- 13.77/13.4, 1983- 13.26, 1984- 13.20/12.7, 1985- 12.89/12.8, 1986- 12.61, 1987- 12.91, 1988- 12.48/12.46w. pb 400mh: 57.9 '83.

Lyubov GURINA b.6 Aug 1957 Matushkino, Kirov region 1.67m 57kg. Kirov Sp. Sports instructor.
At 800m: WCh: '83- 2, '87- 3; ECh: '86- 3. USSR champion 1987. At 1500m: OG: '88- h.
World record 4x800m relay 1984.
Progression at 800m: 1976- 2:15.7, 1977- 2:08.0, 1978- 2:04.6, 1979- 2:00.2, 1980- 1:59.9, 1981- 1:58.72, 1982- 1:57.3, 1983- 1:56.11, 1984- 1:56.26, 1986- 1:57.52, 1987- 1:55.56, 1988- 1:56.56. pbs: 400m: 51.38 '83, 1000m: 2:37.60i '83, 1500m: 4:06.34 '86.

Zoya IVANOVA b.14 Mar 1952 Zaton, North Kazakhstan 1.64m 52kg. Alma-Ata Sp. Teacher.
At Mar: OG: '88- 9; WCh: '83- 23, '87- 2; ECh: '82- 8; WCp: '85- 2, '87- 1; ECp: '81- 1, '88- 3. USSR champion 1981–4. World road 15km: '88- 2.
Four USSR marathon records 1982–7.
Progression at Mar: 1980- 2:45:02, 1981- 2:38:58, 1982- 2:34:26, 1983- 2:36:31, 1984- 2:31:11, 1985- 2:34:17, 1987- 2:27:57, 1988- 2:29:37. pb 10000m: 32:19.50 '88.
Has won 8 of 18 marathons, including Tokyo 1982, Friendship Games 1984. Had a baby in 1986.

Yekaterina KHRAMENKOVA b.6 Oct 1956 Minsk 1.68m 56kg. Minsk TR. University lecturer.
At Mar: WCh: '87- 6; ECh: '86- 3; WCp: '87- 5; ECp: '85- 8, '88- 4. USSR champion 1987. World road 15km: '87- 5, '88- 6.
USSR marathon record 1987.
Progression at Mar: 1984- 2:36:39, 1985- 2:32:24, 1986- 2:34:18, 1987- 2:28:20, 1988- 2:30:27. pbs: 5000m: 15:44.2 '88, 10000m: 31:42.02 '88.

Margarita KHROMOVA b.19 Jun 1963 Balkhash, Kazakhstan 1.78m 58kg. née Ponomaryeva. Leningrad TR. Student of economics.
At 400mh: WCh: '87- sf; ECh: '86- 8; EJ: '81- 3 (2 at 4x400mR); WCp: '85- 6.
World 400mh record 1984.
Progression at 400mh: 1981- 57.45, 1983- 56.9, 1984- 53.58, 1985- 55.48, 1986- 54.57, 1987- 54.58, 1988- 54.95. pb 400m: 52.05 '84, 52.0 '86.

Lyubov KIRYUKHINA b.19 May 1963 Fergana 1.67m 58kg. Moskva SA. Student.
At 800m: WI: '87- 3; ECh: '86- 7; EI: '87- 3; EJ: '81- 3 (2 4x400mR). USSR champion 1986.
WIB 600m 1:26.41 & 1:25.46 '87.
Progression at 800m: 1978- 2:14.0, 1979- 2:05.3, 1980- 2:04.76, 1981- 2:01.36, 1982- 2:00.65, 1983- 1:59.46, 1984- 1:58.87, 1986- 1:57.18, 1987- 1:57.62, 1988- 1:58.56. pbs: 100m: 11.6, 200m: 23.8, 400m: 51.97/51.3 '87, 1000m: 2:39.3i '87, 1500m: 4:07.18 '82.

Svetlana KITOVA b.25 Jun 1960 Dushanbe 1.68m 60kg. Moskva TR.
At 1500m: WCh: '87- 9; ECh: '86- 6; WI: '87- 3; EI: '86- 1, '87- 2; WSG: '85- 1, '87- 2. At 800m: EI: '83- 1; WSG: '85- 4.
Progression at 800m/1500m: 1978- 2:07.1, 1979- 2:06.5, 1980- 2:01.3, 1981- 2:02.1, 1982- 1:59.51, 1983- 1:58.82, 1984- 1:58.08, 1985- 1:59.6/4:05.77, 1986- 2:01.43i/4:01.83, 1987- 2:00.0/4:03.03, 1988- 1:58.1/4:01.02. pb 1000m: 2:37.93i '85.

Yelena KOKONOVA b.4 Aug 1963 1.72m 64kg. née Stetsura. Alma-Ata TR. Student.
At LJ: EI: '86- 3. USSR champion 1984–5.
USSR long jump record 1985.
Progression at LJ: 1981- 6.20, 1982- 6.50, 1983- 6.83, 1984- 7.09, 1985- 7.31, 1986- 7.00i, 1987- 6.95, 1988- 7.29.

Lyudmila KONDRATYEVA b.11 Apr 1958 Shakhty, Rostov 1.68m 57kg. Married to Yuriy Sedykh. Moskva Dyn. Sports instructor.
At 100m/(200m)/R- 4x100m relay: OG: '80- 1, '88- sf/3R; ECh: '78- 6/1/1R, '82- sf; EJ: '75- (4); WCp: '79- 4/3, '81- 3R; ECp: '79- 2/1, '81- 3R, '83- 3R. At 60m: EI: '80- 3. USSR champion 100m & 200m 1979, 200m 1988.

USSR records: 100m (2), 200m (4) 1978–80.
Progression at 100m: 1970- 13.6, 1971- 12.4, 1972- 12.1, 1973- 11.5, 1974- 11.6/11.81, 1975- 11.6, 1976- 11.5/11.72, 1977- 11.3, 1978- 11.35, 1979- 11.15/11.0w/11.1, 1980- 11.06/10.87?, 1981- 11.4, 1982- 11.28, 1983- 11.71, 1984- 11.02, 1987- 11.44/11.2, 1988- 11.05/10.9. pbs: 200m: 22.31 '80, 400m: 51.87 '80, 100mh: 13.7 '76.

Irina KOSTYUCHENKOVA b.11 May 1961 Chelyabinsk 1.71m 78kg. Kharkov Sp.
At JT: OG: '88- 4; WCh: '87- 12; ECh: '86- 8; WSG: '87- 1. USSR champion 1986, 1988.
Progression at JT: 1979- 51.96, 1982- 57.68, 1983- 57.80, 1984- 55.22, 1985- 63.24, 1986- 65.56, 1987- 66.72, 1988- 67.00

Inessa KRAVETS b.5 Oct 1966 1.78m 64kg. Dnepropetrovsk Sp. née Shulyak. Student.
At LJ: OG: '88- 10.
Progression at LJ: 1983- 6.27, 1984- 6.44, 1985- 6.39/6.45i, 1986- 6.61, 1987- 6.72, 1988- 7.27.

Olga KRISHTOP b.8 Oct 1957 Novosibirsk 1.58m 50kg. Novosibirsk Dyn. Engineer.
At 10kmW: WCh: '87- dq; WCp: '85- 3=, '87- 1. At 3kmW: WI: '87- 1.
World 5km walk record 1985, world road bests 10km walk 1986 and 1987, WIB 3km walk 1987.
Progression at 10kmW (road): 1982- 47:06, 1983- 46:08, 1984- 44:52, 1985- 45:02, 1986- 44:43, 1987- 43:22. Track pbs: 3kmW: 12:05.49i '87; 5kmW: 21:36.2 '84, 10kmW: 44:56.0 '86.
Former cross-country skier.

Larisa KUCHUYEVA b.14 Dec 1963 Ashkhabad 1.82m 58kg. née Kositsyna. Student. Moskva Sp.
At HJ: WCh: '83- 17, '87- 5; ECh: '86- 9=; EJ: '81- 3; EI: '83- 2, '86- 3, '88- 2=.
Progression at HJ: 1976- 1.55, 1977- 1.55, 1978- 1.63, 1979- 1.78, 1980- 1.83i, 1981–1.86, 1982- 1.95, 1983- 1.98, 1984- 1.90i, 1985- 1.97, 1986- 1.98i/1.94, 1987- 1.96, 1988- 2.00.

Tatyana KUROCHKINA b.15 Oct 1966 1.74m 58kg. née Matsuta. Minsk Sp.
At OG: '88- 7.
Progression at 400mh: 1984- 60.31, 1985- 57.83, 1986- 58.60, 1987- 58.90, 1988- 54.39.
Improved over three seconds in 1988.

Tatyana LEDOVSKAYA b.21 May 1965 1.71m 60kg. Minsk Sp.
At 400mh/R- 4x400m relay: OG: '88- 2/1R. USSR champion 1988. World record 4x400m relay 1988.
Progression at 400mh: 1987- 56.92, 1988- 53.18. pbs: 200m: 23.32/22.7 '88, 400m: 50.4/50.93 '88.
Made exceptionally rapid progress in 1988, taking 1.3 off her best in Seoul.

Natalya LISOVSKAYA b.16 Jul 1962 Alegazy, Bashkir ASSR 1.86m 100kg. Moskva Sp. Student.
At SP: OG: '88- 1; WCh: '83- 5, '87- 1; WI: '87- 1; ECh: '86- 9; EI: '82- 3; WCp: '85- 1; ECp: '85- 1, '87- 1; WSG: '83- 1, '85–1, '87- 1; WI: '85- 1. USSR champion 1981, 1983, 1985–6, 1988. 2nd GP 1985, 1987.
Three world shot records 1984–7.
Progression at SP: 1978- 13.22, 1979- 14.50, 1980- 14.91, 1981- 18.66, 1982- 19.84, 1983- 20.85, 1984- 22.53, 1985- 21.73, 1986- 21.70, 1987- 22.63, 1988- 22.55. pb DT: 63.44 '82.
Undefeated in 1987 and 1988, when she won all the major titles and made up for her disappointing showing in Stuttgart the previous year. At the Olympics had all six puts better than the silver medallist.

Galina MALCHUGINA b.17 Dec 1962 Bryansk 1.68m 59kg. née Mikheyeva. Bryansk Sp.
At 200m/4x100mR: OG: '88- 8/3R; EJ: '79- 7/2R.
Progression at 200m: 1978- 24.76, 1979- 23.70, 1980- 24.21/24.0, 1981- 23.16, 1982- 23.28/23.2, 1984- 22.74, 1985- 23.06, 1987- 23.15/22.2w, 1988- 22.42. pb 100m: 11.07/10.8 '88.

Marianna MASLENNIKOVA b.17 May 1961 Leningrad 1.73m 66kg. Leningrad Sp. Philology student.
At Hep: WCh: '87- 7; ECh: '86- 5; ECp: '85- 5.
Progression at Hep: 1979- 3925p, 1981- 5333, 1982- 6079, 1983- 5863, 1984- 6374, 1985- 6264, 1986- 6416, 1987- 6456, 1988- 6474. pbs: 200m: 24.07 '88, 800m: 2:04.44 '85, 100mh: 13.29 '87, 13.21w '87, HJ: 1.88 '86, LJ: 6.46 '86, SP: 13.68 '88, JT: 40.42 '88.

Larisa MIKHALCHENKO b.16 May 1963 1.80m 93kg. Kharkov Dyn. Teacher.
At DT: OG: '88- 10; WCh: '87- 7; EJ: '81- 3.
Progression at DT: 1980- 52.14, 1981- 54.74, 1982- 56.28, 1983- 62.00, 1984- 58.22, 1985- 64.92, 1986- 64.48, 1987- 64.88, 1988- 70.80.

Marina MOLOKOVA b.24 Aug 1962 Irkutsk 1.75m 60kg. Irkutsk Sp. Student.
At 200m: ECh: '86- 4. USSR champion 100m 1987, 200m 1986.
Progression at 200m: 1979- 26.9, 1981- 24.5, 1982- 24.02/23.7, 1983- 23.33, 1984- 22.97, 1985- 22.76, 1986- 22.46, 1987- 22.58/22.0, 1988- 22.84. pb 100m: 11.08 '87, 10.8 '88.

Galina MURASHOVA b.22 Dec 1955 Vilnius, Lithuania 1.80m 92kg. Vilnius Dyn. Student.
At DT: OG: '80- 7, '88- nt 12; WCh: '83- 2; ECh: '82- 6; ECp: '83- 2. USSR champion 1983, 1988.
Progression at DT: 1971- 34.00, 1972- 42.00, 1973- 47.64, 1974- 50.04, 1976- 53.56, 1977- 57.82,

1978- 61.80, 1979- 63.38, 1980- 67.52, 1981- 62.52, 1982- 69.06, 1983- 68.86, 1984- 72.14, 1985- 60.92, 1986- 58.34, 1987- 64.12, 1988- 69.86.

Lyudmila NAROZHILENKO b.21 Apr 1964 1.70m 63kg. Michurinsk Sp. Student.
At 100mh: OG: '88- sf.
Progression at 100mh: 1986- 13.41, 1987- 12.98/12.97w, 1988- 12.62/12.3/12.57w. pb 200m: 23.03 '88.
Fell in Olympic semi 1988.

Olga NAZAROVA b.6 May 1965 1.68m 55kg. née Grigoryeva. Moskva SA. Student.
At 400m/R- 4x400m relay: OG: '88- 3/1R; WCh: '87- 8/2R; ECh: '86- sf; WI: '87- 4; ECp: '87- 1R. USSR champion 1987–8.
World record 4x400m relay 1988. WIB 500m 1:07.67 '88.
Progression at 400m: 1983- 54.30, 1984- 53.8i, 1986- 51.44, 1987- 49.96, 1988- 49.11/48.9. pb 200m: 22.68 '87.
Contributed a 48.0 leg to the Soviet WR Olympic win in 1988.

Remigia NAZAROVA b.2 Jun 1967 1.78m 70kg. Vilnius Dyn. née Sablovskaite. Teacher.
At Hep: OG: '88- 5. USSR champion 1988.
Progression at Hep: 1985- 5693, 1986- 5875, 1987- 6241, 1988- 6566. pbs: 200m: 23.92 '88, 23.8 '87; 800m: 2:11.74 '88, 100mh: 13.46 '88, 13.47w/13.3 '87; HJ: 1.84 '87, LJ: 6.47 '88, SP: 15.23 '88, JT: 47.40 '88.

Larisa NIKITINA b.29 Apr 1965 1.77m 70kg. Moskva Sp. Teacher.
At Hep: WCh: '87- 2; EJ: '83- 7. USSR champion 1987.
Progression at Hep: 1981- 5263, 1983- 5674, 1984- 6276, 1985- 6171, 1986- 6316, 1987- 6564, 1988- 6506. pbs: 200m: 24.32 '88, 800m: 2:18.88 '88, 100mh: 13.69/13.5 '87, HJ: 1.87 '87, LJ: 6.66 '87, SP: 15.66 '87, JT: 55.24 '87.

Yelena NIKOLAYEVA b.1 Feb 1966 1.68m 60kg. née Kuznyetsova. Chelyabinsk Sp.
At 10kmW: WCh: '87- 5; WCp: '87- 5. USSR champion 1987–8.
Three world 10km track walk records 1986–8, European 5km records: 21:32.4 '87, 21:08.65 '88.
Progression at 10kmW: 1984- 48:30, 1985- 46:37, 1986- 44:32.50t, 1987- 43:57, 1988- 43:36.41t.

Nadezhda OLIZARENKO b.28 Nov 1953 Bryansk 1.65m 57kg. née Mushta. Married to Sergey Olizarenko (3kmSt 8:24.0 '78). Odessa SA. Sports instructor.
At 800m: OG: '80- 1 (3 at 1500m), '88- sf; WCh: '87- 7; ECh: '78- 2/2 4x400mR, '86- 1; EI: '85- 2; WSG: '79- 1; WCp: '79- 2, '85- 3; ECp: '85- 2/2R. USSR champion 1980, 1988.
Two 800m world records 1980, 1:54.85 and 1:53.43, the latter in winning the Olympic title; and world record 4x800m 1984. WIB: 600m 1:27.3 '80.
Progression at 800m: 1970- 2:11.4, 1972- 2:08.6, 1974- 2:05.0, 1975- 2:03.3, 1976- 2:05.8, 1977- 1:59.76, 1978- 1:55.82, 1979- 1:57.5, 1980- 1:53.43, 1983- 1:58.16, 1984- 1:56.09, 1985- 1:56.25, 1986- 1:57.15, 1987- 1:58.6, 1988- 1:56.03/1:56.0. pbs: 400m: 50.96 '80, 1500m: 3:56.8 '80.

Maria PINIGINA b.9 Feb 1958 Ivanovo, Frunze, Kirghizia 1.71m 58kg. née Kulchunova. Kiev Sp. Sports instructor.
At 400m/R- 4x400m relay: OG: '88- 1R; WCh: '83- 3/3R, '87- 4/2R; ECh: '78- 4/2R, '86- dnc sf; EI: '87- 1; EJ: '75- 4; WSG: '79- 1, '83- 1/1R; WCp: '79- 2, '85- 2R; ECp: '79- 2/2R, '83- 2/2R, '85- 1R, '87- 2/1R. USSR champion 1978–9, 1983, 1986.
Four USSR 400m records 1979–84. World record 4x400m relay 1988.
Progression at 400m: 1971- 64.4, 1972- 64.3, 1973- 57.4, 1974- 54.47, 1975- 52.62, 1976- 51.80, 1977- 52.92, 1978- 50.83, 1979- 49.63, 1980- 51.2/51.45, 1983- 49.19, 1984- 49.74, 1985- 49.61, 1986- 50.29, 1987- 49.87, 1988- 49.74. pbs: 100m: 11.4 '76, 200m: 22.42 '87, 800m: 2:01.35 '88.

Irina PODYALOVSKAYA b.19 Oct 1959 Vishenka, Mogilev region 1.66m 55kg. née Russkikh. Moscow TR. Student.
At 800m: WSG: '83- 1. USSR champion 1983.
World record 4x800m relay 1984.
Progression at 800m: 1975- 2:08.2, 1976- 2:06.03, 1977- 2:03.65, 1979- 2:01.6, 1981- 2:00.2, 1982- 1:59.64, 1983- 1:57.99, 1984- 1:55.69, 1985- 1:57.6, 1986- 1:57.86, 1987- 1:59.13, 1988- 1:58.03. pbs: 400m: 51.67 '84, 1500m: 4:12.36 '87.

Tatyana POLOVINSKAYA b.12 Mar 1965 1.59m 52kg. Simferopol SA. Teacher.
At Mar: OG: '88- 4. USSR champion 1988.
Progression at Mar: 1985- 2:46:06, 1986- 2:36:52, 1987- 2:31:20, 1988- 2:27:05. pbs: 3000m: 9:09.1 '87, 5000m: 15:52.4 '87, 10000m: 32:23.20 '88.

Natalya POMOSHNIKOVA b.9 Jul 1965 1.69m 60kg. Moskva Sp. Student.
At 100m (200m)/4x100mR: OG: '88- 6/3R; WCh: '87- sf/3R; EJ: '83- 1 (4, 2R); ECp: '85- 2R. USSR champion 1984 (tie).
Progression at 100m: 1983- 11.48, 1984- 11.42, 1985- 11.27, 1986- 11.20/11.0, 1987- 11.07, 1988- 10.98. pb 200m: 23.02 '86, 22.6 '85.

Yelena RODIONOVA b.7 May 1965 Chelyabinsk 1.72m 60kg. Chelyabinsk Dyn. Sports student.
At 10kmW: ECh: '86- 4. At 5kmW: WSG: '87- 2.
Progression at 10kmW: 1983- 49:13, 1984- 47:35, 1985- 46:25, 1986- 46:02, 1987- 44:33, 1988- 44:13.75t. Road pbs: 5kmW: 22:00.01 '87, 20kmW: 1:35:06 '87.

Yelena ROMANOVA b.20 Mar 63 1.60m 51kg. née Malykhina. Volgograd SA. Student.
At 3000m: OG: '88- 4; WCh: '87- 5 (h 10000m); WSG: '83- 2. At 1500m: EJ: '81- 2. World CC: '88- 6.
Progression at 3000m: 1981- 8:56.03, 1982- 8:59.18, 1983- 8:59.79, 1985- 9:11.03, 1986- 8:47.79i/8:56.34, 1987- 8:41.15, 1988- 8:30.45. pbs: 800m: 2:04.0, 1500m: 4:04.60 '86.
Ran 3000m pb to win 1987 Grand Prix final.

Tatyana SAMOLENKO b.12 Aug 1961 Sekretarka, Orenburg 1.66m 57kg. née Khamitova. Zaporozhye Sp. Teacher.
At 1500m/3000m: OG: '88- 3/1; WCh: '87- 1/1; WI: '87- 2/1; ECh: '86- 2/5; ECp: '87- 1 800m, 2 1500m. USSR 1500m champion 1986–7.
Progression at 1500m/3000m: 1978- 5:05.0, 1979- 4:28.0, 1980- 4:25.2, 1981- 4:22.4, 1982- 4:17.6, 1983- 4:10.85, 1984- 4:02.41, 1985- 4:02.41, 1986- 3:59.45/8:36.00, 1987- 3:58.56/8:38.73, 1988- 4:00.30/8:26.53. pbs: 400m: 53.5 '86, 800m: 1:58.56 '85, 1000m: 2:39.4i '84.
The European silver medal was her only loss at 1500m in 1986. Added three gold medals and a silver at world championships in 1987. Fast finisher, who had not needed to run very fast times until she took 9.47 sec off her best to win the Olympic 3000m title.

Natalya SHUBENKOVA b.25 Sep 1957 Srosty, Altay province. 1.72m 64kg. Barnaul Dyn. Teacher.
At Hep: OG: '88- 4; WCh: '83- dnf; ECh: '82- 5, '86- 2; ECp: '81- 7, '85- 2. USSR champion 1983–6.
USSR heptathlon record 1984.
Progression at Hep: 1980- 5332, 1981- 5993, 1982- 6524, 1983- 6517, 1984- 6859, 1985- 6510, 1986- 6645, 1988- 6540. pbs: 200m: 23.57 '84, 800m: 2:03.61 '86, 100mh: 12.93 '84, HJ: 1.83 '84, LJ: 6.73 '84, SP: 14.76 '88, JT: 51.42 '85.

Raisa SMEKHNOVA b.16 Sep 1950 Kaltan, Kemerovo 1.66m 50kg. née Katyukova. Minsk Sp. Athletics coach.
At Mar: OG: '88- 16; WCh: '83- 3; WCp: '85- 10; ECp: '88- 2. At 1500m: OG: '76- sf. USSR champion at 3000m 1975, marathon 1985. World CC: '79- 2, '82- 8.
Two USSR marathon records 1983–4.
Progression at Mar: 1981- 2:37:57, 1982- 2:37:04, 1983- 2:31:13, 1984- 2:29:10, 1985- 2:32.00, 1986- 2:32:46, 1987- 2:28:00sh, 1988- 2:28:40. pbs: 800m: 2:01.9 '79, 1500m: 3:59.8 '76, 3000m: 8:41.77 '76, 10000m: 31:59.70 '84.

Irina STRAKHOVA b.4 Mar 1959 Novosibirsk 1.68m 54kg. Novosibirsk Dyn. Sociologist.
At 10kmW: WCh: '87- 1; WCp: '87- 2.
Progression at 10kmW road: 1984- 51:00, 1985- 46:40, 1986- 44:38, 1987- 43:35. pbs road: 5kmW: 21:43 '87, 20kmW: 1:34:31 '87.

Olga TURCHAK b.5 Mar 1967 Alma-Ata 1.90m 60kg. Alma-Ata Sp. Student.
At HJ: OG: '88- 4; WI: '87- 8; ECh: '86- 3; EJ: '85- 2. USSR champion 1986.
World junior high jump record 1984.
Progression at HJ: 1983- 1.84, 1984- 1.96, 1985- 1.95, 1986- 2.01, 1987- 1.94i/1.92, 1988- 2.00.

Galina YERMAKOVA b.15 Jul 1953 Kemerovo 1.82m 98kg. née Savinkova. Moskva Dyn. Sports instructor.
At DT: WCh: '83- 11; ECh: '82- 3, '86- 6; WCp: '81- 3, '85- 2; ECp: '81- 2, '85- 1, '87- 4. USSR champion 1984.
Three USSR discus records 1983–4, including world record in 1983.
Progression at DT: 1971- 33.00, 1972- 41.10, 1973- 55.72, 1974- 59.78, 1976- 76.60, 1977- 61.48, 1978- 62.18, 1979- 65.78, 1980- 67.22, 1981- 69.70, 1982- 69.90, 1983- 73.26, 1984- 73.28, 1985- 72.96, 1986- 68.32, 1987- 68.42, 1988- 64.26. pb SP: 16.50 '80.

Natalya YERMOLOVICH b.29 Apr 1964 Near Gomel, Byelorussia 1.75m 80kg. née Kolenchukova. Mogilev Sp. Engineer.
At JT: OG: '88- 6; WCh: '87- 7; ECh: '86- 6; ECp: '85- 3, '87- 2. USSR champion 1985, 1987.
Progression at JT: 1979- 41.88, 1980- 44.90, 1981- 49.86, 1982- 56.96, 1983- 61.62, 1984- 64.26, 1985- 69.86, 1986- 66.64, 1987- 67.40, 1988- 68.86.

Inna YEVSEYEVA b.14 Aug 1964 1.82m 62kg. Zhitomir Sp. Student.
At 800m: OG: '88- 6.
Progression at 800m: 1983- 2:02.7, 1985- 2:02.7, 1986- 2:00.6, 1988- 1:56.0. pbs: 400m: 50.80/50.6 '86, 600m: 1:25.87i '88, 1500m: 4:12.6 '88, 400mh: 55.85 '86.

Marina ZHIROVA b.6 Jun 1963 Yegoryevsk, Moskva 1.70m 60kg. née Titova. Moskva TR. Student.
At 100m/R- 4x100m relay: OG: '88- sf/3R; WCp: '85- 2=/2R; ECp: '85- 2/2R. At 200m: ECh: '86- 8/3R; WCp: '85- 3. USSR champion 1985, 1988.
USSR 100m record 1985.
Progression at 100m, 200m: 1977- 12.4, 25.4;

1978- 11.9/11.4w, 24.9; 1979- 11.97/11.6/11.72w, 24.31; 1980- 11.8, 24.6; 1981- 11.5, 24.3; 1982- 11.4, 23.4; 1983- 11.80, 23.4/23.71; 1984- 11.24, 23.20; 1985- 10.98, 22.46; 1986- 11.44, 22.93; 1987- 11.22/11.1, 23.27, 1988- 11.10. pb 400m: 52.6 '87.

Elena Joupiua (George Herringshaw/ASP)

Yelena ZHUPIYOVA b.18 Apr 1960 Arkhangelsk 1.63m 51kg. née Durshan. Kharkov Dyn. Engineer.
At 10000m: OG: '88- 3; WCh: '87- 2; ECh: '86- 6 (6 3000m).
Progression at 3000m/10000m: 1979- 9:31.1, 1981- 8:55.8/33:18.12, 1984- 8:39.52, 1985- 8:38.1/ 32:25.37, 1986- 8:40.74/31:42.99, 1987- 8:38.5/ 31:09.40, 1988- 8:44.79/31:19.82. pbs: 200m: 2:03.1 '88, 1500m: 4:04.44 '84, 5000m: 15:23.25 '86.

Ellina ZVERYEVA b.16 Nov 1960 Dolgoprudny 1.82m 90kg. formerly Kisheyeva. Minsk Dyn. Student.
At DT: OG: '88- 5. USSR champion 1986.
Progression at DT: 1981- 59.88, 1982- 62.52, 1983- 65.18, 1984- 68.56, 1985- 66.64, 1986- 68.96, 1987- 60.84, 1988- 71.58.

YUGOSLAVIA

Governing body: Atletski Savez Jugoslavije, Strahinica Bana 73a, 11000 Beograd. Founded in 1921.
National Championships first held in 1920 (men) and 1923 (women)
1988 champions: MEN
100m: Dusko Markovic 10.80, 200m: Slobodan Brankovic 21.18, 400m: Ismail Macev 46.28, 800m: Slobodan Popovic 1:44.85, 1500m: Branko Zorko 3:46.03, 5000m: Dragan Sekulic 14:12.42, 10000m: Mladen Krsek 29:10.45, Mar: Tomislav Askovic 2:33:50, 3kmSt: Vule Maksimovic 8:48.10, 110mh: Zeljko Grabusic 14.15w, 400mh: Branislav Karaulic 49.57, HJ: Mihec Prijon 2.16, PV: Zoran Radovanovic 4.90, LJ: Jovica Petrovic 7.59, TJ: Djordje Kozul 16.44, SP: Jovan Lazarevic 19.08, DT: Dragan Mustapic 56.64, HT: Srecko Stiglic (22nd title) 62.86, JT: Sejad Krdzalic 79.42, Dec: Sasa Karan 7877, 20kmW: Mico Cvjetkovic 1:33:49.
WOMEN
100m: Dijana Istvanovic 11.84, 200m: Kornelija Sinkovic 23.88, 400m/800m: Slobodanka Colovic 52.32/1:57.93, 1500m: Snezana Pajkic 4:24.39, 3000m: Tijana Stojcevic 9:42.61, 10000m: Suzana Ciric 36:00.17, Mar: Slavica Brcic-Marijic 3:07:22, 100mh: Gordana Cotric 13.28, 400mh: Dejana Rakita 58.65, HJ: Amra Temim 1.88, LJ: Tamara Malesev 5.97, SP: Danica Zivanov 16.95, DT: Snezana Golubic 50.16, JT: Vera Cosic 56.58, Hep: Marina Mihajlova 5583.

Sejad KRDZALIC b.5 Jan 1960 Zenica 1.87m 93kg. Partizan, Beograd. Electrician and student of physical education.
At JT: OG: '84- dnq, '88- 12; WCh: '87- dnq; ECh: '86- 7; WSG: '87- 2. Balkan champion 1986, Yugoslav 1983–4, 1987–8.
Four Yugoslav javelin records 1984–5, seven with new javelin 1986–7.
Progression at JT: 1977- 51.06, 1978- 63.86, 1979- 61.26, 1980- 66.24, 1981- 69.16, 1982- 71.90, 1983- 80.86, 1984- 83.70, 1985- 85.10, new: 1986- 82.34, 1987- 83.34, 1988- 82.70.

Slobodan POPOVIC b.28 Sep 1962 Indjija 1.79m 63kg. Crvena Zvezda, Beograd. Law student.
At 800m: OG: '88- sf; WCh: '87- 7; WI: '87- 6; ECh: '86- h; WSG: '87- 1 (2 4x400mR). Balkan champion 1986, Yugoslav 1985–6, 1988. At 400m: EJ: '81- h.
Progression at 800m: 1980- 1:51.2, 1981- 1:50.59, 1983- 1:49.26, 1984- 1:47.35, 1985- 1:46.09, 1986- 1:47.12, 1987- 1:45.07, 1988- 1:44.75. pbs: 100m: 10.6w '86, 200m: 21.6w '86, 400m: 46.5 '87, 46.64 '84, 1000m: 2:25.2 '84, 1500m: 3:47.63 '87.

Women

Slobodanka COLOVIC b.10 Jan 1965 Osijek 1.76m 55kg. Slavonija, Osijek. Student.
At 800m: OG: '88- 4; WCh: '87- 8; WI: '87- 4; ECh: '86- sf; EJ: '83- 4; EI: '86- 3; WSG: '87- 1. Balkan champion 1986, Yugoslav 400m 1986, 1988; 800m 1982–6, 1988.
Yugoslav records: 800m (2), 1500m 1987.
Progression at 800m: 1978- 2:15.8, 1979- 2:13.9, 1980- 2:10.1, 1981- 2:08.21, 1982- 2:04.65, 1983- 2:02.47, 1984- 2:03.04, 1985- 2:01.37, 1986- 1:59.63, 1987- 1:56.51, 1988- 1:57.50. pbs: 100m: 11.7 '87, 200m: 25.29 '83, 400m: 52.32 '88, 1500m: 4:09.14 '87.

METRIC–IMPERIAL CONVERSION TABLES

Throughout this book measurements are given in the metric system. For those readers who are more familiar with imperial units we give a basic conversion table which specifically covers those distances achieved by top class athletes in the field events. This will be hope provide a useful cross check for those wishing to convert.

1.70m –	5ft 7in	17.50m –	57ft 5in	5.60	18ft 4½in	66.00	216ft 6in
1.75	5ft 8¾in	18.00	59ft 0¾in	5.80	18ft 0¼in	68.00	223ft 1in
1.80	5ft 10¾in	18.50	60ft 8½in	6.00	19ft 8¼in	70.00	229ft 8in
1.85	6ft 0¾in	19.00	62ft 4in	6.25	20ft 6¼in	72.00	236ft 3in
1.90	6ft 2¾in	19.50	63ft 11¾in	6.50	21ft 4in	74.00	242ft 9in
1.95	6ft 4¾in	20.00	65ft 7½in	6.75	22ft 1¾in	76.00	249ft 4in
2.00	6ft 6¾in	20.50	67ft 3¼in	7.00	22ft 11¾in	78.00	255ft 11in
2.05	6ft 8¾in	21.00	68ft 10¾in	7.25	23ft 9½in	80.00	262ft 5in
2.10	6ft 10¾in	21.50	70ft 6½in	7.50	24ft 7¼in	82.00	269ft 0in
2.15	7ft 0½in	22.00	72ft 2¼in	7.75	25ft 5¼in	84.00	275ft 7in
2.20	7ft 2½in	22.50	73ft 10in	8.00	26ft 3in	86.00	282ft 2in
2.25	7ft 4½in	23.00	75ft 5½in	8.25	27ft 0¾in	88.00	288ft 8in
2.30	7ft 6½in	50.00	164ft 0in	8.50	27ft 10¾in	90.00	295ft 3in
2.35	7ft 8½in	52.00	170ft 7in	8.75	28ft 8½in	92.00	301ft 10in
2.40	7ft 10½in	54.00	177ft 2in	9.00	29ft 6½in	94.00	308ft 5in
4.60	15ft 1in	56.00	183ft 9in	15.00	49ft 2½in	96.00	314ft 11in
4.80	15ft 9in	58.00	190ft 3in	15.50	50ft 10¼in	98.00	321ft 6in
5.00	16ft 4¾in	60.00	196ft 10in	16.00	52ft 6in	100.00	328ft 1in
5.20	17ft 0¾in	62.00	203ft 5in	16.50	54ft 1¾in	102.00	334ft 8in
5.40	17ft 8½in	64.00	210ft 0in	17.00	55ft 9¼in	104.00	341ft 2in

In the biographies section athletes' weights are given in kilograms, the following guide will help those who are more familiar with weights in pounds:

50kg –	110lbs	100kg –	220lbs
60	132	110	243
70	154	120	265
80	176	130	287
90	198	140	309

INTRODUCTION TO WORLD LIST AND INDEX

RECORDS

World, World Junior, Olympic, Continental and Area records are listed. In running events up to and including 400 metres, only fully automatic times are shown. Marks listed are those which are considered statistically acceptable by the ATFS, and thus may differ from official records where, for instance the performance was set indoors or while the athlete was a professional.

WORLD ALL-TIME AND WORLD YEAR LISTS

These lists are presented in the following format: Mark, Wind reading (where appropriate), Name, Nationality (abbreviated), Date of birth or Year of birth (last two digits), Position in competition, Meeting name (if significant), Venue, Date of performance. Position, meet and venue details have been omitted for reasons of space beyond 100th in year lists.

INDEX

These lists contain the names of all athletes ranked with full details in the world year lists. The format of the index is as follows: Family name, First Name, Nationality, Birthdate, Height (cm) and Weight (kg), 1988 best mark, Lifetime best as at the end of 1987 and the relevant year.

Meeting Abbreviations

The following abbreviations have been used for meetings with, in parentheses, the first year that they were held.

AAA (UK) Amateur Athletic Association Championships (1880)
AAU (USA) Amateur Athletic Union Championships (1888) (now TAC)
AfrC African Championships (1979)
AfG African Games (1965) (or AfrG)
APM Adriaan Paulen Memorial, Hengelo
AsiC Asian Championships (1973)
AsiG Asian Games (1951)
ASV Weltklasse in Köln, ASV Club meeting (1934)
Athl Athletissima, Lausanne
Balk Balkan Games (1929)
Barr (Cuba) Barrientos Memorial (1950)
BGP Budapest Grand Prix (1978) (now HGP)
Bisl Bislett Games, Oslo
BNP BNP meeting, Paris or Lille
CAC Central American and Caribbean Championships (1967)
CAG Central American and Caribbean Games (1926)
CalR California Relays (1942)
CISM International Military Championships (1946)
CG Commonwealth Games (1930) (or CommG)
DNG DN Galan, Stockholm (1966)
Drake Drake Relays (1910)
Drz Druzhba/Friendship Games
EC European Championships (1934)
ECP European Clubs Cup
EI European Indoor Championships (1970, Games from 1966)
EJ European Junior Championships (1970)
EP European Cup – track & field (1965), multi-events (1973)
EsC Eschborn Cup – Women's World Race Walking Cup (1979)
FBK Fanny Blankers-Koen meeting, Hengelo (now APM)
FlaR Florida Relays (1939)
FOT (USA) Final Olympic Trials (1920)
GGala Golden Gala, Roma or Verona (1980)
GO Golden Oval, Dresden
GP IAAF Grand Prix final (1985)
GS Golden Spike, Ostrava (1969)
GWG Goodwill Games, Moskva (1986)
HB Hanns Braun Memorial, München (1930)
HGP Hungalu Budapest Grand Prix
IAAFg IAAF Golden events (1978)

IAC — IAC meeting (1968), formerly Coke meeting, now Miller-Lite
IbAmC — Ibero-American Championships
Int — International meeting
ISTAF — Internationales Stadionfest, Berlin (1921)
Izv — (SU) Izvestia Cup
Jen — Bruce Jenner Classic, San Jose (1979)
Jer — Harry Jerome Track Classic (1984)
JO — Jesse Owens Memorial (1981)
JP — Jan Popper Memorial (1987), formerly 'Journalists' Lath', Praha
-j — Junior Championships
KansR — Kansas Relays, Lawrence (1923)
King — Martin Luther King Games (1969)
Kuso — Janusz Kusocinski Memorial (1954)
Kuts — Vladimir Kuts Memorial
LB — Liberty Bell, Philadelphia
LT — Lugano Trophy, walking (1961)
MedG — Mediterranean Games (1951)
MSR — Mt.San Antonio College Relays (1959)
NC — National Championships
NC-j — National Junior Championships
NC-y — National Youth Championships
NCAA — National Collegiate Athletic Association Championships (1921)
Nik — Nikaia, Nice (1976)
ND — Nina Dumbadze Memorial
NM — Narodna Mladeje, Sofia (1955) (or Nar)
NP — National Cup
Nurmi — Paavo Nurmi Games (1957)
OD — (GDR) Olympischer Tag (Olympic Day)
OG — Olympic Games (1896)
OT — Olympic Trials
PAG — Pan American Games (1951)
PennR — Pennsylvania Relays (1895)
Pepsi — Pepsi Cola Invitational
PG — Peugeot Games (was PTG)
PO — Pre Olympic Meet
Prav — (SU) Pravda Cup
PTG — Peugeot Talbot Games (1980) (now PG)
PTS — Pravda Televizia Slovnaft, Bratislava (1960)
Pre — Steve Prefontaine Memorial (1976)
RomIC — Romanian International Championships (1948)
Ros — Evzen Rosicky Memorial, Praha (1947)
R-W — Rot-Weiss meeting, Koblenz
SGP — Softeland Grand Prix (walking)
SACh — South American Championships (1919) (or SoAmC)
Spart — (SU) Spartakiad (1956)
SW — S & W Invitational, Modesto
TAC — (USA) The Athletics Congress Championships (1980)
TexR — Texas Relays (1925)
USOF — US Olympic Festival
VD — Ivo Van Damme Memorial, Brussels (1977)
WA — West Athletic Meet (AUT/BEL/DEN/HOL/IRL/POR/SPA/SWZ)
WAAA — (UK) Women's Amateur Athletic Association Champs. (1922)
WC — World Championships (1983)
WP — World Cup – track & field (1977), marathon (1985)
WG — World Games, Helsinki (1961)
WI — World Indoor Championships (1987), World Indoor Games (1985)
WJ — World Junior Championships (1986)
WK — Weltklasse, Zürich (1962)
WPT — World Cup Trials (1977)
WUG — World University Games (1923)
Znam — Znamenskiy Brothers Memorial (1958)

Dual and triangular matches are indicated by 'v' (versus) followed by the name(s) of the opposition. Quadrangular and larger inter-nation matches are denoted by the number of nations and -N; viz 8-N designates an 8-nation meeting.

Miscellaneous abbreviations

A — Made at an altitude of 1000m or higher
D — Made in decathlon competition
H — Made in heptathlon competition
h — Made in heat
i — Indoor mark
m — Manual timing in events beyond 400 metres
Q — Mark made in qualifying round
q — Mark made in quarter-final
r — Race number in a series of races
s — Semi-final
w — Wind-assisted
= — Tie (ex-aequo)
* — Converted time from yards to metres:
For 200m: 220 yards less 0.11 second
For 400m: 440 yards less 0.26 second
For 110mh: 120yh plus 0.03 second

GENERAL NOTES

Altitude aid
Marks set at an altitude of 1000m or higher have been prefixed by the letter 'A'.

Although there are not yet separate world records for altitude assisted events, it is understood by experts that in all events up to 400m in length (with the possible exclusion of the 110m hurdles), and in the horizontal jumps, altitude gives a material benefit to performances. As yet there is no scientific formula for quantifying such aid. For events beyond 800m, however, the thinner air of high altitude has a detrimental effect.

Supplementary lists are included in relevant events for athletes with seasonal bests at altitude who have low altitude marks qualifying for the main list.

Automatic timing
In the main lists for sprints and hurdles, only times recorded by fully automatic timing devices are included. Such a timing device is one which is started automatically by the firing of the starter's gun, with the finish recorded photographically with a strip camera or a movie camera and linked back electronically to the start.

Hand timing
In the sprints and hurdles supplementary lists are included for races which are hand timed. Any athlete with a hand timed best 0.01 seconds or more better than his or her automatically timed best has been included. Hand timed lists have been terminated close to the differential levels considered by the IAAF to be equivalent to automatic times, i.e. 0.24 sec. for 100m, 200m, 100mh, 110mh, and 0.14 sec. for 400m and 400mh.

In events beyond 400m, automatically timed marks are integrated with hand timed marks, with the latter designated with the symbol 'm'. All-time lists also include some auto times in tenths of a second, where the 1/100th time is not known, but the reader can differentiate these from hand timed marks as they do not have the suffix 'm'.

Indoor marks
Indoor marks are included in the main lists for field events and straightway track events, but not for other track events. This is because there is no curb for indoor races and theoretically this can enable athletes to run less than full distance, and, more importantly, because track sizes vary in circumference (200m is the international standard) and banking, while outdoor tracks are standardized at 400m. Athletes whose seasonal bests were set indoors are shown in a supplemental list if they also have outdoor marks qualifying for the world list.

Supplementary marks
Non-winning marks in a field event series which, had they been winning marks, would have qualified for the top 30 performances list are included in a supplement at the end of the relevant events.

Wind assistance
In the lists for 100m, 200m, 100mh, 110mh, long jump and triple jump, anemometer readings have been shown where available. The readings are given in metres per second to one decimal place. Where the figure was given originally to two decimal places, it has been rounded to the next tenth upwards, e.g. a wind reading of +2.01 m/s, beyond the IAAF legal limit of 2.0, is rounded to +2.1; or –1.22 m/s is rounded up to –1.2.

Amendments
Keen observers may spot errors in the lists. They are invited to send corrections to the editor, who will pass them on to the relevant compilers:

Peter Matthews,
10 Madgeways Close,
Great Amwell, Ware,
Herts SG12 9RU, England

Event	Record	Name	Nat	Venue	Date

WORLD & CONTINENTAL RECORDS

(as at 31 Dec 1988)

Key: W = World; I = I.A.A.F. (if different); C = Commonwealth
Afr = Africa; Asi = Asia; CAC = Central America & Caribbean
E = Europe; NAm = N.America; Oce = Oceania; SAm = S.America
WJ = World Junior

A = altitude over 1000m; + = timing by photo-electric-cell
* = awaiting ratification; # = not officially ratified

100 METRES

Event	Record	Name	Nat	Venue	Date
W,NAm,C	9.83	Ben JOHNSON	Can	Roma	30 Aug 87
E	9.97	Linford CHRISTIE	UK	Seoul	24 Sep 88
CAC	9.98A	Silvio LEONARD	Cub	Guadalajara	11 Aug 77
Afr	10.00	Chidi IMOH	Nig	W.Berlin	15 Aug 86
SAm	10.00A*	Róbson da SILVA	Bra	Ciudad de México	22 Jul 88
	10.02	Róbson da SILVA	Bra	Habana	27 Sep 86
Oce	10.22	Gerrard KEATING	Aus	Canberra	4 Oct 85
Asi	10.26	LI Tao	Chn	Jakarta	5 Dec 86
WJ	10.07 #	Stanley FLOYD	USA	Austin	24 May 80
	10.08 *	Andre CASON	USA	Tallahassee	24 Jun 88
	10.09A	Mel LATTANY	USA	Colorado Springs	31 Jul 78

200 METRES

Event	Record	Name	Nat	Venue	Date
W,E	19.72A	Pietro MENNEA	Ita	Ciudad de México	12 Sep 79
NAm	19.75	Carl LEWIS	USA	Indianapolis	19 Jun 83
	19.75	Joe DELOACH	USA	Seoul	28 Sep 88
CAC,C	19.86A	Donald QUARRIE	Jam	Cali	3 Aug 71
SAm	20.04A*	Róbson da SILVA	Bra	Ciudad de México	23 Jul 88
	20.04	Róbson da SILVA	Bra	Seoul	28 Sep 88
Oce	20.06A	Peter NORMAN	Aus	Ciudad de México	16 Oct 68
Afr	20.31A#	Tshakile NZIMANDE	RSA	Welkom	21 Nov 87
	20.31	Chidi IMOH	Nig	Bern	23 Aug 88
Asi	20.41	CHANG Jae-Keun	SKo	Jakarta	27 Sep 85
WJ	20.07 #	Lorenzo DANIEL	USA	Starkville	18 May 85
	20.13	Roy Martin	USA	Indianapolis	16 Jun 85

400 METRES

Event	Record	Name	Nat	Venue	Date
W,NAm	43.29	Butch REYNOLDS	USA	Zürich	17 Aug 88
Afr,C	44.17	Innocent EGBUNIKE	Nig	Zürich	19 Aug 87
CAC	44.22A	Roberto HERNANDEZ	Cub	Ciudad de México	22 May 88
E	44.33	Thomas SCHÖNLEBE	GDR	Roma	3 Sep 87
Oce	44.38	Darren CLARK	Aus	Seoul	26 Sep 88
Asi	44.56	Mohamed AL MALKY	Omn	Budapest	12 Aug 88
SAm	45.21	Gérson SOUZA	Bra	Rieti	16 Sep 82
WJ	43.87	Steve LEWIS	USA	Seoul	28 Sep 88

800 METRES

Event	Record	Name	Nat	Venue	Date
W,E,C	1:41.73+	Sebastian COE	UK	Firenze	10 Jun 81
SAm	1:41.77	Joaquim CRUZ	Bra	Köln	26 Aug 84
Afr	1:42.28	Sammy KOSKEI	Ken	Köln	26 Aug 84
NAm	1:42.60	Johnny GRAY	USA	Koblenz	28 Aug 85
CAC	1:43.44	Alberto JUANTORENA	Cub	Sofiya	21 Aug 77
Oce	1:44.3 m	Peter SNELL	NZ	Christchurch	3 Feb 62
Asi	1:45.77	Sri Ram SINGH	Ind	Montréal	25 Jul 76
WJ	1:44.9 ym#	Jim RYUN	USA	Terre Haute	10 Jun 66
	1:44.3 m	Joaquim CRUZ	Bra	Rio de Janeiro	27 Jun 81

Event	Record	Name	Nat	Venue	Date
1500 METRES					
W,Afr	3:29.46	Saïd AOUITA	Mor	W.Berlin	23 Aug 85
E,C	3:29.67	Steve CRAM	UK	Nice	16 Jul 85
NAm	3:29.77	Sydney MAREE	USA	Köln	25 Aug 85
Oce	3:32.4 m	John WALKER	NZ	Oslo	30 Jul 75
SAm	3:34.63	Joaquim CRUZ	Bra	Hengelo	14 Aug 88
Asi	3:38.24	Takashi ISHII	Jap	Düsseldorf	3 Sep 77
CAC	3:38.85	Eduardo CASTRO	Mex	Ciudad Bolívar	14 Aug 81
WJ	3:34.92	Kipkoech CHERUIYOT	Ken	München	26 Jul 83
1 MILE					
W,E,C	3:46.32	Steve CRAM	UK	Oslo	27 Jul 85
Afr	3:46.76	Saïd AOUITA	Mor	Helsinki	2 Jul 87
NAm	3:47.69	Steve SCOTT	USA	Oslo	7 Jul 82
Oce	3:49.08	John WALKER	NZ	Oslo	7 Jul 82
SAm	3:53.00	Joaquim CRUZ	Bra	Los Angeles	13 May 84
CAC	3:57.34	Byron DYCE	Jam	Stockholm	1 Jul 74
Asi	3:59.7 m	Takashi ISHII	Jap	Melbourne	10 Dec 77
WJ	3:51.3 m#	Jim RYUN	USA	Berkeley	17 Jul 66
3000 METRES					
W,Afr,C	7:32.1 m	Henry RONO	Ken	Oslo	27 Jun 78
(W,Afr)	7:32.23 #	Saïd AOUITA	Mor	Köln	17 Aug 86
E	7:32.79	Dave MOORCROFT	UK	London	17 Jul 82
NAm	7:33.37 #	Sydney MAREE	USA	London	17 Jul 82
	7:35.84 *	Doug PADILLA	USA	Oslo	9 Jul 83
	7:36.79	Steve SCOTT	USA	Ingelheim	1 Sep 81
Oce	7:37.49	John WALKER	NZ	London	17 Jul 82
CAC	7:44.63	Arturo BARRIOS	Mex	Stockholm	30 Jun 87
Asi	7:49.92	Shuichi YONESHIGE	Jap	Lappeenranta	5 Jul 88
SAm	7:53.0 m	José da SILVA	Bra	Gateshead	26 Jul 75
WJ	7:43.20	Ari PAUNONEN	Fin	Köln	22 Jun 77
5000 METRES					
W,Afr	12:58.39	Saïd AOUITA	Mor	Roma	22 Jul 87
E,C	13:00.41	Dave MOORCROFT	UK	Oslo	7 Jul 82
NAm	13:01.15	Sydney MAREE	USA	Oslo	27 Jul 85
Oce	13:12.87	Dick QUAX	NZ	Stockholm	5 Jul 77
CAC	13:13.52	Arturo BARRIOS	Mex	Oslo	4 Jul 87
Asi	13:22.97	Shuichi YONESHIGE	Jap	London	8 Jul 88
SAm	13:29.67	Domingo TIBADUIZA	Col	Zürich	16 Aug 78
WJ	13:23.27	Addis ABEBE	Eth	Hengelo	14 Aug 88
10,000 METRES					
W,E	27:13.81	Fernando MAMEDE	Por	Stockholm	2 Jul 84
NAm	27:20.56	Mark NENOW	USA	Bruxelles	5 Sep 86
Afr	27:21.46	Brahim BOUTAYIB	Mor	Seoul	26 Sep 88
C	27:22.47+	Henry RONO	Ken	Wien	11 Jun 78
CAC	27:25.07	Arturo BARRIOS	Mex	Oslo	2 Jul 88
Asi	27:35.33	Takeyuki NAKAYAMA	Jap	Helsinki	2 Jul 87
Oce	27:39.89	Ron CLARKE	Aus	Oslo	14 Jul 65
SAm	27:53.02+	Domingo TIBADUIZA	Col	Wien	11 Jun 78
WJ	27:50.24	Addis ABEBE	Eth	Bruxelles	19 Aug 88

Event	Record	Name	Nat	Venue	Date
LONG JUMP					
W,NAm	8.90A	Bob BEAMON	USA	Ciudad de México	18 Oct 68
E	8.86A	Robert EMMIYAN	SU	Tsakhadzor	22 May 87
CAC	8.51	Jaime JEFFERSON	Cub	Indianapolis	16 Aug 87
SAm	8.36	João Carlos de OLIVEIRA	Bra	Rieti	21 Jul 79
Oce,C	8.27	Gary HONEY	Aus	Budapest	20 Aug 84
Afr	8.26i#	Charlton EHIZUELEN	Nig	Bloomington	7 Mar 75
	8.25	Paul EMORDI	Nig	Baton Rouge	5 Jun 87
Asi	8.23	CHEN Zunrong	Chn	Beijing	12 Apr 86
WJ	8.34	Randy WILLIAMS	USA	München	8 Sep 72
TRIPLE JUMP					
W,NAm	17.97	Willie BANKS	USA	Indianapolis	16 Jun 85
E	17.92	Khristo MARKOV	Bul	Roma	31 Aug 87
SAm	17.89A	João Carlos de OLIVEIRA	Bra	Ciudad de México	15 Oct 75
CAC	17.78	Lázaro BETANCOURT	Cub	Habana	15 Jun 86
C	17.57A	Keith CONNOR	UK	Provo	5 Jun 82
Oce	17.46	Ken LORRAWAY	Aus	London	7 Aug 82
Asi	17.34	ZOU Zhenxian	Chn	Roma	5 Sep 81
Afr	17.26	Ajayi AGBEBAKU	Nig	Edmonton	8 Jul 83
WJ	17.50	Volker MAI	GDR	Erfurt	23 Jun 85
SHOT PUTT					
W,E	23.06	Ulf TIMMERMANN	GDR	Khaniá	22 May 88
NAm	22.86 #	Brian OLDFIELD	USA	El Paso	10 May 75
	22.52 *	John BRENNER	USA	Walnut	26 Apr 87
	22.39	Randy BARNES	USA	Seoul	23 Sep 88
C	21.68	Geoff CAPES	Eng	Cwmbrân	18 May 80
SAm	20.90	Gert WEIL	Chl	Wirges	17 Aug 86
Afr	20.76	Ahmed Kamel SHATTA	Egy	Al Qâhira	24 Mar 88
CAC	20.28	Raúl RUIZ	Cub	Rostock	29 May 88
Oce	19.80	Les MILLS	NZ	Honolulu	3 Jul 67
Asi	19.26	MA Yongfeng	Chn	Tianjing	1 Sep 88
WJ	21.05i#	Terry ALBRITTON	USA	New York	22 Feb 74
	20.65 #	Mike CARTER	USA	Boston	4 Jul 79
	20.38	Terry ALBRITTON	USA	Walnut	27 Apr 74
DISCUS					
W,E	74.08	Jürgen SCHULT	GDR	Neubrandenburg	6 Jun 86
NAm	72.34dq	Ben PLUCKNETT	USA	Stockholm	7 Jul 81
	71.32 #	Ben PLUCKNETT	USA	Eugene	4 Jun 83
CAC	71.06	Luís DELIS	Cub	Habana	21 May 83
Afr	68.48 #	John VAN REENEN	RSA	Stellenbosch	14 Mar 75
	64.72	Christian OKOYE	Nig	Walnut	28 Apr 85
C	67.32	Rob GRAY	Can	Etobicoke	30 Apr 84
Oce	65.62 #	Werner REITERER	Aus	Melbourne	15 Dec 87
	65.08	Wayne MARTIN	Aus	Newcastle	3 Jan 79
Asi	61.06	Djalal-Ali KESHMIRI	Irn	Lancaster	19 May 74
SAm	59.98	José ARAUJO (de Souza)	Bra	Eugene	9 Apr 88
WJ	65.62 #	Werner REITERER	Aus	Melbourne	15 Dec 87
	63.64	Werner HARTMANN	FRG	Strasbourg	25 Jun 78

(dq = retrospectively disqualified by the I.A.A.F. for drug abuse)

Event	Record	Name	Nat	Venue	Date
HAMMER					
W,E	86.74	Yuriy SEDYKH	SU	Stuttgart	30 Aug 86
NAm	81.88	Jud LOGAN	USA	University Park	22 Apr 88
C	77.54	Martin GIRVAN	NI	Wolverhampton	12 May 84
Asi	75.96	Shigenobu MUROFUSHI	Jap	Walnut	15 Jul 84
Oce	75.90	Peter FARMER	Aus	Vanves	14 Aug 79
CAC	74.74	Armando OROZCO	Cub	Habana	25 May 80
Afr	73.86 #	Adam BARNARD	RSA	Johannesburg	26 Mar 76
	71.52	Abdelhakim TUOMI	Alg	Alger	6 Jun 86
SAm	71.34	Andres CHARADIA	Arg	Praha	17 May 87
WJ	78.14	Roland STEUK	GDR	Leipzig	30 Jun 78

Event	Record	Name	Nat	Venue	Date
				110 METRES HURDLES	
W,NAm	12.93	Renaldo NEHEMIAH	USA	Zürich	19 Aug 81
E,C	13.11A	Colin JACKSON	Wal	Sestriere	11 Aug 88
CAC	13.21	Alejandro CASAÑAS	Cub	Sofiya	21 Aug 77
Oce	13.58	Don WRIGHT	Aus	Brisbane	4 Oct 82
Afr	13.63A#	Wessel BOSMAN	RSA	Johannesburg	23 Apr 88
	13.69	Fatwel KIMAIYO	Ken	Christchurch	26 Jan 74
		Godwin OBASOGIE	Nig	Austin	3 Apr 76
SAm	13.62A*	Elvis CEDENO	Ven	Ciudad de México	22 Jul 88
	13.84	Lyndon JOHNSON (Campos)	Bra	São Paulo	16 Aug 87
Asi	13.72	YU Zhicheng	Chn	Guangzhou	28 Nov 87
WJ	13.23	Renaldo NEHEMIAH	USA	Zürich	16 Aug 78
				400 METRES HURDLES	
W,NAm	47.02	Edwin MOSES	USA	Koblenz	31 Aug 83
Afr	47.23	Amadou Dia BÂ	Sen	Seoul	25 Sep 88
E	47.48	Harald SCHMID	FRG	Athínai	8 Sep 82
	#	Harald SCHMID	FRG	Roma	1 Sep 87
C	47.82	John AKII-BUA	Uga	München	2 Sep 72
CAC	48.04	Winthrop GRAHAM	Jam	Seoul	25 Sep 88
Asi	49.20	Ryoichi YOSHIDA	Jap	Zagreb	19 Jul 87
SAm	49.24	António EUZEBIO (Ferreira)	Bra	Kobe	30 Aug 85
Oce	49.32	Bruce FIELD	Aus	Christchurch	29 Jan 74
WJ	48.02	Danny HARRIS	USA	Los Angeles	17 Jun 84
				3000 METRES STEEPLECHASE	
W,Afr,C	8:05.4 m	Henry RONO	Ken	Seattle	13 May 78
	8:05.51 #	Julius KARIUKI	Ken	Seoul	30 Sep 88
E	8:07.62	Joseph MAHMOUD	Fra	Bruxelles	24 Aug 84
NAm	8:09.17	Henry MARSH	USA	Koblenz	28 Aug 85
Oce	8:14.05	Peter RENNER	NZ	Koblenz	29 Aug 84
Asi	8:19.52	Masanari SHINTAKU	Jap	Stockholm	8 Jul 80
SAm	8:23.26	Adauto DOMINGUES	Bra	Indianapolis	12 Aug 87
CAC	8:28.89	Carmelo RIOS	PRc	Indianapolis	17 Jun 83
WJ	8:29.50	Ralf PÖNITZSCH	GDR	Warszawa	19 Aug 76
				HIGH JUMP	
W,CAC	2.43	Javier SOTOMAYOR	Cub	Santander	8 Sep 88
E	2.42	Patrik SJÖBERG	Swe	Stockholm	30 Jun 87
		Carlos THRÄNHARDT	FRG	W.Berlin (i)	26 Feb 88
Asi	2.39	ZHU Jianhua	Chn	Eberstadt	10 Jun 84
NAm	2.37	Thomas McCANTS	USA	Columbus	8 May 88
		Jerome CARTER	USA	Columbus	8 May 88
C	2.34	Nick SAUNDERS	Ber	Seoul	25 Sep 88
Afr	2.28	Othmane BELFAA	Alg	Amman	20 Aug 83
Oce	2.28	John ATKINSON	Aus	Melbourne	31 Mar 84
SAm	2.25	Claudio FREIRE	Bra	Rio de Janeiro	10 Oct 82
	A	Fernando PASTORIZA	Arg	Ciudad de México	23 Jul 88
WJ	2.36	Javier SOTOMAYOR	Cub	Habana	22 Mar 86
				POLE VAULT	
W,E	6.06	Sergiy BUBKA	SU	Nice	10 Jul 88
NAm	5.96	Joe DIAL	USA	Norman	18 Jun 87
SAm	5.76	Tom HINTNAUS	Bra	Zürich	21 Aug 85
C	5.65	Keith STOCK	Eng	Stockholm	7 Jul 81
Asi	5.57	LIANG Xueren	Chn	Anshan	28 Jun 87
Oce	5.53	Don BAIRD	Aus	Long Beach	16 Apr 77
CAC	5.50	Ruben CAMINO	Cub	Indianapolis	15 Aug 87
Afr	5.34	Lakhdar RAHAL	Alg	Paris	4 Jun 79
WJ	5.65	Rodion GATAULLIN	SU	Donetsk	8 Sep 84
		István BAGYULA	Hun	Sudbury	28 Jul 88

Event	Record	Name	Nat	Venue	Date
JAVELIN (1986 MODEL)					
W,E	87.66	Jan ŽELEZNÝ	CS	Nitra	31 May 87
NAm	85.38	Tom PETRANOFF	USA	Helsinki	7 Jul 86
C	85.24	Mick HILL	Eng	Stockholm	30 Jun 87
Asi	84.16	Kazuhiro MIZOGUCHI	Jap	Tokyo	3 May 87
Oce	80.70	Gavin LOVEGROVE	NZ	Auckland	10 Dec 88
CAC	79.24	Ramón GONZALEZ	Cub	Athínai	20 Jun 87
Afr	78.86 #	Johan OOSTHUIZEN	RSA	Johannesburg	24 Apr 88
	76.48	Zakayo MALEKWA	Tan	Arlington	10 May 86
SAm	72.46	Luís LUCUMI	Col	Caracas	26 Jul 87
WJ	80.26	Vladimir OVCHINNIKOV	SU	Seoul	24 Sep 88
DECATHLON (1984 TABLES)					
W,E,C	8847	Daley THOMPSON	Eng	Los Angeles	9 Aug 84
NAm	8634	Bruce JENNER	USA	Montréal	30 Jul 76
SAm	8291m	Tito STEINER	Arg	Provo	23 Jun 83
	8266	Pedro da SILVA	Bra	Walnut	24 Apr 87
Oce	8366m	Simon POELMAN	NZ	Christchurch	22 Mar 87
	8158	Simon POELMAN	NZ	Christchurch	30 Mar 86
Asi	8009m	YANG Chuan-Kuang	Tai	Walnut	28 Apr 63
Afr	7934m	Ahmed MAHOUR BACHA	Alg	Alger	9 Jul 85
	7577	Ahmed MAHOUR BACHA	Alg	Alger	8 May 85
CAC	7749m	Rigoberto SALAZAR	Cub	Habana	25 May 79
	7734	Douglas FERNANDEZ	Ven	Caracas	27 Aug 83
WJ	8397	Torsten VOSS	GDR	Erfurt	7 Jul 82
MARATHON					
W,Afr	2:06:50	Belayneh DINSAMO	Eth	Rotterdam	17 Apr 88
E	2:07:12	Carlos LOPES	Por	Rotterdam	20 Apr 85
C	2:07:13	Steve JONES	Wal	Chicago	20 Oct 85
Asi	2:07:35	Taisuke KODAMA	Jap	Beijing	19 Oct 86
Oce	2:07:51	Rob DE CASTELLA	Aus	Boston	21 Apr 86
NAm	2:08:52	Alberto SALAZAR	USA	Boston	19 Apr 82
CAC	2:08:57	Alejandro CRUZ	Mex	Chicago	30 Oct 88
SAm	2:11:21	Domingo TIBADUIZA	Col	New York	23 Oct 83
WJ	2:15:28	Paul GOMPERS	USA	Huntsville	10 Dec 83
20 KM WALK (ROAD)					
W,E	1:19:08	Mikhail SHCHENNIKOV	SU	Kiyiv	30 Jul 88
Oce,C	1:19:22	Dave SMITH	Aus	Hobart	19 Jul 87
CAC	1:19:24	Carlos MERCENARIO	Mex	New York	3 May 87
SAm	1:20:19	Querubim MORENO	Col	New York	3 May 87
NAm	1:21:13	Guillaume LEBLANC	Can	St.Léonard	5 Oct 86
Asi	1:21:39	LIU Jianli	Chn	Jiading	16 Mar 85
Afr	1:26:17	Abdelwahab FERGUENE	Alg	New York	3 May 87
WJ	1:21:33	Carlos MERCENARIO	Mex	St.Léonard	5 Oct 86
20,000M WALK (TRACK)					
W,CAC	1:18:40.0	Ernesto CANTO	Mex	Fana	5 May 84
E	1:19:22.5	Aleksey PERSHIN	SU	Fana	7 May 88
Oce,C	1:20:51.0	Dave SMITH	Aus	Melbourne	11 Feb 87
NAm	1:23:17 #	Guillaume LEBLANC	Can	Québec	22 May 86
	1:24:58.8	Marcel JOBIN	Can	Québec	12 May 84
Asi	1:24:02.6	JIANG Shaohong	Chn	Jian	8 Mar 86
SAm	1:26:38.0	Marcelo MOREIRO (Palma)	Bra	Curitiba	28 May 88
Afr	1:26:39.93	Benamar KACHKOUCHE	Alg	Thonon-les-Bains	20 Jun 84
WJ	1:22:42	Andrey PERLOV	SU	Donetsk	6 Sep 80

RECORDS

Event	Record	Name	Nat	Venue	Date
		50 KM WALK (ROAD)			
W,E	3:38:17	Ronald WEIGEL	GDR	Potsdam	25 May 86
CAC	3:41:20	Raúl GONZALEZ	Mex	Praha-Podebrady	11 Jun 78
Oce,C	3:44:07	Simon BAKER	Aus	Seoul	30 Sep 88
NAm	3:47:48	Marcel JOBIN	Can	Québec	20 Jun 81
Asi	3:52:51	LI Baojin	Chn	Zhengzhou	25 Oct 87
SAm	4:01:31	Hector MORENO	Col	Seoul	30 Sep 88
Afr	4:14:30 #	Eddie MICHAELS	RSA	Cape Town	11 Mar 67
	4:19:15	H'Mimed RAHOULI	Alg	Bourmerdès	12 Mar 87
		50,000M WALK (TRACK)			
W,CAC	3:41:38.4	Raúl GONZALEZ	Mex	Fana	25 May 79
E	3:46:11 #	Mykola UDOVENKO	SU	Uzhgorod	3 Oct 80
	3:48:59	Vladimir REZAYEV	SU	Fana	2 May 80
C	4:05:47.3	Chris MADDOCKS	Eng	Birmingham	22 Sep 84
Oce	4:06:39	Willi SAWALL	Aus	Melbourne	14 Aug 76
NAm	4:12:44.5	Dan O'CONNOR	USA	Irvine	19 Nov 83
SAm	4:17:11.0	Mauricio CORTEZ	Col	Caracas	16 Nov 86
Asi	4:20:45	Kazuo SHIRAI	Jap	Tokyo	9 Mar 80
Afr	4:21:44.5	Abdelwahab FERGUENE	Alg	Toulouse	25 Mar 84

4×100 METRES RELAY

Event	Record	Nat	Team	Venue	Date
W,NAm	37.83	USA	(Graddy, Brown, C.Smith, Lewis)	Los Angeles	11 Aug 84
E	38.02	SU	(Yevgenyev,Bryzgin,Muravyov,Krylov)	Roma	6 Sep 87
CAC,C	38.39A	Jam	(Stewart, Fray, Forbes, Miller)	C.de México	19 Oct 68
Afr	38.59A	Nig	(Adeyanju, Imoh, Adenikan, Ezinwa)	Bern	23 Aug 88
SAm	38.8 m	Bra	(Oliveira, da Silva, Nakaya, Correia)	São Paulo	1 May 84
	39.02A	Bra	(de Castro, dos Santos, Pegado,Filho)	C.de México	4 Sep 79
Asi	38.90	Jap	(Aoto, Yamauchi, Kurihara, Takano)	Seoul	1 Oct 88
Oce	39.31	Aus	(Lewis, D'Arcy, Ratcliffe, Haskell)	Christchurch	2 Feb 74
WJ	39.00A	USA	(Jessie, Franklin, Blalock, Mitchell)	Col.Springs	18 Jul 83

4×400 METRES RELAY

Event	Record	Nat	Team	Venue	Date
W,NAm	2:56.16A	USA	(Matthews, Freeman, James, Evans)	C.de México	20 Oct 68
	2:56.16	USA	(Everett, Lewis, Robinzine, Reynolds)	Seoul	1 Oct 88
E,C	2:58.86	UK	(Redmond, Akabusi, Black, Brown)	Roma	6 Sep 87
CAC	2:59.16	Cub	(Peñalver, Pavo, Martínez, Hernández)	Roma	6 Sep 87
Afr	2:59.32	Nig	(Uti, Ugbisie, Peters, Egbunike)	Los Angeles	11 Aug 84
Oce	2:59.70	Aus	(Frayne, Clark, Minihan, Mitchell)	Los Angeles	11 Aug 84
Asi	3:02.33	Jap	(Konakatomi,Yamauchi,Kawasumi,Takano)	Seoul	5 Oct 86
SAm	3:02.79	Bra	(da Silva, Barbosa, Guimarães, Souza)	Caracas	28 Aug 83
WJ	3:01.90	USA	(Campbell, Rish, Waddle, Reed)	Athínai	20 Jul 86

Event	Record	Name	Nat	Venue	Date

WORLD & CONTINENTAL RECORDS

(as at 31 Dec 1988)

Key: W = World; I = I.A.A.F. (if different); C = Commonwealth
Afr = Africa; Asi = Asia; CAC = Central America & Caribbean
E = Europe; NAm = N.America; Oce = Oceania; SAm = S.America
WJ = World Junior

A = altitude over 1000m; + = timing by photo-electric-cell
* = awaiting ratification; # = not officially ratified

100 METRES

Event	Record	Name	Nat	Venue	Date
W,NAm	10.49	Florence GRIFFITH JOYNER	USA	Indianapolis	17 Jul 88
E	10.81	Marlies GÖHR	GDR	E.Berlin	8 Jun 83
CAC,C	10.87	Merlene OTTEY	Jam	Walnut	31 May 87
Afr	11.09	Mary ONYALI	Nig	Bauchi	2 Jul 88
Oce	11.20A	Raelene BOYLE	Aus	Ciudad de México	15 Oct 68
Asi	11.22	CHI Cheng	Tai	Wien	18 Jul 70
SAm	11.26	Jennifer INNIS	Guy	Walnut	15 Jul 84
WJ	10.88 *	Marlies OELSNER/GÖHR	GDR	Dresden	1 Jul 77
	10.89	Kathrin KRABBE	GDR	E.Berlin	20 Jul 88

200 METRES

Event	Record	Name	Nat	Venue	Date
W,NAm	21.34	Florence GRIFFITH JOYNER	USA	Seoul	29 Sep 88
E	21.71	Marita KOCH	GDR	Karl-Marx-Stadt	10 Jun 79
	#	Marita KOCH	GDR	Potsdam	21 Jul 84
		Heike DRECHSLER	GDR	Jena	29 Jun 86
	#	Heike DRECHSLER	GDR	Stuttgart	29 Aug 86
CAC,C	21.72	Grace JACKSON	Jam	Seoul	29 Sep 88
Oce	22.35	Denise BOYD	Aus	Sydney	23 Mar 80
Afr	22.42A#	Evette ARMSTRONG	RSA	Johannesburg	18 Apr 86
	22.43	Mary ONYALI	Nig	Seoul	29 Sep 88
Asi	22.62	CHI Cheng	Tai	München	12 Jul 70
SAm	22.94A	Beatriz ALLOCCO	Arg	La Paz	11 Nov 78
WJ	22.19	Natalya BOCHINA	SU	Moskva	30 Jul 80

400 METRES

Event	Record	Name	Nat	Venue	Date
W,E	47.60	Marita KOCH	GDR	Canberra	6 Oct 85
NAm	48.83	Valerie BRISCO	USA	Los Angeles	6 Aug 84
C	49.43	Kathy COOK	UK	Los Angeles	6 Aug 84
CAC	49.57	Grace JACKSON	Jam	Nice	10 Jul 88
Afr	50.12A#	Myrtle BOTHMA	RSA	Germiston	11 Apr 86
	51.56	Rose WAITHERA	Ken	Los Angeles	6 Aug 84
Oce	50.24	Maree HOLLAND	Aus	Seoul	26 Sep 88
Asi	51.2 m	SHIN Keum-Dan	NKo	Pyongyang	31 Oct 64
	51.61	P.T.Usha	Ind	Canberra	6 Oct 85
SAm	51.32	Magnolia FIGUEIREDO	Bra	Seoul	25 Sep 88
WJ	49.77	Christina BREHMER/LATHAN	GDR	Dresden	9 May 76

800 METRES

Event	Record	Name	Nat	Venue	Date
W,E	1:53.28	Jarmila KRATOCHVÍLOVÁ	CS	München	26 Jul 83
CAC	1:55.84	Ana QUIROT	Cub	Roma	31 Aug 87
NAm	1:56.90	Mary SLANEY	USA	Bern	16 Aug 85
C	1:57.42	Kirsty McDERMOTT/WADE	Wal	Belfast	24 Jun 85
Asi	1:58.0 m	SHIN Keum-Dan	NKo	Pyongyang	5 Sep 64
Afr	1:58.1 mA	Francisca CHEPKURUI	Ken	Nairobi	13 Aug 88
Oce	1:59.0 m	Charlene RENDINA	Aus	Melbourne	28 Feb 76
SAm	1:59.92	Soraya TELLES	Bra	Schwechat	15 Jun 88
WJ	1:57.45 *	Hildegard ULLRICH/KÖRNER	GDR	Praha	31 Aug 78
	1:59.17	Birte BRUHNS	GDR	E.Berlin	20 Jul 88

Event	Record	Name	Nat	Venue	Date
1500 METRES					
W,E	3:52.47	Tatyana KAZANKINA	SU	Zürich	13 Aug 80
NAm	3:57.12	Mary DECKER/SLANEY	USA	Stockholm	26 Jul 83
C	3:59.96	Zola BUDD	Eng	Bruxelles	30 Aug 85
Afr	4:01.81 #	Zola BUDD	RSA	Port Elizabeth	21 Mar 84
	4:05.49	Fatima AOUAM	Mor	Köln	17 Aug 85
Oce	4:06.47	Christine PFITZINGER	NZ	San Jose	27 Jun 87
SAm	4:10.07	Soraya TELLES	Bra	Leverkusen	28 Jun 88
Asi	4:12.8 m	ZHENG Lijuan	Chn	Beijing	10 Oct 87
CAC	4:14.7	Charlotte BRADLEY	Mex	Sofiya	23 Aug 77
WJ	3:59.96 *	Zola BUDD	UK	Bruxelles	30 Aug 85
	4:04.39	Zola BUDD	UK	Cwmbrân	28 May 84
1 MILE					
W,E	4:15.8 m#	Natalya ARTYOMOVA	SU	Leningrad	6 Aug 84
I,NAm	4:16.71	Mary SLANEY	USA	Zürich	21 Aug 85
(E)	4:17.44	Maricica PUICA	Rom	Rieti	16 Sep 82
C	4:17.57	Zola BUDD	Eng	Zürich	21 Aug 85
Afr	4:28.4 m#	Sarina CRONJE	RSA	Stellenbosch	15 Nov 80
	4:30.69	Fatima AOUAM	Mor	Bruxelles	5 Sep 86
Oce	4:29.28	Penny JUST	Aus	Oslo	27 Jul 85
SAm	4:30.05	Soraya TELLES	Bra	Praha	9 Jun 88
WJ	4:17.57	Zola BUDD	UK	Zürich	21 Aug 85
3000 METRES					
W,E	8:22.62	Tatyana KAZANKINA	SU	Leningrad	26 Aug 84
NAm	8:25.83	Mary SLANEY	USA	Roma	7 Sep 85
C	8:28.83	Zola BUDD	Eng	Roma	7 Sep 85
Afr	8:37.5 m#	Zola BUDD	RSA	Stellenbosch	29 Feb 84
	8:57.21	Helen KIMAIYO	Ken	Los Angeles	8 Aug 84
Oce	8:44.1 m#	Donna GOULD	Aus	Eugene	13 Jul 84
	8:45.53	Anne AUDAIN	NZ	Brisbane	4 Oct 82
Asi	8:50.68	WANG Xiuting	Chn	Roma	29 Aug 87
SAm	9:15.90 #	Mónica REGONESI	Chl	Santiago	11 Jun 83
	9:16.1 m	Carmen OLIVEIRA	Bra	Curitiba	1 May 87
CAC	9:24.13	Maria-Luisa SERVIN	Mex	Zagreb	17 Jul 87
WJ	8:28.83 *	Zola BUDD	UK	Roma	7 Sep 85
	8:40.22	Zola BUDD	UK	London	6 Jun 84
5000 METRES					
W,E	14:37.33	Ingrid KRISTIANSEN	Nor	Stockholm	5 Aug 86
C	14:48.07	Zola BUDD	UK	London	26 Aug 85
Afr	15:01.83 #	Zola BUDD	RSA	Stellenbosch	5 Jan 84
	15:41.09	Helen KIMAIYO	Ken	Tokyo	6 May 84
NAm	15:06.53 *	Mary SLANEY	USA	Eugene	1 Jun 85
Oce	15:13.23	Anne AUDAIN	NZ	Auckland	17 Mar 82
Asi	15:27.44	WANG Xiuting	Chn	Guangzhou	25 Nov 87
SAm	16:31.2 m	Ena GUEVARAMORA	Per	Tallahassee	21 Apr 85
CAC	16:53.97	Sergía MARTINEZ	Cub	Bratislava	14 Jun 85
WJ	14:48.07	Zola BUDD	UK	London	26 Aug 85
10,000 METRES					
W,E	30:13.74	Ingrid KRISTIANSEN	Nor	Oslo	5 Jul 86
NAm	31:35.3 m	Mary DECKER/SLANEY	USA	Eugene	16 Jul 82
C	31:06.99	Liz LYNCH	Sco	Oslo	2 Jul 88
Asi	31:27.00	WANG Xiuting	Chn	Guangzhou	29 Nov 87
Oce	31:53.31	Anne AUDAIN	NZ	Edinburgh	28 Jul 86
Afr	32:37.51	Marcianne MUKAMURENZI	Rwa	Tours	13 Aug 88
CAC	33:11.8 m	María JIMENEZ	Mex	Walnut	23 Apr 88
SAm	33:48.67	Mónica Regonesi	Mex	Indianapolis	13 Aug 87
WJ	32:12.51 *	Marleen RENDERS	Bel	Roma	4 Sep 87
	32:44.52	Anke SCHÄNING	GDR	Potsdam	8 Jun 88

Event	Record	Name	Nat	Venue	Date

100 METRES HURDLES

Event	Record	Name	Nat	Venue	Date
W,E	12.21	Yordanka DONKOVA	Bul	Stara Zagora	20 Aug 88
NAm	12.61	Gail DEVERS	USA	Los Angeles	21 May 88
	12.61 *	Jackie JOYNER-KERSEE	USA	San Jose	28 May 88
C	12.78A*	Julie ROCHELEAU	Can	Provo	21 May 88
CAC	12.84	Aliuska LOPEZ	Cub	Zagreb	16 Jul 87
Asi	12.89	LIU Huajin	Chn	Guangzhou	25 Nov 87
Oce	12.93	Pam RYAN	Aus	München	4 Sep 72
Afr	13.08A#	Annemarie LE ROUX	RSA	Johannesburg	23 Apr 88
	13.13	Maria USIFO	Nig	Indianapolis	7 Jun 86
SAm	13.16	Nancy VALLECILLA	Ecu	Indianapolis	13 Aug 87
WJ	12.84	Aliuska LOPEZ	Cub	Zagreb	16 Jul 87

400 METRES HURDLES

Event	Record	Name	Nat	Venue	Date
W,E	52.94	Marina STEPANOVA	SU	Tashkent	17 Sep 86
Oce,C	53.17	Debbie FLINTOFF-KING	Aus	Seoul	28 Sep 88
Afr	53.74A	Myrtle BOTHMA	RSA	Johannesburg	18 Apr 86
NAm	54.23	Judy BROWN KING	USA	Indianapolis	12 Aug 87
CAC	54.38	Sandra FARMER/PATRICK	Jam	Roma	3 Sep 87
Asi	55.42	P.T.Usha	Ind	Los Angeles	8 Aug 84
SAm	57.12A*	Liliana CHALA	Ecu	Ciudad de México	24 Jul 88
	57.13	Liliana CHALA	Ecu	Indianapolis	12 Aug 87
WJ	55.20	Leslie MAXIE	USA	San Jose	9 Jun 84

HIGH JUMP

Event	Record	Name	Nat	Venue	Date
W,E	2.09	Stefka KOSTADINOVA	Bul	Roma	30 Aug 87
NAm	2.03	Louise RITTER	USA	Austin	8 Jul 88
	2.03	Louise RITTER	USA	Seoul	30 Sep 88
CAC	2.02	Silvia COSTA	Cub	Nice	10 Jul 88
Afr	2.01 #	Desirée DU PLESSIS	RSA	Johannesburg	15 Sep 86
	1.83	Constance SENGHOR	Sen	Dakar	27 May 84
C	1.99i	Debbie BRILL	Can	Edmonton	23 Jan 82
	1.98	Debbie BRILL	Can	Rieti	2 Sep 84
Oce	1.96	Chris STANTON	Aus	Adelaide	26 Jan 85
		Vanessa BROWNE	Aus	Perth	27 Mar 88
Asi	1.96	YANG Wenqin	Chn	Beijing	26 May 85
SAm	1.90	Liliana ARIGONI	Arg	Santa Fé	5 May 84
		Orlane DOS SANTOS	Bra	São Paulo	21 Jun 87
WJ	2.01 *	Olga TURCHAK	SU	Moskva	7 Jul 86
	2.00	Galina ASTAFEI	Rum	Sudbury	29 Jul 88

LONG JUMP

Event	Record	Name	Nat	Venue	Date
W,E	7.52	Galina CHISTYAKOVA	SU	Leningrad	11 Jun 88
NAm	7.45	Jackie JOYNER-KERSEE	USA	Indianapolis	13 Aug 87
CAC	6.96A	Madeline de JESUS	PRc	Ciudad de México	24 Jul 88
C	6.90	Beverly KINCH	Eng	Helsinki	14 Aug 83
Asi	6.88	Xiong Qiying	Chn	Tianjing	1 Sep 88
Oce	6.87	Nicole BOEGMAN	Aus	Gateshead	14 Aug 88
SAm	6.82	Jennifer INNIS	Guy	Nice	14 Aug 82
Afr	6.80 #	Maryna VAN NIEKERK	RSA	Johannesburg	25 Oct 86
	6.56	Modupe OSHIKOYA	Nig	Knoxville	26 May 78
WJ	7.14 *	Heike DAUTE/DRECHSLER	GDR	Bratislava	4 Jun 83
	6.98	Heike DAUTE/DRECHSLER	GDR	Potsdam	18 Aug 82

SHOT PUTT

Event	Record	Name	Nat	Venue	Date
W,E	22.63	Natalya LISOVSKAYA	SU	Moskva	7 Jun 87
Asi	21.76	LI Meisu	Chn	Shijiazhuang	23 Apr 88
CAC	20.61	María SARRIA	Cub	Habana	22 Jul 82
NAm	20.18	Ramona PAGEL	USA	San Diego	25 Jun 88
C,Oce	19.74	Gael MARTIN	Aus	Berkeley	14 Jul 84
Afr	17.32 #	Mariette VAN HEERDEN	RSA	Germiston	29 Nov 80
	16.60	Souad MALLOUSSI	Mor	Sydney	28 Sep 85
SAm	16.32	María-Nilba FERNANDES	Bra	Manaus	2 Jul 83
WJ	20.52i#	Heidi KRIEGER	GDR	Budapest	8 Feb 84
	20.24 *	Heidi KRIEGER	GDR	Split	20 Apr 84
	20.23	Ilke WYLUDDA	GDR	Karl-Marx-Stadt	16 Jul 88

Event	Record	Name	Nat	Venue	Date
					DISCUS
W,E	76.80	Gabriele REINSCH	GDR	Neubrandenburg	9 Jul 88
CAC	70.50	Maritza MARTEN	Cub	Habana	21 Mar 85
Asi	68.62	YU Houruen	Chn	Beijing	6 May 88
C	67.48	Meg RITCHIE	Sco	Walnut	26 Apr 81
NAm	66.10	Carol CADY	USA	San Jose	31 May 86
Oce	63.00	Gael MULHALL/MARTIN	Aus	Melbourne	11 Jan 79
Afr	58.80 #	Nanette VAN DER WALT	RSA	Port Elizabeth	15 Feb 86
	55.70	Mariette VAN HEERDEN	Zim	Harare	25 May 84
SAm	57.08	María URRUTIA	Col	Indianapolis	10 Aug 87
WJ	74.40	Ilke WYLUDDA	GDR	E.Berlin	13 Sep 88
					JAVELIN
W,E	80.00	Petra FELKE	GDR	Potsdam	9 Sep 88
C	77.44	Fatima WHITBREAD	Eng	Stuttgart	28 Aug 86
CAC	71.82	Ivonne LEAL	Cub	Kobe	30 Aug 85
Oce	69.80	Sue HOWLAND	Aus	Belfast	30 Jun 86
NAm	69.32	Kate SCHMIDT	USA	Fürth	11 Sep 77
Asi	65.50	LI Baolian	Chn	Guangzhou	29 Nov 87
Afr	62.34 #	Susan LION-CACHET	RSA	Pretoria	7 Nov 87
	62.16	Samia DJEMAA	Alg	Alger	19 Jun 87
SAm	60.34	Sueli dos SANTOS	Bra	Curitiba	15 May 88
WJ	71.88	Antoaneta TODOROVA	Bul	Zagreb	15 Aug 81
					HEPTATHLON (1984 TABLES)
W,NAm	7291	Jackie JOYNER-KERSEE	USA	Seoul	24 Sep 88
E	6946	Sabine MÖBIUS	GDR	Potsdam	6 May 84
C	6623	Judy SIMPSON	Eng	Stuttgart	30 Aug 86
Oce	6492	Jane FLEMMING	Aus	Götzis	19 Jun 88
Asi	6211	ZHU Yuqing	Chn	Roma	1 Sep 87
SAm	6017	Conceição GEREMIAS	Bra	Caracas	25 Aug 83
CAC	5930	Hildelise DESPAIGNE	Cub	Praha	17 Aug 84
Afr	5824	Yasmina AZZIZI	Alg	Götzis	19 Jun 88
WJ	6465	Sybille THIELE	GDR	Schwechat	28 Aug 83
					MARATHON
W,E	2:21:06	Ingrid KRISTIANSEN	Nor	London	21 Apr 85
NAm	2:21:21	Joan BENOIT/SAMUELSON	USA	Chicago	20 Oct 85
C,Oce	2:23:51	Lisa MARTIN	Aus	Osaka	31 Jan 88
Asi	2:27:06	ZHAO Youfeng	Chn	Seoul	23 Sep 88
CAC	2:32:09	María TRUJILLO	Mex	Columbus	8 Nov 87
Afr	2:33:39 #	Annette FALKSON	RSA	Cape Town	30 Apr 88
	2:36:52	Marianne MUKAMURENZI	Rwa	Paris	15 May 88
SAm	2:36:17	Elisabeth OBERLI-SCHUH	Ven	Frankfurt/Main	13 May 84
WJ	2:30:30	Akemi MASUDA	Jap	Eugene	11 Sep 83
					5000 METRES WALK (TRACK)
W,Oce,C	20:45.32	Kerry SAXBY	Aus	Perth	27 Mar 88
Asi	21:13.16	CUI Yinzhi	Chn	Jinan	30 Oct 88
E	21:08.65	Yelena NIKOLAYEVA	SU	Portsmouth	19 Jun 88
NAm	22:01.09	Ann PEEL	Can	Zagreb	17 Jul 87
CAC	23:38.25	María DE LA CRUZ/COLIN	Mex	Monterrey	9 Apr 86
Afr	24:45.91	Agnetha CHELIMO	Ken	Sudbury	31 Jul 88
SAm	25:11.55	Liliana BERMEO	Col	Sudbury	31 Jul 88
WJ	21:13.16 *	CUI Yinzhi	Chn	Jinan	30 Oct 88
					10,000 METRES WALK (TRACK)
W,Oce,C	42:14.2 m#	Kerry SAXBY	Aus	Canberra	26 Jan 88
(W),E	43:36.41	Yelena NIKOLAYEVA	SU	Kiyiv	30 Jul 88
Asi	43:52.1 m	CHEN Yaoling	Chn	Zhengzhou	25 Oct 87
(Oce,C)	45:08.13	Kerry SAXBY	Aus	Moskva	7 Jul 86
NAm	46:12.79	Ann PEEL	Can	Karl-Marx-Stadt	13 Jul 86
CAC	47:17.15	María COLIN	Mex	Indianapolis	12 Aug 87
SAm	53:12.00	Elsa ABRIL	Col	Guadalajara	1 Apr 87
Afr	56:54.9	Sabeha MANSOURI	Alg	Alger	11 Apr 85
WJ	43:52.1 m#	CHEN Yaoling	Chn	Zhengzhou	25 Oct 87

Event	Record	Name	Nat	Venue	Date

10 KM WALK (ROAD)

Event	Record	Name	Nat	Venue	Date
W,Oce,C	41:30	Kerry SAXBY	Aus	Canberra	27 Aug 88
E	43:22	Olga KRISHTOP	SU	New York	3 May 87
Asi	43:45	JIN Bingjie	Chn	New York	3 May 87
CAC	45:02	Graciella MENDOZA	Mex	New York	3 May 87
NAm	45:06	Ann PEEL	Can	New York	3 May 87
SAm	48:31	Elsa ABRIL	Col	Xalapa	5 Apr 87
Afr	54:19	Sabeha MANSOURI	Alg	Boumerdès	13 Mar 87
WJ	43:45	JIN Bingjie	Chn	New York	3 May 87

4×100 METRES RELAY

Event	Record	Name	Venue	Date
W, E	41.37	GDR (Gladisch, Rieger, Auerswald, Göhr)	Canberra	6 Oct 85
NAm	41.55*	USA (Brown,Williams,Griffith,Marshall)	W.Berlin	21 Aug 87
C	42.43	Eng (Oakes, Cook, Callender, Lannaman)	Moskva	1 Aug 80
CAC	42.73	Jam (Hodges, Pusey, Cuthbert, Ottey)	Helsinki	10 Aug 83
Oce	43.18	Aus (Wilson, Wells, Boyd, Boyle)	Montréal	31 Jul 76
Afr	43.44	Nig (Utondu, Iheagwam, Onyali, Ogunkoya)	Nairobi	9 Aug 87
Asi	43.68	Chn (Zhang, Liu, Xie, Tian)	Tianjing	1 Sep 88
SAm	44.90A	Arg (Fava, Godoy, Cragno, Allocco)	C.de México	20 Oct 75
WJ	43.33 #	GDR (Breuer, Krabbe, Dietz, Henke)	E.Berlin	20 Jul 88
	43.48	GDR (Breuer, Krabbe, Dietz, Henke)	Sudbury	31 Jul 88

4×400 METRES RELAY

Event	Record	Name	Venue	Date
W,E	3:15.17	Sov (Ledovskaya,Nazarova,Pinigina,Bryzgina)	Seoul	1 Oct 88
NAm	3:15.51	USA (D.Howard,Dixon,Brisco,Griffith Joyner)	Seoul	1 Oct 88
C	3:21.21	Can (Crooks,Richardson,Killingbeck,Payne)	Los Angeles	11 Aug 84
CAC	3:23.13	Jam (Richards, Thomas, Rattray, Powell)	Seoul	1 Oct 88
Oce	3:25.56	Aus (Canty, Burnard, Rendina, Nail)	Montréal	31 Jul 76
Afr	3:27.08	Nig (Usifo, Bakare, Ogunkoya, Onyali)	Nairobi	12 Aug 87
SAm	3:29.22A	Bra (Oliveira, García, Telles, Souza)	C.de México	24 Jul 88
Asi	3:31.55	Ind (Shanbag, Rao, Abraham, Usha)	Roma	5 Sep 87
WJ	3:28.39	GDR (Derr, Fabert, Wöhlk, Breuer)	Sudbury	31 Jul 88

WORLD ALL-TIME LISTS

100 METRES

Mark	Wind	Name		Nat	Yr	Pos	Meet	Venue	Date
9.83	1.0	Ben	Johnson	CAN	61	1	WC	Roma	30 Aug 87
9.92	1.1	Carl	Lewis	USA	61	1	OG	Seoul	24 Sep 88
9.93A	1.4	Calvin	Smith	USA	61	1	USOF	Air Force Academy	3 Jul 83
9.93	1.0		Lewis			2	WC	Roma	30 Aug 87
9.93	1.1		Lewis			1	WK	Zürich	17 Aug 88
9.95A	0.3	Jim	Hines	USA	46	1	OG	Ciudad México	14 Oct 68
9.95	0.8		Johnson			1r1	GWG	Moskva	9 Jul 86
9.95	0.0		Johnson			1	ASV	Köln	16 Aug 87
9.96	0.1	Mel	Lattany	USA	59	1r1		Athens, Ga.	5 May 84
9.96	1.9		Lewis			1h4	FOT	Indianapolis	15 Jul 88
9.96	0.4		Lewis			1q1	FOT	Indianapolis	15 Jul 88
9.97	1.5		Lewis			1	SW	Modesto	14 May 83
9.97	1.6		Smith			1	WK	Zürich	24 Aug 83
9.97	-1.2		Johnson			1	WK	Zürich	19 Aug 87
9.97	1.1		Smith			2	WK	Zürich	17 Aug 88
9.97	0.6		Lewis			1s1	OG	Seoul	24 Sep 88
9.97	1.1	Linford	Christie	UK	60	2	OG	Seoul	24 Sep 88
9.98A	0.6	Silvio	Leonard	CUB	55	1	WPT	Guadalajara	11 Aug 77
9.98	1.6		Lewis			1r1	SW	Modesto	11 May 85
9.98	1.6		Johnson			1	NC	Ottawa	1 Aug 87
9.98A	1.7		Johnson			1		Sestriere	11 Aug 88
9.99	1.3		Lewis			1r1		Houston	6 May 84
9.99	0.2		Lewis			1	OG	Los Angeles	4 Aug 84
9.99	0.9		Lewis			1	WK	Zürich	22 Aug 84
9.99	1.1		Lewis			1q5	OG	Seoul	23 Sep 88
9.99	1.1		Smith			3	OG	Seoul	24 Sep 88
10.00	0.0		Lewis			1		Dallas	16 May 81
10.00	1.9		Lewis			1	CalR	Modesto	15 May 82
10.00	2.0	Marian	Woronin	POL	56	1	Kuso	Warszawa	9 Jun 84
10.00	-0.4		Johnson			1	WP	Canberra	4 Oct 85
10.00	1.0	Chidi	Imoh	NIG	63	1	ISTAF	Berlin	15 Aug 86
10.00	-0.2		Johnson			1	R-W	Koblenz	13 Aug 87
10.00	1.1		Johnson			3	WK	Zürich	17 Aug 88
		(33 performances by 9 athletes)							
10.01A	0.9	Pietro	Mennea (10)	ITA	52	1		Ciudad México	4 Sep 79
10.02A	2.0	Charlie	Greene	USA	44	1q4	OG	Ciudad México	13 Oct 68
10.02	1.0	James	Sanford	USA	57	1	Pepsi	Westwood	11 May 80
10.02	1.8	Robson	da Silva	BRA	64	1	IbAm	Habana	27 Sep 86
10.03A	1.9	Stanley	Floyd	USA	61	1r1	NCAA	Provo	5 Jun 82
10.03	&	Viktor	Bryzgin	SU	62	1RA	Znam	Leningrad	7 Jun 86
10.03	0.4	Joe	DeLoach	USA	67	1	NCAA	Eugene	4 Jun 88
10.03	0.9	Dennis	Mitchell	USA	66	1RA	Athl	Lausanne	24 Jun 88
10.04A	0.3	Lennox	Miller	JAM	46	2	OG	Ciudad México	14 Oct 68
10.04	1.8	Mark	Witherspoon	USA	63	1	TAC	San Jose	27 Jun 87
10.04	0.5	Emmit	King	USA	59	1	TAC	Tampa	17 Jun 88
		(20)							
10.05	-1.1	Steve	Riddick	USA	51	1	WK	Zürich	20 Aug 75
10.05	1.8	Harvey	Glance	USA	57	1r1	FlaR	Tampa	30 Mar 85
10.06	1.1	Bob	Hayes	USA	42	1	OG	Tokyo	15 Oct 64
10.06	0.0	Hasely	Crawford	TRI	50	1	OG	Montreal	24 Jul 76
10.06	1.6	Ron	Brown	USA	61	3	WK	Zürich	24 Aug 83
10.06	2.0	Leandro	Peñalver	CUB	61	1	PAG	Caracas	24 Aug 83
10.06	1.9	Frank	Emmelmann	GDR	61	1		Berlin	22 Sep 85
10.06	0.3	Andrés	Simon	CUB	61	1		Habana	1 Aug 87
10.06A	2.0	Johan	Rossouw	RSA	65	1		Johannesburg	23 Apr 88
10.07	0.0	Valeriy	Borzov	SU	49	1q3	OG	München	31 Aug 72
		(30)							
10.07	0.0	Don	Quarrie	JAM	51	2	OG	Montreal	24 Jul 76

Mark		Name		Nat	Yr	Pos	Meet	Venue	Date
10.07	1.7	Clancy	Edwards	USA	55	1	NCAA	Eugene	2 Jun 78
10.07A	1.8	Eddie	Hart	USA	49	1	USOF	Air Force Academy	30 Jul 78
10.07	-0.1	Steve	Williams	USA	53	1	WK	Zürich	16 Aug 78
10.07A	0.6	Mike	Roberson	USA	56	1s1	WUG	Ciudad México	8 Sep 79
10.07	0.5	Lee	McRae	USA	66	1	WUG	Zagreb	14 Jul 87
10.07	0.5	Brian	Cooper	USA	65	2	TAC	Tampa	17 Jun 88
10.08	0.1	Darrell	Green	USA	60	1		San Angelo	13 Apr 83
10.08	1.6	Terry	Scott	USA	64	1h3	NCAA	Austin	30 May 85
10.08	0.1	Lorenzo	Daniel	USA	66	1h2	SEC	Knoxville	17 May 86
		(40)							
10.08	1.0	Ray	Stewart	JAM	65	3	WC	Roma	30 Aug 87
10.08	0.0	Andre	Cason	USA	69	1	TAC-j	Tallahassee	24 Jun 88
10.09	1.4	Sam	Graddy	USA	64	1h2		Baton Rouge	12 May 84
10.09	1.3	Antoine	Richard	FRA	60	1	NC	Aix-les-Bains	10 Aug 86
10.09	1.5	Max	Morinière	FRA	64	1		Lyon	3 Jul 87
10.09	0.3	Attila	Kovács	HUN	60	1	NC	Miskolc	20 Aug 87
10.09	0.5	Lee	McNeill	USA	64	3	TAC	Tampa	17 Jun 88
10.10A	0.5	Hermes	Ramirez	CUB	48	1q2	OG	Ciudad México	13 Oct 68
10.10A	1.9	Willie	Gault	USA	60	2r1	NCAA	Provo	5 Jun 82
10.10	1.6	Darwin	Cook	USA	62	2r1	SW	Modesto	11 May 85
		(50)							
10.10	-0.4&	Nikolay	Yushmanov	SU	61	1rB	Znam	Leningrad	7 Jun 86
10.10	1.8	Thomas	Schröder	GDR	62	1	NC	Jena	27 Jun 86
10.10	1.9	Stanley	Kerr	USA	67	1	TAC-j	Towson	28 Jun 86

& wind reading of -2.5 almost certainly incorrect, but mark accepted as a national record.

Disqualified for drug abuse

9.79	1.1	Ben	Johnson	CAN	61	-	OG	Seoul	24 Sep 88

Doubtful wind reading

10.02	1.2	Ronald	Desruelles	BEL	55	1		Naimette	11 May 85

Low altitude marks for athletes with best marks at altitude

							alt.best
10.02	1.8	Da Silva	1	IbAmC	Habana	27 Sep 86	9.99
10.03	0.8	Hines	1s1	AAU	Sacramento	20 Jun 68	9.95
10.03		Leonard	1		Habana	13 Sep 77	10.03
10.07	2.0	Floyd	1		Austin	24 May 80	10.03
10.10	0.9	Greene	1s2	AAU	Sacramento	20 Jun 68	10.02

Wind-assisted marks

9.78	5.2	Carl	Lewis	USA	61	1	FOT	Indianapolis	16 Jul 88
9.86	5.2	Dennis	Mitchell	USA	66	2	FOT	Indianapolis	16 Jul 88
9.87	11.2	William	Snoddy	USA	57	1		Dallas	1 Apr 78
9.87	4.9	Calvin	Smith	USA	61	1s2	FOT	Indianapolis	16 Jul 88
9.87	5.2		C.Smith			3	FOT	Indianapolis	16 Jul 88
9.88	2.3	James	Sanford	USA	57	1		Westwood	3 May 80
9.88	5.2	Albert	Robinson	USA	64	4	FOT	Indianapolis	16 Jul 88
9.89	4.2	Ray	Stewart	JAM	65	1s1	PAG	Indianapolis	9 Aug 87
9.90	2.5		Lewis			1	MSR	Walnut	28 Apr 85
9.90	5.2	Joe	DeLoach	USA	67	5	FOT	Indianapolis	16 Jul 88
9.90	3.7		Johnson			1	NC	Ottawa	6 Aug 88
9.91	5.3	Bob	Hayes	USA	42	1s1	OG	Tokyo	15 Oct 64
9.91	2.1		C.Smith			1	vGDR	Karl-Marx-Stadt	9 Jul 82
9.91	4.5		Lewis			1	TAC	Eugene	20 Jun 86
9.91	4.2	Mark	Witherspoon	USA	63	2s1	PAG	Indianapolis	9 Aug 87
9.92A	4.4	Chidi	Imoh	NIG	63	1s1	AfrG	Nairobi	8 Aug 87
9.93	2.3		Lewis			1	MSR	Walnut	24 Apr 83
9.94	4.6		C.Smith			1		Sacramento	21 Jul 84
9.94	4.9		Robinson			2s2	FOT	Indianapolis	16 Jul 88
9.94	5.2	Mike	Marsh	USA	67	6	FOT	Indianapolis	16 Jul 88
9.95	8.9	Willie	Gault	USA	60	1		Knoxville	2 Apr 83
9.95	2.4	Mel	Lattany	USA	59	1		Athens	7 May 83
9.95	2.8		Lewis			1	BNP	Villeneuve D'Ascq	27 Jun 88
9.96	4.9		DeLoach			3s2	FOT	Indianapolis	16 Jul 88
		(24 windy marks to 9.96)							
9.97	7.7	Andrés	Simon	CUB	61	1s1	WUG	Kobe	30 Aug 85

Mark		Name		Nat	Yr	Pos	Meet	Venue	Date
9.97	3.4	Roy	Martin	USA	66	1		Houston	18 May 86
9.98	11.2	Cole	Doty	CAN	55	2		Dallas	1 Apr 78
9.98	5.2	Emmit	King	USA	59	7	FOT	Indianapolis	16 Jul 88
9.99	7.2	Pietro	Mennea	ITA	52	1	vGRE	Bari	13 Sep 78
9.99A	2.7	Leandro	Peñalver	CUB	61	1h2	IbAmC	Ciudad México	22 Jul 88
10.00	2.6	Jeff	Phillips	USA	57	2	NCAA	Baton Rouge	5 Jun 81
10.00	2.6	Lorenzo	Daniel	USA	66	1		Knoxville	18 May 86
10.00	3.7	Desai	Williams	CAN	59	2	NC	Ottawa	6 Aug 88
10.01	2.3	Ron	Brown	USA	61	2	MSR	Walnut	24 Apr 83
10.01A	2.7	José	Arques	SPA	60	2h2	IbAmC	Ciudad México	22 Jul 88
10.02	5.9	Allan	Wells	UK	52	1	CommG	Brisbane	4 Oct 82
10.02	2.9	Terry	Scott	USA	64	1	NCAA	Austin	1 Jun 85
10.02A	6.2	Aaron	Thigpen	USA	64	1		Provo	10 May 86
10.02	4.5	Lee	McRae	USA	66	2	TAC	Eugene	20 Jun 86
10.03	3.5	Harvey	Glance	USA	57	1RA	CalR	Modesto	9 May 87
10.04	11.2	Ray	Brooks	USA	56	3		Dallas	1 Apr 78
10.05	4.2	Brian	Cooper	USA	65	2h4	TAC	San Jose	25 Jun 87
10.06A	8.8	Jerome	Deal	USA	58	1	EL	Paso	6 May 78
10.06	4.3	Stefano	Tilli	ITA	62	1		Cagliari	9 Oct 83
10.06	7.7	Arnaldo S.	de Oliveira	BRA	64	2s1	WUG	Kobe	30 Aug 85
10.06	3.3	Marty	Krulee	USA	56	1rB	MSR	Walnut	24 Apr 88
10.07	3.8	Dwayne	Evans	USA	58	1	CalR	Modesto	16 May 81
10.07	5.9	Cameron	Sharp	UK	58	3	CommG	Brisbane	4 Oct 82
10.07	6.0	Juan	Nuñez	DOM	59	3s2	PAG	Indianapolis	9 Aug 87
Hand timing									
9.8		Harvey	Glance	USA	57	1		Auburn	9 Apr 77
9.8	-0.8		Glance			1	FlaR	Gainesville	28 Mar 81
9.8	0.4	Jeff	Phillips	USA	57	1		Knoxville	22 May 82
Wind-assisted marks									
9.7	3.8	Osvaldo	Lara	CUB	55	1		Santiago de Cuba	24 Feb 82
9.7	3.5	Ben	Johnson	CAN	61	1		Perth	24 Jan87

200 METRES

Mark		Name		Nat	Yr	Pos	Meet	Venue	Date
19.72A	1.8	Pietro	Mennea	ITA	52	1	WUG	Ciudad México	12 Sep 79
19.75	1.5	Carl	Lewis	USA	61	1	TAC	Indianapolis	19 Jun 83
19.75	1.7	Joe	DeLoach	USA	67	1	OG	Seoul	28 Sep 88
19.79	1.7		Lewis			2	OG	Seoul	28 Sep 88
19.80	-0.9		Lewis			1	OG	Los Angeles	8 Aug 84
19.82A	2.0		Lewis			1		Sestriere	11 Aug 88
19.83A	0.9	Tommie	Smith	USA	44	1	OG	Ciudad México	16 Oct 68
19.84	0.2		Lewis			1q3	FOT	Los Angeles	19 Jun 84
19.86A	1.0	Don	Quarrie	JAM	51	1	PAG	Cali	3 Aug 71
19.86	-0.2		Lewis			1	FOT	Los Angeles	21 Jun 84
19.87	0.8	Lorenzo	Daniel	USA	66	1	NCAA	Eugene	3 Jun 88
19.92A	1.9	John	Carlos	USA	45	1	FOT	Echo Summit	12 Sep 68
19.92	1.3		Lewis			1		Madrid	4 Jun 87
19.93	-1.5		Daniel			1	SEC	Auburn	15 May 88
19.95	1.9	Floyd	Heard	USA	66	1	SWC	Lubbock	17 May 87
19.96A	0.2		Mennea			1h9	WUG	Ciudad México	10 Sep 79
19.96	0.0		Mennea			1		Barletta	17 Aug 80
19.96	-0.9	Kirk	Baptiste	USA	63	2	OG	Los Angeles	8 Aug 84
19.96	1.0		DeLoach			1	FOT	Indianapolis	20 Jul 88
19.98	0.2		DeLoach			1	SWC	Austin	15 May 88
19.99	0.6	Calvin	Smith	USA	61	1	WK	Zürich	24 Aug 83
19.99	1.2		Lewis			1		Houston	18 Jun 88
20.00	0.0	Valeriy	Borzov	SU	49	1	OG	München	4 Sep 72
20.01	0.0		Mennea			1	GGala	Roma	5 Aug 80
20.01	1.0		Lewis			2	FOT	Indianapolis	20 Jul 88
20.02	0.3		Lewis			1	Athl	Lausanne	15 Sep 87
20.03	1.6	Clancy	Edwards	USA	55	1		Westwood	29 Apr 78
20.03	0.4		Mennea			1	8-N	Tokyo	20 Sep 80

Mark		Name		Nat	Yr	Pos	Meet	Venue	Date
20.03	-0.1		Mennea			1		Beijing	27 Sep 80
20.03	1.5	Larry	Myricks	USA	56	2	TAC	Indianapolis	19 Jun 83
20.03	1.2		Lewis			1q2	FOT	Indianapolis	18 Jul 88
20.03	0.2		DeLoach			1rA	WK	Zürich	17 Aug 88
20.03	-0.6		DeLoach			1	VD	Bruxelles	19 Aug 88
		(33/13)							
20.04	1.7	Robson C.	da Silva	BRA	64	3	OG	Seoul	28 Sep 88
20.05	1.0	Roy	Martin	USA	66	3	FOT	Indianapolis	20 Jul 88
20.05	1.0	Albert	Robinson	USA	64	4	FOT	Indianapolis	20 Jul 88
20.06A	0.9	Peter	Norman	AUS	42	2	OG	Ciudad México	16 Oct 68
20.06	1.7	Silvio	Leonard	CUB	55	1	Kuso	Warszawa	19 Jun 78
20.07		James	Mallard	USA	57	1		Tuscaloosa	20 Apr 79
20.07	0.2	Mike	Johnson	USA	67	2	SWC	Austin	15 May 88
		(20)							
20.08	0.9	LaMonte	King	USA	59	1	TAC	Walnut	15 Jun 80
20.08A	1.6	Dwayne	Evans	USA	58	1		Albuquerque	13 Jun 87
20.09	1.7	Linford	Christie	UK	60	4	OG	Seoul	28 Sep 88
20.10	1.7	Millard	Hampton	USA	56	1	FOT	Eugene	22 Jun 76
20.11	0.7	Attila	Kovács	HUN	60	1	NC	Miskolc	21 Aug 87
20.14	1.8	James	Gilkes	GUY	52	1		Ingelheim	12 Sep 78
20.15A	0.3	Mike	Miller	USA	59	1h2	NCAA	Provo	2 Jun 82
20.16	-0.1	Steve	Williams	USA	53	1		Stuttgart	26 Aug 75
20.16	1.5	Elliott	Quow	USA	62	3	TAC	Indianapolis	19 Jun 83
20.16	-0.4	Gilles	Quénéhervé	FRA	66	2	WC	Roma	3 Sep 87
		(30)							
20.18	-0.4	John	Regis	UK	66	3	WC	Roma	3 Sep 87
20.18	0.2	Henry	Thomas	USA	67	1		Eagle Rock	14 May 88
20.19	0.0	Larry	Black	USA	51	2	OG	München	4 Sep 72
20.19	0.7	James	Sanford	USA	57	1		Westwood	28 Apr 79
20.19	1.9	Phil	Epps	USA	59	1		College Station	20 Mar 82
20.19	0.6	John	Dinan	AUS	59	1		Canberra	6 Mar 86
20.20	0.7	Greg	Foster	USA	58	2		Westwood	28 Apr 79
20.20	0.8	Atlee	Mahorn	CAN	65	2	NCAA	Eugene	3 Jun 88
20.21	0.9	Allan	Wells	UK	52	2	OG	Moskva	28 Jul 80
20.21	0.1	Mel	Lattany	USA	59	1	WP	Roma	6 Sep 81
		(40)							
20.21	1.3	Mike	Conley	USA	62	2		Fayetteville	18 May 85
20.21A	1.6	Harvey	McSwain	USA	63	2		Albuquerque	13 Jun 87
20.22A	0.4	Tony	Sharpe	CAN	61	1		Colorado Springs	20 Jul 82
20.22A	-0.3	Leandro	Peñalver	CUB	61	2	IbAmC	Ciudad México	23 Jul 88
20.23A	0.3	James	Butler	USA	60	2h2	NCAA	Provo	2 Jun 82
20.23	0.2	Frank	Emmelmann	GDR	61	1	EP	Moskva	18 Aug 85
20.23	0.5	Mike	Timpson	USA	67	1		University Park	16 May 86
20.23	-0.4	Vladimir	Krylov	SU	64	5	WC	Roma	3 Sep 87
20.23	1.2	Danny	Everett	USA	66	2	Pac10	Westwood	22 May 88
20.24A	1.8	Leszek	Dunecki	POL	56	2	WUG	Ciudad México	12 Sep 79
		(50)							
20.24A	-0.3	Roberto	Hernández	CUB	67	3	IbAmC	Ciudad México	23 Jul 88

Low altitude marks for athletes with lifetime bests at high altitude

20.06	0.4	Quarrie	1	WK	Zürich	16 Aug 74	19.86
20.22	1.7	Evans	2	FOT	Eugene	22 Jun 76	20.08

Wind-assisted marks

19.86	4.6	Roy	Martin	USA	66	1		Houston	18 May 86
19.88	3.4	Lorenzo	Daniel	USA	66	1	SEC	Tuscaloosa	17 May 87
19.94	4.0	James	Sanford	USA	57	1s1	NCAA	Austin	7 Jun 80
19.95	3.4	Mike	Roberson	USA	56	1h3	NCAA	Austin	5 Jun 80
19.96	2.8		Roberson			1	NCAA	Austin	7 Jun 80
20.01	2.5	Derald	Harris	USA	58	1		San Jose	9 Apr 77
20.01	2.1		C.Lewis			1	Jen	San Jose	26 May 84
20.05A	3.8	Cyprean	Enweani	CAN	64	1		Calgary	3 Jul 88
20.07A	2.1	James	Butler	USA	60	1r1	NCAA	Provo	4 Jun 82
20.09	3.7	Brady	Crain	USA	56	1	TAC	San Jose	9 Jun 80

Mark		Name		Nat	Yr	Pos	Meet	Venue	Date
20.09	2.2	Dwayne	Evans	USA	58	1		Walnut	1 Jun 86
20.10	4.6	Stanley	Kerr	USA	67	2		Houston	18 May 86
20.11	3.7	Allan	Wells	UK	52	1		Edinburgh	20 Jun 80
20.12	3.6	Mike	Conley	USA	62	1h3	NCAA	Austin	30 May 85
20.14	3.4	Daron	Council	USA	64	2	SEC	Tuscaloosa	17 May 87
20.16	3.9?	Danny	Peebles	USA	66	2	NCAA	Baton Rouge	5 Jun 87
20.20	2.1	Wallace	Spearmon	USA	62	4s2	TAC	San Jose	26 Jun 87
Hand timing									
19.7A		James	Sanford	USA	57	1		El Paso	19 Apr 80
19.8"	1.3	Don	Quarrie	JAM	51	1	Pre	Eugene	7 Jun 75
19.8*	1.3	Steve	Williams	USA	53	2	Pre	Eugene	7 Jun 75
19.8		James	Mallard	USA	57	1		Tuscaloosa	13 May 79
20.0	1.9	Larry	Black	USA	51	1s1		Billings	2 Jun 72
20.0	-0.2	Clancy	Edwards	USA	55	1		Tucson	4 Mar 78
20.0	1.9	LaMonte	King	USA	59	1		San Jose	12 May 79
20.0	-0.8	Mike	Conley	USA	62	1h3		Austin	11 May 84
Wind-assisted marks									
19.8*		Carl	Lawson	JAM	47	1		Moscow	19 May 73
19.8*	3.4	James	Gilkes	GUY	52	1	NCAA	Austin	8 Jun 74
19.8	4.4	Desmond	Ross	USA	61	1		Manhattan	11 May 85
19.9*		Gerald	Tinker	USA	51	1		Kent	5 May 73
19.9*	3.4	Reggie	Jones	USA	53	2	NCAA	Austin	8 Jun 74
19.9		Silvio	Leonard	CUB	55	1		Habana	22 May 77
19.9	4.4	Chidi	Imoh	NIG	63	2		Manhattan	11 May 85

" during 220 yards race, * 220 yards less 0.1 seconds

300 METRES

In 300m races only, not including intermediate times in 400m races

Mark	Name		Nat	Yr	Pos	Meet	Venue	Date
31.70	Kirk	Baptiste	USA	63	1		London	18 Aug 84
31.73	Thomas	Jefferson	USA	62	1		London	22 Aug 87
31.74	Gabriel	Tiacoh	IVC	63	1		La Coruña	6 Aug 86
31.88	Darren	Clark	AUS	65	1		Belfast	30 Jun 86
31.97	Innocent	Egbunike	NIG	61	1	IAC	London	8 Aug 86
32.05	Butch	Reynolds	USA	64	1		Belfast	20 Jul 87
32.08	Roger	Black	UK	66	4	IAC	London	8 Aug 86
32.14	Todd	Bennett	UK	62	2		London	18 Aug 84
32.16	Mel	Lattany	USA	59	1		Gateshead	31 Jul 83
32.16	Walter	McCoy	USA	58	3		London	18 Aug 84
	(10)							
32.17	Darrell	Robinson	USA	63	1		Birmingham	19 Aug 86
32.18	Carl	Lewis	USA	61	4		London	18 Aug 84
32.19	Atlee	Mahorn	CAN	65	5	IAC	London	8 Aug 86
32.22	Dennis	Mitchell	USA	66	1		Jerez	28 Jun 88
32.23	Pietro	Mennea	ITA	52	1		Rieti	21 Jul 79
32.26	Mike	Franks	USA	63	1		Bern	16 Aug 85
32.32	Derek	Redmond	UK	65	1		Gateshead	16 Jul 88
32.34	Roberto	Hernández	CUB	67	1		Canberra	2 Oct 85
32.38	Aldo	Canti	FRA	61	1		Canberra	2 Oct 85
32.38	Mohamed	Al Malky	OMA	62	2		Gateshead	16 Jul 88
	(20)							
32.40	Ken	Randle	USA	54	1		London	4 Jul 75
32.41	Harvey	McSwain	USA	63	2		Belfast	30 Jun 86
32.44	David	Jenkins	UK	52	2		London	4 Jul 75
32.45	Hartmut	Weber	FRG	60	1		Dormagen	4 Jun 82
32.49	Albert	Robinson	USA	64	1		Gateshead	6 Jul 84
32.49	Henry	Thomas	USA	67	2		Edinburgh	23 Jul 85
hand times								
32.1	Jim	Kemp	USA	44	1		Bakersfield	15 May 71
32.2	Alfons	Brijdenbach	BEL	54	1		Bad Durheim	22 Sep 74
32.2	Pietro	Mennea	ITA	52	1		Formia	8 May 75
32.2	Erwin	Skamrahl	FRG	58	1		Rhede	17 May 81
32.3	Karl	Honz	FRG	51	2		Bad Durheim	22 Sep 74

MEN All-time

400 METRES

Mark	Name		Nat	Yr	Pos	Meet	Venue	Date
43.29	Butch	Reynolds	USA	64	1	WK	Zürich	17 Aug 88
43.86A	Lee	Evans	USA	47	1	OG	Ciudad México	18 Oct 68
43.87	Steve	Lewis	USA	69	1	OG	Seoul	28 Sep 88
43.93		Reynolds			1	FOT	Indianapolis	20 Jul 88
43.93		Reynolds			2	OG	Seoul	28 Sep 88
43.97A	Larry	James	USA	47	2	OG	Ciudad México	18 Oct 68
43.98	Danny	Everett	USA	66	2	FOT	Indianapolis	20 Jul 88
44.06A		Evans			1	FOT	Echo Summit	14 Sep 68
44.09		Everett			3	OG	Seoul	28 Sep 88
44.10		Reynolds			1	JO	Columbus	3 May 87
44.11		Lewis			1s2	FOT	Indianapolis	18 Jul 88
44.13		Reynolds			1	NCAA	Baton Rouge	6 Jun 87
44.15		Reynolds			1	PTG	London	10 Jul 87
44.17	Innocent	Egbunike	NIG	61	1rA	WK	Zürich	19 Aug 87
44.19A		James			2	FOT	Echo Summit	14 Sep 68
44.20		Everett			2	WK	Zürich	17 Aug 88
44.22A	Roberto	Hernández	CUB	67	1		Ciudad México	22 May 88
44.23A		Egbunike			1	AfrG	Nairobi	9 Aug 87
44.26	Alberto	Juantorena	CUB	50	1	OG	Montreal	29 Jul 76
44.26		Egbunike			1s1	WC	Roma	1 Sep 87
44.26		Lewis			3	WK	Zürich	17 Aug 88
44.27A		Juantorena			1	CAG	Medellin	16 Jul 78
44.27	Alonzo	Babers	USA	61	1	OG	Los Angeles	8 Aug 84
44.30	Gabriel	Tiacoh	IVC	63	1	NCAA	Indianapolis	7 Jun 86
44.32		Tiacoh			1	Pepsi	Westwood	17 May 86
44.32		Everett			2s2	FOT	Indianapolis	18 Jul 88
44.33	Thomas	Schönlebe	GDR	65	1	WC	Roma	3 Sep 87
44.33		Reynolds			1s2	OG	Seoul	26 Sep 88
44.34		Everett			1	Pac-10	Westwood	22 May 88
44.35		Lewis			1s1	OG	Seoul	26 Sep 88
	(30/11)							
44.38	Darren	Clark	AUS	65	3s1	OG	Seoul	26 Sep 88
44.40	Fred	Newhouse	USA	48	2	OG	Montreal	29 Jul 76
44.41A	Ron	Freeman	USA	47	3	OG	Ciudad México	18 Oct 68
44.45A	Ronnie	Ray	USA	54	1	PAG	Ciudad México	18 Oct 75
44.45	Darrell	Robinson	USA	63	2	Pepsi	Westwood	17 May 86
44.47	Michael	Franks	USA	63	1	WP	Canberra	5 Oct 85
44.48	Roddie	Haley	USA	65	1		Houston	18 May 86
44.50	Erwin	Skamrahl	FRG	58	1		München	26 Jul 83
44.50	Derek	Redmond	UK	65	1s2	WC	Roma	1 Sep 87
	(20)							
44.50	Bert	Cameron	JAM	59	4s1	OG	Seoul	26 Sep 88
44.55	Andrew	Valmon	USA	65	4rA	WK	Zürich	17 Aug 88
44.56	Mohamed	Al Malky	OMA	62	1	HGP	Budapest	12 Aug 88
44.58	Bert	Cameron	JAM	59	1	NCAA	Baton Rouge	6 Jun 81
44.59	Roger	Black	UK	66	1	EC	Stuttgart	29 Aug 86
44.60A	John	Smith	USA	50	1	PAG	Cali	1 Aug 71
44.60	Viktor	Markin	SU	57	1	OG	Moskva	30 Jul 80
44.60	Raymond	Pierre	USA	67	1	PAG	Indianapolis	13 Aug 87
44.60	Ian	Morris	TRI	61	2s2	OG	Seoul	26 Sep 88
44.61	Kevin	Robinzine	USA	66	4	FOT	Indianapolis	20 Jul 88
	(30)							
44.66	Vince	Matthews	USA	47	1	OG	München	7 Sep 72
44.67*	Curtis	Mills	USA	48	1	NCAA	Knoxville	21 Jun 69
44.68	Sunder	Nix	USA	61	1	USOF	Indianapolis	24 Jul 82
44.69	Antonio	McKay	USA	64	4=	WK	Zürich	13 Aug 86
44.70	Karl	Honz	FRG	51	1	NC	München	20 Jul 72
44.70	Cliff	Wiley	USA	55	1	TAC	Sacramento	21 Jun 81
44.71	Andre	Phillips	USA	59	3	Pepsi	Westwood	17 May 86
44.71	Miles	Murphy	AUS	67	1	NC	Perth	26 Mar 88
44.72	Hartmut	Weber	FRG	60	1	EC	Athinai	9 Sep 82
44.73	Willie	Smith	USA	56	1		Tuscaloosa	15 Apr 78

Mark	Name		Nat	Yr	Pos	Meet	Venue	Date
44.73A	James	Rolle	USA	64	1	USOF	Air Force Academy	2 Jul 83
44.73	David	Kitur	KEN	62	3s2	WC	Roma	1 Sep 87
44.75	Clarence	Daniel	USA	61	1q4	FOT	Indianapolis	17 Jul 88
44.76A	El Kashief	Hassan	SUD	56	1h4	NCAA	Provo	3 Jun 82
44.76	Walter	McCoy	USA	58	2	WK	Zürich	22 Aug 84
44.77	Felix	Stevens	CUB	64	1	NC	Santiago de Cuba	23 Feb 86
44.80	Wayne	Collett	USA	49	2	OG	München	7 Sep 72
44.80A	Chris	Whitlock	USA	59	2	USOF	Air Force Academy	2 Jul 83
44.82*	Wendell	Mottley	TRI	41	1	CG	Kingston	11 Aug 66
44.82	Maxie	Parks	USA	51	1	AAU	Westwood	12 Jun 76
	(50)							

* 440 yards less 0.26 seconds
Low altitude mark for athletes with altitude best: Hernández 44.57 2Athl Lausanne 24 Jun 88 44.22

Hand timing

Mark	Name		Nat	Yr	Pos	Meet	Venue	Date	Best auto
44.1	Wayne	Collett	USA	49	1	FOT	Eugene	9 Jul 72	44.80
44.2*	John	Smith	USA	50	1	AAU	Eugene	26 Jun 71	44.60
44.2	Fred	Newhouse	USA	48	1s1	FOT	Eugene	7 Jul 72	44.40
44.4A	Vince	Matthews	USA	47	1		Echo Summit	31 Aug 68	44.66
44.5"	Tommie	Smith	USA	44	1		San José	20 May 67	45.25
44.6	Adolph	Plummer	USA	38	1		Tempe	25 May 63	-
44.7*	Benny	Brown	USA	53	1		Westwood	5 May 73	45.08

* 440 yards less 0.3 seconds, " during 440 yards race

600 METRES

Mark	Name		Nat	Yr	Pos	Meet	Venue	Date
1:12.81	Johnny	Gray	USA	60	1		Santa Monica	24 May 86
1:13.80	Earl	Jones	USA	64	2		Santa Monica	24 May 86
1:14.15	David	Mack	USA	61	3		Santa Monica	24 May 86
1:14.16		Gray			1		Sacramento	21 Jul 84
1:14.3 mA	Lee	Evans	USA	47	1		Echo Summit	31 Aug 68
1:14.6 mA	Larry	James	USA	47	2		Echo Summit	31 Aug 68
1:14.8 mA	Mark	Winzenried	USA	49	3		Echo Summit	31 Aug 68
1:14.84	James	Robinson	USA	54	2		Sacramento	21 Jul 84
1:14.9 m	Martim	McGrady	USA	46	1		Melbourne	17 Mar 70
1:15.0' m+	Sebastian	Coe	UK	56	1		Firenze	10 Jun 81
1:15.14	John	Marshall	USA	63	3		Sacramento	21 Jul 84
	(10)							
1:15.2 m	John	Higham	AUS	51	1		Canberra	30 Nov 77
1:15.3 m	Ralph	Doubell	AUS	45	2		Melbourne	17 Mar 70
1:15.33	Donato	Sabia	ITA	63	1		San Diego	30 Jul 84
1:15.4 m	Garry	Cook	UK	58	2		San Diego	30 Jul 84
1:15.5 m	Robert	Casselman	USA	52	1		Gateshead	3 Aug 74
1:15.6 m	David	Jenkins	UK	52	2		Gateshead	3 Aug 74
1:15.68	Detlef	Wagenknecht	GDR	59	1		East Berlin	31 Jul 83
1:15.70	Olaf	Beyer	GDR	57	1		Potsdam	27 Aug 82
1:15.7 m	Philippe	Dupont	FRA	58	3		San Diego	30 Jul 84
1:15.80i	Chip	Jenkins	USA	64	1		Sherbrooke	1 Feb 87

800 METRES

Mark	Name		Nat	Yr	Pos	Meet	Venue	Date
1:41.73"	Sebastian	Coe	UK	56	1		Firenze	10 Jun 81
1:41.77	Joaquim C.	Cruz	BRA	63	1	ASV	Köln	26 Aug 84
1:42.28	Sammy	Koskei	KEN	61	2	ASV	Köln	26 Aug 84
1:42.33		Coe			1	Bisl	Oslo	5 Jul 79
1:42.34		Cruz			1r1	WK	Zürich	22 Aug 84
1:42.41		Cruz			1	VD	Bruxelles	24 Aug 84
1:42.49		Cruz			1		Koblenz	28 Aug 85
1:42.54		Cruz			1	ASV	Köln	25 Aug 85
1:42.60	Johnny	Gray	USA	60	2		Koblenz	28 Aug 85
1:42.65		Gray			1	WK	Zürich	17 Aug 88
1:42.88	Steve	Cram	UK	60	1r1	WK	Zürich	21 Aug 85
1:42.96		Gray			1		Koblenz	29 Aug 84
1:42.98		Cruz			1r1	ISTAF	Berlin	23 Aug 85
1:43.00		Cruz			1	OG	Los Angeles	6 Aug 84
1:43.06	Billy	Konchellah	KEN	61	1	WC	Roma	1 Sep 87

Mark	Name		Nat	Yr	Pos	Meet	Venue	Date
1:43.07		Coe			2	ASV	Köln	25 Aug 85
1:43.10		Gray			1	APM	Hengelo	14 Aug 88
1:43.19		Cram			1		Rieti	7 Sep 86
1:43.20	José Luiz	Barbosa	BRA	61	2	WK	Zürich	17 Aug 88
1:43.22		Cram			1	CommG	Edinburgh	31 Jul 86
1:43.23		Cruz			2r1	WK	Zürich	21 Aug 85
1:43.28		Gray			2	VD	Bruxelles	24 Aug 84
1:43.28		Gray			3	ASV	Köln	26 Aug 84
1:43.28		Koskei			2		Koblenz	29 Aug 84
1:43.33		Gray			3	ASV	Köln	25 Aug 85
1:43.34		Barbosa			1	R-W	Koblenz	28 Aug 88
1:43.35	David	Mack	USA	61	3r1		Koblenz	28 Aug 85
1:43.39		Konchellah			1rA	WK	Zürich	19 Aug 87
1:43.41	Peter	Elliott	UK	62	2	WC	Roma	1 Sep 87
1:43.42		Cram			3	WK	Zürich	17 Aug 88
1:43.43		Gray			3r1	WK	Zürich	21 Aug 85
1:43.44	Alberto	Juantorena	CUB	50	1	WUG	Sofia	21 Aug 77
	(32/10)							
1:43.45	Paul	Ereng	KEN	67	1	OG	Seoul	26 Sep 88
1:43.5 m*	Rick	Wohlhuter	USA	48	1		Eugene	8 Jun 74
1:43.54	William	Wuyke	VEN	58	2		Rieti	7 Sep 86
1:43.56	Rob	Druppers	HOL	62	4	ASV	Köln	25 Aug 85
1:43.57	Mike	Boit	KEN	49	1	ISTAF	Berlin	20 Aug 76
1:43.62	Earl	Jones	USA	64	2r1	WK	Zürich	13 Aug 86
1:43.63	Agberto	Guimarães	BRA	57	3		Koblenz	29 Aug 84
1:43.65	Willi	Wulbeck	FRG	54	1	WC	Helsinki	9 Aug 83
1:43.7 m	Marcello	Fiascanaro	ITA	49	1	vCS	Milano	27 Jun 73
1:43.84	Olaf	Beyer	GDR	57	1	EC	Praha	31 Aug 78
	(20)							
1:43.86	Ivo	Van Damme	BEL	54	2	OG	Montreal	25 Jul 76
1:43.86	Said	Aouita	MOR	59	1	ASV	Köln	21 Aug 88
1:43.88	Donato	Sabia	ITA	63	1		Firenze	13 Jun 84
1:43.9 m	José	Marajo	FRA	54	1		Saint Maur	12 Sep 79
1:43.91	John	Kipkurgat	KEN	44	1	CommG	Christchurch	29 Jan 74
1:43.92	John	Marshall	USA	63	3	FOT	Los Angeles	19 Jun 84
1:43.92	James	Robinson	USA	54	4	FOT	Los Angeles	19 Jun 84
1:43.95	Philippe	Collard	FRA	60	1	Nik	Nice	13 Jul 87
1:44.03	Peter	Braun	FRG	62	1r1		Koblenz	6 Aug 86
1:44.06	Moussa	Fall	SEN	63	4	WK	Zürich	17 Aug 88
	(30)							
1:44.07	Luciano	Susanj	YUG	48	1	EC	Roma	4 Sep 74
1:44.09	Steve	Ovett	UK	55	2	EC	Praha	31 Aug 78
1:44.10	Vladimir	Graudyn	SU	63	1	Bisl	Oslo	2 Jul 88
1:44.12	Edwin	Koech	KEN	61	2s1	OG	Los Angeles	5 Aug 84
1:44.20	Juma	N'diwa	KEN	60	1		München	26 Jul 83
1:44.24	James	Maina Boi	KEN	54	1	WK	Zürich	15 Aug 79
1:44.25	Vasiliy	Matveyev	SU	62	1	Izv	Kiev	22 Jun 84
1:44.29	Don	Paige	USA	56	1		Rieti	4 Sep 83
1:44.3 m"	Peter	Snell	NZ	38	1		Christchurch	3 Feb 62
1:44.3 m*	Jim	Ryun	USA	47	1	USTFF	Terre Haute	10 Jun 66
	(40)							
1:44.3 m	Dave	Wottle	USA	50	1	FOT	Eugene	1 Jul 72
1:44.38	Ryszard	Ostrowski	POL	61	1	WUG	Kobe	4 Sep 85
1:44.38	Joseph	Chesire	KEN	57	1		Sevilla	1 Jun 88
1:44.40A	Ralph	Doubell	AUS	45	1	OG	Ciudad Mexico	15 Oct 68
1:44.42	Abdi	Bile	SOM	62	1		Kvarnsveden	19 Jun 88
1:44.43	Tracy	Baskin	USA	65	5	WK	Zürich	17 Aug 88
1:44.45	Tom	McKean	UK	63	1	Athl	Lausanne	15 Sep 87
1:44.46	Mark	Everett	USA	68	2	FOT	Indianapolis	18 Jul 88
1:44.47	Abdi	Bile	SOM	62	2	ISTAF	Berlin	21 Aug 87
1:44.5 m	Pekka	Vasala	FIN	48	1	vSWE	Helsinki	20 Aug 72
	(50)							
1:44.5 m*	Danie	Malan	RSA	50	2		Los Angeles	27 May 73
1:44.5m A	Nixon	Kiprotich	KEN	62	1	OT	Nairobi	13 Aug 88

" photo-electric cell time, * 880 yards less 0.6 seconds, " time during 880 yards race

1000 METRES

Mark	Name		Nat	Yr	Pos	Meet	Venue	Date
2:12.18	Sebastian	Coe	UK	56	1	OsloG	Oslo	11 Jul 81
2:12.88	Steve	Cram	UK	60	1		Gateshead	9 Aug 85
2:13.40		Coe			1	Bisl	Oslo	1 Jul 80
2:13.9 m	Rick	Wohlhuter	USA	48	1	King	Oslo	30 Jul 74
2:14.09	Joaquim C.	Cruz	BRA	63	1	Nik	Nice	20 Aug 84
2:14.53	Willi	Wülbeck	FRG	54	2	Bisl	Oslo	1 Jul 80
2:14.54		Cruz			1	Pre	Eugene	21 Jul 84
2:14.90		Coe			1		London (Har.)	16 Jul 86
2:14.95	Sammy	Koskei	KEN	61	1	VD	Bruxelles	30 Aug 85
2:15.09		Cram			1		Edinburgh	23 Jul 85
2:15.11		Cruz			1		Bern	16 Aug 85
2:15.12		Cram			1	Coke	London	17 Sep 82
2:15.16	Said	Aouita	MOR	59	1		London	28 Aug 88
2:15.23	Rob	Druppers	HOL	62	1		Utrecht	17 Aug 85
2:15.25	Andreas	Busse	GDR	59	1		Berlin	31 Jul 83
2:15.28		Cruz			1		Bern	29 Jul 83
2:15.3	Mike	Boit (10)	KEN	49	1		Wattenscheid	23 Sep 77
2:15.33		Druppers			2	VD	Bruxelles	30 Aug 85
2:15.5 m	Ivo	Van Damme	BEL	54	1		Namur	14 Jul 76
2:15.75		Aouita			1		Grosseto	18 Aug 83
2:15.77		Cram			1	PTG	London	11 Jul 86
2:15.81	Agberto	Guimarães	BRA	57	2		Bern	29 Jul 83
2:15.84		Cram			1		London	7 Aug 82
2:15.86		Cram			1		Birmingham	19 Jul 86
2:15.89	Juma	N'diwa	KEN	60	3	VD	Bruxelles	30 Aug 85
2:15.91	Steve	Ovett	UK	55	1		Koblenz	6 Sep 79
2:15.98		Boit			1	Nik	Nice	20 Aug 78
2:15.98		Cram			1		Loughborough	17 Jun 84
2:16.0	Danie	Malan	RSA	49	1	HB	München	24 Jun 73
2:16.0 m	Vladimir	Malozemlin	SU	56	1		Kiev	11 Jun 81
2:16.0 m		Cruz			1	BNP	Paris	13 Jul 85
2:16.03		Boit			1	Nik	Nice	23 Aug 81
	(32/16)							
2:16.1 m	Tom	Byers	USA	55	1		København	6 Aug 81
2:16.2 m	Jürgen	May	GDR	42	1		Erfurt	20 Jul 65
2:16.2 m	Franz-Josef	Kemper	FRG	45	1		Hannover	21 Sep 66
2:16.25	James	Maina Boi	KEN	54	3	R-W	Koblenz	6 Sep 79
	(20)							
2:16.3 m	James	Robinson	USA	54	2		København	6 Aug 81
2:16.3 m	Andreas	Hauck	GDR	60	1		Potsdam	12 Jul 84
2:16.40	Steve	Scott	USA	56	2	Nik	Nice	23 Aug 81
2:16.4	Thomas	Wessinghage	FRG	52	3		Wattenscheid	23 Sep 77
2:16.4 m	Nikolay	Shirokov	SU	55	2		Kiev	11 Jun 81
2:16.47	Peter	Elliott	UK	62	1		Belfast	27 Jun 88
2:16.5 m	Bodo	Tummler	FRG	43	2		Hannover	21 Sep 66
2:16.54	Jim	Spivey	USA	60	2	Pre	Eugene	21 Jul 84
2:16.56	William	Wuyke	VEN	58	3		Bern	29 Jul 83
2:16.57	John	Walker	NZ	52	3	Bisl	Oslo	1 Jul 80
	(30)							
2:16.58	Omer	Khalifa	SUD	56	2		Padova	13 Sep 87
2:16.6 m	Peter	Snell	NZ	38	1		Auckland	12 Nov 64
2:16.6 m	Philippe	Collard	FRA	60	1		Parilly	18 Jul 86
2:16.64	Antonio	Paez	SPA	56	4	Bisl	Oslo	1 Jul 80
2:16.7 m	Siegfried	Valentin	GDR	36	1		Potsdam	19 Jul 60
2:16.7 m	Detlef	Wagenknecht	GDR	59	1		Berlin	26 May 82
2:16.7 m	John	Marshall	USA	63	2		Paris	13 Jul 85
2:16.71	Billy	Konchellah	KEN	61	4	VD	Bruxelles	30 Aug 85
2:16.8 m	José	Marajo	FRA	54	1		Paris	17 Jun 80
2:16.8 m	Vitaliy	Tishchenko	SU	57	3		Kiev	11 Jun 81
	(40)							
2:16.82	Graham	Williamson	UK	60	1		Edinburgh	17 Jul 84
2:16.87	Pierre	Délèze	SWZ	58	4		Bern	29 Jul 83
2:16.88	Ari	Suhonen	FIN	65	1		Lahti	11 Aug 87

1500 METRES

Mark	Name		Nat	Yr	Pos	Meet	Venue	Date
3:29.46	Said	Aouita	MOR	59	1	ISTAF	Berlin	23 Aug 85
3:29.67	Steve	Cram	UK	60	1	Nik	Nice	16 Jul 85
3:29.71		Aouita			2	Nik	Nice	16 Jul 85
3:29.77	Sydney	Maree	USA	56	1	ASV	Köln	25 Aug 85
3:29.77	Sebastian	Coe	UK	56	1		Rieti	7 Sep 86
3:30.15		Cram			1	VD	Bruxelles	5 Sep 86
3:30.69		Aouita			1	Bisl	Oslo	4 Jul 87
3:30.77	Steve	Ovett	UK	55	1		Rieti	4 Sep 83
3:30.92	José Luis	Gonzalez	SPA	57	3	Nik	Nice	16 Jul 85
3:30.95		Cram			1	VD	Bruxelles	19 Aug 88
3:31.01	Jim	Spivey	USA	60	1	R-W	Koblenz	28 Aug 88
3:31.13	José Manuel	Abascal	SPA	58	1		Barcelona	16 Aug 86
3:31.24		Maree			1	ASV	Köln	28 Aug 83
3:31.34		Cram			1	OsloG	Oslo	27 Jun 85
3:31.36		Ovett			1		Koblenz	27 Aug 80
3:31.43		Cram			1rA	WK	Zürich	19 Aug 87
3:31.54		Aouita			1	FBK	Hengelo	6 Jul 84
3:31.57		Ovett			1	BGP	Budapest	29 Jul 81
3:31.58	Thomas	Wessinghage	FRG	52	2		Koblenz	27 Aug 80
3:31.66		Cram			1	VD	Bruxelles	26 Aug 83
3:31.69		Abascal			1		Barcelona	13 Aug 85
3:31.7+		Aouita			1	WK	Zürich	21 Aug 85
3:31.71	Abdi	Bile	SOM	62	1	ASV	Köln	16 Aug 87
3:31.75	Pierre	Délèze	SWZ	58	1	WK	Zürich	21 Aug 85
3:31.76	Steve	Scott	USA	56	4	Nik	Nice	16 Jul 85
3:31.80		Bile			1	VD	Bruxelles	11 Sep 87
3:31.8+ m		Aouita			1	WG	Helsinki	2 Jul 87
3:31.95		Coe			1	DNG	Stockholm	7 Jul 81
3:31.95		Ovett			1		Milano	8 Jul 81
3:31.96	Harald	Hudak	FRG	57	3		Koblenz	27 Aug 80
3:31.96		Scott			1		Koblenz	26 Aug 81
	(31/13)							
3:32.16	Filbert	Bayi	TAN	53	1	CommG	Christchurch	2 Feb 74
3:32.4 m	John	Walker	NZ	52	1	OsloG	Oslo	30 Jul 75
3:32.94	Peter	Elliott	UK	62	2	VD	Bruxelles	19 Aug 88
3:33.07	Kipkoech	Cheruiyot	KEN	64	1		Grosseto	10 Aug 86
3:33.1 m	Jim	Ryun	USA	47	1	vComm	Los Angeles	8 Jul 67
3:33.16	Ben	Jipcho	KEN	43	3	CommG	Christchurch	2 Feb 74
3:33.28	Omer	Khalifa	SUD	56	2		Grosseto	10 Aug 86
	(20)							
3:33.28	Jens-Peter	Herold	GDR	65	1	NC	Potsdam	20 Aug 87
3:33.34	Steve	Crabb	UK	63	3	Bisl	Oslo	4 Jul 87
3:33.39	Mike	Hillardt	AUS	61	4	ISTAF	Berlin	23 Aug 85
3:33.5 m+	Ray	Flynn	IRL	57	2	OsloG	Oslo	7 Jul 82
3:33.54	Dieter	Baumann	FRG	65	2rA	R-W	Koblenz	13 Aug 87
3:33.67+	Mike	Boit	KEN	49	2	VD	Bruxelles	28 Aug 81
3:33.68	Jürgen	Straub	GDR	53	1		Potsdam	31 Aug 79
3:33.74	Willi	Wulbeck	FRG	54	4		Koblenz	27 Aug 80
3:33.79	David	Moorcroft	UK	53	1	FBK	Hengelo	27 Jul 82
3:33.83	John	Robson	UK	57	2	VD	Bruxelles	4 Sep 79
	(30)							
3:33.87	Johan	Fourie	RSA	59	1	NC	Stellenbosch	10 Apr 87
3:33.89	Rod	Dixon	NZ	50	4	CommG	Christchurch	2 Feb 74
3:33.99	Steve	Lacy	USA	56	4	OsloG	Oslo	15 Jul 80
3:33.99	Todd	Harbour	USA	59	2	WK	Zürich	18 Aug 82
3:34.0 m	Jean	Wadoux	FRA	52	1		Colombes	23 Jul 70
3:34.01	Graham	Williamson	UK	60	3	Bisl	Oslo	28 Jun 83
3:34.02	Frank	O'Mara	IRL	61	2	VD	Bruxelles	30 Aug 85
3:34.10	Andreas	Busse	GDR	59	1	OD	Potsdam	21 Jul 84
3:34.11	Markus	Hacksteiner	SWZ	64	3rA	R-W	Koblenz	13 Aug 87
3:34.22	Graham	Crouch	AUS	48	5	CommG	Christchurch	2 Feb 74
	(40)							

Mark	Name		Nat	Yr	Pos	Meet	Venue	Date
3:34.32	Joseph	Chesire	KEN	57	4		Grosseto	10 Aug 86
3:34.49	Igor	Lotarev	SU	64	4	VD	Bruxelles	30 Aug 85
3:34.50	Adrian	Passey	UK	64	4	Bisl	Oslo	4 Jul 87
3:34.52	Philippe	Dien	FRA	57	2		Viareggio	27 Jul 83
3:34.53	Mark	Rowland	UK	63	2		Verona	27 Jul 88
3:34.57	Stefano	Mei	ITA	63	3		Rieti	7 Sep 86
3:34.61	Pat	Scammell	AUS	61	2		Melbourne	17 Mar 88
3:34.63	Joaquim	Cruz	BRA	63	1	APM	Hengelo	14 Aug 88
3:34.66	Tim	Hacker	USA	62	4rA	R-W	Koblenz	13 Aug 87
3:34.7+	Chuck	Aragon	USA	59	3	OsloG	Oslo	21 Jul 84
	(50)							

+ during mile race

1 MILE

Mark	Name		Nat	Yr	Pos	Meet	Venue	Date
3:46.32	Steve	Cram	UK	60	1	Bisl	Oslo	27 Jul 85
3:46.76	Said	Aouita	MOR	59	1	WG	Helsinki	2 Jul 87
3:46.92		Aouita			1	WK	Zürich	21 Aug 85
3:47.33	Sebastian	Coe	UK	56	1	VD	Bruxelles	28 Aug 81
3:47.69	Steve	Scott	USA	56	1	OsloG	Oslo	7 Jul 82
3:47.79	José Luis	Gonzalez	SPA	57	2	Bisl	Oslo	27 Jul 85
3:48.31		Cram			1	Bisl	Oslo	5 Jul 86
3:48.40	Steve	Ovett	UK	55	1	R-W	Koblenz	26 Aug 81
3:48.53		Coe			1	WK	Zürich	19 Aug 81
3:48.53		Scott			1	Bisl	Oslo	26 Jun 82
3:48.73		Scott			2	Bisl	Oslo	5 Jul 86
3:48.8 m		Ovett			1	Bisl	Oslo	1 Jul 80
3:48.83	Sydney	Maree	USA	56	1		Rieti	9 Sep 81
3:48.85		Maree			2	Bisl	Oslo	26 Jun 82
3:48.85		Cram			1	Bisl	Oslo	2 Jul 88
3:48.95		Coe			1	OsloG	Oslo	17 Jul 79
3:49.08	John	Walker	NZ	52	2	OsloG	Oslo	7 Jul 82
3:49.12		Aouita			1	Nik	Nice	13 Jul 87
3:49.20	Peter	Elliott	UK	62	2	Bisl	Oslo	2 Jul 88
3:49.21		Scott			1	ISTAF	Berlin	17 Aug 83
3:49.22		Coe			3	Bisl	Oslo	27 Jul 85
3:49.22	Jens-Peter	Herold	GDR	65	3	Bisl	Oslo	2 Jul 88
3:49.25		Ovett			1	OsloG	Oslo	11 Jul 81
3:49.34	David	Moorcroft	UK	53	3	Bisl	Oslo	26 Jun 82
3:49.40	Abdi	Bile	SOM	62	4	Bisl	Oslo	2 Jul 88
3:49.4m		Walker			1		Göteborg	12 Aug 75
3:49.42		Maree			1		Cork	13 Jul 82
3:49.45	Mike	Boit	KEN	49	2	VD	Bruxelles	28 Aug 81
3:49.49		Scott			1	OsloG	Oslo	9 Jul 83
3:49.49		Cram			1		London	12 Sep 86
	(31/13)							
3:49.77	Ray	Flynn	IRL	57	3	OsloG	Oslo	7 Jul 82
3:49.80	Jim	Spivey	USA	60	3	Bisl	Oslo	5 Jul 86
3:49.98	Thomas	Wessinghage	FRG	52	3	ISTAF	Berlin	17 Aug 83
3:50.34	Todd	Harbour	USA	59	5	OsloG	Oslo	11 Jul 81
3:50.38	Pierre	Délèze	SWZ	58	4	R-W	Koblenz	25 Aug 82
3:50.59	José Manuel	Abascal	SPA	58	2	GP-GG	Roma	10 Sep 86
3:50.64	Graham	Williamson	UK	60	4		Cork	13 Jul 82
	(20)							
3:50.73	Wilson	Waigwa	KEN	49	2	R-W	Koblenz	31 Aug 83
3:50.82	Johan	Fourie	RSA	59	1		Port Elizabeth	11 Mar 87
3:50.84	Tom	Byers	USA	55	6	R-W	Koblenz	25 Aug 82
3:50.98	José	Marajo	FRA	54	4	OsloG	Oslo	9 Jul 83
3:51.0 m	Filbert	Bayi	TAN	53	1	King	Kingston	17 May 75
3:51.02	John	Gladwin	UK	63	2	WK	Zürich	19 Aug 87
3:51.06	Frank	O'Mara	IRL	60	4	GP-GG	Roma	10 Sep 86
3:51.1 m	Jim	Ryun	USA	47	1	AAU	Bakersfield	23 Jun 67
3:51.34	John	Gregorek	USA	60	6	Bisl	Oslo	26 Jun 82
3:51.39	Rich	Harris	USA	59	3	R-W	Koblenz	29 Aug 84
	(30)							

Mark	Name		Nat	Yr	Pos	Meet	Venue	Date
3:51.57	Jack	Buckner	UK	61	4	R-W	Koblenz	29 Aug 84
3:51.59	Eamonn	Coghlan	IRL	52	5	OsloG	Oslo	9 Jul 83
3:51.62	Chuck	Aragon	USA	59	3	OsloG	Oslo	21 Jul 84
3:51.76	Steve	Crabb	UK	63	1hc	IAC	London	14 Aug 87
3:51.82	Mike	Hillardt	AUS	61	1	R-W	Koblenz	28 Aug 85
3:51.94	Suleiman	Nyambui	TAN	53	4		Lausanne	14 Jul 81
3:52.02	Craig	Masback	USA	55	3	OsloG	Oslo	17 Jul 79
3:52.02	Pascal	Thiébaut	FRA	59	4	OsloG	Oslo	21 Jul 84
3:52.14	Joe	Falcon	USA	66	2	WK	Zürich	17 Aug 88
3:52.17	Ben	Jipcho	KEN	43	1	DNG	Stockholm	2 Jul 73
	(40)							
3:52.2 m	Marty	Liquori	USA	49	2	King	Kingston	17 May 75
3:52.24	Dragan	Zdravkovic	UG	59	5	ISTAF	Berlin	17 Aug 83
3:52.31	Vittorio	Fontanella	ITA	53	6	WK	Zürich	19 Aug 81
3:52.36	Uwe	Becker	FRG	55	7	R-W	Koblenz	25 Aug 82
3:52.39	Kipkoech	Cheruiyot	KEN	64	8	Bisl	Oslo	2 Jul 88
3:52.42	Robert	Nemeth	AUT	58	3		Rieti	9 Sep 81
3:52.44	John	Robson	UK	57	8	OsloG	Oslo	11 Jul 81
3:52.50	Marcus	O'Sullivan	IRL	61	3	WK	Zürich	17 Aug 88
3:52.59	Jozef	Plachy	CS	49	2	DNG	Stockholm	3 Jul 78
3:52.78	Alex	Gonzalez	FRA	51	6		Lausanne	14 Jul 81
	(50)							

Crabb's 3:51.76 in handicap race from scratch, next best 3:52.26 (7) Bisl Oslo 2 Jul 88

Indoor marks

Mark	Name		Nat	Yr	Pos	Meet	Venue	Date
3:49.78	Eamonn	Coghlan	IRL	52	1		East Rutherford	27 Feb 83
3:50.94	Marcus	O'Sullivan	IRL	61	1		East Rutherford	13 Feb 88

2000 METRES

Mark	Name		Nat	Yr	Pos	Meet	Venue	Date
4:50.81	Said	Aouita	MOR	59	1	BNP	Paris	16 Jul 87
4:51.39	Steve	Cram	UK	60	1	BGP	Budapest	4 Aug 85
4:51.52	John	Walker	NZ	52	1	Bisl	Oslo	30 Jun 76
4:51.98		Aouita			1	VD	Bruxelles	5 Sep 86
4:52.20	Thomas	Wessinghage	FRG	52	1		Ingelheim	31 Aug 82
4:52.40	José Manuel	Abascal	SPA	58	1		Santander	7 Sep 86
4:52.44	Jim	Spivey	USA	60	1	Athl	Lausanne	15 Sep 87
4:52.82	Peter	Elliott	UK	62	2	Athl	Lausanne	15 Sep 87
4:53.06	Jack	Buckner	UK	61	3	Athl	Lausanne	15 Sep 87
4:53.69	Gary	Staines	UK	63	4	Athl	Lausanne	15 Sep 87
4:54.02		Aouita			1		Rieti	4 Sep 85
4:54.20	Sydney	Maree (10)	USA	56	2		Rieti	4 Sep 85
4:54.46	Pierre	Délèze	SWZ	58	5	Athl	Lausanne	15 Sep 87
4:54.71	Steve	Scott	USA	56	2		Ingelheim	31 Aug 82
4:54.88		Abascal			1		Santander	3 Sep 85
4:54.98		Aouita			1		Madrid	4 Jun 85
4:55.20		Cram			1		London	28 Aug 88
4:55.72		Elliott			2		London	28 Aug 88
4:55.82		Scott			3		Rieti	4 Sep 85
4:56.1 m	Michel	Jazy	FRA	36	1		Saint Maur	12 Oct 66
	(20/13)							
4:56.41	Johan	Fourie	RSA	59	1		Stellenbosch	22 Apr 85
4:56.70	Pascal	Thiébaut	FRA	59	2	BNP	Paris	16 Jul 87
4:57.1 m	Willy	Polleunis	BEL	47	1		Louvain	21 Sep 78
4:57.53	José Luis	Carreira	SPA	62	2		Santander	7 Sep 86
4:57.66	Eamonn	Coghlan	IRL	52	1		London	29 Aug 83
4:57.71	Steve	Ovett	UK	55	1	OsloG	Oslo	7 Jul 82
4:57.8 m	Harald	Norpoth	FRG	42	1		Hagen	10 Sep 66
	(20)							
4:58.08	Marcus	O'Sullivan	IRL	61	3		London	28 Aug 88
4:58.1 m	Francis	Gonzalez	FRA	52	1		Rennes	22 Jun 79
4:58.29	Peter	Wirz	SWZ	60	2		Langenthal	27 Jul 84
4:58.38	Graham	Williamson	UK	60	2		London	29 Aug 83
4:58.51	Peter	Koech	KEN	58	4	BNP	Paris	16 Jul 87
4:58.56	Rémy	Geoffroy	FRA	63	5	BNP	Paris	16 Jul 87
4:58.65	Stefano	Mei	ITA	63	1		Viareggio	15 Aug 84
4:58.84	Sebastian	Coe	UK	56	1		Bordeaux	5 Jun 82

Mark	Name		Nat	Yr	Pos	Meet	Venue	Date
4:58.97	Vincent	Rousseau	BEL	62	1		Hechtel	8 Aug 87
4:59.00	Frank	O'Mara	IRL	60	6	Athl	Lausanne	15 Sep 87
	(30)							
4:59.02	Evgeni	Ignatov	BUL	59	4		Rieti	4 Sep 85
4:59.04	Rich	Harris	USA	59	2		Viareggio	15 Aug 84
4:59.1 m	Peter	Daenens	BEL	60	1		Neerpelt	19 Aug 83
4:59.21	Filbert	Bayi	TAN	53	1		Schaan	17 Sep 78
4:59.28	Todd	Harbour	USA	59	3	Nik	Nice	14 Aug 82
4:59.40	Ray	Flynn	IRL	57	1		Stuttgart	29 Aug 82
4:59.43	Mike	Boit	KEN	49	5		Rieti	4 Sep 85
4:59.54	Markus	Ryffel	SWZ	55	2		Schaan	17 Sep 78
4:59.56	Robert	Nemeth	AUT	58	1		Klagenfurt	8 Aug 84
4:59.56	Mogens	Guldberg	DEN	63	7	Athl	Lausanne	15 Sep 87
	(40)							
4:59.57	Nick	Rose	UK	51	2		London	3 Jun 78
4:59.59	Alex	Gonzalez	FRA	51	2		Bordeaux	5 Jun 82
4:59.6 m	Jürgen	Straub	GDR	53	1		Potsdam	5 Jul 80
4:59.71	Suleiman	Nyambui	TAN	53	3		Schaan	17 Sep 78
4:59.77	Abdi	Bile	SOM	62	1		Fürth	14 Jun 87
4:59.8 m	Emiel	Puttemans	BEL	47	1		Landen	12 Aug 73
4:59.88	Dieter	Baumann	FRG	65	2		Fürth	14 Jun 87
4:59.89	Féthi	Baccouche	TUN	60	6	BNP	Paris	16 Jul 87
Indoor marks								
4:54.07	Eamonn	Coghlan	IRL	52	1		Inglewood	20 Feb 87
4:59.78	Doug	Padilla	USA	56	2		Inglewood	20 Feb 87

3000 METRES

Mark	Name		Nat	Yr	Pos	Meet	Venue	Date
7:32.1 m	Henry	Rono	KEN	52	1	Bisl	Oslo	27 Jun 78
7:32.23	Said	Aouita	MOR	59	1	ASV	Köln	17 Aug 86
7:32.54		Aouita			1	WK	Zürich	13 Aug 86
7:32.79	David	Moorcroft	UK	53	1		London	17 Jul 82
7:32.94		Aouita			1	VD	Bruxelles	30 Aug 85
7:33.3 m		Aouita			1	VD	Bruxelles	24 Aug 84
7:33.37	Sydney	Maree	USA	56	2		London	17 Jul 82
7:35.1 m	Brendan	Foster	UK	48	1		Gateshead	3 Aug 74
7:35.84	Doug	Padilla	USA	56	1	OsloG	Oslo	9 Jul 83
7:36.69	Steve	Scott	USA	56	1		Ingelheim	1 Sep 81
7:36.75	Thomas	Wessinghage	FRG	52	2		Ingelheim	1 Sep 81
7:37.49	John	Walker	NZ	52	3		London	17 Jul 82
7:37.6 m	Emiel	Puttemans (10)	BEL	47	1		Århus	14 Sep 72
7:37.60	Eamonn	Coghlan	IRL	52	1	Bisl	Oslo	1 Jul 80
7:37.70	Rudy	Chapa	USA	57	1		Eugene	10 May 79
7:38.25		Padilla			1		Lausanne	10 Jul 85
7:38.26		Maree			2	WK	Zürich	13 Aug 86
7:38.39		Coghlan			1	VD	Bruxelles	26 Aug 83
7:38.53		Scott			2		Lausanne	10 Jul 85
7:38.79		Maree			1		Malmö	8 Aug 88
7:38.89		Wessinghage			2	Bisl	Oslo	1 Jul 80
7:39.08		Coghlan			1	Bisl	Oslo	5 Jul 79
7:39.09	Peter	Koech	KEN	58	4		London	17 Jul 82
7:39.27	Filbert	Bayi	TAN	53	3	Bisl	Oslo	1 Jul 80
7:39.34		Wessinghage			1	ASV	Köln	22 Aug 82
7:39.38	Paul	Kipkoech	KEN	63	2	ASV	Köln	17 Aug 86
7:39.5 m	Kipchoge	Keino	KEN	40	1		Hälsingborg	27 Aug 65
7:39.69	António	Leitão	POR	58	2	VD	Bruxelles	26 Aug 83
7:39.71		Wessinghage			3	VD	Bruxelles	26 Aug 83
	(29/17)							
7:40.19	Bill	McChesney	USA	59	2	ASV	Köln	22 Aug 82
7:40.25	Dieter	Baumann	FRG	65	1	ISTAF	Berlin	21 Aug 87
7:40.3 m	Suleiman	Nyambui	TAN	53	2	Bisl	Oslo	27 Jun 78
	(20)							
7:40.4 m	Nick	Rose	UK	51	3	Bisl	Oslo	27 Jun 78
7:40.43	Jack	Buckner	UK	61	1	Bisl	Oslo	5 Jul 86
7:40.49	Dragan	Zdravkovic	YUG	59	2	OsloG	Oslo	9 Jul 83
7:40.52	Wilson	Waigwa	KEN	49	4	VD	Bruxelles	26 Aug 83

Mark	Name		Nat	Yr	Pos	Meet	Venue	Date
7:40.64	Wodajo	Bulti	ETH	57	5	VD	Bruxelles	26 Aug 83
7:40.94	Eamonn	Martin	UK	58	3	OsloG	Oslo	9 Jul 83
7:41.00	Francis	Gonzalez	FRA	52	2		Lausanne	18 Jul 79
7:41.00	Markus	Ryffel	SWZ	55	3		Lausanne	18 Jul 79
7:41.0 m	Rod	Dixon	NZ	50	1		Milano	2 Jul 74
7:41.22	Karl	Fleschen	FRG	55	1	ASV	Köln	22 Jun 77
	(30)							
7:41.3 m	Steve	Ovett	UK	55	1		Wattenscheid	23 Sep 77
7:41.60	Ray	Flynn	IRL	57	1	PTG	London	13 Jul 84
7:42.05	Dmitriy	Dmitriyev	SU	56	2	PTG	London	13 Jul 84
7:42.1 m	Boris	Kuznetsov	SU	48	1		Podolsk	20 Aug 78
7:42.11	Ralph	King	USA	56	4		Lausanne	18 Jul 79
7:42.15	Vincent	Rousseau	BEL	62	1	Nik	Nice	15 Jul 86
7:42.24	Dan	Glans	SWE	47	4	Bisl	Oslo	5 Jul 79
7:42.26	Graeme	Fell	UK	59	4	OsloG	Oslo	9 Jul 83
7:42.38	Peter	Weigt	FRG	48	2	ASV	Köln	22 Jun 77
7:42.4 m	Bronislaw	Malinowski	POL	51	3	Bisl	Oslo	4 Jul 74
	(40)							
7:42.4 m	Knut	Kvalheim	NOR	50	4	Bisl	Oslo	4 Jul 74
7:42.47	Dave	Lewis	UK	61	5	OsloG	Oslo	9 Jul 83
7:42.6 m	Steve	Prefontaine	USA	51	2		Milano	2 Jul 74
7:42.73	Francesco	Panetta	ITA	63	1		Cagliari	16 Sep 87
7:42.85	Stefano	Mei	ITA	63	2	Nik	Nice	15 Jul 86
7:42.93	José Luis	Gonzalez	SPA	57	1		Sevilla	28 May 87
7:42.99	Frank	O'Mara	IRL	60	2		Sevilla	28 May 87
7:43.1 m+	Steve	Cram	UK	60	1		London	29 Aug 83
7:43.15	Terry	Brahm	USA	62	2		Paris	22 Jul 86
7:43.18	Eshetu	Tura	ETH	50	1		Viareggio	3 Aug 77
	(50)							
Indoor marks								
7:39.2 m+		Puttemans			1		Berlin	18 Feb 73
7:41.57	Brian	Abshire	USA	63	1		East Rutherford	13 Feb 88
7:42.97	Christoph	Herle	FRG	55	1	NC	Dortmund	16 Feb 85

+ time during 2 miles race

2 MILES

Mark	Name		Nat	Yr	Pos	Meet	Venue	Date
8:13.45	Said	Aouita	MOR	59	1		Torino	28 May 87
8:13.51	Steve	Ovett	UK	55	1	IAC	London	15 Sep 78
8:13.68	Brendan	Foster	UK	48	1		London	27 Aug 73
8:14.0 m	Lasse	Viren	FIN	49	1		Stockholm	14 Aug 72
8:14.05		Aouita			1		Casablanca	11 Jun 88
8:14.32	Rod	Dixon	NZ	50	1		Stockholm	18 Jul 74
8:14.66	Henry	Rono	KEN	52	2	IAC	London	15 Sep 78
8:14.81		Aouita			1		London	12 Sep 86
8:14.93	Steve	Cram	UK	60	1		London	29 Aug 83
8:15.18		Dixon			1	OsloG	Oslo	17 Jul 79
	(10/7)							
8:15.53	Tim	Hutchings	UK	58	2		London	12 Sep 86
8:15.98	Geoff	Turnbull	UK	61	3		London	12 Sep 86
8:16.31	Emiel	Puttemans (10)	BEL	47	1		Stockholm	25 Jul 73
	(10)							
8:16.38	Ben	Jipcho	KEN	43	2		Stockholm	25 Jul 73
8:16.75	David	Moorcroft	UK	53	1		London	20 Aug 82
8:17.05	Peter	Koech	KEN	58	2		London	20 Aug 82
8:17.1 m	Dick	Quax	NZ	48	1	LB	Philadelphia	4 Aug 76
8:17.12	Marty	Liquori	USA	49	1		Stockholm	17 Jul 75
8:17.12	Jack	Buckner	UK	61	4		London	12 Sep 86
8:17.78	Frank	O'Mara	IRL	60	1		Gateshead	16 Jul 88
8:17.8 m	Bronislaw	Malinowski	POL	51	2	ISTAF	Berlin	21 Aug 74
8:18.29	Steve	Prefontaine	USA	51	3		Stockholm	18 Jul 74
8:18.98	Eamonn	Martin	UK	58	3		Gateshead	16 Jul 88
	(20)							
Indoor marks								
8:13.2 m	Emiel	Puttemans	BEL	47	1		Berlin	18 Feb 73
8:15.3 m	Doug	Padilla	USA	56	1		San Diego	15 Feb 85
8:17.9 m	Suleiman	Nyambui	TAN	53	1		San Diego	17 Feb 78
8:18.4 m	Nick	Rose	UK	51	2		San Diego	17 Feb 78

5000 METRES

Mark	Name		Nat	Yr	Pos	Meet	Venue	Date
12:58.39	Said	Aouita	MOR	59	1	GGala	Roma	22 Jul 87
13:00.40		Aouita			1	Bisl	Oslo	27 Jul 85
13:00.41	David	Moorcroft	UK	53	1	OsloG	Oslo	7 Jul 82
13:00.86		Aouita			1		La Coruña	6 Aug 86
13:01.15	Sydney	Maree	USA	56	2	Bisl	Oslo	27 Jul 85
13:04.52		Aouita			1	OsloG	Oslo	27 Jun 85
13:04.78		Aouita			1		Firenze	13 Jun 84
13:05.59		Aouita			1	OG	Los Angeles	11 Aug 84
13:06.20	Henry	Rono	KEN	52	1		Knarvik	13 Sep 81
13:07.29	Wodajo	Bulti	ETH	57	1		Rieti	16 Sep 82
13:07.54	Markus	Ryffel	SWZ	55	2	OG	Los Angeles	11 Aug 84
13:07.70	António	Leitão	POR	60	2		Rieti	16 Sep 82
13:08.4 m		Rono			1		Berkeley	8 Apr 78
13:08.54	Fernando	Mamede	POR	51	1		Tokyo	17 Sep 83
13:08.97		Rono			1	DNG	Stockholm	6 Jul 82
13:09.20		Leitão			3	OG	Los Angeles	11 Aug 84
13:09.50	Peter	Koech	KEN	58	2	DNG	Stockholm	6 Jul 82
13:09.92		Mamede			1		Rieti	4 Sep 83
13:10.06	Alberto	Cova (10)	ITA	58	3	Bisl	Oslo	27 Jul 85
13:10.08		Bulti			2		Firenze	13 Jun 84
13:10.15	Jack	Buckner	UK	61	1	EC	Stuttgart	31 Aug 86
13:10.40	Hansjörg	Kunze	GDR	59	1		Rieti	9 Sep 81
13:10.48		Buckner			1	WK	Zürich	19 Aug 87
13:11.50	Tim	Hutchings	UK	58	4	OG	Los Angeles	11 Aug 84
13:11.57	Stefano	Mei	ITA	63	2	EC	Stuttgart	31 Aug 86
13:11.70	John	Ngugi	KEN	62	1	OG	Seoul	1 Oct 88
13:11.93	Alberto	Salazar	USA	58	3	DNG	Stockholm	6 Jul 82
13:11.99	Valeriy	Abramov	SU	56	2		Rieti	9 Sep 81
13:12.15		Rono			1	R-W	Koblenz	26 Aug 81
13:12.29	Suleiman	Nyambui	TAN	53	1		Stockholm	18 Jun 79
	(30/18)							
13:12.34	José Luis	Gonzalez	SPA	57	1	Bisl	Oslo	4 Jul 87
13:12.49	José Manuel	Abascal	SPA	58	2	Bisl	Oslo	4 Jul 87
	(20)							
13:12.54	Werner	Schildhauer	GDR	59	2	WK	Zürich	18 Aug 82
13:12.78	Thomas	Wessinghage	FRG	52	3	WK	Zürich	18 Aug 82
13:12.86	Dick	Quax	NZ	48	1	DNG	Stockholm	5 Jul 77
13:12.91	Matt	Centrowitz	USA	55	1	Pre	Eugene	5 Jun 82
13:13.0 m	Emiel	Puttemans	BEL	47	1		Bruxelles	20 Sep 72
13:13.02	Frank	O'Mara	IRL	60	3	Bisl	Oslo	4 Jul 87
13:13.15	Evgeni	Ignatov	BUL	59	4	EC	Stuttgart	31 Aug 86
13:13.49	Bruce	Bickford	USA	57	2	OsloG	Oslo	27 Jun 85
13:13.52	Arturo	Barrios	MEX	63	4	Bisl	Oslo	4 Jul 87
13:13.69	Klaus-Peter	Hildenbrand	FRG	52	2		Stockholm	5 Jul 76
	(30)							
13:13.82	Miruts	Yifter	ETH	44	1	WP	Düsseldorf	4 Sep 77
13:13.88	Karl	Fleschen	FRG	55	2	DNG	Stockholm	5 Jul 77
13:13.94	Féthi	Baccouche	TUN	60	5	Bisl	Oslo	4 Jul 87
13:14.3	Ben	Jipcho	KEN	43	1	CommG	Christchurch	29 Jan 74
13:14.40	Paul	Kipkoech	KEN	63	5	OG	Los Angeles	11 Aug 84
13:14.54	Peter	Weigt	FRG	48	3	DNG	Stockholm	5 Jul 77
13:14.60	Pascal	Thiébaut	FRA	59	6	Bisl	Oslo	4 Jul 87
13:14.6	Brendan	Foster	UK	48	2	CommG	Christchurch	29 Jan 74
13:14.80	Bill	McChesney	USA	59	5	WK	Zürich	18 Aug 82
13:15.0	Ilie	Floroiu	RUM	52	1	NC	Bucuresti	23 Jul 78
	(40)							
13:15.01	Vincent	Rousseau	BEL	62	4	GP-GG	Roma	10 Sep 86
13:15.06	Marty	Liquori	USA	49	2	WP	Düsseldorf	4 Sep 77
13:15.31	Dietmar	Millonig	AUT	55	6	WK	Zürich	18 Aug 82
13:15.31	Pierre	Délèze	SWZ	58	1	WG	Helsinki	7 Jul 86
13:15.44	Doug	Padilla	USA	56	1	WG	Helsinki	4 Jul 85
13:15.52	Dieter	Baumann	FRG	65	2	OG	Seoul	1 Oct 88

Mark	Name			Nat	Yr	Pos	Meet	Venue	Date
13:15.59	Julian	Goater		UK	53	2	IAC	London	11 Sep 81
13:15.62	José	Regalo		POR	63	1	VD	Bruxelles	21 Aug 88
13:16.02	Martti	Vainio		FIN	50	2	Bisl	Oslo	28 Jun 84
13:16.09	Domingos	Castro		POR	63	4	OG	Seoul	1 Oct 88
(50)									

10000 METRES

Mark	Name			Nat	Yr	Pos	Meet	Venue	Date
27:13.81	Fernando	Mamede		POR	51	1	DNG	Stockholm	2 Jul 84
27:17.48	Carlos	Lopes		POR	47	2	DNG	Stockholm	2 Jul 84
27:20.56	Mark	Nenow		USA	57	1	VD	Bruxelles	5 Sep 86
27:21.46	Brahim	Boutayeb		MOR	67	1	OG	Seoul	26 Sep 88
27:22.47+	Henry	Rono		KEN	52	1		Wien	11 Jun 78
27:22.95		Mamede				1		Paris	9 Jul 82
27:23.06	Eamonn	Martin		UK	58	1	Bisl	Oslo	2 Jul 88
27:23.44		Lopes				1	OsloG	Oslo	9 Jul 83
27:23.55	Salvatore	Antibo		ITA	62	2	OG	Seoul	26 Sep 88
27:24.39		Lopes				1	Bisl	Oslo	26 Jun 82
27:24.79		Antibo				2	Bisl	Oslo	2 Jul 88
27:24.95	Werner	Schildhauer		GDR	59	1	NC	Jena	28 May 83
27:25.07	Arturo	Barrios		MEX	63	3	Bisl	Oslo	2 Jul 88
27:25.13		Mamede				2	OsloG	Oslo	9 Jul 83
27:25.16	Kipkemboi	Kimeli	(10)	KEN	66	3	OG	Seoul	26 Sep 88
27:25.61	Alberto	Salazar		USA	58	2	Bisl	Oslo	26 Jun 82
27:26.00	Hansjörg	Kunze		GDR	59	4	Bisl	Oslo	2 Jul 88
27:26.11	Said	Aouita		MOR	59	1	Bisl	Oslo	5 Jul 86
27:26.95	Alex	Hagelsteens		BEL	56	3	Bisl	Oslo	26 Jun 82
27:26.95	Francesco	Panetta		ITA	63	1	DNG	Stockholm	30 Jun 87
27:27.7 m		Mamede				1		Lisboa	30 May 81
27:28.67		Rono				4dq	Bisl	Oslo	26 Jun 82
27:28.80		Nenow				2	Bisl	Oslo	5 Jul 86
27:29.06		Salazar				2		Paris	9 Jul 82
27:29.16	Craig	Virgin		USA	55	1		Paris	17 Jul 80
27:29.41	Wodajo	Bulti		ETH	57	1	WG	Helsinki	2 Jul 87
27:29.90		Rono				1		Eugene	10 Apr 82
27:30.00		Salazar				2		Eugene	10 Apr 82
27:30.3	Brendan	Foster		UK	48	1	AAA	London	23 Jun 78
27:30.47	Samson	Kimobwa		KEN	55	1	WG	Helsinki	30 Jun 77
27:30.69	Hansjörg	Kunze		GDR	59	2	NC	Jena	28 May 83
	(31/22)								
27:30.80	Dave	Bedford		UK	49	1	AAA	London	13 Jul 73
27:30.99	Martti	Vainio		FIN	50	1	EC	Praha	29 Aug 78
27:31.19	Nick	Rose		UK	51	3	OsloG	Oslo	9 Jul 83
27:31.48	Venanzio	Ortis		ITA	55	2	EC	Praha	29 Aug 78
27:31.50	Aleksandr	Antipov		SU	55	3	EC	Praha	29 Aug 78
27:34.38	Jaen-Louis	Prianon		FRA	60	2	WG	Helsinki	2 Jul 87
27:34.58	Julian	Goater		UK	53	5	Bisl	Oslo	26 Jun 82
27:35.33	Takeyuki	Nakayama		JAP	59	3	WG	Helsinki	2 Jul 87
	(30)								
27:36.2 m	Gabriel	Kamau		KEN	57	1	MSR	Walnut	24 Apr 82
27:36.27	David	Black		UK	52	5	EC	Praha	29 Aug 78
27:36.64	Gerard	Tebroke		HOL	49	6	EC	Praha	29 Aug 78
27:36.8 m	Karl	Fleschen		FRG	55	1		Troisdorf	28 Apr 79
27:37.17	Bruce	Bickford		USA	57	1	DNG	Stockholm	2 Jul 85
27:37.59	Alberto	Cova		ITA	58	2		Lausanne	30 Jun 83
27:38.1 m	Gidamas	Shahanga		TAN	57	3	MSR	Walnut	24 Apr 82
27:38.35	Lasse	Viren		FIN	49	1	OG	München	3 Sep 72
27:38.6 m	Zakariah	Barie		TAN	53	4	MSR	Walnut	24 Apr 82
27:38.63	Paul	Kipkoech		KEN	62	1	WC	Roma	29 Aug 87
	(40)								
27:39.14	Steve	Jones		UK	55	4	OsloG	Oslo	9 Jul 83
27:39.36	Paul	Arpin		FRA	60	7	OG	Seoul	26 Sep 88
27:39.44	Mohamed	Kedir		ETH	53	2	WP	Roma	4 Sep 81
27:39.52	Salvatore	Antibo		ITA	62	3	Bisl	Oslo	5 Jul 86
27:39.58	Emiel	Puttemans		BEL	47	2	OG	München	3 Sep 72

Mark	Name		Nat	Yr	Pos	Meet	Venue	Date
27:39.65	Xolile	Yawa	RSA	62	1		Port Elizabeth	12 Dec 87
27:39.76	Mike	McLeod	UK	51	1	VD/IAAF	Bruxelles	4 Sep 79
27:39.89	Ron	Clarke	AUS	37	1		Oslo	14 Jul 65
27:40.06	Ilie	Floroiu	ROM	52	7	EC	Praha	29 Aug 78
27:40.36	Boniface	Merande	KEN	62	1		Tokyo	13 May 88
	(50)							

MARATHON

Mark	Name		Nat	Yr	Pos	Meet	Venue	Date
2:06:50	Belayneh	Dinsamo	ETH	65	1		Rotterdam	17 Apr 88
2:07:07	Ahmed	Salah	DJI	56	2		Rotterdam	17 Apr 88
2:07:12	Carlos	Lopes	POR	47	1		Rotterdam	20 Apr 85
2:07:13	Steve	Jones	UK	55	1		Chicago	20 Oct 85
2:07:35	Taisuke	Kodama	JAP	58	1		Beijing	19 Oct 86
2:07:35	Abebe	Mekonnen	ETH	64	1		Beijing	16 Oct 88
2:07:40	Hiromi	Taniguchi	JAP	60	2		Beijing	16 Oct 88
2:07:51	Robert	de Castella	AUS	57	1		Boston	21 Apr 86
2:07:57	Kunimitsu	Itoh	JAP	55	2		Beijing	19 Oct 86
2:08:04	Zithulele	Sinqe	RSA	63	1	NC	Port Elizabeth	3 May 86
	(10)							
2:08:05		Jones			1		Chicago	21 Oct 84
2:08:08	Djama	Robleh	DJI	58	2		Chicago	20 Oct 85
2:08:09		Salah			1	WP	Hiroshima	14 Apr 85
2:08:10	Juma	Ikangaa	TAN	57	1		Tokyo	9 Feb 86
2:08:15	Takeyuki	Nakayama	JAP	59	2	WP	Hiroshima	14 Apr 85
2:08:15	Willie	Mtolo	RSA	65	2	NC	Port Elizabeth	3 May 86
2:08:16		Jones			1		London	21 Apr 85
2:08:18		de Castella			1		Fukuoka	6 Dec 81
2:08:18		Nakayama			1	NC	Fukuoka	6 Dec 87
2:08:20		Jones			1		New York	7 Nov 88
2:08:21		Nakayama			1	AsG	Seoul	5 Oct 86
2:08:26		Robleh			3	WP	Hiroshima	14 Apr 85
2:08:27	Toshihiko	Seko	JAP	56	1		Chicago	26 Oct 86
2:08:29		Dinsamo			2		Tokyo	9 Feb 86
2:08:33	Charles	Spedding	UK	52	2		London	21 Apr 85
2:08:33		Mekonnen			1		Tokyo	14 Feb 88
2:08:34	Derek	Clayton	AUS	42	1		Antwerpen	30 May 69
2:08:37		de Castella			1		Rotterdam	9 Apr 83
2:08:38		Seko			1		Tokyo	13 Feb 83
2:08:39		Lopes			2		Rotterdam	9 Apr 83
2:08:39		Mekonnen			3		Tokyo	9 Feb 86
2:08:39		Ikangaa			3		Beijing	19 Oct 86
	(31/17)							
2:08:43	Ibrahim	Hussein	KEN	58	1		Boston	18 Apr 88
2:08:44	Wodajo	Bulti	ETH	57	3		Rotterdam	17 Apr 88
2:08:47	Jörg	Peter	GDR	55	3		Tokyo	14 Feb 88
	(20)							
2:08:51	Alberto	Salazar	USA	58	1		Boston	19 Apr 82
2:08:52		Seko			1		Fukuoka	4 Dec 83
2:08:54	Dick	Beardsley	USA	56	2		Boston	19 Apr 82
2:08:55	Takeshi	Soh	JAP	53	2		Tokyo	13 Feb 83
2:08:55		Ikangaa			2		Fukuoka	4 Dec 83
2:08:57	Alejandro	Cruz	MEX	68	1		Chicago	30 Oct 88
2:08:58	Mark	Plaatjes	RSA	62	1	NC	Port Elizabeth	4 May 85
2:08:59	Rod	Dixon	NZ	50	1		New York	23 Oct 83
2:09:00	Greg	Meyer	USA	55	1		Boston	18 Apr 83
2:09:01	Gerard	Nijboer	HOL	55	1		Amsterdam	26 Apr 80
2:09:03	Michael	Heilmann	GDR	61	4	WP	Hiroshima	14 Apr 85
2:09:05		Mekonnen			5	WP	Hiroshima	14 Apr 85
2:09:06	Shigeru	Soh	JAP	53	1	Beppu	Oita	5 Feb 78
	(30)							
2:09:08	Geoff	Smith	UK	53	2		New York	23 Oct 83
2:09:12	Ian	Thompson	UK	49	1	CommG	Christchurch	31 Jan 74
2:09:12	Rodolfo	Gomez	MEX	50	3		Tokyo	13 Feb 83
2:09:15	John	Treacy	IRL	57	3		Boston	18 Apr 88
2:09:16	Allister	Hutton	UK	54	3		London	21 Apr 85

Mark	Name		Nat	Yr	Pos	Meet	Venue	Date
2:09:20	Yakov	Tolstikov	SU	59	2		Chicago	30 Oct 88
2:09:23	Christoph	Herle	FRG	55	4		London	21 Apr 85
2:09:24	Hugh	Jones	UK	55	1		London	9 May 82
2:09:26	Li Jong-hyong		NKO	56	1		Pyongyang	19 Oct 83
2:09:27	Bill	Rodgers	USA	47	1		Boston	16 Apr 79
	(40)							
2:09:27	Gelindo	Bordin	ITA	59	4		Boston	18 Apr 88
2:09:28	Ron	Hill	UK	38	1	CommG	Edinburgh	23 Jul 70
2:09:28	John	Graham	UK	56	1		Rotterdam	23 May 81
2:09:30	John	Burra	TAN	62	1		Arusha	12 Mar 88
2:09:31	Ron	Tabb	USA	54	2		Boston	18 Apr 83
2:09:33	Gianni	Poli	ITA	57	5		Boston	18 Apr 88
2:09:39	Gidamis	Shahanga	TAN	57	4		Beijing	19 Oct 86
2:09:39	Richard	Kaitany	KEN	58	3		Chicago	30 Oct 88
2:09:41	Ernest	Seleke	RSA	59	1		Port Elizabeth	31 Mar 84
2:09:43	Mike	Gratton	UK	54	1		London	17 Apr 83
	(50)							
2:09:43	Henrik	Jørgensen	DEN	61	5		London	21 Apr 85
2:09:44	Joseph	Nzau	KEN	50	1		Chicago	16 Oct 83
2:09:51	Masanari	Shintaku	JAP	57	1		Fukuoka	1 Dec 85
2:09:55	Waldemar	Cierpinski	GDR	50	1	OG	Montreal	31 Jul 76
2:09:57	Armand	Parmentier	BEL	54	4		Rotterdam	9 Apr 83
2:09:57	Benji	Durden	USA	51	3		Boston	18 Apr 83

Short course - c.148 metres short

Mark	Name		Nat	Yr	Pos	Meet	Venue	Date
2:08:13	Alberto	Salazar	USA	58	1		New York	25 Oct 81

Note: Downhill point-to-point courses: Port Elizabeth (RSA) has a net drop of 149m between start (203m) and finish (54m). Boston (USA) has a net drop of 116m between start (120m) and finish (4m).

2000 METRES STEEPLECHASE

Mark	Name		Nat	Yr	Pos	Meet	Venue	Date
5:19.68	Samson	Obwocha	KEN	54	1		Birmingham	19 Jul 86
5:19.86	Mark	Rowland	UK	63	1		London	28 Aug 88
5:20.00	Krzysztof	Wesolowski	POL	56	1	Bisl	Oslo	28 Jun 84
5:20.25	Julius	Korir	KEN	60	2		Birmingham	19 Jul 86
5:20.81	Boguslaw	Maminski	POL	55	2	Bisl	Oslo	28 Jun 84
5:21.2 m	Eshetu	Tura	ETH	50	1		Montreal	14 Jul 76
5:21.96	Farley	Gerber	USA	60	3	Bisl	Oslo	28 Jun 84
5:22.2 m	Yohannes	Mohamed	ETH	48	2		Montreal	14 Jul 76
5:22.2 m	Mariano	Scartezzini	ITA	54	1		Udine	20 Sep 81
5:22.24	William	van Dijck	BEL	61	1		Hechtel	8 Aug 87
	(10)							
5:23.6	Roger	Hackney	UK	57	1		Birmingham	10 Jun 82
5:23.71	Colin	Walker	UK	62	2		London	28 Aug 88
5:23.87	Colin	Reitz	UK	60	4	Bisl	Oslo	28 Jun 84
5:24.06	Peter	Renner	NZ	59	3		Birmingham	19 Jul 86
5:24.18	Jorge	Bello	SPA	63	1			16 Aug 86
5:24.64	Joshua	Kipkemboi	KEN	60	2		Birmingham	19 Aug 86
5:24.91	Eddie	Wedderburn	UK	60	3		Birmingham	19 Aug 86
5:24.99	Gábor	Markó	HUN	60	5	Bisl	Oslo	28 Jun 84
5:25.01	Arsenios	Tsiminos	GRE	61	1		Athenai	2 Oct 80
5:25.76	Ivan	Huff	USA	59	4		Birmingham	19 Aug 86
	(20)							

3000 METRES STEEPLECHASE

Mark	Name		Nat	Yr	Pos	Meet	Venue	Date
8:05.4 m	Henry	Rono	KEN	52	1		Seattle	13 May 78
8:05.51	Julius	Kariuki	KEN	61	1	OG	Seoul	30 Sep 88
8:06.79	Peter	Koech	KEN	58	2	OG	Seoul	30 Sep 88
8:07.62	Joseph	Mahmoud	FRA	55	1	VD	Bruxelles	24 Aug 84
8:07.96	Mark	Rowland	UK	63	3	OG	Seoul	30 Sep 88
8:08.02	Anders	Gärderud	SWE	46	1	OG	Montreal	28 Jul 76
8:08.57	Francesco	Panetta	ITA	63	1	WC	Roma	5 Sep 87
8:09.11	Bronislaw	Malinowski	POL	51	2	OG	Montreal	28 Jul 76
8:09.17	Henry	Marsh	USA	54	1	R-W	Koblenz	28 Aug 85
8:09.18	Boguslaw	Maminski	POL	55	2	VD	Bruxelles	24 Aug 84
	(10)							

Mark		Name		Nat	Yr	Pos	Meet	Venue	Date
8:09.70			Gärderud			1	DNG	Stockholm	1 Jul 75
8:09.70			Malinowski			1	OG	Moskva	31 Jul 80
8:10.01		William	van Dijck	BEL	61	1	VD	Bruxelles	5 Sep 86
8:10.32		Hagen	Melzer	GDR	59	2	WC	Roma	5 Sep 87
8:10.36		Frank	Baumgartl	GDR	55	3	OG	Montreal	28 Jul 76
8:10.4 m			Gärderud			1	vGDR,NOR	Oslo	25 Jun 75
8:11.04		Krzysztof	Wesolowski	POL	56	1	VD	Bruxelles	30 Aug 85
8:11.07			Mahmoud			2	VD	Bruxelles	30 Aug 85
8:11.52			van Dijck			1	Nik	Nice	15 Jul 86
8:11.61			Koech			1	Nik	Nice	10 Jul 88
8:11.63			Malinowski			1	ISTAF	Berlin	18 Aug 78
8:11.64			Mahmoud			1	R-W	Koblenz	29 Aug 84
8:11.80		Julius	Korir	KEN	60	1	OG	Los Angeles	10 Aug 84
8:11.93		Rainer	Schwarz	FRG	59	2	R-W	Koblenz	28 Aug 85
8:12.0		George Kip	Rono	KEN	58	1	GGala	Roma	5 Aug 80
8:12.00		Patrick	Sang	KEN	64	2	Nik	Nice	10 Jul 88
8:12.11		Colin	Reitz	UK	60	2	VD	Bruxelles	5 Sep 86
8:12.17		Alessandro	Lambruschini	ITA	65	4	OG	Seoul	30 Sep 88
8:12.18			van Dijck			3	WC	Roma	5 Sep 87
8:12.23			Malinowski			1	DNG	Stockholm	10 Aug 76
		(30/20)							
8:12.48		Filbert	Bayi	TAN	53	2	OG	Moskva	31 Jul 80
8:12.5		Mariano	Scartezzini	ITA	54	2	GGala	Roma	5 Aug 80
8:12.58		Graeme	Fell	CAN	59	3	R-W	Koblenz	28 Aug 85
8:12.60		Tapio	Kantanen	FIN	49	4	OG	Montreal	28 Jul 76
8:13.16		Brian	Diemer	USA	61	2	R-W	Koblenz	29 Aug 84
8:13.57		Eshetu	Tura	ETH	50	3	OG	Moskva	31 Jul 80
8:13.88		Raymond	Pannier	FRA	61	1	Nik	Nice	13 Jul 87
8:13.91		Ben	Jipcho	KEN	43	1	WG	Helsinki	27 Jun 73
8:14.05		Michael	Karst	FRG	52	1	DNG	Stockholm	5 Jul 77
8:14.05		Peter	Renner	NZ	59	3	R-W	Koblenz	29 Aug 84
		(30)							
8:14.13		Joshua	Kipkemboi	KEN	60	1	R-W	Koblenz	6 Aug 86
8:14.17		Samson	Obwocha	KEN	54	2	R-W	Koblenz	6 Aug 86
8:15.06		Patriz	Ilg	FRG	57	1	WC	Helsinki	12 Aug 83
8:15.07		Féthi	Baccouche	TUN	60	1	WG	Helsinki	2 Jul 87
8:15.32		Dan	Glans	SWE	47	3	DNG	Stockholm	10 Aug 76
8:15.74		Domingo	Ramon	SPA	58	4	OG	Moskva	31 Jul 80
8:16.10		Gheorge	Cefan	RUM	47	2		Stockholm	8 Jun 76
8:16.25		Juan	Torres	SPA	57	4	R-W	Koblenz	29 Aug 84
8:16.54		Azzedine	Brahmi	ALG	66	1s2	OG	Seoul	28 Sep 88
8:16.59		Francisco	Sanchez	SPA	58	4	ISTAF	Berlin	17 Aug 83
		(40)							
8:16.59		Ivan	Huff	USA	59	5	VD	Bruxelles	5 Sep 86
8:17.22		Wolfgang	Konrad	AUT	58	2	ISTAF	Berlin	20 Aug 82
8:17.69		Bruno	Le Stum	FRA	59	4	VD	Bruxelles	11 Sep 87
8:17.97		Gábor	Markó	HUN	60	1	OD	Potsdam	21 Jul 84
8:18.02		Hans	Koeleman	HOL	57	2	BGP	Budapest	4 Aug 85
8:18.22		Richard	Tuwei	KEN	54	1	FBK	Hengelo	12 Jul 83
8:18.29		Ismo	Toukonen	FIN	54	3	EC	Praha	3 Sep 78
8:18.32		Eddie	Wedderburn	UK	60	4	DNG	Stockholm	5 Jul 88
8:18.45		John	Gregorek	USA	60	3	FOT	Los Angeles	23 Jun 84
8:18.47		Giuseppe	Gerbi	ITA	55	6	OG	Moskva	31 Jul 80
		(50)							

200 METRES HURDLES

Mark	Wind	Name		Nat	Yr	Pos	Meet	Venue	Date
22.69		Glenn	Davis	USA	34	1		Bern	20 Aug 60
22.79	-0.7	Axel	Schaumann	FRG	61	1		Stuttgart	29 Aug 82
22.92		Dick	Howard	USA	35	2		Bern	20 Aug 60
22.96	1.9	Carlos	Sala	SPA	60	1		Santander	9 Sep 87
22.92w	3.6	Nigel	Walker	UK	63	1		Stoke-on-Trent	7 Sep 86
23.00w	3.6	Jon	Ridgeon	UK	67	2		Stoke-on-Trent	7 Sep 86
Hand timed									
22.5		Martin	Lauer	FRG	37	1		Zürich	7 Jul 59
22.6		Charles	Tidwell	USA	37	1		Berkeley	14 Jun 58

110 METRES HURDLES

Mark	Wind	Name		Nat	Yr	Pos	Meet	Venue	Date
12.93	-0.2	Renaldo	Nehemiah	USA	59	1	WK	Zürich	19 Aug 81
12.97A	2.0	Roger	Kingdom	USA	62	1		Sestriere	11 Aug 88
12.98	1.5		Kingdom			1	OG	Seoul	26 Sep 88
13.00	0.9		Nehemiah			1	Pepsi	Westwood	6 May 79
13.03	-0.2	Greg	Foster	USA	58	2	WK	Zürich	19 Aug 81
13.03	0.3		Kingdom			1		Athinai	3 Sep 88
13.04	0.0		Nehemiah			1		Koblenz	26 Aug 81
13.04	1.6		Kingdom			1	ISTAF	Berlin	26 Aug 88
13.07	-0.1		Nehemiah			1	ASV	Köln	23 Aug 81
13.07	0.3		Nehemiah			1	VD	Bruxelles	28 Aug 81
13.10	0.8		Foster			1	Pepsi	Westwood	10 May 81
13.11	-0.4		Foster			1	Pepsi	Westwood	15 May 83
13.11A	2.0	Colin	Jackson	UK	67	2		Sestriere	11 Aug 88
13.11	0.0		Kingdom			1	WK	Zürich	17 Aug 88
13.14	0.6		Kingdom			1	SW	Modesto	11 May 85
13.14	2.0		Kingdom			1s2	FOT	Indianapolis	23 Jul 88
13.15	-0.7		Foster			1	TAC	Indianapolis	18 Jun 83
13.15	-1.1		Foster			1	WK	Zürich	22 Aug 84
13.15	1.3		Kingdom			1	TAC	Tampa	17 Jun 88
13.16	1.7		Nehemiah			1	Jenner	San Jose	14 Apr 79
13.16	-0.1		Foster			1	ISTAF	Berlin	17 Aug 84
13.16	-1.1		Kingdom			2	WK	Zürich	22 Aug 84
13.17	0.8		Nehemiah			1	AAA	London	8 Aug 81
13.17	-0.4	Sam	Turner	USA	57	2	Pepsi	Westwood	15 May 83
13.17	-0.1		Kingdom			2	ISTAF	Berlin	17 Aug 84
13.17	0.6		Foster			1	Athl	Lausanne	15 Sep 87
13.17	2.0	Mark	McKoy	CAN	61	1	Athl	Lausanne	24 Jun 88
13.17	-2.7		Kingdom			1		San Diego	25 Jun 88
13.17	0.0		McKoy			2	WK	Zürich	17 Aug 88
13.17	0.0	Tonie	Campbell	USA	60	3	WK	Zürich	17 Aug 88
13.17	0.6		Kingdom			1q1	OG	Seoul	25 Sep 88
		(31/7)							
13.20	2.0	Stéphane	Caristan	FRA	64	1	EC	Stuttgart	30 Aug 86
13.20	1.8	Aleksandr	Markin	SU	62	1	Znam	Leningrad	11 Jun 88
13.21	0.6	Alejandro	Casañas	CUB	52	1	WUG	Sofia	21 Aug 77
		(10)							
13.21	1.7	Vladimir	Shishkin	SU	64	2	Znam	Leningrad	11 Jun 88
13.24	0.3	Rod	Milburn	USA	50	1	OG	München	7 Sep 72
13.24	2.0	Arthur	Blake	USA	66	2	Athl	Lausanne	15 Sep 88
13.25	0.1	Andre	Phillips	USA	59	1	USOF	Baton Rouge	28 Jul 85
13.26	1.6	Willie	Gault	USA	60	1	USOF	Indianapolis	25 Jul 82
13.27	1.8	Sergey	Usov	SU	64	3	Znam	Leningrad	11 Jun 88
13.28	1.1	Guy	Drut	FRA	50	1	NC	St. Etienne	29 Jun 75
13.28	1.0	Andrey	Prokofyev	SU	59	1r2	GWG	Moskva	6 Jul 86
13.29	1.9	Rod	Woodson	USA	65	1		Irvine	14 Jun 87
13.29	-0.1	Jonathan	Ridgeon	UK	67	1	WUG	Zagreb	15 Jul 87
		(20)							
13.30	2.0	Cletus	Clark	USA	62	3	Athl	Lausanne	24 Jun 88
13.31		Keith	Talley	USA	64	2r1	GWG	Moskva	6 Jul 86
13.33A	0.0	Willie	Davenport	USA	43	1	OG	Ciudad	17 Oct 68
13.34	1.8	Dedy	Cooper	USA	56	2		Houston	3 May 80
13.35	2.0	Arto	Bryggare	FIN	58	1h1	OG	Los Angeles	5 Aug 84
13.36	0.1	Jack	Pierce	USA	62	2	USOF	Baton Rouge	28 Jul 85
13.37	2.0	Thomas	Munkelt	GDR	52	1	EP	Helsinki	14 Aug 77
13.37	0.2	Milan	Stewart	USA	60	2		Paris	22 Jul 86
13.38A	1.8	Ervin	Hall	USA	47	1s1	OG	Ciudad México	17 Oct 68
13.38	1.6	Jerry	Wilson	USA	50	1	AAU	Eugene	20 Jun 75
		(30)							
13.38	1.4	Igor	Kazanov	SU	63	1	Znam	Moskva	4 Jun 87
13.39	1.9	Larry	Cowling	USA	60	1	vGDR	Karl-Marx-Stadt	10 Jul 82
13.40	2.0	Holger	Pohland	GDR	63	1	vSU	Tallinn	21 Jun 86
13.41	0.0	Charles	Foster	USA	53	4	OG	Montreal	28 Jul 76

Mark		Name		Nat	Yr	Pos	Meet	Venue	Date
13.41	0.5	Al	Joyner	USA	60	2q3	FOT	Indianapolis	22 Jul 88
13.42*	0.0	Tom	Hill	USA	49	1	AAU	Bakersfield	26 Jun 70
13.42	0.8	Javier	Moracho	SPA	57	1	NC	Barcelona	16 Aug 87
13.43	1.8	Earl	McCullough	USA	46	1		Minneapolis	16 Jul 67
13.43*	0.0	Marcus	Walker	USA	49	2	AAU	Bakersfield	26 Jun 70
13.43	1.9	Mark	Holtom	UK	58	2	CommG	Brisbane	4 Oct 82
		(40)							
13.44	0.9	Aleksandr	Puchkov	SU	57	3	OG	Moskva	27 Jul 80
13.44	0.8	Carlos	Sala	SPA	60	2	NC	Barcelona	16 Aug 87
13.45*	0.7	Leon	Coleman	USA	44	1=	AAU	Miami	28 Jun 69
13.45A	1.6	Kerry	Bethel	USA	57	1	USOF	Air Force Academy	30 Jul 78
13.45	1.8	Henry	Andrade	USA	62	3s2	FOT	Los Angeles	19 Jun 84
13.45	1.4	György	Bakos	HUN	60	2	8-N	Tokyo	14 Sep 84
13.45	1.8	Vitaliy	Sklyarov	SU	60	5	Znam	Leningrad	11 Jun 88
13.45	0.8	Tony	Jarrett	UK	68	2h3	OG	Seoul	25 Sep 88
13.46A	0.0	Eddy	Ottoz	ITA	44	3	OG	Ciudad	17 Oct 68
13.46	1.8	James	Owens	USA	55	3	NCAA	Eugene	2 Jun 78
		(50)							
13.46	-0.3	Plamen	Krastev	BUL	58	1	4-N	Athinai	10 Jul 84
13.46	1.4	Al	Lane	USA	62	4		Villanova	9 Jun 85

Doubtful timing

Mark		Name		Nat	Yr	Pos	Meet	Venue	Date
13.41		Viktor	Myasnikov	SU	48	1		Leningrad	4 Jun 80

Low altitude bests for athletes with marks at high altitude

Name	Mark	Wind	Pos	Meet	Venue	Date	High altitude
Jackson	13.23	0.6	1		Belfast	27 Jun 88	13.11A
Davenport	13.38	0.0	3	OG	Montreal	28 Jul 76	13.33A
Hall	13.46*	0.7	3	AAU	Miami	28 Jun 69	13.38A

Wind-assisted marks

Mark		Name		Nat	Yr	Pos	Meet	Venue	Date
12.91	3.5	Renaldo	Nehemiah	USA	59	1	NCAA	Champaign	1 Jun 79
13.00	3.5		Nehemiah			1	USOF	Syracuse	26 Jul 81
13.00	2.7		Kingdom			1		Sacramento	21 Jul 84
13.14	2.9	Igor	Kazanov	SU	63	1r1	Znam	Leningrad	8 Jun 86
13.15	3.1		Foster			1s2	TAC	San Jose	25 Jun 87
13.15	3.1		Kingdom			1s2	TAC	Tampa	17 Jun 88
13.16	2.7	Mark	McKoy	CAN	61	2		Sacramento	21 Jul 84
13.18	2.1		Nehemiah			1	ISTAF	Berlin	21 Aug 81
13.28	2.7	Henry	Andrade	USA	62	3		Sacramento	21 Jul 84
13.33	2.9	Gennadiy	Chugunov	SU	63	3r1	Znam	Leningrad	8 Jun 86
13.33	4.0	Keith	Talley	USA	64	1	SEC	Tuscaloosa	17 May 87
13.35	3.4	Tony	Jarrett	UK	68	2	IAC	Edinburgh	29 Jul 88
13.36*	3.5	Ricky	Stubbs	USA	51	1	TexR	Austin	13 Apr 74
13.38*	2.3	Charles	Foster	USA	53	1	NCAA	Austin	7 Jun 74
13.38	3.4	Al	Lane	USA	62	1h3	NCAA	Eugene	31 May 84
13.38	4.0	Eric	Reid	USA	65	2	SEC	Tuscaloosa	17 May 87
13.39		Colin	Williams	USA		1		Dallas	1 Apr 78
13.40	3.4	Liviu	Giurgian	RUM	62	1		Beograd	27 Jun 86
13.41*	3.5	Efrem	Gipson	USA	49	2	TexR	Austin	13 Apr 74
13.43	3.2	James	McCraney	USA	55	4r1	SW	Modesto	12 May 84

*120 yards time plus 0.03 seconds

Hand timing

Mark		Name		Nat	Yr	Pos	Meet	Venue	Date
12.8	1.0	Renaldo	Nehemiah	USA	59	1		Kingston	11 May 79
13.0	1.8	Guy	Drut	FRA	50	1	ISTAF	Berlin	22 Aug 75
13.0	1.0	Greg	Foster	USA	58	2		Kingston	11 May 79
13.0*	2.0	Rod	Milburn	USA	50	1s1	AAU	Eugene	25 Jun 71
13.0*	1.0		Milburn			1		Eugene	20 Jun 73
13.0A*	0.9		Milburn			1	ITA	El Paso	10 May 75
13.0	0.8	Mark	McKoy	CAN	61	1	Nik	Nice	16 Jul 85
13.0		Stéphane	Caristan	FRA	64	1		Creteil	3 May 86
13.0		Vladimir	Shishkin	SU	64	1		Staiki	13 May 88
13.1		Tonie	Campbell	USA	60	1		Nassau	7 May 83
13.1A*	0.9	Lance	Babb	USA	50	2	ITA	El Paso	10 May 75

Mark		Name		Nat	Yr	Pos	Meet	Venue	Date
13.1		Igor	Kazanov	SU	63	2		Staiki	13 May 88
13.2	0.0	Lee	Calhoun	USA	33	1		Bern	21 Aug 60
13.2	-0.9	Willie	Davenport	USA	43	1		Zürich	4 Jul 69
13.2	1.2	Alejandro	Casanas	CUB	54	1	Kuso	Warszawa	20 Jun 75
13.2	1.8	Charles	Foster	USA	53	2	ISTAF	Berlin	22 Aug 75
13.2	1.7	Karl Werner	Donges	FRG	58	1		Albstadt	14 Jun 81
13.2*	1.7	Tom	Hill	USA	49	1	USTFF	Wichita	13 Jun 70
13.2		Modesto	Castillo	DOM	59	1		Santo Domingo	26 May 84
13.2	0.8	Henry	Andrade	USA	62	2	Nik	Nice	16 Jul 85
13.2	0.8	György	Bakos	HUN	60	3	Nik	Nice	16 Jul 85
Wind-assisted hand times									
13.0		Alejandro	Casañas	CUB	54	1	Barr	Habana	22 May 77
13.0*	2.2		R.Milburn			1		Billings	4 Jun 71
13.0*	3.2		Milburn			1		Lafayette	15 Apr 72
13.0*	2.5		Milburn			1	CalR	Modesto	27 May 72
13.0		Tonie	Campbell	USA	60	1		Los Angeles	16 Jul 86
13.0		Keith	Talley	USA	64	1		Tuscaloosa	26 Mar 88
13.0		James	Walker	USA	57	1		Birmingham	2 May 88
13.1*	3.2	Tom	Hill	USA	49	1s1	USTFF	Wichita	13 Jun 70
13.1*	4.5	Larry	Shipp	USA	54	1	KansR	Lawrence	20 Apr 74
13.1		Ronnie	McCoy	USA	63	1		Naperville	10 May 85
13.2	2.6	Dedy	Cooper	USA	56	1		San Jose	2 May 81
13.2		Gene	Norman	USA	61	1		New York	29 May 83
13.2*		Danny	Smith	BAH	52	1		Baton Rouge	19 Apr 75

* 120 yards time

400 METRES HURDLES

Mark	Name		Nat	Yr	Pos	Meet	Venue	Date
47.02	Edwin	Moses	USA	55	1		Koblenz	31 Aug 83
47.13		Moses			1		Milano	3 Jul 80
47.14		Moses			1		Lausanne	14 Jul 81
47.17		Moses			1	ISTAF	Berlin	8 Aug 80
47.19	Andre	Phillips	USA	59	1	OG	Seoul	25 Sep 88
47.23	Amadou	Dia Bâ	SEN	58	2	OG	Seoul	25 Sep 88
47.27		Moses			1	ISTAF	Berlin	21 Aug 81
47.32		Moses			1		Koblenz	29 Aug 84
47.37		Moses			1	WP	Roma	4 Sep 81
47.37		Moses			1	WK	Zürich	24 Aug 83
47.37		Moses			1	FOT	Indianapolis	17 Jul 88
47.38		Moses			1		Lausanne	2 Sep 86
47.43		Moses			1	ASV	Köln	28 Aug 83
47.45		Moses			1	AAU	Westwood	11 Jun 77
47.46		Moses			1	WC	Roma	1 Sep 87
47.48	Harald	Schmid	FRG	57	1	EC	Athinai	8 Sep 82
47.48	Danny	Harris	USA	65	2	WC	Roma	1 Sep 87
47.48		Schmid			3	WC	Roma	1 Sep 87
47.50		Moses			1	WC	Helsinki	9 Aug 83
47.51		Phillips			1	VD	Bruxelles	5 Sep 86
47.53		Moses			1	WP	Montreal	24 Aug 79
47.53		Moses			1	ISTAF	Berlin	15 Aug 86
47.56		Harris			1		Madrid	4 Jun 87
47.56		Moses			3	OG	Seoul	25 Sep 88
47.58		Moses			1	WP	Dusseldorf	2 Sep 77
47.58		Moses			1s1	FOT	Los Angeles	17 Jun 84
47.58		Phillips			2	FOT	Indianapolis	17 Jul 88
47.59		Moses			1	TAC	Sacramento	21 Jun 81
47.60		Schmid			1	ASV	Köln	16 Aug 87
47.63		Moses			1	OG	Montreal	25 Jul 76
47.63		Harris			1	WK	Zürich	21 Aug 85
	(31/5)							
47.72	Kevin	Young	USA	66	3	FOT	Indianapolis	17 Jul 88
47.75	David	Patrick	USA	60	4	FOT	Indianapolis	17 Jul 88

Mark	Name		Nat	Yr	Pos	Meet	Venue	Date
47.82	John	Akii-Bua	UGA	49	1	OG	München	2 Sep 72
47.92	Aleksandr	Vasilyev	SU	61	2	EP	Moskva	17 Aug 85
48.04	Winthrop	Graham	JAM	65	5	OG	Seoul	25 Sep 88
	(10)							
48.12A	David	Hemery	UK	44	1	OG	Ciudad México	15 Oct 68
48.16	Tony	Rambo	USA	60	3s1	FOT	Los Angeles	17 Jun 84
48.28	Tranel	Hawkins	USA	62	3	FOT	Los Angeles	18 Jun 84
48.34	Vasiliy	Arkhipenko	SU	57	2	EP	Torino	4 Aug 79
48.37	Sven	Nylander	SWE	62	4	WC	Roma	1 Sep 87
48.39	Quentin	Wheeler	USA	55	2	AAU	Walnut	17 Jun 79
48.42	David	Lee	USA	59	4	WK	Zürich	24 Aug 83
48.44A	Harry	Schulting	HOL	56	1	WUG	Ciudad México	12 Sep 79
48.46A	Larry	Cowling	USA	60	2	NCAA	Provo	4 Jun 82
48.48	James	Walker	USA	57	1		Tuscaloosa	13 May 79
	(20)							
48.48	Toma	Tomov	BUL	58	2	BGP	Budapest	11 Aug 86
48.50	Uwe	Ackermann	GDR	60	1	vUSA	Karl-Marx-Stadt	9 Jul 82
48.50	Henry	Amike	NIG	61	4s1	WC	Roma	31 Aug 87
48.51	Ralph	Mann	USA	49	2	OG	München	2 Sep 72
48.52	Reggie	Davis	USA	64	2		Knoxville	23 May 87
48.55	Jim	Bolding	USA	49	1		Paris	8 Jul 75
48.55	Tom	Andrews	USA	54	1	AAU	Westwood	12 Jun 76
48.58	Volker	Beck	GDR	56	3	EP	Torino	4 Aug 79
48.59	Alan	Pascoe	UK	47	1	DNG	Stockholm	30 Jun 75
48.60	Aleksandr	Yatsevich	SU	56	2	EC	Athinai	8 Sep 82
	(30)							
48.63	Bart	Williams	USA	56	2		Lausanne	10 Jul 84
48.64	Jim	Seymour	USA	49	4	OG	München	2 Sep 72
48.64	Kriss	Akabusi	UK	58	3s2	WC	Roma	31 Aug 87
48.65	Edgar	Itt	FRG	67	2	HGP	Budapest	12 Aug 88
48.68	Kevin	Henderson	USA	65	1	TAC	Tampa	18 Jun 88
48.69	Mike	Shine	USA	53	2	OG	Montreal	25 Jul 76
48.71	Vladimir	Budko	SU	65	1	Spart	Tashkent	18 Sep 86
48.72A	Dale	Laverty	USA	65	2		El Paso	20 Apr 86
48.73A	Paul	Montgomery	USA	61	3	NCAA	Provo	4 Jun 82
48.78	Aleksandr	Kharlov	SU	58	1	Spart	Moskva	20 Jun 83
	(40)							
48.80	Athanassios	Kalogiannis	GRE	65	2	WUG	Zagreb	19 Jul 87
48.81A	Hannes	Pienaar	RSA	60	1		Pretoria	15 Feb 86
48.83A	Pat	McGhee	USA	66	2		Sestriere	11 Aug 88
48.94A	Geoff	Vanderstock	USA	46	1	FOT	Echo Summit	11 Sep 68
48.94	Jean-Claude	Nallet	FRA	47	2	EC	Roma	4 Sep 74
48.94	René Meledje	Djédjémel	IVC	58	4	WK	Zürich	13 Aug 86
48.95	Jon	Thomas	USA	63	1		Evanston	19 May 85
48.97A	Shem	Ochako	KEN	64	2	AfrG	Nairobi	9 Aug 87
48.98A	Nikolay	Vasilyev	SU	56	1s2	WUG	Ciudad México	11 Sep 79
48.98	Nikolay	Ilchenko	SU	63	2	Spart	Tashkent	18 Sep 86
	(50)							

Low altitude bests for athletes with high altitude marks

Hemery	48.52	3	OG	München	2 Sep 72	A48.12
Schulting	48.71	2	WK	Zürich	15 Aug 79	A48.44
Cowling	48.87	1		Berkeley	12 Jun 83	A48.46
McGhee	48.98	3		Malmö	8 Aug 88	A48.83

Hand timing

48.1	Jim	Bolding	USA	49	1		Milano	2 Jul 74
48.4	Ralph	Mann	USA	49	1	FOT	Eugene	2 Jul 72
48.5	Aleksandr	Yatsevich	SU	56	1		Kiev	9 Aug 82
48.6	Jean-Claude	Nallet	FRA	47	1	vUSA	Colombes	8 Jul 70
48.6	Dick	Bruggeman	USA	47	2	FOT	Eugene	2 Jul 72
48.7	Aleksandr	Cheshko	SU	58	1		Cherkassy	3 Sep 82
48.7A	Gideon	Yego	KEN	60	1	OT	Nairobi	13 Aug 88
48.9*	Wayne	Collet	USA	49	2	NCAA	Des Moines	20 Jun 70
48.9A	Simon	Kitur	KEN	59	2	OT	Nairobi	13 Aug 88

* 440 yards less 0.3 seconds

HIGH JUMP

Mark	Name		Nat	Yr	Pos	Meet	Venue	Date
2.43	Javier	Sotomayor	CUB	67	1		Salamanca	8 Sep 88
2.42	Patrik	Sjöberg	SWE	65	1	DNG	Stockholm	30 Jun 87
2.42i	Carlo	Thränhardt	FRG	57	1		Berlin	26 Feb 88
2.41	Igor	Paklin	SU	63	1	WUG	Kobe	4 Sep 85
2.41i		Sjöberg			1		Piraeus	1 Feb 87
2.40	Rudolf	Povarnitsin	SU	62	1		Donyetsk	11 Aug 85
2.40i		Thränhardt			1		Simmerath	16 Jan 87
2.40i		Sjöberg			1		Berlin	27 Feb 87
2.39	Zhu Jianhua		CHN	63	1		Eberstadt	10 Jun 84
2.39i	Dietmar	Mögenburg	FRG	61	1		Köln	24 Feb 85
2.39		Sjöberg			1	EP-B	Göteborg	27 Jun 87
2.39i		Sjöberg			1	EI	Budapest	5 Mar 88
2.38		Zhu			1	NC	Shanghai	22 Sep 83
2.38i		Sjöberg			1		Berlin	22 Feb 85
2.38		Sjöberg			1		Eberstadt	16 Jun 85
2.38		Paklin			1		Rieti	7 Sep 86
2.38i		Sjöberg			1	EI	Liévin	21 Feb 87
2.38i		Thränhardt			2		Berlin	27 Feb 87
2.38i		Paklin			1	WC	Indianapolis	7 Mar 87
2.38i	Gennadiy	Avdeyenko	SU	63	2	WC	Indianapolis	7 Mar 87
2.38		Sjöberg			1	WC	Roma	6 Sep 87
2.38		Avdeyenko			2=	WC	Roma	6 Sep 87
2.38		Paklin			2=	WC	Roma	6 Sep 87
2.38		Avdeyenko			1		Seoul	2 Oct 87
2.38i		Sjöberg			1		Genk	7 Feb 88
2.38		Sotomayor			1		Kvarnsveden	19 Jun 88
2.38	Sergey	Malchenko	SU	63	1		Banská Bystrica	4 Sep 88
2.38		Avdeyenko			1	OG	Seoul	25 Sep 88
	(28/9)							
2.37	Valeriy	Sereda	SU	59	1		Rieti	2 Sep 84
2.37	Tom	McCants	USA	62	1	JO	Columbus	8 May 88
2.37	Jerome	Carter	USA	63	2	JO	Columbus	8 May 88
2.37	Sorin	Matei	RUM	63	1		Bucuresti	11 Jun 88
2.36	Gerd	Wessig	GDR	59	1	OG	Moskva	1 Aug 80
2.36	Sergey	Zasimovich	SU	62	1		Tashkent	5 May 84
2.36	Eddy	Annys	BEL	58	1		Ghent	26 May 85
2.36i	Jim	Howard	USA	59	1		Albuquerque	26 Jan 86
2.36i	Jan	Zvara	CS	63	1	vGDR	Jablonec	14 Feb 87
2.36	Hollis	Conway	USA	67	2	OG	Seoul	25 Sep 88
2.35i	Vladimir	Yashchenko	SU	59	1	EI	Milano	12 Mar 78
(	20)							
2.35	Jacek	Wszola	POL	56	1		Eberstadt	25 May 80
2.35i	Aleksandr	Kotovich	SU	61	1		Vilnius	13 Jan 85
2.35	Gerd	Nagel	FRG	57	1		Forbach	7 Aug 88
2.34	Paul	Frommeyer	FRG	57	1		Recke	17 Jun 83
2.34	Dwight	Stones	USA	53	1	FOT	Los Angeles	24 Jun 84
2.34i	Yuriy	Sergiyenko	SU	65	1		Kiev	2 Feb 85
2.34	Dennis	Lewis	USA	59	1		Los Angeles	30 Mar 85
2.34	Doug	Nordquist	USA	58	1	GWG	Moskva	9 Jul 86
2.34	Robert	Ruffini	CS	67	1	v2-N	Praha	3 Jul 88
2.34	Nick	Saunders	BER	63	5	OG	Seoul	25 Sep 88
	(30)							
2.33i	Jeff	Woodard	USA	58	1	TAC	New York	27 Feb 81
2.33	Aleksey	Demyanyuk	SU	58	1		Leningrad	11 Jul 81
2.33	Tyke	Peacock	USA	61	1	ISTAF	Berlin	17 Aug 83
2.33	Vladimir	Granyenkov	SU	59	1		Moskva	5 Aug 84
2.33	Brian	Whitehead	USA	62	1	JO	Columbus	5 May 85
2.33	Milton	Ottey	CAN	59	1	NC	Ottawa	21 Jun 86
2.33	Andrey	Morozov	SU	60	1		Lipetsk	19 Jul 86
2.33	Lee	Balkin	USA	61	1	USOF	Durham	30 Jul 87
2.33	Brian	Stanton	USA	61	1		Walnut	29 May 88
2.33	Tom	Smith	USA	67	1	NCAA	Eugene	4 Jun 88
	(40)							

Mark	Name		Nat	Yr	Pos	Meet	Venue	Date
2.32i	Franklin	Jacobs	USA	57	1		New York	27 Jan 78
2.32i	Janusz	Trzepizur	POL	59	2	EI	Milano	6 Mar 82
2.32i	Roland	Dalhäuser	SWZ	58	3	EI	Milano	6 Mar 82
2.32	Gennadiy	Belkov	SU	56	1		Tashkent	29 May 82
2.32	Del	Davis	USA	60	2	NCAA	Provo	4 Jun 82
2.32	J.Francisco	Centelles	CUB	61	1	PTS	Bratislava	4 Jun 83
2.32	Franck	Verzy	FRA	61	1	EP	London	20 Aug 83
2.32	Thomas	Eriksson	SWE	63	1	NCAA	Austin	1 Jun 85
2.32	Luca	Toso	ITA	64	1		Torino	21 Jul 88
2.32	Krzysztof	Krawczyk	POL	62	1	NC	Lublin	6 Aug 88
	(50)							
2.32	Eugen	Popescu	RUM	62	1	NC	Pitesti	14 Aug 88

Best outdoor marks for athletes with indoor bests

Name	Mark	Pos	Meet	Venue	Date	Indoor
Zvara	2.36	1		Praha	23 Aug 87	2.36i
Howard	2.36	1		Rehlingen	8 Jun 87	2.36i
Yashchenko	2.34	1	Prav	Tbilisi	16 Jun 78	2.35i
Kotovich	2.33	1	Nar	Sofia	20 May 84	2.35i
Woodard	2.32	1	NCAA	Austin	7 Jun 80	2.33i

Ancillary marks

Name	Mark	Date	Name	Mark	Date	Name	Mark	Date
Sotomayor	2.40	8 Sep 88	Sjöberg	2.36i	21 Feb 87	Thränhardt	2.36i	26 Feb 88
Thränhardt	2.38i	16 Jan 87	Paklin	2.36i	7 Mar 87	Sotomayor	2.36	8 Sep 88
Zhu	2.36	10 Jun 84	Avdeyenko	2.36i	7 Mar 87	Avdeyenko	2.36	25 Sep 88

POLE VAULT

Mark	Name		Nat	Yr	Pos	Meet	Venue	Date
6.06	Sergey	Bubka	SU	63	1	Nik	Nice	10 Jul 88
6.05		S.Bubka			1	PTS	Bratislava	9 Jun 88
6.03		S.Bubka			1	Ros	Praha	23 Jun 87
6.01		S.Bubka			1	GWG	Moskva	8 Jul 86
6.00		S.Bubka			1		Paris	13 Jul 85
5.97i		S.Bubka			1		Torino	17 Mar 87
5.96i		S.Bubka			1		Osaka	15 Jan 87
5.96	Joe	Dial	USA	62	1		Norman	18 Jun 87
5.95		S.Bubka			1	Nik	Nice	16 Jul 85
5.95i		S.Bubka			1	TAC	New York	28 Feb 86
5.95	Radion	Gataullin	SU	65	1	ISTAF	Berlin	26 Aug 88
5.94		S.Bubka			1	GGala	Roma	31 Aug 84
5.94i		S.Bubka			1		Inglewood	21 Feb 86
5.94		Dial			1		Albuquerque	13 Jun 87
5.93i	Billy	Olson	USA	58	1		East Rutherford	8 Feb 86
5.92i		S.Bubka			1	NC	Moskva	8 Feb 86
5.91	Thierry	Vigneron	FRA	60	2	GGala	Roma	31 Aug 84
5.91i		Dial			1		Columbia	1 Feb 86
5.91		Dial			1	KansR	Lawrence	18 Apr 87
5.90		S.Bubka			1	PTG	London	13 Jul 84
5.90	Pierre	Quinon	FRA	62	2	Nik	Nice	16 Jul 85
5.90		Dial			1		Norman	25 Apr 86
5.90		Vigneron			1		Paris	22 Jul 86
5.90i	Ferenc	Salbert	FRA	60	1		Grenoble	14 Mar 87
5.90		S.Bubka			1		Donyetsk	1 Jun 87
5.90		Gataullin			1		Bryansk	17 Jul 87
5.90		S.Bubka			1	WK	Zürich	19 Aug 87
5.90		S.Bubka			1		Tokyo	23 Sep 87
5.90i		Gataullin			1		Vilnius	24 Jan 88
5.90		S.Bubka			1		Kvarnsveden	19 Jun 88
5.90	Miroslaw	Chmara	POL	64	1	BNP	Villeneuve d'Ascq	27 Jun 88
5.90		S.Bubka			1		Barcelona	13 Jul 88
5.90		S.Bubka			1	OG	Seoul	28 Sep 88
5.90i		Gataullin			1		Tashkent	26 Dec 88
	(34/8)							
5.89	Kory	Tarpenning	USA	62	1	FOT	Indianopolis	21 Jul 88
5.87	Earl	Bell	USA	55	1		Jonesboro	14 May 88
	(10)							

Mark	Name		Nat	Yr	Pos	Meet	Venue	Date
5.86	Vasiliy	Bubka	SU	60	1		Chelyabinsk	16 Jul 88
5.85	Konstantin	Volkov	SU	60	1	Izv	Kiev	22 Jun 84
5.85	Philippe	Collet	FRA	63	2		Paris	22 Jul 86
5.85	Grigoriy	Yegorov	SU	67	1	NC	Tallinn	4 Jul 88
5.84	Mike	Tully	USA	56	1		Irvine	1 May 88
5.82	Aleksandr	Krupskiy	SU	60	1	BGP	Budapest	20 Aug 84
5.82	Aleksandr	Parnov	SU	59	1		Sumgait	21 Aug 85
5.81	Vladimir	Polyakov	SU	60	1	vGDR	Tbilisi	26 Jun 81
5.81i	Marian	Kolasa	POL	59	1		Praha	13 Feb 86
5.80	Pavel	Bogatyryov	SU	61	1		Schwechat	19 Jun 85
	(20)							
5.80i	Dave	Volz	USA	62	2		New York	14 Feb 86
5.80	Atanas	Tarev	BUL	58	2		Lausanne	2 Sep 86
5.80	Aleksandr	Obizhayev	SU	59	2	NC	Bryansk	17 Jul 87
5.79	Greg	Duplantis	USA	62	1		Tulsa	29 Jun 88
5.78	Wladyslaw	Kozakiewicz	POL	53	1	OG	Moskva	30 Jul 80
5.77	Philippe	Houvion	FRA	57	1		Paris	17 Jul 80
5.77	Doug	Fraley	USA	65	1	MSR	Walnut	27 Apr 86
5.76	Jeff	Buckingham	USA	60	1		Lawrence	16 Jul 83
5.76	Tom	Hintnaus	BRA	58	1	WK	Zürich	21 Aug 85
5.75	Jean-Michel	Bellot	FRA	53	1		Colombes	25 Sep 82
	(30)							
5.75	Brad	Pursley	USA	60	1		Abilene	29 Mar 83
5.75i	Sergey	Kulibaba	SU	59	1		Klaipeda	18 Mar 87
5.75	Tim	Bright	USA	60	3	Athl	Lausanne	15 Sep 87
5.73	Larry	Jessee	USA	52	1		Vanves	27 Apr 84
5.73	Gennadiy	Sukharev	SU	65	1		Minsk	9 Sep 87
5.73	Zdenek	Lubensky	CS	62	1		Praha	13 Sep 87
5.73i	Delko	Lesov	BUL	67	1		Athinai	6 Feb 88
5.72	Dan	Ripley	USA	53	1=	TAC	Knoxville	20 Jun 82
5.72i	Serge	Ferreira	FRA	59	1		Paris	3 Feb 85
5.72	Doug	Lytle	USA	62	1	KansR	Lawrence	19 Apr 86
	(40)							
5.71	Felix	Bohni	SWZ	58	1		Bern	11 Jun 83
5.71	Aleksandr	Chernyayev	SU	60	1		Chernigov	2 Jul 83
5.71	Vladimir	Shulgin	SU	61	3		Riga	2 Jun 85
5.71	Hermann	Fehringer	AUT	62	1		Hainfeld	23 Aug 87
5.70	Dave	Roberts	USA	51	1	FOT	Eugene	22 Jun 76
5.70i	Viktor	Spasov	SU	59	1	EI	Milano	7 Mar 82
5.70	Nikolay	Selivanov	SU	58	1		Moskva	16 Jun 83
5.70	Patrick	Abada	FRA	54	1	VD	Bruxelles	26 Aug 83
5.70	Tadeusz	Slusarski	POL	50	2	VD	Bruxelles	26 Aug 83
5.70	Sergey	Smolyakov	SU	62	3		Moskva	19 Jul 84
	(50)							
5.70	Dale	Jenkins	USA	63	2	SW	Modesto	10 May 86
5.70	Scott	Davis	USA	61	1		Eugene	17 May 86
5.70	Kasimir	Zalar	SWE	57	1		Nyköpping	2 Jul 86
5.70	Vadim	Kodentsev	SU	64	1		Omsk	14 Jul 86
5.70	Stanimir	Penchev	BUL	59	1		Sofia	3 Aug 86
5.70	Aleksandr	Zhukov	SU	65	1		Chelyabinsk	20 Jun 87
5.70	Nikolay	Nikolov	BUL	64	1	Bisl	Oslo	4 Jul 87
5.70	Valeriy	Ishutin	SU	65	2		Chelyabinsk	1 Aug 87
5.70	Philippe	D'Encausse	FRA	67	3	BNP	Villeneuve d'Ascq	27 Jun 88
5.70	Yevgeniy	Bondarenko	SU	66	1		Kiev	14 Aug 88
	(60)							

Best outdoor marks for athletes with lifetime bests indoors

Kolasa	5.80	1		Kamp-Lintfort	1 Sep 86	5.81i
Olson	5.80	1		Dallas	11 Apr 87	5.93i
Volz	5.75	1	Nik	Nice	14 Aug 82	5.80i
Ferreira	5.71	1		Créteil	23 Jun 84	5.72i
Kulibaba	5.70	1	vUSA	Leningrad	10 Jul 81	5.75i

Unsanctiond meeting

5.84 Volkov 1 Irkutsk 2 Aug 81

Extra trial

5.90 S.Bubka 1 Vladivostock 13 Sep 88

Ancillary jumps

S.Bubka	5.90	9 Jun 88
S.Bubka	5.86	10 Jul 88
S.Bubka	5.85	16 Jul 85
S.Bubka	5.85i	28 Feb 86
S.Bubka	5.85	8 Jul 86
Gataullin	5.85	26 Aug 88

Mark	Name		Nat	Yr	Pos	Meet	Venue	Date

Exhibition

Mark	Name	Pos	Venue	Date
5.86i	Jessee	1	Newcastle	16 Oct 85
5.85	S.Bubka	1	St.Ghislain	7 Jul 85
5.71	R.Kolasa	2	Sopot	2 Aug 86
5.71	Slusarski	1	Bologna	7 Sep 83
5.70	Ivo Janshev	2=	Bologna	6 Sep 84
5.70	Kenworthy	1	Mirano	14 Sep 86

LONG JUMP

Mark	Wind	Name		Nat	Yr	Pos	Meet	Venue	Date
8.90A	2.0	Bob	Beamon	USA	45	1	OG	Ciudad México	18 Oct 68
8.86A	1.9	Robert	Emmiyan	SU	65	1		Tsakhkadzor	22 May 87
8.79	1.9	Carl	Lewis	USA	61	1	TAC	Indianapolis	19 Jun 83
8.79i	-		Lewis			1		New York	27 Jan 84
8.76	1.0		Lewis			1	USOF	Indianapolis	24 Jul 82
8.76	0.8		Lewis			1	FOT	Indianapolis	18 Jul 88
8.75	1.7		Lewis			1	PAG	Indianapolis	16 Aug 87
8.74	1.4	Larry	Myricks	USA	56	2	FOT	Indianapolis	18 Jul 88
8.72	-0.2		Lewis			1	OG	Seoul	26 Sep 88
8.71	-0.4		Lewis			1	Pepsi	Westwood	13 May 84
8.71	0.1		Lewis			1	FOT	Los Angeles	19 Jun 84
8.67	0.4		Lewis			1	WC	Roma	5 Sep 87
8.66	0.8		Lewis			-	MSR	Walnut	26 Apr 87
8.66	1.0		Myricks			1		Tokyo	23 Sep 87
8.65	0.2		Lewis			1	VD	Bruxelles	24 Aug 84
8.65	0.7		Lewis			1	TAC	San Jose	26 Jun 87
8.63	2.0		Myricks			2	TAC	San Jose	26 Jun 87
8.62	0.8		Lewis			1	TAC	Sacramento	20 Jun 81
8.62	-0.1		Lewis			1	VD	Bruxelles	30 Aug 85
8.61	0.5		Lewis			1	Pepsi	Westwood	16 May 82
8.61	-0.3		Emmiyan			1	GWG	Moskva	6 Jul 86
8.61	1.2		Myricks			1	HGP	Budapest	12 Aug 88
8.59	1.3		Myricks			1		Rhede	5 Sep 84
8.58	0.0		Lewis			1	WK	Zürich	18 Aug 82
8.58A	1.1		Myricks			1		Sestriere	11 Aug 88
8.56i	-		Lewis			1		East Rutherford	16 Jan 82
8.56	0.5		Myricks			1		Rhede	1 Sep 82
8.56	1.0		Lewis			1	Pepsi	Westwood	15 May 83
8.55i	-		Lewis			1	TAC	New York	26 Feb 82
8.55	1.2		Lewis			1	WC	Helsinki	10 Aug 83
8.55i	-		Lewis			1		East Rutherford	11 Feb 84
		(31/4)							
8.54	0.9	Lutz	Dombrowski	GDR	59	1	OG	Moskva	28 Jul 80
8.51	1.2	Jaime	Jefferson	CUB	62	3	PAG	Indianapolis	16 Aug 87
8.49	1.8	Mike	Powell	USA	63	2	OG	Seoul	26 Sep 88
8.46	1.2	Leonid	Voloshin	SU	66	1	NC	Tallinn	5 Jul 88
8.45	2.0	Nenad	Stekic	YUG	51	1	PO	Montreal	25 Jul 75
8.44	1.7	Eric	Metcalf	USA	68	1	TAC	Tampa	17 Jun 88
		(10)							
8.43	0.8	Jason	Grimes	USA	59	-	TAC	Indianapolis	16 Jun 85
8.43	1.6	Mike	Conley	USA	62	1		Lausanne	10 Jul 85
8.43	1.8	Giovanni	Evangelisti	ITA	61	1		San Giovanni Valdarno	16 May 87
8.38	0.4	Konstantin	Semykin	SU	60	1	Drz	Moskva	17 Aug 84
8.37		Sergey	Rodin	SU	63	1		Moskva	6 Jul 84
8.36	1.0	João Carlos	de Oliveira	BRA	54	1		Rieti	21 Jul 79
8.36	1.6	Frank	Pashchek	GDR	56	1	OD	Berlin	28 May 80
8.35	0.0	Ralph	Boston	USA	39	1	CalR	Modesto	29 May 65
8.35A	0.0	Igor	Ter-Ovanesyan	SU	38	1	PO	Ciudad México	19 Oct 67
8.35	0.8	Josef	Schwarz	FRG	35	1	vUSA	Stuttgart	15 Jul 70
		(20)							
8.35	-0.6	Arnie	Robinson	USA	48	1	OG	Montreal	29 Jul 76
8.35	2.0	Henry	Lauterbach	GDR	57	1		Erfurt	2 Aug 81
8.35	2.0	Sergey	Layevskiy	SU	59	1		Dnepropetrovsk	16 Jul 88
8.34	0.0	Randy	Williams	USA	53	Q	OG	München	8 Sep 72
8.34	0.0	Vladimir	Ochkan	SU	68	1	RigC	Riga	5 Jun 88
8.33i	-	Reggie	Kelly	USA	62	1		Jackson	3 Dec 83
8.32		Ubaldo	Duany	CUB	60	2	NC	Santiago de Cuba	22 Feb 86
8.32A		Ralph	Spry	USA	60	1		Albuquerque	9 Jun 88

Mark		Name		Nat	Yr	Pos	Meet	Venue	Date
8.31	0.7	Atanas	Atanasov	BUL	56	1		Sofia	4 Jul 84
8.31	1.2	Igor	Streltsov	SU	65	2		Dnepropetrovsk	16 Jul 88
		(30)							
8.30	1.8	László	Szálma	HUN	57	1		Budapest	7 Jul 85
8.30	2.0	Andreas	Steiner	AUT	64	1		Innsbruck	5 Jun 88
8.29A		Grigoriy	Petrosyan	SU	58	1		Yerevan	20 Oct 86
8.28		Aleksandr	Beskrovniy	SU	60	1		Moskva	29 May 83
8.28	0.1	Vadim	Kobylyanskiy	SU	61	2	NC	Donyetsk	8 Sep 84
8.28	0.8	Luis Alberto	Bueno	CUB	69	1		Habana	16 Jul 88
8.27	0.5	Grzegorz	Cybulski	POL	51	1	Kuso	Warszawa	20 Jun 75
8.27	2.0	Mike	McRae	USA	55	1	TAC	San Jose	9 Jun 84
8.27	1.2	Gary	Honey	AUS	59	1	BGP	Budapest	20 Aug 84
8.27	1.9	Marco	Delonge	GDR	66	1		Potsdam	6 Jun 87
		(40)							
8.26i	-	Charlton	Ehizuelen	NIG	53	1		Bloomington	7 Mar 75
8.26	1.4	Jacques	Rousseau	FRA	51	-	NC	Lille	26 Jun 76
8.26	1.3	Vladimir	Ratushkov	SU	65	1		Chelyabinsk	16 Jul 88
8.25i	-	Henry	Hines	USA	49	1	ITA	New York	6 Jun 73
8.25	1.7	Gyula	Pálóczi	HUN	62	1	BGP	Budapest	4 Aug 85
8.25	1.9	Luis	Bueno	CUB	69	1	IbAm	Habana	28 Sep 86
8.25	1.9	Paul	Emordi	NIG	65	1	NCAA	Baton Rouge	5 Jun 87
8.25	-0.2	Vladimir	Bobylyov	SU	66	4	Znam	Moskva	7 Jun 87
8.25	1.3	Milan	Mikulás	CS	63	1	NC	Praha	16 Jul 88
8.25	-0.7	Gordon	Laine	USA	58	-	FOT	Indianapolis	18 Jul 88
		(50)							

Low altitude marks for athletes with high altitude bests

Beamon	8.33	1.3	1	AAU	Sacramento	20 Jun 68	8.90A
Ter-Ovanesyan	8.31	-0.1	1		Yerevan	10 Jun 62	8.35A

Note: Sergey Rodin's 8.37 not ratified as USSR record (no wind gauge), but considered wind legal. Next best:

Rodin	8.33	1.0	1		Leningrad	27 Jul 83

Supplementary (non-winning) marks

Lewis	8.71	0.6	19 Jun 83	Lewis	8.60	0.2	5 Sep 87	Lewis	8.73	2.4	18 May 85
Lewis	8.68	0.3	18 Jul 88	Lewis	8.59	0.3	24 Aug 84	Lewis	8.68	3.7	16 Aug 87
Lewis	8.67	-0.2	5 Sep 87	Lewis	8.55		24 Jul 82	Lewis	8.68	4.1	16 Aug 87
Lewis	8.66		26 Apr 87	Myricks	8.55	1.6	18 Jul 88	Lewis	8.66		26 Apr 87
Emmiyan	8.65A		22 May 87	Myricks	8.55	0.6	18 Jul 88	Lewis	8.64		26 Apr 87
Lewis	8.65	0.6	5 Sep 87	Myricks	8.55A		11 Aug 88	Lewis	8.59	3.2	18 Jul 88
Lewis	8.63		26 Apr 87	Wind-assisted:				Lewis	8.56	2.2	26 Sep 88
Lewis	8.61	0.6	16 May 82	Lewis	8.75	2.1	16 Aug 87	Myricks	8.55		26 Jun 87

Wind-assisted marks

8.77	3.9		C.Lewis			1	Pepsi	Westwood	18 May 85
8.77	3.4		Lewis			1	MSR	Walnut	26 Apr 87
8.73	4.6		Lewis			Q	TAC	Sacramento	19 Jun 81
8.73	3.2		Lewis			Q	TAC	Indianapolis	17 Jun 83
8.67	3.3		Lewis			1	TAC	Eugene	20 Jun 86
8.64A	3.1		Myricks			1	USOF	Air Force Academy	2 Jul 83
8.63	2.1		Lewis			1	Pepsi	Westwood	10 May 81
8.63	3.9	Mike	Conley	USA	62	2	TAC	Eugene	20 Jun 86
8.61	3.2		Myricks			1		Shizuoka	3 May 87
8.58	2.4		Myricks			2	PAG	Indianapolis	16 Aug 87
8.57	5.2	Jason	Grimes	USA	59	1	vFRG,AFR	Durham	27 Jun 82
8.56	8.9		Lewis			1		Sacramento	21 Jul 84
8.55	2.5		Myricks			1	SW	Modesto	10 May 86
8.55	2.9		Conley			3	TAC	San Jose	26 Jun 87
8.49	2.6	Ralph	Boston	USA	39	1	FOT	Los Angeles	12 Sep 64
8.46	3.4	Randy	Williams	USA	53	1		Eugene	18 May 73
8.44		Keith	Talley	USA	64	Q		Odessa	16 May 85
8.42		Anthony	Bailous	USA	65	Q		Odessa	16 May 85
8.41	4.3	Shamil	Abbyasov	SU	57	2	vUSA	Indianapolis	3 Jul 82
8.41	3.3	Andre	Ester	USA	65	1	TexR	Austin	4 Apr 87
8.40	4.3	Henry	Hines	USA	49	1	CalR	Modesto	27 May 72
8.39	6.2	Gary	Honey	AUS	59	2		Sacramento	21 Jul 84
8.37	3.5	Arnie	Robinson	USA	48	1	FOT	Eugene	25 Jun 76
8.37	2.8	Jacques	Rousseau	FRA	51	1	NC	Lille	25 Jun 76

Mark		Name		Nat	Yr	Pos	Meet	Venue	Date
8.36	5.2	Ralph	Spry	USA	60	1	NCAA	Houston	3 Jun 83
8.34		Mike	McRae	USA	55	1	SW	Modesto	12 May 84
8.33		Phil	Shinnick	USA	43	1	CalR	Modesto	25 May 63
8.33	2.1	Charlton	Ehizuelen	NIG	53	1	KansR	Lawrence	19 Apr 75
8.33	3.7	Andrzej	Klimaszewski	POL	60	1	Kuso	Warszawa	13 Jun 80
8.33	3.6	Sergey	Vasilenko	SU	65	1B	Znam	Leningrad	11 Jun 88
8.32	3.8	David	Giralt	CUB	59	1	WPT	Québec City	11 Aug 79
8.31		Mike	Davis	USA	64	1		Houston	18 May 86
8.31	3.1	Gordon	Laine	USA	58	4	FOT	Indianapolis	18 Jul 88
8.30A		Yusuf	Alli	NIG	60	1		El Paso	12 Apr 87
8.30	2.6	Jens	Hirschberg	GDR	64	1		Berlin	25 Aug 87
8.29	3.0	Vladimir	Bobylyov	SU	66	2	NC	Bryansk	19 Jul 87
8.28		Yuriy	Samarin	SU	60	1		Kharkov	8 Jul 84
8.27A		Frans	Maas	HOL	64	1		El Paso	17 Apr 88

TRIPLE JUMP

Mark		Name		Nat	Yr	Pos	Meet	Venue	Date
17.97	1.5	Willie	Banks	USA	56	1	TAC	Indianapolis	16 Jun 85
17.92	1.6	Khristo	Markov	BUL	65	1	WC	Roma	31 Aug 87
17.89A	0.0	João Carlos	de Oliveira	BRA	54	1	PAG	Ciudad México	15 Oct 75
17.87	1.7	Mike	Conley	USA	62	1	TAC	San Jose	27 Jun 87
17.86	1.3	Charles	Simpkins	USA	63	1	WUG	Kobe	2 Sep 85
17.81	2.0		Markov			1	Nar	Sofia	31 May 87
17.80	0.6		Markov			1	BGP	Budapest	11 Aug 86
17.78	1.0	Nikolay	Musiyenko	SU	59	1	Znam	Leningrad	7 Jun 86
17.78	0.6	Lazaro	Betancourt	CUB	63	1	Barr	Habana	15 Jun 86
17.77	1.9		Markov			1	EP-B	Budapest	11 Aug 85
17.77	1.0	Aleksandr	Kovalenko	SU	63	1	NC	Bryansk	18 Jul 87
17.77	1.4		Markov			1	NC	Sofia	3 Sep 88
17.76i	-		Conley			1	TAC	New York	27 Feb 87
17.71	1.9		Conley			2	TAC	Indianapolis	16 Jun 85
17.71	2.0		Banks			1		Barcelona	8 Jul 85
17.69	1.0	Oleg	Protsenko	SU	63	1	NC	Leningrad	4 Aug 85
17.69	0.2		Conley			1	GWG	Moskva	9 Jul 86
17.69	1.5	Igor	Lapshin	SU	63	1		Minsk	31 Jul 88
17.68	1.9		Protsenko			1	WG	Helsinki	30 Jun 88
17.67	0.0		Banks			1	Arco	Los Angeles	8 Jun 85
17.67i	-		Protsenko			1		Osaka	15 Jan 87
17.67	-1.0		Conley			2	WC	Roma	31 Aug 87
17.66	1.9		Markov			1	EC	Stuttgart	30 Aug 86
17.65	1.0	Aleksandr	Yakovlev	SU	57	1	Znam	Moskva	6 Jun 87
17.65	0.1		Markov			1		São Paulo	20 Sep 87
17.62			Markov			1	NC	Sofia	14 Aug 86
17.61	0.6		Protsenko			1	EP	Praha	28 Jun 87
17.61	0.7		Markov			1	OG	Seoul	24 Sep 88
17.60	0.6	Vladimir	Plekhanov	SU	58	2	NC	Leningrad	4 Aug 85
17.59	-2.1		Protsenko			1	NC	Kiev	17 Jul 86
17.59	1.6		Conley			1	ISTAF	Berlin	26 Aug 88
		(31/12)							
17.57A	0.0	Keith	Connor	UK	57	1	NCAA	Provo	5 Jun 82
17.56	1.9	Maris	Bruziks	SU	62	1		Riga	3 Sep 88
17.55	0.3	Vasiliy	Grischenkov	SU	58	1	SPA	Moskva	19 Jun 83
17.54i	-	Maris	Bruziks	SU	62	1	EC	Madrid	23 Feb 86
17.53	1.0	Aleksandr	Beskrovniy	SU	60	2	SPA	Moskva	19 Jun 83
17.53	1.6	Zdzislaw	Hoffmann	POL	59	1		Madrid	4 Jun 85
17.53	1.0	Gennadiy	Valyukevich	SU	58	1		Erfurt	1 Jun 86
17.53	1.6	Al	Joyner	USA	60	Q	TAC	San Jose	26 Jun 87
		(20)							
17.53	0.9	Milán	Mikulas	CS	63	1	NC	Praha	17 Jul 88
17.50	0.4	Volker	Mai	GDR	66	1	vSU	Erfurt	23 Jun 85
17.50		Oleg	Sakirkin	SU	66	1		Barcelona	13 Jul 88
17.48	1.9	Jorge	Reyna	CUB	63	1		Santiago de Cuba	27 Feb 87
17.46	1.7	Ken	Lorraway	AUS	56	1		London	7 Aug 82
17.45	1.9	Aleksandr	Leonov	SU	62	1		Sochi	24 May 87
17.44	-0.?	Viktor	Saneyev	SU	45	1		Sukhumi	17 Oct 72

Mark		Name		Nat	Yr	Pos	Meet	Venue	Date
17.44	2.0	Dirk	Gamlin	GDR	63	1		Dresden	7 Jul 85
17.43i	-	Vladimir	Inozemtsev	SU	64	1		Kiev	26 Jan 86
17.43		Peter	Bouschen	FRG	60	1		Düsseldorf	2 Jun 88
		(30)							
17.41	0.0	John	Herbert	UK	62	3	WUG	Kobe	2 Sep 85
17.40A	0.4	Pedro	Perez Duenas	CUB	52	1	PAG	Cali	5 Aug 71
17.37	0.7	Vyacheslav	Bordukov	SU	59	2	Nar	Sofia	19 May 84
17.37i	-	Vasif	Asadov	SU	65	2	NC	Volgograd	12 Feb 88
17.36	1.3	Ray	Kimble	USA	53	1	CalR	Modesto	9 May 87
17.36	1.8	Vladimir	Chernikov	SU	59	1		Odessa	21 Aug 88
17.35	-0.3	Jaak	Uudmäe	SU	54	1	OG	Moskva	25 Jul 80
17.35	1.7	Jacek	Pastusinski	POL	64	5	WC	Roma	31 Aug 87
17.34	0.3	Zou Zhenxian		CHN	55	2	WP	Roma	5 Sep 81
17.34	0.1	Jan	Cado	CS	63	1	PTS	Bratislava	26 May 84
		(40)							
17.33i	-	Grigoriy	Yemets	SU	57	1	EC	Göteborg	3 Mar 84
17.33		Wolfgang	Zinser	FRG	64	1		Düsseldorf	23 Sep 88
17.31	1.5	Jörg	Drehmel	GDR	45	2	OG	München	4 Sep 72
17.31	2.0	Igor	Parygin	SU	67	1	Veet	Tallinn	9 Jul 88
17.30i	-	Shamil	Abbyasov	SU	57	1	EC	Grenoble	21 Feb 81
17.30	1.9	Jörg	Elbe	GDR	64	1		Dresden	2 Aug 85
17.29	-0.6	Ralf	Jaros	FRG	65	1		Rhede	5 Jul 85
17.28	0.2	Juan	Lopez	CUB	67	3		Habana	6 Aug 88
17.27A	2.0	Nelson	Prudencio	BRA	44	2	OG	Ciudad México	17 Oct 68
17.27	1.2	Bedros	Bedrosian	RUM	58	1		Bucuresti	9 Jun 84
		(50)							

Low altitude mark for athlete with high-altitude bests

Connor	17.30	1.2	1		London	9 Jun 82	17.57A

Best outdoor marks for athletes with lifetime bests indoors

Yemets	17.30	0.2	2	NC	Donyetsk	9 Sep 84	17.33i
Abbyasov	17.27		1		Tashkent	15 May 83	17.30i

Wind-assisted marks

18.20	5.2	Willie	Banks	USA	56	1	FOT	Indianapolis	16 Jul 88
17.93	5.2	Charles	Simpkins	USA	63	2	FOT	Indianapolis	16 Jul 88
17.91	3.2		Simpkins			1	TAC	Eugene	21 Jun 86
17.84	2.3		Conley			2	TAC	Eugene	21 Jun 86
17.82	3.6		Banks			1	Jenner	San Jose	31 May 86
17.81	4.6	Keith	Connor	UK	57	1	CommG	Brisbane	9 Oct 82
17.75		Gennadiy	Valyukevich	SU	58	1		Uzhgorod	27 Apr 86
17.72	3.2		Conley			1	NCAA	Austin	1 Jun 85
17.64	3.2		Protsenko			1		São Paulo	11 May 85
17.63	4.3	Robert	Cannon	USA	58	3	FOT	Indianapolis	16 Jul 88
17.62	3.3		Conley			4	FOT	Indianapolis	16 Jul 88
17.60	2.2		Banks			2	TAC	San Jose	27 Jun 87
17.58	5.2	Al	Joyner	USA	60	5	FOT	Indianapolis	16 Jul 88
17.56	3.7	Ron	Livers	USA	55	1	AAU	Walnut	17 Jun 79
17.56	4.9	Kenny	Harrison	USA	65	6	FOT	Indianapolis	16 Jul 88
17.55	3.6	Zdzislaw	Hoffmann	POL	59	1	Kuso	Warszawa	9 Jun 84
17.54	3.2	Ken	Lorraway	AUS	56	2	CommG	Brisbane	9 Oct 82
17.53	4.8	Ray	Kimble	USA	53	7	FOT	Indianapolis	16 Jul 88
17.38	4.2	Milan	Tiff	USA	49	1	AAU	Westwood	11 Jun 77
17.38	2.8	Vyacheslav	Bordukov	SU	59	1		Moskva	16 Aug 87
17.31		Paul	Emordi	NIG	65	1	DrakeR	Des Moines	26 Apr 86
17.31	2.9	Wolfgang	Knabe	FRG	59	1	NC	Frankfurt	23 Jul 88
17.30	3.2	Anatoliy	Piskulin	SU	52	1	WUG	Sofia	22 Aug 77
17.30	3.7	David	McFadgen	USA	60	2	USOCF	Houston	2 Aug 86
17.29	2.9	James	Butts	USA	50	1	FOT	Eugene	26 Jun 76
17.29	3.4	Bela	Bakosi	HUN	57	1		Hiroshima	6 May 82
17.29	3.9	Joseph	Taiwo	NIG	59	6	WC	Roma	31 Aug 87

Ancillary marks

Markov	17.74	1.2	11 Aug 86
Markov	17.73	1.9	31 Aug 87
Markov	17.73	1.6	3 Sep 88
Conley	17.71	1.2	27 Jun 87
Simpkins	17.68	1.0	2 Sep 85
Conley	17.65	1.0	31 Aug 87
Banks	17.64	1.1	16 Jun 85
Markov	17.64	1.4	11 Aug 86
Markov	17.60	1.3	3 Sep 88

Wind-assisted

Banks	18.06	4.9	16 Jul 88
Markov	17.75	2.3	3 Sep 88
Connor	17.72	3.8	9 Oct 82
Simpkins	17.70	3.9	21 Jun 86
Markov	17.70	2.2	31 Aug 87

SHOT

Mark	Name		Nat	Yr	Pos	Meet	Venue	Date
23.06	Ulf	Timmermann	GDR	62	1		Khania	22 May 88
22.91	Alessandro	Andrei	ITA	59	1		Viareggio	12 Aug 87
22.86	Brian	Oldfield	USA	45	1	ITA	El Paso	10 May 75
22.75	Werner	Günthör	SWZ	61	1		Bern	23 Aug 88
22.64	Udo	Beyer	GDR	55	1		Berlin	20 Aug 86
22.62		Timmermann			1		Berlin	22 Sep 85
22.61		Timmermann			1		Potsdam	8 Sep 88
22.60		Timmermann			1	vSU	Tallinn	21 Jun 86
22.56		Timmermann			1		Berlin	13 Sep 88
22.52	John	Brenner	USA	61	1	MSR	Walnut	26 Apr 87
22.51		Timmermann			1		Erfurt	1 Jun 86
22.47		Timmermann			1		Dresden	17 Aug 86
22.47		Günthör			1	WG	Helsinki	2 Jul 87
22.47		Timmermann			1	OG	Seoul	23 Sep 88
22.45		Oldfield			1	ITA	El Paso	22 May 76
22.43		Günthör			1	v3-N	Lüdenscheid	18 Jun 87
22.42	Randy	Barnes	USA	66	1	WK	Zürich	17 Aug 88
22.39		Barnes			2	OG	Seoul	23 Sep 88
22.36+		Timmermann			1		Athinai	16 May 88
22.31		Beyer			1	NC	Potsdam	20 Aug 87
22.28		Oldfield			1	ITA	Edinburgh	18 Jun 75
22.26i		Günthör			1	NC	Magglingen	8 Feb 87
22.26		Brenner			1		Westwood	18 Apr 87
22.25		Günthör			1	WK	Zürich	19 Aug 87
22.24	Sergey	Smirnov	SU	60	2	vGDR	Tallinn	21 Jun 86
22.24i		Timmermann			1	WC	Indianapolis	7 Mar 87
22.23		Günthör			1	WC	Roma	29 Aug 87
22.22		Beyer			1	vUSA	Los Angeles	25 Jun 83
22.22		Günthör			1	EC	Stuttgart	28 Aug 86
22.19		Oldfield			1	Jen	San Jose	26 May 84
22.19i		Timmermann			1	EC	Liévin	21 Feb 87
	(31/8)							
22.10	Sergey	Gavryushin	SU	59	1		Tbilisi	31 Aug 86
22.09	Sergey	Kasnauskas	SU	61	1		Staiki	23 Aug 84
	(10)							
22.02i	George	Woods	USA	43	1		Inglewood	8 Feb 74
22.02	Dave	Laut	USA	56	1		Koblenz	25 Aug 82
22.00	Aleksandr	Baryshnikov	SU	48	1	vFRA	Colombes	10 Jul 76
21.96	Mikhail	Kostin	SU	59	1		Vitebsk	20 Jul 86
21.93	Remigius	Machura	CS	60	1		Praha	23 Aug 87
21.85	Terry	Albritton	USA	55	1		Honolulu	21 Feb 76
21.82	Al	Feuerbach	USA	48	1		San Jose	5 May 73
21.78	Randy	Matson	USA	45	1		College Station	22 Apr 67
21.76	Mike	Carter	USA	60	2	NCAA	Eugene	2 Jun 84
21.74	Janis	Bojars	SU	56	1		Riga	14 Jul 84
	(20)							
21.73	Augie	Wolf	USA	61	1		Leverkusen	12 Apr 84
21.69	Reijo	Ståhlberg	FIN	52	1	WCR	Fresno	5 May 79
21.68	Geoff	Capes	UK	49	1	4-N	Cwmbran	18 May 80
21.68	Edward	Sarul	POL	58	1		Sopot	31 Jul 83
21.67	Hartmut	Briesenick	GDR	49	1		Potsdam	1 Sep 73
21.61	Kevin	Akins	USA	60	1	CalR	Modesto	14 May 83
21.58	Vladimir	Kiselyov	SU	57	3	Drz	Moskva	17 Aug 84
21.53	Yevgeniy	Mironov	SU	49	1	NC	Kiev	24 Jun 76
21.51	Ralf	Reichenbach	FRG	50	1	ISTAF	Berlin	8 Aug 80
21.45	Gregg	Tafralis	USA	58	3	MSR	Walnut	27 Apr 86
	(30)							
21.44	Mikhail	Domorosov	SU	55	2		Staiki	23 Aug 84
21.43	Mike	Lehmann	USA	60	2	Jen	San Jose	28 May 83
21.42i	Fred	DeBernardi	USA	49	1	ITA	Portland	20 Apr 74
21.35	Ron	Semkiw	USA	54	1		Mesa	5 Mar 74
21.33	Hans	Hoglund	SWE	52	1	NCAA	Provo	6 Jun 75
21.32	Heinz-Joachim	Rothenburg	GDR	44	1		Potsdam	3 Jun 72

Mark	Name		Nat	Yr	Pos	Meet	Venue	Date
21.31	Hans-Peter	Gies	GDR	47	2		Potsdam	25 Aug 72
21.30	Helmut	Krieger	POL	58	1	NC	Grudziadz	27 Jun 86
21.29	Jim	Doehring	USA	62	1		Walnut	1 Jun 86
21.25	Hans-Jürgen	Jacobi	GDR	50	2	NC	Cottbus	16 Jul 80
	(40)							
21.24i	Soren	Tallhem	SWE	64	1	NCAA	Syracuse	9 Mar 85
21.22	Lars	Nilsen	NOR	65	1	NCAA	Indianapolis	6 Jun 86
21.22	Klaus	Görmer	GDR	63	3	NC	Potsdam	20 Aug 87
21.20	Josef	Kubes	CS	57	2	NC	Praha	24 Jul 83
21.20	Vyacheslav	Lykho	SU	67	1		Moskva	26 Jul 87
21.19	Wladyslaw	Komar	POL	40	1		Warszawa	17 Aug 74
21.19	Vladimir	Milic	YUG	55	1		Beograd	18 Aug 82
21.16	Vladimir	Kisheyev	SU	58	1		Khabarovsk	18 Sep 88
21.15	Karsten	Stolz	FRG	64	1		Essen	18 Sep 88
21.14	Maris	Petrashko	SU	61	1		Limbazhi	11 Jul 87
	(50)							

+ meeting held under normal competitive conditions, unsanctioned by GDR federation, but included in national lists.
4-N Capes 21.68 Eng v Wal v HUN v HOL * Disqualified for failing dope test

Best outdoor marks for athletes with lifetime bests indoors

Woods	21.63	2	CalR	Modesto	22 May 76	22.02i
DeBernardi	21.41	1	ITA	El Paso	27 Apr 74	21.42i

Ancillary marks

Andrei	22.84	12 Aug 87
Andrei	22.74	12 Aug 87
Andrei	22.72	12 Aug 87
Günthör	22.70	23 Aug 88
Beyer	22.58	20 Aug 86
Timmermann	22.45	22 May 88
Timmermann	22.40	22 May 88
Andrei	22.37	12 Aug 87
Timmermann	22.35	22 May 88
Günthör	22.31	18 Jun 87
Timmermann	22.29	23 Sep 88
Günthör	22.28	2 Jul 87
Oldfield	22.24	10 May 75
Beyer	22.24	20 Aug 86
Günthör	22.23	8 Feb 87
Brenner	22.20	18 Apr 87

DISCUS

Mark	Name		Nat	Yr	Pos	Meet	Venue	Date
74.08	Jürgen	Schult	GDR	60	1		Neubrandenburg	6 Jun 86
71.86	Yuriy	Dumchev	SU	58	1		Moskva	29 May 83
71.32	Ben	Plucknett*	USA	54	1	Pre	Eugene	4 Jun 83
71.26	John	Powell	USA	47	1	TAC	San Jose	9 Jun 84
71.26	Rickard	Bruch	SWE	46	1		Malmö	15 Nov 84
71.26	Imrich	Bugár	CS	55	1	Jen	San Jose	25 May 85
71.18	Art	Burns	USA	54	1		San Jose	19 Jul 83
71.16	Wolfgang	Schmidt	GDR	54	1		Berlin	9 Aug 78
71.14		Plucknett			1		Berkeley	12 Jun 83
71.06	Luis M.	Delís	CUB	57	1	Barr	Habana	21 May 83
71.00		Bruch			1		Malmö	14 Oct 84
70.98	Mac	Wilkins (10)	USA	50	1	WG	Helsinki	9 Jul 80
70.98		Burns			1	Pre	Eugene	21 Jul 84
70.86		Wilkins			1		San Jose	1 May 76
70.82		Plucknett			1		Salinas	1 Jun 83
70.72		Bugár			1	vHUN,AUT	Schwechat	18 Jun 83
70.66		Wilkins			1	AAU	Walnut	16 Jun 79
70.58		Delís			1		Salinas	19 May 82
70.48		Wilkins			1		San Jose	29 Apr 78
70.48		Wilkins			1	Pre	Eugene	31 May 78
70.48		Bruch			1		Malmö	12 Sep 84
70.46		Schult			1		Berlin	13 Sep 88
70.44		Wilkins			2	TAC	San Jose	9 Jun 84
70.38	Jay	Silvester	USA	37	1		Lancaster	16 May 71
70.36		Wilkins			1	SW	Modesto	14 May 83
70.30		Dumchev			1		Bryansk	31 Jul 88
70.26		Bugár			1	vITA	Cagliari	8 Sep 84
70.24		Schmidt			1		Potsdam	18 Aug 78
70.24		Bugár			1		Nitra	26 Aug 84
70.20		Delís			1	CAC	Habana	8 Aug 82
	(30/11)							
70.06	Romas	Ubartas	SU	60	1		Smalininkay	8 May 88
70.00	Juan	Martínez	CUB	58	2	Barr	Habana	21 May 83
69.70	Gejza	Valent	CS	53	2		Nitra	26 Aug 84
69.62	Knut	Hjeltnes	NOR	51	2	Jen	San Jose	25 May 85

Mark	Name		Nat	Yr	Pos	Meet	Venue	Date
69.46	Al	Oerter	USA	36	1	TFA	Wichita	31 May 80
69.44	Georgiy	Kolnootchenko	SU	59	1	vUSA	Indianapolis	3 Jul 82
69.40	Art	Swarts	USA	45	1		Scotch Plains	8 Dec 79
69.26	Ken	Stadel	USA	52	2	AAU	Walnut	16 Jun 79
68.98	Mike	Buncic	USA	62	1		Stanford	20 Jun 87
	(20)							
68.88	Vladimir	Zinchenko	SU	59	1		Dnepropetrovsk	16 Jul 88
68.64	Dmitriy	Kovtsun	SU	55	1		Riga	6 Jul 84
68.52	Igor	Duginyets	SU	56	1	NC	Kiev	21 Aug 82
68.50	Armin	Lemme	GDR	55	1	vUSA	Karl-Marx-Stadt	10 Jul 82
68.48	John	van Reenen	RSA	47	1		Stellenbosch	14 Mar 75
68.44	Vaclavas	Kidikas	SU	61	1		Sochi	1 Jun 88
68.30	Stefan	Fernholm	SWE	59	1		Västerås	15 Jul 87
68.12	Markku	Tuokko	FIN	51	1	WCR	Fresno	5 May 79
68.12	Iosif	Nagy	RUM	46	2		Zaragoza	22 May 83
68.08	Hein-Direck	Neu	FRG	44	1		Bremerhaven	27 May 77
	(30)							
68.00	Svein Inge	Valvik	NOR	56	1		Juarez	31 May 82
67.82	Velko	Velev	BUL	48	1		Riga	13 Aug 78
67.80	Alwin	Wagner	FRG	50	1		Melsungen	1 Jul 87
67.76	Vitaliy	Pishchalnikov	SU	58	1		Stavropol	9 May 84
67.62	Randy	Heisler	USA	61	1		Bloomington	29 Jun 87
67.60	Rolf	Danneberg	FRG	53	1		Berlin	30 May 87
67.56	Wolfgang	Warnemunde	GDR	53	1		Rostock	2 Jun 80
67.54	Siegfried	Pachale	GDR	49	1		Karl-Marx-Stadt	29 May 76
67.54	Hilmar	Hossfeld	GDR	54	2	OT	Jena	17 May 80
67.54	Werner	Hartmann	FRG	59	1		Georgsheil	29 Apr 82
	(40)							
67.38	Tim	Vollmer	USA	46	2		Lancaster	16 May 71
67.38	Ferenc	Tégla	HUN	47	1		Szentes	12 Oct 77
67.32	Rob	Gray	CAN	56	1		Etobicoke	30 Apr 84
67.30	Ion	Zamfirache	RUM	53	1		Bucuresti	19 May 85
67.22	Mitch	Crouser	USA	57	1		Eugene	5 Aug 85
67.18	Ludvík	Danek	CS	37	1		Praha	10 Jul 74
67.14	Borislav	Tashev	BUL	56	1		Pleven	31 Jul 82
67.14	Igor	Avrunin	SU	57	1		Smolininkay	9 May 84
67.10	Brad	Cooper	BAH	57	1	NC	Nassau	14 Jun 86
66.98	Greg	McSeveney	USA	59	1		Walnut	2 Jun 85
	(50)							
*** Subsequent to drugs disqualification**								
72.34!	Ben	Plucknett	USA	54	1	DNG	Stockholm	7 Jul 81
71.20		Plucknett			1	CalR	Modesto	16 May 81
! recognised as US record								
Technical irregularity								
67.02	Lothar	Milde	GDR	34	1		Halle	27 May 72
Sloping ground								
72.08	John	Powell	USA	47	1		Klagshamn	11 Sep 87
69.80	Stefan	Fernholm	SWE	59	1		Klagshamn	13 Aug 87
67.20	Vestein	Hafsteinsson	ICE	60	1		Klagshamn	17 Jul 87

Ancillary marks

Plucknett 71.10 4 Jun 83 | Wilkins 70.24 1 May 76 | Wilkins 70.20 9 Jul 80
Wilkins 70.40 31 May 78

HAMMER

Mark	Name		Nat	Yr	Pos	Meet	Venue	Date
86.74	Yuriy	Sedykh	SU	55	1	EC	Stuttgart	30 Aug 86
86.66		Sedykh			1	vGDR	Tallinn	22 Jun 86
86.34		Sedykh			1		Cork	3 Jul 84
86.04	Sergey	Litvinov	SU	58	1	OD	Dresden	3 Jul 86
85.74		Litvinov			2	EC	Stuttgart	30 Aug 86
85.68		Sedykh			1	BGP	Budapest	11 Aug 86
85.60		Sedykh			1	PTG	London	13 Jul 84
85.60		Sedykh			1	Drz	Moskva	17 Aug 84
85.20		Litvinov			2		Cork	3 Jul 84
85.14		Litvinov			1	PTG	London	11 Jul 86
85.14		Sedykh			1		Moskva	4 Sep 88

Mark	Name		Nat	Yr	Pos	Meet	Venue	Date
85.02		Sedykh			1	BGP	Budapest	20 Aug 84
84.92		Sedykh			2	OD	Dresden	3 Jul 86
84.88		Litvinov			1	GP-GG	Roma	10 Sep 86
84.80		Litvinov			1	OG	Seoul	26 Sep 88
84.72		Sedykh			1	GWG	Moskva	9 Jul 86
84.64		Litvinov			2	GWG	Moskva	9 Jul 86
84.60		Sedykh			1		Tokyo	14 Sep 84
84.58		Sedykh			1	Znam	Leningrad	8 Jun 86
84.46		Sedykh			1		Vladivostock	14 Sep 88
84.40	Juri	Tamm	SU	57	1		Banská Bystrica	9 Sep 84
84.36		Litvinov			2	vGDR	Tallinn	22 Jun 86
84.26		Sedykh			1	Nik	Nice	15 Jul 86
84.16		Tamm			1		Kharkov	19 Jun 88
84.14		Litvinov			1	Spart	Moskva	21 Jun 83
84.14		Sedykh			1	WG	Helsinki	7 Jul 86
84.08		Tamm			1	BGP	Budapest	4 Aug 85
84.04		Litvinov			1		Sochi	1 Jun 88
84.02		Litvinov			2	WG	Helsinki	7 Jul 86
83.98		Litvinov			1		Moskva	4 Jun 82
	(30/3)							
83.78	Igor	Nikulin	SU	60	1		Leningrad	18 Jun 88
83.44	Igor	Astapkovich	SU	63	1		Minsk	31 Jul 88
83.40+	Ralf	Haber	GDR	62	1		Athinai	16 May 88
82.64	Günther	Rodehau	GDR	59	1		Dresden	3 Aug 85
82.52	Heinz	Weis	FRG	63	1		Leverkusen	28 Jun 88
82.24	Benjaminas	Viluckis	SU	61	1		Klaipeda	24 Aug 86
82.24	Vyacheslav	Korovin	SU	62	1		Chelyabinsk	20 Jun 87
	(10)							
82.16	Vitaliy	Alisevich	SU	67	1		Parnu	13 Jul 88
82.08	Ivan	Tanev	BUL	57	1	NC	Sofia	3 Sep 88
81.88	Jud	Logan	USA	59	1		University Park	22 Apr 88
81.70	Plamen	Minev	BUL	65	1		Sofia	4 Jun 88
81.68	Tibor	Gécsek	HUN	64	1		Szombathely	13 Sep 88
81.56	Christoph	Sahner	FRG	63	1		Rehlingen	27 May 85
81.52	Juha	Tiainen	FIN	55	1		Tampere	11 Jun 84
81.52	Sergey	Alay	SU	65	1		Siauliai	22 May 88
81.44	Yuriy	Tarasyuk	SU	57	1		Minsk	10 Aug 84
81.32	Klaus	Ploghaus	FRG	56	1		Paderborn	25 May 86
	(20)							
81.20	Igor	Grigorash	SU	59	1		Kiev	23 Aug 84
81.18	Albert	Sinka	HUN	62	1		Székesfehérvár	7 Aug 88
81.10	Sergey	Ivanov	SU	62	1		Chelyabinsk	27 Jun 87
80.92	Matthias	Moder	GDR	63	1		Halle	11 Jun 85
80.80	Karl-Hans	Riehm	FRG	51	1		Rhede	30 Jul 80
80.70	Vasiliy	Sidorenko	SU	61	1		Tiraspol	9 Aug 86
80.68	Viktor	Litvinenko	SU	57	2		Kiev	23 Aug 84
80.64	Emanuil	Dyulgherov	BUL	55	1		Sofia	25 Aug 84
80.60	Imre	Szitás	HUN	61	1		Szombathely	11 Jul 88
80.54	Viktor	Apostolov	BUL	62	2	NC	Sofia	3 Sep 88
	(30)							
80.50	Detlef	Gerstenberg	GDR	57	1		Berlin	15 Jul 84
80.48	Boris	Zaychuk	SU	47	2		Sochi	24 May 80
80.38	Frantisek	Vrbka	CS	58	2	EP	Moskva	18 Aug 85
80.38	Andrey	Abduvaliyev	SU	66	1		Chelyabinsk	16 Jul 88
80.32	Nikolay	Lysenko	SU	66	1		Ordzhonikidze	24 Sep 88
80.24	Grigoriy	Shevtsov	SU	58	1		Volgograd	9 May 83
80.20	Igor	Shchegolev	SU	60	1		Volgograd	6 Sep 86
80.18	Zdzislaw	Kwasny	POL	60	2	EP	London	21 Aug 83
80.16	Anatoliy	Chyuzhas	SU	56	2		Klaipeda	27 May 84
80.12	Viktor	Apostolov	BUL	62	1		Sofia	22 Aug 87
	(40)							
80.02	Ken	Flax	USA	63	1	CalR	Modesto	7 May 88
79.92	Jörg	Schaefer	FRG	59	1	ISTAF	Berlin	15 Aug 86
79.90	Roland	Steuk	GDR	59	1		Sofia	16 Jun 84
79.70	Johann	Lindner	AUT	56	1		Schwerin	24 Jun 87

Mark	Name		Nat	Yr	Pos	Meet	Venue	Date
79.66	Donatas	Plunge	SU	60	2		Klaipeda	24 Aug 86
79.56	Anatoliy	Yefimov	SU	56	1		Adler	24 Apr 83
79.46	Mariusz	Tomaszewski	POL	56	1		Zabrze	1 Jul 84
79.30	Walter	Schmidt	FRG	48	1		Frankfurt am Main	14 Aug 75
79.22	Igor	Kuprishchenkov	SU	59	1		Smolensk	20 Jul 85
79.16	Manfred	Huning	FRG	53	1		Dortmund	22 Aug 79
	(50)							
Extra trial								
81.04	Mariusz	Tomaszewski	POL	56	-		Zabrze	1 Jul 84
Chain exceeding maximum legal length								
81.12	Grigoriy	Shevtsov	SU	58	1		Sochi	12 May 83
Questionable measurement								
82.40	Plamen	Minev	BUL	65	1		Sofia	8 Aug 87

Ancillary marks to 84.50

Sedykh	86.68	30 Aug 86	Sedykh	85.42	11 Aug 86	Sedykh	84.98	4 Sep 88
Sedykh	86.62	30 Aug 86	Litvinov	85.42	3 Jul 86	Litvinov	84.92	3 Jul 86
Sedykh	86.00	3 Jul 84	Sedykh	85.28	30 Aug 86	Litvinov	84.84	3 Jul 84
Sedykh	86.00	22 Jun 86	Sedykh	85.26	11 Aug 86	Litvinov	84.76	26 Sep 88
Sedykh	85.82	22 Jun 86	Sedykh	85.24	11 Aug 86	Sedykh	84.84	17 Aug 84
Sedykh	85.52	13 Jul 84	Sedykh	85.20	3 Jul 84	Sedykh	84.64	11 Aug 86
Sedykh	85.46	30 Aug 86	Sedykh	85.04	13 Jul 84	Sedykh	84.58	14 Sep 84
						Litvinov	84.58	11 Jul 86

JAVELIN

Mark	Name		Nat	Yr	Pos	Meet	Venue	Date
87.66	Ján	Zelezny	CS	66	1		Nitra	31 May 87
86.88		Zelezny			1		Leverkusen	28 Jun 88
86.64	Klaus	Tafelmeier	FRG	58	1	NC	Gelsenkirchen	12 Jul 87
86.62		Zelezny			1	GS	Ostrava	10 Jun 87
86.50	Tapio	Korjus	FIN	61	1		Lahti	25 Aug 88
85.96		Tafelmeier			1		Tokyo	13 May 88
85.90		Zelezny			Q	OG	Seoul	24 Sep 88
85.76		Zelezny			1		Kvarnsveden	19 Jun 88
85.74		Tafelmeier			1		Como	21 Sep 86
85.74		Zelezny			1	PTS	Bratislava	8 Jun 88
85.38	Tom	Petranoff	USA	58	1	WG	Helsinki	7 Jul 86
85.24	Mike	Hill	UK	64	1	DNG	Stockholm	30 Jun 87
85.20		Zelezny			1		Banska Bystrica	9 May 87
85.18		Korjus			1	vNOR	Oyestad	16 Jun 88
85.16	Viktor	Yevsyukov	SU	56	1	vGDR	Karl-Marx-Stadt	21 Jun 87
84.86		Yevsyukov			1	EP	Praha	27 Jun 87
84.76		Tafelmeier			1	EC	Stuttgart	27 Aug 86
84.76		Zelezny			1		Tokyo	7 Oct 88
84.66	Einar	Vilhjálmsson	ICE	60	1	NC	Reykjavik	25 Jun 88
84.50		Yevsyukov			1	OD	Berlin	8 Jul 87
84.38		Korjus			1	NC	Hameenlinna	7 Aug 88
84.34		Zelezny			1		Praha	2 Jun 88
84.30	Lev	Shatilo	SU	62	1	Znam	Moskva	7 Jun 87
84.28		Korjus			1	OG	Seoul	25 Sep 88
84.16	Kazuhiro	Mizoguchi	JAP	62	1		Tokyo	3 May 87
84.14	Silvio	Warsönke	GDR	67	1		Rostock	29 May 88
84.12		Zelezny			2	OG	Seoul	25 Sep 88
84.06	Detlef	Michel	GDR	55	1		Berlin	13 Sep 88
84.02		Yevsyukov			1	VD	Bruxelles	11 Sep 87
84.00		Mizoguchi			1	Jen	San Jose	30 May 87
	(30/11)							
83.84	Roald	Bradstock	UK	62	1		Tucson	2 May 87
83.54	Seppo	Räty	FIN	62	1	WC	Roma	30 Aug 87
83.52	Detlef	Michel	GDR	55	1		Berlin	18 Jun 86
83.34	Sejad	Krdzalic	YUG	60	1		Beograd	30 May 87
83.30	Gerald	Weiss	GDR	60	1		Jena	3 Jun 88
83.20	Heino	Puuste	SU	55	2	vGDR	Tallinn	22 Jun 86
83.00	Brian	Crouser	USA	62	1		Corvallis	16 May 87
82.74	Duncan	Atwood	USA	55	1	TAC	San Jose	26 Jun 87
82.64	Dag	Wennlund	SWE	63	1	TexR	Austin	4 Apr 87
	(20)							

Mark	Name		Nat	Yr	Pos	Meet	Venue	Date
82.20	Andreas	Linden	FRG	65	1		Bad Ems	3 Oct 87
82.18	Vladislav	Grib	SU	64	1		Banská Bystrica	4 Sep 88
82.06 *	Chris	de Beer	RSA	61	1	NC	Stellenbosch	11 Apr 87
82.06	Mike	Barnett	USA	61	1	BR	Holmdel	29 Jul 87
82.00	Marek	Kaleta	SU	61	1	NC	Kiev	15 Jul 86
81.94	Viktor	Zaitsev	SU	66	1		Alma-Ata	16 May 88
81.92	Normunds	Pildavs	SU	64	1		Riga	3 Sep 88
81.74	Sergey	Gavras	SU	57	3	vGDR	Karl-Marx-Stadt	21 Jun 87
81.48	Pascal	Lefévre	FRA	65	1	NC	Tours	14 Aug 88
81.38	Peter	Borglund	SWE	64	1		Sodertälje	13 Jun 88
(30)								
81.30	Wolfram	Gambke	FRG	59	1	NC	W.Berlin	13 Jul 86
81.38	Yuriy	Rybin	SU	63	1		Adler	11 Feb 88
81.26	Volker	Hadwich	GDR	64	1	vITA	Neubrandenberg	9 Jul 88
81.26	Charlus-Michel	Bertimon	FRA	57	2	NC	Tours	14 Aug 88
81.16	Nicu	Roata	RUM	61	2	Ros	Praha	23 Jun 87
80.98	David	Ottley	UK	55	Q	OG	Seoul	24 Sep 88
80.94	Sergey	Glebov	SU	64	1	Spart	Tashkent	17 Sep 86
80.92	Mark	Roberson	UK	67	1		London	12 Jun 88
80.84	Sigurdur	Einarsson	ICE	62	5	OD	Berlin	8 Jul 87
80.84	Peter	Blank	FRG	62	1	NC	Frankfurt am Main	24 Jul 88
(40								
80.82	Zbigniew	Bednarski	POL	60	1		Slupsk	1 May 88
80.78	Zdenek	Nenadál	CS	64	2		Praha	2 Jun 88
80.76	Stéphane	Laporte	FRA	66	1		Dijon	11 Jun 88
80.72	Constantin	Miclea	RUM	63	1	Nar	Sofia	25 Jun 88
80.70	Gavin	Lovegrove	NZ	67	1		Auckland	10 Dec 88
80.66	Masami	Yoshida	JAP	58	1		Kawasaki	23 Sep 86
80.66	Yuriy	Zhirov	SU	60	2	NC	Bryansk	19 Jul 87
80.62	Vladimir	Gavrilyuk	SU	61	1		Ternopol	5 Jul 87
80.60	Dave	Stephens	USA	62	1		Sacramento	27 Aug 88
80.56	László	Stefán	HUN	63	1	v3-N	Linz	29 Jun 86
(50)								
80.56	Jorma	Markus	FIN	52	3		Pihtipudas	13 Jul 86

* later disqualified for drug abuse

Ancillary marks

85.50	Zelezny	28 Jun 88
84.88	Hill	30 Jun 87
84.80	Zelezny	28 Jun 88
84.72	Hill	30 Jun 87
84.66	Zelezny	7 Oct 88
84.36	Yevsyukov	21 Jun 87
84.18	Yevsyukov	27 Jun 87

DECATHLON

Mark	Name		Nat	Yr	Pos	Meet	Venue	Date
8847	Daley	Thompson	UK	58	1	OG	Los Angeles	9 Aug 84
	10.44 8.01 15.72 2.03 46.97 14.33 46.56 5.00 65.24 4:35.00							
8832	Jürgen	Hingsen	FRG	58	1		Mannheim	9 Jun 84
	10.70w 7.76 16.42 2.07 48.05 14.07 49.36 4.90 59.86 4:19.75							
8825		Hingsen			1		Filderstadt	5 Jun 83
	10.92 7.74 15.94 2.15 47.89 14.10 46.80 4.70 67.26 4:19.74							
8811		Thompson			1	EC	Stuttgart	28 Aug 86
	10.26 7.72 15.73 2.00 47.02 14.04 43.38 5.10 62.78 4:26.16							
8792	Uwe	Freimuth	GDR	61	1	OD	Potsdam	21 Jul 84
	11.06 7.79 16.30 2.03 48.43 14.66 46.58 5.15 72.42 4:25.19							
8774		Thompson			1	EC	Athinai	8 Sep 82
	10.51 7.80 15.44 2.03 47.11 14.39 45.48 5.00 63.56 4:23.71							
8762	Siegfried	Wentz	FRG	60	2		Filderstadt	5 Jun 83
	10.89 7.49 15.35 2.09 47.38 14.00 46.90 4.80 70.68 4:24.90							
8741		Hingsen			1		Ulm	15 Aug 82
	10.74w 7.85 16.00 2.15 47.65 14.64 44.92 4.60 63.10 4:15.13							
8730		Thompson			1		Götzis	23 May 82
	10.50w 7.95 15.31 2.08 46.86 14.31 44.34 4.90 60.52 4:30.55							
8730		Hingsen			2	EC	Stuttgart	28 Aug 86
	10.87w 7.89w 16.46 2.12 48.79 14.52 48.42 4.60 64.38 4:21.61							
8714		Thompson			1	WC	Helsinki	13 Aug 83
	10.60 7.88 15.35 2.03 48.12 14.37w 44.46 5.10 65.24 4:29.72							

Mark	Name		Nat	Yr	Pos	Meet	Venue	Date
8709	Aleksandr	Apaychev	SU	61	1	vGDR	Neubrandenburg	3 Jun 84
	10.96 7.57 16.00 1.97 48.72 13.93 48.00 4.90 72.24 4:26.51							
8698	Grigoriy	Degtyarov	SU	58	1	NC	Kiev	22 Jun 84
	10.87 7.42 16.03 2.10 49.75 14.53 51.20 4.90 67.08 4:23.09							
8695		Hingsen			2	OG	Los Angeles	9 Aug 84
	10.91 7.80 15.87 2.12 47.69 14.29 50.82 4.50 60.44 4:22.60							
8680	Torsten	Voss	GDR	63	1	WC	Roma	4 Sep 87
	10.69 7.88 14.98 2.10 47.96 14.13 43.96 5.10 58.02 4:25.93							
8676		Wentz			3	EC	Stuttgart	28 Aug 86
	10.83 7.60 15.45 2.12 47.57 14.07 45.66 4.90 65.34 4:35.00							
8667	Guido	Kratschmer	FRG	53	1		Filderstadt	14 Jun 80
	10.58w 7.80 15.47 2.00 48.04 13.92 45.52 4.60 66.50 4:24.15							
8667		Thompson			1	vFRA	Arles	18 May 86
	10.56 7.81 15.39 1.98 47.52 14.35 47.62 4.90 63.68 4:30.04							
8663		Thompson			1	CommG	Edinburgh	28 Jul 86
	10.37 7.70w 15.01 2.08 47.30 14.22 43.72 5.10 60.82 4:39.63							
8648	1	Thompson			1		Götzis	18 May 80
	10.55 7.72 14.46 2.11 48.04 14.37 42.98 4.90 65.38 4:25.49							
8645		Wentz			1		Götzis	24 May 87
	10.85w 7.49w 15.82 2.05 47.55 13.96 48.20 4.80 65.50 4:34.58							
8634	Bruce	Jenner	USA	49	1	OG	Montreal	30 Jul 76
	10.94 7.22 15.35 2.03 47.51 14.8 50.04 4.80 68.52 4:12.61							
8617		Degtyarov			1		Götzis	20 May 84
	11.05 7.73 16.14 2.08 49.76 14.45 49.40 4.90 60.70 4:20.49							
8616		Freimuth			2	vSU	Neubrandenburg	3 Jun 84
	11.10 7.79 16.42 1.94 48.93 14.54 51.54 4.90 66.32 4:27.95							
8599		Hingsen			2	WC	Helsinki	13 Aug 83
	10.95 7.75 15.66 2.00 48.08 14.36w 43.30 4.90 67.42 4:21.59							
8597		Freimuth			1	NC	Potsdam	6 May 84
	11.06 7.69 16.06 1.97 48.78 14.75 47.54 4.80 73.02 4:24.46							
8592		Apaychev			1		Kiev	6 May 84
	10.97 7.61 15.91 1.95 48.40 14.11 45.08 4.80 68.88 4:18.78							
8590		Wentz			1		Filderstadt	15 Jun 86
	10.97 7.17 16.03 2.06 48.09 14.11 48.16 4.90 67.42 4:32.25							
8580		Degtyarov			1	Spart	Moskva	19 Jun 83
	11.13 7.75 15.97 2.09 49.40 14.51 49.66 5.00 58.56 4:25.53							
8572		Degtyarov			1	Drz	Moskva	18 Aug 84
	10.99 7.58 15.54 2.09 50.29 14.60 49.20 5.10 63.20 4:27.14							
	(30/9)							
8547	Igor	Sobolevskiy	SU	62	2	NC	Kiev	22 Jun 84
	10.64 7.71 15.93 2.01 48.24 14.82 50.54 4.40 67.40 4:32.84							
	(10)							
8534	Siegfried	Stark	GDR	55	1		Halle	4 May 80
	11.10w 7.64 15.81 2.03 49.53 14.86w 47.20 5.00 68.70 4:27.70							
8519	Yuriy	Kutsenko	SU	52	3	NC	Kiev	22 Jun 84
	11.07 7.54 15.11 2.13 49.07 14.94 50.38 4.60 61.70 4:12.68							
8512	Christian	Plaziat	FRA	63	1		Talence	17 Jul 88
	10.69 7.74 13.51 2.16 48.16 14.15 43.74 4.90 55.76 4:24.01							
8506	Valter	Külvet	SU	64	1		Staiki	3 Jul 88
	11.05 7.35 15.78 2.00 48.08 14.55 52.04 4.60 61.72 4:15.93							
8491	Aleksandr	Nevskiy	SU	58	2		Götzis	20 May 84
	10.97 7.24 15.04 2.08 48.44 14.67 46.06 4.70 69.56 4:19.62							
8488	Christian	Schenk	GDR	65	1	OG	Seoul	29 Sep 88
	11.25 7.43 15.48 2.27 48.90 15.13 49.28 4.70 61.32 4:28.95							
8485	Konstantin	Akhapkin	SU	56	1	NC	Moskva	2 Aug 82
	11.10 7.72 15.25 2.02 49.14 14.38 45.68 4.90 62.42 4:19.60							
8466	Nikolay	Avilov	SU	48	1	OG	München	8 Sep 72
	11.00 7.68 14.36 2.12 48.45 14.31 46.98 4.55 61.66 4:22.82							
8447	Robert	De Wit	HOL	62	1	NC	Eindhoven	22 May 88
	11.07 6.98 15.88 2.04 48.80 14.32 46.20 5.00 63.94 4:20.98							
8437	Richaras	Malakhovskis	SU	65	2		Staiki	3 Jul 88
	10.93 7.04 14.94 2.09 47.77 14.34 44.04 4.90 59.58 4:13.67							
	(20)							
8417	Sergey	Zhelanov	SU	57	4	NC	Kiev	22 Jun 84
	11.04 7.50 14.31 2.13 48.94 14.40 43.44 5.00 65.90 4:37.24							

Mark	Name		Nat	Yr	Pos	Meet	Venue	Date
8415	Dave	Steen	CAN	59	3		Talence	17 Jul 88
	11.02 7.56 13.99 1.98 48.22 14.95 44.08 5.20 65.36 4:21.46							
8400h	Aleksandr	Grebenyuk	SU	51	1	NC	Riga	3 Jul 77
	10.7 7.12 15.50 2.02 48.8 14.3 45.52 4.70 71.52 4:27.3							
8397	Fred	Dixon	USA	49	1	vSU	Bloomington	14 Aug 77
	10.85 7.44 15.20 2.04 48.54 14.94 47.14 4.60 67.88 4:30.21							
8387	Alain	Blondel	FRA	62	4		Talence	17 Jul 88
	11.03 7.58 13.70 1.98 47.99 14.15 45.28 5.10 56.80 4:19.67							
8381W	John	Sayre	USA	61	1	TAC	Indianapolis	18 Jun 85
	10.86W 7.41w 14.22 2.00 49.98 14.84W 46.08 5.30 67.68 4:37.07							
8375	Pavel	Tarnavetskiy	SU	61	3	WC	Roma	4 Sep 87
	11.01 7.43 15.32 2.07 49.22 14.86 47.66 4.90 58.60 4:23.96							
8366	Vadim	Podmaryov	SU	58	1		Tashkent	26 May 85
	11.09 7.56 15.28 2.08 50.00 14.89 48.58 4.60 67.46 4:32.31							
8366h	Simon	Poelman	NZ	63	1	NC	Christchurch	22 Mar 87
	10.6 7.34 15.11 2.06 49.4 14.1 46.66 4.95 56.94 4:27.2							
8364	Igor	Maryin	SU	65	2	NC	Kiev	31 Jul 88
	10.91 7.79 15.10 2.04 49.22 15.71 43.16 5.00 67.70 4:32.19							
	(30)							
8362	Thomas	Fahner	GDR	66	3		Götzis	19 Jun 88
	11.04 7.55w 13.01 1.93 47.94 14.54 46.66 4.60 68.40 4:27.77							
8356	Viktor	Gruzenkin	SU	51	5	NC	Kiev	22 Jun 84
	10.92 7.67 15.98 2.07 50.06 14.65 46.70 4.60 65.74 4:43.00							
8340	Tim	Bright	USA	60	1	NC	San Jose	24 Jun 87
	10.90 7.31 14.35 2.11 49.24 14.16 41.12 5.50 57.68 4:44.49							
8334	Rainer	Pottel	GDR	53	1	EP	Birmingham	30 Aug 81
	11.06 7.68 14.38 2.01 48.35 14.57 39.52 4.80 67.46 4:22.67							
8334	Stefan	Niklaus	SWZ	58	1	NC	Lausanne	3 Jul 83
	10.82 7.32 15.44 2.01 47.47 14.79 48.68 4.40 67.84 4:41.29							
8330	Mikhail	Medved	SU	64	3	NC	Kiev	31 Jul 88
	11.24 7.46 15.73 2.07 50.13 14.40 45.32 5.00 64.50 4:41.26							
8327W	William	Motti	FRA	64	1	EP-B	Arles	5 Jul 87
	10.98W 7.39 15.13 2.13 48.83 14.57w 47.66 4.40 61.82 4:30.39							
8326	Andreas	Rizzi	FRG	59	4		Filderstadt	5 Jun 83
	10.52 7.71 14.78 2.00 46.82 14.91 43.62 4.70 50.92 4:21.04							
8322	Mike	Ramos	USA	62	1		Los Angeles	21 May 86
	10.77 7.39 14.67 2.16 50.16 14.98 49.04 4.80 63.52 4:48.06							
8322	Andrey	Nazarov	SU	65	1		Sochi	17 May 87
	10.71 7.69 13.73 2.16 49.21 13.88 41.68 4.70 56.60 4:36.36							
	(40)							
8309h	Bill	Toomey	USA	39	1		Los Angeles	11 Dec 69
	10.3 7.76 14.38 1.93 47.1 14.3 46.49 4.27 65.74 4:39.4							
8304W	Tito	Steiner	ARG	52	1	NCAA	Baton Rouge	3 Jun 81
	11.19W 7.37 15.20 2.09 49.85 14.97 45.28 4.70 70.28 4:31.98							
8293	Gary	Kinder	USA	62	1	FOT	Indianapolis	21 Jul 88
	10.82 7.20 16.34 2.02 49.74 14.95 47.72 5.00 66.32 4:55.39							
8289	Veroslav	Valenta	CS	65	1		Praha	29 May 88
	11.07 7.47w 15.47 2.00 49.67 14.49 48.84 4.80 60.68 4:35.27							
8288	Valeriy	Kachanov	SU	54	2	NC	Moskva	21 Jun 80
	11.08 7.54 14.53 2.08 48.70 14.61 46.10 4.50 58.10 4:17.4							
8282	Aleksandr	Shablenko	SU	57	1	vGDR	Potsdam	1 Jun 80
	10.95 7.25 15.23 2.03 48.85 14.25 47.14 5.00 50.64 4:25.9							
8326	Andreas	Rizzi	FRG	59	4		Filderstadt	5 Jun 83
	10.95 7.25 15.23 2.03 48.85 14.25 47.14 5.00 50.64 4:25.9							
8267	Mark	Anderson	USA	58	1	MSR	Walnut	22 Apr 83
	11.11 7.03 14.86 2.10 49.21 15.77 42.50 4.70 76.42 4:21.75							
8266	Pedro F.	Da Silva	BRA	66	1	MSR	Walnut	23 Apr 87
	11.07 7.61 14.30 2.10 48.97 14.00 49.04 4.70 56.12 4:48.25							
8261	Steffen	Grummt	GDR	59	1		Halle	20 Jun 82
	10.99w 7.62 16.32 1.91 49.16 14.38w 48.76 4.40 63.56 4:24.68							
	(50)							

w wind-aided between 2.0 and 4.0 metres per second
W wind-aided in excess of 4 metres per second
Dates given are those of second day of competition, all pre-1986 marks achieved with old javelin

4 x 100 METRES RELAY

Mark	Name		Pos	Meet	Venue	Date
37.83	USA	(Graddy, R.Brown, C.Smith, Lewis)	1	OG	Los Angeles	11 Aug 84
37.86	USA	(E.King, Gault, C.Smith, Lewis)	1	WC	Helsinki	10 Aug 83
37.90	USA	(McRae, L.McNeill, Glance, Lewis)	1	WC	Roma	6 Sep 87
37.98	USA	(McRae, Heard, Glance, Lewis)	1	GWG	Moskva	9 Jul 86
38.02	SU	(Yevgenyev, Bryzgin, Muravyov, Krylov)	2	WC	Roma	6 Sep 87
38.03	USA	(Collins, Riddick, Wiley, S.Williams)	1	WP	Düsseldorf	3 Sep 77
38.10	USA	(Glance, Baptiste, C.Smith, Evans)	1	WP	Canberra	5 Oct 85
38.13	USA	(Lattany, Floyd, C.Smith, Lewis)	1	WK	Zürich	18 Aug 82
38.18	USA	(McRae, L.McNeill, Glance, Lewis)	1	ISTAF	Berlin	21 Aug 87
38.19	USA	(Black, R.Taylor, Tinker, Hart)	1	OG	München	10 Sep 72
38.19	SU	(Yevgenyev, Yushmanov, Muravyev, Bryzgin)	2	GWG	Moskva	9 Jul 86
38.19	SU	(Bryzgin, Krylov, Muravyov, Savin)	1	OG	Seoul	1 Oct 88
38.22	USA	(T.Wright, M.Miller, Cook, C.Smith)	1	vGDR	Karl-Marx-Stadt	9 Jul 82
38.24A	USA	(Greene, Pender, R.R.Smith, Hines)	1	OG	Ciudad México	20 Oct 68
38.24	USA	(Lattany, Floyd, C.Smith, Lewis)	1	ISTAF	Berlin	20 Aug 82
38.26	SU	(Muravyev, Sidorov, Aksinin, Prokofyev)	1	OG	Moskva	1 Aug 80
38.27	US South	(M.Miller, Lewis, C.Smith, Floyd)	1	USOF	Indianapolis	24 Jul 82
38.28	SU	(Shlyapnikov, Semenov, Yevgenyev, Muravyev)	1	EP	Moskva	17 Aug 85
38.28	USA	(Glance, Baptiste, C.Smith, Lewis)	1	vSU, JAP	Tokyo	21 Sep 85
38.28	UK	(Bunney, Regis, McFarlane, Christie)	2	OG	Seoul	1 Oct 88
38.29	GDR	(Schröder, Kübeck, Prenzler, Emmelmann)	2	vUSA	Karl-Marx-Stadt	9 Jul 82
38.29	SU	(Yevgenyev, Yushmanov, Muravyev, Bryzgin)	1	EC	Stuttgart	31 Aug 86
38.29	SU	(Yevgenyev, Bryzgin, Muravyov, Krylov)	1s1	WC	Roma	5 Sep 87
38.30A	US South	(Roberson, Glance, Collins, Lattany)	1	USOF	A.F Academy	30 Jul 79
38.30	GDR	(Schröder, Bringmann, Prenzler, Emmelmann)	1	OD	Berlin	8 Jun 83
38.31A	USA	(C.Edwards, L.Brown, Merrick, Collins)	1	PAG	Ciudad México	20 Oct 75
38.31	Americas	(D.Williams, Simon, R.da Silva, Johnson)	2	WP	Canberra	5 Oct 85
38.32	SU	(Yevgenyev, Fedoriv, Muravyev,				
38.33	USA	(Glance, J.Jones, Hampton, Riddick)	1	OG	Montreal	31 Jul 76
38.33	POL	(Zwolinski, Licznerski, Dunecki, Woronin)	2	OG	Moskva	1 Aug 80
	(30/5)					
38.37	ITA	(Tilli, Simionato, Pavoni, Mennea)	2	WC	Helsinki	10 Aug 83
38.39A	JAM	(Stewart, Fray, Forbes, L.Miller)	1s1	OG	Ciudad México	19 Oct 68
38.40A	CUB	(Ramirez, Morales, Montes, Figuerola)	2	OG	Ciudad México	20 Oct 68
38.40	FRA	(Marie-Rose, Sangouma, Quénéhervé, Morinière)	3	OG	Seoul	1 Oct 88
38.43A	CAN	(Johnson, Sharpe, D.Williams, S.Hinds)	1		Colorado Springs	19 Jul 82
	(10)					
38.54	FRG	(Heer, Haas, Klein, Schweisfurth)	1	R-W	Koblenz	28 Aug 88
38.59	NIG	(Adeyanju, Imoh, Adeniken, Ezinwa)	1		Bern	23 Aug 88
38.67	HUN	(Karaffa, Nagy, Tatár, Kovács)	1	BGP	Budapest	16 Jun 86
38.73A	IvC	(Ouré, Meité, Nogboum, Kablan)	2	WUG	Ciudad México	13 Sep 79
38.82	CS	(Matousek, Demec, Kynos, Bohman)	4	OG	München	10 Sep 72
38.90	JAP	(Aoto, Yamauchi, Kurihara, Takano)	5s1	OG	Seoul	1 Oct 88
38.97A	TRI	(Fabien, Short, Archer, Roberts)	3h1	OG	Ciudad México	19 Oct 68
38.99	BUL	(Pavlov, Ivanov, Karaniotov, Petrov)	5	OG	Moskva	1 Aug 80
39.02A	BRA	(de Castro, dos Santos, Pegado, Araujo)	1		Ciudad México	4 Sep 79
39.05	CHN	(Li Tao, Cai, Li Feng, Zheng Chen)	4s2	WC	Roma	5 Sep 87
	(20)					
39.13	GHA	(Akogyiram, Gariba, Mills, Tuffour)	3h2	OG	Seoul	30 Sep 88
39.19	SWZ	(Fähndrich, U.Gisler, Muster, Ziegler)	1		Bern	5 Aug 78
39.20A	SPA	(Gascon, Talavera, Rocando, Arques)	1h1	IbA	Ciudad México	24 Jul 88
39.20	QAT	(Suliman, Marzouk, Muftah, Mansour)	1	AsCh	Singapore	26 Jul 87
39.30	FIN	(RajamUaki, Vilen, Gustafsson, Juhola)	5s2	OG	München	9 Sep 72
39.31	AUS	(G.Lewis, D'Arcy, Ratcliffe, Haskell)	1	CG	Christchurch	2 Feb 74
39.43	KOR	(Sung, Shim, Kim, Chang)	7s1	OG	Seoul	1 Oct 88
39.45A	BAH	(Wisdom, Robinson, Nottage, Johnson)	4h1	OG	Ciudad México	19 Oct 68
39.47	KEN	(Nyangau, Ondiek, Kipkemboi, Wekesa)	6s2	OG	Seoul	1 Oct 88
39.53	VEN	(Herrera, Murad, Romero, Fusil)	6	OG	Tokyo	21 Oct 64
	(30)					
39.54A	CON	(Ntsana, Kanza, Nkounkou, Pauletto)	1s1	WUG	Ciudad México	12 Sep 79
39.54A	RSA	(Bosman, Oosthuizen, Nzimande, Rossouw)	1		Johannesburg	23 Apr 88
39.56	DOM	(Mendez, Suero, Reynoso, Nunez)	3	CAG	Santiago, Dom	3 Jul 86

4 x 400 METRES RELAY

Mark	Name	Nat Yr	Pos	Meet	Venue	Date
2:56.16A	USA	(Matthews 45.0, Freeman 43.2, James 43.9, Evans 44.1)	1	OG	Ciudad México	20 Oct 68
2:56.16	USA	(Everett 44.0, S.Lewis 43.6, Robinzine 44.7, Reynolds 43.9)	1	OG	Seoul	1 Oct 88
2:57.29	USA	(Everett 45.1, Haley 44.0, McKay 44.20, Reynolds 44.00)	1	WC	Roma	6 Sep 87
2:57.91	USA	(Nix 45.59, Armstead 43.97, Babers 43.75, McKay 44.60)	1	OG	Los Angeles	11 Aug 84
2:58.65	USA	(Frazier 45.3, B.Brown 44.62, Newhouse 43.8, Parks 45.00)	1	OG	Montreal	31 Jul 76
2:58.86	UK	(Redmond 45.2, Akabusi 44.5, Black 44.81, Brown 44.34)	2	WC	Roma	6 Sep 87
2:59.06	USA	(Everett 45.3, Franks 44.6, Pierre 44.7, McKay 44.5)	1s2	WC	Roma	5 Sep 87
2:59.12	USA	(McCoy 45.20, Wiley 44.41, W.Smith 44.58, Darden 44.93)	1	WP	Roma	6 Sep 81
2:59.13	UK	(Akabusi 45.87, Cook 44.74, T.Bennett 44.17, P.Brown 44.35)	2	OG	Los Angeles	11 Aug 84
2:59.16	Cuba	(Peñalver 45.2, Pavó 45.2, Martínez 44.90, Hernández 43.88)	3	WC	Roma	6 Sep 87
2:59.32	Nigeria	(Uti 45.34, Ugbisie 44.48, Peters 44.94, Egbunike 44.56)	3	OG	Los Angeles	11 Aug 84
2:59:52	USA	(Frazier 45.5, B.Brown 45.3, Newhouse 43.63, Parks 45.1)	1h1	OG	Montreal	30 Jul 76
2:59.54	USA	(Rowe 45.8, Robinzine 45.0, Pierre 43.67, Haley 45.04)	1	PAG	Indianapolis	16 Aug 87
2:59.6m	USA	(Frey 46.3, Evans 44.5, T.Smith 43.8, T.Lewis 45.0)	1		Los Angeles	24 Jul 66
2:59.64A	Kenya	(Asati 44.6, Nyamau 45.5, Bon 45.1, Rudisha 44.4)	2	OG	Ciudad México	20 Oct 68
2:59.70	Australia	(Frayne 45.38, Clark 43.86, Minihan 45.07, Mitchell 45.39)	4	OG	Los Angeles	11 Aug 84
2:59.71A	Cuba	(Martínez, Valentín, Stevens, Hernández)	1	IbAmC	Ciudad México	24 Jul 88
2:59.72	Cuba	(Penalver 45.6, Pavo 45.3, Martínez 44.1, Hernández 44.7)	2	PAG	Indianapolis	16 Aug 87
2:59.83	Kenya	(Asati 45.3, Nyamau 45.8, Ouko 45.2, Sang 43.5)	1	OG	München	10 Sep 72
2:59.84	UK	(Redmond 45.4, Akabusi 45.4, Whittle 45.2, Black 43.9)	1	EC	Stuttgart	31 Aug 86
2:59.84	US South	(McCoy 46.0, Robinzine 44.7, Pierre 44.5, Haley 44.7)	1	USOF	Durham	26 Jul 87
2:59.86	GDR	(Möller 45.8, Schersing 44.8, Carlowitz 45.3, Schönlebe 44.1)	1	vSU	Erfurt	23 Jun 85
2:59.86	US North	(Franks 45.5, Simon 44.7, Lowery 44.8, Nix 44.9)	2	USOF	Durham	26 Jul 87
2:59.91A	US South	(L.Brown, Brooks, Rolle, McCoy)	1	USOF	A.F. Academy	3 Jul 83
2:59.91	UCLA (USA)	(S.Lewis 45.0, Young 44.4, Everett 45.3, Thomas 45.2)	1	NCAA	Eugene	4 Jun 88
2:59.96	FRG	(Dobeleit 45.7, Henrich 44.3, Tt 45.12, Schmid 44.93)	4	WC	Roma	6 Sep 87
3:00.04	US North	(Franks 45.0, Armstead 45.2, Dixson 44.8, Harris 45.1)	1	USOF	Baton Rouge	28 Jul 85
3:00.07	GDR	(Lieske, Schersing, Carlowitz, Schönlebe)	1		Erfurt	3 Jun 84
3:00.11	USA	(W.Smith, Armstead, Babers, McCoy)	1		Berkeley	14 Jul 84
3:00.16	USSR	(Lovachov, Lomtyev, Kurochkin, Markin 43.9)	1	Drz	Moskva	18 Aug 84
(30/9)						
3:00.58A	Poland	(Gredzinski 46.8, Balachowski 44.7, Werner 44.5, Badenski 44.5)	4	OG	Ciudad México	20 Oct 68
3:00.65	France	(Bertould 46.2, Velasquez 45.0, Kerbiriou 45.2, Carette 44.3)	3	OG	München	10 Sep 72
3:01.08	Jamaica	(Senior, Morris, Graham, Cameron)	3s2	WC	Roma	5 Sep 87
3:01.12	Finland	(Lönnqvist 46.7, Salin 45.1, Karttunen 44.8, Kukkoaho 44.5)	6	OG	München	10 Sep 72
3:01.37	Italy	(Bongiorni 46.2, Zuliani 45.0, Petrella 45.3, Ribaud 44.9)	4	EC	Stuttgart	31 Aug 86
3:01.59	Yugoslavia	(Karaulic, Popovic, Brankovic, Macev)	5s2	OG	Seoul	30 Sep 88

Mark	Name	Nat	Yr	Pos	Meet	Venue	Date
3:01.60	Barbados (Louis 46.67, Peltier 44.97, Edwards 45.04, Forde 44.92)			6	OG	Los Angeles	11 Aug 84
3:01.7	Trinidad & Tobago (Skinner 46.0, Bernard 45.3, Roberts 45.4, Mottley 45.0)			3	OG	Tokyo	21 Oct 64
3:02.09	Uganda (Govile 46.72, Kyeswa 44.60, Rwamu 46.40, Okot 44.37)			7	OG	Los Angeles	11 Aug 84
3:02.33	Japan (Konakatoni, Yamauchi, Kawasumi, Takano)			1	AsG	Seoul	5 Oct 86
3:02.57	Sweden (Carlgren 46.0, Faager 45.5, Öhlman 45.3, Rönner 45.8)			7	OG	München	10 Sep 72
	(20)						
3:02.64	Canada (Seale 47.0, Domansky 45.3, Hope 45.5, Saunders 44.8)			4	OG	Montreal	31 Jul 76
3:02.79	Brazil (E.da Silva, Barbosa, Guimarães, Gerson Souza)			2	PAG	Caracas	28 Aug 83
3:02.82	Czechoslovakia (Brecka 46.9, Malovec 44.9, Zahorak 45.4, Sajdok 45.6)			5	EC	Athinai	11 Sep 82
3:03.18A	Netherlands (Pont, Gijsbers, Klarenbeek, Schulting)			2	WUG	Ciudad México	13 Sep 79
3:03.36	South Africa (Reinach, Myburgh, Kotze, J.Oosthuizen)			1		Stellenbosch	25 Apr 83
3:03.50	Ivory Coast (Kablam 46.5, Nogboum 46.3, Melejde 46.3, Tiacoh 44.4)			3h3	OG	Los Angeles	10 Aug 84
3:03.68	Belgium (DeLeeuw, Roelandt, Van den Berghe, Brijdenbach)			2	EP/s	Lille	5 Jul 81
3:04.04	Spain (Prado, Sanchez, Heras, Alonso)			1	EP-B	Budapest	11 Aug 85
3:04.29	Switzerland (Strittmatter, Haas, Vost, R.Gisler 45.56)			4	EC	Praha	3 Sep 78
3:04.56A	Venezuela (Bodington, Phillips, Aguiar, Malave)			2	IbAmC	Ciudad México	24 Jul 88
	(30)						

20 KILOMETRES WALK (Track)

Mark	First name	Name	Nat	Yr	Pos	Meet	Venue	Date
1:18:40.0	Ernesto	Canto	MEX	59	1	SGP	Fana	5 May 84
1:19:22.5	Aleksey	Pershin	SU	62	1	SGP	Fana	7 May 88
1:20:06.8	Daniel	Bautista	MEX	52	1		Montreal	17 Oct 79
1:20:36.7	Erling	Andersen	NOR	60	2	SGP	Fana	5 May 84
1:20:37.8	Valdas	Kazlauskas	SU	58	1		Moskva	16 Sep 83
1:20:41.6	Yevgeniy	Misyulya	SU	64	1	SGP	Fana	26 Apr 86
1:20:47.0		Bautista			1		Formia	13 Apr 80
1:20:51.0	David	Smith	AUS	55	1		Melbourne	11 Feb 87
1:20:54.9	Ronald	Weigel	GDR	59	1		East Berlin	27 Mar 83
1:20:57.8		Andersen			1		Trois-Rivières	24 Sep 80
	(10/8)							
1:20:58.6	Domingo	Colin	MEX	52	1	SGP	Fana	26 May 79
1:21:00.0	Aleksandr	Boyarshinov	SU	63	1		Bryansk	14 Aug 86
1:21:21.3	Roland	Wieser	GDR	56	1		Leipzig	23 Jun 79
1:21:23.5	Pavol	Blazek	CS	58	3	SGP	Fana	5 May 84
1:21:24.5	Felix	Gómez	MEX	55	2		Montreal	17 Oct 79
1:21:30.0	Pyotr	Pochenchuk	SU	54	1		Leningrad	16 Aug 80
1:21:39.2	Jozef	Pribilinec	CS	60	2	SGP	Fana	3 May 80
1:21:47.0	Nikolay	Vinnichenko	SU	58	1		Donetsk	6 Sep 80
1:21:47.8	Maurizio	Damilano	ITA	57	2		Formia	13 Apr 80
1:21:48.8	Raul	González	MEX	52	4	SGP	Fana	5 May 84
1:21:56.0	Yevgeniy	Yevsyukov	SU	50	2		Donetsk	6 Sep 80

20 KILOMETRES WALK (Road)

Mark	First name	Name	Nat	Yr	Pos	Meet	Venue	Date
1:19:08	Mikhail	Shchennikov	SU	67	1	NC	Kiev	30 Jul 88
1:19:12	Axel	Noack	GDR	61	1	vSU	Karl-Marx-Stadt	21 Jun 87
1:19:16	Yevgeniy	Misyulya	SU	64	2	NC	Kiev	30 Jul 88
1:19:22	David	Smith	AUS	55	1		Hobart	19 Jul 87
1:19:24	Carlos	Mercenario	MEX	67	1	LT	New York	3 May 87
1:19:30	Jozef	Pribilinec	CS	60	1	LT	Bergen	24 Sep 83
1:19:32	Viktor	Mostovik	SU	63	2	LT	New York	3 May 87
1:19:35	Domingo	Colin	MEX	52	1		Cherkassy	27 Apr 80
1:19:37	Ernesto	Canto	MEX	59	1		Xalapa	5 Apr 87
1:19:39	Frants	Kostyukevich	SU	63	1	Znam	Leningrad	11 Jun 88
1:19:41		Canto			2	LT	Bergen	24 Sep 83
1:19:43	Anatoliy	Solomin	SU	52	3	LT	Bergen	24 Sep 83
1:19:47		Mostovik			3	NC	Kiev	30 Jul 88
1:19:49		Pribilinec			1		Barcelona	17 Apr 83
1:19:50		Mostovik			2	vGDR	Karl-Marx-Stadt	21 Jun 87
1:19:52		Smith			1		Jiading	16 Mar 85
1:19:52	Reima	Salonen	FIN	55	1	IM	Pihtipudas	21 Jun 86

Mark	Name		Nat	Yr	Pos	Meet	Venue	Date
1:19:53	Yevgeniy	Yevsyukov	SU	50	2		Cherkassy	27 Apr 80
1:19:56	Ronald	Weigel	GDR	59	1		East Berlin	27 Jul 84
1:19:57		Mostovik			1		Sochi	22 Feb 87
1:19:57		Pribilinec			1	OG	Seoul	23 Sep 88
1:20:00	José	Marin	SPA	50	2		Barcelona	17 Apr 83
1:20:00		Canto			3		Cherkassy	27 Apr 80
1:20:00		Weigel			2	OG	Seoul	23 Sep 88
1:20:02		Salonen			1	GP	Russe	20 Apr 86
1:20:04	Anatoliy	Gorshkov	SU	53	3	LT	New York	3 May 87
1:20:06	Sergey	Protsyshin	SU	59	4	NC	Kiev	30 Jul 88
1:20:08	Valdas	Kazlauskas	SU	58	5	NC	Kiev	30 Jul 88
1:20:09	Maurizio	Damilano	ITA	57	1		Piacenza	13 May 84
1:20:10		Damilano			4	LT	Bergen	24 Sep 83
1:20:10	Igor	Lyubomirov	SU	61	2	Znam	Leningrad	11 Jun 88
	(31/20)							
1:20:14	Georgiy	Korneyev	SU	61	6	NC	Kiev	30 Jul 88
1:20:17	Pavol	Blazek	CS	58	1		L'Hospitalet	24 Apr 88
1:20:18	Alessandro	Pezzatini	ITA	57	2		Piacenza	13 May 84
1:20:19	Querubin	Moreno	COL	59	4	LT	New York	3 May 87
1:20:19	Vyacheslav	Smirnov	SU	57	3	Znam	Leningrad	11 Jun 88
1:20:31	Ralf	Kowalsky	GDR	62	1	IM	Potsdam	24 May 86
1:20:40	Marcelino	Colin	MEX	61	6	LT	Bergen	24 Sep 83
1:20:40	Aleksey	Pershin	SU	62	1		Sochi	21 Feb 88
1:20:43	Ljubomir	Ivanov	BUL	60	1	NM	Sofia	26 Jun 88
1:20:43	Roman	Mrazek	CS	62	5	OG	Seoul	23 Sep 88
	(30)							
1:20:50	Nikolay	Polozov	SU	51	5		Cherkassy	27 Apr 80
1:20:51	Hartwig	Gauder	GDR	54	3	JLC	Värnamo	29 May 87
1:20:53	Aivars	Rumbenieks	SU	51	6		Cherkassy	27 Apr 80
1:20:53	Artur	Shmak	SU	63	8	NC	Kiev	30 Jul 88
1:20:58	Valeriy	Borisov	SU	66	6	Znam	Leningrad	11 Jun 88
1:21:00	Daniel	Bautista	MEX	52	1		Xalapa	30 Mar 80
1:21:10	Pyotr	Kakhnovich	SU	61	1		Novopolotsk	25 Apr 87
1:21:11	Carlo	Mattioli	ITA	54	7	LT	Bergen	24 Sep 83
1:21:11	Oleg	Plastun	SU	63	7	Znam	Leningrad	11 Jun 88
1:21:13	Guillaume	Leblanc	CAN	62	1	PAC	St.Leonard	5 Oct 86
	(40)							
1:21:16	Andrey	Perlov	SU	61	7		Cherkassy	27 Apr 80
1:21:18	Nikolay	Matveyev	SU	55	1		Ruse	17 Apr 83
1:21:18	Giovanni	Di Benedictis	ITA	68	9	OG	Seoul	23 Sep 88
1:21:19	Felix	Gómez	MEX	55	2		Vretstorp	9 Jun 79
1:21:19	Simon	Baker	AUS	58	1	NC	Canberra	27 Aug 88
1:21:21	Aleksandr	Potashov	SU	62	8		Cherkassy	27 Apr 80
1:21:28	Vyacheslav	Ivanenko	SU	61	1		Novopolotsk	12 Jul 87
1:21:33	Nikolay	Vinnichenko	SU	58	4		Sochi	21 Feb 88
1:21:34	Sandor	Urbanik	HUN	64	1		Szeged	10 Jul 88
1:21:35	Pyotr	Pochenchuk	SU	54	2		Novopolotsk	25 Apr 87
	(50)							

50 KILOMETRES WALK (Track)

Mark	Name		Nat	Yr	Pos	Meet	Venue	Date
3:41:38.4	Raúl	González	MEX	52	1	SGP	Fana	25 May 79
3:43:42.4		González			1	SGP	Fana	2 May 80
3:45:38.0		González			1	SGP	Fana	14 May 82
3:46:11.0	Nikolay	Udovenko	SU	56	1		Uzhgorod	3 Oct 80
3:48:59.0	Vadim	Rezayev	SU	50	2	SGP	Fana	2 May 80
3:50:39.9	Jaen-Marie	Neff	FRA	61	1		Caen	17 Apr 88

50 KILOMETRES WALK (Road)

Mark	Name		Nat	Yr	Pos	Meet	Venue	Date
3:38:17	Ronald	Weigel	GDR	59	1	IM	Potsdam	25 May 86
3:38:29	Vyacheslav	Ivanenko	SU	61	1	OG	Seoul	30 Sep 88
3:38:31		Weigel			1		East Berlin	20 Jul 84
3:38:56		Weigel			2	OG	Seoul	30 Sep 88
3:39:45	Hartwig	Gauder	GDR	54	3	OG	Seoul	30 Sep 88
3:39:47	Andrey	Perlov	SU	61	1		Leningrad	3 Aug 85
3:40:07		Perlov			1		Kharkov	5 Sep 87

Mark	Name		Nat	Yr	Pos	Meet	Venue	Date
3:40:46	José	Marin	SPA	50	1		Valencia	13 Mar 83
3:40:53		Gauder			1	WC	Roma	5 Sep 87
3:40:55		Gauder			1	EC	Stuttgart	31 Aug 86
3:41:00	Aleksandr	Potashov	SU	62	4	OG	Seoul	30 Sep 88
3:41:20	Raul	González	MEX	52	1		Podebrady	11 Jun 78
3:41:24		Gauder			2		East Berlin	20 Jul 84
3:41:30		Weigel			2	WC	Roma	5 Sep 87
3:41:31		Weigel			1		Naumberg	1 May 83
3:41:51	Venyamin	Nikolayev	SU	58	2		Leningrad	3 Aug 85
3:41:54		Ivanenko			2	EC	Stuttgart	31 Aug 86
3:42:04	Yevgeniy	Yevsyukov	SU	50	3		Leningrad	3 Aug 85
3:42:20	Pavel	Szikora (10)	CS	52	1		Dudince	4 Apr 87
3:42:26		Weigel			1	LT	New York	2 May 87
3:42:33		Weigel			1		Naumburg	1 May 88
3:42:36	Reima	Salonen	FIN	55	1	NC	Vantaa	24 May 86
3:42:37	Valeriy	Suntsov	SU	55	4		Leningrad	3 Aug 85
3:42:38		Suntsov			3	EC	Stuttgart	31 Aug 86
3:42:52		Gauder			2	LT	New York	2 May 87
3:43:03		Marin			5	OG	Seoul	30 Sep 88
3:43:06		Perlov			1		Moskva	17 Aug 84
3:43:08		Weigel			1	WC	Helsinki	12 Aug 83
3:43:14	Dietmar	Meisch	GDR	59	3	LT	New York	2 May 87
3:43:23		Gauder			2		Naumberg	1 May 83
	(30/13)							
3:43:36	Martín	Bermúdez	MEX	58	1	LT	Eschborn	30 Sep 79
3:43:59	Enrique	Vera-Ybánez	MEX	54	2	LT	Eschborn	30 Sep 79
3:44:07	Simon	Baker	AUS	58	6	OG	Seoul	30 Sep 88
3:44:08	Viktor	Dorovskikh	SU	50	5		Leningrad	3 Aug 85
3:44:24	Erling	Andersen	NOR	60	2	WCp-s	Borås	15 Jun 85
3:44:27	Raffaello	Ducceschi	ITA	62	1	NC	Barletta	17 Apr 88
3:44:33	Jorge	Llopart	SPA	52	1		Reus	26 Aug 79
	(20)							
3:44:49	Bo	Gustafsson	SWE	54	7	OG	Seoul	30 Sep 88
3:45:51	Uwe	Dünkel	GDR	60	1		East Berlin	18 Jul 81
3:45:51	Sergey	Protsyshin	SU	59	4	EC	Stuttgart	31 Aug 86
3:46:28	Valeriy	Yarets	SU	56	6		Leningrad	3 Aug 85
3:46:30	Vitaliy	Popovich	SU	57	3	NC	Vilnius	29 May 88
3:46:34	Willi	Sawall	AUS	41	1		Adelaide	6 Apr 80
3:46:55	Vyächeslav	Fursov	SU	54	5	LT	Eschborn	30 Sep 79
3:46:57	Vladimir	Rezayev	SU	50	2		Moskva	27 Jul 79
3:47:13	Pyotr	Gaus	SU	52	3		Moskva	3 Jul 82
3:47:14	Giovanni	Perricelli	ITA	67	11	OG	Seoul	30 Sep 88
	(30)							
3:47:16	Sergey	Yung	SU	55	4		Moskva	3 Jul 82
3:47:18	Domingo	Colin	MEX	52	1		Valencia	20 May 79
3:47:20	Nikolay	Frolov	SU	56	7		Leningrad	3 Aug 85
3:47:25	Aleksandr	Starchenko	SU	51	2		Sochi	17 Apr 83
3:47:30	Bernd	Gummelt	GDR	63	2		Berlin	14 May 88
3:47:31	Pavol	Blazek	CS	58	12	OG	Seoul	30 Sep 88
3:47:48	Marcel	Jobin	CAN	42	2		Québec	20 Jun 81
3:47:59	Viktor	Shchernov	SU	52	1		Cherkassy	8 Oct 82
3:48:08	Alessandro	Bellucci	ITA	55	3	NC	Barletta	17 Apr 88
3:48:15	François	Lapointe	CAN	61	14	OG	Seoul	30 Sep 88
	(40)							
3:48:19	Pyotr	Melnyk	SU	51	4		Moskva	27 Jul 79
3:49:00	Viliulfo	Andablo	MEX	65	—			30 Jul 88
3:49:06	Felix	Gómez	MEX	55	2		Mixhuca	18 Apr 82
3:49:08	Vladimir	Nefyodov	SU	55	1		Kiev	29 Aug 83
3:49:25	Nikolay	Udovenko	SU	56	3		Mixhuca	18 Apr 82
3:49:52	Ivan	Tikhonov	SU	50	3		Sochi	17 Apr 83
3:49:58	Viktor	Grodovchuk	SU	52	5		Moskva	3 Jul 82
3:49:58	Artur	Shumak	SU	63	4		Zhitomir	30 Sep 84
3:50:15	Grigoriy	Korneyev	SU	61	7	NC	Vilnius	29 May 88
3:50:24	Yevgeniy	Ivchenko	SU	38	5		Moskva	27 Jul 79
3:50:24	Leonid	Sivakov	SU	56	9		Leningrad	3 Aug 85
	(51)							

MEN'S WORLD LISTS 1988

100 METRES

Mark	Wind	Name		Nat	Born	Pos	Meet	Venue	Date
9.92	1.1	Carl	Lewis	USA	1.7.61	1	OG	Seoul	24 Sep
9.93	1.1		Lewis			1rA	WK	Zürich	17 Aug
9.96	1.9		Lewis			1h4	FOT	Indianapolis	15 Jul
9.96	0.4		Lewis			1q1	FOT	Indianapolis	15 Jul
9.97	1.1	Calvin	Smith	USA	8.1.61	2rA	WK	Zürich	17 Aug
9.97	0.6		Lewis			1s1	OG	Seoul	24 Sep
9.97	1.1	Linford	Christie	UK	2.4.60	2	OG	Seoul	24 Sep
9.98A	1.7	Ben	Johnson	CAN	30.12.61	1rA		Sestriere	11 Aug
9.99	1.1		Lewis			1q5	OG	Seoul	23 Sep
9.99	1.1		Smith			3	OG	Seoul	24 Sep
10.00A	1.6	Robson C.	da Silva	BRA	4.9.64	1h3	IbAmC	Ciudad México	22 Jul
10.00	1.1		Johnson			3rA	WK	Zürich	17 Aug
10.03	0.4	Joe	DeLoach	USA	5.6.67	1	NCAA	Eugene	4 Jun
10.03	0.9	Dennis	Mitchell	USA	20.2.66	1rA	Athl	Lausanne	24 Jun
10.04	0.5	Emmit	King	USA	24.3.59	1	TAC	Tampa	17 Jun
10.04	1.1	Chidi	Imoh	NIG	27.8.63	4rA	WK	Zürich	17 Aug
10.04	-0.6		Lewis			1	VD	Bruxelles	19 Aug
10.04	1.1		Mitchell			4	OG	Seoul	24 Sep
10.05	1.4		Lewis			1		Houston	4 May
10.06A	2.0	Johan	Rossouw	RSA	20.10.65	1		Johannesburg	23 Apr
10.07	0.5	Brian	Cooper	USA	21.8.65	2	TAC	Tampa	17 Jun
10.07	1.4		Smith			1	PTS	Bratislava	9 Jun
10.07	1.1		Christie			5rA	WK	Zürich	17 Aug
10.08	0.0	Andre	Cason	USA	13.1.69	1	TAC-Jr	Tallahassee	24 Jun
10.08		Ray	Stewart	JAM	18.3.65	1	NC	Kingston	15 Jul
10.08A	1.1		daSilva			1	IbAmC	Ciudad México	22 Jul
10.08	0.9		Stewart			1		Linz	15 Aug
10.08	1.1		Mitchell			6rA	WK	Zürich	17 Aug
10.09	0.5	Lee	McNeill	USA	2.12.64	3	TAC	Tampa	17 Jun
10.09	1.3		Imoh			1		Malmö	8 Aug
10.09	1.1		Stewart			7rA	WK	Zürich	17 Aug
10.09	0.4		Lewis			1		Tokyo	8 Oct
		(32 performances by14 athletes)							
10.11A	2.0	Tshakile	Nzimande	RSA	19.11.61	2		Johannesburg	23 Apr
10.11	0.5	Lee	McRae	USA	23.1.66	4	TAC	Tampa	17 Jun
10.11	0.4	Albert	Robinson	USA	28.11.64	2q1	FOT	Indianapolis	15 Jul
10.11	1.1	Desai	Williams	CAN	12.6.59	7	OG	Seoul	24 Sep
10.12	0.9	Mike	Marsh	USA	4.8.67	1		LosAngeles	14 May
10.12A	0.7	Arnaldo	Oliveira	BRA	26.3.64	1h1	IbAmC	Ciudad México	22 Jul
		(20)							
10.12A	1.1	Leandro	Peñalver	CUB	23.5.61	2	IbAmC	Ciudad México	22 Jul
10.13	2.0	Vladimir	Krylov	SU	26.2.64	1rA		Sochi	31 May
10.13A	1.6	Andrés	Simon	CUB	15.9.61	2h3	IbAmC	Ciudad México	22 Jul
10.14		Victor	Edet	NIG	24.2.66	1h		Waco	22 Apr
10.14		Andrew	Smith	JAM	29.1.64	2		Kingston	7 May
10.14	2.0	Sven	Matthes	GDR	23.8.69	1		Berlin	13 Sep
10.15	0.0	Lorenzo	Daniel	USA	23.3.66	2h2	SEC	Auburn	14 May
10.15	2.0	Nikolay	Yushmanov	SU	18.12.61	2rA		Sochi	31 May
10.15	-1.8	Vitaliy	Savin	SU	23.1.66	1	Znam	Leningrad	12 Jun
10.15	0.9	Andreas	Berger	AUT	9.6.61	3		Linz	15 Aug
		(30)							
10.17	0.9	Mark	Witherspoon	USA	3.9.63	2rA	MSR	Walnut	24 Apr
10.17	1.5	Daron	Council	USA	26.12.64	2s2	TAC	Tampa	17 Jun
10.20		Jason	Leach	USA	11.3.66	1		Austin	26 Mar
10.20A	2.0	Eugene	van Niekerk	RSA	26.8.65	3		Johannesburg	23 Apr
10.20	0.5	Greg	Barnes	USA	10.8.65	6	TAC	Tampa	17 Jun
10.20		Ronnell	Barclay	TRI	25.10.66	1	NC	Port of Spain	10 Jul
10.20	0.5	Harvey	Glance	USA	28.3.57	1rB	WK	Zürich	17 Aug
10.20		Viktor	Bryzgin	SU	22.8.62	1rB		Vilnius	27 Aug
10.21	0.2	Steffen	Bringmann	GDR	11.3.64	2	NC	Rostock	25 Jun
10.21	1.3	Marian	Woronin	POL	13.8.56	1		Lublin	6 Aug
		(40)							

Mark		Name		Nat	Born	Pos	Meet	Venue	Date
10.21	0.3	John	Myles-Mills	GHA	19.4.66	1q6	OG	Seoul	23 Sep
10.22	-0.9	James	Butler	USA	21.6.60	1	Barr	Habana	5 Mar
10.22	1.7	Derrick	Florence	USA	19.6.68	2h2	NCAA	Eugene	2 Jun
10.22	1.9	Greg	Sholars	USA	8.2.66	3h4	FOT	Indianapolis	15 Jul
10.22	1.6	Valentin	Atanasov	BUL	7.5.61	1	NC	Sofia	2 Sep
10.23	0.9	Henry	Thomas	USA	10.7.67	2		LosAngeles	14 May
10.23	2.0	Andrey	Fedoriv	SU	11.8.63	3rA		Sochi	31 May
10.23	0.5	Stanley	Floyd	USA	23.6.61	2rB	WK	Zürich	17 Aug
10.24A	0.7	Enrique	Talavera	SPA	15.6.67	2h1	IbAmC	Ciudad México	22 Jul
10.25		John	Drummond	USA	9.9.68	1h1	JUCO	Odessa	19 May
		(40)							
10.25		Garfield	Campbell	JAM	1.11.67	1	JUCO	Odessa	20 May
10.25	1.7	Ahmed	deKom	HOL	15.2.59	1h3	PTS	Bratislava	9 Jun
10.25	1.9	Roscoe	Tatum	USA	13.2.66	5s1	TAC	Tampa	17 Jun
10.25	1.4	Sergey	Deminov	SU	.64	1		Bryansk	11 Jul
10.25A	1.3	Bruno	Marie-Rose	FRA	20.5.65	1		Font-Romeu	20 Jul
10.25A	0.7	Carlos	Moreno	CHL	28.10.67	3h1	IbAmC	Ciudad México	22 Jul
10.25	1.5	Charles-Louis	Seck	SEN	11.5.65	1		La Chaux De Fonds	21 Aug
10.25	1.9	Marty	Krulee	USA	4.11.56	1		Lohja	28 Aug
10.26		Tony	Jones	USA	30.12.65	2		Austin	26 Mar
10.26	0.6	Deion	Sanders	USA	9.8.67	1		Tallahassee	23 Apr
		(50)							
10.26	1.5	Norm	McGee	USA	23.3.66	3s2	TAC	Tampa	17 Jun
10.26	0.2	Frank	Emmelmann	GDR	15.9.61	3	NC	Rostock	25 Jun
10.26		Peter	Ifeduba	NIG	.69	1s2	OT/NC	Bauchi	1 Jul
10.26	-0.3	Ron	Brown	USA	31.3.61	5q4	FOT	Indianapolis	15 Jul
10.26	1.0	Attila	Kovács	HUN	2.9.60	1		Budapest	3 Sep
10.27		Clive	Wright	JAM	18.11.65	2		Kingston	16 Apr
10.27	0.0	Walter	Cranford	USA	16.4.67	1		Arcata, Cal.	7 May
10.27		Robert	Ligans	USA	27.6.68	1s1	JUCO	Odessa	20 May
10.27A	1.1	José	Arques	SPA	16.5.60	4	IbAmC	Ciudad México	22 Jul
10.27	1.3	Andrey	Razin	SU	10.5.62	1	NC	Tallinn	4 Jul
		(60)							
10.27	1.4	Ezio	Madonia	ITA	7.8.66	3		Cagliari	3 Sep
10.28	-1.5	Atlee	Mahorn	CAN	27.10.65	2		Westwood	22 May
10.28	1.7	Walker	Watkins	USA	29.9.67	3h2	NCAA	Eugene	2 Jun
10.28		Ricardo	Chacón	CUB	30.4.63	1		Puerto Ordaz	4 Jul
10.28	1.4	Shinji	Aoto	JAP	7.5.66	1		Tokyo	11 Sep
10.29		Kermit	Ward	USA	.68	2s1	JUCO	Odessa	20 May
10.29		Woody	Holman	USA	2.5.68	2	JUCO	Odessa	20 May
10.29		Aleksey	Graudyn	SU	28.4.68	1		Moskva	4 Jun
10.29	1.3	Vladimir	Muravyov	SU	30.9.59	4	NC	Tallinn	4 Jul
10.29	0.5	Olapade	Adeniken	NIG	19.8.69	1		Bern	23 Aug
		(70)							
10.30	0.1	Robert	Hackett	USA	3.8.64	1		Rehlingen	23 May
10.30	0.2	Stefano	Tilli	ITA	22.8.62	2		Formia	19 Jun
10.30		Iziaq	Adeyanju	NIG	24.2.59	1h1	OT/NC	Bauchi	30 Jun
10.31	0.9	William	Jackson	USA	2.2.69	1h1		Winter Park	28 May
10.31	0.4	Leroy	Burrell	USA	21.2.67	5	NCAA	Eugene	4 Jun
10.31		Nivaldo	Torres	CUB	7.12.63	1		Habana	11 Jun
10.31	1.9	Dmitriy	Bartenyev	SU	8.3.69	1	NC-j	Bryansk	6 Jul
10.31	1.3	John	Regis	UK	13.10.66	2	AAA	Birmingham	5 Aug
10.31		Ronald	Desruelles	BEL	14.2.55	1		Hasselt	27 Aug
10.31	0.8	Emmanuel	Tuffour	GHA	2.12.66	1h4	OG	Seoul	23 Sep
		(80)							
10.32		Calvin	Long	USA	2.7.66	1		Gainesville	16 Apr
10.32A		Frankie	Fredericks	RSA	2.10.67	1		Provo	23 Apr
10.32	0.1	Danny	Peebles	USA	30.5.66	2		Knoxville	21 May
10.32		John	Mair	JAM	20.11.63	1		Holmdel	25 Jun
10.32	1.4	Rafis	Nigmatulin	SU	.64	2		Bryansk	11 Jul
10.32	-0.3	Max	Morinière	FRA	16.2.64	1	NC	Tours	13 Aug
10.32	-0.6	Jiri	Valik	CS	26.7.66	1		Praha	6 Sep
10.32	0.3	Afdiharto	Mardi	INA	19.1.68	2q6	OG	Seoul	23 Sep
10.33		Tim	Williams	USA	27 .5.62	1		San Diego	26 Mar
10.33	0.0	Boris	Goins	USA	7.4.67	3h2	SEC	Auburn	14 May
		(90)							

Mark	Wind	Name		Nat	Born	Pos	Meet	Venue	Date
10.33		Derwin	Hall	USA	27.7.69	1h3	JUCO	Odessa	19 May
10.33	0.1	Manley	Waller	USA	21.7.64	2		Tallahassee	28 May
10.33	-0.1	Sergey	Klenov	SU	11.6.67	1rB		Sochi	31 May
10.33	1.2	Mel	Lattany	USA	10.8.59	1		Ljubljana	20 Jun
10.33	1.9	Fabian	Whymns	BAH	11.6.61	3		Helsinki	28 Aug
10.33	1.0	István	Tatár	HUN	24.3.58	2		Budapest	3 Sep
10.33	0.0	Talal	Mansour	QAT	.64	1		Seoul	19 Sep
10.33	0.4	Juan	Nunez	DOM	19.11.59	2q3	OG	Seoul	23 Sep
10.33	1.4	PierFrancesco	Pavoni	ITA	21.2.63	4q5	OG	Seoul	23 Sep

Mark	Wind	Name	Nat	Born	Date
10.34	1.7	Augustine Olobia	NIG	67	26 Mar
		(100)			
10.34		Tarrell Carpenter	USA	67	1 Apr
10.34		Harlan Davis	USA	67	9 Apr
10.34	0.6	Sammie Smith	USA	67	23 Apr
10.34		Art Caswell	USA		19 May
10.34	-0.1	Aleksey Knoroz	SU	63	31 May
10.34	0.8	Sergey Kudryavtsev	SU	66	18 Jun
10.34	0	Wallace Spearmon	USA	62	15 Jul
10.34	1.3	Barrington Williams	UK	55	5 Aug
10.34A	1.6	Michele Lazazzera	ITA	68	11 Aug
10.35	1.1	Mike Haynes	USA	65	23 Apr
10.35	1.9	Reggie McCray	USA	66	19 May
		(110)			
10.35	1.9	Titus Dixon	USA	66	19 May
10.35	0.9	Yuriy Mizera	SU	66	4 Jun
10.35	1.9	David Brown	USA	67	15 Jul
10.36	1.5	Anri Grigorov	BUL	64	15 Jun
10.36		Joel Isasi	CUB	67	24 Jun
10.36		Chris Faulknor	JAM	62	
10.36	2.0	Aleksandr Goremykin	SU	71	6 Jul
10.36A	0.7	Luis Cunha	POR	64	22 Jul
10.36		Lubos Chochlik	CS	59	25 Jul
10.36	1.3	Elliot Bunney	UK	66	5 Aug
		(120)			
10.36	-1.5	Pedro Agostinho	POR	65	13 Aug
10.36	1.3	Thomas Jefferson	USA	62	28 Aug
10.37		Jaime Jefferson	CUB	62	5 Feb
10.37		Dwayne Evans	USA	58	2 Apr
10.37	0.7	Devlon Dunn	USA	67	16 Jun
10.37	1.5	Matthias Schlicht	FRG	67	2 Jul
10.37	-2.7	Aleksandr Shlychkov	SU	70	28 Jul
10.37	1.9	Tatsuo Sugimoto	JAP	70	2 Aug
10.37	1.3	Jacek Marlicki	POL	68	6 Aug
10.37	1.5	Samuel Nchinda	CMR	67	21 Aug
		(130)			
10.37	-0.6	Amadou M.Mbaye	SEN	64	29 Aug
10.38	0.6	Eric Smith	USA	68	18 Mar
10.38	0.1	Dwight Frazier	USA	67	26 Mar
10.38		Kirk Baptiste	USA	63	2 Apr
10.38		DeAngelo Newsom	USA	70	30 Apr
10.38	1.2	Claude Magee	USA	62	8 May
10.38	1.5	Kaoru Matsubara	JAP	60	21 May
10.38		Marvin Setzer	USA	69	26 May
10.38	1.7	Roland Barclay	TRI	66	2 Jun
10.38	0.8	Vadim Samoilenko	SU	63	18 Jun
		(140)			
10.38	1.3	Ernest Obeng	UK	56	24 Jun
10.38		Abdullahi Tetengi	NIG	69	30 Jun
10.38	1.4	Viktor Malchugin	SU	61	11 Jul
10.38A	1.3	Alain Mazella	FRA	66	20 Jul
10.38	1.3	Mike McFarlane	UK	60	5 Aug
10.38	1.3	Clarence Callender	UK	61	5 Aug
10.38	0.2	Tallal Mansour	QAT	64	23 Sep
10.39	0.1	Kevin Braunskill	USA	69	26 Mar
10.39	1.7	Victor Omagbemi	NIG		26 Mar
10.39		Keith Stanford	USA	64	26 Mar
		(150)			
10.39		Anthony Barnes	USA	65	9 Apr
10.39	0.7	Rex Brown	USA	64	7 May
10.39	0.3	Michael Bates	USA	69	11 Jun
10.39	-3.0	Sergey Kiyevskiy	SU	68	17 Jun
10.39	1.3	Andrzej Popa	POL	68	17 Jun
10.39	1.8	Joachim Helbik	POL	62	19 Jun
10.39	-0.1	Tony Lee	USA	69	24 Jun
10.39A	1.3	Jean Charles Trouabal	FRA	65	20 Jul
10.39	-1.9	Nikolay Antonov	BUL	68	6 Aug
10.39	0.9	Patrick Stevens	BEL	68	15 Aug
		(160)			
10.39	0.3	Li Tao	CHN	68	26 Oct
10.39		M.Lestari	INA		10 Nov
10.40		Kenny Glenn	USA	68	9 Apr
10.40		Eugene McNeill	USA	65	9 Apr
10.40A		Gerhard Barnard	RSA	67	23 Apr
10.40		Vadim Davydov	SU	60	7 May
10.40	-1.5	Markus Kessler	FRG	62	15 May
10.40	0.6	Sergey Konstantinov	SU	61	31 May
10.40		Mustapha Selmi	ALG	65	- .Jun
10.40	0.2	Mark McKoy	CAN	61	19 Jun
		(170)			
10.40		R.Williams	USA		10 Jul
10.40	1.3	Michael Rosswess	UK	65	5 Aug

Disqualified for drugs abuse

Mark	Wind	Name		Nat	Born	Pos	Meet	Venue	Date
9.79	1.1	Ben	Johnson	CAN	30.12.61	-	OG	Seoul	24 Sep
10.03	-1.2		Johnson			1s2	OG	Seoul	24 Sep

Low altitude marks for athletes with altitude bests

Mark	Wind	Name	Pos	Meet	Venue	Date	Altitude best
10.11	1.1	Da Silva	6	OG	Seoul	24 Sep	10.08A
10.19	1.5	Simon	1		Schwechat	15 Jun	10.13A
10.22	1.5	Peñalver	3		Schwechat	15 Jun	10.12A
10.23	1.4	Oliveira	3	PTS	Bratislava	9 Jun	10.12A
10.26	0.9	Marie-Rose	5rA	Athl	Lausanne	24 Jun	10.25A
10.38	1.7	Fredericks				19 Mar	10.32A
10.39	0.9	Trouabal				23 Sep	10.39A
10.40	1.0	Lazazzera				13 Aug	10.34A

Wind assisted

Mark	Wind	Name		Nat	Born	Pos	Meet	Venue	Date
9.78	5.2	Carl	Lewis	USA	1.7.61	1	FOT	Indianapolis	16 Jul
9.86	5.2	Dennis	Mitchell	USA	20.2.66	2	FOT	Indianapolis	16 Jul
9.87	4.9	Calvin	Smith	USA	8.1.61	1s2	FOT	Indianapolis	16 Jul
9.87	5.2		Smith			3	FOT	Indianapolis	16 Jul
9.88	5.2	Albert	Robinson	USA	28.11.64	4	FOT	Indianapolis	16 Jul
9.90	5.2	Joe	DeLoach	USA	5.6.67	5	FOT	Indianapolis	16 Jul
9.90	3.7	Ben	Johnson	CAN	30.12.61	1	NC/OT	Ottawa	6 Aug
9.94	4.9		Robinson			2s2	FOT	Indianapolis	16 Jul

Mark		Name		Nat	Born	Pos	Meet	Venue	Date
9.94	5.2	Mike	Marsh	USA	4.8.67	6	FOT	Indianapolis	16 Jul
9.95	2.8		Lewis			1	BNP	Villeneuve d'Ascq	27 Jun
9.96	4.9		DeLoach			3s2	FOT	Indianapolis	16 Jul
9.98	5.2	Emmit	King	USA	24.3.59	7	FOT	Indianapolis	16 Jul
9.99A	2.7	Leandro	Peñalver	CUB	23.5.61	1h2	IbAmC	Ciudad México	22 Jul
10.00		Lorenzo	Daniel	USA	23.3.66	1		Starkville	26 Mar
10.00	3.7	Desai	Williams	CAN	12.6.59	2	NC/OT	Ottawa	6 Aug
10.01	2.4	Ray	Stewart	JAM	18.3.65	1	SWC	Austin	15 May
10.01A	2.7	José Javier	Arques	SPA	16.5.60	2h2	IbAmC	Ciudad México	22 Jul
10.02	2.6		Lewis			1s1	FOT	Indianapolis	16 Jul
10.03	2.8		Smith			2	BNP	Villeneuve d'Ascq	27 Jun
10.04	4.9		King			4s2	FOT	Indianapolis	16 Jul
10.05	3.4		Stewart			1h1	SWC	Austin	14 May
10.05	2.5		Mitchell			1		Kvarnsveden	19 Jun
10.05	4.9	Lee	McRae	USA	23.1.66	5s2	FOT	Indianapolis	16 Jul
10.06A	6.2		King			1rA		El Paso	17 Apr
10.06	3.3	Marty	Krulee	USA	4.11.56	1rB	MSR	Walnut	24 Apr
10.07	3.1		DeLoach			1h1	FOT	Indianapolis	15 Jul
10.07	2.6		Mitchell			2s1	FOT	Indianapolis	16 Jul
		(25/15)							
10.08	5.2	Lee	McNeill	USA	2.12.64	8	FOT	Indianapolis	16 Jul
10.09	3.3	Leroy	Burrell	USA	21.2.67	2rB	MSR	Walnut	24 Apr
10.10		Roscoe	Tatum	USA	13.2.66	1h1		Houston	18 Mar
10.11	2.5	Bruno	Marie-Rose	FRA	20.5.65	1rA		Strasbourg	25 Jun
10.12A	8.4	Devlon	Dunn	USA	1.4.67	1rC		El Paso	17 Apr
10.12	3.6	Andrew	Smith	JAM	29.1.64	1rB	Athl	Lausanne	24 Jun
10.15	2.8	Derrick	Florence	USA	19.6.68	1h2	SWC	Austin	14 May
10.16	5.2	Clayton	Kearney	AUS	11.4.64	1		Sydney	29 Oct
10.17	3.3	Dwayne	Evans	USA	13.10.58	3rB	MSR	Walnut	24 Apr
10.17	3.7	Attila	Kovács	HUN	2.9.60	1		Budapest	8 Sep
10.19A		Wessel	Oosthuizen	RSA	23.2.61	1		Secunda	20 Feb
10.19	2.2	Augustine	Olobia	NIG	.67	1		College Station	16 Apr
10.19	2.2	Mike	Johnson	USA	13.9.67	1rA		Austin	7 May
10.20A	3.4	Anthony	Barnes	USA	23.12.65	1		Logan	14 May
10.20	2.1	Norm	McGee	USA	23.3.66	1		San Angelo	21 May
10.20	3.7	Atlee	Mahorn	CAN	27.10.65	3	NC/OT	Ottawa	6 Aug
10.21	3.2	Antonio	Smith	USA	.66	1h1		Arlington	7 May
10.21	2.4	Greg	Sholars	USA	8.2.66	6	SWC	Austin	15 May
10.22		Roland	Barclay	TRI	25.10.66	h		Houston	18 Mar
10.24		Robert	Ligans	USA	27.6.68	h		Houston	18 Mar
10.24		Craig	Taylor	JAM	.68	1		Plainview	2 Apr
10.24	2.4	Ray	Hill	USA	24.6.66	1	KansR	Lawrence	23 Apr
10.24	3.9	Manley	Waller	USA	21.7.64	1		Athens	7 May
10.25	2.8	Tony	Jones	USA	30Dec65	4h2	SWC	Austin	14 May
10.26	2.8	Stanley	Kerr	USA	19.6.67	6h2	SWC	Austin	14 May
10.26	3.7	István	Tatár	HUN	24.3.58	2		Budapest	8 Sep
10.27		Ricky	Huell	USA	10.11.69	2		Starkville	26 Mar
10.27	2.3	Barrington	Williams	UK	11.9.55	1		Edinburgh	2 Jul
10.28	4.4	Patrick	Nwankwo	NIG	.66	2		Azusa	26 Mar
10.28A		Mike	Haynes	USA	24.12.65	1		Flagstaff	14 May
10.28	3.2	Brian	Bridgewater	USA	7.9.70	1		Van Nuys	21 May
10.28	3.6	Anri	Grigorov	BUL	18.10.64	5rB	Athl	Lausanne	24 Jun
10.30	3.7	Andrew	Mowatt	CAN	25.5.64	4	NC/OT	Ottawa	6 Aug
10.30	3.7	Brian	Morrison	CAN	25.8.68	5	NC/OT	Ottawa	6 Aug
10.31	3.9	Reggie	McCray	USA	7.8.66	2		Athens	7 May
10.31	2.3	Clarence	Callender	UK	16.11.61	2		Edinburgh	2 Jul
10.32		Ron	McCree	USA	21.3.68	1h		Fullerton	30 Apr
10.32	2.7	Victor	Omagbemi	NIG		1		Houston	7 May
10.32	2.6	Lester	Benjamin	ANT	14.9.63	1		New York City	5 Jun
10.32	3.0	Alain	Mazella	FRA	13.11.66	1rB		Strasbourg	25 Jun

Mark	Wind	Name	Nat	Born	Date
10.34		Stanley Howard	USA	65	1 Apr
10.34	2.1	Titus Dixon	USA	66	21 May
10.34	4.4	Eric Tatum	USA	67	7 May
10.34	4.5	Darren Braithwaite	UK	69	25 Jun

Mark	Wind	Name	Nat	Born	Date
10.34	2.4	Andre Love	USA	66	26 Jun
10.34	2.3	Elliot Bunney	UK	66	2 Jul
10.35	2.4	Kenny Glenn	USA	68	28 May
10.35	3.3	Jacek Marlicki	POL	68	19 Jun
10.35A	2.7	Marcos Belizaire	PAN	63	22 Jul
10.35	3.0	Amadou M. Mbaye	SEN	64	21 Aug
10.36		Derek Butler	USA		9 Apr
10.36	2.3	Rex Brown	USA	64	1 May
10.36	5.8	Tatsuo Sugimoto	JAP	70	2 Aug
10.37	4.4	Lucius Miller	USA	63	26 Mar
10.37	2.9	Andre Freeman	USA	64	23 Apr
10.37	3.2	Marvin Brown	USA	65	19 May
10.37	4.5	Courtney Rumbolt	UK	69	25 Jun
10.37	3.5	Valentin Rocandio	SPA	63	16 Jul
10.37	3.7	Lászlo Karaffa	HUN	64	8 Sep
10.38	3.9	Fred Martin	AUS	66	13 Mar
10.38	4.4	Benny Cureton	USA	65	30 Apr
10.39A		Anthony Monroe	TRI	64	14 May
10.38	2.4	Roy Martin	USA	66	18 Jun
10.38	2.4	Ray Brown	USA	66	26 Jun
10.38A	2.7	Pedro Curvelo	POR	60	22 Jul
10.39		Ray Ethridge	USA	68	30 Apr
10.39	3.2	Garry Henry	USA	67	7 May
10.39	3.9	Mark Pickens	USA	66	7 May
10.39	2.6	Mike Franks	USA	63	5 Jun
10.39	2.5	Bertrand Chatam	FRA	67	25 Jun
10.39	4.1	György Bakos	HUN	60	23 Jul
10.39	5.2	Koichi Igarashi	JAP	68	15 Sep

Hand timing

Mark	Wind	First name	Name	Nat	Born	Pos	Meet	Venue	Date
9.9		Iziaq	Adeyanju	NIG	24.2.59	1	OT/NC	Bauchi	2 Jul
9.9		Olapade	Adeniken	NIG	19.8.69	2	OT/NC	Bauchi	2 Jul
9.9	0.7	Vitaliy	Savin	SU	23.1.66	1		Vladivostok	13 Sep
10.0		Abdullahi	Tetengi	NIG	15.7.69	3	OT/NC	Bauchi	2 Jul
10.0	0.0	Oleg	Borov	SU	.68	1		Alma-Ata	16 Jun
10.0A	1.6	Robson C	daSilva	BRA	4.9.64	1h3	IbAmC	Ciudad México	22 Jul
10.0A		Peter	Wekesa	KEN	22.9.61	1		Eldoret	18 Aug

Mark	Wind	Name	Nat	Born	Date
10.1		Shane Naylor	AUS	67	16 Feb
10.1		Albert Robinson	USA	64	9 Apr
10.1		Zheng Chen	CHN	65	23 Apr
10.1		Cai Jianming	CHN	63	23 Apr
10.1		Thomas Jefferson	USA	62	7 May
10.1	0.5	Mark Witherspoon	USA	63	7 May
10.1	0.5	Kirk Baptiste	USA	63	7 May
10.1		Aleksandr Starovoitov	SU	63	12 May
10.1		Garfield Campbell	JAM	67	18 May
10.1	1.3	Deion Sanders	USA	67	21 May
10.1	1.4	Shinji Aoto	JAP	66	28 May
10.1	1.9	Kenji Yamauchi	JAP	64	31 May
10.1	0.0	Yuriy Yazynin	SU	66	16 Jun
10.1		Rimantas Skrabulis	SU	67	18 Jun
10.1		Sergey Khilko	SU	63	18 Jun
10.1		Victor Nwankwo	NIG	69	2 Jul
10.1	0.0	Bruno Marie-Rose	FRA	65	2 Jul
10.1A		Kennedy Ondiek	KEN	66	13 Aug
10.1		John Myles-Mills	GHA	66	20 Aug
10.1	0.7	Igor Groshev	SU	64	13 Sep

Doubtful timing

Mark	Wind	Name	Nat	Born	Date
10.1		Giovanni DeLucia	ITA	69	21 May

Wind assisted

Mark	First name	Name	Nat	Born	Pos	Meet	Venue	Date
9.8	Ricardo	Chacón	CUB	30.4.63	1		Caracas	24 Jun
9.9	William	Trott	BER	20.3.65	1h2	Big8	Ames	14 May
9.9	Clive	Wright	JAM	18.11.65	1		Kings Point	14 May
9.9	Joel	Isasi	CUB	31.7.67	2		Caracas	24 Jun
9.9	Nivaldo	Torres	CUB	7.12.63	3		Caracas	24 Jun
10.0	John	Drummond	USA	9.9.68	1		Odessa	22 Apr
10.0	Lee	McNeill	USA	2.12.64	1		Harrisonburg	23 Apr
10.0	Peter	Ifeduba	NIG	.69	1h1	Big8	Ames	14 May
10.0	Victor	Edet	NIG	24.2.66	2h2	Big8	Ames	14 May

Mark	Wind	Name	Nat	Born	Date
10.1		James Trapp	USA		Apr
10.1		Keith Bly	USA		Apr
10.1		James Walker	USA	70	20 Apr
10.1	5.1	Valentin Rocandio	SPA	63	30 Apr
10.1		Pat Williams	JAM		30 Apr
10.1		Sam Rice	USA	70	May
10.1		Sergey Klenov	SU	67	11 May
10.1		Kenny Brokenburr	USA	68	14 May
10.1	4.3	José Carbonnell	SPA	57	6 Aug

100 Metres Year List Progression

Year	Best	10th	20th	50th	100th	Under 10.30	Under 10.40	Ave.100
1958	10.29	10.3	10.3+	10.4+	10.5	1	4	
1968	9.95	10.18	10.28	10.2	10.3	22	42	
1978	10.07	10.15	10.23	10.36	10.45	26	62	10.334
1979	10.01	10.16	10.22	10.34	10.44	38	67	10.323
1980	10.02	10.18	10.21	10.33	10.44	32	71	10.322
1981	10.00	10.18	10.23	10.35	10.43	33	77	10.330
1982	10.00	10.15	10.20	10.32	10.40	41	91	10.292
1983	9.93	10.15	10.19	10.30	10.37	48	111	10.266
1984	9.96	10.14	10.20	10.29	10.36	53	129	10.269
1985	9.98	10.11	10.20	10.27	10.35	62	132	10.256
1986	9.95	10.10	10.14	10.26	10.36	65	139	10.238
1987	9.83	10.09	10.17	10.25	10.34	79	157	10.229
1988	9.92	10.06	10.12	10.25	10.33	80	173	10.217

(+ Imperial mark converted)

200 METRES

Mark		Name		Nat	Born	Pos	Meet	Venue	Date
19.75	1.7	Joe	DeLoach	USA	5.6.67	1	OG	Seoul	28 Sep
19.79	1.7	Carl	Lewis	USA	1.7.61	2	OG	Seoul	28 Sep
19.82A	2.0		Lewis			1		Sestriere	11 Aug
19.87	0.8	Lorenzo	Daniel	USA	23.3.66	1	NCAA	Eugene	3 Jun
19.93	1.5		Daniel			1	SEC	Auburn	15 May
19.96	1.0		DeLoach			1	FOT	Indianapolis	20 Jul
19.98	0.2		DeLoach			1	SWC	Austin	15 May
19.99	1.2		Lewis			1		Houston	17 Jun
20.01	1.0		Lewis			2	FOT	Indianapolis	20 Jul
20.03	1.2		Lewis			1q2	FOT	Indianapolis	19 Jul
20.03	0.2		DeLoach			1	WK	Zürich	17 Aug
20.03	-0.6		DeLoach			1	VD	Bruxelles	19 Aug
20.04	1.7	Robson C.	da Silva	BRA	4.9.64	3	OG	Seoul	28 Sep
20.05	1.0	Roy	Martin	USA	25.12.66	3	FOT	Indianapolis	20 Jul
20.05	1.0	Albert	Robinson	USA	28.11.64	4	FOT	Indianapolis	20 Jul
20.05A	-0.3		da Silva			1	IbAmC	Ciudad México	23 Jul
20.06	1.6		DeLoach			1s2	OG	Seoul	28 Sep
20.07	0.2	Mike	Johnson	USA	13.9.67	2	SWC	Austin	15 May
20.08	0.2	Calvin	Smith	USA	8.1.61	2	WK	Zürich	17 Aug
20.09	2.0		Johnson			1rA		College Station	16 Apr
20.09	1.7	Linford	Christie	UK	2.4.60	4	OG	Seoul	28 Sep
20.17	1.7		Smith			1	BNP	Villeneuve d'Ascq	27 Jun
20.18	0.2	Henry	Thomas (10)	USA	10.7.67	1		Eagle Rock	14 May
20.20	0.8	Atlee	Mahorn	CAN	27.10.65	2	NCAA	Eugene	3 Jun
20.20	-0.7		Martin			1s1	FOT	Indianapolis	20 Jul
20.20A	2.0	Gilles	Quénéhervé	FRA	17.5.66	2		Sestriere	11 Aug
20.21	1.2		Mahorn			1	Pac-10	Westwood	22 May
20.22A	-0.3	Leandro	Peñalver	CUB	23.5.61	2	IbAmC	Ciudad México	23 Jul
20.23	1.2	Danny	Everett	USA	1.11.66	2	Pac-10	Westwood	22 May
20.23A	2.0		Robinson			3		Sestriere	11 Aug
20.23	1.5		Lewis			1s1	OG	Seoul	28 Sep
		(31/14)							
20.24A	-0.3	Roberto	Hernández	CUB	6.3.67	3	IbAmC	Ciudad México	23 Jul
20.27	0.8	Danny	Peebles	USA	30.5.66	4	NCAA	Eugene	3 Jun
20.29	0.0	Dennis	Mitchell	USA	20.2.66	1h1	SEC	Auburn	14 May
20.30	1.8	Marty	Krulee	USA	4.11.56	2rA	MSR	Walnut	24 Apr
20.31	0.5	Chidi	Imoh	NIG	27.8.63	1		Bern	23 Aug
20.32	0.4	John	Regis	UK	13.10.66	1		Athinai	3 Sep
		(20)							
20.34	0.4	Harlan	Davis	USA	4.8.67	1		Bakersfield	21 May
20.35	0.2	Mike	Marsh	USA	4.8.67	2		Eagle Rock	14 May
20.35	0.4	Eugene	McNeill	USA	10.12.65	1s1	TAC	Tampa	18 Jun
20.36	1.5	James	Butler	USA	21.6.60	1	Barr	Habana	6 Mar
20.37	1.7	Frank	Emmelmann	GDR	15.9.61	1	NC	Rostock	26 Jun
20.40	0.2	Stanley	Kerr	USA	19.6.67	3	SWC	Austin	15 May
20.41	0.8	Ray	Stewart	JAM	18.3.65	5	NCAA	Eugene	3 Jun
20.41	1.2	Dwayne	Evans	USA	13.10.58	2q3	FOT	Indianapolis	18 Jul
20.41A	2.0	Stefano	Tilli	ITA	22.8.62	5		Sestriere	11 Aug
20.42	0.0	Reggie	McCray	USA	7.8.66	1		Tallahassee	28 May
		(30(							
20.44	2.0	Robert	Stone	AUS	5.1.65	1		Canberra	13 Mar
20.44A		Willie	Caldwell	USA	25.9.63	1		Albuquerque	9 Jun
20.45A	1.3	Bruno	Marie-Rose	FRA	20.5.65	1		Font-Romeu	20 Jul
20.46	1.7	Daniel	Sangouma	FRA	7.2.65	3	BNP	Villeneuve d'Ascq	27 Jun
20.48A	1.7	Johan	Rossouw	RSA	20.10.65	1		Johannesburg	23 Apr
20.50	-1.2	Larry	Myricks	USA	10.3.56	1	TAC	Tampa	18 Jun
20.50	1.2	Floyd	Heard	USA	24.3.66	3q3	FOT	Indianapolis	18 Jul
20.51A		Tshakile	Nzimande	RSA	19.11.61	1		Windhoek	23 Jan
20.51	-0.1	Andre	Phillips	USA	5.9.59	1		Tucson	11 Jun
20.51	1.6	Derrick	Florence	USA	19.6.68	1		Austin	22 Jun
		(40)							
20.51	1.6	Michael	Rosswess	UK	11.6.65	4s2	OG	Seoul	26 Sep
20.52	-0.4	Thomas	Jefferson	USA	6.8.62	3		Monaco	2 Aug
20.53	0.1	Mike	Timpson	USA	6.6.67	1		Pittsburgh	14 May

Mark		Name		Nat	Born	Pos	Meet	Venue	Date
20.53	1.4	Brian	Bridgewater	USA	7.9.70	1h		Van Nuys	20 May
20.54	0.4	Daron	Council	USA	26.12.64	2s1	TAC	Tampa	18 Jun
20.55	0.2	Tony	Jones	USA	30.12.65	4	SWC	Austin	15 May
20.55	2.0	Kevin	Little	USA	3.4.68	1		Lincoln	25 May
20.55		Edgardo	Guilbe	PR	10.3.66	1		San Juan	10 Jul
20.55A	1.3	Jean Charles	Trouabal	FRA	10.5.65	2		Font-Romeu	20 Jul
20.57	1.6	Frankie	Fredericks	RSA	2.10.67	1		Tucson	19 Mar
		(50)							
20.57	0.2	Jason	Leach	USA	11.3.66	5	SWC	Austin	15 May
20.57	1.6	Cyprean	Enweani	CAN	19.3.64	5s2	OG	Seoul	28 Sep
20.59	1.8	Miles	Murphy	AUS	19.5.67	1		Canberra	5 Mar
20.59	1.6	Devlon	Dunn	USA	1.4.67	1rB	MSR	Walnut	24 Apr
20.59A		Greg	Moore	USA	8.11.59	1		Flagstaff	14 May
20.60	0.6	Robert	Hackett	USA	3.8.64	1		Rehlingen	23 May
20.60	1.7	Igor	Streltsov	SU	1.5.65	1	Znam	Leningrad	11 Jun
20.61A		Wessel	Oosthuizen	RSA	23.2.61	1		Pretoria	13 Feb
20.62	1.5	Walker	Watkins	USA	29.9.67	1		Eugene	16 Apr
20.62	1.8	Mike	Franks	USA	23.9.63	4rA	MSR	Walnut	24 Apr
		(60)							
20.62	-0.4	Don	Quarrie	JAM	25.2.51	1		Eagle Rock	18 Jun
20.62	1.3	Vladimir	Krylov	SU	26.2.64	1	NC	Tallinn	6 Jul
20.63	0.6	Kevin	Braunskill	USA	31.3.69	1		Raleigh	25 May
20.63	1.7	Aleksandr	Starovoitov	SU	31.8.63	2	Znam	Leningrad	11 Jun
20.64A	1.5	Anthony	Barnes	USA	23.12.65	1		Logan	14 May
20.64	0.4	Juan	Tobin	USA	4.1.68	2		Bakersfield	21 May
20.64	-0.6	Wallace	Spearmon	USA	3.9.62	3		Leverkusen	28 Jun
20.64A	1.5	Luis	Barroso	POR	27.6.66	3h1	IbAmC	Ciudad México	23 Jul
20.65		Darrell	Hadden	USA	14.11.64	1		Natchotoches	30 Apr
20.67		Iziak	Adeyanju	NIG	24.2.59	1		Fayetteville	16 Apr
		(70)							
20.67		Devon	Morris	JAM	22.1.61	1		Plainview	14 May
20.67	1.6	Quincy	Watts	USA	19.6.70	1h		Van Nuys	20 May
20.67	0.6	Mike	Brooks	USA	.67	2		Raleigh	25 May
20.67	1.6	Olapade	Adeniken	NIG	19.8.69	6s2	OG	Seoul	28 Sep
20.68	-0.1	Mike	Bates	USA	19.12.69	3		Tucson	11 Jun
20.70	1.1	Troy	Douglas	BER	30.11.62	3q2	OG	Seoul	26 Sep
20.71		Calvin	Long	USA	2.7.66	1		Gainesville	16 Apr
20.71	2.0	Courtney	Brown	CAN	21.4.65	1rB		Baton Rouge	23 Apr
20.71	1.7	Lee	McNeill	USA	2.12.64	1		Harrisonburg	23 Apr
20.71	1.5	Ian	Morris	TRI	30.11.61	1		San Angelo	20 May
		(80)							
20.71	0.9	Deion	Sanders	USA	9.8.67	1		Tallahassee	21 May
20.71A		Luis	Cunha	POR	5.12.64	1rB	IbAmC	Ciudad México	23 Jul
20.72A		Gerhard	Barnard	RSA	8.5.67	1		Pietersburg	5 Mar
20.72	0.7	Patrick	Stevens	BEL	31.1.68	1	NC	Bruxelles	4 Sep
20.72	2.0	Abdullahi	Tetengi	NIG	15.7.69	1rB		Seoul	19 Sep
20.73	1.6	David	Campbell	USA	23.5.66	2		Austin	22 Jun
20.73	0.2	Chris	Barnes	USA	21.7.69	1	TAC-Jr	Tallahassee	25 Jun
20.73	1.7	Olaf	Prenzler	GDR	24.8.58	2	NC	Rostock	26 Jun
20.75	-0.4	Rex	Brown	USA	12.2.64	2		Eagle Rock	18 Jun
20.75		Clive	Wright	JAM	18.11.65	1	NC	Kingston	16 Jul
		(90)							
20.75	0.4	Aldo	Canti	FRA	9.3.61	6		Athinai	3 Sep
20.76	0.5	Greg	Meghoo	JAM	11.8.65	3		Champaign	28 May
20.76	1.7	Nikolay	Razgonov	SU	16.1.64	3	Znam	Leningrad	11 Jun
20.76	0.9	Andrew	Carrott	UK	1.1.66	1		Cork	5 Jul
20.76	-0.6	Ralf	Lübke	FRG	17.6.65	1	NC	Frankfurt	24 Jul
20.77		Ahmed	de Kom	HOL	15.2.59	2		Rehlingen	23 May
20.77	0.9	Arthur	Blake	USA	19.8.66	2		Tallahassee	21 May
20.78	1.4	Kirk	Baptiste	USA	20.6.63	1		Houston	19 Mar
20.79		Tim	Williams	USA	27.5.62	1		San Diego	12 Mar
20.79	0.2	Eric	Tatum	USA	11.12.67	7	SWC	Austin	15 May
		(100)							
20.79	0.7	Maurice	Draper	USA	.69	1		Natchitoches	11 May
20.79		Victor	Nwankwo	NIG	18.9.69	1s	OT/NC	Bauchi	30 Jun
20.79	1.5	Norbert	Dobeleit	FRG	17.7.64	1		Lüdenscheid	6 Aug
20.79	0.0	Kennedy	Ondiek	KEN	12.12.66	1h6	OG	Seoul	26 Sep

Mark		Name	Nat	Born	Date
20.80	0.3	Mel Lattany	USA	59	4 Jun
20.80		Félix Stevens	CUB	64	5 Jul
20.81	1.5	Norm McGee	USA	66	20 May
20.81	-0.9	Jirí Valík	CS	66	17 Jul
20.82	1.7	Mark Garner	AUS	69	16 Jan
20.82A	1.7	Eugene van Niekerk	RSA	65	23 Apr
		(110)			
20.82	1.5	Sammie Smith	USA	67	23 Apr
		(also 20.82 +0.9 21 May)			
20.82		Derwin Hall	USA	69	19 May
20.83	2.0	Dino Napier	USA	69	14 May
20.83	0.4	Erwin Skamrahl	FRG	58	1 Jun
20.84		Roscoe Tatum	USA	66	
20.84		Mike Murphy	USA	67	30 Apr
20.84		Jeroen Fischer	BEL	66	21 May
20.84		Dazel Jules	TRI	67	21 May
20.84		Sergio Menezes	BRA	65	1 Jun
20.84	1.7	Aleksey Graudyn	SU	68	11 Jun
		(120)			
20.84	1.2	David Campbell	USA	66	18 Jun
20.84	1.0	Peter Klein	FRG	59	24 Jul
20.84	0.4	Aleksandr Shlychkov	SU	70	14 Aug
20.85	1.8	Leroy Burrell	USA	67	4 May
20.85		Terrence Warren	USA	69	11 Jun
20.85	1.5	Dmitriy Bartenyev	SU	69	8 Jul
20.85		John Myles-Mills	GHA	66	27 Jul
20.85	0.5	Brian Cooper	USA	65	23 Aug
20.86	-1.8	Steffen Bringmann	GDR	64	20 Jun
20.86	0.2	Sandro Floris	ITA	65	22 Jun
		(130)			
20.86		Henriko Atkins	BAR	66	18 Jul
20.86	-1.5	Marcus Adam	UK	68	7 Aug
20.87	1.8	Pietro Mennea	ITA	52	5 Mar
20.87		Marvin Setzer	USA	69	11 Jun
20.87	0.0	György Fetter	HUN	63	5 Jun
20.87	1.8	Ivan Ryashko	SU	62	11 Jun
20.87	0.6	Sergio Querol	CUB	65	19 Jun
20.87	1.7	Thierry Tribondeau	FRA	62	31 Jul
20.88		Vincent Coleman	USA	65	28 May
20.88	1.6	Heiko Truppel	GDR	64	12 Jun
		(140)			
20.88	2.0	Yoshiuki Okuyama	JAP	70	19 Jun
20.89	1.6	Phil Ferguson	JAM	67	19 Mar
20.89	1.7	Torsten Heimrath	GDR	63	26 Jun
20.89	0.5	Oleg Fatun	SU	59	12 Jul
20.90		Clifton Campbell	USA	67	9 Apr
20.90A	1.8	Carlos Turro	SPA	64	23 Jul
20.90	1.8	Todd Bennett	UK	62	29 Jul
20.91	0.2	Sergey Klenov	SU	67	1 Jun
20.91	0.2	Marcello Pantone	ITA	65	22 Jun
20.91	0.5	Stanley Floyd	USA	61	23 Aug
		(150)			

Low altitude marks for athletes with altitude bests

Mark	Wind	Name	Pos	Meet	Venue	Date	Best
20.40	1.7	Quénéhervé	6	OG	Seoul	28 Sep	20.20A
20.48	1.1	Marie-Rose	2q2	OG	Seoul	26 Sep	20.45A
20.53		Hernández	2		St.Denis	6 Jun	20.24A
20.55	0.2	Tilli	1		Potenza	22 Jun	20.41A
20.61	1.8	Peñalver	2		Habana	6 Aug	20.22A
20.61	0.4	Trouabal	5		Athinai	3 Sep	20.55A
20.81	-0.4	Barroso	26Sep		20.64A		

Wind assisted

Mark	Wind	Name		Nat	Born	Pos	Meet	Venue	Date
20.05A	3.8	Cyprean	Enweani	CAN	19.3.64	1		Calgary	3 Jul
20.14	2.6		DeLoach			1q4	FOT	Indianapolis	18 Jul
20.15	2.2		Daniel			1h3	NCAA	Eugene	1 Jun
20.35A		Wessel	Oosthuizen	RSA	23.2.61	1		Secunda	20 Feb
20.47		Clive	Wright	JAM	18.11.65	1	JUCO	Odessa	21 May
20.50	3.0	Phil	Snoddy	IRL	3.2.66	1	NC	Dublin	24 Jul
20.58A	4.1	Andrew	Smith	JAM	29.1.64	2rA		El Paso	17 Apr
20.58	3.8	Walker	Watkins	USA	29.9.67	5h2	NCAA	Eugene	1 Jun
20.65A	2.3	Gerhard	Barnard	RSA	8.5.67	1	NC-U21	Secunda	9 Apr
20.65	2.6	Tony	Dees	USA	6.8.63	4q4	FOT	Indianapolis	18 Jul
20.67		Bernard	Chatman	USA					
20.67		Ronnie	Green	USA	28.11.66	1		Lubbock	1 May
20.67		Norm	McGee	USA	23.3.66	1h3		San Angelo	18 May
20.68		Victor	Omagbemi	NIG		1		Houston	6 May
20.68		Barry	Smith	USA	22.2.71	1		Eugene	24 Jul
20.71	3.7	Kermit	Ward	USA	.68	1rB		Austin	7 May
20.71		David	Lawyer	USA		1h1		Moscow	20 May
20.72	3.3	Steffen	Bringmann	GDR	11.3.64	1		Karl-Marx-Stadt	12 Jun
20.74	3.1	Kenny	Brokenburr	USA	29.10.68	1		Arlington	7 May
20.74	2.6	David	Jones	USA	.69	1		Houston	7 May
20.75		Ronnell	Barclay	TRI	25.10.66	2		Houston	6 May
20.76		Vincent	Coleman	USA	28.6.65	1h1		Houston	28 May
20.78	3.3	Torsten	Heimrath	GDR	14.5.63	2		Karl-Marx-Stadt	12 Jun

Mark	Wind	Name	Nat	Born	Date
20.79	2.8	Ade Mafe	UK	66	1 May
20.79	2.8	Sunday Uti	NIG	62	1 May
20.79		Mike Haynes	USA	65	20 May
20.79	3.3	Sven Matthes	GDR	69	12 Jun
20.80		Reggie Jones	USA		20 May
20.82A	2.3	Paul van Wyk	RSA	68	9 Apr
20.83	2.8	Rex Brobby	GHA	61	1 May
20.85A	4.1	Pat Williams	JAM		17 Apr
20.86	3.3	Steffen Lassler	GDR	65	12 Jun
20.86	2.5	Kenji Yamauchi	JAP	64	18 Jun
20.87	2.2	Cayetano Cornet	SPA	63	14 Aug
20.88		Dushon Orr	USA		
20.89	2.3	Yoshito Hanada	JAP	67	5 Jun
20.89	3.6	Czeslaw Pradzynski	POL	60	7 Aug

Mark		Name		Nat	Born	Pos	Meet	Venue	Date
Hand timing									
20.1		Thomas	Jefferson	USA	6.8.62	1		Port of Spain	7 May
20.1		Dazel	Jules	TRI	10.8.67	2		Port of Spain	7 May
20.3A	-1.1	Kennedy	Ondiek	KEN	12.12.66	1	OT	Nairobi	13 Aug
20.4		Wessel	Oosthuizen	RSA	23.2.61	1		Port Elizabeth	9 Mar
20.4		Daron	Council	USA	26.12.64	1		Raleigh	14 May
20.4	1.3	Derrick	Florence	USA	19.6.68	1=		College Station	25 May
20.4	0.1	Larry	Myricks	USA	10.3.56	1		Walnut	29 May
20.5		Tshakile	Nzimande	RSA	19.11.61	2		Port Elizabeth	9 Mar
20.5		Ian	Morris	TRI	30.11.61	3		Port of Spain	7 May
20.5	0.1	Greg	Moore	USA	8.11.59	2		Walnut	29 May

Mark		Name	Nat	Born	Date
20.6		Clive Wright	JAM	65	14 May
20.6		Dmitriy Bartenyev	SU	69	29 Jun
20.6A	-1.1	Simon Kipkemboi	KEN	60	13 Aug
20.6A	-1.1	Elkana Nyangau	KEN	63	13 Aug
20.6		John Myles-Mills	GHA	66	20 Aug

Mark	Name		Nat	Born	Pos	Meet	Venue	Date
Wind assisted								
20.1	Sergey	Klenov	SU	11.7.67	1		Leningrad	12 May
20.1	Jeff	Reynolds	USA	25.1.66	1h2	Big 8	Ames	14 May
20.1	Iziak	Adeyanju	NIG	24.2.59	1h3	Big 8	Ames	14 May
20.3	Mark	Perry	USA	25.7.67	2h3	Big 8	Ames	14 May
20.4	Kyle	Hargett	USA	14.1.67	2h2	Big 8	Ames	14 May
20.4	Devlon	Dunn	USA	1.4.67	3h2	Big 8	Ames	14 May
20.4	Clyde	Bishop	USA	29.5.62	1		Houston	5 Aug
20.5	Victor	Edet	NIG	24.2.66	1h1	Big 8	Ames	14 May
20.5	Peter	Ifeduba	NIG	.69	2h1	Big 8	Ames	14 May
20.5	Aleksey	Fyodorov	SU	3.5.65	2		Leningrad	12 May
20.6	Carmel	Waldron	USA	Apr				
Indoor marks								
20.62	Nikolay	Razgonov	SU	16.1.64	1	EC	Budapest	6 Mar
20.65	Nikolay	Antonov	BUL	17.8.68	2	EC	Budapest	6 Mar
20.79	John	Drummond	USA	9.9.68	1		Lubbock	5 Mar
20.85	Andreas	Berger	AUT	9.6.61	4	EC	Budapest	6 Mar

200 Metres Year List Progression

Year	Best	10th	20th	50th	100th	Under 20.70	Under 20.90	Ave.100
1958	20.6	20.8+	21.0	21.2+	21.4+			
1968	19.83	20.2	20.5	20.8	20.9			
1978	20.03	20.44	20.61	20.77	21.02	35	63	20.752
1979	19.72	20.34	20.47	20.79	20.96	35	75	20.703
1980	19.96	20.36	20.55	20.76	20.94	43	82	20.700
1981	20.20	20.46	20.60	20.79	20.96	35	78	20.742
1982	20.15	20.39	20.47	20.74	20.88	43	108	20.672
1983	19.75	20.32	20.46	20.65	20.85	53	117	20.611
1984	19.80	20.34	20.41	20.62	20.78	79	144	20.565
1985	20.07	20.32	20.41	20.59	20.80	72	140	20.573
1986	20.12	20.33	20.48	20.60	20.79	68	129	20.606
1987	19.92	20.23	20.38	20.54	20.75	85	142	20.511
1988	19.75	20.18	20.32	20.57	20.79	75	144	20.494

400 METRES

Mark	Name		Nat	Born	Pos	Meet	Venue	Date
43.29	Butch	Reynolds	USA	8.6.64	1rA	WK	Zürich	17 Aug
43.87	Steve	Lewis	USA	16.5.69	1	OG	Seoul	28 Sep
43.93		Reynolds			1	FOT	Indianapolis	20 Jul
43.93		Reynolds			2	OG	Seoul	28 Sep
43.98	Danny	Everett	USA	1.11.66	2	FOT	Indianapolis	20 Jul
44.09		Everett			3	OG	Seoul	28 Sep
44.11		Lewis			1s2	FOT	Indianapolis	18 Jul
44.20		Everett			2rA	WK	Zürich	17 Aug
44.22A	Roberto	Hernández	CUB	6.3.67	1		Ciudad México	22 May
44.26		Lewis			3rA	WK	Zürich	17 Aug
44.32		Everett			2s2	FOT	Indianapolis	18 Jul
44.33		Reynolds			1s2	OG	Seoul	26 Sep
44.34		Everett			1	Pac-10	Westwood	22 May
44.35		Lewis			1s1	OG	Seoul	26 Sep
44.36		Everett			2s1	OG	Seoul	26 Sep

Mark	Name		Nat	Born	Pos	Meet	Venue	Date
44.37		Lewis			3	FOT	Indianapolis	20 Jul
44.38	Darren	Clark	AUS	6.9.65	3s1	OG	Seoul	26 Sep
44.40		Everett			1		Lausanne	24 Jun
44.41		Lewis			1q3	OG	Seoul	25 Sep
44.44A		Hernández			1	IbAmC	Ciudad México	22 Jul
44.46		Reynolds			1q4	OG	Seoul	25 Sep
44.50	Bert	Cameron	JAM	16.11.59	4s1	OG	Seoul	26 Sep
44.52		Everett			1	NCAA	Eugene	4 Jun
44.53A		Everett			1		Sestriere	11 Aug
44.54		Reynolds			1q3	FOT	Indianapolis	17 Jul
44.55	Andrew	Valmon	USA	1.1.65	4rA	WK	Zürich	17 Aug
44.55		Clark			4	OG	Seoul	28 Sep
44.56	Mohamed	Al Malky	OMA	1.12.62	1	HGP	Budapest	12 Aug
44.57		Hernández			2	Athl	Lausanne	24 Jun
44.60	Ian	Morris	TRI	30.11.61	2s2	OG	Seoul	26 Sep
44.61		Lewis			1q1	FOT	Indianapolis	17 Jul
44.61	Kevin	Robinzine	USA	12.4.66	4	FOT	Indianapolis	20 Jul
44.61		Everett			1	VD	Bruxelles	19 Aug
	(33/10)							
44.62A	Thomas	Schönlebe	GDR	6.8.65	2		Ciudad México	22 May
44.67	Derek	Redmond	UK	3.9.65	1rB	WK	Zürich	17Aug
44.71	Miles	Murphy	AUS	19.5.67	1	NC	Perth	26 Mar
44.72	Innocent	Egbunike	NIG	30.1.61	5	OG	Seoul	28 Sep
44.75	Clarence	Daniel	USA	11.6.61	1q4	FOT	Indianapolis	17 Jul
44.76	Roddie	Haley	USA	6.12.65	1	Pepsi	Westwood	5 Jun
44.79	Antonio	McKay	USA	9.2.64	5	FOT	Indianapolis	20 Jul
44.82	Mike	Franks	USA	23.9.63	1	Drake	Des Moines	30 Apr
44.84	Walter	McCoy	USA	15.11.58	2		Athinai	3 Sep
44.88	Tim	Simon	USA	11.9.66	3q1	FOT	Indianapolis	17 Jul
	(20)							
44.88	Mark	Rowe	USA	28.7.60	4q1	FOT	Indianapolis	17 Jul
44.90	Susumu	Takano	JAP	21.5.61	5s1	OG	Seoul	26 Sep
44.92	Willie	Smith	USA	28.2.56	2q4	FOT	Indianapolis	17 Jul
44.93	Kriss	Akabusi	UK	28.11.58	1	AAA	Birmingham	7Aug
44.98	Robert	Stone	AUS	5.1.65	1		Melbourne	6 Mar
44.98	Jeff	Reynolds	USA	25.1.66	5q1	FOT	Indianapolis	17 Jul
44.99	Darrell	Robinson	USA	23.12.63	5s2	FOT	Indianapolis	18 Jul
45.08	Jens	Carlowitz	GDR	8.8.64	1		Potsdam	8 Sep
45.10	Andre	Phillips	USA	5.9.59	1		Tucson	11 Jun
45.20	Ralf	Lübke	FRG	17.6.65	3	R-W	Koblenz	28 Aug
	(30)							
45.20	Mathias	Schersing	GDR	7.10.64	2		Potsdam	8 Sep
45.22	Brian	Whittle	UK	24.4.64	3q1	OG	Seoul	25 Sep
45.23	Mike	Johnson	USA	13.9.67	1		Waco	22 Apr
45.24	Darrell	Hadden	USA	14.11.64	1		San Angelo	16 Apr
45.27	Todd	Bennett	UK	6.7.62	3	AAA	Birmingham	7 Aug
45.27	Tomasz	Jedrusik	POL	3.2.69	4q1	OG	Seoul	25 Sep
45.27	Gerson A.	Souza	BRA	2.1.59	7s1	OG	Seoul	26 Sep
45.29	Ray	Armstead	USA	27.5.60	4q2	FOT	Indianapolis	17 Jul
45.30	Devon	Morris	JAM	22.1.61	4q3	OG	Seoul	25 Sep
45.32	Clifton	Campbell	USA	18.6.67	3h2	NCAA	Eugene	2 Jun
	(40)							
45.32	Chris	Whitlock	USA	18.5.59	3q3	FOT	Indianapolis	17 Jul
45.33	Sunday	Uti	NIG	23.10.62	5q1	OG	Seoul	25 Sep
45.34	Howard	Davis	JAM	27.4.67	1rB	MSR	Walnut	24 Apr
45.35	Peter	Howard	USA	17.10.63	4	TAC	Tampa	18 Jun
45.36	Antonio	Pettigrew	USA	3.11.67	1		Tallahassee	28 May
45.37A	Alonzo	Babers	USA	31.10.61	1		Albuquerque	9 Jun
45.39	Howard	Burnett	JAM	8.3.61	1h2		San Angelo	19 May
45.39	Cayetano	Cornet	SPA	22.8.63	5q3	OG	Seoul	25 Sep
45.40	Gary	Duncan	USA	25.5.64	1	SEC	Auburn	15 May
45.43	Calvin	Long	USA	2.7.66	2	SEC	Auburn	14 May
	(50)							
45.43	Edgar	Itt	FRG	8.6.67	5rA	ASV	Köln	21 Aug
45.44	Simon	Kipkemboi	KEN	15.4.60	5q2	OG	Seoul	25 Sep

Mark	Name		Nat	Born	Pos	Meet	Venue	Date
45.46A	Henry	Mohoanyane	LES	11.8.63	1		Bloemfontein	18 Mar
45.49	Raymond	Pierre	USA	19.9.67	5	TAC	Tampa	18 Jun
45.49	Gabriel	Tiacoh	IVC	10.9.63	5q4	OG	Seoul	25 Sep
45.53	Larry	Cantrell	USA	4.7.67	3	SEC	Auburn	14 May
45.55	Lázaro	Martínez	CUB	11.11.62	2	Barr	Habana	5 Mar
45.58A	Willie	Caldwell	USA	25.9.63	2		Albuquerque	9 Jun
45.59	Winthrop	Graham	JAM	17.11.65	2rA		Westwood	3 Sep
45.61A	Jesús	Malave	VEN	24.10.65	3	IbAmC	Ciudad México	22 Jul
	(60(							
45.62	Sergio	Menezes	BRA	27.4.65	3		São Paulo	22 May
45.63	Norbert	Dobeleit	FRG	17.7.64	1rC	ASV	Köln	21 Aug
45.64	Paul	Harmsworth	UK	28.9.63	4	AAA	Birmingham	7 Aug
45.64	Yevgeniy	Lomtyev	SU	20.10.61	1		Kiev	15 Aug
45.65	Kyle	Hargett	USA	14.1.67	3	Drake	Des Moines	30 Apr
45.65A	Patrick	Barré	FRA	12.4.59	1		Font-Romeu	24 Jul
45.67	Kevin	Young	USA	16.9.66	2		Malmö	7 Aug
45.68	Patrick	Gordon	JAM	20.8.65	4	Drake	Des Moines	30 Apr
45.68A	Thomas	Johnson	USA	7.6.65	3		Albuquerque	9 Jun
45.69	Oliver	Bridges	USA	30.6.62	5s1	TAC	Tampa	17 Jun
	(70)							
45.69	Troy	Douglas	BER	30.11.62	2h10	OG	Seoul	24 Sep
45.72	Lucas	Sang	KEN	12.2.61	6q2	OG	Seoul	25 Sep
45.75	Juha	Pyy	FIN	12.6.63	1=	WG	Helsinki	30 Jun
45.75	Patrick	Delice	TRI	12.11.67	7q2	OG	Seoul	25 Sep
45.76	Harry	Ellerby	USA	4.5.69	1		Lincoln, PA.	7 May
45.77	Bernard	Chatman	USA	22.9.65	1		Fresno	9 Apr
45.77	Bodo	Kuhn	FRG	9.8.67	1		Ulm	6 Aug
45.77	António	Sanchez	SPA	22.9.63	3		Salamanca	8 Sep
45.78	Jorge	Valentín	CUB	16.8.64	1	Nar	Sofia	25 Jun
45.79	Lee	Bridges	USA	20.3.67	2	Big 10	Ann Arbor	22 May
	(80)							
45.80	Chris	Nelloms	USA	14.8.71	1		Columbus	4 May
45.81	Tim	Hesse	GHA	7.3.68	1		Tucson	19 Mar
45.82	Arkadiy	Kornilov	SU	25.2.63	1	Znam	Leningrad	11 Jun
45.84	Amadou	Dia Bâ	SEN	22.9.58	1		Dijon	11 Jun
45.84	Nordin M.	Jadi	MAL	12.6.62	3rA		Westwood	3 Sep
45.86	Vladimir	Prosin	SU	15.8.59	2		Sochi	31 May
45.87	Félix	Stevens	CUB	8.3.64	1		Habana	11 Jun
45.87	Moses	Ugbisie	NIG	11.12.64	1s1	AfrC	Annaba	29 Aug
45.88	Mark	Garner	AUS	30.6.69	4	NC	Perth	26 Mar
45.88	Sunder	Nix	USA	2.12.61	1h4	FOT	Indianapolis	16 Jul
	(90)							
45.89	Samuel	Matete	ZAM	25.7.69	2s1	AfrC	Annaba	29 Aug
45.91	Mark	Everett	USA	2.9.68	1rB		Westwood	3 Sep
45.92	Ken	Lowery	USA	13.8.61	1		Indianapolis	12 Jun
45.92	Aleksandr	Minakov	SU	28.8.59	2		Kiev	15 Aug
45.94	Marlin	Cannon	USA	9.12.70	1		Austin	14 May
45.94	Anthony	Washington	USA	22.12.66	2h1	Pac-10	Westwood	21 May
45.94	Aleksandr	Kurochkin	SU	23.7.61	3		Sochi	31 May
45.95	Anthony	Christie	JAM	22.2.67	1		Baton Rouge	23 Apr
45.95	Charles	Bruce	USA	18.4.67	1		Houston	7 May
45.96	Moses	Kyeswa	UGA	12.4.58	2		Kvarnsveden	19 Jun
	(100)							
45.99	Tamás	Molnár	HUN	23.7.68	2 v	2-N	Athinai	4 Jun
45.99	Lubos	Balosák	CS	5.4.65	1		Budapest	11 Jul

Mark	Name		Nat	Born	Date
46.00	Mike	Cannon	USA	64	2 Jun
46.01A	Samuel	van Aswegen	RSA	65	15 Apr
46.02	Roger	Hunter	UK	65	22 May
46.02	Alemayehu	Gudeta	ETH	60	29 Aug
46.03	Ismail	Macev	YUG	60	16 Jun
46.04	Felix	Sandy	SLE	64	9 Apr
46.05	Thierry	Diagana	FRA	66	19 Jun
46.05A	Aldo	Canti	FRA	61	24 Jul
	(110)				
46.06	Gustav	Menczer	HUN	59	16 Jul
46.06	Trevor	Graham	JAM	63	16 Jul
46.07	Dries	Vorster	RSA	62	6 Apr
46.07	Harlan	Davis	USA	67	21 May
46.08	Anton	Skerritt	CAN	64	25 Sep
46.09	Elkana	Nyangau	KEN	63	25 Sep
46.10	Ben	Cureton	USA	65	14 May
46.10	Vyacheslav	Kocheryagin	SU	62	11 Jun
46.10	Jörg	Vaihinger	FRG	62	7 Aug
46.11	Leandro	Penalver	CUB	61	1 Jun
	(120)				
46.12	Bruce	Phillip	DMN	66	19 Mar
46.12	Slobodan	Brankovic	YUG	67	16 Jul

Mark	Name		Nat	Born	Date
46.13	Mark	Henrich	FRG	61	19 Jun
46.14	Seyba	Yaya	MLI	57	20 Jul
46.15	Robert	Louis	USA	66	21 May
46.15	Phil	Brown	UK	62	7 Aug
46.15A	Vito	Petrella	ITA	65	11 Aug
46.15	Aivar	Ojastu	SU	61	15 Aug
46.16	Rod	Eleby	USA	67	16 Apr
46.16	Kevin	Henderson	USA	65	8 Jun
	(130)				
46.19	Angel	Heras	SPA	58	1 Jun
46.19	Robert	Ballard	AUS	64	19 Sep
46.20	Roberto	Ribaud	ITA	61	20 Jul
46.21	Steve	Perry	AUS	70	28 Jul
46.22	Elvis	Forde	BAR	59	22 May
46.22	Mike	Spangler	USA	66	28 May
46.23	Ousmane	Diarra	SEN	64	25 Sep
46.24	Terron	Wright	USA	58	28 May
46.24	Jeroen	Fischer	BEL	66	3 Sep
46.25	Kris	Durr	USA	64	22 May
	(140)				
46.26	Seymour	Fagen	JAM		7 May
46.26	Paul	Sanders	UK	62	7 Aug
46.26	Pat	McGhee	USA	66	4 Aug
46.26	Tony	Eziuka	NIG	71	19 Sep
46.28	Jerome	Williams	USA	69	25 Jun
46.29	Anthony	Wallace	USA		
46.29	Jesse	Carr	USA	69	25 Jun
46.29	Wayne	McDonald	UK	70	28 Jul
46.30	Jürgen	Koffler	FRG	60	11 Jun
46.32	Joseph Kiptanui	Chepsiror	KEN	71	28 Jul
	(150)				
46.33A	Japie	de Jongh	RSA	64	1 Nov
46.34	Mark	Senior	JAM	63	23 Apr
46.35	Eddie	Miller	USA	69	21 May
46.35	Dawda	Jallow	GAM	69	25 Sep
46.36	Rob	Collier	USA	68	19 Mar
46.36	Frank	Müller	GDR	60	13 Sep
46.37	Takahiro	Watanabe	JAP	70	1 Aug
46.38	Pat	Lanning	USA	66	9 Apr
46.38	David	Lawyer	USA		21 May
46.39	Calvin	Smith	USA	61	2 Apr
	(160)				
46.39	Eric	Jösjö	SWE	61	3 Sep
46.40A	Leon	van Biljoen	RSA	67	15 Apr
46.40A	Carlos	Morales	CHL	66	22 Jul
46.40	Dimitar	Rangelov	BUL	63	2 Sep
46.41	Yann	Quentrec	FRA	62	2 Aug
46.42	Roy	Martin	USA	66	7 May
46.43	Mark	Richardson	UK	72	28 Jul
46.43	Momchil	Kharizanov	BUL	62	16 Jul
46.43A	Mauro	Zuliani	ITA	59	11 Aug
46.44	Lorenzo	McGill	USA		
	(170)				
46.44A	Demetrius	Carter	USA	67	14 May
46.44	Wojciech	Lach	POL	68	15 Sep

Low altitude marks for athletes with altitude bests

44.90	Schönlebe	5s2	OG	Seoul	26 Sep	44.62A
45.39	Babers	4q3	FOT	Indianapolis	17 Jul	45.37A
45.72	Barré	1	NC	Tours	14 Aug	45.65A

46.05	Malave	25 Jun	45.61A
46.17	Petrella	20 Jul	46.15A
46.24	Stevens	6 Aug	45.94A
46.28	Caldwell	16 Jul	45.58A

Hand timing

45.0A	Simon	Kipkemboi	KEN	15.4.60	1h2	OT	Nairobi	12 Aug
45.1A	Elkana	Nyangau	KEN	63	1		Nairobi	21 May
45.2	Pat	Gordon	JAM	20.8.65	1	SWC	Austin	15 May
45.3A	Lucas	Sang	KEN	12.2.61	1h1	OT	Nairobi	12 Aug
45.5A	Joseph	Saina	KEN	3.1.66	2h1	OT	Nairobi	12 Aug
45.6	Mike	Cannon	USA	26.10.64	3	SWC	Austin	15 May
45.7A	Stephen	Mwanzia	KEN	65	2h2	OT	Nairobi	12 Aug
45.8A	Samuel	van Aswegen	RSA	5.11.65	1		Germiston	24 Mar
45.8	Tamás	Molnár	HUN	23.7.68	1	NC	Budapest	16 Jul
45.8A	Tito	Sawe	KEN	10.7.60	5	OT	Nairobi	13 Aug

45.9A	Thomas	Koech	KEN	65	13 Aug
46.0	Terrence	Sheppard	USA	68	23 Apr
46.0	Felipe	Lomba	POR	59	8 May
46.0A	David	Kitur	KEN	62	12 Aug
46.2A	Marius	Erlank	RSA	68	24 Mar
46.2	Larry	Gardner	USA	66	7 May
46.2	Maurice	Holt	USA	67	15 May
	(46.27 per Texas A&M)				
46.2	Albert	Ransom	USA	71	28 May
46.2	Allen	Ingraham	BAH	62	19 Jun
46.3	Mike	Greene	USA	66	23 Apr
46.3A	Jafter	Keter	KEN	63	21 May

400 Metres Year List Progression

Year	Best	10th	20th	50th	100th	Under 46.00	Under 46.30	Ave.100
1958	45.4	46.3	46.6	47.2	47.6	3	5	
1968	43.86	45.2	45.6	46.2	46.7	42	60	
1978	44.27	45.37	45.65	46.15	46.60	37	62	46.041
1979	44.92	45.24	45.73	46.10	46.47	39	70	46.005
1980	44.60	45.33	45.57	46.03	46.35	45	86	45.910
1981	44.58	45.18	45.54	46.02	46.31	46	96	45.871
1982	44.68	45.09	45.46	45.89	46.23	65	106	45.764
1983	44.50	44.98	45.29	45.74	46.16	80	117	45.627
1984	44.27	44.83	45.19	45.62	46.03	98	157	45.511
1985	44.47	44.91	45.11	45.52	45.99	102	139	45.477
1986	44.30	44.72	45.02	45.61	46.01	99	139	45.463
1987	44.10	44.72	45.04	45.59	46.00	99	155	45.470
1988	43.29	44.61	44.88	45.40	45.96	102	147	45.336

Mark	Name		Nat	Born	Pos	Meet	Venue	Date

800 METRES

Mark	Name		Nat	Born	Pos	Meet	Venue	Date
1:42.65	Johnny	Gray	USA	19.6.60	1rA	WK	Zürich	17 Aug
1:43.10		Gray			1	APM	Hengelo	14 Aug
1:43.20	José Luiz	Barbosa	BRA	27.5.61	2rA	WK	Zürich	17 Aug
1:43.34		Barbosa			1rA	R W	Koblenz	28 Aug
1:43.42	Steve	Cram	UK	14.10.60	3rA	WK	Zürich	17 Aug
1:43.45	Paul	Ereng	KEN	22.8.67	1	OG	Seoul	26 Sep
1:43.49		Barbosa			2	APM	Hengelo	14 Aug
1:43.70		Gray			1	Jerome	Burnaby	5 Jun
1:43.86	Said	Aouita	MOR	2.11.59	1	ASV	Köln	21 Aug
1:43.90	Joaquim	Cruz	BRA	12.3.63	2	OG	Seoul	26 Sep
1:43.93	Sebastian	Coe	UK	29.9.56	2rA	R W	Koblenz	28 Aug
1:43.96		Gray			1	FOT	Indianapolis	18 Jul
1:44.06	Moussa	Fall	SEN	28.8.63	4rA	WK	Zürich	17 Aug
1:44.06	Sam	Koskei	KEN	14.5.61	3rA	R W	Koblenz	28 Aug
1:44.06		Aouita			3	OG	Seoul	26 Sep
1:44.10	Vladimir	Graudyn	SU	26.8.63	1	Bisl	Oslo	2 Jul
1:44.12	Peter	Elliott	UK	9.10.62	4	OG	Seoul	26 Sep
1:44.16		Cram			1	OT	Birmingham	6 Aug
1:44.19		Elliott			1		Rieti	31 Aug
1:44.21	Peter	Braun	FRG	1.8.62	2	Bisl	Oslo	2 Jul
1:44.27		Cruz			2	ASV	Köln	21 Aug
1:44.36		Aouita			1	VD	Bruxelles	19 Aug
1:44.38	Joseph	Chesire	KEN	12.11.57	1rA		Sevilla	1 Jun
1:44.42	Abdi	Bile	SOM	28.12.62	1		Kvarnsveden	19 Jun
1:44.43	Tracy	Baskin	USA	3.11.65	5rA	WK	Zürich	17 Aug
1:44.43		Gray			2	VD	Bruxelles	19 Aug
1:44.46	Mark	Everett	USA	2.9.68	2	FOT	Indianapolis	18 Jul
1:44.47		Barbosa			3	ASV	Köln	21 Aug
1:44.5mA	Nixon	Kiprotich	KEN	4.12.62	1	OT	Nairobi	13 Aug
1:44.51		Elliott			6rA	WK	Zürich	17 Aug
	(30/17)							
1:44.59	Tony	Morrell	UK	30.5.62	3	Bisl	Oslo	2 Jul
1:44.75	Slobodan	Popovic	YUG	28.9.62	2		Linz	15 Aug
1:44.8mA	Juma	Ndiwa	KEN	28.11.60	2	OT	Nairobi	13 Aug
	(20)							
1:44.82	Dieudonné	Kwizéra	BUR	6.6.67	1rB	R W	Koblenz	28 Aug
1:44.90	Donato	Sabia	ITA	11.9.63	3s1	OG	Seoul	25 Sep
1:44.92	Ibrahim	Okash	SOM	18.9.64	3		Kvarnsveden	19 Jun
1:44.98	Rob	Druppers	HOL	29.4.62	2rA		Sevilla	1 Jun
1:45.05	Tom	McKean	UK	27.10.63	1rB	WK	Zürich	17 Aug
1:45.06	Ocky	Clark	USA	14.11.60	2rA		Bern	23 Aug
1:45.09	Babacar	Niang	SEN	9.9.58	5s1	OG	Seoul	25 Sep
1:45.11	Faouzi	Lahbi	MOR	2.3.58	3	APM	Hengelo	14 Aug
1:45.12	Alvaro	Silva	POR	21.4.65	5s2	OG	Seoul	25 Sep
1:45.14	Ari	Suhonen	FIN	19.12.65	1	WG	Helsinki	30 Jun
	(30)							
1:45.17	Rob	van Helden	HOL	6.2.65	4	APM	Hengelo	14 Aug
1:45.20	Stanley	Redwine	USA	10.4.61	5	APM	Hengelo	14 Aug
1:45.29	Andrey	Sudnik	SU	11.3.67	4	Bisl	Oslo	2 Jul
1:45.32	Steve	Heard	UK	29.4.62	3	AAA	Birmingham	6 Aug
1:45.35	George	Kersh	USA	3.7.68	4	FOT	Indianapolis	18 Jul
1:45.4m	Simon	Hoogewerf	CAN	11.5.63	1		Victoria,BC	23 Jul
1:45.47	Mike	Okot	UGA	25.12.58	5		Kvarnsveden	19 Jun
1:45.50	James	Robinson	USA	27.8.54	1	Jenner	San Jose	28 May
1:45.58	William	Wuyke	VEN	21.5.58	7	APM	Hengelo	14 Aug
1:45.6m	Sergey	Afanasyev	SU	28.4.64	1		Kiev	25 Jun
	(40)							
1:45.64	Paul	Herbert	UK	20.12.66	1	NC	Derby	5 Jun
1:45.65	Réda	Abdenouz	ALG	29.12.68	2		Grosseto	10 Aug
1:45.69	Steve	Crabb	UK	30.11.63	4rB	WK	Zürich	17 Aug
1:45.70	Barry	Acres	AUS	9.7.65	1		Canberra	26 Jan
1:45.70	David	Sharpe	UK	8.7.67	5	Bisl	Oslo	2 Jul
1:45.70	Edgar	Itt	FRG	8.6.67	2rB	R W	Koblenz	28 Aug

Mark	Name		Nat	Born	Pos	Meet	Venue	Date
1:45.72	Tonino	Viali	ITA	16.9.60	4		Rieti	31 Aug
1:45.74	Getahun	Ayana	ETH	10.9.65	8	APM	Hengelo	14 Aug
1:45.79	Charlton	Hamer	USA	7.8.66	3	TAC	Tampa	18 Jun
1:45.79	John	Marshall	USA	5.11.63	4rA		Athinai	3 Sep
	(50)							
1:45.8m	Viktor	Kalinkin	SU	23.2.60	2		Kiev	25 Jun
1:45.88	Piotr	Piekarski	POL	10.4.64	1		Sopot	20 Aug
1:45.9mA	Sisa	Kirati	KEN	.57	3		Nairobi	20 May
1:45.91	Ray	Brown	USA	11.8.61	3rB	R W	Koblenz	28 Aug
1:45.92	Oslen	Barr	GUY	3.4.61	1		Houston	7 May
1:45.92	Agberto	Guimarães	BRA	18.8.57	6rB	WK	Zürich	17 Aug
1:45.93	Cheikh Tidiane	Boye	SEN	10.8.61	6s2	OG	Seoul	25 Sep
1:45.96	Rainer	Thau	FRG	2.12.62	1		Menden	15 Jun
1:45.98	Pablo	Squella	CHL	14.8.63	2rB		Bern	23 Aug
1:46.0m	Andrey	Kraminskiy	SU	27.3.63	1		Kharkov	4 Jul
	(60)							
1:46.0m	Stephen	Ole Marai	KEN	11.11.62	5	OT	Nairobi	13 Aug
1:46.06	Martin	Enholm	SWE	7.2.65	6		Kvarnsveden	19 Jun
1:46.08	Ryszard	Ostrowski	POL	6.2.61	3rB		Bern	23 Aug
1:46.1m	Mike	Hillardt	AUS	22.1.61	1		Melbourne	4 Feb
1:46.11	Markus	Trinkler	SWZ	11.10.62	7rB	WK	Zürich	17 Aug
1:46.13	Gary	Marlow	UK	26.11.63	7		Verona	27 Jul
1:46.21	Thomas	Johnson	USA	7.6.65	2	MSR	Walnut	24 Apr
1:46.25	Ikem	Billy	UK	25.1.64	6	Bisl	Oslo	2 Jul
1:46.26	Ian	Gaudry	AUS	20.3.64	1		Melbourne	17 Mar
1:46.26	Paul	Osland	CAN	1.1.64	3	Jerome	Burnaby	5 Jun
	(70)							
1:46.29	Ahmed	Belkessam	ALG	27.3.62	5		Grosseto	10 Aug
1:46.38	Terrence	Herrington	USA	31.7.66	3h2	NCAA	Eugene	1 Jun
1:46.42	Geryl	House	USA	18.8.65	1s1	FOT	Indianapolis	17 Jul
1:46.44	Mike	Stahr	USA	9.12.64	4	TAC	Tampa	18 Jun
1:46.44	Hauke	Fuhlbrügge	GDR	21.3.66	2 v	FRG	Düsseldorf	20 Jun
1:46.47	Luc	Bernaert	BEL	24.6.66	1		Hechtel	30 Jul
1:46.49	Jack	Armour	USA	10.2.61	1rB		Athinai	3 Sep
1:46.50	David	Patrick	USA	12.6.60	4	MSR	Walnut	24 Apr
1:46.50	Esko	Parpala	FIN	2.7.65	6	WG	Helsinki	30 Jun
1:46.55	Rafal	Jerzy	POL	27.4.66	1		Sopot	30 Jul
	(80)							
1:46.57A	Daniel	Makoena	RSA	9.9.58	1		Germiston	24 Mar
1:46.57	António	Abrantes	POR	15.5.68	2rB		Athinai	3 Sep
1:46.58	Colomán	Trabado	SPA	2.1.58	1		Jerez	28 Jun
1:46.6m	Mauricio	Hernández	MEX	30.11.61	1		Ciudad Victoria	10 Jul
1:46.66	Peter Kip	Rono	KEN	31.7.67	2		Leverkusen	28 Jun
1:46.70	Atle	Douglas	UK	9.6.68	1		Sandnes	9 Jun
1:46.7mA	Robert	Kibet	KEN	.65	6	OT	Nairobi	13 Aug
1:46.71	Thomas	Giessing	FRG	19.3.61	5		Linz	15 Aug
1:46.74	Miroslav	Chochkov	BUL	26.12.67	1		Stara Zagora	28 Aug
1:46.78	Gert	Kilbert	SWZ	21.9.65	9rA	Athl	Lausanne	24 Jun
	(90)							
1:46.80	Tomas	De Teresa	SPA	5.9.68	3rB		Athinai	3 Sep
1:46.84	Roosevelt	Jackson	USA	4.4.62	3	Pepsi	Westwood	5 Jun
1:46.88	Simon	Doyle	AUS	.66	3		Canberra	26 Jan
1:46.88	Ian	Newhouse	CAN	25.12.56	5	Jerome	Burnaby	5 Jun
1:46.89	Teofilo	Benito	SPA	22.7.66	1rB		Sevilla	1 Jun
1:46.9mA	Jonah	Birir	KEN	27.12.71	2h2	NC	Nairobi	17 Jun
1:46.9m	Leonid	Masunov	SU	5.5.62	4		Kiev	25 Jun
1:46.9m	Mike	Birke	CAN	14.1.68	2		Montreal	11 Aug
1:46.91A	David	Hlabahlaba	RSA	9.10.61	2		Germiston	24 Mar
1:46.91	Petru	Dragoescu	RUM	22.7.62	1		Bucuresti	12 Jun
	(100)							
1:46.92	Harald	Andrä	FRG	3.9.60	1rC	R W	Koblenz	28 Aug
1:46.93	Holger	Böttcher	FRG	27.7.63	3		Essen	2 Sep
1:46.94	Vadim	Laushkin	SU	5.2.65	3	NC	Kiev	2 Aug
1:46.95	Martin	Steele	UK	30.9.62	2		Cork	5 Jul
1:46.97	Bret	Garrett	USA	8.8.66	1		Champaign	28 May
1:46.97	Ado	Maude	NIG	15.2.67	1	OT/NC	Bauchi	1 Jul

Mark	Name		Nat	Born	Pos	Meet	Venue	Date
1:46.98	Axel	Harries	FRG	19.9.64	8	WG	Helsinki	30 Jun
1:46.99	Valeriy	Starodubtsev	SU	14.2.62	4	NC	Kiev	2 Aug

Mark	First name	Name	Nat	Born	Date
1:47.0m	Peter	Bourke	AUS	58	4 Feb
1:47.0m	Terrence	Goods	USA	64	
	(110)				
1:47.0mA	Wilson	Kipketer	KEN	70	17 Jun
1:47.0m	Andrey	Vamishin	SU	67	25 Jun
1:47.0m	Anatoliy	Legeda	SU	62	4 Jul
1:47.0A	Edwin	Koech	KEN	61	12 Aug
1:47.01	Claude	Diomar	FRA	61	7 Jun
1:47.03A	Karel	Mouton	RSA	67	14 Mar
1:47.03	Sotirios	Moutsanas	GRE	58	1 Jun
1:47.03	Chuck	Aragon	USA	59	17 Jun
1:47.04	Chris	McGeorge	UK	62	5 Jun
1:47.04	Jose	Arconada	SPA	64	28 Jun
	(120)				
1:47.04	Eckhardt	Rüter	FRG	63	2 Sep
1:47.05	Bo	Breigan	NOR	58	2 Jul
1:47.06A	Deon	Brummer	RSA	59	24 Mar
1:47.08	Stephan	Plätzer	FRG	66	28 Aug
1:47.09	Leonardo	de Villiers	RSA	65	9 Mar
1:47.09	Marin	Rados	RUM	62	12 Jun
1:47.10	Ismail	Yousuf	QAT	67	21 Aug
1:47.1m	Igor	Lotarev	SU	64	25 Jun
1:47.1m	Yuriy	Bukin	SU	66	4 Jul
1:47.15	Fabio	Di Vito	ITA	67	10 Aug
	(130)				
1:47.15	Alex	Geissbühler	SWZ	64	4 Sep
1:47.18	Milan	Drahonovsky	CS	66	30 Jul
1:47.19	Massimo	Martelli	ITA	64	29 Jun
1:47.20	Luis Karim	Toledo	MEX	64	24 Apr
1:47.2m	Pat	Scammell	AUS	61	4 Feb
1:47.2m	Ernest	Barrett	JAM		12 May
1:47.2m	John	Cook	USA	64	12 May
1:47.2mA	Francis	Mbuvi	KEN	59	17 Jun
1:47.2mA	David	Ngeny	KEN	59	17 Jun
1:47.2mA	B.	Kiplimo	KEN		18 Jun
	(140)				
1:47.2m	Wilfred Oanda	Kirochi	KEN	69	Jul
1:47.22	Kevin	McKay	UK	69	5 Jun
1:47.25	Han	Kulker	HOL	59	2 Sep
1:47.26	Lewis	Johnson	USA	62	14 May
1:47.26	Richie	Martinez	USA	63	20 May
1:47.26	Ralph	Schumann	GDR	66	8 Jun
1:47.29	Anthony	Christie	JAM	67	7 May
1:47.3mA	William	Tanui	KEN	64	18 Jun
1:47.3m	Ivan	Bondaryuk	SU	67	4 Jul
1:47.32	Dariusz	Odya	POL	65	19 Jun
	(150)				
1:47.32	Regis	Humphrey	USA	65	17 Jul
1:47.32	Joseph	Lucas	RSA	63	12 Nov
1:47.33	Bodo	Kuhn	FRG	67	23 May
1:47.33	Jens-Peter	Herold	GDR	65	11 Jun
1:47.34	Marco	Leenders	HOL	64	30 Jul
1:47.34	Matthias	Assmann	FRG	57	28 Aug
1:47.35	Aaron	Baynes	USA	67	15 May
1:47.35	Lennart	Skoog	SWE	64	19 Jun
1:47.36	Melfort	Homela	ZIM	70	23 Sep
1:47.38	Gert	de Bruyn	RSA	65	9 Mar
	(160)				
1:47.40	Ousmane	Diarra	SEN	64	0 Aug
1:47.4m	David	Strang	UK	68	23 Apr
1:47.4mA	Paul	Ruto	KEN	60	17 Jun
1:47.4m	Nikolay	Dobrovolskiy	SU	66	25 Jun
1:47.4m	Vladimir	Rudyuk	SU	63	4 Jul
1:47.4m	Pierre	Leveille	CAN	62	11 Aug
1:47.41	Doug	Consiglio	CAN	64	8 Jun
1:47.41	Jim	Maton	USA	66	17 Jun
1:47.41	Alexander	Adam	FRG	68	21 Aug
1:47.43	André	Lavie	FRA	59	7 Jun
	(170)				
1:47.43	Stuart	Paton	UK	63	6 Aug
1:47.45	Franzwa	Woldemariam	ETH	69	22 May
1:47.45	Markus	Trines	FRG	63	4 Sep
1:47.46	Ismail	Macev	YUG	60	4 Sep
1:47.48	Hector	Herrera	CUB	59	8 Jul
1:47.5m	Dennis	Stewart	JAM	67	9 Jun
1:47.5m	Hervé	Phelippeau	FRA	62	15 Jun
1:47.5mA	Kip	Jumo	KEN		18 Jun
1:47.51	Matt	Favier	AUS	65	17 Mar
1:47.51	Doug	Herron	USA	66	17 Jun
	(180)				
1:47.54	Alan	Ozolins	AUS	64	17 Mar
1:47.56	Pavel	Hujer	CS	69	16 Sep
1:47.58	Dietmar	Stephan	FRG	67	2 Sep
1:47.58	Jarmo	Kokkola	FIN	68	4 Sep
1:47.58	Johann	Bekker	RSA	65	12 Nov
1:47.60	Costel	Ene	RUM	62	12 Jun
1:47.60	Torsten	Kallweit	FRG	68	2 Sep
1:47.6m	Paul	Gambrah	GHA		12 May
1:47.6m	Stanislav	Varvyanskiy	SU	66	4 Jul
	(190)				
1:47.61	Giuseppe	D'Urso	ITA	69	25 Jun
1:47.62	Kraig	Cesar	USA	65	15 May
1:47.66A	Manuel	Balmaceda	CHL	67	24 Jul
1:47.67	Ton	Baltus	HOL	65	2 Sep
1:47.67	Sergey	Timofeyev	SU	68	4 Sep
1:47.67	Yoshikazu	Tachi	JAP	69	10 Oct
1:47.69	Didier	Le Guillou	FRA	60	11 Jun
1:47.70	Yves	Gardes	FRA	65	7 Jun
1:47.7m	Konstantin	Russkikh	SU	62	25 Jun
1:47.7m	Samir	Benfares	FRA	68	3 Aug
	(200)				
1:47.73	Denis	Badie	FRA	65	7 Jun

800 Metres Year List Progression

Year	Best	10th	20th	50th	100th	Under 1:46.0	Under 1:47.0	Ave.100
1958	1:46.7	1:47.6	1:48.4	1:49.6	1:50.5	-	5	
1968	1:44.40	1:46.5	1:46.9	1:47.8	1:48.7	6	22	
1978	1:43.84	1:45.7	1:46.09	1:47.24	1:48.0	19	40	1:46.92
1979	1:42.33	1:45.54	1:46.3	1:46.9	1:47.85	16	52	1:46.91
1980	1:44.53	1:45.6	1:46.11	1:46.9	1:47.85	17	52	1:46.79
1981	1:41.73	1:45.30	1:46.0	1:46.89	1:47.66	19	55	1:46.60
1982	1:44.45	1:45.05	1:45.44	1:46.5	1:47.33	31	76	1:46.29
1983	1:43.61	1:44.32	1:45.13	1:46.29	1:47.14	42	89	1:45.97
1984	1:41.77	1:43.93	1:44.87	1:46.04	1:46.97	46	101	1:45.73
1985	1:42.49	1:44.15	1:45.21	1:46.08	1:47.17	46	91	1:45.89
1986	1:43.19	1:44.59	1:45.14	1:46.18	1:47.12	40	90	1:46.00
1987	1:43.06	1:44.72	1:45.17	1:46.36	1:46.94	33	103	1:46.04
1988	1:42.65	1:44.10	1:44.8	1:45.79	1:46.91	59	109	1:45.64

1000 METRES

Mark	Name		Nat	Born	Pos	Meet	Venue	Date
2:15.16	Said	Aouita	MOR	2.11.59	1		London	28 Aug
2:16.47	Peter	Elliott	UK	9.10.62	1		Belfast	27 Jun
2:16.86	Sam	Koskei	KEN	14.5.61	2		Belfast	27 Jun
2:16.99	Tony	Morrell	UK	30.5.62	2		London	28 Aug
2:17.18	Eckhardt	Rüter	FRG	24.10.63	1		Hamm	9 Sep
2:17.67	Mike	Hillardt	AUS	22.1.61	1		Melbourne	14 Jan
2:17.75	Abdi	Bile	SOM	28.12.62	1	PG	London	8 Jul
2:17.76	Joaquim	Cruz	BRA	12.3.63	1		San Diego	25 Jun
2:17.80	Steve	Cram	UK	14.10.60	2	PG	London	8 Jul
2:17.84	Maurice	Smith	USA	20.11.62	3		Belfast	27 Jun
(10)								
2:17.89	Hauke	Fuhlbrügge	GDR	21.3.66	1		Berlin	13 Sep
2:17.95	Ibrahim	Okash	SOM	18.9.64	4		Belfast	27 Jun
2:18.03	Benny	Greyling	RSA	1.2.65	1		Stellenbosch	8 Feb
2:18.12	Alessandro	Lambruschini	ITA	7.1.65	2		Viareggio	3 Aug
2:18.22	Miroslav	Chochkov	BUL	26.12.67	1		Stara Zagora	20 Aug
2:18.34	Deon	Brummer	RSA	4.4.59	2		Stellenbosch	8 Feb
2:18.34	Joseph	Chesire	KEN	12.11.57	4	PG	London	8 Jul
2:18.44	George	Kersh	USA	3.7.68	2		San Diego	25 Jun
2:18.44	Lewis	Johnson	USA	13.12.62	5		Belfast	27 Jun
2:18.52	Ocky	Clark	USA	14.11.60	3		Viareggio	3 Aug
(20)								
2:18.61	Jens Peter	Herold	GDR	25.10.65	2		Berlin	13 Sep
2:18.72	Ari	Suhonen	FIN	19.12.65	5	PG	London	8 Jul
2:18.94	Wilfred Oanda	Kirochi	KEN	12.12.69	2		Gateshead	16 Jul
2:18.95	Rob	Druppers	HOL	29.4.62	1		Madrid	7 Jun
Indoor mark								
2:16.62	Rob	Druppers	HOL	29.4.62	1		Den Haag	20 Feb

1500 METRES

Mark	Name		Nat	Born	Pos	Meet	Venue	Date
3:30.95	Steve	Cram	UK	14.10.60	1	VD	Bruxelles	19 Aug
3:31.01	Jim	Spivey	USA	7.3.60	1	R W	Koblenz	28 Aug
3:32.69	Said	Aouita	MOR	2.11.59	1	Nik	Nice	10 Jul
3:32.94	Peter	Elliott	UK	9.10.62	2	VD	Bruxelles	19 Aug
3:33.33	Jens Peter	Herold	GDR	25.10.65	1		Potsdam	8 Jun
3:33.6m	Abdi	Bile	SOM	28.12.62	1+	Bisl	Oslo	2 Jul
3:33.7m		Herold			2+	Bisl	Oslo	2 Jul
3:33.7m		Cram			3+	Bisl	Oslo	2 Jul
3:33.8m		Elliott			4+	Bisl	Oslo	2 Jul
3:33.95	Steve	Crabb	UK	30.11.63	1	GGala	Verona	27 Jul
3:34.06	Mike	Hillardt	AUS	22.1.61	1		Melbourne	17 Mar
3:34.53	Mark	Rowland	UK	7.3.63	2	GGala	Verona	27 Jul
3:34.61	Pat	Scammell	AUS	15.4.61	2		Melbourne	17 Mar
3:34.63	Joaquim	Cruz	BRA	12.3.63	1	APM	Hengelo	14 Aug
3:34.72	Gennaro	Di Napoli	ITA	5.3.68	1		Rieti	31 Aug
3:34.8m		Spivey			5+	Bisl	Oslo	2 Jul
3:34.8m		Crabb			6+	Bisl	Oslo	2 Jul
3:34.82	Dieter	Baumann	FRG	9.2.65	1	WK	Zürich	17 Aug
3:34.9m	Steve	Scott	USA	5.5.56	7+	Bisl	Oslo	2 Jul
3:34.96		Herold			1		Jena	3 Jun
3:34.97		Baumann			2	APM	Hengelo	14 Aug
3:35.14	Adrian	Passey	UK	2.9.64	2		Rieti	31 Aug
3:35.20		Spivey			2	WK	Zürich	17 Aug
3:35.22		Cruz			3	WK	Zürich	17 Aug
3:35.32	Mogens	Guldberg	DEN	2.8.63	3	APM	Hengelo	14 Aug
3:35.54		Guldberg			2	Nik	Nice	10 Jul
3:35.59	Peter Kip	Rono	KEN	31.7.67	1	Jerome	Burnaby	5 Jun
3:35.61	Pascal	Thiébaut	FRA	6.6.59	3	Nik	Nice	10 Jul
3:35.65+		Aouita			1	WK	Zürich	17 Aug
3:35.70		Aouita			1	DNG	Stockholm	5 Jul
3:35.70	Abdelmajid	Moncef	MOR	10.5.61	3	GGala	Verona	27 Jul
	(31/19)							

Mark	Name		Nat	Born	Pos	Meet	Venue	Date
3:35.72	Sebastian	Coe	UK	29.9.56	3		Rieti	31 Aug
3:35.78	Mustapha	Lachaal	MOR	10.2.64	4	GGala	Verona	27 Jul
3:35.81	Terry	Brahm	USA	21.11.62	4	APM	Hengelo	14 Aug
3:35.82	Doug	Consiglio	CAN	10.1.64	2	Jerome	Burnaby	5 Jun
3:35.83	Mark	Deady	USA	2.1.67	5	APM	Hengelo	14 Aug
3:35.84	Joe	Falcon	USA	23.6.66	1		Fayetteville	16 Apr
3:36.04	Marcus	O'Sullivan	IRL	22.12.61	3	VD	Bruxelles	19 Aug
3:36.07	Wilfred Oanda	Kirochi	KEN	12.12.69	4		Rieti	31 Aug
3:36.10	Jeff	Atkinson	USA	24.2.63	6	APM	Hengelo	14 Aug
3:36.18	Rémy	Geoffroy	FRA	22.3.63	5	GGala	Verona	27 Jul
3:36.2m	Kipkoech	Cheruiyot	KEN	2.12.64	8+	Bisl	Oslo	2 Jul
	(30)							
3:36.2m	Joseph	Chesire	KEN	12.11.57	9+	Bisl	Oslo	2 Jul
3:36.26	Rachid	Kram	ALG	5.4.63	6	GGala	Verona	27 Jul
3:36.3m	John	Walker	NZ	12.1.52	10+	Bisl	Oslo	2 Jul
3:36.41	José Luis	Gonzalez	SPA	8.12.57	2	R W	Koblenz	28 Aug
3:36.42	Tim	Hacker	USA	27.12.62	1		Athinai	3 Sep
3:36.47	Sydney	Maree	USA	9.9.56	2	ASV	Köln	21 Aug
3:36.47	Jan	Kubista	CS	27.5.60	6		Rieti	31 Aug
3:36.62	Hauke	Fuhlbrügge	GDR	21.3.66	1	vFRG	Düsseldorf	19 Jun
3:36.63	Peter	Wirz	SWZ	29.7.60	4	R W	Koblenz	28 Aug
3:36.79	Andreas	Busse	GDR	6.5.59	3		Potsdam	8 Jun
	(40)							
3:36.81	Vincent	Rousseau	BEL	29.7.62	5	Nik	Nice	10 Jul
3:36.84	Hervé	Phelippeau	FRA	16.9.62	5	R W	Koblenz	28 Aug
3:36.90	Steve	Ovett	UK	9.10.55	7	APM	Hengelo	14 Aug
3:36.9m	Sergey	Afanasyev	SU	28.4.64	1		Kiev	24 Jun
3:36.99	Han	Kulker	HOL	15.8.59	8	APM	Hengelo	14 Aug
3:37.07	Markus	Hacksteiner	SWZ	18.11.64	2	Bisl	Oslo	2 Jul
3:37.1m	Viktor	Kalinkin	SU	23.2.60	2		Kiev	24 Jun
3:37.2m	Igor	Lotarev	SU	30.8.64	3		Kiev	24 Jun
3:37.23	Marco	Rapp	SWZ	23.9.57	9	WK	Zürich	17 Aug
3:37.29	Davide	Tirelli	ITA	12.8.66	7		Rieti	31 Aug
	(50)							
3:37.3m	Anatoliy	Legeda	SU	27.10.62	4		Kiev	24 Jun
3:37.31	Ari	Suhonen	FIN	19.12.65	1		Lohja	28 Aug
3:37.33	Branko	Zorko	YUG	1.7.67	7	Nik	Nice	10 Jul
3:37.38	Eckhardt	Rüter	FRG	24.10.63	6	R W	Koblenz	28 Aug
3:37.4mA	Sisa	Kirati	KEN	.57	2	NC	Nairobi	18 Jun
3:37.57	Paul	Larkins	UK	19.5.63	1	WG	Helsinki	30 Jun
3:37.73	Bruno	Levant	FRA	24.1.60	10	Nik	Nice	10 Jul
3:37.83	Klaus Peter	Nabein	FRG	10.5.60	4	Bisl	Oslo	2 Jul
3:37.89	José	Moreira	POR	6.7.64	2		Athinai	3 Sep
3:38.02	Julius	Kariuki	KEN	12.6.61	5	Bisl	Oslo	2 Jul
	(60)							
3:38.02	Gerry	O'Reilly	IRL	1.7.64	9		Rieti	31 Aug
3:38.07	Dave	Reid	CAN	26.3.63	10		Rieti	31 Aug
3:38.13	Dieudonné	Kwizéra	BUR	6.6.67	4		Malmö	8 Aug
3:38.17	Charles	Cheruiyot	KEN	2.12.64	2		Budapest	11 Jul
3:38.17	Mahmoud	Kalboussi	TUN	9.2.65	1		Bern	23 Aug
3:38.21	Abel	Anton	SPA	24.10.62	9	R W	Koblenz	28 Aug
3:38.22	Dave	Campbell	CAN	31.8.60	8	Bisl	Oslo	2 Jul
3:38.24	Peter	O'Donoghue	NZ	1.10.61	2		Bern	23 Aug
3:38.3m	Alessandro	Lambruschini	ITA	7.1.65	1		Viareggio	13 Jul
3:38.40	Omer	Khalifa	SUD	18.12.56	3s2	OG	Seoul	30 Sep
	(70)							
3:38.44	Frank	O'Mara	IRL	17.7.60	1		Lappeenranta	5 Jul
3:38.50	Mika	Maaskola	FIN	15.9.66	9	Bisl	Oslo	2 Jul
3:38.50	Pavel	Yakovlev	SU	20.1.58	3		Budapest	11 Jul
3:38.51	Nikos	Vousis	GRE	16.1.66	1		Drama	25 Jun
3:38.56	Mário	Silva	POR	23.7.61	4s2	OG	Seoul	30 Sep
3:38.59	Tom	Hanlon	UK	2.5.67	3		Dijon	12 Jun
3:38.65	Rainer	Thau	FRG	2.12.62	10	R W	Koblenz	28 Aug
3:38.70	Steffen	Brand	FRG	10.3.65	10	Bisl	Oslo	2 Jul
3:38.75	M.Brahim	Boutayeb	MOR	15.8.67	5		La Coruña	4 Aug
3:38.79	Neil	Horsfield	UK	7.12.66	5	PG	London	8 Jul
	(80)							

Mark	Name		Nat	Born	Pos	Meet	Venue	Date
3:38.80	Espen	Borge	NOR	8.9.61	11	Bisl	Oslo	2 Jul
3:38.84	José Luiz	Barbosa	BRA	27.5.61	4		Bern	23 Aug
3:38.86	Lars	Bogh	DEN	29.9.64	2		Växjö	25 Aug
3:39.0m	Ilya	Korobkov	SU	.66	5		Kiev	24 Jun
3:39.02	Jari	Venäläinen	FIN	21.8.67	2		Lappeenranta	5 Jul
3:39.05	Richard	Martinez	USA	31.7.63	2		Stockholm	4 Aug
3:39.07	Mario	Neumann	GDR	7.9.68	2		Potsdam	8 Sep
3:39.08	Kai	Jenkel	SWZ	24.2.64	5		Bern	23 Aug
3:39.1m	Brendan	Matthias	CAN	12.8.69	1		Montreal	11 Aug
3:39.25	Ove	Talsnes	NOR	22.6.62	12	Bisl	Oslo	2 Jul
	(90)							
3:39.26	Marc	Olesen	CAN	13.10.64	1		Stanford	23 Apr
3:39.31	Rob	Druppers	HOL	29.4.62	4		Jerez	28 Jun
3:39.34	Teófilo	Benito	SPA	22.7.66	5		Bilbao	9 Jul
3:39.36	Barnabas	Korir	KEN	.65	4		Århus	6 Jul
3:39.39	José Manuel	Abascal	SPA	17.3.58	6		Bilbao	9 Jul
3:39.39	László	Tóth	HUN	31.8.55	3		Budapest	11 Jul
3:39.4mA	Joshua	Kipkemboi	KEN	22.2.60	1		Nairobi	22 May
3:39.41	Radim	Kuncicky	CS	18.5.67	2		Berlin	29 Jun
3:39.42	Ray	Flynn	IRL	22.1.57	3		Victoria	8 Jun
3:39.46	Pierre	Délèze	SWZ	25.9.58	4		Lappeenranta	5 Jul
	(100)							
3:39.46	Lorenzo	Hidalgo	SPA	7.1.65	7		Bilbao	9 Jul
3:39.47	Andrés	Vera	SPA	31.12.60	8	ASV	Köln	21 Aug

Mark	Name		Nat	Born	Date
3:39.5m	Andrew	McGuigan	CAN	66	11 Aug
3:39.51	Maurice	Smith	USA	62	18 Jun
3:39.52	Walter	Merlo	ITA	65	10 Jul
3:39.54	Angel	Fariñas	SPA	67	9 Jul
3:39.56	Manuel	Pancorbo	SPA	66	4 Aug
3:39.57	Mal	Edwards	UK	58	8 Jul
3:39.61	Ivo	Schutte	GDR	66	10 Jul
3:39.61	Vasiliy	Matveyev	SU	62	31 Jul
	(110)				
3:39.66	Adelino	Hidalgo	SPA	63	28 Jun
3:39.69	Eduardo	Henriques	POR	68	20 Aug
3:39.73	Sándor	Serfözö	HUN	66	11 Jul
3:39.78	Peter	Bourke	AUS	58	9Feb
3:39.8m	Roman	Punda	SU	64	24 Jun
3:39.8m	João	Campos	POR	58	13 Aug
3:39.88	Ronny	Olsson	SWE	61	19 Jun
3:39.9m	Harvey	Mitro	CAN	64	11 Aug
3:39.91	Charles	Marsala	USA	65	4 Jun
3:39.91	Jama	Aden	SOM	62	28 Aug
	(120)				
3:39.97	Mike	Stahr	USA	64	4 Jun
3:40.0m	Gawain	Guy	USA	62	16 Jul
3:40.06A	Deon	Brummer	RSA	59	15Apr
3:40.1m	José	Regalo	POR	63	2 Jul
3:40.11	António	Monteiro	POR	63	28 Jun
3:40.11	Abdelaziz	Sahere	MOR	67	28 Jun
3:40.15	Domingos	Castro	POR	63	30 Jul
3:40.16	Dionisio	Castro	POR	63	30 Jul
3:40.17	Ferenc	Reichnach	HUN	64	11 Jul
3:40.18	Bob	Dielis	HOL	65	30 Jul
	(130)				
3:40.19	Steve	Balkey	USA	65	2 Jul
3:40.22	John	Hinton	USA	62	18 Jun
3:40.30	Mark	Kirk	UK	63	8 Jul
3:40.31	Jaime	Villalonga	SPA	65	20 Aug
3:40.32	Roosevelt	Jackson	USA	62	11 Jun
3:40.33	Bennie	Greyling	RSA	65	26Apr
3:40.36	Ross	Donoghue	USA	59	2 Jul
3:40.38	Atle	Karlsen	NOR	65	2 Jul
3:40.41	Nourredine	Morceli	ALG	70	16 Jul
3:40.42	Stefano	Mei	ITA	63	13 Jun
	(140)				
3:40.43	Tony	Morrell	UK	62	21 May
3:40.47	Igor	Kristensen	NOR	61	2 Jul
3:40.47	Rafal	Jerzy	POL	66	11 Jul
3:40.47	Constantin	Gavrila	RUM	67	16 Jul
3:40.49	Rui	Moreira	POR	65	20 Aug
3:40.5m	Valeriy	Abramov	SU	56	24 Jun
3:40.56	Monde	Tutani	RSA	62	26Apr
3:40.56	Aleksandr	Lysenko	SU	55	31 Jul
3:40.58	Philippe	Fargère	FRA	64	11 Jun
3:40.60	Greg	Whiteley	USA	67	22 May
	(150)				
3:40.60	Alfredo	Rodelas	SPA	61	28 Jun
3:40.60	Luca	Vandi	ITA	62	27 Jul
3:40.65	Steve	Ave	USA	63	18 Jun
3:40.66	Jacky	Carlier	FRA	61	21 May
3:40.70	Simon	Hoogewerf	CAN	63	9 Aug
3:40.73	Tom	Moloney	IRL	60	8 Aug
3:40.78	Zeki	Oztürk	TUR	65	28 Aug
3:40.80	Mike	Michno	USA	62	2 Jul
3:40.80	Enda	Fitzpatrick	IRL	65	10 Aug
3:40.8m	Jim	Norris	USA	63	6 Jul
	(160)				
3:40.81	Eddy	Stevens	BEL	61	27 Jun
3:40.83	Stephen	Halliday	UK	68	16 Jul
3:40.85	Jan	Persson	SWE	61	5 Jul
3:40.9m	Dave	Mather	CAN	65	11 Aug
3:40.91	Dub	Myers	USA	64	21 Jul
3:40.92	Gary	Staines	UK	63	21 Jun
3:40.94	Robert	Denmark	UK	68	31 Jul
3:41.0A	Jackson	Lokol	KEN	64	13 Aug
3:41.01	Waldemar	Lisicki	POL	62	13 Aug
3:41.04	Terrence	Herrington	USA	66	21 Jul
	(170)				
3:41.12	Adrian	Callan	UK	62	16 Jul
3:41.12	José Luis	Carreira	SPA	62	8 Sep
3:41.13	Darryl	Frerker	USA	63	18 Jun
3:41.13	Spyros	Spyrou	CYP	58	3 Sep

Indoor Marks

Mark	Name		Nat	Born	Pos	Venue	Date
3:35.4m	Marcus	O'Sullivan	IRL	22.12.61	1+	East Rutherford	13 Feb
3:38.06	Rüdiger	Horn	GDR	28.7.67	2	Wien	13-Feb

Mark	Name		Nat	Born	Pos	Meet	Venue	Date

1500 Metres Year List Progression

Year	Best	10th	20th	50th	100th	Under 3:38.0	Under 3:40.0	Ave.100
1958	3:36.0	3:41.1	3:42.5	3:46.4	3:49.4	1	4	
1968	3:34.94	3:38.9	3:40.3	3:42.0	3:44.3	6	16	
1978	3:35.48	3:37.0	3:37.7	3:39.4	3:40.9	24	67	3:39.33
1979	3:32.03	3:36.05	3:37.4	3:38.7	3:40.6	30	87	3:38.43
1980	3:31.36	3:34.11	3:36.3	3:38.64	3:40.41	35	83	3:37.99
1981	3:31.57	3:34.96	3:36.6	3:38.87	3:40.86	33	82	3:38.27
1982	3:32.12	3:34.40	3:37.02	3:38.88	3:40.3	30	86	3:38.26
1983	3:30.77	3:34.01	3:35.2	3:38.18	3:39.86	49	100	3:37.43
1984	3:31.54	3:34.20	3:35.16	3:37.1	3:38.89	65	136	3:36.86
1985	3:29.46	3:33.91	3:35.29	3:38.38	3:40.32	47	84	3:37.59
1986	3:29.77	3:34.01	3:35.50	3:37.75	3:39.9	54	105	3:37.18
1987	3:30.69	3:33.66	3:34.85	3:37.40	3:39.52	59	118	3:36.97
1988	3:30.95	3:34.61	3:35.72	3:37.29	3:39.46	59	121	3:37.14

1 MILE

Mark	Name		Nat	Born	Pos	Meet	Venue	Date
3:48.85	Steve	Cram	UK	14.10.60	1	Bisl	Oslo	2 Jul
3:49.20	Peter	Elliott	UK	9.10.62	2	Bisl	Oslo	2 Jul
3:49.22	Jens Peter	Herold	GDR	25.10.65	3	Bisl	Oslo	2 Jul
3:49.40	Abdi	Bile	SOM	28.12.62	4	Bisl	Oslo	2 Jul
3:50.09	Steve	Scott	USA	5.5.56	5	Bisl	Oslo	2 Jul
3:50.57	Jim	Spivey	USA	7.3.60	6	Bisl	Oslo	2 Jul
3:50.82	Said	Aouita	MOR	2.11.59	1	WK	Zürich	17 Aug
3:52.14	Joe	Falcon	USA	23.6.66	2	WK	Zürich	17 Aug
3:52.26	Steve	Crabb	UK	30.11.63	7	Bisl	Oslo	2 Jul
3:52.39	Kipkoech	Cheruiyot	KEN	2.12.64	8	Bisl	Oslo	2 Jul
	(10)							
3:52.48	John	Walker	NZ	12.1.52	9	Bisl	Oslo	2 Jul
3:52.50	Marcus	O'Sullivan	IRL	22.12.61	3	WK	Zürich	17 Aug
3:52.80	Jeff	Atkinson	USA	24.2.63	4	WK	Zürich	17 Aug
3:52.85	Sydney	Maree	USA	9.9.56	5	WK	Zürich	17 Aug
3:53.09	Joseph	Chesire	KEN	12.11.57	10	Bisl	Oslo	2 Jul
3:53.6m		Scott			1	Pepsi	Westwood	6 Jun
3:53.6m	Joaquim	Cruz	BRA	12.3.63	2	Pepsi	Westwood	5 Jun
	(16/15)							
3:54.4m	Chuck	Aragon	USA	29.3.59	3	Pepsi	Westwood	5 Jun
3:55.31	Rémy	Geoffroy	FRA	22.3.63	6	WK	Zürich	17 Aug
3:55.42	Bennie	Greyling	RSA	1.2.65	1		Stellenbosch	12 Nov
3:55.57	Deon	Brummer	RSA	4.4.59	2		Stellenbosch	12 Nov
3:55.7m	Tim	Hacker	USA	27.12.62	4	Pepsi	Westwood	5 Jun
	(20)							
3:55.76	Jean	Verster	RSA	23.4.65	3		Stellenbosch	12 Nov
3:56.02	Klaus Peter	Nabein	FRG	10.5.60	7	WK	Zürich	17 Aug
3:56.2m	Dub	Myers	USA	4.4.64	5	Pepsi	Westwood	5 Jun
3:56.63	Tom	Moloney	IRL	11.3.60	2		Cork	5 Jul
3:56.67	José Luis	Gonzalez	SPA	8.12.57	3	ISTAF	Berlin	26 Aug
3:56.67	Ray	Wicksell	USA	11.4.57	4		Stellenbosch	12 Nov
3:56.71	Chris	McGeorge	UK	13.1.62	3		Cork	5 Jul
3:56.81	Markus	Hacksteiner	SWZ	18.11.64	4	ISTAF	Berlin	26 Aug
3:56.85	Mark	Rowland	UK	7.3.63	3		Gateshead	16 Jul
3:56.91	Peter Kip	Rono	KEN	31.7.67	4		Gateshead	16 Jul
	(30)							
3:57.00	Pierre	Délèze	SWZ	25.9.58	8	WK	Zürich	17 Aug
3:57.15	Gary	Taylor	UK	1.6.63	4		Cork	5 Jul
3:57.18	Mogens	Guldberg	DEN	2.8.63	5	ISTAF	Berlin	26 Aug
3:57.21	Gary	Staines	UK	3.7.63	5		Gateshead	16 Jul
3:57.39	Monde	Tutani	RSA	22.2.62	2		Port Elizabeth	9 Mar
3:57.42	Colin	Ridding	UK	1.11.61	5		Cork	5 Jul
3:57.46	Mike	Blackmore	USA	19.12.61	2		Eugene	7 May
3:57.6m	Tim	Hutchings	UK	4.12.58	1		Hornchurch	7 Sep
3:57.7m	Doug	Consiglio	CAN	10.1.64	3	Pre	Eugene	2 Jul
3:57.88	Dieter	Baumann	FRG	9.2.65	1	PTS	Bratislava	9 Jun
	(40)							

Mark	Name		Nat	Born	Date
3:58.10	Victor	Radebe	RSA	61	9 Mar
3:58.23	Deon	Fouche	RSA	67	12 Nov
3:58.43	Glen	Ritchie	AUS	62	5 Jul
3:58.5m	Tony	Morrell	UK	62	9 Sep
3:58.59	Wilfred Oanda	Kirochi	KEN	69	13 Jul
3:58.61	Enda	Fitzpatrick	IRL	65	5 Jul
3:58.69	M.Brahim	Boutayeb	MOR	67	7 Jun
3:58.71	Steve	Ovett	UK	55	5 Jul
3:58.82	Frank	Conway	IRL	67	5 Jul
3:58.86	Rachid	Kram	ALG	63	9 Jun
	(50)				
3:58.89	Han	Kulker	HOL	59	7 Jun
3:58.90	Rudolph	Greyling	RSA	67	9 Mar
3:58.90	Mario	Silva	POR	61	13 Jul

2000 METRES

Mark	Name		Nat	Born	Pos	Meet	Venue	Date
4:55.20	Steve	Cram	UK	14.10.60	1		London	28 Aug
4:55.72	Peter	Elliott	UK	9.10.62	2		London	28 Aug
4:58.08	Marcus	O'Sullivan	IRL	22.12.61	3		London	28 Aug
5:01.48	Paul	Larkins	UK	19.5.63	1		Riihimäki	5 Jun
5:02.5m	Gennaro	Di Napoli	ITA	5.3.68	1		Milano	16 Sep
5:03.46	Patrick	Sang	KEN	11.4.64	2		Riihimäki	5 Jun
5:04.00	Bennie	Greyling	RSA	1.2.65	1		Stellenbosch	1 Feb
5:04.1m+	Yobes	Ondieki	KEN	21.2.61	1		Malmö	8 Aug
5:04.1m	Francesco	Panetta	ITA	10.1.63	2		Milano	16 Sep
5:04.3m+	Sydney	Maree	USA	9.9.56	2		Malmö	8 Aug
5:06.45	Jean-Pierre	N'Dayisenga	BEL	12.12.64	1		Duffel	7 Aug
5:06.51	Miko	Maaskola	FIN	15.9.66	3		Riihimäki	5 Jun
5:06.91	Deon	Brummer	RSA	4.4.59	2		Stellenbosch	1 Feb

Mark	Name		Nat	Born	Date
5:07.02	Abdi	Bile	SOM	62	9 Jun
5:07.56	Eddy	De Pauw	BEL	60	7 Aug
5:07.87	Peter Van de Kerkhove		BEL	65	7 Aug
5:08.90	Jonny	Danielson	SWE	64	5 Jun
5:09.0	Alejandro	Gomez	SPA	67	17 Sep

+ time during 3000metres race

3000 METRES

Mark	Name		Nat	Born	Pos	Meet	Venue	Date
7:38.79	Sydney	Maree	USA	9.9.56	1		Malmö	8 Aug
7:42.94		Maree			1		Monaco	2 Aug
7:43.22	M.Brahim	Boutayeb	MOR	15.8.67	1	ASV	Köln	21 Aug
7:43.46	Pierre	Délèze	SWZ	25.9.58	2		Monaco	2 Aug
7:43.58	Paul	Arpin	FRA	20.2.60	1		La Coruña	4 Aug
7:44.08	Vincent	Rousseau	BEL	29.7.62	3		Monaco	2 Aug
7:44.12		Rousseau			1		Tessenderlo	10 Sep
7:44.31	Yobes	Ondieki	KEN	21.2.61	2	ASV	Köln	21 Aug
7:44.36		Maree			1		Victoria	8 Jun
7:44.85	John	Doherty	IRL	22.7.61	2		La Coruña	4 Aug
7:45.40	William	van Dijck	BEL	24.1.61	2		Tessenderlo	10 Sep
7:45.45	Steve	Cram	UK	14.11.60	1		Sevilla	1 Jun
7:45.48		Délèze			1		Bern	23 Aug
7:45.59	Frank	O'Mara (10)	IRL	17.7.60	1		Belfast	27 Jun
7:45.82	Raymond	Pannier	FRA	12.2.61	3		La Coruña	4 Aug
7:46.05	Gary	Staines	UK	3.7.63	2		Belfast	27 Jun
7:46.22	Paul	Williams	CAN	7.8.56	2		Victoria	8 Jun
7:46.33	Peter	Koech	KEN	18.2.58	2		Sevilla	1 Jun
7:46.34		Arpin			2		Malmö	8 Aug
7:46.57	Joe	Falcon	USA	23.6.66	2		Bern	23 Aug
7:46.76		Rousseau			1		Nivelles	22 May
7:46.84	Cyrille	Laventure	FRA	29.3.64	3		Bern	23 Aug
7:46.85	Jonny (23/17)	Danielson	SWE	4.9.64	3		Malmö	8 Aug
7:47.12	Simon	Mugglestone	UK	24.1.68	3		Belfast	27 Jun
7:47.13	Juan Carlos	Paul	SPA	6.5.64	1		Jerez	28 Jun
7:47.79	Féthi (20)	Baccouche	TUN	16.11.60	2		Jerez	28 Jun
7:47.85	João	Campos	POR	22.9.58	4		Bern	23 Aug
7:47.91	Pascal	Thiébaut	FRA	6.6.59	4		Malmö	8 Aug
7:48.11	António	Serrano	SPA	8.3.65	3		Jerez	28 Jun
7:48.16	Dietmar	Millonig	AUT	1.6.55	5		Bern	23 Aug
7:48.19	Joshua	Kipkemboi	KEN	22.2.60	3		Sevilla	1 Jun
7:48.38	Alejandro	Gomez	SPA	11.4.67	4		La Coruña	4 Aug
7:48.4m	Bruce	Bickford	USA	12.3.57	1		Chiba	14 Sep
7:48.47	Terry	Brahm	USA	21.11.62	5		Malmö	8 Aug

Mark	Name		Nat	Born	Pos	Meet	Venue	Date
7:48.48	Stefano	Mei	ITA	3.2.63	1		Cagliari	3 Sep
7:48.61	Jim	Spivey	USA	7.3.60	1		Lappeenranta	5 Jul
	(30)							
7:48.78	Jacky	Carlier	FRA	8.11.61	4		Monaco	2 Aug
7:49.11	Mike	McLeod	UK	25.1.52	5		Jerez	28 Jun
7:49.2+	Eamonn	Martin	UK	9.10.58	3		Gateshead	16 Jul
7:49.36	William	Musyoki	KEN	.66	6		Monaco	2 Aug
7:49.36	Steve	Scott	USA	5.5.56	1		Sacramento	27 Aug
7:49.41	Joël	Lucas	FRA	11.3.52	7		Monaco	2 Aug
7:49.45	Tim	Hutchings	UK	4.12.58	3		Cagliari	3 Sep
7:49.89	Risto	Ulmala	FIN	7.5.63	2		Lappeenranta	5 Jul
7:49.92	Shuichi	Yoneshige	JAP	24.6.61	3		Lappeenranta	5 Jul
7:49.98	Pascal	Clouvel	FRA	12.11.60	8		Monaco	2 Aug
	(40)							
7:49.99	Mário	Silva	POR	23.7.61	1		Lisboa	29 May
7:50.11	Domingos	Castro	POR	22.11.63	2		Lisboa	29 May
7:50.25	John	Halvorsen	NOR	17.8.66	6		Malmö	8 Aug
7:50.27	Dave	Lewis	UK	15.10.61	4		Belfast	27 Jun
7:50.30	Dieter	Baumann	FRG	9.2.65	1	vGDR	Düsseldorf	20 Jun
7:50.72	Arturo	Barrios	MEX	12.12.63	2		Sacramento	27 Aug
7:50.98	Mark	Nenow	USA	16.11.57	5		Belfast	27 Jun
7:51.0+	Eddie	Wedderburn	UK	6.12.60	5		Gateshead	16 Jul
7:51.0m	Pat	Porter	USA	31.5.59	2		Chiba	14 Sep
7:51.05	Greg	Lautenslager	USA	15.10.57	6		Bern	23 Aug
	(50)							
7:51.17	Andreas	Busse	GDR	6.5.59	2	vFRG	Düsseldorf	20 Jun
7:51.44	Bill	Krohn	USA	9.3.58	7		Malmö	8 Aug
7:51.61	Kiprotich	Rono	KEN	4.1.58	6		Belfast	27 Jun
7:51.63	Lars Ove	Strømø	NOR	7.5.63	1	vFIN	Øyestad	16 Jun
7:51.65	Jim	Farmer	USA	14.8.65	7		Belfast	27 Jun

Mark	Name		Nat	Born	Date
7:52.03	Boguslaw	Maminski	POL	55	23 Aug
7:52.07	Gerry	Curtis	IRL	59	27 Jun
7:52.09	Julius	Kariuki	KEN	61	26 Jun
7:52.21	Are	Nakkim	NOR	64	8 Aug
7:52.50	Patric	Nilsson	SWE	64	8 Aug
	(60)				
7:52.53	Raf	Wijns	BEL	64	10 Sep
7:52.56	Mauricio	Gonzalez	MEX	60	7 Jun
7:52.63	Seamus	McCann	UK	66	27 Jun
7:52.77	Patrick	Sang	KEN	64	26 Jun
7:52.82	Nat	Muir	UK	59	29 May
7:52.88	Fernando	Couto	POR	59	29 May
7:52.89	Marcus	O'Sullivan	IRL	61	12 Jul
7:52.95	Steffen	Brand	FRG	65	25 May
7:53.0m+	Steve	Plasencia	USA	56	2 Jul
7:53.05	Mark	Rowland	UK	63	24 Jun
	(70)				
7:53.05	Mats	Erixon	SWE	58	8 Aug
7:53.1m	Emmanuel	Goulin	FRA	62	1 Jun
7:53.12	Gino	Van Geyte	BEL	67	10 Sep
7:53.20	Joaquim	Pinheiro	POR	60	29 May
7:53.21	Abdelaziz	Sahere	MOR	67	4 Aug
7:53.26	Herbert	Stephan	FRG	59	27 Jun
7:53.26	Frank	Bialluch	FRG	62	2 Aug
7:53.30	Juma	Mnyampanda	TAN	67	8 Aug
7:53.30	Bjorn	Nordheggen	NOR	61	8 Aug
7:53.33	Peter	Wirz	SWZ	60	1 Jun
	(80)				
7:53.40	Paul	O'Callaghan	IRL	64	2 Aug
7:53.51	José Manuel	Abascal	SPA	58	4 Aug
7:53.52	Geoff	Turnbull	UK	61	29 Jul
7:53.56	Jean Louis	Prianon	FRA	60	2 Aug
7:53.57	Eamonn	Coghlan	IRL	52	12 Jul
7:53.71	Marcos	Barreto	MEX	60	7 Jun
7:53.71	David	Moorcroft	UK	53	23 Aug
7:53.74	Antonio	Rapisarda	FRA	65	2 Aug
7:53.78	Barnabas	Korir	KEN	65	26 Jun
7:53.8m	Brian	Diemer	USA	61	14 Sep
	(100)				
7:54.10	Bruno	Levant	FRA	60	29 Jun
7:54.19	Arnold	Mächler	SWZ	64	23 Aug
7:54.2m	Brian	Abshire	USA	63	14 Sep
7:54.3m	Henry	Marsh	USA	54	14 Sep
7:54.39	Tony	Rodgers	NZ	57	2 Aug
7:54.52	Antonio	Prieto	SPA	58	4 Aug
7:54.56	Harri	Hänninen	FIN	63	16 Jun
7:54.63	Jim	Cooper	USA	59	27 Jun
7:54.67	Gerry	O'Reilly	IRL	64	12 Jul
7:54.7m	Mohamed	Choumassi	MOR	69	30 Jun
	(110)				
7:54.88	João	Junqueira	POR	65	29 May
7:54.9m	Phil	Clode	NZ	65	30 Jun
7:54.94	Kozo	Akutsu	JAP	60	5 Jul

+ time during 2 miles race

Indoor marks

Mark	Name		Nat	Born	Pos	Meet	Venue	Date
7:41.57	Brian	Abshire	USA	14.11.63	1		East Rutherford	13 Feb
7:47.54	José Luis	Gonzalez	SPA	8.12.57	1		Oviedo	12 Mar
7:47.55	Terry	Brahm	USA	21.11.62	3		East Rutherford	13 Feb
7:50.57	Markus	Hacksteiner	SWZ	18.11.64	1		Stuttgart	30 Jan
7:51.48	Branko	Zorko	YUG	1.7.67	2	v2 N	Torino	10 Feb
7:51.82	Doug	Padilla	USA	4.10.56	5		East Rutherford	13 Feb

Mark	Name		Nat	Born	Date
7:53.12	Abel	Anton	SPA	62	30 Jan
7:53.51	Mogens	Guldberg	DEN	63	31 Jan
7:53.70	Maik	Dreissigacker	GDR	64	13 Feb
7:54.00	Mark	Junkermann	USA	65	10 Mar
7:54.07	Heiner	Mebes	GDR	64	13 Feb
7:54.15	Radim	Kuncicky	CS	67	6 Feb

2 MILES

Mark	Name		Nat	Born	Pos	Meet	Venue	Date
8:14.05	Said	Aouita	MOR	2.11.59	1		Casablanca	11 Jun
8:17.78	Frank	O'Mara	IRL	17.7.60	1		Gateshead	16 Jul
8:17.79	Steve	Cram	UK	14.11.60	2		Gateshead	16 Jul
8:18.98	Eamonn	Martin	UK	9.10.58	3		Gateshead	16 Jul
8:19.45	John	Doherty	IRL	22.7.61	4		Gateshead	16 Jul
8:21.18	Terry	Brahm	USA	21.11.62	1	Pre	Eugene	2 Jul
8:24.82	Eddie	Wedderburn	UK	6.12.60	5		Gateshead	16 Jul
8:24.86	M.Brahim	Boutayeb	MOR	15.8.67	2		Casablanca	11 Jun
8:26.04	Steve	Plasencia	USA	28.10.56	2	Pre	Eugene	2 Jul
8:26.09	Paul	Davies Hale	UK	21.6.62	2		London	28 Aug
8:26.37	Gary	Staines	UK	3.7.63	3		London	28 Aug
8:26.52	Jack	Buckner	UK	22.9.61	4		London	28 Aug
8:26.65	Tim	Hutchings	UK	4.12.58	5		London	28 Aug

5000 METRES

Mark	Name		Nat	Born	Pos	Meet	Venue	Date
13:11.70	John	Ngugi	KEN	10.5.62	1	OG	Seoul	1 Oct
13:15.52	Dieter	Baumann	FRG	9.2.65	2	OG	Seoul	1 Oct
13:15.62	José	Regalo	POR	22.11.63	1	VD	Bruxelles	19 Aug
13:15.73	Hansjörg	Kunze	GDR	28.12.59	3	OG	Seoul	1 Oct
13:15.85	Sydney	Maree	USA	9.9.56	1	APM	Hengelo	14 Aug
13:16.09	Domingos	Castro	POR	22.11.63	4	OG	Seoul	1 Oct
13:16.1m	Salvatore	Antibo	ITA	7.2.62	1		Palermo	5 Sep
13:17.06	Yobes	Ondieki	KEN	21.2.61	2	VD	Bruxelles	19 Aug
13:17.14	John	Doherty	IRL	22.7.61	1	DNG	Stockholm	5 Jul
13:17.48	Pascal	Thiébaut	FRA	6.6.59	1	Bisl	Oslo	2 Jul
	(10)							
13:17.82	Arturo	Barrios	MEX	12.12.63	2	DNG	Stockholm	5 Jul
13:17.95		Ngugi			2	Bisl	Oslo	2 Jul
13:18.18		Doherty			3	VD	Bruxelles	19 Aug
13:18.29	Cyrille	Laventure	FRA	29.3.64	4	VD	Bruxelles	19 Aug
13:18.43		Baumann			3	DNG	Stockholm	5 Jul
13:18.68	M.Brahim	Boutayeb	MOR	15.8.67	4	DNG	Stockholm	5 Jul
13:18.69		Castro			5	DNG	Stockholm	5 Jul
13:18.69	Dionisio	Castro	POR	22.11.63	6	DNG	Stockholm	5 Jul
13:19.16	Vincent	Rousseau	BEL	29.7.62	7	DNG	Stockholm	5 Jul
13:19.92		Ngugi			1		Sevilla	1 Jun
13:19.95		Ondieki			3	Bisl	Oslo	2 Jul
13:20.29	Jonny	Danielson	SWE	4.9.64	4	Bisl	Oslo	2 Jul
13:20.32		Maree			5	Bisl	Oslo	2 Jul
13:20.62		Regalo			1		St.Denis	7 Jun
13:20.67	Abel	Anton	SPA	24.10.62	6	Bisl	Oslo	2 Jul
13:20.75	Lars Ove	Strømø	NOR	7.5.63	7	Bisl	Oslo	2 Jul
13:20.91		Ondieki			2		Sevilla	1 Jun
13:21.02	Alejandro	Gomez	SPA	11.4.67	8	Bisl	Oslo	2 Jul
13:21.3m	Mikhail	Dasko	SU	26.1.61	1		Kiev	25 Jun
13:21.60	Paul	Davies Hale	UK	21.6.62	1	PG	London	8 Jul
	(30/21)							
13:21.83	Mark	Rowland	UK	7.3.63	3		Sevilla	1 Jun
13:22.03	Paul	Arpin	FRA	20.2.60	2		St.Denis	7 Jun
13:22.68	Paul	Williams	CAN	7.8.56	9	Bisl	Oslo	2 Jul
13:22.88	Eamonn	Martin	UK	9.10.58	2	ISTAF	Berlin	26 Aug
13:22.97	Shuichi	Yoneshige	JAP	24.6.61	4	PG	London	8 Jul
13:23.24	Tim	Hutchings	UK	4.12.58	5	PG	London	8 Jul
13:23.27	Addis	Abebe	ETH	.70	2	APM	Hengelo	14 Aug
13:23.71	Steve	Binns	UK	25.8.60	4		Sevilla	1 Jun
13:23.8 *	Jack	Buckner	UK	22.9.61	7s1	OG	Seoul	29 Sep
	(30)							
13:24.01	Douglas	Wakiihuri	KEN	26.9.63	6	PG	London	8 Jul
13:24.20	Stefano	Mei	ITA	3.2.63	1s2	OG	Seoul	29 Sep
13:24.51	Gary	Staines	UK	3.7.63	4s2	OG	Seoul	29 Sep
13:24.76	Evgeni	Ignatov	BUL	25.6.59	6s2	OG	Seoul	29 Sep
13:26.27	Charles	Cheruiyot	KEN	2.12.64	7	PG	London	8 Jul
13:26.75	Mark	Nenow	USA	16.11.57	7	Athl	Lausanne	24 Jun
13:26.75	Frank	O'Mara	IRL	17.7.60	11	Bisl	Oslo	2 Jul

Mark	Name		Nat	Born	Pos	Meet	Venue	Date
13:27.30	José Luis	Gonzalez	SPA	8.12.57	2	WK	Zürich	17 Aug
13:27.65	Mauricio	Gonzalez	MEX	16.10.60	9	PG	London	8 Jul
13:27.89	António	Pinto	POR	22.3.66	6	VD	Bruxelles	19 Aug
	(40)							
13:28.29	Simon	Mugglestone	UK	24.1.68	10	PG	London	8 Jul
13:28.94	Antonio	Rapisarda	FRA	6.1.65	4		St.Denis	7 Jun
13:29.20	Fernando	Couto	POR	4.12.59	5		St.Denis	7 Jun
13:29.37	Paul	O'Callaghan	IRL	1.6.64	6		St.Denis	7 Jun
13:29.57	Francesco	Panetta	ITA	10.1.63	10	DNG	Stockholm	5 Jul
13:29.68	John	Gregorek	USA	15.4.60	1		Dedham	2 Jul
13:30.03	Markus	Ryffel	SWZ	5.2.55	7	WK	Zürich	17 Aug
13:30.21	Dietmar	Millonig	AUT	1.6.55	8	WK	Zürich	17 Aug
13:30.69	Dave	Lewis	UK	15.10.61	11	PG	London	8 Jul
13:31.03	Bruno	Levant	FRA	24.1.60	7		St.Denis	7 Jun
	(50)							
13:31.05	Kiprotich	Rono	KEN	4.1.58	2	WG	Helsinki	30 Jun
13:31.17	Risto	Ulmala	FIN	7.5.63	1		Lahti	25 Aug
13:31.18	Ezequiel	Canário	POR	10.4.60	8		St.Denis	7 Jun
13:31.55	Steve	Moneghetti	AUS	26.9.62	1		Melbourne	17 Mar
13:31.64	Hagen	Melzer	GDR	16.6.59	11	DNG	Stockholm	5 Jul
13:31.66	Craig	Mochrie	UK	6.11.62	12	PG	London	8 Jul
13:31.82	Jon	Richards	UK	19.5.64	1		Sandnes	9 Jun
13:32.12	João	Campos	POR	22.9.58	4	NC	Maia	7 Aug
13:32.16	Kozo	Akutsu	JAP	11.11.60	13	PG	London	8 Jul
13:32.28	Eamonn	Coghlan	IRL	24.11.52	8	VD	Bruxelles	19 Aug
	(60)							
13:32.34	John	Treacy	IRL	4.6.57	3	APM	Hengelo	14 Aug
13:32.42	Joël	Lucas	FRA	11.3.52	10		St.Denis	7 Jun
13:32.46	Terry	Brahm	USA	21.11.62	1	Jerome	Burnaby	5 Jun
13:32.64	Pierre	Délèze	SWZ	25.9.58	9	VD	Bruxelles	19 Aug
13:32.66	Are	Nakkim	NOR	13.2.64	1	NC	Byrkjelo	12 Aug
13:32.8m	Valeriy	Abramov	SU	22.8.56	2		Kiev	25 Jun
13:32.81	Doug	Padilla	USA	4.10.56	2	Jerome	Burnaby	5 Jun
13:33.00	Ralf	Salzmann	FRG	6.2.55	2	vGDR	Düsseldorf	19 Jun
13:33.57	Graeme	Fell	CAN	19.3.59	3		Hamamatsu	8 May
13:33.57	Herbert	Stephan	FRG	6.10.59	3	vGDR	Düsseldorf	19 Jun
	(70)							
13:33.62	Martin	ten Kate	HOL	16.12.58	4	APM	Hengelo	14 Aug
13:33.68	Wodajo	Bulti	ETH	11.3.57	2	Znam	Leningrad	12 Jun
13:33.85	Alberto	Cova	ITA	1.12.58	13	DNG	Stockholm	5 Jul
13:33.91	Pat	Porter	USA	31.5.59	2		Dedham	2 Jul
13:34.13	Dave	Murphy	USA	4.3.57	3		Dedham	2 Jul
13:34.50	Paolo	Donati	ITA	22.1.62	5		Rieti	31 Aug
13:34.62	John	Halvorsen	NOR	17.8.66	2	NC	Byrkjelo	12 Aug
13:34.63	Jan	Huruk	POL	27.1.60	1		Sopot	30 Jul
13:34.70	Gerry	Curtis	IRL	18.5.59	1		Hechtel	30 Jul
13:34.71	António	Serrano	SPA	8.3.65	5	Nik	Nice	10 Jul
	(80)							
13:34.90	Geoff	Turnbull	UK	15.4.61	1		Barcelona	13 Jul
13:34.96	Steve	Plasencia	USA	28.10.56	3	Jerome	Burnaby	5 Jun
13:34.96	Juan Carlos	Paul	SPA	6.5.64	6		Rieti	31 Aug
13:35.32	Kipkemboi	Kimeli	KEN	30.11.66	1+	OG	Seoul	26 Sep
13:35.33	Giuseppe	Miccoli	ITA	21.11.61	7		Rieti	31 Aug
13:35.49	Leszek	Beblo	POL	8.7.66	2		Sopot	30 Jul
13:35.56	José Manuel	Albentosa	SPA	21.1.64	8		Rieti	31 Aug
13:35.60	Dominique	Delattre	FRA	12.10.58	12		St.Denis	7 Jun
13:35.71	Raymond	Pannier	FRA	12.2.61	2	R W	Koblenz	28 Aug
13:36.15	Andrew	Lloyd	AUS	14.2.59	1	NC	Melbourne	4 Feb
	(90)							
13:36.16	Arnold	Mächler	SWZ	11.5.64	2		Essen	2 Sep
13:36.25	Matti	Valkonen	FIN	17.9.60	1	NC	Hameenlinna	5 Aug
13:36.31	Féthi	Baccouche	TUN	16.11.60	4		Hamamatsu	8 May
13:36.48	Ray	Wicksell	USA	11.4.57	4		Dedham	2 Jul
13:36.74	Moses	Tanui	KEN	20.8.65	3+	OG	Seoul	26 Sep
13:36.93	Jay	Marden	USA	22.3.63	5	Jerome	Burnaby	5 Jun
13:36.95	Bjørn	Nordheggen	NOR	24.8.61	3	NC	Byrkjelo	12 Aug

Mark	Name		Nat	Born	Pos	Meet	Venue	Date
13:37.08	Zhang Guowei		CHN	27.4.59	14	PG	London	8 Jul
13:37.10	Jesus	Herrera	MEX	22.3.62	4	Znam	Leningrad	12 Jun
13:37.20	Kenji	Ayabe	JAP	25.3.68	15	PG	London	8 Jul
	(100)							

Mark	Name		Nat	Born	Date
13:37.22	Patriz	Ilg	FRG	57	1 Jun
13:37.24	John	Castellano	CAN	66	5 Jun
13:37.28	Gerry	O'Reilly	IRL	64	11 Jun
13:37.31	Gerhard	Hartmann	AUT	55	1 Jun
13:37.53	Greg	Whiteley	USA	67	11 Jun
13:37.62	Martti	Vainio	FIN	50	5 Aug
13:37.76	Jim	Farmer	USA	65	11 Jun
13:37.94	Leonid	Tikhonov	SU	59	4 Sep
13:37.95	Carlos	Patricio	POR	64	26 Jun
13:38.17	Harri	Hänninen	FIN	63	5 Aug
	(110)				
13:38.19	Steve	Harris	UK	61	19 Jun
13:38.7m	Alain	Capovani	ITA	63	19 Jun
13:38.75	Alberto	Maravilha	POR	65	7 Aug
13:38.94	Haji	Bulbula	ETH	61	16 Jun
13:38.99	Steffen	Brand	FRG	65	24 Jul
13:39.20	Eirik	Hansen	NOR	63	12 Aug
13:39.29	Haruo	Urata	JAP	62	18 Jun
13:39.30	Mike	McLeod	UK	52	8 May
13:39.4m	Angelo	Carosi	ITA	64	19 Jun
13:39.41	Greg	Lautenslager	USA	57	11 Jun
	(120)				
13:39.41	Debebe	Demisse	ETH	68	16 Jun
13:39.46	Axel	Krippschock	GDR	62	19 Jun
13:39.46	Joaquim	Pinheiro	POR	60	7 Aug
13:39.47	Kazuya	Nishimoto	JAP	62	8 May
13:39.53	Jacky	Carlier	FRA	61	5 Jun
13:39.6m	Doug	Tolson	USA	62	20 May
13:39.63	Marcus	O'Sullivan	IRL	61	5 Jul
13:39.74	Kamel	Bouhaloufa	FRA	67	7 Jun
13:39.79	John	Walker	NZ	52	16 Mar
13:39.82	Steven	Tunstall	FRA	64	7 Jun
	(130)				
13:40.1m	Salvatore	Nicosia	ITA	63	19 Jun
13:40.19	Andy	Bristow	UK	61	8 Jul
13:40.2m	Joaquim	Silva	POR	61	23 Jul
13:40.59	Ignacio	Fragoso	MEX	68	16 Jun
13:40.9m	Mohamed	Issengar	MOR		27 Jul
13:40.94	João	Junqueira	POR	65	7 Aug
13:40.97	Manuel	Garcia	SPA	62	25 Aug
13:41.0m	Oleg	Strizhakov	SU	63	25 Jun
13:41.1m	William	van Dijck	BEL	61	11 Jun
13:41.20	Bidelu	Kibret	ETH	69	14 Aug
13:41.26	Ray	Flynn	IRL	57	5 Jun
	(140)				
13:41.3m	Marco	Gozzano	ITA	63	19 Jun
13:41.31	Elisio	Rios	POR	61	25 Aug
13:41.36	Raf	Wijns	BEL	64	30 Apr
13:41.4m	Julius	Kariuki	KEN	61	8 Apr
13:41.42	Vitaliy	Tishchenko	SU	57	2 Aug
13:41.60	Jim	Hill	USA	61	4 Aug
13:41.73	Ivan	Uvizl	CS	58	8 Jul
13:41.89	Mark	Harris	UK	64	8 Jul
13:41.95	Mohamed	Choumassi	MOR	69	10 Jul
13:41.98	Rainer	Schwarz	FRG	59	1 Jun
	(150)				
13:42.00	Carlos	Monteiro	POR	65	25 Aug
13:42.03	William	Musyoki	KEN	66	27 Jul
13:42.05	Farid	Khairullin	SU	65	2 Aug
13:42.1m	Patrick	Carroll	AUS	61	13 Feb
13:42.18	Juma	Mnyampanda	TAN	67	4 Aug
13:42.30	Didier	Bernard	FRA	58	31 Jul
13:42.37	John	Andrews	AUS	58	4 Feb
13:42.4m	Severino	Bernardini	ITA	66	19 Jun
13:42.48	Francois	Barreau	FRA	60	7 Jun
13:42.51	Bill	Krohn	USA	58	4 Aug
	(160)				
13:42.58	Wang	Helin	CHN	65	27 Jul
13:42.76	Patrick	Sang	KEN	64	19 Jun
13:42.80	Geoff	Wightman	UK	60	2 Sep
13:42.90	Paul	McCloy	CAN	63	5 Jun
13:42.90	Phil	Clode	NZ	65	6 Jul
13:42.94	Lars-Erik	Nilsson	SWE	61	4 Aug
13:43.0m	Mario	D'Ovidio	ITA	65	19 Jun
13:43.0m	Robert	Lonergan	CAN	59	2 Sep
13:43.11	Patrick	Cross	USA	60	11 Jun
13:43.26	Pascal	Clouvel	FRA	60	31 Jul
	(170)				
13:43.30	Yevgeniy	Leontyev	SU	63	4 Sep
13:43.40	Suleiman	Nyambui	TAN	53	6 Jul
13:43.4m	Greg	Beardsley	USA	61	11 Jun
13:43.5m	Aleksandr	Burtsev	SU	65	25 Jun
13:43.60	Grant	Whitney	USA	64	5 Jun
13:43.88	Vince	Draddy	USA	61	5 Jun
13:43.91	Francisco	Pacheco	MEX	61	16 Jun
13:44.09	Ahmed	Warsama	QAT	66	1 Jun
13:44.13	Patrick	Umbe	TAN	67	4 Aug
13:44.38	Pablo	Ceron	MEX	59	23 Apr
	(180)				
13:44.41	Rob	de Brouwer	HOL	62	1 Jun
13:44.58	Theo	Van den Abeele	BEL	60	30 Jul
13:44.74	Musa	Jouda	SUD	57	27 Jul
13:44.9m	Carey	Nelson	CAN	63	16 Mar

Indoor mark

Mark	Name		Nat	Born	Date
13:37.3	Richard	Nerurkar	UK	64	10 Dec

* Buckner's official time was 13:23.17, but all times in this semi-final were too fast by approximately 0.6 seconds, according to a study made by A.Lennart Julin, ATFS. Buckner also 13:23.85 6 OG Seoul 1 Oct

5000 Metres Year List Progression

Year	Best	10th	20th	50th	100th	Under 13:40	Under 13:50	Ave.100
1958	13:38.5*	13:57.2	14:05.2	14:12.2	14:21.6	-	1	
1968	13:27.8	13:35.8	13:45.6	13:51.0	13:59.0	3	14	
1978	13:08.4	13:21.9	13:25.41	13:32.8	13:38.8	36	105	13:30.90
1979	13:12.29	13:19.87	13:23.2	13:31.4	13:39.6	44	105	13:29.77
1980	13:16.34	13:19.8	13:22.1	13:29.47	13:40.1	51	97	13:29.51
1981	13:06.20	13:19.74	13:23.79	13:31.52	13:38.4	45	110	13:29.51
1982	13:00.41	13:12.91	13:19.62	13:30.88	13:39.74	41	103	13:29.11
1983	13:08.54	13:20.94	13:22.67	13:31.43	13:38.8	39	109	13:30.15
1984	13:04.78	13:16.81	13:23.56	13:27.95	13:35.1	57	144	13:27.17
1985	13:00.40	13:18.47	13:21.13	13:32.7	13:38.5	40	117	13:29.44
1986	13:06.86	13:15.86	13:21.73	13:28.7	13:35.34	62	146	13:26.83
1987	12:58.39	13:17.44	13:22.37	13:28.62	13:37.31	55	129	13:28.21
1988	13:11.70	13:17.48	13:21.3	13:31.03	13:37.20	46	130	13:28.54

10000 METRES

Mark	Name			Nat	Born	Pos	Meet	Venue	Date
27:21.46	M.Brahim	Boutayeb		MOR	15.8.67	1	OG	Seoul	26 Sep
27:23.06	Eamonn	Martin		UK	9.10.58	1	Bisl	Oslo	2 Jul
27:23.55	Salvatore	Antibo		ITA	7.2.62	2	OG	Seoul	26 Sep
27:24.79		Antibo				2	Bisl	Oslo	2 Jul
27:25.07	Arturo	Barrios		MEX	12.12.63	3	Bisl	Oslo	2 Jul
27:25.16	Kipkemboi	Kimeli		KEN	30.11.66	3	OG	Seoul	26 Sep
27:26.00	Hansjörg	Kunze		GDR	28.12.59	4	Bisl	Oslo	2 Jul
27:33.14	Francesco	Panetta		ITA	10.1.63	1	VD	Bruxelles	19 Aug
27:36.43	Jean-Louis	Prianon		FRA	22.2.60	4	OG	Seoul	26 Sep
27:39.12		Boutayeb				5	Bisl	Oslo	2 Jul
27:39.32		Barrios				5	OG	Seoul	26 Sep
27:39.35		Kunze				6	OG	Seoul	26 Sep
27:39.36	Paul	Arpin		FRA	20.2.60	7	OG	Seoul	26 Sep
27:40.36	Boniface	Merande	(10)	KEN	13.2.62	1		Tokyo	13 May
27:40.59	Moses	Tanui		KEN	20.8.65	2		Tokyo	13 May
27:42.84	Dionisio	Castro		POR	22.11.63	3		Tokyo	13 May
27:43.04	Shuichi	Yoneshige		JAP	24.6.61	4		Tokyo	13 May
27:43.30	Domingos	Castro		POR	22.11.63	5		Tokyo	13 May
27:43.64	Mauricio	Gonzalez		MEX	16.10.60	1	MSR	Walnut	23 Apr
27:45.58		Gonzalez				6	Bisl	Oslo	2 Jul
27:46.16	Kozo	Akutsu		JAP	11.11.60	6		Tokyo	13 May
27:46.48		Prianon				7	Bisl	Oslo	2 Jul
27:46.80	Pat	Porter		USA	31.5.59	2	MSR	Walnut	23 Apr
27:47.23		Tanui				8	OG	Seoul	26 Sep
27:47.40	John	Halvorsen		NOR	17.8.66	8	Bisl	Oslo	2 Jul
27:49.22		Arpin				2	VD	Bruxelles	19 Aug
27:50.24	Addis	Abebe		ETH	.70	3	VD	Bruxelles	19 Aug
27:50.30	Martin	ten Kate		HOL	16.12.58	9	OG	Seoul	26 Sep
27:50.95	Marcos	Barreto		MEX	25.4.60	3	MSR	Walnut	23 Apr
27:51.35	John	Ngugi		KEN	10.5.62	1	BNP	Villeneuve d'Ascq	27 Jun
27:51.38		Akutsu				9	Bisl	Oslo	2 Jul
	(31/22)								
27:52.27	Ezequiel	Canário		POR	10.4.60	4	VD	Bruxelles	19 Aug
27:52.78	Antonio	Prieto		SPA	11.1.58	10	OG	Seoul	26 Sep
27:52.80	Alberto	Cova		ITA	1.12.58	5	VD	Bruxelles	19 Aug
27:54.33	Rolando	Vera		ECU	27.4.65	7	VD	Bruxelles	19 Aug
27:56.26	Evgeni	Ignatov		BUL	25.6.59	10	Bisl	Oslo	2 Jul
27:56.35	Wodajo	Bulti		ETH	11.3.57	1	Znam	Leningrad	11 Jun
27:56.75	Ravil	Kashapov		SU	15.11.56	2	Znam	Leningrad	11 Jun
27:56.96	Paul	Williams		CAN	7.8.56	1		Abbotsford	11 Jun
	(30)								
27:57.06	Stefano	Mei		ITA	3.2.63	11	Bisl	Oslo	2 Jul
27:57.68	Axel	Krippschock		GDR	5.2.62	13	Bisl	Oslo	2 Jul
27:57.93	Jesús	Herrera		MEX	22.3.62	4	MSR	Walnut	23 Apr
27:59.60	Douglas	Wakiihuri		KEN	26.9.63	14	Bisl	Oslo	2 Jul
28:00.38	Jay	Marden		USA	22.3.63	5	MSR	Walnut	23 Apr
28:00.60	Steve	Harris		UK	17.11.61	15	Bisl	Oslo	2 Jul
28:01.00	António	Pinto		POR	22.3.66	3	BNP	Villeneuve d'Ascq	27 Jun
28:01.74	Takeyuki	Nakayama		JAP	20.12.59	16	Bisl	Oslo	2 Jul
28:02.04	Martti	Vainio		FIN	30.12.50	17	Bisl	Oslo	2 Jul
28:02.37	Ralf	Salzmann		FRG	6.2.55	4	BNP	Villeneuve d'Ascq	27 Jun
	(40)								
28:02.4m	José	Regalo		POR	22.11.63	1	NC	Lisboa	23 Apr
28:03.5m	Paul	McCloy		CAN	6.11.63	6	MSR	Walnut	23 Apr
28:03.78	Haji	Bulbula		ETH	.61	1	PTS	Bratislava	9 Jun
28:05.37	Bruce	Bickford		USA	12.3.57	1rA	PennR	Philadelphia	28 Apr
28:08.44	Dave	Lewis		UK	15.10.61	1	NC	Derby	5 Jun
28:08.44	Carl	Thackery		UK	14.10.62	6	BNP	Villeneuve d'Ascq	27 Jun
28:08.49	Joaquim	Pinheiro		POR	20.12.60	8	VD	Bruxelles	19 Aug
28:09.39	Mark	Dalloway		UK	28.10.63	2	NC	Derby	5 Jun
28:09.70	José Manuel	Albentosa		SPA	21.1.64	9	VD	Bruxelles	19 Aug
28:10.4m	Xolile	Yawa		RSA	29.9.62	1		Port Elizabeth	9 Mar
	(50)								

Mark	Name		Nat	Born	Pos	Meet	Venue	Date
28:10.4m	Luis	Horta	POR	14.1.58	3	NC	Lisboa	23 Apr
28:10.4m	Manuel	Vera	MEX	19.3.51	7	MSR	Walnut	23 Apr
28:10.93	Gabriel	Kamau	KEN	20.3.57	2		Abbotsford	11 Jun
28:11.0m	Terry	Cotton	USA	7.8.54	8	MSR	Walnut	23 Apr
28:12.67	Mike	McLeod	UK	25.1.52	8		Tokyo	13 May
28:12.77	Jean-Pierre	N'Dayisenga	BEL	12.12.64	10	VD	Bruxelles	19 Aug
28:12.78	Bidelu	Kibret	ETH	.69	11	VD	Bruxelles	19 Aug
28:12.93	Gary	Staines	UK	3.7.63	3	NC	Derby	5 Jun
28:13.32	Markus	Ryffel	SWZ	5.2.55	7	BNP	Villeneuve d'Ascq	27 Jun
28:13.5m	Brian	Sheriff	ZIM	11.11.61	9	MSR	Walnut	23 Apr
	(60)							
28:13.75	Tsukasa	Endo	JAP	9.11.61	9		Tokyo	13 May
28:15.01	Yutaka	Kanai	JAP	16.10.59	10		Tokyo	13 May
28:16.00	Giuseppe	Miccoli	ITA	21.11.61	8	BNP	Villeneuve d'Ascq	27 Jun
28:16.28	Matthews	Temane	RSA	14.12.60	1		Stellenbosch	26 Apr
28:16.32	Joël	Lucas	FRA	11.3.52	9	BNP	Villeneuve d'Ascq	27 Jun
28:16.37	John	Treacy	IRL	4.6.57	12	VD	Bruxelles	19 Aug
28:16.86	Thierry	Pantel	FRA	6.7.64	10	BNP	Villeneuve d'Ascq	27 Jun
28:17.00	Debebe	Demisse	ETH	.68	2	PTS	Bratislava	9 Jun
28:17.13	Keith	Brantly	USA	23.5.62	2rA	PennR	Philadelphia	28 Apr
28:17.59	Andy	Bristow	UK	2.9.61	11	BNP	Villeneuve d'Ascq	27 Jun
	(70)							
28:17.78	Kazuya	Nishimoto	JAP	2.6.62	12		Tokyo	13 May
28:18.1m	António	Serrano	SPA	8.3.65	1		Pontevedra	3 Sep
28:18.2m	Zephaniah	Ncube	TAN	10.1.57	1		Gaborene	19 Jul
28:18.98	Steve	Moneghetti	AUS	26.9.62	1	NC	Canberra	11 Mar
28:19.6m	Harry	Green	USA	18.7.67	10	MSR	Walnut	23 Apr
28:19.8m	Martin	Pitayo	MEX	10.1.60	11	MSR	Walnut	23 Apr
28:19.88	Gennadiy	Fishman	SU	7.9.59	3	Znam	Leningrad	11 Jun
28:19.94	Rainer	Wachenbrunner	GDR	11.1.62	3	NC	Potsdam	8 Jun
28:20.0m	Bo	Reed	USA	15.3.66	12	MSR	Walnut	23 Apr
28:20.4m	Carey	Nelson	CAN	4.6.63	13	MSR	Walnut	23 Apr
	(80)							
28:20.46	Jim	Hill	USA	1.7.61	1		Eugene	30 Apr
28:20.7m	Carlos	Retiz	MEX	13.8.61	14	MSR	Walnut	23 Apr
28:21.50	Leonid	Tikhonov	SU	23.3.59	4	Znam	Leningrad	11 Jun
28:22.0m	Rick	Robirds	USA	18.9.66	15	MSR	Walnut	23 Apr
28:23.13	Rafael	Zepeda	MEX	22.8.61	3		Abbotsford	11 Jun
28:23.8m	Joaquim	Silva	POR	13.1.61	1		Maia	3 Jul
28:24.03	Karl	Harrison	UK	16.10.56	4	NC	Derby	5 Jun
28:24.38	Oleg	Syroyezhko	SU	9.12.62	5	Znam	Leningrad	11 Jun
28:24.80	Ken	Velasquez	USA	3.11.62	4		Abbotsford	11 Jun
28:24.82	Matti	Valkonen	FIN	17.9.60	1		Helsinki	26 May
	(90)							
28:24.89	Dmitriy	Dmitriyev	SU	3.3.56	6	Znam	Leningrad	11 Jun
28:25.00	Andrew	Lloyd	AUS	14.2.59	19	Bisl	Oslo	2 Jul
28:25.13	Sergey	Maksimov	SU	13.12.63	7	Znam	Leningrad	11 Jun
28:25.4m	José	Rocha	USA	7.12.64	3rA	PennR	Philadelphia	28 Apr
28:25.77	Mohamed	Choumassi	MOR	.69	21	Bisl	Oslo	2 Jul
28:25.8m	Alberto	Maravilha	POR	27.12.65	5	NC	Lisboa	23 Apr
28:26.0m	David	Barney	USA	18.1.60	16	MSR	Walnut	23 Apr
28:26.27	Fernando	Couto	POR	4.12.59	13	BNP	Villeneuve d'Ascq	27 Jun
28:27.20	Sergey	Smirnov	SU	26.11.65	1rB	NC	Kiev	30 Jul
28:27.26	Steve	Spence	USA	9.5.62	5		Abbotsford	11 Jun
	(100)							
28:27.28	Chris	Fox	USA	22.10.58	4rA	PennR	Philadelphia	28 Apr
28:27.28	Tony	Milovsorov	UK	4.11.58	5	NC	Derby	5 Jun
28:27.29	Oleg	Strizhakov	SU	18.7.63	1rA	NC	Kiev	30 Jul
28:27.4m	John	Tuttle	USA	16.10.58	5rB	PennR	Philadelphia	28 Apr

Mark	Name		Nat	Born	Date
28:28.58	Kenji	Ayabe	JAP	68	13 May
28:28.84	Valeriy	Abramov	SU	56	30 Jul
28:28.94	Jonny	Danielson	SWE	64	23 May
28:29.0m	Richard	Nerurkar	UK	64	2 Jul
28:29.18	Vladimir	Gusev	SU	61	30 Jul
28:29.8m	Carlos	Patricio	POR	64	23 Apr
	(110)				
28:29.95	Aleksandr	Zagoruyko	SU	55	30 Jul
28:30.55	Pat	Carroll	AUS	61	11 Mar
28:30.66	Juan Carlos	Paul	SPA	64	9 Apr
28:30.71	Mikhail	Khramov	SU	63	5 Sep
28:31.30	Pierre	Levisse	FRA	52	27 Jun
28:31.9m	Manuel	Matias	POR	62	23 Apr

Mark	Name		Nat	Born	Date
28:32.29	Spiridon	Andriopoulos	GRE	62	2 Jul
28:32.3m	Randy	Reina	USA	59	20 May
28:32.36	Alain	Capovani	ITA	63	27 Jun
28:32.47	André	Wessel	GDR	65	8 Jun
	(120)				
28:32.75	Michael	Heilmann	GDR	61	8 Jun
28:33.91	Francisco	Pacheco	MEX	61	9 Jun
28:34.0m	Sam	Montoya	USA		23 Apr
28:34.22	Vladimir	Maifat	SU	63	30 Jul
28:35.2m	Dave	Cuadrado	USA	62	23 Apr
28:35.21	Jon	Richards	UK	64	2 Jul
28:35.6m	Dirk	Lakeman	USA	58	4 Jun
28:35.72	Hisatoshi	Shintaku	JAP	57	13 May
28:35.82	Severino	Bernardini	ITA	66	27 Jun
28:36.0m	Maurilio	Castillo	MEX	62	23 Apr
	(130)				
28:36.9m	Greg	Meyer	USA	55	4 Jun
28:36.47	Takao	Nakamura	JAP	58	13 May
28:37.00	Paolo	Donati	ITA	62	8 Sep
28:37.08	John	Andrews	AUS	58	11 Mar
28:37.24	Marco	Gozzano	ITA	63	8 Sep
28:37.55	Juan Carlos	Montero	SPA	61	9 Apr
28:37.68	Hiromi	Taniguchi	JAP	60	1 May
28:37.96	Carlos	Monteiro	POR	65	13 Jul
28:38.1m	Dan	Dillon	USA	57	4 Jun
28:38.11	Zhang	Guowei	CHN	59	2 Jul
	(140)				
28:38.2m	Dennis	Simonaitis	USA	62	4 Jun
28:38.39	Sanshiro	Kasama	JAP	64	13 May
28:38.64	Steven	Tunstall	FRA	64	27 Jun
28:38.67	Paulo	Ferreira	POR	65	13 Jul
28:39.2m	Juvenal	Ribeiro	POR	64	13 Jul
28:39.66	Gennadiy	Temnikov	SU	61	30 Jul
28:39.7m	Keith	Hanson	USA	64	4 Jun
28:39.8m	Henrique	Crisostomo	POR	62	13 Jul
28:39.82	Kazuya	Wakakura	JAP	62	13 May
28:39.87	Tadayoshi	Kametaka	JAP		22 Oct
	(150)				
28:39.9m	Juan José	Rosario	SPA	62	31 Jul
28:40.00	Alessio	Faustini	ITA	60	8 Sep
28:40.14	Steve	Binns	UK	60	6 Aug
28:40.63	Frank	Powers	USA	61	2 Jul
28:40.70	Simon	Malibeng	RSA	62	26 Apr
28:41.1m	António	Salvador	POR	67	13 Jul
28:41.8m	Kenji	Ide	JAP	59	17 Apr
28:41.88	Jim	Sapienza	USA	63	28 Apr
28:42.2m	Steve	Taylor	USA	65	28 Apr
28:42.35	Tom	Ansberry	USA	63	11 Jun
	(160)				
28:42.43	Haruo	Urata	JAP	62	19 Jun
28:42.5m	Ken	Halla	USA	63	4 Jun
28:42.51	Bob	Kempainen	USA	66	2 Jul
28:42.55	Jamie	Harrison	AUS	63	15 Dec
28:42.8m	Charley	Bevier	USA	59	4 Jun
28:43.12	Michael	McDermott	RSA	64	26 Apr
28:43.2m	Manuel O.	Moreira	POR	62	13 Jul
28:43.63	Marnix	Goegebeur	BEL	62	19 Aug
28:44.01	Malcolm	Norwood	AUS	64	11 Mar
28:44.01	Pablo	Martin	SPA	60	9 Apr
	(170)				
28:44.1m	Manuel C.	Moreira	POR	66	13 Jul
28:44.66	Mike	Musyoki	KEN	56	2 Jul
28:45.05	Toshio	Watanabe	JAP	63	22 Oct
28:45.11	Darren	Wilson	AUS	68	15 Dec
28:45.31	Masayuki	Nishi	JAP	64	8 Oct
28:45.57	Francisco Javier	Fontaneda	SPA	64	13 Aug
28:45.6m	Paulo	Catarino	POR	63	13 Jul
28:45.63	Lars Erik	Nilsson	SWE	61	11 Mar
28:45.79	Martin	Vrabel	CS	55	15 Jul
28:45.83	Ivan	Uvizl	CS	58	15 Jul
	(180)				
28:46.47	Vicente	Polo	SPA	55	13 Aug
28:46.53	Mike	O'Reilly	IRL	58	11 Mar
28:46.74	Kenji	Ide	JAP	59	13 May
28:46.9m	John	Castellano	USA/CAN	66	2 Jul
28:47.18	David	Chawane	RSA		26 Apr
28:47.64	José E.	Montiel	SPA	62	13 Aug
28:47.78	Vincent	Rousseau	BEL	62	1 Jun
28:47.98	Jan	Hagelbrand	SWE	54	23 May
28:48.3m	Bill	McChesney	USA	59	9 Jul
28:48.45	Chris	Borsa	USA	67	2 Jul
	(190)				
28:48.6m	Wally	Collins	USA	59	2 Jul
28:48.95	Jan	Tau	RSA	60	9 Mar
28:49.1m	Doug	Tolson	USA	62	23 Apr
28:49.26	Gerry	Curtis	IRL	59	23 Jul
28:49.3m	Pat	Davey	USA	56	2 Jul
28:49.4m	Gerry	Clapper	USA	61	2 Jul
28:49.75	Kurt	Hürst	SWZ	51	1 Jun
28:49.84	Hamid	Zouhair	FRA	63	1 Jun
28:49.95	Gusman	Abdullin	SU	58	30 Jul

MEN 1988

10000 metres Year List Progression

Year	Best	10th	20th	50th	100th	Under 28:00	Under 28:30	Ave.100
1958	28:56.0	29:06.4	29:31.4	29:55.8	30:22.7*	-	-	
1968	27:49.4	28:23.4*	28:39.8	28:59.0	29:19.6	1	13	
1978	27:22.47	27:41.26	27:57.2	28:17.61	28:39.8	25	62	28:15.78
1979	27:36.8	27:47.4	28:01.7	28:20.6	28:40.82	16	74	28:16.83
1980	27:29.16	27:46.71	27:55.41	28:16.12	28:36.6	22	84	28:13.12
1981	27:27.7	27:47.54	28:00.58	28:26.31	28:41.8	19	59	28:20.04
1982	27:22.95	27:38.1	28:01.00	28:17.71	28:35.01	19	87	28:14.67
1983	27:23.44	27:46.93	27:59.15	28:19.97	28:38.40	22	68	28:15.14
1984	27:13.81	27:47.0	27:57.68	28:07.49	28:26.1	25	115	28:07.38
1985	27:37.17	27:49.36	27:58.56	28:23.40	28:39.2	21	66	28:17.49
1986	27:20.56	27:45.45	27:54.8	28:09.4	28:29.41	32	102	28:07.53
1987	27:26.95	27:47.05	28:05.16	28:20.24	28:33.77	17	77	28:16.18
1988	27:21.46	27:40.36	27:50.30	28:10.4	28:27.28	34	109	28:05.53

Long Distance Track Events

Although there are world records for a number of long distance track events, these are run very rarely.
The only top-class marks in 1988 were by
Pierre Levisse FRA 52 at St.Maur on 9 July - 20,187m for 1 hour, passing 20km in 59:28.7

MARATHON

Mark	Name		Nat	Born	Pos	Meet	Venue	Date
2:06:50	Belayneh	Dinsamo	ETH	28.6.57	1		Rotterdam	17 Apr
2:07:07	Ahmed	Salah	DJI	31.12.56	2		Rotterdam	17 Apr
2:07:35	Abebe	Mekonnen	ETH	9.1.64	1		Beijing	16 Oct
2:07:40	Hiromi	Taniguchi	JAP	4.4.60	2		Beijing	16 Oct
2:08:20	Stephen	Jones	UK	4.8.55	1		New York	6 Nov
2:08:33		Mekonnen			1		Tokyo	14 Feb
2:08:42	Juma	Ikangaa	TAN	19.7.57	2		Tokyo	14 Feb
2:08:43	Ibrahim	Hussein	KEN	3.6.58	1		Boston	18 Apr
2:08:44	Wodajo	Bulti	ETH	11.3.57	3		Rotterdam	17 Apr
2:08:44		Ikangaa			2		Boston	18 Apr
2:08:47	Jörg	Peter	GDR	23.10.55	3		Tokyo	14 Feb
2:08:49	Robert	de Castella (10)	AUS	27.2.57	4		Tokyo	14 Feb
2:08:57	Alejandro	Cruz	MEX	10.2.68	1		Chicago	30 Oct
2:09:15	John	Treacy	IRL	4.6.57	3		Boston	18 Apr
2:09:20	Yakov	Tolstikov	SU	20.5.59	2		Chicago	30 Oct
2:09:27	Gelindo	Bordin	ITA	2.4.59	4		Boston	18 Apr
2:09:30	John	Burra	TAN	20.11.65	1		Arusha	13 Mar
2:09:33		Mekonnen			4		Rotterdam	17 Apr
2:09:33	Pier Giovanni	Poli	ITA	5.11.57	5		Boston	18 Apr
2:09:39	Richard	Kaitany	KEN	17.6.58	3		Chicago	30 Oct
2:10:10	Ralf	Salzmann	FRG	6.2.55	5		Tokyo	14 Feb
2:10:18	Willie	Mtolo	RSA	24.4.64	1		Kaapstad	30 Apr
2:10:19	Martin	Mondragon (20)	MEX	11.11.53	1		Los Angeles	6 Mar
2:10:19	Manuel	Matias	POR	30.3.62	4		Chicago	30 Oct
2:10:20	Henrik	Jørgensen	DEN	10.10.61	1	NC	London	17 Apr
2:10:32		Bordin			1	OG	Seoul	2 Oct
2:10:40	Jesús	Herrera	MEX	22.3.62	2		Los Angeles	6 Mar
2:10:40	Takeshi	Soh	JAP	9.1.53	3		Beijing	16 Oct
2:10:41	Mark	Plaatjes	USA/RSA	1.6.62	3		Los Angeles	6 Mar
2:10:44	Patrick (30/26)	Carroll	AUS	17.8.61	1		Surfer's Paradise	24 Jul
2:10:47	Douglas	Wakiihuri	KEN	26.9.63	2	OG	Seoul	2 Oct
2:10:52	Kevin	Forster	UK	27.9.58	2	NC	London	17 Apr
2:10:59	Isamu	Sennai	JAP	11.8.60	6		Tokyo	14 Feb
2:10:59	Kazuyoshi (30)	Kudo	JAP	27.2.61	3	NC	London	17 Apr
2:11:04	Toshihiro	Shibutani	JAP	30.8.62	1		Fukuoka	4 Dec
2:11:05	Takeyuki	Nakayama	JAP	20.12.59	4	OG	Seoul	2 Oct
2:11:08	Hugh	Jones	UK	1.11.55	4	NC	London	17 Apr
2:11:08	John	Campbell	NZ	6.2.49	6		Boston	18 Apr
2:11:19	Ravil	Kashapov	SU	15.11.56	3		Fukuoka	4 Dec
2:11:30	Carlos	Retiz	MEX	15.11.61	4		Los Angeles	6 Mar
2:11:30	John	Woods	IRL	8.12.55	1	NC	Wexford	24 Apr
2:11:33	David	Long	UK	21.11.60	5	NC	London	17 Apr
2:11:34	Michael	Heilmann	GDR	26.10.61	1	NC	Nové Mesto	9 Jul
2:11:38	Taisuke (40)	Kodama	JAP	26.7.58	4		Fukuoka	4 Dec
2:11:41	Salvatore	Bettiol	ITA	28.11.61	2		New York	6 Nov
2:11:42	Allister	Hutton	UK	18.7.54	6	NC	London	17 Apr
2:11:44	Geir	Kvernmo	NOR	29.10.44	1		Houston	17 Jan
2:11:45	Suleiman	Nyambui	TAN	13.2.53	1		Berlin (West)	9 Oct
2:11:49	Martin	ten Kate	HOL	16.12.58	5		Rotterdam	17 Apr
2:11:49	Stephen	Moneghetti	AUS	26.9.62	5	OG	Seoul	2 Oct
2:11:50	Salvador	Garcia	MEX	29.10.60	2		Houston	17 Jan
2:11:50	Michael	O'Reilly	IRL	23.4.58	5		Chicago	30 Oct
2:11:50	Steven	Brace	UK	7.7.61	6		Chicago	30 Oct
2:11:51	Hideki (50)	Kita	JAP	28.9.52	5		Fukuoka	4 Dec
2:11:52	Alessio	Faustini	ITA	10.6.60	2	ECp	Huy	30 Apr
2:11:54	Herbert	Steffny	FRG	5.9.53	7	NC	London	17 Apr
2:11:57	Fumiake	Abe	JAP	31.7.58	6		Fukuoka	4 Dec
2:11:58	Bruno	Lafranchi	SWZ	19.7.55	1		Oita	7 Feb

Mark	Name		Nat	Born	Pos	Meet	Venue	Date
2:11:58	Cai Shangyan		CHN	25.9.62	8	NC	London	17 Apr
2:12:00	Futoshi	Shinohara	JAP	14.4.62	2		Oita	7 Feb
2:12:04	Kebede	Balcha	ETH	7.9.51	6		Rotterdam	17 Apr
2:12:04	Spiridon	Andriopoulos	GRE	1.8.62	2		Berlin (West)	9 Oct
2:12:06	Dominique	Chauvelier	FRA	3.8.56	4		Beijing	16 Oct
2:12:08	Carlos	Rivas	MEX	4.11.62	1		San Diego	11 Dec
	(60)							
2:12:11	Gerardo	Alcala	MEX	28.6.61	7		Chicago	30 Oct
2:12:13	John	Wheway	UK	8.8.51	9	NC	London	17 Apr
2:12:14	Koichi	Takahashi	JAP	7.6.62	3		Oita	7 Feb
2:12:14	Toru	Mimura	JAP	1.12.62	8		Tokyo	14 Feb
2:12:14	David	Tsebe	RSA		2		Kaapstad	30 Apr
2:12:19	Omar	Aguilar	CHL	1.12.59	8		Rotterdam	17 Apr
2:12:19	Richard	Hooper	IRL	26.8.56	2	NC	Wexford	24 Apr
2:12:19	Charles	Spedding	UK	19.5.52	6	OG	Seoul	2 Oct
2:12:22	Toshihiro	Inahara	JAP	8.9.58	4		Oita	7 Feb
2:12:23	Tadesse	Belayneh	ETH	24.4.66	2		Arusha	13 Mar
	(70)							
2:12:24	Alain	Lazare	FRA	23.3.52	3	ECp	Huy	30 Apr
2:12:26	Wiktor	Sawicki	POL	20.5.55	1	NC	Debno	27 Mar
2:12:26	Mark	Conover	USA	28.5.60	1	NC	Jersey City	24 Apr
2:12:27	Allan	Zachariassen	DEN	4.11.55	9		Rotterdam	17 Apr
2:12:28	Stephan	Freigang	GDR	27.9.67	8		Fukuoka	4 Dec
2:12:29	Tulu	Mekonnen	ETH	68	3		Berlin (West)	9 Oct
2:12:32	Orlando	Pizzolato	ITA	30.7.58	7		Boston	18 Apr
2:12:33	Nikolay	Tabak	SU	15.4.56	4	ECp	Huy	30 Apr
2:12:37	Boguslav	Psujek	POL	22.11.56	4		Berlin (West)	9 Oct
2:12:38	Gerard	Nijboer	HOL	18.8.55	1	NC	Amsterdam	8 May
	(80)							
2:12:40	Derek	Froude	NZ	30.4.59	8		Chicago	30 Oct
2:12:41	Toshihiko	Seko	JAP	15.7.56	1	NC	Otsu	13 Mar
2:12:41	Kim Won-tak		SKO	21.7.64	1		Seoul	20 Mar
2:12:42	Toru	Kozasu	JAP	4.7.64	5		Oita	7 Feb
2:12:42	John	Vermeule	HOL	4.12.61	10		Rotterdam	17 Apr
2:12:45	Richard	McCandless	USA	16.12.55	1		Sacramento	4 Dec
2:12:49	Ryu Chae-song		KOR	20.3.60	2		Seoul	20 Mar
2:12:49	Edward	Eyestone	USA	15.6.61	2	NC	Jersey City	24 Apr
2:12:49	Tesfayi	Dadi	ETH	69	5		Berlin (West)	9 Oct
2:12:50	Vicente	Anton	SPA	16.10.59	5		Beijing	16 Oct
	(90)							
2:12:51	Chae Song-rak		SKO	29.5.51	3		Seoul	20 Mar
2:12:51	Yutaka	Kanai	JAP	16.10.59	9		Fukuoka	4 Dec
2:12:52	Alexandre	Gonzalez	FRA	16.3.61	5	ECp	Huy	30 Apr
2:12:53	Elísio	Rios	POR	3.4.61	9		Chicago	30 Oct
2:12:56	Jerzy	Skarzynski	POL	13.1.56	2	NC	Debno	27 Mar
2:12:56	Ernest	Tjela	LES	16.10.54	1		München	8 May
2:12:59	Pavel	Klimes	CS	27.10.58	1		Sevilla	6 Mar
2:13:02	John	Sebata	RSA	7.1.56	3		Kaapstad	30 Apr
2:13:06	Han Chae-ho		SKO	6.3.65	4		Seoul	20 Ma
2:13:08	Radames	Gonzales	CUB	56	1		Palma de Mallorca	11 Dec
	(100)							
2:13:08	Kim Yong-gil		SKO		5		Seoul	20 Mar
2:13:08	Helmuth	Stuhlpfarrer	AUT	19.3.59	1	Lille	3 Sep	
2:13:08	Walter	Bassi	ITA	12.7.64				18 Dec

Mark	Name		Nat	Born	Date
2:13:09	Peter	Pfitzinger	USA	57	24 Apr
2:13:09	Sergey	Rozum	SU	62	9 Oct
2:13:12	Manuel	Vera	MEX	51	6 Mar
2:13:12	Cornelius	Saelmans	BEL	60	9 Apr
2:13:13	Diamantino	Dos Santos	BRA	61	8 May
2:13:16	Jos	Sasse	HOL	57	30 Oct
2:13:17	Honorato	Hernández	SPA	56	30 Apr
	(110)				
2:13:17	Liu Wen-Jun		CHN	66	16 Oct
2:13:18	Nada	Saktay	TAN	59	13 Mar
2:13:20	Tadeusz	Lawicki	POL	56	27 Mar
2:13:21	Masayuki	Nishi	JAP	64	4 Dec
2:13:25	Alfonso	Abellan	SPA	51	30 Apr
2:13:27	Wieslaw	Furmanek	POL	59	27 Mar
2:13:31	Igor	Braslavskiy	SU	59	17 Apr
2:13:32	Steve	Binns	UK	60	30 Oct
2:13:33	Gerhard	Hartmann	AUT	55	17 Apr
2:13:33	Dirk	Vanderherten	BEL	57	30 Apr
	(120)				
2:13:33	Gerard	Barrett	AUS	56	22 Jul
2:13:33	Tadesse	Gebre	ETH		16 Oct
2:13:35	Jean-Pierre	Paumen	BEL	56	6 Mar
2:13:36	Kenny	Stuart	UK	57	17 Apr
2:13:38	Stephens	Morake	RSA	54	30 Apr
2:13:42	Igor	Yefimov	SU	58	17 Apr
2:13:42	José	da Silva	BRA	53	17 Apr

Mark	Name		Nat		Date
2:13:44	Yevgeniy	Okorokov	SU	59	17 Apr
2:13:44	Aleksandr	Khlynin	SU	56	17 Apr
2:13:44	Arthur	Boileau	CAN	57	17 Apr
	(130)				
2:13:46	Martin	Grüning	FRG	62	30 Oct
2:13:48	Emiliano	Garcia	SPA	61	16 Oct
2:13:49	Viktor	Taratukhin	SU	58	17 Apr
2:13:50	Gidamis	Shahanga	TAN	57	6 Nov
2:13:52	Japhet	Mashishanga	TAN	60	13 Mar
2:13:52	Yoo Jin-hong		SKO		30 Oct
2:13:57	Tomohiro	Imamura	JAP	63	4 Dec
2:13:58	Cornelius	Lambregts	HOL	58	15 May
2:13:59	Edward	Rydzewski	POL	59	27 Mar
2:14:00	Juan Carlos	Montero	SPA	61	6 Nov
	(140)				
2:14:01	Aleksandr	Shevchenko	SU	61	17 Apr
2:14:02	Tony	Milovsorov	UK	58	30 Oct
2:14:03	Bertrand	Itsweire	FRA	65	27 Jun
2:14:04	John	Makanya	TAN	64	18 Apr
2:14:05	Ieuan	Ellis	UK	60	30 Oct
2:14:06	Muhamet	Nazhipov	SU	64	17 Apr
2:14:06	Michel	Constant	FRA	56	3 Sep
2:14:08	Bjørn	Sivertsen	DEN	57	16 Oct
2:14:09	Dimitry	Troc	SU	62	17 Apr
2:14:10	David	Edge	CAN	54	17 Apr
	(150)				
2:14:10	Daniel	Boltz	AUS	62	2 Oct

Downhill Point-to-Point Courses

Note that Boston (USA) has a net drop of 116 m between start (120 m) and finish (4 m)

Marathon Year List Progression

Year	Best	10th	20th	50th	100th	Under 2:12:00	Under 2:14:00
1958	2:15.17	2:21.51				-	-
1968	2:10.48	2:14.29	2:16.41	2:19.12	2:20.52	1	8
1978	2:09.06	2:11.58	2:12.49	2:14.45	2:16.21	12	32
1979	2:09.27	2:11.13	2:12.19	2:14.13	2:15.46	18	45
1980	2:09.01	2:10.23	2:11.00	2:12.50	2:14.25	33	85
1981*	2:08.13*	2:10.53	2:11.36	2:13.15	2:14.24	24	77
1982	2:08.51	2:11.08	2:11.44	2:12.54	2:14.32	25	82
1983	2:08.37	2:09.12	2:10.07	2:11.44	2:13.22	55	124
1984	2:08.05	2:10.05	2:10.53	2:12.00	2:13.20	49	132
1985	2:07.12	2:09.05	2:10.23	2:11.55	2:13.39	52	119
1986	2:07.35	2:09.57	2:11.03	2:12.22	2:13.38	42	124
1987	2:08.18	2:10.34	2:11.21	2:12.26	2:13.34	38	141
1988	2:06.50	2:08.49	2:10.19	2:11.51	2:13.08	55	139

* including short New York course, next best 2:08:18

3000 METRES STEEPLECHASE

Mark	Name		Nat	Born	Pos	Meet	Venue	Date
8:05.51	Julius	Kariuki	KEN	12.6.61	1	OG	Seoul	30 Sep
8:06.79	Peter	Koech	KEN	18.2.58	2	OG	Seoul	30 Sep
8:07.96	Mark	Rowland	UK	7.3.63	3	OG	Seoul	30 Sep
8:11.61		Koech			1	Nik	Nice	10 Jul
8:12.00	Patrick	Sang	KEN	11.4.64	2	Nik	Nice	10 Jul
8:12.17	Alessandro	Lambruschini	ITA	7.1.65	4	OG	Seoul	30 Sep
8:13.99	William	van Dijck	BEL	24.1.61	5	OG	Seoul	30 Sep
8:14.39	Henry	Marsh	USA	15.3.54	6	OG	Seoul	30 Sep
8:15.22		Sang			7	OG	Seoul	30 Sep
8:15.63		van Dijck			1s1	OG	Seoul	28 Sep
8:15.68		Koech			2s1	OG	Seoul	28 Sep
8:15.71		Kariuki			1	PG	London	8 Jul
8:15.72		Koech			1	DNG	Stockholm	5 Jul
8:15.97	Boguslaw	Maminski	POL	18.12.55	8	OG	Seoul	30 Sep
8:16.01	Raymond	Pannier	FRA	12.2.61	1		St.Denis	7 Jun
8:16.04	Francesco	Panetta (10)	ITA	10.1.63	1	WK	Zürich	17 Aug
8:16.07		Sang			2	DNG	Stockholm	5 Jul
8:16.17		Kariuki			1	WG	Helsinki	30 Jun
8:16.27	Hagen	Melzer	GDR	16.6.59	3s1	OG	Seoul	28 Sep
8:16.33		Rowland			3	DNG	Stockholm	5 Jul
8:16.54	Azzedine	Brahmi	ALG	13.9.66	1s2	OG	Seoul	28 Sep
8:16.70		Sang			4s1	OG	Seoul	28 Sep
8:16.92		Lambruschini			2s2	OG	Seoul	28 Sep
8:17.23		Panetta			5s1	OG	Seoul	28 Sep
8:17.28		Melzer			2	WG	Helsinki	30 Jun
8:17.49		Pannier			1	NC	Tours	13 Aug
8:17.55		Pannier			1	VD	Bruxelles	19 Aug
8:17.79		Panetta			9	OG	Seoul	30 Sep

Mark	Name		Nat	Born	Pos	Meet	Venue	Date
8:18.02	Joshua	Kipkemboi	KEN	22.2.60	2		St.Denis	7 Jun
8:18.09		Koech			2	PG	London	8 Jul
	(30/13)							
8:18.12	Féthi	Baccouche	TUN	16.11.60	3	Nik	Nice	10 Jul
8:18.32	Eddie	Wedderburn	UK	6.12.60	4	DNG	Stockholm	5 Jul
8:18.91	Roger	Hackney	UK	2.9.57	2		Hechtel	30 Jul
8:19.15	Bruno	LeStum	FRA	25.12.59	2	VD	Bruxelles	19 Aug
8:19.99	Graeme	Fell	CAN	19.3.59	6s2	OG	Seoul	28 Sep
8:20.44	Brian	Diemer	USA	10.10.61	1	R W	Koblenz	28 Aug
8:20.56	Hans	Koeleman	HOL	5.10.57	1	APM	Hengelo	14 Aug
	(20)							
8:20.73	Tom	Hanlon	UK	2.5.67	7	Nik	Nice	10 Jul
8:21.10	Kiprotich	Rono	KEN	4.1.58	3		Hechtel	30 Jul
8:21.48	Miroslaw	Zerkowski	POL	20.8.56	2	APM	Hengelo	14 Aug
8:21.48	Bélá	Vágó	HUN	3.10.63	1		Budapest	9 Sep
8:21.64	José	Regalo	POR	22.11.63	2	WA	Bruxelles	18 Jun
8:22.35	Ivan	Huff	USA	31.7.59	3		Monaco	2 Aug
8:22.45	Abdelaziz	Sahere	MOR	.67	9	Nik	Nice	10 Jul
8:22.76	Joseph	Mahmoud	FRA	13.12.55	10	Nik	Nice	10 Jul
8:22.85	Jens	Volkmann	FRG	31.5.67	5	VD	Bruxelles	19 Aug
8:23.19	Patriz	Ilg	FRG	5.12.57	1	NC	Frankfurt	24 Jul
	(30)							
8:23.40	Boniface	Merande	KEN	13.2.62	1		Barcelona	13 Jul
8:23.64	Brian	Abshire	USA	14.11.63	1	FOT	Indianapolis	22 Jul
8:23.70	Henryk	Jankowski	POL	15.10.61	1		Sopot	30 Jul
8:24.13	Are	Nakkim	NOR	13.2.64	3	R W	Koblenz	28 Aug
8:24.14	Mark	Smith	USA	22.2.63	4		Hechtel	30 Jul
8:24.38	Adauto	Domingues	BRA	20.5.61	2		Barcelona	13 Jul
8:24.98	Rainer	Schwarz	FRG	5.6.59	6	DNG	Stockholm	5 Jul
8:25.06	Franco	Boffi	ITA	2.11.58	7	WG	Helsinki	30 Jun
8:26.0m	Bret	Hyde	USA	3.7.59	2	Jenner	San Jose	28 May
8:26.08	Jim	Cooper	USA	6.10.59	5	FOT	Indianapolis	22 Jul
	(40)							
8:26.38	Engelbert	Franz	FRG	24.11.63	2	vGDR	Düsseldorf	20 Jun
8:26.56	Brendan	Quinn	IRL	26.7.60	7		Hechtel	30 Jul
8:26.76	Julius	Korir	KEN	21.4.60	2		La Coruña	4 Aug
8:27.30	Gábor	Markó	HUN	7.2.60	2	ASV	Köln	21 Aug
8:27.36	Tomasz	Zimny	POL	24.12.63	3	NC	Grudziadz	12 Aug
8:27.60	Pascal	Debacker	FRA	8.4.60	4		St.Denis	7 Jun
8:28.34	Kregg	Einspahr	USA	19.4.60	7	FOT	Indianapolis	22 Jul
8:28.9m	Martin	Fiz	SPA	3.3.63	1		Bilbao	18 Jun
8:28.99	Ivan	Danu	SU	17.10.59	1rA	Znam	Leningrad	12 Jun
8:29.30	Czeslaw	Mojzysz	POL	3.8.58	4	NC	Grudziadz	12 Aug
	(50)							
8:29.48	Micah	Boinett	KEN	19.12.65	2		Århus	6 Jul
8:29.85	Aivar	Tsarskiy	SU	15.6.62	3rA	Znam	Leningrad	12 Jun
8:29.94	Vasiliy	Koromyslov	SU	15.5.57	1	Kuts	Moskva	4 Sep
8:29.95	Herman	Hofstee	HOL	17.7.63	6		St.Denis	7 Jun
8:30.13	Karl	Van Calcar	USA	11.1.65	1	Pac 10	Westwood	21 May
8:30.32	Dmitriy	Ryzhukhin	SU	.67	3	Kuts	Moskva	4 Sep
8:30.41	Juan	Azkueta	SPA	2.7.67	4		La Coruña	4 Aug
8:30.61	Colin	Walker	UK	29.10.62	3		Sandnes	9 Jun
8:30.61	Dan	Reese	USA	15.10.63	4	TAC	Tampa	18 Jun
8:30.68	Vitaliy	Surin	SU	5.1.63	4	Kuts	Moskva	4 Sep
	(60)							
8:30.84	Mohamed	Mestour	MOR	.61	5		Barcelona	13 Jul
8:30.94	Frank	Ruhkieck	GDR	23.11.61	3	vFRG	Düsseldorf	20 Jun
8:31.04	Piotr	Zgarda	POL	18.6.56	3		Sopot	30 Jul
8:31.18	Joseph	Chelelgo	KEN	24.4.63	1	PNG	Turku	28 Jul
8:31.29	Mark	Souza	USA	14.12.63	5s1	FOT	Indianapolis	20 Jul
8:31.29	Matthias	Kohls	FRG	23.2.61	3	APM	Hengelo	14 Aug
8:31.35	Gatis	Deksnis	SU	21.7.64	5	Kuts	Moskva	4 Sep
8:31.58	Mauro	Pregnolato	ITA	21.10.64	11	VD	Bruxelles	19 Aug
8:31.67	Dave	Daniels	USA	28.10.58	7s1	FOT	Indianapolis	20 Jul
8:31.71	Juan	Conde	CUB	30.4.65	6	PTS	Bratislava	9 Jun
	(70)							

Mark	Name		Nat	Born	Pos	Meet	Venue	Date
8:31.76	Slawomir	Gurny	POL	2.9.64	5	NC	Grudziadz	12 Aug
8:31.93	Lubos	Gaisl	CS	11.3.63	8	PTS	Bratislava	9 Jun
8:32.12	Ivan	Konovalov	SU	6.7.59	2		Odessa	19 Aug
8:32.18	Patric	Nilsson	SWE	26.2.64	2		Karlskrona	16 Jun
8:32.40	Juan	Espino	SPA	24.6.59	6		Barcelona	13 Jul
8:32.42	Jirí	Svec	CS	14.8.64	9	PTS	Bratislava	9 Jun
8:32.51	JUorgen	Salo	FIN	14.1.66	2	PNG	Turku	28 Jul
8:32.64	Lev	Glinskikh	SU	25.7.62	3		Odessa	19 Aug
8:32.80	Aaron	Ramirez	USA	29.7.64	8s1	FOT	Indianapolis	20 Jul
8:32.94	Mark	Junkermann	USA	27.6.65	8	FOT	Indianapolis	22 Jul
	(80)							
8:33.22	Andreas	Fischer	FRG	11.4.68	3	NC	Frankfurt	24 Jul
8:33.39	Hubert	Karl	FRG	24.12.63	4	NC	Frankfurt	24 Jul
8:33.79	Francisco	Sanchez	SPA	18.5.58	8	R W	Koblenz	28 Aug
8:33.87	Thierry	Brusseau	FRA	22.7.64	8		St.Denis	7 Jun
8:33.88	Anton	Nicolaisen	RSA	25.1.68	1		Stellenbosch	12 Nov
8:33.97	Kazuhito	Yamada	JAP	3.2.64	1	NC	Tokyo	19 Jun
8:34.03	Shigeyuki	Aikyo	JAP	29.1.64	2	NC	Tokyo	19 Jun
8:34.39	Djamel	Lahlali	FRA	21.3.63	4	NC	Tours	13 Aug
8:34.46	Christian	Schieber	FRG	18.9.59	6	APM	Hengelo	14 Aug
8:34.47	Johan	Schnetler	RSA	1.2.66	2		Stellenbosch	6 Apr
	(90)							
8:34.6mA	William	Mutwol	KEN	.67	3	NC	Nairobi	18 Jun
8:34.73	Marian	Huncík	CS	30.1.66	10	PTS	Bratislava	9 Jun
8:34.93	Benito	Nogales	SPA	1.8.65	2		Casablanca	11 Jun
8:35.0m	Volker	Welzel	FRG	23.9.61	9		Hechtel	30 Jul
8:35.09	Hector	Begeo	PHI	19.6.64	12s1	OG	Seoul	28 Sep
8:35.14	Dan	Bell	USA	23.1.65	10	FOT	Indianapolis	22 Jul
8:35.16	Dan	Nelson	USA	15.5.64	8	TAC	Tampa	18 Jun
8:35.17	Michael	Heist	FRG	2.5.65	3		Essen	2 Sep
8:35.24	Jon	Thanos	USA	4.1.65	1h2	TAC	Tampa	16 Jun
8:35.29	Aleksandr	Saprykin	SU	.66	6	Kuts	Moskva	4 Sep
	(100)							
8:35.46	Mike	Fadil	USA	22.6.63	4h2	TAC	Tampa	16 Jun
8:35.47	Rickey	Pittman	USA	4.10.61	5h2	TAC	Tampa	16 Jun
8:35.49	Valeriy	Vandyak	SU	9.1.61	5rA	Znam	Leningrad	12 Jun
8:35.6m	Colin	Reitz	UK	6.4.60	10		Hechtel	30 Jul
8:35.74	Daniel	Gottschall	FRG	16.1.63	2		Koblenz	1 Jun
8:35.80	Csaba	Szücs	HUN	29.1.65	4	NC	Miskolc	16 Jul
8:35.88	António	Peula	SPA	21.3.66	4	NC	Vigo	13 Aug

Mark	Name		Nat	Born	Date
8:36.04	Viktor	Shevlyakov	SU	67	12 Jun
8:36.06	Marc	Fourny	FRA	63	13 Jul
8:36.21	Angel	Rodriguez	CUB	67	4 Jun
	(110)				
8:36.28	Paul	Henderson	USA	62	30 Apr
8:36.28	Tom	Stevens	USA	61	18 Jun
8:36.40	Burkhard	Dahm	FRG	65	24 Jul
8:36.4m	William Kipkosgei	Chemitei	KEN	70	18 Jun
8:36.53	Valeriy	Gryaznov	SU	61	19 Aug
8:36.74	Carlos	Pereira	POR	60	6 Aug
8:36.8m	Nikolay	Polyukhovich	SU	64	24 Jun
8:37.06	Inocencio	Lopez	SPA	66	20 Aug
8:37.10	Anatoliy	Reznik	SU	68	12 Jun
8:37.14	Chris	Griffith	RSA	65	12 Nov
	(120)				
8:37.3m	Igor	Pavlov	SU	60	24 Jun
8:37.37	Neil	Smart	UK	63	5 Jun
8:37.4m	Mateo	Domingues	SPA	55	25 Jun
8:37.49	Domingo	Ramon	SPA	58	13 Jul
8:37.52	Peter	McColgan	UK	63	5 Jun
8:37.57	César	Sanchez	SPA	63	9 Jul
8:37.60	Marcelo	Cascabello	ARG	64	16 Oct
8:37.82	Uwe	Pflügner	GDR	66	12 Aug
8:37.94	Masashi	Otokita	JAP	62	3 May
8:37.98	Richard	Cooper	USA	65	30 Apr
	(130)				
8:38.21	Rusty	Korhonen	USA	65	18 Jun
8:38.21	Kamel	Benyakhlef	ALG	60	1 Sep
8:38.24	Jonas	Lundström	SWE	.65	13 Aug
8:38.32	Andonis	Vouzis	GRE	66	28 May
8:38.53	Ted	Mecham	USA	65	2 Jul
8:38.6m	Bruno	Coutant	FRA	63	28 May
8:38.6m	Peter	Daenens	BEL	60	30 Jul
8:38.71	Teofil	Ciobanu	RUM	61	19 Jun
8:38.72	Wiktor	Pietrzyk	POL	65	12 Aug
8:38.8mA	Phillip	Barkutwo	KEN		18 Jun
8:38.92	António	Rodrigues	POR	62	6 Aug
8:38.97	Tom	Nohilly	USA	66	30 Apr
8:39.01	Maricel	Martinas	RUM	63	19 Jun
	(140)				
8:39.08	Gavin	Gaynor	USA	65	16 Jun
8:39.15	Volker	Werner	FRG	66	24 Jul
8:39.25	Yevgeniy	Agarkov	SU	64	19 Aug
8:39.40	Marian	Borcz	POL	59	12 Aug
8:39.42	Masaru	Matsuda	JAP	58	19 Jun
8:39.54	Mustapha	Badjaoui	MOR	65	11 Jun
8:39.55	Nikolay	Karpovich	SU	67	12 Jun
8:39.55	Robert	Banai	HUN	67	16 Jul
8:39.77	David	Baptiste	UK	65	5 Jun
8:39.82	Manuel	de Oliveira	FRA	59	13 Aug
	(150)				
8:39.9m	Marcelo	Cascabello	ARG	64	7 Aug
8:39.93	Steve	Chipman	USA	60	16 Jun
8:40.00	Rusty	Knowles	USA	63	16 Jun
8:40.1m	Ricardo	Vera	URU	62	7 Aug
8:40.12	Terry	Perrault	USA	61	30 Apr

Mark	Name		Nat		Born	Mark	Name		Nat		Born
8:40.12	Stan	Zevedei	RUM	63	19 Jun	8:40.64	Steve	Conwell	CAN	67	20 Aug
8:40.13	Jim	Gibson	USA	68	30 Apr	8:40.65	Roger	Gjøvåg	NOR	56	13 Aug
8:40.47	Corrie	Muller	RSA	64	12 Nov	8:40.7m	Michel	De Coster	BEL	64	30 Jul
8:40.54	Panayot	Kachanov	BUL	57	25 Jun	8:40.83	Hassan	Ouhrouch	MOR	61	11 Jun
8:40.59	Radiy	Ivanov	SU	66	26 Aug	8:40.93	Thomas	Peucker	GDR	66	30 Jun
	(160)					8:40.98	Igor	Zimin	SU	66	4 Sep

3000 Metres Steeplechase Year List Progression

Year	Best	10th	20th	50th	100th	Under 8:30	Under 8:35	Ave.100
1958	8:32.0	8:42.4	8:50.0	8:59.2	9:09.6		1	
1968	8:24.2	8:33.8	8:37.0	8:41.4	8:48.4	4	12	
1978	8:05.4	8:22.5	8:26.4	8:32.0	8:38.8	36	71	8:31.07
1979	8:17.92	8:23.41	8:26.67	8:32.4	8:37.18	32	75	8:31.19
1980	8:09.70	8:18.78	8:22.81	8:29.1	8:36.3	55	87	8:28.17
1981	8:13.32	8:21.93	8:25.79	8:30.7	8:37.1	45	75	8:30.24
1982	8:16.17	8:21.15	8:23.94	8:31.0	8:35.7	42	94	8:29.30
1983	8:12.37	8:19.38	8:21.72	8:28.77	8:36.09	60	94	8:28.76
1984	8:07.62	8:17.27	8:20.40	8:28.95	8:35.35	55	97	8:27.22
1985	8:09.17	8:18.02	8:21.99	8:30.23	8:35.95	49	87	8:28.44
1986	8:10.01	8:16.59	8:19.88	8:29.00	8:35.65	62	95	8:26.83
1987	8:08.57	8:16.46	8:20.83	8:30.29	8:37.2	46	84	8:28.12
1988	8:05.51	8:16.04	8:20.56	8:29.08	8:35.29	54	93	8:26.90

110 METRES HURDLES

Mark	Wind	Name		Nat	Born	Pos	Meet	Venue	Date
12.97A	2.0	Roger	Kingdom	USA	26.8.62	1		Sestriere	11 Aug
12.98	1.5		Kingdom			1	OG	Seoul	26 Sep
13.03	0.3		Kingdom			1		Athinai	3 Sep
13.04	1.6		Kingdom			1	ISTAF	Berlin	26 Aug
13.11A	2.0	Colin	Jackson	UK	18.2.67	2		Sestriere	11 Aug
13.11	0.0		Kingdom			1	WK	Zürich	17 Aug
13.14	2.0		Kingdom			1s2	FOT	Indianapolis	23 Jul
13.15	1.3		Kingdom			1	TAC	Tampa	17 Jun
13.17	2.0	Mark	McKoy	CAN	10.12.61	1	Athl	Lausanne	24 Jun
13.17	-2.7		Kingdom			1		San Diego	25 Jun
13.17	0.0		McKoy			2	WK	Zürich	17 Aug
13.17	0.0	Tonie	Campbell	USA	14.6.60	3	WK	Zürich	17 Aug
13.17	0.6		Kingdom			1q1	OG	Seoul	25 Sep
13.20	1.8	Aleksandr	Markin	SU	8.9.62	1	Znam	Leningrad	11 Jun
13.20	0.5		Kingdom			1		Jerez	28 Jun
13.21	1.8	Vladimir	Shishkin	SU	16.6.64	2	Znam	Leningrad	11 Jun
13.21A	2.0		McKoy			3		Sestriere	11 Aug
13.23	0.6		Jackson			1		Belfast	27 Jun
13.24	2.0	Arthur	Blake	USA	19.8.66	2	Athl	Lausanne	24 Jun
13.25	2.0		Blake			2s2	FOT	Indianapolis	23 Jul
13.25	1.3		McKoy			1	OT	Ottawa	6 Aug
13.27	1.8	Sergey	Usov	SU	14.1.64	3	Znam	Leningrad	11 Jun
13.27	1.8		Jackson			1h1		Birmingham	7 Aug
13.28	1.3		Campbell			2	TAC	Tampa	17 Jun
13.28	1.6		Campbell			2	ISTAF	Berlin	26 Aug
13.28	1.5		Jackson			2	OG	Seoul	26 Sep
13.29	1.3		Blake			3	TAC	Tampa	17 Jun
13.29	-0.8		Jackson			1	OT	Birmingham	7 Aug
13.29	1.2		Campbell			1		Seoul	19 Sep
13.30	0.0		Kingdom			1	Pepsi	Westwood	5 Jun
13.30	2.0	Cletus	Clark	USA	20.1.62	3	Athl	Lausanne	24 Jun
		(31/9)							
13.36	2.0	Andre	Phillips	USA	5.9.59	3s2	FOT	Indianapolis	23 Jul
13.38	1.8	Igor	Kazanov	SU	24.9.63	4	Znam	Leningrad	11 Jun
13.39	0.0	Greg	Foster	USA	4.8.58	2	Pepsi	Westwood	5 Jun
13.41	1.6	Jack	Pierce	USA	23.9.62	1h2	FOT	Indianapolis	22 Jul
13.41	0.5	Al	Joyner	USA	19.1.60	1h6	FOT	Indianapolis	22 Jul
13.41	0.5	Milan	Stewart	USA	31.10.60	2h6	FOT	Indianapolis	22 Jul
13.43	2.0	Renaldo	Nehemiah	USA	24.3.59	4s2	FOT	Indianapolis	23 Jul

Mark		Name		Nat	Born	Pos	Meet	Venue	Date
13.45	1.8	Vitaliy	Sklyarov	SU	31.1.60	5	Znam	Leningrad	11 Jun
13.45	0.8	Tony	Jarrett	UK	13.8.68	2h3	OG	Seoul	25 Sep
13.47	1.2	Stéphane	Caristan	FRA	31.3.64	1h1	NC	Tours	13 Aug
13.49	2.0	Igor	Khitryakov	SU	15.7.65	3	NC	Tallinn	5 Jul
		(20)							
13.49	2.0	Eric	Reid	USA	17.2.65	6s2	FOT	Indianapolis	23 Jul
13.50	0.4	Keith	Talley	USA	28.1.64	1		Indianapolis	2 Jul
13.50	1.2	Florian	Schwarthoff	FRG	7.5.68	1	NC	Frankfurt-am-Main	23 Jul
13.52A	1.4	Steve	Kerho	USA/CAN	24.3.64	1		Provo	21 May
13.52	0.6	Liviu	Giurgian	RUM	22.7.62	1		Bucuresti	18 Jun
13.52	0.5	Jirí	Hudec	CS	15.8.64	1		Barcelona	13 Jul
13.52	1.5	Jonathan	Ridgeon	UK	14.2.67	5	OG	Seoul	26 Sep
13.54A		Mike	Benjamin	USA	17.5.61	1		Albuquerque	9 Jun
13.54	-0.1	Tony	Dees	USA	6.8.63	2q4	FOT	Indianapolis	22 Jul
13.56	1.3	James	Purvis	USA	4.9.66	4	TAC	Tampa	17 Jun
		(30)							
13.57A		Mike	Profit	USA	17.10.66	2		Albuquerque	9 Jun
13.58A		Charles	James	USA	19.7.64	3		Albuquerque	9 Jun
13.58	1.8	Andrey	Dydalin	SU	28.2.66	6=	Znam	Leningrad	11 Jun
13.58	1.8	Sergey	Krasovskiy	SU	18.5.63	6=	Znam	Leningrad	11 Jun
13.60	-0.2	Emilio	Valle	CUB	21.4.67	2	PTS	Bratislava	8 Jun
13.60A	0.8	Javier	Moracho	SPA	18.8.57	1h2	IbAmC	Ciudad México	22 Jul
13.61	2.0	György	Bakos	HUN	6.7.60	2		Schwechat	15 Jun
13.61	1.7	Krzysztof	Platek	POL	13.1.62	1	Kuso	Warszawa	19 Jun
13.61	0.9	Tomasz	Nagorka	POL	2.10.67	1		Lodz	28 Jun
13.61	0.5	Gianni	Tozzi	ITA	6.5.62	2		Barcelona	13 Jul
		(40)							
13.62	-0.8	Andrey	Koroteyev	SU	6.10.66	1		Kharkov	18 Jun
13.62A	0.8	Elvis	Cedeño	VEN	25.1.64	2h2	IbAmC	Ciudad México	22 Jul
13.62	0.4	Philippe	Tourret	FRA	8.7.67	1	NC	Tours	13 Aug
13.63A	1.4	Wessel	Bosman	RSA	24.6.58	1		Johannesburg	23 Apr
13.63	1.3	Thomas	Wilcher	USA	11.4.64	6	TAC	Tampa	17 Jun
13.64A	1.4	Ralph	Schroeder	RSA	6.11.62	2		Johannesburg	23 Apr
13.64	1.8	Rod	Jett	USA	28.10.66	2	NCAA	Eugene	4 Jun
13.64		Alex	Washington	USA	28.12.62	1		Indianapolis	12 Jun
13.64	1.9	Mikael	Ylöstalo	FIN	2.5.63	1		Lohja	28 Aug
13.65	-1.4	Andreas	Oschkenat	GDR	9.6.62	2	vFRG	Düsseldorf	20 Jun
		(50)							
13.65A	0.8	LyndonJohnson	Pereira	BRA	8.5.66	3h2	IbAmC	Ciudad México	22 Jul
13.65A		Kobus	Schoeman	RSA	16.11.65	2		Pretoria	15 Oct
13.67	1.4	Holger	Pohland	GDR	5.4.63	1	NC	Rostock	24 Jun
13.67	1.7	Yuriy	Pleshko	SU	6.11.63	1		Bryansk	12 Jul
13.68	0.4	Philippe	Aubert	FRA	5.10.57	2	NC	Tours	13 Aug
13.69		Richard	Bucknor	JAM	6.11.66	1	NC	Kingston	16 Jul
13.69		Andrew	Parker	JAM	11.1.65	2	NC	Kingston	16 Jul
13.69	-1.7	Carlos	Sala	SPA	20.3.60	2		Salamanca	8 Sep
13.69	-0.9	Gela	Veshapidze	SU	5.9.66	1		Baku	10 Sep
13.70		Robert	Reading	USA	9.6.67	2		Fresno	9 Apr
		(60)							
13.70	1.9	Anton	Isayev	SU	25.6.62	2h2	Znam	Leningrad	11 Jun
13.70	-1.4	Gennadiy	Dakshevich	SU	15.3.66	1		Kharkov	18 Jun
13.72A		John	Lenstrohm	USA	27.2.61	2		Flagstaff	14 May
13.72	1.1	David	Nelson	UK	11.3.67	2	vUSA	Birmingham	24 Jun
13.73	2.0	Timur	Yudakov	SU	25.3.66	3h1	Znam	Leningrad	11 Jun
13.73	1.7	Sergey	Strelchenko	SU	21.12.61	2		Bryansk	12 Jul
13.73	0.2	Alain	Cuypers	BEL	29.11.67	1h1	NC	Bruxelles	3 Sep
13.74		James	McCraney	USA	28.3.55	2		Santa Monica	12 Jun
13.74	0.8	Georghe	Boroi	RUM	26.8.64	1	BalkG	Ankara	16 Jul
13.74	1.7	Chris	Lancaster	USA	23.12.65	2h1	FOT	Indianapolis	22 Jul
		(70)							
13.74	1.6	Dietmar	Koszewski	FRG	26.7.67	3	ISTAF	Berlin	26 Aug
13.74	1.2	Pascal	Boussemart	FRA	29.4.59	2h1	NC	Tours	13 Aug
13.75	0.7	Yu Zhicheng		CHN	23.7.63	3		Tokyo	13 May
13.75	0.9	William	Skinner	USA	30.9.64	3rB		Sevilla	1 Jun
13.75	1.9	Pavel	Sáda	CS	26.1.64	1		Praha	2 Jun
13.75	0,5	Mikhail	Edel	SU	7.9.69	1		Bryansk	23 Jun

Mark		Name		Nat	Born	Pos	Meet	Venue	Date
13.76	1.1	Kevin	Savoie	USA	31.7.67	3h1	FOT	Indianapolis	22 Jul
13.76	-0.3	Eric	Cannon	USA	2.3.67	3q1	FOT	Indianapolis	22 Jul
13.77		Terry	Johnson	USA	7.12.66	1		Los Angeles	19 Mar
13.77		Earl	Diamond	USA	21.7.66	1s1	JUCO	Odessa	20 May
		(80)							
13.77	0.8	Plamen	Krastev	BUL	18.11.58	3	BalkG	Ankara	16 Jul
13.77	1.6	Jailto S.	Bonfim	BRA	4.1.64	1		Sao Paulo	14 Aug
13.77	1.5	Fabian	Niederhäuser	SWZ	15.7.61	1		La Chaux de Fonds	21 Aug
13.78		Terry	Reese	USA	20.6.67	1		Raleigh	14 May
13.78	1.2	Stefan	Mattern	FRG	11.5.65	3=	NC	Frankfurt	23 Jul
13.78	1.2	Jürgen	Schoch	FRG	10.4.62	3=	NC	Frankfurt	23 Jul
13.79		Derrick	Knowles	BAH	22.3.66	2		Durham	1 Apr
13.79	0.0	Vladimir	Belokon	SU	13.2.69	1		Simferopol	28 May
13.80	0.1	Mike	Timpson	USA	6.6.67	1		Pittsburgh	14 May
13.80	0.1	Steve	Brown	USA	6.1.69	1	TAC j	Tallahassee	24 Jun
		(90)							
13.80	1.5	Franck	Chevallier	FRA	3.1.64	2		La Chaux de Fonds	20 Aug
13.81	0.1	Roget	Ware	USA	5.9.68	2		Pittsburgh	14 May
13.81	1.8	Lawrence	Felton	USA	21.2.67	4	NCAA	Eugene	4 Jun
13.81	0.8	Venzislav	Radev	BUL	9.1.61	4	BalkG	Ankara	16 Jul
13.81A	0.8	Robert	Carmona	MEX	17.9.69	4h2	IbAmC	Ciudad México	22 Jul
13.82		Kenny	Morris	JAM	19.11.66	2s1	JUCO	Odessa	21 May
13.82	2.0	Anatoliy	Titov	SU	3.3.56	7	NC	Tallinn	5 Jul
13.82	0.8	Jacinto	Alvarez	CUB	16.5.66	2		Habana	5 Aug
13.83	1.2	Heiko	Buss	FRG	6.1.63	5	NC	Frankfurt	23 Jul
13.83	-0.1	Erik	Jensen	DEN	4.6.62	1	NC	Aalborg	6 Aug
		(100)							
13.83	1.3	Jeff	Glass	CAN	21.4.62	2	OT	Ottawa	6 Aug

Mark	Wind	Name	Nat	Yr	Date
13.84	1.9	Dirk Morris	TRI	65	23 Apr
13.84	0.1	Calvin Holmes	USA	65	14 May
13.84	1.6	Rod Lawson	USA	67	21 May
13.84	1.9	Anthony Norris	USA	65	28 May
13.84	1.0	João Lima	POR	61	29 May
13.84	0.3	Jeff Smith	USA	64	18 Jun
13.85	0.5	Arto Bryggare	FIN	58	9Feb
13.85	1.1	Hugh Teape	UK	63	24 Jun
13.85	0.8	Herwig Röttl	AUT	68	11 Aug
		(110)			
13.86	-0.9	Aivars Ikaunieks	SU	59	19 May
13.86	2.0	Viktor Batrachenko	SU	63	11 Jun
13.86	0.9	Vladimir Mozharovskiy	SU	64	11 Jun
13.86	2.0	Ulf Söderman	SWE	63	4 Jun
13.87		David Ashford	USA	64	12 Jun
13.88	0.8	Nigel Walker	UK	63	7 May
13.88	1.3	Kevin Reid	CAN	66	6 Aug
13.88	0.6	Daniel Darien	FRA	61	13 Aug
13.88	1.0	Jamie Horn	USA		11 May
13.89	0.3	Derek Knight	USA	67	22 May
		(120)			
13.89	1.8	Aleksandr Gorshenin	SU	69	7 Jul
13.89	0.8	Stelios Bisbas	GRE	68	16 Jul
13.90	2.0	Harri Ylinen	FIN	64	15 Jun
13.90	-1.6	Mikhail Ryabukhin	SU	67	18 Jun
13.90	0.0	Olivier St.Gilles	FRA	63	29 Jun
13.91	-0.9	Don Wright	AUS	59	17 Mar
13.91		Judex Lefou	MAU	66	19 May
13.91	1.9	John Martin	USA	68	28 May
13.91	2.0	Thomas Weimann	AUT	67	15 Jun
13.91	1.7	Rafal Ciesla	POL	67	19 Jun
		(130)			
13.91	1.2	Martin Wiechert	FRG	65	23 Jul
13.91	1.7	Reinaldo Quintero	CUB	69	30 Jul
13.91	-1.1	Piotr Wojcik	POL	65	13 Aug
13.91		Thomas Kearns	IRL	66	20 Aug
13.92	1.8	Shannon Daugherty	USA	65	28 May
13.92		Wu Chin Jing	TAI	58	28 May
13.92	0.5	Al Lane	USA	62	22 Jul
13.93		John Elliott	USA	64	13 May
13.93A	0.0	Jailto S. Bonfim	BRA	64	22 Jul
13.94		Brett Fortune	USA		16 Apr
		(140)			
13.94	0.1	Don Moore	USA	68	15 May
13.94	0.0	Ales Höffer	CS	62	25 Jun
13.94	0.1	Elbert Ellis	USA	69	24 Jun
13.94	1.8	Piotr Klewenhagen	POL	69	8 Sep
13.95	1.9	John Caligari	AUS	62	6 Mar
13.95	0.0	Carter Jefferson	USA	68	21 Apr
13.95	-1.0	Bernard Williams	USA	65	21 May
13.95	1.7	Charles Powell	USA	64	16 Jun
13.95	2.0	Oleg Arlov	SU	69	7 Jul
13.95		Patrick Duffy	USA	65	11 Jul
		(150)			
13.96		Pat McGhee	USA	66	7 May
13.96	0.1	George Ifill	USA	66	14 May
13.96	-0.4	Vernon George	USA	64	2 Jun
13.96	1.8	Mircea Oeida	RUM	69	10 Jul
13.96	0.5	Angel Martin	SPA	64	13 Jul
13.96	0.0	Laisvunas Sankauskas	SU	64	16 Aug
13.96	1.4	Ysbrand Visser	HOL	61	4 Sep
13.97	2.0	Valdis Norins	SU	65	11 Jun
13.97	0.6	Lajos Sárközi	HUN	67	15 Jul
13.97	0.0	Mark Thomas	USA		22 Jul
		(160)			
13.97	1.7	Paul Gray	UK	69	30 Jul
13.97	1.3	Patrice Procope	FRA	62	31 Jul
13.97	1.2	Eric Chauchoy	FRA	63	13 Aug
13.98		Joe Galeano	USA	69	23 Apr
13.98	0.1	Kelly Carter	USA	69	15 May
13.98	1.0	Aleksandr Apaychev	SU	61	22 May
13.98	-0.5	Vyacheslav Ivashchenko	SU	67	18 Jun
13.98	0.8	Grigorios Zagoras	GRE	68	16 Jul
13.98	0.5	Mark Floyd	USA	64	22 Jul
13.98	1.2	Vincent Clarico	FRA	66	13 Aug
		(170)			
13.98	1.9	Kai Kyllonen	FIN	65	28 Aug
13.99	-0.1	Charles Johnson	USA	69	19 May
13.99	0.8	Ales Kolar	YUG	64	16 Jul

Reese (13.78) also 13.78 0.9 2h1 Knoxville 20 May
Morris (13.84) also 13.84 1.8 5 NCAA Eugene 4 Jun
Elliott (13.93) also 13.93 1.9 28 May

Mark	Wind	Name	Nat	Born	Date
14.00		Kevin Young	USA	66	16 Apr
14.00	0.0	John Owens	USA		14 May
14.00	1.9	Arthur Smith	USA	69	15 May
14.00		Glenn Patterson	USA	62	25 Jun
14.00	0.9	Thierry Richard	FRA	61	31 Jul
14.00	0.6	Kim Jin Tae	KOR	64	25 Sep
14.01		Rodney Belk	USA		20 May
(180)					
14.01	0.8	Yang Guang	CHN	63	25 Sep
14.01	1.3	Olivier Vallaeys	FRA	66	31 Jul

Best low altitude marks for athletes with altitude bests

Mark	Wind	Name	Pos	Meet	Venue	Date	Alt. best
13.61	0.0	Kerho	4		Westwood	5 Jun	13.52A
13.71	0.5	Moracho	3		Barcelona	13 Jul	13.60A
13.75		Bosman	1		Stellenbosch	6 Apr	13.63A
13.78	1.7	Benjamin	3h1	TAC	Tampa	17 Jun	13.54A
13.78	1.1	James	4h1	FOT	Indianapolis	22 Jul	13.58A
13.87		Schroeder				6 Apr	13.64A
13.95		Schoeman				26 Apr	13.64A
13.89	0.5	Johnson Pereira				13 Jul	13.65A

Wind assisted marks

Mark	Wind	Name		Nat	Born	Pos	Meet	Venue	Date
13.15	3.1		Kingdom			1s2	TAC	Tampa	16 Jun
13.21	2.2		Jackson			1		Oslo	21 Jun
13.21	2.5		Kingdom			1	FOT	Indianapolis	23 Jul
13.21	3.4		Jackson			1		Edinburgh	29 Jul
13.24	2.3		Campbell			1s1	TAC	Tampa	16 Jun
13.25	2.5		Campbell			2	FOT	Indianapolis	23 Jul
13.28	2.5		Blake			3	FOT	Indianapolis	23 Jul
13.33	2.5	Andre	Phillips	USA	.5.9.59	4	FOT	Indianapolis	23 Jul
13.35	3.4	Tony	Jarrett	UK	13.8.68	2		Edinburgh	29 Jul
13.36	2.1	Keith	Talley	USA	28.1.64	1		Knoxville	21 May
13.45	3.4	Jonathan	Ridgeon	UK	14.2.67	3		Edinburgh	29 Jul
13.46	3.2	James	Purvis	USA	4.9.66	2		Austin	7 May
13.46	2.6	Robert	Thomas	USA	25.7.60	1		Austin	22 Jun
13.50	4.7	Derrick	Knowles	BAH	22.3.66	1		San Angelo	21 May
13.51A	5.1	Steve	Kerho	USA/CAN	24.3.64	1		Provo	20 May
13.51	2.1	Tony	Dees	USA	6.8.63	2		Knoxville	21 May
13.53	2.1	Mikael	Ylöstalo	FIN	2.5.63	1	NC	Hämeenlinna	7 Aug
13.56	2.6	Mark	Floyd	USA	11.2.64	2		Austin	22 Jun
13.58	3.7	György	Bakos	HUN	6.7.60	1rB		Budapest	8 Sep
13.60	2.1	Terry	Reese	USA	20.6.67	3		Knoxville	21 May
13.61	2.8	James	McCraney	USA	28.3.55	2		Irvine	1 May
13.63		Lawrence	Felton	USA	21.2.67	1h		Houston	18 Mar
13.65	2.8	David	Nelson	UK	11.3.67	2		London	20 Aug
13.66	3.7	Andrew	Parker	JAM	11.1.65	2		Sacramento	27 Aug
13.67		Eric	Cannon	USA	2.3.67	1		Pittsburgh	9 Apr
13.67	2.2	Carlos	Sala	SPA	20.3.60	1	NC	Vigo	14 Aug
13.69	2.5	Dietmar	Koszewski	FRG	26.7.67	1		Strasbourg	.25 Jun
13.69	2.6	Kevin	Reid	CAN	15.3.66	3		Austin	26 Jun
13.70	3.3	Albert	Jones	USA	8.10.62	1		Arlington	7 May
13.71	3.0	Vernon	George	USA	6.10.64	1		Houston	7 May
13.71	3.1	Reinaldo	Quintero	CUB	10.7.69	1	WJ	Sudbury	30 Jul
13.73	3.1	Steve	Brown	USA	6.1.69	2	WJ	Sudbury	30 Jul
13.75		Lemuel	Stinson	USA	10.5.66	1h2		Houston	18 Mar
13.76		Earl	Diamond	USA	21.7.66	1		Odessa	22 Apr
13.78	3.1	Elbert	Ellis	USA	23.6.69	3	WJ	Sudbury	30 Jul
13.79	3.6	Ulf	Söderman	SWE	18.3.63	1		Västerås	30 Jun
13.80	4.7	Brett	Fortune	USA		2		San Angelo	21 May
13.80	3.0	Hugh	Teape	UK	26.12.63	1		London	18 Jun
13.80	2.5	Piotr	Wojcik	POL	7.2.65	1h1		Lublin	6 Aug
13.82		Robert	Johnson	USA	.61	1		Plainview	14 Mar
13.82		Felton	Nails	USA		1		Brenham	26 Mar
13.83		Dennis	Brantley	USA	13.7.61	3rB		Houston	21 May

Mark	Wind	Name	Nat	Born	Date
13.84	4.7	Charles Johnson	USA	69	21 May
13.84	3.0	István Simon Balla	HUN	58	8 Sep
13.87	2.4	Don Wright	AUS	59	13 Mar
13.87	2.8	Reggie Pate	USA		7 May
13.88	2.7	John Caligari	AUS	62	27 Feb
13.88	3.5	Charles Powell	USA	64	24 Apr
13.88	5.5	Rafal Ciesla	POL	67	19 Jun
13.89	2.5	Ron Stewart	USA	63	16 Jun
13.89	3.1	Olivier Vallaeys	FRA	66	25 Jun
13.90		Kason Jewell	USA	67	26 Mar

Mark	Wind	Name	Nat	Born	Date	Mark	Wind	Name	Nat	Born	Date
13.90		Ikechukwu Mbadugha	NIG	68		13.96	2.7	Courtney Hawkins	USA	67	23 Apr
13.90	3.7	Thomas Kearns	IRL	66	25 Aug	13.96	2.1	Beat Rutishauser	SWZ	64	12 May
13.91	3.3	Arthur Smith	USA	69	14 May	13.96	2.1	Cliff Bishop	USA		28 May
13.91	4.3	Sheldon Blockberger	USA	64	24 May	13.97	2.4	- House	USA		23 Apr
13.92		Mike Cole	USA	61	1 May	13.97	2.4	Brett St.Louis	UK	68	30 Jul
13.92	2.5	Dan Philibert	FRA	70	30 Jul	13.99	3.5	Henry Andrade	USA	62	24 Apr
13.94	4.7	Darryl Gilliams	USA		21 May	13.99	2.1	Randy Simmons	USA		19 May
13.94	2.7	Leslaw Hyjek	POL	66	6 Aug	13.99	5.5	Andrzej Siwek	POL	58	19 Jun
13.94	2.1	Petri Keskitalo	FIN	67	7 Aug	14.00		Victor Colter	USA		7 May
13.95	2.1	Harold Morton	USA	64	28 May	14.01	3.2	Robert de Wit	HOL	62	10 Jul

Hand times

Mark	Wind	Name		Nat	Born	Pos	Venue	Date
13.0		Vladimir	Shishkin	SU	16.6.64	1	Staiki	13 May
13.1		Igor	Kazanov	SU	24.9.63	2	Staiki	13 May
13.4	1.0	Sergey	Krasovskiy	SU	18.5.63	1h	Voroshilovgrad	14 May
13.4		Milan	Stewart	USA	31.10.60	1	Irvine	26 Jun
13.4		Robert	Reading	USA	9.6.67	2	Los Angeles	29 Jun
13.4		Mike	Profit	USA	17.10.66	3	Los Angeles	29 Jun
13.5	-0.9	Derrick	Knowles	BAH	22.3.66	1	Raleigh	26 Mar
13.5		Yu	Zhicheng	CHN	23.7.63	1	Shijiazhuang	23 Apr
13.5	-3.0	Philippe	Tourret	FRA	8.7.67	1	Franconville	6 May
13.5	-0.5	Gennadiy	Dakshevich	SU	15.3.66	1	Voroshilovgrad	14 May
13.5	-0.5	Igor	Borisov	SU	12.8.67	2	Staiki	1 Aug
13.5	1.2	Gela	Veshapidze	SU	5.9.66	1	Tbilisi	12 Oct
13.6i		Anton	Isayev	SU	25.6.62	1h	Leningrad	7 Feb
13.6	-0.9	Eric	Cannon	USA	2.3.67	2	Raleigh	26 Mar
13.6	-0.9	Terry	Reese	USA	20.6.67	3	Raleigh	26 Mar
13.6		Mikhail	Ryabukhin	SU	25.3.67	2	Voroshilovgrad	14 May
13.6		Chris	Lancaster	USA	23.12.65	1rA	Champaign	28 May
13.6	0.1	Viktor	Batrachenko	SU	6.1.63	1	Chernigov	24 Jul
13.6	0.1	Andrey	Koroteyev	SU	6.10.66	2	Chernigov	24 Jul
13.6	-0.6	Anatoliy	Titov	SU	3.3.56	2	Vladivostock	13 Sep

Mark	Wind	Name	Nat	Born	Date	Mark	Wind	Name	Nat	Born	Date
13.7i	-	Yuriy Myshkin	SU	63	6Mar	13.8	-0.9	Calvin Holmes	USA	65	26Mar
13.7		Shannon Daugherty	USA	65	16Apr	13.8	0.2	Kevin Young	USA	66	9Apr
13.7	-0.5	Oleg Degtyar	SU	64	14May	13.8		Lawrence Felton	USA	67	16Apr
13.7	1.0	Oleg Shiman	SU	68	14May	13.8		Mark Floyd	USA	64	16Apr
13.7		Igor Podmaryov	SU	61	17May	13.8		Hubertus Kaiser	FRG	64	11May
13.7	0.0	Aleksandr Gorshenin	SU	69	28May	13.8		Yuriy Yemelyanov	SU	64	17May
13.7	0.0	Mikhail Edel	SU	69	28May	13.8	-0.1	Vladimir Mozharovskiy	SU	64	4Jun
13.7	0.0	Vladimir Belokon	SU	69	28May	13.8		Vyacheslav Ustinov	SU	57	9Jul
13.7		Patrick Duffy	USA	65	11Jun	13.8		Marco Todsechini	ITA	67	10Jul
13.7		Jacinto Alvarez	CUB	66	25Jun	13.8		Willie Gault	USA	60	15Jul
13.7	1.9	John Caligari	AUS	62	28Jun	13.8		Oleg Likhachev	SU	64	6Aug
13.7		Laisvunas Sankauskas	SU	64	4Sep	13.8		Yang Guang	CHN	63	23Jul

Wind assisted hand times

Mark	Wind	Name		Nat	Born	Pos	Venue	Date
13.0		Keith	Talley	USA	28.1.64	1	Tuscaloosa	26 Mar
13.0		James	Walker	USA	25.10.57	1	Birmingham	2 May

Mark	Wind	Name	Nat	Born	Date	Mark	Wind	Name	Nat	Born	Date
13.7	3.9	Sergey Strelchenko	SU	61	18Jun	13.7		Yang Guang	CHN	63	12Aug

110 Metres Hurdles Year List Progression

Year	Best	10th	20th	50th	100th	Under 13.80	Under 14.00	Ave.100
1958	13.6	13.9	14.1*	14.3*	14.5*			
1968	13.33	13.5	13.7	13.9	14.1	14	34	
1978	13.22	13.56	13.72	13.96	14.14	31	59	13.895
1979	13.200	13.56	13.76	13.92	14.09	23	68	13.870
1980	13.21	13.53	13.68	13.90	14.07	31	77	13.844
1981	12.93	13.59	13.70	13.87	14.04	39	83	13.822
1982	13.22	13.46	13.65	13.82	14.01	45	94	13.776
1983	13.11	13.50	13.60	13.79	13.96	50	106	13.752
1984	13.15	13.45	13.55	13.74	13.91	59	138	13.701
1985	13.14	13.46	13.59	13.75	13.94	57	115	13.720
1986	13.20	13.40	13.51	13.72	13.90	65	138	13.683
1987	13.17	13.39	13.51	13.70	13.86	77	148	13.649
1988	12.97	13.36	13.49	13.65	13.83	88	171	13.618

400 METRES HURDLES

Mark	Name		Nat	Born	Pos	Meet	Venue	Date
47.19	Andre	Phillips	USA	5.9.59	1	OG	Seoul	25 Sep
47.23	Amadou	Dia Bâ	SEN	22.9.58	2	OG	Seoul	25 Sep
47.37	Edwin	Moses	USA	31.8.55	1	FOT	Indianapolis	17 Jul
47.56		Moses			3	OG	Seoul	25 Sep
47.58		Phillips			2	FOT	Indianapolis	17 Jul
47.72	Kevin	Young	USA	16.9.66	3	FOT	Indianapolis	17 Jul
47.74		Young			1=	WK	Zürich	17 Aug
47.74	Danny	Harris	USA	7.9.65	1=	WK	Zürich	17 Aug
47.75	David	Patrick	USA	12.6.60	4	FOT	Indianapolis	17 Jul
47.76		Harris			5	FOT	Indianapolis	17 Jul
47.85		Young			1	NCAA	Eugene	3 Jun
47.89		Moses			1		Malmö	8 Aug
47.89		Phillips			1	VD	Bruxelles	19 Aug
47.89		Moses			1s1	OG	Seoul	24 Sep
47.94		Young			4	OG	Seoul	25 Sep
48.04	Winthrop	Graham	JAM	17.11.65	5	OG	Seoul	25 Sep
48.06		Patrick			3	WK	Zürich	17 Aug
48.09		Harris			1		Athinai	3 Sep
48.19		Phillips			1s2	OG	Seoul	24 Sep
48.23	Harald	Schmid	FRG	29.9.57	1	NC	Frankfurt	24 Jul
48.27		Moses			1		Irvine	26 Jun
48.27		Young			1h1	FOT	Indianapolis	15 Jul
48.32		Young			1	Athl	Lausanne	24 Jun
48.32		Young			1	BNP	Villeneuve d'Ascq	27 Jun
48.34		Moses			1s2	FOT	Indianapolis	16 Jul
48.37		Harris			1	ASV	Köln	21 Aug
48.37		Graham			2s2	OG	Seoul	24 Sep
48.38		Moses			1		Tucson	11 Jun
48.42		Dia Bâ			1	HGP	Budapest	12 Aug
48.44		Dia Bâ			1	Nik	Nice	10 Jul
	(30/8)							
48.65	Tranel	Hawkins	USA	17.9.62	6	FOT	Indianapolis	17 Jul
48.65	Edgar	Itt	FRG	8.6.67	2	HGP	Budapest	12 Aug
	(10)							
48.67	Kriss	Akabusi	UK	28.11.58	4	WK	Zürich	17 Aug
48.68	Kevin	Henderson	USA	4.2.65	1	TAC	Tampa	18 Jun
48.83A	Pat	McGhee	USA	24.6.66	2		Sestriere	11 Aug
48.90	Toma	Tomov	BUL	21.5.58	5s2	OG	Seoul	24 Sep
49.00	Aleksandr	Vasilyev	SU	26.7.61	1	NC	Tallinn	6 Jul
49.03	Nat	Page	USA	26.1.57	1		Granada	28 May
49.20A	José	Alonso	SPA	12.2.57	1	IbAmC	Ciudad México	24 Jul
49.30	Gordon	Bugg	USA	24.6.66	2	Pac 10	Westwood	22 May
49.32	Theron	Brown	USA	18.1.63	2	TAC	Tampa	18 Jun
49.33	Aleksey	Bazarov	SU	14.10.63	1rB	Znam	Leningrad	12 Jun
	(20)							
49.35	Sven	Nylander	SWE	1.1.62	4	DNG	Stockholm	5 Jul
49.36	Athanassios	Kalogiannis	GRE	10.9.65	1	BalkG	Ankara	17 Jul
49.36	Henry	Amike	NIG	4.10.61	2	AfrC	Annaba	2 Sep
49.40	German	Petrov	SU	26.3.67	2	NC	Tallinn	6 Jul
49.40	Jozef	Kucej	CS	23.3.65	3	HGP	Budapest	12 Aug
49.47	Nikolay	Ilchenko	SU	12.8.63	1rC	Znam	Leningrad	12 Jun
49.48	Krasimir	Demirev	BUL	28.8.62	2	Nar	Sofia	26 Jun
49.49	George	Porter	USA	19.12.66	3	TAC	Tampa	18 Jun
49.50	Kelly	Carter	USA	15.2.69	1	WJ	Sudbury	29 Jul
49.50	Joseph	Maritim	KEN	22.10.68	5s1	OG	Seoul	24 Sep
	(30)							
49.50A	Dries	Vorster	RSA	25.10.62	1		Germiston	22 Oct
49.54	Kevin	Mason	USA	17.6.67	1h4	FOT	Indianapolis	15 Jul
49.57	Reggie	Davis	USA	17.1.64	1	FlaR	Gainesville	26 Mar
49.57	Branislav	Karaulic	YUG	8.4.63	1	NC	Sarajevo	4 Sep
49.61A	Domingo	Cordero	PR	17.10.65	2	IbAmC	Ciudad México	24 Jul
49.64	Stanislav	Návesnák	CS	1.1.65	1	NC	Praha	17 Jul
49.66	Bernard	Williams	USA	23.5.65	2h4	FOT	Indianapolis	15 Jul

Mark	Name		Nat	Born	Pos	Meet	Venue	Date
49.67	Tony	Valentine	USA	6.9.64	1		New Haven	22 May
49.68	Yuriy	Chashchin	SU	8.6.63	1		Sochi	20 May
49.74	Simon	Kitur	KEN	12.6.59	6s2	OG	Seoul	24 Sep
	(40)							
49.75	Alain	Cuypers	BEL	29.11.67	7s2	OG	Seoul	24 Sep
49.76	Rok	Kopitar	YUG	5.5.59	2	BalkG	Ankara	17 Jul
49.80	John	Branch	USA	2.10.67	1	PennR	Philadelphia	29 Apr
49.80	Aleksandr	Kharlov	SU	18.3.58	4	NC	Tallinn	6 Jul
49.80	Gideon	Yego	KEN	6.5.60	3h4	OG	Seoul	23 Sep
49.85	Leigh	Miller	AUS	19.8.63	1	NC	Perth	27 Mar
49.85	Shem	Ochako	KEN	12.12.64	2		Barcelona	13 Jul
49.86	Uwe	Schmitt	FRG	17.8.61	1		Berlin	29 May
49.86	Klaus	Ehrle	AUT	11.3.66	3		Linz	15 Aug
49.90	Al	Washington	USA	29.6.67	1		Knoxville	16 Apr
	(50)							
49.95	Chris	Lancaster	USA	23.12.65	1		Champaign	28 May
49.95	Petr	Marincic	CS	15.3.65	2	NC	Praha	17 Jul
50.00	Oleg	Azarov	SU	16.2.62	2rC	Znam	Leningrad	12 Jun
50.01	Phil	Harries	UK	7.4.66	1	NC	Derby	5 Jun
50.03	Ralph	Carrington	USA	30.6.69	2	TAC j	Tallahassee	25 Jun
50.03	Dale	Laverty	USA	30.4.65	4		Västerås	30 Jun
50.03	Max	Robertson	UK	27.12.63	2	PG	London	8 Jul
50.04	Nikolay	Taletskiy	SU	.62	6	NC	Tallinn	6 Jul
50.04	Martin	Briggs	UK	4.1.64	1	IsrCh	Tel Aviv	10 Jul
50.04	István	Simon Balla	HUN	9.2.58	1rB	HGP	Budapest	12 Aug
	(60)							
50.06	Francisco	Velazco	CUB	4.10.61	1		Caracas	25 Jun
50.08	Carsten	Köhrbrück	FRG	26.6.66	2		Berlin	29 May
50.08	Thomas	Nyberg	SWE	17.4.62	1	NC	Eskilstuna	14 Aug
50.12A	Antônio Diaz	Ferreira	BRA	2.3.60	3	IbAmC	Ciudad México	24 Jul
50.15	Uwe	Ackermann	GDR	12.9.60	1	NC	Rostock	25 Jun
50.17	Dale	Burrage	USA	30.5.67	1	TexR	Austin	8 Apr
50.17	Bryan	Leturgez	USA	3.8.62	2		Champaign	28 May
50.19	Marc	Dollendorf	BEL	7.2.66	2	NC	Bruxelles	4 Sep
50.21	Tony	Rambo	USA	30.5.60	4h4	FOT	Indianapolis	15 Jul
50.22	Ulf	Sedlacek	SWE	10.6.65	4		Kvarnsveden	19 Jun
	(70)							
50.22	Patrick	Mann	USA	24.4.66	3		Indianapolis	2 Jul
50.22	Hamidou	Mbaye	SEN	21.4.64	2h2	AfrC	Annaba	1 Sep
50.24	Elbert	Ellis	USA	23.6.69	3	TAC j	Tallahassee	25 Jun
50.25	McClinton	Neal	USA	11.7.68	1		Natchitoches	30 Apr
50.25	Ryoichi	Yoshida	JAP	2.3.65	1		Tokyo	11 Sep
50.27	Vladimir	Budko	SU	4.2.65	1	RigC	Riga	5 Jun
50.28	Pedro	Chiamulera	BRA	29.6.64	3		Bern	23 Aug
50.29	Olivier	Gui	FRA	20.1.62	1		Limoges	13 Jul
50.30	Darren	Wright	AUS	16.7.65	2	NC	Perth	27 Mar
50.30	John	Graham	CAN	20.11.65	3h1	OG	Seoul	23 Sep
	(80)							
50.31	David	Jones	USA	7.7.66	2		New Haven	22 May
50.31	Olider	Pérez	CUB	6.11.63	2	Barr	Habana	6 Mar
50.33	Sebron	Flenaugh	USA	15.9.65	1		Northridge	4 Jul
50.36A	Johan	Jonker	RSA	19.3.70	1		Germiston	22 Oct
50.37	Pat	Griffin	USA	22.4.67	2		Natchitoches	30 Apr
50.38	Ahmed	Hamada	BHN	18.9.61	1		Doha	18 Feb
50.40	Shannon	Daugherty	USA	11.2.65	3		Natchitoches	30 Apr
50.40	Sylvain	Moreau	FRA	13.6.66	1		Tarare	22 Jul
50.40	Lloyd	Guss	CAN	22.1.59	2	vITA	Cesenatico	14 Aug
50.41	Bart	Williams	USA	20.9.56	4		Tucson	11 Jun
	(90)							
50.42	Allan	Phillips	USA	16.9.67	2	Big 10	Ann Arbor	22 May
50.42	Thomas	Futterknecht	AUT	24.12.62	7		Linz	15 Aug
50.43	Mugur	Mateescu	RUM	13.6.69	1		Ternopol	25 Sep
50.44	Ahmed Abdul	Ghanem	EGY	2.1.59	4h2	OG	Seoul	23 Sep
50.45	Gilles	Vimbert	FRA	27.7.66	1		Poitiers	3 Jun
50.46	Randy	Cox	TRI	22.12.64	1		Princeton	14 May
50.47	Rik	Tommelein	BEL	1.11.62	1		Hechtel	30 Jul

Mark	Name		Nat	Born	Pos	Meet	Venue	Date
50.50A	Eric	Chesley	USA	.66	1		Provo	7 May
50.51	Jesús	Arino	SPA	5.8.63	2	NC	Vigo	14 Aug
50.52	Paul	Steele	JAM	10.7.66	1		Notre Dame	28 May
	(100)							
50.52	Pierre	Leveille	CAN	19.2.62	3	NC/OT	Ottawa	7 Aug
50.52	Hong Chul-hwang		KOR	27.2.66	4h1	OG	Seoul	23 Sep

Mark	Name		Nat	Born	Date
50.53	James	Purvis	USA	66	23 Apr
50.53	Valeriy	Vikhrov	SU	61	5 Jun
50.53	Michel	Zimmerman	BEL	60	
50.54	Mike	Timpson	USA	67	29 Apr
50.54	Bernard	Ellison	USA	67	21 May
50.55	Juan	Hernández	CUB	68	25 Jun
50.57	David	Charlton	BAH	62	21 May
50.60A	Shaun	McAlmont	CAN	65	7 May
	(110)				
50.60	Olaf	Hense	FRG	67	24 Jul
50.60	Igor	Kurochkin	SU	66	27 Aug
50.61	Yassem	Al Duaill	KUW	63	18 Feb
50.61	Ken	Gordon	AUS	62	27 Mar
50.63	Marvin	Parnell	USA	66	29 Apr
50.63A	Japie	de Jongh	RSA	64	22Oct
50.65	Daniel	Hejret	CS	62	7 Jun
50.65	Sansiski	Daniels	USA	64	8 Jul
50.65	Carsten	Fischer	FRG	62	24 Jul
50.67	Atsushi	Yamamoto	JAP	70	2 Aug
	(120)				
50.68	Hans-Jürgen	Ende	GDR	62	25 Jun
50.68	Antonio	Smith	VEN	67	9 Jul
50.69	Philippe	Gonigam	FRA	63	2 Jul
50.70	Mike	Graham	USA	67	28 May
50.70	Mauro	Maurizi	ITA	68	5Oct
50.71	Dirk	Morris	TRI	65	23 Apr
50.71	Derrick	Adkins	USA	70	25 Jun
50.74	Samuel	Matete	ZAM	69	1 Sep
50.75	Shigeru	Yamaguchi	JAP	69	13 May
50.75	Kevin	McKinley	USA	64	27 Jun
	(130)				
50.75	Robert	Zajkowski	POL	65	20 Aug
50.76	Said	Aberkan	MOR	63	31 Jul
50.77	Martin	Gillingham	UK	63	8 Jul
50.78	Steve	Jackson	USA	65	22 May
50.78	Jon	Thomas	USA	63	15 Jul
50.79	Pawel	Wozniak	POL	69	20 Aug
50.80	Vesa-Pekka	Pihlavisto	FIN	65	4 Sep
50.81	Vadim	Zadoinov	SU	69	19 Jun
50.82	Kevin	Oakey	AUS	64	27 Mar
50.82	Vladimir	Shmaryov	SU	66	13 Jul
	(140)				
50.83	Craig	Calk	USA	65	25 May
50.84	Keith	Wheeler	USA	69	25 May
50.84	Krzysztof	Swierczynski	POL	63	16 Jun
50.85	James	Stephenson	AUS		29 May
50.86	Koen	Verlinde	BEL	62	4 Sep
50.88	Valeriy	Dauksha	SU	66	5 Jun
50.89	Greg	Rolle	BAH	59	17 Jun
50.89	Alberto	Von Hellens	FIN	63	4 Sep
50.90	Derek	Knight	USA	67	21 May
50.90	Oleg	Tverdokhleb	SU	69	25 Sep
	(150)				
50.91	Shigenobu	Ohmori	JAP	60	17 Jun
50.91	Hiroshi	Kakimori	JAP	68	17 Jun
50.91	Pel	v.d.Kerkhof	HOL	68	23 Jul
A50.91	Ferrins	Pieterse	RSA	67	15 Oct
50.92	Richard	Bucknor	JAM	66	15 Jul
50.93	Luca	Cosi	ITA	63	21 Jul
50.94	Markku	Karvonen	FIN	66	5 Jun
50.94	Dominique	Duvigneau	FRA	60	22 Jul
50.95	Izel	Jenkins	USA	64	26 Mar
50.95	Allan	Ince	BAR	67	15 May
	(160)				
50.95	Niklas	Wallenlind	SWE	68	28 Aug
50.96	Charles	Moss	USA	63	28 May
50.97	Carl	Johnson	USA	66	28 May
50.97	Yao	Yongzhi	CHN	62	7 Jun
50.97	Gianluca	Piazzola	ITA	65	27 Jul
50.97A	Koos	Pretorius	RSA	66	15 Oct
50.98	Michael	Grün	FRG	68	2 Sep
50.99	Song Xingliang		CHN	64	5 Sep
51.00	Udo	Schiller	FRG	67	29 May
51.00	Yuriy	Malenko	SU	65	31 May
	(170)				
51.00	Javier	Poumier	CUB	69	17 Jul
51.01	Thomas	Bürkle	FRG	58	7 Aug
51.02	Pablo	Squella	CHL	63	7 May
51.02	Oleg	Zhdanov	SU	62	20 May
51.02	Giorgios	Vamvakas	GRE	60	4 Jun
51.03	Toshifumi	Yasui	JAP	67	21 May
51.04	Trevor	Burton	UK	61	9 Jun
51.04	Emmanuel	Gonigam	FRA	63	26 Jul

Best at low altitude if with altitude best

Mark	Name	Pos	Venue	Date	Alt best
48.98	McGhee	3	Malmö	8 Aug	48.83A
49.48	Alonso	4	Madrid	7 Jun	49.20A
49.78	Vorster	1	Stellenbosch	24 Apr	49.50A
50.65	Ferreira			29 May	50.12A

Disqualified for trailing leg infraction

Mark	Name		Nat	Born	Pos	Meet	Venue	Date
48.89	Reggie	Davis	USA	17.1.64		TAC	Tampa	18 Jun

Hand times

Mark	Name		Nat	Born	Pos	Meet	Venue	Date
48.7A	Gideon	Yego	KEN	6.5.60	1	OT	Nairobi	13 Aug
48.9A	Simon	Kitur	KEN	12.6.59	2	OT	Nairobi	13 Aug
49.3A	Shem	Ochako	KEN	12.12.64	1	NC	Nairobi	18 Jun
49.3A	Joseph	Maritim	KEN	22.10.68	3	OT	Nairobi	13 Aug
49.6	Klaus	Ehrle	AUT	11.3.66	1		Innsbruck	11 Jun
49.8	Elbert	Ellis	USA	23.6.69	1		Villanova	8 May
49.8	Randy	Cox	TRI	22.12.64	1		Washington	28 May
49.9	Nikolay	Taletskiy	SU	.62	1		Staiki	1 Aug
50.1	Ryoichi	Yoshida	JAP	2.3.65	1		Mito	29 May
50.2A	Barnabas	Kinyor	KEN	.61	3	NC	Nairobi	18 Jun
50.3	Thomas	Futterknecht	AUT	24.12.62	2		Innsbruck	11 Jun

Mark	Name		Nat	Born	Date
50.4	Valeriy	Dauksha	SU	66	1 Aug
50.5A	Samuel	Matete	ZAM	69	13 Aug
50.5A	Paul	Rop	KEN	62	13 Aug
50.6	Greg	Rolle	BAH	59	12 Aug
50.8	Sergey	Filipyev	SU	64	28 May
50.9A	Gideon	Biwott	KEN	67	18 Jun

Mark	Name		Nat	Born	Pos	Meet	Venue	Date

400 metres Hurdles Year List Progression

Year	Best	10th	20th	50th	100th	Under 50.00	Under 51.00	Ave.100
1958	49.2	51.2	51.7	52.7	53.5	2	5	
1968	48.12	49.47	50.1	51.1	51.6	18	38	
1978	47.94	49.55	49.85	50.58	51.23	24	81	50.407
1979	47.53	49.30	49.69	50.63	51.24	25	83	50.350
1980	47.13	49.24	49.69	50.25	50.99	28	100	50.279
1981	47.14	49.33	49.72	50.41	50.94	23	109	50.217
1982	47.48	48.90	49.64	50.19	50.89	34	111	50.040
1983	47.02	49.03	49.35	50.02	50.72	48	137	49.900
1984	47.32	48.74	49.40	49.92	50.53	52	162	49.759
1985	47.63	49.03	49.34	49.91	50.65	56	144	49.826
1986	47.63	48.71	49.13	49.81	50.41	63	174	49.661
1987	47.46	48.56	49.03	49.82	50.54	61	168	49.661
1988	47.19	48.65	49.33	49.90	50.52	52	154	49.719

HIGH JUMP

2.43	Javier	Sotomayor	CUB	13.10.67	1		Salamanca	8 Sep
2.42i	Carlo	Thränhardt	FRG	5.7.57	1		Berlin	26 Feb
2.39i	Patrik	Sjöberg	SWE	5.1.65	1	EI	Budapest	5 Mar
2.38i		Sjöberg			1		Genk	7 Feb
2.38		Sotomayor			1		Kvarnsveden	19 Jun
2.38	Sergey	Malchenko	SU	2.11.63	1		Banská Bystrica	4 Sep
2.38	Gennadiy	Avdeyenko	SU	4.11.63	1	OG	Seoul	25 Sep
2.37i	Dietmar	Mögenburg	FRG	15.8.61	2	EI	Budapest	5 Mar
2.37	Tom	McCants	USA	27.11.62	1	JO	Columbus	8 May
2.37	Jerome	Carter	USA	25.3.63	2	JO	Columbus	8 May
2.37	Sorin	Matei	RUM	6.7.63	1		Bucuresti	11 Jun
2.37		Sjöberg			1	Nik	Nice	10 Jul
2.36i		Malchenko			1		Moskva	9 Jan
2.36i		Mögenburg			2		Berlin	26 Feb
2.36i		Matei			1	HunCh	Budapest	27 Feb
2.36		Matei			1		Hamamatsu	8 May
2.36	Rudolf	Povarnitsyn	SU	13.6.62	1	PTS	Bratislava	9 Jun
2.36		Avdeyenko			1	NC	Tallinn	6 Jul
2.36		Malchenko			1		Dnepropetrovsk	17 Jul
2.36	Igor	Paklin	SU	15.6.63	1		Vilnius	28 Aug
2.36	Hollis	Conway	USA	8.1.67	2	OG	Seoul	25 Sep
2.36		Povarnitsyn			3=	OG	Seoul	25 Sep
2.36		Sjöberg			3=	OG	Seoul	25 Sep
2.35i		Thränhardt			1		Wuppertal	24 Jan
2.35i		Sjöberg			1		Madrid	2 Feb
2.35i		Matei			3	EI	Budapest	5 Mar
2.35		Sotomayor			1	Barr	Habana	6 Mar
2.35		McCants			1		Tuscaloosa	27 Mar
2.35		Sotomayor			1	IbAmC	Ciudad.México	23 Jul
2.35	Gerd	Nagel	FRG	22.10.57	1		Forbach	7 Aug
2.35		Sotomayor			1		Athinai	3 Sep
2.35		Malchenko			1		Vladivostok	14 Sep
2.35		Povarnitsyn			2		Vladivostok	14 Sep
	(33/13)							
2.34i	Jim	Howard	USA	11.9.59	1		East Rutherford	13 Feb
2.34	Doug	Nordquist	USA	20.12.58	1	TAC	Tampa	18 Jun
2.34	Robert	Ruffíni	CS	26.1.67	1	vBUl,GRE	Praha	3 Jul
2.34	Nick	Saunders	BER	14.9.63	5	OG	Seoul	25 Sep
2.33	Brian	Stanton	USA	19.2.61	1		Walnut	29 May
2.33	Tom	Smith	USA	10.7.67	1	NCAA	Eugene	4 Jun
2.32i	Aleksandr	Kotovich	SU	6.1.61	2		Vilnius	23 Jan
	(20)							
2.32i	Andrey	Morozov	SU	14.6.60	3	NC	Volgograd	12 Feb
2.32	Luca	Toso	ITA	15.2.64	1		Torino	21 Jul
2.32	Krzysztof	Krawczyk	POL	28.1.62	1		Lublin	6 Aug
2.32	Eugen	Popescu	RUM	12.8.62	1	NC	Pitesti	14 Aug

Mark	Name		Nat	Born	Pos	Meet	Venue	Date
2.31i	James	Lott	USA	13.10.65	1		New York	5 Feb
2.31i	Mark	Reed	USA	22.5.65	1		Bloomington	5 Feb
2.31i	Gerd	Wessig	GDR	16.7.59	1		Wien	13 Feb
2.31i	Milton	Ottey	CAN	29.12.59	3		East Rutherford	13 Feb
2.31i	Vladimir	Korniyenko	SU	28.1.66	1		Moskva	20 Feb
2.31	Brent	Harken	USA	1.12.61	1	Jerome	Burnaby	5 Jun
	(30)							
2.31	J.Francisco	Centelles	CUB	26.1.61	2	IbAmC	Ciudad.México	23 Jul
2.31	Dalton	Grant	UK	8.4.66	7=	OG	Seoul	25 Sep
2.30i	Valeriy	Sereda	SU	30.6.59	1		Leipzig	16 Jan
2.30i	Sergey	Serebryanskiy	SU	24.12.62	1		Zaporozhye	23 Jan
2.30i	Dennis	Lewis	USA	20.3.59	1		Ypsilanti	28 Jan
2.30i	Brian	Brown	USA	6.6.67	1		Baton Rouge	19 Feb
2.30i	Georgi	Dakov	BUL	21.10.67	2	HunCh	Budapest	27 Feb
2.30i	Fabrizio	Borellini	ITA	5.7.68	4	EI	Budapest	5 Mar
2.30i	Troy	Kemp	BAH	18.3.66	2	NCAA	Oklahoma City	12 Mar
2.29i	Aleksey	Yemelin	SU	13.12.68	2		Moskva	20 Feb
	(40)							
2.29	Jake	Jacoby	USA	24.9.61	6	FOT	Indianapolis	16 Jul
2.29	Jacek	Wszola	POL	30.12.56	1	NC	Grudziadz	14 Aug
2.28	Brian	Marshall	CAN	1.4.65	1	Pac 10	Westwood	22 May
2.28	Artur	Partyka	POL	25.7.69	1		Spala	28 May
2.28	Torsten	Marschner	GDR	17.11.68	1	vITA	Neubrandenburg	9 Jul
2.28	Jean-Charles	Gicquel	FRA	24.2.67	8	Nik	Nice	10 Jul
2.28	Panagiotis	Kontaxakis	GRE	16.8.64	3	BalkG	Ankara	16 Jul
2.28	Geoff	Parsons	UK	14.8.64	1	AAA	Birmingham	6 Aug
2.28	Arturo	Ortiz	SPA	18.9.66	Q	OG	Seoul	24 Sep
2.27i	Daniele	Pagani	ITA	11.6.66	7	EI	Budapest	5 Mar
	(50)							
2.27	Marcello	Benvenuti	ITA	26.4.64	1		Viareggio	3 Aug
2.27	Christian	Schenk	GDR	9.2.65	D	OG	Seoul	28 Sep
2.26i	Mike	Pascuzzo	USA	8.11.61	1		West Point	2 Jan
2.26i	Yevgeniy	Dosayev	SU	12.8.63	1		Zaporozhye	16 Jan
2.26i	Jon	Baer	USA	30.9.65	1		Madison	16 Jan
2.26i	Rick	Noji	USA	22.10.67	1		Portland	23 Jan
2.26i	Greg	Jones	USA	21.8.65	2		Moscow, ID.	19 Feb
2.26	Neal	Guidry	USA	3.4.67	2		Lafayette, LA.	19 Mar
2.26	David	Anderson	AUS	8.12.65	1	NC	Perth	26 Mar
2.26	Marc	Howard	AUS	5.11.66	2	NC	Perth	26 Mar
	(60)							
2.26	Jon	Shelton	USA	5.12.67	1	DrakeR	Des Moines	30 Apr
2.26	Bob	Sundell	USA	27.1.67	1		Cape Girardeau	7 May
2.26	Ben	Lucero	USA	22.6.62	1		Flagstaff	14 May
2.26	Mike	Vukovich	USA	7.1.65	1		Minneapolis	28 May
2.26	Ján	Zvara	CS	12.2.63	1		Praha	2 Jun
2.26	Lee	Balkin	USA	7.6.61	2	Pepsi	Westwood	5 Jun
2.26	Oleg	Palashevskiy	SU	.62	1eB	Znam	Leningrad	12 Jun
2.26	Sergey	Zasimovich	SU	6.9.62	2eB	Znam	Leningrad	12 Jun
2.26	Lambros	Papakostas	GRE	20.10.69	1	NC	Thessaloniki	12 Jun
2.26	Kenny	Banks	USA	12.11.66	4	TAC	Tampa	18 Jun
	(70)							
2.26	John	Morris	USA	20.1.64	5	TAC	Tampa	18 Jun
2.26	Dariusz	Zielke	POL	21.10.60	2	Kuso	Warszawa	19 Jun
2.26	Bernhard	Bensch	FRG	22.9.64	1		Dortmund	3 Jul
2.26	Leo	Williams	USA	28.4.60	1		Northridge	11 Jul
2.26	Dwight	Stones	USA	6.12.53	2		Northridge	11 Jul
2.26	Eric	Monnerais	FRA	4.4.65	1		Tours	23 Jul
2.25i	Yuriy	Gotovskiy	SU	31.5.61	2		Leningrad	17 Jan
2.25i	Oleg	Azizmuradov	SU	20.1.62	2		Zaporozhye	23 Jan
2.25i	Andrey	Mukhin	SU	1.6.65	1		Leningrad	30 Jan
2.25i	Yuriy	Shevchenko	SU	18.4.60	3		Kiev	30 Jan
	(80)							
2.25i	Hrvoje	Fizuleto	YUG	15.1.63	3	HunCh	Budapest	27 Feb
2.25i	Saso	Apostolovski	YUG	20.1.63	4	HunCh	Budapest	27 Feb
2.25i	Dothel	Edwards	USA	9.9.66	1	SEC	Baton Rouge	28 Feb
2.25	Thomas	Eriksson	SWE	1.5.63	D		Houston	5 Mar

Mark	Name		Nat	Born	Pos	Meet	Venue	Date
2.25	Brian	Whitehead	USA	24.2.62	1		Naperville, IL.	20 May
2.25	Zhu Jianhua		CHN	29.5.63	1		Anshan	6 Jun
2.25	Kosmas	Michalopoulos	GRE	6.3.66	1	NC	Thessaloniki	11 Jun
2.25	Lubomír	Rosko	CS	9.10.62	1		Budapest	11 Jul
2.25	Konstantin	Galkin	SU	25.3.65	2		Grodno	17 Jul
2.25	Fernando	Pastoriza	ARG	1.2.65	3	IbAmC	Ciudad México	23 Jul
	(90)							
2.25	Sergey	Dymchenko	SU	23.8.67	1		Kharkov	5 Aug
2.25	Robert	Marinov	BUL	1.2.67	1		Sofia	6 Aug
2.25	Cho Hyun-wook		KOR	15.3.62	1		Seoul	12 Aug
2.25	Dominique	Hernandez	FRA	1.8.60	1	NC	Tours	13 Aug
2.25	Floyd	Manderson	UK	5.3.61	2		London	20 Aug
2.25	Ralf	Sonn	FRG	17.1.67	1		New Delhi	6 Sep
2.24i	Vladimir	Sokolov	SU	5.10.63	5		Moskva	20 Feb
2.24i	Carsten	Siebert	GDR	24.11.62	1	NC	Senftenberg	27 Feb
2.24i	Gyula	Németh	HUN	2.12.59	8=	EI	Budapest	5 Mar
2.24i	Håkon	Särnblom	NOR	3.3.66	10=	EI	Budapest	5 Mar
	(100)							
2.24	Franck	Verzy	FRA	13.5.61	1		Genéve	6 Aug
2.24	Gustavo	Becker	SPA	17.6.66	2	NC	Vigo	14 Aug
2.24	Grigoriy	Fyodorkov	SU	.64	2		Kiev	15 Aug
2.24	Jouko	Kilpi	FIN	21.4.61	1		Lohja	28 Aug

Mark	Name		Nat	Yr	Date
2.23	Kenneth	Smith	USA	62	9 Jun
2.23	Markus	Einberger	AUT	64	15 Jun
2.23	Marcello	Furlani	ITA	63	16 Jun
2.23	Joe	Radan	USA	57	15 Jul
2.23	Jindrich	Vondra	CS	57	11 Aug
2.23	Takahisa	Yoshida	JAP	70	19 Oct
	(110)				
2.23	Satoru	Nonaka	JAP	63	3 Nov
2.22i	Vadim	Oganyan	SU	63	10 Jan
2.22i	Bill	Bluethmann	USA	68	16 Jan
2.22i	Oleg	Kulikovskiy	SU	63	23 Jan
2.22i	Bill	Jasinski	USA	64	29 Jan
2.22i	Oleg	Urmakayev	SU	65	30 Jan
2.22i	Gennadiy	Balandinskiy	SU	65	30 Jan
2.22i	Yuriy	Sergiyenko	SU	65	30 Jan
2.22i	Igor	Samylov	SU	62	30 Jan
2.22i	Constantin	Militaru	RUM	63	13 Feb
	(120)				
2.22i	Dave	Glassburn	USA	63	19 Feb
2.22	Mike	Harris	USA	67	5 Mar
2.22	Tony	Brown	USA	66	23 Apr
2.22	Darren	Burton	USA	63	30 Apr
2.22	Obie	Martin	USA	64	30 Apr
2.22	Vladimir	Granenkov	SU	59	3 May
2.22	Paul	Wiechern	USA	67	7 May
2.22	Dave	Sampson	USA	63	7 May
2.22	Troy	Glasgow	BER	66	14 May
2.22	Jeff	Rogers	USA	67	14 May
	(130)				
2.22	Dimitrios	Kattis	GRE	56	25 May
2.22	Mikko	Levola	FIN	59	5 Jun
2.22	Andrea	Liverani	ITA	64	12 Jun
2.22	Konstantin	Kozyryov	SU	65	17 Jun
2.22	Takao	Sakamoto	JAP	58	18 Jun
2.22	Fernando	Moreno	ARG	67	3 Jul
2.22	Matti	Viitala	FIN	66	17 Jul
2.22	Sergey	Shinkaryov	SU	64	22 Jul
2.22	Andre	Schneider	FRG	58	24 Jul
2.22	Park Jae hong		KOR	70	24 Jul
	(140)				
2.22	Timo	Ruuskanen	FIN	68	31 Jul
2.22	Jaroslaw	Kotewicz	POL	69	31 Jul
2.22	Alain	Metellus	CAN	65	6 Aug
2.22	Veli Pekka	Kokkonen	FIN	66	7 Aug
2.22	Krzysztof	Przybyla	POL	62	14 Aug
2.22	Michael	Mikkelsen	DEN	66	21 Aug
2.22	Patrice	Legrand	FRA	68	30 Sep
2.22i	Joe	Patrone	USA	62	28 Dec
2.21i	Gunnar	Schipper	GDR	65	16 Jan
2.21i	Sergey	Malyi	SU	65	16 Jan
	(150)				
2.21i	Gennadiy	Golubyov	SU	66	23 Jan
2.21i	Matthias	Grebenstein	GDR	64	30 Jan
2.21i	Aleksey	Khabarov	SU	69	7 Feb
2.21i	Sergey	Ilnitskiy	SU	62	4 Mar
2.21i	Vladimir	Stalmach	CS	65	8 Mar
2.21i	Mike	Fairchild	USA		11 Mar
2.21	Eddie	McGill	USA	68	25 Mar
2.21	Walter	Barney	USA	69	2 Apr
2.21	Darrin	Moore	USA	68	9 Apr
2.21	Novica	Canovic	YUG	61	15 May
	(160)				
2.21	Sergey	Ryzhikov	SU	66	12 Jun
2.21	Gisle	Ellingsen	NOR	65	12 Jun
2.21	Juha	Isolehto	FIN	68	16 Jun
2.21	Maris	Reinsons	SU	64	17 Jun
2.21	Kevin	Clements	USA	70	18 Jun
2.21	Vincent	Gouzalch	FRA	63	2 Jul
2.21	Miguel	Moral	SPA	61	2 Jul
2.21	Volker	Wieland	FRG	64	3 Jul
2.21	Milan	Machotka	CS	63	9 Jul
2.21	John	Holman	UK	68	23 Jul
	(170)				
2.21	Enrico	Zanti	ITA	65	27 Jul
2.21	Dimitri	Maenhoudt	BEL	69	7 Aug
2.21	Andrey	Sankovich	SU	66	15 Aug
2.21	Marat	Sharipov	SU	65	15 Aug
2.21	Kosmas	Mihalopoulos	GRE	66	28 Aug

Exhibition

Mark	Name		Nat	Born	Pos	Meet	Venue	Date
2.30	Jacek	Wszola	POL	30.12.56	-		Patria, GRE	4 Sep
2.25	Enrico	Zanti	ITA	17.4.65	-		Padova	13 Oct

Unknown Irregularity

Mark	Name		Nat	Born	Pos	Meet	Venue	Date
2.35		Thränhardt			1		Bensheim	15 May
2.25	Ralf	Neunzling	FRG	24.7.67	3		Bensheim	15 May

Disqualified due to earlier time fault

Mark	Name		Nat	Born	Pos	Meet	Venue	Date
2.35		Thränhardt			-	EI	Budapest	5 Mar

Mark	Name	Nat	Born	Pos	Meet	Venue	Date

Best outdoor marks for athletes with indoor seasonal bests

2.34	Thränhardt	1		Eberstadt	26 Jun	2.42i
2.34	Howard	1	FOT	Indianapolis	16 Jul	2.34i
2.34	Mögenburg	1	OG	Seoul	25 Sep	2.37i
2.32	Morozov	3	NC	Tallinn	6 Jul	2.32i
2.31	Lott	1	Pepsi	Westwood	5 Jun	2.31i
2.30	Dakov	1		Sofia	5 Jun	2.30i
2.28	Lewis	1		Indianapolis	2 Jul	2.30i
2.28	Borellini	1		Roma	8 May	2.30i
2.28	Wessig	2	vITA	Neubrandenburg	9 Jul	2.31i
2.28	Yemelin	1		Moskva	7 Aug	2.29i
2.28	Ottey	6=	WK	Zürich	17 Aug	2.31i
2.27	Kemp	1		Boise, ID.	2 Apr	2.30i
2.27	Korniyenko	1	RigC	Riga	5 Jun	2.31i
2.26	Brown	1		Monroe	26 Mar	2.30i
2.26	Pascuzzo	1		Tampa	30 Apr	2.26i
2.26	Reed	1		Houston	21 May	2.31i
2.26	Jones	Q	FOT	Indianapolis	15 Jul	2.26i
2.26	Pagani	2	vCAN	Cesenatico	14 Aug	2.27i
2.25	Edwards	1	SEC	Auburn	15 May	2.25i
2.25	Azizmuradov	1		Alma-Ata	16 May	2.25i
2.25	Noji	2	Pac-10	Westwood	22 May	2.26i
2.25	Kotovich	2	RigC	Riga	5 Jun	2.32i
2.25	Apostolovski	1		Kranj	6 Jul	2.25i
2.25	Shevchenko	2		Dnepropetrovsk	17 Jul	2.25i
2.24	Siebert	1		Karl-Marx-Stadt	12 Jun	2.24i
2.23	Baer				14 May	2.26i
2.22	Jasinski				16 Apr	2.22i
2.22	Sokolov				24 Apr	2.24i
2.22	Glassburn				30 Apr	2.22i
2.21	Schipper				7 Jul	2.21i
2.21	Ilnitskiy				15 Aug	2.21i
2.21	Mukhin				15 Aug	2.25i

Ancillary jumps

Heights cleared prior to competition bests

Sotomayor	2.40	8 Sep
Thränhardt	2.36i	26 Feb
Sotomayor	2.36	8 Sep
Avdeyenko	2.36	25 Sep
Sjöberg	2.35i	5 Mar

High Jump Year List Progression

Year	Best	10th	20th	50th	100th	Over 2.25	Over 2.21	Ave.100
1958	2.12	2.09	2.06	2.02	2.00	-	-	
1968	2.24	2.175	2.15	2.12	2.09	4	-	
1978	2.35	2.27	2.25	2.21	2.185	20	57	2.222
1979	2.32	2.28	2.26	2.22	2.20	27	79	2.230
1980	2.36	2.29	2.27	2.24	2.20	35	94	2.240
1981	2.33	2.30	2.27	2.24	2.21	35	122	2.246
1982	2.34	2.31	2.28	2.25	2.22	57	146	2.258
1983	2.38	2.32	2.30	2.27	2.24	83	187	2.274
1984	2.39	2.33	2.31	2.28	2.24	98	184	2.282
1985	2.41	2.35	2.32	2.27	2.24	85	171	2.284
1986	2.38	2.34	2.31	2.27	2.23	75	163	2.279
1987	2.42	2.34	2.31	2.27	2.24	87	167	2.281
1988	2.43	2.36	2.32	2.28	2.24	96	175	2.289

POLE VAULT

6.06	Sergey	Bubka	SU	4.12.63	1	Nik	Nice	10 Jul
6.05		S.Bubka			1	PTS	Bratislava	9 Jun
5.95	Rodion	Gataullin	SU	23.11.65	1	ISTAF	Berlin	26 Aug
5.90i		Gataullin			1		Vilnius	24 Jan
5.90		S.Bubka			1		Kvarnsveden	19 Jun
5.90	Miroslaw	Chmara	POL	9.5.64	1	BNP	Villeneuve d'Ascq	27 Jun
5.90		S.Bubka			1		Barcelona	13 Jul
5.90		S.Bubka			1	OG	Seoul	28 Sep
5.90i		Gataullin			1		Tashkent	24 Dec
5.89	Kory	Tarpenning	USA	27.2.62	1	FOT	Indianapolis	21 Jul
5.87	Earl	Bell	USA	25.8.55	1		Jonesboro	14 May
5.86i		Gataullin			1		Los Angeles	19 Feb
5.86	Vasiliy	Bubka	SU	26.11.60	1		Chelyabinsk	16 Jul
5.85i		S.Bubka			1		Moskva	21 Feb
5.85		Gataullin			1eA	Znam	Leningrad	11 Jun
5.85		S.Bubka			1	Athl	Lausanne	24 Jun
5.85		Tarpenning			1	Pre	Eugene	2 Jul
5.85	Grigoriy	Yegorov	SU	12.1.67	1	NC	Tallinn	5 Jul
5.85		Gataullin			2	OG	Seoul	28 Sep
5.84	Mike	Tully	USA	21.10.56	1		Irvine	1 May

Mark	Name		Nat	Born	Pos	Meet	Venue	Date
5.81i	Thierry	Vigneron	FRA	9.3.60	1		New York	5 Feb
5.81i		Bell			2		New York	5 Feb
5.81		Tully			1	Pepsi	Westwood	5 Jun
5.80i		S.Bubka			1		Stuttgart	31 Jan
5.80i		Gataullin			1		Fairfax	14 Feb
5.80i		Chmara			1		Grenoble	12 Mar
5.80i	Philippe	Collet	FRA	13.12.63	2		Grenoble	12 Mar
5.80		Tully			1	CalR	Modesto	7 May
5.80		Yegorov			1		St.Denis	7 Jun
5.80		Collet			2	Athl	Lausanne	24 Jun
5.80		Collet			2	BNP	Villeneuve d'Ascq	27 Jun
5.80		Chmara			2		Barcelona	13 Jul
5.80		S.Bubka			2	ISTAF	Berlin	26 Aug
5.80		Yegorov			3	OG	Seoul	28 Sep
	(34/10)							
5.79	Greg	Duplantis	USA	22.1.62	1		Tulsa	29 Jun
5.75	Tim	Bright	USA	28.7.60	1		Hamamatsu	8 May
5.73i	Delko	Lesov	BUL	6.1.67	1		Athinai	6 Feb
5.72	Billy	Olson	USA	19.7.58	1		Abilene	12 May
5.71	Joe	Dial	USA	26.10.62	1		São Paulo	22 May
5.71	Atanas	Tarev	BUL	31.1.58	1		Bern	22 Jun
5.70i	Aleksandr	Zhukov	SU	25.1.65	1		Minsk	17 Jan
5.70i	Valeriy	Ishutin	SU	5.9.65	1	NC	Volgograd	11 Feb
5.70i	Scott	Davis	USA	12.12.61	2		Valencia	23 Feb
5.70i	Nikolay	Nikolov	BUL	15.10.64	2	EC	Budapest	6 Mar
	(20)							
5.70	Doug	Fraley	USA	7.3.65	1	MSR	Walnut	24 Apr
5.70	Vadim	Kodentsev	SU	2.2.64	1		Sochi	19 May
5.70	Marian	Kolasa	POL	12.8.59	2	Kuso	Warszawa	19 Jun
5.70	Philippe	D'Encausse	FRA	24.3.67	3	BNP	Villeneuve d'Ascq	27 Jun
5.70	Aleksandr	Obizhayev	SU	16.9.59	1		Pärnu	13 Jul
5.70	Vladimir	Polyakov	SU	17.4.60	1		Dnepropetrovsk	16 Jul
5.70	Pierre	Quinon	FRA	20.2.62	1		La Teste	6 Aug
5.70	Yevgeniy	Bondarenko	SU	8.10.66	1		Kiev	15 Aug
5.67	Scott	Shaffer	USA	31.5.64	2		Jonesboro	14 May
5.67	Asko	Peltoniemi	FIN	7.2.63	1		Nokia	10 Aug
	(30)							
5.66	Vladimir	Bukreyev	SU	15.6.64	1		Odessa	20 Aug
5.65i	Igor	Potapovich	SU	6.9.67	2	NC	Volgograd	11 Feb
5.65	Scott	Huffman	USA	30.11.64	1		Lawrence	26 Mar
5.65	Pat	Manson	USA	29.11.67	2		Lawrence	26 Mar
5.65	Pavel	Bogatyryov	SU	19.3.61	1		Sochi	23 Apr
5.65	Todd	Cooper	USA	4.3.63	2		Abilene	12 May
5.65	Jean-Marc	Tailhardat	FRA	12.4.66	1		Clermont Ferrand	18 Jun
5.65	István	Bagyula	HUN	2.1.69	1	WJ	Sudbury	28 Jul
5.65	Gennadiy	Sukharev	SU	3.2.65	1		Staiki	31 Jul
5.65	Zdenek	Lubensky	CS	3.12.62	1		London	28 Aug
	(40)							
5.65i	Denis	Petushinskiy	SU	29.6.67	1		Kemerovo	24 Dec
5.65i	Vasiliy	Trofimenko	SU	28.1.62	1		Leningrad	24 Dec
5.64i	Dave	Kenworthy	USA	27.6.60	2	TAC	New York	26 Feb
5.64	Steve	Glander	USA	3.9.61	1		Waco	9 Jun
5.62	Harri	Palola	FIN	29.10.66	1		Parkano	12 Jun
5.60i	Rumen	Stoyanov	BUL	21.4.59	1		Sofia	6 Feb
5.60i	Aleksandr	Morozov	SU	27.2.63	4	NC	Volgograd	11 Feb
5.60	Andrey	Grudinin	SU	3.5.69	1		Simferopol	27 May
5.60	Viktor	Ryzhenkov	SU	25.8.66	1B	Znam	Leningrad	11 Jun
5.60	Serge	Ferreira	FRA	11.8.59	1		Dijon	11 Jun
	(50)							
5.60	Igor	Trandenkov	SU	17.8.66	2	Ros	Praha	16 Jun
5.60	Stoyan	Peev	BUL	12.5.65	3	Ros	Praha	16 Jun
5.60	Gennadiy	Kachkovskiy	SU	12.3.64	1		Kishinev	19 Jun
5.60	Uwe	Langhammer	GDR	12.6.65	1	NC	Rostock	24 Jun
5.60	Valentin	Videv	BUL	20.1.63	1		Sofia	23 Jul
5.60	Maxim	Tarasov	SU	2.12.70	2	WJ	Sudbury	28 Jul

Mark	Name		Nat	Born	Pos	Meet	Venue	Date
5.60	Pyotr	Bochkaryov	SU	18.6.67	2		Moskva	30 Jul
5.60	Alain	Donias	FRA	15.1.60	2	NC	Tours	14 Aug
5.60	Hermann	Fehringer	AUT	8.12.62	1		Vöcklabruck	20 Aug
5.60	Bernhard	Zintl	FRG	16.6.65	1	R W	Koblenz	28 Aug
	(60)							
5.59	Jeff	Ward	USA	4.8.60	6=	FOT	Indianapolis	21 Jul
5.59	Lane	Lohr	USA	10.9.64	8	FOT	Indianapolis	21 Jul
5.58	Greg	West	USA	19.5.67	1	SWC	Austin	14 May
5.57i	Dean	Starkey	USA	27.3.67	1		Oklahoma City	13 Feb
5.57	Cam	Miller	USA	13.11.66	1		Lubbock	1 May
5.57	Doug	Wicks	USA	6.11.63	2		Irvine	1 May
5.57	Steve	Thaxton	USA	29.7.64	1		Knoxville	20 May
5.57	Steve	Klassen	USA	15.2.65	1		Northridge	22 May
5.57	Jerry	Mulligan	USA	9.4.58	2		Northridge	22 May
5.57	Craig	Hagan	USA	7.4.64	2		Champaign	28 May
	(70)							
5.57	Kelly	Riley	USA	29.12.68	1	NCAA	Eugene	3 Jun
5.57	Bobby	Williams	USA	23.5.61	2		Waco	9 Jun
5.57	Roy	Hix	USA	16.11.64	3		Waco	9 Jun
5.57	Tim	McMichael	USA	22.12.67	2		Tulsa	22 Jun
5.55i	Wladyslaw	Kozakiewicz	FRG	8.12.53	1		Hannover	24 Jan
5.55i	Ferenc	Salbert	FRA	5.8.60	2		Liévin	24 Jan
5.55i	Christoph	Pietz	GDR	15.7.64	1	v2 N	Torino	10 Feb
5.55i	Roman	Barabashov	SU	13.9.68	6		Moskva	21 Feb
5.55	Javier	Garcia	SPA	22.7.66	1		Vic	6 Aug
5.55	Marco	Andreini	ITA	8.10.61	1		Grosseto	10 Aug
	(80)							
5.52	Miro	Zalar	SWE	24.3.57	1=		Tampere	23 Aug
5.51	Tim	Canfield	USA	16.11.63	1A		Corvallis	11 Jun
5.50i	Steve	Stubblefield	USA	30.12.61	1		Lawrence	23 Jan
5.50i	Aleksandr	Chernyayev	SU	19.5.60	2		Kiev	31 Jan
5.50i	Tom	Hintnaus	BRA	15.2.58	3		Gent	17 Feb
5.50i	Enzo	Brichese	ITA	17.11.65	1	NC	Firenze	23 Feb
5.50i	Giorgio	Grassi	ITA	8.1.63	2	NC	Firenze	23 Feb
5.50i	Jürgen	Winkler	FRG	1.3.59	3		Berlin	26 Feb
5.50	Matt	Kolb	USA	4.2.64	1		Commerce	2 Mar
5.50	Jay	Davis	USA	29.7.67	1		Eugene	16 Apr
	(90)							
5.50	Paul	Babits	USA	24.12.60	2		Knoxville	21 May
5.50	Ryszard	Kolasa	POL	17.4.64	1		Khania	22 May
5.50	Rainer	Lewin	GDR	5.3.67	1		Potsdam	26 May
5.50	Marko	Schröder	GDR	5.2.68	2		Potsdam	26 May
5.50	Monte	Weller	USA	22.8.66	3		Champaign	28 May
5.50	Igor	Yanchevskiy	SU	11.3.68	4	RigC	Riga	5 Jun
5.50	Sergey	Gavrikov	SU	19.4.64	5	RigC	Riga	5 Jun
5.50	Arkadiy	Shkvira	SU	18.10.60	6	RigC	Riga	5 Jun
5.50	Oleg	Shkerdin	SU	9.6.68	3		Alma Ata	17 Jun
5.50	Aleksey	Starushchenko	SU	5.5.66	2		Kharkov	18 Jun
	(100)							
5.50	Riccardo	Orioli	ITA	23.4.65	1		Foggia	23 Jun
5.50	Anthony	Curran	USA	27.6.59	1		Northridge	3 Jul
5.50	Paul	Benavides	USA	5.11.64	6		Barcelona	13 Jul
5.50	Konstantin	Adnachev	SU	15.2.66	4		Chelyabinsk	16 Jul
5.50	Yuriy	Kazeka	SU	.68	7		Chelyabinsk	16 Jul
5.50	Felix	Böhni	SWZ	14.2.58	1		Zürich	10 Sep
5.50	Andrey	Skvortsov	SU	.68	1		Ordzhonikidze	24 Sep
5.50i	Vladislav	Lutkowskiy	SU	12.12.67	2		Kemerovo	24 Dec

Mark	Name		Nat	Born	Date
5.49	David	Swezey	USA	59	18 Jun
5.48	Lee Jae-bok		KOR	61	29 Jul
	(110)				
5.45i	Dirk	Ledegen	BEL	66	21 Feb
5.45	Jari	Holttinen	FIN	65	3 Jul
5.45	Kim Chul-kyun		KOR	69	15 Jul
5.44i	Troy	Smith	USA	66	20 Feb
5.43	Bob	Babits	USA	59	2 Jul
5.43	Doug	Lytle	USA	62	2 Jul
5.42i	Gian Franco	Beda	ITA	61	17 Feb
5.42	Gerhard	Schmidt	FRG	61	10 Jul
5.41	Steve	Horvath	USA	66	21 May
5.41	Alberto	Ruíz	SPA	61	28 Jun
	(120)				
5.40i	Gerard	Pineau	FRA	62	5 Jan
5.40i	Aleksey	Nikitin	SU	58	8 Jan
5.40i	Vitaliy	Stepanov	SU	65	24 Jan
5.40i	Gábor	Molnár	HUN	64	29 Jan
5.40i	Viktor	Loshchev	SU	65	29 Jan
5.40i	Andrey	Fomin	SU	69	6 Feb

Mark	Name		Nat	Born	Date
5.40i	Daniel	Ivanov	BUL	65	6 Feb
5.40i	Jerome	Fréhaut	FRA	66	13 Feb
5.40i	Kimmo	Pallonen	FIN	59	14 Feb
5.40i	Anton	Paskalev	BUL	58	14 Feb
	(130)				
5.40i	Stanimir	Penchev	BUL	59	14 Feb
5.40i	Pavel	Sluka	CS	64	17 Feb
5.40i	Sergey	Yesipchuk	SU	67	20 Feb
5.40i	Frantisek	Jansa	CS	62	20 Feb
5.40i	Nayden	Yordanov	BUL	62	21 Feb
5.40i	Aleksandr	Gorbatenko	SU	66	5 Mar
5.40	Tadeusz	Slusarski	POL	50	4 May
5.40	Igor	Zaytsev	SU	70	14 May
5.40	Andrey	Kravchenko	SU	71	27 May
5.40	Yuan	Shunen	CHN	66	5 Jun
	(140)				
5.40	Viktor	Spasov	SU	59	5 Jun
5.40	Jeff	Hanoch	USA	67	18 Jun
5.40	Sergey	Fomenko	SU	67	18 Jun
5.40	Andy	Ashurst	UK	65	19 Jun
5.40	Enrico	Mann	GDR	65	24 Jun
5.40	Patrik	Johansson	SWE	68	6 Jul
5.40	Bob	Ferguson	CAN	62	17 Jul
5.40	Georgiy	Nalgiyev	SU	67	30 Jul
5.40	Vyacheslav	Polonitskiy	SU	64	30 Jul
5.40	Paul	Just	CAN	64	6 Aug
	(150)				
5.40	Peter	Widen	SWE	67	25 Aug
5.40	Peter	Volmer	FRG	58	28 Aug
5.40	Qin Cheng		CHN	65	4 Sep
5.40	Ge Yun		CHN	68	4 Sep
5.37i	Tom	Reither	CHL	64	21 Jan
5.36i	Dan	Burton	USA	67	16 Jan

Mark	Name		Nat	Born	Date
5.36i	David	Wooten	USA	67	20 Feb
5.35i	Petri	Peltoniemi	FIN	70	30 Jan
5.35i	Lance	Adams	USA	64	4 Mar
5.35	Marc	Maes	BEL	59	12 May
	(160)				
5.35	Alain	Morineau	FRA	60	11 Jun
5.35	Helmar	Schmidt	FRG	61	29 Jun
5.35	Pat	Frederick	USA	69	8 Jul
5.35	Wojciech	Dakiniewicz	POL	67	3 Sep
5.34	Tim	Bihm	USA	68	23 Apr
5.34	John	Finney	USA	67	21 May
5.34	Mike	Thornton	USA	66	
5.34	Eric	Forney	USA	62	
5.33i	Jimm	Stack	USA	68	19 Feb
5.33i	John	Coyne	USA	68	11 Mar
	(170)				
5.33i	Chris	Bohanan	USA	65	11 Mar
5.33	Dave	Brannan	USA	68	9 Apr
5.33	Mark	Strawderman	USA	60	16 Apr
5.33	Bill	Payne	USA	67	22 Apr
5.33	Jim	Mours	USA	65	23 Apr
5.33	Brian	Wicks	USA		5 May
5.33	Brent	Burns	USA	69	19 Mar
5.33	Phil	Yuska	USA	65	
5.33	Ken	Miller	USA		7 May
5.33	Malcolm	Hunsacker	USA	64	21 May
	(180)				
5.33	Todd	Verbick	USA	65	22 May
5.33	Ricky	Wright	USA	64	23 Aug
5.33	António	Colella	ITA	64	22 Sep
5.32	Xu Yueliang		CHN	60	28 Apr
5.32	Ignacio	Paradinas	SPA	66	25 Aug
5.31	Anastasios	Tzonis	GRE	58	12 Jun

Extra Trial (5th attempt)

5.90 S.Bubka - Vladivostok 13 Sep

Exhibition

5.80 Chmara - Sopot 22 Aug

Ancillary marks

S.Bubka	5.90	9 Jun
S.Bubka	5.86	10 Jul
Gataullin	5.85	26 Aug
Chmara	5.80	27 Jun

Best outdoor marks for athletes with indoor seasonal bests

Mark	Name	Pos	Meet	Venue	Date	Indoor
5.70	Vigneron	1		Nice	4 Apr	5.81i
5.70	S.Davis	3	CalR	Modesto	7 May	5.70i
5.65	Potapovich	2		Chelyabinsk	16 Jul	5.65i
5.60	Lesov	1		Sofia	6 Aug	5.73i
5.60	Nikolov	2		Sofia	6 Aug	5.70i
5.57	Starkey	1		Indianapolis	2 Jul	5.57i
5.55	Kenworthy	4		Dijon	12 Jun	5.64i
5.52	Kozakiewicz	3		Ylivieska	3J ul	5.55i
5.50	Pietz	1		Cottbus	28 May	5.55i
5.50	Ishutin	7A	Znam	Leningrad	11 Jun	5.70i
5.50	Stoyanov	1		Sofia	11 Jun	5.60i
5.50	Chernyayev	3		Kharkov	18 Jun	5.50i
5.50	Trofimenko	1		Leningrad	12 Jul	5.65i
5.50	Zhukov	2		Dnepropetrovsk	17Jul	5.70i
5.50	Winkler	2	R-W	Koblenz	28 Aug	5.50i

Mark	Name	Date	Indoor
5.40	Salbert	9 Apr	5.55i
5.40	Hintnaus	9 Apr	5.50i
5.40	Brichese	15 May	5.50i
5.40	Yesipchuk	27 May	5.40i
5.40	Jansa	2 Jun	5.40i
5.40	Yordanov	11 Jun	5.40i
5.40	Grassi	23 Jun	5.50i
5.40	Pestushinskiy	27 Jun	5.65i
5.40	Fréhaut	3 Jul	5.40i
5.40	Fomin	7 Jul	5.40i
5.40	Ledegen	15 Aug	5.45i
5.35	Sluka	20 Aug	5.40i
5.33	Reither	9 Apr	5.37i
5.33	Wooten	7 May	5.36i

Pole Vault Year List Progression

Year	Best	10th	20th	50th	100th	Over 5.50	Over 5.40	Ave.100
1958	4.68	4.56	4.47	4.36	4.26	-	-	
1968	5.41	5.25	5.15	5.00	4.85	-	3	
1978	5.71	5.50	5.45	5.30	5.20	15	61	5.341
1979	5.65	5.56	5.50	5.35	5.25	21	83	5.384
1980	5.78	5.65	5.57	5.41	5.28	39	98	5.451
1981	5.81	5.65	5.55	5.48	5.30	49	124	5.471
1982	5.75	5.70	5.60	5.51	5.33	63	135	5.509
1983	5.83	5.71	5.60	5.50	5.36	65	97	5.537
1984	5.94	5.75	5.66	5.55	5.41	84	129	5.573
1985	6.00	5.80	5.71	5.60	5.40	84	124	5.595
1986	6.01	5.80	5.70	5.60	5.50	103	152	5.622
1987	6.03	5.80	5.71	5.60	5.44	92	143	5.607
1988	6.06	5.80	5.70	5.60	5.50	106	144	5.626

LONG JUMP

Mark		Name		Nat	Born	Pos	Meet	Venue	Date
8.76	0.8	Carl	Lewis	USA	1.7.61	1	FOT	Indianapolis	18 Ju
8.74	1.4	Larry	Myricks	USA	10.3.56	2	FOT	Indianapolis	18 Ju
8.72	-0.2		Lewis			1	OG	Seoul	26 Se
8.61	1.2		Myricks			1	HGP	Budapest	12 Au
8.58A	1.1		Myricks			1		Sestriere	11 Au
8.51	1.6		Myricks			1	BNP	Villeneuve d'Ascq	27 Ju
8.50	-0.7		Myricks			1		Monaco	2 Au
8.49	1.8	Mike	Powell	USA	10.11.63	2	OG	Seoul	26 Se
8.47	-1.2		Lewis			1		Houston	21 Ma
8.47	1.5		Myricks			1		Bern	23 Au
8.46	1.2	Leonid	Voloshin	SU	30.3.66	1	NC	Tallinn	5 Ju
8.44	1.7	Eric	Metcalf	USA	23.1.68	1	TAC	Tampa	17 Ju
8.43	1.5		Lewis			1	Athl	Lausanne	24 Ju
8.41	0.2		Myricks			1		Rhede	1 Ju
8.38i	-		Myricks			1		Karlsruhe	7 Fe
8.38	-0.4		Myricks			1	WK	Zürich	17 Au
8.37A	0.2	Jaime	Jefferson	CUB	17.1.62	1	IbAmC	Ciudad México	22 Ju
8.35	2.0	Sergey	Layevskiy	SU	3.3.59	1		Dnepropetrovsk	16 Ju
8.34	0.0	Vladimir	Ochkan	SU	13.1.68	1	RigC	Riga	5 Ju
8.34	-0.3		Powell			1	VD	Bruxelles	19 Au
8.34	1.1		Jefferson			1	R-W	Koblenz	28 Aug
8.33	0.6		Myricks			2	Athl	Lausanne	24 Jun
8.33	0.6		Jefferson			1		Habana	5 Aug
8.33	0.6		Myricks			1		Linz	15 Aug
8.33	-0.3		Powell			2	WK	Zürich	17 Aug
8.33			Ochkan			1		Vilnius	27 Aug
8.32i	-		Ochkan			1		Vilnius	10 Jan
8.32A		Ralph	Spry	USA	16.6.60	1		Albuquerque	9 Jun
8.32A	1.9		Powell			2		Sestriere	11 Aug
8.32	0.2		Myricks			2	VD	Bruxelles	19 Aug
8.32	0.6		Powell			2		Bern	23 Aug
		(31/9)							
8.31	1.2	Igor	Streltsov	SU	1.5.65	2		Dnepropetrovsk	16 Jul
		(10)							
8.30	2.0	Andreas	Steiner	AUT	31.3.64	1		Innsbruck	4 Jun
8.28	0.8	Luis Alberto	Bueno	CUB	22.5.69	1		Habana	16 Jul
8.28	0.6	Ubaldo	Duany	CUB	16.5.60	2		Habana	5 Aug
8.26	1.3	Vladimir	Ratushkov	SU	1.1.65	1		Chelyabinsk	16 Jul
8.25	1.3	Milan	Mikulás	CS	1.4.63	1	NC	Praha	16 Jul
8.25	-0.7	Gordon	Laine	USA	24.2.58	-	FOT	Indianapolis	18 Jul
8.23i	-	Vladimir	Bobylyov	SU	15.7.66	1	NC	Volgograd	10 Feb
8.23	0.0	Mike	Conley	USA	5.10.62	5	FOT	Indianapolis	18 Jul
8.23	1.9	Ron	Beer	GDR	29.8.65	1A		Berlin	20 Jul
8.23	0.8	Marco	Delonge	GDR	16.6.66	2A		Berlin	20 Jul
		(20)							
8.22		Dezalya	Manns	USA	9.11.64	1		Harrisonburg	23 Apr
8.22	1.8	Sergey	Zaozerskiy	SU	27.1.64	1		Bryansk	11 Jul
8.22	2.0	Gary	Honey	AUS	26.7.59	2	HGP	Budapest	12 Aug
8.22	1.6	Norbert	Brige	FRA	9.1.64	1		Nimes	4 Sep
8.19		Ray	Humphrey	USA	31.8.65	1	IC4A	New Haven	21 May
8.19	-0.4	Emiel	Mellaard	HOL	21.3.66	1	NC	Groningen	17 Jul
8.18	1.3	Vasiliy	Sokov	SU	7.4.68	2	NC	Tallinn	5 Jul
8.16		Andre	Ester	USA	27.4.65	1		Monroe	26 Mar
8.16		Sergey	Vasilenko	SU	27.9.65	1		Alma-Ata	18 Jun
8.16	1.1	Antonio	Corgos	SPA	10.3.60	1		Salamanca	8 Sep
		(30)							
8.15i	-	Yusuf	Alli	NIG	28.7.60	1	TAC	New York	26 Feb
8.15A		Francois	Fouche	RSA	5.6.63	1		Johannesburg	23 Apr
8.14		Mike	McRae	USA	9.7.55	1		Berkeley	13 Feb
8.14A		Tyrus	Jefferson	USA	14.9.65	1		Germiston	22 Oct
8.13	1.5	David	Culbert	AUS	17.3.67	2		Melbourne	6 Mar
8.13		Vernon	George	USA	6.10.64	2		Houston	21 May
8.13	0.2	Pang Yan		CHN	15.1.63	1		Tianjin	1 Sep

Mark		Name		Nat	Born	Pos	Meet	Venue	Date
8.12	2.0	Chen Zunrong		CHN	25.8.62	5A	Znam	Leningrad	11 Jun
8.12	0.7	Juan	Ortiz	CUB	13.8.64	3		Habana	5 Aug
8.12	1.5	Christian	Thomas	FRG	31.3.65	2	R-W	Koblenz	28 Aug
		(40)							
8.11	1.6	Igor	Kharitonov	SU	7.12.62	1		Baku	11 Sep
8.10	1.6	Kenny	Harrison	USA	13.2.65	Q	NCAA	Eugene	1 Jun
8.09		Martí	Digno	CUB	21.10.65	1		Habana	6 Feb
8.09		Ray	Hawkins	USA	14.6.65	2	IC4A	New Haven	21 May
8.08	-0.4	Boris	Goins	USA	7.4.67	1	SEC	Auburn	14 May
8.08		Sergey	Kravchenko	SU	20.5.66	1		Kharkov	19 Aug
8.07	1.5	Giovanni	Evangelisti	ITA	11.9.61	1		Padova	13 Jun
8.06i	-	Frans	Maas	HOL	13.7.64	1	EC	Budapest	5 Mar
8.06	0.0	Sergey	Kargin	SU	3.7.62	3	RigC	Riga	5 Jun
8.06	0.6	Junichi	Usui	JAP	5.10.57	2	NC	Tokyo	19 Jun
		(50)							
8.06	1.5	Teddy	Steinmayr	AUT	4.2.64	1		Ebensee	24 Jul
8.05		Eduard	Belozerskikh	SU	7.3.65	2		Alma-Ata	18 Jun
8.05	1.7	Robert	Széli	CS	29.5.65	1		Budapest	6 Jul
8.04i	-	Dietmar	Haaf	FRG	6.3.67	1	NC	Dortmund	20 Feb
8.04		Gordon	McKee	USA	12.10.66	1		San Angelo	15 Apr
8.04	0.0	Hiroyuki	Shibata	JAP	29.4.63	-	NC	Tokyo	19 Jun
8.04	0.2	Jarmo	Kärnä	FIN	4.8.58	1		Lahti	25 Aug
8.03i	-	Aleksandr	Aushev	SU	1.7.60	2		Klaipeda	5 Mar
8.03i	-	László	Szalma	HUN	21.10.57	2	EC	Budapest	5 Mar
8.03	2.0	Joakim	Assenmacher	FRG	10.1.63	1		Bensheim	15 May
		(60)							
8.03		Arunas	Voitovich	SU	31.3.65	1		Siauliai	21 May
8.03	0.0	Vladimir	Puzyrev	SU	17.3.62	4	RigC	Riga	5 Jun
8.03	1.9	Llewellyn	Starks	USA	10.2.67	Q	FOT	Indianapolis	17 Jul
8.03	-0.5	Grigoriy	Petrosyan	SU	3.12.58	2		Baku	11 Sep
8.03i	-	Vladimir	Zubrilin	SU	15.6.63	1		Kemerovo	24 Dec
8.02i	-	Keith	Talley	USA	28.1.64	1		Johnson City	21 Jan
8.02A	1.5	Bruny	Surin	CAN	12.7.67	1		Provo	21 May
8.01	1.9	Glenroy	Gilbert	CAN	30.4.68	-	NC/OT	Ottawa	6 Aug
8.00i	-	Robert	Emmiyan	SU	16.2.65	2		Stuttgart	30 Jan
8.00		Alvin	Thomas	USA	16.9.65	1		Jonesboro	29 Apr
		(70)							
8.00	1.1	Ian	James	CAN	17.7.63	1		Etobicoke	14 May
8.00	0.9	Vladimir	Amidzhinov	BUL	7.9.63	2	Nar	Sofia	26 Jun
8.00	1.9	Sergey	Novozhilov	SU	21.4.69	1	NC-J	Bryansk	7 Jul
8.00	2.0	Vladimir	Pilyutin	SU	.65	2		Bryansk	29 Jul
8.00		Kim Yong-il		KOR	11.9.62	1		Seoul	12 Aug
8.00	0.7	Peter	Rouhi	FRG	12.3.66	3	R-W	Koblenz	28 Aug
7.99i	-	Miroslaw	Hydel	POL	24.7.63	1		Warszawa	7 Feb
7.99		Trevor	Black	JAM	.66	3	IC4A	New Haven	21 May
7.99	1.6	Juha	Plosila	FIN	21.6.65	2		Vesanto	3 Jul
7.99	2.0	Vadim	Kobylyanskiy	SU	8.8.61	3		Baku	11 Sep
		(80)							
7.98i	-	George	Ogbeide	NIG	8.4.68	4	NCAA	Oklahoma City	11 Mar
7.98		Andreja	Marinkovic	YUG	23.1.65	1		Beograd	2 Jul
7.98		Igor	Lapshin	SU	8.8.63	1		Vitebsk	10 Jul
7.98	1.6	Stewart	Faulkner	UK	19.2.69	1	AAA	Birmingham	6 Aug
7.97i	-	Igor	Dovoino	SU	29.7.64	1		Kiev	30 Jan
7.97		Billy	Coleman	USA	26.7.67	1		Fresno	9 Apr
7.97		Lester	Benjamin	ANT	14.9.63	1		Knoxville	16 Apr
7.97		Russell	Adams	USA	18.5.67	1		Waco	22 Apr
7.97		Vince	Martin	USA	22.8.67	1		Knoxville	27 May
7.96	1.1	Andrzej	Klimaszewski	POL	14.5.60	2		Granada	28 May
		(90)							
7.96	0.0	Yuriy	Samarin	SU	27.12.60	5	RigC	Riga	5 Jun
7.96	1.4	Krzysztof	Kaniecki	POL	23.5.65	1		Wroclaw	25 Jun
7.95i	-	Heiko	Reski	FRG	22.8.63	1		Dortmund	13 Jan
7.95	0.4	Franck	Lestage	FRA	20.4.68	1		Narbonne	3 Jul
7.95	0.7	Georgi	Pomashki	BUL	10.1.60	1		Pleven	10 Jul
7.95	0.2	Mark	Forsythe	UK	10.8.65	1	IsrCh	Tel Aviv	10 Jul
7.95	2.0	Ivo	Krsek	CS	21.3.67	2	NC	Praha	16 Jul

Mark		Name		Nat	Born	Pos	Meet	Venue	Date
7.94		Reginaldas	Stasaitis	SU	.67	2		Siauliai	21 May
7.94		Craig	Stewart	USA	5.5.62	1		Santa Monica	1 Jul
7.94	0.9	André	Müller	GDR	15.11.70	1eB		Berlin	20 Jul
		(100)							

Mark	Wind	Name	Nat	Born	Date
7.93i	-	Ralf Jaros	FRG	65	17 Jan
7.93	0.8	Latin Berry	USA	67	21 May
7.93		Bill Ayears	USA	66	26 May
7.93	-0.3	Milan Gombala	CS	68	16 Jun
7.93	0.6	Saúl Isalgué	CUB	69	16 Jul
7.93	0.6	Ian Hilton	CAN	67	5 Aug
7.92		Joshua Kio	NIG	57	15Jan
7.92		Matt Rose	USA	67	21 May
7.92A		David Lamai	KEN	64	18 Jun
7.92	2.0	Aleksey Tkachenko	SU	63	29 Jul
		(110)			
7.92	0.5	Stanislaw Jaskulka	POL	58	31 Jul
7.91i	-	Konstantinos Koukodimos	GRE	69	29 Jan
7.91i	-	Oleg Kurbatov	SU	67	14 Feb
7.91i	-	Barrington Williams	UK	55	12 Mar
7.91	1.3	John King	UK	63	6 Aug
7.91		Volker Mai	GDR	66	27 Aug
7.90i	-	Aleksey Starkov	SU	64	10 Feb
7.90		Laurent Broothaerts	BEL	66	11 Jun
7.90		Lahor Marinkovic	YUG	67	11 Jun
7.90		Wlodzimierz Wlodarczyk	POL	57	18 Jun
		(120)			
7.90		Sinisa Ergotic	YUG	68	2 Jul
7.90	0.5	Derrick Brown	UK	63	11 Jul
7.90	2.0	Gyula Páloczi	HUN	62	8 Sep
7.89i	-	Scott Sanders	USA	67	5 Feb
7.89	-0.5	Dimitrios Hatzopoulos	GRE	67	28 May
7.89		Allen Turner	USA	69	24 Jul
7.88		Obinna Eregbu	NIG	69	15 Jan
7.88		Joe Greene	USA	67	8 May
7.88		Gian Carlo Biscarini	ITA	62	15 May
7.88		Michael Arnold	AUT	67	11 Jun
		(130)			
7.88	1.8	Csaba Almási	HUN	66	8 Sep
7.87i	-	Thomas Fahner	GDR	66	3 Feb
7.87i	-	Claude Morinière	FRA	60	21 Feb
7.87	0.9	Mathias Koch	GDR	62	11 Jun
7.87		Peller Phillips	USA	70	11 Jun
7.87		Viktor Rudenik	SU	64	18 Jun
7.86Ai	-	Percy Knox	USA	69	20 Feb
7.86		Dennis Harris	USA	68	19 May
7.86		Nenad Stekic	YUG	51	2 Jun
7.86		Derek McKinley	USA	60	27 Jun
		(140)			
7.86A		Kevin Adkins	USA	68	15 Oct
7.85A		Wessel Bosman	RSA	58	24 Mar
7.85		Chris Walker	USA	65	29 Apr
7.85	1.7	Igor Lysenko	SU	70	7 Jul
7.85A	1.9	Angel Tovar	VEN	66	22 Jul
7.85	1.8	Attila Szekeres	HUN	67	19 Aug
7.84i	-	Aleksandr Yakovlev	SU	57	10 Feb
7.84i	-	Michael Becker	FRG	65	20 Feb
7.84		Spencer Williams	USA	67	26 Mar
		(150)			
7.84		J.J. Birden	USA	65	9 Apr
7.84		Johnny Cleveland	USA	66	20 May
7.84		Nugent Cotton	USA	68	21 May
7.84		John Alexander	USA	66	25 May
7.84	-0.2	Dimitrios Delifotis	GRE	57	28 May
7.84	1.8	Leroy Burrell	USA	67	3 Jun
7.84	0.9	Alfonz Hertelendi	HUN	62	26 Jun
7.84		Gianni Becatti	ITA	63	2 Jul
7.84		Guo Haili	CHN	57	23 Jul
7.84	1.7	Andrey Ignatov	SU	68	29 Jul
		(160)			
7.84		Vyacheslav Bordukov	SU	59	19 Aug
7.84	1.0	Nai Hui-Fang	TAI	69	11 Sep
7.83		McArthur Anderson	USA	69	5 Mar
7.83		Valeriy Misko	SU	63	6 Aug
7.82i	-	Winfried Klepsch	FRG	56	20 Feb
7.82i	-	Giuseppe Bertozzi	ITA	64	24 Feb
7.82		Paul Jones	USA	68	7 May
7.82	1.6	Yutaka Fukazawa	JAP	66	19 Jun
7.82	0.5	Petri Keskitalo	FIN	67	28 Jun
7.82	1.0	Moses Kiyai	KEN	60	1 Jul
		(170)			
7.82	1.8	Jörg Pohl	GDR	66	20 Jul
7.81i	-	Frederic Ebong-Salle	CAM	64	20 Feb
7.81i	-	Kenny Brokenburr	USA	68	27 Feb
7.81		Philmore Morris	JAM	64	21 May
7.81	1.2	Oleg Konovalov	SU	67	28 May
7.81	0.0	Oleg Mamayev	SU	58	5 Jun
7.81	1.6	Milko Campus	ITA	69	19 Jun
7.81	1.5	Xavier Donaldson	USA	68	17 Jul
7.81	1.8	Serge Hélan	FRA	64	30 Jul
7.80i	-	Brian Bradley	USA	66	26 Feb
		(180)			
7.80		Keith Holley	USA	69	8 May
7.80		Tarrell Carpenter	USA	67	14 May
7.80		Dion Bentley	USA	71	19 May
7.80		Phil Morris	JAM	64	21 May
7.80	2.0	Yevgeniy Semenyuk	SU	69	7 Jul
7.80	2.0	Andrey Yegorov	SU	69	7 Jul
7.80	1.2	Theodoros Tantanozis	GRE	64	30 Jul
7.80	0.4	Borut Bilac	YUG	65	20Aug
7.80		Dirk Hering	FRG	61	10 Sep

Best outdoor marks for athletes with indoor seasonal bests

Mark	Wind	Name	Pos	Meet	Venue	Date	Indoor
8.13	1.8	Bobylyov	2		Bryansk	11 Jul	8.23i
8.06		Alli	-		Sestriere	11 Aug	8.15i
8.04	0.7	Haaf	1		Düsseldorf	2 Jun	8.04i
8.02	1.0	Szalma	3	HGP	Budapest	12 Aug	8.03i
8.01A		Maas	-		El Paso	17 Apr	8.06i
7.98		Aushev	4		Vilnius	27 Aug	8.03i
7.96	1.3	Emmiyan	Q	NC	Tallinn	4 Jul	8.00i

Mark	Wind	Name	Date	Indoor
7.92	1.4	Reski	27Jun	7.95i
7.91		Hydel	7 Aug	7.99i
7.90	-0.3	Dovoino	11 Jun	7.97i
7.87	1.4	Koukodimos	10 Jul	7.91i
7.84	0.0	B.Williams	16 Jul	7.91i
7.83	0.0	Zubrilin	13 Sep	8.03i
7.82		Ayears	30 Apr	7.85i
7.81	0.2	Starkov	10 Jul	7.90i

Best low altitude marks

Mark	Wind	Name	Pos	Meet	Venue	Date	Altitude best
8.05	1.4	Alli	1		St.Denis	7Jun	8.06A
8.04	1.0	Jefferson	7	FOT	Indianapolis	18 Jul	8.14A
7.97	0.5	Spry	-	TAC	Tampa	17 Jun	8.32A
7.97	0.4	Surin	2		Jerez	27 Jun	8.02A
7.97		Fouche	1		Stellenbosch	18 Oct	8.15A

Mark	Wind	Name		Nat	Born	Pos	Meet	Venue	Date
Downhill runway									
8.16		Lester	Benjamin	ANT	14.9.63	1		St.Johns	8 May
7.80		Orde	Ballantyne	STV	8 May				
Wind-assisted marks									
8.44	2.6		Powell			Q	FOT	Indianapolis	17 Jul
8.44	3.9		Powell			1		Sapporo	3 Sep
8.37	5.1	Giovanni	Evangelisti	ITA	11.9.61	1		San Giov..Valdarno	21 May
8.36	2.8		Powell			3	FOT	Indianapolis	18 Jul
8.34	2.3		Powell			Q	OG	Seoul	25 Sep
8.33	3.6	Sergey	Vasilenko	SU	27.9.65	1eB	Znam	Leningrad	11 Jun
8.31	3.1	Gordon	Laine	USA	24.2.58	4	FOT	Indianapolis	18 Jul
8.30	5.8	Gary	Honey	AUS	26.7.59	1	NC	Perth	27 Mar
8.27A		Frans	Maas	HOL	13.7.64	1		El Paso	17 Apr
8.26A	3.4	Yusuf	Alli	NIG	28.7.60	3		Sestriere	11 Aug
8.23		Kenny	Harrison	USA	13.2.65	1	Big-8	Ames	14 May
8.23	4.4	Peller	Phillips	USA	23.6.70	1		Sacramento	11 Jun
8.21	2.5	Emiel	Mellaard	HOL	21.3.66	1		Tel Aviv	8 May
8.19	2.7	Bruny	Surin	CAN	12.7.67	1		Hamamatsu	8 May
8.19	5.2	Vernon	George	USA	6.10.64	Q	FOT	Indianapolis	17 Jul
8.15	2.2	Tyrus	Jefferson	USA	14.9.65	3	TAC	Tampa	17 Jun
8.13A		George	Ogbeide	NIG	.69	2		El Paso	17 Apr
8.12	2.4	Llewellyn	Starks	USA	10.2.67	3	NCAA	Eugene	3 Jun
8.12	3.9	Reginaldas	Stasaitis	SU	.67	2eB	Znam	Leningrad	11 Jun
8.11		Edrick	Floreal	CAN	5.10.66	2	SWC	Austin	15 May
8.10	2.3	Matt	Rose	USA	29.1.67	5	NCAA	Eugene	3 Jun
8.10	2.2	Glenroy	Gilbert	CAN	30.4.68	1	NC/OT	Ottawa	6 Aug
8.08		Leroy	Burrell	USA	21.2.67	3	SWC	Austin	15 May
8.06	2.6	Hiroyuki	Shibata	JAP	29.4.63	1	NC	Tokyo	19 Jun
8.05	2.2	Grigoriy	Petrosyan	SU	3.12.58	4	NC	Tallinn	5 Jul
8.04A	4.0	Andreja	Marinkovic	YUG	23.1.65	4		Sestriere	11 Aug
8.04	3.2	Stewart	Faulkner	UK	19.2.69	1		London	20 Aug
8.03	2.3	Russell	Adams	USA	18.5.67	Q	NCAA	Eugene	1 Jun
7.99	4.0	Andrzej	Klimaszewski	POL	14.5.60	1		Lublin	6 Aug
7.98	5.0	Yutaka	Fukazawa	JAP	.66	1		Tokyo	3 Jun
7.98	4.2	Gyula	Páloczi	HUN	13.9.62	2		Budapest	6 Jul
7.98	2.8	Bill	Ayears	USA	6.4.66	Q	FOT	Indianapolis	17 Jul
7.97	2.9	Xavier	Donaldson	USA	12.12.68	1		San Angelo	21 May
7.96	2.4	Viktor	Rudenik	SU	30.3.64	8	NC	Tallinn	5 Jul
7.96	3.1	Frederic	Ebong-Salle	CMR	10.9.64	2		London	20 Aug
7.96	3.8	Attila	Szekeres	HUN	24.8..67	1		Zalaegerszeg	28 Aug

Mark	Wind	Name	Nat	Born	Date	Mark	Wind	Name	Nat	Born	Date
7.93		Dennis Harris	USA	68	17 May	7.87	2.5	Bernhard Kelm	FRG	67	15 May
7.92		J.J. Birden	USA	65	9 Apr	7.86		Don Nixon	USA	68	4 May
7.92		Kenny Brokenburr	USA	68	1 May	7.86		Julius Meekins	USA	59	7 May
7.91		James Morris	USA	66	14 May	7.86	7.2	Manabu Sato	JAP	67	15 Sep
7.91	2.1	Derrick Brown	UK	63	4 Jun	7.85	5.1	Masaki Sumitani	JAP	67	3 May
7.91	2.2	Olivier Cadier	BRA	60	13 Jul	7.84		Rod Terry	USA	64	25 Mar
7.91		Rey Quinones	PR	58	27 Aug	7.83		John Register	USA	65	15 May
7.90A		Wessel Bosman	RSA	58	26 Mar	7.82		Teddy Palacios	USA	66	7 May
7.90		Chris Walker	USA	65	28 May	7.82		Sharrief Hazim	USA	64	14 May
7.90	5.7	Hisanori Yasuda	JAP	65	3 Jun	7.82		A.J. Hodges	USA	67	20 May
7.89		Curtis Rogers	USA	68	30 Apr	7.81		Chris Sims	USA	66	1 May
7.89	2.5	Carlos Casar	MEX	60	26 Jun	7.81	3.7	Kyle McDuffie	CAN	60	6 Aug
7.87		Paul Johnson	UK	68	15 May						

Series for best marks

Mark	Name	Date						
8.76	Lewis	18 Jul	(8.34	8.59w	8.76	x	8.68	6.77w)
8.74	Myricks	18 Jul	(8.43	8.55	8.74	8.55	8.06	x)
8.72	Lewis	26 Sep	(8.41	8.56w	8.52	8.72	8.52	x)
8.61	Myricks	12 Aug	(8.31w	8.49	x	x	8.34	8.61)
8.58A	Myricks	11 Aug	(8.43	x	8.55	8.58	8.52	x)
8.51	Myricks	27 Jun	(8.30w	8.07	p	p	x	8.51)
8.50	Myricks	2 Aug	(x	8.41	p	p	x	8.50)
8.49	Powell	26 Sep	(8.23	8.11	8.49	x	p	x)
8.47	Lewis	21 May	(8.47w	x	x	8.40	8.44	8.47)
8.47	Myricks	23 Aug	(8.31	8.29	8.36	8.47	8.34	8.12)
8.46	Voloshin	5 Jul	(8.46	x	5.60	8.12	7.90	x)
8.44	Metcalf	17 Jun	(7.78	x	8.07	8.22	8.03	8.44)

Mark	Name	Date						
8.43	Lewis	24 Jun	(8.32	x	8.31	8.43	x	8.23)
8.41	Myricks	1 Jul	(8.11	8.31	x	8.34	x	8.41)
8.38i	Myricks	7 Feb	(7.97	x	x	8.28	8.24	8.38)
8.38	Myricks	17 Aug	(7.98	8.17	8.21	8.28	8.38	8.08)
8.37A	Jefferson	22 Jul	(8.17	8.22	8.35	8.20	8.37	x)
8.35	Layevskiy	16 Jul	(7.99	8.00	8.04	8.35	8.07	8.00)
8.34	Ochkan	5 Jun	(7.90	8.00	x	x	8.34	x)
8.34	Powell	19 Aug	(x	8.16	x	8.34	x	x)
8.34	Jefferson	28 Aug	(7.61w	7.75	7.90	8.34	8.03	8.32)
8.33	Myricks	24 Jun	(x	x	8.26	x	8.33	x)
8.33	Jefferson	5 Aug	(7.97	8.09	8.19	8.25	8.33	x)
8.33	Myricks	15 Aug	(8.31	x	x	8.33	x	8.09)
8.33	Powell	17 Aug	(7.93	8.26	x	x	8.30	8.33)
8.32	Myricks	19 Aug	(8.13	x	8.07	8.20	8.21	8.32)
8.32	Powell	23 Aug	(8.30	x	8.25	8.32	x	8.23)

Long Jump Year List Progression

Year	Best	10th	20th	50th	100th	Over 8.00	Over 7.80	Ave.100
1958	8.00	7.69	7.64	7.47	7.36	1	7	
1968	8.90	8.07	7.93	7.73	7.63	18	37	
1978	8.32	8.07	8.00	7.86	7.77	20	84	7.900
1979	8.52	8.13	8.03	7.88	7.77	25	85	7.922
1980	8.54	8.13	8.09	7.91	7.78	36	91	7.949
1981	8.62	8.12	8.08	7.91	7.77	30	82	7.946
1982	8.76	8.19	8.12	7.95	7.85	41	124	8.005
1983	8.79	8.19	8.10	7.99	7.86	47	135	8.016
1984	8.79	8.27	8.14	8.02	7.90	58	157	8.063
1985	8.62	8.23	8.14	8.03	7.89	60	149	8.051
1986	8.61	8.24	8.16	8.04	7.90	61	154	8.063
1987	8.86	8.25	8.18	8.06	7.92	74	172	8.096
1988	8.76	8.31	8.23	8.06	7.94	76	189	8.109

TRIPLE JUMP

Mark	Wind	First name	Name	Nat	Born	Pos	Meet	Venue	Date
17.77	1.4	Khristo	Markov	BUL	27.1.65	1	NC	Sofia	3 Sep
17.69	1.5	Igor	Lapshin	SU	8.8.63	1		Staiki	31 Jul
17.68	1.9	Oleg	Protsenko	SU	11.8.63	1	WG	Helsinki	30 Jun
17.61	0.7		Markov			1	OG	Seoul	24 Sep
17.59	1.6	Mike	Conley	USA	5.10.62	1	ISTAF	Berlin	26 Aug
17.56	1.9	Maris	Bruziks	SU	25.8.62	1		Riga	3 Sep
17.55	0.5		Protsenko			1	PTS	Bratislava	9 Jun
17.53	0.9	Milan	Mikulás	CS	1.4.63	1	NC	Praha	17 Jul
17.52	1.6		Lapshin			-	Znam	Leningrad	12 Jun
17.52	0.1		Lapshin			2	OG	Seoul	24 Sep
17.50		Oleg	Sakirkin	SU	23.1.66	1		Barcelona	13 Jul
17.48	1.5		Lapshin			1	Kuts	Moskva	4 Sep
17.47	0.3	Aleksandr	Kovalenko	SU	8.5.63	1	NC	Tallinn	7 Jul
17.45i	-		Markov			1		Athinai	6 Feb
17.44		Gennadiy	Valyukevich	SU	1.6.58	1		Jena	4 Jun
17.43	2.0		Kovalenko			1		Sochi	1 Jun
17.43	0.0	Peter	Bouschen (10)	FRG	16.5.60	1		Düsseldorf	2 Jun
17.42	-0.8		Kovalenko			3	OG	Seoul	24 Sep
17.39i	-	Aleksandr	Leonov	SU	7.2.62	1	NC	Volgograd	12 Feb
17.39	1.0		Protsenko			2	ISTAF	Berlin	26 Aug
17.38	1.8	Lázaro	Betancourt	CUB	18.3.63	1		Habana	6 Aug
17.38	0.0		Protsenko			4	OG	Seoul	24 Sep
17.37i	-	Vasif	Asadov	SU	27.8.65	2	NC	Volgograd	12 Feb
17.37	0.1		Lapshin			Q	OG	Seoul	23 Sep
17.36	1.8	Vladimir	Chernikov	SU	3.8.59	1		Odessa	21 Aug
17.35	0.0		Conley			1	TAC	Tampa	18 Jun
17.34	0.4	Jorge	Reyna	CUB	10.1.63	2		Habana	6 Aug
17.33	1.6	Wolfgang	Zinser	FRG	26.3.64	1		Düsseldorf	23 Sep
17.32	0.0		Conley			1	WK	Zürich	17 Aug
17.32	-1.0		Protsenko			1	ASV	Köln	21 Aug
		(30/16)							

Mark		Name		Nat	Born	Pos	Meet	Venue	Date
17.31	2.0	Igor	Parygin	SU	3.2.67	1	Veet	Tallinn	9 Jul
17.29i	-	Vladimir	Inozemtsev	SU	25.5.64	1		Moskva	21 Feb
17.29	0.2	Charles	Simpkins	USA	19.10.63	5	OG	Seoul	24 Sep
17.28	0.2	Juan	Lopez	CUB	7.4.67	3		Habana	6 Aug
		(20)							
17.25i	-	Béla	Bakosi	HUN	18.6.57	2	EC	Budapest	6 Mar
17.25	0.3	Nikolay	Musiyenko	SU	16.12.59	1		Dnepropetrovsk	17 Jul
17.23		Andrey	Kayukov	SU	12.4.64	1		Sukhumi	15 May
17.23	2.0	Volker	Mai	GDR	3.5.66	1	vITA	Neubrandenburg	9 Jul
17.23		Aleksandr	Maletskiy	SU	13.6.66	1		Chernigov	24 Jul
17.22	1.3	Igor	Dovoino	SU	19.8.64	2		São Paulo	22 May
17.22		Joseph	Taiwo	NIG	24.8.59	1	OT	Bauchi	30 Jun
17.19	1.7	Ivan	Slanar	CS	11.1.61	1		Praha	6 Sep
17.19	0.4	Willie	Banks	USA	11.3.56	2	WK	Zürich	19 Aug
17.17	0.4	Vyacheslav	Bordukov	SU	1.1.59	1		Vladivostock	14 Sep
		(30)							
17.15i	-	Ray	Kimble	USA	19.4.53	1	TAC	New York	26 Feb
17.15	0.6	Aleksandr	Yakovlev	SU	8.9.57	-		São Paulo	22 May
17.15		Kenny	Harrison	USA	13.2.65	1		San Diego	25 Jun
17.12		Frank	Rutherford	BAH	23.11.64	1	CalR	Modesto	7 May
17.12	1.6	John	Herbert	UK	20.4.62	1	AAA	Birmingham	7 Aug
17.12		Wolfgang	Knabe	FRG	12.7.59	2		Düsseldorf	23 Sep
17.11	0.8	Dirk	Gamlin	GDR	26.10.63	1	GO	Dresden	11 Jun
17.11	1.7	Nikolay	Mamchur	SU	9.10.63	3		Odessa	21 Aug
17.03	0.8	Georgi	Pomashki	BUL	10.1.60	4	HGP	Budapest	12 Aug
17.01	1.0	Robert	Cannon	USA	9.7.58	-	FOT	Indianapolis	16 Jul
		(40)							
17.01		Serge	Hélan	FRA	24.2.64	1		Salamanca	8 Sep
17.01	0.7	Chen Yanping		CHN	.66	1		Tianjin	2 Sep
16.96	1.8	Vladimir	Zubrilin	SU	15.6.63	2	RigC	Riga	4 Jun
16.96		Oleg	Grokhovskiy	SU	.68	1		Alma-Ata	17 Jun
16.96		Djordje	Kozul	YUG	31.12.63	1	BalkG	Ankara	16 Jul
16.95i	-	John	Tillman	USA	11.2.65	2	TAC	New York	26 Feb
16.95		Erich	Gotman	SU	16.10.63	2		Alma-Ata	17 Jun
16.94	-0.9	Lucian	Sfia	RUM	10.9.63	1		Bucuresti	19 Jun
16.94		Patterson	Johnson	BAH	26.8.64	1	OT	Nassau	17 Jun
16.93i	-	Dario	Badinelli	ITA	10.8.60	1	NC	Firenze	23 Feb
		(50)							
16.93	1.0	Parkev	Grigoryan	SU	.65	6	Znam	Leningrad	12 Jun
16.92	1.4	Andrzej	Grabarczyk	POL	12.1.64	-		Lublin	6 Aug
16.89		Norbert	Elliott	BAH	6.11.62	2	OT	Nassau	17 Jun
16.89		Vyacheslav	Shkarpov	SU	6.9.66	1		Chernigov	24 Jul
16.89	1.9	Nikolay	Ivanov	BUL	6.8.63	2	NC	Sofia	3 Sep
16.88i	-	Mihai	Bran	RUM	12.1.62	1	NC	Bacau	14 Feb
16.88i	-	Marios	Hadjiandreou	CYP	19.9.62	1		Athinai	20 Feb
16.87	0.5	Lazaro	Balcindes	CUB	8.2.63	4		Habana	6 Aug
16.86i	-	Dainis	Berzins	SU	24.4.66	6	NC	Volgograd	12 Feb
16.85	1.5	Mamed	Akhundov	SU	9.10.64	2		Chelyabinsk	17 Jul
		(60)							
16.84		Steve	Hanna	BAH	30.10.58	1		Bridgetown	21 May
16.84A		Ernesto	Torres	PR	26.12.59	2	IbAmC	Ciudad.México	22 Jul
16.83	0.9	Vladimir	Plekhanov	SU	11.4.58	1		Moskva	17 Jun
16.81A		Jorge T.	Da Silva	BRA	4.1.66	3	IbAmC	Ciudad.México	22 Jul
16.79		Wendell	Lawrence	BAH	.67	-		Boise	16 Apr
16.79	1.0	Al	Joyner	USA	19.1.60	Q	FOT	Indianapolis	15 Jul
16.79	1.0	Pierre	Camara	FRA	10.9.65	1	NC	Tours	13 Aug
16.78		Konstantin	Bykov	SU	11.1.66	1		Voroshilovgrad	14 May
16.77	1.4	Dmitriy	Litvinenko	SU	12.8.63	5		Odessa	21 Aug
16.76	0.2	Vladimir	Melikhov	SU	30.3.69	1		Simferopol	29 May
		(70)							
16.76	1.5	Edrick	Floreal	CAN	5.10.66	-	NCAA	Eugene	4 Jun
16.76	0.9	Valeriy	Stankevich	SU	.67	3	RigC	Riga	4 Jun
16.75		Joshua	Kio	NIG	7.9.57	1		Port Harcourt	15 Jan
16.75	0.5	Vernon	Samuels	UK	5.10.64	2	OT	Birmingham	7 Aug
16.74		Jonathan	Edwards	UK	10.5.66	1		Newcastle	23 Jul
16.73	0.8	Nikolay	Avramov	BUL	25.2.67	1		Pleven	10 Jul
16.73		Didier	Falise	BEL	3.3.61	1		Hechtel	30 Jul

Mark		Name		Nat	Born	Pos	Meet	Venue	Date
16.72	-0.6	Jacek	Pastusinski	POL	8.9.64	8	OG	Seoul	24 Sep
16.71	0.3	Zoran	Djurdjevic	YUG	3.4.68	1		Beograd	3 Jul
16.70	0.5	Aleksandr	Beskrovniy	SU	5.4.60	2		Sochi	20 May
		(80)							
16.68	1.7	Ajayi	Agbebaku	NIG	6.12.56	1		Västerås	30 Jun
16.68	0.8	Arne	Holm	SWE	22.12.61	3	DNG	Stockholm	5 Jul
16.68		Du Benzhong		CHN	15.5.67	1		Anshan	6 Jun
16.67i	-	Gennadiy	Kakhno	SU	3.4.64	3		Kiev	31 Jan
16.66		Henry	Ellard	USA	21.7.61	1		Fresno	26 May
16.66		Sergey	Frolenkov	SU	11.2.62	1		Tula	20 Jun
16.66	1.1	Héctor	Marquetti	CUB	7.4.68	5		Habana	6 Aug
16.65		Theodoros	Tantanozis	GRE	29.9.64	3	BalkG	Ankara	16 Jul
16.64	0.0	Damir	Tashpulatov	SU	29.1.64	2		Alma-Ata	16 May
16.64	1.6	Abcelvio	Rodrigues	BRA	26.5.57	2		Barcelona	13 Jul
		(90)							
16.64		Virginius	Daukshis	SU	14.7.67	1		Vilnius	12 Aug
16.62	-0.3	Francis	DoDoo	GHA	13.4.60	5	DNG	Stockholm	5 Jul
16.62	0.9	Esa	Viitasalo	FIN	19.5.60	1	NC	Hämeenlinna	7 Aug
16.62	0.3	Yuriy	Gorbachenko	SU	19.7.66	6		Vladivostok	13 Sep
16.61		Robin	Hernández	CUB	21.10.69	3		Habana	19 Feb
16.61		Gregorio	Hernández	CUB	2.6.68	4		Habana	19 Feb
16.61	0.3	Reggie	Jackson	USA	5.7.69	1	TAC-j	Tallahassee	25 Jun
16.60i	-	Mike	Patton	USA	20.6.66	2	NCAA	Oklahoma City	12 Mar
16.60	0.2	George	Wright	CAN	20.2.63	1		Etobicoke	14 May
16.60	2.0	Michael	Makin	UK	1.3.62	3	OT	Birmingham	7 Aug
		(100)							

Mark		Name	Nat	Born	Date
16.59	0.1	Norifumi Yamashita	JAP	62	13 May
16.59A		Benson Mugun	KEN	62	18 Jun
16.58	1.2	Peter Beames	AUS	63	13 Mar
16.57i	-	Aleksandr Vinokurov	SU	63	30 Jan
16.57	-0.1	Alfred Stummer	AUT	62	13 Jul
16.56i	-	Mihai Ene	RUM	60	13 Feb
16.56i	-	Carroll Cobb	USA	63	26 Feb
16.56i	-	Zdzislaw Hoffmann	POL	59	6 Mar
16.56		William Beasley	USA	66	9 Apr
16.56	1.8	Trevor Black	JAM	66	4 Jun
		(110)			
16.56	1.2	Krzysztof Zuch	POL	62	31 Jul
16.54		Tony Anderson	US	65	8 May
16.54		Johnny Washington	USA	65	22 Jun
16.54		Ján Cado	exCS	63	9 Jul
16.53		Arturs Apinis	SU	64	17 Jun
16.52i	-	Gyula Páloczi	HUN	62	14 Feb
16.52		Artyom Semyonov	SU	66	20 Aug
16.52	0.7	Atanas Atanasov	BUL	68	28 Aug
16.52		Kerstin Wolters	FRG	65	2 Sep
16.51	-1.1	Marcus Hooks	USA	68	26 Mar
		(120)			
16.50		Zou Sixin	CHN	67	6 Jun
16.50	1.5	Maksim Gerasimov	SU	66	4 Sep
16.50	0.6	Piotr Weremczuk	POL	66	8 Sep
16.49i	-	Sergey Tarasov	SU	62	31 Jan
16.48		Spiros Kormoussis	GRE	65	5 Jun
16.48		Eric McCalla	UK	60	8 Jul
16.48		Nai Hui-Fang	TAI	69	10 Sep
16.47		Francisco A. Santos	BRA	60	30 Apr
16.47		Mikhail Kusturov	SU	62	20 Jun
16.47	-0.6	Aleksey Blokhin	SU	65	13 Jul
		(130)			
16.46	1.3	Santiago Moreno	SPA	64	12 Aug
16.45		Haralambis Giannoulis	GRE	63	16 Aug
16.44		Andrey Stepin	SU	67	20 Jun
16.44	0.0	Dmitriy Byzov	SU	67	25 Sep
16.43	1.5	Andre Ernst	GDR	67	9 Jul
16.43	2.0	António Santos	ANG	64	2 Sep
16.43		Kestutis Leskauskas	SU	67	4 Sep
16.42	1.3	Garfield Anselm	FRA	66	19 Mar
16.42	0.4	Vadim Kobylyanskiy	SU	61	22 May
16.42	1.9	Aleksey Fatyanov	SU	69	6 Jul
		(140)			
16.41	1.2	Juan Carlos Ibanez	CUB	69	25 Mar
16.41	0.2	Toussaint Rabenala	MAD	65	14 May
16.41		Shamil Abbyasov	SU	57	16 May
16.40	0.4	Jörg Elbe	GDR	64	9 Jul
16.40	1.4	Vladimir Davydov	SU	64	13 Jul
16.40	1.3	David McFadgen	USA	60	15 Jul
16.40		Daniele Buttiglione	ITA	66	13 Aug
16.39	1.6	Wolfgang Mai	FRG	61	23 Jul
16.38		Brian Wellman	BER	67	29 May
16.38		Csaba Földessy	HUN	66	2 Jul
		(150)			
16.37		José Salazar	VEN	57	5 Jun
16.35	1.7	Latin Berry	USA	67	22 May
16.35		Joe Greene	USA	67	28 May
16.35	1.0	Vladimir Frolov	SU	68	19 Jun
16.35	1.5	Ravil Aminov	SU	63	13 Jul
16.35A		Japhet Tipis	KEN		13 Aug
16.35	1.2	Ivo Bilík	CS	62	6 Sep
16.34i	-	Daniel Ciobanu	RUM	65	13 Feb
16.34	0.0	Alain René-Corail	FRA	62	22 Apr
16.34		Andrey Kruzhakov	SU	61	28 Aug
		(160)			
16.33		Carlos Vizcaino	CUB	69	13 Feb
16.33		Sun Xiao	CHN	69	29 Jun
16.32i	-	Boris Khokhlov	SU	58	24 Jan
16.32i	-	Claes Rahm	SWE	64	31 Jan
16.32A		Greg Foster	USA	61	14 May
16.32		Mike Hanks	USA	64	14 May
16.32		He Miyuan	CHN	64	6 Jun
16.32		Darryl Taylor	USA	62	8 Jul
16.32		Jörg Friess	GDR	68	27 Aug
16.31i	-	James Morris	USA	66	13 Feb
		(170)			
16.31	0.8	Tikhomir Todorov	BUL	68	10 Jul
16.30	1.8	Matt Sweeney	AUS	66	6 Mar
16.30		Yuriy Avdeyenko	SU	64	20 Apr
16.30	0.6	William Turner	USA	67	4 Jun
16.30	1.1	Femi Abejide	UK	65	14 Aug
16.29	1.4	Stoicho Tsonov	BUL	69	2 Jul
16.29	1.9	Timo Utriainen	FIN	64	7 Aug
16.28		Sun Changjiang	CHN	64	17 Apr
16.28		Warren Posey	USA	67	14 May
16.28	-0.9	José Leitão	POR	65	20 Aug
16.28		Péter Kárpáti	HUN	68	18 Sep

Mark		Name		Nat	Born	Pos	Meet	Venue	Date

Best outdoor marks for athletes with indoor seasonal bests

Mark	Wind	Name	Pos	Meet	Venue	Date	Indoor
17.04		Inozemtsev	1		Voroshilovgrad	15.May	17.29i
16.95	1.2	Kimble	5	HGP	Budapest	12.Aug	17.15i
16.92	0.0	Tillman	3	TAC	Tampa	18.Jun	16.95i
16.85	0.8	Bran	1		Bucuresti	12.Jun	16.88i
16.85A	0.1	Badinelli	1		Sestriere	11.Aug	16.93i
16.80	1.7	Asadov	5		Sochi	1.Jun	17.37i
16.80	1.1	Hadjiandreou	2		Athinai	4.Sep	16.88i
16.76	0.9	Berzins	3	RigC	Riga	4.Jun	16.86i

Mark	Wind	Name	Date	Indoor	Mark	Wind	Name	Date	Indoor
16.57		Vinokurov	1.Jun	16.57i	16.31	0.9	Páloczi	28.Jun	16.52i
16.42	1.3	Kakhno	4.Jun	16.67i	16.30	1.2	Hoffmann	6.Aug	16.56i
16.37	-0.9	Cobb	15.Jul	16.56i	16.28	1.5	Khokhlov	21.Aug	16.32i

Best low altitude marks

Mark	Name	Pos	Meet	Venue	Date	Altitude
16.78	Badinelli	2	GG	Verona	27.Jul	16.85A
16.64	Da Silva	1		São Paulo	16.Aug	16.81A

Wind-assisted marks

Mark	Wind	Name		Nat	Born	Pos	Meet	Venue	Date
18.20	5.2	Willie	Banks	USA	11.3.56	1	FOT	Indianapolis	16 Jul
17.93	5.2	Charles	Simpkins	USA	19.10.63	2	FOT	Indianapolis	16 Jul
17.63	4.3	Robert	Cannon	USA	9.7.58	3	FOT	Indianapolis	16 Jul
17.62	3.3	Mike	Conley	USA	5.10.62	4	FOT	Indianapolis	16 Jul
17.58	5.2	Al	Joyner	USA	19.1.60	5	FOT	Indianapolis	16 Jul
17.56	4.9	Kenny	Harrison	USA	13.2.65	6	FOT	Indianapolis	16 Jul
17.54	3.0		Lapshin			1	Znam	Leningrad	12 Jun
17.53	4.8	Ray	Kimble	USA	19.4.53	7	FOT	Indianapolis	16 Jul
17.42	2.4	Aleksandr	Yakovlev	SU	8.9.57	1		São Paulo	22 May
17.31	2.9	Wolfgang	Knabe	FRG	12.7.59	1	NC	Frankfurt	23 Jul
17.19	2.1	Edrick	Floreal	CAN	5.10.66	1	NCAA	Eugene	4 Jun
17.08	2.6	Andrzej	Grabarczyk	POL	12.1.64	1	NC	Grudziadz	14 Aug
17.06	5.2	Arne	Holm	SWE	22.12.61	1		Riihimäki	5 Jun
17.00A	3.5	Dario	Badinelli	ITA	10.8.60	1		Sestriere	6 Aug
16.93	2.6	Jacek	Pastusinski	POL	8.9.64	2	NC	Grudziadz	14 Aug
16.91		Wendell	Lawrence	BAH		1		Boise	16 Apr
16.87	2.2	Garfield	Anselm	FRA	7.6.66	2		Dijon	11 Jun
16.73	3.6	Francis	DoDoo	GHA	13.4.60	2		Riihimäki	5 Jun
16.64	2.1	Warren	Posey	USA	26.3.67	2	NCAA	Eugene	4 Jun

Mark	Wind	Name	Nat	Born	Date	Mark	Wind	Name	Nat	Born	Date
16.60	3.1	Trevor Black	JAM	66	4 Jun	16.45	2.5	Yuriy Avdeyenko	SU	64	24 Apr
16.60		Spiros Kormoussis	GRE	65	12 Jun	16.45A	3.0	Daniele Buttiglione	ITA	66	6 Aug
16.58		William Beasley	USA	66	23 Apr	16.44	3.7	Ivo Bilík	CS	62	6 Sep
16.57		David McFadgen	USA	60	6 Aug	16.43	2.1	William Turner	USA	67	4 Jun
16.55	5.4	Francis Agyepong	UK	65	12 Jun	16.40	3.1	Alex Norca	FRA	69	10 Jul
16.54	2.6	Timo Utriainen	FIN	64	7 Aug	16.34		Bannon Hayes	USA	67	28 May
16.52	2.2	Matt Sweeney	AUS	66	26 Mar	16.34	2.5	Tuomas Sallinen	FIN	58	7 Aug
16.52	2.1	Yuriy Avdeyenko	SU	64	10 Sep	16.33	4.0	Andrew Murphy	AUS	69	26 Mar
16.49		Rayfield Dupree	USA	53	7 Jul	16.33	2.7	Mike Hanks	USA	64	17 Jun
16.47	2.4	Piotr Weremczuk	POL	66	14 Aug	16.31		Péter Tóth	HUN	59	

Series for best marks

Mark	Name	Date	1	2	3	4	5	6
17.77	Markov	3 Sep	(17.60	x	x	17.75w	17.77	17.73)
17.69	Lapshin	6 Aug	(16.98	x	17.69	16.90	p	p)
17.68	Protsenko	30 Jun	(16.82w	x	17.68	x	17.38	x)
17.61	Markov	24 Sep	(17.61	x	15.71	17.54	x	17.10)
17.59	Conley	26 Aug	(16.55	16.74	16.87	17.09	x	17.59)
17.56	Bruziks	3 Sep	(16.84	x	x	17.30	17.22	17.56)
17.55	Protsenko	9 Jun	(17.19	16.89	17.29	17.55	x	17.47)
17.53	Mikulás	17 Jul	(16.54	17.29	x	17.53	p	17.33)
17.52	Lapshin	12 Jun	(17.54w	17.48	17.52	x	p	p)
17.52	Lapshin	24 Sep	(16.75	17.00	x	x	x	17.52)
17.50	Sokirkin	13 Jul	(16.64	17.50	x	p	16.60	17.21)
17.48	Lapshin	4 Sep	(17.04	17.48	17.30	x	x	17.22)
17.47	Kovalenko	7 Jul	(16.34	17.32	16.88	16.89	17.47	16.76)
17.45i	Markov	6 Feb	(17.40	17.45	p	p	p	p)
17.44	Valyukevich	4 Jun						
17.43	Kovalenko	1 Jun	(x	17.07	17.39	17.43	17.14	17.34)
17.43	Bouschen	2 Jun	(16.20	16.49	x	x	16.68	17.43)
17.42	Kovalenko	24 Sep	(17.42	17.40	x	x	p	x)
17.39i	Leonov	12 Feb	(16.55	16.89	17.39	16.79	17.02	x)

Mark	Name	Nat	Born	Pos	Meet	Venue	Date
17.39	Protsenko	26 Aug	(14.63	16.59	x	17.39	14.96	17.36)
17.38	Betancourt	6 Aug	(17.01	17.38	x	x	x	16.47)
17.38	Protsenko	24 Sep	(17.38	x	x	17.31	x	16.61)
17.37i	Asadov	12 Feb	(16.77	14.96	x	16.86	x	17.37)
17.37	Lapshin	23 Sep	(17.37	p	p)			
17.36	Chernikov	20 Aug	(16.47	x	16.31	16.61	17.36	17.04)
17.35	Conley	18 Jun	(x	16.35	15.78	16.86	x	17.35)
17.34	Reyna	6 Aug	(16.65	16.90	17.34	16.82	16.97	16.93)
17.33	Zinser	23 Sep	(			16.69	17.29	17.33)
17.32	Conley	17 Aug	(16.45	16.86	17.24	17.32	17.24	17.20)
17.32	Protsenko	21 Aug	(16.72	x	17.32	x	17.18	17.05)
Wind assisted marks							
18.20	Banks	16 Jul	(18.06w	17.62w	17.25w	p	p	18.20w)
17.93	Simpkins	16 Jul	(x	x	16.87w	17.19w	16.50w	17.93w)
17.63	Cannon	16 Jul	(17.30w	17.63w	x	17.61w	17.55w	17.01)
17.62	Conley	16 Jul	(16.85w	16.99w	17.32w	17.36w	17.62w	17.55w)
17.58	Joyner	16 Jul	(x	16.86w	17.58w	p	17.29w	17.56w)
17.56	Harrison	16 Jul	(17.50w	x	17.05w	x	17.49w	17.56w)
17.54	Lapshin	12 Jun	see 17.52 legal.					
17.53	Kimble	16 Jul	(17.20w	x	17.37w	x	17.53w	x)
17.42	Yakovlev	22 May	(17.12	16.69	16.37	17.15	17.42w	x)

Triple Jump Year List Progression

Year	Best	10th	20th	50th	100th	Over 17.00	Over 16.50	Ave.100
1958	16.59	15.92	15.70	15.43	15.07	-	1	
1968	17.39	16.73	16.35	16.04	15.71	5	13	
1978	17.44	16.94	16.69	16.46	16.18	8	45	16.513
1979	17.29	17.00	16.76	16.47	16.14	10	46	16.520
1980	17.35	17.03	16.81	16.51	16.22	11	51	16.564
1981	17.56	17.13	16.97	16.59	16.30	18	68	16.671
1982	17.57	17.16	17.02	16.69	16.38	24	74	16.735
1983	17.55	17.27	17.12	16.74	16.43	33	87	16.826
1984	17.52	17.34	17.19	16.78	16.42	32	91	16.851
1985	17.97	17.48	17.29	16.88	16.51	31	103	16.943
1986	17.80	17.43	17.17	16.93	16.52	39	102	16.939
1987	17.92	17.39	17.24	16.86	16.50	35	102	16.940
1988	17.77	17.43	17.28	16.93	16.60	42	123	16.984

SHOT

Mark	First	Name	Nat	Born	Pos	Meet	Venue	Date
23.06	Ulf	Timmermann	GDR	1.11.62	1		Khania	22 May
22.75	Werner	Günthör	SWZ	11 .7.61	1		Bern	23 Aug
22.61		Timmermann			1		Potsdam	8 Sep
22.56		Timmermann			1		Berlin	13 Sep
22.47		Timmermann			1	OG	Seoul	23 Sep
22.42	Randy	Barnes	USA	16 .6.66	1	WK	Zürich	17 Aug
22.39		Barnes			2	OG	Seoul	23 Sep
22.36+		Timmermann			1		Athinai	16 May
22.15		Timmermann			1		Berlin	27 Apr
22.11		Barnes			1	MSR	Walnut	24 Apr
22.10	Udo	Beyer	GDR	9 .8.55	2		Potsdam	8 Sep
22.05		Beyer			1		Karl-Marx-Stadt	12 Jun
22.01		Barnes			1		San Diego	25 Jun
21.99		Günthör			3	OG	Seoul	23 Sep
21.94+		Beyer			2		Athinai	16 May
21.91		Günthör			1	NC	Zug	13 Aug
21.88		Timmermann			1	NC	Rostock	24 Jun
21.88		Barnes			1	FOT	Indianapolis	15 Jul
21.88	Sergey	Smirnov	SU	17.9.60	1		Vilnius	28 Aug
21.87		Beyer			1		Rostock	29 May
21.86		Timmermann			1	vITA	Neubrandenburg	10 Jul
21.84		Beyer			2		Berlin	13 Sep
21.83		Smirnov			1		Moskva	4 Sep
21.82		Günthör			2	WK	Zürich	17 Aug
21.80		Smirnov			1		Sochi	31 May

Mark	Name		Nat	Born	Pos	Meet	Venue	Date
21.78		Timmermann			1	vFRG	Düsseldorf	20 Jun
21.76		Barnes			1		College Station	16 Apr
21.75		Beyer			1		Jena	3 Jun
21.72i		Barnes			1		Dallas	6 Feb
21.71i	Remigius	Machura	CS	3 .7.60	1		Jablonec	30 Jan
21.71		Günthör			Q	NC	Zug	12 Aug
21.63		Günthör			1		Luzern	11 Jun
	(32/6)							
21.39i	Mikhail	Kostin	SU	10 .5.59	1		Minsk	31 Jan
21.39	Sergey	Gavryushin	SU	27 .6.59	1	NC	Tallinn	7 Jul
21.36	Gregg	Tafralis	USA	9 .4.58	1		Los Gatos	7 Jul
21.16	Vladimir	Kisheyev	SU	4.12.58	1		Khabarovsk	18 Sep
	(10)							
21.15	Karsten	Stolz	FRG	23 .7.64	1		Essen	18 Sep
21.04	Jim	Doehring	USA	27.1.62	1		Irvine	20 Aug
21.03	Helmut	Krieger	POL	17 .7.58	1		Lublin	4 Sep
21.02	Ron	Backes	USA	19.2.63	1	Jenner	San Jose	28 May
21.01	Georgi	Todorov	BUL	7.3.60	1	NC	Sofia	2 Sep
20.99	Dave	Laut	USA	21.12.56	2		San Diego	25 Jun
20.96	Vyacheslav	Lykho	SU	16.1.67	1		Banská Bystrica	4 Sep
20.95i	Andrey	Nemchaninov	SU	27.11.66	1		Kiev	31 Jan
20.89	Mikhail	Kulish	SU	20.3.64	1		Kharkov	17 Jun
20.79	Janis	Bojars	SU	12 .5.56	1		Riga	2 May
	(20)							
20.76	Ahmed K.	Shatta	EGY	23.1.61	1		Cairo	24 Mar
20.76	Maris	Petrashko	SU	6.3.61	1		Riga	5 Aug
20.76	August	Wolf	USA	3.9.61	1		Sacramento	27 Aug
20.74	Gert	Weil	CHL	3.1.60	1		Köln	3 Sep
20.71	Karel	Sula	CS	30 .6.59	1		Praha	2 Jun
20.68	Sergey	Rubtsov	SU	.65	2		Moskva	7 Aug
20.65i	Aleksandr	Bagach	SU	21.11.66	1		Klaipeda	5 Mar
20.63	Georg	Andersen	NOR	7.1.63	1	NC	Byrkjelo	14 Aug
20.61	Alessandro	Andrei	ITA	3.1.59	1		Tirrenia	21 Aug
20.59	Klaus	Görmer	GDR	5 .7.63	1		Leipzig	25 May
	(30)							
20.54	Nikolay	Borodkin	SU	4 .4.55	2		Baku	10 Sep
20.53i	Sergey	Sinnitsa	SU	21.12.66	1		Minsk	27 Feb
20.52i	Vladimir	Yaryshkin	SU	28.2.63	2		Moskva	20 Feb
20.52	John	Brenner	USA	4.1.61	1		Auckland	27 Feb
20.52	Richard	Navara	CS	11.9.64	2		Liberec	21 Aug
20.43	Janne	Ronkainen	FIN	5.2.63	1		Kotka	24 May
20.40	Saulius	Kleiza	SU	2 .4.64	1		Leselidze	23 May
20.37	Tariel	Bitsadze	SU	12.1.66	5	NC	Tallinn	7 Jul
20.36	Ventsislav	Khristov	BUL	18 .5.62	2	Nar	Sofia	26 Jun
20.30i	Erik	De Bruin	HOL	25 .5.63	1	NC	Den Haag	20 Feb
	(40)							
20.30	Brian	Faul	USA	5.3.60	2		Los Gatos	7 Jul
20.29	Dimitrios	Koutsoukis	GRE	8.12.62	1		Herakleion	27 Aug
20.28	Paul	Ruiz	CUB	21.9.62	3		Rostock	29 May
20.26	Sergey	Kot	SU	7.1.60	1		Alma-Ata	17 May
20.25i	Klaus	Bodenmüller	AUT	6.9.62	1	v2-N	Wien	13 Feb
20.23	Zlatan	Saracevic	YUG	27 .7.56	1		Celje	10 Jun
20.20i	Marty	Kobza	USA	6.3.62	2		Johnson City	21 Jan
20.13	Radoslav	Despotov	BUL	8 .8.68	3		Sofia	12 Jun
20.13	Wolfgang	Schmidt	FRG	16.1.54	2		Weiler	10 Jul
20.09	Torsten	Pelzer	GDR	26 .6.63	2		Rostock	29 May
	(50)							
20.03i	Udo	Gelhausen	FRG	5 .7.56	1		Düsseldorf	31 Jan
20.03	Pétur	Gudmundsson	ICE	9.3.62	1		Reykjavik	18 Jun
20.03	Jovan	Lazarevic	YUG	3 .5.52	1		Ljubljana	20 Jun
19.98i	Zsigmond	Ladányi	HUN	4 .8.61	1		Budapest	13 Feb
19.98	Janusz	Gassowski	POL	1.3.58	1		Stargard	10 Sep
19.97i	Randy	Heisler	USA	7 .8.61	1		Bloomington	13 Feb
19.97	Sergey	Nikolayev	SU	12.11.66	2		Leselidze	23 May
19.97	Igor	Palchikov	SU	19 .6.60	2		Khabarovsk	18 Sep
19.92	Dragan	Peric	YUG	8 .5.64	1		Osijek	20 Aug

Mark	Name		Nat	Born	Pos	Meet	Venue	Date
19.91	Jim	Banich	USA	12.9.63	1		Los Angeles	1 Jul
	(60)							
19.90i	Ed	Wade	USA	10.12.64	1		New York	12 Feb
19.88	Jim	Camp	USA	16.12.63	1		Flagstaff	14 May
19.82i	Aleksandr	Baryshnikov	SU	11.11.48	1		Leningrad	17 Jan
19.81	John	Frazier	USA	27 .4.63	1		Northridge	10 Jul
19.81	Paul	Edwards	UK	16.2.59	1		Sandhurst	15 Jul
19.81	Jari	Kuoppa	FIN	25 .6.60	1		Seinajäki	29 Aug
19.81	Valeriy	Sotin	SU	12 .6.60	3		Moskva	4 Sep
19.78	Sören	Tallhem	SWE	16.2.64	1		Provo	2 Apr
19.78	Mohamed	Achouche	EGY	18.11.55	2		Leningrad	10 Aug
19.74i	Kevin	Akins	USA	27.1.60				
	(70)							
19.72	Brian	Muir	USA	18.12.60	2		Irvine	26 Jun
19.60	Tom	Huminik	USA	18.10.66	1		Raleigh	25 May
19.56	Jan	Pienaar	RSA	19.1.66	1		Pretoria	29 Nov
19.54	László	Szabó	HUN	6.1.55	1	NC	Miskolc	16 Jul
19.53	Peter	Kassubek	FRG	10 .6.59	1		Düsseldorf	9 Jul
19.52	Kalman	Konya	FRG	27.10.61	1		Bensheim	15 May
19.48i	Lars	Sundin	SWE	21 .7.61	1		Karlstad	23 Jan
19.48i	Nikolay	Gemizhev	BUL	4 .8.56	1		Sofia	23 Jan
19.46	Sergey	Donskikh	SU	25.1.56	3		Leningrad	10 Aug
19.45	John	Minns	AUS	31 .5.67	1		Canberra	26 Jan
	(80)							
19.44	Mike	Stulce	USA	14 .7.69	1	SWC	Austin	14 May
19.43	Jozef	Lacika	CS	8 .6.61	Q	NC	Praha	16 Jul
19.42	Eugene	Nysschen	RSA	27 .4.64	1		Johannesburg	7 Mar
19.40	Virginius	Mitkus	SU	.66	2		Smolininkay	8 May
19.38	Tony	Harlin	USA	4.9.59	1		Paramus	1 Jul
19.37	Piotr	Perzylo	POL	15.11.61	2	NC	Grudziadz	14 Aug
19.35	Aleksey	Lukashenko	SU	29.3.67	3		Siauliai	21 May
19.33	Luc	Viudes	FRA	31.1.56	1		St.Denis	7 Jun
19.32	Ben	Plucknett	USA	13 .4.54	1		Westwood	13 Sep
19.29	Scott	Eriksson	USA	1 .7.61	1		Auburn	9 Apr
	(90)							
19.26	Ma Yongfeng		CHN	28.11.62	1		Tianjin	1 Sep
19.24	Valeriy	Krizhanovskiy	SU	6.3.62	1		Zhitomir	6 Aug
19.23i	Pyotr	Pogorelyi	SU	28 .4.68	4		Kiev	31 Jan
19.22	David	Wilson	USA	19.9.66	1		Santa Monica	7 Aug
19.20i	Viktor	Belyi	SU	.64	1		Donyetsk	5 Mar
19.20	German	Geiger	SU	8.12.62	1		Novosibirsk	27 Jun
19.19	Narciso	Boue	CUB	28.11.63	7	PTS	Bratislava	9 Jun
19.18i	Aleksandr	Klimenko	SU	27.3.70	1	NC-j	Chelyabinsk	7 Feb
19.18	Mikhail	Ivanov	SU	26.12.62	2		Sochi	24 Apr
19.17i	Dmitriy	Kovtsun *	SU	29.9.55	5		Kiev	30 Jan
	(100)							

Mark	Name		Nat	Born	Date
19.15	Brian	Oldfield	USA	45	18 Jun
19.14	Jack	Trahan	USA	66	10 Dec
19.12	John	Bender	USA	66	1 Jul
19.11	Claus-Dieter	Föhrenbach	FRG	55	10 Jul
19.11	Konstantin	Strangov	BUL	64	20 Aug
19.09	Jannie	Van der Merwe	RSA	66	30 Jan
19.09	Terry	Strouf	USA		
19.09	Yevgeniy	Palchikov	SU	68	13 Jul
19.08	Gennadiy	Vlasyuk	SU	61	5 Mar
19.05	Sven	Buder	GDR	66	8 Sep
	(110)				
19.04i	Marius	Andrusca	RUM	61	30 Jan
19.03i	Mike	Buncic	USA	62	5 Feb
18.98	Georgiy	Panfilov	SU	65	13 May
18.97	Costel	Grasu	RUM	67	12 Aug
18.96i	Jeff	Braun	USA	57	20 Feb
18.94	Michael	Mertens	FRG	65	26 Jun
18.89i	Steve	Muse	USA	66	5 Mar
18.88i	Roar	Hoff	NOR	65	6 Feb
18.87	Stefan	Schröfel	FRG	61	17 Jul
18.84i	Dave	Brown	USA	64	5 Mar
	(120)				
18.83	Yuriy	Kharchenko	SU	59	17 May
18.82	Yevgeniy	Mironov	SU	49	14 Aug
18.81i	Dmitriy	Vasilyev	SU	69	20 Feb
18.81	Edward	Sarul	POL	58	14 Aug
18.76	Werner	Hartmann	FRG	59	31 Jul
18.75	Sergey	Belkin	SU	62	2 May
18.74i	Mark	Colligan	USA	63	19 Feb
18.74	Ron	McKee	USA	59	7 Jul
18.74	Andrey	Malakhov	SU	61	2 Aug
18.71	Sergey	Martyshin	SU	66	20 Aug
	(130)				
18.70	Gong	Yitian	CHN	63	21 May
18.68	Adewale	Olukoji	NIG	68	12Mar
18.66	Ivo	Rahnel	SU	63	18 Jun
18.65i	Aleksandr	Klimov	SU	69	7 Feb
18.64	Peter	Dajia	CAN	64	29 Apr
18.63i	Bo	Hendriksson	SWE	63	30Jan
18.63	Jaroslav	Malinin	SU	61	3 Jun
18.63	Ivars	Logins	SU	66	5 Aug
18.62	Daniel	Chernev	BUL	64	26 Jun
18.61	Marco	Montelatici	ITA	53	22 May
	(140)				

Mark	Name	Nat	Born	Pos	Meet	Venue	Date

\+ meeting held under normal competitive conditions, unsanctioned by GDR federation, but included in national lists.
* athlete disqualified by national federation during outdoor season.

Unsanctioned meeting

20.48i	Lars	Sundin	SWE	21 Jul 61	1	Lidingö	30 Jan

Best outdoor marks for athletes with seasonal bests indoors

Mark	Name	Pos	Meet	Venue	Date	Indoor
21.19	Kostin	2	Znam	Leningrad	12 Jun	21.39i
20.94	Machura	1		Liberec	21 Aug	21.71i
20.21	Bagach	2		Kharkov	17 Jun	20.65i
20.20	Yaryshkin	6	Znam	Leningrad	12 Jun	20.52i
20.16	De Bruin	1		Leiden	12 May	20.30i
19.92	Bodenmüller	5		Bern	23 Aug	20.25i
19.89	Nemchaninov	3		Kharkov	17 Jun	20.95i
19.79	Gelnhausen	1		Pomona	16 Apr	20.03i
19.66	Ladányi	4	PTG	London	8 Jul	19.98i
19.53	Sinnitsa	2		Vitebsk	12 Jul	20.53i
19.48	Akins	1		Wickliffe	27 Jun	19.60i
19.41	Wade	1	TAC	Tampa	18 Jun	19.75i
19.37	Gemizhev	4		Sofia	12 Jun	19.48i
19.18	Klimenko	1		Simferopol	27 May	19.18i
19.16	Belyi	2		Kharkov	20 Aug	19.20i
19.12	Kobza	3	TAC	Tampa	18 Jun	20.20i

Mark	Name	Date
19.09	Heisler	8 May
18.94	Buncic	27 Feb
18.81	Sundin	7 Aug
18.80	Shtrangov	12 Jun
18.79	Hoff	16 Jun

Series for top marks

Mark	Name	Date	1	2	3	4	5	6
23.06	Timmermann	22 May	(22.40	23.06	x	x	22.35	22.45)
22.75	Günthör	23 Aug	(21.73	x	21.84	22.70	x	22.75)
22.61	Timmermann	8 Sep	(21.86	21.93	22.17	22.61	22.11	21.96)
22.56	Timmermann	13 Sep	(21.82	22.10	22.56	p	p	x)
22.47	Timmermann	23 Sep	(22.02	21.31	22.16	21.90	22.29	22.47)
22.42	Barnes	17 Aug	(20.48	21.52	22.42	21.82	x	20.63)
22.39	Barnes	23 Sep	(20.17	20.72	x	21.31	21.01	22.39)
22.36+	Timmermann	16 May						
22.15	Timmermann	27 Apr	(21.38	21.49	21.67	21.65	22.15	21.67)
22.11	Barnes	24 Apr	(19.99	x	21.64	22.03	22.11	x)
22.10	Beyer	8 Sep	(21.88	22.10	21.49	21.84	p	p)
22.05	Beyer	12 Jun	(21.52	22.05	21.73	21.10	x	x)
22.01	Barnes	25 Jun	(20.99	x	22.01	x	p	p)
21.99	Günthör	23 Sep	(21.45	21.59	21.70	20.98	21.99	21.61)
21.94+	Beyer	16 May						
21.91	Günthör	13 Aug	(x	x	20.77	21.76	21.25	21.91)
21.88	Timmermann	24 Jun	(21.88	21.85	21.88	21.72	21.71	21.69)
21.88	Barnes	15 Jul	(18.34	21.06	21.36	x	21.88	x)
21.88	Smirnov	28 Aug						
21.87	Beyer	29 May						
21.86	Timmermann	10 Jul	(21.45	20.96	21.83	x	21.37	21.86)
21.84	Beyer	13 Sep	(21.80	21.84	21.71	21.70	21.51	p)
21.83	Smirnov	4 Sep	(21.30	21.01	x	21.83	x	x)
21.82	Günthör	17 Aug	(21.82	21.80	21.75	21.57	x	x)
21.80	Smirnov	31 May	(20.76	x	20.84	x	21.04	21.80)
21.78	Timmermann	20 Jun	(21.61	x	21.21	21.68	21.78	21.19)
21.76	Barnes	16 Apr	(20.70	21.76	x	21.62	21.53	x)
21.75	Beyer	3 Jun						
21.72i	Barnes	6 Feb	(x	20.48	21.47	21.72	x	x)
21.71i	Machura	30 Jan						
21.71	Günthör	12 Aug	(21.71	p	p	)		
21.63	Günthör	11 Jun						

Shot Year List Progression

Year	Best	10th	20th	50th	100th	Over 20.00	Over 19.00	Ave.100
1958	19.23	17.72	17.37	16.68	16.22	-	1	
1968	21.30	19.90	19.32	18.40	17.56	7	26	
1978	22.15	20.68	20.15	19.58	18.84	28	86	19.685
1979	21.74	20.68	20.39	19.63	18.98	32	96	19.764
1980	21.98	21.10	20.67	19.90	19.15	43	116	20.059
1981	22.02	20.60	20.33	19.88	19.06	38	107	19.877
1982	22.02	21.04	20.62	19.98	19.22	47	133	20.054
1983	22.22	21.20	20.81	20.13	19.37	64	149	20.261
1984	22.19	21.63	21.09	20.23	19.48	66	145	20.412
1985	22.62	21.32	20.98	20.07	19.34	54	119	20.245
1986	22.64	21.49	20.90	20.24	19.33	61	127	20.337
1987	22.91	21.22	20.82	20.11	19.09	56	110	20.247
1988	23.06	21.16	20.79	20.09	19.17	53	112	20.194

DISCUS

Mark	Name		Nat	Born	Pos	Meet	Venue	Date
70.46	Jürgen	Schult	GDR	11.5.60	1		Berlin	13 Sep
70.30	Yuriy	Dumchev	SU	5.8.58	1		Bryansk	31 Jul
70.06	Romas	Ubartas	SU	26.5.60	1		Smolininkay	9 May
69.80+		Schult			1		Athinai	16 May
68.92	Mike	Buncic	USA	25.7.62	1		Salinas	25 May
68.88	Vladimir	Zinchenko	SU	25.7.59	1		Dnepropetrovsk	16 Jul
68.82		Schult			1	OG	Seoul	1 Oct
68.56		Ubartas			1		Vilnius	27 Aug
68.44	Vaclavas	Kidikas	SU	17.10.61	1		Sochi	1 Jun
68.24	Stefan	Fernholm	SWE	2.7.59	1		Logan	30 Apr
68.22		Ubartas			1		Leselidze	15 May
68.22	Wolfgang	Schmidt	FRG	16.1.54	1		Hafnarfirdi	22 Jun
68.14		Schult			1		Potsdam	8 Sep
67.96	Mac	Wilkins	USA	15.11.50	1	MSR	Walnut	24 Apr
67.92		Fernholm			1		Fort Williams	7 Aug
67.90		Kidikas			2		Smolininkay	9 May
67.72		Ubartas			1	v2-N	Portsmouth	19 Jun
67.62		Schult			1		Rostock	29 May
67.54		Kidikas			2	v2-N	Portsmouth	19 Jun
67.48		Schult			1		Jena	4 Jun
67.48		Ubartas			2	OG	Seoul	1 Oct
67.40		Schult			1	vFRG	Düsseldorf	20 Jun
67.38	Rolf	Danneberg	FRG	1.3.53	3	OG	Seoul	1 Oct
67.28		Ubartas			1	Znam	Leningrad	11 Jun
67.20		Ubartas			2		Sochi	1 Jun
67.20		Danneberg			1	NC	Frankfurt	23 Jul
67.12		Danneberg			1		Stade	7 May
67.10		Buncic			1		Los Gatos	14 Jul
67.04		Schult			1		Khania	22 May
67.00		Wilkins			2		Salinas	25 May
	(30/10)							
66.96	Alwin	Wagner	FRG	11.8.50	1		Wabern	17 Jul
66.42	Wulf	Brunner	FRG	20.3.62	1		Kassel	3 Jul
66.42	Gejza	Valent	CS	3.10.53	1		Nitra	28 Aug
66.42	Imrich	Bugár	CS	14.4.55	2		Nitra	28 Aug
66.40	Göran	Svensson	SWE	8.3.59	2		Fort Williams	7 Aug
66.36	Vitaliy	Gaslenko	SU	15.3.62	1		Kharkov	13 Aug
66.30	Igor	Duginyets	SU	20.5.56	1		Leningrad	11 May
66.26	Andrey	Kuzyanin	SU	25.6.60	2		Bryansk	31 Jul
66.24	Juan	Martínez	CUB	17.5.58	1		Madrid	7 Jun
66.12	Aleksandr	Mishakov	SU	7.5.64	1		Baku	11 Sep
	(20)							
66.08	Erik	De Bruin	HOL	25.5.63	1		Hilversum	22 May
66.02	Georgi	Georgiev	BUL	16.7.61	1		Sofia	4 Jun
66.02	Werner	Hartmann	FRG	20.4.59	1		Wirdum	1 Jun
66.00	Georgi	Taushanski	BUL	26.12.57	1		Sofia	11 Jun
65.90	Alois	Hannecker	FRG	10.7.61	1		Bensheim	15 May
65.80	Luis M.	Delís	CUB	6.12.57	2		Madrid	7 Jun
65.60	Georgiy	Kolnootchenko	SU	7.5.59	3		Leselidze	15 May
65.60	Vésteinn	Hafsteinsson	ICE	12.12.60	2		Hafnarfjirdi	22 Jun
65.50	Olaf	Többen	FRG	19.12.62	1A		Norden	18 Sep
65.40	Knut	Hjeltnes	NOR	8.12.51	3		Salinas	25 May
	(30)							
65.16	Marco	Martino	ITA	21.2.60	1		Spoleto	19 Aug
65.08	Yevgeniy	Karpov	SU	6.11.66	3		Bryansk	31 Jul
64.94	Randy	Heisler	USA	7.8.61	3	FOT	Indianapolis	23 Jul
64.94	Carsten	Kufahl	FRG	14.11.67	1B		Norden	18 Sep
64.82	Kamen	Dimitrov	BUL	18.1.62	3		Stara Zagora	28 Aug
64.68	József	Ficsor	HUN	29.7.65	1		Budapest	8 Sep
64.58	Yuriy	Seskin	SU	8.7.66	1		Leningrad	12 Jul
64.54	Olav	Jenssen	NOR	11.5.62	1		Spikketsad	7 Sep
64.44	Brad	Cooper	BAH	30.6.57	1	OT	Nassau	19 Jun

Mark	Name		Nat	Born	Pos	Meet	Venue	Date
64.40	Roger	Bakowski	FRG	9.7.64	2B		Norden	18 Sep
	(40)							
64.36	Csaba	Holló	HUN	6.7.58	1		Budapest	25 Jun
64.30	Svein-Inge	Valvik	NOR	20.9.56	1		Sandnes	9 Jun
64.28	Valeriy	Murashov	SU	5.5.64	3		Smolininkay	9 May
64.18	Mitch	Crouser	USA	30.12.57	1		Gresham	9 Jul
64.18	Attila	Horváth	HUN	28.7.67	1		Szombathely	15 Oct
64.10	Vlad	Slavnic	AUS	10.9.58	1		Melbourne	20 Jan
64.10	John	Powell	USA	25.6.47	2		Stanford	3 Jul
64.04	Christian	Erb	SWZ	14.2.59	3B		Norden	18 Sep
63.62	Judd	Binley	USA	4.1.55	1		Los Angeles	1 Jul
63.60	Adewale	Olukoju	NIG	27.7.68	2		Gateshead	14 Aug
	(50)							
63.56	Manfred	Schmitz	FRG	13.3.60	4B		Norden	18 Sep
63.54	Raimo	Vento	FIN	15.9.54	1		Lappeenranta	6 Jun
63.54	James	Parman	USA	28.1.64	1		Arlington	1 Jul
63.48	Ben	Plucknett	USA	13.4.54	4	FOT	Indianapolis	23 Jul
63.48	Lars	Sundin	SWE	21.7.61	1		Karlstad	6 Aug
63.38	Ray	Lazdins	CAN	25.9.64	1		Toronto	19 Jul
63.26	Raúl	Calderón	CUB	27.11.62	1		Habana	11 Jun
63.22	Erwin	Weitzl	AUT	17.7.60	1	NC	Schwechat	3 Jul
63.20	Yevgeniy	Burin	SU	4.3.64	2		Leningrad	11 May
63.16	Werner	Reiterer	AUS	27.1.68	1		Melbourne	13 Feb
	(60)							
63.02	Patrick	Journoud	FRA	27.4.64	1		Sorgues	14 Jul
62.96	Greg	McSeveney	USA	29.5.59	2		Los Angeles	1 Jul
62.96	Art	McDermott	USA	7.11.61	2		Santa Monica	8 Jul
62.94	Marcus	Gordien	USA	29.4.55	1		Santa Monica	12 Jun
62.92	Dariusz	Juzyszyn	POL	20.3.57	1		Lublin	6 Aug
62.78	Andrey	Kokhanovskiy	SU	11.1.68	1		Moskva	4 May
62.74	Mieczyslaw	Szpak	POL	10.7.61	1		Stargard	10 Sep
62.64	Eggert	Bogasson	ICE	19.7.60	4		Hafnarfirdi	22 Jun
62.64	Sergey	Lyakhov	SU	68	2		Vladivostok	14 Sep
62.60	Andreas	Becker	GDR	15.8.62	2	NC	Rostock	26 Jun
	(70)							
62.52	John	Nichols	USA	23.8.69	1		Baton Rouge	23 Apr
62.52	Edward	Rikert	POL	22.8.61	1		Bialystok	8 Sep
62.26	George	Tossel	RSA	21.2.61	1		Stellenbosch	29 Feb
62.26	Lars	Riedel	GDR	28.6.67	2		Berlin	13 Sep
62.20	Art	Swarts	USA	14.2.45	1		New York	5 Jun
62.14	Ron	Harrer	USA	5.2.65	1		Carbondale	8 May
62.10	Rosen	Velinov	BUL	7.8.67	3		Sofia	12 Aug
61.92	Frédéric	Selle	FRA	13.3.57	4	v2-N	Portsmouth	19 Jun
61.90	Gary	Kostrubala	USA	30.6.64	1		Indianapolis	2 Jul
61.86	Tony	Washington	USA	16.1.66	1		Emmitsburg	30 Apr
	(80)							
61.84	Andreas	Seelig	GDR	6.7.70	1		Halle	15 May
61.78	Thoralf	Fiedler	GDR	8.7.66	2		Berlin	21 May
61.74	Dimitrios	Koutsoukis	GRE	8.12.62	1		Athinai	12 May
61.62	Lutz	Friedrich	GDR	8.8.61	1	GO	Dresden	11 Jun
61.60	Vasiliy	Kaptyukh	SU	27.6.67	1		Siauliai	21 May
61.40	Anatoliy	Letyuchiy	SU	8.6.64	1		Zhitomir	11 Jun
61.36	Kevin	Carr	USA	19.7.64	1		Corvallis	26 May
61.32	Vladimir	Kisheyev	SU	4.12.58	5		Odessa	19 Aug
61.30	Rob	James	USA	3.5.61	1		Cape Girardeau	11 Jun
61.22	Mike	Gravelle	USA	3.4.65	4		Salinas	16 Apr
	(90)							
61.22	Jacek	Strychalski	POL	6.3.62	2		Bialystok	8 Sep
61.20	Roberto	Moya	CUB	11.2.65	3		Habana	27 Feb
61.16	Paul	Mardle	UK	10.11.62	1		London	27 Jul
61.12	Stanislav	Kovár	CS	6.5.64	1		Praha	15 May
61.00	Klaus	Weiffenbach	FRG	21.1.45	1		Rottershausen	24 Jul
60.94	Scott	Eriksson	USA	1.7.61	1		Hillsdale	30 Apr
60.92	Tomás	Panácek	CS	28.3.67	3	NC	Praha	17 Jul
60.90	August	Wolf	USA	3.9.61	5		Salinas	16 Apr
60.88	Sergey	Fyodorov	SU	66	4		Moskva	8 Jul

Mark	Name		Nat	Born	Pos	Meet	Venue	Date
60.84	Bernd (100)	Kneissler	FRG	13.9.62	1		Ludwigsburg	23 Apr
60.84	Miroslaw	Jasinski	FRG	5.5.59	1		Dortmund	21 May
60.82+	Rüdiger	Pudenz	GDR	22.12.66	2		Athinai	16 May
60.82	Costel	Grasu	RUM	5.7.67	1	NC	Pitesti	14 Aug

Mark	Name		Nat	Born	Date
60.76	Ken	Stadel	USA	52	23 Apr
60.70	Mika	Muukka	FIN	66	26 May
60.66	Konstantinos	Georgakopoulos	GRE	63	16 Jul
60.62	Sergey	Kot	SU	60	19 Aug
60.60	Pavel	Popov	SU	65	11 May
60.60	Sergey	Pachin	SU	68	18 Jun
60.60	Mohamed (110)	Naguib	EGY	53	25 Jun
60.54	Ed	Wade	USA	64	23 Apr
60.52	Rick	Meyer	USA	61	24 Apr
60.48	JR (Jon)	Quinn	USA	64	27 May
60.46	Ferenc	Tégla	HUN	47	8 Jun
60.40	Zhang Jinglong		CHN	61	26 Mar
60.32	Todd	Kaufman	USA	61	7 May
60.30	Lutz	Hager	FRG	64	9 Apr
60.16	Jonas	Siaudinis	SU	58	21 May
60.14	Yu Wenge		CHN	66	5 Jun
60.12	Ferenc (120)	Szegletes	HUN	58	7 Aug
60.06	Zdenek	Kohout	CS	67	7 Sep
60.04	Göran	Bergqvist	SWE	60	24 Jun
60.00	Kari	Nisula	FIN	63	22 May
60.00	Li Weinan		CHN	57	2 Sep
59.98	José A.	de Souza	BRA	65	9 Apr
59.98	Steve	Davis	USA	60	7 May
59.90	Gennadiy	Kostyuchenko	SU	62	10 Sep
59.86	Vesselin	Yefremov	BUL	67	11 Jun
59.84	Tim	Taylor	USA	60	30 Jun
59.78	Glenn (130)	Schneider	USA	67	23 Apr
59.76	Valeriy	Yagovdik	SU	63	26 Feb
59.76	Maris	Petrashko	SU	61	4 Sep
59.70	Frantisek	Petrovic	CS	65	1 Jul
59.68	Dmitriy	Shevchenko	SU	68	6 Apr
59.68	Scott	Lofquist	USA	62	14 May
59.68	Bo	Henriksson	SWE	63	16 Sep
59.64	Johnny	Mitchell	USA	64	8 May
59.62	Gunnar	Minstedt	GDR	68	9 Jul
59.60	Milan	Gavor	CS	66	15 May
59.58	Vladimir (140)	Turanok	SU	57	11 Jul
59.58	Dragan	Peric	YUG	64	17 Jul
59.52	Paul	Nandapi	AUS	61	6 Jan
59.52	Marcel	Tirle	RUM	66	20 Feb
59.52	Jörg	Gatzsch	GDR	64	4 Jun
59.46	Aleksandras	Ciupkovas	SU	66	11 Sep
59.42	Wim	de Wolff	HOL	58	5 Aug
59.38	László	Kerekes	HUN	64	14 May
59.36	J.R.	Hanley	USA	59	11 Jun
59.32	Stanislaw	Grabowski	POL	55	28 Jul
59.26	Michael (150)	Möllenbeck	FRG	69	3 Jul
59.18	Vasiliy	Petrov	SU	66	18 Jun
59.04	Doc	Luckie	USA	59	23 Apr
59.04	Vyacheslav	Pachin	SU	64	11 Jun
59.00	Pertti	Valta	FIN	60	15 Jun
58.98	Tadeusz	Majewski	POL	54	11 Sep
58.96	John	Brenner	USA	61	27 Feb
58.90	Adriano	Coos	ITA	59	28 Aug
58.84	Christos	Papadopoulos	GRE	65	30 Jul
58.84	Saulius	Kleiza	SU	64	11 Aug
58.82	Marek (160)	Majkrzak	POL	65	11 Sep
58.60	Angelos	Nikolaidis	GRE	56	13 Jul
58.58	Brian	Blutreich	USA	67	12 Mar
58.58	Gian Paolo	Cretoni	ITA	60	19 Aug
58.54i	Steve	Muse	USA	66	23 Jan
58.54	Peter	Thompson	USA	67	26 Mar
58.50	Angelos	Nikolaidis	GRE	56	5 Jun
58.44	Al	Oerter	USA	36	

\+ meeting held under normal competitive conditions, unsanctioned by GDR federation, but included in national lists.

Light Implement

Mark	Name		Nat	Born	Pos	Meet	Venue	Date
64.92	Edward	Rikert	POL	22.8.61	1		Bydgoszcz	3 Sep
62.04	Eligiusz	Pukownik	POL	30.6.62	2		Bydgoszcz	3 Sep

Unconfirmed mark

Mark	Name		Nat	Born	Pos	Meet	Venue	Date
64.12	Adewale	Olukoju	NIG	27.7.68	1	OT	Bauchi	1 Jul

Sloping ground

Mark	Name		Nat	Born	Pos	Meet	Venue	Date
63.56	Ken	Stadel	USA	19.2.52	1		Emporia	8 Jun

Disqualified for drug abuse

Mark	Name		Nat	Born	Pos	Meet	Venue	Date
67.06	Dmitriy	Kovtsun	SU	29.9.55	1		Kiev	3 May

Series of top marks

Mark	Name	Date	1	2	3	4	5	6
70.46	Schult	13 Sep	(67.28	70.46	69.76	68.22	69.86	p)
70.30	Dumchev	31 Jul	(67.60	67.80	70.30	68.50	68.68	68.60)
70.06	Ubartas	9 May	(70.06	68.78	x	67.70	x	66.98)
68.88	Zinchenko	16 Jul	(66.24	62.26	x	68.10	x	68.88)
68.82	Schult	1 Oct	(68.82	67.92	65.76	68.18	65.70	68.26)
68.44	Kidikas	1 Jun	(x	68.08	66.44	68.44	x	65.22)
68.24	Fernholm	30 Apr	(68.24, 68.20, 67.30)					
68.22	Schmidt	22 Jun	(60.44	67.48	x	68.22	67.00	65.62)
68.14	Schult	8 Sep	(64.66	66.70	67.26	67.50	x	68.14)
67.96	Wilkins	24 Apr	(67.96	x	x	64.08	x	59.88)
67.92	Fernholm	7 Aug	(x	x	x	67.92	x	x)
67.72	Ubartas	19 Jun	(62.66	x	67.72	x	x	67.02)
67.54	Kidikas	19 Jun	(65.28	x	66.00	67.40	67.54	66.36)
67.48	Ubartas	1 Oct	(66.86	66.20	66.24	64.40	63.74	67.48)
67.38	Danneberg	1 Oct	(65.58	63.60	x	63.88	67.38	62.56)
67.28	Ubartas	11 Jun	(63.26	61.90	67.02	65.26	65.84	67.28)

Mark	Name		Nat	Born	Pos	Meet	Venue	Date
67.20	Ubartas	1 Jun	(64.96	67.20	66.24	x	x	65.82)
67.20	Danneberg	23 Jul	(57.60	55.84	64.44	61.64	62.46	67.20)
67.04	Schult	22 May	(66.26	63.50	64.10	67.02	x	67.04)

Series not known for: Buncic 69.92 and 67.10, Schult 69.90, 67.62, 67.48 and 67.40, Ubartas 68.56 and 68.22, Kidikas 67.90, Danneberg 67.12

Discus Year List Progression

Year	Best	10th	20th	50th	100th	Over 62.00	Over 60.00	Ave.100
1958	57.42	55.94	54.63	51.88	49.82	-	-	
1968	68.40	62.68	60.78	57.90	55.08	12	28	
1978	71.16	64.92	63.94	61.98	59.72	49	95	62.390
1979	70.66	66.52	64.84	62.28	59.78	52	96	62.993
1980	70.98	67.68	66.34	62.86	60.32	70	108	63.760
1981	72.34	67.26	65.62	62.00	60.02	51	104	62.883
1982	70.58	68.20	66.36	62.92	60.26	62	104	63.598
1983	71.86	68.12	66.24	62.98	60.48	73	119	63.813
1984	71.26	67.76	66.90	63.66	60.96	80	129	64.383
1985	71.26	67.36	66.38	63.02	60.54	70	121	63.848
1986	74.08	67.02	65.86	63.24	60.96	77	128	63.833
1987	69.52	67.22	65.82	62.92	60.40	62	113	63.340
1988	70.46	67.38	66.12	63.60	60.84	77	124	64.055

HAMMER

Mark	First	Name	Nat	Born	Pos	Meet	Venue	Date
85.14	Yuriy	Sedykh	SU	11.6.55	1	Kuts	Moskva	4 Sep
84.80	Sergey	Litvinov	SU	23.1.58	1	OG	Seoul	26 Sep
84.46		Sedykh			1		Vladivostok	14 Sep
84.16	Jüri	Tamm	SU	5.2.57	1		Kharkov	19 Jun
84.04		Litvinov			1		Adler	1 Jun
83.78	Igor	Nikulin	SU	14.8.60	1		Leningrad	18 Jun
83.76		Sedykh			2	OG	Seoul	26 Sep
83.62		Litvinov			2		Vladivostok	14 Sep
83.44	Igor	Astapkovich	SU	4.1.63	1		Staiki	31 Jul
83.40+	Ralf	Haber	GDR	18.8.62	1		Athinai	16 May
83.36		Tamm			1		Kiev	4 May
83.18		Litvinov			1		Rostov on Don	8 May
83.18		Tamm			3		Vladivostok	14 Sep
83.12		Sedykh			1	Znam	Leningrad	12 Jun
82.66		Sedykh			1	Athl	Lausanne	24 Jun
82.66		Tamm			1		Odessa	21 Aug
82.54		Tamm			2		Adler	1 Jun
82.54		Haber			1		Potsdam	9 Sep
82.52	Heinz	Weis	FRG	14.7.63	1		Leverkusen	28 Jun
82.42		Litvinov			2	Znam	Leningrad	12 Jun
82.40		Astapkovich			1		Grodno	6 Aug
82.36		Haber			1	GO	Dresden	11 Jun
82.34		Tamm			1	NC	Tallinn	6 Jul
82.34		Nikulin			2	NC	Tallinn	6 Jul
82.32		Nikulin			1	Nik	Nice	10 Jul
82.28		Tamm			2	Kuts	Moskva	4 Sep
82.22		Haber			1		Jena	3 Jun
82.16	Vitaliy	Alisevich	SU	15.6.67	1		Pärnu	13 Jul
82.10		Tamm			1		Leselidze	15 May
82.08	Ivan	Tanev	BUL	1.5.57	1	NC	Sofia	3 Sep
81.88	Jud	Logan	USA	19.7.59	1		University Park	22 Apr
	(30/10)							
81.82	Gunther	Rodehau	GDR	6.7.59	1		Berlin	13 Sep
81.78	Christoph	Sahner	FRG	23.9.63	1		Wemmetsweiler	11 Sep
81.70	Plamen	Minev	BUL	28.4.65	1		Sofia	4 Jun
81.68	Tibor	Gécsek	HUN	22.9.64	1		Szombathely	13 Sep
81.52	Sergey	Alay	SU	11.6.65	1		Siauliai	22 May
81.18	Albert	Sinka	HUN	22.11.62	1		Székesfehérvár	7 Aug
80.60	Imre	Szitás	HUN	4.9.61	1		Szombathely	11 Jul
80.54	Viktor	Apostolov	BUL	1.10.62	2	NC	Sofia	3 Sep

Mark	Name		Nat	Born	Pos	Meet	Venue	Date
80.52	Vasiliy	Sidorenko	SU	1.5.61	1		Adler	24 Apr
80.38	Andrey	Abduvaliyev	SU	30.6.66	1		Chelyabinsk	16 Jul
	(20)							
80.32	Nikolay	Lysenko	SU	14.7.66	1		Ordzhonikidze	24 Sep
80.04	Benjaminas	Viluckis	SU	20.3.61	6	Znam	Leningrad	12 Jun
80.02	Ken	Flax	USA	20.4.63	1	CalR	Modesto	7 May
79.24	Vyacheslav	Korovin	SU	8.9.62	2		Leselidze	15 May
78.94	Sergey	Dorozhon	SU	17.2.64	1		Alushta	24 Jan
78.80	Aleksandr	Seleznyev	SU	25.1.63	2		Bryansk	11 Jul
78.72	József	Vida	HUN	9.1.63	2		Zalaegerszeg	12 Jun
78.64	Kjell	Bystedt	SWE	24.5.60	1		Västerås	6 Aug
78.48	Tore	Gustafsson	SWE	11.2.62	1		Provo	21 May
78.46	Juha	Tiainen	FIN	5.12.55	1		Savonlinna	31 Jul
	(30)							
78.30	Boris	Kotelnikov	SU	65	1		Bryansk	31 Jul
78.28	Norbert	Radefeld	FRG	3.3.62	Q	NC	Frankfurt	23 Jul
78.18	Valeriy	Gubkin	SU	11.1.67	3		Staiki	31 Jul
78.12	Valeriy	Kocherga	SU	12.9.63	1		Voroshilovgrad	14 May
78.10	Viktor	Baygush	SU	16.12.63	2		Dnepropetrovsk	16 Jul
78.04	Igor	Shchogolev	SU	26.10.60	1		Taganrog	18 Jun
78.04	Yuriy	Tarasyuk	SU	11.4.57	4		Staiki	31 Jul
78.02	Lucio	Serrani	ITA	11.3.61	1	NC	Milano	6 Sep
77.96	Jörg	Schaeffer	FRG	17.7.59	3		Rhede	1 Jul
77.90	Mikhail	Popel	SU	25.5.66	5		Staiki	31 Jul
	(40)							
77.88	Klaus	Ploghaus	FRG	31.1.56	1		Aschaffenburg	15 Jul
77.88	Sergey	Ivanov	SU	3.1.62	3	Kuts	Moskva	4 Sep
77.80	Sándor	Vörös	HUN	19.1.58	1		Szeged	19 Aug
77.78	Harri	Huhtala	FIN	13.8.52	1		Imatra	28 Jul
77.76	Marc	Odenthal	FRG	19.2.63	1		Düsseldorf	7 Jul
77.70	Johann	Lindner	AUT	3.5.59	2		Linz	15 Aug
77.64	Sergey	Dvoretskiy	SU	30.4.57	2		Chelyabinsk	16 Jul
77.42	Yuriy	Chernega	SU	18.2.67	2		Orzhonikidze	24 Sep
77.40	Yevgeniy	Gribov	SU	18.4.62	2		Taganrog	18 Jun
77.02	Enrico	Sgrulletti	ITA	24.4.65	1		Caorle	30 Jul
	(50)							
76.98	Aleksandr	Drigol	SU	25.4.66	4		Vladivostok	14 Sep
76.94	Vladimir	Styopochkin	SU	3.7.64	4		Odessa	21 Aug
76.50	Emanuil	Dyulgerov	BUL	7.2.55	3	Nar	Sofia	26 Jun
76.42	Aivar	Räni	SU	4.3.63	1		Tallinn	18 May
76.40	Fyodor	Makovskiy	SU	64	4		Adler	24 Apr
76.26	Nicolae	Bindar	RUM	14.3.56	1		Bucuresti	2 Jun
76.00	Vasiliy	Rymaruk	SU	9.3.61	1		Ivano-Frankovsk	2 Jun
75.98	Sergey	Gula	SU	2.6.63	4		Voroshilovgrad	14 May
75.74	Eduard	Piskunov	SU	26.9.67	1		Ternopol	25 Sep
75.64	Lance	Deal	USA	21.8.61	1		Corvallis	11 Jun
	(60)							
75.58	René	Fox	FRG	9.11.67	1		Darmstadt	12 Jun
75.56	Donatas	Plunge	SU	11.11.60	2		Vilnius	3 Sep
75.52	Walter	Ciofani	FRA	17.2.62	1		Antony	25 Jun
75.24	Raphael	Piolanti	FRA	14.11.67	1		Franconville	9 Oct
75.14	Rumen	Koprivichin	BUL	2.10.62	Q	NC	Sofia	2 Sep
75.00	Dave	Smith	UK	21.6.62	1	BNP	Villeneuve d'Ascq	27 Jun
74.96	Valeriy	Reshetnikov	SU	25.3.59	4		Dnepropetrovsk	16 Jul
74.88	Aleksandr	Puchkov	SU	30.4.60	5	RigC	Riga	5 Jun
74.84	Sándor	Füzesi	HUN	15.12.59	3		Székesfehérvár	7 Aug
74.76	Mariusz	Tomaszewski	POL	23.4.56	1		Warzawa	20 Aug
	(70)							
74.66	Claus	Dethloff	FRG	4.9.68	1		Wunstorf	18 Sep
74.62	Georgi	Minchev	BUL	8.9.62	5		Sofia	20 Aug
74.60	Jörn	Hübner	GDR	27.1.68	1		Cottbus	7 Jun
74.48	Stefan	Jönsson	SWE	14.2.64	2		Västerås	6 Aug
74.46	Sean	Carlin	AUS	29.11.67	3		Auckland	27 Feb
74.46	Pasi	Heikkilä	FIN	31.5.65	1		Mäntyharju	5 Jun
74.44	Joe	Quigley	AUS	5.12.61	1		Melbourne	15 Mar
74.30	Ivan	Petkov	BUL	15.2.60	6		Sofia	20 Aug

Mark	Name		Nat	Born	Pos	Meet	Venue	Date
74.16	Conor	McCullough	IRL	22.3.61	1	NC	Dublin	24 Jul
74.04	Ajet	Toska	ALB	61	2	BalkG	Ankara	17 Jul
	(80)							
74.02	Ari	Taavitsainen	FIN	12.4.58	1		Anjalankoski	5 Sep
73.76	Ralf	Jossa	GDR	2.11.66	1		Cottbus	18 May
73.70	Mikhail	Pyryalov	SU	63	1		Smolensk	26 Jun
73.66	Frantisek	Vrbka	CS	23.7.58	1		Praha	25 Jun
73.58	Milan	Malát	CS	10.3.67	1		Praha	9 Jul
73.44	Björn-Peter	Fuhrmann	GDR	4.9.67	3	GO	Dresden	11 Jun
73.40	Thomas	Grogorick	GDR	10.5.62	4	NC	Rostock	24 Jun
73.32	Oleg	Polyushin	SU	23.4.69	1		Simferopol	29 May
73.28	Sergey	Pribytkin	SU	68	5		Grodno	18 Jun
73.24	Frédéric	Kuhn	FRA	10.7.68	1	NC	Tours	13 Aug
	(90)							
73.20	Sergey	Vorobyov	SU	29.1.64	6		Kiev	14 Aug
72.62	Vadim	Kolesnik	SU	29.1.69	1	NC-j	Bryansk	6 Jul
72.62	Matt	Mileham	UK	27.12.56	1		Harrow	23 Aug
72.62	Vadim	Kalugin	SU	3.7.68	3		Ordzhonikidze	25 Sep
72.62	Bi Zhong		CHN	68	1		Jinan	26 Oct
72.52	Sabin	Khristov	BUL	21.2.67	6	Nar	Sofia	26 Jun
72.40	Waclaw	Filek	POL	2.4.59	2		Mielec	1 Sep
72.40	Lech	Kowalski	POL	17.1.61	3		Mielec	1 Sep
72.34	Stefan	Fischer	FRG	19.1.69	1		Leverkusen	16 Jul
72.28	Francisco	Fuentes	SPA	6.2.63	2		Sevilla	1 Jun
	(100)							

Mark	Name		Nat	Born	Date
72.26	Miroslav	Vrican	CS	66	2 Sep
72.18	Sergey	Gavrilov	SU	70	18 Jun
72.16	Pavel	Sedlácek	CS	68	2 Sep
72.14	Mike	Maynard	USA	.59	14 May
72.12	Jukka	Olkkonen	FIN	58	1 May
72.12	Dave	Huxley	AUS	58	7 Aug
72.10	Mike	Jones	UK	63	27 Aug
71.94	Lutz	Amme	GDR	66	17 Jun
71.92	Aleksandr	Gribachenko	SU	67	1 May
71.90	Sergey	Pribytkin	SU	65	12 Jul
	(110)				
71.82	John	McArdle	USA	57	28 May
71.68	Károly	Povászon	HUN	60	2 Jul
71.60	Vladimir	Poleshko	SU	65	6 May
71.58	Yuriy	Alatorskikh	SU	66	14 May
71.46	Panagiotis	Kremastiotis	GRE	60	28 May
71.44	Hakim	Toumi	ALG	61	16 Jun
71.40	Aleksandr	Krykoun	SU	68	5 Mar
71.38	Paul	Head	UK	65	25 Aug
71.32	Vilnis	Sudars	SU	63	17 Jun
71.30	Yu Guangming		CHN	64	13 Aug
	(120)				
71.28	Ryszard	Jakubowski	POL	59	15 Sep
71.20	Christoph	Koch	FRG	65	16 Jul
71.20	Sergey	Kirmasov	SU	70	24 Sep
71.18	Mario	Tschierschwitz	FRG	62	24 Aug
71.14	Michael	Beierl	AUT	63	29 May
71.12	Aleksandr	Muravskiy	SU	70	15 May
71.10	Gary	Halpin	IRL	66	2 Apr
71.10	Jaroslav	Chmyr	SU	66	19 Jun
71.04	Sven	Schulze	GDR	68	18 May
71.00	Vladimir	Knigin	SU	64	10 Jul
	(130)				
70.98	Klaus-Bernd	Leitges	FRG	66	7 Jul
70.82	Vladimir	Zotov	SU	63	16 Jul
70.82	Angus	Cooper	NZ	64	17 Dec
70.74	Valeriy	Kobarenkov	SU	69	13 Aug
70.70	Thomas	Hommel	GDR	69	21 Jul
70.70	Sergey	Lebonta	SU	69	11 Sep
70.48	Vicente	Sanchez	CUB	66	2 Jul
70.40	Ruslan	Yaroshenko	SU	68	21 Aug
70.38	Vadim	Poklonov	SU	63	30 Jul
70.34	Yuriy	Lebedev	SU	67	24 Sep
	(140)				
70.30	Stewart	Rogerson	UK	62	14 Aug
70.28	Vladimir	Glubokov	SU	64	18 Jun
70.28	Xie Yingqi		CHN	58	5 Jun
70.24	Dmitriy	Sukharev	SU	69	28 Jun
70.06	Doug	Gillard	USA	60	7 May
70.02	Iosif	Shaverdashvili	SU	68	21 Aug
70.00	Peter	Baxevanis	AUS	67	17 Dec

Irregular conditions

Mark	Name		Nat	Born	Date
71.56	Hakim	Toumi	ALG	61	2 Jun

Light implement

Mark	Name		Nat	Born	Pos	Venue	Date
73.72	Leszek	Woderski	POL	4.4.58	1	Bydgoszcz	3 Sep

+ meeting held under normal competitive conditions, unsanctioned by GDR federation, but included in nationallists

Series of top marks

Mark	Name	Date	Series					
85.14	Sedykh	4 Sep	(84.98	84.18	x	x	85.14	x)
84.80	Litvinov	26 Sep	(84.76	83.82	83.86	83.98	84.80	83.80)
84.46	Sedykh	14 Sep	(82.18	84.46	82.86	x	83.62	x)
84.16	Tamm	19 Jun	(79.32	82.04	82.82	81.14	84.16	83.02)
84.04	Litvinov	1 Jun	(79.48	82.54	82.22	84.04	83.08	p)
83.76	Sedykh	26 Sep	(80.96	83.62	83.44	83.44	x	83.76)
83.62	Litvinov	14 Sep	(x	83.62	65.28	82.82	x	p)
83.40+	Haber	16 May	(81.22	x	83.40	80.08	81.72	82.12)
83.18	Tamm	14 Sep	(79.76	x	83.18	83.12	79.70	82.18)
83.12	Sedykh	12 Jun	(83.02	80.80	83.10	x	x	83.12)
82.66	Sedykh	24 Jun	(81.00	82.60	81.94	82.66	81.04	x)
82.66	Tamm	21 Aug	(x	79.52	80.56	78.96	82.42	82.66)
82.54	Tamm	1 Jun	(79.58	81.20	80.70	82.54	x	81.10)

Mark	Name	Date						
82.54	Haber	9 Sep	(x	82.54	79.40	78.80	79.88	82.34)
82.52	Weis	28 Jun	(79.44	80.10	81.86	x	82.52	82.04)
82.42	Litvinov	12 Jun	(81.92	82.42	x	81.62	80.06	x)
82.34	Tamm	6 Jul	(79.90	81.94	82.30	81.34	82.34	x)
82.34	Nikulin	6 Jul	(80.80	81.68	82.18	82.34	81.12	x)
82.32	Nikulin	10 Jul	(80.26	81.80	x	x	82.32	81.74)
82.28	Tamm	4 Sep	(82.28	x	x	x	82.12	81.60)

Series not known for Nikulin 83.78, Astapkovich 83.44 and 82.40, Tamm 83.36 and 82.10, Litvinov 83.18, Haber 82.36 and 82.22, Alisevich 82.16, Tanev 82.08

Hammer Year List Progression

Year	Best	10th	20th	50th	100th	Over 75.00	Over 72.00	Ave.100
1958	68.68	64.59	63.12	60.01	57.21	-	-	
1968	73.76	69.78	68.48	64.92	62.62	-	3	
1978	80.32	75.64	73.84	71.46	69.00	13	43	72.066
1979	79.82	76.36	75.18	72.66	69.26	23	56	72.831
1980	81.80	77.96	76.02	73.08	69.98	31	63	73.667
1981	80.56	76.84	75.90	72.32	69.88	22	58	73.016
1982	83.98	77.92	76.60	74.56	71.62	43	94	74.839
1983	84.14	80.00	77.98	75.30	72.40	55	109	75.969
1984	86.34	80.50	79.06	76.34	73.08	64	122	76.502
1985	84.08	80.20	78.50	76.48	72.96	69	116	76.633
1986	86.74	80.68	79.30	76.14	72.36	61	106	76.538
1987	83.48	80.74	79.36	76.52	72.00	63	106	76.685
1988	85.14	81.88	80.38	77.02	72.28	66	107	77.114

JAVELIN

Mark		Name	Nat	Born	Pos	Meet	Venue	Date
86.88	Jan	Zelezny	CS	16.6.66	1		Leverkusen	28 Jun
86.50	Tapio	Korjus	FIN	10.2.61	1		Lahti	25 Aug
85.96	Klaus	Tafelmeier	FRG	12.4.58	1		Tokyo	13 May
85.90		Zelezny			Q	OG	Seoul	24 Sep
85.76		Zelezny			1		Kvarnsveden	19 Jun
85.74		Zelezny			1	PTS	Bratislava	8 Jun
85.18		Korjus			1	vNOR	Oyestad	16 Jun
84.76		Zelezny			1		Tokyo	7-Oct
84.66	Einar	Vilhjálmsson	ICE	1.6.60	1	NC	Reykjavik	25 Jun
84.38		Korjus			1	NC	Hämeenlinna	7 Aug
84.34		Zelezny			1		Praha	2 Jun
84.28		Korjus			1	OG	Seoul	25 Sep
84.14	Silvio	Warsönke	GDR	2.8.67	1		Rostock	29 May
84.12		Zelezny			2	OG	Seoul	25 Sep
84.06	Detlef	Michel	GDR	13.10.55	1		Berlin	13 Sep
83.44		Vilhjálmsson			1	DNG	Stockholm	5 Jul
83.40		Tafelmeier			2		Leverkusen	28 Jun
83.38		Zelezny			1		Auckland	27 Feb
83.36		Viljhalmsson			1		Austin	7 May
83.36		Korjus			1eA		Pihtipudas	24 Jul
83.30	Gerald	Weiss	GDR	8.1.60	1		Jena	3 Jun
83.26	Seppo	Räty	FIN	27.4.62	3	OG	Seoul	25 Sep
83.12		Zelezny			1	Ros	Praha	16 Jun
82.78		Michel			1		Khania	22 May
82.76	Viktor	Yevsyukov	SU	6.10.56	1		Moskva	5 Sep
82.74		Warsönke			1		Potsdam	9 Sep
82.72		Tafelmeier			4	OG	Seoul	25 Sep
82.70	Sejad	Krdzalic	YUG	5.1.60	1		Beograd	14 May
82.68		Warsönke			2		Jena	3 Jun
82.68		Vilhjálmsson			1	WG	Helsinki	30 Jun
	(30/10)							
82.34	Kazuhiro	Mizoguchi	JAP	18.3.62	2		Tokyo	13 May
82.22	Lev	Shatilo	SU	21.10.63	1		Adler	14 Feb
82.18	Vladislav	Grib	SU	8.5.64	1		Banská Bystrica	4 Sep
81.94	Viktor	Zaitsev	SU	6.6.66	1		Alma-Ata	16 May
81.92	Normunds	Pildavs	SU	12.4.64	1		Riga	3 Sep
81.86	Mike	Barnett	USA	21.5.61	1		Knoxville	21 May

Mark	Name		Nat	Born	Pos	Meet	Venue	Date
81.48	Pascal	Lefévre	FRA	25.1.65	1	NC	Tours	14 Aug
81.38	Yuriy	Rybin	SU	5.5.63	1	NC-w	Adler	11 Feb
81.38	Peter	Borglund	SWE	29.1.64	1		Södertalje	13 Jun
81.30	Dag	Wennlund	SWE	9.10.63	1		Västerås	30 Jun
	(20)							
81.30	Mike	Hill	UK	22.10.64	2	DNG	Stockholm	5 Jul
81.26	Volker	Hadwich	GDR	23.9.64	1	vITA	Neubrandenburg	9 Jul
81.26	Charlus-Michel	Bertimon	FRA	1.1.57	2	NC	Tours	14 Aug
81.22	Marek	Kaleta	SU	17.12.61	1		Savonlinna	31 Jul
81.22	László	Stefán	HUN	4.11.63	1		Budapest	16 Sep
80.98	Dave	Ottley	UK	5.8.55	Q	OG	Seoul	24 Sep
80.94	Tom	Petranoff	USA	8.4.58	1		Stellenbosch	18-Oct
80.92	Mark	Roberson	UK	13.3.67	1		London	12 Jun
80.84	Peter	Blank	FRG	10.4.62	1	NC	Frankfurt	24 Jul
80.82	Zbigniew	Bednarski	POL	4.6.60	1		Slupsk	18 May
	(30)							
80.78	Zdenek	Nenadál	CS	12.2.64	2		Praha	2 Jun
80.76	Stéphane	Laporte	FRA	17.7.66	1		Dijon	11 Jun
80.72	Constantin	Miclea	RUM	13.4.63	1	Nar	Sofia	25 Jun
80.70	Gavin	Lovegrove	NZ	21.10.67	1		Auckland	10 Dec
80.60	Dave	Stephens	USA	8.2.62	1		Sacramento	27 Aug
80.48	Duncan	Atwood	USA	11.10.55	1		San Diego	25 Jun
80.40	Andrey	Novikov	SU	12.4.63	3		Sochi	31 May
80.32	Marcis	Shtrobinders	SU	12.6.66	1		Kiev	15 Aug
80.26	Vladimir	Ovchinnikov	SU	2.8.70	Q	OG	Seoul	24 Sep
80.24	Kimmo	Kinnunen	FIN	31.3.68	Q	OG	Seoul	24 Sep
	(40)							
80.20	Nikolay	Kosyanok	SU	25.2.58	2	NC-w	Adler	11 Feb
80.08	Emil	Tsvetanov	BUL	14.3.63	1		Pleven	9 Jul
80.06	Reidar	Lorentzen	NOR	22.9.56	1	NC	Byrkjelo	14 Aug
79.90	Marko	Hyytiäinen	FIN	27.11.66	3		Lahti	29 Aug
79.88	Brian	Crouser	USA	9.7.62	1		Corvallis	11 Jun
79.86	Oleg	Pakhol	SU	64	3	NC-w	Adler	11 Feb
79.80	Vladimir	Furdylo	SU	6.4.58	Q	NC	Tallinn	6 Jul
79.64	Ivan	Mustapic	YUG	9.7.66	1		Zagreb	14 May
79.62	Stanislaw	Witek	POL	24.4.60	1		Slupsk	3 Sep
79.58	Yki	Laine	FIN	16.5.65	2		Mäntyharju	5 Jun
	(50)							
79.58	Sulev	Lepik	SU	22.7.66	2		Riga	3 Sep
79.56	Mike	Mahovlich	CAN	27.8.60	1		Burnaby	29 Jun
79.50	Stephen	Backley	UK	12.2.69	1	NC	Derby	5 Jun
79.50	Roald	Bradstock	UK	24.4.62	2	AAA	Birmingham	7 Aug
79.32	Milan	Stjepovic	YUG	8.3.68	1	BalkG	Ankara	16 Jul
79.28	Vladimir	Sasimovich	SU	9.6..68	1		Vilnius	3 Sep
79.24	Rudolf	Steiner	SWZ	16.1.51	1		Bulle	19 Aug
79.22	Uwe	Trinks	GDR	19.2.62	3		Jena	3 Jun
79.18	Yuriy	Zhirov	SU	1.1.60	3		Adler	14 Feb
79.12	Miroslaw	Witek	POL	24.4.67	2		Slupsk	3 Sep
	(60)							
79.06	Dainis	Kula	SU	28.4.59	1		Ventspils	25 Sep
79.00	Valeriy	Nosov	SU	20.2.68	5	NC-w	Adler	11 Feb
78.92	Jeroen	Van der Meer	HOL	7.4.59	1		Vught	7 Jun
78.92	Sergey	Gavras	SU	16.4.57	3		Vilnius	28 Aug
78.88	Jean-Paul	Lakafia	FRA	29.6.61	3	NC	Tours	14 Aug
78.84	Johan	Oosthuizen	RSA	8.8.54	1		Stellenbosch	26 Apr
78.76	Dumitru	Negoita	RUM	9.2.60	1	NC	Pitesti	12 Aug
78.74	Eero	Heikkinen	FIN	22.7.55	2eA		Pihtipudas	24 Jul
78.32	Juan	de la Garza	MEX	20.9.61	1		New Orleans	25 Jun
78.28	Sigurdur	Einarsson	ICE	28.9.62	1		Tallahassee	23 Apr
	(70)							
78.28	István	Csider	HUN	21.10.64	1		Budapest	6 Sep
78.14	Masami	Yoshida	JAP	14.6.58	4		Tokyo	8-Oct
78.10	Lee Wook-Jong		KOR	26.10.66	Q	OG	Seoul	24 Sep
77.96	Hannu	Holopainen	FIN	25.6.58	4A		Pihtipudas	24 Jul
77.92	Bogdan	Patelka	POL	6.12.66	1		Sopot	28 May
77.88	Kenneth	Petersen	DEN	18.12.65	3		Växjö	25 Aug

Mark	Name		Nat	Born	Pos	Meet	Venue	Date
77.82	Steve	Feraday	CAN	5.4.59	1		North York	22 Jun
77.78	Stefan	König	FRG	25.8.66	1	APM	Hengelo	14 Aug
77.74	Igor	Adeyev	SU	63	1		Volgograd	12 Jun
77.60	Craig	Christianson	USA	1.4.61	4		Knoxville	21 May
	(80)							
77.58	Mike	O'Rourke	NZ	21.8.55	2		Auckland	7 Feb
77.54	Libor	Kverek	CS	14.3.67	3		Praha	2 Jun
77.52	Radovan	Scekic	YUG	1.10.67	3	NC	Sarajevo	3 Sep
77.22	Yuriy	Subbotin	SU	56	2		Moskva	7 Aug
77.08	Juha	Laukkanen	FIN	6.1.69	2		Kuortane	28 May
76.82	Eduard	Budnik	SU	21.1.61	1		Kiev	3 May
76.80	Tamás	Bolgár	HUN	24.8.55	2	v4-N	Forli	22 May
76.80	Mikko	Anttonen	FIN	5.7.63	7A		Pihtipudas	23 Jul
76.80	Philippe	Lecurieux	FRA	22.5.58	4	NC	Tours	14 Aug
76.76	Ramón	González	CUB	24.8.65	1		Habana	5 Aug
	(90)							
76.74	Kari	Siuvatti	FIN	3.2.62	1		Rukki	10 Jul
76.70	Sergey	Glebov	SU	26.1.64	1	Veet	Tallinn	10 Jul
76.68	Mark	Babich	USA	7.8.63	6		Knoxville	21 May
76.64	Vladimir	Grinchenko	SU	14.3.65	2		Kharkov	18 Jun
76.64	Steffen	Kauerauf	GDR	9.5.66	3	NC	Rostock	26 Jun
76.58	Janusz	Jakubczyk	POL	20.7.59	1		Sopot	2 Jul
76.58	Miroslaw	Szybowski	POL	25.3..60	3		Slupsk	3 Sep
76.52	Patrik	Bodén	SWE	30.6.67	3		Karlstad	30 Aug
76.48	Aleksandr	Gorbatov	SU	66	Q	NC-w	Adler	10 Feb
76.48	Vladimir	Gavrilyuk	SU	17.6.61	3		Kharkov	18 Jun
	(100)							

Mark	Name		Nat	Born	Date
76.46	Terry	McHugh	IRL	63	24 Sep
76.32	Kauko	Koivuniemi	FIN	58	31 Jul
76.30	Orlando	Hernández	CUB	62	20 Feb
76.28	Jean-Pol	Schlatter	BEL	57	12 Aug
76.06	Kimmo	Solehmainen	FIN	69	1 Jun
76.06	Kari	Ihalainen	FIN	54	10 Jul
76.04	Markus	Galanski	FRG	67	28 Aug
76.02	Peter	Schreiber	FRG	64	11 Jun
75.92	Gerhard	Burger	RSA	69	15Oct
75.86	Fabio	De Gaspari	ITA	66	13 Jun
	(110)				
75.84	Andreas	Linden	FRG	65	14 Aug
75.82	Attila	Bereith	HUN	62	16 Jul
75.80	Klaus-Peter	Schneider	FRG	58	15 May
75.80	Jukka	Miettinen	FIN	54	25 Aug
75.72	Tom	Pukstys	USA	68	18 Mar
75.72	Jan-Olov	Johansson	SWE	62	30 Aug
75.66	Andreas	Lang	GDR	65	26 Jun
75.60	Georgiy	Shapkin	SU	66	14 Feb
75.58	Vince	Labosky	USA	67	30 Apr
75.56	Juan	Quinones	CUB	64	28 Feb
	(120)				
75.56	Alfred	Grossenbacher	SWZ	59	7 May
75.54	Andrey	Chikov	SU	64	11 May
75.52	Justin	Arop	UGA	64	6 Aug
75.50	Fabianao	Fakataulavelua	FRA	62	30 Apr
75.50	Toivo	Moorast	SU	52	24 Jul
75.48	Nigel	Bevan	UK	68	9 Sep
75.46	Jens	Reimann	GDR	69	14 May
75.38	Arto	Manninen	FIN	62	28 May
75.32	Nicu	Roata	RUM	61	7 May
75.26	Wang	Wenzhong	CHN	67	28 Jun
	(130)				
75.20	Arto	Pulkkanen	FIN	64	25 Aug
75.20	Johan	van Lieshout	HOL	69	2 Sep
75.14	Knut	Hempel	FRG	65	24 Jul
75.06	Tommi	Huotilainen	FIN	67	3 Jul
75.06	Aleksandr	Fingert	SU	65	10 Aug
75.02	Chris	Athanasia	USA	68	22 May
75.02	Slawomir	Grzegorzyk	POL	64	28 May
75.02	Leons	Lapukis	SU	62	25 Sep
75.00	Ken	Asakura	JAP	61	8 May
75.00	Juha	Hentunen	FIN	60	7 Aug
	(140)				
74.96	Ferenc	Paragi	HUN	53	11 Jul
74.96	Francois	Demontigny	FRA	65	14 Aug
74.94	Aleksey	Gritskevich	SU	62	15 Aug
74.90	Jean-Baptiste	Siselo	FRA	62	21 May
74.90	Jouni	Seppälä	FIN	61	3 Jul
74.90	Steve	Roller	USA	54	16 Jul
74.84	Jan	Stark	GDR	70	6 Feb
74.82	Karl-Friedrich	Michel	FRG	65	21 May
74.80	Ivan	Soffiato	ITA	68	21 Feb
74.76	Janis	Zirnis	SU	47	2 Jul
	(150)				
74.70	Gary	Jenson	UK	67	5 Jun
74.68	Yuriy	Turlayev	SU	61	22 Jul
74.66	Tom	Jadwin	USA	58	9 Apr
74.66	Dariusz	Adamus	POL	57	4 Sep
74.66	Czeslaw	Uhl	POL	58	6 Sep
74.62	Aimo	Aho	FIN	51	25 Jun
74.58	Stanislaw	Gorak	POL	59	7 Aug
74.52	Aleksandr	Zaitsev	SU	57	2 May
74.52	Dmitriy	Polyunik	SU	69	20 Aug
74.52	Igor	Kosteryov	SU	65	28 Aug
	(160)				
74.50	Yuriy	Smirnov	SU	61	4 Jun
74.48	Andrey	Maznichenko	SU	66	10 Feb
74.38	Miroslaw	Baraniak	POL	64	13 Aug
74.32	John	Stapylton-Smith	NZ	61	19 Nov
74.30	Martín	Alvarez	CUB	60	13 Feb
74.26	Angel	Mandzhukov	BUL	69	25 Jun
74.26	Oistein	Slettvold	NOR	62	30 Jul
74.26	Mathias	Lillehelm	NOR	59	14 Aug
74.26	Arnt	Pedersen	DEN	56	3 Sep
74.24	Mikael	Olander	SWE	63	15 May
	(170)				
74.22	Constantin	Chiriac	RUM	64	22 Feb
74.18	Mizuharu	Abui	JAP		11 Sep
74.14	Colin	Mackenzie	UK	63	11 Jun
74.08	Harri	Hirvonen	FIN	64	10 Sep
74.06	Donald	Sild	SU	68	30 May
74.06	Vladimír	Danek	CS	64	2 Jun
74.04	Miroslaw	Ketrzynski	POL	65	13 Aug
74.02	Gennadiy	Ardevanidze	SU	66	26 Feb
74.00	Jim	Lothrop	USA	55	17 Jun

Mark	Name	Nat	Born	Pos	Meet	Venue	Date

Series of top marks

Mark	Name	Date	Series					
86.88	Zelezny	28 Jun	(83.10	83.52	86.88	85.50	84.80	x)
86.50	Korjus	25 Aug						
85.96	Tafelmeier	13 May	(82.32	78.64	85.96	p	p	p)
85.90	Zelezny	24 Sep	(85.90	p	p	)		
85.76	Zelezny	19 Jun	(71.12	82.04	85.76	81.52	p	80.24)
85.74	Zelezny	8 Jun	(80.56	x	x	x	84.24	85.74)
85.18	Korjus	16 Jun	(x	85.18	p	p	p	p)
84.76	Zelezny	7 Oct	(81.10	75.34	82.48	84.76	84.66	77.88)
84.66	Viljhálmsson	25 Jun						
84.38	Korjus	7 Aug						
84.34	Zelezny	2 Jun						
84.28	Korjus	25 Sep	(82.74	76.20	p	p	x	84.28)
84.14	Warsönke	29 May	(80.76	78.60	84.14	77.98	81.98	x)
84.12	Zelezny	25 Sep	(x	82.32	81.60	83.46	77.88	84.12)
84.06	Michel	13 Sep						
83.44	Viljhálmsson	5 Jul	(79.20	76.74	76.78	83.34	82.18	83.44)
83.40	Tafelmeier	28 Jun	(75.60	79.20	83.40	x	80.60	79.30)
83.38	Zelezny	27 Feb						
83.36	Viljhálmsson	7 May						
83.36	Korjus	23 Jul						
83.30	Weiss	3 Jun						
83.26	Räty	25 Sep	(80.00	76.26	83.26	78.74	80.66	80.44)
83.12	Zelezny	16 Jun	(77.58	p	x	83.12	68.64	p)
82.78	Michel	22 May						
82.76	Yevsyukov	5 Sep	(78.00	80.74	82.76	x	x	x)
82.74	Warsönke	9 Sep	(x	x	82.74	82.34	76.22	81.18)
82.72	Tafelmeier	25 Sep	(80.14	78.72	78.28	x	77.76	82.72)
82.70	Krdzalic	14 May						
82.68	Warsönke	3 Jun						
82.68	Viljhálmsson	30 Jun	(81.32	x	82.68	x	79.72	78.20)

Series not known for Korjus 86.50, 84.38 and 83.36, Viljhálmsson 84.66 and 83.36, Zelezny 84.34 and 83.38, Michel 84.06 and 82.78, Weiss 83.30, Krdzalic 82.70, Warsönke 82.68

Javelin Year List Progression (old specification)

Year	Best	10th	20th	50th	100th	Over 85.00	Over 80.00	Ave.100
1958	84.90	78.36	76.53	73.23	70.20	-	6	
1968	91.98	84.40	81.24	77.94	75.31	8	32	
1978	94.22	88.32	86.00	82.60	79.78	28	96	83.424
1979	93.84	89.74	86.50	82.42	79.56	33	87	83.734
1980	96.72	89.46	87.90	84.32	80.68	41	107	84.804
1981	92.48	89.48	88.02	83.66	80.24	39	107	84.492
1982	95.80	88.40	86.78	84.00	80.48	41	108	84.486
1983	99.72	90.58	87.80	84.56	81.14	42	125	85.065
1984	104.80	90.94	87.68	84.60	81.52	42	135	85.401
1985	96.96	91.56	88.58	84.70	81.40	46	135	85.649
(new specification)								
1986	85.74	81.86	80.66	77.38	75.30	2	25	
1987	87.66	83.24	81.74	79.04	76.68	4	34	
1988	86.88	82.70	81.30	79.58	76.48	3	43	

DECATHLON

Mark	First name	Name	Nat	Born	Pos	Meet	Venue	Date
8512	Christian	Plaziat	FRA	28.10.63	1	Int	Talence	17 Jul
		10.69 7.74 13.51 2.16 48.16			14.15 43.74 4.90 55.76 4:24.01			
8506	Valter	Külvet	SU	19.2.64	1		Staiki	2 Jul
		11.05 7.35 15.78 2.00 48.08			14.55 52.04 4.60 61.72 4:15.93			
8488	Christian	Schenk	GDR	9.2.65	1	OG	Seoul	29 Sep
		11.25 7.43 15.48 2.27 48.90			15.13 49.28 4.70 61.32 4:28.95			
8475		Schenk			2	Int	Talence	17 Jul
		11.10 7.63 15.17 2.22 49.50			15.09 47.60 4.70 60.08 4:21.41			
8447	Robert	de Wit	HOL	7.7.63	1	NC	Eindhoven	22 May
		11.07 6.98 15.88 2.04 48.80			14.32 46.20 5.00 63.94 4:20.98			
8441		Plaziat			1	NC	Tours	14 Aug
		10.81 7.65 14.12 2.13 47.78			14.24 43.38 5.10 52.70 4:31.20			
8437	Richardas	Malakhovskis	SU	28.4.65	2		Staiki	2 Jul
		10.93 7.21 14.94 2.09 47.77			14.34 44.04 4.90 59.58 4:13.67			

Mark		Name	Nat	Born	Pos	Meet	Venue	Date
8424	Aleksandr	Apaychev	SU	6.5.61	1	NC	Kiev	31 Jul
		11.07 7.42 15.46 1.95 49.28 14.05 45.88 4.90 67.64 4:28.57						
8415	Dave	Steen	CAN	14.11.59	3	Int	Talence	17 Jul
		11.02 7.56 13.99 1.98 48.22 14.95 44.08 5.20 65.36 4:21.46						
8403m	Siegfried	Wentz	FRG	7.3.60	1		Schwäb. Gmünd	26 Jun
		10.6 7.19 15.91 2.02 48.4 14.0 50.18 4.60 62.64 4:35.4						
8399	Torsten	Voss	GDR	24.3.63	2	OG	Seoul	29 Sep
		10.87 7.45 14.97 1.97 47.71 14.46 44.36 5.10 61.76 4:33.02						
8395		Apaychev			3		Staiki	2 Jul
		11.00 7.38 15.90 1.91 49.12 14.01 47.06 4.60 67.52 4:24.17						
8387	Alain	Blondel	FRA	7.12.62	4	Int	Talence	17 Jul
		11.03 7.58w 13.70 1.98 47.99 14.15 45.28 5.10 56.80 4:19.67						
8387		Voss			1		Berlin	20 Jul
		10.69w 7.61w 15.61 1.99 49.61 14.17 46.52 5.00 59.96 4:41.40						
8381	Uwe	Freimuth	GDR	10.9.61	1	Int	Götzis	19 Jun
		11.18w 7.68w 15.80 1.96 48.77 14.88 47.96 4.90 62.84 4:29.37						
8364	Igor	Maryin	SU	28.4.65	2	NC	Kiev	31 Jul
		10.91 7.79 15.10 2.04 49.22 15.71 43.16 5.00 67.70 4:32.19						
8362		Steen			2	Int	Götzis	19 Jun
		11.01w 7.78 13.35 1.99 47.70 14.71 42.86 5.10 60.06 4:21.10						
8362	Thomas	Fahner	GDR	18.7.66	3	Int	Götzis	19 Jun
		11.04 7.55w 15.01 1.93 47.94 14.54 46.66 4.60 68.40 4:27.77						
8360	Jürgen	Hingsen	FRG	25.1.58	1		Lage	21 Aug
		11.26 7.44 15.62 2.01 49.46 14.28 46.80 4.80 63.86 4:26.63						
8349		Plaziat			4	Int	Götzis	19 Jun
		10.81 7.53w 14.57 2.08 47.73 14.34 43.02 4.90 53.70 4:27.73						
8348		Apaychev			1		Sochi	22 May
		10.95 7.24 16.19 1.90 49.98 13.98 44.78 4.90 68.02 4:31.60						
8330		Schenk			5	Int	Götzis	19 Jun
		11.36 7.71w 14.76 2.20 49.23 14.99 44.86 4.40 61.38 4:16.02						
8330	Mikhail	Medved	SU	30.1.64	3	NC	Kiev	31 Jul
		11.24 7.46 15.73 2.07 50.13 14.40 45.32 5.00 64.50 4:41.26						
8328		Steen			3	OG	Seoul	29 Sep
		11.18 7.44 14.20 1.97 48.29 14.81 43.66 5.20 64.16 4:23.20						
8306		de Wit			5	Int	Talence	17 Jul
		11.06 7.02 14.45 1.98 48.35 14.25 46.00 5.00 61.42 4:20.19						
8306	Daley	Thompson	UK	30.7.58	4	OG	Seoul	29 Sep
		10.62 7.38 15.02 2.03 49.06 14.72 44.80 4.90 64.04 4:45.11						
8299	Pavel	Tarnavetskiy	SU	22.2.61	6	Int	Götzis	19 Jun
		11.03w 7.35w 15.49 1.99 48.19 14.90 45.86 5.00 58.72 4:28.09						
8293	Gary	Kinder	USA	25.10.62	1	FOT	Indianapolis	21 Jul
		10.82 7.20 16.34 2.02 49.74 14.95 47.72 5.00 66.32 4:55.39						
8290		Freimuth			1	NC	Cottbus	29 May
		11.34 7.45 15.67 1.93 49.17 14.78 49.34 5.00 64.06 4:34.36						
8289	Veroslav	Valenta	CS	25.3.65	1		Praha	29 May
		11.07 7.47w 15.47 2.00 49.67 14.49 48.84 4.80 60.68 4:35.27						
	(30/19)							
8287	Tim	Bright	USA	28.7.60	2	FOT	Indianapolis	21 Jul
		10.95 7.38 13.59 2.05 49.44 14.40 41.62 5.60 60.54 4:45.12						
	(20)							
8250	Karl-Heinz	Fichtner	FRG	16.8.62	7	Int	Götzis	19 Jun
		11.11 7.75w 15.39 1.99 49.19 15.03 43.50 5.10 56.44 4:29.22						
8245m	Anatoliy	Gazyura	SU	17.3.64	1		Kharkov	5 Jul
		10.8 7.15 15.94 1.93 48.0 14.2 47.70 4.80 60.18 4:33.4						
8245	Dave	Johnson	USA	7.4.63	3	FOT	Indianapolis	21 Jul
		11.14 7.36 14.63 2.05 49.27 14.84 45.64 4.70 68.22 4:33.92						
8244	Beat	Gähwiler	SWZ	26.1.65	8	Int	Götzis	19 Jun
		11.23 7.57 13.49 1.99 48.70 14.56 43.82 4.70 64.24 4:14.77						
8226w	Mike	Ramos	USA	1.11.62	1	vCAN	Saskatoon	14 Aug
		10.80 7.39W 15.57 2.08 50.50 14.78 44.98 5.00 60.86 4:50.82						
8209	Deszö	Szabó	HUN	4.9.67	1	NC	Budapest	7 Aug
		10.91w 7.65w 12.54 2.02 48.22 15.11 39.14 5.30 55.94 4:16.96						
8203	Aleksey	Lyach	SU	4.5.62	2		Sochi	22 May
		11.16 7.58 15.69 2.02 50.76 14.69 46.20 5.00 61.98 4:47.88						

Mark	Name		Nat	Born	Pos	Meet	Venue	Date
8203	Mike	Gonzalez	USA	13.3.64	2	vCAN	Saskatoon	14 Aug
		11.07 7.30 13.69 2.05 49.91 14.68 42.30 5.20 62.62 4:29.91						
8183	Ivan	Babiy	SU	22.7.63	9	Int	Götzis	19 Jun
		10.90 7.56w 14.51 2.02 48.72 14.07 41.50 4.80 54.12 4:29.58						
8143	Petri	Keskitalo	FIN	10.3.67	11	OG	Seoul	29 Sep
		10.94 7.56 15.34 1.97 49.94 14.25 41.86 4.80 66.64 4:55.89						
	(30)							
8141	Roman	Hraban	CS	28.6.62	2		Praha	29 May
		10.78 7.53w 16.88 1.91 49.45 15.04 47.18 4.90 60.86 5:04.81						
8126	Mikael	Olander	SWE	11.6.63	1	SEC	Auburn	13 May
		11.27w 6.79w 16.02 1.97 49.61 15.89 50.90 4.86 71.90 4:40.05						
8114	Sergey	Popov	SU	2.12.57	4		Staiki	2 Jul
		11.09 7.19 14.25 1.94 49.84 15.03 48.90 5.00 66.56 4:29.35						
8109	Bart	Goodell	USA	4.10.61	1		Santa Barbara	22 May
		10.92 7.05 15.66 1.98 49.56 14.36 48.32 4.60 60.88 4:44.8						
8107	Staffan	Blomstrand	SWE	3.8.60	1		Kessel-Lo	7 Aug
		11.10 7.34 15.15 1.87 47.89 15.79 48.20 4.70 67.62 4:35.24						
8083	Mike	Smith	CAN	16.9.67	14	OG	Seoul	29 Sep
		10.99 7.37 13.61 1.97 47.83 14.70 43.88 4.30 66.54 4:28.97						
8079	Rainer	Sonnenburg	FRG	2.10.60	11	Int	Götzis	19 Jun
		10.88 7.69w 15.24 1.96 50.00 14.51 45.16 4.20 62.68 4:38.15						
8076	Shannon	Sullivan	USA	15.10.59	4	FOT	Indianapolis	21 Jul
		11.24 6.91 13.40 1.99 49.41 14.81 46.66 5.20 57.46 4:26.46						
8075	Derek	Huff	USA	26.11.66	1		Tucson	13 Mar
		10.94 7.15 14.89 2.11 51.06 15.03 44.56 4.90 62.42 4:46.88						
8073	Igor	Samylov	SU	22.2.62	5	NC	Kiev	31 Jul
		10.98 7.47 14.18 2.19 48.15 14.58 39.32 4.50 53.18 4:35.34						
	(40)							
8063	Steve	Erickson	USA	13.1.61	1	vCAN	Saskatoon	14 Aug
		11.12 7.01 13.85 1.96 49.23 14.75 43.56 5.00 66.86 4:35.65						
8050	Dariusz	Grad	POL	7.4.63	1	NC	Grudziadz	14 Aug
		11.04 6.94w 14.23 2.04 48.60 14.60 45.16 4.80 52.98 4:23.71						
8036	Simon	Shirley	AUS	3.8.66	15	OG	Seoul	29 Sep
		11.03 7.45 14.20 1.97 48.84 15.44 41.68 4.70 64.00 4:27.48						
8023	René	Günther	GDR	7.2.65	9	Int	Talence	17 Jul
		11.46 7.24 14.93 2.04 50.55 15.03 47.84 4.80 54.78 4:22.36						
8022	Igor	Pupchonok	SU	20.5.60	1		Tashkent	4 Sep
		11.35 7.39 15.37 2.08 50.35 14.98 44.44 4.50 61.34 4:34.45						
8021	Simon	Poelman	NZ	27.5.63	16	OG	Seoul	29 Sep
		11.09 7.08 14.51 2.03 49.89 14.78 43.20 4.90 57.18 4:28.54						
8013	Chris	Branham	USA	24.1.62	1		Long Beach	12 Jun
		11.11w 7.25w 14.75 1.97 51.38 14.11 47.32 4.90 54.74 4:38.86						
7994	Lars	Warming	DEN	21.6.63	13	Int	Götzis	19 Jun
		11.08 7.31 13.54 1.93 48.03 14.34 42.60 4.70 51.94 4:17.35						
7989	Igor	Drobyshevskiy	SU	17.10.66	3		Sochi	22 May
		11.06 7.13w 11.45 2.14 48.25 14.54 42.32 4.70 54.12 4:20.88						
7976	Yevgeniy	Ovsyannikov	SU	10.7.63	4		Sochi	22 May
		10.97 7.35 15.67 2.05 50.45 14.86 46.30 4.80 49.00 4:44.46						
	(50)							
7959	Valeriy	Urbanskiy	SU	6.7.68	5		Staiki	2 Jul
		10.93 7.18 13.76 2.03 48.99 14.35 40.54 4.30 54.28 4:13.19						
7955	Hans-Ullrich	Riecke	GDR	3.10.63	2		Cottbus	18 Jun
		11.06 7.42 14.94 1.94 50.65 14.82 43.50 4.50 64.00 4:35.68						
7946	Jay	Thorson	USA	25.2.63	2	MSR	Walnut	22 Apr
		11.14 6.56 12.89 1.99 48.99 14.20 46.76 5.10 54.30 4:30.32						
7946	Patrick	Vetterli	SWZ	6.10.61	1		Balgach	17 Jul
		11.33 6.99 14.72 2.07 49.26 14.59 45.44 4.70 56.80 4:41.25						
7936	Severin	Moser	SWZ	23.10.62	2		Balgach	17 Jul
		10.88 7.13 12.93 1.86 48.78 14.59 40.46 5.10 53.42 4:16.55						
7922	Stephan	Kallenberg	FRG	4.7.63	14	Int	Götzis	19 Jun
		10.99 7.62w 14.10 1.87 48.87 15.34 47.26 4.50 63.58 4:47.76						
7922	Roman	Terekhov	SU	31.3.63	6	NC	Kiev	31 Jul
		11.31 7.26 13.42 1.95 48.91 14.78 41.76 4.70 57.42 4:15.64						
7916	Georg	Werthner	AUT	7.4.56	1	NC	Kapfenberg	21 Aug
		11.35 7.33 14.37 2.03 49.46 15.25 41.36 4.60 62.08 4:29.43						
7913	Norbert	Demmel	FRG	10.5.63	1		Dillingen	11 Sep
		11.28 6.88 15.72 1.97 49.48 14.92 49.08 4.40 57.68 4:31.25						

Mark	Name		Nat	Born	Pos	Meet	Venue	Date
7910m	Sven	Reintak	SU	17.6.63	1		Pärnu	6 Aug
		11.2 7.10 13.93 2.00 52.5 14.6 45.66 5.10 65.68 4:42.0						
	(60)							
7907	Christian	Gugler	SWZ	1.8.60	3	NC	Olten	21 Aug
		11.60 7.22 13.55 2.04 51.17 14.82 42.48 4.70 63.44 4:19.88						
7900w	Bruce	Reid	USA	10.2.67	1		Baton Rouge	24 May
		10.82W 7.43w 15.79 2.14 49.54 14.60 45.22 4.06 56.80 5:14.61						
7899m	Heinz	Hinrichs	USA	22.3.62	1		Los Angeles	28 May
		10.6 7.30 14.57 1.92 48.6 15.1 44.74 4.60 59.04 4:42.5						
7891	António	Peñalver	SPA	1.12.68	1	v4-N	Lorca	19 Jun
		11.14 7.39w 15.37 2.05 48.88 15.10 44.18 4.20 54.30 4:35.07						
7891	Dan	O'Brien	USA	18.7.66	1		Santa Barbara	26 Jun
		10.72w 7.45w 13.70 2.01 48.77 14.54 43.44 4.20 52.44 4:35.1						
7887	Gerald	Borchert	FRG	3.9.66	3	NC	Rhede	10 Jul
		11.14 6.78 13.29 2.06 49.59 14.26 41.74 4.50 63.74 4:31.99						
7882	Carlos	O'Connell	IRL	21.6.63	1		Emmitsburg	5 Jun
		10.89 7.50 13.05 1.92 48.84 14.59 41.70 4.40 54.96 4:21.75						
7881	John	Schwepker	USA	24.9.65	1		Cape Girardeau	5 Jun
		10.84 7.25 13.15 2.03 49.54 14.96 40.10 5.18 57.68 4:57.02						
7878	Andrey	Atsuta	SU	20.1.62	1		Irkutsk	26 Jun
		11.20 7.10 15.82 1.80 48.74 14.93 47.12 4.90 54.32 4:40.01						
7877	Sasa	Karan	YUG	7.4.65	1	NC	Beograd	5 Jun
		11.15 6.89 14.17 2.00 49.16 14.74 49.56 4.30 54.22 4:26.04						
	(70)							
7873w	John	Sayre	USA	25.3.61	2		Santa Barbara	26 Jun
		11.12w 6.71W 14.59 1.98 50.07 15.02 46.12 4.90 63.90 4:50.1						
7872	Jim	Connolly	USA	24.3.63	8	FOT	Indianapolis	21 Jul
		11.20 6.83 13.95 1.99 50.03 15.10 40.00 4.70 57.64 4:34.10						
7866	Sergey	Zhelanov	SU	14.6.57	7	NC	Kiev	31 Jul
		11.37 7.31 13.86 2.07 49.43 15.07 41.92 4.90 57.00 4:44.70						
7861	Kris	Szabadhegy	USA	23.7.64	2		San Francisco	31 Mar
		11.32 7.31 14.22 1.94 49.63 14.60 41.22 4.60 57.70 4:25.23						
7856	Steve	Odgers	USA	9.11.61	2		Lage	21 Aug
		11.09 6.89 14.61 1.92 48.13 14.92 44.78 4.40 61.40 4:34.46						
7853	André	Preysing	GDR	6.10.66	1	v3-N	Praha	3 Sep
		11.17 7.09 13.10 2.10 48.51 14.67 40.46 5.00 48.66 4:37.16						
7845w	Rusty	Hunter	USA	4.9.65	1	SWC	Austin	13 May
		10.92w 7.09 12.25 1.95 49.25 14.76W 39.90 5.00 60.02 4:34.9						
7833	Kevin	McGorty	USA	12.4.65	1		Tallahassee	20 Jun
		11.39 7.27 12.65 2.07 49.93 14.70 38.22 4.77 56.94 4:21.61						
7822	Christian	Deick	FRG	8.6.65	1	v2-N	Lage	21 Aug
		11.10 7.65 14.73 1.95 50.73 15.25 47.08 4.30 55.54 4:37.36						
7821w	Ed	Brown	USA	20.7.58	3		Santa Barbara	26 Jun
		11.34w 7.20W 12.66 2.10 50.00 14.78 38.52 4.50 58.36 4:17.1						
	(80)							
7807	Nikolay	Zayats	SU	3.2.67		2	Irkutsk	26 Jun
		10.89 7.21 14.70 1.98 48.62 14.37 41.80 5.00 50.12 5:11.64						
7805	Gary	Armstrong	USA	31.12.60	2		Tallahassee	20 Jun
		11.30 7.12 13.23 1.98 49.79 15.52 43.14 4.87 59.20 4:27.05						
7796	Tiit	Pahker	SU	22.12.58	7		Sochi	22 May
		10.85 7.05w 13.23 2.02 50.78 15.12 43.28 5.00 54.36 4:42.64						
7795	Frank	Müller	FRG	18.6.68	1		Hannover	29 May
		10.92 7.27 12.98 2.01 48.46 15.30 42.34 4.20 59.52 4:30.18						
7790	Michael	Kohnle	FRG	3.5.70	1	vPOL-j	Wattenscheid	26 Jun
		10.91 7.03 13.14 2.02 49.27 14.71 40.24 4.90 56.18 4:48.76						
7779	Bruno	Chirco	FRG	7.4.66	5	NC	Rhede	10 Jul
		11.28 7.22 14.41 1.97 49.61 15.84 46.24 4.60 52.60 4:22.83						
7778	Patrick	Gellens	FRA	8.2.59	14	Int	Talence	17 Jul
		10.95 7.29 13.45 1.95 50.25 15.65 43.00 5.00 52.46 4:31.81						
7762	Jann	Trefny	SWZ	10.1.66	4		Balgach	17 Jul
		11.21 6.84 13.04 1.98 48.57 14.35 40.96 4.30 55.70 4:15.01						
7761	Marco	Rossi	ITA	7.7.63	18	Int	Götzis	19 Jun
		10.94 7.05w 13.80 1.96 49.11 14.52 42.34 4.30 51.30 4:22.95						
7760	Michael	Rückel	FRG	24.9.63	7	NC	Rhede	10 Jul
		11.22 7.03 16.35 1.94 51.00 15.00 49.58 3.80 69.10 4:55.49						
	(90)							

Mark	Name		Nat	Born	Pos	Meet	Venue	Date
7753m	Vilnis	Valkins	SU	5.7.62	1		Riga	29 Jun
		11.1 7.00 14.00 1.95 49.6 14.4 39.52 4.70 54.18 4:18.6						
7752	Vladimir	Kryuchkov	SU	28.7.62	1		Odessa	20 Aug
		11.33 7.08 14.46 2.05 50.78 15.20 43.54 4.80 54.00 4:39.23						
7748	Tony	Allen-Cooksey	USA	7.7.56	2		San Diego	21 May
		11.33 7.68 14.23 1.92 50.72 14.67 42.02 4.35 55.72 4:31.07						
7739	Lee Fu-An		TAI	6.4.64				16 Apr
7719m	Aleksey	Kostenich	SU	30.10.66	2		Kharkov	5 Jul
		11.3 7.34 12.44 2.14 50.0 14.8 39.50 4.50 56.10 4:26.8						
7714	Ramil	Ganeyev	SU	23.9.68	7		Staiki	2 Jul
		10.96 7.03 13.16 2.09 50.09 14.78 42.06 4.60 53.18 4:46.42						
7711	Stuart	Andrews	AUS	17.1.62	1		Adelaide	6 Feb
		11.12 7.22 12.83 1.86 50.4 15.1 48.06 4.70 59.44 4:37.2						
7707	Alex	Kruger	UK	18.11.63	2	v4-N	Lorca	19 Jun
		11.64 7.27 13.51 2.20 49.8115.23 41.02 4.50 52.80 4:37.55						
7703	Knut	Gundersen	NOR	24.9.64	2		San Angelo	18 May
		11.19w 7.27w 15.03 1.98 50.42 15.12 41.86 4.30 56.64 4:35.68						
7702	Sergey	Lisitskiy	SU	23.7.63	8		Sochi	22 May
		11.29 6.93 15.86 1.99 50.50 15.99 49.48 4.60 54.90 4:47.72						
	(100)							

Mark	Name		Nat	Born	Date
7694	Sergey	Tomshin	SU	67	26 Jun
7684	Andrzej	Wyzykowski	POL	60	24 Jul
7683	Aleksandr	Tsyoma	SU	61	12 Jun
7677w	Mark	Sanders	USA	63	26 Jun
7676	Marko	Vunder	SU	67	22 May
7670	Luis	Milanes	CUB	63	26 Feb
7667	Oleg	Semyonov	SU	67	4 Sep
7659	Igor	Asmetkin	SU	66	22 May
7659	Robert	Zmelík	CS	69	28 Jul
7654m	Alben	Kardamov	BUL	66	19 Jun
	(110)				
7648	Aleksandr	Areshin	SU	61	16 Aug
7637w	Jari	Näkki	FIN	67	3 Jul
7629	Csaba	Fábián	HUN	67	7 Aug
7628	Viktor	Radchenko	SU	68	22 May
7619	Lajos	Sárközi	HUN	67	7 Aug
7610	Greg	Richards	UK	56	23 Aug
7599	Sten	Ekberg	SWE	64	17 Jul
7596	Eduard	Hämäläinen	SU	69	28 Jul
7594	Michael	Kühne	GDR	68	18 Jun
7592	Sergey	Mikish	SU	66	22 May
	(120)				
7590	Ralf	Oberhofer	FRG	66	16 May
7588	Goran	Kabic	YUG	65	17 Jul
7581	Jürgen	Hoppe	FRG	65	21 Aug
7579	Mark	Luscombe	UK	64	8 May
7578	Viktor	Shmalko	SU	67	2 Jul
7577	Gernot	Kellermayr	AUT	66	19 Jun
7559m	Aleksandr	Stavro	SU	63	16 Jun
7548	Katsuhika	Matsuda	JAP	65	4 Sep
7544	Olivier	Dekernavanois	FRA	63	13 Aug
7542m	Borislav	Kolov	BUL	65	7 Aug
	(130)				
7538	Edgar	Maihöfer	FRG	65	10 Jul
7538	Eugene	Gilkes	UK	62	21 Aug
7529	Henrik	Dagård	SWE	69	3 Jul
7527	Alfred	Stummer	AUT	62	21 Aug
7525	Craig	Branstrom	USA	64	21 Apr
7519	Santiago	Wellado	ESA	63	29 Sep
7515	Steve	Degner	USA	62	28 May
7510	Peter	Neumaier	FRG	67	11 Sep
7504	Janusz	Lesniewicz	POL	55	24 Jul
7503	Jerzy	Holowenko	POL	65	28 Aug
	(140)				
7501	Sergey	Kolmakov	SU	69	7 Jul
7501	Jean-Bernard	Royer	FRA	62	13 Aug
7499	Ernesto	Betancourt	CUB	62	26 Feb
7499m	Asen	Aleksandrov	BUL	69	7 Aug
7498	Miroslav	Kvasov	SU	66	20 Aug
7496	Athanassios	Pampliaris	GRE	63	28 Aug
7487m	Jens	Hohaus	FRG	67	17 Jun
7484	Aivar	Haller	SU	63	12 Jul
7483	Thomas	Stewens	FRG	66	10 Jul
7482	Kip	Janvrin	USA	65	26 May
	(150)				
7482	Kaj	Ekman	FIN	64	6 Aug
7479	Igor	Oleynik	SU	65	31 Jul
7473	Miguel	Quintero	CUB	66	21 May
7473m	Vladimir	Romanov	SU	61	5 Jul
7472	Rich	Schindelar	USA		20 Mar
7471m	Falk	Schade	FRG	67	17 Jun
7469m	Ivan	Kirdoda	SU	66	16 Jun
7466m	Mikhail	Romanyuk	SU	62	24 Apr
7465	Peter	Hunt	USA	66	28 May
7464	Norbert	Lampe	GDR	70	13 Aug
	(160)				
7460	Andrey	Chernyavskiy	SU	68	28 May
7453	Frédéric	Sacco	FRA	61	17 Jul
7450	Stefan	Haigis	FRG	67	10 Jul

Decathlon Year List Progression

Year	Best	10th	20th	50th	100th	Over	Over
1984	8847	8491	8207	7946	7630	39	c181
1985	8559	8317	8132	7883	7676	30	151
1986	8811	8302	8170	7920	7686	40	140
1987	8680	8304	8144	7918	7631	40	135
1988	8512	8387	8287	7976	7702	47	142

4 x 100 METRES RELAY

Mark	Name		Pos	Meet	Venue	Date
38.19	USSR	(Bryzgin, Krylov, Muravyov, Savin)	1	OG	Seoul	1 Oct
38.28	UK	(Bunney, Regis, McFarlane, Christie)	2	OG	Seoul	1 Oct
38.40	France	(Marie Rose, Sangouma, Quenéhérvé, Morinière)	3	OG	Seoul	1 Oct
38.47	Jamaica	(Faulknor, Meghoo, Wright, Mair)	4	OG	Seoul	1 Oct
38.48	Cuba	(Simón, Peñalver, Querol, Jefferson)	1		Habana	30 Jul
38.49	France	(Marie Rose, Sangouma, Quenéhérvé, Morinière)	1s1	OG	Seoul	1 Oct
38.52	UK	(Bunney, Regis, McFarlane, Christie)	2s1	OG	Seoul	1 Oct
38.53	GDR	(Matthes, Bringmann, Prenzler, Emmelmann)	1	vFRG	Düsseldorf	19 Jun
38.54	FRG	(Heer, Haas, Klein, Schweisfurth)	1	R W	Koblenz	28 Aug
38.54	Italy	(Madonia, Floris, Pavoni, Tilli)	5	OG	Seoul	1 Oct
38.55	USSR	(Bryzgin, Krylov, Muravyov, Savin)	1s2	OG	Seoul	1 Oct
38.55	FRG	(Heer, Haas, Klein, Schweisfurth)	6	OG	Seoul	1 Oct
38.57	Cuba	(Simón, Peñalver, Querol, Jefferson)	1		Sevilla	1 Jun
38.58	Canada	(McKoy, Mahorn, Williams, Johnson)	1	vITA	Cesenatico	13 Aug
38.59	UCLA (USA)	(Marsh, Everett, S.Lewis, Thomas)	1	Pac 10	Westwood	22 May
38.59	Nigeria	(Adeyanju, Imo, Adeniken, Ezinwa)	1rB		Bern	23 Aug
38.62	GDR	(Matthes, Heimrath, Prenzler, Emmelmann)	1	OD	Berlin	29 Jun
38.63	Santa Monica TC (USA)	(Marsh, Witherspoon, DeLoach, C.Lewis)	1	APM	Hengelo	14 Aug
38.65	USA	(Robinson, L.McNeill, Smith, Mitchell)	1	VD	Bruxelles	19 Aug
38.65	Italy	(Madonia, Floris, Pavoni, Tilli)	2s2	OG	Seoul	1 Oct
38.66A	Santa Monica TC (USA)	(Marsh, Witherspoon, DeLoach, C.Lewis)	1		Sestriere	11 Aug
38.68	Italy	(Madonia, Floris, Pavoni, Tilli)	2	vCAN	Cesenatico	13 Aug
38.71	Texas A&M Un. (USA)	(Felton, Florence, Cason, Kerr)	1h2	NCAA	Eugene	2 Jun
38.75	France	Marie Rose, Sangouma, Quenéhérvé, Trouabal)	2rB		Bern	23 Aug
38.75	Jamaica	(Faulknor, Meghoo, Wright, Mair)	3s1	OG	Seoul	1 Oct
38.75	FRG	(Heer, Haas, Klein, Schweisfurth)	4s1	OG	Seoul	1 Oct
38.76	Cuba	(Simón, Peñalver, Querol, Jefferson)	1		Schwechat	16 Jun
38.77	FRG	(Heer, Haas, Klein, Schweisfurth	1	ASV	Köln	21 Aug
38.78	GDR	(Lassler, Heimrath, Schwabe, Schröder)	1		Cottbus	17 Jun
38.79	TCU (USA/JAM)	(Tatum, Allen, Stewart/JAM, Sholars)	1h1	NCAA	Eugene	2 Jun
38.79	UCLA (USA)	(Marsh, Everett, S.Lewis, Thomas)	1h3	NCAA	Eugene	2 Jun
	(31/11)					
38.80	Hungary	(Tatár, Kovács, Fetter, Havas)	1	v2 N	Athinai	4 Jun
38.90	Japan	(Aoto, Yamauchi, Kurihara, Takano)	5s1	OG	Seoul	1 Oct
39.03	Czechoslovakia	(Hudec, Roun, Belosek, Valík)	1	v2 N	Praha	2 Jul
39.10	Poland	(Helbik, Popa, Pradzynski, Kamenicki)	1	Nar	Sofia	26 Jun
39.13	Ghana	(Akogyiram, Gariba, Mills, Tuffour)	3h2	OG	Seoul	30 Sep
39.20A	Spain	(Gascon, Talavera, Rocandio, Arques)	1h1	IbAmC	Ciudad México	24 Jul
39.20A	Brasil	(Jailto Bonfim, Pereira, Menezes, da Silva)	2h1	IbAmC	Ciudad México	24 Jul
39.43	Korea	(Sung, Shim, Kim, Chang)	7s1	OG	Seoul	1 Oct
39.47	Kenya	(Nyangau, Ondiek, Kipkemboi, Wekesa)	6s2	OG	Seoul	1 Oct
	(20)					
39.49	Bulgaria	(Lyubikov, Atanasov, Karadimov, Grigorov)	2	v2 N	Praha	2 Jul
39.54A	RSA	(Bosman, Oosthuizen, Nzimande, Rossouw)	1		Johannesburg	23 Apr
39.61	Portugal	(Abrantes, Curvelo, Agostinho, Barroso)	3h4	OG	Seoul	30 Sep
39.66	Sénegal	(Seck, Dias, Tamba, Mbaye)	3	AfrC	Annaba	1 Sep
39.67	China	(Cai, Li Feng, Li Tao, Zheng)	4h2	OG	Seoul	30 Sep
39.73	Holland	(Kroch, von der Klundert, Ooievaar, de Kom)	5	APM	Hengelo	14 Aug
39.74A	México	(Adam, Nava, Ruiz, Elizondo)	3h1	IbAmC	Ciudad México	24 Jul
39.75	Belgium	(Desruelles, Cuypers, Stevens, Fischer)	1		Bruxelles	3 Sep
39.93	Greece	(Genovelis, Papanikolau, Vagenas, Stratos)	2	BalkG	Ankara	16 Jul
	(29 nations)					

4 x 400 METRES RELAY

Mark	Name		Pos	Meet	Venue	Date
2:56.16	USA		1	OG	Seoul	1 Oct
		(Everett 43.79, S.Lewis 43.69, Robinzine 44.74, Reynolds 43.94)				
2:59.71A	CUBA	(Martínez, Valentín, Stevens, Hernández)	1	IbAmC	Ciudad México	24 Jul
2:59.91	UCLA (USA)		1	NCAA	Eugene	4 Jun
		(S.Lewis 45.0, Young 44.4, Everett 45.3, Thomas 45.2)				
3:00.30	Jamaica		2	OG	Seoul	1 Oct
		(Davis 45.1, Morris 44.8, Graham 45.8, Cameron 44.6)				
3:00.56	FRG		3	OG	Seoul	1 Oct
		(Dobeleit 45.8, Itt 44.2, Vaihinger 45.9, Lübke 44.6)				

Mark	Name	Nat	Born	Pos	Meet	Venue	Date
3:00.60	GDR			1s2	OG	Seoul	30 Sep
	(Carlowitz 44.9, Müller 45.5, Schersing 44.9, Schönlebe 45.3)						
3:00.66	FRG			2s2	OG	Seoul	30 Sep
	(Dobeleit, Henrich, Vaihinger 44.9, Lübke 44.9)						
3:00.68	Florida (USA)			2	NCAA	Eugene	4 Jun
	(Long 45.6, Mitchell 44.4, T.Johnson 45.5, M.Everett 45.2)						
3:00.81	UCLA (USA)			1	MSR	Walnut	24 Apr
	(S.Lewis 45.9, Young 44.9, Thomas 45.2, Everett 44.8)						
3:00.88	Athletics West (USA)			2	MSR	Walnut	24 Apr
	(Baptiste, Redwine , Haley 45.1, Reynolds 44.4)						
3:00.92	GDR (Schober, Carlowitz, Schersing, Schönlebe)			1	vFRG	Düsseldorf	20 Jun
3:00.94	Jamaica (Graham, Morris, Cameron, Davis)			3s2	OG	Seoul	30 Sep
3:01.13	Nigeria (Uti, Ugbisie, Amike, Egbunike 44.7)			4s2	OG	Seoul	30 Sep
3:01.13	GDR			4	OG	Seoul	1 Oct
	(Carlowitz 45.0, Schersing 44.8, Müller 46.6, Schönlebe 44.7)						
3:01.59	Yugoslavia (Karaulic, Popovic, Brankovic, Macev)			5s2	OG	Seoul	30 Sep
3:02.00	UK			5	OG	Seoul	1 Oct
	(Whittle 45.7, Akabusi 44.8, Bennett 46.1, Brown 45.4)						
3:02.00	GDR (Schimmer, Schersing, Carlowitz, Schönlebe)			1	vITA	Neubrandenburg	10 Jul
3:02.16	USA			1h3	OG	Seoul	30 Sep
	(Valmon 45.3, Robinzine 45.6, McKay 45.1, S.Lewis 46.2)						
3:02.44	Florida (USA) (T.Johnson, Mitchell , Long , M.Everett)			1	FlaR	Gainesville	26 Mar
3:02.49	Australia			6	OG	Seoul	1 Oct
	(Ballard 46.4, Garner 45.1, Murphy 46.6, Clark 44.4)						
3:02.50	Nigeria			7	OG	Seoul	1 Oct
	(Uti 45.0, Ugbisie 45.3, Amike 46.2, Egbunike 46.0)						
3:02.51	Baylor (USA) (Thompson, Stanford, Johnson, Pierre)			1	SWC	Austin	15 May
3:02.52	Mazda TC (USA) (McCoy, T.Johnson, D.Davis, Rambo)			2	FlaR	Gainesville	26 Mar
3:02.53	Sports TC (USA/JAM)			3	MSR	Walnut	24 Apr
	(W.Smith, Senior/JAM, Page, Franks)						
3:02.80	USA (UCLA)			1		Tempe	2 Apr
	(Washington 46.1, Young 45.3, S.Lewis 45.6, Everett 45.8)						
3:02.84	USA			1s1	OG	Seoul	30 Sep
	(Valmon 45.3, Robinzine 45.2, McKay 45.3, S.Lewis 47.0)						
3:03.05	Un. of Illinois (USA			1	DrakeR	Des Moines	30 Apr
	(Tolbert 46.6, Bridges 45.4, Hamer 46.6, Simon 44.5)						
3:03.12	FRG (Koffler, Dobeleit, Itt, Schlepütz)			2	vGDR	Düsseldorf	20 Jun
3:03.13	USSR			1	v2 N	Portsmouth	19 Jun
	(Bazarov 46.5, Kornilov 45.3, Lomtyev 45.6, Prosin 45.8)						
3:03.18	Florida Un. (USA)			1h1	TexR	Austin	9 Apr
	(Johnson 46.8, Mitchell 45.6, Long 45.2, M.Everett 45.6)						
	(30/10)						
3:03.24	Kenya (Sawe, Sang, Ereng, Kipkemboi)			2s1	OG	Seoul	30 Sep
3:03.68	Italy (Ribaud, Zuliani, Petrella, Sabia)			2		Rieti	31 Aug
3:03.80	Japan (Koike, Yamauchi, Kawasumi, Takano)			6s2	OG	Seoul	30 Sep
3:04.56A	Venezuela (Bodington, Phillips, Aguilar, Malave)			2	IbAmC	Ciudad México	24 Jul
3:04.92	France (Boussemart, Diagana, Lauret, Pat.Barré)			1		Talence	17 Jul
3:05.14A	Portugal (Curvela, Lomba, Abrantes, A.Silva)			3	IbAmC	Ciudad México	24 Jul
3:05.34	Bulgaria (Kharizanov, Rangelov, Tomov, Demirev)			2	BalkG	Ankara	17 Jul
3:05.41A	Nord Transvaal (RSA)			1		Bloemfontein	16 Apr
3:06.03	Barbados (Straughn, Louis, Ince, Forde)			5h1	OG	Seoul	30 Sep
3:06.16	Greece (Arhentidis, V.Kalliposis, S.Kalliposis, Kalogiannis)			3	BalkG	Ankara	17 Jul
	(20)						
3:06.74	Czechoslovakia (Navesnák, Hysek, Roun, Kucej)			1	v2 N	Praha	3 Jul
3:06.86	Hungary (Katona, Molnár, Németh, Menczer)			2	v2 N	Athinai	5 Jun
3:06.93	Sénegal (Diarra, Niang, Fall, Dia Bâ)			4h3	OG	Seoul	30 Sep
3:07.11	Ethiopia (Tesfaye, Worku, Ojulu, Gudeta)			1	AfrC	Annaba	2 Sep
3:07.13	Canada (Smith, Folkes, Graham, Skerrit)			2	vITA	Cesenatico	14 Aug
3:07.15	Ivory Coast (Kpidi, Djédjémel, Djetnan, Tiacoh)			6s1	OG	Seoul	30 Sep
3:07.72	Spain (Moreno, Sanchez, Alonso, Cornet)			1	WA	Bruxelles	18 Jun
3:07.73	Ireland			2		Talence	17 Jul
3:08.11	Zambia (Matete, Musonda, Douglas, Jonathan)			1h1	AfrC	Annaba	1 Sep
3:08.13	Sweden (Avebäck, Sedlacek, Granat, Josjö)			1	vFIN	Helsinki	4 Sep
	(30 nations						

5000 METRES TRACK WALK

Mark	Name		Nat	Born	Pos	Meet	Venue	Date
18:11.41i	Ronald	Weigel	GDR	8.8.59	1		Wien	13 Feb
18:25.94i	Frants	Kostyukevich	SU	4.4.63	1		Minsk	29 Jan
18:37.54io	Jozef	Pribilinec	CS	6.7.60	1		Jablonec	20 Feb
18:38.6i		Kostyukevich			1		Mimck	29 Jan
18:39.2i	Yevgeniy	Misyulya	SU	13.3.64	2		Minsk	29 Jan
18:42.55io	Roman	Mrázek	CS	21.1.62	2	NC	Jablonec	20 Feb
18:44.40		Pribilinec			1	EI	Budapest	6 Mar
18:44.93i		Mrazek			2	EI	Budapest	6 Mar
18:45.50i	Pavol	Blazek	CS	9.7.58	2		Wien	13 Feb
18:45.91i	Sandor	Urbanik	HUN	15.12.64	3	EI	Budapest	6 Mar
18:49.10i	Erling	Andersen	NOR	22.9.60	4	EI	Budapest	6 Mar
18:49.49i	Zdzislaw	Szlapkin	POL	18.1.61	5	EI	Budapest	6 Mar
18:52.55i		Weigel			1		Torino	10 Feb
18:53.25i	Guillaume	Leblanc	(10)CAN	14.4.62	1	TAC	New York	26 Feb
18:54.67i	Jos	Martens	BEL	64	6	EI	Budapest	6 Mar
18:58.40i	Giovanni	Di Benedictis	ITA	8.1.68	7	EI	Budapest	6 Mar
18:59.30i	Ján	Záhoncík	CS	23.4.65	3		Wien	13 Feb
18:59.67i	Hartwig	Gauder	GDR	10.11.54	2		Torino	10 Feb
	(18/14)							
19:00.02	Lyubomir	Ivanov	BUL	9.3.60	8	EI	Budapest	6 Mar
19:09.73i	Jean-Claude	Corre	FRA	14.9.62	1	NC	Liévin	21 Feb
19:11.73i	Carlo	Mattioli	ITA	23.10.54	3		Torino	10 Feb
19:13.2	David	Smith	AUS	24.7.55	1		Brisbane	26 Feb
19:15.0'i	Reima	Salonen	FIN	19.11.55	1		Truku	9 Mar
19:15.92i	Mikhail	Shchennikov (20)	SU	24.12.67	1		Valencia	17 Feb
19:17.48io	Igor	Kollár	CS	25.6.55	4	NC	Jablonec	20 Feb
19:18.30i	Sergey	Protsyshin	SU	26.2.59	10	EI	Budapest	6 Mar
19:21.59i	Igor	Plotnikov	SU	12.7.64	2		Minsk	6 Mar
19:21.81i	Jan	Staaf	SWE	11.1.62	12	EI	Budapest	6 Mar

io indicates infoors and on a track over 200m in circumference

10000 METRES TRACK WALK

Mark	Name		Nat	Born	Pos	Meet	Venue	Date
38:46.0i	Reima	Salonen	FIN	19.11.55	1		Turku	9 Mar
38:51.04i	Ronald	Weigel	GDR	8.8.59	1	NC	Senftenberg	26 Feb
39:05.8	Maurizio	Damilano	ITA	4.6.57	1		Limbiate	25 Oct
39:07.38	Axel	Noack	GDR	23.9.61	1	vITA	Neubrandenburg	10 Jul
39:13.0	Jozef	Pribilinec	CS	6.7.60	1		Lomelo	18 Jun
39:13.15i	Hartwig	Gauder	GDR	10.11.54	2	NC	Senftenberg	26 Feb
39:27.59	Mikhail	Shchennikov	SU	24.12.67	1	vUK,Fra	Portsmouth	19 Jun
39:28.0i	Frants	Kostyukevich	SU	4.4.63	1		Minsk	4 Mar
39:32.0i	Igor	Plotnikov	SU	12.7.64	2		Minsk	4 Mar
39:42.64	Zdzislaw	Szlapkin	POL	18.1.61	1		Stargard	10 Sep
	(10)							
39:46.84		Damilano			2	vGDR	Neubrandenburg	10 Jul
39:48.54		Szlapkin			1		Lublin	6 Aug
39:49.56	Ljubomir	Ivanov	BUL	9.3.60	1	NC	Sofia	3 Sep
40:04.7i	Vladimir	Zoiko	SU	65	3		Minsk	4 Mar
40:11.0i	Andrey	Popov	SU	28.4.64	1		Leningrad	31 Jan
40:13.83	Giovanni	Di Benedictis	ITA	8.1.68	3	vGDR	Neubrandenburg	10 Jul
40:14.5i	Nikolay	Matveyev	SU	15.1.55	4		Minsk	4 Mar
40:19.0i	Sergey	Abiralo	SU	22.1.61	5		Minsk	4 Mar
40:21.44	Pavol	Blazek	CS	9.7.58	2	PTS	Bratislava	8 Jun
40:22.0i	Vitaliy	Matsko	SU	60	2		Leningrad	31 Jan
40:23.0i	Oleg	Troshin	SU	65	2		Moskva	31 Jan
40:23.85	Dietmar	Meisch	GDR	10.2.59	4	vITA	Neubrandenburg	10 Jul

20 KILOMETRES WALK

Mark	Name		Nat	Born	Pos	Meet	Venue	Date
1:19:08	Mikhail	Shchennikov	SU	24.12.67	1	NC	Kiev	30 Jul
1:19:16	Yevgeniy	Misyulya	SU	13.3.64	2	NC	Kiev	30 Jul
1:19:22.5t	Aleksey	Pershin	SU	23.9.62	1	SGP	Fana	7 May
1:19:39	Frants	Kostyukevich	SU	4.4.63	1	Znam	Leningrad	11 Jun
1:19:47	Viktor	Mostovik	SU	7.1.63	3	NC	Kiev	30 Jul
1:19:57	Jozef	Pribilinec	CS	6.7.60	1	OG	Seoul	23 Sep
1:20:00	Ronald	Weigel	GDR	8.8.59	2	OG	Seoul	23 Sep

Mark	Name		Nat	Born	Pos	Meet	Venue	Date
1:20:06	Sergey	Protsyshin	SU	26.2.59	4	NC	Kiev	30 Jul
1:20:08	Valdas	Kazlauskas	SU	7.8.58	5	NC	Kiev	30 Jul
1:20:10	Igor	Lyubomirov	SU	9.11.61	2	Znam	Leningrad	11 Jun
	(10)							
1:20:14	Georgiy	Korneyev	SU	61	6	NC	Kiev	30 Jul
1:20:14	Maurizio	Damilano	ITA	4.6.57	3	OG	Seoul	23 Sep
1:20:17	Pavol	Blazek	CS	9.7.58	1		L'Hospitalet	24 Apr
1:20:19	Vyacheslav	Smirnov	SU	57	3	Znam	Leningrad	11 Jun
1:20:26		Damilano			1	NC	Piacenza	9 Oct
1:20:34	José	Marin	SPA	20.1.50	4	OG	Seoul	23 Sep
1:20:39	Axel	Noack	GDR	23.9.61	1		Naumburg	1 May
1:20:40	Ralf	Kowalsky	GDR	22.3.62	2		Naumburg	1 May
1:20:40		Pershin			1	NC-w	Sochi	21 Feb
1:20:43	Anatoliy	Solomin	SU	2.7.52	4	Znam	Leningrad	11 Jun
1:20:43	Ljubomir	Ivanov	BUL	9.3.60	1	NM	Sofia	26 Jun
1:20:43	Roman	Mrázek (20)	CS	21.1.62	5	OG	Seoul	23 Sep
1:20:47		Protsyshin			5	Znam	Leningrad	11 Jun
1:20:47		Shchennikov			6	OG	Seoul	23 Sep
1:20:49		Kazlauskas			2	NC-w	Sochi	21 Feb
1:20:50		Kostyukevich			7	NC	Kiev	30 Jul
1:20:52	Zdzislaw	Szlapkin	POL	18.1.61	1		Warszawa	19 Jun
1:20:53	Artur	Shumak	SU	63	8	NC	Kiev	30 Jul
1:20:53	Carlos	Mercenario	MEX	3.5.67	7	OG	Seoul	23 Sep
1:20:57		Weigel			1	NC	Rostock	24 Jun
1:20:58	Valeriy	Borisov	SU	18.9.66	6	Znam	Leningrad	11 Jun
	(31/24)							
1:21:11	Oleg	Plastun	SU	20.9.63	7	Znam	Leningrad	11 Jun
1:21:18?	Ernesto	Canto	MEX	18.10.59	1		Montreal	7 May
	1:22:52				2		Värnamo	13 May
1:21:18	Giovanni	Di Benedictis	ITA	8.1.68	9	OG	Seoul	23 Sep
1:21:19	Simon	Baker	AUS	6.2.58	1	NC	Canberra	27 Aug
1:21:29	Guillaume	Leblanc	CAN	14.4.62	10	OG	Seoul	23 Sep
1:21:33	Nikolay	Vinnichenko	SU	12.11.58	4		Sochi	21 Feb
	(30)							
1:21:34	Sandor	Urbanik	HUN	15.12.64	1		Szeged	10 Jul
1:21:45	Bernd	Gummelt	GDR	21.12.63	2	NC	Rostock	24 Jun
1:21:53	Daniel	Plaza	SPA	3.7.66	12	OG	Seoul	23 Sep
1:21:58	Andrey	Popov	SU	28.4.64	8	Znam	Leningrad	11 Jun
1:22:00	Ricardo	Pueyo	SPA	1.3.67	1		Llinars Valles	7 Feb
1:22:00	Joel	Sanchez	MEX	15.9.66				7 May
1:22:03	Ian	McCombie	UK	11.1.61	13	OG	Seoul	23 Sep
1:22:06	Vitaliy	Popovich	SU	57	1		Moskva	30 Apr
1:22:07	Igor	Plotnikov	SU	12.7.64	9	Znam	Leningrad	11 Jun
1:22:07	Yevgeniy	Zaikin	SU	20.7.57	11	NC	Kiev	30 Jul
	(40)							
1:22:09	Vladimir	Druchik	SU	25.6.65	12	NC	Kiev	30 Jul
1:22:10	Walter	Arena	ITA	30.5.64	2		Porto San Giórgio	26 Jun
1:22:10	Carlo	Mattioli	ITA	23.10.54	3		Porto San Giórgio	26 Jun
1:22:12	German	Skurygin	SU	63	10	Znam	Leningrad	11 Jun
1:22:15	Dietmar	Meisch	GDR	10.2.59	3	NC	Rostock	24 Jun
1:22:22	Aleksandr	Turov	SU	11.2.62	11	Znam	Leningrad	11 Jun
1:22:28.0t	Anatoliy	Gorshkov	SU	4.8.58	2	SGP	Fana	7 May
1:22:29	Andrew	Jachno	AUS	13.4.62	2	NC	Canberra	27 Aug
1:22:36	Vladimir	Zoyko	SU	65	5	NC-w	Sochi	21 Feb
1:22:38	Aleksey	Rodionov	SU	57	12	Znam	Leningrad	11 Jun
	(50)							
1:22:42	Reima	Salonen	FIN	19.11.55	2		Ruse	17 Apr
1:22:43	Mauricio	Villegas	MEX					7 May
1:22:43	Martial	Fesselier	FRA	9.10.61	16	OG	Seoul	23 Sep
1:22:45	Jimmy	McDonald	IRL	11.4.64	17	OG	Seoul	23 Sep
1:22:50	Oleg	Troshin	SU	65	2		Moskva	10 Jul
1:22:54	Gianni	Perricelli	ITA	25.8.67	3	NC	Piacenza	9 Oct
1:22:55	Antanas	Grigaliunas	SU	14.10.61	13	NC	Kiev	30 Jul
1:22:55	Thierry	Toutain	FRA	14.2.62	18	OG	Seoul	23 Sep
1:22:56	Vladimir	Bolotov	SU	20.8.63	14	NC	Kiev	30 Jul

Mark	Name		Nat	Born	Pos	Meet	Venue	Date
1:23:00	Viliulfo	Andablo	MEX	65	3		Värnamo	13 May
	(60)							
1:23:00	Vladimir	Ostrovskiy	SU	67	15	NC	Kiev	30 Jul
1:23:05	Sergey	Abiralo	SU	22.1.61	6	NC-w	Sochi	21 Feb
1:23:09	Jean-Claude	Corre	FRA	14.9.62	20	OG	Seoul	23 Sep
1:23:13	Jos	Martens	BEL					10 Apr
1:23:14	Vitaliy	Matsko	SU	60	7	NC-w	Sochi	21 Feb
1:23:15	Hartwig	Gauder	GDR	10.11.54	4	NC	Rostock	24 Jun
1:23:20	Hector	Moreno	COL	63	6		L'Hospitalet	24 Apr
1:23:24	Hirofumi	Sakai	JAP	10.2.65	1		Wajima	24 Apr
1:23:30	Erling	Andersen	NOR	22.9.60	22	OG	Seoul	23 Sep
1:23:33	Nikolay	Matveyev	SU	15.1.55	1		Novopolotsk	23 Apr
	(70)							
1:23:33	Pyotr	Kakhnovich	SU	12.4.61	3		Novopolotsk	23 Apr
1:23:43	Aleksandr	Zhukov	SU	14.7.64	2		Kherson	8 May
1:23:45	Chris	Maddocks	UK	28.3.57	2	Hun Ch	Békéscsaba	10 Apr
1:23:47	Vyacheslav	Cherepanov	SU	2.11.64	8	NC-w	Sochi	21 Feb
1:23:51	Stefan	Johansson	SWE	11.4.67	25	OG	Seoul	23 Sep
1:24:00	Mechislav	Vezhel	SU	62	4		Novopolotsk	23 Apr
1:24:06	Andrey	Plotnikov	SU	12.8.64	8	NC-w	Sochi	21 Feb
1:24:11	Dimitris	Orfanopoulos	GRE	9.5.64	3		Ruse	17 Apr
1:24:14	Ján	Záhoncík	CS	23.4.65	3	6N	Trnava	8 May
1:24:16	Nikolay	Frolov	SU	57	12	Znam	Leningrad	11 Jun
	(80)							
1:24:17	Anatoliy	Stepanenko	SU	65	3		Kherson	8 May
1:24:17	Zbigniew	Sadlej	POL	13.12.61	2		Warszawa	19 Jun
1:24:22	Jan	Staaf	SWE	11.1.62				13 May
1:24:24	Sergio	Spagnulo	ITA	7.10.62	4		Porto San Giórgio	26 Jun
1:24:25	Anatoliy	Kozlov	SU	2.10.67	4		Kherson	8 May
1:24:32	Massimo	Quiriconi	ITA	8.1.63	5		Porto San Giórgio	26 Jun
1:24:33	Andrey	Gnussarov	SU	6.12.62	13	Znam	Leningrad	11 Jun
1:24:35	Mikhail	Kurushin	SU	27.11.67	14	Znam	Leningrad	11 Jun
1:24:36	Jozef	Hudák	CS	17.9.62	2	NM	Sofia	26 Jun
1:24:38	Francisco	Vargas	COL	12.11.67	4		Naumburg	1 May
	(90)							
1:24:40	Miguel	A.Prieto	SPA	20.9.64	6	6N	La Coruña	5 Jun
1:24:43	Dmitriy	Ossipov	SU	12.8.66	15	Znam	Leningrad	11 Jun
1:24:45	Nikolay	Panfilov	SU	63	3		Adler	31 Jan
1:24:46	Andrei	Rubarth	GDR	28.1.62	7	6N	La Coruña	5 Jun
1:24:47	Marcello	Villa	ITA		4	NC	Piacenza	9 Oct
1:24:50t	Tim	Lewis	USA	7.1.60	1		Seattle	7 May
1:24:52	Bo	Gustafsson	SWE	29.9.54	7		Värnamo	13 May
1:24:54	Sandro	Bellucci	ITA	21.2.55	6		Porto San Giórgio	26 Jun
1:24:54	Kari	Ahonen	FIN	66	2	NC	Hämeenlinna	5 Aug
1:24:56	Christos	Karagiorgos	GRE	3.5.53	4		Ruse	17 Apr
	(100)							
1:24:56	José	Urbano	POR	1.3.66	29	OG	Seoul	23 Sep

t indicates track walk, all others on road courses

50 KILOMETRES WALK

Mark	Name		Nat	Born	Pos	Meet	Venue	Date
3:38:29	Vyacheslav	Ivanenko	SU	1.3.61	1	OG	Seoul	30 Sep
3:38:56	Ronald	Weigel	GDR	8.8.59	2	OG	Seoul	30 Sep
3:39:45	Hartwig	Gauder	GDR	10.11.54	3	OG	Seoul	30 Sep
3:41:00	Aleksandr	Potashov	SU	12.3.62	4	OG	Seoul	30 Sep
3:42:33		Weigel			1		Naumburg	1 May
3:43:03	José	Marin	SPA	21.1.50	5	OG	Seoul	30 Sep
3:44:01		Ivanenko			1	NC	Vilnius	29 May
3:44:07	Simon	Baker	AUS	6.2.58	6	OG	Seoul	30 Sep
3:44:27	Raffaello	Ducceschi	ITA	25.2.62	1	NC	Barletta	17 Apr
3:44:49	Bo	Gustafsson	SWE	29.9.54	7	OG	Seoul	30 Sep
3:44:57	Reima	Salonen	FIN	19.11.55	1		Turku	24 Jul
3:45:11		Potashov			2	NC	Vilnius	29 May
3:45:43		Ducceschi			8	OG	Seoul	30 Sep
3:45:44		Gustafsson			1		Arras	21 Aug
3:46:30		Gauder			1		Berlin	14 May

Mark	Name		Nat	Born	Pos	Meet	Venue	Date
3:46:30	Vitaliy	Popovich	(10) SU	22.10.62	3	NC	Vilnius	29 May
3:46:31	Dietmar	Meisch	GDR	10.2.59	9	OG	Seoul	30 Sep
3:46:50		Meisch			2		Naumburg	1 May
3:46:52	Pavel	Szikora	CS	26.3.52	1		Podebrady	5 Jun
3:47:04		Szikora			10	OG	Seoul	30 Sep
3:47:14	Giovanni	Perricelli	ITA	25.8.67	11	OG	Seoul	30 Sep
3:47:27		Perricelli			2	NC	Barletta	17 Apr
3:47:30	Bernd	Gummelt	GDR	21.12.63	2		Berlin	14 May
3:47:31	Pavol	Blazek	CS	9.7.58	12	OG	Seoul	30 Sep
3:48:08	Alessandro	Bellucci	ITA	2.9.55	3	NC	Barletta	17 Apr
3:48:09	Jorge	Llopart	SPA	5.5.52	13	OG	Seoul	30 Sep
3:48:15	François	Lapointe	CAN	23.8.61	14	OG	Seoul	30 Sep
3:48:39	Nikolay	Frolov	SU	57	4	NC	Vilnius	29 May
3:48:53	Valeriy	Suntsov	SU	10.5.55	5	NC	Vilnius	29 May
	(29/20)							
3:49:00?	Viliulfo	Andablo	MEX	65	—			30 Jul
3:49:10	Erling	Andersen	NOR	22.9.60	1		Pollensa	20 Mar
3:49:14	Andrey	Perlov	SU	12.12.61	6	NC	Vilnius	29 May
3:49:22	Martín	Bermúdez	MEX	19.7.58	15	OG	Seoul	30 Sep
3:49:38	Herman	Andrade	MEX	1.11.60	1		Ciudad México	3 Apr
3:50:15	Grigoriy	Korneyev	SU	61	7	NC	Vilnius	29 May
3:50:28	Alain	Lemercier	FRA	11.1.57	16	OG	Seoul	30 Sep
		3:53:15.1t			2		Caen	17 Apr
3:50:39.9t	Jaen-Marie	Neff	FRA	29.9.61	1		Caen	17 Apr
3:50:43	Vitaliy	Matsko	SU	60	8	NC	Vilnius	29 May
3:50:46	Roman	Mrázek	CS	21.1.62	17	OG	Seoul	30 Sep
	(30)							
3:51:24	Aleksandr	Volgin	SU	68	10	NC	Vilnius	29 May
3:51:34	Jacek	Bednarek	POL	27.1.64	1		Södertälje	31 Jul
3:51:55	Godfried	De Jonckheere	BEL	1.7.52	1	NC	Fleurus	2 Jul
3:53:15.3t	Eric	Neisse	FRA	27.11.64	3		Caen	17 Apr
3:53:20	Sergey	Tsimbalyuk	SU	2.3.58	11	NC	Vilnius	29 May
3:53:23	Manuel	Alcalde	SPA	31.12.56	3		Pollensa	20 Mar
3:53:23	Andrew	Jachno	AUS	13.4.62	19	OG	Seoul	30 Sep
3:53:34	Stefan	Johansson	SWE	11.4.67	20	OG	Seoul	30 Sep
3:53:42	Andrey	Plotnikov	SU	10.8.67	1		Alushta	2 Oct
3:53:58	Vladimir	Zoika	SU	65	12	NC	Vilnius	29 May
	(40)							
3:54:06.5t	René	Piller	FRA	23.4.65	4		Caen	17 Apr
3:54:39	Valeriy	Yarets	SU	56	13	NC	Vilnius	29 May
3:54:56	Giuseppe	DeGaetano	ITA	66	4	NC	Barletta	17 Apr
3:55:57	José	Pinto	POR	19.6.56	21	OG	Seoul	30 Sep
3:56:14	Alfons	Schwarz	FRG	14.7.54	1	NC	Eschborn	24 Apr
3:56:44	Stanislav	Vezhel	SU	58	3		Alushta	2 Oct
3:56:55	Marco	Evoniuk	USA	30.9.57	22	OG	Seoul	30 Sep
3:57:05	Hubert	Sonnek	CS	11.2.62	1		Békéscsaba	10 Apr
3:57:21	Sergey	Shildkret	SU	25.10.62	14	NC	Vilnius	29 May
3:57:44	Carl	Schueler	USA	26.2.56	23	OG	Seoul	30 Sep
	(50)							
3:57:45	Anatoliy	Tikhonov	SU	14.5.65	15	NC	Vilnius	29 May
3:57:58	Sergey	Titov	SU	25.11.63	16	NC	Vilnius	29 May
3:58:20	Ján	Záhoncík	CS	23.4.65	1		Dudince	10 Apr
3:58:23	Jan	Cortenbach	HOL	59	1	NC	Goirle	5 Jun
3:58:25	Les	Morton	UK	1.7.58	5		Pollensa	20 Mar
3:58:39.0t	Philippe	Lafleur	FRA	11.2.60	5		Caen	17 Apr
3:58:43	LI Baojin		CHN	2.11.59	1		Xuzhou	20 Mar
3:58:57	Anatoliy	Grigartsev	SU	61	17	NC	Vilnius	29 May
3:59:04.0t	Denis	Terraz	FRA	5.2.58	6		Caen	17 Apr
3:59:13	Jaroslav	Makovec	CS	11.1.60	3		Podebrady	5 Jun
	(60)							
3:59:17	Félix	Gómez	MEX	55			Ciudad México	3 Apr
3:59:35	Massimo	Quiriconi	ITA	8.1.63	5	NC	Barletta	17 Apr
3:59:40	László	Sátor	HUN	9.5.53	1	NC	Békéscsaba	10 Apr
3:59:55	Ionat	Olikh	SU	58	6		Alushta	2 Oct
4:00:07	Paul	Blagg	UK	23.1.60	28	OG	Seoul	30 Sep

Mark	Name		Nat	Born	Pos	Meet	Venue	Date
4:00:15.5t	Christos	Karagiorgos	GRE	3.5.53	1	SGP	Fana	7 May
4:01:04	Arturo	Bravo	MEX	19.5.58				8 May
4:01:13	Patrizio	Parcesepe	ITA		6	NC	Barletta	17 Apr
4:01:31	Hector	Moreno	COL	8.6.63	30	OG	Seoul	30 Sep
4:01:44	Robert	Illiy	SU	64	19	NC	Vilnius	29 May
	(70)							
4:01:50	Aleksandr	Turov	SU	11.2.62	1		Leningrad	13 Aug
4:02:07	Valeriy	Berechnyuk	SU	62	20	NC	Vilnius	29 May
4:02:08	Thierry	Toutain	FRA	14.2.62			Houdain	7 May
4:02:21	Antonio	Gonzalez	SPA	22.7.62	6		Naumburg	1 May
4:02:32	Peter	Scholle	GDR	19.1.66	3		Berlin	14 May
4:02:42	Aleksandr	Aleksandrov	SU	63	2		Odessa	20 Aug
4:02:57	Leonid	Sivakov	SU	21.6.56	21	NC	Vilnius	29 May
4:03:12	Tadahiro	Kosaka	JAP	10.2.60	31	OG	Seoul	30 Sep
4:03:13	Jerzy	Wroblewicz	POL	21.8.61	1	NC	Gdynia	16 Apr
4:03:29	Igor	Pasteruk	SU	61	22	NC	Vilnius	29 May
	(80)							
4:03:40	Roman	Parolek	CS	21.4.65	2		Dudince	10 Apr
4:03:53	Ton	van Andel	HOL	58	2	NC	Goirle	5 Jun
4:04:08	Zoltán	Czukor	HUN	18.12.62	2	NC	Békéscsaba	10 Apr
4:04:27	Bruno	Penocchio	ITA	62	7	NC	Barletta	17 Apr
4:04:44	Oleg	Troshin	SU	64	23	NC	Vilnius	29 May
4:04:46	Kestutis	Ezepcikas	SU	65	24	NC	Vilnius	29 May
4:04:48	Adam	Urbanowski	POL	24.12.59	2	NC	Gdynia	16 Apr
4:04:53	Igor	Volchen	SU	62	25	NC	Vilnius	29 May
4:05:07	Andy	Kaestner	USA	25.8.64	3	FOT	Indianapolis	24 Apr
4:05:09	Andrés	Marin	SPA	18.7.61	7		Naumburg	1 May
	(90)							
4:05:30	Edel	Oliva	CUB	12.2.65	1	NC	Caibarién	1 Feb

At the time of going to press in mid-March no walks lists had been received from our walks experts, so I have compiled my own lists. I therefore apologies if, in having to do these extremely quickly, there are omissions or inaccuracies. This applies to men's and women's lists for 1988 and for all-time.

Peter Matthews

Mark		Name		Nat	Born	Pos	Meet	Venue	Date

WORLD JUNIOR MEN'S ALL-TIME LISTS

100 METRES

Mark	Wind	Name		Nat	Born	Pos	Meet	Venue	Date
10.07	2.0	Stanley	Floyd	USA	23.6.61	1		Austin	24 May 80
10.08	0.0	Andre	Cason	USA	13.1.69	1	TAC-j	Tallahassee	24 Jun 88
10.09A	1.8	Mel	Lattany	USA	10.8.59	2	USOF	Colorado Springs	30 Jul 78
10.10	1.9	Stanley	Kerr	USA	19.6.67	1	TAC-j	Towson	28 Jun 86
10.11	1.9	Harvey	Glance	USA	28.3.57	1	FOT	Eugene	20 Jun 76
10.13	1.9	Derrick	Florence	USA	19.6.68	2	TAC-j	Towson	28 Jun 86
10.14	0.8	Ronnie Ray	Smith	USA	28.3.49	2s1	AAU	Sacramento	20 Jun 68
10.14	2.0	Sven	Matthes	GDR	23.8.69	1		Berlin	13 Sep 88
10.16i	-	Eugen	Ray	GDR	26.7.57	1		Berlin	25 Jan 76
10.16	1.9	Houston	McTear	USA	12.2.57	2	FOT	Eugene	20 Jun 76
Wind-assisted									
10.07	2.9	Lee	McRae	USA	23.1.66	2h5	NCAA	Austin	30 May 85
10.08	4.0	Johnny	Jones	USA	4.4.58	1		Austin	20 May 77
10.09	4.1	Stanley	Blalock	USA	18.3.64	1		Athens	19 Mar 83
10.11	4.0	Rod	Richardson	USA	17.9.62	1		Austin	22 May 81
10.12	3.7	Calvin	Smith	USA	8.1.61	1h5	NCAA	Austin	5 Jun 80
10.12A		Jerome	Harrison	USA	17.2.62	1		Colorado Springs	25 Jul 81
10.14	3.6	Thomas	Schröder	GDR	23.8.62	1	EJ	Utrecht	20 Aug 81
10.14	4.0	Roy	Martin	USA	25.12.66	1	TexR	Austin	6 Apr 84
10.14	4.8	Lorenzo	Daniel	USA	23.2.66	1h2		Starkvile	17 May 85

200 METRES

Mark	Wind	Name		Nat	Born	Pos	Meet	Venue	Date
20.07	1.5	Lorenzo	Daniel	USA	23.2.66	1		Starkville	18 May 85
20.13	1.7	Roy	Martin	USA	25.12.66	1		Austin	11 May 85
20.22	1.7	Dwayne	Evans	USA	13.10.58	2	FOT	Eugene	22 Jun 76
20.23	0.5	Michael	Timpson	USA	6.6.67	1		University Park	16 May 87
20.24	0.2	Joe	DeLoach	USA	5.6.67	3		Los Angeles	8 Jun 85
20.29	1.5	Clinton	Davis	USA	17.8.65	1	TAC-j	University Park	26 Jun 83
20.37	1.0	Jürgen	Evers	FRG	29.4.65	1	EJ	Schwechat	28 Aug 83
20.37	0.2	Roberto	Hernández	CUB	6.3.67	1		Sevilla	24 May 86
20.39A	1.0	Marshall	Dill	USA	9.8.52	2	PAm	Cali	3 Aug 71
20.39	0.9	Stanley	Kerr	USA	19.6.67	1	TAC-j	Towson	29 Jun 87
Wind-assisted									
20.01	2.5	Derald	Harris	USA	5.4.58	1		San Jose	9 Apr 77
20.10	4.6	Stanley	Kerr	USA	19.6.67	2r2		Houston	18 May 86
20.34A	2.2	Marshall	Dill	USA	9.8.52	1s2	PAm	Cali	3 Aug 71

400 METRES

Mark		Name		Nat	Born	Pos	Meet	Venue	Date
43.87		Steve	Lewis	USA	16.5.59	1	OG	Seoul	28 Sep 88
44.69		Darrell	Robinson	USA	23.12.63	2	USOF	Indianapolis	24 Jul 82
44.73A		James	Rolle	USA	2.2.64	1	USOF	Colorado Springs	2 Jul 83
44.75		Darren	Clark	AUS	6.9.65	4	OG	Los Angeles	8 Aug 84
45.01		Thomas	Schönlebe	GDR	6.8.65	1		Berlin	15 Jul 84
45.04A		Wayne	Collett	USA	20.10.49	1q2	FOT	Echo Summit	13 Sep 68
45.05		Roberto	Hernández	CUB	6.3.67	2		Santiago de Cuba	21 Feb86
45.09		Kevin	Robinzine	USA	12.4.66	4	TAC	Indianapolis	16 Jun 85
45.09		Henry	Thomas	USA	10.7.67	2r2	ISTAF	Berlin	23 Aug 85
45.17		William	Reed	USA	1.4.70	1	TAC-j	Tucson	20 Jul 87
Hand timing									
44.9'A		Steve	Williams	USA	13.11.53	1		El Paso	13 May 72

800 METRES

Mark		Name		Nat	Born	Pos	Meet	Venue	Date
1:44.3m* (88oy less 0.6)		Jim	Ryun	USA	29.4.47	1	USTFF	Terre Haute	10 Jun 66
1:44.3m		Joaquim	Cruz	BRA	12.3.63	1		Rio de Janeiro	27 Jun 81
1:45.45		Andreas	Busse	GDR	6.5.59	1	GS	Ostrava	7 Jun 78
1:45.64		David	Sharpe	UK	8.7.67	5	VD	Bruxelles	5 Sep 86
1:45.77		Steve	Ovett	UK	9.10.55	2	EC	Roma	4 Sep 74
1:45.84		Detlef	Wagenknecht	GDR	3.1.59	1	NC	Leipzig	2 Jul 78
1:45.96A		Jozef	Plachy	CS	28.2.49	3s2	OG	Ciudad México	14 Oct 68
1:46.17		József	Bereczki	HUN	1.7.62	1	EJ	Utrecht	13 Aug 81
1:46.3m		Josef	Schmid	FRG	15.2.53	2		Waiblingen	2 Aug 72
1:46.37		Gheorge	Ghipu	RUM	30.9.54	3	EP/s	Nice	5 Aug 73
1:46.37		Igor	Lotarev	SU	30.8.64	3	SPA	Moskva	20 Jun 83

Mark	Name		Nat	Born	Pos	Meet	Venue	Date
1500 METRES								
3:34.92	Kipkoech	Cheruiyot	KEN	2.12.64	1		München	26 Jul 83
3:36.07	Wilfred Oanda	Kirochi	KEN	12.12.69	4		Rieti	31 Aug 88
3:36.1m+	Jim	Ryun	USA	29.4.47	1		Berkeley	17 Jul 66
3:36.6m+	Graham	Williamson	UK	15.6.60	3	OsloG	Oslo	17 Jul 79
3:37.5m	Tom	Byers	USA	12.4.55	3		Torino	24 Jul 74
3:38.07	Ari	Paunonen	FIN	10.3.58	1	NC	Tampere	31 Jul 77
3:38.2m	José	M.Abascal	SPA	17.3.58	1		Barcelona	10 Sep 77
3:38.3m	Igor	Lotarev	SU	30.8.64	1		Krasnodar	7 Aug 83
3:38.9m	Filbert	Bayi	TAN	23.6.53	1		Dar-es-Salaam	3 Dec 72
3:38.92	Téofilo	Benito	SPA	22.7.66	2		Barcelona	13 Aug 85
+ during 1 mile race								
3000 METRES								
7:43.20	Ari	Paunonen	FIN	10.3.58	3		Köln	22 Jun 77
7:47.47	Charles	Cheruiyot	KEN	2.12.64	3	ISTAF	Berlin	17 Aug 83
7:48.28	Jon	Richards	UK	19.5.64	9	OsloG	Oslo	9 Jul 83
7:51.84	Steve	Binns	UK	25.8.60	2		Gateshead	8 Sep 79
7:53.4m	Eddy	De Pauw	BEL	8.6.60	2		Bornem	3 Aug 79
7:54.2m	Raf	Wijns	BEL	7.1.64	4		Bosvoorde	4 Aug 83
7:54.7m	Mohamed	Choumassi	MOR	.69	1		Västerås	30 Jun 88
7:55.3m	Jean-Pierre	N'dayisenga	BEL	13.12.62	1		Louvain	12 Jul 81
7:56.28	John	Doherty	UK	22.7.61	10		London	13 Jul 80
7:56.4m	Hansjörg	Kunze	GDR	28.12.59	2		Karl-Marx-Stadt	27 Jun 76
5000 METRES								
13:23.27	Addis	Abebe	ETH	.70	2	APM	Hengelo	14 Aug 88
13:25.33	Charles	Cheruiyot	KEN	2.12.64	1		München	26 Jul 83
13:26.88	Terry	Thornton	RSA	23.9.67	1		Stellenbosch	8 Nov86
13:27.04	Steve	Binns	UK	25.8.60	3	IAC	London	14 Sep 79
13:33.6	Berhanu	Girma	ETH	.60	2r1		Sochi	8 Jun 79
13:35.06	Ibrahim	Juma/Kivina	TAN	25.2.58	4		Den Haag	25 Jun 77
13:35.95	Paul	Davies-Hale	UK	21.6.62	6	IAC	London	11 Sep 81
13:37.4	David	Black	UK	2.10.52	4	IAC	London	10 Sep 71
13:38.74	Jean-Pierre	N'Dayisenga	BEL	12.12.62	7	VD	Bruxelles	28 Aug 81
13:39.6	Steve	Prefontaine	USA	25.1.51	2	vFRG	Stuttgart	16 Jul 70
Notable 3 Miles time								
13:04.0	Gerry	Lindgren	USA	9.3.46	2	AAA	London	10 Jul 65
10000 METRES								
27:50.24	Addis	Abebe	ETH	.70	3	VD	Bruxelles	19 Aug 88
28:12.78	Bidelu	Kibret	ETH	.69	11	VD	Bruxelles	19 Aug 88
28:25.77	Mohamed	Choumassi	MOR	.69	21	Bis	Oslo	2 Jul 88
28:29.32	Habte	Negash	ETH	.67	2	Znam	Moskva	9 Jun 85
28:31.29	Debede	Demisse	ETH	.68	2	PTS	Bratislava	12 Jun 87
28:31.39	John	Ngeno	KEN	11.4.53	6	CG	Edinburgh	18 Jul 70
28:32.7	Rudy	Chapa	USA	7.11.57	5		Des Moines	24 Apr 76
28:35.02	Salvatore	Nicosia	ITA	8.3.63	11		Firenze	25 May 82
28:39.20	Gábor	K.Szabó	HUN	19.6.62	4		Warszawa	4 Jul 81
28:39.4	Walter	Merlo	ITA	18.7.65	1		Torino	13 Oct 84
3000 METRES STEEPLECHASE								
8:29.50	Ralf	Pönitzsch	GDR	20.10.57	4	vPOL,SU	Warszawa	19 Aug 76
8:29.85	Paul	Davies-Hale	UK	21.6.62	3	vPOL,SWZ	London	31 Aug 81
8:30.29	Anton	Nicolaisen	RSA	25.1.68	1		Durban	7 Dec 87
8:31.27	Shigeyuki	Aikyo	JAP	29.1.64	9h1	WC	Helsinki	9 Aug 83
8:31.85	Arsenios	Tsiminos	GRE	19.1.61	3	vSPA,BEL-j	Barcelona	31 Aug 80
8:33.24	Francesco	Panetta	ITA	10.1.63	2		Firenze	25 May 82
8:33.8	John	Gregorek	USA	15.4.60	2	IC4A	Philadelphia	20 May 79
8:34.84	Anders	Carlsson	SWE	17.4.59	2	NC	Stockholm	5 Aug 78
8:35.99	Frank	Baumgartl	GDR	29.5.55	4	vFIN,SU	Helsinki	16 Sep 73
8:36.2	Gyula	Balogh	HUN	15.2.61	1	NC	Budapest	30 Aug 80

Mark		Name		Nat	Born	Pos	Meet	Venue	Date
110 METRES HURDLES									
13.23	0.0	Renaldo	Nehemiah	USA	24.3.59	1r2	WK	Zürich	16 Aug 78
13.44	-0.8	Colin	Jackson	UK	18.2.67	1	WJ	Athinai	19 Jul 86
13.46	1.8	Jon	Ridgeon	UK	14.2.67	1	EJ	Cottbus	23 Aug 85
13.47	1.9	Holger	Pohland	GDR	5.4.63	2	vUSA	Karl-Marx-Stadt	10 Jul 82
13.57	1.4	Robert	Gaines	USA	14.4.57	2s1	FOT	Eugene	24 Jun 76
13.57*	0.5	Greg	Foster	USA	4.8.58	1	WCR	Fresno	7 May 77
13.66	2.0	Arto	Bryggare	FIN	26.5.58	4	EP	Helsinki	14 Aug 77
13.67	1.7	James	Walker	USA	25.10.57	1	vFRG-j	Lüdenscheid	8 Jul 76
13.69	1.7	Florian	Schwarthoff	FRG	7.5.68	1	vUK-j	Ipswich	27 Jun 87
13.71	0.6	Rod	Wilson	USA	24.9.61	1	PAG-j	Sudbury	31 Aug 80
13.71	1.3	Jörg	Naumann	GDR	2.1.63	1		Potsdam	10 Jun 82
13.71		Rod	Woodson	USA	10.3.65	2		Tallahassee	17 Mar 84
Wind-assisted									
13.42	4.5	Colin	Jackson	UK	18.2.67	2	CG	Edinburgh	27 Jun 86
13.54	4.1	Rod	Wilson	USA	24.9.61	1h2	NCAA	Austin	6 Jun 80
13.55	3.1	Arto	Bryggare	FIN	26.5.58	1	vUK	Oulu	10 Jul 77
13.70	4.0	Milan	Stewart	USA	31.10.60	3h1	NCAA	Champaign	31 May 79

* 120 yards hurdles time plus 0.03 sec.

Mark	Name		Nat	Born	Pos	Meet	Venue	Date
400 METRES HURDLES								
48.02	Danny	Harris	USA	7.9.65	2s1	FOT	Los Angeles	17 Jun 84
48.74	Vladimir	Budko	SU	4.2.65	2	DRZ	Moskva	18 Aug 84
49.33A	Joseph	Maritim	KEN	22.10.68	4	AfrG	Nairobi	9 Aug 87
49.45	Belfred	Clark	USA	19.8.65	1	TAC-j	Los Angeles	23 Jun 84
49.50	Kelly	Carter	USA	15.2.69	1	WJ	Sudbury	29 Jul 88
49.61	Harald	Schmid	FRG	29.9.57	1	vUSA-j	Lüdenscheid	7 Jul 76
49.62	Dennis	Otono	NIG	16.4.58	2	NCAA	Champaign	4 Jun 77
49.64	Jószef	Szalai	HUN	8.3.61	3	BGP	Budapest	11 Aug 80
49.66	Edgar	Itt	FRG	8.6.67	1	NC-j	Wetzlar	7 Sep 86
49.71	Ruslan	Mishchenko	SU	24.4.64	1	EJ	Schwechat	28 Aug 83
HIGH JUMP								
2.36	Javier	Sotomayor	CUB	13.10.67	1		Santiago de Cuba	23 Feb 86
2.35i	Vladimir	Yashchenko	SU	12.1.59	1	EI	Milano	12 Mar 78
2.35	Dietmar	Mögenburg	FRG	15.8.61	1		Rehlingen	26 May 80
2.33	Zhu	Jianhua	CHN	29.5.63	1	AsiG	New Delhi	1 Dec 82
2.33	Patrik	Sjöberg	SWE	5.1.65	1	OsloG	Oslo	9 Jul 83
2.31	Jörg	Freimuth	GDR	10.9.61	3	OG	Moskva	1 Aug 80
2.30	Dothel	Edwards	USA	9.9.66	1	v3-N	Pullman	21 Jul 85
2.29	Yuriy	Sergiyenko	SU	19.3.65	1		Tashkent	25 Sep 83
2.29	Hollis	Conway	USA	8.1.67	1		Lafayette	12 Apr 86
2.29	Georgi	Dakov	BUL	27.10.67	2	Nar	Sofia	1 Jun 86
POLE VAULT								
5.65	Rodion	Gataullin	SU	23.11.65	2	NC	Donyetsk	8 Sep 84
5.65	István	Bagyula	HUN	2.1.69	1	WJ	Sudbury	28 Jul 88
5.61	Thierry	Vigneron	FRA	9.3.60	1		Longwy	30 Sep 79
5.61i	Grigoriy	Yegorov	SU	12.1.67	1	vGDR-j	Moskva	16 Feb 86
5.60	Konstantin	Volkov	SU	28.2.60	1	EP	Torino	5 Aug 79
5.60	Andrey	Grudinin	SU	3.5.69	1		Simferopol	27 May 88
5.60	Maxim	Tarasov	SU	2.12.70	2	WJ	Sudbury	28 Jul 88
5.57	Dave	Volz	USA	2.5.62	1		Bloomington	18 Apr 81
5.55	Sergey	Bubka	SU	4.12.63	1		Kharkov	4 Sep 82
5.55	Delko	Lesev	BUL	6.1.67	2	Nar	Sofia	31 May 86
5.55	Roman	Barabashov	SU	13.9.68	1		Alma-Ata	12 Sep 87

Mark		Name		Nat	Born	Pos	Meet	Venue	Date
LONG JUMP									
8.34	0.0	Randy	Williams	USA	23.8.53	Q	OG	München	8 Sep 72
8.28	0.8	Luis	A.Bueno	CUB	22.5.69	1		Habana	16 Jul 88
8.24	0.2	Eric	Metcalf	USA	23.1.68	1	NCAA	Indianapolis	6 Jun 86
8.24	1.8	Vladimir	Ochkan	SU	13.1.68	1	vGDR-j	Leningrad	21 Jun 87
8.22		Larry	Doubley	USA	15.3.58	1	NCAA	Champaign	3 Jun 77
8.21A	2.0	Vance	Johnson	USA	13.3.63	1	NCAA	Provo	4 Jun 82
8.18		LaMonte	King	USA	18.12.59	2	CalR	Modesto	20 May 78

Mark		Name		Nat	Born	Pos	Meet	Venue	Date
8.15	1.2	Leroy	Burrell	USA	21.2.67	1		Los Angeles	19 Apr 86
8.13		Carl	Lewis	USA	1.7.61	3	PAG	San Juan	7 Jul 79
8.13	1.1	Robert	Emmiyan	SU	16.2.65	1		Baku	14 Sep 84
Wind assisted									
8.35	2.2	Carl	Lewis	USA	1.7.61	1	NCAA	Austin	6 Jun 80
8.23	4.4	Peller	Phillips	USA	23.6.70	1		Sacramento	11 Jun 88

TRIPLE JUMP

Mark		Name		Nat	Born	Pos	Meet	Venue	Date
17.50	0.3	Volker	Mai	GDR	3.5.66	1	vSU	Erfurt	23 Jun 85
17.42	1.3	Khristo	Markov	BUL	27.1.65	1	Nar	Sofia	19 May 84
17.40A	0.4	Pedro	Perez Duenas	CUB	23.2.52	1	PAG	Cali	5 Aug 71
17.00		Gustavo	Platt	CUB	29.7.54	1		Habana	5 May 73
16.97	0.2	Igor	Parigin	SU	3.2.67	1	WJ	Athinai	20 Jul 86
16.91		Héctor	Marquetti	CUB	7.4.68	1	CAC	Caracas	26 Jul 87
16.86	1.5	Yuriy	Gorbachenko	SU	19.7.66	1		Odessa	15 Sep 85
16.83	0.8	Aleksandr	Beskrovniy	SU	5.4.60	Q	EJ	Bydgoszcz	18 Aug 79
16.81A	0.0	Greg	Neal	USA	22.1.63	3	NCAA	Provo	5 Jun 82
16.81	-0.1	Ralf	Jaros	FRG	13.12.65	1	NC	Düsseldorf	23 Jun 84
Disqualified for drugs usage									
16.94	2.2	Juan	M.Lopez	CUB	7.4.67	2	WJ	Athinai	22 Jul 86

SHOT

Mark	Name		Nat	Born	Pos	Meet	Venue	Date
21.05i	Terry	Albritton	USA	14.1.55	1	AAU	New York	22 Feb 74
20.65	Mike	Carter	USA	29.10.60	1	vSU-j	Boston	4 Jul 79
20.20	Randy	Matson	USA	5.3.45	2	OG	Tokyo	17 Oct 64
20.20	Udo	Beyer	GDR	9.8.55	2	NC	Leipzig	6 Jul 74
19.99	Karl	Salb	USA	19.5.49	4	FOT	Echo Summit	10 Sep 68
19.74	Andreas	Horn	GDR	31.1.62	2	vSU-j	Cottbus	24 Jun 81
19.71	Vladimir	Kiselyov -1	SU	1.1.57	1		Yalta	15 May 76
19.68	Ron	Semkiw	USA	28.3.54	1	vAFR	Dakar	4 Aug 73
19.53i	Vyacheslav	Lykho	SU	16.1.67	1		Moskva	28 Dec 86
19.51	Viktor	Beliy	SU	.64	6		Leningrad	26 Jul 83

DISCUS

Mark	Name		Nat	Born	Pos	Meet	Venue	Date
65.62	Werner	Reiterer	AUS	27.1.68	1		Melbourne	15 Dec 87
63.64	Werner	Hartmann	FRG	20.4.59	1	vFRA	Strasbourg	25 Jun 78
63.62	Sergey	Pachin	SU	24.5.68	2		Moskva	25 Jul 87
62.52	John	Nichols	USA	23.8.69	1		Baton Rouge	23 Apr 88
62.04	Kenth	Gardenkrans	SWE	2.10.55	2		Helsingborg	11 Aug 74
61.84	Attila	Horváth	HUN	28.7.67	2		Budapest	18 May 85
61.84	Andreas	Seelig	GDR	6.7.70	1		Halle	15 May 88
61.30	Wolfgang	Schmidt	GDR	16.1.54	4	NC	Dresden	22 Jul 73
60.60	Vladimir	Zinchenko	SU	25.7.59	1		Yalta	28 Sep 77
60.60	Vasil	Baklarov	BUL	1.1.67	1	WJ	Athinai	17 Jul 86

HAMMER

Mark	Name		Nat	Born	Pos	Meet	Venue	Date
78.14	Roland	Steuk	GDR	5.3.59	1	NC	Leipzig	30 Jun 78
78.00	Sergey	Dorozhon	SU	17.2.64	1		Moskva	7 Aug 83
76.54	Valeriy	Gubkin	SU	3.9.67	2		Minsk	27 Jun 86
75.24	Christoph	Sahner	FRG	23.9.63	1	vPOL-j	Göttingen	26 Jun 82
75.22	Jaroslav	Chmyr	SU	29.11.66	1		Kiev	7 Sep 85
75.20	Igor	Nikulin	SU	14.8.60	2		Leselidze	1 Jun 79
75.10	Eduard	Piskunov	SU	26.9.67	1		Grodno	5 Jul 86
74.78	Matthias	Moder	GDR	17.6.63	1	NC-j	Cottbus	24 Jul 82
74.32	Sergey	Litvinov	SU	23.1.58	1		Simferopol	7 Aug 77
73.60	Marc	Odenthal	GDR	19.2.63	2	vPOL-j	Göttingen	26 Jun 82

JAVELIN

Mark	Name		Nat	Born	Pos	Meet	Venue	Date
80.26	Vladimir	Ovchinnikov	SU	2.8.70	Q	OG	Seoul	24 Sep 88
79.58	Gavin	Lovegrove	NZ	21.10.67	2		Noumea	26 Oct 86
79.50	Stephen	Backley	UK	12.12.69	1	NC	Derby	5 Jun 88
79.46	Juha	Laukkanen	FIN	6.1.69	1		Joutsa	19 Jul 87
78.84	Vladimir	Zasimovich	SU	14.9.68	1	WJ	Athinai	18 Jul 86
76.06	Kimmo	Solehmainen	FIN	22.3.69			Helsinki	1 Jun 88
75.92	Gerhard	Burger	RSA	21.12.69	1		Pretoria	15 Oct 88

Mark	Name		Nat	Born	Pos	Meet	Venue	Date
75.90	Raymond	Hecht	GDR	11.11.68	1	vSU-j	Leningrad	20 Jun 87
75.46	Jens	Reimann	GDR	21.3.69	1		Halle	14 May 88
75.40	Kim Jae-sang		SKO	23.9.68	1	Asi-j	Djakarta	4 Dec 86

DECATHLON

Second day

Mark	Name		Nat	Born	Pos	Meet	Venue	Date
8397	Torsten	Voss	GDR	24.3.63	1	NC	Erfurt	7 Jul 82
	10.76 7.66 14.41 2.09 48.37 14.37 41.76 4.80 62.90 4:34.04							
8104w	Valter	Külvet	SU	19.2.64	1		Viimsi	23 Aug 81
	10.7w 7.26w 13.86 2.09 48.5 14.8 47.92 4.50 60.34 4:37.8							
8082	Daley	Thompson	UK	30.7.58	1	EP/s	Sittard	31 Jul 77
	10.70 7.54 13.84 2.01 47.31 15.26 41.70 4.70 54.48 4:30.4							
8036	Christian	Schenk	GDR	9.2.65	5		Potsdam	21 Jul 84
	11.54 7.18 14.26 2.16 49.23 15.06 44.74 4.20 65.98 4:24.11							
7868	Mikhail	Romanyuk	SU	6.2.62	1	EJ	Utrecht	21 Aug 81
	11.26 7.11 13.50 1.98 49.98 14.72 42.94 4.90 59.74 4:30.63							
7827	Igor	Maryin	SU	28.4.65	1		Frunze	9 Sep 84
	11.30 7.25 13.55 2.04 50.65 15.21 43.70 4.70 62.92 4:42.05							
7815	Thomas	Fahner	GDR	18.7.66	1	EJ	Cottbus	23 Aug 85
	11.13 7.17 13.33 2.00 49.31 15.18 42.02 4.90 62.02 4:51.46							
7790	Michael	Kohnle	FRG	3.8.70	1	vPOL-j	Bochum	26 Jun 88
	10.91 7.03 13.14 2.02 49.27 14.71 40.24 4.90 56.18 4:48.76							
7776	Sepp	Zeilbauer	AUT	24.9.52	5	EC	Helsinki	12 Aug 71
	10.96 7.38 13.49 2.04 48.8 15.06 39.70 4.00 48.96 4:27.5							
7775	Siegfried	Wentz	FRG	7.3.60	1	EJ	Bydgoszcz	17 Aug 79
	11.29 7.15 14.75 2.01 49.95 15.08 42.74 4.00 64.52 4:30.6							

10000 METRES WALK

Mark	Name		Nat	Born	Pos	Meet	Venue	Date
38:54.75	Ralf	Kowalsky	GDR	22.3.62	1		Cottbus	24 Jun 81
39:44.71	Giovanni	De Benedictis	ITA	8.12.68	1	EJ	Birmingham	7 Aug 87
40:27.2	Andrey	Perlov	SU	12.12.61	1		Ryazan	1 Jul 80
40:38.01	Mikhail	Shchennikov	SU	24.12.67	1	WJ	Athinai	18 Jul 86
40:40.73	Salvatore	Cacia	ITA	15.6.67	2	WJ	Athinai	18 Jul 86
40:41.05	Ricardo	Pueyo	SPA	1.3.67	3	WJ	Athinai	18 Jul 86
40:47.60	Walter	Arena	ITA	30.5.64	2		Milano	22 Jun 83
40:50.0	Erling	Andersen	NOR	22.9.60	1		Oslo	3 Aug 79
40:55.4	Jozef	Pribilinec	CS	6.7.60	1		Zilina	4 May 79
40:57.6	Vladimir	Pyshko	SU	12.8.62	2		Ryazan	1 Jul 80

4 x 100 METRES RELAY

Mark	Nat	Team	Pos	Meet	Venue	Date
39.00A	USA	Jessie, Franklin, Blalock, Mitchell	1		Colorado Springs	18 Jul 83
39.25	FRG	Dobeleit, Klameth, Evers, Lübke	1	EJ	Schwechat	28 Aug 83
39.54	NIG	Tetengi, Ezinwa, Nwankwo, Adeniken	1h2	WJ	Sudbury	30 Jul 88
39.62	SU	Shlychkov, Kuchmuradov, Goremykin, Ivanov	1	Druzh	Nyiregyháza	13 Aug 88
39.69	GDR	Malke, Hoff, Thiele, Prenzler	1		Potsdam	10 Aug 77
39.69	FRA	Thessard, Patrick Barré, Panzo, Pascal Barré	1		Dôle	6 Aug 77
39.80	UK	McKenzie, Bunney, Ashby, Regis	1	EJ	Cottbus	25 Aug 85
39.93	POL	Konopka, Kaniecki, Jedrusik, Parjaszewski	1h3	WJ	Athinai	19 Jul 86
39.99	JAP	Okuyama, Sugimoto, Kato, Nakamichi	1	AsiC-j	Singapore	11 Sep 88
40.21	ITA	Angelini, Tiziani, Colombo, Simionato	3	EJ	Bydgoszcz	19 Aug 79
40.21	CUB	Isasi, Valle, González, Martínez	3h2	WJ	Athinai	19 Jul 86

4 x 400 METRES RELAY

Mark	Nat	Team	Pos	Meet	Venue	Date
3:01.90	USA	Campbell, Rish, Waddle, Reed	1	WJ	Athinai	20 Jul 86
3:04.22	CUB	Cadogan, Mordoche, González, Hernández	2	WJ	Athinai	20 Jul 86
3:04.58	GDR	Preusche, Löper, Trylus, Carlowitz	1	EJ	Utrecht	23 Aug 81
3:05.16	JAM	Christie, Mason, Davis, Patterson	3	WJ	Athinai	20 Jul 86
3:05.77	FRG	Gruber, Seybold, Mikisch, Just	2	EJ	Schwechat	28 Aug 83
3:05.89	UK	Patterson, Bakewell, Crampton, Tyler	4	WJ	Athinai	20 Jul 86
3:06.45	SU	Filipev, Mishchenko, Tatoyev, Budko	3	EJ	Schwechat	28 Aug 83
3:06.95	ITA	Campana, Petrella, Milocco, D'Amico	5	EJ	Schwechat	28 Aug 83
3:07.10	NIG	Falaye, Vincent, Bosso, Bakare	2h3	WJ	Athinai	19 Jul 86
3:07.39	POL	Jedrusik, Szymkowicz, Rychter, Sidowski	6	WJ	Athinai	20 Jul 86

WORLD JUNIOR MEN'S LISTS 1988

100 METRES

Mark		Name		Nat	Born	Pos	Meet	Venue	Date
10.08	0.0	Andre	Cason	USA	13.1.69	1	NC-j	Tallahassee	24 Jun
		10.17	+0.1			1h4	NC-j	Tallahassee	24 Jun
		10.17	+0.7			1h8	WJ	Sudbury	27 Jul
		10.18	+1.9			2h4		Indianapolis	16 Jul
		10.22	-2.7			1	WJ	Sudbury	28 Jul
		10.23	+1.7			1		College Station	26 Mar
		10.17w	+2.4			3	SWC	Austin	15 May
		10.20w	+3.4			3h1		Austin	14 May
10.14	+2.0	Sven	Matthes	GDR	23.8.69	1		Berlin	13 Sep
		10.18	+0.3			1s1	NC	Rostock	25 Jun
		10.19	+0.2			1	NC	Rostock	25 Jun
		10.19				1r2		Berlin	20Jul
10.26		Peter	Ifeduba	NIG	69	1s2	OT/NC	Bauchi	1 Jul
10.29	+0.5	Oladape	Adeniken	NIG	19.8.69	1rA		Bern	23 Aug
10.31	+0.9	William	Jackson	USA	2.2.69	1h1		Winter Park	28 May
10.31	+1.9	Dmitriy	Bartenyev	SU	8.3.69	1	NC-j	Bryansk	6 Jul
10.33		Derwin	Hall	USA	27.7.69	1h3	JUCO	Odessa	19 May
10.36	+2.0	Aleksandr	Goremykin	SU	3.3.71	1s	NC-j	Bryansk	6 Jul
10.37	-2.7	Aleksandr	Shlychkov	SU	31.3.70	3	WJ	Sudbury	28 Jul
10.37	+1.9	Tatsuo	Sugimoto	JAP	25.11.70	1		Kobe	2 Aug
10.38		D'Angelo	Newsom	USA	30.1.70	1		Mesquite	30 Apr
10.38		Marvin	Setzer	USA	16.12.69	1		Gary	26 May
10.38		Abdullahi	Tetengi	NIG	15.7.69	2s		Bauchi	30 Jun
10.39	+0.1	Kevin	Braunskill	USA	31.3.69	3		Raleigh	26 Mar
10.39	+0.3	Michael	Bates	USA	19.12.69	3		Tucson	11 Jun
10.39	-0.1	Tony	Lee	USA	23.10.69	2	NC-j	Tallahassee	24 Jun
10.41	+1.9	Anvar	Kuchmuradov	SU	5.1.69	2		Bryansk	6 Jul
10.42		Leonardo	Prevot	CUB	13.6.71	1		Jalisco	24 Jun
10.43A		Albert	Ransom	USA	27.8.71	1		Greenwood	21 May
10.44	+0.4	Chris	Barnes	USA	21.7.69	1		Austin	14 May
10.44	+2.0	Jamie	Henderson	UK	28.3.69	1		Haringey	20 Aug
10.44		Davison	Enzinwa	NIG	22.11.71	1rB		Bern	23 Aug
10.44	+1.6	Eric	Akogyiram	GHA	25.6.69	2rD		Seoul	19 Apr
Wind assisted									
10.27		Ricky	Huell	USA	10.11.69	2		Starkville	26 Mar
10.28	+3.2	Brian	Bridgewater	USA	7.9.70	1		Van Nuys	20 May
10.34	+4.5	Darren	Braithwaite	UK	20.7.69	1	NC-j	Stoke-on-Trent	25 Jun
10.36	+5.8	Tatsuo	Sugimoto	JAP	25.11.70	1s2		Kobe	2 Aug
10.37	+4.5	Courtney	Rumbolt	UK	26.7.69	2	NC-j	Stoke-on-Trent	25 Jun
10.39		Ray	Ethridge	USA	69	2		Fullerton	30 Apr
10.41	6.8	Tim	Jackson	AUS	4.7.69	1		Sydney	29 Oct
10.42		Benari	Burroughs	USA	70	1		San Jose	21 May
Hand timing									
9.9		Oladape	Adeniken	NIG	19.8.69	2	OT/NC	Bauchi	2 Jul
10.0		Abdullahi	Tetengi	NIG	15.7.69	3	OT/NC	Bauchi	2 Jul
10.1		Victor	Nwankwo	NIG	18.9.69	4	OT/NC	Bauchi	2 Jul
10.2		Raghib	Ismail	USA		1h		Wilkes-Barre	20 May
10.2		Randy	Jordan	USA		1		Apex	21 May
10.2	+1.0	Mitsushige	Sugimoto	JAP	21.8.70	1h		Odawara	2 May
10.2	+1.9	Masahiro	Nagura	JAP	5.5.69	1		Ageo	2 May
10.2		Quincy	Watts	USA	19.6.70	1		Huntington Beach	12 Jun
10.2	1.9	David	Branle	BEL	29.10.69	1		Aalst	25 Jun
10.2		Anvar	Kuchmuradov	SU	5.1.69	1		Fergana	10 Sep
Wind assisted									
10.0		Peter	Ifeduba	NIG	69	1h1	Big8	Ames	14 May
10.1		James	Trapp	USA				Moore	Apr
10.1		Keith	Bly	USA				Stillwater	Apr
10.1		James	Walker	USA	70	1		Killeen	15 Apr
10.1		Sam	Rice	USA	70				May
10.2		six men							
Doubtful timing									
10.1		Giovanni	De Lucia	ITA	9.769	1		Portici	21 May

Mark		Name		Nat	Born	Pos	Meet	Venue	Date
200 METRES									
20.53	+1.4	Brian	Bridgewater	USA	7.9.70	1h		Van Nuys	20 May
20.63	+0.6	Kevin	Braunskill	USA	31.3.69	1		Raleigh	25 May
20.67	+1.6	Quincy	Watts	USA	19.6.70	1h		Van Nuys	20 May
20.67	+1.6	Oladape	Adeniken	NIG	19.8.69	6s2	OG	Seoul	28 Sep
20.68	-0.1	Michael	Bates	USA	19.12.69	3		Tucson	11 Jun
20.72	+2.0	Abdullahi	Tetengi	NIG	15.7.69	1rB		Seoul	19 Sep
20.73	+0.2	Chris	Barnes	USA	21.7.69	1	NC-j	Tallahassee	25 Jun
		20.75				1s2	NC-j	Tallahassee	25 Jun
20.79	+0.7	Maurice	Draper	USA	69	1		Natchitoches	11 May
20.79		Victor	Nwankwo	NIG	18.9.69	1s	OT/NC	Bauchi	1 Jul
20.82	+1.7	Mark	Garner	AUS	30.6.69	1		Sydney	16 Jan
20.82		Derwin	Hall	USA	27.7.69			Odessa	19 May
20.83	+2.0	Dino	Napier	USA	24.11.69	1		Austin	14 May
20.84	+0.4	Aleksandr	Shlychkov	SU	31.3.70	1	Druzh	Nyiregyháza	14 Aug
20.85?		Terrence	Warren	USA	2.8.69			Pasadena	11 Jun
20.85	+1.5	Dmitriy	Bartenyev	SU	8.3.69	1	NC-j	Bryansk	8 Jul
20.87		Marvin	Setzer	USA	16.12.69	1		Indianapolis	11 Jun
20.88	+2.0	Yoshuki	Okuyama	JAP	3.5.70	1		Yamagata	19 Jun
20.92		Davison	Ezinwa	NIG	22.11.71	2		Bauchi	2 Jul
20.96		Steve	Lewis	USA	16.5.69	4		Göteberg	21 Jun
20.98	1.2	Tomasz	Jedrusik	POL	3.2.69	2rB		Sevilla	1 Jun
Wind assisted									
20.68		Barry	Smith	USA	22.2.71	1		Eugene	24 Jul
20.74	+2.6	David	Jones	USA	69	1		Houston	7 May
20.79	+3.3	Sven	Matthes	GDR	23.8.69	3		Karl Marx Stadt	12 Jun
		20.81	+3.1			1s3	WJ	Sudbury	29 Jul
20.88		Dushon	Orr	USA					
Hand timing									
20.6		Dmitry	Bartenyev	SU	8.3.69	1	NC-j	Bryansk	29 Jun
20.7?		Carey	Johnson	JAM	1.3.69	1		Kingston	9 May
20.7	+2.0	Aundre	Reese	USA	3.7.70	2		Austin	14 May
Wind assisted									
20.5		Peter	Ifeduba	NIG	69	2h1		Ames	14 May

400 METRES

Mark	Name		Nat	Born	Pos	Meet	Venue	Date
43.87	Steve	Lewis	USA	16.5.69	1	OG	Seoul	28 Sep

Mark	Pos	Meet	Venue	Date	Mark	Pos	Meet	Venue	Date
44.11	1s2	FOT	Indianapolis	18 Jul	44.61	1q1	FOT	Indianapolis	17 Jul
44.26	3rA	WK	Zürich	17 Au	44.65	2	Pac-10	Westwood	22 May
44.35	1s1	OG	Seoul	28 Sep	44.65	3	Athl	Lausanne	24 Jun
44.37	3	FOT	Indianapolis	20 Jul	44.75	1		Malmö	8 Aug
44.41	1q3	OG	Seoul	25 Sep					

Mark	Name		Nat	Born	Pos	Meet	Venue	Date
45.27	Tomasz	Jedrusik	POL	3.2.69	4q1	OG	Seoul	25 Sep
45.76	Harry	Ellerbe	USA	4.5.69	1		Lincoln, Pa.	7 May
45.80	Chris	Nelloms	USA	14.8.71	1		Columbus	4 Jun
45.88	Mark	Garner	AUS	3.6.69	4	NC	Perth	26 Mar
45.89	Samuel	Matete	ZIM	27.7.69?	2s1		Annaba	29 Aug
45.94	Marlin	Cannon	USA	9.12.70	1		Austin	14 May
46.21	Stephen	Perry	AUS	23.9.70	1s1	WJ	Sudbury	28 Jul
46.26	Anthony	Eziuka	NIG	8.5.71	1rB		Seoul	19 Sep
46.28	Jerome	Williams	USA	14.5.69	1	NC-j	Tallahassee	25 Jun
46.29	Jesse	Carr	USA	18.6.69	2	NC-j	Tallahassee	25 Jun
46.29	Wayne	McDonald	UK	5.10.70	1s2	WJ	Sudbury	28 Jul
46.32	Joseph Kiptanui	Chepsiror	KEN	20.10.71	2s2	WJ	Sudbury	28 Jul
46.35	Eddie	Miller	USA	20.6.69	1		Tallahassee	21 May
46.35	Dawda	Jallow	GAM	22.12.69	7q1	OG	Seoul	25 Sep
46.37	Takahiro	Watanabe	JAP	8.4.70	1		Kobe	1 Aug
46.43	Mark	Richardson	UK	26.7.72	2s1	WJ	Sudbury	28 Jul
46.51	Derrick	Cunningham	USA	15.3.70	1		Dallas	2 Apr
46.58	Jean-Charles	Thierry	FRA	12.2.70	1		Créteil	10 Jul
46.59	Ibrahim	Esmael	QAT	69	1	AsiC-j	Singapore	10 Sep
Hand timing								
46.2	Albert	Ransom	USA	27.8.71	1		Tempe	28 May

800 METRES

Mark	Name		Nat	Born	Pos	Meet	Venue	Date
1:46.40i	Pedrag	Melnjak	YUG	17.3.69	1		Torino	10 Feb
		1:47.97			3		Sarajevo	4 Sep
1:46.9 A	Jonah K	Birir	KEN	27.12.71	2h2	NC	Nairobi	17 Jun
		1:47.0 A			4	NC	Nairobi	18 Jun
1:47.0 A	Wilson Kosgei	Kipketer	KEN	12.12.70	1h1	NC	Nairobi	17 Jun
		1:47.2 A			5	NC	Nairobi	18 Jun
1:47.2	Wilfred Oanda	Kirochi	KEN	12.12.69				Jul
1:47.22	Kevin	McKay	UK	9.2.69	5	NC	Derby	5 Jun
1:47.36	Melfort	Homela	ZIM	3.6.70	3h9	OG	Seoul	23 Sep
1:47.45	Franzwa	Woldemariam	ETH	69	4		São Paolo	22 May
1:47.56	Pavel	Hujer	CS	16.12.69	2		Saloniki	16 Sep
1:47.61	Giuseppe	D'Urso	ITA	15.9.69	2		Palermo	25 Jun
1:47.67	Yoshikazu	Tachi	JAP	7.8.69	1		Tokyo	10 Oct
1:47.89	Luis M	Cadogan	CUB	23.2.69	2rB		Habana	8 Jul
1:48.27	Nourredine	Morceli	NIG	20.2.70	2rB	PTS	Bratislava	9 Jun
1:48.42	Steffen	Weissgerber	GDR	5.3.69	4		Potsdam	8 Jun
1:48.45	Nick	Smith	UK	15.5.69	3		Edinburgh	2 Jul
1:48.57	Victor	Ngubeni	RSA	28.9.69	5		Indianapolis	5 May
1:48.59	Paul	Burgess	UK	10.11.70	7	NC	Derby	5 Jun
1:48.63	Odd Magne	Øgreid	NOR	7.7.70	6		Sandnes	9 Jun
1:48.71	Pedro J	Canete	CUB	21.1.69	4		Habana	8 Jul
1:48.75	Sergey	Mitov	BUL	12.5.70	4		Sofia	25 Jul
1:48.92	Colin	Mathieson	CAN	19.6.69				

1500 METRES

Mark	Name		Nat	Born	Pos	Meet	Venue	Date
3:36.07	Wilfred Oanda	Kirochi	KEN	12.12.69	4		Rieti	31 Aug
		3:38.2 A			3	NC	Nairobi	18 Jun
		3:39.62			1		Rovereto	29 Jun
3:39.1	Brendan	Matthias	CAN	12.8.69	1		Montreal	11 Aug
3:40.41	Nourredine	Morceli	ALG	20.2.70	2	Kodak	Gateshead	16 Jul
		3:41.85			2r1		Ostrava	7 Jun
3:41.4	Alesandro	Cellai	ITA	17.3.69	2		Viareggio	13 Jul
3:41.6 A	Atoi	Boru	KEN	25.10.73	h?	NC	Nairobi	17 Jun
3:42.56	Fermin	Cacho	SPA	16.2.69	2		Pontevedra	16 Aug
3:42.68	Franzwa	Woldemariam	ETH	69			São Paulo	May
3:42.88	Christoph	Impens	BEL	9.12.69	3		Bruxelles	4 Sep
3:43.07	Siegfried	Sacher	GDR	2.11.69	8		Potsdam	8 Jun
3:43.41	Victor	Ngubeni	RSA	28.9.69	6		Knoxville	21 May
3:43.45	Jason	Pyrah	USA	6.4.69	1		Columbus	24 Jul
3:43.54	Hirokazu	Tatsumi	JAP	23.4.69	1		Odwara	10 Jul
3:43.6 A	Joseph	Kiprobon	KEN	70	7	NC	Nairobi	18 Jun
3:43.6	Bill	Mullaney	IRE	5.5.69			Dedham	2 Jul
3:43.85	Mohamed	Sulaiman	QAT	69	2h3	WJ	Sudbury	30 Jul
3:43.95	Amado	Ramos	CUB	30.1.69	1		Habana	25 Feb
3:43.95	John	Bowden	CAN	69			Ottawa	28 Jul
3:44.04	Fermin Cacho	Ruiz	SPA	16.2.69	3h3	WJ	Sudbury	30 Jul
3:44.40	Zoltán	Káldy	HUN	7.1.69	3		Budapest	3 Sep
3:45.37	Paul	Vandegrift	USA	16.5.69	2	NC-j	Tallahassee	25 Jun

1 MILE

Mark	Name		Nat	Born	Pos	Meet	Venue	Date
3:58.59	Wilfred Oanda	Kirochi	KEN	12.12.69	2		Barcelona	13 Jul

3000 METRES

Mark	Name		Nat	Born	Pos	Meet	Venue	Date
7:54.7	Mohamed	Choumassi	MOR	69	1		Västerås	30 Jun
7:57.22	Morgan	Tollofsén	SWE	9.12.70	2		Umeå	14 Jun
8:00.35i	Zoltán	Kaády	HUN	7.1.69	3		Budapest	27 Feb
8:02.0	Hancene	Morcelli	MOR				Annaba	5 May
8:05.1	Jon	Dennis	UK	25.6.70	4		Colindale	4 Aug
8:11.03	Viktor	Karpenko	SU	69	1	Druzh	Nyiregyháza	14 Aug
8:11.27	Michal	Bartoszak	POL	21.6.70	2	Druzh	Nyiregyháza	14 Aug
8:13.0	Aleksey	Nizyayev	SU	27.7.69			Tartu	20 Jul
8:13.0	Cândido	Maia	POR	8.2.69	4		Lisboa	13 Aug
8:13.52	Carsten	Eich	GDR	9.1.70	3	Druzh	Nyiregyháza	14 Aug

Mark	Name		Nat	Born	Pos	Meet	Venue	Date
5000 METRES								
13:23.27	Addis	Abebe	ETH	70	2	APM	Hengelo	14 Aug
		13:58.08			3	WJ	Sudbury	30 Jul
		14:00.04			1h1	WJ	Sudbury	28 Jul
13:41.20	Bedelu	Kibret	ETH	69	6	APM	Hengelo	14 Aug
13:41.95	Mohamed	Choumassi	MOR	69	8	Nik	Nice	10 Jul
		13:45.70			1		Århus	6 Jul
		13:54.36			2	WJ	Sudbury	30 Jul
13:51.96	Demeke	Bekele	ETH	69	2		São Paulo	22 May
13:52.78	Zoltán	Káldy	HUN	17.1.69	2		Miskolc	17 Jul
13:54.29	Henry Kipyegon	Kirui	KEN	5.4.72	1	WJ	Sudbury	30 Jul
13:59.35	Norbert	Kilimali	TAN	69	4	WJ	Sudbury	30 Jul
14:03.42	Aleksey	Nizyayev	SU	27.7.69	2		Kiev	2 Aug
14:03.7	Juan Manuel	Abad	SPA	19.2.69	1		La Coruña	27 Aug
14:07.66	Jon	Dennis	UK	25.6.70	23	NC	Derby	4 Jun
14:08.0	Paul	Bitok	KEN	26.6.70			Nakuru	11 Jun
14:08.74	Viktor	Karpenko	SU	12.6.70			??	
14:10.9	Michael	Dufermont	FRA	27.5.69			St Maur	22 Jun
14:11.00	Mohamed Ahmed Hussein		SOM	69			Hargeisa	3 Mar
14:11.38	Dean	Livingston	AUS	24.11.70	10		Melbourne	17 Mar
14:12.2	Ryuji	Takei	JAP	18.5.71			Kawaguchi	23 Sep
14:13.16	Yasunari	Oba	JAP	1			Tokyo	21 May
14:13.66	Jun	Hiratsuka	JAP	8.1.69	1		Nagoya	2 Jul
14:13.85	Boay	Akonay	TAN		4h2	WJ	Sudbury	28 Jul
14:14.60	Morgan	Tollofsén	SWE	9.12.70	5h2	WJ	Sudbury	28 Jul
10000 METRES								
27:50.24	Addis	Abebe	ETH	70	3	VD	Bruxelles	19 Aug
		28:42.13			1	WJ	Sudbury	27 Jul
28:12.78	Bedelu	Kibret	ETH	69	11	VD	Bruxelles	19 Aug
		28:48.55			2	WJ	Sudbury	27 Jul
28:25.77	Mohamed	Choumassi	MOR	69	21	Bisl	Oslo	2 Jul
28:50.42	James	Songok	KEN	23.7.70	3	WJ	Sudbury	27 Jul
		28:58.0 A			2	NC	Nairobi	17 Jun
28:51.00	Norbert	Kilimiali	TAN		4	WJ	Sudbury	27 Jul
29:01.73	Zoltán	Káldy	HUN	7.1.69	3	NC	Budapest	22 May
29:02.7	Boay	Akunay	TAN		2		Morogoro	28 Aug
29:03.6	Stephenson G	Nyamu	KEN	21.11.71	3	EAfrC	Kasarani	2 Jul
29:15.6 A	Abel	Gisemba	KEN	69	4	NC	Nairobi	17 Jun
29:17.7	Joseph Mongabi Otwori		KEN	69	1		Hachioji	2 Oct
29:20.1	Terunobu	Iwamoto	JAP				Kawaguchi	23 Sep
29:30.6	Mike	Le Valle	USA	12.12.69	12	PennR	Philadelphia	28 Apr
29:34.6	Takashi	Inuzuka	JAP				Hachioji	10 Oct
29:38.9	Hideyuki	Matsumoto	JAP				Kawaguchi	23 Sep
29:39.3	Rene	Guillen	USA	27.8.69			San Antonio	19 Mar
29:43.51	Jörg	Albert	GDR	22.8.69	9	NC	Potsdam	8 Jun
29:43.9	Hiroyuki	Itabashi	JAP	27.6.69			Hachioji	10 Oct
29:47.44	Masaki	Kido	JAP	10.10.70	1		Kyoto	19 Oct
29:49.55	Yang Fudou		CHN	69			Anshan	7 Jun
29:50.01	Vítor	Barbosa	POR	5.6.69	15		Maia	13 Jul
3000 METRES STEEPLECHASE								
8:36.4 A	William Kipkosgei Chemitei		KEN	29.12.70	4		Nairobi	18 Jun
		8:41.0					Kasarani	2 Jul
		8:41.61			1	WJ	Sudbury	31 Jul
8:43.4	Mathew	Birir	KEN	25.11.69	2		Kasarani	2 Jul
		8:44.54			2	WJ	Sudbury	31 Jul
8:43.70	Leonid	Schvetsov	SU	28.3.69				19 Jun
8:45.25	Horst	Vangermain	GDR	13.9.70	2		Jena	4 Jun
8:45.42	Arto	Kuusisto	FIN	1.3.69	3		Hämeenlinna	6 Aug
		8:46.42			3	WJ	Sudbury	31 Jul
8:48.16	Wander Do Prado Moura		BRA	22.2.69	4	WJ	Sudbury	31 Jul
8:48.57	Richard	Jürgenson	SU	7.1.69	1		Pärnu	13 Jul
8:49.68	Lars	Richter	FRG	31.1.69	3		Koblenz	1 Jun

Mark		Name		Nat	Born	Pos	Meet	Venue	Date
8:50.68		Joseba	González	SPA	27.3.69	8h2	NC	Vigo	11 Aug
8:52.14		Yuriy	Sychov	USR	69				
8:52.4		Giuseppe	D'Urso	ITA	15.9.69			Vigna di Valle	19 May
8:53.53		Kim-Lars	Bauermeister	FRG	20.11.70	6		Koblenz	1 Jun
8:53.72		Carlos	Pinto	POR	16.1.69	4A		Lisboa	11 Jun
8:54.0		Ramiro	Morán	SPA	17.5.69	1		Pontevedra	3 Sep
8:54.36A		Shimeretu	Alemayehu	ETH	70			Addis Abeba	May
8:54.5		Romain	Berthier	FRA	19.10.69			St.Maur	22 Jun
8:54.92		Mark	Wortley	UK	1.6.69	6h1	NC	Derby	4 Jun
8:54.97		Norbert	Wildner	FRG	9.11.69	9		Koblenz	1 Jun
8:55.48		Akihiko	Muramatsu	JAP	21.1.72	1		Nagoya	3 Jul
8:55.54		Markku	Kyyrönen	FIN	31.5.69	2	v4N	Leipzig	6 Jul

110 METRES HURDLES

Mark		Name		Nat	Born	Pos	Meet	Venue	Date
13.75		Mikhail	Edel	SU	7.9.69	1	NC-j	Bryansk	23 Jun
13.79	0.0	Vladimir	Belokon	SU	13.2.69	1		Simferopol	28 May
		13.82w	+3.1			4	WJ	Sudbury	30 Jul
13.80	+0.1	Steve	Brown	USA	6.1.69	1	NC-j	Tallahassee	25 Jun
		13.81	-0.1			1h1	NC-j	Tallahassee	24 Jun
13.81A	+0.8	Roberto	Carmona	MEX	17.9.69	4h2	IbAmC	Cuidad México	22 Jul
13.89	+1.8	Alexandr	Gorshenin	SU	11.5.69	1	NC-j	Bryansk	7 Jul
		13.90				1h	NC-j	Bryansk	7 Jul
13.91	+1.7	Reinaldo	Quintero	CUB	10.7.69	1s2	WJ	Sudbury	30 Jul
		13.93	+0.9			2		Sofia	26 Jun
		13.94				1r2		Columbus	24 Jul
13.94	+0.1	Elbert	Ellis	USA	23.6.69	2	NC-j	Tallahassee	25 Jun
13.94	+1.8	Piotr	Klewenhagen	POL	15.4.69	2		Lublin	8 Sep
13.95	+0.2	Oleg	Arlov	SU	8.1.69	1h	NC-j	Bryansk	7 Jul
13.96	+1.8	Mircea	Oaida	RUM	20.9.69	1	Balk-j	Alexandroúpolis	10 Jul
13.97	+1.7	Paul	Gray	UK	25.5.69	3s2	WJ	Sudbury	30 Jul
13.98		Joe	Galeano	USA	31.7.69	1	KenR	Lexington	23 Apr
13.98	+0.1	Kelly	Carter	USA	15.2.69	2	SEC	Auburn	15 May
13.99	-0.1	Charles	Johnson	USA	69	h		San Angelo	19 May
14.00	+1.9	Arthur	Smith	USA	16.5.69	2	SWC	Austin	15 May
14.04A		Ras	Dotsey	USA	11.4.69	2		Provo	7 May
14.04	+1.8	Robert	Zmelík	CS	18.4.69	3r1		Ostrava	7 Jun
14.08	+0.5	Dan	Philibert	FRA	6.8.70	1		Reims	4 Jun
14.10	+1.8	Pawel	Raczka	POL	15.7.70	1	Druzh	Nyiregyháza	12 Aug
14.12	0.6	Igor	Kovác	CS	12.5.69	1		Banská Bystrica	28 May
Wind assisted									
13.71	+3.1	Reinaldo	Quintero	CUB	10.7.69	1	WJ	Sudbury	30 Jul
13.73	+3.1	Steve	Brown	USA	6.1.69	2	WJ	Sudbury	30 Jul
		13.91	+2.5			1s1	WJ	Sudbury	30 Jul
13.78	+3.1	Elbert	Ellis	USA	23.6.69	3	WJ	Sudbury	30 Jul
13.84	+4.7	Charles	Johnson	USA	69	3	NCAA II	San Angelo	21 May
13.91	+3.3	Arthur	Smith	USA	16.5.69	1h1		Austin	14 May
13.92	+2.4	Dan	Philibert	FRA	6.8.70	2s1	WJ	Sudbury	30 Jul
14.03	+2.5	Diego	Puppo	ITA	4.7.69	4s1	WJ	Sudbury	30 Jul
14.05	+4.1	Theorachis	Varitimidis	GRE	69	2h2	Balk-j	Alexandroúpolis	9 Jul
14.11	+2.5	Hans-Peter	Lott	FRG	9.3.69	5s1	WJ	Sudbury	
Hand timing									
13.7	0.0	Alexandr	Gorshenin	SU	11.5.69	1s		Simferopol	28 May
13.7	0.0	Vladimir	Belokon	SU	13.2.69	1s		Simferopol	28 May
13.7	0.0	Mikhail	Edel	SU	7.9.69	5		Simferopol	28 May
13.9i	-	Oleg	Arlov	SU	8.1.69	2		Chelyabinsk	7 Feb
13.9	-0.8	Vladimir	Dobrydnyev	SU	14.1.70	h		Dnepropetrovsk	30 Apr
13.9	0.0	Boris	Shamash	SU	70	s		Simferopol	28 May

400 METRES HURDLES

Mark		Name		Nat	Born	Pos	Meet	Venue	Date
49.50		Kelly	Carter	USA	15.2.69	1	WJ	Sudbury	29 Jul
			49.90			1	NC-j	Tallahassee	25 Jun
50.03		Ralph	Carrington	USA	30.6.69	2	NC-j	Tallahassee	25 Jun
			50.48			1		Austin	25 Mar
			50.55			1		Austin	6 May
			50.63			1s1		Odessa	20 May

Mark	Name		Nat	Born	Pos	Meet	Venue	Date
50.24	Elbert	Ellis	USA	23.6.69	3	NC-j	Tallahassee	25 Jun
		50.46			3		New Haven	22 May
50.36A	Johan	Jonker	RSA	19.3.70	2		Germiston	22 Oct
50.43	Mugur	Mateescu	RUM	13.6.69	1		Ternopol	25 Sep
50.67	Atsuhi	Yamamoto	JAP	14.9.70	1		Kobe	2 Aug
50.71	Derrick	Adkins	USA	2.7.70	4	NC-j	Tallahassee	25 Jun
50.74	Samuel	Matete	ZAM	25.7.69	3h2	AfrC	Annaba	1 Sep
50.75	Shigeru	Yamaguchi	JAP	16.7.69	3		Tokyo	13 May
50.79	Pawel	Wozniak	POL	5.3.69	3		Poznan	20 Aug
50.81	Vadim	Zadoynov	SU	24.5.69	4	vGB,FRA	Portsmouth	19 Jun
50.84	Keith	Wheeler	USA	1.3.69	2		College Station	25 May
50.90	Oleg	Tverdokhleb	SU	3.1.69	2		Ternopol	25 Sep
51.00	Javier	Paumier	CUB	13.3.69	1		Habana	17 Jul
51.07	Valeriy	Kosobokov	SU	7.11.69	1	NC-j	Bryansk	23 Jul
51.09	Asen	Markov	BUL	27.6.69	1	NC-j	Sofia	3 Jul
51.17A	Dirk	Spies	RSA	30.6.69	2		Pretoria	3 Dec
51.26	Brian	Wright	USA	5.10.69	3		Eugene	29 May
51.29	David	Niare	FRA	27.9.69	1h1		Créteil	9 Jul
51.31	Masanori	Sawano	JAP		2		Kobe	2 Aug
Hand timing								
49.8	Elbert	Ellis	USA	23.6.69	1		Villanova	8 May
50.5A	Samuel	Matete	ZAM	25.7.69	6	Trials	Nairobi	13 Aug
51.2	Sergey	Matveyev	SU	69			Dushanbe	8 May

HIGH JUMP

Mark	Name		Nat	Born	Pos	Meet	Venue	Date
2.28	Artur	Partyka	POL	25.7.69	1		Spala	28 May
		2.28			1	WJ	Sudbury	31 Jul
		2.27i			1		Lodz	16 Jan
		2.26			1		Warszawa	19 Jun
		2.25			1		Ruse	21 May
		2.25			1		Lublin	8 Sep
2.26	Labros	Papakostas	GRE	20.10.69	1	NC	Thesaloniki	11 Jun
		2.25			2	WJ	Sudbury	31 Jul
2.23	Takahisa	Yoshida	JAP	17.2.70	1		Kyoto	19 Oct
2.22	Park Jae-Hong		SKO	8.11.70	1		Columbus	24 Jul
2.22	Jaroslaw	Kotewicz	POL	16.3.69	2=	WJ	Sudbury	31 Jul
2.21i	Aleksandr	Khabarov	SU	29.10.69	1	NC-j	Chelyabinsk	7 Feb
		2.20			2		Moskva	5 Sep
2.21	Walter	Barney	USA	29.3.69	1		Northridge	2 Apr
2.21	Kevin	Clements	USA	28.9.70	1		Elmhurst	18 Jun
2.21	Dimitri	Maenhoudt	BEL	24.3.69	1		Duffel	7 Aug
2.20i	Herman	Moore	USA	20.10.69	1		Johnson City	20 Feb
2.20	Mihec	Prijon	YUG	11.1.71	1		Postojna	21 Aug
2.20	Vladimir	Kostenko	SU	31.8.70	1		Berdichev	21 Sep
2.19	Darren	Plab	USA	26.9.70	1			12 May
2.19	Vyacheslav	Tyrtyshnik	SU	16.1.71	1		Simferopol	27 May
2.19	Carsten	Korth	GDR	3.1.69	5		Jena	3 Jun
2.19	Konstantin	Matusevich	SU	71			Kiev	7 Jun
2.19	Joël	Vincent	FRA	19.1.69	6	NC	Tours	13 Aug
2.19	Hiroyuki	Sakaida	JAP	15.9.71	5	WJ	Sudbury	31 Jul
2.18i	Jacek	Bialobrzewski	POL	8.5.69	1		Warszawa	17 Jan
2.18	Reggie	Betton	USA	14.3.70	1		Arcadia	9 Apr
2.18	Gert	Pieterse	RSA	3.1.69	1		Bloemfontein	16 Apr
2.18	Scott	Benson	USA		1		Sioux Falls	May
2.18	Eric	Hannah	USA	1.3.70	1		Sacramento	11 Jun
2.18	Darwin	Van De Hoef	USA		2		Elmhurst	18 Jun
2.18	Takeki	Uchida	JAP	29.9.70	1		Kobe	3 Aug
2.18	Georgios	Tsoungos	GRE	2.5.69	2		Iráklion	27 Aug
2.18	Ian	Garrett	AUS	70	1		Canberra	11 Dec

POLE VAULT

Mark	Name		Nat	Born	Pos	Meet	Venue	Date
5.65	István	Bagyula	HUN	2.1.69	1	WJ	Sudbury	28 Jul
		5.60			7	OHG	Seoul	28 Sep
		5.56			1	v4N	Leipzig	6 Jul
		5.53						2 Sep
		5.50 on 15 May, 23 Aug, 26 Aug, 9 Sep						
5.60	Andrey	Grudinin	SU	3.5.69	1		Simferopol	27 May
5.60	Maxim	Tarasov	SU	2.12.70	2	WJ	Sudbury	28 Jul
		5.60			3		Odessa	20 Aug
		5.50i on 12 Feb, 5.50 on 6 Aug						
5.45	Kim Chul-Kyun		SKO	28.2.69	1		Seoul	15 Jul
5.40i	Andrey	Fomin	SU	69	2	NC-j	Chelyabinsk	6 Feb
5.40	Dmitriy	Zaytsev	SU	70	1		Nikolayev	14 May
5.40	Andrey	Kravchenko	SU	4.1.71	2		Simferopol	27 May
5.35i	Petri	Peltoniemi	FIN	6.3.70	1		Jablonec	30 Jan
5.35	Patrick	Frederick	USA	21.2.69	1		Austin	8 Jul
5.33	Brent	Burns	USA	2.5.69				19 Mar
5.30	Konstantin	Semyonov	URS	69	1		Fergana	10 Sep
5.20i	Gianni	Iapichino	ITA	2.3.69	5		Firenze	23 Feb
5.20	Matt	Warwick	USA		1			21 Apr
5.20	Yevgeniy	Chistyakov	SU	70	4		Simferopol	29 May
5.20	Martin	Amann	FRG	23.11.70	1		Schwäbisch.Gmünd	29 May
5.20	Miroslav	Dukov	BUL	21.3.71	7		Sofia	4 Jun
5.20	Greg	Fenza	USA	14.11.69	2	NC-j	Tallahassee	24 Jun
5.20	Jayson	Lavender	USA	71	3	NC-j	Tallahassee	24 Jun
5.20	Tadeusz	Tomaszewski	POL	21.1.70	1		Bochum	26 Jun
5.20	Aleksandr	Ivanyets	SU	69	1		Bryansk	28 Jun
5.20	Marc	Osenberg	FRG	15.3.69	1		Lübeck	9 Jul
5.20	Erki	Nool	SU	25.6.70	4		Pärnu	13 Jul

Best outdoor marks

Mark	Name	Pos	Venue	Date
5.40	Fomin	3	Bryansk	7 Jul
5.30	Peltoniemi	1	Vammala	11 Jun
5.20	Iapichino	1	M. Carrara	14 May

LONG JUMP

Mark	Wind	Name		Nat	Born	Pos	Meet	Venue	Date
8.28	0.8	Luis Alberto	Bueno	CUB	22.5.69	1		Habana	16 Jul
		8.25A				Q	IbAmC	Ciudad México	22 Jul
		8.10				1		Columbus	24 Jul
		7.99	-1.0			1	WJ	Sudbury	29 Jul
8.00	1.9	Sergey	Novozhilov	SU	21.4.69	1	NC-j	Bryansk	7 Jul
7.98	1.6	Stewart	Faulkner	UK	19.2.69	1	AAA	Birmingham	6 Aug
		7.93	+0.2			1		Athens	3 Sep
7.94	0.9	André	Müller	GDR	15.11.70	3		Berlin	20 Jul
7.93	0.6	Saúl	Isalgué	CUB	3.11.70	2		Habana	16 Jul
7.91i	-	Konstandinos	Koukodimos	GRE	14.9.69	1		Piraeus	29 Jan
		7.87	1.4			1	Balk-j	Alexandroúpolis	10 Jul
7.89		Alan	Turner	USA	19.3.69	2		Columbus	24 Jul
7.88		Obinna	Eregbu	NIG	11.9.69	2		Port Harcourt	14 Jan
7.87	1.2	Peller	Phillips	USA	23.6.70	-		Sacramento	11 Jun
7.86Ai	-	Percy	Knox	USA	14.10.69	1		Flagstaff	20 Feb
7.85	1.7	Igor	Lysenko	SU	28.9.70	2	NC-j	Bryansk	7 Jul
7.84	1.0	Nai Hui-fang		TAI	26.2.69	1	AsiC-j	Singapore	8 Sep
7.83		McArthur	Anderson	USA	25.10.69	1		San Diego	5 Mar
7.81	1.6	Milko	Campus	ITA	4.2.69	1		Formia	19 Jun
7.80		Keith	Holley	USA	8.11.69	4		Columbus	8 May
7.80		Dion	Bentley	USA	26.8.71	1		Pittsburgh	19 May
7.80	2.0	Yevgeniy	Semenyuk	SU	11.12.69	3	NC-j	Bryansk	7 Jul
7.80	2.0	Andrey	Yegorov	SU	7.2.69	5	NC-j	Bryansk	7 Jul
7.79	0.0	Bogdan	Tudor	RUM	1.2.70	1		Resita	2 Oct

Wind assisted

Mark	Wind	Name		Nat	Born	Pos	Meet	Venue	Date
8.23	4.4	Peller	Phillips	USA	23.6.70	1		Sacramento	11 Jun
8.04	3.2	Stewart	Faulkner	UK	19.2.69	1		Haringey	20 Aug
7.80	2.2	Ilya	Sablin	SU	69	4	NC-j	Bryansk	7 Jul

Mark		Name		Nat	Born	Pos	Meet	Venue	Date
TRIPLE JUMP									
16.76	0.2	Vladimir	Melikhov	SU	30.3.69	1		Simferopol	29 May
		16.69	+1.6			1	WJ	Sudbury	31 Jul
		16.52w	+2.4			Q	WJ	Sudbury	30 Jul
16.61		Robin	Hernández	CUB	21.10.69	3		Habana	19 Feb
16.61	0.3	Reggie	Jackson	USA	5.7.69	1	NC-j	Tallahassee	25 Jun
16.48		Nai Hui-fang		TAI	26.2.69	1	AsiC-j	Singapore	10 Sep
16.42	1.9	Aleksey	Fatyanov	SU	69	1	NC-j	Bryansk	6 Jul
16.41	1.2	Juan Carlos	Ibanez	CUB	24.11.69	1		Habana	25 Mar
16.33		Carlos	Vizcaino	CUB	29.7.69	1		Camaguey	13 Feb
16.33		Sun Xiao		CHN	69			Qingdao	29 Jun
16.29	1.4	Stoicho	Tsonov	BUL	6.5.69	1	NC-j	Sofia	2 Jul
16.25i	-	Ilya	Yashchuk	SU	18.5.70	1	NC-j	Chelyabinsk	6 Feb
16.22i		Yuriy	Osipenko	SU	12.7.69	2	NC-j	Chelyabinsk	6 Feb
16.22		Andrius	Raiznis	SU	69	2		Siauliai	22 May
16.21		Anisio	Souza Silva	BRA	18.6.69	1		Columbus	24 Jul
16.20	0.8	Georges	Sainte-Rose	FRA	3.9.69	3	NC	Tours	13 Aug
16.18	1.8	Galin	Georgiev	BUL	23.3.70	2	WJ	Sudbury	31 Jul
16.16	1.2	Eugene	Greene	BAH	24.3.69	3	WJ	Sudbury	31 Jul
16.15	0.7	Alex	Norca	FRA	18.1.69	-		Creteil	10 Jul
16.12		Saúl	Isalgué	CUB	3.11.70	1		Guantanamo	13 Feb
16.10	1.8	Vladlen	Trutayev	SU	19.4.70	2	NC-j	Bryansk	6 Jul
16.09		Germain	Martial	FRA	69	1		Kingston	8Apr
Wind assisted									
16.40	3.1	Alex	Norca	FRA	18.1.69	1		Créteil	10 Jul
16.33	4.0	Andrew	Murphy	AUS	18.12.69	3		Perth	26 Mar
16.23	2.6	Li Hong		CHN	18.4.69	q	WJ	Sudbury	30 Jul
16.19	2.2	Giorgos	Dalousis	GRE	4.6.69	1		Athinai	11 Sep
16.10	+3.2	Germain	Martial	FRA	69	3		Créteil	10Jul
SHOT									
19.44		Michael	Stulce	USA	14.7.69	1	SWC	Austin	14 May
			19.08			1		Columbus	24Jul
			19.04			Q	NCAA	Eugene	2Jun
			18.99			1	NCAA	Eugene	4 Jul
			18.95					Houston	25 May
			18.91			2		College Station	16 Apr
			18.84			1		Houston	4 May
19.18i		Aleksander	Klimenko	SU	27.3.70	1	NC-j	Chelyabinsk	7 Feb
			19.18			1		Simferopol	27 May
			18.92			1	WJ	Sudbury	30 Jul
18.81i		Dmitriy	Vasilyev	SU	24.3.69	7		Moskva	20 Feb
18.65i		Aleksandr	Klimov	SU	25.6.69	2	NC-j	Chelyabinsk	7 Feb
18.26		Shane	Collins	USA	11.4.69	2	Pac-10	Westwood	21 May
18.12		Mikhail	Luvochenko	SU	69	1			25Sep
18.08		Dmitriy	Slasten	SU	69	4		Simferopol	27 May
17.73		Frank	Werth	GDR	20.4.70	1		Schwerin	1 Jun
17.73		Leonid	Tikhonyuk	SU	69	3		Bryansk	24 Jun
17.69		Paolo	Dal Soglio	ITA	29.7.70			Vicenza	4 Oct
17.68		Robert	Sehnert	USA	20.2.69	1	PennR	Philadelphia	30 Apr
17.62		Mika	Halvari	FIN	13.2.70			Huddinge	27 Aug
17.60i		Matthew	Simson	UK	28.5.70	1	NC-j	Cosford	19 Mar
17.53		Dirk	Preuss	GDR	8.1.70	3		Halle	11 Jun
17.53		David	Bultman	USA	6.3.69	2	NC-j	Tallahassee	25 Jun
17.44		Andreas	Vlasny	AUT	12.9.69	1		Bad Ischl	25 Sep
17.40		Cui Guangyuan	CHN	30.6.69			Jinan	30 Oct	
17.39		Jordy	Reynolds	USA	69	6	SWC	Austin	14 May
17.39		Dirk	Urban	FRG	14.1.69	1		Bochum	26 Jun
17.36		Igor	Smolyakov	SU	25.5.69			Bryansk	29 Jun
Best outdoor marks									
18.71		Vasilyev	1	Fergana			10 Sep		
18.20		Klimov	1	Bryansk			6 Jul		
17.54		Simson	1	Thurrock			9 Sep		

Mark	Name		Nat	Born	Pos	Meet	Venue	Date
DISCUS								
62.52	John	Nichols	USA	23.8.69	1		Baton Rouge	23 Apr
		61.90			1		Eugene	16 Apr
		59.72			1		Tempe	2 Apr
		59.32			1	DrakeR	Des Moines	29 Apr
61.84	Andreas	Seelig	GDR	6.7.70	1		Halle	15 May
		60.54			1	vSU	Halle	11 Jun
		60.46					Berlin	18 Jul
		60.16			3		Seville	1 Jun
		59.18			6		Jena	4 Jun
59.26	Michael	Möllenbeck	FRG	12.12.69	1		Bonn	2 Jul
57.50	Andrey	Balashov	SU	69			Moskva	8 Jul
56.50	Kari	Keshmiri	USA	23.1.69	1		Los Gatos	27 Feb
56.32	Yuriy	Nesteryets	SU	26.2.69	2	vGDR-j	Halle	11 Jun
56.16	Pedro J.	Acosta	CUB	15.1.70	1		Jalisco	25 Jun
55.60	Vitaliy	Sidorov	SU	70	1	NC-j	Bryansk	6 Jul
55.02	Nikolay	Shidlovskiy	SU	23.2.69	1		Nikolayev	13 May
55.02	Artur	Astapenko	SU	69			Leningrad	10 Aug
54.76	Andrey	Ganatobvsliy	SU	69	1		Bryansk	29 Jun
54.74	Ma Wei		CHN	10.3.69			Beijing	17 Apr
54.46	Valeriy	Shimanskiy	SU	30.1.69	1		Adler	26 Feb
54.22	Joachim	Tidow	FRG	4.2.69	3	vPOL-j	Bochum	26 Jun
54.16	Péter	Tamás	HUN	19.4.71	2		Osijek	16 Apr
54.00	Jordy	Reynolds	USA	69	2	PennR	Philadelphia	29 Apr
53.36	Dariusz	Kosinski	POL	16.6.70	1		Pila	16 Jul
53.08	Steve	Yates	USA	69	3	PennR	Philadelphia	29 Apr
53.08	János	Verebes	HUN	25.2.69			Pecs	18 Sep
52.90	Tapani	Alentola	FIN	14.5.69			Forssa	9 Jun
HAMMER								
73.32	Oleg	Polyushin	SU	23.4.69	1		Simferopol	29 May
		71.70			1		Sudbury	23 Jul
72.62	Vadim	Kolesnik	SU	29.4.69	1	NC-j	Bryansk	6 Jul
		70.72			2		Simferopol	29May
72.34	Stefan	Fischer	FRG	19.1.69	1		Leverkusen	16 Jul
72.18	Sergey	Gavrilov	SU	70	1		Moskva	18 Jun
71.20	Sergey	Kumasov	SU	70	4		Ordzhonikidze	24 Sep
71.12	Aleksandr	Muravskiy	SU	70	1		Dnepropetrovsk	15 May
70.74	Valeriy	Kobarenkov	SU	69				13 Aug
70.70	Thomas	Hommel	GDR	16.8.69	1		Potsdam	21 Jul
70.70	Sergey	Lebonta	SU	11.6.69			Fergana	11 Sep
70.24	Dmitriy	Sukharev	SU	69	1		Bryansk	28 Jun
69.78	Aleksandr	Yeroshin	SU	12.4.69	2		Bryansk	28 Jun
69.74	Giovanni	Sanguin	ITA	14.5.69	1		Verona	20 Jul
69.62	Emilio	Calabro	ITA	4.2.69	1		Latina	2 Oct
69.60	Janos	Verebes	HUN	25.2.69	1		Budapest	19 Jun
69.48	Andrey	Dvoretskiy	SU	6.1.69	1		Sochi	26 Feb
69.08	Steffen	Burdack	GDR	30.6.70	3	vSU-j	Halle	12 Jun
68.94	Hannes	Pinter	AUT	69			Wolfsberg	4 Jun
68.92	Georgios	Nalzaziadis	GRE	29.1.69	1		Iráklion	27 Aug
68.44	Eleonor	Rosca	RUM	15.3.69			Bucuresti	5 Jun
68.14	Andrey	Mityushin	SU	70	1		Nikolayev	14 May
JAVELIN								
80.26	Vladimir	Ovchinnikov	SU	2.8.70	q	OG	Seoul	24 Sep
		80.18			2		Vilnius	28 Aug
		79.56			1		Vladivostok	14 Sep
		79.12			7	OG	Seoul	24 Sep
		78.96			1	Druzh	Nyiregyháza	13 Aug
		78.80			1		Bucaresti	18 Jun
		78.20			1		Adler	27 Feb
		78.04			1		Adler	13 Feb
79.50	Stephen	Backley	UK	12.2.69	1	NC	Derby	5 Jun
		78.00			4	AAA	Birmingham	7 Aug

Mark	Name		Nat	Born	Pos	Meet	Venue	Date
77.08	Juha	Laukkanen	FIN	6.1.69	2		Kuortane	28 May
76.06	Kimmo	Solehmainen	FIN	22.3.69	2		Helsinki	1 Jun
75.92	Gerhard	Burger	RSA	21.12.69	1		Pretoria	15 Oct
75.46	Jens	Reimann	GDR	21.3.69	1		Halle	14 May
75.20	Johan	van Lieshout	HOL	8.3.69	1		Helmond	2 Sep
74.84	Jan	Stark	GDR	4.4.70	1		Berlin	6 Feb
74.52	Dmitriy	Polyunik	SU	6.4.69	3		Odessa	20 Aug
74.26	Angel	Mandzhukov	BUL	3.3.69	4		Sofia	25 Jun
73.94	Juha	Mattila	FIN	11.1.69	1		Pattijoki	10 Aug
73.80	Tommi	Viskari	FIN	3.2.71	1		Lappeenranta	2 Jun
73.08	Park Yong-Young		SKO	30.12.69			Seoul	21 Apr
73.04	Ján	Garaj	CS	23.3.70	1		Bratislava	3 Sep
72.74	Michael	Kettner	GDR	4.7.70	3	v4N	Leipzig	6 Jul
72.66	Alexey	Shurkhal	SU	17.9.70	1		Ternopol	24 Sep
72.54	Gert	Beyer	GDR	24.6.70	1		Jena	3 Jun
72.52	Kimio	Morisawa	JAP	26.10.70	1		Nagoya	3 Jul
72.30	Hansie	Rothman	RSA	3.7.69	1		Sasolburg	16 Nov
72.08	Petri	Castren	FIN	2.6.69	1		Pihtipudas	19 Jul

DECATHLON

Mark	Name		Nat	Born	Pos	Meet	Venue	Date
7790	Michael	Kohnle	FRG	3.5.70	1	vPOL-j	Bochum	26 Jun
	10.91 7.03 13.14 2.02 49.27 14.71 40.24 4.90 56.18 4:48.76							
		7729			1	WJ	Sudbury	28 Jul
	10.78 6.97 13.25 2.01 48.96 14.60 36.50 4.50 58.38 4:38.65							
7659	Robert	Zmelík	CS	18.4.69	2	WJ	Sudbury	28 Jul
	11.08 7.29 12.33 2.07 51.08 14.61 38.98 4.50 56.08 4:37.78							
		7488			1		Leipzig	7 Jul
	11.10 7.53 12.15 2.05 50.82. 14.78 36.26 4.30 55.76 4:49.16							
7596	Eduard	Hämäläinen	SU	21.1.69	3	WJ	Sudbury	28 Jul
	11.42 6.99 13.57 2.01 50.21 14.91 39.84 4.70 53.18 4:33.22							
		7480			1	vGDR	Halle	12 Jun
	11.44 6.99 13.36 1.90 49.97 15.01 40.64 4.60 55.62 4:33.26							
7529	Henrik	Dagård	SWE	7.8.69	3		Fredriksberg	3 Jul
	10.69w 7.19 12.32 1.89 47.83 15.29w 35.40 4.20 62.38 4:43.66							
7501	Sergey	Kolmakov	SU	69	1	NC-j	Bryansk	7 Jul
	11.07 7.32 12.85 1.97 51.69 14.79 40.04 4.50 50.82 4:38.22							
7499	Asen	Alexandrov	BUL	5.5.69	2		Sofia	7 Aug
	10.9 7.16 14.84 2.00 51.0 14.4 40.04 4.40 53.54 5:19.8							
7464	Norbert	Lampe	GDR	9.1.70	1	Druzh	Nyiregyháza	14 Aug
	11.05 6.97 12.39 1.87 48.77 15.39 41.36 4.20 56.10 4:26.03							
7425	Aleksandr	Zhdanovich	SU	15.11.69	2		Bryansk	7 Jul
	11.02 6.95 12.77 1.94 49.64 15.40 40.00 4.20 52.12 4:25.51							
7406	Jochen	Ackermann	FRG	24.5.69	1		Ahlen	29 May
	10.99 7.00 13.13 1.84 48.93 15.37 39.70 4.20 55.86 4:34.47							
7370	Alvaro	Burrell	SPA	29.4.69	2	v3N	Lorca	19 Jun
	11.34 6.75 14.19 1.99 48.88 15.27 41.70 3.90 51.54 4:35.16							
7283	Sergey	Pustovit	SU	70	3		Simferopol	28 May
7267	Christian	Jacquart	FRA	6.8.69			Bordeaux	1 May
	11.44 6.93 13.70 1.86 49.96 14.80 42.72 4.00 50.52 4:37.93							
7247w	Radek	Bartakovic	CS	16.3.70	4		Praha	29 May
	11.03 7.17W 12.14 1.91 48.21 16.44 33.98 4.50 47.02 4:26.19							
7247	Sándor	Munkácsi	HUN	24.7.69	5		Budapest	7 Aug
	11.36 7.03 11.13 2.02 49.91 15.31 35.58 4.30 46.28 4:17.86							
7226w	Thomas	Neumann	GDR	11.7.69	1		Jena	4 Jun
	11.39 6.92w 12.45 1.92 50.62 15.46 38.08 4.20 57.44 4:35.19							
7224	Mirko	Spada	SWZ	26.1.69	13		Landquart	12 Jun
	11.25w 6.77 14.58 1.83 50.24 15.23 44.16 3.80 54.20 4:44.51							
7215	Aleksandr	Kostyubenko	SU	70	3	NC-j	Bryansk	7 Jul
	11.53 6.92 12.84 1.94 50.78 15.47 37.00 4.50 51.46 4:33.56							
7207	Raimonds	Gausins	SU	4.2.71	2		Murjani	9 May
	11.0 6.78 12.32 1.95 50.4 15.2 41.40 3.80 52.90 4:24.8							
7201	Lars-Erik	Geisel	FRG	22.1.69	2		Bochum	26 Jun
	11.39 6.90 12.80 1.87 50.91 15.47 37.78 4.40 54.66 4:34.28							
7178	Udo	Jacobasch	GDR	30.8.70	2		Dresden	8 May
	11.65 6.92 12.50 1.92 50.62 15.20w 39.72 4.70 46.32 4:41.52							

Mark	Name		Nat	Born	Pos	Meet	Venue	Date

10000 METRES WALK

Mark	Name		Nat	Born	Pos	Meet	Venue	Date
40:59.48	Mikhail	Khmelnitskiy	SU	24.7.69	1	vGDR-j	Halle	11 Jun
	41:24.6				1		Simferopol	27 May
	41:38.86				3	WJ	Sudbury	29 Jul
40:59.50	Andrey	Sapnikas	SU	13.11.69	2	vGDR-j	Halle	11 Jun
	41:30.2				2		Simferopol	27 May
41:10.90	Yuriy	Mostovik	SU	12.2.71	1	NC-j	Bryansk	7 Jul
41:13.00	Ralf	Weise	GDR	15.9.69	3	vSU-j	Halle	11 Jun
41:16.11	Alberto	Cruz	MEX	6.6.72	1	WJ	Sudbury	29 Jul
41:33.95	Valentin	Massana	SPA	5.7.70	2	WJ	Sudbury	29 Jul
41:39.79	Olaf	Möldner	GDR	12.12.69	1		Karl-Marx-Stadt	15 Jul
41:41.4	Juan	Rojas	ECU	20569	1	SAm-j	São Paulo	2 Jul
41:46.41	Germán	Nieto	SPA	7.4.70	4	WJ	Sudbury	29 Jul
41:47.6	Károly	Kirszt	HUN	23.7.69	1	vYUG-j	Zalaegerszeg	26 Jun
41:51.20	Volker	Jahn	GDR	19.7.69	2	NC-j	Karl-Marx-Stadt	15 Jul
42:03.3	Nick	A'Hern	AUS	6.1.69	2		Canberra	26 Jan
42:05.9	Chen Baowen		CHN				Xuzhou	19 Mar
42:08.8	Leszek	Pazio	POL	17.5.70	5		Sopot	22 May
42:09.9	Wang Feng		CHN				Xuzhou	19 Mar
42:13.4	Kong Tao		CHN				Xuzhou	19 Mar
42:22.0	Fanis	Shaikhudzhinov	SU	69	2		Bryansk	24 Jun
42:23.2	Rishat	Shafikov	SU	70	3		Simferopol	27 May
42:23.8	Bernardo	Cartoni	ITA	13.7.69	2		Roma	13 Apr
42:25.6	Yevgeniy	Bocharov	SU	69	3		Bryansk	24 Jun
Indoor mark								
42:12.0	Rishat	Shafikov	SU	70	2	NC-j	Chelyabinsk	7 Feb

4 x 100 METRES RELAY

Mark	Nat	Team	Pos	Meet	Venue	Date
39.27	USA	Braunskill, Watts, Cason, Warren	1	WJ	Sudbury	31 Jul
		39.40 Braunskill, Watts, Cason, Warren	1h	WJ	Sudbury	30 Jul
		39.41 Braunskill, Watts, Cason, Warren	1		Columbus	24 Jul
39.54	NIG	Tetengi, Ezinwa, Nwankwo, Adeniken	1h2	WJ	Sudbury	30 Jul
39.62	SU	Shlychkov, Kuchmuradov, Goremykin, Ivanov	1	Druzh	Nyiregyháza	13 Aug
		39.88	1	VGDR-j	Halle	11 Jun
39.96	GDR	Olbrich, Matthes, Gratz, Huke	1		Cottbus	29 May
	unsanctioned race	39.48 Olbrich, Matthes, Gratz, Löchle	1		Berlin	20 Jul
39.99	JAP	Okuyama, Sugimoto, Kato, Nakamichi	1	AsiC-j	Singapore	11 Sep
40.06	UK	Rumbolt, Stapleton, Braithwaite, Henderson	3	WJ	Sudbury	31 Jul
40.1	AUS	Bennett, Garner, Jackson, Johnson	1		Hobart	5 Jan
		40.30 Johnson,Bennett,Garner,Jackson	1		Leipzig	6 Jul
40.47	JAM	Moore, Dobson, Mowatt, Allen	4h2	WJ	Sudbury	30 Jul
40.49	TAI		2	AsiC-j	Singapore	11 Sep
40.50	BEL		4		Bruxelles	19 Aug
40.51	FRA	Lecerf, Théophile, Ceryl, Perrot	5h2	WJ	Sudbury	30 Jul
40.51	CAN	Clarke, McCuaig, Pierre, Ogilvie	6h2	WJ	Sudbury	30 Jul
40.71	FRG	Peters, Terlinden, Schulte-Mäter, Reinicke	1	vPOL-j	Bochum	25 Jun

4 x 400 METRES RELAY

Mark	Nat	Team	Pos	Meet	Venue	Date
3:05.09	USA	Carr, Nelloms, J.Williams, Carrington	1	WJ	Sudbury	31 Jul
		3:06.12 Carr, Nelloms, J.Williams, Carrington	1h2	WJ	Sudbury	30 Jul
		3:07.44 Nelloms, Carr, J.Williams, Carrington	1		Columbus	24 jul
3:07.60	JAM	Pryce, England, Johnson, Campbell	2		Columbus	24 Jul
3:07.60	AUS	Ryan, Garner, Capobianco, Perry	2	WJ	Sudbury	31 Jul
3:08.02	CUB	Cadogan, Díaz, Carmensolta, Cañete	1h1	WJ	Sudbury	30 Jul
3:08.15	FRA	Noirot, Landre, Blancquart, Jean-Charles	2h1	WJ	Sudbury	30 jul
3:08.24	NIG	Omokheghuele, Oritse, Omokaro, Eziuka	3h2	WJ	Sudbury	30 Jul
3:08.57	JAP	Matsunaga, Komori, Yamaguchi, Tachi	4h2	WJ	Sudbury	30 Jul
3:09.80	POL	Jazwinski, Oraczewski, Wozniak, Jedrusik	1		Bochum	26 Jun
3:10.13	CAN	Dicker, Jones, Fidelak, Jackson	5h2	WJ	Sudbury	30 Jul
3:11.23	SPA	Cuesta, Navarro, Mohedano, Mañas	6h2	WJ	Sudbury	30 Jul
3:11.23	SU	Gabidullin, Barakhov, Kosobokov, Goremykin	1	Druzh	Nyiregyháza	14 Aug
3:11.41	GDR	Schmidt, Baxmann, Lieder, Tschida	2	Druzh	Nyiregyháza	14 Aug
3:11.51	CS	Lysek, Hujer, Sendler, Josták	2		Leipzig	7 Jul
3:11.71	KEN	Kosgei, Tengelei, Birir, Kirochi	7h2	WJ	Sudbury	30 Jul
3:11.81	UK	Roberts, Lill, McDonald, Richardson	1	vCS-j	Praha	19 Jun

WOMEN'S ALL-TIME LISTS

100 METRES

Mark	Wind	Name		Nat	Yr	Pos	Meet	Venue	Date
10.49	0.0	Florence	Griffith-Joyner	USA	59	1q1	FOT	Indianapolis	16 Jul 88
10.61	1.2		Griffith-Joyner			1	FOT	Indianapolis	17 Jul 88
10.62	1.0		Griffith-Joyner			1q3	OG	Seoul	24 Sep 88
10.70	1.6		Griffith-Joyner			1s1	FOT	Indianapolis	17 Jul 88
10.76	1.7	Evelyn	Ashford	USA	57	1	WK	Zürich	22 Aug 84
10.79A	0.6		Ashford			1	USOF	Colo Springs	3 Jul 83
10.81	1.7	Marlies	Göhr'	GDR	58	1	OD	Berlin	8 Jun 83
10.81	1.2		Ashford			2	FOT	Indianapolis	17 Jul 88
10.83	1.7	Marita	Koch	GDR	57	2	OD	Berlin	8 Jun 83
10.83	0.0	Sheila	Echols	USA	64	1q2	FOT	Indianapolis	16 Jul 88
10.84	1.7		Göhr			2	WK	Zürich	22 Aug 84
10.85	1.6		Ashford			2s1	FOT	Indianapolis	17 Jul 88
10.85	2.0	Anelia	Nuneva	BUL	62	1s1	NC	Sofia	2 Sep 88
10.86	0.4		Göhr			1		Potsdam	5 May 84
10.86	2.0		Göhr			1		Berlin	22 Sep 85
10.86	0.8		Nuneva'			1		Beograd	17 Jun 87
10.86	0.6	Silke	Gladisch'	GDR	64	1	NC	Potsdam	20 Aug 87
10.86	0.0	Diane	Williams	USA	60	2q1	FOT	Indianapolis	16 Jul 88
10.87	1.9		Göhr			1		Dresden	26 Jul 84
10.87	1.1	Merlene	Ottey	JAM	60	1		Walnut	31 May 87
10.87	0.2		Nuneva			1	NC	Sofia	2 Sep 88
10.88	2.0		Oelsner'			1	NC	Dresden	1 Jul 77
10.88	1.9		Göhr			1	v USA	Karl-Marx-Stadt	9 Jul 82
10.88	1.9		Ashford			1		Rieti	7 Sep 86
10.88	1.0		Griffith-Joyner			1h7	OG	Seoul	24 Sep 88
10.88	1.6		Ashford			1q2	OG	Seoul	24 Sep 88
10.89	0.7		Göhr			1	NC	Erfurt	1 Jun 84
10.89	-0.1		Griffith-Joyner			1		San Diego	25 Jun 88
10.89	2.0		Göhr			1	v Ita	Neubrandenburg	9 Jul 88
10.89	1.8	Katrin	Krabbe	GDR	69	1		Berlin	20 Jul 88
		(30 performances by 10 athletes)							
10.91	0.2	Heike	Drechsler'	GDR	64	2	GWG	Moskva	6 Jul 86
10.91	1.2	Gwen	Torrence	USA	65	3	FOT	Indianapolis	17 Jul 88
10.92	0.0	Alice	Brown	USA	60	2q2	FOT	Indianapolis	16 Jul 88
10.93	1.8	Ewa	Kasprzyk	POL	57	1	NC	Grudziadz	27 Jun 86
10.95	1.0	Barbel	Wöckel'	GDR	55	2	NC	Dresden	1 Jul 82
10.97	0.0	Angella	Issajenko'	CAN	58	3	ASV	Köln	16 Aug 87
10.97	0.0	Gail	Devers-Roberts	USA	66	3q1	FOT	Indianapolis	16 Jul 88
10.98	0.1	Marina	Zhirova	SU	63	2	EP	Moskva	17 Aug 85
10.98	0.8	Angela	Bailey	CAN	62	2	BGP	Budapest	6 Jul 87
10.98	1.6	Natalya	Pomoshchnikova	SU	65	2q2	OG	Seoul	24 Sep 88
		(20)							
10.99	1.3	Valerie	Brisco-Hooks	USA	69	1	Pepsi	Westwood	17 May 86
11.01	0.6	Annegret	Richter	FRG	50	1s1	OG	Montreal	25 Jul 76
11.01	0.8	Pam	Marshall	USA	60	2	Athl	Lausanne	15 Sep 87
11.02	2.0	Romy	Müller'	GDR	58	3	OT	Dresden	24 May 80
11.02	-0.2	Lyudmila	Kondratyeva	SU	58	2	Drz	Praha	16 Aug 84
11.03	2.0	Monika	Hamann'	GDR	54	2	NC	Dresden	1 Jul 77
11.03	1.0	Juliet	Cuthbert	JAM	64	2q3	OG	Seoul	24 Sep 88
11.04	0.6	Inge	Helten	FRG	50	1h1		Fürth	13 Jun 76
11.04	1.7	Ingrid	Auerswald'	GDR	57	4	WK	Zürich	22 Aug 84
11.05	1.0	Kerstin	Behrendt	GDR	67	3	OT	Potsdam	8 Sep 88
	(30)								
11.07	-0.2	Renate	Stecher'	GDR	50	1	OG	München	2 Sep 72
11.07	1.8	Galina	Malchugina	SU	62	1	Znam	Leningrad	11 Jun 88
11.08A	1.2	Wyomia	Tyus	USA	45	1	OG	Ciudad México	15 Oct 68
11.08	2.0	Brenda	Morehead	USA	57	1	FOT	Eugene	21 Jun 76
11.08	-0.1	Jeanette	Bolden	USA	60	2	WK	Zürich	13 Aug 86
11.08	0.8	Nelli	Cooman-Fiere	HOL	64	3	ECh	Stuttgart	27 Aug 86
11.08		Marina	Molokova	SU	62	1		Sochi	16 May 87

Mark		Name		Nat	Yr	Pos	Meet	Venue	Date
11.08		Grace	Jackson	JAM	61	2s1	NC	Kingston	15 Jul 88
11.08	0.0	Maya	Azarashvili	SU	64	1		Kiev	14 Aug 88
11.09	1.7	Jarmila	Kratochvílová	CS	51	1	PTS	Bratislava	6 Jun 81
		(40)							
11.09	1.7	Nadezhda	Georgieva	BUL	61	1	NC	Sofia	4 Jun 83
11.09	-1.4	Irina	Slyusar	SU	63	1	Znam	Leningrad	7 Jun 86
11.09		Mary	Onyali	NIG	68	1	NC	Bauchi	2 Jul 88
11.10	0.1	Kathy	Smallwood'	UK	60	2	WP	Roma	5 Sep 81
11.10	1.6	Dannette	Young	USA	64	3s1	FOT	Indianapolis	17 Jul 88
11.11	1.7	Bärbel	Schölzel	GDR	59	5	OD	Berlin	8 Jun 83
11.11A	0.6	Jackie	Washington	USA	62	3	USOF	Colorado Springs	3 Jul 83
11.11	0.0	Carlette	Guidry	USA	68	4q1	FOT	Indianapolis	16 Jul 88
11.12A	0.6	Barbara	Ferrell	USA	47	1q1	OG	Ciudad México	14 Oct 68
11.12	0.2	Elvira	Barbashina'	SU	63	3	GWG	Moskva	6 Jul 86
	(50)								

Semi-automatic timing

Mark		Name		Nat	Yr	Pos	Meet	Venue	Date
10.87	1.9	Lyudmila	Kondratyeva	SU	58	1	Leningrad		3 Jun 80
10.99	1.9	Natalya	Bochina	SU	62	2	Leningrad		3 Jun 80

Marks made with assisting wind > 2m/s

Mark		Name		Nat	Yr	Pos	Meet	Venue	Date
10.54	3.0		Griffith-Joyner			1	OG	Seoul	25 Sep 88
10.60	3.2		Griffith-Joyner			1h1	FOT	Indianapolis	16 Jul 88
10.70	2.6		Griffith-Joyner			1s2	OG	Seoul	25 Sep 88
10.78	3.1		Ashford			1		Modesto	12 May 84
10.78	5.0	Gwen	Torrence	USA	65	1q3	FOT	Indianapolis	16 Jul 88
10.79	3.3	Marlies	Göhr'	GDR	58	1	NC	Cottbus	16 Jul 80
10.80	2.9	Pam	Marshall	USA	60	1	TAC	Eugene	20 Jun 86
10.80	2.8	Heike	Drechsler'	GDR	64	1	Bisl	Oslo	5 Jul 86
10.82	2.2	Silke	Gladisch'	GDR	64	1s1	WCh	Roma	30 Aug 87
10.83	3.9		Echols			1h2	FOT	Indianapolis	16 Jul 88
10.83	3.0		Ashford			2	OG	Seoul	25 Sep 88
10.84	2.9	Alice	Brown	USA	60	2	TAC	Eugene	20 Jun 86
10.85	5.2		Ashford			1		Norwalk	14 Jun 81
10.85	2.4		Ashford			1		Modesto	14 May 83
10.85	2.9		Ashford			3	TAC	Eugene	20 Jun 86
10.85	4.7	Gail	Devers	USA	66	1s1	PAG	Indianapolis	9 Aug 87
10.85	3.0		Drechsler			3	OG	Seoul	25 Sep 88
10.86	3.0		Devers			1	NCAA	Eugene	4 Jun 88
10.87	3.5		Torrence			1	Pre	Eugene	2 Jul 88
10.88	3.0		Ashford			1	MSR	Walnut	29 Apr 84
10.88	3.9		Brown			2h2	FOT	Indianapolis	16 Jul 88
		(21/10)							
10.89	3.1	Kerstin	Behrendt	GDR	67	2		Berlin	13 Sep 88
10.92	3.3	Bärbel	Wöckel'	GDR	55	2	NC	Cottbus	16 Jul 80
10.92	3.4	Angella	Taylor'	CAN	58	1s2	CG	Brisbane	4 Oct 82
10.93	3.8	Sonia	Lannaman	UK	56	1	EP/sf	Dublin	17 Jul 77
10.93	3.3	Ingrid	Auerswald'	GDR	57	3	NC	Cottbus	16 Jul 80
10.94	3.9	Jackie	Washington	USA	62	1		Houston	18 May 86
10.95	2.1	Juliet	Cuthbert	JAM	64	1h2	TAC	San Jose	25 Jun 87
10.96	2.9	Brenda	Morehead	USA	57	1s2	AAU	Walnut	16 Jun 79
10.97	3.3	Gesine	Walther	GDR	62	4	NC	Cottbus	16 Jul 80
10.97	3.0	Grace	Jackson	JAM	61	4	OG	Seoul	25 Sep 88
10.99	2.4	Chandra	Cheeseborough	USA	59	2		Modesto	14 May 83
11.01	4.0	Heather	Hunte'	UK	59	1		London	21 May 80
11.02	5.0	Jennifer	Inniss	USA	59	3q3	FOT	Indianapolis	16 Jul 88
11.04	3.0	Michelle	Finn	USA	65	1	NCAA	Austin	1 Jun 85
11.05A	2.2	Silvia	Chivas	CUB	54	1	WPT	Guadalajara	12 Aug 77
11.05	2.5	Ulrike	Sarvari	FRG	64	2rB	WK	Zürich	17 Aug 88
11.06	2.8	Linda	Haglund	SWE	56	1	ISTAF	Berlin	21 Aug 81
11.06	3.7	Randy	Givens	USA	62	1	NCAA	Eugene	1 Jun 84
11.08	2.9	Kathy	Cook'	UK	60	4	WK	Zürich	24 Aug 83
11.08	2.5	Nadezhda	Georgieva	BUL	61	2		Schwechat	15 Jun 88
11.09	2.7	Olga	Antonova'	SU	60	1		Leningrad	26 Jul 83
11.09		Angela	Williams	TRI	65	1		Nashville	14 Apr 84
11.09		Wanda	Fort	USA	63	2		Nashville	14 Apr 84

200 METRES

Mark	Wind	Name		Nat	Yr	Pos	Meet	Venue	Date
21.34	1.3	Florence	Griffith-Joyner	USA	59	1	OG	Seoul	29 Sep 88
21.56	1.7		Griffith-Joyner			1s1	OG	Seoul	29 Sep 88
21.71	0.7	Marita	Koch	GDR	57	1	v Can	Karl-Marx-Stadt	10 Jun 79
21.71	0.3		Koch			1	OD	Potsdam	21 Jul 84
21.71	1.2	Heike	Drechsler'	GDR	64	1	NC	Jena	29 Jun 86
21.71	-0.8		Drechsler			1	ECh	Stuttgart	29 Aug 86
21.72	1.3	Grace	Jackson	JAM	61	2	OG	Seoul	29 Sep 88
21.74	0.4	Marlies	Göhr'	GDR	58	1	NC	Erfurt	3 Jun 84
21.74	1.2	Silke	Gladisch'	GDR	64	1	WCh	Roma	3 Sep 87
21.76	0.3		Koch			1	NC	Dresden	3 Jul 82
21.76	0.7		Griffith-Joyner			1q1	OG	Seoul	28 Sep 88
21.77	-0.1		Griffith-Joyner			1q2	FOT	Indianapolis	22 Jul 88
21.78	-1.3		Koch			1	NC	Leipzig	11 Aug 85
21.79	1.7		Gladisch			1	NC	Potsdam	22 Aug 87
21.81	-0.1	Valerie	Brisco	USA	60	1	OG	Los Angeles	9 Aug 84
21.82	1.3		Koch			1	NC	Karl-Marx-Stadt	18 Jun 83
21.83	-0.2	Evelyn	Ashford	USA	57	1	WP	Montreal	24 Aug 79
21.84	-1.1		Ashford			1	VD	Bruxelles	28 Aug 81
21.84	1.0		Drechsler			1	NC	Rostock	26 Jun 88
21.85	0.3	Bärbel	Wöckel'	GDR	55	2	OD	Potsdam	21 Jul 84
21.85	1.3		Griffith-Joyner			1	FOT	Indianapolis	23 Jul 88
21.87	0.0		Koch			1	WK	Zürich	22 Aug 84
21.88	0.9		Ashford			1	TAC	Indianapolis	19 Jun 83
21.90	1.9		Koch			1		Dresden	3 Aug 85
21.90	-0.7		Koch			1	WP	Canberra	4 Oct 85
21.91A	1.9		Koch			1	WUG	Ciudad México	12 Sep 79
21.93	0.9	Merlene	Ottey	JAM	60	1	TAC	Indianapolis	16 Jun 85
21.93	1.3	Pam	Marshall	USA	60	2	FOT	Indianapolis	23 Jul 88
21.94	-1.3		Drechsler			1	v FRG	Düsseldorf	20 Jun 88
21.95	1.3		Drechsler			3	OG	Seoul	29 Sep 88
		(30/11))							
21.97	1.9	Jarmila	Kratochvílová	CS	51	1	PTS	Bratislava	6 Jun 81
21.99	0.9	Chandra	Cheeseborough	USA	59	2	TAC	Indianapolis	19 Jun 83
22.01	-0.5	Anelia	Nuneva'	BUL	62	1	NC	Sofia	16 Aug 87
22.02	1.3	Gwen	Torrence	USA	65	3	FOT	Indianapolis	23 Jul 88
22.10	-0.1	Kathy	Cook'	UK	60	4	OG	Los Angeles	9 Aug 84
22.13	1.2	Ewa	Kasprzyk	POL	57	2	GWG	Moskva	8 Jul 86
22.19	1.5	Natalya	Bochina	SU	62	2	OG	Moskva	30 Jul 80
22.21	1.9	Irena	Szewinska'	POL	46	1		Potsdam	13 Jun 74
22.23	-0.2	Dannette	Young	USA	64	1	Herc	Monaco	2 Aug 88
		(20)							
22.24	0.3	Gesine	Walther	GDR	62	2	NC	Dresden	3 Jul 82
22.24	0.1	Maya	Azarashvili	SU	64	1		Kiev	16 Aug 88
22.25A	0.8	Angella	Taylor'	CAN	58	1		Colorado Springs	20 Jul 82
22.27	1.2	Elvira	Barbashina'	SU	63	3	GWG	Moskva	8 Jul 86
22.30	0.0	Jackie	Joyner-Kersee	USA	62	1H	FOT	Indianapolis	15 Jul 88
22.31	0.1	Lyudmila	Kondratyeva	SU	58	1		Moskva	12 Jun 80
22.31	0.9	Randy	Givens	USA	62	4	TAC	Indianapolis	19 Jun 83
22.32	-0.8	Marie-Christine	Cazier	FRA	63	2	ECh	Stuttgart	29 Aug 86
22.35	1.8	Denise	Boyd'	AUS	52	1	NC	Sydney	23 Mar 80
22.36	1.7	Kerstin	Behrendt	GDR	67	3		Karl-Marx-Stadt	12 Jun 88
		(30)							
22.37	1.3	Sabine	Rieger'	GDR	63	2	v SU	Cottbus	26 Jun 82
22.38	1.6	Renate	Stecher'	GDR	50	1	NC	Dresden	21 Jul 73
22.38	1.7	Brenda	Morehead	USA	57	1		Nashville	12 Apr 80
22.38	2.0	Lillie	Leatherwood'	USA	64	1		Tuscaloosa	17 May 87
22.39	0.6	Mona-Lisa	Pursiainen'	FIN	51	1	WUG	Moskva	20 Aug 73
22.39	0.0	Annegret	Richter	FRG	50	2	OG	Montreal	28 Jul 76
22.39	1.3	Alice	Brown	USA	60	5	FOT	Indianapolis	23 Jul 88
22.42	1.2	Nadezhda	Georgieva	BUL	61	1	NarM	Sofia	22 May 83
22.42A		Evette	Armstrong'	RSA	65	1		Johannesburg	18 Apr 86
22.42A	1.7	Maria	Pinigina'	SU	58	1		Tsakhkadzor	23 May 87
		(40)							

Mark		Name		Nat	Yr	Pos	Meet	Venue	Date
22.42	1.3	Galina	Malchugina	SU	62	8	OG	Seoul	29 Sep 88
22.43	1.7	Mary	Onyali	NIG	68	5s1	OG	Seoul	29 Sep 88
22.44	1.3	Olga	Vladykina'	SU	63	1		Donyetsk	29 Aug 85
22.45	1.1	Raelene	Boyle	AUS	51	2	OG	München	7 Sep 72
22.46	0.2	Marina	Zhirova	SU	63	1	v Jap,USA	Tokyo	22 Sep 85
22.46	0.1	Marina	Molokova	SU	62	1	NC	Kiev	16 Jul 86
22.47	1.5	Romy	Müller'	GDR	58	4	OG	Moskva	30 Jul 80
22.47	0.2	Tatána	Kocembova'	CS	62	1		Barcelona	8 Jul 84
22.47	0.5	Natalya	German	SU	63	1		Chelyabinsk	21 Jun 87
22.49	2.0	Pauline	Davis	BAH	66	3		Tuscaloosa	17 May 87
		(50)							
22.49A	1.7	Vineta	Ikauniece	SU	62	2		Tsakhkadzor	23 May 87
Marks made with assisting wind > 2 m/s									
21.85	2.6		Koch			1		Karl-Marx-Stadt	27 May 79
21.85	2.6	Bärbel	Wöckel'	GDR	55	1	v USA	Karl-Marx-Stadt	10 Jul 82
21.90	2.4		Griffith-Joyner			1s2	FOT	Indianapolis	23 Jul 88
22.19A	3.1	Angella	Taylor'	CAN	58	1		Colorado Springs	21 Jul 82
22.21	2.7	Dannette	Young	USA	64	2	Athl	Lausanne	24 Jun 88
22.25	2.6	Juliet	Cuthbert	JAM	64	1s2	TAC	San Jose	26 Jun 87
22.33	3.7	Alice	Brown	USA	60	3s1	FOT	Indianapolis	23 Jul 88
22.34	2.3	Katrin	Krabbe	GDR	69	1	WJ	Sudbury	30 Jul 88
22.39A	2.9	Evette	Armstrong'	RSA	65	1h	NC	Germiston	12 Apr 86
22.48	4.0	Michelle	Scutt'	UK	60	1	WA	Dublin	4 Jul 82

400 METRES

Mark	Name		Nat	Yr	Pos	Meet	Venue	Date
47.60	Marita	Koch	GDR	57	1	WP	Canberra	6 Oct 85
47.99	Jarmila	Kratochvílová	CS	51	1	WCh	Helsinki	10 Aug 83
48.16		Koch			1	ECh	Athinai	8 Sep 82
48.16		Koch			1	Drz	Praha	16 Aug 84
48.22		Koch			1	ECh	Stuttgart	28 Aug 86
48.26		Koch			1		Dresden	27 Jul 84
48.27	Olga	Vladykina'	SU	63	2	WP	Canberra	6 Oct 85
48.45		Kratochvílová			1	NC	Praha	23 Jul 83
48.59	Tatána	Kocembová'	CS	62	2	WCh	Helsinki	10 Aug 83
48.60		Koch			1	EP	Torino	4 Aug 79
48.60		Vladykina			1	EP	Moskva	17 Aug 85
48.61		Kratochvílová			1	WP	Roma	6 Sep 81
48.65		Bryzgina'			1	OG	Seoul	26 Sep 88
48.73		Kocembová			2	Drz	Praha	16 Aug 84
48.77		Koch			1	v USA	Karl-Marx-Stadt	9 Jul 82
48.82		Kratochvílová			1	Ros	Praha	23 Jun 83
48.83	Valerie	Brisco	USA	60	1	OG	Los Angeles	6 Aug 84
48.85		Kratochvílová			2	ECh	Athinai	8 Sep 82
48.86		Kratochvílová			1	WK	Zürich	18 Aug 82
48.86		Koch			1	NC	Erfurt	2 Jun 84
48.87		Koch			1	VD	Bruxelles	27 Aug 82
48.88		Koch			1	OG	Moskva	28 Jul 80
48.89		Koch			1		Potsdam	29 Jul 79
48.89		Koch			1		Berlin	15 Jul 84
48.94		Koch			1	ECh	Praha	31 Aug 78
48.96		Vladykina			1	NC	Leningrad	3 Aug 85
48.97		Koch			1	WP	Montreal	26 Aug 79
48.97		Koch			1		Berlin	22 Sep 85
48.98		Vladykina			1		Kiev	22 Jun 84
49.01		Kratochvílová			1	ASV	Köln	23 Aug 81
	(30/5))							
49.05	Chandra	Cheeseborough	USA	59	2	OG	Los Angeles	6 Aug 84
49.11	Olga	Nazarova	SU	65	1s1	OG	Seoul	25 Sep 88
49.19	Maria	Pinigina'	SU	58	3	WCh	Helsinki	10 Aug 83
49.24	Sabine	Busch	GDR	62	2	NC	Erfurt	2 Jun 84
49.28	Irena	Szewinska'	POL	46	1	OG	Montreal	29 Jul 76
	(10)							

Mark	Name		Nat	Yr	Pos	Meet	Venue	Date
49.30	Petra	Müller'	GDR	65	1		Jena	3 Jun 88
49.43	Kathy	Cook'	UK	60	3	OG	Los Angeles	6 Aug 84
49.47	Aelita	Yurchenko	SU	65	2	Kuts	Moskva	4 Sep 88
49.56	Bärbel	Wöckel'	GDR	55	1		Erfurt	30 May 82
49.57	Grace	Jackson	JAM	61	1	Nik	Nice	10 Jul 88
49.58	Dagmar	Rubsam'	GDR	62	3	NC	Erfurt	2 Jun 84
49.62A	Ana Fidelia	Quirot	CUB	63	1		Ciudad México	22 May 88
49.66	Christina	Lathan'	GDR	58	3	OG	Moskva	28 Jul 80
49.75	Gaby	Bussmann	FRG	59	4	WCh	Helsinki	10 Aug 83
49.84	Diane	Dixon	USA	64	3s1	OG	Seoul	25 Sep 88
	(20)							
49.87	Denean	Howard	USA	64	4s1	OG	Seoul	25 Sep 88
49.91	Marita	Payne'	CAN	60	4	OG	Los Angeles	6 Aug 84
49.91	Jillian	Richardson	CAN	65	5s1	OG	Seoul	25 Sep 88
49.95	Lillie	Leatherwood'	USA	64	1	TAC	San Jose	27 Jub 87
49.99	Pam	Marshall	USA	60	1	Pepsi	Westwood	17 May 86
50.03	Gesine	Walther	GDR	62	2		Jena	13 May 84
50.07	Irina	Nazarova'	SU	57	4	OG	Moskva	28 Jul 80
50.07	Kirsten	Emmelmann'	GDR	61	2	ISTAF	Berlin	23 Aug 85
50.12A	Myrtle	Bothma'	RSA	64	1	NC	Germiston	11 Apr 86
50.14	Riita	Salin	FIN	50	1	ECh	Roma	4 Sep 74
	(30)							
50.15	Ellen	Streidt'	GDR	52	2		Berlin	10 Jul 76
50.17	Nina	Zyuskova	SU	52	5	OG	Moskva	28 Jul 80
50.19	Irina	Baskakova	SU	56	2	Spart	Moskva	21 Jun 83
50.24	Maree	Holland	AUS	63	3s2	OG	Seoul	25 Sep 88
50.26	Brigitte	Rohde'	GDR	54	1rB	v UK,Yug	Split	1 May 76
50.28	Lilia	Novoseltsova'	SU	62	2		Moskva	20 Jul 84
50.28	Ute	Thimm'	FRG	58	6s1	OG	Seoul	25 Sep 88
50.34	Doris	Maletzki	GDR	52	4	OT	Berlin	10 Jul 76
50.36	Helga	Arendt	FRG	64	4s2	OG	Seoul	25 Sep 88
50.40	Sherri	Howard	USA	62	4	FOT	Los Angeles	19 Jun 84
	(40)							
50.45	Charmaine	Crooks	CAN	61	7	OG	Los Angeles	6 Aug 84
50.49	Tatyana	Goyshchik'	SU	52	3	Spart	Moskva	24 Jul 79
50.55	Iolanda	Oanta	RUM	65	1	NC	Pitesti	13 Aug 88
50.56	Pirjo	Häggman	FIN	51	4	OG	Montreal	29 Jul 76
50.56A	Aurelia	Penton	CUB	43	1	CAG	Medellin	16 Jul 78
50.57A	Evette	Armstrong'	RSA	65	1		Germiston	2 Apr 86
50.60	Larisa	Krylova	SU	55	1		Kiev	14 Aug 82
50.61	Lyudmila	Dzhigalova	SU	62	4rA	Znam	Leningrad	12 Jun 88
50.62	Rosalyn	Bryant	USA	56	1s2	OG	Montreal	28 Jul 76
50.62	Karoline	Kafer	AUT	54	1		Klagenfurt	18 Jun 77
	(50)							
Hand timing								
48.9	Olga	Nazarova	SU	65	1	NP	Vladivostok	13 Sep 88
49.9	Lyudmila	Dzhigalova	SU	62	1		Kiev	24 Jun 88
50.3	Olga	Mineyeva	SU	52	1		Kharkov	9 Aug 80
50.4	Tatyana	Ledovskaya	SU	66	1		Staiki	28 May 88
50.6	Tatyana	Prorochenko	SU	52	1		Alushta	8 Sep 77
50.6	Inna	Yevseyeva	SU	64	1		Kiev	29 Aug 86

800 METRES

Mark	Name		Nat	Yr	Pos	Meet	Venue	Date
1:53.28	Jarmila	Kratochvilová	CS	51	1		München	26 Jul 83
1:53.43	Nadezhda	Olizarenko'	SU	53	1	OG	Moskva	27 Jul 80
1:54.68		Kratochvilová			1	WCh	Helsinki	9 Aug 83
1:54.81	Olga	Mineyeva	SU	52	2	OG	Moskva	27 Jul 80
1:54.85		Olizarenko			1	Prav	Moskva	12 Jun 80
1:54.94	Tatyana	Kazankina	SU	51	1	OG	Montreal	26 Jul 76
1:55.04		Kratochvilová			1		Oslo	23 Aug 83
1:55.05	Doina	Melinte	RUM	56	1	NC	Bucuresti	1 Aug 82
1:55.1		Mineyeva			1	Znam	Moskva	6 Jul 80
1:55.26	Sigrun	Wodars'	GDR	65	1	WCh	Roma	31 Aug 87
1:55.32	Christine	Wachtel	GDR	65	2	WCh	Roma	31 Aug 87
1:55.41		Mineyeva			1	ECh	Athinai	8 Sep 82
1:55.42	Nikolina	Shtereva	BUL	55	2	OG	Montreal	26 Jul 76

Mark	Name		Nat	Yr	Pos	Meet	Venue	Date
1:55.46	Tatyana	Providokhina	SU	53	3	OG	Moskva	27 Jul 80
1:55.5 m		Mineyeva			1	Kuts	Podolsk	21 Aug 82
1:55.56	Lyubov	Gurina	SU	57	3	WCh	Roma	31 Aug 87
1:55.60	Elfi	Zinn	GDR	53	3	OG	Montreal	26 Jul 76
1:55.68	Ella	Kovacs	RUM	64	1	RomIC	Bucuresti	2 Jun 85
1:55.69	Irina	Podyalovskaya	SU	59	1	Izv	Kiev	22 Jun 84
1:55.74	Anita	Weiss'	GDR	55	4	OG	Montreal	26 Jul 76
1:55.80		Providokhina			1	ECh	Praha	31 Aug 78
1:55.82		Mushta'			2	ECh	Praha	31 Aug 78
1:55.84	Ana Fidelia	Quirot	CUB	63	4	WCh	Roma	31 Aug 87
1:55.86		Wachtel			1	NC	Potsdam	21 Aug 87
1:55.9		Providokhina			2	Znam	Moskva	6 Jul 80
1:55.91		Kratochvilová			1	EP	Moskva	17 Aug 85
1:55.96	Lyudmila	Veselkova	SU	50	2	ECh	Athinai	8 Sep 82
1:55.96	Yekaterina	Podkopayeva'	SU	52	1		Leningrad	27 Jul 83
1:56.0 m	Valentina	Gerasimova	SU	48	1	NC	Kiev	12 Jun 76
1:56.0 m	Inna	Yevseyeva	SU	64	1		Kiev	25 Jun 88
1:56.0 m		Olizarenko			1		Kharkov	4 Jul 88
1:56.03		Olizarenko			1	NC	Kiev	1 Aug 88
	(32/19)							
1:56.1 m	Ravilya	Agletdinova	SU	60	2	Kuts	Podolsk	21 Aug 82
	(20)							
1:56.2	Totka	Petrova	BUL	56	1		Paris	6 Jul 79
1:56.2 m	Tatyana	Mishkel	SU	52	3	Kuts	Podolsk	21 Aug 82
1:56.21	Martina	Kämpfert'	GDR	59	4	OG	Moskva	27 Jul 80
1:56.21	Zamira	Zaytseva	SU	53	2		Leningrad	27 Jul 83
1:56.42	Paula	Ivan	RUM	63	1	Balk	Ankara	16 Jul 88
1:56.44	Svetlana	Styrkina	SU	49	5	OG	Montreal	26 Jul 76
1:56.51	Slobodanka	Colovic	YUT	65	1		Beograd	17 Jun 87
1:56.57	Zoya	Rigel	SU	52	3	ECh	Praha	31 Aug 78
1:56.6 m	Tamara	Sorokina'	SU	50	5	Kuts	Podolsk	21 Aug 82
1:56.67	Fita	Lovin'	RUM	51	2	Prav	Moskva	12 Jun 80
	(30)							
1:56.7 m	Dalia	Matuseviciene	SU	62	2		Kiev	25 Jun 88
1:56.78	Lyudmila	Borisova	SU	59	3	Izv	Kiev	22 Jun 84
1:56.82	Lyudmila	Rogachova	SU	66	1		Parnu	13 Jul 88
1:56.84	Nina	Ruchayeva	SU	56	2		Moskva	19 Jul 84
1:56.90	Mary	Decker-Slaney	USA	58	1		Bern	16 Aug 85
1:56.9 m	Olga	Dvirna	SU	53	6	Kuts	Podolsk	21 Aug 82
1:56.91	Kim	Gallagher	USA	64	3	OG	Seoul	26 Sep 88
1:56.95	Jolanta	Januchta	POL	55	1	BGP	Budapest	11 Aug 80
1:56.96	Zuzana	Moravciková	CS	56	1		Leipzig	27 Jul 83
1:56.97	Valentina	Zhukova'	SU	59	5	Izv	Kiev	22 Jun 84
	(40)							
1:57.0	Olga	Vakhrusheva	SU	47	3	Prav	Moskva	12 Jun 80
1:57.06	Ulrike	Klapezynski'	GDR	53	1		Berlin	10 Jul 76
1:57.08	Galina	Zakharova	SU	56	1	NP	Baku	16 Sep 84
1:57.18	Lyubov	Kiryukhina	SU	63	1	NC	Kiev	16 Jul 86
1:57.20	Hildegard	Ullrich'	GDR	59	5	OG	Moskva	27 Jul 80
1:57.2	Nadezhda	Loboyko	SU	61	3		Kiev	25 Jun 88
1:57.21	Svetla	Zlateva-Koleva	BUL	52	6	OG	Montreal	26 Jul 76
1:57.22	Margrit	Klinger	FRG	60	3	ECh	Athinai	8 Sep 82
1:57.26	Elzbieta	Katolik	POL	49	2	BGP	Budapest	11 Aug 80
1:57.28	Milena	Matejkovicová'	CS	61	2		Leipzig	27 Jul 83
	(50)							

1000 METRES

Mark	Name		Nat	Yr	Pos	Meet	Venue	Date
2:30.6	Tatyana	Providokhina	SU	53	1		Podolsk	20 Aug 78
2:30.85	Martina	Kämpfert'	GDR	59	1		Berlin	9 Jul 80
2:31.5 m	Maricica	Puica	RUM	50	1		Poiana Brasov	1 Jun 86
2:31.6	Beate	Liebich	GDR	58	2		Berlin	9 Jul 80
2:31.65	Olga	Dvirna	SU	53	1		Athinai	1 Sep 82
2:31.74	Anita	Weiss'	GDR	55	1		Potsdam	13 Jul 80
2:31.8		Dvirna			1	Kuts	Podolsk	5 Aug 79
2:31.95	Ulrike	Bruns'	GDR	53	1	ISTAF	Berlin	18 Aug 78

Mark	Name		Nat	Yr	Pos	Meet	Venue	Date
2:32.29	Christiane	Wartenberg'	GDR	56	2		Potsdam	13 Jul 80
2:32.6	Raisa	Byelousova	SU	52	2	Kuts	Podolsk	5 Aug 79
2:32.70	Jolanta	Januchta	POL	55	1	WK	Zürich	19 Aug 81
	(11/10)							
2:32.8 m	Tamara	Sorokina'	SU	50	1		Podolsk	24 Jul 76
2:32.9	Lyudmila	Kalnitskaya	SU	53	2		Podolsk	20 Aug 78
2:33.0 m	Totka	Petrova	BUL	56	1		Sofia	13 Aug 78
2:33.2 m	Gabriella	Dorio	ITA	57	1		Formia	28 Aug 82
2:33.4 m	Andrea	Lange'	GDR	66	1		Potsdam	28 May 87
2:33.44	Brigitte	Kraus	FRG	56	1	ISTAF	Berlin	17 Aug 79
2:33.6	Svetlana	Ulmasova	SU	53	3	Kuts	Podolsk	5 Aug 79
2:33.70	Kirsty	McDermott'	UK	62	1		Gateshead	9 Aug 85
2:33.8 m	Nikolina	Shtereva	BUL	55	1		Sofia	4 Jul 76
2:34.1	Valentina	Ilyinykh	SU	56	4	Kuts	Podolsk	5 Aug 79
	(20)							
2:34.13	Tatyana	Pozdnyakova	SU	56	2		Athinai	1 Sep 82
2:34.6 m	Heike	Oehme	GDR	63	1		Cottbus	14 May 86
2:34.65	Mary	Slaney'	USA	58	1	AP	Hengelo	14 Aug 88
2:34.8 m	Christina	Liebetrau'	GDR	53	1		Dresden	7 Aug 77
2:34.8 m	Hildegard	Ullrich'	GDR	59	2		Potsdam	12 Jul 84
2:34.92	Christina	Boxer'	UK	57	2		Gateshead	9 Aug 85
2:34.94	Margrit	Klinger	FRG	60	1		Letter	8 Sep 83

1500 METRES

Mark	Name		Nat	Yr	Pos	Meet	Venue	Date
3:52.47	Tatyana	Kazankina	SU	51	1	WK	Zürich	13 Aug 80
3:53.96	Paula	Ivan'	RUM	63	1	OG	Seoul	1 Oct 88
3:54.23	Olga	Dvirna	SU	53	1	NC	Kiev	27 Jul 82
3:55.0		Kazankina			1	Znam	Moskva	6 Jul 80
3:56.0 m		Kazankina			1		Podolsk	28 Jun 76
3:56.14	Zamira	Zaytseva	SU	53	2	NC	Kiev	27 Jul 82
3:56.22		Ivan			1	WK	Zürich	17 Aug 88
3:56.50	Tatyana	Pozdnyakova	SU	56	3	NC	Kiev	27 Jul 82
3:56.56		Kazankina			1	OG	Moskva	1 Aug 80
3:56.63	Nadezhda	Ralldugina	SU	57	1	Drz	Praha	18 Aug 84
3:56.65	Yekaterina	Podkopayeva'	SU	52	1		Rieti	2 Sep 84
3:56.7	Lyubov	Smolka	SU	52	2	Znam	Moskva	6 Jul 80
3:56.7 m	Doina	Melinte	RUM	56	1		Bucuresti	12 Jul 86
3:56.8	Nadezhda	Olizarenko'	SU	53	3	Znam	Moskva	6 Jul 80
3:56.9		Zaytseva			4	Znam	Moskva	6 Jul 80
3:57.05	Svetlana	Guskova	SU	59	4	NC	Kiev	27 Jul 82
3:57.12	Mary	Decker-Slaney	USA	58	1	vNord	Stockholm	26 Jul 83
3:57.22	Maricica	Puica	RUM	50	1		Bucuresti	1 Jul 84
3:57.24		Decker			1	VD	Bruxelles	30 Aug 85
3:57.4	Totka	Petrova	BUL	56	1	Balk	Athinai	11 Aug 79
3:57.4		Podkopayeva			5	Znam	Moskva	6 Jul 80
3:57.48		Puica			1	NC	Bucuresti	31 Jul 82
3:57.70		Pozdnyakova			2		Rieti	2 Sep 84
3:57.71	Christiane	Wartenberg'	GDR	56	2	OG	Moskva	1 Aug 80
3:57.72	Galina	Zakharova	SU	56	1	NP	Baku	14 Sep 84
3:57.73		Puica			2	VD	Bruxelles	30 Aug 85
3:57.78		Dvirna			1	BGP	Budapest	29 Jul 81
3:57.80		Dvirna			1	ECh	Athinai	11 Sep 82
3:57.82		Puica			1		Tirrenia	25 Aug 82
3:58.1 m		Melinte			1	RomIC	Bucuresti	9 Jun 84
	(30/16)							
3:58.2	Natalia	Marasescu'	RUM	52	1	NC	Bucuresti	13 Jul 79
3:58.37	Tatyana	Providokhina	SU	53	1	Kuts	Podolsk	22 Aug 82
3:58.40	Ravilya	Agletdinova	SU	60	1	EP	Moskva	18 Aug 85
3:58.5	Ileana	Silai	RUM	41	2	NC	Bucuresti	13 Jul 79
	(20)							
3:58.56	Tatyana	Samolyenko'	SU	61	1	WCh	Roma	5 Sep 87
3:58.65	Gabriella	Dorio	ITA	57	2		Tirrenia	25 Aug 82
3:58.67	Hildegard	Körner'	GDR	59	2	WCh	Roma	5 Sep 87
3:58.76	Svetlana	Ulmasova	SU	53	2	Kuts	Podolsk	22 Aug 82

Mark	Name		Nat	Yr	Pos	Meet	Venue	Date
3:58.89	Tamara	Sorokina'	SU	50	1	Znam	Leningrad	26 Jul 81
3:59.01	Giana	Romanova	SU	55	1	ECh	Praha	3 Sep 78
3:59.06	Sandra	Gasser *	SWZ	62	3	WCh	Roma	5 Sep 87
3:59.28	Natalya	Artyomova	SU	63	2	NC	Leningrad	2 Aug 85
3:59.48	Yelena	Sipatova	SU	55	4	Kuts	Podolsk	22 Aug 82
3:59.67	Anna	Bukis	POL	53	3	BGP	Budapest	29 Jul 81
	(30)							
3:59.8 m	Raisa	Katyukova'	SU	50	2		Podolsk	28 Jun 76
3:59.90	Angelika	Zauber	GDR	58	1	NC	Jena	9 Aug 81
3:59.90	Cornelia	Bürki	SWZ	53	5	WCh	Roma	5 Sep 87
3:59.9 m	Ulrike	Klapezynski'	GDR	53	1		Potsdam	14 Jul 76
3:59.9 m	Beate	Liebich	GDR	58	1	OT	Potsdam	5 Jul 80
3:59.96	Zola	Budd	UK	66	3	VD	Bruxelles	30 Aug 85
4:00.07	Andrea	Lange'	GDR	66	2	NC	Potsdam	22 Aug 87
4:00.12	Fita	Lovin'	RUM	51	1	RomIC	Bucuresti	4 Jun 83
4:00.18	Valentina	Ilyinykh	SU	56	4	ECh	Praha	3 Sep 78
4:00.18	Irina	Nikitina'	SU	61	5	Kuts	Podolsk	22 Aug 82
	(40)							
4:00.18	Ruth	Wysocki	USA	57	1	FOT	Los Angeles	24 Jun 84
4:00.24	Laima	Baikauskaite	SU	56	2	OG	Seoul	1 Oct 88
4:00.26	Alla	Yushina	SU	58	3	Znam	Leningrad	26 Jul 81
4:00.27	Lynn	Williams	CAN	60	4	VD	Bruxelles	30 Aug 85
4:00.3	Lyudmila	Shestyerova	SU	56	7	Znam	Moskva	6 Jul 80
4:00.42	Lyudmila	Medvedyeva	SU	57	3	NP	Baku	14 Sep 84
4:00.46	Regina	Jacobs	USA	63	2	FOT	Indianapolis	23 Jul 88
4:00.53	Svetlana	Popova	SU	59	6	NC	Kiev	27 Jul 82
4:00.55	Grete	Waitz'	NOR	53	5	ECh	Praha	3 Sep 78
4:00.57	Christina	Boxer'	UK	57	1		Gateshead	6 Jul 84
	(50)							

1 MILE

Mark	Name		Nat	Yr	Pos	Meet	Venue	Date
4:15.8 m	Natalya	Artyomova	SU	63	1		Leningrad	5 Aug 84
4:16.71	Mary	Decker-Slaney	USA	58	1	WK	Zürich	21 Aug 85
4:17.33	Maricica	Puica	RUM	50	2	WK	Zürich	21 Aug 85
4:17.44		Puica			1		Rieti	16 Sep 82
4:17.57	Zola	Budd	UK	66	3	WK	Zürich	21 Aug 85
4:18.08		Decker			1		Paris	9 Jul 82
4:18.25		Puica			1	Nik	Nice	15 Jul 86
4:19.18		Decker			1	Bisl	Oslo	27 Jul 85
4:19.41	Kirsty	McDermott'	UK	62	2	Bisl	Oslo	27 Jul 85
4:19.59		Decker			1	IAC	London	2 Aug 85
4:20.89	Lyudmila	Veselkova	SU	50	1		Bologna	12 Sep 81
4:20.89		Puica			1		Paris	22 Jul 86
4:21.25		Slaney			1	Pre	Eugene	2 Jul 88
4:21.40	Fita	Lovin'	RUM	51	2		Bologna	12 Sep 81
4:21.46		Decker			1	Bisl	Oslo	26 Jun 82
4:21.52	Vesela	Yatzinska	BUL	51	1	BGP	Budapest	30 Jun 82
4:21.59	Ulrike	Bruns'	GDR	53	4	WK	Zürich	21 Aug 85
4:21.61		Wade'			1	VD	Bruxelles	5 Sep 86
4:21.65		Decker			1	Pepsi	Westwood	15 may 83
4:21.68		Decker			1		Auckland	26 Jan 80
4:21.78	Vanya	Stoyanova	BUL	58	2	BGP	Budapest	30 Jun 82
	21/(10)							
4.21.78	Ruth	Wysocki	USA	57	1	IAC	London	7 Sep 84
4:21.88	Doina	Melinte	RUM	56	2	VD	Bruxelles	5 Sep 86
4:21.89	Tamara	Sorokina'	SU	50	3	BGP	Budapest	30 Jun 82
4:22.09	Natalia	Marasescu'	RUM	52	1		Auckland	27 Jan 79
4:22.40	Elly	van Hulst	HOL	59	4	VD	Bruxelles	5 Sep 86
4:22.5 m	Zamira	Zaytseva	SU	53	1		Kiev	15 Jun 81
4:22.64	Christina	Boxer'	UK	57	2	IAC	London	7 Sep 84
4:22.82	Ivana	Walterova'	CS	62	5	VD	Bruxelles	5 Sep 84
4:23.08	Yvonne	Murray	UK	64	6	VD	Bruxelles	5 Sep 84
4:23.29	Gabriella	Dorio	ITA	57	1		Viareggio	14 Aug 80
	(20)							
4:23.38	Sandra	Gasser *	SWZ	62	1	VD	Bruxelles	11 Sep 87
4:23.8 m	Svetlana	Ulmasova	SU	53	2		Kiev	15 Jun 81

2000 METRES

Mark	Name		Nat	Yr	Pos	Meet	Venue	Date
5:28.69	Maricica	Puica	ROM	50	1	PTG	London	11 Jul 86
5:28.72	Tatyana	Kazankina	SU	51	1		Moskva	4 Aug 84
5:29.58	Yvonne	Murray	UK	64	2	PTG	London	11 Jul 86
5:29.64	Tatyana	Pozdnyakova	SU	56	2		Moskva	4 Aug 84
5:30.19	Zola	Budd	UK	66	3	PTG	London	11 Jul 86
5:30.92	Galina	Zakharova	SU	56	3		Moskva	4 Aug 84
5:32.7	Mary	Decker-Slaney	USA	58	1		Eugene	3 Aug 84
5:33.85	Christina	Boxer	UK	57	2	PTG	London	13 Jul 84
5:35.59	Cornelia	Burki	SWZ	53	4	PTG	London	11 Jul 86
5:37.00	Christine	Benning	UK	55	3	PTG	London	13 Jul 84
(10)								
5:37.55	Zamira	Zaitseva	SU	53	4		Moskva	4 Aug 84
5:37.62	Ulrike	Bruns	GDR	53	1		Berlin	22 Sep 85
5:37.86	Lesley	Welch	USA	63	5	PTG	London	11 Jul 86
5:39.0	Natalia	Marasescu	ROM	52	1		Auckland	13 Jan 79
5:39.00	Annette	Sergent	FRA	62	6	PTG	London	11 Jul 86
5:39.52	Elly	van Hulst	HOL	59	7	PTG	London	11 Jul 86
5:39.96	Debbie	Bowker	CAN	58	1		Gateshead	5 Aug 86
Disqualified								
5:39.19	Sue	Addison	USA	56	-	PTG	London	11 Jul 86

3000 METRES

Mark	Name		Nat	Yr	Pos	Meet	Venue	Date
8:22.62	Tatyana	Kazankina	SU	51	1		Leningrad	26 Aug 84
8:25.83	Mary	Decker-Slaney	USA	58	1	GG	Roma	7 Sep 85
8:26.53	Tatyana	Samolyenko'	SU	61	1	OG	Seoul	25 Sep 88
8:26.78	Svetlana	Ulmasova	SU	53	1	NC	Kiev	25 Jul 82
8:27.12	Lyudmila	Bragina	SU	43	1	v USA	Colllege Park	7 Aug 76
8:27.15	Paula	Ivan'	RUM	63	2	OG	Seoul	25 Sep 88
8:27.83	Maricica	Puica	RUM	50	2	GG	Roma	7 Sep 85
8:28.83	Zola	Budd	UK	59	3	GG	Roma	7 Sep 85
8:29.02	Yvonne	Murray	UK	64	3	OG	Seoul	25 Sep 88
8:29.36	Svetlana	Guskova	SU	59	2	NC	Kiev	5 Jul 82
8:29.59		Guskova			1		Moskva	6 Aug 84
8:29.69		Decker			1	ASV	Köln	25 Aug 85
8:29.71		Decker			1		Oslo	7 Jul 82
8:30.28		Ulmasova			1	ECh	Athinai	9 Sep 82
8:30.32		Puica			2	ASV	Köln	25 Aug 85
8:30.45	Yelena	Romanova	SU	63	4	OG	Seoul	25 Sep 88
8:31.67		Puica			1	Balk	Bucuresti	14 Aug 82
8:31.67	Natalya	Artyomova	SU	63	5	OG	Seoul	25 Sep 88
8:31.75	Grete	Waitz'	NOR	53	1		Oslo	17 Jul 79
8:32.0 m	Tatyana	Pozdnyakova	SU	56	1		Ryazan	11 Aug 84
8:32.08		Kazankina			1		Leningrad	27 Jul 83
8:32.1 m		Waitz			1		Oslo	27 Jun 78
8:32.91		Decker			1	PTG	London	20 Jul 85
8:33.01		Kazankina			1	Drz	Praha	16 Aug 84
8:33.16		Ulmasova			1	ECh	Praha	29 Aug 78
8:33.33		Puica			2	ECh	Athinai	9 Sep 82
8:33.40	Galina	Zakharova	SU	56	3	NC	Kiev	25 Jul 82
8:33.53	Natalia	Marasescu'	RUM	52	2	ECh	Praha	29 Aug 78
8:33.53	Yelena	Sipatova	SU	55	1		Moskva	12 Jul 80
8:33.57		Puica			1	NC	Bucuresti	10 Jul 84
	(30/17)							
8:33.9	Tatyana	Sychova	SU	57	2		Moskva	12 Jul 80
8:33.97	Elly	van Hulst	HOL	59	1	WK	Zürich	17 Aug 88
8:33.99	Olga	Bondarenko'	SU	60	1	ECh	Stuttgart	28 Aug 86
	(20)							
8:34.0	Faina	Krasnova'	SU	57	3		Moskva	12 Jul 80
8:34.02	Alla	Yushina	SU	58	2		Leningrad	27 Jul 83
8:34.10	Ingrid	Kristiansen'	NOR	58	1	WK	Zürich	13 Aug 86
8:35.11	Brigitte	Kraus	FRG	56	2	WCh	Helsinki	10 Aug 83
8:35.74	Alla	Libutina	SU	53	6	NC	Kiev	25 Jul 82
8:35.74	Zamira	Zaytseva	SU	53	2	EP	Moskva	17 Aug 85
8:36.0	Lyubov	Smolka	SU	52	4		Moskva	12 Jul 80

Mark	Name		Nat	Yr	Pos	Meet	Venue	Date
8:36.38	Ulrike	Bruns'	GDR	53	1	OD	Berlin	20 Jul 84
8:36.40	Olga	Dvirna	SU	53	1		Sochi	30 May 82
8:37.06	Wendy	Sly'	UK	59	5	WCh	Helsinki	10 Aug 83
	(30)							
8:37.11	Doina	Melinte	RUM	56	1	v Eng,Rus	Bucuresti	15 Jun 86
8:37.25	Vicki	Huber	USA	67	6	OG	Seoul	25 Sep 88
8:37.30	Lynn	Williams	CAN	60	3	WK	Zürich	17 Aug 88
8:37.96	Agnese	Possamai	ITA	53	6	WCh	Helsinki	10 Aug 83
8:38.1 m	Yelena	Zhupiyova	SU	60	1		Kharkov	11 Aug 85
8:38.22	Olga	Kuzyukova	SU	53	8		Leningrad	27 Jul 83
8:38.60	Cindy	Bremser	USA	53	2	WK	Zürich	22 Aug 84
8:38.71	Cornelia	Bürki	SWZ	53	2	PTG	London	20 Jul 85
8:38.83	Mariana	Stanescu	RUM	64	1	GWG	Moskva	6 Jul 86
8:39.25	Regina	Chistyakova	SU	61	3	GWG	Moskva	6 Jul 86
	(40)							
8:39.85	Elizabeth	Lynch'	UK	64	1	Nik	Nice	13 Jul 87
8:40.4	Nina	Yapeyeva	SU	56	5		Moskva	12 Jul 80
8:41.05	Raisa	Sadreydinova	SU	52	9		Leningrad	27 Jul 83
8:41.07	Zhanna	Tursunova	SU	57	6	Izv	Kiev	20 Jun 84
8:41.43	Joan	Hansen	USA	58	3	FOT	Los Angeles	23 Jun 84
8:41.54	Iulia	Besliu	RUM	65	1	v Rus	Bucuresti	19 Jun 88
8:41.77	Raisa	Katyukova'	SU	50	2	v USA	Colllege Park	7 Aug 76
8:41.8	Giana	Romanova	SU	55	6		Moskva	12 Jul 80
8:42.16	Elena	Fidatov	RUM	60	2	RomIC	Bucuresti	14 Jun 87
8:42.3 m	Loa	Olafsson	DEN	58	2		Oslo	17 Jun 78
	(50)							

5000 METRES

Mark	Name		Nat	Yr	Pos	Meet	Venue	Date
14:37.33	Ingrid	Kristiansen'	NOR	56	1		Stockholm	5 Aug 86
14:48.07	Zola	Budd	UK	66	1		London	26 Aug 85
14:54.08	Natalya	Artyomova	SU	63	1		Podolsk	9 Sep 85
14:55.76	Olga	Bondarenko'	SU	60	2		Podolsk	9 Sep 85
14:57.43		Kristiansen			2		London	26 Aug 85
14:58.70		Kristiansen			1	FBK	Hengelo	27 Jul 86
14:58.89		Kristiansen			1	Bisl	Oslo	28 Jun 84
15:01.08	Elizabeth	Lynch'	UK	64	1		Oslo	5 Aug 87
15:01.83		Budd			1		Stellenbosch	5 Jan 84
15:02.12	Svetlana	Guskova	SU	59	1	v GDR	Tallinn	21 Jun 86
15:03.29		McColgan'			1	ISTAF	Berlin	26 Aug 88
15:03.51		Bondarenko			1	GWG	Moskva	8 Jul 86
15:05.31		Bondarenko			1	NC	Leningrad	1 Aug 85
15:05.50	Svetlana	Ulmasova	SU	53	2	GWG	Moskva	8 Jul 86
15:06.04	Maricica	Puica	RUM	50	1	WG	Helsinki	4 Jul 85
15:06.18		Bondarenko			2	v GDR	Tallinn	21 Jun 86
15:06.53	Mary	Decker-Slaney	USA	58	1	Pre	Eugene	1 Jun 85
15:06.96	Aurora	Cunha	POR	59	2	WG	Helsinki	4 Jul 85
15:07.56	Cathy	Branta-Easker	USA	63	3	WG	Helsinki	4 Jul 85
15:07.71	Lynn	Williams	CAN	60	4	WG	Helsinki	4 Jul 85
15:07.89#		Kristiansen			1	ECh	Stuttgart	30 Aug 86
15:08.26		Decker			1	Pre	Eugene	5 Jun 82
15:08.36	Lynn	Jennings	USA	60	2	FBK	Hengelo	27 Jun 86
15:08.80	Grete	Waitz'	NOR	53	1	Bisl	Oslo	26 Jun 82
15:09.07		Cunha			2	Bisl	Oslo	28 Jun 84
15:09.86		Budd			1		Port Elizabeth	7 Mar 84
	(26/14)							
15:11.78	Cindy	Bremser	USA	53	3	GWG	Moskva	8 Jul 86
15:12.62	Irina	Bondarchuk	SU	52	1	Znam	Moskva	11 Jun 82
15:12.7 m	Lynn	Nelson	USA	62	1	Pre	Eugene	2 Jul 88
15:13.22	Anne	Audain'	NZ	55	1		Auckland	17 Mar 82
15:13.22	Angela	Tooby	UK	60	2		Oslo	5 Aug 87
15:14.51	Paula	Fudge	UK	52	1		Knarvik	13 Sep 81
	(20)							
15:15.2 m	Francie	Larrieu Smith	USA	52	2	Pre	Eugene	2 Jul 88
15:16.27	Lyudmila	Matveyeva	SU	57	2	NC	Leningrad	1 Aug 85

Mark	Name		Nat	Yr	Pos	Meet	Venue	Date
15:16.83	Natalya	Sorokivskaya	SU	62	2	Kuts	Moskva	5 Sep 88
15:17.02	Cathie	Twomey	USA	56	2	AP	Hengelo	14 Aug 88
15:17.77	Jill	Hunter	UK	66	3	ISTAF	Berlin	26 Aug 88
15:18.24	Annette	Sergent	FRA	62	4	ISTAF	Berlin	26 Aug 88
15:18.71	Brenda	Webb	USA	54	1	TAC	Tampa	17 Jun 88
15:19.0 m	Anna	Domoratskaya	SU	53	1		Kiev	30 Sep 83
15:19.26	Marina	Rodchenkova	SU	61	3	NC	Leningrad	1 Aug 85
15:19.54	Charlotte	Teske	FRG	49	2	Bisl	Oslo	26 Jun 82
	(30)							
15:20.23	Kathrin	Ullrich	GDR	67	1	v FRG	Düsseldorf	20 Jun 88
15:20.88	PattiSue	Plumer	USA	62	5	GWG	Moskva	8 Jul 86
15:21.0	Margherita	Gargano	ITA	52	1		Partinico	22 Sep 82
15:21.45	Wendy	Sly'	UK	59	3		Oslo	5 Aug 87
15:21.90	Gabriele	Veith'	GDR	56	6	GWG	Moskva	8 Jul 86
15:21.92	Anna	Pedan	SU	61	5	NC	Leningrad	1 Aug 85
15:22.33	Mary	Knisely'	USA	59	3	GP	Roma	10 Sep 86
15:22.96	Sue	French-Lee	CAN	60	5	Pre	Eugene	1 Jun 85
15:22.97	Rosa	Mota	POR	58	3		Oslo	27 Jun 85
15:23.03	Kathy	Hayes	USA	62	1		Eugene	4 May 85
	(40)							
15:23.12	Tatyana	Kazankina	SU	51	1		Paris	4 Sep 84
15:23.25	Yelena	Zhupiyova	SU	60	7	GWG	Moskva	8 Jul 86
15:23.54	Erika	Veréb	HUN	63	4	GP	Moskva	10 Sep 86
15:24.22	Sabrina	Dornhoefer	USA	63	2	AP	Hengelo	19 Jul 87
15:24.6 m	Yelena	Sipatova	SU	55	1	Kuts	Podolsk	6 Sep 81
15:25.13	Yelena	Tsukhlo	SU	54	2	Znam	Moskva	11 Jun 82
15:25.24	Betty	Springs'	USA	61	7	Pre	Eugene	1 Jun 85
15:25.84	Martine	Oppliger'	SWZ	57	5	ISTAF	Berlin	26 Aug 88
15:27.05	Ines	Bibernell	GDR	65	1	OD	Dresden	3 Jul 86
15:27.44	Wang Xiuting		CHN	65	1	NC	Guangzhou	25 Nov 87
	(50)							

10 000 METRES

Mark	Name		Nat	Yr	Pos	Meet	Venue	Date
30:13.74	Ingrid	Kristiansen'	NOR	56	1	Bisl	Oslo	5 Jul 86
30:23.25		Kristiansen			1	ECh	Stuttgart	30 Aug 86
30:57.21	Olga	Bondarenko'	SU	60	2	ECh	Stuttgart	30 Aug 86
30:59.42		Kristiansen			1	Bisl	Oslo	27 Jul 85
31:05.21		Bondarenko			1	OG	Seoul	30 Sep 88
31:05.85		Kristiansen			1	WCh	Roma	4 Sep 87
31:08.44		McColgan			2	OG	Seoul	30 Sep 88
31:09.40	Yelena	Zhupiyova	SU	60	2	WCh	Roma	4 Sep 87
31:06.99	Elizabeth	Lynch-McColgan	UK	64	1	Bisl	Oslo	2 Jul 88
31:11.34	Kathrin	Ullrich	GDR	67	3	WCh	Roma	4 Sep 87
31:13.78		Bondarenko			1	Izv	Kiev	24 Jun 84
31:15.00	Galina	Zakharova	SU	56	2	Izv	Kiev	24 Jun 84
31:15.66		Kristiansen			1	Bisl	Oslo	4 Jul 87
31:18.38		Bondarenko			4	WCh	Roma	4 Sep 87
31:19.76	Ulrike	Bruns'	GDR	53	3	ECh	Stuttgart	30 Aug 86
31:19.82		Lynch			5	WCh	Roma	4 Sep 87
31:19.82		Zhupiyova			3	OG	Seoul	30 Sep 88
31:25.18		Bondarenko			1	Znam	Moskva	9 Jun 85
31:26.79		Ullrich			1	NC	Potsdam	8 Jun 88
31:27.00	Wang Xiuting		CHN	65	1	NC	Guangzhou	29 Nov 87
31:27.58	Raisa	Sadreydinova	SU	52	1	NC	Odessa	7 Sep 83
31:27.99	Hou Juhua		CHN	67	2	NC	Guangzhou	29 Nov 87
31:29.27		Ullrich			4	OG	Seoul	30 Sep 88
31:29.41	Aurora	Cunha	POR	59	2	Bisl	Oslo	5 Jul 86
31:31.37		Kristiansen			2	Bis!	Oslo	2 Jul 88
31:35.01	Lyudmila	Baranova	SU	50	1		Krasnodar	29 May 83
31:35.16		Bondarenko			1	NC	Bryansk	19 Jul 87
31:35.3 m	Mary	Decker-Slaney	USA	58	1		Eugene	16 Jul 82
31:35.45		Cunha			2	Bisl	Oslo	27 Jul 85
31:35.52	Francie	Larrieu Smith	USA	52	5	OG	Seoul	30 Sep 88
	(30/14)							

WOMEN All-time

Mark	Name		Nat	Yr	Pos	Meet	Venue	Date
31:38.02	Lyudmila	Matveyeva	SU	57	1	NC	Kiev	2 Aug 88
31:39.93	Lynn	Jennings	USA	60	6	OG	Seoul	30 Sep 88
31:42.02	Yekaterina	Khramenkova	SU	56	4	NC	Kiev	2 Aug 88
31:42.43	Svetlana	Guskova	SU	59	5	ECh	Stuttgart	30 Aug 86
31:42.8 m	Lesley	Welch-Lehane	USA	63	1		Dedham	11 Jun 88
31:44.73	Wang	Qinghuan	CHN	65	3	NC	Guangzhou	29 Nov 87
	(20)							
31:45.4 m	Loa	Olafsson	DEN	58	1mx		København	6 Apr 78
31:46.43	Natalya	Sorokivskaya	SU	62	5	NC	Kiev	2 Aug 88
31:46.61	Maria Albertina	Machado	POR	61	7	WCh	Roma	4 Sep 87
31:48.23	Anna	Domoratskaya	SU	53	1	NC	Kiev	27 Jul 82
31:48.94	Tatyana	Pozdnyakova	SU	56	3	NC	Odessa	7 Sep 83
31:50.51	Sue	Lee'	CAN	60	8	OG	Seoul	30 Sep 88
31:51.27	Lynn	Nelson	USA	62	1	FOT	Indianapolis	22 Jul 88
31:53.31	Anne	Audain'	NZ	55	2	CG	Edinburgh	28 Jul 86
31:53.36	Wendy	Sly	UK	59	3	Super	Tokyo	8 Oct 88
31:53.53	Zhanna	Tursunova	SU	57	3	Izv	Kiev	24 Jun 84
	(30)							
31:55.30	Angela	Tooby	UK	60	9	WCh	Roma	4 Sep 87
31:55.67	Chen Qingmei		CHN	63	4	Super	Tokyo	8 Oct 88
31:55.93	Karolina	Szabó	HUN	61	8	ECh	Stuttgart	30 Aug 86
31:56.01	Lyubov	Konyukhova	SU	56	4	Izv	Kiev	24 Jun 84
31:56.33	Natalya	Artyomova	SU	63	6	NC	Kiev	2 Aug 88
31:56.80	Kerstin	Pressler	FRG	62	10	WCh	Roma	4 Sep 87
31:59.70	Raisa	Smekhnova'	SU	50	6	Izv	Kiev	24 Jun 84
32:00.26	Charlotte	Teske	FRG	49	2	IAAFg	Knarvik	4 Sep 83
32:02.89	Dorthe	Rasmussen	DEN	60	3	IAAFg	Knarvik	4 Sep 83
32:04.34	Maria	Curatolo	ITA	63	10	ECh	Stuttgart	30 Aug 86
	(40)							
32:04.78	Annette	Sergent	FRA	62	4	Bisl	Oslo	2 Jul 88
32:06.14	Collette	Goudreau	USA	65	1	Penn	Philadelphia	28 Apr 88
32:06.76	Rosanna	Munerotto	ITA	62	9h1	OG	Seoul	26 Sep 88
32:07.13	Maria Albertina	Dias	POR	65	10	OG	Seoul	30 Sep 88
32:07.41	Joan	Benoit'	USA	57	1	FOT	Los Angeles	17 Jun 84
32:07.49	Martine	Oppliger'	SWZ	57	11	WCh	Roma	4 Sep 87
32:08.32	Malin	Wästlund	SWE	64	5	Bisl	Oslo	2 Jul 88
32:09.08	Carole	Rouillard	CAN	60	10h1	OG	Seoul	26 Sep 88
32:10.05	Carolyn	Schuwalow	AUS	65	11h1	OG	Seoul	26 Sep 88
32:11.49	Marleen	Renders	BEL	68	13h1	OG	Seoul	26 Sep 88
	(50)							

MARATHON

Mark	Name		Nat	Yr	Pos	Meet	Venue	Date
2:21:06	Ingrid	Kristiansen	NOR	56	1		London	21 Apr 85
2:21:21	Joan	Benoit'	USA	57	1		Chicago	20 Oct 85
2:22:43		Benoit			1		Boston	18 Apr 83
2:22:48		Kristiansen			1		London	10 May 87
2:23:05		Kristiansen			2		Chicago	20 Oct 85
2:23:29	Rosa	Mota	POR	58	3		Chicago	20 Oct 85
2:23:51	Lisa	Martin	AUS	60	1		Osaka	31 Jan 88
2:24:26		Kristiansen			1		London	13 May 84
2:24:30		Mota			1		Boston	18 Apr 88
2:24:52		Benoit			1	OG	Los Angeles	5 Aug 84
2:24:54	Grete	Waitz	NOR	53	1		London	20 Apr 86
2:24:55		Kristiansen			1		Boston	21 Apr 86
2:25:17		Mota			1	WC	Roma	29 Aug 87
2:25:21		Mota			1		Boston	20 Apr 87
2:25:24	Katrin	Dörre	GDR	61	1		Tokyo	15 Nov 87
2:25:29		Waitz			1		London	17 Apr 83
2:25:40		Mota			1	OG	Seoul	23 Sep 88
2:25:41		Kristiansen			1	NC	London	17 Apr 88
2:25:42		Waitz			1		New York	26 Oct 80
2:25:53		Martin			2	OG	Seoul	23 Sep 88
2:26:01		Mota			1		Chicago	21 Oct 84
2:26:07		Martin			1	CommG	Edinburgh	1 Aug 86

Mark	Name		Nat	Yr	Pos	Meet	Venue	Date
2:26:11		Benoit			1		Eugene	12 Sep 82
2:26:18		Waitz			2	OG	Los Angeles	5 Aug 84
2:26:21		Dörre			3	OG	Seoul	23 Sep 88
2:26:26	Julie	Brown	USA	55	1		Los Angeles	5 Jun 83
2:26:34	Carolina	Beurskens	HOL	52	2		Tokyo	15 Nov 87
2:26:46	Allison	Roe	NZ	56	1		Boston	20 Apr 81
2:26:51	Priscilla	Welch (10)	UK	44	2		London	10 May 87
2:26:52		Dörre			1		Berlin (East)	21 Jul 84
	(30/10)							
2:27:05	Tatyana	Polovinskaya	SU	65	4	OG	Seoul	23 Sep 88
2:27:06	Zhao You-Feng		CHN	65	5	OG	Seoul	23 Sep 88
2:27:49	Laura	Fogli	ITA	59	6	OG	Seoul	23 Sep 88
2:27:51	Patricia	Catalano	USA	53	2		Boston	20 Apr 81
2:27:57	Zoya	Ivanova	SU	52	3		Tokyo	15 Nov 87
2:28:04	Veronique	Marot	UK	55	4		Chicago	20 Oct 85
2:28:06	Sarah	Rowell	UK	62	2		London	21 Apr 85
2:28:07	Carey	May	IRL	59	1		Osaka	27 Jan 85
2:28:11	Ria	Van Landeghem	BEL	57	1		St. Paul	2 Oct 88
2:28:17	Lorraine	Moller	NZ	55	2	CommG	Edinburgh	1 Aug 86
	(20)							
2:28:20	Mary	O'Connor	NZ	55	2		London	17 Apr 83
2:28:20	Yekaterina	Khramenkova	SU	54	1	NC	Mogilyov	7 Jun 87
2:28:32	Charlotte	Teske	FRG	49	1		Frankfurt	15 May 83
2:28:36	Sylvia	Ruegger	CAN	61	1		Houston	6 Jan 85
2:28:38	Sally-Ann	Hales	UK	61	3		London	21 Apr 85
2:28:40	Raisa	Smekhnova	SU	50	2	ECp	Huy	30 Apr 88
2:28:51	Agnes	Öze Sipka	HUN	54	1		Budapest	26 Oct 86
2:28:53	Yelena	Tsukhlo	SU	54	2	NC	Mogilyov	7 Jun 87
2:29:16	Renata	Kokowska	POL	58	1		Berlin (West)	9 Oct 88
2:29:17	Lisa	Weidenbach	USA	61	1		Chicago	30 Oct 88
	(30)							
2:29:19	Birgit	Stephan	GDR	64	3		Nagoya	6 Mar 88
2:29:23	Danièe	Kaber	LUX	60	7	OG	Seoul	23 Sep 88
2:29:26	Tuija	Jousimaa	FIN	58	2		Boston	18 Apr 88
2:29:27	Jacqueline	Gareau	CAN	53	2		Boston	18 Apr 83
2:29:37	Misako	Miyahara	JAP	62	2		Osaka	31 Jan 88
2:29:43	Joyce	Smith	UK	37	1		London	9 May 82
2:29:46	Emma	Scaunich	ITA	54	2		Chicago	30 Oct 88
2:29:47	Paula	Fudge	UK	52	3		Chicago	30 Oct 88
2:29:49	Alevtina	Chasova	SU	61	1		Uzhgorod	17 Apr 88
2:29:50	Agnes	Pardaens	BEL	56	2		Boston	20 Apr 87
	(40)							
2:29:50	Margaret	Groos	USA	59	1	NC	Pittsburgh	1 May 88
2:29:51	Maria	Lelut	FRA	56	2		Chicago	26 Oct 86
2:30:09	Vera	Sukhova	SU	63	1		Belaja Cerkov	7 Oct 88
2:30:11	Sylvie	Bornet	FRA	60	1		St. Paul	11 Oct 87
2:30:14	Nancy	Ditz	USA	54	2	NC	Pittsburgh	1 May 88
2:30:14	Maria	Curatolo	ITA	63	8	OG	Seoul	23 Sep 88
2:30:18	Cathy	O'Brien	USA	67	3	NC	Pittsburgh	1 May 88
2:30:23	Deborah	Raunig	USA	55	2		St. Paul	2 Oct 88
2:30:25	Lyutsia	Belyaeva	SU	57	3	NC	Mogilyov	7 Jun 87
2:30:30	Akemi	Masuda	JAP	64	1		Eugene	11 Sep 83
	(50							

WORLD BESTS - NON-STANDARD EVENTS OUTDOORS

Event	Mark	Athlete	Venue	Date
60 metres	6.9	Alice Annum (Gha)	Mainz	17 Jun 1975
150 metres	16.10	Florence Griffith-Joyner (USA)	Seoul (in 200m)	29 Sep 1988
300 metres	34.1	Marita Koch (GDR)	Canberra (in 400m)	6 Oct 1985
500 metres	1:09.9	Colette Besson (Fra)	Font Romeu	16 Aug 1970
600 metres	1:23.5	Doina Melinte (Rom)	Poiana Brasov	27 Jul 1986
2000m Steeple	6:16.41	Marina Pluzhnikova (SU)	Kiev	2 Aug 1988
200m hurdles	25.7	Pamela Ryan (Aus)	Melbourne	25 Nov 1971
Pole vault	3.75	Zhang Chunzhen (Chn)	Nanjing	10 Jun 1988
Hammer (4kg)	58.98	Lyubov Vasilyeva (SU)	Vilnius	28 Aug 1988

100 METRES HURDLES

Mark		Name		Nat	Yr	Pos	Meet	Venue	Date
12.21	0.7	Yordanka	Donkova	BUL	61	1		Stara Zagora	20 Aug 88
12.24	0.9		Donkova			1s		Stara Zagora	28 Aug 88
12.25	1.4	Ginka	Zagorcheva	BUL	58	1	v CS,Gre	Drama	8 Aug 87
12.26	1.5		Donkova			1	Balk	Ljubljana	7 Sep 86
12.27	-1.2		Donkova			1		Stara Zagora	28 Aug 88
12.29	-0.4		Donkova			1	ASV	Köln	17 Aug 86
12.33	1.4		Donkova			1		Fürth	14 Jun 87
12.34	-0.5		Zagorcheva			1	WCh	Roma	4 Sep 87
12.35	0.1		Donkova			1h2	ASV	Köln	17 Aug 86
12.36	1.9	Grazyna	Rabsztyn	POL	52	1	Kuso	Warszawa	13 Jun 80
12.36	-0.6		Donkova			1	NC	Sofia	13 Aug 86
12.36	1.1		Donkova			1		Schwechat	15 Jun 88
12.37	1.4		Donkova			1	ISTAF	Berlin	15 Aug 86
12.38	0.0		Donkova			1	BGP	Budapest	11 Aug 86
12.38	-0.7		Donkova			1	ECh	Stuttgart	29 Aug 86
12.38	0.2		Donkova			1	OG	Seoul	30 Sep 88
12.39	1.5	Vera	Komisova'	SU	53	1	GG	Roma	5 Aug 80
12.39	1.5		Zagorcheva			2	Balk	Ljubljana	7 Sep 86
12.40	0.4		Donkova			1	GWG	Moskva	8 Jul 86
12.42	1.8	Bettine	Jahn	GDR	58	1	OD	Berlin	8 Jun 83
12.42	1.0		Zagorcheva			1		Sofia	14 Aug 85
12.42	-0.2		Donkova			1	VD	Bruxelles	5 Sep 86
12.43	-0.9	Lucyna	Kalek'	POL	56	1		Hannover	19 Aug 84
12.43	0.7		Zagorcheva			1	BGP	Budapest	6 Jul 87
12.44	1.9		Langer'			2	Kuso	Warszawa	13 Jun 80
12.44	1.0		Donkova			1		Sofia	7 Aug 82
12.44	-0.5	Gloria	Uibel'	GDR	64	2	WCh	Roma	4 Sep 87
12.45	1.5		Kalek			1h1	ECh	Athinai	8 Sep 82
12.45	0.4		Kalek			1	ECh	Athinai	9 Sep 82
12.45	1.3	Cornelia	Oschkenat'	GDR	61	1		Neubrandenburg	11 Jun 87
12.45	0.0		Donkova			1	BGP	Budapest	12 Aug 88
		(31/8)							
12.48	-1.0	Natalya	Grigoryeva	SU	61	1	Znam	Leningrad	12 Jun 88
12.50	0.0	Vera	Akimova'	SU	59	1		Sochi	19 May 84
		(10)							
12.54	0.4	Kerstin	Knabe	GDR	59	3	ECh	Athinai	9 Sep 82
12.54	0.9	Sabine	Paetz'	GDR	57	1		Berlin	15 Jul 84
12.56	1.2	Johanna	Klier'	GDR	52	1	NC	Cottbus	17 Jul 80
12.59	-0.6	Anneliese	Ehrhardt	GDR	50	1	OG	München	8 Sep 72
12.61	0.3	Svetlana	Gusarova	SU	59	2	NC	Leningrad	3 Aug 85
12.61	1.1	Gail	Devers	USA	66	1h1		Westwood	21 May 88
12.61	0.2	Jackie	Joyner-Kersee	USA	62	1	Jenn	San Jose	28 May 88
12.62	0.9	Lyudmila	Narozhilenko	SU	64	1		Sochi	1 Jun 88
12.63	1.8	Zofia	Bielczyk	POL	58	1h1	Kuso	Warszawa	18 Jun 79
12.63	1.4	Heike	Theele'	GDR	64	2	NC	Jena	27 Jun 86
		(20)							
12.65A	0.0	Danuta	Perka	POL	56	1h3	WUG	Ciudad México	9 Sep 79
12.65	0.0	Nadezhda	Korshunova	SU	61	2		Sochi	19 May 84
12.66	0.0	Yelena	Biserova	SU	62	3		Sochi	19 May 84
12.67	0.6	Tatyana	Anisimova	SU	49	2	ECh	Praha	2 Sep 78
12.69	0.2	Laurence	Elloy	FRA	59	2h1	GWG	Moskva	8 Jul 86
12.70	1.6	Mihaela	Pogacean'	RUM	58	1		Tel Aviv	9 May 87
12.71	-0.7	Yelena	Politika	SU	64	2	NC	Kiev	15 Jul 86
12.73	0.6	Gudrun	Berend'	GDR	55	3	ECh	Praha	2 Sep 78
12.76		Nina	Derbina'	SU	56	1		Leningrad	22 Jun 80
12.76	1.7	Xenia	Siska	HUN	57	3	BGP	Budapest	20 Aug 84
		(30)							
12.76	0.0	Lynda	Tolbert	USA	67	1rA	WK	Zürich	17 Aug 88
12.78	-0.7	Yelizaveta	Chernysheva	SU	58	4	NC	Kiev	15 Jul 86
12.78A	1.3	Julie	Rocheleau	CAN	64	1		Provo	21 May 88
12.79	1.9	Stephanie	Hightower	USA	58	3	v GDR	Karl-Marx-Stadt	10 Jul 82
12.80	0.0	Natalya	Lebedyeva	SU	49	3	OG	Montreal	29 Jul 76
12.80	1.9	Elzbieta	Rabsztyn	POL	56	5	Kuso	Warszawa	13 Jun 80

Mark		Name		Nat	Yr	Pos	Meet	Venue	Date
12.80	1.3	LaVonna	Martin	USA	66	1	TAC	San Jose	26 Jun 87
12.80	0.4	Tatyana	Reshetnikova	SU	66	1		Leningrad	5 Jul 87
12.80	-0.2	Claudia	Zaczkiewicz'	FRG	62	1	NC	Gelsenkirchen	11 Jul 87
12.81	1.0	Maria	Merchuk'	SU	59	3	v GDR	Cottbus	26 Jun 82
		(40)							
12.82	0.7	Eva	Sokolova	SU	61	1	NC	Bryansk	18 Jul 87
12.82	-0.5	Anne	Piquereau	FRA	64	5	WCh	Roma	4 Sep 87
12.82	0.8	Sally	Gunnell	UK	66	1rB	WK	Zürich	17 Aug 88
12.83	1.5	Natalya	Petrova	SU	57	2s2	WCh	Helsinki	13 Aug 83
12.83	-0.3	Svetlana	Buraga	SU	65	H		Staiki	1 Jul 88
12.83	1.9	Patricia	Davis	USA	65	1s1	FOT	Indianapolis	22 Jul 88
12.83	1.4	Jackie	Humphrey	USA	65	1s2	FOT	Indianapolis	22 Jul 88
12.83	-0.4	Marjan	Olyslager	HOL	62	1	VD	Bruxelles	19 Aug 88
12.84	0.0	Valeria	Bufanu	RUM	46	1s1	OG	Munchen	7 Sep 72
12.84	1.2	Irina	Litovchenko'	SU	50	3s2	OG	Moskva	28 Jul 80
		(50)							
12.84	1.1	Benita	Fitzgerald-Brown	USA	61	1	NCAA	Houston	4 Jun 83
12.84	1.1	Ulrike	Denk	FRG	64	1	NC	Stuttgart	3 Aug 85
12.84	1.5	Aliuska	Lopez	CUB	69	2	WUG	Zagreb	16 Jul 87
12.84	1.5	Florence	Colle	FRA	65	3	WUG	Zagreb	16 Jul 87
12.84	0.5	Kim	McKenzie	USA	61	1	TAC	Tampa	17 Jun 88

Low altitude best A-best

12.69	1.9	Perka	4	Kuso	Warszawa	13 Jun 80	12.65A

Wind assisted

Mark		Name		Nat	Yr	Pos	Meet	Venue	Date
12.28	2.7	Cornelia	Oschkenat'	GDR	61	1		Berlin	25 Aug 87
12.29	3.5		Donkova			1	Athl	Lausanne	24 Jun 88
12.35	2.4	Bettine	Jahn	GDR	58	1	WCh	Helsinki	13 Aug 83
12.37	2.7	Gloria	Uibel'	GDR	64	2		Berlin	25 Aug 87
12.39	2.8		Rabsztyn			1	4-N	Bremen	24 Jun 79
12.42	2.4	Kerstin	Knabe	GDR	59	2	WCh	Helsinki	13 Aug 83
12.46	2.6	Natalya	Grigoryeva	SU	61	1	NC	Tallinn	5 Jul 88
12.51	3.2	Johanna	Klier'	GDR	52	1	NC	Cottbus	17 Jul 80
12.51	3.6	Sabine	Paetz'	GDR	57	1		Dresden	27 Jul 84
12.57	2.6	Lyudmila	Narozhilenko	SU	64	2	NC	Tallinn	5 Jul 88
12.66	2.6	Yelena	Politika	SU	64	3	NC	Tallinn	5 Jul 88
12.67	2.4	Natalya	Petrova	SU	57	4	WCh	Helsinki	13 Aug 83
12.70	4.1	Rhonda	Blanford	USA	63	1	NCAA	Austin	1 Jun 85
12.75	3.6	Lynda	Tolbert	USA	67	1s2	TAC	Tampa	16 Jun 88
12.78	4.5	Shirley	Strong	UK	58	1	CG	Brisbane	8 Oct 82
12.78	4.6	Stephanie	Hightower	USA	58	1		Modesto	12 May 84
12.78	3.5	Florence	Colle	FRA	65	2	Athl	Lausanne	24 Jun 88
12.80	3.3	Sally	Gunnell	UK	66	1	IAC	Edinburgh	29 Jul 88
12.81	3.0	Benita	Fitzgerald-Brown	USA	61	1q1	FOT	Indianapolis	21 Jul 88
12.83	3.2	Lidia	Okolo-Kulak	SU	58	2s2	NC	Tallinn	5 Jul 88

400 METRES HURDLES

Mark	Name		Nat	Yr	Pos	Meet	Venue	Date
52.94	Marina	Styepanova'	SU	50	1s	Spart	Tashkent	17 Sep 86
53.17	Debbie	Flintoff-King	AUS	60	1	OG	Seoul	28 Sep 88
53.18	Tatyana	Ledovskaya	SU	66	2	OG	Seoul	28 Sep 88
53.24	Sabine	Busch	GDR	62	1	NC	Potsdam	21 Aug 87
53.32		Styepanova			1	ECh	Stuttgart	30 Aug 86
53.55		Busch			1		Berlin	22 Sep 85
53.58	Margarita	Ponomaryova'	SU	63	1		Kiev	22 Jun 84
53.58	Cornelia	Ullrich'	GDR	63	2	NC	Potsdam	21 Aug 87
53.60		Busch			2	ECh	Stuttgart	30 Aug 86
53.62		Busch			1h2	NC	Jena	27 Jun 86
53.62		Busch			1	WCh	Roma	3 Sep 87
53.63	Ellen	Fiedler'	GDR	58	3	OG	Seoul	28 Sep 88
53.64		Busch			1	VD	Bruxelles	5 Sep 86
53.67		Styepanova			1	Drz	Praha	17 Aug 84
53.69		Busch			4	OG	Seoul	28 Sep 88
53.72		Styepanova			1h	Spart	Tashkent	16 Sep 86

Mark	Name		Nat	Yr	Pos	Meet	Venue	Date
53.74A	Myrtle	Bothma'	RSA	64	1		Johannesburg	18 Apr 86
53.75		Busch			1		Jena	31 May 86
53.76		Flintoff-King			1	Bisl	Oslo	5 Jul 86
53.80		Busch			1	v SU	Karl-Marx-Stadt	20 Jun 87
53.81		Styepanova			1	GWG	Moskva	7 Jul 86
53.83		Busch			1		Jena	12 Jun 85
53.83		Styepanova			1s2	ECh	Stuttgart	29 Aug 86
53.84		Styepanova			1	NC	Kiev	16 Jul 86
53.85		Busch			1	NC	Jena	28 Jun 86
53.92		Styepanova			1h	Znam	Leningrad	7 Jun 86
53.93		Busch			1	v SU	Erfurt	23 Jun 85
53.95A		Bothma			1	NC	Germiston	12 Apr 86
53.95		Flintoff			1	ASV	Köln	16 Aug 87
53.95		Busch			1h1	NC	Potsdam	20 Aug 87
	(30/8)							
54.02	Anna	Ambraziene'	SU	55	1	Znam	Moskva	11 Jun 83
54.03	Sally	Gunnell	UK	66	5	OG	Seoul	28 Sep 88
	(10)							
54.04	Gudrun	Abt	FRG	62	6	OG	Seoul	28 Sep 88
54.14	Yekaterina	Fesenko-Grun	SU	58	1	WCh	Helsinki	10 Aug 83
54.15	Ann-Louise	Skoglund	SWE	62	4	ECh	Stuttgart	30 Aug 86
54.23	Judi	Brown King	USA	61	1	PAG	Indianapolis	12 Aug 87
54.24	Susanne	Losch	GDR	66	1	v FRG	Düsseldorf	19 Jun 88
54.27	Genowefa	Blaszak'	POL	57	1	DNG	Stockholm	2 Jul 85
54.28	Karin	Rossley	GDR	57	1		Jena	17 May 80
54.34	Tatyana	Pavlova'	SU	58	1h1	NC	Leningrad	2 Aug 85
54.36	LaTanya	Sheffield	USA	63	3s1	OG	Seoul	26 Sep 88
54.38	Sandra	Farmer'	USA/JAM	62	4	WCh	Roma	3 Sep 87
	(20)							
54.39	Tatyana	Kurochkina'	SU	67	7	OG	Seoul	28 Sep 88
54.55	Barbel	Broschat	GDR	57	1	WCh	Sittard	16 Aug 80
54.55	Cristieana	Matei'	RUM	62	2	GWG	Moskva	7 Jul 86
54.56	Yelena	Filipishina	SU	62	2		Moskva	20 Jul 84
54.56	Anita	Protti	SWZ	64	5s1	OG	Seoul	26 Sep 88
54.61	Nawal	el Moutawakil	MOR	62	1	OG	Los Angeles	8 Aug 84
54.62	Tuija	Helander-Kuusisto	FIN	61	5	WCh	Roma	3 Sep 87
54.64	Petra	Pfaff	GDR	60	4	WCh	Helsinki	10 Aug 83
54.68	Birgit	Uibel	GDR	61	1		Dresden	19 May 84
54.76	Petra	Krug	GDR	63	5	WCh	Helsinki	10 Aug 83
	(30)							
54.78	Marina	Sereda'	SU	64	2	Spart	Tashkent	18 Sep 86
54.80	Tatyana	Storozheva	SU	54	1		Moskva	12 Jun 80
54.82	Schowonda	Williams	USA	66	4s1	WCh	Roma	1 Sep 87
54.86	Tonja	Brown	USA	60	3	GG	Roma	7 Sep 85
54.89	Tatyana	Zelentsova	SU	48	1	ECh	Praha	2 Sep 78
54.90	Sharrieffa	Barksdale	USA	61	1		Knoxville	24 May 86
54.93	Chantal	Réga	FRA	55	3	ECh	Athinai	10 Sep 82
54.93	Yelena	Goncharova	SU	63	1		Sochi	18 May 86
55.02	Margarita	Navickaite'	SU	61	6	Izv	Kiev	22 Jun 84
55.05	Jackie	Joyner'	USA	62	4	VD	Bruxelles	30 Aug 85
	(40)							
55.14	Silvia	Hollmann	FRG	55	2	ECh	Praha	2 Sep 78
55.16	Nicoleta	Carutasu'	RUM	64	2		Bucuresti	24 May 86
55.16	Maria	Usifo	NIG	64	1	NCAA	Indianapolis	6 Jun 86
55.19	Mary	Wagner	FRG	61	1		Fürth	21 May 83
55.20	Leslie	Maxie	USA	67	2	TAC	San Jose	9 Jun 84
55.23	Cristina	Perez	SPA	65	5s2	OG	Seoul	26 Sep 88
55.26	Yelena	Mitrukova	SU	64	1r2	NC	Bryansk	18 Jul 87
55.33	Angela	Wright-Scott	USA	64	2	FOT	Los Angeles	21 Jun 84
55.40	Sophia	Hunter	USA	64	5	TAC	San Jose	27 Jun 87
55.42	Pillavulakandi	Usha	IND	64	4	OG	Los Angeles	8 Aug 84
	(50)							

HIGH JUMP

Mark	Name		Nat	Yr	Pos	Meet	Venue	Date
2.09	Stefka	Kostadinova	BUL	65	1	WCh	Roma	30 Aug 87
2.08		Kostadinova			1	NarM	Sofia	31 May 86
2.07	Lyudmila	Andonova	BUL	60	1	OD	Berlin	20 Jul 84
2.07		Kostadinova			1		Sofia	25 May 86
2.07		Kostadinova			1		Cagliari	16 Sep 87
2.07		Kostadinova			1	NC	Sofia	3 Sep 88
2.06		Kostadinova			1	EP	Moskva	18 Aug 85
2.06		Kostadinova			1		Fürth	15 Jun 86
2.06		Kostadinova			1		Cagliari	14 Sep 86
2.06		Kostadinova			1		Worrstadt	6 Jun 87
2.06		Kostadinova			1		Rieti	8 Sep 87
2.06i		Kostadinova			1		Athinai	20 Feb 88
2.05	Tamara	Bykova	SU	58	1	Izv	Kiev	22 Jun 84
2.05		Kostadinova			1		Wörrstadt	14 Jun 86
2.05		Kostadinova			1		Rieti	7 Sep 86
2.05i		Kostadinova			1	WCh	Indianapolis	8 Mar 87
2.05		Kostadinova			1	Bisl	Oslo	4 Jul 87
2.05		Kostadinova			1		Padova	13 Sep 87
2.05		Kostadinova			1	BGP	Budapest	12 Aug 88
2.04		Bykova			1		Pisa	25 Aug 83
2.04		Kostadinova			1	VD	Bruxelles	30 Aug 85
2.04		Kostadinova			1		Rieti	4 Sep 85
2.04		Kostadinova			1		Bern	20 Aug 86
2.04i		Kostadinova			1	v Ita,Spa	Genova	31 Jan 87
2.04		Kostadinova			1	v CS,Gre	Drama	8 Aug 87
2.04		Bykova			2	WCh	Roma	30 Aug 87
2.04i		Kostadinova			1	4-N	Athinai	6 Feb 88
2.04i		Kostadinova			1	EI	Budapest	6 Mar 88
2.04		Kostadinova			1		Formia	19 Jun 88
2.03i		Bykova			1	EI	Budapest	6 Mar 83
2.03	Ulrike	Meyfarth	FRG	56	1	EP	London	21 Aug 83
2.03		Bykova			2	EP	London	21 Aug 83
2.03		Bykova			1		Moskva	6 Aug 84
2.03		Andonova			1		Rieti	2 Sep 84
2.03		Kostadinova			1	GWG	Moskva	7 Jul 86
2.03		Kostadinova			1		Formia	11 Jul 87
2.03i		Kostadinova			1		Sindelfingen	5 Feb 88
2.03		Kostadinova			1		Sofia	22 May 88
2.03	Louise	Ritter	USA	58	1		Austin	8 Jul 88
2.03		Ritter			1	OG	Seoul	30 Sep 88
	(40/5)							
2.02i	Susanne	Beyer'	GDR	61	2	WCh	Indianapolis	8 Mar 87
2.02	Silvia	Costa	CUB	64	1	Nik	Nice	10 Jul 88
2.01	Sara	Simeoni	ITA	53	1	v Pol	Brescia	4 Aug 78
2.01	Olga	Turchak	SU	67	2	GWG	Moskva	7 Jul 86
2.01	Desiré	du Plessis	RSA	65	1		Johannesburg	16 Sep 86
	(10)							
2.01i	Gabriele	Günz	GDR	61	2		Stuttgart	31 Jan 88
2.00	Rosemarie	Ackermann'	GDR	52	1	ISTAF	Berlin	26 Aug 77
2.00i	Coleen	Sommer'	USA	60	1		Ottawa	14 Feb 82
2.00	Charmaine	Gale	RSA	64	1		Pretoria	25 Mar 85
2.00i	Emilia	Dragieva'	BUL	65	3	WCh	Indianapolis	8 Mar 87
2.00	Lyudmila	Avdyeyenko'	SU	63	1	NC	Bryansk	17 Jul 87
2.00	Svetlana	Isaeva	BUL	67	2	v CS,Gre	Drama	8 Aug 87
2.00i	Larisa	Kositsyna	SU	63	2	NC	Volgograd	11 Feb 88
2.00	Galina	Astafei	RUM	69	1	WJ	Sudbury	29 Jul 88
1.99i	Debbie	Brill	CAN	53	1		Edmonton	23 Jan 82
	(20)							
1.99i	Andrea	Bienias'	GDR	59	2	ECh	Milano	7 Mar 82
1.99i	Katalin	Sterk	HUN	61	3	ECh	Milano	7 Mar 82
1.99	Kerstin	Brandt'	GDR	61	3	EP	London	21 Aug 83
1.98i	Andrea	Mátay	HUN	55	1	NC	Budapest	17 Feb 79

Mark	Name		Nat	Yr	Pos	Meet	Venue	Date
1.98	Valentina	Poluyko	SU	55	1		Leningrad	26 Jul 83
1.98	Lyudmila	Butuzova	SU	57	2	Znam	Sochi	10 Jun 84
1.98	Niculina	Vasile	RUM	58	1	RomIC	Bucuresti	2 Jun 85
1.98	Heike	Redetzky	FRG	64	1	v GDR	Dusseldorf	20 Jun 88
1.98	Yelena	Yelesina	SU	70	1	Druzh	Nyiregyháza	13 Aug 88
1.97	Pam	Spencer	USA	57	1	VD	Bruxelles	28 Aug 81
	(30)							
1.97i	Zhanna	Nyekrasova	SU	57	1	NP	Moskva	13 Feb 82
1.97	Jutta	Kirst	GDR	54	1	v USA	Karl-Marx-Stadt	10 Jul 82
1.97	Yelena	Popkova	SU	55	2	NC	Kiev	21 Aug 82
1.97	Olga	Juha	HUN	62	4	EP	London	21 Aug 83
1.97i	Marina	Doronina	SU	61	1		Vilnius	14 Jan 84
1.97	Danuta	Bulkowska	POL	59	2		Wörrstadt	9 Jun 84
1.97	Olga	Byelkova	SU	55	2	Izv	Kiev	22 Jun 84
1.97	Joni	Huntley	USA	56	3	OG	Los Angeles	10 Aug 84
1.97i	Lisa	Bernhagen	USA	66	1		Flagstaff	21 Feb 87
1.97	Jan	Wohlschlag'	USA	58	1	TAC	Tampa	17 Jun 88
	(40)							
1.96	Nina	Serbina	SU	52	1		Chernigov	3 Jun 80
1.96	Chris	Stanton'	AUS	59	H		Adelaide	26 Jan 85
1.96	Yang Wenqin		CHN	60	1		Beijing	26 May 85
1.96	Maryse	Ewanje-Epée	FRA	64	1	NC	Colombes	21 Jul 85
1.96	Galina	Brigadnaya	SU	58	1	NP	Alma-Ata	13 Sep 85
1.96	Albina	Kazakova	SU	62	1	Znam	Moskva	7 Jun 87
1.96	Marina	Degtyar	SU	62	3	Znam	Moskva	7 Jun 87
1.96	Gabriela	Mihalcea	RUM	64	1	EP-B	Göteborg	28 Jun 87
1.96i	Madely	Beaugendre	FRA	65	1		Paris	7 Feb 88
1.96	Vanessa	Browne	AUS	63	1	NC	Perth	27 Mar 88
	(50)							
1.96	Biljana	Petrovic	YUG	61	1	Balk	Ankara	16 Jul 88
1.96	Trish	King	USA	62	2	FOT	Indianapolis	23 Jul 88

Best outdoor marks

Mark	Name	Pos	Meet	Venue	Date	Indoor
1.99	Beyer'	3	WCh	Roma	30 Aug 87	2.02i
1.98	Sommer	1	v FRG,Afr	Durham	26 Jun 82	2.00i
1.98	Kositsyna	2	NarM	Sofia	21 May 83	2.00i
1.98	Brill	2		Rieti	2 Sep 84	1.99i
1.98	Sterk	1	NC	Budapest	17 Aug 86	1.99i
1.97	Bienias	1		Leipzig	27 Jul 83	1.99i
1.97	Günz	1		Halle	26 Jun 87	2.01i
1.96	Doronina	2	NC	Donyetsk	7 Sep 84	1.97i

LONG JUMP

Mark	Wind	Name		Nat	Yr	Pos	Meet	Venue	Date
7.52	1.4	Galina	Chistyakova	SU	62	1	Znam	Leningrad	11 Jun 88
7.48	1.2	Heike	Drechsler	GDR	64	1	v Ita	Neubrandenburg	9 Jul 88
7.45	0.9		Drechsler'			1	v SU	Tallinn	21 Jun 86
7.45	1.1		Drechsler			1	OD	Dresden	3 Jul 86
7.45	0.6	Jackie	Joyner-Kersee	USA	62	1	PAG	Indianapolis	13 Aug 87
7.45	1.6		Chistyakova			1	BGP	Budapest	12 Aug 88
7.44	2.0		Drechsler			1		Berlin	22 Sep 85
7.43	1.4	Anisoara	Cusmir'	RUM	62	1	RomIC	Bucuresti	4 Jun 83
7.40	1.8		Daute'			1		Dresden	26 Jul 84
7.40	0.7		Drechsler			1	NC	Potsdam	21 Aug 87
7.40	0.9		Joyner-Kersee			1	OG	Seoul	29 Sep 88
7.39	0.3		Drechsler			1	WK	Zürich	21 Aug 85
7.39	0.5	Yelena	Byelevskaya'	SU	63	1	NC	Bryansk	18 Jul 87
7.39			Joyner-Kersee			1		San Diego	25 Jun 88
7.37i	-		Drechsler			1	v Aut,Yug	Wien	13 Feb 88
7.36	0.4		Joyner			1	WCh	Roma	4 Sep 87
7.36	1.8		Byelevskaya			2	Znam	Leningrad	11 Jun 88
7.34	1.6		Daute'			1		Dresden	19 May 84
7.34	1.4		Chistyakova			2	v GDR	Tallinn	21 Jun 86
7.34			Byelevskaya			1		Sukhumi	17 May 87
7.34	0.7		Drechsler			1	v SU	Karl-Marx-Stadt	20 Jun 87
7.33	0.4		Drechsler			1	v SU	Erfurt	22 Jun 85

Mark		Name		Nat	Yr	Pos	Meet	Venue	Date
7.33	2.0		Drechsler			1		Dresden	2 Aug 85
7.32	-0.2		Daute'			1	OD	Berlin	20 Jul 84
7.32i	-		Drechsler			1	TAC	New York	27 Feb 87
7.31	1.5	Yelena	Kokonova	SU	63	1	NP	Alma-Ata	12 Sep 85
7.31	1.3		Drechsler			1		Jena	31 May 86
7.31	-0.2		Byelevskaya			1	NC	Kiev	15 Jul 86
7.31	1.1		Byelevskaya			1		Moskva	16 Aug 87
		(30/6)							
7.27		Inessa	Kravets'	SU	66	1		Kiev	22 May 88
7.21	1.6	Helga	Radtke	GDR	62	2		Dresden	26 Jul 84
7.20	-0.5	Valy	Ionescu	RUM	60	1	NC	Bucuresti	1 Aug 82
7.20	2.0	Irena	Ozhenko'	SU	62	1		Budapest	12 Sep 86
		(10)							
7.19	1.3	Larisa	Berezhnaya	SU	61	1		Krasnodar	22 Jun 86
7.17	1.8	Irina	Valyukevich	SU	59	2	NC	Bryansk	18 Jul 87
7.16		Yolanda	Chen	SU	61	1		Moskva	30 Jul 88
7.14	1.8	Niole	Medvedyeva	SU	60	1		Riga	4 Jun 88
7.12	1.6	Sabine	Paetz'	GDR	57	2		Dresden	19 May 84
7.09	0.0	Vilma	Bardauskiene	SU	53	Q	ECh	Praha	29 Aug 78
7.07	0.0	Svetlana	Zorina	SU	60	1		Krasnodar	15 Aug 87
7.06	0.4	Tatyana	Kalpakova	SU	59	1	OG	Moskva	31 Jul 80
7.05	0.8	Yelena	Ivanova	SU	61	2	Znam	Moskva	7 Jun 87
7.04	0.5	Brigitte	Wujak'	GDR	55	2	OG	Moskva	31 Jul 80
		(20)							
7.04	0.9	Tatyana	Proskuryakova'	SU	56	1		Kiev	25 Aug 83
7.04	2.0	Yelena	Yatsuk	SU	61	1	Znam	Moskva	8 Jun 85
7.04	0.3	Carol	Lewis	USA	63	5	WK	Zürich	21 Aug 85
7.01	-0.4	Tatyana	Skachko	SU	54	3	OG	Moskva	31 Jul 80
7.01	-0.3	Eva	Murková	CS	62	1	PTS	Bratislava	26 May 84
7.01	-1.0	Marina	Kibakina'	SU	60	1		Krasnoyarsk	10 Aug 85
7.00	2.0	Jodi	Anderson	USA	57	1	FOT	Eugene	28 Jun 80
7.00		Margarita	Butkiene	SU	49	1		Vilnius	25 May 83
7.00	-0.2	Birgit	Grösshennig	GDR	65	2		Berlin	9 Jun 84
7.00	0.6	Silvia	Khristova'	BUL	65	1		Sofia	3 Aug 86
		(30)							
6.99	2.0	Siegrun	Siegl'	GDR	54	1	OD	Dresden	19 May 76
6.98	1.1	Marieta	Ilcu	RUM	62	2	NC	Pitesti	14 Aug 88
6.97	2.0	Agata	Karczmarek	POL	63	1		Lublin	6 Aug 88
6.96	2.0	Anna	Wlodarczyk	POL	51	1	NC	Lublin	22 Jun 84
6.96	1.8	Christine	Schima	GDR	62	3		Dresden	26 Jul 84
6.96A	0.0	Madeline	de Jesus	PR	57	1	IbAC	Ciudad México	24 Jul 88
6.94	1.3	Yelena	Chicherova	SU	58	2	Izv	Kiev	21 Jun 84
6.94	-1.0	Sheila	Echols	USA	64	1	NCAA	Baton Rouge	5 Jun 87
6.92	1.6	Angela	Voigt'	GDR	51	1		Dresden	9 May 76
6.92		Vera	Olenchenko	SU	59	1		Baku	22 Sep 85
		(40)							
6.92	1.6	Heike	Grabe	GDR	62	2	PTS	Bratislava	13 Jun 87
6.91	1.8	Heike	Duwe	GDR	60	3		Berlin	9 Jun 84
6.90	1.8	Ramona	Neubert	GDR	58	-	v UK	Dresden	14 Jun 81
6.90		Tatyana	Turulina	SU	58	1		Krasnodar	26 May 83
6.90	1.4	Beverley	Kinch	UK	64	-	WCh	Helsinki	14 Aug 83
6.90	1.7	Jolanta	Bartzak	POL	64	1	PTS	Bratislava	9 Jun 88
6.89	-0.3	Sigrid	Ulbricht	GDR	58	2	NC	Jena	9 Aug 81
6.89	1.8	Jarmila	Strejckova'	CS	53	1		Praha	18 Sep 82
6.89	0.0	Yelena	Pershina	SU	63	2		Alma-Ata	18 Jun 88
6.88	0.6	Natalya	Shevchenko	SU	66	2		Sochi	26 May 84
		(50)							
6.88	-0.8	Lyudmila	Ninova	BUL	60	1	NC	Sofia	14 Aug 86
6.88	1.6	Galina	Salo	SU	59	2		Volgograd	6 Sep 86
6.88	1.5	Carmen	Sirbu	RUM	67	2	NC	Pitesti	9 Aug 87
6.88	0.3	Xiong Qiying		CHN	67	2		Tianjin	1 Sep 88
Wind assisted									
7.45	2.6	Jackie	Joyner-Kersee	USA	62	1	FOT	Indianapolis	23 Jul 88
7.35	3.4		Drechsler			1	NC	Jena	29 Jun 86
7.33	3.5		Drechsler			1		Jena	12 Jun 85
7.33	2.1		Drechsler			1	Bisl	Oslo	4 Jul 87

Mark		Name		Nat	Yr	Pos	Meet	Venue	Date
7.17	3.6	Eva	Murková	CS	62	1		Nitra	26 Aug 84
7.00	3.8	Ramona	Neubert	GDR	58	1	v UK	Dresden	14 Jun 81
7.00	4.2	Sue	Hearnshaw'	UK	58	1	NC	Cwmbran	27 May 84
6.99	4.6	Beverley	Kinch	UK	64	5	WCh	Helsinki	14 Aug 83
6.98	3.4	Ines	Schmidt	GDR	60	2		Nitra	26 Aug 84
6.97	2.7	Anna	Wlodarczyk	POL	51	1	4-N	Warszawa	15 Jul 84
6.96		Tatyana	Shchelkanova	SU	37	P	NC	Dnepropetrovsk	14 Aug 66
6.91		Kathy	McMillan	USA	57	1		Houston	3 May 80
6.91	2.7	Shonel	Ferguson	BAH	57	1	CG	Brisbane	8 Oct 82
6.90	2.6	Robyn	Lorraway'	AUS	61	1		Adelaide	4 Feb 84

TRIPLE JUMP

Mark		Name		Nat	Yr	Pos	Meet	Venue	Date
14.16		Li Huirong		CHN	65	1		Shijiazhuang	23 Apr 88
14.04	+0.3	Li Huirong						Hamamatsu	11 Oct 87
13.98i	-	Galina	Chistyakova	SU	62	1		Moskva	25 Jan 87
13.93i	-	Valy	Ionescu	RUM	60	1		Inglewood	21 Feb 87
13.85	+1.7	Sheila	Hudson	USA	67	1	TAC	San Jose	26 Jun 87
13.82	+1.8	Wendy	Brown	USA	66	1	TAC	Tampa	17 Jun 88
13.79i	-	Yvette	Bates	USA	65	1	NCAA	Oklahoma City	14 Mar 87
13.79			Hudson			1		Modesto	7 May 88
13.73		Flora	Hyacinth	UVI	66	1		Tuscaloosa	17 May 87
13.71		Brown				1		Los Angeles	2 May 87
		(10/7)							
13.68	0.0	Esmeralda	Garcia	BRA	59	q	NCAA	Indianapolis	5 Jun 86
13.68	0.0	Terri	Turner	USA	63	q	NCAA	Indianapolis	5 Jun 86
13.56i	-	Renita	Robinson	USA	67	1		Lincoln	13 Feb 88
13.55		Eloina	Echevarria	CUB	61	1		Habana	24 Feb 87
		(11)							
Wind assisted									
13.92	+3.8	Sheila	Hudson	USA	67	1	NCAA	Eugene	4 Jun 88
13.78	+3.2		Brown			1	TAC	Eugene	20 Jun 86

SHOT

Mark	Name		Nat	Yr	Pos	Meet	Venue	Date
22.63	Natalya	Lisovskaya	SU	62	1	Znam	Moskva	7 Jun 87
22.55		Lisovskaya			1	NC	Tallinn	5 Jul 88
22.53		Lisovskaya			1		Sochi	27 May 84
22.53		Lisovskaya			1		Kiev	14 Aug 88
22.50i	Helena	Fibingerová	CS	49	1		Jablonec	19 Feb 77
22.45	Ilona	Slupianek'	GDR	56	1		Potsdam	11 May 80
22.41		Slupianek			1	OG	Moskva	24 Jul 80
22.40		Slupianek			1		Berlin	3 Jun 83
22.38		Slupianek			1		Karl-Marx-Stadt	25 May 80
22.36		Slupianek			1		Celje	2 May 80
22.34		Slupianek			1		Berlin	7 May 80
22.34		Slupianek			1	NC	Cottbus	18 Jul 80
22.32		Fibingerová			1		Nitra	20 Aug 77
22.24		Lisovskaya			1	OG	Seoul	1 Oct 88
22.22		Slupianek			1		Potsdam	13 Jul 80
22.19	Claudia	Losch	FRG	60	1		Hainfeld	23 Aug 87
22.14i		Lisovskaya			1	NC	Penza	7 Feb 87
22.13		Slupianek			1		Split	29 Apr 80
22.06		Slupianek			1		Berlin	15 Aug 78
22.06		Lisovskaya			1		Moskva	6 Aug 88
22.05		Slupianek			1	OD	Berlin	28 May 80
22.05		Slupianek			1		Potsdam	31 May 80
22.04		Slupianek			1		Potsdam	4 Jul 79
22.04		Slupianek			1		Potsdam	29 Jul 79
21.99		Fibingerová			1		Opava	26 Sep 76
21.98		Slupianek			1		Berlin	17 Jul 79
21.96		Fibingerová			1	GS	Ostrava	8 Jun 77
21.96		Lisovskaya			1	Drz	Praha	16 Aug 84
21.96		Lisovskaya			1		Vilnius	28 Aug 88
21.95		Lisovskaya			1	IAC	Edinburgh	29 Jul 88
	(30/4)							

Mark	Name		Nat	Yr	Pos	Meet	Venue	Date
21.89	Ivanka	Khristova	BUL	41	1		Belmeken	4 Jul 76
21.86	Marianne	Adam	GDR	51	1	v SU	Leipzig	23 Jun 79
21.76	Li Meisu		CHN	59	1		Shijiazhuang	23 Apr 88
21.73	Natalya	Akhremenko	SU	55	1		Leselidze	21 May 88
21.61	Verzhinia	Veselinova	BUL	57	1		Sofia	21 Aug 82
21.58	Margitta	Droese'	GDR	52	1		Erfurt	28 May 78
	(10)							
21.57 @	Ines	Muller'	GDR	59	1		Athinai	16 May 88
21.53	Nunu	Abashidze	SU	55	2	Izv	Kiev	20 Jun 84
21.45	Nadezhda	Chizhova	SU	45	1		Varna	29 Sep 73
21.43	Eva	Wilms	FRG	52	2	HB	München	17 Jun 77
21.42	Svetlana	Krachevskaya'	SU	44	2	OG	Moskva	24 Jul 80
21.31 @	Heike	Hartwig'	GDR	62	2		Athinai	16 May 88
21.28	Huang Zhihong		CHN	65	2		Shijiazhuang	23 Apr 88
21.27	Liane	Schmuhl	GDR	61	1		Cottbus	26 Jun 82
21.21	Kathrin	Neimke	GDR	66	2	WCh	Roma	5 Sep 87
21.19	Helma	Knorscheidt	GDR	56	1		Berlin	24 May 84
	(20)							
21.10	Heidi	Krieger	GDR	65	1	ECh	Stuttgart	26 Aug 86
21.08	Valentina	Fedyushina	SU	65	1		Leselidze	15 May 88
21.05	Zdenka	Silhava'	CS	54	2	NC	Praha	23 Jul 83
21.01	Ivanka	Petrova-Stoycheva	BUL	51	1	NC	Sofia	28 Jul 79
21.00	Mihaela	Loghin	RUM	52	1		Formia	30 Jun 84
21.00	Cordula	Schulze	GDR	59	4	OD	Potsdam	21 Jul 84
20.99	Larisa	Peleshenko'	SU	64	1		Leselidze	13 May 87
20.95	Elena	Stoyanova	BUL	52	2	Balk	Sofia	14 Jun 80
20.91	Svetla	Mitkova	BUL	64	1		Sofia	24 May 87
20.80	Sona	Vasicková	CS	62	1		Praha	2 Jun 88
	(30)							
20.72	Grit	Haupt'	GDR	66	3		Neubrandenburg	11 Jun 87
20.61	María Elena	Sarría	CUB	54	1		Habana	22 Jul 82
20.60	Marina	Antonyuk	SU	62	1		Chelyabinsk	10 Aug 86
20.53	Iris	Plotzitzka	FRG	66	1	ASV	Köln	21 Aug 88
20.47	Nina	Isayeva	SU	50	1		Bryansk	28 Aug 82
20.47	Cong Yuzhen		CHN	63	2	IntC	Tianjin	3 Sep 88
20.44	Tatyana	Orlova	SU	55	1		Staiki	28 May 83
20.27	Danguole	Bimbaite'	SU	62	2		Leselidze	13 May 87
20.27	Lyudmila	Voyevudskaya	SU	59	1		Nikolayev	7 Aug 87
20.23	Ilke	Wyludda	GDR	69	1	NC-j	Karl-Marx-Stadt	16 Jul 88
	(40)							
20.22	Margitta	Gummel'	GDR	41	2	OG	München	7 Sep 72
20.21	Svetlana	Melnikova	SU	51	1		Riga	5 Jun 82
20.21	Lyudmila	Savina	SU	55	2	Znam	Sochi	9 Jun 84
20.18	Ramona	Pagel	USA	61	1		San Diego	25 Jun 88
20.12	Vera	Tsapkalenko	SU	54	2	Prav	Sochi	29 May 77
20.12	Rimma	Muzikeviciene	SU	52	1		Vilnius	16 Aug 80
20.08	Sui Xinmei		CHN	65	2		Tianjin	1 Sep 88
20.07	Tatyana	Shcherbanos	SU	60	4	NC	Donyetsk	7 Sep 84
20.06	Raisa	Taranda	SU	47	2	NC	Kiev	23 Jun 76
20.04	Gabriele	Retzlaff	GDR	54	5	NC	Cottbus	18 Jul 80
	(50)							

@ made in unsanctioned meeting but included in national ranking lists

DISCUS

Mark	Name		Nat	Yr	Pos	Meet	Venue	Date
76.80	Gabriele	Reinsch	GDR	63	1	v Ita	Neubrandenburg	9 Jul 88
74.56	Zdenka	Silhavá'	CS	54	1		Nitra	26 Aug 84
74.44		Reinsch			1		Berlin	13 Sep 88
74.40	Ilke	Wyludda	GDR	69	2		Berlin	13 Sep 88
74.08	Diana	Gansky'	GDR	63	1	v SU	Karl-Marx-Stadt	20 Jun 87
73.90		Gansky			1	EP	Praha	27 Jun 87
73.84	Daniela	Costian	RUM	65	1		Bucuresti	30 Apr 88
73.78		Costian			1		Bucuresti	24 Apr 88
73.42		Reinsch			1		Karl-Marx-Stadt	12 Jun 88
73.36	Irina	Meszynski	GDR	62	1	Drz	Praha	17 Aug 84
73.32		Gansky			1		Neubrandenburg	11 Jun 87
73.28	Galina	Savinkova'	SU	53	1	NC	Donyetsk	8 Sep 84

Mark		Name	Nat	Yr	Pos	Meet	Venue	Date
73.26		Savinkova			1		Leselidze	21 May 83
73.26		Sachse'			1		Neubrandenburg	6 Jun 86
73.24		Gansky			1		Leipzig	29 May 87
73.22	Tsvetanka	Khristova	BUL	62	1		Kazanlak	19 Apr 87
73.10	Gisela	Beyer	GDR	60	1	OD	Berlin	20 Jul 84
73.04		Gansky			1		Potsdam	6 Jun 87
72.96		Savinkova			1	v GDR	Erfurt	23 Jun 85
72.94		Gansky			2	v Ita	Neubrandenburg	9 Jul 88
72.92	Martina	Hellmann'	GDR	60	1	NC	Potsdam	20 Aug 87
72.90		Costian			1		Bucuresti	14 May 88
72.78		Hellmann			2		Neubrandenburg	11 Jun 87
72.78		Reinsch			1	OD	Berlin	29 Jun 88
72.70		Wyludda			1	NC-j	Karl-Marx-Stadt	15 Jul 88
72.54		Gansky			1	NC	Rostock	25 Jun 88
72.52		Hellmann			1		Frohburg	15 Jun 86
72.52		Khristova			1	BGP	Budapest	11 Aug 86
72.44		Gansky			1		Potsdam	7 Jul 87
72.38		Gansky			1		Berlin	25 Aug 87
	(30/10)							
72.14	Galina	Murashova	SU	55	2	Drz	Praha	17 Aug 84
71.80	Maria	Vergova-Petkova	BUL	50	1	NC	Sofia	13 Jul 80
71.58	Ellina	Zveryeva'	SU	60	1	Znam	Leningrad	12 Jun 88
71.50	Evelin	Jahl'	GDR	56	1		Potsdam	10 May 80
71.22	Ria	Stalman	HOL	52	1		Walnut	15 Jul 84
70.80	Larisa	Mikhalchenko	SU	63	1		Kharkov	18 Jun 88
70.50	Faina	Melnik	SU	45	1	Znam	Sochi	24 Apr 76
70.50	Maritza	Marten	CUB	63	1		Habana	21 Mar 85
70.34 @	Silvia	Madetzky	GDR	62	3		Athinai	16 May 88
69.86	Valentina	Kharchenko	SU	49	1		Feodosia	16 May 81
	(20)							
69.72	Svetla	Mitkova	BUL	64	2	NC	Sofia	15 Aug 87
69.50	Florenta	Craciunescu'	RUM	55	1	Balk	Stara Zagora	2 Aug 85
69.08	Carmen	Romero	CUB	50	1	NC	Habana	17 Apr 76
69.08	Mariana	Lengyel'	RUM	53	1		Constanta	19 Apr 86
68.92	Sabine	Engel	GDR	54	1	v SU,Pol	Karl-Marx-Stadt	25 Jun 77
68.64	Margitta	Pufe'	GDR	52	1	ISTAF	Berlin	17 Aug 79
68.62	Yu Hourun		CHN	62	1		Beijing	6 May 88
68.62	Hou Xuemei		CHN	62	1	IntC	Tianjin	4 Sep 88
68.60	Nadezhda	Kugayevskikh	SU	60	1		Oryol	30 Aug 83
68.58	Lyubov	Zverkova	SU	55	1	Izv	Kiev	22 Jun 84
	(30)							
68.18	Tatyana	Lesovaya	SU	56	1		Alma-Ata	23 Sep 82
68.18	Irina	Khval	SU	62	1		Moskva	8 Jul 88
67.96	Argentina	Menis	RUM	48	1	RomIC	Bucuresti	15 May 76
67.92	Hilda Elisa	Ramos	CUB	64	2	NarM	Sofia	31 May 86
67.90	Petra	Sziegaud	GDR	58	1		Berlin	19 May 82
67.82	Tatyana	Byelova	SU	62	1		Irkutsk	10 Aug 87
67.64	Irina	Shabanova	SU	64	1		Krasnodar	15 Aug 87
67.54	Svetlana	Petrova	SU	51	1		Brest	20 Sep 78
67.48	Meg	Ritchie	UK	52	1	MSR	Walnut	26 Apr 81
67.44	Irina	Yatchenko	SU	65	6	Znam	Leningrad	12 Jun 88
	(40)							
67.40	Brigitte	Michel	GDR	56	2		Halle	14 Jun 79
67.32	Natalya	Gorbachova	SU	47	1		Leningrad	4 Jun 83
67.26	Svetla	Bozhkova	BUL	51	2		Sofia	5 Jul 80
67.16	Simona	Andrusca	RUM	62	2	RomIC	Bucuresti	1 Jun 85
67.06	Ingra-Anne	Manecke	FRG	56	1		Fürth	29 May 82
67.02	Gabriele	Hinzmann	GDR	47	1		Potsdam	1 Sep 73
67.02	Ulla	Lundholm	FIN	57	1		Helsinki	23 Aug 83
67.00	Jana	Günther	GDR	68	6	NC	Potsdam	20 Aug 87
66.94	Nadezhda	Yerokha	SU	52	1		Leselidze	23 Mar 80
66.60	Astrid	Kumbernuss	GDR	70	1		Berlin	20 Jul 88
	(50)							
Unofficial meeting								
78.14	Martina	Hellmann	GDR	60	-		Berlin	6 Sep

JAVELIN

Mark	Name		Nat	Yr	Pos	Meet	Venue	Date
80.00	Petra	Felke	GDR	59	1		Potsdam	9 Sep 88
78.90		Felke			1		Leipzig	29 Jul 87
78.14		Felke			1	OT	Jena	3 Jun 88
77.52		Felke			1	Super	Tokyo	8 Oct 88
77.44	Fatima	Whitbread	UK	61	Q	ECh	Stuttgart	28 Aug 86
76.82		Felke			1	v FRG	Düsseldorf	19 Jun 88
76.80		Felke			1		Chania	22 May 88
76.76		Felke			1		Berlin	27 Aug 88
76.64		Whitbread			1	WCh	Roma	6 Sep 87
76.50		Felke			1		Rostock	29 May 88
76.34		Whitbread			1	Bisl	Oslo	4 Jul 87
76.32		Whitbread			1	ECh	Stuttgart	29 Aug 86
75.62		Whitbread			1	NC	Derby	25 May 87
75.40		Felke			1		Schwerin	4 Jun 85
75.16		Felke			1	Bisl	Oslo	2 Jul 88
75.04		Felke			1	GO	Dresden	17 Aug 86
74.94		Felke			1	v SU	Erfurt	22 Jun 85
74.92		Felke			1	OD	Berlin	29 Jun 88
74.90		Felke			1	OD	Berlin	27 Jun 85
74.76	Tiina	Lillak	FIN	61	1		Tampere	13 Jun 83
74.74		Whitbread			1		Crawley	26 Aug 87
74.72		Felke			1		Celje	5 May 84
74.70		Felke			1		Berlin	22 Sep 85
74.68		Felke			1	OG	Seoul	26 Sep 88
74.62		Felke			1		Berlin	13 Sep 88
74.56		Felke			1	ISTAF	Berlin	23 Aug 85
74.32		Felke			1		Neubrandenburg	11 Jun 87
74.24		Lillak			1		Fresno	7 Apr 84
74.24		Felke			1	OD	Potsdam	21 Jul 84
74.20	Sofia	Sakorafa	GRE	57	1	NC	Chania	26 Sep 82
	(30/4)							
73.58	Tessa	Sanderson	UK	56	1		Edinburgh	26 Jun 83
72.70	Anna	Verouli	GRE	56	1		Chania	20 May 84
72.16	Antje	Kempe-Zollkau	GDR	63	2		Celje	5 May 84
71.88	Antoaneta	Todorova'	BUL	63	1	EP	Zagreb	15 Aug 81
71.82	Ivonne	Leal	CUB	66	1	WUG	Kobe	30 Aug 85
71.00	Silke	Renk	GDR	67	2	NC	Rostock	25 Jun 88
	(10)							
70.14	Mayra	Vila	CUB	60	2		Madrid	14 Jun 85
70.14	María	Caridad Colón	CUB	58	1	Barr	Habana	15 Jun 86
70.08	Tatyana	Biryulina	SU	55	1		Podolsk	12 Jul 80
69.96	Ruth	Fuchs	GDR	46	1		Split	29 Apr 80
69.86	Natalya	Kolenchuková'	SU	64	1	NC	Leningrad	3 Aug 85
69.80	Sue	Howland	AUS	60	2		Belfast	30 Jun 86
69.68	Ingrid	Thyssen	FRG	56	1	ISTAF	Berlin	21 Aug 87
69.60	Susanne	Jung	GDR	63	2	NC	Potsdam	22 Aug 87
69.56	Beate	Peters	FRG	59	1	NC	Berlin	12 Jul 86
69.32	Kate	Schmidt	USA	53	1		Fürth	11 Sep 77
	(20)							
69.28	Petra	Rivers	AUS	52	1	NC	Brisbane	20 Mar 82
68.94	Trine	Solberg	NOR	66	1	v SU	Oslo	16 Jul 85
68.80	Eva	Raduly-Zörgö	RUM	54	1	Znam	Moskva	5 Jul 80
68.80	Beate	Koch	GDR	67	2		Potsdam	9 Sep 88
68.28	Saida	Gunba	SU	59	2	Znam	Moskva	5 Jul 80
67.90	Dulce M.	García	CUB	65	3	Barr	Habana	15 Jun 86
67.84	Jadviga	Putiniene	SU	45	3	Znam	Moskva	5 Jul 80
67.40	Tuula	Laaksalo	FIN	53	2		Pihtipudas	24 Jul 83
67.32	Regine	Kempter	GDR	67	2	NC	Jena	27 Jun 86
67.24	Ute	Hommola	GDR	52	1	v UK	Dresden	13 Jun 81
	(30)							
67.24	Svetlana	Pestretsova	SU	61	1	Kuts	Moskva	5 Sep 88
67.20	Fausta	Quintavalla	ITA	59	1		Milano	22 Jun 83
67.18	Zsuzsa	Malovecz	HUN	62	1	5-N	Forli	22 May 88

Mark	Name		Nat	Yr	Pos	Meet	Venue	Date
67.00	Corina	Girbea'	RUM	59	1	v Hun	Debrecen	13 Jun 82
67.00	Zinaida	Gavrilina	SU	61	1	NC	Donyetsk	9 Sep 84
67.00	Irina	Kostyuchenkova	SU	61	2	Znam	Leningrad	12 Jun 88
66.96	Ute	Richter	GDR	58	1		Neubrandenburg	21 May 83
66.80	Olga	Gavrilova	SU	57	1	WP	Canberra	4 Oct 85
66.80	Jana	Kopping	GDR	66	3	NC	Jena	27 Jun 86
66.56	Elena	Burgarová	CS	52	2		Nitra	26 Aug 84
	(40)							
66.52	Alexandra	Beck	GDR	68	1		Chania	24 May 86
66.48	Eva	Helmschmidt	FRG	57	1	v Hol,Bel	Bielefeld	4 Jun 83
66.48	Natalya	Shikolenko	SU	64	2	v Fra,GB	Portsmouth	19 Jun 88
66.08	Rositha	Potreck	GDR	59	1	NC	Jena	9 Aug 81
65.74	Pam	Matthews	AUS	58	1		Brisbane	16 Dec 79
65.68	Yelena	Medvedyeva	SU	65	2	NC	Leningrad	3 Aug 85
65.52	Genowefa	Olejarz'	POL	62	1		Zabrze	20 May 84
65.50	Li Baolian		CHN	63	1	NC	Guangzhou	29 Nov 87
65.46	Sabine	Sebrowski	GDR	51	1	OT	Karl-Marx-Stadt	30 May 76
65.38	Ivanka	Vancheva	BUL	53	5	OG	Moskva	25 Jul 80
	(50)							

HEPTATHLON

Mark	Name				Nat	Yr	Pos	Meet	Venue		Date
7291	Jackie	Joyner-Kersee			USA	62	1	OG	Seoul		24 Sep 88
	12.69/+0.5	1.86	15.80	22.56/+1.6			7.27/+0.7		45.66	2:08.51	
7215		Joyner-Kersee					1	FOT	Indianapolis		16 Jul 88
	12.71/-0.9	1.93	15.65	22.30/ 0.0			7.00/-1.3		50.08	2:20.70	
7158		Joyner-Kersee					1	USOF	Houston		2 Aug 86
	13.18/-0.5	1.88	15.20	22.85/+1.2			7.03/+2.9		50.12	2:09.69	
7148		Joyner					1	GWG	Moskva		7 Jul 86
	12.85/+0.2	1.88	14.76	23.00			7.01/-0.5		49.86	2:10.02	
7128		Joyner-Kersee					1	WCh	Roma		1 Sep 87
	12.91/+0.2	1.90	16.00	22.95/+1.2			7.14/+0.9		45.68	2:16.29	
6979		Joyner-Kersee					1	TAC	San Jose		24 Jun 87
	12.90/+2.0	1.85	15.17	23.02/+0.4			7.25/+2.3		40.24	2:13.07	
6946	Sabine	Paetz'			GDR	57	1	NC	Potsdam		6 May 84
	12.64/+0.3	1.80	15.37	23.37/+0.7			6.86/-0.2		44.62	2:08.93	
6935	Ramona	Neubert			GDR	58	1	v SU	Moskva		19 Jun 83
	13.42	1.82	15.25	23.49			6.79/+0.7		49.94	2:07.51	
6910		Joyner					1	MSR	Walnut		25 Apr 86
	12.9	1.86	14.75	23.24/+2.8			6.85/+2.1		48.30	2:14.11	
6897		John'					2	OG	Seoul		24 Sep 88
	12.85/+0.5	1.80	16.23	23.65/+1.6			6.71/ 0.0		42.56	2:06.14	
6859	Natalya	Shubenkova			SU	57	1	NC	Kiev		21 Jun 84
	12.93/+1.0	1.83	13.66	23.57/-0.3			6.73/+0.4		46.26	2:04.60	
6858	Anke	Behmer'			GDR	61	3	OG	Seoul		24 Sep 88
	13.20/+0.5	1.83	14.20	23.10/+1.6			6.68/+0.1		44.54	2:04.20	
6845		Neubert					1	v SU	Halle		20 Jun 82
	13.58	1.83	15.10	23.14			6.84w	42.54	2:06.16		
6841		Joyner					1	Int	Götzis		25 May 86
	13.09/-1.3	1.87	14.34	23.63/-0.8			6.76/-0.3		48.88	2:14.58	
6813		Paetz					1	OD	Potsdam		21 Jul 84
	12.71/+0.4	1.74	16.16	23.23w			6.58		41.94	2:07.03	
6805		Behmer					1	Int	Götzis		19 Jun 88
	13.28/+1.6	1.84	14.38	22.73/+4.0			6.62/+1.1		40.48	2:04.64	
6803	Jane	Frederick			USA	52	1	Int	Talence		16 Sep 84
	13.27/+1.2	1.87	15.49	24.15/+1.6			6.43/+0.2		51.74	2:13.55	
6789		Neubert					2	OD	Potsdam		21 Jul 84
	13.48/+0.4	1.74	15.03	23.47w			6.71		47.88	2:04.73	
6788		Neubert					1	v SU	Kiev		28 Jun 81
	13.70	1.86	15.41	23.58			6.82/+0.2		40.62	2:06.72	
6775		Vater'					3	OD	Potsdam		21 Jul 84
	13.30/+0.4	1.86	14.86	23.20w			6.84/+0.5		34.04	2:03.76	
6772		Neubert					1	EP-A	Sofia		11 Sep 83
	13.39	1.78	15.21	23.52			6.69	45.30	2:06.70		
6770		Neubert					1	WCh	Helsinki		9 Aug 83
	13.29/+0.3	1.80	15.38	23.27/-0.1			6.67/-0.4		45.12	2:11.34	

Mark	Name		Nat	Yr	Pos	Meet	Venue	Date
6733		Behmer			1	Int	Talence	17 Jul 88
	13.11/+0.8	1.75 14.31 23.14/+0.6			6.79/+0.6		40.48 2:04.29	
6718		Joyner			1	USOF	Baton Rouge	28 Jul 85
	13.32/-2.2	1.82 14.72 23.59/-1.3			6.69		45.04 2:11.46	
6717		Behmer			1	ECh	Stuttgart	30 Aug 86
	13.25/+0.8	1.77 14.50 23.46/-0.1			6.79/+1.4		40.24 2:03.96	
6713		Paetz			2	WCh	Helsinki	9 Aug 83
	13.11/+0.3	1.83 14.23 23.60/-0.1			6.68/-0.9		44.52 2:11.59	
6702	Chantal	Beaugeant	FRA	61	2	Int	Götzis	19 Jun 88
	13.10/+1.6	1.78 13.74 23.96/+3.5			6.45/+0.2		50.96 2:07.09	
6692		Behmer			1	Int	Götzis	24 May 87
	13.41/+1.5	1.87 14.06 23.30/+0.3			6.85/+2.2		35.10 2:06.36	
6678		Frederick			4	OD	Potsdam	21 Jul 84
	13.76	1.86 15.91 24.86			6.21		52.74 2:10.25	
6670		Neubert			1	NC	Halle	24 May 81
	13.58	1.80 14.75 23.70			6.82/+2.0		40.98 2:07.55	
	(30/7)							
6660	Ines	Schulz	GDR	65	3	Int	Götzis	19 Jun 88
	13.56/+0.4	1.84 13.95 23.93/+2.8			6.70/+0.7		42.82 2:06.31	
6646	Natalya	Grachova	SU	52	1	NC	Moskva	2 Aug 82
	13.80	1.80 16.18 23.86			6.65/+3.5		39.42 2:06.59	
6635	Sibylle	Thiele	GDR	65	2	GWG	Moskva	7 Jul 86
	13.14/+0.6	1.76 16.00 24.18			6.62		45.74 2:15.30	
	(10)							
6623	Judy	Simpson'	UK	60	3	ECh	Stuttgart	30 Aug 86
	13.05/+0.8	1.92 14.73 25.09/+0.0			6.56/+2.5		40.92 2:11.70	
6616	Malgorzata	Nowak'	POL	59	1	WUG	Kobe	31 Aug 85
	13.27/+4.0	1.95 15.35 24.20/+0.0			6.37/+3.9		43.36 2:20.39	
6597	Svetlana	Buraga'	SU	65	1		Staiki	2 Jul 88
	12.83/-0.3	1.82 13.78 23.82/+0.3			6.46/+0.1		40.96 2:08.45	
6569	Heike	Tischler	GDR	64	4	Int	Götzis	19 Jun 88
	14.42/+1.3	1.78 13.73 23.62/+3.5			6.68/+1.3		49.24 2:08.16	
6566	Remigia	Sablovskaite	SU	67	1	NC	Kiev	2 Aug 88
	13.46/+0.4	1.77 15.13 24.29/+0.8			6.47/+0.3		47.40 2:11.74	
6564	Larisa	Nikitina	SU	65	2	WCh	Roma	1 Sep 87
	13.77/-0.3	1.87 15.66 24.48/+1.9			6.33/-0.1		55.24 2:27.01	
6552	Nadezhda	Vinogradova'	SU	58	2	NC	Kiev	21 Jun 84
	13.92/+1.0	1.80 15.19 23.84/+0.2			6.67/+0.1		38.60 2:06.80	
6551	Yelena	Martsenyuk	SU	61	2		Staiki	2 Jul 88
	13.54/-0.4	1.82 15.32 24.25/+0.3			6.25/+0.7		47.56 2:12.72	
6541	Mila	Kolyadina	SU	60	4	v GDR	Moskva	19 Jun 83
	14.05	1.82 16.28 24.81			6.48/+0.8		48.26 2:15.26	
6539	Tatyana	Shpak	SU	60	3		Staiki	2 Jul 88
	13.57/-0.4	1.76 15.30 23.61/+0.5			6.52/-0.6		39.28 2:07.25	
	(20)							
6536	Yekaterina	Smirnova	SU	56	3	v GDR	Moskva	19 Jun 83
	13.41	1.82 14.82 24.84			6.56/+1.1		45.66 2:13.38	
6523	Sabine	Everts	FRG	61	1	v SU	Mannheim	10 Jun 82
	13.45	1.89 12.39 23.73			6.75		36.02 2:07.73	
6493	Svetlana	Filatyeva	SU	64	1		Kiev	14 Aug 88
	13.77	1.89 13.89 24.94			6.30		48.44 2:11.89	
6492	Jane	Flemming	AUS	65	5	Int	Götzis	19 Jun 88
	13.33/+0.4	1.81 13.65 23.37/+4.0			6.29/+0.8		43.52 2:11.85	
6487	Birgit	Dressel	FRG	60	4	ECh	Stuttgart	30 Aug 86
	13.56/-1.6	1.92 14.12 24.68/+0.0			6.28/+1.1		45.70 2:15.78	
6474	Marianna	Maslennikova	SU	61	2	NC	Kiev	2 Aug 88
	13.37/+0.4	1.83 13.68 24.07/-0.0			6.28/+0.2		40.42 2:05.60	
6461	Valentina	Kurochkina	SU	59	1		Tallinn	11 Aug 83
	13.89	1.85 14.40 24.51			6.63/+1.2		43.98 2:15.94	
6453	Valentina	Dimitrova	BUL	56	2	Int	Götzis	29 May 83
	14.31/+0.8	1.86 16.07 24.78/+1.0			6.26/+1.4		42.26 2:08.74	
6442	Marion	Reichelt'	GDR	62	2	EP	Arles	5 Jul 87
	13.47/+3.2	1.87 12.91 23.62/+1.9			6.68/+0.2		37.80 2:15.15	
6436	Sabine	Braun	FRG	65	1	v Bul	Mannheim	9 Jun 84
	13.68	1.78 13.09 23.88			6.03		52.14 2:09.41	
	(30)							

Mark	Name		Nat	Yr	Pos	Meet	Venue	Date
6427m	Antonina	Sukhova	SU	59	1		Tula	26 Aug 84
	13.0	1.82 13.79 24.8			6.41		45.88 2:13.5	
6424	Jodi	Anderson	USA	57	2	FOT	Los Angeles	17 Jun 84
	13.52	1.80 13.40 24.49			6.36		48.52 2:13.20	
6424	Irina	Matyusheva'	SU	65	3	NC	Kiev	2 Aug 88
	13.40/+0.4	1.86 13.54 24.40/-0.0			6.28/+0.3		40.20 2:08.24	
6423m	Lyubov	Racu	SU	61	1		Kishinyev	28 Aug 83
	13.6	1.80 14.75 24.2			6.53		41.86 2:11.6	
6403	Emilia	Dimitrova	BUL	67	6	GWG	Moskva	7 Jul 86
	13.73	1.76 13.46 23.17			6.29		43.30 2:09.85	
6399	Olga	Yakovleva	SU	57	1	NP	Tashkent	27 Sep 82
	13.53	1.79 15.14 24.26			6.13		41.42 2:09.20	
6387	Glynis	Nunn'	AUS	60	1	OG	Los Angeles	4 Aug 84
	13.02/-1.5	1.80 12.82 24.06/-1.3			6.66/-0.8		35.58 2:10.57	
6377	Kristine	Nitzsche	GDR	59	4	EP-A	Sofia	11 Sep 83
	13.96	1.90 16.10 24.28			6.10		41.54 2:20.16	
6364	Liliana	Nastase	RUM	62	1	WUG	Zagreb	14 Jul 87
	13.10	1.77 13.90 24.12			6.39		40.58 2:13.90	
6349w	Valda	Ruskite	SU	62	7	GWG	Moskva	7 Jul 86
	13.34	1.70 14.63 24.74			6.45W		43.48 2:11.16	
	(40)							
6343	Petra	Vaideanu'	RUM	65	1		Bucuresti	22 May 88
	13.63	1.75 14.98 24.82			6.34		44.20 2:12.45	
6333	Nadine	Debois	FRA	61	1		Clamart	27 Apr 86
	13.62	1.81 13.74 24.37			6.59		32.48 2:05.77	
6319m	Tamara	Moshicheva	SU	62	1		Kharkov	7 Jul 85
	13.7	1.78 12.78 24.2			6.35		44.96 2:07.3	
6307	Vera	Yurchenko	SU	59	1	NP	Dnepropetrovsk	7 Sep 86
	13.68/+1.5	1.66 15.45 24.47/+0.5			6.48/+0.6		42.42 2:12.02	
6297	Cindy	Greiner	USA	57	8	OG	Seoul	24 Sep 88
	13.55/+1.2	1.80 14.13 24.48/-0.7			6.47/+0.1		38.00 2:13.65	
6295	Yekaterina	Gordiyenko	SU	51	1	v USA	Leningrad	2 Aug 81
	13.58	1.74 15.37 24.44			6.45		34.80 2:09.67	
6289	Svetlana	Chistyakova	SU	61	2	NP	Lvov	20 Sep 87
	13.24w	1.83 13.12 24.92			6.43		41.14 2:15.83	
6289	Svetla	Dimitrova	BUL	70	1	WJ	Sudbury	30 Jul 88
	13.47/+1.1	1.77 13.07 23.78/-1.6			6.45/+3.1		39.98 2:14.39	
6272	Yelena	Davydova	SU	67	2	WUG	Zagreb	14 Jun 87
	14.33	1.89 12.77 25.07			6.37		47.14 2:15.56	
6269	Olga	Nemogayeva'	SU	59	7	v GDR	Moskva	19 Jun 83
	13.53	1.82 13.15 24.56			6.34		37.40 2:08.79	
	(50)							
6268	Zuzana	Lajbnerová	CS	63	7	Int	Götzis	19 Jun 88
	13.79/+0.5	1.84 14.92 24.72/+2.8			6.14/-1.2		43.10 2:18.68	

4 x 100 METRES RELAY

Mark	Nat	Team	Pos	Meet	Venue	Date
41.37	GDR	(Gladisch, Rieger, Auerswald, Göhr)	1	WP	Canberra	6 Oct 85
41.53	GDR	(Gladisch, Koch, Auerswald, Göhr)	1		Berlin	31 Jul 83
41.55	USA	(Brown, Williams, Griffith, Marshall)	1	ISTAF	Berlin	21 Aug 87
41.58	USA	(Brown, Williams, Griffith, Marshall)	1	WCh	Roma	6 Sep 87
41.60	GDR	(Müller, Wöckel, Auerswald, Göhr)	1	OG	Moskva	1 Aug 80
41.61A	USA	(Brown, Williams, Cheeseborough, Ashford)	1	USOF	Colorado Springs	3 Jul 83
41.63	USA	(Brown, Williams, Cheeseborough, Ashford)	1	v GDR	Los Angeles	25 Jun 83
41.65	USA	(Brown, Bolden, Cheeseborough, Ashford)	1	OG	Los Angeles	11 Aug 84
41.65	GDR	(Gladisch, Koch, Auerswald, Göhr)	1	EP	Moskva	17 Aug 85
41.69	GDR	(Gladisch, Koch, Auerswald, Göhr)	1	OD	Potsdam	21 Jul 84
41.73	GDR	(Möller, Behrendt, Lange, Göhr)	1		Berlin	13 Sep 88
41.76	GDR	(Gladisch, Koch, Auerswald, Göhr)	1	WC	Helsinki	10 Aug 83
41.79	GDR	(Gladisch, Drechsler, Auerswald, Göhr)	1	v SU	Karl-Marx-Stadt	20 Jun 87
41.84	GDR	(Gladisch, Gunther, Auerswald, Göhr)	1	EC	Stuttgart	31 Aug 86
41.85	GDR	(Müller, Wöckel, Auerswald, Göhr)	1	OT	Potsdam	13 Jul 80
41.85	GDR	(Gladisch, Koch, Auerswald, Göhr)	1	WK	Zurich	22 Aug 84
41.94	GDR	(Müller, Wöckel, Auerswald, Göhr)	1	NC	Cottbus	17 Jul 80
41.94	GDR	(Gladisch, Drechsler, Auerswald, Göhr)	1	EP	Praha	27 Jun 87
41.95	GDR	(Gladisch, Oschkenat, Behrendt, Göhr)	2	WCh	Roma	6 Sep 87
41.96	USA	(Brown, Williams, Griffith, Marshall)	1h2	WCh	Roma	5 Sep 87

Mark	Nat	Name	Pos	Meet	Venue	Date
41.97	GDR	(G.Walther, Wöckel, Schölzel, Göhr)	1		Potsdam	28 Aug 82
41.97	GDR	(Gladisch, Koch, Auerswald, Göhr)	1		Leipzig	27 Jul 83
41.98	GDR	(Gladisch, Günther, Auerswald, Göhr)	1	GO	Dresden	17 Aug 86
41.98	USA	(Brown, Echols, Griffith-Joyner, Ashford)	1	OG	Seoul	1 Oct 88
41.99	GDR	(G.Walther, Wöckel, Schölzel, Göhr)	1	v USA	Karl-Marx-Stadt	9 Jul 82
42.00	SU	(Nastoburko, Pomoshchnikova, Zhirova, Barbashina)	2	EP	Moskva	17 Aug 85
42.01	SU	(Kondratyeva, Malchugina, Zhirova, Pomoshchnikova)	1s1	OG	Seoul	1 Oct 88
42.04	GDR	(Gladisch, Drechsler, Behrendt, Göhr)	1		Berlin	25 Aug 87
42.07	GDR	(Gladisch, Koch, Auerswald, Göhr)	1	v SU	Erfurt	22 Jun 85
42.08	USA II.	(Echols, Torrence, Finn, Devers)	2	ISTAF	Berlin	21 Aug 87
(30 performances by 3 national teams)						
42.09	BUL	(Zagorcheva, Nuneva, Georgieva, Donkova)	2	EP	Praha	27 Jun 87
42.43	UK	(Hunte, Smallwood, Goddard, Lannaman)	3	OG	Moskva	1 Aug 80
42.59	FRG	(Possekel, Helten, Richter, Kroniger)	2	OG	Montreal	31 Jul, 76
42.58	FRA	(Bily, Cazier, Bacoul, Gaschet)	3	ECh	Athinai	11 Sep 82
42.71	POL	(Tomczak, Pakula, Pisiewicz, Kasprzyk)	3	EP	Moskva	17 Aug 85
42.73	JAM	(Hodges, Pusey, Cuthbert, Ottey)	3	WCh	Helsinki	10 Aug 83
42.77	CAN	(Bailey, Payne, Taylor, Gareau)	2	OG	Los, Angeles	11 Aug 84
	(10)					
42.98	CS	(Sokolová, Soborová, Kocembová, Kratochvilová)	1	WK	Zürich	18 Aug 82
43.18	AUS	(Wilson, Wells, Robertson, Boyle)	5	OG	Montreal	31 Jul, 76
43.36A	CUB	(Elejalde, Romay, Quesada, Cobian)	2	OG	Ciudad México	20 Oct, 68
43.44A	HOL	(van, den, Berg, Sterk, Hennipman, Bakker)	4	OG	Ciudad México	20 Oct 84
43.44A	NIG	(Utondu, Iheagwam, Onyali, Ogunkoya)	1	AfrG	Nairobi	9 Aug 87
43.68	CHN	(Zhang Xiaoqiong, Liu Shaomei, Xie Zhiling, Zhang Caihua)	1		Tianjin	1 Sep 88
43.87	ITA	(Angotzi, Tarolo, Ferrian, Masullo)	1		Bolzano	9 Jun 88
43.95	FIN	(Rautanen, Pursiainen, Häggman, Salin)	2	v SU	Helsinki	30 Aug, 75
44.10	RSA	(Orange Free State) (Basson, Naude, du Toit, Rademeyer)	1	NC	Stellenbosch	11 Apr 87
44.12	GHA	(Bawuah, Yankey, Addy, Appiah)	5h3	OG	Seoul	30 Sep 88
	(20)					

4 x 400 METRES RELAY

Mark	Nat	Name	Pos	Meet	Venue	Date
3:15.17	SU	(Ledovskaya, O.Nazarova, Pinigina, Bryzgina)	1	OG	Seoul	1 Oct 88
3:15.51	USA	(D.Howard, Dixon, Brisco, Griffith-Joyner)	2	OG	Seoul	1 Oct 88
3:15.92	GDR	(G.Walther, Busch, Rübsam, Koch)	1	NC	Erfurt	3 Jun 84
3:16.87	GDR	(Emmelmann, Busch, Müller, Koch)	1	ECh	Stuttgart	31 Aug 86
3:18.29	USA	(Leatherwood, S.Howard, Brisco-Hooks, Cheeseborough)	1	OG	Los Angeles	11 Aug 84
3:18.29	GDR	(Neubauer, Emmelmann, Busch, Müller)	3	OG	Seoul	1 Oct 88
3:18.58	SU	(I.Nazarova, Olizarenko, Pinigina, Vladykina)	1	EP	Moskva	18 Aug 85
3:18.63	GDR	(Neubauer, Emmelmann, Müller, Busch)	1	WCh	Roma	6 Sep 87
3:19.04	GDR	(Siemon', Busch, Rübsam, Koch)	1	ECh	Athinai	11 Sep 82
3:19.12	SU	(Baskakova, I.Nazarova, Pinigina, Vladykina)	1	Drz	Praha	18 Aug 84
3:19.23	GDR	(Maletzki, Rohde, Streidt, Brehmer)	1	OG	Montreal	31 Jul 76
3:19.49	GDR	(Emmelmann, Busch, Neubauer, Koch)	1	WP	Canberra	4 Oct 85
3:19.50	SU	(Yurchenko, O.Nazarova, Pinigina, Bryzgina)	2	WCh	Roma	6 Sep 87
3:19.60	USA	(Leatherwood, S.Howard, Brisco-Hooks, Cheeseborough)	1		Walnut	25 Jul 84
3:19.62	GDR	(Kotte, Brehmer, Köhn, Koch)	1	EP	Torino	5 Aug 79
3:19.66	GDR	(Losch, Emmelmann, Neubauer, Müller)	1	v FRG	Düsseldorf	20 Jun 88
3:19.73	GDR	(K.Walther, Busch, Koch, Rübsam)	1	WCh	Helsinki	14 Aug 83
3:19.83	GDR	(Rübsam, Steuk, Wöckel, Koch)	1	EP	Zagreb	16 Aug 81
3:20.10	GDR	(Emmelmann, Busch, Neubauer, Müller)	2	EP	Moskva	18 Aug 85
3:20.12	SU	(Prorochenko, Goyshchik, Zyuskova, I.Nazarova)	1	OG	Moskva	1 Aug 80
3:20.21	GDR	(Emmelmann, Busch, Müller, Neubauer)	1	v SU	Erfurt	23 Jun 85
3:20.23	GDR	(Siemon, Busch, Rübsam, Koch)	1	v USA	Karl-Marx-Stadt	10 Jul 82
3:20.32	CS	(Kocembová, Moravciková, Matejkovicová, Kratochvilová)	2	WCh	Helsinki	14 Aug 83
3:20.35	GDR	(Löwe, Krug, Lathan, Koch)	2	OG	Moskva	1 Aug 80
3:20.37	GDR	(Kotte, Brehmer, Köhn, Koch)	1	WP	Montreal	24 Aug 79
3:20.39	SU	(Bagryantseva, Zyuskova, Prorochenko, Kulchunova)	2	EP	Torino	5 Aug 79
3:20.41	SU	(Ikauniece, Pinigina, Dzhigalova, O.Nazarova)	1	EP	Praha	28 Jun 86
3:20.60	SU	(Alexeyeva, I.Nazarova, Pinigina, Vladykina)	2	WP	Canberra	4 Oct 85
3:20.60	GDR	(Emmelmann, Busch, Drechsler, Müller)	2	EP	Praha	28 Jun 87
3:20.62	GDR	(Rübsam, Steuk, Wöckel, Koch)	1	WP	Roma	4 Sep 81
(30 performances by 4 national teams)						
3:21.21	CAN	(Crooks, Richardson, Killingbeck, Payne)	2	OG	Los Angeles	11 Aug 84

Mark		Name	Nat Yr	Pos	Meet	Venue	Date
3:22.49	FRG	(Thimm, Arendt, Thomas, Abt)		4	OG	Seoul	1 Oct 88
3:23.13	JAM	(Richards, Thomas, Rattray-Williams, Powell)		5	OG	Seoul	1 Oct 88
3:24.65	POL	(Kasprzyk, Wojdecka, Kapusta, Blaszak)		3	ECh	Stuttgart	31 Aug 86
3:25.51	UK	(Scutt, Barnett, Taylor, Hoyte-Smith)		4	OG	Los Angeles	11 Aug 84
3:25.56	AUS	(Canty, Burnard, Rendina, Nail)		4	OG	Montreal	31 Jul 76
	(10)						
3:25.7a	FIN	(Eklund, Pursiainen, Wilmi, Salin)		2	ECh	Roma	8 Sep 74
3:25.81	BUL	(Ilieva, Stamenova, Penkova, Damyanova)		1	v Hun,Pol	Sofia	24 Jul 83
3:27.08A	NIG	(Usifo,, Bakare,, Ogunkoya,, Onyali)		1	AfrG	Nairobi	12 Aug 87
3:27.52	FRA	(Duvivier, Besson, Martin, Duclos)		4	OG	München	10 Sep 72
3:27.7a	RUM	(Korodi, Lazarciuc, Samungi, Tarita)		4	OG	Moskva	1 Aug 80
3:27.9a	HUN	(Orosz, Forgács, Tóth, Pál)		5	OG	Moskva	1 Aug 80
3:28.94A	KEN	(Shitandayi, Wanjiru, Kavaya, Chepkurui)		2	AfrG	Nairobi	12 Aug 87
3:29.22A	BRA	(Montalvao, Oliveira, Telles, Figueiredo)		1	IbAC	Ciudad México	24 Jul 88
3:29.37	SPA	(Lacambra, Perez, Pujol, Lahoz)		1	v Fra,Pol	Epinal	5 Jul 86
3:29.70	CUB	(Petitón, Alvarez, Fernández, Quirot)		4	PAG	Indianapolis	16 Aug 87
	(20)						

3000 METRES TRACK WALK

Mark	First name	Surname	Nat	Yr	Pos	Meet	Venue	Date
12:14.48	Kerry	Saxby	AUS	61	1		Sydney	20 Feb88
12:20.07		Saxby			1		Canberra	20 Jan 87
12:20.07		Saxby			1mx		Canberra	26 Jan 88
12:29.0	Sari	Essayeh	FIN	67	1		Kuopio	23 Jul 88
12:31.0	Aleksandra	Grigoryeva	SU	60	1		Lapinlahti	22 Jun 86
12:31.79	Giuliana	Salce	ITA	55	1		Udine	14 Sep 87
12:32.37'	Yelena	Nikolayeva	SU	66	1	vUK,Fra	Portsmouth	19 Jun 88
12:35.6		Essayeh			1		Lapinlaxa	26 Jun 88
12:39.1	Wang Yan		CHN	71	1		Beijing	29 Mar 86
12:39.8'	Guan Ping		CHN	66	1	NC	Qingdao	17 Oct 86
12:42.33		Salce			1		Ancona	17 Jul 84
12:42.8'	Li Sujie		CHN	66	2	NC	Qingdao	17 Oct 86
12:46.8	Lidiya	Levandovskaya	SU	62	2		Lapinlahti	22 Jun 86
12:49.4	Olga	Yarutkina	SU	60	1		Lapinlahti	24 Jun 84
12:51.24'	Beate	Anders	GDR	68	1	NC	Rostock	26 Jun 88
12:52.3	Anne	Jansson	SWE	58	1		Östersund	1 Jul 87
12:53.97	Kathrin	Born	GDR	70	1		Karl-Marx-Stadt	15 Jul 88
12:54.61	Dana	Vavracová	CS	54	2		Lapinlahti	21 Jun 87
Indoor marks								
12:05.49	Olga	Krishtop	SU	57	1	WI	Indianapolis	6 Mar 87
12:26.69	Natalya	Spiridonova	SU	63	1	NC	Volgograd	10 Feb 88
12:28.64	Sada	Eidikite	SU	67	2	NC	Volgograd	10 Feb 88
12:30.13	Svetlana	Kaburkina	SU	67	3	NC	Volgograd	10 Feb 88
12:31.57	Giuliana	Salce	ITA	55	1		Firenze	6 Feb 85
12:36.31	Beate	Anders	GDR	68	1		Turin	10 Feb 88
12:36.76		Salce			2	WI	Indianapolis	6 Mar 87
12:38.97	Ann	Peel	CAN	61	3	WI	Indianapolis	6 Mar 87
12:45.38	Maryanne	Torrellas	USA	58	1	TAC	New York	26 Feb 88
12:46.8	Olga	Yarutkina	SU	60	1		Moskva	4 Mar 84
12:47.32	Teresa	Vaill	USA	62	2	TAC	New York	26 Feb 88
12:47.49	Dana	Vavracová	CS	54	4	WI	Indianapolis	6 Mar 87
12:48.82	Maria	Cruz Diaz	SPA	69	2		Valencia	17 Feb 88
12:48.99	Maria	Reyes Sobrino	SPA	67	1	EI	Budapest	6 Mar 88

' time during longer track walk

5000 METRES TRACK WALK

Mark	First name	Surname	Nat	Yr	Pos	Meet	Venue	Date
20:45.32	Kerry	Saxby	AUS	61	1	NC	Perth	27 Mar 88
20:55.76		Saxby			1		Sydney	10 Jan 88
21:08.5	Yelena	Nikolayeva	SU	66	1	vUK,Fra	Portsmouth	19 Jun 88
21:13.16	Cui Yingzi		CHN	71	1		Jinan	30 Oct 88
21:16.4		Saxby			1mx		Sydney	4 Apr 87
21:20.2	Yan Hong		CHN	66	1		Xinglong	29 Mar 87
21:25.5'		Nikolayeva			1	SGP	Fana	7 May 88
21:26.5	Guan Ping		CHN	66	1	NC	Qingdao	17 Oct 86
21:29.0'		Nikolayeva			1		Kiev	30 Jul 88
21:30.92	Oksana	Shchastnaya	SU	71	1	EJ	Birmingham	7 Aug 87

Mark	Name		Nat	Yr	Pos	Meet	Venue	Date
21:31.06		Saxby			1	NC	Sydney	29 Mar 87
21:31.7	Chen Yueling		CHN	68	1	NC	Guangzhou	23 Oct 87
21:32.1	Xu Yongjiu		CHN	64	2	NC	Guangzhou	23 Oct 87
21:32.4'		Nikolayeva'			1		Cheboksary	7 Jun 87
21:33.2	Xiong Yan		CHN	67	3	NC	Guangzhou	23 Oct 87
21:33.8	Wang Yan		CHN	71	1		Jian	9 Mar 86
21:34.37	Li Sujie		CHN	66	1		Beijing	9 Sep 86
21:35.25	Giuliana	Salce	ITA	55	1	IM	Verona	19 Jun 86
21:35.28	Beate	Anders	GDR	68	1	NC	Rostock	26 Jun 88
21:36.2	Olga	Krishtop'	SU	57	1	NC	Penza	4 Aug 84
	(20/14)							
21:36.92	Maria	Cruz Diaz	SPA	69	2	EJ	Birmingham	7 Aug 87
21:42.2	Olga	Yarutkina	SU	60	2	NC	Penza	4 Aug 84
21:43.27	Kathrin	Born	GDR	70	1	NC-j	Karl-Marx-Stadt	15 Jul 88
21:48.4	Alina	Ivanova	SU	70	1		Simferopol	27 May 88
21:49.0	Zhang Min		CHN	67	4	NC	Guangzhou	23 Oct 87
21:49.19	Vera	Osipova	SU	57	1		Poznan	19 Sep 87
	(20)							
21:53.0'	Vera	Molokova	SU	66	2		Kiev	30 Jul 88
21:54.81	Li Chunxiu		CHN	69	2		Jinan	30 Oct 88
21:55.0'	Nadezhda	Ryashkina	SU	67	3		Kiev	30 Jul 88
21:55.99	Aleksandra	Grigoryeva'	SU	60	1		Lapinlahti	23 Jun 85
21:56.1	An Limei		CHN	68	6	NC	Guangzhou	23 Oct 87
21:57.54	Gao Hongmiao		CHN	74	3		Jinan	30 Oct 88
21:58.17	Olga	Sánchez	SPA	70	2	WJ	Sudbury	31 Jul 88
21:58.8	Tatyana	Titova	SU	69	2		Simferopol	27 May 88
21:59.0	Natalya	Serbinenko'	SU	59	3	SGP	Fana	5 May 84
21:59.1	Chen Zhimin		CHN	67	3	NC	Qingdao	17 Oct 86
	(30)							
22:00.0'	Yelena	Rodionova	SU	68	4		Kiev	30 Jul 88
22:00.0'	Sada	Eidikite	SU	67	5		Kiev	30 Jul 88
22:01.09	Ann	Peel	CAN	61	3	WUG	Zagreb	17 Jul 87
22:01.09	Sari	Essayeh	FIN	67	1		Sipoo	4 Jun 88
22:01.38	Ines	Estedt	GDR	67	2		Potsdam	19 Sep 87
22:01.9'	Anne	Jansson	SWE	58	1		Ornsöldsvik	4 Jul 87

' during 10,000 metres walk

Indoor mark

Mark	Name		Nat	Yr	Pos	Meet	Venue	Date
21:44.52	Giulliana	Salce	ITA	55	1		Turin	20 Feb 85

5000 METRES ROAD WALK

Leading performances, and then thletes with marks superior to track bests

Mark	Name		Nat	Yr	Pos	Meet	Venue	Date
20:34	Kerry	Saxby	AUS	65	1		Hildesheim	24 Sep 87
20:52		Saxby			1		Adelaide	16 Oct 88
20:59		Saxby			1		Bad Krozingen	22 Aug 87
21:01		Saxby			1		Fürth	8 Aug 87
21:03		Saxby			1		Mexidon	8 May 88
21:04	Tamara	Kovalenko	SU	64	1		Odessa	20 Aug 88
21:07		Saxby			1		Canberra	7 Jun 87
21:12'		Saxby			1		Hobart	19 Jul 87
21:14		Saxby			1		Vaxjö	29 May 88
21:17		Saxby			1		Hospitalet	12 Sep 87
21:25	Maria	Reyes Sobrino	SPA	67	1		La Coruña	16 May 87
21:26	Irina	Shumak'	SU	65	2		Odessa	20 Aug 88
21:29	Olga	Kardopoltseva	SU	66	3		Odessa	20 Aug 88
21:31	Natalya	Spiridonova	SU	63	1		Moskva	7 Aug 88
21:33		Saxby			1		Hospitalet	24 Apr 88
21:34	Vera	Osipova	SU	57	1		Ruse	21 Apr 85
21:36'	Xu Yongjiu		CHN	64	1	EsC	New York	3 May 87
21:36	Anne	Jansson	SWE	58	2		La Coruña	16 May 87
21:37'	Olga	Krishtop'	SU	57	2=	EsC	New York	3 May 87
21:37'		Saxby			2=	EsC	New York	3 May 87
	(20/10)							
21:37'	Yan Hong		CHN	66	2=	EsC	New York	3 May 87
21:38	Olga	Yarutkina	SU	60	2		Ruse	21 Apr 85
21:39	Rimma	Underova	SU	55	3		Ruse	21 Apr 85

Mark	Name		Nat	Yr	Pos	Meet.	Venue	Date
21:42	Aleksandra	Grigoryeva'	SU	60	2		Hospitalet	11 May 86
21:43'	Irina	Strakhova	SU	59	6	EsC	New York	3 May 87
21:46'	Guan Ping		CHN	66	7	EsC	New York	3 May 87
21:51	Natalya	Yermolenko	SU	57	2		Chelyabinsk	29 Jul 87
21:53'	Jin Bingjie		CHN	71	8	EsC	New York	3 May 87
21:53	Sada	Eidikite	SU	67	1		Alushta	8 May 88
21:54'	Svetlana	Kaburkina	SU	67	1		Naumburg	1 May 88
21:57	Susan	Cook'	AUS	58	2		Hildesheim	24 Sep 87
21:59	Raisa	Sinyavina	SU	58	1		Mogilyov	2 Jun 85

' during 10,000 metres road walk

10 000 METRES TRACK WALK

Mark	Name		Nat	Yr	Pos	Meet.	Venue	Date
42:14.2	Kerry	Saxby	AUS	61	1mx		Canberra	26 Jan 88
43:36.41	Yelena	Nikolayeva'	SU	66	1	NC	Kiev	30 Jul 88
43:36.5		Nikolayeva			1	SGP	Fana	7 May 88
43:52.1	Chen Yaoling		CHN	68	1	NC	Guangzhou	24 Oct 87
44:07.97	Nadezhda	Ryashkina	SU	67	2	NC	Kiev	30 Jul 88
44:08.30	Vera	Mokolova	SU	66	3	NC	Kiev	30 Jul 88
44:13.75	Yelena	Rodionova	SU	65	4	NC	Kiev	30 Jul 88
44:19.5	Xu Jongjiu		CHN	64	2	NC	Guangzhou	24 Oct 87
44:26.5		Xu Jongjiu			1		Xinglong	31 Mar 87
44:26.7	Jin Bingjie		CHN	71	2		Xinglong	31 Mar 87
44:27.1	Xiong Yan		CHN	67	3	NC	Guangzhou	24 Oct 87
44:28.37	Tamara	Kovalenko	SU	64	5	NC	Kiev	30 Jul 88
44:32.50		Nikolayeva			1		Bryansk	16 Aug 86
44:38.9	Guan Ping		CHN	66	1		Amagasaki	27 Nov 88
44:42.2		Guan Ping			1	NC	Qingdao	18 Oct 86
44:42.3	Li Sujie		CHN	66	2	NC	Qingdao	18 Oct 86
44:50.28	Lyubov	Kolesnikova	SU	70	6	NC	Kiev	30 Jul 88
44:50.7	Natalya	Spiridonova	SU	63	2	SGP	Fana	7 May 88
44:56.23	Svetlana	Kaburkina	SU	67	1		Cheboksary	7 Jun 87
44:59.2		Xu Yongjiu			1		Fuxin	30 Mar 86
	(20/15)							
44:59.3	Wang Yang		CHN	72	2		Fuxin	30 Mar 86
45:04.80	Natalya	Serbinenko	SU	59	7	NC	Kiev	30 Jul 88
45:13.50	Valentina	Shmer	SU	64	8	NC	Kiev	30 Jul 88
45:20.8	Lidiya	Levandovskaya	SU	62	1		Zhitomir	6 Sep 86
45:21.1	Fu Liqin		CHN	70	4	NC	Guangzhou	24 Oct 87
	(20)							
45:23.7	Gui Jiangzi		CHN	64	3		Fuxin	30 Mar 86
45:29.0	Raisa	Sinyavina	SU	58	2		Zhitomir	6 Sep 86
45:31.53	Nina	Galyanina	SU	66	9	NC	Kiev	30 Jul 88
45:32.4	Yan Hong		CHN	66	3		Jian	10 Mar 86
45:32.5	Olga	Veremeychuk	SU	59	3		Zhitomir	6 Sep 86
45:35.22	Sada	Eidikite	SU	67	10	NC	Kiev	30 Jul 88
45:43.14	Tamara	Torshina	SU	67	11	NC	Kiev	30 Jul 88
45:43.44	Irina	Shumak'	SU	65	12	NC	Kiev	30 Jul 88
45:45.44	Galina	Kuchma	SU	67	13	NC	Kiev	30 Jul 88
45:47.0	Susan	Cook'	AUS	58	1		Leicester	14 Sep 83
	(30)							
45:49.88	Yelena	Zayko	SU	67	15	NC	Kiev	30 Jul 88
45:51.9	Shi Xiaoling		CHN	60	5	NC	Guangzhou	24 Oct 87
45:53.76	Ruzhina	Ivoylova	SU	66	16	NC	Kiev	30 Jul 88
45:54.64	Leonarda	Yukhnevich	SU	63	17	NC	Kiev	30 Jul 88
45:58.1	Ileana	Salvador	ITA	62	1		Bergamo	8 Oct 88
45:58.56	Vera	Osipova	SU	58	18	NC	Kiev	30 Jul 88
45:59.8	Svetlana	Kashina	SU	62	1		Kiev	5 Oct 86

10 000 METRES ROAD WALK

Leading performances, and then thletes with marks superior to track bests

Mark	Name		Nat	Yr	Pos	Meet.	Venue	Date
41:30	Kerry	Saxby	AUS	61	1	NC	Canberra	27 Aug 88
42:52		Saxby			1	NC	Hobart	19 Jul 87
43:22	Olga	Krishtop'	SU	57	1	EsC	New York	3 May 87

Mark	Name		Nat	Yr	Pos	Meet	Venue	Date
43:26	Svetlana	Kaburkina	SU	67	1		Bucaresti	19 Jun 88
43:29	Vera	Mokolova	SU	63	1		Alushta	1 Oct 88
43:35	Irina	Strakhova	SU	59	2	EsC	New York	3 May 87
43:43	Tamara	Kovalenko	SU	64	2		Alushta	1 Oct 88
43:44		Saxby			1		Järna	4 Jun 88
43:45	Jin Bingjie		CHN	71	3	EsC	New York	3 May 87
43:53	Natalya	Spiridonova	SU	63	1	Znam	Leningrad	11 Jun 88
43:57		Saxby			4	EsC	New York	3 May 87
43:57	Yelena	Nikolayeva'	SU	66	5	EsC	New York	3 May 87
43:59		Saxby			1mx		Värnamo	13 May 88
44:04		Nikolayeva'			1	NC	Novopolotsk	12 Jul 87
44:10		Kovalenko			2		Bucaresti	19 Jun 88
44:12		Strakhova			1	WC	Roma	1 Sep 87
44:13	Nadezhda	Ryashkina	SU	67	2	Znam	Leningrad	11 Jun 88
44:14	Yan Hong		CHN	66	1	NC	Jian	16 Mar 85
44:15		Saxby			1		Ätran	15 May 88
44:16	Natalya	Serbinenko'	SU	59	1		Kherson	8 May 88
44:20	Sada	Eidikite	SU	67	3	Znam	Leningrad	11 Jun 88
44:21	Yelena	Veremeychuk	SU	59	2		Kherson	8 May 88
44:23		Saxby			2	WC	Roma	1 Sep 87
44:26		Kaburkina			1	NC-w	Sochi	21 Feb 88
44:26	Sari	Essayeh	FIN	67	1		Vaasassa	21 May 88
44:27		Kaburkina			1		Naumburg	1 May 88
44:28	Guan Ping		CHN	66	2	NC	Jian	16 Mar 85
44:30		Kovalenko			1		Odessa	18 Aug 88
44:33	Yelena	Rodionova	SU	65	1		Kharkov	5 Sep 87
44:33		Nikolayeva			2	NC-w	Sochi	21 Feb 88
	(30/17)							
44:33	Beate	Anders	GDR	68	1		Berlin	14 May 88
44:45	Xu Jongjiu		CHN	64	3	NC	Jian	16 Mar 85
44:45	Lidiya	Levandovskaya	SU	62	2		Kharkov	5 Sep 87
	(20)							
44:48	Maria	Cruz Diaz	SPA	69	4	WC	Roma	1 Sep 87
44:54	Mirva	Hämäläinen	FIN	62	2		Vaasassa	21 May 88
44:55	Lyudmila	Khrushchova	SU	55	2		Donetsk	7 Jul 85
44:55	Vera	Osipova	SU	57	1	NC	Leningrad	4 Aug 85
44:57	Lyudmila	Lyubmirova	SU	62	4	Znam	Leningrad	11 Jun 88
44:59	Victoria	Oprea	ROM	65	1		Pitesti	12 Aug 88
45:01	Valentina	Shmer	SU	64	5	Znam	Leningrad	11 Jun 88
45:02	Graciella	Mendoza	MEX	63	6	EsC	New York	3 May 87
45:04	Olga	Yarutkina	SU	60	2	NC	Penza	5 Aug 84
45:06	Ann	Peel	CAN	61	7	EsC	New York	3 May 87
	(30)							
45:07	Natalya	Yermolenko	SU	57	5		Kharkov	5 Sep 87
45:09	Dana	Vavracová	CS	54	1	NC	Trinec	17 Aug 87
45:09	Monica	Gunnarsson	SWE	65	6	WC	Roma	1 Sep 87
45:12	Natalya	Dmitrochenko	SU	66	4	NC	Leningrad	4 Aug 85
45:15	Olympiada	Ivanova	SU	70	6		Kharkov	5 Sep 87
45:17	Li Sujie		CHN	66	4	NC	Jian	16 Mar 85
45:17	Natalya	Storozhenko	SU	63	3		Kherson	8 May 88
45:19	Susan	Cook'	AUS	58	1		Canberra	19 Jul 86
45:19	Yelena	Zayko	SU	67	7	Znam	Leningrad	11 Jun 88
45:20	Irina	Lutkova	SU	65	8	Znam	Leningrad	11 Jun 88
45:24	Anne	Jansson	SWE	58	9	EsC	New York	3 May 87
45:24	Zaliya	Sinekeyeva	SU	65	9	Znam	Leningrad	11 Jun 88
45:27	Olga	Kardapoltseva	SU	66	10	Znam	Leningrad	11 Jun 88
45:29	Olga	Ossyko	SU	66	11	Znam	Leningrad	11 Jun 88
45:33	Aleksandra	Grigoryeva'	SU	60	1		Sochi	21 Feb 86
45:33	Maria	de la Cruz'/Colin	MEX	66	3	PAC	St.Leonard	4 Oct 86
45:35	Galina	Mudryk	SU	67	9		Kharkov	5 Sep 87
45:37	Maria	Reyes Sobrino	SPA	67	9	WC	Roma	1 Sep 87
45:37	Tatyana	Titova	SU	69	3		Alitus	1 Oct 88
45:38	Sally	Pierson	AUS	63	1		Melbourne	8 May 82

Indicated by ' in the all-time lists are women who have competed with distinction at two or more names. This list shows the names for these competitors.

ORIGINAL NAME	MARRIED NAME
Agapova	Peleshenko
Andersen	Waitz
Andrei	Marasescu
Annison	Stanton
Auerswald	Lange I.
Bagryantseva	Nazarova I.
Barbashina	Tkachenko E.
Barkusky	Weiss
Bartonová	Silhavá
Benoit	Samuelson
Berend	Wakan
Besprozvannaya	Buraga
Bimbaite	Urbikiene
Bondaryeva	Litovchenko
Boxer	Cahill
Brehmer	Lathan
Chesbro	Wohlschlag
Christensen	Kristiansen
Cojocaru	Matei
Cusmir	Stanciu
Daute	Drechsler
Dedner	Brandt
de Klerk	Armstrong E.
de la Cruz	Colin
Derevinskaya	Grigoryeva
Dittrich	Hartwig
Dolzhenko	Krachevskaya
Droese	Pufe
Dukhnovich	Ozhenko
Eckert	Wöckel
Farmer S.	Patrick
Feuerbach	Ullrich C.
Finger	Thimm
French	Lee S.
Garrett	Audain
Gîrbea	Ivan C.
Gladisch	Möller
Gustavsson	Vera-Ybanez
Guzowska	Nowak M.
Haupt	Hammer
Hearnshaw	Telfer
Helm	Beyer S.
Helmbold	Gummel
Hunte	Oakes H.
Ilie	Ivan P.
Ionescu	Lengyel M.
Joyner	Kersee
Kämpfert	Steuk
Kastetskaya	Ambraziene
Katyukova	Smekhnova
Kazachkova	Sorokina
Kemenchendzhi	Merchuk
Khamitova	Samolyenko
Khristova S.	Moneva
Kibakina	Sluzhkina
Kirszenstein	Szewinska

ORIGINAL NAME	MARRIED NAME
Klapezynski	Bruns
Kleinová	Walterová
Kocembová	Slaninová
Kolenchukova	Yermolovich
Kotenyeva	Sereda
Kovarik	Uibel
- Siebert	
Krasnova	Andreyeva F.
Krentser, O	Bondarenko
Kulchunova	Pinigina
Künzel	Wujak
Kuragina	Nemogayeva
Kushenko	Matyusheva
Kuznyetsova Y	Nikolayeva
Lange A.	Hahmann
Langer	Kalek
Leatherwood	King L.
Lind-Petersen	McRoberts
Livermore	Simpson J.
Ludwigs	Wodars
Lynch E.	McColgan
Makeyeva, M	Styepanova
Matekovicová	Strnadová
Matsuta	Kurochkina
McDermott	Wade
Meinel	Lehmann
- Veith	
Meissner	Stecher
Meyer	Hamann
Mihalache	Vaideanu
Mityayeva	Byelevskaya
Möbius	Paetz
- John	
Morgulina	Derbina
Müller P.	Schersing
Mushta	Olizarenko
Nasonova O.	Antonova
Nasonova T.	Goyshchik
Navickaite	Jesaviciene
Neumann E.	Fiedler E.
Neumann C.	Liebetrau
Nikitina V.	Komisova
Nikitina I.	Lebedinskaya
Nowaczyk	Blaszak
Nuneva	Vechernikova
Nygrynová	Strejcková
Oelsner	Göhr
Olejarz	Patla
Opitz	Hellmann
Oppliger	Bouchonneau
Orr	Cook
Parkhuta	Zhukova
Payne M.	Wiggins
Petkanova	Dragieva
Petrus	Avdyeyenko
Ponomaryova M.	Khromova

ORIGINAL NAME	MARRIED NAME
Poryvkina	Podkopayeva
Probert	Scutt
Proskuryakova	Rodionova
Rafira	Lovin
Reichenbach	Müller I.
Reichstein	Bienias
Reidick	Zaczkiewicz
Riefstahl	Oschkenat
Rieger S.	Günther S.
Rienstra	Sommer
Robertson	Boyd
Röhde	Köhn
Rübsam	Neubauer
Sachse	Gansky
Saunders	Nunn
Savinkova	Yermakova
Schaller	Klier
Schilly M.	Knisely
Schlaak	Jahl
Schmalfeld	Voigt
Schneider	Müller R.
Schoknecht	Slupianek
- Briesenick	
Sharipova	Serbinenko
Shulyak	Kravets
Siemon	Emmelmann
Simpson M.	Bothma
Smallwood	Cook K.
Smith W.	Sly
Springs	Geiger
Stoica	Pogacean
Stoll	Wartenberg
Strandvall	Pursiainen
Strong R.	Lorraway
Stropahl	Streidt
Tacu	Craciunescu
Taylor A.	Issajenko
Terpe	Theele

WOMEN'S WORLD LISTS 1988

100 METRES

Mark	Wind	Name		Nat	Born	Pos	Meet	Venue	Date
10.49	0.0	Florence	Griffith-Joyner	USA	59	1q1	FOT	Indianapolis	16 Jul
10.61	1.2		Griffith-Joyner			1	FOT	Indianapolis	17 Jul
10.62	1.0		Griffith-Joyner			1q3	OG	Seoul	24 Sep
10.70	1.6		Griffith-Joyner			1s1	FOT	Indianapolis	17 Jul
10.81	1.2	Evelyn	Ashford	USA	57	2	FOT	Indianapolis	17 Jul
10.83	0.0	Sheila	Echols	USA	64	1q2	FOT	Indianapolis	16 Jul
10.85	1.6		Ashford			2s1	FOT	Indianapolis	17 Jul
10.85	2.0	Anelia	Nuneva	BUL	62	1s1	NC	Sofia	2 Sep
10.86	0.0	Diane	Williams	USA	60	2q1	FOT	Indianapolis	16 Jul
10.87	0.2		Nuneva			1	NC	Sofia	2 Sep
10.88	1.0		Griffith-Joyner			1h7	OG	Seoul	24 Sep
10.88	1.6		Ashford			1q2	OG	Seoul	24 Sep
10.89	-0.1		Griffith-Joyner			1		San Diego	25 Jun
10.89	2.0	Marlies	Göhr	GDR	58	1	v Ita	Neubrandenburg	9 Jul
10.89	1.8	Katrin	Krabbe	GDR	69	1		Berlin	20 Jul
10.91	1.7	Heike	Drechsler	GDR	64	1	Bisl	Oslo	2 Jul
10.91	1.2	Gwen	Torrence	USA	65	3	FOT	Indianapolis	17 Jul
10.91	1.4		Griffith-Joyner			1	Int	Tokyo	7 Oct
10.92	1.1		Nuneva			1	Hanz	Beograd	2 Jun
10.92	0.9		Drechsler			1	GO	Dresden	11 Jun
10.92	0.0	Alice	Brown (10)	USA	60	2q2	FOT	Indianapolis	16 Jul
10.94A	2.0		Ashford			1	Int	Sestriere	11 Aug
10.94	1.0		Göhr			1		Potsdam	8 Sep
10.96			Nuneva			1		Kvarnsveden	19 Jun
10.96	0.9		Drechsler			1	DNG	Stockholm	5 Jul
10.96	0.5		Drechsler			1q1	OG	Seoul	24 Sep
10.96	0.0		Nuneva			1q4	OG	Seoul	24 Sep
10.97	0.0	Gail	Devers	USA	66	3q1	FOT	Indianapolis	16 Jul
10.98	1.6	Natalya	Pomoshchnikova	SU	65	2q2	OG	Seoul	24 Sep
10.99	1.1		Griffith-Joyner			1		Santa Monica	12 Jul
10.99	1.3		Echols			1s2	FOT	Indianapolis	17 Jul
10.99	1.0		Drechsler			2		Potsdam	8 Sep
10.99	1.6		Göhr			3q2	OG	Seoul	24 Sep
10.99	0.0		Torrence			2q4	OG	Seoul	24 Sep
10.99	0.5		Ashford			1s1	OG	Seoul	25 Sep
		(35 Performances by 12 Athletes)							
11.00	-0.9	Merlene	Ottey	JAM	60	1	Int	St. Denis	7 Jun
11.01	0.8	Angella	Issajenko	CAN	58	1	NC	Ottawa	6 Aug
11.03	1.0	Juliet	Cuthbert	JAM	64	2q3	OG	Seoul	24 Sep
11.05	1.0	Kerstin	Behrendt	GDR	67	3	OT	Potsdam	8 Sep
11.05	1.0	Lyudmila	Kondratyeva	SU	58	3q3	OG	Seoul	24 Sep
11.06	0.9	Silke	Möller	GDR	64	2	GO	Dresden	11 Jun
11.07	1.8	Galina	Malchugina	SU	62	1	Znam	Leningrad	11 Jun
11.08		Grace	Jackson	JAM	61	2s1	NC	Kingston	15 Jul
		(20)							
11.08	0.0	Maya	Azarashvili	SU	64	1		Kiev	14 Aug
11.08	1.6	Nelli	Cooman	HOL	64	4q2	OG	Seoul	24 Sep
11.09		Mary	Onyali	NIG	68	1	NC	Bauchi	2 Jul
11.10	0.6	Marina	Zhirova	SU	63	1	NarM	Sofia	26 Jun
11.10	1.6	Dannette	Young	USA	64	3s1	FOT	Indianapolis	17 Jul
11.11	-0.7	Nadezhda	Georgieva	BUL	61	1	Balk	Ankara	16 Jul
11.11	0.0	Carlette	Guidry	USA	68	4q1	FOT	Indianapolis	16 Jul
11.11	0.8	Angela	Bailey	CAN	62	2	NC	Ottawa	6 Aug
11.13	1.2	Julie	Rocheleau	CAN	64	1	Jenn	San Jose	28 May
11.14	1.8	Marina	Molokova	SU	62	3	Znam	Leningrad	11 Jun
		(30)							
11.15	1.6	Jennifer	Inniss	USA	59	4s1	FOT	Indianapolis	17 Jul
11.16	0.5	Ulrike	Sarvari	FRG	64	3q1	OG	Seoul	24 Sep
11.17	-1.1	Pauline	Davis	BAH	66	1	SEC	Auburn	15 May

Mark		Name		Nat	Born	Pos	Meet	Venue	Date
11.17	2.0	Ingrid	Lange	GDR	57	2	v Ita	Neubrandenburg	9 Jul
11.18	-0.1	Pam	Marshall	USA	60	2		San Diego	25 Jun
11.18	0.6	Liliana	Allen	CUB	70	3	NarM	Sofia	26 Jun
11.18	-0.4	Diana	Dietz	GDR	69	1	WJ	Sudbury	28 Jul
11.19		Falilat	Ogunkoya	NIG	68	1h	NC	Bauchi	30 Jun
11.19	0.0	Dawn	Sowell	USA	66	5q1	FOT	Indianapolis	16 Jul
11.21	1.1	Olga	Antonova	SU	60	1		Sochi	31 May
		(40)							
11.21	1.8	Svetlana	Chervyakova	SU	63	1h4	Znam	Leningrad	11 Jun
11.21	0.0	Tatyana	Papilina	SU	67	2		Kiev	14 Aug
11.22		Angela	Williams	TRI	65	1		Washington	9 Apr
11.22	0.0	Esther	Jones	USA	69	4q2	FOT	Indianapolis	16 Jul
11.22	0.3	Nadezhda	Rashchupkina	SU	63	2s		Kiev	14 Aug
11.23	1.4	Natalya	German	SU	63	2h3	Znam	Leningrad	11 Jun
11.23	1.5	Olga	Zolotaryova	SU	61	3	NC	Tallinn	4 Jul
11.24	1.2	Laurence	Bily	FRA	63	1	NC	Tours	13 Aug
11.26	1.5	Paula	Dunn	UK	64	1	WAAA	Birmingham	5 Aug
11.27	1.0	Annette	Kersten	GDR	67	7	OT	Potsdam	8 Sep
		(50)							
11.28	1.4	Antonina	Nastoburko	SU	59	3h3	Znam	Leningrad	11 Jun
11.28	-0.1	Jeanette	Bolden	USA	60	4		San Diego	25 Jun
11.28	0.0	Angela	Burnham	USA	71	5q2	FOT	Indianapolis	16 Jul
11.28	1.9	Kerry	Johnson	AUS	63	1		Chiba	15 Sep
11.29	1.6	Natalya	Kovtun	SU	64	2		Bryansk	11 Jul
11.30	1.6	Valerie	Brisco	USA	60	3		Irvine	26 Jun
11.30A	1.7	Sandra	Myers	SPA	61	1h1	IbAC	Ciudad México	22 Jul
11.31	1.7	Marina	Markina	SU	62	2h1	Znam	Leningrad	11 Jun
11.31	1.0	Simmone	Jacobs	UK	66	5q3	OG	Seoul	24 Sep
11.32	1.2	Zhang Caihua		CHN	64	4	Jenn	San Jose	28 May
		(60)							
11.32	0.6	Michelle	Finn	USA	65	3	TAC	Tampa	17 Jun
11.32		Els	Vader	HOL	59	3	AP	Hengelo	14 Aug
11.33	0.4	Ewa	Pisiewicz	POL	62	1	NC	Grudziadz	12 Aug
11.34		Ethlyn	Tate	JAM	66	1		Kingston	16 Apr
11.34	-0.9	Marie-Josée	Pérec	FRA	68	2	Int	St. Denis	7 Jun
11.34		Tayami	Martinez	CUB	72	1		Jalisco	24 Jun
11.34		Rufina	Uba	NIG	59	.h	NC	Bauchi	30 Jun
11.34	0.4	Andrea	Thomas	FRG	63	2		Sindelfingen	3 Jul
11.34	0.4	Jolanta	Janota	POL	64	2	NC	Grudziadz	12 Aug
11.34		Evette	de Klerk	RSA	65	1		Durban	10 Dec
		(70)							
11.35	0.0	Andrea	Thompson	USA	66	6q1	FOT	Indianapolis	16 Jul
11.35	1.6	Joanna	Smolarek	POL	65	6q2	OG	Seoul	24 Sep
11.36	1.7	Olga	Frolova	SU	64	3h1	Znam	Leningrad	11 Jun
11.36	1.2	Marieta	Ilcu	RUM	62	1		Bucuresti	9 Jul
11.36	0.4	Agnieszka	Siwek	POL	62	4	NC	Grudziadz	12 Aug
11.36	0.0	Olga	Voronova	SU	68	4		Kiev	14 Aug
11.36	2.0	Rita	Angotzi	ITA	67	2	Int	Cagliari	3 Sep
11.37	1.7	Rochelle	Stevens	USA	66	2		Atlanta	14 May
11.37	0.9	Sabine	Günther	GDR	63	5	GO	Dresden	11 Jun
11.38		Tina	Iheagwam	NIG	68	2	S&W	Modesto	7 May
		(80)							
11.38	1.3	Wendy	Vereen	USA	66	6s2	FOT	Indianapolis	17 Jul
11.39	0.1	Cristina	Perez	SPA	65	1	Int	Barcelona	13 Jul
11.39	-0.8	Patricia	Girard	FRA	68	1h2	NC-j	Montgeron	16 Jul
11.39	1.8	Kathrin	Henke	GDR	69	3		Berlin	20 Jul
11.40	1.1	Yelena	Kelchevskaya	SU	55	5rA		Sochi	31 May
11.40	1.2	Laloa	Ravaonirina	MAD	63	2	FraC	Tours	13 Aug
11.40	1.0	Marisa	Masullo	ITA	59	1		Sestriere	25 Aug
11.41	1.0	Antonina	Slyusar	SU	63	1rC		Sochi	31 May
11.41	0.8	Angela	Phipps	CAN	64	3	NC	Ottawa	6 Aug
11.41	1.7	Vivienne	Spence	JAM	65	2		Sacramento	27 Aug
		(90)							
11.42	-0.1	Marie-Christine	Cazier	FRA	63	1		Abymes	22 Apr
11.42	0.6	Krasimira	Pencheva	BUL	58	5	NarM	Sofia	26 Jun
11.42	0.1	Esmie	Lawrence	CAN	61	3	Int	Barcelona	13 Jul

Mark		Name		Nat	Born	Pos	Meet	Venue	Date
11.42	0.8	Keturah	Anderson	CAN	68	4	NC	Ottawa	6 Aug
11.43	1.4	Natalya	Merzlyakova	SU	65	1		Yaroslavl	4 Jun
11.43	0.7	Valya	Demireva	BUL	61	1		Sofia	11 Jun
11.43	1.8	Vera	Sychugova	SU	63	1	v Rom	Bucuresti	18 Jun
11.43	0.1	Blanca	Lacambra	SPA	65	4	Int	Barcelona	13 Jul
11.43	0.5	Tsvetanka	Ilieva	BUL	63	2		Stara Zagora	20 Aug
11.43		Olga	Naumkina	SU	64	.h		Vilnius	27 Aug
		(100)							

Mark		Name	Nat	Born	Date
11.44	0.0	Olga Rypakova	SU	64	18 Jun
11.44	1.5	Magali Seguin	FRA	64	25 Jun
11.44A	1.7	Susana Armenteros	CUB	61	22 Jul
11.45	2.0	Irena Gurskaite	SU	69	6 Jul
11.45	0.0	LaMonda Miller	USA	67	16 Jul
11.46	0.7	Silke-Beate Knoll	FRG	67	25 May
11.46	1.7	Jeanette Düring	GDR	65	25 Jun
11.46	1.2	Muriel Leroy	FRA	68	13 Aug
11.46	1.9	Sue Butler	AUS	63	29 Oct
11.47	1.5	Nadezhda Rotach	SU	70	6 Jul
		(110)			
11.47	0.8	Françoise Leroux	FRA	61	13 Aug
11.47	0.0	Irina Kot	SU	67	14 Aug
11.47	2.0	Sisko Hanhijoki	FIN	62	25 Aug
11.48	·	Michelle Freeman	JAM	69	7 Apr
11.48	0.6	Diane Dixon	USA	64	5 Jun
11.48	1.4	Yelena Bykova	SU	66	11 Jun
11.48	1.6	Natalya Tochilova	SU	64	11 Jul
11.48A	1.6	Beverly Kinch	UK	64	11 Aug
11.49		Laurel Johnson	JAM	67	19 May
11.49	0.8	Lynda Tolbert	USA	67	21 May
		(120)			
11.49	1.1	Olga Kvast	SU	63	31 May
11.49	1.1	Sabine Richter	FRG	66	24 Sep
11.50	1.2	Chryste Gaines	USA	70	8 Apr
11.50		Dionne Smith	USA	..	9 Apr
11.50	0.0	Celena Mondie	USA	68	2 Jul
11.50A		Alma D.Vazquez	MEX	62	8 Jul
11.50	0.8	Helen Miles	UK	67	5 Aug
11.50	-0.0	Yelena Petrova	SU	62	14 Aug
11.50	1.9	Jane Flemming	AUS	65	15 Sep
11.51	1.8	Galina Syomkina	SU	61	11 Jun
		(130)			
11.51	0.9	Heike Morgenstern	GDR	62	25 Jun
11.51	0.0	Regula Aebi	SWZ	65	23 Aug
11.51	0.4	Ingrid Verbruggen	BEL	64	4 Sep
11.52		Tatyana Plakhova	SU	60	7 May
11.52		Claudia Schuster	GDR	67	23 May
11.52A	1.7	Claudilea M. Santos	BRA	65	22 Jul
11.52		Ansie Basson	RSA	66	26 Nov
11.53	0.9	Grit Breuer	GDR	72	20 May
11.53	2.0	Rossella Tarolo	ITA	64	9 Jul
11.53	0.1	Lourdes Valdor	SPA	54	13 Jul
		(140)			
11.54	1.5	Sallyanne Short	UK	68	26 May
11.54		Lynda Eseimokumo	NIG	66	30 Jun
11.54A	1.7	Claudia Acerenza	URU	66	22 Jul
11.55	1.3	Lisa Ford	USA	66	15 May
11.55	0.9	Karina Knuhr	GDR	69	20 May
11.55	0.3	Michaela Schabinger	FRG	61	2 Jul
11.55	0.8	Olga Vasina	SU	65	14 Aug
11.55	0.0	Martha Grössenbacher	SWZ	59	23 Aug
11.55	0.5	Tian Yumei	CHN	65	24 Sep
11.56	1.1	Diane Holden	AUS	63	5 Mar
		(150)			
11.56	-0.1	Anita Howard	USA	69	24 Jun
11.57	1.4	Terri Dendy	USA	65	26 Mar
11.57		Marina Vladimirova	SU	67	7 May
11.57	1.5	Zelda Johnson	USA	64	29 May
11.57	1.3	Elvira Barbashina	SU	63	31 May
11.57	0.0	Cecile Peyre	FRA	69	9 Jul
11.57	-0.4	Eusebia Riquelme	CUB	69	28 Jul
11.57	0.8	Yelena Nasonkina	SU	62	14 Aug
11.58	1.7	Kendra Mackey	USA	69	2 Apr
11.58	0.7	Beatrice Utondu	NIG	69	4 May
		(160)			
11.58	0.8	Pam Reynolds	USA	66	21 May
11.58	-1.1	Maria V. Gomes	POR	64	9 Jul
11.58	1.2	Odile Singa	FRA	67	13 Aug
11.59A		Elinda Rademeyer	RSA	65	15 Apr
11.59		Lorna Johnson	JAM		16 Apr
11.59	0.0	Magalie Seguin	FRA	64	12 Jun
11.59		Marbella Washington	USA	62	10 Jul
11.59		Stephanie Douglas	UK	69	24 Jul
11.59	1.5	Janis Neilson	UK	63	5 Aug
11.59	0.0	Amparo Caicedo	COL	65	24 Sep
		(170)			
11.60	1.8	Corina Rosioru	RUM	68	18 Jun
11.60	1.5	Pippa Windle	UK	61	5 Aug
11.60	0.8	Ute Thimm	FRG	58	9 Sep

Handicap race (possible rolling start)

Mark		Name	Nat	Born	Date
11.49		Wendy Hoyte	UK	57	20 Jul

Wind assisted

Mark		Name		Nat	Born	Pos	Meet	Venue	Date
10.54	3.0		Griffith-Joyner			1	OG	Seoul	25 Sep
10.60	3.2		Griffith-Joyner			1h1	FOT	Indianapolis	16 Jul
10.70	2.6		Griffith-Joyner			1s2	OG	Seoul	25 Sep
10.78	5.0	Gwen	Torrence	USA	65	1q3	FOT	Indianapolis	16 Jul
10.83	3.9		Echols			1h2	FOT	Indianapolis	16 Jul
10.83	3.0		Ashford			2	OG	Seoul	25 Sep
10.85	3.0	Heike	Drechsler	GDR	64	3	OG	Seoul	25 Sep
10.86	3.0	Gail	Devers	USA	66	1	NCAA	Eugene	4 Jun
10.87	3.5		Torrence			1	Pre	Eugene	2 Jul
10.88	3.9	Alice	Brown	USA	60	2h2	FOT	Indianapolis	16 Jul
10.89	3.1		Göhr			1		Berlin	13 Sep
10.89	3.1	Kerstin	Behrendt	GDR	67	2		Berlin	13 Sep
10.91	5.0		Ashford			2q3	FOT	Indianapolis	16 Jul
10.91	2.6		Drechsler			2s2	OG	Seoul	25 Sep
10.93	2.7		Torrence			1h3	FOT	Indianapolis	16 Jul
10.95	2.5		Nuneva			1	Int	Schwechat	15 Jun
10.96	2.5	Juliet	Cuthbert	JAM	64	1rB	WK	Zürich	17 Aug
10.97	2.1		Devers			1h1	Pac10	Westwood	21 May
10.97	3.0	Grace	Jackson	JAM	61	4	OG	Seoul	25 Sep

Mark		Name		Nat	Born	Pos	Meet	Venue	Date
10.97	3.0		Torrence			5	OG	Seoul	25 Sep
		(20 Performances by 12 Athletes)							
11.02	5.0	Jennifer	Inniss	USA	59	3q3	FOT	Indianapolis	16 Jul
11.04	3.1	Ingrid	Lange	GDR	57	3		Berlin	13 Sep
11.05	2.5	Ulrike	Sarvari	FRG	64	2rB	WK	Zürich	17 Aug
11.08	2.5	Nadezhda	Georgieva	BUL	61	2	Int	Schwechat	15 Jun
11.10	3.9	Jeanette	Bolden	USA	60	3h2	FOT	Indianapolis	16 Jul
11.12	2.8	Tatyana	Papilina	SU	67	1s		Kiev	14 Aug
11.12	2.6	Pauline	Davis	BAH	66	6s2	OG	Seoul	25 Sep
11.13	2.5	Paula	Dunn	UK	64	1	NP	Haringey	20 Aug
11.13	3.1	Annette	Kersten	GDR	67	4		Berlin	13 Sep
11.18	3.0	Esther	Jones	USA	69	3	NCAA	Eugene	4 Jun
11.18	2.8	Olga	Frolova	SU	64	2s		Kiev	14 Aug
11.18	3.5	Olga	Zolotaryova	SU	61	1		Odessa	18 Aug
11.19	2.8	Els	Vader	HOL	59	1		Den Haag	10 Jul
11.19	5.0	Wendy	Vereen	USA	66	4q3	FOT	Indianapolis	16 Jul
11.22	4.6	Diane	Holden	AUS	64	#	mix	Sydney	6 Feb
11.22	5.0	Michelle	Finn	USA	65	5q3	FOT	Indianapolis	16 Jul
11.22A	4.3	Laloa	Ravaonirina	MAD	63	1		Font Romeu	20 Jul
11.26	3.9	Angela	Burnham	USA	71	4h2	FOT	Indianapolis	16 Jul
11.26	2.5	Regula	Aebi	SWZ	65	5rB	WK	Zurich	17 Aug
11.27	2.5	Krasimira	Pencheva	BUL	58	3	Int	Schwechat	15 Jun
11.28	3.2	Yelena	Kelchevskaya	SU	55	2h2	Znam	Leningrad	11 Jun
11.28	3.6	Ewa	Pisiewicz	POL	62	1		Lublin	6 Aug
11.29	2.5	Celena	Mondie	USA	68	1	Big10	Ann Arbor	22 May
11.30	4.5	Vivienne	Spence	JAM	65	1	NCAA/II	San Agelo	21 May
11.31	3.5	Tina	Iheagwam	NIG	68	6	MSR	Walnut	24 Apr
11.32	2.7	Rufina	Uba	NIG	59	1	KansR	Lawrence	23 Apr
11.32	3.2	Olga	Voronova	SU	68	3h2	Znam	Leningrad	11 Jun
11.34	3.9	LaMonda	Miller	USA	67	5h2	FOT	Indianapolis	16 Jul
11.34A	2.4	Cristina	Perez	SPA	65	1h2	IbAC	Mexico	22 Jul
11.34	3.6	Joanna	Smolarek	POL	65	2		Lublin	6 Aug
11.36	6.4	Lisa	Ford	USA	66	1		Arlington	7 May
11.36	2.5	Wendy	Hoyte	UK	57	2	NP	Haringey	20 Aug
11.38	2.5	Valya	Demireva	BUL	61	6	Int	Schwechat	15 Jun
11.41A		Lynda	Tolbert	USA	67	1		Flagstaff	14 May
11.41	2.8	Irina	Kot	SU	67	3s		Kiev	14 Aug
11.41	2.5	Helen	Miles	UK	67	3	NP	Haringey	20 Aug
11.42A		Evette	de Klerk	RSA	65	1		Johannesburg	23 Apr
11.42	2.6	Zina	Age	USA	65	2		Pasadena	11 Jun
11.42	2.9	Muriel	Leroy	FRA	68	1		Nantes	24 Jun
11.42	3.1	Kornelija	Sinkovic	YUG	64	1	NP	Beograd	2 Jul
11.43		Inger	Miller	JAM	72	2		Norwalk	21 May

Mark	Wind	Name	Nat	Born	Date
11.44	5.0	LaVonna Martin	USA	66	22 Jun
11.44	2.5	Martha Grössenbacher	SWZ	59	17 Aug
11.45	2.4	Teresa Foster	USA	72	7 May
11.45	3.2	Elvira Tkachenko	SU	63	11 Jun
11.45	4.8	Stephanie Douglas	UK	69	25 Jun
11.45	3.5	Olga Kvast	SU	63	18 Aug
11.46	2.3	Teresa Neighbors	USA	67	28 May
11.47	5.0	Dyan Webber	USA	66	22 Jun
11.48	3.9	Maree Holland	AUS	63	6 Feb
11.48	2.7	Jakki Harman	UK	67	23 Jul
11.48A	2.4	Maria V.Gomes	POR	64	22 Jul
11.51	3.3	Magalie Simioneck	FRA	70	9 Jul
11.52		Sherri Howard	USA	62	14 May
11.52		Lorinda Richardson	USA	65	15 May
11.53	3.1	Dijana Istvanovic	YUG	57	2 Jul
11.54		Bridgette Tate	USA	66	22 Apr
11.54	2.7	Davera Taylor	USA	65	23 Apr
11.54	5.8	Carol Bailey	USA	..	27 May
11.54	2.3	Ursula Younger	USA	67	28 May
11.54	3.5	Anita Howard	USA	69	16 Jul
11.54	3.5	Rimma Nurmukhomyatova	SU	59	18 Aug
11.55	3.5	Pam Reynolds	USA	66	24 Apr
11.55		Kim Dunlap	USA	64	28 May
11.55	2.8	Maria Fernström	SWE	67	30 Jul
11.55	2.8	Ena Waldo	UK	63	30 Jul
11.56	2.4	Yvette Green	USA	68	2 Apr
11.56A	2.4	Ines A. Ribeiro	BRA	63	22 Jul
11.57A	3.1	Marcel Winkler	RSA	70	23 Apr
11.57A	2.4	Idania Pino	CUB	67	22 Jul
11.57	2.8	Marie-Christine Dubois	FRA	67	30 Jul
11.58	2.4	Caroline Nwajei	NIG	68	2 Apr
11.58	2.3	Ximena Restrepo	COL	69	27 Jul
11.59A	4.3	Martine Cassin	FRA	62	20 Jul
11.59	2.5	Lynne Draper	UK	67	20 Aug
11.60	4.5	Sharon Hudson	USA	68	21 May
11.60	2.5	Angela McClatchey	USA	67	22 May
11.60	5.0	Benita Fitzgerald-Brown	USA	61	22 Jun
11.60	2.5	Marita Payne	CAN	60	17 Aug

Mark		Name		Nat	Born	Pos	Meet	Venue	Date
Hand timing									
10.7		Merlene	Ottey	JAM	60	1h	NC	Kingston	15 Jul
10.8	0.6	Galina	Malchugina	SU	62	1h	NP	Vladivostok	13 Sep
10.8	1.0	Marika	Molokova	SU	62	1h	NP	Vladivostok	13 Sep
10.9		Zhang Caihua		CHN	64	1		Shijiazhuang	23 Apr
10.9	0.5	Lyudmila	Kondratyeva	SU	58	1h	NP	Vladivostok	13 Sep
10.9	0.8	Maya	Azarashvili	SU	64	1	NP	Vladivostok	13 Sep
11.0		Kerstin	Behrendt	GDR	67	1		Leipzig	26 May
11.0	0.1	Irina	Kot	SU	67	1		Chernigov	23 Jul
11.0	0.6	Marina	Zhirova	SU	63	2h	NP	Vladivostok	13 Sep
11.1		Yelena	Kelchevskaya	SU	55	1		Staiki	12 May
11.1	1.0	Antonina	Slyusar	SU	63	2h	NP	Vladivostok	13 Sep

Mark		Name	Nat	Born	Date
11.2		Liu Shaomei	CHN	63	12 Aug
11.2		Marina Vladimirova	SU	67	5 Apr
11.2		Tian Yumei	CHN	65	23 Apr
11.2		Irina Slyusar	SU	63	15 May
11.2		Laloa Ravaonirina	MAD	63	2 Jun
11.2	0.0	Olga Kvast	SU	63	17 Jun
11.2	-0.1	Esther Jones	USA	69	24 Jun
11.2		Lidia Okolo-Kulak	SU	67	10 Jul
11.2	1.3	Marina Markina	SU	62	16 Jul
11.2	0.4	Yelena Zhirkova	SU	67	28 Jul
11.2	1.0	Olga Voronova	SU	68	13 Sep
11.2	0.6	Tatyana Papilina	SU	67	13 Sep
11.2	0.5	Galina Syomkina	SU	61	13 Sep
11.3		Yelena Ruzina	SU	64	5 Apr
11.3		Tatyana Alexeyeva	SU	63	5 Apr
11.3		Ge Weidong	CHN	69	23 Apr
11.3		Gudrun Abt	FRG	62	29 May
11.3		Marieta Ilcu	RUM	62	4 Jun
11.3		Diane Dixon	USA	64	10 Jun
11.3		Ingrid Verbruggen	BEL	64	25 Jun
11.3		Marbella Washington	USA	62	6 Jul
11.3		Tatyana Plakhova	SU	60	8 Jul
11.3	-0.1	Irina Ivanova	SU	66	9 Jul
11.3	0.9	Nelli Bulgakova	SU	69	26 Jul
11.3	1.2	Olga Rizina	SU	66	31 Jul
11.3	-1.6	Yelena Nasonkina	SU	62	6 Aug
11.3	0.0	Helga Arendt	FRG	64	7 Sep
11.3	0.0	Bettina Braag	FRG	65	7 Sep

Wind assisted

Mark		Name		Nat	Born	Pos	Venue	Date
11.0		Tracy	Mayfield	USA	68	1	Abilene	28 Apr
11.0	4.5	Yelena	Kelchevskaya	SU	55	1s	Staiki	31 Jul

Mark		Name	Nat	Born	Date
11.2		Teresa Foster	USA	72	11 Mar
11.2		Karen Kruger	RSA	63	14 May
11.2	2.5	Sisko Hanhijoki	FIN	62	4 Jun
11.2	4.5	Olga Rizina	SU	66	31 Jul
11.2A	2.1	Marisa Masullo	ITA	59	6 Aug
11.3	4.6	Jane Flemming	AUS	65	21 Jan
11.3	3.1	Lisa Ford	USA	66	7 May
11.3		Lorinda Richardson	USA	65	14 May
11.3		LaBerta Carter	USA	72	
11.3	2.8	Karine Gambier	FRA	67	26 Jun
11.3		Marinella Signori	ITA	63	24 Jul

Doubtful timing

Mark	Name	Nat	Born	Date
11.2	Diane Holden	AUS	63	27 Feb

Year List Progression

Year	100 Metres Best	10th	20th	50th	100th	200 Metres Best	10th	20th	50th	100th
1968	11.1	11.4	11.5	11.6	11.8	22.7	23.4	23.7	24.0	24.3
1978	10.94	11.23	11.35	11.52	11.4	22.06	22.77	23.03	23.52	23.76
1979	10.97	11.23	11.36	11.53	11.67	21.71	22.80	23.03	23.41	23.70
1980	10.93	11.20	11.28	11.43	11.65	22.01	22.47	22.82	23.28	23.64
1981	10.90	11.21	11.29	11.51	11.66	21.84	22.72	22.98	23.43	23.71
1982	10.88	11.14	11.28	11.43	11.58	21.76	22.39	22.91	23.23	23.56
1983	10.79	11.09	11.22	11.41	11.54	21.82	22.42	22.79	23.15	23.54
1984	10.76	11.10	11.21	11.36	11.51	21.71	22.36	22.65	22.98	23.39
1985	10.86	11.11	11.21	11.38	11.54	21.78	22.55	22.75	23.19	23.58
1986	10.88	11.08	11.20	11.33	11.51	21.71	22.39	22.60	23.02	23.36
1987	10.86	11.01	11.13	11.34	11.48	21.74	22.40	22.55	23.07	23.35
1988	10.49	10.92	11.08	11.27	11.44	21.34	22.24	22.59	22.93	23.32

200 METRES

Mark	Wind	Name		Nat	Born	Pos	Meet	Venue	Date
21.34	+1.3	Florence	Griffith-Joyner	USA	59	1	OG	Seoul	29 Sep
21.56	+1.7		Griffith-Joyner			1s1	OG	Seoul	29 Sep
21.72	+1.3	Grace	Jackson	JAM	61	2	OG	Seoul	29 Sep
21.76	+0.7		Griffith-Joyner			1q1	OG	Seoul	28 Sep
21.77	-0.1		Griffith-Joyner			1q2	FOT	Indianapolis	22 Jul
21.84	+1.0	Heike	Drechsler	GDR	64	1	NC	Rostock	26 Jun
21.85	+1.3		Griffith-Joyner			1	FOT	Indianapolis	23 Jul
21.93	+1.3	Pam	Marshall	USA	60	2	FOT	Indianapolis	23 Jul
21.94	-1.3		Drechsler			1	v FRG	Düsseldorf	20 Jun
21.95	+1.3		Drechsler			3	OG	Seoul	29 Sep
21.96	+0.6		Griffith-Joyner			1h1	FOT	Indianapolis	22 Jul
21.99	+1.7		Drechsler			1		Karl-Marx-Stadt	12 Jun
21.99	+1.3	Merlene	Ottey	JAM	60	4	OG	Seoul	29 Sep

Mark		Name		Nat	Born	Pos	Meet	Venue	Date
22.02	+1.3	Gwen	Torrence	USA	65	3	FOT	Indianapolis	23 Jul
22.07	+1.7		Ottey			2s1	OG	Seoul	29 Sep
22.08	+2.0		Drechsler			1		Berlin	13 Sep
22.09	+1.3	Silke	Möller	GDR	64	5	OG	Seoul	29 Sep
22.11	+1.3	Valerie	Brisco	USA	60	4	FOT	Indianapolis	23 Jul
22.13	+1.8		Jackson			1s2	OG	Seoul	29 Sep
22.15	+1.4		Griffith-Joyner			1		Santa Monica	12 Jun
22.15	+1.7		Möller			3s1	OG	Seoul	29 Sep
22.17	+1.3		Torrence			6	OG	Seoul	29 Sep
22.19	+2.0		Möller			2		Berlin	13 Sep
22.23	+0.6		Ottey			1	Int	Sevilla	1 Jun
22.23	-0.2	Dannette	Young	USA	64	1	Herc	Monaco	2 Aug
22.24	+0.1	Maya	Azarashvili (10)	SU	64	1		Kiev	16 Aug
22.24	+0.3		Jackson			1q3	OG	Seoul	28 Sep
22.25	+0.7		Torrence			1q2	OG	Seoul	28 Sep
22.26	+1.6		Torrence			1q3	FOT	Indianapolis	22 Jul
22.26	0.0		Young			1	ASV	Köln	21 Aug
		(30/10)							
22.28	+1.7	Marlies	Göhr	GDR	58	2		Karl-Marx-Stadt	12 Jun
22.30	0.0	Jackie	Joyner-Kersee	USA	62	1H	FOT	Indianapolis	15 Jul
22.36	+1.7	Kerstin	Behrendt	GDR	67	3		Karl-Marx-Stadt	12 Jun
22.39	+1.3	Alice	Brown	USA	60	5	FOT	Indianapolis	23 Jul
22.42	+1.3	Galina	Malchugina	SU	62	8	OG	Seoul	29 Sep
22.43	+1.7	Mary	Onyali	NIG	68	5s1	OG	Seoul	29 Sep
22.51	+2.0	Katrin	Krabbe	GDR	69	3		Berlin	13 Sep
22.53	+0.8	Nadezhda	Georgieva	BUL	61	1	Int	Schwechat	15 Jun
22.58	+1.8	Diane	Dixon	USA	64	1		New York	5 Jun
22.59	-0.4	Juliet	Cuthbert	JAM	64	1	BGP	Budapest	12 Aug
		(20)							
22.65	+1.7	Heike	Morgenstern	GDR	62	4		Karl-Marx-Stadt	12 Jun
22.65	+0.7	Lyudmila	Kondratyeva	SU	58	1	NC	Tallinn	6 Jul
22.67	0.0	Aelita	Yurchenko	SU	65	1h		Simferopol	28 May
22.67	-0.1	Diane	Williams	USA	60	2q1	FOT	Indianapolis	22 Jul
22.67	+1.7	Pauline	Davis	BAH	66	7s1	OG	Seoul	29 Sep
22.72	-0.2	Marie-Josée	Pérec	FRA	68	2	Herc	Monaco	2 Aug
22.73	+0.9	Yelena	Ruzina	SU	64	1		Sochi	19 May
22.74	+0.7	Andrea	Thomas	FRG	63	1		Ravensburg	27 Aug
22.74	+0.3	Olga	Nazarova	SU	65	1h	Kuts	Moskva	5 Sep
22.78	+0.2	Marie-Christine	Cazier	FRA	63	1	Perr	Fort-de-France	30 Apr
		(30)							
22.79	+1.7	Sabine	Günther	GDR	63	5		Karl-Marx-Stadt	12 Jun
22.79	+1.2	Paula	Dunn	UK	64	1	DNG	Stockholm	5 Jul
22.80	-0.2	Lillie	Leatherwood	USA	64	3	Herc	Monaco	2 Aug
22.80	+1.0	Agnieszka	Siwek	POL	62	1		Lublin	6 Aug
22.82	+1.4	Iolanda	Oanta	RUM	65	1	NC	Pitesti	14 Aug
22.82	+1.7	Kerry	Johnson	AUS	63	1		Chiba	15 Sep
22.83	+1.7	Maree	Holland	AUS	63	2		Chiba	15 Sep
22.83A		Myrtle	Bothma	RSA	64	1		Sasolburg	16 Nov
22.84	+0.2	Marina	Molokova	SU	62	1h1	NC	Tallinn	6 Jul
22.86	+0.6	Cristina	Perez	SPA	65	2	Int	Sevilla	1 Jun
		(40)							
22.87	+1.9	Alice	Jackson	USA	58	2	Owens	Columbus	8 May
22.88	-1.0	Anelia	Nuneva	BUL	62	1		Sofia	5 Jun
22.88	-0.4	Regula	Aebi	SWZ	65	1	NC	Zug	14 Aug
22.88	-0.9	Maria	Pinigina	SU	58	2	NP	Vladivostok	14 Sep
22.88	+0.7	Falilat	Ogunkoya	NIG	68	5q2	OG	Seoul	28 Sep
22.89	+0.9	Tatyana	Papilina	SU	67	2		Sochi	19 May
22.91	+0.8	Rochelle	Stevens	USA	66	3	NCAA	Eugene	3 Jun
22.92	+0.2	Marina	Markina	SU	62	2h1	NC	Tallinn	6 Jul
22.93	+1.5	Marina	Kharlamova	SU	62	1		Bryansk	12 Jul
22.93	+1.3	Wendy	Vereen	USA	66	7	FOT	Indianapolis	23 Jul
		(50)							
22.94	+1.3	Els	Vader	HOL	59	1	ECC	Lisboa	5 Jun
22.95	-0.2	Olga	Bryzgina	SU	63	1h	NP	Vladivostok	14 Sep
22.99	-0.1	Carlette	Guidry	USA	68	3q1	FOT	Indianapolis	22 Jul

Mark	Wind	Name		Nat	Born	Pos	Meet	Venue	Date
22.99		Maria	M. Figueiredo	BRA	63	1		Americana	8 Sep
23.00		Natalya	Kovtun	SU	64	1		Leningrad	24 Jul
23.00	-0.2	Ute	Thimm	FRG	58	2	NC	Frankfurt	24 Jul
23.01	+1.8	Lisa	Ford	USA	66	2	SWC	Austin	15 May
23.01	-0.6	Petra	Müller	GDR	65	1	v Ita	Neubrandenburg	10 Jul
23.02	+1.0	Olga	Sychugova	SU	63	1	v Rom	Bucuresti	19 Jun
23.03	+0.9	Lyudmila	Narozhilenko	SU	64	3		Sochi	19 May
		(60)							
23.04	+1.3	Grit	Breuer	GDR	72	1		Jena	20 May
23.04A	0.0	Blanca	Lacambra	SPA	65	1	IbAC	Mexico	23 Jul
23.05	+0.8	Esther	Jones	USA	69	6	NCAA	Eugene	3 Jun
23.05	+1.8	Marita	Payne	CAN	65	3	BNP	Villeneuve d'Ascq	27 Jun
23.06		Silke-Beate	Knoll	FRG	67	1		Saarbrücken	2 Jun
23.06		Galina	Syomkina	SU	61	1		Vilnius	28 Aug
23.06		Ansie	Basson	RSA	66	1		Welkom	26 Nov
23.07	+1.5	Ana	Fidelia Quirot	CUB	63	1		Habana	6 Aug
23.08	+1.0	Jillian	Richardson	CAN	65	1	Int	Barcelona	13 Jul
23.09	+0.9	Ethlyn	Tate	JAM	66	1		Washington	28 May
		(70)							
23.09	+1.8	Evelyn	Ashford	USA	57	5	BNP	Villeneuve d'Ascq	27 Jun
23.10	+1.6	Anke	Behmer	GDR	61	H	OG	Seoul	23 Sep
23.11		Olga	Zolotaryova	SU	61	1		Odessa	19 Aug
23.13	+1.6	Dawn	Sowell	USA	66	4q3	FOT	Indianapolis	22 Jul
23.13	-0.2	Helga	Arendt	FRG	64	3	NC	Frankfurt	24 Jul
23.13	+1.5	Liliana	Allen	CUB	70	2		Habana	6 Aug
23.14	+0.9	Angela	Williams	TRI	65	3		Washington	28 May
23.14	+1.0	Jolanta	Janota	POL	64	2		Lublin	6 Aug
23.15	+0.9	Olga	Frolova	SU	64	4		Sochi	19 May
23.26y		Chryste	Gaines	USA	70	1h		Mesquite	29 Apr
		(80)							
23.18	+0.6	Angella	Issajenko	CAN	58	4	Int	Sevilla	1 Jun
23.18	+0.4	Lyudmila	Dzhigalova	SU	62	2h	Kuts	Moskva	5 Sep
23.19	+1.5	Celena	Mondie	USA	68	1	Big10	Ann Arbor	22 May
23.19	+1.5	Bridgette	Tate	USA	66	2	Big10	Ann Arbor	22 May
23.19	+0.7	Maicel	Malone	USA	69	1	Pac10	Westwood	22 May
23.19	+0.7	Muriel	Leroy	FRA	68	3h5	OG	Seoul	28 Sep
23.20A		Evette	de Klerk	RSA	65	1		Pretoria	13 Feb
23.20	+1.0	Jeanette	Düring	GDR	65	4	NC	Rostock	26 Jun
23.20	-0.1	Terri	Dendy	USA	65	4q2	FOT	Indianapolis	22 Jul
23.21	-0.6	Annette	Kersten	GDR	67	2	v Ita	Neubrandenburg	10 Jul
		(90)							
23.21		Irina	Kot	SU	67	2		Vilnius	28 Aug
23.22	+0.1	Olga	Petrova	SU	62	3		Kiev	16 Aug
23.24	-0.4	Sisko	Hanhijoki	FIN	62	1	Int	Lapinlahti	26 Jun
23.24	-1.1	Ingrid	Verbruggen	BEL	64	1	NC	Bruxelles	4 Sep
23.26	+1.6	Nadezhda	Chistyakova	SU	69	1	NC-j	Bryansk	8 Jul
23.27	-0.6	Marisa	Masullo	ITA	59	3	v GDR	Neubrandenburg	10 Jul
23.29	+1.0	Esmie	Lawrence	CAN	61	3	Int	Barcelona	13 Jul
23.31	+0.3	Svetla	Dimitrova	BUL	70	1	NC-j	Sofia	3 Jul
23.31	-0.5	Ina	Cordes	FRG	68	1	IntC	Tel Aviv	10 Jul
23.32	+0.9	Kendra	Mackey	USA	69	1		Athens, Ga.	7 May
		(100)							
23.32	0.0	Tatyana	Ledovskaya	SU	66	1	Int	Riga	5 Jun
23.32	+0.1	Angela	Bailey	CAN	62	1		North York	16 Jul

Mark	Wind	Name	Nat	Born	Date
23.33	+1.3	Michelle Finn	USA	65	2 Jul
23.33	+1.2	Simone Jacobs	UK	66	5 Jul
23.33	+1.6	Irena Gurskaite	SU	69	8 Jul
23.33	+0.1	Ewa Pisiewicz	POL	62	31 Jul
23.33	+0.7	Rita Angotzi	ITA	67	28 Sep
23.34	-1.1	Daniela Plescan	RUM	69	5 Jun
23.34	+1.0	Sandra Myers	SPA	61	13 Jul
23.34	-0.2	Fabienne Ficher	FRA	66	2 Aug
		(110)			
23.35		Kim Dunlap	USA	64	28 May
23.37	+0.1	Gudrun Abt	FRG	62	2 Jul
23.40		Denise Mitchell	USA	66	2 Apr
23.40		Diana Dietz	GDR	69	12 Jun
23.40	-0.4	Marieta Ilcu	RUM	62	10 Jul
23.40A	0.8	Martine Cassin	FRA	62	20 Jul
23.41A	0.8	Nathalie Simon	FRA	62	20 Jul
23.42	+1.8	Ximena Restrepo	COL	69	5 Jun
23.42	+0.5	Xie Zhiling	CHN	63	4 Sep
23.43	+1.2	Svetlana Chervyakova	SU	63	24 Apr
		(120)			
23.43	+0.9	Magali Seguin	FRA	64	12 Jun
23.43	-1.7	Tsvetanka Ilieva	BUL	63	17 Jul
23.44	+0.6	Denean Howard	USA	64	7 May
23.45	+1.0	Angela Burnham	USA	71	4 Jun
23.46	+0.7	Yelena Nasonkina	SU	62	6 Jul
23.47		Kirsten Emmelmann	GDR	61	3 Jul

Mark		Name	Nat	Born	Date	Mark		Name	Nat	Born	Date
23.47	-0.2	Louise Stuart	UK	67	28 Aug	23.55	+0.8	Angelika Haggenmüller	FRG	69	10 Jul
23.48	0.0	Vineta Ikauniece	SU	62	22 Jun	23.55	-0.1	Nadezhda Rashchupkina	SU	63	1 Sep
23.48	-0.4	Manuela Derr	GDR	71	14 Aug	23.57	+1.2	Jocelyn Joseph	ANT	64	28 Sep
23.48	+0.1	Olga Voronova	SU	68	16 Aug	23.58	+0.7	Urszula Jaros	POL	56	11 Jun
		(130)				23.58		Revolie Campbell	JAM	72	24 Jul
23.49		Anita Howards	USA	69	6 May	23.58	-0.4	Jana Schönenberger	GDR	71	14 Aug
23.49	+0.8	Milena Saracheva	BUL	67	15 Jun	23.58	-0.2	Pat Beckford	UK	65	28 Aug
23.49A		Ines A. Ribeiro	BRA	63	23 Jul			(150)			
23.50		Cathy Rattray	JAM	63	18 Jun	23.59	+1.6	Lisa Horton	USA	68	7 May
23.50	+1.4	Joanna Smolarek	POL	65	13 Aug	23.59	+0.9	Inger Miller	JAM	72	21 May
23.51		Doreen Fahrendorff	GDR	68	29 May	23.59	+1.0	Simone Cain	USA	70	4 Jun
23.52	-0.4	Molly Killingbeck	CAN	59	24 Jun	23.59	-0.7	Karin Janke	FRG	63	26 Jun
23.53	+0.8	Sallyanne Short	UK	68	26 May	23.59	+1.1	Yelena Kelchevskaya	SU	55	6 Jul
23.54	+1.8	LaShawn Haythe	USA	68	15 May	23.59	+0.7	Odile Singa	FRA	67	14 Aug
23.54		Marina Shmonina	SU	65	19 Jun	23.59	-0.7	Jane Flemming	AUS	65	23 Sep
		(140)				23.59	+1.6	Svetlana Buraga	SU	65	23 Sep
23.54	+1.5	Martha Grössenbacher	SWZ	59	10 Sep	23.60	+0.1	LaMonda Miller	USA	67	2 Apr
23.55		Virgie Bullie	USA	65	21 May	23.60	+1.6	Tanya McIntosh	USA	66	7 May
23.55		Angela McClatchey	USA	67	28 May			(160)			
						23.60	+0.7	Jacinta Bartholomew	GRN	65	22 May

Wind assisted

Mark	Wind	First name	Name	Nat	Born	Pos	Meet	Venue	Date
21.90	+2.4		Griffith-Joyner			1s2	FOT	Indianapolis	23 Jul
22.12	+3.7		Torrence			1s1	FOT	Indianapolis	23 Jul
22.17	+2.7		Jackson			1	Athl	Lausanne	24 Jun
22.21	+2.7	Dannette	Young	USA	64	2	Athl	Lausanne	24 Jun
22.24	+3.7		Marshall			2s1	FOT	Indianapolis	23 Jul
		(5/5)							
22.33	+3.7	Alice	Brown	USA	60	3s1	FOT	Indianapolis	23 Jul
22.34	+2.3	Katrin	Krabbe	GDR	69	1	WJ	Sudbury	30 Jul
22.69	+2.7	Evelyn	Ashford	USA	57	3	Athl	Lausanne	24 Jun
22.73	+4.0	Anke	Behmer	GDR	61	1H	Int	Götzis	18 Jun
22.77	+3.7	Wendy	Vereen	USA	66	4s1	FOT	Indianapolis	23 Jul
22.85	+3.7	Rochelle	Stevens	USA	66	5s1	FOT	Indianapolis	23 Jul
22.87	+2.7	Angella	Issajenko	CAN	58	5	Athl	Lausanne	24 Jun
22.88	+2.3	Diana	Dietz	GDR	69	2	WJ	Sudbury	30 Jul
22.96	+3.0	Carlette	Guidry	USA	68	3rA		Austin	7 May
22.97	+2.3	Liliana	Allen	CUB	70	3	WJ	Sudbury	30 Jul
23.00	+2.3	Esther	Jones	USA	69	4	WJ	Sudbury	30 Jul
23.04	+2.1	Jolanta	Janota	POL	64	2		Lublin	8 Sep
23.09		Vivienne	Spence	JAM	65	1h1	NCAA/II	San Angelo	18 May
23.17A	2.5	Marisa	Masullo	ITA	59	2	Int	Sestriere	11 Aug
23.18A	2.5	Terri	Dendy	USA	65	3	Int	Sestriere	11 Aug
23.20	+2.1	Ewa	Pisiewicz	POL	62	3		Lublin	8 Sep
23.24	+2.1	Joanna	Smolarek	POL	65	4		Lublin	8 Sep
23.26	+2.2	Angelika	Haggenmuller	FRG	69	2s1	WJ	Sudbury	29 Jul
23.27		Sharon	Powell	JAM	65	1h1	Big8	Ames	14 May

Mark		Name	Nat	Born	Date	Mark		Name	Nat	Born	Date
23.34		Yolande Straughn	BAR	68	18 May	23.48	+2.8	Diane Holden	AUS	63	6 Mar
23.35	+2.8	Gudrun Abt	FRG	62	21 May	23.48		Laurel Johnson	JAM	67	20 May
23.37	+4.0	Jane Flemming	AUS	65	18 Jun	23.51		Natasha Kaiser	USA	67	14 May
23.38		Darlena Morganfield	USA	69	14 May	23.51		Jearl Miles	USA	66	20 May
23.40	+2.1	Sally Gunnell	UK	66	20 Aug	23.51	+4.0	Liliana Nastase	RUM	62	18 Jun
23.41A	2.5	Dagmar Neubauer	GDR	62	11 Aug	23.51A	+2.7	Marcel Winkler	RSA	70	8 Oct
23.45	+2.6	Sue Alton	AUS	66	6 Mar	23.56	+2.3	Oksana Kovalyova	SU	69	29 Jul
23.47	>4.0	Patricia Amond	IRL	62	24 Jul	23.57	+2.3	Tanya McIntosh	USA	66	14 May

Hand timing

Mark	Wind	First name	Name	Nat	Born	Pos	Meet	Venue	Date
22.3		Kerstin	Behrendt	GDR	67	1		Leipzig	26 May
22.6		Aelita	Yurchenko	SU	65	1		Voroshilovgrad	14 May
22.7	+1.0	Tatyana	Ledovskaya	SU	66	1		Staiki	29 May
22.7	+1.6	Carlette	Guidry	USA	68	1		Austin	22 Jun
22.8	+1.7	Gail	Devers-Roberts	USA	66	1		Los Angeles	16 Apr
22.8		Tatyana	Papilina	SU	67	1		Chelyabinsk	17 Jul
22.9		Tatyana	Alexeyeva	SU	63	1		Novosibirsk	28 Jun
22.9		Olga	Frolova	SU	64	2		Chelyabinsk	17 Jul
22.9	+2.0	Irina	Kot	SU	67	1		Chernigov	24 Jul
23.0		Lyudmila	Dzhigalova	SU	62	2		Voroshilovgrad	14 May
23.0	+1.6	Dyan	Webber	USA	66	2		Austin	22 Jun
23.0		Vineta	Ikauniece	SU	62	1		Pärnu	13 Jul

Mark		Name		Nat	Born	Date	Mark		Name	Nat	Born	Date
23.1		Natalya Pomoshchnikova		SU	65	8 May	23.3	0.0	Rita Angotzi	ITA	67	17 Jul
23.2	+0.1	Sherri Howard		USA	62	23 Apr	23.3A	-0.8	Joyce Odhiambo	KEN	63	13 Aug
23.2	+0.1	Michelle Finn		USA	65	21 May	Wind assisted					
23.2	+2.0	Yelena Petrova		SU	62	24 Jul	23.2	+4.0	Yulia Kharitoshina	SU	66	12 May
23.3	+0.1	Tina Iheagwam		NIG	68	23 Apr	23.3	+3.9	Sallyanne Short	UK	68	25 Jun
23.3		Yelena Kelchevskaya		SU	55	13 May	23.3	+3.8	Simone Jacobs	UK	66	29 Jul
23.3		Svetla Dimitrova		BUL	70	29 May						

Indoor marks

Mark	Wind	Name		Nat	Born	Pos	Meet	Venue	Date
22.69	-	Ewa	Kasprzyk	POL	57	1	EC	Budapest	6 Mar
22.79	-	Tatyana	Papilina	SU	67	2	EC	Budapest	6 Mar
22.97	-	Silke-Beate	Knoll	FRG	67	1		Dortmund	20 Feb
23.04	-	Tsvetanka	Ilieva	BUL	63	1	v CS	Sofia	14 Feb
23.05	-	Ingrid	Auerswald-Lange	GDR	57	1	NC	Senftenberg	27 Feb
23.07	-	Natalya	German	SU	63	2	NP	Moskva	21 Feb
23.15	-	Marina	Krivosheina	SU	67	1h		Minsk	5 Mar
23.24	-	Kirsten	Emmelmann	GDR	61	1		Senftenberg	3 Feb

Mark		Name	Nat	Born	Date	Mark		Name	Nat	Born	Date
23.38	-	Natalya Pomoshchnikova	SU	65	26 Feb	23.44	-	Vineta Ikauniece	SU	62	21 Feb
23.43	-	Dagmar Neubauer	GDR	62	6 Feb	23.46	-	Kornelija Sinkovic	YUG	64	6 Mar

400 METRES

Mark	Name			Nat	Born	Pos	Meet	Venue	Date
48.65	Olga	Bryzgina		SU	63	1	OG	Seoul	26 Sep
49.11	Olga	Nazarova		SU	65	1s1	OG	Seoul	25 Sep
49.18		Bryzgina				1	Kuts	Moskva	4 Sep
49.30	Petra	Müller		GDR	65	1		Jena	3 Jun
49.33		Bryzgina				1s2	OG	Seoul	25 Sep
49.45		Müller				2	OG	Seoul	26 Sep
49.47	Aelita	Yurchenko		SU	65	2	Kuts	Moskva	4 Sep
49.50		Müller				2s1	OG	Seoul	25 Sep
49.57	Grace	Jackson		JAM	61	1	Nik	Nice	10 Jul
49.58		Müller				1	Int	Karl-Marx-Stadt	12 Jun
49.62A	Ana Fidelia	Quirot		CUB	63	1		Ciudad México	22 May
49.65		Müller				1	v FRG	Düsseldorf	19 Jun
49.74	Maria	Pinigina		SU	58	3	Kuts	Moskva	4 Sep
49.75		Yurchenko				1h		Simferopol	28 May
49.79		Yurchenko				1rA	Znam	Leningrad	12 Jun
49.81		Quirot				2	Nik	Nice	10 Jul
49.84		Jackson				1rA	ASV	Köln	21 Aug
49.84	Diane	Dixon		USA	64	3s1	OG	Seoul	25 Sep
49.87	Denean	Howard		USA	64	4s1	OG	Seoul	25 Sep
49.90	Valerie	Brisco	(10)	USA	60	2s2	OG	Seoul	25 Sep
49.90		Nazarova				3	OG	Seoul	26 Sep
49.91	Jillian	Richardson		CAN	65	5s1	OG	Seoul	25 Sep
49.98		Müller				1		Potsdam	8 Sep
50.00		Bryzgina				2rA	Znam	Leningrad	12 Jun
50.09		Nazarova				1	NC	Tallinn	5 Jul
50.10		Richardson				2rA	ASV	Köln	21 Aug
50.10		Quirot				1	Int	Salamanca	8 Sep
50.13		Müller				1	OD	Berlin	29 Jun
50.14		Dixon				3rA	ASV	Köln	21 Aug
50.16		Quirot				1	PTS	Bratislava	8 Jun
50.16		Brisco				4	OG	Seoul	26 Sep
	(31/11)								
50.24	Maree	Holland		AUS	63	3s2	OG	Seoul	25 Sep
50.28	Ute	Thimm		FRG	58	6s1	OG	Seoul	25 Sep
50.29	Marita	Payne-Wiggins		CAN	60	7s1	OG	Seoul	25 Sep
50.36	Helga	Arendt		FRG	64	4s2	OG	Seoul	25 Sep
50.39	Kirsten	Emmelmann		GDR	61	5s2	OG	Seoul	25 Sep
50.45	Dagmar	Neubauer		GDR	62	2	v FRG	Düsseldorf	19 Jun
50.55	Iolanda	Oanta		RUM	65	1	NC	Pitesti	13 Aug
50.61	Lyudmila	Dzhigalova		SU	62	4rA	Znam	Leningrad	12 Jun
50.68	Lillie	Leatherwood		USA	64	4	FOT	Indianapolis	18 Jul
	(20)								
50.71	Vineta	Ikauniece		SU	62	4	Kuts	Moskva	4 Sep
50.75	Marina	Kharlamova		SU	62	1	BGP	Budapest	12 Aug

Mark	Name		Nat	Born	Pos	Meet	Venue	Date
50.82	Cathy	Rattray-Williams	JAM	63	6s2	OG	Seoul	25 Sep
50.93	Tatyana	Ledovskaya	SU	66	5rA	Znam	Leningrad	12 Jun
50.96	Maicel	Malone	USA	69	1s1	FOT	Indianapolis	17 Jul
51.02	Debbie	Flintoff-King	AUS	60	5rA	ASV	Köln	21 Aug
51.10	Marina	Shmonina	SU	65	2	vGB,FRA	Portsmouth	19 Jun
51.11	Pauline	Davis	BAH	66	1	DrakeR	Des Moines	30 Apr
51.14A	Madelé	Naude	RSA	63	1		Pretoria	14 Mar
51.14	Grit	Breuer	GDR	72	3		Jena	3 Jun
	(30)							
51.16	Charmaine	Crooks	CAN	62	2	McVit	London	28 Aug
51.23	Rochelle	Stevens	USA	66	1	NCAA	Eugene	4 Jun
51.28	Jearl	Miles	USA	66	3s1	FOT	Indianapolis	17 Jul
51.29A	Myrtle	Bothma	RSA	64	1	NC	Bloemfontein	15 Apr
51.29	Merlene	Ottey	JAM	60	3	MSR	Walnut	24 Apr
51.32	Maria M.	Figueiredo	BRA	63	5q1	OG	Seoul	24 Sep
51.35	Maria-Josée	Pérec	FRA	68	1	NC	Tours	14 Aug
51.44	Rositsa	Stamenova	BUL	55	1		Stara Zagora	20 Aug
51.45	Celena	Mondie	USA	68	4	TAC	Tampa	18 May
51.45	Terri	Dendy	USA	65	3rB	ASV	Köln	21 Jun
	(40)							
51.46	Yelena	Vinogradova	SU	64	2rB	Znam	Leningrad	12 Jun
51.62	Sandie	Richards	JAM	68	2		Kingston	16 Apr
51.63	Sherri	Howard	USA	62	5	FOT	Indianapolis	18 Jul
51.64	Vera	Sychugova	SU	63	6	NC	Tallinn	5 Jul
51.65	Linda	Keough	UK	63	1	WAAA	Birmingham	6 Aug
51.67	Sharon	Powell	JAM	65	4	NCAA	Eugene	4 Jun
51.72	Dalia	Matuseviciene	SU	62	1	Int	Schwechat	13 Aug
51.73	Blanca	Lacambra	SPA	65	2	Int	Madrid	7 Jun
51.73	Natasha	Kaiser	USA	67	6s1	FOT	Indianapolis	17 Jul
51.76	Tanya	McIntosh	USA	66	5	TAC	Tampa	18 Jun
	(50)							
51.76	Norfalia	Carabali	COL	67	3q3	OG	Seoul	24 Sep
51.79	Evelyne	Elien	FRA	64	2	NC	Tours	14 Aug
51.80	Nadezhda	Loboyko	SU	61	1		Baku	10 Sep
51.81	Fabienne	Ficher	FRA	66	3	NC	Tours	14 Aug
51.83	Nadezhda	Olizarenko	SU	53	4rB	Znam	Leningrad	12 Jun
51.84	Gwen	Torrence	USA	65	2	DrakeR	Des Moines	30 Apr
51.84	Camelia	Jianu	RUM	67	2	v Rus	Bucuresti	18 Jun
51.88	Sandra	Farmer-Patrick	USA	62	1	Int	Athinai	3 Sep
51.98	Galina	Moskvina	SU	68	1		Sochi	20 May
52.01	Uta	Rohländer	GDR	69	1		Halle	14 May
	(60)							
52.03	Delisa	Walton-Floyd	USA	61	1		Houston	28 May
52.03	Milena	Saracheva	BUL	67	1		Stara Zagora	28 Aug
52.04	Alice	Jackson	USA	58	1h3	TAC	Tampa	16 Jun
52.04	Tsvetanka	Ilieva	BUL	63	3	NarM	Sofia	26 Jun
52.04	Célestine	N'Drin	IVC	63	4q4	OG	Seoul	24 Sep
52.05	Denise	Mitchell	USA	66	1	SEC	Auburn	15 May
52.08	Tatyana	Alekseyeva	SU	63	2		Sochi	24 Apr
52.08	Gisela	Kinzel	FRG	61	4	PTS	Bratislava	9 Jun
52.08	Yelena	Golesheva	SU	66	1		Kiev	15 Aug
52.12	Nathalie	Simon	FRA	62	4	NC	Tours	14 Aug
	(70)							
52.12	Malena	Andonova	BUL	57	3		Stara Zagora	20 Aug
52.12	Anita	Protti	SWZ	60	1	LieC	Schaan	10 Sep
52.13	Maya	Azarashvili	SU	64	6rA	Znam	Leningrad	12 Jun
52.13	Stefanie	Fabert	GDR	69	2		Berlin	20 Jul
52.15	Airat	Bakare	NIG	68	1	AfrC	Annaba	30 Aug
52.18	Tudorita	Chidu	RUM	67	1		Bucuresti	9 Jul
52.20	Michaela	Schabinger	FRG	61	8rA	ASV	Köln	21 Aug
52.21	Lilia	Nurutdinova	SU	63	3		Sochi	24 Apr
52.22	Gudrun	Abt	FRG	62	3		Dormagen	4 Sep
52.23	Lyubov	Kiryukhina	SU	63	3		Moskva	6 Aug
	(80)							
52.26	Patricia	Beckford	UK	65	2	Int	Gateshead	14 Aug
52.26	Martha	Grossenbacher	SWZ	59	4rB	ASV	Köln	21 Aug

Mark	Name		Nat	Born	Pos	Meet	Venue	Date
52.29	Yordanka	Stoyanova	BUL	59	4		Stara Zagora	20 Aug
52.32	Slobodanka	Colovic	YUG	65	1	NC	Sarajevo	3 Sep
52.33	Nicoleta	Carutasu	RUM	64	2	Balk	Ankara	16 Jul
52.33	Aissatou	Tandian	SEN	66	6q4	OG	Seoul	24 Sep
52.34	Marcia	Tate	JAM	61	2		Los Angeles	3 Sep
52.36	Cristina	Perez	SPA	65	4	Int	Madrid	7 Jun
52.38	Inna	Yevseyeva	SU	64	5rB	Znam	Leningrad	12 Jun
52.38	Michelle	Taylor	USA	67	4h1	TAC	Tampa	16 Jun
	(90)							
52.38	Sigrun	Wodars	GDR	65	3		Berlin	13 Sep
52.42	Leslie	Hardison	USA	67	5h1	FOT	Indianapolis	15 Jul
52.44	Essie	Washington	USA	57	2		Houston	28 May
52.45	Genowefa	Blaszak	POL	57	7rA	Znam	Leningrad	12 Jun
52.45	Ronny	Uebel	GDR	63	3	BGP	Budapest	12 Aug
52.46	Dannette	Young	USA	64	1		Tallahassee	23 Apr
52.46	Daniela	Spasova	BUL	69	1	Balk-j	Alexandroúpolis	9 Jul
52.46	Ann-Louise	Skoglund	SWE	62	3	McVit	London	28 Aug
52.48	Daniela	Plescan	RUM	69	6rB	Znam	Leningrad	12 Jun
52.50	Florence	Griffith-Joyner	USA	59	1		Los Angeles	14 May
	(100)							
52.50	Anna	Ambraziene	SU	55	1	Int	St. Denis	7 Jun
52.50	Tamara	Kuprianovich	SU	64	1		Leningrad	24 Jul

Mark	Name		Nat	Born	Date
52.53	Suzete G.	Montalvao	BRA	65	16 Jun
52.54	Barbara	Flowers	USA	66	15 Jul
52.55	Victoria	Fulcher	USA	65	22 May
52.55	Irina	Vasilyeva	SU	64	11 Jul
52.56	Anke	Wöhlk	GDR	70	20 Jul
52.58A	Evette	de Klerk	RSA	65	29 Nov
52.59	Karin	Janke	FRG	63	23 Jul
52.59	Lyudmila	Borisova I.	SU	59	31 Jul
	(110)				
52.60	Sally	Fleming	AUS	61	28 Jun
52.60	Andrea	Thomas	JAM	68	15 Jul
52.62	Manuela	Derr	GDR	71	20 Jul
52.64A	Zelda	Botes	RSA	68	29 Nov
52.66	Alena	Paríková	CS	61	17 Jul
52.66	Natalya	Knyazkova	SU	63	15 Aug
52.68	Irina	Radeyeva	SU	68	15 Aug
52.69	Angela	Springer	BAR		21 May
52.70	Doreen	Fahrendorf	GDR	68	3 Jun
52.70	Daniela	Gamalie	RUM	67	13 Aug
	(120)				
52.71	Lilia	Nurutdinova	SU	63	24 Apr
52.71	Teresa	Zuñiga	SPA	64	7 Jun
52.71	Loreen	Hall	UK	67	18 Jun
52.71	Christine	Wachtel	GDR	65	13 Sep
52.72	Larisa	Glavenko	SU	63	12 Jun
52.72	Molly	Killingbeck	CAN	59	27 Jun
52.72	Olga	Moroz	SU	70	6 Jul
52.73	Joetta	Clark	USA	62	5 Jun
52.74	Linetta	Wilson	USA	67	15 May
52.75	Janeene	Vickers	USA	68	22 May
	(130)				
52.81	Schowonda	Williams	USA	66	27 Jun
52.84	Tania	van Heer	AUS	70	27 Mar
52.84	Yvonne	van Dorp	HOL	66	23 Sep
52.85	Bonka	Peneva	BUL	56	20 Aug
52.88	Mercy	Addy	GHA	64	30 Aug
52.89	Marlyn	Dewarder	GUY	60	7 May
52.89	Janet	Smith	UK	68	6 Aug
52.92	Ellen	Fiedler	GDR	58	9 Sep
52.94	Rosie	Edeh	CAN	66	24 Jul
52.95	Danyel	Wofford-Simmons	BAR	66	15 May
	(140)				
52.95	Tamika	Foster	USA	65	22 May
52.96	Kehinde	Vaughan	NIG	61	30 Aug
52.97	LaTanya	Sheffield	USA	63	27 May
53.01	Wendy	Vereen	USA	66	16 Jun
53.02	Mary	Onyali	NIG	68	28 May
53.03	Sun	Sumei	CHN	68	10 Jun
53.04	Meredith	Rainey	USA	68	17 Jun
53.04	Sadia	Sowunmi	NIG	64	30 Jun
53.05	Nadine	Debois	FRA	61	8 May
53.05	Erzsébet	Szabó	HUN	63	21 Jun
	(150)				
53.05	Jennifer	Stoute	UK	65	5 Aug
53.05	Angela	Piggford	UK	63	28 Aug
53.06	Galina	Selivanova	SU	60	20 May
53.07	Michelle	Milling	USA	66	30 Apr
53.07	Gervaise	McCraw	USA	64	28 Jun
53.07	Viktoria	Miloserdova	SU	70	7 Jul
53.07	Larisa	Mitina	SU	64	15 Aug
53.09	Gerda	Haas	AUT	65	3 Jul
53.13	Svetlana	Yurlina	SU	64	31 Jul
53.14	Michele	Felder	USA	67	16 Apr
	(160)				
53.14	Nadezda	Tomsová	CS	71	28 Jul
53.15	Christina	Sussiek	FRG	60	7 May
53.15	Teri	Smith	USA	69	15 May
53.15	Helena	Dziurová	CS	65	2 Jul
53.16	Tara	Coleman	USA	68	14 May
53.16	Lilia	Ship	SU	66	15 Aug
53.17	Stephanie	Saleem	USA	69	16 Jun
53.17	Lyudmila	Kashchey	SU	68	17 Jun
53.17	Sonja	Finell	FIN	68	7 Aug
53.18	Kendra	Mackey	USA	69	25 May
	(170)				
53.18	Elzbieta	Kapusta	POL	60	5 Jun
53.18	Gabriela	Lesch	FRG	64	26 Jun
53.19A	Rose	Blake	USA		14 May
53.19	Sabine	Alber	FRG	65	3 Jul
53.19	Alla	Malchenko	SU	61	18 Aug

Hand Timing

Mark	Name		Nat	Born	Pos	Meet	Venue	Date
48.9	Olga	Nazarova	SU	65	1	NP	Vladivostok	13 Sep
49.9	Lyudmila	Dzhigalova	SU	62	1		Kiev	24 Jun
50.1		Yurchenko			1h		Voroshilovgrad	15 May
50.4	Tatyana	Ledovskaya	SU	66	1		Staiki	28 May
51.1	Gwen	Torrence	USA	65	3	Pepsi	Westwood	6 Jun
51.2	Sherri	Howard	USA	62	4	Pepsi	Westwood	6 Jun

Mark	Name		Nat	Born	Pos	Meet	Venue	Date
51.3	Dalia	Matuseviciene	SU	62	3		Kiev	24 Jun
51.8	Tamara	Kuprianovich	SU	64	1		Staiki	31 Jul
51.9	Yelena	Cherepanova	SU	65	.h		Smolensk	25 Jun
52.0	Lyudmila	Borisova I.	SU	59	5		Kiev	24 Jun
52.1	Leslie	Hardison	USA	67	1	SWC	Austin	15 May
52.2	Natalya	Knyazkova	SU	63	1		Bryansk	28 Jul
52.3	Erzsébet	Szabó	HUN	63	1	NC	Miskolc	16 Jul

Mark	Name		Nat	Born	Date
52.4	Alla	Malchenko	SU	61	13 Sep
52.5	Barbara	Flowers	USA	66	15 May
52.6	Sun	Sumei	CHN	68	13 Aug
52.7A	Francisca	Chepkurui	KEN	63	10 Jun
52.9	Olga	Marshavina	SU	62	11 Jul
53.0	Irina	Gayduk	SU	63	27 Jun
53.0	Yelena	Goncharova	SU	63	28 Jul
53.0A	Esther	Kavaya	KEN	58	13 Aug

Indoor Marks

Mark	Name		Nat	Born	Pos	Meet	Venue	Date
51.77	Sally	Gunnell	UK	66	4	EC	Budapest	6 Mar
51.96	Gisela	Kinzel	FRG	61	2	NC	Dortmund	20 Feb
52.47	Erzsébet	Szabó	HUN	63	4s1	EI	Budapest	5 Mar

Mark	Name		Nat	Born	Date
52.51	Christina	Sussiek	FRG	60	20 Feb
52.52	Linetta	Wilson	USA	66	13 Feb
52.68	Judith	Forgács	HUN	59	28 Feb
52.74	Cornelia	Ullrich	GDR	63	25 Feb
52.97	Michelle	Milling	USA	67	13 Feb
53.18	Margarita	Khromova	SU	63	11 Feb

400 Metres — Year List Progression — 800 Metres

Year	400 Best	400 10th	400 20th	400 50th	400 100th	800 Best	800 10th	800 20th	800 50th	800 100th
1968	52.4	53.8	54.4	55.3	56.1	2:01.0	2:04.6	2:05.8	2:07.9	2:09.9
1978	48.94	51.11	51.59	52.88	53.54	1:55.80	1:58.7	1:59.8	2:01.99	2:03.73
1979	48.60	51.00	51.55	52.49	53.30	1:56.2	1:57.92	1:59.0	2:00.9	2:02.90
1980	48.88	51.00	51.31	52.12	53.00	1:53.43	1:57.0	1:58.51	2:00.5	2:02.5
1981	48.61	51.43	51.77	52.52	53.28	1:56.98	1:58.22	1:59.22	2:01.00	2:02.82
1982	48.16	50.63	51.18	52.08	52.95	1:55.05	1:57.3	1:59.0	2:00.9	2:02.8
1983	47.99	50.63	50.99	51.89	52.77	1:53.28	1:57.4	1:58.5	2:00.1	2:01.91
1984	48.16	49.74	50.56	51.89	52.63	1:55.69	1:57.20	1:58.08	1:59.6	2:01.50
1985	47.60	50.38	51.12	52.21	52.89	1:55.68	1:57.42	1:58.42	2:00.73	2:02.43
1986	48.22	50.29	50.92	51.74	52.50	1:56.2	1:58.11	1:58.80	2:00.60	2:02.04
1987	49.38	50.41	51.11	51.88	52.64	1:55.26	1:57.46	1:58.6	2:00.06	2:01.79
1988	48.65	49.90	50.68	51.76	52.50	1:56.0	1:56.91	1:58.1	1:59.97	2:01.66

800 METRES

Mark	Name		Nat	Born	Pos	Meet	Venue	Date
1:56.0	Inna	Yevseyeva	SU	64	1		Kiev	25 Jun
1:56.0	Nadezhda	Olizarenko	SU	53	1	RC	Kharkov	4 Jul
1:56.03		Olizarenko			1	NC	Kiev	1 Aug
1:56.10	Sigrun	Wodars	GDR	65	1	OG	Seoul	26 Sep
1:56.36	Ana Fidelia	Quirot	CUB	63	1	BNP	Villeneuve d'Ascq	27 Jun
1:56.42	Paula	Ivan	RUM	63	1	Balk	Ankara	16 Jul
1:56.56	Lyubov	Gurina	SU	57	1	NP	Vladivostok	14 Sep
1:56.64	Christine	Wachtel	GDR	65	2	OG	Seoul	26 Sep
1:56.7	Dalia	Matuseviciene	SU	62	2		Kiev	25 Jun
1:56.82	Lyudmila	Rogachova	SU	66	1		Pärnu	13 Jul
1:56.91	Kim	Gallagher (10)	USA	64	3	OG	Seoul	26 Sep
1:56.96		Quirot			1	WK	Zürich	17 Aug
1:57.09		Wachtel			1		Jena	3 Jun
1:57.2	Nadezhda	Loboyko	SU	61	3		Kiev	25 Jun
1:57.21		Wodars			1s1	OG	Seoul	25 Sep
1:57.30		Wodars			2		Jena	3 Jun
1:57.39		Gallagher			2s1	OG	Seoul	25 Sep
1:57.45	Teresa	Zuñiga	SPA	64	1	Int	Sevilla	1 Jun
1:57.46		Matuseviciene			2		Pärnu	13 Jul
1:57.50	Slobodanka	Colovic	YUG	65	4	OG	Seoul	26 Sep
1:57.57		Loboyko			3		Pärnu	13 Jul
1:57.64	Tudorita	Chidu	RUM	67	2	Balk	Ankara	16 Jul
1:57.73		Wachtel			1		Potsdam	8 Jun
1:57.77	Yelena	Afanasyeva	SU	66	4		Pärnu	13 Jul
1:57.80		Chidu			1	NC	Pitesti	12 Aug
1:57.80	Delisa	Walton-Floyd	USA	61	5	OG	Seoul	26 Sep
1:57.81		Wodars			2		Potsdam	8 Jun
1:57.88		Gurina			1	Kuts	Moskva	4 Sep

Mark	Name		Nat	Born	Pos	Meet	Venue	Date
1:57.90		Matuseviciene			1s1	NC	Kiev	31 Jul
1:57.93		Colovic			1	NC	Sarajevo	4 Sep
	(30/16)							
1:58.03	Irina	Podyalovskaya	SU	59	2s1	NC	Kiev	31 Jul
1:58.10	Ella	Kovacs	RUM	64	1		Bucuresti	12 Jun
1:58.1	Svetlana	Kitova	SU	60	1		Moskva	8 Jul
1:58.1 A	Francisca	Chepkurui	KEN	63	1	OT/NC	Nairobi	13 Aug
	(20)							
1:58.12	Vera	Chuvashova	SU	59	3s1	NC	Kiev	31 Jul
1:58.48	Galina	Reznikova	SU	61	3s2	NC	Kiev	31 Jul
1:58.56	Lyubov	Kiryukhina	SU	63	5s1	NC	Kiev	31 Jul
1:58.61	Laima	Baikauskaite	SU	56	6		Pärnu	13 Jul
1:58.70	Tatyana	Grebenchuk	SU	62	1		Sochi	31 May
1:58.70	Vera	Dodika	SU	59	2		Sochi	31 May
1:58.72	Mitica	Constantin	RUM	62	2	NC	Pitesti	12 Aug
1:58.84	Marina	Yachmenyeva	SU	61	2h1	NC	Kiev	30 Jul
1:58.85	Lyudmila	Derevyankina	SU	66	3h1	NC	Kiev	30 Jul
1:58.86	Tatyana	Samolyenko	SU	61	1	v Fra,UK	Portsmouth	19 Jun
	(30)							
1:58.96	Viorica	Niga	RUM	68	3	NC	Pitesti	12 Aug
1:59.17	Birte	Bruhns	GDR	70	1		Berlin	20 Jul
1:59.31	Olga	Nelyubova	SU	64	3		Sochi	31 May
1:59.33	Sabine	Zwiener	FRG	67	3	v GDR	Düsseldorf	19 Jun
1:59.35	Violeta	Beclea	RUM	65	2	NP	Bucuresti	28 Aug
1:59.4	Yelena	Zavadskaya	SU	64	2		Kharkov	4 Jul
1:59.42	Gabriela	Lesch	FRG	64	4	v GDR	Düsseldorf	19 Jun
1:59.5	Natalya	Knyazkova	SU	63	1		Krasnodar	10 Jul
1:59.66	Diane	Edwards	UK	66	4s2	OG	Seoul	25 Sep
1:59.70	Essie	Washington	USA	57	1		San Diego	25 Jun
	(40)							
1:59.7	Lyubov	Kremlyova	SU	62	.		Kiev	25 Jun
1:59.78	Christina	Cahill	UK	57	2	Int	Rieti	31 Aug
1:59.79	Joetta	Clark	USA	62	1	TAC	Tampa	18 Jun
1:59.8	Svetlana	Prodan	SU	62	3		Kharkov	4 Jul
1:59.84	Natalya	Artyomova	SU	63	2	NP	Vladivostok	14 Sep
1:59.9	Tatyana	Kalina	SU	63	.		Kiev	25 Jun
1:59.92	Soraya	Vieira Telles	BRA	58	1	Int	Schwechat	15 Jun
1:59.94	Shireen	Bailey	UK	60	6s2	OG	Seoul	26 Sep
1:59.95	Martina	Steuk	GDR	59	3	NC	Rostock	25 Jun
1:59.97	Debbie	Marshall	USA	65	4	TAC	Indianapolis	18 Jul
	(50)							
2:00.10	Lilia	Nurutdinova	SU	63	4h1	NC	Kiev	30 Jul
2:00.30	Alisa	Harvey	USA	65	1	Int	Athinai	3 Sep
2:00.3	Svetlana	Yurlina	SU	64	2		Chelyabinsk	17 Jul
2:00.35	Gabriela	Sedláková	CS	68	2	Int	Koblenz	28 Aug
2:00.36	Andrea	Hahmann	GDR	66	1	Int	Potsdam	30 Jun
2:00.39	Beverley	Nicholson	UK	67	2	McVit	London	28 Aug
2:00.39	Olga	Dogadina	SU	59	7	Kuts	Moskva	4 Sep
2:00.5	Olga	Ignatyeva	SU	68	1		Orenburg	19 Jun
2:00.53	Catalina	Gheorghiu	RUM	69	1		Bucuresti	10 Jul
2:00.59	Julie	Jenkins	USA	64	1	Pepsi	Westwood	6 Jun
	(60)							
2:00.6	Galina	Bochkayeva	SU	63	.		Kiev	25 Jun
2:00.61	Kirsty	Wade	UK	62	3	Nik	Nice	10 Jul
2:00.7	Natalya	Betekhtina	SU	61	1		Chelyabinsk	17 Jul
2:00.71	Nathalie	Thoumas	FRA	62	4	v SU,UK	Portsmouth	19 Jun
2:00.84	Tatyana	Minogenkova	SU	64	1		Bryansk	13 Jul
2:00.89	Ute	Lix	FRG	65	5	v GDR	Düsseldorf	19 Jun
2:00.93	Margrit	Klinger	FRG	60	3	Int	Koblenz	28 Aug
2:01.03	Karol	Davidson	USA	65	4	TAC	Tampa	18 Jun
2:01.06	Hildegard	Körner	GDR	59	1		Potsdam	9 Sep
2:01.1	Tatyana	Lebonda	SU	64	4		Moskva	8 Jul
	(70)							
2:01.13	Regina	Jacobs	USA	63	1		Northridge	3 Jul
2:01.16	Rosa	Colorado	SPA	54	3	Int	Sevilla	1 Jun
2:01.16	Irina	Gayduk	SU	63	2		Bryansk	13 Jul

Mark	Name		Nat	Born	Pos	Meet	Venue	Date
2:01.20	Patricia	Wellman	CAN	64	1	Jer	Burnaby	5 Jun
2:01.20	Yvonne	Grabner	GDR	65	1	Int	New Delhi	5 Sep
2:01.2	Alla	Upyr	SU	62	4		Kharkov	4 Jul
2:01.22	Dorota	Dziak	POL	63	1		Zabrze	1 Aug
2:01.23	Yelena	Ryazanova	SU	62	5		Sochi	31 May
2:01.26	Sharon	Powell	JAM	65	2		Westwood	3 Sep
2:01.28	Madelé	Naude	RSA	63	1		Pretoria	14 Mar
	(80)							
2:01.30	Ellen	Kiessling	GDR	68	1		Cottbus	17 Jun
2:01.30	Lyudmila	Borisova II.	SU	66	2		Vilnius	28 Aug
2:01.3	Antonina	Babushkina	SU	62	.		Kiev	25 Jun
2:01.3	Tamara	Koba	SU	57	1		Zhitomir	7 Aug
2:01.31	Barbara	Gourdet	FRA	65	4	Int	Koblenz	28 Aug
2:01.35	Maria	Pinigina	SU	58	1	Veet	Tallinn	10 Jul
2:01.36	Heike	Oehme	GDR	63	4		Jena	3 Jun
2:01.36	Lyudmila	Borisova I	SU	59	3	Int	Riga	5 Jun
2:01.37	Malgorzata	Rydz	POL	67	2		Zabrze	1 Aug
2:01.37	Yekaterina	Podkopayeva	SU	52	4		Odessa	20 Aug
	(90)							
2:01.38	Camille	Cato	CAN	63	3	Int	Formia	19 Jun
2:01.40	Sharon	Stewart	AUS	65	1	Int	Melbourne	17 Mar
2:01.40	Zelda	Botes	RSA	68	1		Stellenbosch	6 Apr
2:01.40	Erzsébet	Szabó	HUN	63	3	Int	Schwechat	15 Jun
2:01.46	Kathi	Harris	USA	64	5	TAC	Tampa	18 Jun
2:01.47	Montserrat	Pujol	SPA	61	2	Int	Madrid	7 Jun
2:01.5	Wendy	Old	AUS	60	#	mix	Adelaide	20 Feb
2:01.51	Anushka	Dimitrova	BUL	62	1	4-N	Praha	3 Jul
2:01.61	Luminita	Avasiloaie	RUM	69	5	RomIC	Bucuresti	19 Jun
2:01.66	Renée	Bélanger	CAN	62	1		Abbotsford	12 Jun
	(100)							

Mark	Name		Nat	Born	Date
2:01.67	Maria	Akraka	SWE	60	8 Aug
2:01.7	Svetlana	Agapova	SU	59	4 Jul
2:01.72	Lynn	Williams	CAN	60	9 Aug
2:01.82	Rose	Monday	USA	59	5 Jun
2:01.83	Letitia	Vriesde	SUR	64	25 Sep
2:01.87	Dawn	Gandy	UK	65	19 Jun
2:01.94	Christine	Hanon	FRA	60	14 Aug
2:01.98	Yvonne	Murray	UK	64	23 Jul
2:02.00	Olga	Politova	SU	64	31 May
2:02.00	Andrea	Thomas	JAM	68	16 Jul
	(110)				
2:02.0	Zoya	Kaznovskaya	SU	66	4 Jul
2:02.0	Tatyana	Mamayeva	SU	62	17 Aug
2:02.02	Maria	Pîntea	RUM	67	11 Aug
2:02.03	Olga	Burkanova	SU	69	14 May
2:02.05	Svetlana	Andreyeva	SU	65	13 Jul
2:02.09	Hassiba	Boulmerka	ALG	68	25 Jun
2:02.19	Grace	Verbeek	CAN	58	12 Jun
2:02.20	Tatyana	Tokina	SU	66	5 Jun
2:02.23	Ciska	Swart	RSA	59	6 Apr
2:02.27	Snezana	Pajkic	YUG	70	2 Jun
	(120)				
2:02.27	Janet	Bell	UK	59	19 Jun
2:02.30	Petya	Strashilova	BUL	65	25 Jun
2:02.34	Daniela	Steinecke	GDR	69	3 Jun
2:02.34	Angela	Chalmers	CAN	63	9 Aug
2:02.35	Tiina	Pakkala	FIN	62	3 Sep
2:02.43	Grazyna	Kowina	POL	62	30 Jul
2:02.44	Claudette	Groenendaal	USA	63	24 Apr
2:02.44	Dorota	Buczkowska	POL	69	26 Jun
2:02.5	Irina	Kolmakova	SU	64	28 Jun
2:02.5	Olga	Parlyuk	SU	63	17 Jul
	(130)				
2:02.5	Rose	Tata-Muya	KEN	60	13 Aug
2:02.5	Mary	Chepkemboi	KEN	68	13 Aug
2:02.52	Nina	Ruchayeva	SU	56	13 Jul
2:02.58	Elly	van Hulst	HOL	59	15 Jun
2:02.58	Joanna	Siemieniuk	POL	65	27 Jul
2:02.64	Vesna	Bajer	YUG	63	5 Jun
2:02.66	Aurica	Mitrea	RUM	59	12 Aug
2:02.67	Denisa	Zavelca	RUM	70	5 Jun
2:02.68	Toril	Hatling	NOR	67	28 Aug
2:02.71	Celeste	Halliday	USA	67	17 Jul
	(140)				
2:02.76	Marjorie	van der Merwe	RSA	68	14 Mar
2:02.83	Katja	Prochnow	GDR	68	30 Jun
2:02.85	Nadine	Debois	FRA	61	27 Jun
2:02.89	Gail	Millar	AUS	63	26 Jan
2:02.89	Fatima	Aouam	MOR	59	20 Aug
2:02.85	Linda	Sheskey	USA	62	27 Jun
2:02.85	Mary	Burzminski	CAN	60	24 Sep
2:02.9	Carlene	Dillimore	NZ	66	22 Mar
2:02.9	Tatyana	Varfolomeyeva	SU	66	17 Aug
2:02.93	Gail	Harris	CAN	66	5 Jun
	(150)				
2:02.96	Astrid	Bartels	FRG	63	22 Jul
2:02.97	Evelyn	Adiru	UGA	64	1 Jun
2:02.98	Regine	Berg	BEL	58	30 Jul
2:03.05	Svetlana	Mashkova	SU	62	27 Aug
2:03.06	Claudia	Riedel	GDR	67	3 Jun
2:03.06	Helen	Thorpe	UK	63	6 Aug
2:03.08	Diana	Richburg	USA	63	2 Jul
2:03.1	Yelena	Zhupiyova	SU	60	4 Jul
2:03.12	Olivera	Stankov	BUL	67	3 Jul
2:03.14	Galina	Afonina	SU	63	5 Jun
	(160)				
2:03.16	Lyn	Foreman	AUS	57	17 Mar
2:03.18	Edith	Nakiyngi	UGA	68	30 Apr
2:03.20	Yelena	Storchovaya	SU	66	30 Jul
2:03.2	Yelena	Cherepanova	SU	65	12 Jul
2:03.23	Nonna	Novozhilova	SU	63	28 Aug
2:03.26	Wanda	Wojtowiec	POL	60	30 Jul
2:03.26	Jolanta	Wieprzkowicz	POL	66	7 Aug
2:03.26	Shiny	Abraham	IND	65	24 Sep
2:03.30	Lesley	Noll	USA	67	9 Apr
2:03.3	Lyudmila	Kolomeyets	SU	66	4 Jul
	(170)				
2:03.31	Aisling	Molloy	IRL	64	7 May

Unconfirmed mark

Mark	Name		Nat	Born	Date
2:01.84	Nadia	Ouaziz	MOR	72	

Mark		Name	Nat	Born	Pos	Meet	Venue	Date
Indoor marks								
1:56.40	Christine	Wachtel	GDR	65	1	v Aut,Yug	Wien	13 Feb
1:57.64		Wachtel			1	v Ita	Torino	10 Feb
1:57.67		Wodars			2	v Aut,Yug	Wien	13 Feb
2:00.62	Katrin	Wühn	GDR	65	1		Senftenberg	6 Feb
2:00.7	Doina	Melinte	RUM	56	1	LAT	Los Angeles	19 Feb
2:00.81	Yvonne	Grabner	GDR	65	2		Senftenberg	6 Feb
2:01.51	Gaby	Bussmann	FRG	59	1	Int	Karlsruhe	7 Feb

2:02.58 Vera Michallek FRG 58 7 Feb | 2:02.66 Galina Afonina SU 63 23 Jan
2:02.63 Brigitte Brückner FRG 56 13 Feb

1000 METRES

Mark		Name	Nat	Born	Pos	Meet	Venue	Date
2:34.65	Mary	Slaney	USA	58	1	APM	Hengelo	14 Aug
2:35.7	Heike	Oehme	GDR	63	1		Cottbus	25 May
2:36.34	Julie	Jenkins	USA	64	2	APM	Hengelo	14 Aug
2:37.02	Diana	Richburg	USA	63	3	APM	Hengelo	14 Aug
2:37.60	Diane	Edwards	UK	66	1	Int	Gateshead	16 Jul
2:37.90	Essie	Washington	USA	57	4	APM	Hengelo	14 Aug
2:37.91	Linda	Sheskey	USA	62	5	APM	Hengelo	14 Aug
2:38.01	Kirsty	Wade	UK	62	2	Int	Gateshead	16 Jul
2:38.04	Christina	Cahill	UK	57	3	Int	Gateshead	16 Jul
2:38.16	Elly	van Hulst	HOL	59	6	APM	Hengelo	14 Aug
2:38.17	Claudette	Groenendaal	USA	63	7	APM	Hengelo	14 Aug
2:38.68	Zelda	Botes	RSA	68	1		Stellenbosch	6 Jan
2:38.91	Yvonne	van der Kolk	HOL	69	8	APM	Hengelo	14 Aug
2:38.96	Shireen	Bailey	UK	59	4	Int	Gateshead	16 Jul
2:39.40	Ciska	Swart	RSA	59	2		Stellenbosch	6 Jan
2:40.25	Lynne	MacIntyre	UK	65	5	Int	Gateshead	16 Jul
2:40.45	Ruth	Wysocki	USA	57	9	APM	Hengelo	14 Aug
2:40.51	Lynn	Williams	CAN	60	1		Chiba	15 Sep
Indoor marks								
2:35.5	Laima	Baikauskaite	SU	56	1		Vilnius	31 Jan
2:36.02	Marina	Yachmenyova	SU	61	1	NP	Moskva	20 Feb
2:37.89	Lyubov	Kremlyova	SU	62	2	NP	Moskva	20 Feb
2:38.06	Michelle	Marter-Rohl	USA	65	1		Kansas City	27 Feb
2:38.45	Doina	Melinte	RUM	56	1	Int	Sherbrooke	24 Jan
2:39.62	Tatyana	Samolyenko	SU	61	3	NP	Moskva	20 Feb
2:40.01	Lyudmila	Rogachova	SU	67	4	NP	Moskva	20 Feb

1500 METRES

Mark		Name	Nat	Born	Pos	Meet	Venue	Date
3:53.96	Paula	Ivan	RUM	63	1	OG	Seoul	1 Oct
3:56.22		Ivan			1	WK	Zürich	17 Aug
3:58.80		Ivan			1	GG	Verona	27 Jul
3:58.92	Mary	Slaney	USA	58	1	FOT	Indianapolis	23 Jul
3:59.17		Ivan			1	VD	Bruxelles	19 Aug
4:00.14		Ivan			1	Nik	Nice	10 Jul
4:00.24		Ivan			1	ISTAF	West Berlin	26 Aug
4:00.24	Laima	Baikauskaite	SU	56	2	OG	Seoul	1 Oct
4:00.30	Tatyana	Samolyenko	SU	61	3	OG	Seoul	1 Oct
4:00.46	Regina	Jacobs	USA	63	2	FOT	Indianapolis	23 Jul
4:00.64	Christina	Cahill	UK	57	4	OG	Seoul	1 Oct
4:00.66		Baikauskaite			1	NC	Kiev	2 Aug
4:00.85	Doina	Melinte	RUM	56	2	VD	Bruxelles	19 Aug
4:00.86	Lynn	Williams	CAN	60	5	OG	Seoul	1 Oct
4:00.96	Andrea	Hahmann	GDR	66	6	OG	Seoul	1 Oct
4:01.02	Svetlana	Kitova	(10) SU	60	2	NC	Kiev	2 Aug
4:01.24		Melinte			2	WK	Zürich	17 Aug
4:01.31		Hahmann			1		Potsdam	8 Sep
4:01.49		Kitova			1		Moskva	6 Aug
4:02.32	Shireen	Bailey	UK	59	7	OG	Seoul	1 Oct
4:02.34		Melinte			1	ASV	Köln	21 Aug
4:02.41	Lyubov	Kremlyova	SU	62	3	NC	Kiev	2 Aug

Mark	Name		Nat	Born	Pos	Meet	Venue	Date
4:02.49		Slaney			8	OG	Seoul	1 Oct
4:02.76	Viorica	Ghican	RUM	65	1		Bucuresti	11 Jun
4:02.84		Hahmann			1	GO	Dresden	11 Jun
4:02.84	Marina	Yachmenyeva	SU	61	4	NC	Kiev	2 Aug
4:02.89		Melinte			9	OG	Seoul	1 Oct
4:03.0		Kremlyova			1		Kiev	24 Jun
4:03.29	Kim	Gallagher	USA	64	1		Westwood	3 Sep
4:03.33		Ivan			1h2	OG	Seoul	29 Sep
	(30/15)							
4:03.49	Mitica	Constantin	RUM	62	1	Herc	Monaco	2 Aug
4:03.74	Hildegard	Körner	GDR	59	2		Potsdam	8 Sep
4:04.03	Natalya	Artyomova	SU	63	2	Kuts	Moskva	5 Sep
4:04.25	Ruth	Wysocki	USA	57	3	WK	Zürich	17 Aug
4:04.29	Lyudmila	Rogachova	SU	66	5	NC	Kiev	2 Aug
	(20)							
4:04.36	Iulia	Besliu	RUM	65	2		Bucuresti	11 Jun
4:04.57	Yekaterina	Podkopayeva	SU	52	7	NC	Kiev	2 Aug
4:04.69	Nikolina	Shtereva	BUL	55	1		Stara Zagora	28 Aug
4:04.8	Nadezhda	Olizarenko	SU	53	2	NP	Vladivostok	13 Sep
4:04.87	Heike	Oehme	GDR	63	2	v FRG	Düsseldorf	20 Jun
4:04.88	Elly	van Hulst	HOL	59	3	Nik	Nice	10 Jul
4:04.96	Yelena	Romanova	SU	63	5	Kuts	Moskva	5 Sep
4:05.33	Kirsty	Wade	UK	62	1	v Fra,SU	Portsmouth	19 Jun
4:05.62	Fatima	Aouam	MOR	59	5	WK	Zürich	17 Aug
4:05.78	Angela	Chalmers	CAN	63	2	NC	Ottawa	7 Aug
	(30)							
4:05.89	Lyudmila	Derevyankina	SU	66	8	NC	Kiev	2 Aug
4:05.90	Tamara	Koba	SU	57	9	NC	Kiev	2 Aug
4:05.96	Regina	Chistyakova	SU	61	6	Kuts	Moskva	5 Sep
4:06.18	Vera	Michallek	FRG	58	4	GG	Verona	27 Jul
4:06.2	Olga	Bondarenko	SU	60	4	NP	Vladivostok	13 Sep
4:06.30	Cindy	Grant	CAN	63	3	NC	Ottawa	7 Aug
4:06.34	Yvonne	Murray	UK	64	1	DNG	Stockholm	5 Jul
4:06.40	Ella	Kovacs	RUM	64	5	Nik	Nice	10 Jul
4:06.41	Olga	Nelyubova	SU	64	2	v Fra,UK	Portsmouth	19 Jun
4:06.44	Teresa	Zuñiga	SPA	64	5	Bisl	Oslo	2 Jul
	(40)							
4:06.59	Margrit	Klinger	FRG	60	6	Nik	Nice	10 Jul
4:06.62	Debbie	Bowker	CAN	58	2	Jer	Burnaby	5 Jun
4:06.66	Julie	Jenkins	USA	64	5	FOT	Indianapolis	23 Jul
4:06.94	Lyudmila	Borisova II.	SU	66	7	Kuts	Moskva	5 Sep
4:07.27	Katrin	Wühn	GDR	65	3	v FRG	Düsseldorf	20 Jun
4:07.40	Vicki	Huber	USA	67	1	TAC	Tampa	18 Jun
4:07.41	Linda	Sheskey	USA	62	1	Pepsi	Westwood	6 Jun
4:07.42	Lenuta	Prescura	RUM	66	3		Bucuresti	11 Jun
4:07.51	Brigitte	Kraus	FRG	56	1	Int	Koblenz	1 Jun
4:07.55	Birgit	Barth	GDR	62	2	Int	Rieti	31 Aug
	(50)							
4:07.6	Svetlana	Prodan	SU	61	1		Kharkov	5 Jul
4:07.72	Elena	Fidatov	RUM	60	4	RomIC	Bucuresti	18 Jun
4:07.8	Yelena	Afanasyeva	SU	66	5		Kiev	24 Jun
4:07.94	Violeta	Beclea	RUM	65	5	RomIC	Bucuresti	18 Jun
4:08.05	Olga	Dogadina	SU	59	8	Kuts	Moskva	5 Sep
4:08.08	Cornelia	Bürki	SWZ	53	7	Nik	Nice	10 Jul
4:08.15	Liz	McColgan	UK	64	4	v Ita,SU	Portsmouth	19 Jun
4:08.25	Patricia	Demilly	FRA	59	6	Herc	Monaco	2 Aug
4:08.33	Hassiba	Boulmerka	ALG	68	9h2	OG	Seoul	29 Sep
4:08.35	Tatyana	Pozdnyakova	SU	55	1		Odessa	18 Aug
	(60)							
4:08.46	Beverley	Nicholson	UK	67	4	PTG	London	8 Jul
4:08.56	Margareta	Keszeg	RUM	65	4		Bucuresti	11 Jun
4:08.56	Diana	Richburg	USA	63	4	ASV	Köln	21 Aug
4:08.59	Lyubov	Gurina	SU	57	7h1	OG	Seoul	29 Sep
4:08.8	Zoya	Kaznovskaya	SU	66	2		Kharkov	5 Jul
4:08.86	Yvonne	Grabner	GDR	65	4	OD	Berlin	29 Jun
4:08.90	Galina	Bochkayeva	SU	63	3h1	NC	Kiev	1 Aug

Mark	Name		Nat	Born	Pos	Meet	Venue	Date
4:08.92	Roberta	Brunet	ITA	65	5	OD	Berlin	29 Jun
4:09.15	Sabrina	Dornhoefer	USA	63	2	TAC	Tampa	18 Jun
4:09.20	Mary	Knisely	USA	59	4	Jer	Burnaby	5 Jun
	(70)							
4:09.35	Natalya	Betekhtina	SU	61	1		Bryansk	13 Jul
4:09.37	Robyn	Meagher	CAN	67	5	Jer	Burnaby	5 Jun
4:09.50	Debbie	Marshall	USA	65	5s1	FOT	Indianapolis	21 Jul
4:09.5	Yelena	Zhupiyova	SU	60	1		Kharkov	30 May
4:09.63	Ciska	Swart	RSA	59	1		Port Elizabeth	9 Mar
4:09.68	Nadezhda	Kornyeva	SU	60	11	NC	Kiev	2 Aug
4:09.73	Alisa	Harvey	USA	65	7	FOT	Indianapolis	23 Jul
4:09.74	Liliana	Palade	RUM	67	6		Bucuresti	11 Jun
4:09.80	Paula	Schnurr	CAN	64	1		Victoria	8 Jun
4:09.87	Vera	Nozicková	CS	66	7	OD	Berlin	29 Jun
	(80)							
4:09.93	Ellen	Kiessling	GDR	68	3	NC	Rostock	24 Jun
4:10.04	Valentina	Tauceri	ITA	66	8	GG	Verona	27 Jul
4:10.07	Soraya	Vieira Telles	BRA	58	2	Int	Leverkusen	28 Jun
4:10.13	Susan	Sirma	KEN	66	10h2	OG	Seoul	29 Sep
4:10.33	Darlene	Beckford	USA	61	7s1	FOT	Indianapolis	21 Jul
4:10.4	Rose	Monday	USA	59	1		Santa Monica	1 Jul
4:10.54	Birute	Skurdelite	SU	63	5h1	NC	Kiev	1 Aug
4:10.55	Luminita	Zaituc	RUM	68	7		Bucuresti	11 Jun
4:10.74	Doina	Homneac	RUM	69	7	RomIC	Bucuresti	18 Jun
4:10.81	Vera	Chuvashova	SU	59	10	Kuts	Moskva	5 Sep
	(90)							
4:10.76	Natalya	Sorokivskaya	SU	61	3		Odessa	18 Aug
4:11.03	Marina	Rodchenkova	SU	61	2		Kiev	14 Aug
4:11.11	Svetlana	Meleshkova	SU	62	2		Moskva	6 Aug
4:11.16	Alison	Wyeth	UK	64	7	ISTAF	West Berlin	26 Aug
4:11.2	Sylvia	Mosqueda	USA	66	1		Santa Monica	8 Jul
4:11.4	Leah	Pells	CAN	64	1		Montreal	11 Aug
4:11.41	Elana	van Zyl	RSA	66	2		Port Elizabeth	9 Mar
4:11.46	Lyudmila	Medvedyeva	SU	57	6h1	NC	Kiev	1 Aug
4:11.70	Katalin	Rácz	HUN	65	14	Znam	Leningrad	12 Jun
4:11.71	Malin	Ewerlöf	SWE	72	1	v Fin	Helsinki	4 Sep
	(100)							

Mark	Name		Nat	Born	Date
4:11.75	Kaisa	Siitonen	FIN	60	4 Sep
4:11.86	Marjorie	van der Merwe	RSA	68	9 Mar
4:11.86	Larisa	Zemlyanova	SU	67	1 Aug
4:11.9	Olga	Sinitsyna	SU	64	11 Jul
4:11.9	Sue	Lee	CAN	60	11 Aug
4:12.12	Olga	Parlyuk	SU	63	14 Aug
4:12.16	Sonia	McGeorge	UK	64	8 Jul
4:12.20	Antonina	Babushkina	SU	62	1 Aug
4:12.27	Svetlana	Mashkova	SU	62	6 Aug
4:12.28	Ulla	Marquette	CAN	58	5 Jun
	(110)				
4:12.29	Evelyn	Adiru	UGA	64	18 Jun
4:12.30	Sissel	Grottenberg	NOR	56	2 Jul
4:12.39	Lesley	Lehane	USA	63	4 Jun
4:12.41	Sue	Addison	USA	56	21 Jul
4:12.44	Leslie	Seymour	USA	60	21 Jul
4:12.46	Florence	Giolitti	FRA	66	11 Jun
4:12.47	Tatyana	Nefyodova	SU	66	1 Aug
4:12.49	Marie-Pierre	Duros	FRA	67	2 Aug
4:12.50	Lynne	MacIntyre	UK	65	7 Aug
4:12.6	Tatyana	Lebonda	SU	64	16 Jul
	(120)				
4:12.6	Inna	Yevseyeva	SU	64	13 Jul
4:12.64	Ana	Padurean	RUM	69	18 Jun
4:12.67	Gabriella	Dorio	ITA	57	23 Aug
4:12.72	Wendy	Sly	UK	59	31 Jul
4:12.80	Zita	Agoston	HUN	65	28 Jun
4:12.88	Anette	Westerberg	SWE	60	14 Aug
4:12.95	Carita	Sunell	FIN	68	4 Sep
4:13.12	Gitte	Karlshøj	DEN	59	5 Jun
4:13.21	Alena	Mocáriová	CS	64	25 Jun
4:13.3	Yulia	Galimova	SU	60	11 Jul
	(130)				
4:13.33	Slobodanka	Colovic	YUG	65	26 Jun
4:13.38	Collette	Goudreau	USA	65	16 Apr
4:13.4	Nina	Byelikova	SU	63	11 Jul
4:13.42	Rosalind	Taylor	USA	67	18 Jun
4:13.47	Tatyana	Kalina	SU	63	4 Jun
4:13.5	Svetlana	Agapova	SU	59	14 May
4:13.6	Nathalie	Rouillard	CAN	69	11 Aug
4:13.64	PattiSue	Plumer	USA	62	5 Jun
4:13.72	Annika	Ericson	SWE	60	2 Jul
4:13.73	Yekaterina	Skvortsova	SU	61	5 Sep
	(140)				
4:13.76	Margareta	Ghile	RUM	61	27 Aug
4:13.77	Jana	Kuceríková	CS	64	25 Jun
4:13.78	Slobodanka	Colovic	YUG	65	26 Jun
4:13.84	Claudette	Groenendaal	USA	63	8 Jun
4:13.85	Farida	Sultanova	SU	61	26 Aug
4:13.86	Nela	Vlad	RUM	66	11 Jun
4:13.89	Sue	Foster	USA	61	21 Jul
4:13.90	Tania	Merchiers	BEL	66	30 Jul
4:13.91	Suzy	Favor	USA	68	4 Jun
4:13.98	Yvonne	van der Kolk	HOL	69	28 Jun
	(150)				
4:14.00	Nathalie	Thoumas	FRA	62	24 Jun
4:14.00	Malgorzata	Rydz	POL	67	12 Aug
4:14.02	Vanya	Stoyanova	BUL	58	2 Jul
4:14.07	Montserrat	Pujol	SPA	61	9 Jul
4:14.10	Pam	Raglin	USA	65	18 Jun
4:14.3	Tatyana	Inzhevatova	SU	64	16 Jul
4:14.4	Jill	Purola	CAN	63	11 Aug
4:14.43	Grazyna	Kowina	POL	62	12 Aug

Mark	Name		Nat	Born	Pos	Meet	Venue	Date
Indoor marks								
4:02.3#		Melinte			1	Inv	East Rutherford	13 Feb
4:05.67	Katrin	Wuhn	GDR	65	2	v Ita	Torino	10 Feb
4:06.16	Birgit	Barth	GDR	62	3	v Ita	Torino	10 Feb
4:06.19	Kathrin	Ullrich	GDR	67	4	v Ita	Torino	10 Feb
4:07.06	Brigitte	Kraus	FRG	56	3	EC	Budapest	6 Mar
4:07.88	Katalin	Rácz	HUN	65	1	NC	Budapest	28 Feb
4:09.69	Zita	Agoston	HUN	65	2	NC	Budapest	28 Feb
4:10.68	Vanya	Stoyanova	BUL	58	1	NC	Sofia	20 Feb

Mark	Name		Nat	Born	Date
4:12.63	Rita	Csordós	HUN	67	6 Mar
4:12.72	Anushka	Dimitrova	BUL	62	20 Feb
4:13.79	Christine	Toonstra	HOL	66	14 Feb
4:12.26	Galina	Afonina	SU	63	29 Jan
4:12.4	Zhanna	Tursunova	SU	57	31 Jan

Year List Progression

	1500 Metres					3000 Metres				
Year	Best	10th	20th	50th	100th	Best	10th	20th	50th	100th
1968	4:15.6	4:23.6	4:28.6	4:36.1	4:44.6	9:59.6				
1978	3:59.01	4:02.8	4:04.73	4:11.9	4:16.1	8:32.1	8:46.13	9:00.9	9:12.4	9:20.2
1979	3:57.4	4:01.53	4:05.4	4:09.6	4:14.2	8:31.75	8:46.8	8:55.2	9:08.0	9:16.0
1980	3:52.47	3:59.82	4:02.98	4:07.3	4:13.2	8:33.53	8:44.7	8:52.2	9:00.6	9:16.21
1981	3:57.78	4:01.44	4:03.88	4:08.78	4:13.60	8:34.30	8:49.61	8:53.10	9:01.55	9:11.74
1982	3:54.23	3:59.24	4:03.05	4:07.72	4:13.25	8:26.78	8:36.54	8:46.01	8:55.98	9:08.02
1983	3:57.12	4:01.4	4:03.36	4:08.32	4:12.2	8:32.08	8:37.40	8:47.36	8:55.09	9:05.7
1984	3:56.63	4:00.18	4:01.83	4:06.09	4:10.22	8:22.62	8:37.36	8:42.14	8:52.49	9:01.5
1985	3:57.24	4:02.05	4:04.73	4:09.54	4:12.3	8:25.83	8:42.19	8:48.52	8:58.55	9:05.94
1986	3:56.7	4:02.92	4:04.56	4:06.81	4:12.00	8:33.99	8:39.25	8:46.94	8:56.34	9:04.04
1987	3:58.56	4:01.20	4:04.48	4:07.68	4:11.59	8:38.1	8:42.16	8:46.88	8:56.33	9:03.64
1988	3:53.96	4:01.02	4:04.29	4:07.55	4:11.71	8:26.53	8:37.70	8:44.81	8:52.09	9:01.71

1 MILE

Mark	Name		Nat	Born	Pos	Meet	Venue	Date
4:21.25	Mary	Slaney	USA	58	1	Pre	Eugene	2 Jul
4:22.86		Slaney			1	Int	Malmö	8 Aug
4:25.80	Paula	Ivan	RUM	63	1	IAC	Edinburgh	29 Jul
4:28.24	Ruth	Wysocki	USA	57	2	Int	Malmö	8 Aug
4:28.77	Vicki	Huber	USA	67	3	Int	Malmö	8 Aug
	(5/5)							
4:30.05	Soraya	Vieira Telles	BRA	58	1	PTS	Bratislava	9 Jun
4:30.26	Nikolina	Shtereva	BUL	55	2	PTS	Bratislava	9 Jun
4:30.82	Lyubov	Kremlyova	SU	62	3	PTS	Bratislava	9 Jun
4:31.67	Yekaterina	Podkopayeva	SU	52	4	PTS	Bratislava	9 Jun
4:31.92	Regina	Jacobs	USA	63	2	IAC	Edinburgh	29 Jul
4:32.12	Vera	Michallek	FRG	58	5	PTS	Bratislava	9 Jun
	(10)							

Mark	Name		Nat	Born	Date
4:32.53	Mariana	Stanescu	RUM	64	9 Jun
4:34.00	Katalin	Rácz	HUN	65	9 Jun
4:34.02	Christien	Toonstra	HOL	66	9 Jun
4:34.37	Beverley	Nicholson	UK	67	16 Oct
4:34.68	Lesley	Lehane	USA	63	28 May
4:34.91	Alison	Wyeth	UK	64	29 Jul
4:35.52	Lynne	MacIntyre	UK	65	29 Jul
4:35.54	Leslie	Seymour	USA	60	2 Jul
4:35.57	Marjorie	van der Merwe	RSA	68	1 Feb
4:35.61	Shireen	Bailey	UK	59	16 Oct
4:37.20	Elana	van Zyl	RSA	66	1 Feb
4:38.03	Claudette	Groedendaal	USA	63	2 Jul
4:38.19	Annette	Hand	USA	65	2 Jul
4:38.59	Anette	Westerberg	SWE	60	8 Aug

Mark	Name		Nat	Born	Pos	Meet	Venue	Date
Indoor marks								
4:18.86	Doina	Melinte	RUM	56	1	Inv	East Rutherford	13 Feb
4:21.45		Melinte			1	MillG	New York	5 Feb
4:23.86	Kirsty	Wade	UK	62	2	MillG	New York	5 Feb
4:27.17		Wade			2	Inv	East Rutherford	13 Feb
4:28.08	Elly	van Hulst	HOL	59	1	Int	Sindelfingen	5 Feb
4:28.29	Vera	Michallek	FRG	58	2	Int	Sindelfingen	5 Feb
4:28.31	Vicki	Huber	USA	67	3	MillG	New York	5 Feb
4:31.28	Alisa	Harvey	USA	65	4	MillG	New York	5 Feb
4:31.55	Mitica	Junghiatu	RUM	62	5	MillG	New York	5 Feb
4:31.75	Wendy	Sly	UK	59	6	MillG	New York	5 Feb

Mark	Name		Nat	Born	Date
4:35.97	Suzy	Favor	USA	68	27 Feb
4:36.12	Lynn	Williams	CAN	60	16 Jan
4:36.42	Angela	Chalmers	CAN	63	19 Feb
4:36.91	Christine	Toonstra	HOL	66	5 Feb
4:37.19	Christina	Cahill	UK	57	19 Feb
4:37.99	Debbie	Bowker	CAN	58	23 Jan
4:38.07	Kim	Betz	USA	68	27 Feb
4:38.08	Uta	Eckhardt	FRG	67	5 Feb
4:38.21	Collette	Goudreau	USA	65	30 Jan
4:38.35	Britt	Lind-Petersen	CAN	57	23 Jan
4:38.81	Teena	Colebrook	UK	56	6 Feb
4:38.91	Kathy	Franey	USA	67	12 Mar

Mark	Name		Nat	Born	Pos	Meet	Venue	Date

2000 METRES

Mark	Name		Nat	Born	Pos	Meet	Venue	Date
5:28.63#	Liz	McColgan	UK	64	1'	Nik	Nice	10 Jul
5:36.65	Mary	Slaney	USA	58	1		San Diego	25 Jun
5:41.99	Mary	Knisely	USA	59	2		San Diego	25 Jun
5:44.08#	Vicki	Huber	USA	67	1'	OG	Seoul	25 Sep
5:44.13#	Yvonne	Murray	UK	64	2'	OG	Seoul	25 Sep
5:44.24#	Paula	Ivan	RUM	63	3'	OG	Seoul	25 Sep
5:44.41#	Elly	van Hulst	HOL	59	4'	OG	Seoul	25 Sep
5:44.42#		Slaney			5'	OG	Seoul	25 Sep
5:44.43#	Tatyana	Samolyenko	SU	61	6'	OG	Seoul	25 Sep
5:44.55#	Lynn	Williams	CAN	60	7'	OG	Seoul	25 Sep
5:44.67#	Yelena	Romanova	SU	63	8'	OG	Seoul	25 Sep
	(10)							
5:44.71#	Natalya	Artyomova	SU	63	9'	OG	Seoul	25 Sep
5:45.86#	Wendy	Sly	UK	59	10'	OG	Seoul	25 Sep
5:49.92	Angela	Chalmers	CAN	63	3		San Diego	25 Jun
5:50.27	Monica	Joyce	IRL	58	4		San Diego	25 Jun

time during 3000 metres race

3000 METRES

Mark	Name		Nat	Born	Pos	Meet	Venue	Date
8:26.53	Tatyana	Samolyenko	SU	61	1	OG	Seoul	25 Sep
8:27.15	Paula	Ivan	RUM	63	2	OG	Seoul	25 Sep
8:29.02	Yvonne	Murray	UK	64	3	OG	Seoul	25 Sep
8:30.45	Yelena	Romanova	SU	63	4	OG	Seoul	25 Sep
8:31.67	Natalya	Artyomova	SU	63	5	OG	Seoul	25 Sep
8:33.97	Elly	van Hulst	HOL	59	1	WK	Zürich	17 Aug
8:34.69	Mary	Slaney	USA	58	2	WK	Zürich	17 Aug
8:37.22		Murray			1	Nik	Nice	10 Jul
8:37.25	Vicki	Huber	USA	67	6	OG	Seoul	25 Sep
8:37.30	Lynn	Williams	CAN	60	3	WK	Zürich	17 Aug
8:37.70	Wendy	Sly (10)	UK	59	7	OG	Seoul	25 Sep
8:38.43		Williams			8	OG	Seoul	25 Sep
8:39.28		Williams			2	Nik	Nice	10 Jul
8:41.54	Iulia	Besliu	RUM	65	1	v Rus	Bucuresti	19 Jun
8:42.19		Artyomova			1rA	NC	Kiev	30 Jul
8:42.39	Viorica	Ghican	RUM	54	1		Bucuresti	12 Jun
8:42.44		Romanova			2rA	NC	Kiev	30 Jul
8:42.50	Liz	McColgan	UK	64	1	Int	Belfast	27 Jun
8:42.53		Slaney			1	FOT	Indianapolis	17 Jul
8:42.99		McColgan			3	Nik	Nice	10 Jul
8:43.09	Regina	Chistyakova	SU	61	3rA	NC	Kiev	30 Jul
8:43.10		Ivan			1h2	OG	Seoul	23 Sep
8:43.48		Samolyenko			1	WG	Helsinki	30 Jun
8:43.59	Ingrid	Kristiansen	NOR	56	2	Int	Belfast	27 Jun
8:43.70		Ghican			2	v Rus	Bucuresti	19 Jun
8:43.73		McColgan			1	vD	Bruxelles	19 Aug
8:43.73		Murray			2h2	OG	Seoul	23 Sep
8:43.81	Debbie	Bowker	CAN	58	3h2	OG	Seoul	23 Sep
8:43.82		Artyomova			2	WG	Helsinki	30 Jun
8:43.92		van Hulst			9	OG	Seoul	25 Sep
	(30/16)							
8:43.95	Olga	Bondarenko	SU	60	4rA	NC	Kiev	30 Jul
8:44.19	Annette	Sergent	FRA	62	4	Nik	Nice	10 Jul
8:44.79	Yelena	Zhupiyova	SU	60	1	Kuts	Moskva	4 Sep
8:44.81	Kathrin	Ullrich	GDR	67	4	WG	Helsinki	30 Jun
	(20)							
8:44.91	Sabrina	Dornhoefer	USA	63	1		Victoria	8 Jun
8:45.21	PattiSue	Plumer	USA	62	7h2	OG	Seoul	23 Sep
8:45.69	Marina	Rodchenkova	SU	61	6rA	NC	Kiev	30 Jul
8:45.81	Cornelia	Bürki	SWZ	53	4	DNG	Stockholm	5 Jul
8:46.28	Mariana	Stanescu	RUM	64	3	RomIC	Bucuresti	19 Jun
8:47.36	Jill	Hunter	UK	66	6	WK	Zürich	17 Aug
8:47.45	Mary	Knisely	USA	59	3		Victoria	8 Jun

Mark	Name		Nat	Born	Pos	Meet	Venue	Date
8:47.53	Yulia	Galimova	SU	60	7rA	NC	Kiev	30 Jul
8:47.59	Angela	Tooby	UK	60	5	DNG	Stockholm	5 Jul
8:47.62	Vera	Michallek	FRG	58	6	DNG	Stockholm	5 Jul
	(30)							
8:47.66	Roberta	Brunet	ITA	65	1	Int	Rieti	31 Aug
8:47.7	Christine	Pfitzinger	NZ	59	1		Auckland	15 Mar
8:47.9	Marie-Pierre	Duros	FRA	67	1		Saint Maur	20 Jul
8:47.94	Natalya	Lagunkova	SU	59	8rA	NC	Kiev	30 Jul
8:48.19	Lynn	Jennings	USA	60	2	VD	Bruxelles	19 Aug
8:48.2	Natalya	Sorokivskaya	SU	61	1		Odessa	20 Aug
8:48.60	Angela	Chalmers	CAN	63	3h1	OG	Seoul	23 Sep
8:49.98	Marina	Pluzhnikova	SU	62	4	v Rum	Bucuresti	19 Jun
8:49.98	Yelena	Plastinina	SU	63	9rA	NC	Kiev	30 Jul
8:50.24	Elena	Fidatov	RUM	60	1		Bucuresti	10 Jul
	(40)							
8:50.26	Lenuta	Pescura	RUM	66	2		Bucuresti	12 Jun
8:50.67	Tamara	Koba	SU	57	2		Kiev	16 Aug
8:50.74	Tatyana	Pozdnyakova	SU	56	10rA	NC	Kiev	30 Jul
8:50.94	Andrea	Hahmann	GDR	66	1		Jena	3 Jun
8:51.04	Birgit	Barth	GDR	62	1	v FRG	Düsseldorf	19 Jun
8:51.07	Tuija	Jousimaa	FIN	58	5	WG	Helsinki	30 Jun
8:51.53	Chen	Qingmei	CHN	63	11h2	OG	Seoul	23 Sep
8:51.84	Francie	Larrieu Smith	USA	52	1		Chiba	11 Sep
8:51.96	Margareta	Keszeg	RUM	65	6	RomIC	Bucuresti	19 Jun
8:52.09	Lyubov	Kremlyova	SU	62	1		Tallinn	10 Jul
	(50)							
8:52.39	Nadezhda	Styepanova	SU	59	3	v Fra,UK	Portsmouth	19 Jun
8:53.00	Eva	Kadas	RUM	59	7	RomIC	Bucuresti	19 Jun
8:53.85	Maricica	Puica	RUM	50	2	Int	Rieti	31 Aug
8:54.62	Farida	Sultanova	SU	61	3	Znam	Leningrad	11 Jun
8:54.82	Ilinca	Oprita	RUM	64	3		Bucuresti	12 Jun
8:54.84	Elana	van Zyl	RSA	66	1		Stellenbosch	18 Mar
8:55.11	Lynn	Nelson	USA	62	5	VD	Bruxelles	19 Aug
8:55.12	Zita	Agoston	HUN	65	8	RomIC	Bucuresti	19 Jun
8:55.45	Cindy	Grant	CAN	63	1		Montreal	9 Aug
8:55.69	Claudia	Borgschulze	FRG	64	2	Int	Koblenz	1 Jun
	(60)							
8:55.85	Ruth	Wysocki	USA	57	6	WG	Helsinki	30 Jun
8:55.93	Cathie	Twomey	USA	56	6	VD	Bruxelles	19 Aug
8:56.48	Veronique	Collard	BEL	63	7	VD	Bruxelles	19 Aug
8:56.48	Päivi	Tikkanen	FIN	60	1		Tampere	23 Aug
8:56.51	Alison	Wiley	CAN	63	2		Montreal	9 Aug
8:56.90	Irina	Matrosova	SU	62	12rA	NC	Kiev	30 Jul
8:56.99	Lyudmila	Borisova II.	SU	66	3		Kiev	16 Aug
8:57.0	Sue	Lee	CAN	60	1		Victoria	23 Jul
8:57.25	Collette	Goudreau	USA	65	1	MSR	Walnut	23 Apr
8:57.56	Sirje	Eichelmann	SU	55	3		Tallinn	10 Jul
	(70)							
8:57.69	Carole	Rouillard	CAN	60	3		Montreal	9 Aug
8:57.88	Angelines	Rodriguez	SPA	69	2	Int	Barcelona	13 Jul
8:58.19	Yvonne	Grabner	GDR	65	3	v FRG	Düsseldorf	19 Jun
8:58.2	Svetlana	Poltorak	SU	60	2		Kiev	24 Jun
8:58.28	Elena	Murgoci	RUM	60	4	NC	Pitesti	11 Aug
8:59.0	Sylvia	Mosqueda	USA	66	1		Santa Monica	29 Jul
8:59.04	Rosario	Murcia	FRA	64	5	BNP	Villeneuve d'Ascq	27 Jun
8:59.15	Annette	Hand	USA	65	2	NCAA	Eugene	3 Jun
8:59.19	Fatima	Aouam	MOR	59	1	AfrC	Annaba	1 Sep
8:59.19	Ulrike	Bruns	GDR	53	1		Potsdam	9 Sep
	(80)							
8:59.21	Yelena	Tolstoguzova	SU	62	2		Bryansk	13 Jul
8:59.41	Radka	Naplatanova	BUL	57	1	PTS	Bratislava	9 Jun
8:59.56	Ulla	Marquette	CAN	58	9	DNG	Stockholm	5 Jul
8:59.65	Kathy	Hayes	USA	62	7		Victoria	8 Jun
8:59.78	Jana	Kuceriková	CS	64	2	PTS	Bratislava	9 Jun
8;59.78	Doina	Homneac	RUM	69	9	RomIC	Bucuresti	19 Jun
9:00.0	Erika	Veréb	HUN	63	2	NC	Miskolc	17 Jul

Mark	Name		Nat	Born	Pos	Meet	Venue	Date
9:00.23	Natalya	Boborova	SU	59	4rB	NC	Kiev	30 Jul
9:00.29	Joan	Nesbit	USA	62	2		Dedham	2 Jul
9:00.36	Sonia	McGeorge	UK	64	6	Int	Belfast	27 Jun
	(90)							
9:00.38	Fernanda	Ribeiro	POR	69	2	Int	Saint Denis	7 Jun
9:00.40	M. Albertina	Dias	POR	65	3	Int	Saint Denis	7 Jun
9:00.74	Jane	Shields	UK	60	2	Int	Dublin	12 Jul
9:00.88	Ann	Keenan-Buckley	IRL	62	7	Int	Belfast	27 Jun
9:00.93	Lyubov	Fyodorova	SU	65	5rB	NC	Kiev	30 Jul
9:01.00	Anne	Schweitzer	USA	65	5	Jenn	San Jose	28 May
9:01.5	M. Albertina	Machado	POR	61	1		Pontevedra	3 Sep
9:01.60	Nina	Byelikova	SU	63	6	Znam	Leningrad	11 Jun
9:01.67	Melissa	Watson	UK	64	8	Int	Belfast	27 Jun
9:01.71	Maria	Curatolo	ITA	63	10	DNG	Stockholm	5 Jul
	(100)							

Mark	Name		Nat	Born	Date
9:01.76	Sabine	Kunkel	FRG	64	25 Jun
9:01.82	Jackie	Perkins	AUS	65	23 Sep
9:02.18	Andri	Avraam	CYP	63	23 Sep
9:02.23	Nicola	Morris	UK	62	16 Jul
9:02.32	Malin	Ewerlöf	SWE	72	19 Jun
9:02.53	Vera	Nozicková	CS	66	8 Sep
9:02.59	Gitte	Karlshoj	DEN	59	8 Jun
9:02.63	Ana I.	Alonso	SPA	63	28 Aug
9:02.66	Monika	Hamhalterová	CS	66	9 Jun
9:02.91	Tania	Merchiers	BEL	66	11 Jun
	(110)				
9:02.94	Susan	Tooby	UK	60	13 Jul
9:03.10	Antje	Winkelmann	FRG	65	9 Jun
9:03.10	Agnes	Sergent	FRA	59	13 Aug
9:03.45	Li Suni		CHN	62	23 Oct
9:03.46	Christin	Sørum	NOR	68	19 Jun
9:03.51	Olga	Sinitsyna	SU	64	13 Jul
9:03.72	Maree	McDonagh	AUS	67	17 Mar
9:04.1	Aurora	Cunha	POR	59	-3 Jul
9:04.15	Malin	Wästlund	SWE	64	19 Jun
9:04.32	M.Conceição	Ferreira	POR	62	7 Aug
	(120)				
9:04.46	Corine	Debaets	BEL	63	4 Sep
9:04.5	Dolores	Rizo	SPA	68	3 Sep
9:04.56	Farida	Fates	FRA	62	13 Aug
9:04.69	Kristina	Ljungberg	SWE	64	19 Jun
9:04.90	Robyn	Meagher	CAN	67	9 Jul
9:05.15	Christien	Toonstra	HOL	66	28 Aug
9:05.37	Alena	Mocariova	CS	64	16 Jul
9:05.5	Natalya	Solomiskaya	SU	61	20 Aug
9:05.53	Miyoko	Asahina	JAP	69	23 Oct
9:05.67	Anke	Schäning	GDR	70	20 Jul
	(130)				
9:05.87	Ellen	Kiessling	GDR	68	26 Jun
9:06.0	Alisa	Harvey	USA	65	21 May
9:06.01	Rosanna	Munerotto	ITA	62	6 Sep
9:06.03	Lisa	Weidenbach	USA	61	9 Jul
9:06.16	Helen	Titterington	UK	69	19 Jun
9:06.16	Olga	Nazarkina	SU	70	14 Aug
9:06.43	Monica	Joyce	IRL	58	5 Jul
9:06.64	Mary	Donohue	IRL	62	27 Jun
9:06.7	Susan	Sirma	KEN	66	12 Aug
9:06.99	Lieve	Slegers	BEL	65	11 Jun
	(140)				
9:07.00	Gulnara	Faizullina	SU	65	30 Jul
9:07.13	Gabriele	Veith	GDR	56	26 Jun
9:07.23	Monika	Lieske	GDR	66	19 Jun
9:07.5	Tatyana	Sokolova	SU	58	27 Aug
9:07.67	Karen	Hartmann	GDR	70	20 Jul
9:07.68	Lisa	Welch	USA	63	2 Jul
9:07.79	Nedka	Keremedzhieva	BUL	60	3 Jul
9:07.86	Penny	Graves	USA	66	7 May
9:07.88	Stefa	Statkuviene	SU	63	10 Jul
9:08.00	Isabella	Moretti	SWZ	63	28 Jun
	(150)				
9:08.05	Martine	Oppliger	SWZ	57	28 Jun
9:08.06	Nadia	Dandolo	ITA	62	6 Sep
9:08.07	Rita	Delnoye	HOL	66	23 Apr
9:08.31	Ingrid	Delagrange	BEL	58	5 Jun
9:08.33	Tanya	Peckham	RSA	66	12 Nov
9:08.47	Yvonne	Lichtenfeld	GDR	69	20 Jul
9:08.63	Nina	Anikiyenko	SU	58	30 Jul
9:08.95	Trina	Leopold	USA	66	18 Jun

Indoor marks

Mark	Name		Nat	Born	Pos	Meet	Venue	Date
8:41.79	Kathrin	Ullrich	GDR	67	1	v Aut,Yug	Wien	13 Feb
8:45.00	Andrea	Lange-Hahmann	GDR	66	2	v Aut,Yug	Wien	13 Feb
8:46.97	Vera	Michallek	FRG	58	2	EI	Budapest	6 Mar
8:49.90	Brenda	Webb	USA	54	1	Inv	Johnson City	22 Jan

Mark	Name		Nat	Born	Date
9:01.82	Kirsty	Wade	UK	62	6 Mar
9:05.81	Christine	McMiken	NZ	63	26 Feb
9:07.02	Ragnheidur	Olafsdóttir	ICE	63	12 Mar
9:07.30	Vanya	Stoyanova	BUL	58	6 Mar

5000 METRES

Mark	Name		Nat	Born	Pos	Meet	Venue	Date
15:03.29	Liz	McColgan	UK	64	1	ISTAF	West Berlin	26 Aug
15:10.17		McColgan			1	NC	Derby	5 Jun
15:10.89	Ingrid	Kristiansen	NOR	56	2	ISTAF	West Berlin	26 Aug
15:11.16	Olga	Bondarenko	SU	60	1	Kuts	Moskva	5 Sep
15:11.83	Lynn	Jennings	USA	60	1	AP	Hengelo	14 Aug
15:12.7	Lynn	Nelson	USA	62	1	Pre	Eugene	2 Jul
15:15.2	Francie	Larrieu Smith	USA	52	2	Pre	Eugene	2 Jul
15:16.83	Natalya	Sorokivskaya	SU	61	2	Kuts	Moskva	5 Sep
15:17.02	Cathie	Twomey	USA	56	2	AP	Hengelo	14 Aug
15:17.77	Jill	Hunter	UK	66	3	ISTAF	West Berlin	26 Aug
15:17.89	Angela	Tooby	UK	60	2	NC	Derby	5 Jun
15:18.24	Annette	Sergent	FRA	62	4	ISTAF	West Berlin	26 Aug

Mark	Name		Nat	Born	Pos	Meet	Venue	Date
15:18.71	Brenda	Webb	USA	54	1	TAC	Tampa	17 Jun
15:19.06#		Kristiansen			1'	Bisl	Oslo	2 Jul
15:19.2 #		McColgan			2'	Bisl	Oslo	2 Jul
15:20.23	Kathrin	Ullrich	GDR	67	1	v FRG	Düsseldorf	20 Jun
15:23.77	Natalya	Artyomova	SU	63	1		Leningrad	19 Jun
15:24.12		Nelson			3	AP	Hengelo	14 Aug
15:25.53		A.Tooby			1	GG	Verona	27 Jul
15:25.84	Martine	Oppliger	SWZ	57	5	ISTAF	West Berlin	26 Aug
15:26.2	Sue	Lee	CAN	60	3	Pre	Eugene	2 Jul
15:27.4		Twomey			4	Pre	Eugene	2 Jul
	(22/16)							
15:30.95	Sabrina	Dornhoefer	USA	63	4	AP	Hengelo	14 Aug
15:31.0	Kellie	Cathey	USA	61	5	Pre	Eugene	2 Jul
15:32.34	Jane	Shields	UK	60	3	NC	Derby	5 Jun
15:32.6	PattiSue	Plumer	USA	62	6	Pre	Eugene	2 Jul
	(20)							
15:33.3	Nan	Davis	USA	62	7	Pre	Eugene	2 Jul
15:34.55	Annette	Hand	USA	65	1		Eugene	30 Apr
15:34.78	Viorica	Ghican	RUM	65	2	GG	Verona	27 Jul
15:35.4	Kathy	Hayes	USA	62	8	Pre	Eugene	2 Jul
15:36.05	Yelena	Tolstoguzova	SU	62	3	Kuts	Moskva	5 Sep
15:37.70	Marina	Pluzhnikova	SU	63	1	Znam	Leningrad	12 Jun
15:38.08	Radka	Naplatanova	BUL	57	3	Znam	Leningrad	12 Jun
15:38.17#	Yelena	Zhupiyova	SU	60	2'	OG	Seoul	30 Sep
15:38.81	Kerstin	Pressler	FRG	62	2	v GDR	Düsseldorf	20 Jun
15:40.14	Gabriele	Veith	GDR	56	3=	v FRG	Düsseldorf	20 Jun
	(30)							
15:40.14	Antje	Winkelmann	FRG	65	3=	v GDR	Düsseldorf	20 Jun
15:40.25	Lyudmila	Matveyeva	SU	57	5		Leningrad	18 Jun
15:40.48	Marina	Rodchenkova	SU	61	6	Znam	Leningrad	12 Jun
15:41.36	Erika	Veréb	HUN	63	1	NC	Miskolc	15 Jul
15:41.42	Jackie	Goodman	NZ	68	2	NCAA	Eugene	4 Jun
15:42.40	Irina	Matrosova	SU	62	8	Znam	Leningrad	12 Jun
15:42.67	Wanda	Panfil	POL	59	1	Mal	Grudziadz	21 Jun
15:43.05	Nadezhda	Styepanova	SU	59	9	Znam	Leningrad	12 Jun
15:43.67	Alena	Mocáriová	CS	64	2	Mal	Grudziadz	21 Jun
15:44.0 #	Lesley	Lehane	USA	63	1'		Dedham	11 Jun
	(40)							
15:44.11	Monika	Hamhalterová	CS	66	3	Mal	Grudziadz	21 Jun
15:44.15	Elana	van Zyl	RSA	66	1		Stellenbosch	6 Jan
15:44.16	Lizanne	Bussières	CAN	61	1		Sherbrooke	18 Jun
15:44.2 #	Yekaterina	Khramenkova	SU	56	.'	NC	Kiev	2 Aug
15:44.25	Rita	Delnoye	HOL	66	1	Int	Hechtel	30 Jul
15:44.98	Gulnara	Faizullina	SU	65	11	Znam	Leningrad	12 Jun
15:45.2	Lisa	Weidenbach	USA	61	9	Pre	Eugene	2 Jul
15:45.23	Monica	Joyce	IRE	58	1		Santa Monica	20 May
15:45.28	Lieve	Slegers	BEL	65	2	Int	Hechtel	30 Jul
15:45.96	Jackie	Perkins	AUS	65	2	BGP	Budapest	12 Aug
	(50)							

Mark	Name		Nat	Born	Date
15:46.22	Márta	Visnyei	HUN	62	24 Aug
15:46.3	Marty	Cooksey	USA	54	2 Jul
15:46.50	Betty	Geiger	USA	61	17 Jun
15:47.07	Akemi	Matsuno	JAP	68	22 Oct
15:48.0	Yelena	Plastinina	SU	63	25 Jun
15:48.22	Zhong Huandi		CHN	66	10 Jun
15:48.61	Kristina	Ljungberg	SWE	64	4 Jun
15:49.22#	M. Albertina	Machado	POR	61	30 Sep
15:49.26	Angelines	Rodriguez	SPA	69	9 Apr
15:49.4	Natalya	Boborova	SU	59	25 Jun
	(60)				
15:49.68#	Wang Xiuting		CHN	65	30 Sep
15:49.85	Nina	Anikiyenko	SU	58	12 Jun
15:50.41	Penny	Graves	USA	66	4 Jun
15:50.60	Rosanna	Munerotto	ITA	62	10 Jul
15:51.10	Nadezhda	Tatarenkova	SU	68	12 Jun
15:51.40	Vera	Michallek	FRG	58	25 May
15:51.61	Iulia	Negura	RUM	67	21 Jun
15:52.17	Trina	Leopold	USA	66	4 Jun
15:52.28	Georgeta	State	RUM	65	21 Jun
15:52.61	Christine	McMiken	NZ	63	30 Apr
	(70)				
15:53.4	Irina	Yagodina	SU	64	17 Jul
15:53.73	Nadezhda	Ilyina	SU	64	12 Jun
15:53.91	Tatyana	Polovinskaya	SU	65	5 Sep
15:54.01	Sylvia	Mosqueda	USA	66	4 Jun
15:54.10	Grethe	Fosse	NOR	59	14 Aug
15:55.33	Maria	Lantsova	SU	62	14 Sep
15:55.34#	Wang Qinghuan		CHN	65	30 Sep

time during 10000 metres race

Indoor mark

Mark	Name	Pos	Meet	Venue	Date
15:25.02	Webb	1	Inv	Gainesville	30 Jan

Unverified mark: 15:29.0 Anne Hannam NZ 61 1 Auckland 30 Nov

10 000 METRES

Mark	Name		Nat	Born	Pos	Meet	Venue	Date
31:05.21	Olga	Bondarenko	SU	60	1	OG	Seoul	30 Sep
31:06.99	Liz	McColgan	UK	64	1	Bisl	Oslo	2 Jul
31:08.44		McColgan			2	OG	Seoul	30 Sep
31:19.82	Yelena	Zhupiyova	SU	60	3	OG	Seoul	30 Sep
31:26.79	Kathrin	Ullrich	GDR	67	1	NC	Potsdam	8 Jun
31:29.27		Ullrich			4	OG	Seoul	30 Sep
31:31.37	Ingrid	Kristiansen	NOR	56	2	Bisl	Oslo	2 Jul
31:35.52	Francie	Larrieu Smith	USA	52	5	OG	Seoul	30 Sep
31:38.02	Lyudmila	Matveyeva	SU	57	1	NC	Kiev	2 Aug
31:38.63		Bondarenko			2	NC	Kiev	2 Aug
31:39.93	Lynn	Jennings	USA	60	6	OG	Seoul	30 Sep
31:40.23	Wang Xiuting		CHN	65	7	OG	Seoul	30 Sep
31:40.88		Zhupiyova			3	NC	Kiev	2 Aug
31:42.02	Yekaterina	Khramenkova (10)	SU	56	4	NC	Kiev	2 Aug
31:42.8	Lesley	Lehane	USA	63	1		Dedham	11 Jun
31:44.69		Kristiansen			1h1	OG	Seoul	26 Sep
31:46.43	Natalya	Sorokivskaya	SU	62	5	NC	Kiev	2 Aug
31:46.72		Bondarenko			1	Int	Tokyo	8 Oct
31:47.67		Bondarenko			2h1	OG	Seoul	26 Sep
31:47.99		Zhupiyova			3h1	OG	Seoul	26 Sep
31:48.63		Zhupiyova			2	Int	Tokyo	8 Oct
31:49.6		Sorokivskaya			1		Kiev	24 Jun
31:50.51	Sue	Lee	CAN	60	8	OG	Seoul	30 Sep
31:51.27	Lynn	Nelson	USA	62	1	FOT	Indianapolis	22 Jul
31:51.40		Ullrich			4h1	OG	Seoul	26 Sep
31:51.42		Lee			5h1	OG	Seoul	26 Sep
31:52.02		Larrieu Smith			6h1	OG	Seoul	26 Sep
31:52.04	M. Albertina	Machado	POR	61	7h1	OG	Seoul	26 Sep
31:53.36	Wendy	Sly	UK	59	3	Int	Tokyo	8 Oct
31:55.67	Chen Qingmei		CHN	63	4	Int	Tokyo	8 Oct
	(30/17)							
31:56.33	Natalya	Artyomova	SU	63	6	NC	Kiev	2 Aug
32:04.52	Wang Qinghuan	CHN	65	8h1	OG	Seoul	26 Sep	
32:04.78	Annette	Sergent	FRA	62	4	Bisl	Oslo	2 Jul
	(20)							
32:05.8	Anne	Audain	NZ	55	1		Auckland	1 Mar
32:06.14	Collette	Goudreau	USA	65	1rA	Penn	Philadelphia	28 Apr
32:06.76	Rosanna	Munerotto	ITA	62	9h1	OG	Seoul	26 Sep
32:07.13	M. Albertina	Dias	POR	65	10	OG	Seoul	30 Sep
32:08.32	Malin	Wästlund	SWE	64	5	Bisl	Oslo	2 Jul
32:09.08	Carole	Rouillard	CAN	60	10h1	OG	Seoul	26 Sep
32:10.05	Carolyn	Schuwalow	AUS	65	11h1	OG	Seoul	26 Sep
32:11.49	Marleen	Renders	BEL	68	13h1	OG	Seoul	26 Sep
32:11.62	Päivi	Tikkanen	FIN	60	6	Bisl	Oslo	2 Jul
32:12.2	Yelena	Tolstoguzova	SU	62	2		Kiev	24 Jun
	(30)							
32:14.05	Nan	Davis	USA	62	4	FOT	Indianapolis	22 Jul
32:14.05	Nancy	Tinari	CAN	59	13	OG	Seoul	30 Sep
32:14.50	Erika	Veréb	HUN	63	7	Bisl	Oslo	2 Jul
32:15.88	Lisa	Weidenbach	USA	61	5	FOT	Indianapolis	22 Jul
32:16.50	Natalya	Boborova	SU	59	7	NC	Kiev	2 Aug
32:17.58	Natalya	Lagunkova	SU	59	8	NC	Kiev	2 Aug
32:17.74	Natalya	Solominskaya	SU	61	9	NC	Kiev	2 Aug
32:19.50	Zoya	Ivanova	SU	52	8	Bisl	Oslo	2 Jul
32:12.57	Akemi	Matsuno	JAP	68	9h2	OG	Seoul	26 Sep
32:19.62	Nadezhda	Styepanova	SU	59	10	NC	Kiev	2 Aug
	(40)							
32:19.77	Maria	Curatolo	ITA	63	9	Bisl	Oslo	2 Jul
32:20.39	Christine	McMiken	NZ	63	10h2	OG	Seoul	26 Sep
32:20.7	Elena	Murgoci	RUM	60	1		Bucuresti	10 Jul
32:20.95	Susan	Tooby	UK	60	10	Bisl	Oslo	2 Jul
32:23.11	Nadezhda	Ilyina	SU	64	11	NC	Kiev	2 Aug

Mark	Name		Nat	Born	Pos	Meet	Venue	Date
32:23.20	Tatyana	Polovinskaya	SU	65	1		Sochi	1 Jun
32:28.26	Martine	Oppliger	SWZ	57	14h1	OG	Seoul	26 Sep
32:28.57	Sylvia	Mosqueda	USA	66	1	NCAA	Eugene	1 Jun
32:28.6	M. Conceição	Ferreira	POR	62	.	NC	Lisboa	23 Apr
32:28.7	Ana I.	Alonso	SPA	63	1		Vigo	30 Jul
	(50)							
32:33.04	Betty	Geiger	USA	61	6	FOT	Indianapolis	22 Jul
32:33.9	Aurora	Cunha	POR	59	2		Vigo	30 Jul
32:34.05	Evy	Palm	SWE	42	1	v Fin	Helsinki	4 Sep
32:34.68	Midde	Hamrin	SWE	57	2	v Fin	Helsinki	4 Sep
32:35.33	Kerstin	Pressler	FRG	62	12	Bils	Oslo	2 Jul
32:36.3	Monica	Joyce	IRL	58	2	MSR	Walnut	23 Apr
32:37.51	Marciana	Mukamurenzi	RWA	59	1	FraC	Tours	13 Aug
32:38.11	Cathie	Twomey	USA	56	7	FOT	Indianapolis	22 Jul
32:38.88	Maria	Lelut	FRA	56	2	NC	Tours	13 Aug
32:40.17	Lorraine	Moller	NZ	55	1		Dedham	2 Jul
	(60)							
32:40.35	Marty	Cooksey	USA	54	8	FOT	Indianapolis	22 Jul
32:42.0	Jane	Shields	UK	60	2	???	London	24 Aug
32:42.25	Kathy	Hayes	USA	62	9	FOT	Indianapolis	22 Jul
32:42.69	Yelena	Plastinina	SU	63	13	NC	Kiev	2 Aug
32:44.16	Stepanie	Herbst	USA	65	2	NCAA	Eugene	1 Jun
32:44.52	Anke	Schäning	GDR	70	2	NC	Potsdam	8 Jun
32:45.42	Lizanne	Bussières	CAN	61	14	Bisl	Oslo	2 Jul
32:47.54	Veronique	Collard	BEL	63	16	Bisl	Oslo	2 Jul
32:47.86	Sirje	Eichelmann	SU	55	14	NC	Kiev	2 Aug
32:48.15	Elly	van Hulst	HOL	59	5	Int	Tokyo	8 Oct
	(70)							
32:49.78	Lieve	Slegers	BEL	65	17	Bisl	Oslo	2 Jul
32:50.01	Raisa	Smekhnova	SU	50	15	NC	Kiev	2 Aug
32:51.37	Jocelyne	Villeton	FRA	54	3	NC	Tours	13 Aug
32:51.61	Danièle	Kaber	LUX	60	18	Bisl	Oslo	2 Jul
32:52.86	Kirsten	O'Hara	USA	65	3	NCAA	Eugene	1 Jun
32:55.16	Tuija	Jousimaa	FIN	58	1	NC	Hameenlinna	5 Aug
32:55.55	Teresa	Ornduff	USA	56	10	FOT	Indianapolis	22 Jul
32:55.73	Françoise	Bonnet	FRA	57	4	NC	Tours	13 Aug
32:57.38	Patty	Murray	USA	65	1	DrakeR	Des Moines	30 Apr
32:58.33	Zita	Agoston	HUN	65	2	NC	Budapest	22 May
	(80)							
32:58.60	Kellie	Cathey	USA	61	11	FOT	Indianapolis	22 Jul
32:59.30	Andri	Avraam	CYP	63	12h2	OG	Seoul	26 Sep
32:59.6	Kathy	Pfiefer	USA	59	3	MSR	Walnut	23 Apr
33:01.5	Lisa	Welch	USA	63	2		Dedham	11 Jun
33:01.52	Hassania	Darami	MOR	56	13h2	OG	Seoul	26 Sep
33:01.6	Judy	Chamberlin	USA	58	6	MSR	Walnut	23 Apr
33:02.4	Tatyna	Zuyeva	SU	58	1		Odessa	18 Aug
33:03.2	Antje	Winkelmann	FRG	65	1		Obersuhl	12 Oct
33:03.8	Kazue	Kojima	JAP	65	1		Mito	29 May
33:04.2	Farida	Sultanova	SU	61	3		Kiev	24 Jun
	(90)							
33:04.75	Yuki	Tamura	JAP	66	2	NC	Tokyo	18 Jun
33:05.02	Eleanor	Simonsick	USA	58	12	FOT	Indianapolis	22 Jul
33:05.07	Izumi	Maki	JAP	68	2		Kyoto	18 Oct
33:05.13	Janet	Smith	USA	65	4	NCAA	Eugene	1 Jun
33:05.43	Elspeth	Turner	UK	65	5	NCAA	Eugene	1 Jun
33:07.08	Renata	Kokowska	POL	58	1		Sopot	30 Jul
33:08.1	Kim	Jones	USA	58	1		Seattle	8 Jun
33:09.3	Jana	Kucerίková	CS	64	1		Banská Bystrica	26 Aug
33:10.82	Radka	Naplatanova	BUL	57	1	NC	Plovdiv	22 May
33:11.31	Barbara	Moore	NZ	57	1	NC	Hamilton	11 Mar
	(100)							

Mark	Name		Nat	Born	Date
33:11.58	Anuta	Catuna	RUM	68	19 Jun
33:11.8	Martha	Jimenez	MEX	65	23 Apr
33:12.56	Kumi	Araki	JAP	65	1 May
33:12.70	Isabella	Moretti	SWZ	63	22 Aug
33:13.38	Carol	Gray	USA	68	1 Jun
33:13.95	Angela	Tooby	UK	60	7 Aug
33:14.0	Hiromi	Satoyama	JAP	67	29 May
33:14.98	Susan	Sirma	KEN	66	1 May
33:16.4	Irina	Matrosova	SU	62	18 Aug
33:17.00	Naomi	Watanabe	JAP	68	18 Oct
	(110)				
33:17.5	Olga	Nazarkina	SU	70	27 May

Mark	Name		Nat	Born	Date
33:18.8	Alena	Mocáriová	CS	64	26 Aug
33:19.08	Rebecca	Rivkin	USA	68	1 Jun
33:19.8	Marina	Pluzhnikova	SU	62	24 Jun
33:20.09	Liz	Natale	USA	64	28 Apr
33:20.52	Zhong Huandi		CHN	67	12 Jun
33:21.38	Zhao Youfeng		CHN	65	18 Jun
33:21.75	Grete	Kirkeberg	NOR	64	2 Jul
33:22.19	Maria	Starovská	CS	59	15 Jul
33:22.81	Monika (120)	Hamhalterová	CS	66	15 Jul
33:23.4	Marjan	Freriks	HOL	61	3 Sep
33:23.75	Svetlana	Poltorak	SU	60	2 Aug
33:25.19	Sirkku	Kumpulainen	FIN	56	4 Sep
33:25.2	Iulia	Negura	RUM	67	10 Jul
33:25.3	Monica	Gama	POR	70	23 Apr
33:25.4	Ana Paula	Oliveira	POR	70	23 Apr
33:26.96	Li Xiuxia		CHN	65	12 Jun
33:27.48	Karen	Lutzke	USA	62	30 Apr
33:27.9	Cyndie	Welte	USA	61	11 Jun
33:27.93	Vanya (130)	Stoyanova	BUL	58	22 May
33:28.13	Xie Lihua		CHN	64	30 Sep
33:28.67	Sinikka	Keskitalo	FIN	51	5 Aug
33:29.33	Birgit	Jerschabek	GDR	69	8 Jun
32:29.97	Márta	Visnyei	HUN	62	22 May
33:30.00	Svetlana	Kuznyetsova	SU	61	12 Jul
33:30.16	Patty	Matava	USA	65	22 Jul
33:31.25	Anna	Iskra	POL	62	30 Jul
33:31.35	Sue	Schroeder	USA	63	20 May
33:31.96	Eileen	Donaghy	USA	66	1 Jun
33:32.00	Irena (140)	Czuta	POL	66	30 Jul
33:32.73	Naomi	Yoshida	JAP	69	18 Oct
33:33.6	Elena	Evanoff	CAN	64	23 Apr
33:33.74	Satoe	Minegishi	JAP	62	18 Oct
33:33.91	Yelena	Tsukhlo	SU	54	2 Aug
33:33.95	Diane	Rodger	NZ	56	11 Mar
33:34.1	Genoveva	Dominguez	MEX	65	23 Apr
33:34.7	Maria Luisa	Servin	MEX	62	23 Apr
33:34.99	Xiao Hongyan		CHN	65	12 Jun
33:35.1	Linda	Begley	USA	59	11 Jun
33:35.1	Martha (150)	Geissler	USA	63	11 Jun
33:35.41	Ragnheidur	Olafsdóttir	ICE	63	27 Mar
33:35.90	Nedka	Keremedzhieva	BUL	60	22 May
33:35.96	Suzanne	Eberle	USA	62	28 Apr
33:36.4	Emma	Scaunich	ITA	54	6 Jul
33:37.0	Jennifer	Christiansen	CAN	68	23 Apr
33:37.04	Tatyana	Gridnyeva	SU	58	2 Aug
33:37.4	Aisling	Ryan	IRL	69	23 Apr
33:37.8	Mary	Alico	USA	63	23 Apr
33:39.0	Nancy	Ditz	USA	51	Mar
33:39.07	Alevtina (160)	Chasova	SU	61	2 Aug

Unconfirmed: 32:04.0 Malin Wästlund SWE 64

WOMEN 1988

10000 Metres — Year List Progression — Marathon

Year	Best	10th	20th	50th	100th	Marathon Best	10th	50th	100th
1978	31:45.4	34:41.0				2:32:30	2:44:52	2:53:15	
1979	32:52.5	34:32.8				2:27:33	2:39:37	2:47:33	2:53:46
1980	32:57.17	33:48.49	34:25.3			2:25:42	2:35:06	2:44:28	2:49:08
1981	32:17.19	33:01.5	33:28.20			2:25:29	2:33:13	2:42:12	2:45:47
1982	31:35.3	32:36.96	33:14.6	34:15.5		2:26:11	2:33:36	2:38:44	2:43:19
1983	31:27.58	32:23.04	33:02.37	33:40.5	34:43.8	2:22:43	2:31:12	2:36:31	2:38:52
1984	31:13.78	32:30.91	32:50.6	33:34.7	34:26.36	2:24:26	2:29:10	2:34:49	2:37:29
1985	30:59.42	32:25.62	32:45.58	33:28.36	33:59.39	2:21:06	2:28:38	2:35:27	2:38:17
1986	30:13.74	31:56.59	32:22.63	32:47.25	33:29.46	2:24:54	2:29:51	2:34:41	2:37:58
1987	31:05.85	31:46.61	32:18.24	32:46.14	33:19.20	2:22:48	2:29:56	2:33:22	2:37:06
1988	31:05.21	31:42.02	32:04.78	32:28.7	33:11.31	2:23:51	2:28:40	2:31:56	2:35:29

MARATHON

Mark	Name		Nat	Born	Pos	Meet	Venue	Date
2:23:51	Lisa	Martin	AUS	12.5.60	1		Osaka	31 Jan
2:24:30	Rosa	Mota	POR	29.6.58	1		Boston	18 Apr
2:25:40		Mota			1	OG	Seoul	23 Sep
2:25:41	Ingrid	Kristiansen	NOR	21.3.56	1	NC	London	17 Apr
2:25:53		Martin			2	OG	Seoul	23 Sep
2:26:21	Katrin	Dörre	GDR	6.10.61	3	OG	Seoul	23 Sep
2:27:05	Tatyana	Polovinskaya	SU	14.3.65	4	OG	Seoul	23 Sep
2:27:06	Zhao Youfeng		CHN	5.5.65	5	OG	Seoul	23 Sep
2:27:49	Laura	Fogli	ITA	5.10.59	6	OG	Seoul	23 Sep
2:27:56		Zhao			1		Nagoya	6 Mar
2:28:02		Polovinskaya			1	NC	Tallinn	26 Jun
2:28:07	Grete	Waitz	NOR	1.10.53	1		New York	6 Nov
2:28:11	Ria	Van Landeghem	BEL	19.7.57	1		St. Paul	2 Oct
2:28:24		Waitz			1	NC	Stockholm	4 Jun
2:28:28		Dörre			1	ECp	Huy	30 Apr
2:28:40	Raisa	Smekhnova (10)	SU	16.9.50	2	ECp	Huy	30 Apr
2:28:58	Carolina	Beurskens	HOL	10.2.52	2		Nagoya	6 Mar
2:29:16	Renata	Kokowska	POL	4.12.58	1		Berlin (West)	9 Mar
2:29:17	Lisa	Weidenbach	USA	13.12.61	1		Chicago	30 Oct
2:29:19	Birgit	Stephan	FRG	27.9.64	3		Nagoya	6 Mar
2:29:23	Danièle	Kaber	LUX	20.4.60	7	OG	Seoul	23 Sep
2:29:26	Tuija	Jousimaa	FIN	22.9.58	2		Boston	18 Apr
2:29:37	Misako	Miyahara	JAP	29.5.62	2		Osaka	31 Jan

Mark	Name		Nat	Born	Pos	Meet	Venue	Date
2:29:37	Zoya	Ivanova	SU	14.3.52	3	ECp	Huy	30 Apr
2:29:46	Emma	Scaunich	ITA	1.3.54	2		Chicago	30 Oct
2:29:47	Paula	Fudge (20)	UK	30.3.52	3		Chicago	30 Oct
2:29:49	Alevtina	Chasova	SU	16.1.61	1		Uzhgorod	17 Apr
2:29:50	Margaret	Groos	USA	21.9.59	1	NC	Pittsburgh	1 May
2:30:09	Vera	Sukhova	SU	9.7.63	1		Belaja Cerkov	7 Oct
2:30:14	Nancy	Ditz	USA	25.6.54	2	NC	Pittsburgh	1 May
	(30/24)							
2:30:14	Maria	Curatolo	ITA	12.10.63	8	OG	Seoul	23 Sep
2:30:18	Cathy	O'Brien	USA	19.7.67	3	NC	Pittsburgh	1 May
2:30:23	Charlotte	Teske	FRG	23.11.49	1	NC	Hamburg	24 Apr
2:30:23	Deborah	Raunig	USA	23.9.55	2		St. Paul	2 Oct
2:30:27	Yekaterina	Khramenkova	SU	6.10.54	2	NC	Tallinn	26 Jun
2:30:35	Odette	Lapierre	CAN	28.1.55	3		Boston	18 Apr
	(30)							
2:30:37	Kerstin	Pressler	FRG	2.2.62	2	NC	Hamburg	24 Apr
2:30:38	Ann	Ford	UK	30.3.52	2	NC	London	17 Apr
2:30:51	Angela	Pain	UK	8.2.62	10	OG	Seoul	23 Sep
2:30:53	Priscilla	Welch	UK	22.11.44	4		Boston	18 Apr
2:30:57	Karolina	Szabó	HUN	17.11.61	1	NC	Szeged	26 Mar
2:30:57	Lizanne	Bussières	CAN	20.8.61	5		Boston	18 Apr
2:30:59	Valentina	Yegorova	SU	16.2.54	1		Ufa	10 Sep
2:31:08	Margherita	Marchisio	ITA	13.2.50	1		Carpi	9 Oct
2:31:09	Julie	Isphording	USA	5.12.61	1		Columbus	13 Nov
2:31:19	Tani	Ruckle	AUS	25.6.62	4		Chicago	30 Oct
	(40)							
2:31:21	Antonella	Bizioli	ITA	29.3.57	1		Cesano Boscone	13 Nov
2:31:23	Silvana	Cucchietti	ITA	30.12.57	2		Carpi	9 Oct
2:31:26	Aurora	Cunha	POR	31.5.59	1		Tokyo	20 Nov
2:31:33	Susan	Tooby	UK	24.10.60	12	OG	Seoul	23 Sep
2:31:35	Evy	Palm	SWE	31.1.42	3	NC	London	17 Apr
2:31:35	Hélène	Rochefort	CAN	22.11.54	6		Boston	18 Apr
2:31:40	Kumi	Araki	JAP	11.10.65	3		Osaka	31 Jan
2:31:43	Xie Lihua		CHN	19.7.65	4		Nagoya	6 Mar
2:31:44	Li Juan		CHN	10.10.66	1		Tianjin	4 Mar
2:31:56	Gabriela	Wolf	FRG	28.10.60	3	NC	Hamburg	24 Apr
	(50)							
2:32:03	Kim	Jones	USA	2.5.58	5		Chicago	30 Oct
2:32:11	Lesley	Lehane	USA	12.3.63	3		St. Paul	2 Oct
2:32:13	Eriko	Asai	JAP	20.10.59	4		Osaka	31 Jan
2:32:20	Uta	Pippig	GDR	7.9.65	2		Tokyo	20 Nov
2:32:23	Wanda	Panfil	POL	26.1.59	1	NC	Debno	27 Mar
2:32:29	Kellie	Cathey	USA	24.11.61	6		Chicago	30 Oct
2:32:30	Irina	Yagodina	SU	24.4.64	3	NC	Tallinn	26 Jun
2:32:31	Francie	Larrieu-Smith	USA	23.11.52	2		Columbus	13 Nov
2:32:36	Françoise	Bonnet	FRA	8.4.57	14	OG	Seoul	23 Sep
2:32:40	Joan	Samuelson	USA	16.5.57	3		New York	6 Nov
	(60)							
2:32:48	Yelena	Tsukhlo	SU	13.5.54	5	ECp	Huy	30 Apr
2:32:51	Lee Mi-ok		SKO	10.3.68	15	OG	Seoul	23 Sep
2:32:53	Maureen	Roben	USA	31.8.55	4		St. Paul	2 Oct
2:32:53	Maria	Lelut	FRA	29.1.56	3		Tokyo	20 Nov
2:33:03	Elena	Murgoci	RUM	20.5.60	1	NC	Bucuresti	22 Sep
2:33:19	Li Yemei		CHN	25.5.66	2		Tianjin	4 Mar
2:33:31	Lynn	Nelson	USA	8.1.62	8	NC	Pittsburgh	1 May
2:33:36	Veronique	Marot	FRA	16.6.55	3		Columbus	13 Nov
2:33:39	Annette	Falkson	RSA	8.10.57	1		Kaapstad	30 Apr
2:33:44	Sheila	Catford	UK	29.8.60	2		Berlin (West)	9 Oct
	(70)							
2:33:54	Malgorzata	Birbach	POL	17.2.60	3		Berlin (West)	9 Oct
2:33:56	Marie-Louise	Hamrin	SWE	19.4.57	9		Chicago	30 Oct
2:33:58	Agnes	Öze Sipka	HUN	14.8.54	2	NC	Szeged	26 Mar
2:34:02	Jocelyne	Villeton	FRA	17.9.54	19	OG	Seoul	23 Sep
2:34:04	Ludmila	Melicherová	CS	6.6.64	5		Nagoya	6 Mar
2:34:09	Sirye	Eichelmann	SU	16.7.55	2		Belaja Cerkov	7 Oct
2:34:12	Sinikka	Keskitalo	FIN	29.1.51	7		Boston	18 Apr

Mark	Name		Nat	Born	Pos	Meet	Venue	Date
2:34:18	Janis	Klecker	USA	18.7.60	1		Sacramento	4 Dec
2:34:23	Conçeicão	Ferreira	POR	13.3.52	20	OG	Seoul	23 Sep
2:34:25	Irina	Sklyarenko	SU	7.11.61	2		Uzhgorod	17 Apr
	(80)							
2:34:26	Susan	Marchiano	USA	5.11.54	10	NC	Pittsburgh	1 May
2:34:26	Heather	MacDuff	UK	17.5.58	1		Eindhoven	16 Oct
2:34:30	Lyutsia	Belyayeva	SU	22.6.57	3		Uzhgorod	17 Apr
2:34:33	Irina	Petrova	SU	12.1.62	4		Uzhgorod	17 Apr
2:34:35	Chen	Qingmei	CHN	4.4.63	5		Tokyo	20 Nov
2:34:36	Luzia	Sahli	SWZ	27.5.56	1		Zürich	24 Apr
2:34:38	Yoshiko	Hidaka	JAP	30.12.65	8		Osaka	31 Jan
2:34:41	Marguerite	Buist	NZ	29.12.62	6		Tokyo	20 Nov
2:34:43	Genoveva	Eichenmann	SWZ	12.9.57	2		Zürich	24 Apr
2:34:52	Linda	Zeman	USA	4.11.60	1		Houston	17 Jan
	(90)							
2:34:59	Annette	Fincke	GDR	10.10.63	9	ECp	Huy	30 Apr
2:35:00	Tatyana	Fedorova	SU	18.5.60	3		Belaja Cerkov	7 Oct
2:35:06	Jeanette	Hain	GDR	7.12.66	10	ECp	Huy	30 Apr
2:35:10	Susan	Crehan	UK	12.9.56	5	NC	London	17 Apr
2:35:12	Irina	Ruban	SU	4.8.62	4	NC	Tallinn	26 Jun
2:35:23	Laurie	Crisp	USA	28.3.61	11	NC	Pittsburgh	1 May
2:35:24	Sirkku	Kumpulainen	FIN	12.1.56	8		Boston	18 Apr
2:35:26	Rosmarie	Müller	SWZ	27.3.58	3		Zurich	24 Apr
2:35:26	Ursula	Starke	FRG	16.4.56	5	NC	Hamburg	24 Apr
2:35:29	Krystyna	Chylinska	POL	18.11.64	2	NC	Debno	27 Mar
	(100)							

Mark	Name		Nat	Born	Date
2:35:36	Magda	Ilands	BEL	50	30 Apr
2:35:37	Teresa	Ornduff	USA	56	1 May
2:35:44	Grete	Kirkeberg	NOR	64	30 Oct
2:35:45	Irina	Bogacheva	SU	62	20 Nov
2:35:52	Tove	Lorentzen	DEN	60	17 Apr
2:36:02	Graziella	Striuli	ITA	49	3 Jul
2:36:02	Zhong Huan-Di		CHN	67	23 Sep
2:36:04	Jacqueline	Gareau	CAN	53	17 Apr
2:36:08	Jane	Welzel	USA	55	1 May
2:36:11	Blanca	Jaime	MEX	65	6 Mar
	(110)				
2:36:12	Yu Qiuli		CHN	67	4 Mar
2:36:30	Márta	Visnyei	HUN	62	9 Oct
2:36:45	Rita	Borralho	POR	54	17 Jan
2:36:48	Dagmar	Knudsen	FRG	56	24 Apr
2:36:49	Glynis	Penny	UK	51	10 Apr
2:36:50	Terry	Puckett	USA	56	30 Oct
2:36:51	Ewa	Szydlowska	POL	60	27 Mar
2:36:53	Marcianne	Mukamurenzi	RWA	59	15 May
2:36:58	Gabriela	Gorzynska	POL	56	9 Oct
2:36:59	Sylviane	Geffray	ITA	53	30 Apr
	(120)				
2:36:59	Sonja	Laxton	RSA	48	28 Aug
2:37:03	Jennifer	Colgrove	USA	61	1 May
2:37:04	Dimitra	Papaspirou	GRE	64	9 Oct
2:37:06	Moira	O'Neill	UK	56	31 Oct
2:37:10	Rosemary	Ellis	UK	53	17 Apr
2:37:11	Cesarina	Taroni	ITA	49	9 Oct
2:37:12	Jillian	Costley	NZ	61	6 Mar
2:37:12	Lyubov	Svirskaya	SU	60	9 Oct
2:37:13	Leatrice	Hayer	USA	55	1 May
2:37:19	Czeslawa	Mentlewicz	POL	56	24 Apr
	(130)				
2:37:21	Rosella	Di Dionisio	ITA	63	9 Oct
2:37:24	Annabel	Holtkamp	FRG	55	30 Oct
2:37:28	Maria	Trujillo	USA	59	1 May
2:37:34	Miho	Yamauchi	JAP	63	31 Jan
2:37:36	Sandra	Mewett	UK	49	17 Jan
2:37:36	Tatyana	Gridneva	SU	58	30 Oct
2:37:37	Lyudmila	Petrova	SU	66	10 Sep
2:37:38	Angelicade	Almeida	BRA	63	26 Jun
2:37:42	Wang Qing-Huan		CHN	65	17 Apr
2:37:44	Gordon	Bakoulis	USA	61	1 May
	(140)				
2:37:46	Xiao Hong-Yan		CHN	65	17 Apr
2:37:49	Allison	Gooderham	UK	60	17 Apr
2:37:50	Yasuko	Hashimoto	JAP	65	31 Jan
2:37:52	Christa	Vahlensieck	FRG	49	10 Apr
2:37:52	Lorraine	Moller	NZ	55	23 Sep
2:37:55	Marie	Rollins	IRL	59	6 Feb
2:37:59	Ngaire	Drake	NZ	49	6 Mar
2:38:00	Sally	Ellis	UK	58	31 Jan
2:38:00	Madina	Biktagirova	SU	64	25 Apr
2:38:13	Gizella	Molnár	HUN	58	26 Mar
	(150)				
2:38:13	Mary	Alico	USA	63	1 May
2:38:15	Zoya	Gavrilyuk	SU	59	17 Apr
2:38:16	Lisa	Brady	USA	63	10 Oct
2:38:21	Lim Eun-joo		SKO	61	23 Sep
2:38:24	Ann	Roden	UK	46	9 Oct
2:38:31	Nadezhda	Yerokhina	SU	56	17 Apr
2:38:35	Marty	Cooksey	USA	54	
2:38:42	Janice	Ettle	USA	58	1 May
2:38:42	Angelike	Dunke	FRG	55	9 Oct
2:38:44	Sandra	Branney	UK	54	31 Oct
	(160)				
2:38:48	Susan	Stone	CAN	60	18 Apr
2:38:56	Irina	Kazakova	SU	68	17 Apr
2:39:01	Cindy	Girard	USA	61	1 May
2:39:11	Glenys	Quick	NZ	57	6 Mar
2:39:23	Maija	Vuorinen	FIN	52	24 Apr
2:39:23	Kamila	Gradus	POL	67	27 Mar
2:39:25	Chiemi	Kashiwagi	JAP	60	31 Jan
2:39:28	Jenni	Peters	USA	55	17 Jan
2:39:30	Machiko	Inoguchi	JAP	66	6 Mar
2:39:30	Susan	Jackson	USA	58	1 May
	(170)				

Downhill Point-to-Point Courses

Boston (USA) has a net drop of 116 m between start (120 m) and finish (4 m)

Notable Altitude Performances

Mark	Name		Nat	Born	Pos	Venue	Date
2:41:16	Sonja	Laxton	RSA	6.8.48	1	Johannesburg (1753m)	10 Oct
2:42:49	Frith	van der Merwe	RSA		2	Johannesburg	10 Oct

100 METRES HURDLES

Mark		Name		Nat	Born	Pos	Meet	Venue	Date
12.21	0.7	Yordanka	Donkova	BUL	61	1		Stara Zagora	20 Aug
12.24	0.9		Donkova			1s		Stara Zagora	28 Aug
12.27	-1.2		Donkova			1		Stara Zagora	28 Aug
12.36	1.1		Donkova			1	Int	Schwechat	15 Jun
12.38	0.2		Donkova			1	OG	Seoul	30 Sep
12.45	0.0		Donkova			1	BGP	Budapest	12 Aug
12.47	1.2		Donkova			1	PTS	Bratislava	9 Jun
12.47	0.5		Donkova			1	NarM	Sofia	26 Jun
12.47	1.3		Donkova			1q2	OG	Seoul	29 Sep
12.48	0.6		Donkova			1=	Int	Reims	4 Jun
12.48	0.6	Ginka	Zagorcheva	BUL	58	1=	Int	Reims	4 Jun
12.48	-0.5	Gloria	Siebert	GDR	64	1h3	Znam	Leningrad	12 Jun
12.48	-1.0	Natalya	Grigoryeva	SU	61	1	Znam	Leningrad	12 Jun
12.50	1.2		Zagorcheva			2	PTS	Bratislava	9 Jun
12.50	-1.0		Siebert			2	Znam	Leningrad	12 Jun
12.50	0.9		Donkova			1	4-N	Praha	2 Jul
12.52	1.4		Siebert			1		Cottbus	29 May
12.52	2.0	Cornelia	Oschkenat	GDR	61	1	NC	Rostock	24 Jun
12.53	-0.2		Donkova			1	Int	Saint Denis	7 Jun
12.58	-1.9		Oschkenat			1	v FRG	Düsseldorf	20 Jun
12.58	0.5		Donkova			1s1	OG	Seoul	30 Sep
12.59	-0.7		Zagorcheva			1h2	Int	Saint Denis	7 Jun
12.59	1.7		Oschkenat			1rA	GO	Dresden	11 Jun
12.59	0.8		Oschkenat			1	OD	Berlin	29 Jun
12.60	0.5		Siebert			2s1	OG	Seoul	30 Sep
12.60	-0.2		Donkova			1	Int	Tokyo	8 Oct
12.61	1.1	Gail	Devers	USA	66	1h1	Pac10	Westwood	21 May
12.61	0.2	Jackie	Joyner-Kersee	USA	62	1	Jenn	San Jose	28 May
12.61	0.2		Siebert			2	OG	Seoul	30 Sep
12.62	0.9	Lyudmila	Narozhilenko	SU	64	1		Sochi	1 Jun
12.62	0.9		Oschkenat			1rB	GO	Dresden	11 Jun
12.62	1.2		Donkova			1h2	Int	Schwechat	15 Jun
12.62	1.3		Narozhilenko			2q1	OG	Seoul	29 Sep
		(33/8)							
12.70	0.8	Kerstin	Knabe	GDR	59	2	OD	Berlin	29 Jun
12.73	-1.0	Yelena	Politika	SU	64	4	Znam	Leningrad	12 Jun
		(10)							
12.75	0.4	Claudia	Zaczkiewicz	FRG	62	2s2	OG	Seoul	30 Sep
12.76	0.0	Lynda	Tolbert	USA	67	1rA	WK	Zürich	17 Aug
12.78A	1.3	Julie	Rocheleau	CAN	64	1		Provo	21 May
12.79	1.0	Mihaela	Pogacian	RUM	58	1	Int	Hamamatsu	8 May
12.82	0.8	Sally	Gunnell	UK	66	1rB	WK	Zürich	17 Aug
12.83	-0.3	Svetlana	Buraga	SU	65	1H		Staiki	1 Jul
12.83	1.9	Patricia	Davis	USA	65	1s1	FOT	Indianapolis	22 Jul
12.83	1.4	Jackie	Humphrey	USA	65	1s2	FOT	Indianapolis	22 Jul
12.83	-0.4	Marjan	Olyslager	HOL	62	1	VD	Bruxelles	19 Aug
12.84	0.5	Kim	McKenzie	USA	61	1	TAC	Tampa	17 Jun
		(20)							
12.84	1.0	Florence	Colle	FRA	65	1h1	NC	Tours	14 Aug
12.85	0.1	LaVonna	Martin	USA	66	2	NCAA	Eugene	4 Jun
12.85	0.5	Benita	Fitzgerald-Brown	USA	61	2	TAC	Tampa	17 Jun
12.85	0.5	Sabine	John	GDR	57	2H	OG	Seoul	23 Sep
12.87	1.7	Yelizaveta	Chernysheva	SU	58	1h		Bryansk	12 Ju
12.87	1.6	Natalya	Tochilova	SU	64	1		Bryansk	12 Ju
12.87	1.0	Monique	Ewanje-Epée	FRA	67	2h1	NC	Tours	14 Aug
12.89	1.9	Pam	Page	USA	58	2q2	FOT	Indianapolis	21 Ju
12.91	0.2	Laurence	Elloy	FRA	59	2	Nik	Nice	10 Ju
12.93	-0.1	Liu Huajin		CHN	60	6	Znam	Leningrad	12 Jun
		(30)							
12.94	0.8	Kerstin	Patzwahl	GDR	65	3	OD	Berlin	29 Jun
12.94	-0.4	Anne	Piquereau	FRA	64	1	Herc	Monaco	2 Aug
12.94	0.1	Galina	Khaustova	SU	65	.s		Kiev	14 Aug

Mark		Name		Nat	Born	Pos	Meet	Venue	Date
12.95	-0.5	Ulrike	Denk	FRG	64	2	NC	Frankfurt	23 Jul
12.96	0.7	Liliana	Nastase	RUM	62	1	Int	Auckland	27 Feb
12.96	1.6	Aliuska	López	CUB	69	1s1	WJ	Sudbury	29 Jul
12.99	-1.9	Lidia	Okolo-Kulak	SU	67	4h2	Znam	Leningrad	12 Jun
13.00	0.8	Irina	Svetonosova	SU	68	2h1	NC	Tallinn	5 Jul
13.00	1.6	Marina	Azyabina	SU	63	3		Bryansk	12 Jul
13.00	1.4	Stephanie	Hightower	USA	59	3s2	FOT	Indianapolis	22 Jul
		(40)							
13.01	2.0	Heike	Theele	GDR	64	4	NC	Rostock	24 Jun
13.07	-0.9	Natalya	Kolovanova	SU	64	2		Kharkov	18 Jun
13.08A	1.3	Annemarie	le Roux	RSA	63	1		Johannesburg	23 Apr
13.08	0.8	Rosalind	Council	USA	65	3	Gator	Knoxville	21 May
13.08	-0.8	Natalya	Shubenkova	SU	57	H		Staiki	1 Jul
13.08	1.2	Carla	Tuzzi	ITA	67	5	v GDR	Neubrandenburg	9 Jul
13.09	1.4	Rhonda	Blanford	USA	63	4s2	FOT	Indianapolis	22 Jul
13.09	0.3	Gabriele	Lippe	FRG	67	2s2	NC	Frankfurt	23 Jul
13.10A	1.3	Ina	van Rensburg	RSA	56	2		Johannesburg	23 Apr
13.10	1.6	Chantal	Beaugeant	FRA	61	H	Int	Götzis	18 Jun
		(50)							
13.10	0.2	Rita	Heggli	SWZ	62	5	Nik	Nice	10 Jul
13.11	-0.9	Tatyana	Styepanova	SU	67	3		Kharkov	18 Jun
13.11	0.8	Anke	Behmer	GDR	61	H	Int	Talence	16 Jul
13.12		Marina	Grishina	SU	62	.h		Moskva	7 May
13.13	0.5	Donna	Waller	USA	64	4	TAC	Tampa	17 Jun
13.14	1.9	Yolanda	Johnson	USA	68	4q2	FOT	Indianapolis	21 Jul
13.16	0.4	Lyudmila	Oliyar	SU	62	1		Pärnu	13 Jul
13.17	0.8	Jane	Flemming	AUS	65	H	Int	Talence	16 Jul
13.18	-1.1	Eva	Sokolova	SU	62	3h2	Znam	Leningrad	12 Jun
13.18		Galina	Makarova	SU	60	1		Odessa	19 Aug
		(60)							
13.19	-1.7	Lesley-Ann	Skeete	UK	67	2	WAAA	Birmingham	7 Aug
13.20		Odalys	Adams	CUB	66	1		Habana	11 Jun
13.20	-0.9	Irina	Matyusheva	SU	65	H		Staiki	1 Jul
13.21	-0.9	Alla	Knyazeva	SU	64	4		Kharkov	18 Jun
13.21	2.0	Yulia	Filippova	SU	70	1h	NC-j	Bryansk	6 Jul
13.22	-0.8	Tananjalyn	Stanley	USA	67	1h2	SEC	Auburn	14 May
13.22	2.0	Nadezhda	Chistyakova	SU	69	2h	NC-j	Bryansk	6 Jul
13.23		Irina	Dobrenko	SU	65	.h		Moskva	7 May
13.23		Elisabeta	Anghel	RUM	67	H		Bucuresti	21 May
13.24	1.2	Svetla	Dimitrova	BUL	70	1H	OG	Seoul	23 Sep
		(70)							
13.25	1.9	Sabine	Everts	FRG	61	1H	NC	Rhede	9 Jul
13.27	-0.9	Lyudmila	Khristosenko	SU	66	5		Kharkov	18 Jun
13.27	0.8	Sibylle	Thiele	GDR	65	H	Int	Talence	16 Jul
13.27	1.4	Gayle	Watkins	USA	58	7s2	FOT	Indianapolis	22 Jul
13.27	-0.5	Angelika	Kuhmann	FRG	57	4	NC	Frankfurt-am-Main	23 Jul
13.27	1.0	Isabelle	Kaftandjian	FRA	64	3h1	NC	Tours	14 Aug
13.28	0.4	Birgit	Wolf	FRG	69	2		Sindelfingen	2 Jul
13.28	1.1	Gordana	Cotric	YUG	68	1	NC	Sarajevo	3 Sep
13.29A		Ilse	Luneburg	RSA	65	3		Germiston	24 Mar
13.29	1.2	Sylvia	Dethier	BEL	65	1		Genève	6 Aug
		(80)							
13.29	0.0	Marianna	Maslennikova	SU	61	5		Kiev	14 Aug
13.30	0.9	Kim	Hagger	UK	61	1		Irvine	1 May
13.30	1.0	Lyubov	Stolyar	SU	65	4h2	NC	Tallinn	5 Jul
13.30	1.4	Dawn	Bowles	USA	69	8s2	FOT	Indianapolis	22 Jul
13.31	1.8	Zhanna	Gurbanova	SU	69	2	NC-j	Bryansk	6 Jul
13.31		Gretha	Tromp	HOL	64	.s	NC	Groningen	17 Jul
13.31	0.1	Yekaterina	Gorbatova	SU	68	.s		Kiev	14 Aug
13.32	0.1	Schowonda	Williams	USA	66	5	NCAA	Eugene	4 Jun
13.32	1.2	Irina	Tyukhay	SU	67	H	NC	Kiev	1 Aug
13.32	1.2	Xénia	Siska	HUN	57	1		Budapest	5 Aug
		(90)							
13.32	0.5	Wendy	Jeal	UK	60	2	Int	Athinai	3 Sep
13.35	-0.1	Jitka	Tesárková	CS	65	1		Praha	9 Jul
13.35	-1.2	Vera	Ordina	SU	68	1		Leningrad	12 Aug

Mark		Name		Nat	Born	Pos	Meet	Venue	Date
13.36	1.1	Sabine	Seitl	AUT	65	3	Int	Schwechat	15 Jun
13.36	0.2	Candy	Young	USA	62	3h2	TAC	Tampa	16 Jun
13.37	-0.1	Irina	Antonova	SU	60	2		Moskva	7 Aug
13.38		Ine	Langehuizen	HOL	68	.s	NC	Groningen	17 Jul
13.38		Tatyana	Dolgaya	SU	64	H	NP	Tashkent	3 Sep
13.39	-2.4	Du Juan		CHN	68	2h1	Znam	Leningrad	12 Jun
13.39	1.2	Patricia	Lombardo	ITA	58	8	v GDR	Neubrandeburg	9 Jul
		(100)							
13.39	0.5	Karen	Nelson	CAN	64	1		Burnaby	27 Jul
13.39	-1.2	Svetlana	Yermilova	SU	59	2		Leningrad	12 Aug
13,39	1.6	Ilona	Dumitrascu	RUM	62	2	NC	Pitesti	14 Aug

Mark		Name	Nat	Born	Date
13.40A	1.3	Riana Raath	RSA	61	23 Apr
13.40A		Sandra Tavares	MEX	62	21 May
13.41	1.9	Alicia Bass	USA	65	2 Jun
13.42	0.9	Patricia Girard	FRA	68	1 Jul
13.43	1.3	Peggy Beer	GDR	69	29 May
13.43	-1.6	Feng Yinghua	CHN	66	1 Sep
13.44	0.0	Kerstin Poltrock	FRG	64	2 Jun
		110)			
13.44	1.9	Ulrike Kleindl	AUT	63	15 Jun
13.44	1.1	Svetla Trichkova	BUL	68	15 Jun
13.44	1.6	Lyudmila Kustyumova	SU	67	12 Jul
13.44		Tineke Hidding	HOL	59	23 Jul
13.46	0.4	Remigia Sablovskaite	SU	67	1 Aug
13.46		Dinah Yankey	GHA	67	19 Sep
13.47	1.8	Petra Vaideanu	RUM	65	16 Jul
13.47	0.7	Monica Pellegrinelli	SWZ	65	21 Aug
13.47	1.1	Margita Papic	YUG	61	3 Sep
13.48	1.1	Leticia Beverly	USA	67	8 May
		(120)			
13.48A	1.3	LaTanya Sheffield	USA	63	21 May
13.48	-0.5	Bridgette Tate	USA	66	2 Jun
13.48	0.1	Silke Nahler	FRG	66	23 Jul
13.48	1.4	Gudrun Lattner	FRG	59	23 Jul
13.49	0.0	Elisavet Pantazi	GRE	56	8 May
13.49	0.3	Margit Palombi	HUN	61	18 Jun
13.49	2.0	Tatyana Kryukova	SU	70	6 Jul
13.49	0.4	Maryse Ewanje-Epée	FRA	64	16 Jul
13.49	0.5	Karen Cannon	USA	58	3 Sep
13.50A		Janet Harvey	USA	61	14 May
		(130)			
13.50		Mary Cobb	USA	68	19 May
13.50	1.2	Nancy Vallecilla	ECU	57	9 Jun
13.50	0.7	Valda Ruskite	SU	62	1 Aug
13.50	0.1	Maria Usifo	NIG	64	29 Sep
13.51		Ionica Domniteanu	RUM	69	21 May
13.51A	-1.0	Natalie Day	USA	63	23 May
13.52	1.3	Ilka Rönisch	GDR	72	29 May
13.53	0.4	Grazyna Tadrzak	POL	67	5 Jun
13.53	-0.6	Lynne Green	UK	64	27 Jun
13.53	0.7	Svetlana Chistyakova	SU	61	1 Aug
		(140)			
13.53	1.9	Daniela Bizbac	RUM	67	14 Aug
13.54	-0.4	Yelena Martsenyuk	SU	61	1 Jul
13.54	0.6	Veronique Truwant	FRA	65	31 Jul
13.54	1.2	Debbie Baker	UK	62	7 Aug
13.54	1.2	Judith Robinson	UK	64	21 Aug
13.54		Sabine Braun	FRG	65	20 Aug
13.55	1.1	Yvette Bates	USA	65	21 May
13.55	-0.3	Viktoria Ryzhova	SU	68	1 Jul
13.55	1.5	Christine Hurtlin	FRA	67	9 Jul
13.55		Rhonda Brady	USA	59	9 Jul
		(150)			
13.55A	0.0	Beatriz Capotosto	ARG	62	23 Jul
13.55	1.1	Yelena Petushkova	SU	69	29 Jul
13.55	1.6	Gabriela Zaharia	RUM	67	14 Aug
13.55	-0.2	Kathy Freeman	USA	62	15 Aug
13.55	-0.5	Claudia Dickow	FRG	63	17 Sep
13.55	1.2	Cindy Greiner	USA	57	23 Sep
13.56	0.4	Ines Schulz	GDR	65	18 Jun
13.57	1.2	Arnita Epps	USA	64	23 Apr
13.57		Birgit Gautzsch	GDR	67	17 Jun
13.57	0.0	Lisa Wells	USA	70	25 Jun
		(160)			
13.57	-0.4	Tatyana Shpak	SU	60	1 Jul
13.57	1.6	Svetlana Demeshonkova	SU	66	12 Jul
13.57	0.1	Karen Jung	FRG	68	23 Jul
13.57		Judy Simpson	UK	60	20 Aug
13.58	0.4	Sylwia Bednarska	POL	66	5 Jun
13.58	0.1	Michaela Hübel	FRG	69	26 Jun
13.58	1.7	Irina Pimentyeva	SU	60	12 Jul
13.58	0.6	Ivanka Valkova	BUL	65	16 Jul
13.58	0.1	Alla Motina	SU	67	14 Aug
13.59	1.9	Tanya Davis	USA	68	28 May
		(170)			

Wind assisted

Mark		Name		Nat	Born	Pos	Meet	Venue	Date
12.29	3.5		Donkova			1	Athl	Lausanne	24 Jun
12.46	2.6	Natalya	Grigoryeva	SU	61	1	NC	Tallinn	5 Jul
12.47	4.4	Gloria	Siebert	GDR	64	1rA		Berlin	13 Sep
12.49	3.1		Donkova			1	BNP	Villeneuve d'Ascq	27 Jun
12.50	3.2	Cornelia	Oschkenat	GDR	61	1rB		Berlin	13 Sep
12.51	4.4		Oschkenat			2rA		Berlin	13 Sep
12.57	2.6	Lyudmila	Narozhilenko	SU	64	2	NC	Tallinn	5 Jul
12.61	2.6		Narozhilenko			1s1	NC	Tallinn	5 Jul
		(8/5)							
12.66	2.6	Yelena	Politika	SU	64	3	NC	Tallinn	5 Jul
12.71	4.4	Sabine	John	GDR	57	3rA		Berlin	13 Sep
12.75	3.6	Lynda	Tolbert	USA	67	1s2	TAC	Tampa	16 Jun
12.78	3.5	Florence	Colle	FRA	65	2	Athl	Lausanne	24 Jun
12.80	3.3	Sally	Gunnell	UK	66	1	IAC	Edinburgh	29 Jul
12.81	3.0	Benita	Fitzgerald-Brown	USA	61	1q1	FOT	Indianapolis	21 Jul
12.83	3.5	Laurence	Elloy	FRA	59	3	Athl	Lausanne	24 Jun
12.83	3.2	Lidia	Okolo-Kulak	SU	58	2s2	NC	Tallinn	5 Jul
12.83	2.4	Anne	Piquereau	FRA	64	1	NC	Tours	14 Aug
12.86	2.4	Monique	Ewanje-Epée	FRA	67	2	NC	Tours	14 Aug

Mark		Name		Nat	Born	Pos	Meet	Venue	Date
12.88	2.6	Irina	Svetonosova	SU	58	5	NC	Tallinn	5 Jul
12.94	2.8	Liliana	Nastase	RUM	62	H	Int	Auckland	24 Feb
12.98	3.2	Natalya	Kolovanova	SU	64	3s2	NC	Tallinn	5 Jul
12.99	3.6	Donna	Waller	USA	64	3s2	TAC	Tampa	16 Jun
13.00	3.2	Marina	Grishina	SU	62	4s2	NC	Tallinn	5 Jul
13.01	3.5	Rita	Heggli	SWZ	62	7	Athl	Lausanne	24 Jun
13.03	3.2	Lyudmila	Oliyar	SU	58	5s2	NC	Tallinn	5 Jul
13.06	3.6	Rhonda	Blanford	USA	63	4s2	TAC	Tampa	16 Jun
13.07A		Annemarie	le Roux	RSA	63	1		Secunda	20 Feb
13.07	2.6	Lyudmila	Khristosenko	SU	66	4s1	NC	Tallinn	5 Jul
13.08A		Ina	van Rensburg	RSA	56	2		Secunda	20 Feb
13.09	2.4	Tananjalyn	Stanley	USA	67	3s1	TAC	Tampa	16 Jun
13.10	3.6	Dawn	Bowles	USA	69	2		New York	5 Jun
13.10	3.5	Eva	Sokolova	SU	62	8	Athl	Lausanne	24 Jun
13.16	2.6	Lyubov	Stolyar	SU	61	6s1	NC	Tallinn	5 Jul
13.18	6.2	Du Juan		CHN	68	1h2		Warszawa	18 Jun
13.24		Bridgette	Tate	USA	66	1		Oxford	22 Apr
13.24	3.0	Candy	Young	USA	62	4q1	FOT	Indianapolis	21 Jul
13.24	2.4	Isabelle	Kaftandjian	FRA	64	4	NC	Tours	14 Aug
13.25	2.8	Schowonda	Williams	USA	66	2		Baton Rouge	23 Apr
13.25	2.8	Kathy	Freeman	USA	62	3		Baton Rouge	23 Apr
13.25	3.7	Grazyna	Tadrzak	POL	67	1		Bialystok	11 Jun
13.25	6.2	Sylwia	Bednarska	POL	66	2h2		Warszawa	18 Jun
13.27	3.8	Ionica	Domniteanu	RUM	69	1	Balk-j	Alexandroúpolis	10 Jul
13.32	4.4	Karen	Nelson	CAN	64	1	SWC	Austin	15 May
13.34	2.5	Kay	Morley	UK	63	1	vNor	Nesbyen	3 Sep

Mark	Wind	Name	Nat	Born	Date
13.39	3.1	Cindy Greiner	USA	57	7 May
13.39	3.3	Debbie Baker	UK	62	29 Jul
13.44	5.1	Kim Kilpatrick	USA	66	14 May
13.44	5.6	Maureen Wiltshire	JAM.		21 May
13.46	2.6	Lorna Boothe	UK	54	29 May
13.47	2.6	Cheryl Dickey	USA	66	6 May
13.47	2.6	Sylvia Dyer	JAM	66	19 May
13.48	3.6	Yvette Bates	USA	65	16 Jun
13.48	2.4	Albertine An (50)	FRA	63	14 Aug
13.49	4.0	Malgorzata Urbanowicz	POL	68	7 Aug
13.51	5.1	Carla Wilson	CAN	66	14 May
13.51	2.9	Christine Hurtlin	FRA	67	26 Jun
13.51	2.9	Simone Schon	FRG	65	26 Jun
13.52	2.4	Véronique Truwant	FRA	65	14 Aug
13.52	8.1	Chizuko Akimoto	JAP	60	15 Sep
13.54	2.4	Nikki Williams	USA	67	29 May
13.56A	3.4	Tanya Davis	USA	68	14 May
13.56	3.7	Lenuta Birzu	RUM	69	10 Jul
13.56	3.8	Zdravka Georgieva (60)	BUL	69	10 Jul
13.56	3.8	Brigita Bukovec	YUG	70	10 Jul
13.58A	2.2	Mary Massarin	ITA	63	11 Aug
13.59	2.6	Hope Obika	NIG	70	6 May
13.59	4.0	Donna Smellie	CAN	64	12 Jun

Hand timing

Mark		Name		Nat	Born	Pos	Meet	Venue	Date
12.3	1.1	Lyudmila	Narozhilenko	SU	64	1h	NP	Vladivostok	13 Sep
12.3	1.0		Narozhilenko			1	NP	Vladivostok	13 Sep
12.4	0.0	Natalya	Grigoryeva	SU	62	1h		Simferopol	28 May
12.5	1.7	Lidia	Okolo-Kulak	SU	67	1		Staiki	28 May
12.5	1.0		Grigoryeva			2	NP	Vladivostok	13 Sep
12.5		Liu Huajin		CHN	60	1		Beijing	17 Sep
12.6	1.1		Grigoryeva			2h	NP	Vladivostok	13 Sep
12.7	-1.3	Yelizaveta	Chernysheva	SU	58	1		Chelyabinsk	16 Jul
12.8	0.5	Kim	McKenzie	USA	61	2		Tallahassee	23 Apr
12.8		Feng Yinghua		CHN	66	.		Beijing	14 May
12.8	1.0	Svetlana	Buraga	SU	65	3	NP	Vladivostok	13 Sep
12.9	-1.3	Marina	Grishina	SU	62	2		Chelyabinsk	16 Jul
12.9	-0.2	Irina	Svetonosova	SU	58	1		Staiki	31 Jul
12.9		Du Juan		CHN	68	.		Beijing	12 Aug
13.0	2.0	Natalya	Kolovanova	SU	64	2		Voroshilovgrad	14 May
13.0		Ludmila	Oliyar	SU	58	1		Riga	16 Jun
13.0	2.0	Sylvia	Dethier	BEL	65	1		Aalst	25 Jun
13.0	0.2	Irina	Tyukhay	SU	67	1		Novosibirsk	27 Jun
13.0	1.0	Vera	Ordina	SU	68	4	NP	Vladivostok	13 Sep
13.1 i	-	Yelena	Biserova	SU	62	2		Minsk	5 Mar
13.1A	1.6	Donna	Waller	USA	64	1		El Paso	17 Apr
13.1		Lorna	Boothe	UK	54	2		Santa Monica	1 Jul
13.1	1.0	Yekaterina	Gorbatova	SU	68	6	NP	Vladivostok	13 Sep

Mark		Name	Nat	Born	Date	Mark		Name	Nat	Born	Date
13.2	0.5	Mary Hawkins	USA	65	23 Apr	13.2	1.1	Xénia Siska	HUN	57	17 Jul
13.2	0.5	Terry Robinson	USA	69	23 Apr	13.2		Margita Papic	YUG	61	20 Aug
13.2	0.5	Andrea Thompson	USA	66	23 Apr	13.3	0.4	Zhanna Gurbanova	SU	69	28 May
13.2		Tatyana Dolgaya	SU	64	13 May	13.3	0.7	Valda Ruskite	SU	62	15 Jun
13.2	0.5	Yulia Filippova	SU	70	28 May	13.3		Larisa Nikitina	SU	65	8 Jul
13.2		Alla Knyazeva	SU	64	12 Jun	13.3	1.1	Margit Palombi	HUN	61	17 Jul
13.2		Tatyana Pantyukhova	SU	65	18 Jun	13.3	0.1	Alla Motina	SU	67	24 Jul
13.2		Karen Cannon	USA	58	1 Jul	13.3	0.1	Irina Antipova	SU	69	24 Jul

Wind assisted

Mark	Wind	Name	Nat	Born	Pos	Venue	Date
12.9		Svetla Dimitrova	BUL	70	1H	Sofia	18 Jun
13.1A	5.0	Patricia Lombardo	ITA	58	1	Sestriere	6 Aug

Mark		Name	Nat	Born	Date	Mark		Name	Nat	Born	Date
13.2	4.2	Karen Nelson	CAN	63	17 Jul	13.3	4.5	Maureen Wiltshire	JAM		29 Apr
13.3		Kathy Freeman	USA	62	18 Mar						

100 Metres Hurdles — Year List Progression — 400 Metres Hurdles

Year	Best	10th	20th	50th	100th	Best	10th	20th	50th	100th
1978	12.48	13.02	13.25	13.56	13.81	54.89	56.67	57.43	59.18	60.02
1979	12.48	12.91	13.13	13.52	13.83	54.78	56.46	57.56	58.83	59.95
1980	12.36	12.80	13.10	13.42	13.77	54.28	56.16	56.96	58.48	59.69
1981	12.68	13.14	13.25	13.51	13.75	54.79	56.36	56.93	58.10	59.24
1982	12.44	12.88	13.09	13.42	13.68	54.57	55.76	56.48	57.86	58.79
1983	12.42	12.86	13.00	13.25	13.55	54.02	55.49	56.03	57.00	58.20
1984	12.43	12.74	13.01	13.33	13.48	53.58	54.93	55.60	56.86	58.07
1985	12.42	12.85	12.99	13.24	13.48	53.55	54.95	55.48	56.86	58.00
1986	12.26	12.75	12.95	13.23	13.47	52.94	54.76	55.62	56.79	57.89
1987	12.25	12.80	12.91	13.22	13.45	53.24	55.05	55.55	56.92	57.87
1988	12.21	12.73	12.84	13.10	13.39	53.17	54.49	55.30	56.40	57.50

400 METRES HURDLES

Mark	First name	Name	Nat	Born	Pos	Meet	Venue	Date
53.17	Debbie	Flintoff-King	AUS	60	1	OG	Seoul	28 Sep
53.18	Tatyana	Ledovskaya	SU	66	2	OG	Seoul	28 Sep
53.63	Ellen	Fiedler	GDR	58	3	OG	Seoul	28 Sep
53.69	Sabine	Busch	GDR	62	4	OG	Seoul	28 Sep
54.00		Flintoff-King			1s1	OG	Seoul	26 Sep
54.01		Ledovskaya			2s1	OG	Seoul	26 Sep
54.03	Sally	Gunnell	UK	66	5	OG	Seoul	28 Sep
54.04	Gudran	Abt	FRG	62	6	OG	Seoul	28 Sep
54.05		Flintoff-King			1	Int	Bern	23 Aug
54.11		Busch			1	NC	Rostock	25 Jun
54.18		Busch			1		Potsdam	8 Sep
54.24	Susanne	Losch	GDR	66	1	vFRG	Düsseldorf	19 Jun
54.28		Fiedler			1s2	OG	Seoul	26 Sep
54.36	LaTanya	Sheffield	USA	63	3s1	OG	Seoul	26 Sep
54.39	Tatyana	Kurochkina	SU	67	7	OG	Seoul	28 Sep
54.42		Busch			1	OD	Berlin	29 Jun
54.46		Kurochkina			2s2	OG	Seoul	26 Sep
54.48		Ledovskaya			1h		Vilnius	27 Aug
54.48		Gunnell			4s1	OG	Seoul	26 Sep
54.49	Sandra	Farmer-Patrick	USA	62	1	APM	Hengelo	14 Aug
	(10)							
54.52		Fiedler			1	vIta	Neubrandenburg	9 Jul
54.52		Abt			3s2	OG	Seoul	26 Sep
54.56	Anita	Protti	SWZ	64	5s1	OG	Seoul	26 Sep
54.58		Fiedler			1h3	OG	Seoul	25 Sep
54.71		Fiedler			2		Potsdam	8 Sep
54.71		Busch			4s2	OG	Seoul	26 Sep
54.73		Losch			1	GO	Dresden	11 Jun
54.74		Fiedler			2	NC	Rostock	25 Jun
54.75		Kurochkina			1		Kiev	14 Aug
54.76		Losch			2	OD	Berlin	29 Jun
	(30/11)							
54.81	Cornelia	Ullrich	GDR	63	1		Jena	3 Jun
54.93	Schowonda	Williams	USA	66	1	FOT	Indianapolis	20 Jul
54.95	Margarita	Khromova	SU	63	.h		Vilnius	27 Aug
55.13A	Myrtle	Bothma	RSA	64	1		Germiston	22 Oct
55.14	Genowefa	Blaszak	POL	57	2	WG	Helsinki	30 Jun

Mark	Name		Nat	Born	Pos	Meet	Venue	Date
55.22	Yelena	Filipishina	SU	62	1		Sochi	20 May
55.23	Cristina	Pérez	SPA	65	5s2	OG	Seoul	26 Sep
55.29	Leslie	Maxie	USA	67	2	FOT	Indianapolis	20 Jul
55.30	Judi	Brown King	USA	61	1	Pre	Eugene	2 Jul
	(20)							
55.31	Anna	Ambraziene	SU	55	.h		Vilnius	27 Aug
55.41	Yelena	Goncharova	SU	63	2		Kiev	14 Aug
55.44	Iolanda	Oanta	RUM	65	1		Bucuresti	10 Jul
55.47	Olga	Nazarova I	SU	62	1		Sochi	31 May
55.55	Sally	Fleming	AUS	61	1		Ylivieska	3 Jul
55.57	Hélène	Huart	FRA	65	3rA	Int	Bern	23 Aug
55.59	Gretha	Tromp	HOL	64	1	Int	Hechtel	30 Jul
55.60	Linetta	Wilson	USA	67	2	NCAA	Eugene	3 Jun
55.63	Marina	Sereda	SU	64	3	Znam	Leningrad	11 Jun
55.74	Jackie	Joyner-Kersee	USA	62	1		Los Angeles	14 May
	(30)							
55.74	Irmgard	Trojer	ITA	64	4h4	OG	Seoul	25 Sep
55.76	Chantal	Beaugeant	FRA	61	2	NC	Tours	14 Aug
55.77	Olga	Petrova	SU	65	2	Kuts	Moskva	4 Sep
55.85	Nicoleta	Carutasu	RUM	64	1	Balk	Ankara	17 Jul
55.88	Victoria	Fulcher	USA	65	3	TAC	Tampa	18 Jun
55.90	Tuija	Helander-Kuusisto	FIN	61	1	PTS	Bratislava	Jun
55.91	Elaine	McLaughlin	UK	63	6s2	OG	Seoul	26 Sep
55.93	Sofia	Sabeva	BUL	69	1	NC-j	Sofia,	3 Jul
55.97	Natalya	Kalinnikova	SU	63	3		Kiev,	14 Aug
55.99	Karen	Wilkenson	RSA	66	2		Stellenbosch	26 Apr
	(40)							
55.99	Maria	Usifo	NIG	64	5h3	OG	Seoul	25 Sep
56.10	Janeen	Vickers	USA	68	4	NCAA	Eugene	3 Jun
56.10	Alla	Malchenko	SU	61	4	Kuts	Moskva	4 Sep
56.14	Natalya	Dudina	SU	66	4		Tallinn	5 Jul
56.18	Rose	Tata-Muya	KEN	60	4h1	OG	Seoul	25 Sep
56.26	Rosie	Edeh	CAN	62	1	NC	Ottawa	7 Aug
56.29	Christine	Wennberg	SWE	63	2rB	Int	Bern	23 Aug
56.34	Leisa	Knowles	USA	63	1		Austin	7 May
56.39	Galina	Selivanova	SU	60	1		Odessa	20 Aug
56.40	Tania	Fernández	CUB	67	2	PTS	Bratislava	8 Jun
	(50)							
56.44	Jenny	Laurendet	AUS	62	4h2	OG	Seoul	25 Sep
56.46	Camelia	Jianu	RUM	67	1	v2N	Bucaresti	19 Jun
56.54	Yelena	Mitrukova	SU	64	4	vUK	Portsmouth	19 Jun
56.54	Helga	Halldórsdóttir	ICE	63	2		Los Angeles	3 Sep
56.55	Natalya	Borisova	SU	66	4		Kiev	14 Aug
56.56	Yelena	Stas	SU	65	6	Znam	Leningrad	11 Jun
56.56	Zuzana	Machotková	CS	65	1	NC	Praha	17 Jul
56.57	Kathy	Freeman	USA	62	4	TAC	Tampa	18 Jun
56.59	Gayle	Kellon	USA	65	1		Northridge	3 Jul
56.64	Alina	Buhus	RUM	67	2	NC	Pitesti	12 Aug
	(60)							
56.68	Nadeen	Bridgeforth	USA	66	1		Fairfax	15 May
56.71	Margarita	Jesaviciené	SU	61	5		Kiev	14 Aug
56.72	Sabine	Alber	FRG	65	4	v GDR	Düsseldorf	19 Jun
56.78	Tonja	Brown	USA	60	2		Eagle Rock	14 May
56.79	Sharon	Hanson	USA	65	2		Northridge	3 Jul
56.80	Arnita	Epps	USA	64	5	TAC	Tampa	18 Jun
56.82	Lori	McCauley	USA	61	6s1	FOT	Indianapolis	18 Jul
56.84	Olga	Mikushina	SU	59	4h1	Znam	Leningrad	11 Jun
56.85	Wendy	Cearns	UK	60	2	vHun	Gateshead	14 Aug
56.88	Yelena	Klimova	SU	66	6		Kiev	14 Aug
	(70)							
56.89	Monika	Klebe	SWE	64	1	Gator	Knoxville	21 May
56.96	Connie	Ellerbe	USA	68	2		Fairfax	15 May
57.00	Simone	Laidlow	UK	65	3	WAAA	Birmingham	6 Aug
57.02	Christine	Wynn	CAN	62	2	NC	Ottawa	7 Aug
57.05	Ann-Louise	Skoglund	SWE	62	3		Gävle	2 Aug
57.05	Maria-Luisa	Cilimbini	ITA	67	2	vCan	Cesenatico	14 Aug
57.10	Antje	Axmann	GDR	69	1	NC-j	Karl-Marx-Stadt	16 Jul

Mark	Name		Nat	Born	Pos	Meet	Venue	Date
57.12A	Liliana	Chala	ECU	65	2	IbAC	Ciudad México	24 Jul
57.13	Sandra	Seuser	FRG	66	13	NC	Frankfurt-am-Main	24 Jul
57.20	Semra	Aksu	TUR	62	6h5	OG	Seoul	25 Sep
	(80)							
57.26A	Marna	van den Burgh	RSA	57	2		Pretoria	21 Mar
57.26	Sylvie	Levecq	FRA	62	1		Antony	25 Jun
57.29A	Jill	McDermid	CAN	68	1		Calgary	23 Jun
57.29	Ulrike	Heinz	FRG	67	1		Dortmund	14 Aug
57.32	Marian	Knijn	HOL	66	3		Fairfax	15 May
57.32	Ruth	Kyalisima	UGA	55	2	AfrC	Annaba	1 Sep
57.33	Cristeana	Matei	RUM	62	1	Int	Reims	4 Jun
57.35	Bonka	Peneva	BUL	56	2	vCS,UK	Praha	3 Jul
57.35	Ewa	Johansson	SWE	64	2	vFin	Helsinki	4 Sep
	(90)							
57.35	Marie Gnebele	Womplou	IVC	69	5h1	OG	Seoul	25 Sep
57.36A	Irma	Swart	RSA	65	3	NC	Bloemfontein	16 Apr
57.37	Christiane	Beinhauear	FRG	68	4	NC	Frankfurt-am-Main	24 Jul
57.41	Jennifer	Pearson	UK	62	5	WAAA	Birmingham	5 Aug
57.43	Malgorzata	Platek	POL	63	2	RomIC	Bucaresti	19 Jun
57.45	Jacqui	Parker	UK	66	2h3	WAAA	Birmingham	5 Aug
57.47	Caroline	Fortin	CAN	70	3	NC	Ottawa	7 Aug
57.49	Margit	Grötzinger	FRG	67	3		Dortmund	14 Aug
57.50	Vera	Ordina	SU	68	4s1	NC	Tallinn	5 Jul
57.50	Giuseppina	Cirulli	ITA	59	5	Int	Sestriere	11 Aug
	(100)							

Mark	Name		Nat	Born	Date
57.52	Aura	Cracea	RUM	70	21 May
57.52	Monika	Schediwy	SWZ	64	23 Aug
57.54	Odalys	Hernández	CUB	66	21 Jun
57.54	Lorraine	Hanson	UK	65	6 Aug
57.57	Corinne	Pierre-Joseph	FRA	66	26 Jun
57.57	Gwen	Wall	CAN	63	13 Jul
57.58	Ann	Maenhout	BEL	69	29 Jul
57.60	Monica	Westén	SWE	66	14 Aug
57.63	Liu Guihua		CHN	58	30 Aug
57.64A	Maria	Ferreira	BRA	60	24 Jul
	(110)				
57.66	Anna	Chuprina	SU	70	27 Jun
57.74A	Lorraine	du Toit	RSA	64	21 Mar
57.74	Jill	Irizarry	USA	66	21 May
57.75	Yaroslava	Gaba	SU	55	31 May
57.75	Annie	Moelo	FRA	62	27 Jun
57.78	DeDe	Nathan	USA	68	28 Apr
57.78	Marina	Matyakina	SU	69	7 Jul
57.78	Iris	Gauch	FRG	67	14 Aug
57.79	Larisa	Turshina	SU	61	12 Jul
57.81	Catalina	Gheorghiu	RUM	69	21 May
	(120)				
57.82A	Ame	Ice	USA	67	14 May
57.83	Erika	Szopori	HUN	63	6 Jul
57.84	Rachel	Clary	USA	62	21 May
57.84	Svetlana	Slavcheva	BUL	70	14 Aug
57.85	Jennifer	Harlan	USA	66	17 Jun
57.85	Teodora	Khristova	BUL	67	3 Jul
57.85	Lisa	Kueneman	CAN	67	2 Aug
57.87	Tamara	Kuprianovich	SU	64	11 Sep
57.88	Silvia	Rieger	FRG	70	29 Jul
	(130)				
57.93	Barbara	Johnson	IRL	62	24 Jul
57.95	Julie	Harrison	USA	67	26 Jun
57.98A	Lana	Uys	RSA	68	22 Oct
57.99	Flora	Hyacinth	UVI	I66	14 May
57.99	Beata	Knapczyk	POL	64	12 Aug
58.00	Sara	Robitaille	USA	64	21 May
58.04	Dejana	Rakita	YUG	68	17 Jul
58.05	Katrin	Schreiter	GDR	69	20 May
58.06A	Maria João	Lopes	POR	62	24 Jul
58.07A	Dana	Wright	CAN	59	23 May
	(140)				
58.08	Ann	Hall	USA	65	20 May
58.08	Nadine	Debois	FRA	61	4 Jun
58.08	Valbona	Sina	ALB	70	17 Jul
58.14	Karen	Koellner	USA	66	30 Apr
58.15	Gerda	Haas	AUT	66	15 Jun
58.15	Jolanta	Stalmach	POL	60	24 Jul
58.19	Lumina	Trandafir	RUM	67	2 Aug
58.20	Yelena	Pavlova	SU	69	8 Jul
58.25	Leslie	Nixon	USA	66	29 Apr
58.26	Anzhela	Bologan	SU	66	20 Aug
	(150)				
58.31	Kim	Batten	USA	69	7 May
58.32	Angelica	Sirbu	RUM	70	27 Aug
58.37	Frida	Johansson	SWE	70	14 Aug
58.38	Bridget	Kehoe	CAN	64	9 Aug
58.38	Qiu Aihua		CHN	66	4 Sep
58.38	Lyudmila	Myachikova	SU	64	14 Sep
58.39	Nelli	Voronkova	SU	72	26 Aug
58.41	Lynn	Parry	UK	65	18 Jun
58.44	Margaret	Still	UK	65	18 Jun
58.44	Petra	Schellenbeck	FRG	70	26 Jun
	(160				
58.48	Michelle	Martinot	HOL	69	12 May
58.48	Natalya	Cherkashina	SU	70	8 Jul
58.49	Barbara	Gourdet	FRA	65	11 Sep

Hand timing

Mark	Name		Nat	Born	Pos	Meet	Venue	Date
55.5	Anna	Ambraziene	SU	55	1		Vilnius	10 Aug
55.71A	Rose	Tata-Muya	KEN	60	1	NC/OT	Nairobi	12 Aug
56.3	Yelena	Stas	SU	65	1		Alma-Ata	18 Jun
56.6	Larisa	Turshinma	SU	61	1h		Bryansk	12 Jul
56.7	Cheyn	Dongmei	CHN	60	1		Beijing	23 Sep
57.3	Natalya	Rudina	SU	66	.		Staiki	29 May

Mark	Name		Nat	Born	Date
57.8A	Marcella	Mbunde	KEN	65	12 Aug
58.0	Yelena	Pavlova	SU	69	28 May
58.1	Lyudmila	Yushchenko	SU	64	13 May
58.2	Natalya	Cherkashina	SU	70	28 May
58.3	Irina	Dorofeyeva	SU	62	17 Jul
58.4	Sharrieffa	Barksdale	USA	61	10 Jun
58.4	Tamara	Golikova	SU	65	17 Jul

HIGH JUMP

Mark	Name		Nat	Born	Pos	Meet	Venue	Date
2.07	Stefka	Kostadinova	BUL	65	1	NC	Sofia	3 Sep
2.06i		Kostadinova			1	Int	Athinai	20 Feb
2.05		Kostadinova			1	BGP	Budapest	12 Aug
2.04i		Kostadinova			1	4-N	Athinai	6 Feb
2.04i		Kostadinova			1	EI	Budapest	6 Mar
2.04		Kostadinova			1	Int	Formia	19 Jun
2.03i		Kostadinova			1	Int	Sindelfingen	5 Feb
2.03		Kostadinova			1		Sofia	22 May
2.03	Louise	Ritter	USA	58	1		Austin	8 Jul
2.03		Ritter			1	OG	Seoul	30 Sep
2.02	Silvia	Costa	CUB	64	1	Nik	Nice	10 Jul
2.01i		Kostadinova			1	Int	Stuttgart	31 Jan
2.01i	Gabriele	Günz	GDR	61	2	Int	Stuttgart	31 Jan
2.01		Costa			1	NarM	Sofia	26 Jun
2.01		Kostadinova			2	OG	Seoul	30 Sep
2.00i		Günz			1		Leipzig	16 Jan
2.00i		Kostadinova			1	Int	Madrid	2 Feb
2.00i	Lyudmila	Avdyeyenko	SU	63	1	NC	Volgograd	11 Feb
2.00i	Larisa	Kositsyna	SU	63	2	NC	Volgograd	11 Feb
2.00i		Kostadinova			1	v CS	Sofia	13 Feb
2.00i		Kositsyna			1	Int	West Berlin	26 Feb
2.00		Kostadinova			1	Int	Saint Denis	7 Jun
2.00		Kostadinova			1		Sorgues	9 Jun
2.00		Kostadinova			1		Sofia	12 Jun
2.00	Olga	Turchak	SU	67	1	v Fra,UK	Portsmouth	19 Jun
2.00		Kositsyna			1		Chelyabinsk	16 Jul
2.00		Kostadinova			1		Sofia	23 Jul
2.00	Galina	Astafei	RUM	69	1	WJ	Sudbury	29 Jul
2.00		Kostadinova			1	Int	Viareggio	3 Aug
1.99i		Gunz			1		Schwendt	23 Jan
1.99		Ritter			1	FOT	Indianapolis	23 Jul
1.99	Tamara	Bykova	SU	58	3	OG	Seoul	30 Sep
	(32/9)							
1.98	Coleen	Sommer	USA	60	1	Inv	Austin	7 May
	(10)							
1.98	Heike	Redetzky	FRG	64	1	v GDR	Düsseldorf	20 Jun
1.98	Yelena	Yelesina	SU	70	1	Druzh	Nyiregyháza	13 Aug
1.97i	Susanne	Beyer	GDR	61	2	v Ita,Yug	Torino	10 Feb
1.97	Charmaine	Gale	RSA	64	1		Pretoria	30 Mar
1.97	Jan	Wohlschlag	USA	58	1	TAC	Tampa	17 Jun
1.96i	Madely	Beaugendre	FRA	65	1		Paris	7 Feb
1.96	Vanessa	Browne	AUS	63	1	NC	Perth	27 Mar
1.96	Biljana	Petrovic	YUG	61	1	Balk	Ankara	16 Jul
1.96	Trish	King	USA	62	2	FOT	Indianapolis	23 Jul
1.95i	Yelena	Panikarovskikh	SU	59	1		Vilnius	23 Jan
	(20)							
1.95i	Emilia	Dragieva	BUL	65	1	JP	Praha	29 Jan
1.95	Lyudmila	Andonova	BUL	60	1		Sofia	4 Jun
1.95	Maryse	Ewanje-Epée	FRA	64	1	NC	Tours	14 Aug
1.94i	Lyudmila	Sukhoroslova	SU	62	1		Zaporozhye	24 Jan
1.94	Svetlana	Ruban	SU	65	1		Alma-Ata	17 May
1.94	Heike	Balck	GDR	70	2		Jena	4 Jun
1.94	Megumi	Satoh	JAP	66	1	NC	Tokyo	19 Jun
1.94	Yelena	Rodina	SU	67	1	NC	Tallinn	7 Jul
1.94	Galina	Balgurina	SU	65	1		Staiki	1 Aug
1.94	Amra	Temim	YUG	68	1	4-N	Thessaloniki	16 Sep
	(30)							
1.93	Desiré	du Plessis	RSA	65	1		Stellenbosch	6 Jan
1.93	Chris	Stanton	AUS	59	2	NC	Perth	27 Mar
1.93	Ute	Seidler-Kuhn	GDR	65	1		Halle	4 May
1.93	Jane	Clough	USA	63	2	Jenn	San Jose	28 May
1.93	Svetlana	Isaeva	BUL	67	1	Int	Wörrstadt	4 Jun
1.93	Jackie	Joyner-Kersee	USA	62	H	FOT	Indianapolis	15 Jul

Mark	Name		Nat	Born	Pos	Meet	Venue	Date
1.93	Jin Ling		CHN	67	1	Int	Tianjin	1 Sep
1.92i	Jeannie	Cockcroft	CAN	65	1	Int	Vancouver	16 Jan
1.92i	Jolanta	Komsa	POL	58	1	NC	Zabrze	21 Feb
1.92i	Irina	Barinova	SU	61	2		Klaipeda	5 Mar
	(40)							
1.92	Galina	Brigadnaya	SU	58	1	RigaC	Riga	4 Jun
1.92	Amber	Welty	USA	67	1	NCAA	Eugene	4 Jun
1.92	Inga	Butkus	SU	67	1		Volgograd	12 Jun
1.92	Diana	Davies	UK	61	3	v Fra,SU	Portsmouth	19 Jun
1.92	Klara	Kosenko	SU	66	1		Bryansk	13 Jul
1.92	Karen	Scholz	GDR	69	3	WJ	Sudbury	29 Jul
1.92	Lyubov	Pakhomchik	SU	63	2		Staiki	1 Aug
1.92	Irina	Prisyazhnyuk	SU	64	1		Kharkov	5 Aug
1.92	Svetlana	Mokrak	SU	67	1		Odessa	19 Aug
1.92	Kim Hee-Sun		SKO	63	q	OG	Seoul	29 Sep
	(50)							
1.92	Janet	Boyle	UK	63	q	OG	Seoul	29 Sep
1.91	Hanne	Haugland	NOR	67	1		Sandnes	9 Jun
1.91	Candy	Cashell	USA	63	1		Trenton	10 Jun
1.91	Kerstin	Brandt	GDR	61	3	NC	Rostock	26 Jun
1.91	Klodeta	Gjini	ALB	64	1		Tirane	29 Jul
1.91	Ni Xiuling		CHN	62	2	IntC	Tianjin	4 Sep
1.90i	Svetlana	Boroday	SU	59	1		Voroshilovgrad	13 Jan
1.90i	Danuta	Bulkowska	POL	59	2	NC	Zabrze	21 Feb
1.90i	Debbie	Brill	CAN	53	2	TAC	New York	26 Feb
1.90i	Sigrid	Kirchmann	AUT	66	1	NC	Wien	28 Feb
	(60)							
1.90	Deann	Bopf	AUS	62	1	Int	Brisbane	13 Mar
1.90	Gai	Kapernick	AUS	70	1	Int	Melbourne	17 Mar
1.90	Sharon	Barber	AUS	65	3	NC	Perth	27 Mar
1.90	Valentina	Gotovskaya	SU	65	1		Sochi	20 May
1.90	Camille	Jampolsky	USA	65	1		Westwood	21 May
1.90	Cristina	Fink-Sisniega	MEX	64	2		Westwood	21 May
1.90	Marina	Dyuzhova	SU	65	1		Smolensk	26 Jun
1.90	Dimitrinka	Borislavova	BUL	65	1		Pleven	9 Jul
1.90	Terri	Turner	USA	63	H	FOT	Indianapolis	15 Jul
1.90	Rita	Graves	USA	64	4	FOT	Indianapolis	23 Jul
	(70)							
1.90	Latrese	Johnson	USA	66	5=	FOT	Indianapolis	23 Jul
1.90	Yelena	Zavalishcheva	SU	60	2		Baku	11 Sep
1.90	Jo	Jennings	UK	69	13=	OG	Seoul	29 Sep
1.89i	Svetlana	Lavrova	SU	71	4		Vilnius	10 Jan
1.89i	Natalya	Golodnova	SU	67	4	Bul	Minsk	17 Jan
1.89i	Marina	Kuporosova	SU	62	1		Baku	24 Jan
1.89i	Svetlana	Odintsova	SU	62	2		Kiev	30 Jan
1.89	Jolanda	Jones	USA	65	1	TexR	Austin	9 Apr
1.89	Yolanda	Henry	USA	64	2	TexR	Austin	9 Apr
1.89	Ute	Demming	FRG	68	1	v UK	Birmingham	25 Jun
	(80)							
1.89	Sarka	Kaspárková	CS	71	1	5-N-j	Leipzig	6 Jul
1.89	Svetlana	Filatyeva	SU	64	H	NC	Kiev	1 Aug
1.89	Olga	Starik	SU	65	2		Zhitomir	6 Aug
1.89	Octavia	Iacob	RUM	65	2	NC	Pitesti	12 Aug
1.89	Niculina	Ilie	RUM	58	3	NC	Pitesti	12 Aug
1.89	Marita	Pakarinen	FIN	67	1	Int	Lahti	25 Aug
1.88i	Deborah	McDowell	UK	64	1		Glasgow	17 Jan
1.88i	Yvona	Tichopádová	CS	64	3	JP	Praha	29 Jan
1.88i	Kerstin	Kraeft	GDR	63	1		Senftenberg	3 Feb
1.88i	Linda	McCurdy-Cameron	CAN	63	1	NC	Windsor	21 Feb
	(90)							
1.88i	Coralea	Brown	CAN	72	2	NC	Windsor	21 Feb
1.88i	Vicki	Borsheim	USA	66	1		Seattle	21 Feb
1.88i	Angie	Bradburn	USA	68	1	NCAA	Oklahoma City	11 Mar
1.88i	Tonya	Mendonca	USA	65	1B		Flagstaff	27 Feb
1.88i	Shelley	Fehrman	USA	65	2B		Flagstaff	27 Feb
1.88i	Andrea	Mátay	HUN	55	7=	ECh	Budapest	6 Mar

Mark	Name		Nat	Born	Pos	Meet	Venue	Date
1.88	Tammy	Thurman	USA	65	1		Eugene	16 Apr
1.88	Charles-Line	Scaron	FRA	62	1	Perr	Fort-de-France	30 Apr
1.88	Maria del Carmen Garcia		CUB	69	2	Int	Sevilla	1 Jun
1.88	Britta	Vörös	GDR	68	1		Cottbus	17 Jun
	(100)							
1.88	Silvia	Oswald	FRG	68	2	NC	Frankfurt-am-Main.	23 Jul
1.88	Christiane	Mergemann	FRG	65	3	NC	Frankfurt-am-Main	23 Jul
1.88	Viktoria	Yupatova	SU	66	5		Moskva	6 Aug
1.88	Sabine	De Wachter	BEL	64	1		Kessel-Lo	6 Aug
1.88	Sharon	Hutchings	UK	62	3	WAAA	Birmingham	7 Aug
1.88	Maria Orlane Lima dos Santos		BRA	66	1		São Paulo	7 Aug
1.88	Katalin	Sterk	HUN	61	1		Debrecen	20 Aug

Mark	First name	Name	Nat	Born	Date
1.87i	Bettina	Braag	FRG	65	16 Jan
1.87i	Niki	Bakogianni	GRE	68	6 Feb
1.87i	Thordis	Gisladóttir	ICE	61	28 Feb
	(110)				
1.87i	Sarka	Nováková	CS	71	8 Mar
1.87	Mazel	Thomas	JAM	67	28 Apr
1.87	Mary	Moore	USA	65	14 May
1.87	Cindy	Greiner	USA	57	15 Jul
1.87	Darja	Lihteneger	YUG	62	16 Jul
1.87	Felicia	Hodges	USA	67	23 Jul
1.87	Yulia	Shkuratova	SU	66	30 Jul
1.87	Natalja	Jonckheere	BEL	70	4 Sep
1.87	Barbara	Fiammengo	ITA	67	6 Sep
1.86i	Svetlana	Melnikova	SU	65	24 Jan
	(120)				
1.86i	Nathalie	Said	FRA	66	24 Jan
1.86i	Anke	Behmer	GDR	61	30 Jan
1.86i	Natalya	Zamyatina	SU	70	6 Feb
1.86i	Lisa	Bernhagen	USA	66	7 Feb
1.86i	Yelena	Obukhova	SU	69	19 Feb
1.86i	Urszula	Kielan	POL	60	21 Feb
1.86i	Marion	Reichelt	GDR	62	25 Feb
1.86	Jane	Buchan	USA	64	12 Mar
1.86	Tia	Hensler	USA	64	29 Apr
1.86	Melinda	Stott	USA	66	15 May
	(130)				
1.86	Niki	Gavera	GRE	67	22 May
1.86	Tatyana	Shevchik	SU	69	27 May
1.86	Debra	Larsen	USA	64	27 May
1.86	Olga	Bolshova	SU	68	1 Jun
1.86	Dania	Fernández	CUB	67	1 Jun
1.86	Jane	Frederick	USA	52	17 Jun
1.86	Malgorzata	Orlowska	POL	63	26 Jun
1.86	Alica	Checová	CS	69	2 Jul
1.86	Krisztina	Solti	HUN	68	6 Jul
1.86	Masami	Matsui	JAP	63	9 Jul
	(140)				
1.86	Phyllis	Bluntson	USA	59	22 Jul
1.86	Odile	Lesage	FRA	69	29 Jul
1.86	Irina	Byelova	SU	68	1 Aug
1.86	Irina	Matyusheva	SU	65	1 Aug
1.86	Marion	Goldkamp	FRG	67	3 Aug
1.86	Olga	Panchuk	SU	63	6 Aug
1.86	Jayne	Barnetson	UK	68	21 Aug
1.86	Alessandra	Bonfiglioli	ITA	63	27 Aug
1.86	Tatyana	Gulevich	SU	71	26 Aug
1.86	Irina	Tyukhay	SU	67	3 Sep
	(150)				
1.86	Wang Hui		CHN	68	4 Sep
1.86	Birgit	Kähler	FRG	70	4 Sep
1.86	Oana	Musunoi	RUM	72	11 Sep
1.86	Galina	Mikhailova	SU	66	21 Sep
1.86	Dong Yuping		CHN	63	23 Sep
1.86	Corine	Schneider	SWZ	62	23 Sep
1.86	Marjon	Wijnsma	HOL	65	23 Sep

Best outdoor marks

Mark	Name	Pos	Meet	Venue	Date	Indoor
1.98	Avdyeyenko	1	NP	Vladivostok	13 Sep	2.00i
1.94	Beyer	1		Jena	4 Jun	1.97i
1.94	Günz	1		Neubrandenburg	10 Jul	2.01i
1.94	Panikarovskikh	2		Vilnius	27 Aug	1.95i
1.93	Beaugendre	2	NC	Tours	14 Aug	1.96i
1.92	Sukhoroslova	3	Znam	Leningrad	11 Jun	1.94i
1.90	Barinova	2=		Chelyabinsk	16 Jul	1.92i
1.89	Komsa	2	PTS	Bratislava	8 Jun	1.92i
1.88	Brill	2	MSR	Walnut	24 Apr	1.90i
1.88	Fehrmann	5		Austin	7 May	1.88i
1.88	Bulkowska	1	Int	Chania	22 May	1.90i
1.88	Golodnova	q	NC	Tallinn	6 Jul	1.89i

Mark	Name	Date	Indoor
1.87	Mendonca	23 Jul	1.89i
1.87	Kirchmann	3 Sep	1.90i
1.86	Borsheim	21 May	1.88i
1.86	Bernhagen	4 Jun	1.86i
1.86	Nováková	2 Jul	1.87i
1.86	Odintsova	16 Jul	1.89i
1.86	Bakogianni	27 Aug	1.87i

High Jump — Year List Progression — Long Jump

Year	HJ Best	10th	20th	50th	100th	LJ Best	10th	20th	50th	100th
1968	1.82	1.74	1.72	1.70	1.65	6.63	6.42	6.30	6.14	5.99
1978	2.01	1.91	1.88	1.85	1.83	7.09	6.69	6.58	6.40	6.28
1979	1.99	1.93	1.90	1.86	1.84	6.90	6.67	6.58	6.44	6.31
1980	1.98	1.94	1.92	1.88	1.85	7.06	6.81	6.72	6.54	6.34
1981	1.97	1.94	1.92	1.88	1.85	6.96	6.78	6.66	6.51	6.39
1982	2.02	1.97	1.93	1.89	1.86	7.20	6.86	6.79	6.57	6.44
1983	2.04	1.97	1.93	1.90	1.87	7.43	6.90	6.79	6.59	6.47
1984	2.07	1.97	1.95	1.90	1.87	7.40	7.01	6.88	6.69	6.48
1985	2.06	1.96	1.94	1.90	1.87	7.44	7.00	6.81	6.64	6.48
1986	2.08	1.97	1.94	1.91	1.88	7.45	7.01	6.85	6.65	6.48
1987	2.09	1.97	1.95	1.92	1.88	7.45	7.01	6.85	6.62	6.46
1988	2.07	1.98	1.95	1.92	1.88	7.52	7.07	6.88	6.67	6.53

LONG JUMP

Mark		Name		Nat	Born	Pos	Meet	Venue	Date
7.52	1.4	Galina	Chistyakova	SU	62	1	Znam	Leningrad	11 Jun
7.48	1.2	Heike	Drechsler	GDR	64	1	v Ita	Neubrandenburg	9 Jul
7.45	1.6		Chistyakova			1	BGP	Budapest	12 Aug
7.40	0.9	Jackie	Joyner-Kersee	USA	62	1	OG	Seoul	29 Sep
7.39			Joyner-Kersee			1		San Diego	25 Jun
7.37i	-		Drechsler			1	v Aut,Yug	Wien	13 Feb
7.36	1.8	Yelena	Byelevskaya	SU	63	2	Znam	Leningrad	11 Jun
7.30i	-		Drechsler			1	EI	Budapest	5 Mar
7.29	0.9		Chistyakova			1		Sochi	1 Jun
7.29	0.0	Yelena	Kokonova	SU	63	1		Alma-Ata	18 Jun
7.27		Inessa	Kravets	SU	66	1		Kiev	22 May
7.27	0.7		Joyner-Kersee			H	OG	Seoul	24 Sep
7.24i	-		Drechsler			1		Berlin	20 Feb
7.24i	-		Chistyakova			2	EI	Budapest	5 Mar
7.23i	-		Chistyakova			1	NC	Volgograd	10 Feb
7.23	2.0		Kravets			1	NC	Tallinn	6 Jul
7.22	1.5		Joyner-Kersee			q	FOT	Indianapolis	22 Jul
7.22	0.5		Drechsler			2	OG	Seoul	29 Sep
7.21			Byelevskaya			1		Sukhumi	16 May
7.21	2.0		Byelevskaya			2		Sochi	1 Jun
7.21	0.1		Chistyakova			1	NP	Vladivostok	14 Sep
7.20	0.8		Drechsler			1	NC	Rostock	25 Jun
7.18	0.6		Drechsler			1		Jena	3 Jun
7.18	0.4		Chistyakova			1	Ros	Praha	16 Jun
7.17	-0.4		Drechsler			1	OD	Berlin	29 Jun
7.17	2.0		Drechsler			1		Berlin	13 Sep
7.16	0.0		Kravets			1		Kharkov	18 Jun
7.16		Yolanda	Chen	SU	61	1		Moskva	30 Jul
7.14	1.8	Niole	Medvedyeva	SU	60	1	RigaC	Riga	4 Jun
7.13i	-		Chistyakova			1	NP	Moskva	20 Feb
7.12	0.8		Drechsler			1	v FRG	Düsseldorf	19 Jun
7.09	0.0		Drechsler			1		Potsdam	9 Sep
		(32/8)							
7.08	0.4	Valy	Ionescu	RUM	60	1	RomIC	Bucuresti	19 Jun
7.07	1.0	Larisa	Berezhnaya	SU	61	4	Znam	Leningrad	11 Jun
		(10)							
6.98	1.1	Marieta	Ilcu	RUM	62	2	NC	Pitesti	14 Aug
6.97	2.0	Agata	Karczmarek	POL	63	1		Lublin	6 Aug
6.96A	0.0	Madeline	de Jesus	PR	57	1	IbAC	Ciudad México	24 Jul
6.90	1.7	Jolanta	Bartzak	POL	64	1	PTS	Bratislava	9 Jun
6.89	0.0	Yelena	Pershina	SU	63	2		Alma-Ata	18 Jun
6.88	0.2	Irina	Valyukevich	SU	59	1		Tallinn	26 Jun
6.88	0.2	Vera	Olenchenko	SU	59	1		Dnepropetrovsk	17 Jul
6.88	2.0	Sheila	Echols	USA	64	2	FOT	Indianapolis	23 Jul
6.88	1.6	Carol	Lewis	USA	63	3	FOT	Indianapolis	23 Jul
6.88	0.3	Xiong Qiying		CHN	67	2	Int	Tianjin	1 Sep
		(20)							
6.87	0.1	Nicole	Boegman	AUS	67	1	Int	Gateshead	14 Aug
6.86	0.5	Yelena	Semiraz	SU	65	2		Kharkov	18 Jun
6.85i	-	Sylvia	Moneva	BUL	65	1	NC	Sofia	21 Feb
6.85	1.6	Lyudmila	Ninova	BUL	60	1		Sofia	4 Jun
6.83	0.0	Yelena	Sevastyanova	SU	67	3		Alma-Ata	18 Jun
6.82i	-	Yelena	Chicherova	SU	58	1		Shahkty	9 Jan
6.82	0.2	Alla	Nechiporets	SU	64	2		Dnepropetrovsk	17 Jul
6.82	1.8	Fiona	May	UK	69	-	WJ	Sudbury	30 Jul
6.81		Meledy	Smith	USA	64	1		Houston	6 May
6.81	1.0	Sabine	John	GDR	57	q	OG	Seoul	28 Sep
		(30)							
6.80i	-	Anke	Behmer	GDR	61	P	NC	Senftenberg	3 Feb
6.79		Liu Shuzhen		CHN	66	1		Shijiazhuang	23 Apr
6.78	1.3	Tsetska	Kancheva	BUL	63	1		Pleven	9 Jul
6.77	-1.6	Gail	Devers	USA	66	1		Westwood	16 Apr
6.76i	-	Helga	Radtke	GDR	62	2	NC	Senftenberg	27 Feb

Mark		Name		Nat	Born	Pos	Meet	Venue	Date
6.76	0.7	Svetlana	Zorina	SU	60	5		Sochi	1 Jun
6.74	0.1	Tatyana	Shpak	SU	60	H	NC	Kiev	2 Aug
6.72i	-	Antonella	Capriotti	ITA	62	1	NC	Firenze	24 Feb
6.70	2.0	Liao Wenfen		CHN	63	1	Int	Hamamatsu	8 May
6.70	0.7	Ines	Schulz	GDR	65	H	Int	Götzis	19 Jun
		(40)							
6.70	1.4	Jennifer	Inniss	USA	59	q	FOT	Indianapolis	22 Jul
6.70	1.4	Sofia	Bozhanova	BUL	67	2		Sofia	12 Aug
6.69		Valentina	Kravchenko	SU	63	3		Zhitomir	6 Aug
6.68i	-	Sandra	Myers	SPA	64	1		Oviedo	30 Jan
6.68	2.0	Inna	Lasovskaya	SU	69	1	NC-j	Bryansk	7 Jul
6.68	1.3	Heike	Tischler	GDR	64	H	Int	Götzis	19 Jun
6.68	1.2	Yvette	Bates	USA	65	-	FOT	Indianapolis	23 Jul
6.67	1.8	Tatyana	Pavlova	SU	60	6		Sochi	1 Jun
6.67	1.2	Ringa	Ropo	FIN	66	1		Sipoo	4 Jun
6.67	0.8	Ulrike	Kleindl	AUT	63	1		Ebensee	24 Jul
		(50)							
6.66	1.0	Svetlana	Shtatnova	SU	69	2	NC-j	Bryansk	7 Jul
6.66	0.9	Estera	Szabo	RUM	67	3	NC	Pitesti	14 Aug
6.66	1.7	Nina	Perevedentseva	SU	64	4		Baku	11 Sep
6.65	1.0	Liliana	Nastase	RUM	62	H	Int	Götzis	19 Jun
6.64	0.4	Sabine	Everts	FRG	61	H	NC	Rhede	10 Jul
6.64	1.6	Irina	Osipova	SU	63	1		Bryansk	29 Jul
6.63	1.8	Claire	Connor	USA	66	q	FOT	Indianapolis	22 Jul
6.63		Tatyana	Ter-Mesrobian	SU	68	1		Leningrad	28 Jul
6.62	-0.4	Niurka	Montalvo	CUB	68	1	NP	Habana	27 Feb
6.62		Sheila	Hudson	USA	67	1		Berkeley	23 Apr
		(60)							
6.62		Almagul	Adilova	SU	66	2		Alma-Ata	17 May
6.62	1.9	Valentina	Uccheddu	ITA	66	1		Trento	4 Jun
6.62	0.0	Yelena	Garbuz	SU	70	5		Alma-Ata	18 Jun
6.62	1.9	Stefanie	Hühn	FRG	66	H	NC	Rhede	10 Jul
6.62	0.9	Lene	Demsitz	DEN	59	1		Frederiksberg	24 Jul
6.61		Tineke	Hidding	HOL	56	-	v Bel,Eng	Roosendaal	23 Jul
6.60i	-	Irena	Ozhenko	SU	62	2		Vilnius	30 Jan
6.60i	-	Octavia	Iacob	RUM	65	.		Bacau	30 Jan
6.59		Beatrice	Utondu	NIG	69	1		Austin	7 May
6.59	1.5	Ivanka	Valkova	BUL	65	4		Sofia	4 Jun
		(70)							
6.59A		Wendy	Brown	USA	66	1	Int	Sestriere	11 Aug
6.58		Deng Shifen		CHN	66	.		Beijing	7 May
6.58	0.7	Tamara	Moshicheva	SU	62	H		Irkutsk	26 Jun
6.58	0.6	Mirela	Belu	RUM	70	1	Balk-j	Alexandroúpolis	9 Jul
6.58	-0.2	Nadine	Fourcade	FRA	63	1		Clamart	27 Jul
6.57i	-	Gaby	Ehlert	GDR	64	2		Senftenberg	3 Feb
6.57i	-	Eva	Murková	CS	62	2	4-N	Athinai	6 Feb
6.57		Zsuzsa	Vanyek	HUN	60	1		Budapest	5 Aug
6.57	1.3	Adelina	Polledo	CUB	66	1		Habana	5 Aug
6.57		Marjon	Wijnsma	HOL	65	2	AP	Hengelo	14 Aug
		(80)							
6.56	1.6	Tracy	Smith	CAN	64	-	NC	Ottawa	6 Aug
6.55i	-	Anke	Schmidt	GDR	68	P	NC	Senftenberg	3 Feb
6.55i	-	Monika	Hirsch	FRG	59	1	NC	Dortmund	20 Feb
6.55		Li Huirong		CHN	65	.		Shijiazhuang	23 Apr
6.55	1.2	Patricia	Bille	GDR	68	2		Dresden	11 Jun
6.55	0.5	Nadezhda	Miromanova	SU	58	H		Irkutsk	26 Jun
6.55		Natalya	Shmelyova	SU	66	1		Moskva	10 Jul
6.55	1.2	Anna	Derevyankina	SU	67	3		Chelyabinsk	17 Jul
6.55	1.2	Andrea	Hannemann	FRG	64	1	NC	Frankfurt-am-Main	23 Jul
6.55	1.4	Tatyana	Zhuravlyova	SU	67	H	NC	Kiev	2 Aug
		(90)							
6.55		Jayne	Mitchell	NZ	64	1		Auckland	26 Nov
6.54i	-	Inna	Romanchenkova	SU	58	P		Lipetsk	16 Jan
6.54	0.3	Edine	van Heezik	HOL	61	1		West Berlin	29 May
6.54	1.8	Yelena	Selina	SU	64	5		Baku	11 Sep
6.53	1.1	Mary	Berkeley	UK	65	1	NC	Derby	5 Jun

Mark	Wind	Name		Nat	Born	Pos	Meet	Venue	Date
6.53	2.0	Yelena	Volf	SU	69	3	NC-j	Bryansk	7 Jul
6.53	0.7	Galina	Salo	SU	59	3		Bryansk	11 Jul
6.53	1.9	Ivonne	Mathesius	GDR	71	1	NC-j	Berlin	20 Jul
6.53		Irina	Onopriyenko	SU	67	7		Vilnius	27 Aug
6.53		Larisa	Nikitina	SU	65	H	NP	Tashkent	4 Sep
		(100)							

Mark	Wind	Name	Nat	Born	Date
6.52	1.1	Deirdre McKinley	USA	62	9 Apr
6.51i	-	Marion Reichelt	GDR	62	13 Feb
6.51A		Carole Jones	USA	65	17 Apr
6.51		Nena Gage	USA	66	1 Jun
6.51	1.2	Mirela Dulgheru	RUM	66	14 Aug
6.50i	-	Patricia Davis	USA	65	5 Feb
6.50i	-	Elisabeth Anghel	RUM	67	15 Feb
6.50		Tatyana Kotova	SU	70	14 May
6.50		Zhuang Ping	CHN	66	21 May
6.50	0.8	Heike Grabe	GDR	62	11 Jun
		(110)			
6.50	2.0	Tatyana Morozova	SU	64	29 Jul
6.50	2.0	Maria Lambrou	CYP	53	21 Aug
6.49	0.8	Rita Heggli	SWZ	62	24 Jul
6.48i	-	Sabine Braun	FRG	65	28 Feb
6.48	0.9	Svetlana Buraga	SU	65	22 May
6.48		Yelizaveta Galkina	SU	72	1 Jul
6.48		Dong Yuping	CHN	63	10 Jul
6.48	0.9	Cindy Greiner	USA	57	22 Jul
6.48	0.1	Satomi Kawazu	JAP	62	1 Sep
6.47i	-	Irina Konyukhova	SU	59	30 Jan
		(120)			
6.47	0.6	Anu Kaljurand	SU	69	12 Jun
6.47		Anita Chesnakova	SU	68	16 Jun
6.47	0.2	Natalya Frolova	SU	65	18 Jun
6.47	1.8	Gwen Loud	USA	61	22 Jul
6.47	1.5	Joanne Wise	UK	71	30 Jul
6.47	0.3	Remigia Sablovskaite	SU	67	2 Aug
6.46A		Jolanda Jones	USA	65	17 Apr
6.46	1.2	Jasmin Feige +	FRG	59	11 Jun
6.46		Petra Vaideanu	RUM	65	19 Jun
6.46	0.5	Anisoara Ghebuta	RUM	70	19 Jun
		(130)			
6.46	0.9	Olimpia Constantea	RUM	68	14 Aug
6.46	1.9	Lena Wallin	SWE	58	14 Aug
6.45	0.2	Chantal Beaugeant	FRA	61	19 Jun
6.44		Jacinta Bartholomew	GRN	65	1 Jun
6.44	0.0	Lyudmila Kharenko	SU	68	18 Jun
6.44	1.8	Silke Harms	FRG	67	10 Jul
6.44	-1.0	Mieke van den Kolk	HOL	68	17 Jul
6.44		Wang Chunfang	CHN	70	21 Aug
6.43		Julie Lewis	USA	66	22 Jun
6.43	0.4	Edith Oker	FRG	61	1 Jul
		(140)			
6.43	-0.2	Viktoria Ryzhova	SU	68	2 Jul
6.42i	-	Terri Turner	USA	63	22 Jan
6.42i	-	Irina Tyukhay	SU	67	6 Feb
6.42i	-	Kerstin Poltrock	FRG	64	20 Feb
6.42i	-	Carlette Guidry	USA	68	11 Mar
6.42		Karen Kruger	RSA	63	22 Apr
6.42		Alla Kozlova	SU	69	28 Jun
6.42	2.0	Sabrina Williams	USA	63	22 Jul
6.42	1.0	Emilia Dimitrova	BUL	67	29 Aug
6.41		Menka Scott	USA	66	27 May
		(150)			
6.41	1.2	Iwona Ciolkowska	POL	71	24 Jul
6.40A		Sanet Fouché	RSA	64	16 Apr
6.40		Pam Smith	USA	66	29 Apr
6.40		Galina Baranovskaya	SU	66	21 May
6.40	0.4	Maria C. Moroni	ITA	69	19 Jun
6.40	1.9	Julie Goodrich	USA	65	22 Jul
6.40		Yelena Bykova	SU	67	21 Sep
6.40	0.1	Hiroko Okumura	JAP	64	18 Oct

Best outdoor marks

Mark	Wind	Name	Pos	Meet	Venue	Date	Indoor
6.79	0.6	Behmer	H	Int	Talence	17 Jul	6.80i
6.79	1.4	Chicherova	1		Baku	11 Sep	6.82i
6.73	0.9	Radtke	1	GO	Dresden	11 Jun	6.76i
6.70	0.0	Capriotti	1		Brescia	12 Jun	6.72i
6.69	2.0	Moneva	-		Sofia	4 Jun	6.85i
6.60	0.0	Myers	1	Int	Sevilla	1 Jun	6.68i
6.59	0.5	Iacob	4	RomIC	Bucuresti	19 Jun	6.60i

Mark	Wind	Name	Date	Indoor
6.53	0.6	Ehlert	4 Jun	6.57i
6.51	0.0	Hirsch	26 Jun	6.55i
6.48		Reichelt	18 Jun	6.51i
6.46		Cornateanu	14 Aug	6.69i
6.42		Tyukhay	4 Sep	6.42i
6.41		Turner	7 May	6.42i
6.41		Schmidt	29 May	6.55i

Wind assisted

Mark	Wind	Name		Nat	Born	Pos	Meet	Venue	Date
7.45	2.6	Jackie	Joyner-Kersee	USA	62	1	FOT	Indianapolis	23 Jul
7.07	2.7	Irina	Valyukevich	SU	59	5	Znam	Leningrad	11 Jun
6.88	3.3	Yvette	Bates	USA	65	4	FOT	Indianapolis	23 Jul
6.88	2.1	Fiona	May	UK	69	1	WJ	Sudbury	30 Jul
6.87	3.1	Anke	Behmer	GDR	61	2		Berlin	13 Sep
6.84	2.8	Anu	Kaljurand	SU	69	2	RigaC	Riga	4 Jun
6.81		Adelina	Polledo	CUB	66	1		Caracas	24 Jun
6.72	3.3	Sofia	Bozhanova	BUL	67	1		Sofia	23 Jul
6.69	4.7	Joanne	Wise	UK	71	3	WJ	Sudbury	30 Jul
6.67	2.8	Tatyana	Ter-Mesrobian	SU	67	8	Znam	Leningrad	11 Jun
6.65		Claire	Connor	USA	66	1	DrakeR	Dei Moines	30 Apr
6.64	2.2	Tineke	Hidding	HOL	56	1	v Bel,Eng	Roosendaal	23 Jul
6.64	2.1	Tracy	Smith	CAN	64	1	NC	Ottawa	6 Aug
6.62		Nena	Gage	USA	66	1	NCAA	Eugene	3 Jun
6.59	2.3	Arja	Jusilla	FIN	53	1	Int	Savonlinna	31 Jul
6.58	2.2	Gaby	Ehlert	GDR	65	2	v Ita	Neubrandenburg	9 Jul
6.58	2.9	Cindy	Greiner	USA	57	7	FOT	Indianapolis	23 Jul
6.58	2.3	Mary	Berkeley	UK	65	1	Int	Hechtel	30 Jul
6.54		Jacinta	Bartholomew	GRN	65	3	NCAA	Eugene	3 Jun
6.54	3.8	Beverly	Kinch	UK	64	2	NP	Haringey	20 Aug
6.54	2.6	Jane	Flemming	AUS	65	2		Chiba	15 Sep

Mark	Wind	Name	Nat	Born	Date
6.52	2.5	Satomi Kawazu	JAP	62	29 May
6.51		Lorinda Richardson	USA	66	30 Apr
6.51		Karen Kruger	RSA	63	14 May
6.50		Beatrice Mau	GDR	71	12 Jun
6.47		Jearl Miles	USA	66	30 Apr
6.46		Mazel Thomas	JAM	67	20 May
6.45		Alissa Bell	USA	68	4 May
6.45	2.2	Janet Harvey	USA	61	22 Jul
6.45	3.1	Svetla Dimitrova	BUL	70	30 Jul
6.43		DeDe Nathan	USA	68	23 Apr
6.43		Catherine Richards	BAR	..	6 May
6.43	2.6	Julie Goodrich	USA	65	23 Jul
6.41		Camille Jampolsky	USA	65	9 Apr

Best series

Mark	Name	Date						
7.52	Chistyakova	11 Jun	(7.21	7.38w	7.21	7.45	x	7.52)
7.48	Drechsler	9 Jul	(7.01	6.87	7.26	7.37	7.16w	7.48)
7.45	Chistyakova	12 Aug	(7.05	7.13w	7.24	7.28w	7.45	x)
7.40	Joyner-Kersee	29 Sep	(7.00	x	7.16	x	7.40	x)
7.39	Joyner-Kersee	25 Jun	(7.39	x	x	-	-	-)
7.37i	Drechsler	13 Feb	(4.51	x	6.71	6.97	x	7.37)
7.36	Byelevskaya	11 Jun	(7.03w	7.36	7.08	7.25	x	7.20w)
7.30i	Drechsler	5 Mar	(6.96	7.17	7.03	7.22	x	7.24)
7.29	Chistyakova	1 Jun	(7.23	7.29	x	6.88	x	7.11)
7.27	Joyner-Kersee	24 Sep	(7.27	-	-	)		
7.24i	Drechsler	20 Feb	(x	7.07	7.11	7.12	x	7.24)
7.24i	Chistyakova	5 Mar	(7.01	7.24	6.94	7.14	x	7.15)
7.23i	Chistyakova	10 Feb	(6.98	7.03	6.83	7.23	7.21	x)
7.23	Kravets	6 Jul	(6.70	6.87	6.70	6.89	7.00	7.23)
7.22	Joyner-Kersee	22 Jul	(7.22	-	-	)		
7.22	Drechsler	29 Sep	(6.92	7.06	7.18	7.22	7.16	7.17)
7.21	Byelevskaya	1 Jun	(x	7.08	6.87	7.21	x	7.05)
7.21	Chistyakova	14 Sep	(7.03	7.21	6.59	7.07	7.10	x)
7.20	Drechsler	25 Jun	(7.02	6.93	7.20	7.17	x	x)
7.18	Chistyakova	16 Jun	(7.18	6.96	x	x	6.98	7.11)
7.17	Drechsler	29 Jun	(6.83	7.03	6.64	6.73	6.71	7.17)
7.16	Kravets	18 Jun	(6.90	6.97	7.14	6.98	7.16	6.78)
7.14	Medvedyeva	4 Jun	(x	6.83	x	7.14	6.98	7.05)
7.13i	Chistyakova	20 Feb	(6.90	7.13	-	-	-	-)
7.12	Drechsler	19 Jun	(6.71	7.10	6.89	x	x	7.12)
7.45w	Joyner-Kersee	23 Jul	(7.04w	7.45w	5.51	x	x	6.40w)

Series not known for Kokonova 7.29, Kravets 7.27, Byelevskaya 7.21, Drechsler 7.18 and 7.17 (13 Sep), Chen 7.16

TRIPLE JUMP

Mark	Wind	Name		Nat	Born	Pos	Meet	Venue	Date
14.16		Li Huirong		CHN	65	1		Shijiazhuang	23 Apr
13.82	1.8	Wendy	Brown	USA	66	1	TAC	Tampa	17 Jun
13.79		Sheila	Hudson	USA	67	1	S&W	Modesto	7 May
13.64i	-	Yvette	Bates	USA	65	1	NCAA	Oklahoma City	12 Mar
13.59			Brown			1		Westwood	22 May
13.56i	-	Renita	Robinson (Nb)	USA	67	1	Inv	Lincoln	13 Feb
13.54			Hudson			2		Westwood	22 May
13.48i	-		Brown			2	NCAA	Oklahoma City	12 Mar
13.46i	-		Robinson			1		Lincoln	30 Jan
13.46		Hudson (10/5)				1		Fresno	9 Apr
13.30i	-	Flora	Hyacinth	UVI	66	1		Baton Rouge	28 Feb
13.25		Diana	Wills	USA	67	1	NCAA/II	San Angelo	21 May
13.19		Li Shuhua		CHN	68	.		Tianjin	5 Sep
13.08	-0.1	Tatyana	Fyodorova	SU	..	1		Sochi	23 Apr
13.07		Cheng Xianhong (10)		CHN	68	.		Tianjin	5 Sep

Mark	Wind	Name	Nat	Born	Date
13.06		Lavern Clark	CAN	67	15 May
13.01		Carina Kjellman	FIN	63	4 Jun
13.00i	-	Tamara Compton	USA	65	12 Mar
12.98	1.3	Nena Gage	USA	66	17 Jun
12.94	1.1	Angela Goodman	USA	66	17 Jun
12.94		Wei Wein	CHN	68	5 Sep
12.93	-0.6	Galina Pavlova	SU		23 Apr
12.92		Jackie Anderson	USA	69	16 Apr
12.91		Felicia Curry	USA	66	2 Jun
12.83i	-	LaKeta Ziegler (20)	USA	68	6 Mar
12.83		Fu Xiaorong	CHN	68	10 Jun
12.80		Julie Lewis	USA	66	15 May
12.79i	-	Janeen Bonner	USA	67	11 Dec
12.77	1.2	Starlite Williams	USA	64	7 May
12.76		Zhao Mei	CHN	66	5 Sep
12.75		Sylvia Dyer	JAM	66	15 Apr
12.75	-0.2	Irina Oreshkina	SU	63	23 Apr
12.75i	-	Evette Finikin	UK	63	11 Dec
12.75	-0.5	Irina Osipova	SU	63	23 Apr
12.73	-0.1	Natalya Kayukova (30)	SU		23 Apr

Best outdoor mark

Mark	Name	Pos	Venue	Date
13.40	Bates	1	Los Angeles	9 Apr

WOMEN 1988

Mark		Name		Nat	Born	Pos	Meet	Venue	Date
Wind assisted									
13.92	3.8	Sheila	Hudson	USA	67	1	NCAA	Eugene	4 Jun
13.55	2.8		Brown			2	NCAA	Eugene	4 Jun
13.53	2.2		Robinson			1		Indianapolis	21 Jul
13.51			Hudson			1		Stanford	26 Mar
13.48	2.4		Bates			3	NCAA	Eugene	4 Jun
13.47A			Bates			1		El Paso	17 Apr

Mark	Name	Nat	Born	Date	Mark	Name	Nat	Born	Date
13.03	Billie Butler	USA	68	9 Apr	12.91	Sylvia Dyer	JAM	66	21 May
13.03	Felicia Curry	USA	66	23 Apr	12.88	Mazel Thomas	JAM	67	21 May
12.99	Nena Gage	USA	66	28 Apr	12.75	Robyne Johnson	USA	63	7 May
					12.75	Yolanda Taylor	USA	67	15 May

SHOT

Mark	Name		Nat	Born	Pos	Meet	Venue	Date
22.55	Natalya	Lisovskaya	SU	62	1	NC	Tallinn	5 Jul
22.53		Lisovskaya			1		Kiev	14 Aug
22.24		Lisovskaya			1	OG	Seoul	1 Oct
22.06		Lisovskaya			1		Moskva	6 Aug
21.96		Lisovskaya			1		Vilnius	28 Aug
21.95		Lisovskaya			1	IAC	Edinburgh	29 Jul
21.92		Lisovskaya			1		Sochi	1 Jun
21.76	Li Meisu		CHN	59	1		Shijiazhuang	23 Apr
21.73	Natalya	Akhrimenko	SU	55	1		Leselidze	21 May
21.73		Lisovskaya			1	v Fra,UK	Portsmouth	19 Jun
21.60i		Lisovskaya			1	NC	Volgograd	11 Feb
21.60i		Lisovskaya			1	NP	Moskva	21 Feb
21.57 @	Ines	Müller	GDR	59	1		Athinai	16 May
21.49		Li Meisu			1	Int	Tianjin	1 Sep
21.44i		Lisovskaya			1	v Ita,Spa	Valencia	17 Feb
21.43		Lisovskaya			1	PTS	Bratislava	8 Jun
21.42		Akhrimenko			2	NC	Tallinn	5 Jul
21.38		Li Meisu			1	NC	Nanjing	11 Jun
21.31 @	Heike	Hartwig	GDR	62	2		Athinai	16 May
21.30		Akhrimenko			1	NP	Vladivostok	14 Sep
21.28	Huang Zhihong		CHN	65	2		Shijiazhuang	23 Apr
21.27		Hartwig			1	Int	Chania	22 May
21.20		Lisovskaya			1	Znam	Leningrad	11 Jun
21.17		Hartwig			1		Karl-Marx-Stadt	12 Jun
21.14		Müller			1		Potsdam	30 Jun
21.11	Kathrin	Neimke	GDR	66	1		Berlin	13 Sep
21.08i		Li Meisu			1	NC	Beijing	25 Mar
21.08	Valentina	Fedyushina	SU	65	1		Leselidze	15 May
21.08		Müller			1		Rostock	29 May
21.07		Neimke			2	OG	Seoul	1 Oct
	(30/8)							
20.89	Larisa	Peleshenko	SU	64	2		Kiev	14 Aug
20.81	Ilona	Briesenick	GDR	56	1		Berlin	27 Aug
	(10)							
20.80	Sona	Vasicková	CS	62	1		Praha	2 Jun
20.58	Svetla	Mitkova	BUL	64	1	NC	Sofia	3 Sep
20.57	Claudia	Losch	FRG	60	2	v GDR	Düsseldorf	19 Jun
20.53	Iris	Plotzitzka	FRG	66	1	ASV	Köln	21 Aug
20.51	Marina	Antonyuk	SU	62	3		Sochi	1 Jun
20.50	Grit	Hammer	GDR	66	4	NC	Rostock	25 Jun
20.47	Cong Yuzhen		CHN	63	2	IntC	Tianjin	3 Sep
20.23	Ilke	Wyludda	GDR	69	1	NC-j	Karl-Marx-Stadt	16 Jul
20.18	Ramona	Pagel	USA	61	1		San Diego	25 Jun
20.08	Sui Xinmei		CHN	65	2	Int	Tianjin	1 Sep
	(20)							
19.85	Helena	Fibingerová	CS	49	1		Kamp-Linfort	27 Aug
19.80	Lyudmila	Voyevudskaya	SU	59	1		Dnepropetrovsk	17 Jul
19.79	Mihaela	Loghin	RUM	52	1	NC	Pitesti	14 Aug
19.78	Zdenka	Silhavá	CS	54	2	5-N	Nitra	28 Aug
19.73	Stephanie	Storp	FRG	68	2	NC	Frankfurt	24 Jul
19.68	Vera	Schmidt	FRG	61	2		München	3 Jul
19.65	Heidi	Krieger	GDR	65	6	NC	Rostock	25 Jun
19.55	Danguole	Urbikiene	SU	62	5	NC	Tallinn	5 Jul

Mark	Name		Nat	Born	Pos	Meet	Venue	Date
19.55	Livia	Mehes	RUM	65	2	NC	Pitesti	14 Aug
19.50	Zhou Tianhua		CHN	66	4	Int	Tianjin	1 Sep
	(30)							
19.49	Bonnie	Dasse	USA	59	2		San Diego	25 Jun
19.36	Judith	Oakes	UK	58	1	v Hun	Gateshead	14 Aug
19.34	Belsis	Laza	CUB	67	1	Hanz	Zagreb	2 Jun
19.28	Verzhinia	Veselinova	BUL	57	2		Sofia	5 Jun
19.23	Jana	Ciobanu	RUM	68	1		Bucuresti	12 Jun
19.19	Christa	Wiese	GDR	67	1		Schwerin	1 Jun
19.15	Connie	Price	USA	62	1	TAC	Tampa	18 Jun
19.13i	Alena	Vitoulová	CS	60	2	NC	Jablonec	20 Feb
19.06	Anna	Romanova	SU	68	4		Vilnius	28 Aug
18.94	Heike	Rohrmann	GDR	69	1		Halle	14 May
	(40)							
18.80	Ines	Wittich	GDR	69	2	NC-j	Karl-Marx-Stadt	16 Jul
18.80	Sabine	Kruse	FRG	66	1		Ulm	6 Aug
18.73	Astrid	Kumbernuss	GDR	70	3	NC-j	Karl-Marx-Stadt	16 Jul
18.70i	Galina	Kuzhel	SU	59	1		Volgograd	30 Jan
18.60i	Tatyana	Khorkhulyova	SU	64	1		Minsk	30 Jan
18.60i	Viktória	Horváth	HUN	56	1	5-N	Athinai	6 Feb
18.58	Tatyana	Byelova	SU	62	1		Bryansk	29 Jul
18.49	Asta	Hovi	FIN	63	1	Int	Tampere	23 Aug
18.47i	Lyubov	Vasilyeva	SU	57	5	NP	Moskva	21 Feb
18.42	Yelena	Byelovolova	SU	65	1		Smolensk	27 Jun
	(50)							
18.35	Svetlana	Krivelyova	SU	69	1	NC-j	Bryansk	6 Jul
18.35	Tatyana	Orlova	SU	55	1		Staiki	2 Aug
18.30i	Malgorzata	Wolska	POL	66	1	NC	Zabrze	20 Feb
18.30	Marina	Burina	SU	62	2		Leningrad	11 May
18.29	Myrtle	Augee	UK	65	2		Waltham Forest	3 Sep
18.20	Lilia	Shults	SU	64	2		Sochi	24 Apr
18.18	Annette	Gerlach	GDR	69	3		Jena	20 May
18.07i	Pam	Dukes	USA	64	2	TAC	Princeton	26 Jan
18.07	Lyubov	Khvostikova	SU	64	1		Leningrad	3 Jun
18.04	Astra	Etienne	AUS	60	1		Canberra	26 Jan
	(60)							
18.04	Nadezhda	Frantseva	SU	61	3		Odessa	18 Aug
18.02	Ursula	Stäheli	SWZ	57	1	NC	Zug	14 Aug
18.01	Nadezhda	Lukiniv	SU	68	2		Kharkov	17 Jun
18.00	Hajnal	Vörös-Herth	HUN	59	2	Int	Budapest	11 Jul
17.94i	Yelena	Kakushkina	SU	63	1		Minsk	9 Jan
17.90	Lyudmila	Novikova	SU	64	4		Kiev	14 Aug
17.73	Zheng Liuhong		CHN	69	1		Changsha	24 May
17.72	Svetlana	Melnikova	SU	51	.		Moskva	28 Aug
17.64	Zhou Shuqin		CHN	68	.		Nanjing	26 Aug
17.61i	Eha	Rünne	SU	63	1		Tallinn	6 Feb
	(70)							
17.53i	Monika	Andris	SU	65	2		Zaporozhye	24 Jan
17.52	Irina	Khudorozhkina	SU	68	3		Sochi	24 Apr
17.52	Ella	Polyakova	SU	70	2	NC-j	Bryansk	6 Jul
17.51	Svetlana	Dorokhova	SU	64	4		Odessa	18 Aug
17.51	Yelena	Ortina	SU	61	5		Odessa	18 Aug
17.50	Mihaela	Oana	RUM	68	2		Bucuresti	2 Jun
17.50	Diana	Stoyanova	BUL	69	1	NC-j	Sofia	2 Jul
17.48	Leng Molian		CHN	67	2		Jinan	27 Oct
17.47	Regina	Cavanaugh	USA	64	5	FOT	Indianapolis	23 Jul
17.47	Zhen Wenhua		CHN	67	5	IntC	Tianjin	3 Sep
	(80)							
17.46i	Alexandra	Kuznyetsova	SU	66	2		Baku	24 Jan
17.46	Mariana	Lengyel	RUM	53	2	Int	Auckland	27 Feb
17.45	Peggy	Pollock	USA	60	2		Los Angeles	19 Feb
17.45	Liliana	Isac	RUM	63	4	NC	Pitesti	14 Aug
17.39i	Anastasia	Pavlova	SU	68	3		Klaipeda	6 Mar
17.33	Wang Hong		CHN	70	2		Changsha	24 May
17.28	Simona	Andrusca	RUM	62	1		Suceava	8 May
17.24	Katja	Weiser	FRG	66	1		Lüdenscheid	8 Oct

Mark	Name		Nat	Born	Pos	Meet	Venue	Date
17.22	Dot	Jones	USA	64	1		Bakersfield	13 Feb
17.22	Yvonne	Hanson-Nortey	UK	64	1		Cleckheaton	22 May
	(90)							
17.22	Petya	Zhecheva	BUL	69	2	Balk-j	Alexandroúpolis	9 Jul
17.18	Natalya	Kozlova	SU	67	1		Kharkov	19 Aug
17.07	Lyudmila	Koptyakevich	SU	65	3		Moskva	9 Jul
17.05i	Tatyana	Vinogradova	SU	66	1		Donyetsk	5 Mar
17.05	Yelena	Lyapunova	SU	70	4		Sochi	24 Apr
17.04	Lisette	Martínez	CUB	66	2	NP	Habana	28 Feb
17.03	Zhanna	Babikova	SU	69	1		Ordzhonikidze	25 Sep
17.02	Carol	Cady	USA	62	q	FOT	Indianapolis	22 Jul
17.01	Wang Wei		CHN	67	6	IntC	Tianjin	3 Sep
16.95	Danica	Zivanov	YUG	67	1	NC	Sarajevo	4 Sep
	(100)							

Mark	Name		Nat	Born	Date
16.94i	Iveta	Garancha	SU	64	30 Jan
16.94	Jennifer	Ponath	USA	65	14 May
16.93	Min Chunfeng		CHN	69	27 Oct
16.89	Gabriele	Völkl	FRG	70	9 Jul
16.85	Carla	Garrett	USA	67	22 Jul
16.84	Jackie	Joyner-Kersee	USA	62	26 Jun
16.80i	Svetlana	Buryak	SU	67	12 Jan
16.80	Debbie	St.Phard	HAI	64	27 Jun
16.80	Dörte	Warbelow	GDR	70	2 Jul
16.79	Viktoria	Kochetova	SU	67	29 Jul
	(110)				
16.76	Márta	Bácskai	HUN	60	8 Jun
16.73	Irena	Car	POL	66	20 Aug
16.70i	Elmira	Urusova	SU	66	24 Jan
16.67	Annette	Bohach	USA	61	8 May
16.64i	Larisa	Baranova	SU	61	10 Jan
16.63	Birgit	Petsch	FRG	63	13 Jun
16.61i	Angie	Barker	USA	65	20 Feb
16.61	Tünde	Elekes	HUN	63	14 May
16.60i	Natalya	Zubekhina	SU	51	30 Jan
16.60	Deborah	Dunant	HOL	66	19 Jun
	(120)				
16.58	Agnese	Maffeis	ITA	65	4 Jun
16.57	Herminia	Fernández	CUB	67	28 Feb
16.54	Hana	Mísarová	CS	67	15 May
16.41	Kathy	Picknell	USA	58	3 Jul
16.39	Yelena	Chibisova	SU	69	10 Sep
16.37	Margaret	Lynes	UK	63	30 Apr
16.37	Melody	Torcolacci	CAN	60	27 May
16.36i	Margarita	Ramos	SPA	66	21 Feb
16.30	Galabina	Koleva	BUL	71	13 Aug
16.29	Lada	Kirillova	SU	69	2 May
	(130)				
16.29	Malda	Lange	SU	61	10 Sep
16.28	Viktoria	Pavlysh	SU	69	27 May
16.27	Oksana	Popova	SU	71	10 Apr
16.26i	Nathalie	Ganguillet	SWZ	67	21 Feb
16.26	Elena	Ghilencea	RUM	69	15 May
16.23	Sabine	John	GDR	57	23 Sep
16.22	Remigia	Sablovskaite	SU	67	3 Aug
16.22	Wang Yurong		CHN		3 Sep
16.20	Natalya	Cheshkina	SU	68	19 Jun
16.18i	Natalya	Lisetskaya	SU	68	9 Jan
	(140)				
16.18	Larisa	Kostyrskaya	SU	68	11 Jun
16.18	Chen Yingli		CHN		27 Oct
16.17i	Sonja	Payne	USA	68	12 Mar
16.17	Julieta	Zheleva	BUL	70	13 Aug
16.16i	Iveta	Kudrnová	CS	66	6 Feb
16.14	Lisa	Vizaniari	AUS	69	29 Oct
16.12	Yelena	Kovalyova	SU	63	27 Jun
16.11i	Nina	Korsunskaya	SU	54	9 Jan
16.10	Yelena	Bolshakova	SU	71	26 Aug
16.08	Svetlana	Bystrova	SU	67	2 Aug
	(150)				
16.07	Agnes	Deselaers	FRG	68	1 May
16.06	Martine	Jean-Michel	FRA	64	19 Jun
16.05	Yelena	Dementiy	SU	69	25 Jun
16.03i	Miglena	Meleshkova	BUL	67	20 Feb
16.03	Anna	Salinska	POL	63	4 Jun
16.03	Caroline	Isgren	SWE	66	21 Sep
16.02	Shirley	Ross	USA	65	6 May
16.02	Valérie	Hanicque	FRA	64	1 Jun
16.02	Cornelia	Heinrich	FRG	60	18 Jun
16.01i	Concetta	Milanese	ITA	62	9 Jan
	(160)				
16.01	Léone	Bertimon	FRA	50	11 Jun

Best outdoor marks

Mark	Name	Pos	Meet	Venue	Date	Indoor
18.62	Kuzhel	4	v Rum	Bucuresti	19 Jun	18.70i
18.57	Horváth	2	v UK	Gateshead	14 Aug	18.60i
18.35	Khorkhulyova	1		Grodno	19 Jun	18.60i
18.32	Vasilyeva	1		Chelyabinsk	17 Jul	18.47i
18.18	Vitoulová	3	GS	Ostrava	7 Jun	19.13i
17.88	Wolska	2		Poznan	20 Aug	18.30i
17.78	Kakushkina	2		Grodno	19 Jun	17.94i
17.70	Dukes	2	TAC	Tampa	18 Jun	18.07i
17.24	Andris	2		Baku	10 Sep	17.53i

Mark	Name	Date	Indoor
16.92	Kuznyetsova	12 Jul	17.46i
16.84	Pavlova	14 Jun	17.39i
16.77	Runne	30 May	17.61i
16.72	Vinogradova	19 Aug	17.05i
16.70	Garancha	3 Sep	16.94i
16.30	Ramos	2 Jun	16.36i
16.23	Barker	20 Mar	16.61i

Best series

Mark	Name	Date	Series					
22.55	Lisovskaya	5 Jul	(20.70	21.62	22.55	20.95	22.19	21.16)
22.53	Lisovskaya	14 Aug	(21.94	22.40	22.04	22.53	21.60	x)
22.24	Lisovskaya	1 Oct	(21.69	21.49	21.24	21.74	21.11	22.24)
22.06	Lisovskaya	6 Aug	(21.10	x	22.06	21.89	21.44	21.86)
21.95	Lisovskaya	29 Jul	(21.95	21.01	21.19	21.37	x	21.70)
21.92	Lisovskaya	1 Jun	(19.68	21.73	21.13	21.92	21.35	x)
21.60i	Lisovskaya	11 Feb	(21.41	21.31	x	20.76	21.00	21.60)
21.60i	Lisovskaya	21 Feb	(20.04	20.71	20.77	21.60	21.09	20.86)
21.43	Lisovskaya	8 Jun	(x	20.86	x	x	21.43	21.41)
21.42	Akhrimenko	5 Jul	(20.91	x	x	x	x	21.42)
21.30	Akhrimenko	14 Sep	(19.47	21.30	-	-	-	-)

Mark	Name		Nat	Born	Pos	Meet	Venue	Date
21.27	Hartwig	22 May	(21.27	20.68	19.89	20.63	20.93	x)
21.20	Lisovskaya	11 Jun	(20.68	20.86	21.06	21.20	x	x)
21.07	Neimke	1 Oct	(19.64	20.07	19.82	20.37	20.72	21.07)

Series not known for other top 30 performances

	Shot		Year List Progression			Discus				
Year	Best	10th	20th	50th	100th	Best	10th	20th	50th	100th
1968	18.34	16.60	15.74	14.93	14.27	61.26	55.10	53.00	50.06	48.00
1978	22.06	19.92	19.01	17.25	16.09	70.72	64.34	62.40	59.34	55.06
1979	22.04	20.21	19.18	17.46	16.35	69.82	65.06	63.80	59.86	56.00
1980	22.45	20.54	19.36	17.58	16.33	71.80	66.02	65.26	61.80	56.46
1981	21.61	19.54	18.75	17.41	16.47	71.46	66.80	64.20	60.82	56.42
1982	21.80	20.55	19.62	17.96	16.82	71.40	68.18	65.04	60.90	57.04
1983	22.40	20.54	19.61	18.19	17.00	73.26	67.32	65.10	61.98	58.52
1984	22.53	20.55	19.94	18.42	17.18	74.56	68.56	66.02	62.10	58.50
1985	21.73	20.39	19.47	18.13	16.92	72.96	67.52	65.20	60.92	57.14
1986	21.70	20.60	19.59	18.54	17.12	73.26	67.92	65.44	60.66	57.48
1987	22.63	20.85	20.27	18.55	17.19	74.08	67.90	66.34	61.30	57.78

DISCUS

Mark	Name		Nat	Born	Pos	Meet	Venue	Date
76.80	Gabriele	Reinsch	GDR	63	1	v Ita	Neubrandenburg	9 Jul
74.44		Reinsch			1		Berlin	13 Sep
74.40	Ilke	Wyludda	GDR	69	2		Berlin	13 Sep
73.84	Daniela	Costian	RUM	65	1		Bucuresti	30 Apr
73.78		Costian			1		Bucuresti	24 Apr
73.42		Reinsch			1	Int	Karl-Marx-Stadt	12 Jun
72.94	Diana	Gansky	GDR	63	2	v Ita	Neubrandenburg	9 Jul
72.90		Costian			1		Bucuresti	14 May
72.78		Reinsch			1	OD	Berlin	29 Jun
72.70		Wyludda			1	NC-j	Karl-Marx-Stadt	15 Jul
72.54		Gansky			1	NC	Rostock	25 Jun
72.30	Martina	Hellmann	GDR	60	1	OG	Seoul	29 Sep
72.24		Wyludda			3	v Ita	Neubrandenburg	9 Jul
72.06		Costian			1		Bucuresti	7 May
72.02		Hellmann			1	Int	Chania	22 May
72.02		Costian			1		Bucuresti	4 Jun
71.98		Wyludda			2	Int	Karl-Marx-Stadt	12 Jun
71.88 @		Wyludda			1		Athinai	16 May
71.88		Reinsch			2	NC	Rostock	25 Jun
71.88		Gansky			2	OG	Seoul	29 Sep
71.68	Zdenka	Silhavá	CS	54	1		Praha	15 May
71.64		Reinsch			1		Potsdam	12 May
71.64 @		Gansky			2		Athinai	16 May
71.64		Reinsch			1		Jena	4 Jun
71.64		Silhava			1		Litomysl	6 Aug
71.58	Ellina	Zveryeva	SU	60	1	Znam	Leningrad	12 Jun
71.54		Wyludda			1	Int	Rostock	29 May
71.38		Hellmann			4	v Ita	Neubrandenburg	9 Jul
71.26		Hellmann			2		Jena	4 Jun
71.22		Zveryeva			1		Leselidze	22 May
	(30/7)							
71.06	Tsvetanka	Khristova	BUL	61	1		Stara Zagora	28 Aug
70.80	Larisa	Mikhalchenko	SU	63	1		Kharkov	18 Jun
70.34 @	Silvia	Madetzky	GDR	62	3		Athinai	16 May
	(10)							
69.86	Galina	Murashova	SU	55	1		Vilnius	11 Aug
69.14	Irina	Meszynski	GDR	62	1		Berlin	27 Aug
69.14	Svetla	Mitkova	BUL	64	4	OG	Seoul	29 Sep
68.62	Yu Hourun		CHN	62	1		Beijing	6 May
68.62	Hou Xuemei		CHN	62	1	IntC	Tianjin	4 Sep
68.18	Irina	Khval	SU	62	1		Moskva	8 Jul
67.62	Mariana	Lengyel	RUM	53	1	Int	Hamilton	20 Feb
67.44	Irina	Yatchenko	SU	65	6	Znam	Leningrad	12 Jun
67.02	Maritza	Marten	CUB	63	1	GG	Verona	27 Jul

Mark	Name		Nat	Born	Pos	Meet	Venue	Date
66.84	Jana	Günther	GDR	68	1		Budapest	2 Jul
	(20)							
66.60	Astrid	Kumbernuss	GDR	70	1		Berlin	20 Jul
66.58	Hilda	Ramos	CUB	64	1	ISTAF	West Berlin	26 Aug
66.48	Tatyana	Byelova	SU	62	1		Krasnoyarsk	10 Jul
66.18	Renata	Katewicz	POL	65	1		Lodz	7 Aug
66.08	Larisa	Korotkevich	SU	67	1		Siauliai	21 May
65.68	Andrea	Thieme	GDR	64	1		Leipzig	25 May
65.64	Elisabeta	Neamtu	RUM	60	2		Bucuresti	14 May
65.56	Franka	Dietzsch	GDR	68	5		Berlin	13 Sep
65.42	Xin Ailan		CHN	65			Beijing	30 Apr
65.34	Olga	Davydova	SU	62	4		Sochi	31 May
	(30)							
65.06	Malda	Lange	SU	61	1		Valmiera	11 Sep
64.58	Cristina	Boit	RUM	68	1		Bucuresti	9 Jul
64.32	Antonina	Patoka	SU	64	1		Chelyabinsk	16 Jul
64.26	Galina	Yermakova	SU	53	5		Sochi	31 May
64.22	Lyudmila	Platonova	SU	64	1		Odessa	2 May
63.82	Carol	Cady	USA	62	1		Stellenbosch	18 Oct
63.52	Ilga	Smeikste	SU	66	1		Pärnu	13 Jul
63.34	Barbara	Beuge	FRG	60	1		Schwabmünchen	31 Jul
63.32	Becky	Levi	USA	62	1		Tucson	11 Jun
63.18	Eha	Rünne	SU	63	2		Pärnu	13 Jul
	(40)							
63.16	Dagmar	Galler	FRG	61	1		Leverkusen	22 Aug
63.06	Irina	Shabanova	SU	64	1		Krasnodar	5 Apr
63.06	Vilia	Zubaitite	SU	63	1		Smalinikai	9 May
63.02	Valentina	Ivanova	SU	63	3		Vilnius	27 Aug
62.58	Viktoria	Kochetova	SU	67	4	Kuts	Moskva	4 Sep
62.54	Connie	Price	USA	62	2	Int	Hamilton	20 Feb
62.44	Larisa	Baranova	SU	61	2		Bryansk	12 Jul
62.42	Lyudmila	Novikova	SU	64	1		Leningrad	12 May
62.30	Mette	Bergmann	NOR	62	1		Alavieska	24 Jul
62.26	Tatyana	Berezhnaya	SU	56	1		Grodno	16 Jul
	(50)							
62.22	Galina	Kvachova	SU	65	13	Znam	Leningrad	12 Jun
62.20	Lacy	Barnes	USA	64	1		Logan	13 May
61.98	Natalya	Lisovskaya	SU	62	2	v UK,Fra	Portsmouth	19 Jun
61.80	Li Yan		CHN	64		NC	Nanjing	12 Jun
61.62	Olga	Nikishina	SU	66	3	RC	Kharkov	18 Jun
61.54	Stefenia	Simova	BUL	63	3		Stara Zagora	28 Aug
61.38	Márta	Bacskai	HUN	60	1		Budapest	18 Jun
61.36	Anne	Känsäkangas	FIN	59	1		Kokkola	2 Aug
61.34	Martina	Polisenská	CS	66	1		Olomouc	9 May
61.34	Sonja	Rust	GDR	66	8		Rostock	29 May
	(60)							
61.28	Ramona	Pagel	USA	61	2	FOT	Indianapolis	21 Jul
61.18	Olga	Cinibulková	CS	60	2		Litomysl	6 Aug
61.08	Penny	Neer	USA	60	1		Salinas	25 May
60.94	Jana	Lauren	GDR	70	2		Berlin	20 Jul
60.88	Ewa	Siepsiak	POL	57	2	Wal	Krakow	5 Jun
60.60	Agnes	Herczeg	HUN	50	1	v UK	Gateshead	14 Aug
60.60	Min Chunfeng		CHN	69	1		Jinan	26 Oct
60.28	Ursula	Kreutel	FRG	65	1		Stuttgart	20 Jul
60.26	Bárbara	Echevarría	CUB	66	7	NarM	Sofia	26 Jun
60.14	Lorna	Griffin	USA	56	1		Eagle Rock	18 Jun
	(70)							
60.10	Vita	Sileikite	SU	66	2		Vilnius	11 Aug
60.02	Svetlana	Dorokhova	SU	64	1	Kiev	3 May	
59.98	Svetlana	Savchenko	SU	65	1		Odessa	19 Aug
59.92	Irina	Yurchenko	SU	68	5	RigaC	Riga	4 Jun
59.82	Dai Mei		CHN	65	4	IntC	Tianjin	4 Sep
59.64	Iveta	Garancha	SU	64	2		Ozolnieki	23 Jul
59.60	Floarea	Vieru	RUM	67	3	NC	Pitesti	12 Aug
59.28	Proletka	Voycheva	BUL	70	1	Balk-j	Alexandroúpolis	10 Jul
59.18	Yelena	Kovalyova	SU	61	3		Moskva	2 May

Mark	Name		Nat	Born	Pos	Meet	Venue	Date
59.18	Zsuzsa	Pallay	HUN	48	1		Hatvan	23 Sep
	(80)							
59.10	Ingrid	Belz	FRG	67	q	NC	Frankfurt-am-Main	22 Jul
59.06	Becky	Fettig	USA	63	1		St. Paul	25 Jun
59.00	Olga L.	Gómez	CUB	66	3	Barr	Habana	5 Mar
58.82	Tatyana	Lugovskaya	SU	69	1		Kharkov	20 May
58.76	Li Xiaohui		CHN	57	1		Hiratsuka	23 Oct
58.72	Kelly	Landry	USA	63	1		New York	5 Jun
58.70	Carla	Garrett	USA	67	2		Tucson	11 Jun
58.38	Agnese	Maffeis	ITA	65	1		Trento	4 Jun
58.24	Manuela	Tirneci	RUM	69	1		Craiova	7 May
58.10	Dörte	Warbelow	GDR	70	1		Berlin	9 Jul
	(90)							
57.94	Svetlana	Melnikova	SU	51	3		Tula	21 Jun
57.82	Laura	Lavine	USA	66	3		Tucson	11 Jun
57.70	Zhang Hui		CHN	67	4	Int	Tianjin	1 Sep
57.70	Gale	Dolegiewicz	CAN	60	1		Saskatoon	8 Sep
57.60	Ursula	Weber	AUT	60	1		Baden	20 Aug
57.56	Zilia	Akhmetova	SU	61	3		Odessa	19 Aug
57.40	Sandra	Willms	RSA	60	1		Stellenbosch	29 Feb
57.40	Yelena	Rogachevskaya	SU	63	1		Zhitomir	12 Jun
57.40	Tatyana	Byelyakova	SU	69	1		Tula	21 Jun
57.40	Nanette	van der Walt	RSA	59	2		Stellenbosch	18 Oct
	(100)							

Mark	Name		Nat	Born	Date
57.28	Ilona	Zakharchenko	SU	67	6 Aug
57.12	Nadezhda	Frantseva	SU	61	5 Mar
57.10	Irina	Merkusheva	SU	67	16 May
57.10	Larisa	Zakorko	SU	64	16 Jul
57.08	Maria	Marello	ITA	61	14 Aug
56.98	Kathy	Picknell	USA	58	1 May
56.72	Stephanie	Storp	FRG	68	8 May
56.70	Astra	Etienne	AUS	60	13 Feb
56.58	Natalya	Bevzyuk	SU	66	9 Jan
56.56	Cheng Xiaohong		CHN	68	19 Jun
	(110)				
56.54	Kris	Larson	USA	65	22 May
56.50	Valérie	Hanicque	FRA	64	19 Mar
56.44	Patricia	Katona	FRA	61	26 Jun
56.28	Pinkie	Suggs	USA	64	7 May
56.28	Virginia	Tsutsurika	SU	68	8 Jul
56.22	Alla	Kokhan	SU	69	29 May
56.20	Svetlana	Buryak	SU	67	24 Jan
56.18	Marie-Paule Geldhof		BEL	59	27 Aug
56.10	Venissa	Head	UK	56	19 Jun
56.04	Rouxnel	White	RSA	63	18 Oct
	(120)				
56.00	Katalin	Csöke	HUN	57	9 Jun
55.86	Agnes	Deselaers	FRG	68	14 May
55.82	Irina	Grachova	SU	63	16 Jul
55.72	Vera	Schmidt	FRG	61	7 May
55.68	Zhao Yonghua		CHN	69	14 May
55.54	Pia	Iacovo	USA	61	16 Apr
55.32	Francine	Kaylor	USA	59	22 May
55.32	Lidia	Kolesnikova	SU	70	13 Aug
55.28	Anzhela	Baralyuk	SU	70	29 May
55.28	Zsuzsa	Lipl	HUN	65	7 Aug
	(130)				
55.22	Iveta	Kudrnova	CS	66	2 Jun
55.20	Larisa	Sudnitsina	SU	68	28 Jul
55.18	Angeles	Barreiro	SPA	63	13 Jul
55.16	Irina	Mikheyeva	SU	63	9 May
55.16	Ikuko	Kitamori	JAP	63	17 Jun
55.14	Yelena	Byelovolova	SU	65	4 Sep
55.12	Nadezhda	Glazova	SU	66	16 May
55.10	Mary	Dentinger	USA	64	16 Apr
55.00	Tracie	Millett	USA	69	3 Jun
54.74	Yevgenia	Nechayeva	SU	69	15 May
	(140)				
54.66	Janet	Hill	USA	70	18 May
54.64	Jennifer	Ponath	USA	65	22 May
54.58	Austrite	Mikelite	SU	69	14 Aug
54.54	Zheng Liping		CHN	65	9 Apr
54.46	Ines	Wittich	GDR	69	8 Jul
54.44	Svetlana	Golubic	YUG	62	2 Jul
54.38	Silke	Hachenberg	FRG	68	11 Jun
54.36	Colleen	Rosensteel	USA	67	16 Apr
54.32	Danuta	Zrajkowska	POL	67	9 Jul
54.32	Alla	Fyodorova	SU	66	27 Aug
	(150)				
54.28	Galina	Nikityayeva	SU	68	11 Jul
54.26	Heidi	Krieger	GDR	65	27 Aug
54.22	Isabel	Urrutia	COL	64	22 Jul
54.18	Sabine	Kruse	FRG	66	22 Jun
54.06	China	Blockton	USA	66	13 May
54.02	Pam	Dukes	USA	64	20 Mar
54.02	Catherine	Beauvais	FRA	65	12 Aug

Unofficial meeting

Mark	Name		Nat	Born	Pos	Venue	Date
78.14	Martina	Hellmann	GDR	60	-	Berlin	6 Sep

Best series

Mark	Name	Date	1	2	3	4	5	6
76.80	Reinsch	9 Jul	(76.80	73.10	x	70.56	70.86	71.98)
74.44	Reinsch	13 Sep	(66.62	74.44	68.80	73.32	x	71.06)
74.40	Wyludda	13 Sep	(73.16	70.58	72.74	74.40	72.00	x)
72.94	Gansky	9 Jul	(71.74	71.56	x	72.94	67.32	70.90)
72.90	Costian	14 May	(69.80	70.22	70.90	72.28	x	72.90)
72.78	Reinsch	29 Jun	(69.38	71.00	72.78	71.04	x	71.06)
72.70	Wyludda	15 Jul	(69.04	x	69.54	65.20	70.28	72.70)
72.54	Gansky	25 Jun	(59.36	67.76	72.50	72.32	70.94	72.54)
72.30	Hellmann	29 Sep	(71.84	64.80	68.70	72.30	69.66	67.50)
72.24	Wyludda	9 Jul	(69.94	69.48	70.00	70.64	70.86	72.24)
72.06	Costian	7 May	(x	72.06	69.90	69.50	?	?)

Mark	Name		Nat	Born	Pos	Meet	Venue	Date
72.02	Hellmann	22 May	(70.66	72.02	x	68.80	67.10	x)
71.88	Reinsch	25 Jun	(70.88	69.20	65.44	66.90	70.76	71.88)
71.88	Gansky	29 Sep	(65.58	66.14	x	65.82	71.88	68.08)
71.68	Silhava	15 May	(68.00	x	70.90	x	x	71.68)
71.64	Reinsch	12 May	(69.60	71.62	67.66	71.64	70.64	66.70)
71.64	Silhava	6 Aug	(66.80	69.38	68.70	71.58	71.64	x)
71.58	Zveryeva	12 Jun	(68.08	67.88	70.90	x	63.36	71.58)
71.38	Hellmann	9 Jul	(x	68.66	69.92	70.94	71.38	68.50)
78.14u	Hellmann	6 Sep	(76.92	78.14	70.52	76.56	75.66	74.04)

Series not known for Costian 73.84, 73.78 and 72.02; Reinsch 73.42 and 71.64; Wyludda 71.98, 71.88 and 71.54; Gansky 71.64; Hellmann 71.26; Zveryeva 71.22

JAVELIN

Mark	Name		Nat	Born	Pos	Meet	Venue	Date
80.00	Petra	Felke	GDR	59	1		Potsdam	9 Sep
78.14		Felke			1	OT	Jena	3 Jun
77.52		Felke			1	Int	Tokyo	8 Oct
76.82		Felke			1	v FRG	Düsseldorf	19 Jun
76.80		Felke			1	Int	Chania	22 May
76.76		Felke			1		Berlin	27 Aug
76.50		Felke			1		Rostock	29 May
75.16		Felke			1	Bisl	Oslo	2 Jul
74.92		Felke			1	OD	Berlin	29 Jun
74.68		Felke			1	OG	Seoul	26 Sep
74.62		Felke			1		Berlin	13 Sep
74.02		Felke			1	Znam	Leningrad	12 Jun
73.86		Felke			1	NC	Rostock	25 Jun
73.86		Felke			1	WG	Helsinki	30 Jun
73.30	Tiina	Lillak	FIN	61	1		Lappeenranta	10 Sep
71.70	Tessa	Sanderson	UK	56	1		Crawley	16 Jul
71.66		Felke			1	v Ita	Neubrandenburg	10 Jul
71.60		Felke			1	DNG	Stockholm	5 Jul
71.00	Silke	Renk	GDR	67	2	NC	Rostock	25 Jun
70.48	Ivonne	Leal	CUB	66	1	NP	Habana	27 Feb
70.32	Fatima	Whitbread	UK	61	2	OG	Seoul	26 Sep
70.10		Whitbread			1	NC	Derby	5 Jun
69.40		Whitbread			1	McVit	London	28 Aug
69.22		Leal			1	Barr	Habana	6 Mar
69.22		Renk			1	GO	Dresden	11 Jun
69.12		Renk			2	Int	Chania	22 May
69.06		Sanderson			2	McVit	London	28 Aug
69.00		Felke			1	PTG	London	8 Jul
68.86	Natalya	Yermolovich	SU	64	1		Vitebsk	10 Jul
68.80	Beate (30/8)	Koch	GDR	67	2		Potsdam	9 Sep
68.76	Anna	Verouli	GRE	56	1	Balk	Ankara	16 Jul
68.42	Antoaneta (10)	Selenska	BUL	63	1		Sofia	5 Jun
68.12 @	Susanne	Jung	GDR	63	1		Athinai	16 May
67.50	Trine	Solberg	NOR	66	1		Odda	31 Jul
67.44	María Caridad	Colón	CUB	58	1	Int	Kvarnsveden	19 Jun
67.24	Svetlana	Pestretsova	SU	61	1	Kuts	Moskva	5 Sep
67.18	Zsuzsa	Malovecz	HUN	62	1	5-N	Forli	22 May
67.00	Irina	Kostyuchenkova	SU	61	2	Znam	Leningrad	12 Jun
67.00	Tuula	Laaksalo	FIN	53	2		Lappeenranta	10 Sep
66.48	Natalya	Shikolenko	SU	64	2	v Fra,UK	Portsmouth	19 Jun
66.00	Ingrid	Thyssen	FRG	56	1	NC	Frankfurt-am-Main	23 Jul
65.34	Manuela (20)	Alizadeh	FRG	63	1		Dormagen	4 Sep
64.94	Genowefa	Olejarz-Patla	POL	62	1	5-N	Nitra	28 Aug
64.80	Katalin	Hartai	HUN	63	1	IAC	Edinburgh	29 Jul
64.70	Tatyana	Shikolenko	SU	68	2		Sochi	31 May
64.68	Karen	Forkel	GDR	70	1	Druzh	Nyiregyháza	12 Jun
64.64	Herminia	Bouza	CUB	65	1		Maturin	1 Jul
64.48	Dulce M.	García	CUB	65	2	NP	Habana	27 Feb

Mark	Name		Nat	Born	Pos	Meet	Venue	Date
64.42	Terese	Nekrosaite	SU	61	6	Znam	Leningrad	12 Jun
64.04	Yekaterina	Slyadnyeva	SU	64	1		Leningrad	10 Aug
63.66	Donna	Mayhew	USA	60	1	FOT	Indianapolis	18 Jul
63.62	Denise	Thiémard	SWZ	60	1	v Hun,Swe	Gävle	28 Jun
	(30)							
63.42	Britta	Heydrich	GDR	70	2		Berlin	20 Jul
63.32	Han Jinli		CHN	66	1		Beijing	14 May
63.30	Nadine	Auzeil	FRA	64	1		Brive	12 May
63.22	Aurica	Bujnita	RUM	68	1	NC	Pitesti	13 Aug
63.18	Paivi	Alafrantti	FIN	64	3		Lappeenranta	10 Sep
63.16	Sofia	Sakorafa	GRE	57	4	Int	Chania	22 May
63.16	Heike	Galle	GDR	67	4	NC	Rostock	25 Jun
62.94	Larisa	Avdyeyeva	SU	61	1		Adler	14 Feb
62.84	Zhang Li		CHN	61	.		Shijiazhuang	23 Apr
62.84	Brigitte	Graune	FRG	61	2	NC	Frankfurt-am-Main	23 Jul
	(40)							
62.58	Anja	Reiter	GDR	69	2		Halle	14 May
62.26	Zhou Yuanxiang		CHN	64	.		Guangzhou	8 May
62.26	Galya	Nikolova	BUL	65	2	NarM	Sofia	25 Jun
62.16	Carla	Dumitru	RUM	67	1		Bucuresti	20 Feb
62.14	Beate	Peters	FRG	59	2	ISTAF	West Berlin	26 Aug
62.06	Katerina	Kotmelová	CS	56	1		Praha	4 May
62.02	Iris	Grönfeldt	ICE	63	1		Oslo	19 May
61.60	Elisabet	Nagy	SWE	60	2	IAC	Edinburgh	29 Jul
61.54	Susan	Lion-Cachet	RSA	62	1		Potchefstroom	4 Mar
61.50	Li Guohua		CHN	61	.		Beijing	7 May
	(50)							
61.50	Saida	Gunba	SU	59	8	Znam	Leningrad	12 Jun
61.40	Maria	Dzhaleva	BUL	64	1		Sofia	24 Jul
61.36	Alyona	Bezdyenezhnykh	SU	68	3	NC-w	Sochi	27 Feb
61.30	Xin Xiaoli		CHN	66	.		Beijing	14 May
61.30	Li Baolian		CHN	63	.		Beijing	21 May
61.14	Ingrid	Lammertsma	HOL	67	1		Amstelveen	11 Sep
61.06	Xu Demei		CHN	67	1	Int	Tianjin	1 Sep
61.02	Karin	Bergdahl	SWE	64	1		Karlstad	12 Jun
60.92	Natalya	Balabayeva	SU	66	q		Adler	13 Feb
60.72	Zoya	Karepina	SU	62	2		Odessa	20 Aug
	(60)							
60.70	Lynda	Sutfin	USA	62	1		Westwood	3 Sep
60.68	Helena	Laine	FIN	55	4	Int	Lahti	25 Aug
60.52	Isel	López	CUB	70	4		Habana	20 Feb
60.44	Elizabeth	Fernández	CUB	67	2		Habana	11 Jun
60.42	Ding Fenghua		CHN	64	.		Nanjing	28 Aug
60.40	Jana	Köpping	GDR	66	5	NC	Rostock	25 Jun
60.40	Nóra	Rockenbauer	HUN	66	1		Klagenfurt	6 Aug
60.34	Sueli Pereira dos Santos		BRA	65	1		Curitiba	15 May
60.34	Dorit	Dräger	GDR	71	2		Berlin	16 Jan
60.24	Emi	Matsui	JAP	63	1	Int	Tokyo	13 May
	(70)							
60.02	Laverne	Eve	BAH	65	q	OG	Seoul	25 Sep
60.00	Song Ruiling		CHN	66	.	IntC	Tianjin	2 Sep
59.90	Sharon	Gibson	UK	61	2	NC	Derby	5 Jun
59.62	Tang Lishuang		CHN	68	.	IntC	Tianjin	2 Sep
59.32	Ansie	Rogers	RSA	64	2		Stellenbosch	26 Apr
59.30	Elena	Revayová	CS	56	2		Praha	25 Jun
59.18	Tatyana	Kazantseva	SU	63	1		Baku	10 Sep
58.98	Yulia	Lichagina	SU	65	1		Bryansk	11 Jul
58.96	Kristina	Jazbinsek	YUG	65	4	Balk	Ankara	16 Jul
58.94	Stefania	Galbiati	ITA	69	1		Grosseto	9 Oct
	(80)							
58.88	Natalya	Nasedkina	SU	63	1		Alushta	24 Jan
58.86	Celine	Chartrand	CAN	62	1		Montreal	21 May
58.80	Olga	Gavrilova	SU	57	4		Moskva	6 Aug
58.58	Erica	Wheeler	USA	67	1		Westwood	21 May
58.56	Dagmar	Kosche	GDR	70	3		Halle	14 May
58.50	Malgorzata	Kielczewska	POL	69	3	Kuso	Warszawa	19 Jun

Mark	Name		Nat	Born	Pos	Meet	Venue	Date
58.48	Rita	Romanauskaite	SU	70	1	NC-j	Bryansk	8 Jul
58.44	Yelena	Zhilichkina	SU	63	q		Adler	26 Feb
58.40	Cristina	Dobronoiu	RUM	62	3		Bucuresti	20 Feb
58.40	Mayra	Vila	CUB	60	3		Habana	11 Jun
	(90)							
58.36	Kinga	Zsigmond	HUN	64	1		Jaszbereny	8 Oct
58.34	Marilyn	Senz	USA	61	1		Gainesville	30 Jan
58.30	Zinaida	Gavrilina	SU	61	1		Zhitomir	7 Aug
58.28	Sonia	Bisset	CUB	71	5		Habana	5 Aug
58.24	Simone	Frandsen	DEN	61	1		Vejle	29 May
58.24	Wang Lianyun		CHN	69	1		Tianjin	21 Aug
58.20	Fausta	Quintavalla	ITA	59	4	5-N	Forli	22 May
58.18	Anna-Lena	Pihl	SWE	64	4	v Fin	Helsinki	4 Sep
58.14	Éva	Placsintár	HUN	65	2		Budapest	19 Jun
58.12	Cherry	Harvey	AUS	66	1	Int	Hamilton	20 Feb
	(100)							
58.12	Luo Zhonghua		CHN	69	1	NC-j	Changsha	23 May

Mark	Name		Nat	Born	Date
57.94	Karin	Smith	USA	55	25 Sep
57.88	Zsuzsa	Csizmadia	HUN	67	7 Aug
57.86	Marina	Ovsyannikova	SU	64	31 May
57.82	Mandy	Uhlig	GDR	69	11 May
57.64	Ieva	Skrastina	SU	69	27 Feb
57.56	Anna	Chorinou	GRE	70	4 Sep
57.38	Natalya	Cherniyenko	SU	65	17 Jun
57.04	Jette	Jeppesen	DEN	64	24 Jul
56.98	Valeria	Ivanova	SU	69	28 May
	(110)				
56.94	Durelle	Schimek	USA	68	21 May
56.90	Kate	Farrow	AUS	67	27 Feb
56.84	Zhanna	Penkova	SU	65	5 Jun
56.84	Marie-Danielle	Teanyouen	FRA	70	25 Jun
56.82	Christine	Gravier	FRA	63	25 Jun
56.78	Yelena	Medvedyeva	SU	65	18 Jun
56.76	Sonya	Radicheva	BUL	68	5 Jun
56.66	Marina	Kochnyeva	SU	63	7 Jul
56.58	Vera	Cosic	YUG	67	4 Sep
56.36	Marina	Terenchenko	SU	61	14 Feb
	(120)				
56.36	Iris E.	de Grasse	CUB	64	20 Feb
56.34	Anna	Chugunova	SU	69	26 Jun
56.12	Eva	Raduly-Zörgö	RUM	54	13 Aug
56.12	Nathalie	Teppe	FRA	72	8 Oct
56.08	Chie	Katoh	JAP	64	22 Oct
56.04	Rita	Knoll	FRG	64	27 Jul
55.98	Jill	Smith	USA	67	2 Jul
55.98	Mariola	Dankiewicz	POL	64	16 Jul
55.98	Artemis	Kandrevitiou	GRE	65	20 Jul
55.88	Svetlana	Samunova	SU	68	12 Jun
	(130)				
55.82	Gerda	Blokziel	HOL	61	16 Jul
55.78	Julie	Abel	UK	66	2 May
55.70	Konstanze	Zahn	FRG	59	11 Jun
55.62	Katrin	Kirm	SU	69	30 Jul
55.62	Lisbeth	Mischkounig	AUT	60	10 Sep
55.60	Akiko	Miyajima	JAP	66	5 Jun
55.58	Nicki	Nye	USA	65	9 Apr
55.50	Naomi	Tokuyama	JAP	68	8 May
55.42	Tatyana	Korablina	SU	64	14 Feb
55.42	György	Csontos	HUN	68	6 Sep
	(140)				
55.40	Krystyna	Maczka	POL	63	14 Aug
55.38	Yelena	Burgiman	SU	68	7 Jul
55.26	Heike	Hopfer	GDR	71	14 May
55.26	Katja	Hausmann	FRG	69	13 Aug
55.22	Wilma	Vidotto	ITA	65	13 Jun
55.14	Liz	Mueller	USA	62	17 Jul
55.06	Daniela	Coman	RUM	70	22 May
55.04	Nadezhda	Motorina	SU	63	12 Jun
55.02	Svetlana	Koltygina	SU	67	26 Feb
55.00	Yelena	Tarkhunova	SU	68	12 Jun
	(150)				
54.98	Margot	Kruber	FRG	69	23 Aug
54.86	Shelly	Sanford	USA	67	7 May
54.82	Oksana	Chernyenko	SU	71	13 Feb
54.76	Deanna	Carr	USA	61	7 May
54.64	Oksana	Yarygina	SU	72	25 Aug
54.62	Meg	Foster	USA	65	17 Jul
54.60	Yelena	Fedotova	SU	67	14 Feb
54.60	Cheryl	Coker	CAN	65	4 Jun
54.54	Jeanne	Villegas	USA	67	26 Mar
54.54	Atsuko	Shiraishi	JAP	63	13 May
	(160)				

New javelin

Mark	Name	Pos	Venue	Date
73.40	Felke	-	Berlin	27 Aug

Best series

Mark	Name	Date	Series					
80.00	Felke	9 Sep	(77.16	x	x	73.92	77.62	80.00)
78.14	Felke	3 Jun	(75.20	73.94	78.14	66.24	75.18	73.32)
77.52	Felke	8 Oct	(68.60	77.72	x	x	72.44	70.64)
76.82	Felke	19 Jun	(x	72.62	76.82	74.02	71.60	73.92)
76.80	Felke	22 May	(71.56	71.32	71.78	74.14	76.80	71.02)
75.16	Felke	2 Jul	(71.10	64.74	66.60	x	75.16	x)
74.92	Felke	29 Jun	(69.38	69.62	72.70	53.06	74.86	74.92)
74.68	Felke	26 Sep	(72.62	74.68	68.12	66.76	71.12	68.38)
74.62	Felke	13 Sep	(72.14	65.68	x	72.08	73.34	74.62)
74.02	Felke	12 Jun	(70.64	74.02	72.02	71.02	72.82	73.66)
73.86	Felke	25 Jun	(68.36	73.86	x	71.34	64.04	68.80)
73.86	Felke	30 Jun	(x	64.78	x	64.38	73.86	67.24)
71.66	Felke	10 Jul	(62.56	69.48	x	64.64	x	71.66)
71.60	Felke	5 Jul	(65.66	x	x	x	68.04	71.60)
71.00	Renk	25 Jun	(x	x	62.88	68.02	71.00	65.80)
70.48	Leal	27 Feb	(58.48	70.48	62.70	60.66	x	x)

Mark Name Nat Born Pos Meet Venue Date

Mark	Name	Date						
70.32	Whitbread	26 Sep	(61.98	67.46	66.58	64.88	67.82	70.32)
70.10	Whitbread	5 Jun	(59.54	70.10	63.10	x	-	x)
69.40	Whitbread	28 Aug	(69.40	63.10	65.98	x	-	x)
69.22	Leal	6 Mar	(69.22	67.42	65.72	x	x	x)
69.12	Renk	22 May	(67.28	x	64.00	69.12	62.38	64.60)
69.06	Sanderson	28 Aug	(63.08	61.92	69.06	-	-	-)

Series not known for Felke 76.76, 76.50, 69.00; Lillak 73.30, Sanderson 71.70; Renk 69.22

	Javelin		Year List Progression			Heptathlon				
Year	**Best**	**10th**	**20th**	**50th**	**100th**	**Best**	**10th**	**20th**	**50th**	**100th**
1968	60.68	55.54	54.51	51.40	49.06					
1978	69.16	63.32	59.74	56.64	53.56	Heptathlon replaced pentathlon from 1981				
1979	69.52	63.04	60.90	57.04	54.36	Table incomplete as pre-1985 only top 20				
1980	70.08	66.40	62.92	58.42	55.08	rescored on current tables				
1981	71.88	64.62	63.10	59.00	55.30	6788	6181	5964		
1982	74.20	66.64	64.00	59.70	56.20	6895	6371	6123		
1983	74.76	67.20	64.60	60.70	56.82	6935	6461	6170		
1984	74.72	66.56	64.26	60.68	57.74	6946	6424	6276	c.5925	c.5590
1985	75.40	68.20	64.18	60.66	57.44	6718	6368	6223	5921	5566
1986	77.44	67.80	64.92	60.74	57.20	7158	6403	6250	5966	5654
1987	78.90	67.64	65.18	61.20	57.82	7128	6364	6254	5989	5701
1988	80.00	68.42	65.34	61.50	58.12	7291	6540	6343	6056	5741

HEPTATHLON

Mark		Name	Nat	Born	Pos	Meet	Venue	Date
7291	Jackie	Joyner-Kersee	USA	62	1	OG	Seoul	24Sep
	12.69/+0.5	1.86 15.80 22.56/+1.6			7.27/+0.7		45.66 2:08.51	
7215		Joyner-Kersee			1	FOT	Indianapolis	16 Jul
	12.71/-0.9	1.93 15.65 22.30/0.0			7.00/-1.3		50.08 2:20.70	
6897	Sabine	John	GDR	57	2	OG	Seoul	24 Sep
	12.85/+0.5	1.80 16.23 23.65/+1.6			6.71/0.0		42.56 2:06.14	
6858	Anke	Behmer	GDR	61	3	OG	Seoul	24 Sep
	13.20/+0.5	1.83 14.20 23.10/+1.6			6.68/+0.1		44.54 2:04.20	
6805		Behmer			1	Int	Götzis	19 Jun
	13.28/+1.6	1.84 14.38 22.73/+4.0			6.62/+1.1		40.48 2:04.64	
6733		Behmer			1	Int	Talence	17 Jul
	13.11/+0.8	1.75 14.31 23.14/+0.6			6.79/+0.6		40.48 2:04.29	
6702	Chantal	Beaugeant	FRA	61	2	Int	Götzis	19 Jun
	13.10/+1.6	1.78 13.74 23.96/+3.5			6.45/+0.2		50.96 2:07.09	
6660	Ines	Schulz	GDR	65	3	Int	Götzis	19 Jun
	13.56/+0.4	1.84 13.95 23.93/+2.8			6.70/+0.7		42.82 2:06.31	
6659		John			1		Berlin	19 Jul
	13.12	1.81 16.05 24.84			6.73w 44.08 2:14.45			
6643		Beaugeant			2	Int	Talence	17 Jul
	13.17/+0.8	1.84 13.99 24.59/+0.I8			6.25/+0.4		48.86 2:05.44	
6597	Svetlana	Buraga	SU	65	1		Staiki	2Jul
	12.83/-0.3	1.82 13.78 23.82/+0.I3			6.46/+0.1		40.96 2:08.45	
6569	Heike	Tischler	GDR	64	4	Int	Götzis	19 Jun
	14.42/+1.3	1.78 13.73 23.62/+3.I5			6.68/+1.3		49.24 2:08.16	
6566	Remigia	Sablovskaite	SU	67	1	NC	Kiev	2 Aug
	13.46/+0.4	1.77 15.13 24.29/+0.8			6.47/+0.3		47.40 2:11.74	
6551	Yelena	Martsenyuk	SU	61	2		Staiki	2 Jul
	13.54/-0.4	1.82 15.32 24.25/+0.3			6.25/+0.7		47.56 2:12.72	
6540	Natalya	Shubenkova (10)	SU	57	4	OG	Seoul	24 Sep
	13.51/+0.5	1.74 14.76 23.93/+1.6			6.32/-0.3		47.46 2:07.90	
6539	Tatyana	Shpak	SU	60	3		Staiki	2 Jul
	13.57/-0.4	1.76 15.30 23.61/+0.5			6.52/-0.6		39.28 2:07.25	
6526	Sibylle	Thiele	GDR	65	3	Int	Talence	17 Jul
	13.27/+0.8	1.75 15.31 24.48/+0.8			6.37/0.0		46.68 2:11.13	
6506	Larisa	Nikitina	SU	65	1	NP	Tashkent	4 Sep
	13.81	1.77 15.66 24.32			6.53		49.44 2:18.88	
6500		Shubenkova			4		Staiki	2 Jul
	13.08/-0.8	1.70 14.52 23.88/+0.3			6.08/-0.8		45.80 2:03.71	
6493	Svetlana	Filatyeva	SU	64	1		Kiev	14 Aug
	13.77	1.89 13.89 24.94			6.30		48.44 2:11.89	

Mark	Name		Nat	Born	Pos	Meet	Venue	Date
6492	Jane	Flemming	AUS	65	5	Int	Götzis	19 Jun
	13.33/+0.4	1.81 13.65 23.37/+4.0			6.29/+0.8		43.52 2:11.85	
6485		Shubenkova			4	Int	Talence	17 Jul
	13.42/+0.8	1.69 14.35 24.20/+0.6			6.31/+0.6		47.92 2:05.20	
6474	Marianna	Maslennikova	SU	61	2	NC	Kiev	2 Aug
	13.37/+0.4	1.83 13.68 24.07/-0.0			6.28/+0.2		40.42 2:05.60	
6456		Sablovskaite			5	OG	Seoul	24 Sep
	13.61/+0.5	1.80 15.23 23.92/+1.6			6.25/+0.7		42.78 2:12.24	
6442		Flemming			5	Int	Talence	17 Jul
	13.17/+0.8	1.81 13.07 23.71/+0.6			6.32/0.0		42.92 2:11.75	
6432	Sabine	Braun	FRG	65	1		Lage	21Aug
	13.54	1.84 13.92 24.72			6.38		49.30 2:18.73	
6424	Irina	Matyusheva	SU	65	3	NC	Kiev	2 Aug
	13.40/+0.4	1.86 13.54 24.40/-0.0			6.28/+0.3		40.20 2:08.24	
6411		Schulz			6	OG	Seoul	24 Sep
	13.75/+0.5	1.83 13.50 24.65/+1.6			6.33/+0.6		42.82 2:05.79	
6404		Tischler			1		Cottbus	29 May
	14.48	1.78 12.96 24.23			6.46		52.52 2:09.93	
6399m		Flemming			1		Brisbane	14 Feb
	13.8	1.83 14.01 23.6			6.35/+0.5		44.46 2:14.0	
	(30/18)							
6352	Liliana	Nastase	RUM	62	6	Int	Götzis	19Jun
	13.09/+1.6	1.72 12.44 23.51/+4.0			6.65/+1.0		40.84 2:14.12	
6343	Petra	Vaideanu	RUM	65	1		Bucuresti	22 May
	13.63	1.75 14.98 24.82			6.34		44.20 2:12.45	
	(20)							
6337m	Valda	Ruskite	SU	62	1		Tallinn	16 Jun
=6.335	13.3	1.73 15.60 24.9			6.29		47.20 2:16.1	
6306	Sabine	Everts	FRG	61	1	NC	Rhede	10 Jul
	13.25/+1.9	1.78 13.09 24.33/-1.3			6.64/+0.4		35.78 2:11.43	
6297	Cindy	Greiner	USA	57	8	OG	Seoul	24 Sep
	13.55/+1.2	1.80 14.13 24.48/-0.7			6.47/+0.1		38.00 2:13.65	
6289	Svetla	Dimitrova	BUL	70	1	WJ	Sudbury	30 Jul
	13.47/+1.1	1.77 13.07 23.78/-1.6			6.45/+3.1		39.98 2:14.39	
6268	Zuzana	Lajbnerová	CS	63	7	Int	Götzis	19 Jun
	13.79/+0.5	1.84 14.92 24.72/+2.8			6.14/-1.2		43.10 2:18.68	
6213	Marjon	Wijnsma	HOL	65	1	NC	Eindhoven	22 May
	13.68	1.80 12.98 24.56			6.46		37.32 2:11.19	
6213	Nadezhda	Miromanova	SU	58	1		Irkutsk	26 Jun
	14.63/-1.5	1.60 15.40 24.29			6.55/+0.5		46.22 2:12.04	
6204	Birgit	Clarius	FRG	65	2	NC	Rhede	10 Jul
	14.00	1.78 14.43 25.01			5.99		45.90 2:11.92	
6187m	Marina	Shcherbina	SU	68	1		Kharkov	5 Jul
	13.7	1.82 13.32 24.3			6.33		41.96 2:17.3	
6176	Tineke	Hidding	HOL	59	2	NC	Eindhoven	22 May
	13.57	1.74 13.86 24.20			6.30		36.06 2:10.94	
	(30)							
6157	Corinne	Schneider	SWZ	62	13	OG	Seoul	24 Sep
	13.85/+0.2	1.86 11.58 24.87/+1.6			6.05/0.0		47.50 2:14.93	
6156	Tatyana	Zhuravlyeva	SU	67	7	NC	Kiev	2 Aug
	13.91/+1.1	1.77 12.56 24.41/-0.4			6.55/+1.4		36.80 2:10.68	
6149	Corina	Tifrea	RUM	58	2	RomIC	Bucuresti	19 Jun
	13.96	1.69 13.82 25.06			6.33		41.60 2:07.00	
6146	Birgit	Gautzsch	GDR	67	3		Cottbus	29 May
	13.85	1.72 12.96 23.61			6.21w		42.44 2:14.85	
6140	Marion	Reichelt	GDR	62	2		Cottbus	18 Jun
	13.83	1.78 13.54 24.90			6.48		36.88 2:13.35	
6129	Irina	Tyukhay	SU	67	4	NP	Tashkent	4 Sep
=6.127	13.43	1.86 12.66 24.57			6.42		34.54 2:19.00	
6116	Svetlana	Bystrova	SU	66	8	NC	Kiev	2 Aug
	14.01/+0.8	1.74 16.08 25.54/+0.8			6.14/+0.1		44.74 2:20.67	
6109	Tamara	Moshicheva	SU	62	2		Irkutsk	26Jun
	14.38/-1.5	1.60 15.05 24.92			6.58/+0.7		47.42 2:18.26	
6102	Yelena	Petushkova	SU	69	2	WJ	Sudbury	30 Jul
	13.55/+1.1	1.80 13.27 24.86/-1.6			5.90/+2.8		41.68 2:13.29	

Mark	Name		Nat	Born	Pos	Meet	Venue	Date
6101	Satu	Ruotsalainen	FIN	66	15	OG	Seoul	24 Sep
	13.79/+0.2	1.80 12.32	24.61/+1.6		6.08/0.0		45.44 2:17.06	
	(40)							
6087	Dong Yuping		CHN	63	16	OG	Seoul	24 Sep
	13.93/+1.2	1.86 14.21	25.00/-0.7		6.40/+0.4		38.60 2:26.67	
6082m	Yelena	Zaytseva	SU	67	2		Kharkov	5 Jul
	13.9	1.82 13.37	23.7		6.01		34.34 2:09.6	
6081	Beatrice	Mau	GDR	71	1	vSU-j	Halle	12 Jun
	14.35	1.74 12.52	25.46		6.50w		48.84 2:17.15	
6079	Wendy	Brown	USA	66	3	FOT	Indianapolis	16 Jul
	13.77	1.81 12.86	24.76		6.36		45.88 2:28.80	
6079	Svetlana	Chistyakova	SU	61	5	NP	Tashkent	4 Sep
	13.68	1.77 13.16	24.82		6.22		37.62 2:12.20	
6072	Olga	Abramova	SU	64	9	NC	Kiev	2 Aug
	13.89/+1.2	1.77 14.24	25.52/+0.5		6.35/+0.2		42.80 2:21.25	
6067w	Peggy	Beer	GDR	69	3	WJ	Sudbury	29 Jul
	13.65/+1.1	1.77 13.13	24.45/0.8		6.17/+4.7		38.06 2:15.02	
6063	Svetlana	Vasilyeva	SU	67	4		Sochi	22 May
	14.03/+0.8	1.82 11.63	24.68/+1.2		6.24/+1.0		40.68 2:12.43	
6061	Viktoria	Ryzhova	SU	68	6		Staiki	2 Jul
	13.55/-0.3	1.79 13.48	25.32/+0.5		6.43/-0.2		40.56 2: 23.82	
6056	Irina	Byelova	SU	68	5		Sochi	22 May
	13.94/+0.8	1.85 12.31	24.26/+0.2		6.20/+0.5		32.18 2:10.31	
	(50)							
6048	Jane	Frederick	USA	52	4	FOT	Indianapolis	16 Jul
	13.69/+2.7	1.72 15.11	24.89		6.17/0.0		46.26 2:30.12	
6048	Tatyana	Dolgaya	SU	64	6	NP	Tashkent	4 Sep
	13.38	1.68 12.96	24.46		6.19		40.68 2:14.51	
6047	Ellina	Kolobova	SU	68	7		Staiki	2 Jul
	13.81/-0.9	1.67 13.00	24.49/-0.9		6.08/+1.5		46.30 2:14.49	
6041	Taisia	Prokhorenko	SU	67	10	NC	Kiev	2 Aug
	13.78/+2.2	1.71 13.15	24.32/+0.5		5.97/+0.1		41.04 2:11.02	
6037	Anita	Behrbaum	USA	64	1		Azusa	22 Apr
	13.84	1.68 13.36	24.58		5.70		52.62 2:17.42	
6028	Grit	Colditz	GDR	66	6		Cottbus	29 May
	13.81	1.81 13.98	25.87		6.03		44.76 2:20.85	
6020m	Tatyana	Morozova	SU	64	1		Bryansk	28 Jul
=6.026	13.8	1.84 12.65	24.9		6.50/+2.0		36.28 2:18.6	
6020	Larisa	Zakharova	SU	64	7	NP	Tashkent	4 Sep
	14.13	1.71 13.54	25.08		6.29		46.30 2:20.13	
6016	Anke	Schmidt	GDR	68	3		Cottbus	18 Jun
	13.91	1.75 13.20	24.41		6.30		32.50 2:10.37	
6016	Helga	Nusko	FRG	65	11	Int	Götzis	19 Jun
	14.06/+1.3	1.75 15.47	25.00/+2.5		6.10/0.0		44.16 2:27.58	
	(60)							
6016	Khodizha	Kabanova	1					
				25.18		6.03	44.64 2:14.77	
6007	Ionica	Domniteanu	RUM	69	3	RomIC	Bucuresti	19 Jun
	13.63	1.72 13.78	24.50		5.80		42.08 2:15.24	
6006	Ragne	Kytölä	FIN	65	11	Int	Talence	17 Jul
	13.88/+0.8	1.75 11.73	25.28/+0.9		6.12/0.0		45.68 2:12.58	
5997	Yelena	Chicherova	SU	58	8	NP	Tashkent	4 Sep
	13.62	1.77 11.59	24.30		6.59		32.62 2:16.25	
5990	Emilia	Dimitrova	BUL	67	1	NC	Stara Zagora	29 Aug
	13.87	1.77 14.42	23.81		6.42		32.26 2:27.00	
5975	Kim	Hagger	UK	61	17	OG	Seoul	24 Sep
	13.47/+0.2	1.80 12.75	25.47/+1.6		6.34/0.0		35.78 2:18.48	
5969	Helena	Otáhalová	CS	59	13	Int	Talence	17 Jul
	14.04/+0.4	1.78 14.01	25.12/+0.1		5.94/+1.4		43.86 2:21.80	
5948	Christine	Höss	FRG	62	4	NC	Rhede	10 Jul
	14.44	1.72 12.56	25.83		5.83		48.52 2:10.32	
5928	Jacqueline	Hautenauve	BEL	62	1	NC	Kessel-lo	7 Aug
							43.94 2:15.87	

Mark	Name		Nat	Born	Pos	Meet	Venue	Date
5926	Liliane	Menissier	FRA	60	1		Montpellier	5 Jun
	13.80	1.81 11.59 25.71			6.23		44.54 2:22.11	
	(70)							
5906	Sylvia	Tornow	FRG	69	1	vPol-j	Bochum	26 Jun
	14.02	1.75 13.88 24.82			5.54		45.52 2:18.90	
5905	Judy	Simpson	UK	60	4		Lage	21 Aug
	13.57	1.75 14.71 25.67			5.87		39.68 2:20.93	
5892m	Irina	Oleynik	SU	63	3		Kharkov	5 Jul
	14.0	1.70 14.17 25.0			6.20		39.50 2:17.9	
5883	Irina	Stassenko	SU	66	9	NP	Tashkent	4 Sep
	14.32	1.59 14.31 25.18			5.83		46.32 2:10.78	
5881w	Sheila	Tarr	USA	64	1	TAC	Tampa	16 Jun
	14.08/+1.0	1.71 13.99 25.21/+5.3			5.81/+2.4		50.36 2:27.27	
5873m	Odile	Lesage	FRA	69	1		Antony	15 May
	13.7	1.78 12.19 24.8			5.90		42.20 2:18.3	
5864	Tatyana	Blokhina	SU	70	2		Simferopol	29 May
=5.861	14.15/-0.4	1.78 14.40 25.03			5.55		44.46 2:23.4	
5862	Claudia	Dickow	FGR	63	5	NC	Rhede	10 Jul
	13.79/+0.2	1.72 11.74 24.23/+0.2			6.09/+2.0		35.74 2:13.82	
5861w	Cathy	Tyree	USA	64	2	TAC	Tampa	16 Jun
	14.21/+0.1	1.71 14.20 25.02/+4.8			6.06/0.0		40.06 2:20.50	
5857	Renate	Pfeil	FRG	63	6	NC	Rhede	10 Jul
	13.98/+1.9	1.78 14.09 25.77/-1.3			5.90/+0.8		38.76 2:18.58	
	(80)							
5825	Urszula	Wlodarczyk	POL	65	1		Slupsk	24 Jul
	14.28/+0.6	1.72 13.78 25.29/+0.9			6.10/+1.4		39.68 2:19.77	
5824	Yasmina	Azzizi	ALG	66	16	Int	Götzis	19 Jun
	13.72/+0.4	1.69 13.88 24.81/+3.5			5.50/+2.2		47.10 2: 24.03	
5824	Cornelia	Günthner	FRG	71	2	vPol-j	Bochum	26 Jun
	13.77	1.84 10.69 23.97			6.00		32.74 2:18.35	
5824	Lilia	Fastivets	SU	64	12	NP	Tashkent	4 Sep
	13.93	1.74 14.79 24.75			5.56		32.42 2:11.99	
5823	Nadine	Debois	FRA	61	4	NC	Tours	13 Aug
	13.74/+0.5	1.75 12.46 24.75/+0.4			5.99/+1.0		29.34 2:08.96	
5815m	Jocelyn	Millar-Cubit	AUS	62	1		Launceston	21Feb
	14.0	1.77 11.89 24.1			6.09		34.88 2:15.8	
5815	Anne Brit	Skjæveland	NOR	62	1	5N	København	3 Jul
	13.81/+2.4	1.84 11.16 24.96/+2.3			5.91/-0.2		36.52 2:17.20	
5809	Antje	Schmuck	FRG	64	8	NC	Rhede	10 Jul
	14.06/+0.2	1.84 12.14 25.46			5.95		35.14 2:15.43	
5796	Yelena	Miron	SU	65	9		Staiki	2 Jul
	13.82	1.67 13.30 25.07			5.95		42.34 2:21.65	
5795m	Svetlana	Demeshonkova	SU	66	3		Bryansk	29 Jul
	14.0	1.55 13.54 24.3			6.37		34.82 2:11.2	
	(90)							
5790w	Bettina	Braag	FRG	65	5		Lage	21 Aug
	13.86	1.81 11.62 24.22			5.94		35.44 2:22.19	
5783	Monica	Westén	SWE	66	18	Int	Götzis	19 Jun
	13.96/1.3	1.84 10.96 24.74w/2.5			5.80/0.7		30.64 2:08.37	
5767	Rita	Ináncsi	HUN	71	19	Int	Götzis	19 Jun
	14.38/-0.7	1.75 12.87 25.18/1.9			6.00/1.5		39.34 2:19.36	
5764	Natalya	Knyazeva	SU	64	10		Sochi	22 May
	14.19/0.9	1.73 12.91 25.95/+0.2			5.74/+0.8		45.00 2:17.05	
5763	Esther	Suter	SWZ	62	2	NC	Hochdorf	21 Aug
	14.02/+0.2	1.71 11.89 25.26/-0.2			5.65/+0.2		44.70 2:14.42	
5762	Olga	Shabalina	SU	64	16	NC	Kiev	2 Aug
	14.59/+1.1	1.74 15.07 25.20/+0.9			5.92/-0.2		37.70 2: 23.30	
5747	Stefanie	Huhn	FRG	66	9	NC	Rhede	10 Jul
	13.78	1.69 11.67 25.02			6.62/1.9		27.96 2:15.43	
5746	Wu Pin		CHN	65			Nanjing	12 Jun
5746	Joanne	Mulliner	UK	66	19	OG	Seoul	24 Sep
	14.39/+0.2	1.71 12.68 24.92/+1.6			6.10/+0.1		37.76 2:18.02	
5741	Crystal	Young	USA	65	1		Moscow, Id	19 May
	14.38	1.77 13.47 25.74			5.77		41.34 2:20.01	
	(100)							

Mark	Name		Nat	Born	Date
5720	Christiane	Scharf	FRG	70	26 Jun
5706	Vanda	Nováková	CS	58	17 Jul
5697m	Isabelle	Kaftandjian	FRA	64	23 May
5690	Tina	Rattyä	FIN	68	3 Jul
5680	Svetlana	Kozharko	SU	66	14 Aug
5679	Ivanka	Valkova	BUL	65	22 May
5679	Sabine	Köhler	FRG	68	10 Jul
5678	Maryse	Ewanje-Epée	FRA	64	17 Jul
5669w	Jolanda	Jones	USA	65	22 Apr
5668	Janet	Nichols	USA	63	22 Apr
	(110)				
5667	Shi Guiking		CHN	68	5 Sep
5665	Camelia	Cornateanu	RUM	67	19 Jun
5664	Inga	Mikhailova	SU	66	4 Sep
5661	Marcela	Podracká	CS	70	13 Aug
5654	Lyubov	Polyakova	SU	66	26 Jun
5645 (5647?)	Olga	Rudoy	SU	68	12 Jun
5637	Donna	Smellie	CAN	64	14 Aug
5636	Margit	Palombi	HUN	61	7 Aug
5635	Bettina	Beinhauer	FRG	65	24 Feb
5629	Sharon	Hanson	USA	65	22 Apr
	(120)				
5625mw	Sharon	Jaklofsky-Smith	AUS	68	10 Jan
5618m	Tamara	Mamonova	SU	58	29 Jul
5616	Nadezhda	Zakharova	SU	62	26 Jun
5611	Trish	King	USA	62	16 Jul
5610	Dagmar	Federwisch	FRG	68	10 Jul
5606	Jayne	Barnetson	UK	68	4 Sep
5604	Terri	Turner	USA	63	16 Jul
5600	Maryline	Becquet	FRA	69	3 Jul
5597	Heidrun	Wellhöfer	FRG	64	10 Jul
	(130)				
5597	Heidrun	Wellhöfer	FRG	64	10 Jul
5595	Connie	Polman-Tuin	CAN	63	3 Jun
5590	Jamie	McNeair	USA	69	2 Jun
5583	Marina	Mihajlova	YUG	62	5 Jun
5581	Anoeschka	Daans	HOL	65	3 Jul
5577m	Kylie	Coombe	AUS	67	10 Jan
5577	Karin	Wiesel	FRG	64	10 Jul
5572	Iustina	Nicolescu	RUM	69	19 Jun
5570	Herta	Steiner	ITA	64	21 Aug
5565	Ye Lianying		CHN	60	5 Sep
	(140				
5564	Hélène	Léfèvre	FRA	67	4 Sep
5560	Natalya	Koritskaya	SU	67	4 Sep
5555	Ingrid	Didden	BEL	68	22 May
5553	Alessandra	Becatti	ITA	65	21 Aug
5546	Malgorzata	Lisowska	POL	62	14 Aug
5545	Heléne	Friberg	SWE	66	3 Jul
5545	Silke	Harms	FRG	67	10 Jul
5544m	Debra	Larsen	USA	64	28 May
5537	Minako	Isogai	JAP	67	24 Apr
5537	Sabine	Schwarz	FRG	67	19 Jun
	(150)				
5533	Svetlana	Korobkina	SU	67	12 Jun
5533w	Patricia	Nadler	SWZ	69	12 Jun
5530	Elida María	Aveillé	CUB	61	6 Aug
5525	Stefania	Frisiero	ITA	67	21 Aug
5524	Teri	LeBlanc	USA	66	14 May
5517	Shona	Urquhart	UK	63	21 Aug
5518m (5518?)	Svetlana	Akimova	SU	69	11 Sep
5514	Svetlana	Bagreyeva	SU	61	12 Jun
5513m	Natalya	Sergeyeva	SU	71	17 May
5513w	Jill	Lancaster	USA	59	16 Jun
	(160)				

Best non-windy performances

Mark	Name		Nat	Born	Pos	Meet	Venue	Date
6007	Peggy	Beer	GDR	69	2	vSU-j	Halle	12 Jun
	13.95	1.74 12.97 24.66		6.08		41.24	2:13.74	
5773	Sheila	Tarr	USA	64	1		Los Angeles	28 May
	14.2	1.74 14.48 25.5		5.90		47.10	2:30.7	
5762m	Cathy	Tyree	USA	64	1		Los Angeles	28 May
	14.0	1.74 13.90 25.4		5.90		43.66	2:26.2	

4 x 100 METRES RELAY

Mark	Nat	Team	Pos	Meet	Venue	Date
41.73	GDR	Möller, Behrendt, Lange, Göhr	1		Berlin	13 Sep
41.98	USA	Brown, Echols, Griffith-Joyner, Ashford	1	OG	Seoul	1 Oct
42.01	SU	Kondratyeva, Malchugina, Zhirova, Pomoshchnikova	1s1	OG	Seoul	1 Oct
42.09	GDR	Möller, Behrendt, Lange, Göhr	2	OG	Seoul	1 Oct
42.12	USA	Brown, Echols, Griffith-Joyner, Ashford	1s2	OG	Seoul	1 Oct
42.23	GDR	Möller, Behrendt, Lange, Göhr	2s1	OG	Seoul	1 Oct
42.29	Bulgaria	Pencheva, Nuneva, Georgieva, Donkova	1		Sofia	26 Jun
42.30	GDR	Kersten, Möller, Lange, Göhr	1		Berlin	29 Jun
42.39	USA	Brown, Echols, Young, Ashford	1h3	OG	Seoul	30 Sep
42.87	Bulgaria	T.Ilieva, Nuneva, Georgieva, Demireva	1	NC	Sofia	3 Sep
42.50	GDR	Möller, Behrendt, Lange, Göhr	1		Potsdam	9 Sep
42.53	GDR	Möller, Günther, Lange, Göhr	1	v FRG	Düsseldorf	19 Jun
42.59	GDR	Behrendt, Günther, Lange, Göhr	1		Karl-Marx-Stadt	12 Jun
42.64	Bulgaria	T.Ilieva, Nuneva, Georgieva, Demireva	1		Stara Zagora	20 Aug
42.69	FRG	Richter, Sarvari, Thomas, Thimm	2s2	OG	Seoul	1 Oct
42.70	GDR	Möller, Behrendt, Lange, Göhr	1rA		Cottbus	17 Jun
42.75	GDR	Möller, Behrendt, Lange, Göhr	1	Int	Sestriere	11 Aug
42.75	SU	Kondratyeva, Malchugina, Zhirova, Pomoshchnikova	3	OG	Seoul	1 Oct
42.76	FRG	Richter, Sarvari, Thomas, Thimm	4	OG	Seoul	1 Oct
42.77	GDR	Möller, Behrendt, Lange, Göhr	1rB		Cottbus	17 Jun
42.88	SU	Azarashvili, Malchugina, Zhirova, Pomoshchnikova	1h1	OG	Seoul	30 Sep
42.89	Bulgaria	Nuneva, T.Ilieva, Georgieva, Demireva	1	Balk	Ankara	16 Jul
42.92	GDR	Behrendt, Göhr, Lange, Möller	1h2	OG	Seoul	30 Sep
42.97	USA		1	VD	Bruxelles	19 Aug
42.99	FRG	Richter, Sarvari, Thomas, Thimm	2h1	OG	Seoul	30 Sep

Mark	Name	Nat Born	Pos	Meet	Venue	Date
43.02	Bulgaria	T.Ilieva, Demireva, Georgieva, Donkova	5	OG	Seoul	1 Oct
43.06	GDR "B"	Kersten, Krabbe, Dietz, Günther	2		Berlin	13 Sep
43.07	Bulgaria	T.Ilieva, Demireva, Georgieva, Donkova	3s2	OG	Seoul	1 Oct
43.12	FRG	Zaczkiewicz, Sarvari, Thomas, Knoll	1	ASV	Köln	21 Aug
43.16	Bulgaria	Zagorcheva, Nuneva, Georgieva, Donkova	1	PTS	Bratislava	9 Jun
	(30/5 nations)					
43.19	Poland	Smolarek, Janota, Siwek, Pisiewicz	1		Mielec	1 Sep
43.30	Jamaica	E.Tate, Jackson, Cuthbert, Ottey	3s1	OG	Seoul	1 Oct
43.41	France	Girard, Leroy, Seguin, Pérec	1	v UK,SU	Portsmouth	19 Jun
43.46	UK	Miles, Baptiste, Jacobs, Dunn	2	v Fra,SU	Portsmouth	19 Jun
43.48	Holland	Cooman, Tromp, Olyslager, Vader	5s1	OG	Seoul	1 Oct
	(10)					
43.68	China	Zhang Xiaoqiong, Liu Shaomei, Xie Zhiling, Zhang Caihua	1	Int	Tianjin	1 Sep
43.72	Canada	Anderson, Phipps, Bailey, Richardson	1	v Ita	Cesenatico	13 Aug
43.87	Italy	Angotzi, Tarolo, Ferrian, Masullo	1	Int	Bolzano	9 Jun
44.04	Cuba Juniors	Riquelme, López, Valdivia, Allen	2	WJ	Sudbury	31 Jul
44.12	Ghana	Bawuah, Yankey, Addy, Appiah	5h3	OG	Seoul	30 Sep
44.41	Greece	Tsoni, Patoulidou, Zouganeli, Skordi	2	Balk	Ankara	16 Jul
44.47A	Spain	Myers, Perez, Diaz, Valdor	1	IbAC	Ciudad México	24 Jul
44.54	Switzerland	Haug, Colemberg, Aebi, Albonico	1		Luzern	11 Jun
44.84	Czechoslovakia	Spicková, Weegerová, Cernochová, Niková	2	4-N	Praha	2 Jul
45.08	Finland	Painilainen, Hanhijoki, Raumala Marttinen	1	v Swe	Helsinki	3 Sep
	(20)					
45.13	Benfica (POR)		3	ECC	Lisboa	5 Jun
45.20	Mexico	Tavares, Vazquez, Flores, G.Garcia	2	IbAC	Ciudad México	24 Jul
45.23	Crvena Zvezda (YUG)	Cotric, Zivkovic, Sinkovic, Istvanovic	1		Beograd	2 Jul
45.24	Rapid Bucuresti (ROM)		1	NC	Pitesti	13 Aug
45.25	New South Wales (AUS)	Holland, Sullivan, Sambell, Butler	1	NC	Perth	26 Mar
45.28	Brazil	Pereira, da Silva, Matos, dos Santos	3	IbAC	Mexico	24 Jul
45.46	Colombia	Caicedo, Carabali, Escalante, Restrepo	5h1	OG	Seoul	30 Sep
45.51	Belgium		3	WA	Bruxelles	18 Jun
45.53	Hungary	Barati, Könye, Kozary, Acs	2	Int	Schwechat	15 Jun
45.59	Ivory, Coast	Alimata, Koré, Woumplou, Foufouet	2	AfrC	Annaba	1 Sep
	(30)					
45.83	South Korea	Yoon Mi-kyong, Woo Yang-ja, Park Mi-sun, Lee Young-sook	7h2	OG	Seoul	30 Sep
45.88	SolK Hellas (SWE)	Hjertman, Lindqvist, H.Fernström, M.Fernström	1	NC	Sollentuna	11 Jun
45.93	Nord Transvaal (RSA)		1	NC	Bloemfontein	16 Apr
45.93	Norway	Solbakken, Riisnes, Olsen, Kleive	1	v Wal	Nesbyen	3 Sep

4 x 200 METRES RELAY

Mark	Name	Nat Born	Pos	Meet	Venue	Date
1:33.03	Arizona State Un.	Bartholomew', Tolbert, Foster, Malone	1rA	PennR	Philadelphia	30 Apr
1:33.31	Morgan State Un.(USA)	B.Tate, Stevens, G.Harris, Vereen	1rB	PennR	Philadelphia	30 Apr
1:33.72	UK	Keough, Stuart, Douglas, Short	1	Int	Gateshead	16 Jul
1:33.74	Illinois Un. (USA)	Mondie, McClatchey, Beverly, Fulcher	1	DrakeR	Des, Moines	30 Apr
1:33.86	World Class AC (USA)	Joyner-Kersee, Bolden, Griffith-Joyner, Marshall	1	MSR	Walnut	23 Apr
1:33.93	Abilene Christian Un.	Mayfield, Hudson, Straughn', Titus	2	MSR	Walnut	23 Apr
Indoor mark						
1:32.55	SC Eintracht Hamm (FRG)	Arendt, Knoll, Kluth, Kinzel	1		Dortmund	20 Aug

4 x 400 METRES RELAY

Mark	Name	Nat Born	Pos	Meet	Venue	Date
3:15.17	SU	Ledovskaya, Nazarova, Pinigina, Bryzgina	1	OG	Seoul	1 Oct
3:15.51	USA	D.Howard, Dixon, Brisco, Griffith-Joyner	2	OG	Seoul	1 Oct
3:18.29	GDR	Neubauer, Emmelmann, Busch, Müller	3	OG	Seoul	1 Oct
3:19.66	GDR	Losch, Emmelmann, Neubauer, Müller	1	v FRG	Düsseldorf	20 Jun
3:22.49	FRG	Thimm, Arendt, Thomas, Abt	4	OG	Seoul	1 Oct
3:23.13	Jamaica	Richards, Thomas, Rattray-Williams, Powell	5	OG	Seoul	1 Oct
3:24.13	FRG	Thimm, Arendt, Abt, Kinzel	2	v GDR	Düsseldorf	20 Jun
3:25.86	USA	Leatherwood, S.Howard, D.Howard, Dixon	1h2	OG	Seoul	30 Sep
3:25.94	Ukraine (USSR)	Sereda, Dzhigalova, Pinigina, Yurchenko	1	NC	Tallinn	7 Jul
3:26.01	SU	Shmonina, Grebenchuk, Ambraziene, Bryzgina	1	v Fra,UK	Portsmouth	19 Jun
3:26.83	Jamaica	M.Tate, Thomas, Rattray-Williams, Powell	2h2	OG	Seoul	30 Sep
3:26.84	GDR	Fiedler, Uebel, Emmelmann, Müller	1	v Ita	Neubrandenburg	10 Jul
3:26.89	UK	Keough, Stoute, Piggford, Gunnell	6	OG	Seoul	1 Oct
3:27.14	SU	Dzhigalova, Nazarova, Pinigina, Bryzgina	3h2	OG	Seoul	30 Sep
3:27.37	GDR	Breuer, Neubauer, Emmelmann, Müller	1h1	OG	Seoul	30 Sep

Mark	Name		Pos	Meet	Venue	Date
3:27.63	Canada	Crooks, Lawrence, Payne-Wiggins, Richardson	2h1	OG	Seoul	30 Sep
3:27.7 m	Ukraine	Dzhigalova, Bryzgina, Kashchey, Olizarenko	1		Sochi	1 Jun
3:27.75	FRG	Arendt, Schabinger, Kinzel, Abt	3s1	OG	Seoul	30 Sep
3:28.1 m	RSFSR	Vinogradova, Nurutdinova, Moskvina, Kharlamova	2		Sochi	1 Jun
3:28.39	RSFSR	Sychugova, Kharlamova, Ruzina, Kovtun	2	NC	Tallinn	7 Jul
3:28.39	GDR Juniors	Derr, Fabert, Wöhlk, Breuer	1	WJ	Sudbury	31 Jul
3:28.4 m	Moskva	Nazarova, Balukhina, Golesheva, Radeyeva	3		Sochi	1 Jun
3:28.48	Moskva	Dudina, Selivanova, Golesheva, Nazarova	3	NC	Tallinn	7 Jul
3:28.52	UK	Keough, Stoute, Smith, Gunnell	4h1	OG	Seoul	30 Sep
3:28.56	Byelorussia	Kuprianovich, Ledovskaya, Kurochkina, Kalinnikova	4	NC	Tallinn	7 Jul
3:28.98	World Class AC (USA)	Kellon, Joyner-Kersee, Brisco, Griffith-Joyner	1	MSR	Walnut	24 Apr
3:29.12	SC Turbine Erfurt (GDR)	Schreiter, Neubauer, Steinecke, Losch	1		Jena	3 Jun
3:29.21	Bulgaria	Saracheva, T.Ilieva, Stoyanova, Stamenova	1	4-N	Praha	3 Jul
3:29.22	Brazil	Montalvao, Oliveira, Telles, Figueiredo	1	IbAC	Mexico	24 Jul
3:29.37	France	Ficher, Simon, Debois, Elien	7	OG	Seoul	1 Oct
	(30/10 nations)					
3:29.66	Romania	Oanta, Jianu, Carutasu, Plescan	1	v Rus	Bucuresti	19 Jun
3:30.21	Nigeria	Ogunkoya, Vaughan, Bakare, Onyali	6h1	OG	Seoul	30 Sep
3:31.77	Czechoslovakia	Slaninová, Dziurová, Machotková, Paríková	3	4-N	Praha	3 Jul
3:31.83	Spain	Pujol, Lahoz, Zuñiga, Lacambra	1	WA	Bruxelles	19 Jun
3:32.77	Cuba	Alvarez, Vinent, Hernández, Quirot	3	IbAC	Mexico	24 Jul
3:33.46	India	Kuttan, Rao, Shanbagh, Abraham	7h1	OG	Seoul	30 Sep
3:33.68	Nord Transvaal (RSA)		1	NC	Bloemfontein	16 Apr
3:33.68	Italy	Furlan, Campana, Morabito, Rossi	2	v Can	Cesenatico	14 Aug
3:33.72	Holland	Tromp, van Steennis, de Leeuw, van Dorp	2	WA	Bruxelles	19 Jun
3:34.25	Sweden	Wennberg, Akraka, E.Johansson, Skoglund	1	v Fin	Helsinki	4 Sep
	(20)					
3:34.83	Finland	Haikkonen, Uunimaki, Pakkala, Finell	2	v Swe	Helsinki	4 Sep
3:35.77	Yugoslavia	Sinkovic, Colovic, Paskulin, Rakita	3	Balk	Ankara	17 Jul
3:35.84	Hungary	Kozáry, Forgács, Szopori, Szabó	1	v Swe,Swi	Gävle	28 Jun
3:35.94	Poland	Sosin, Keller, Kurach, Spizak	1	4-N	Thessaloniki	16 Sep
3:37.74	Uganda	Ajilo, Kyalisima, Buzu, Kyakutema	1	AfrC	Annaba	1 Sep
3:37.78	Switzerland	Schediwy, Vogt, Scalabrin, Albonico	3	WA	Bruxelles	19 Jun
3:38.30	Ivory, Coast	Womplou, Alimata, Koré, N'Drin	2	AfrC	Annaba	1 Sep
3:39.00	Belgium		4	WA	Bruxelles	19 Jun
3:39.10	Austria	Haas, Lindner, Drda, Zenz	5	WA	Bruxelles	19 Jun
3:39.52	South Australia (AUS)	Harris, Causby, Millar, van, Heer	1	NC	Perth	27 Mar
	(30)					
3:39.72	Ireland	Amond, Walsh, Johnson, Molloy	6	WA	Bruxelles	19 Jun

4 x 800 METRES RELAY

Mark	Name		Pos	Meet	Venue	Date
8:25.25	Villanova Univ (USA)	Franey, Huber, DiMuro, Halliday	1	PennR	Philadelphia	30 Apr

3000 METRES TRACK WALK

Mark	Name		Nat	Born	Pos	Meet	Venue	Date
12:14.48	Kerry	Saxby	AUS	2.6.61	1		Sydney	20 Feb
12:20.07		Saxby			1mx		Canberra	26 Jan
12:29.0	Sari	Essayeh	FIN	21.2.67	1		Kuopio	23 Jul
12:32.37'	Yelena	Nikolayeva	SU	1.2.66	1	vUK,Fra	Portsmouth	19 Jun
12:35.6		Essayeh			1		Lapinlaxa	26 Jun
12:51.24'	Beate	Anders	GDR	4.2.68	1	NC	Rostock	26 Jun
12:52.0'		Nikolayeva			1	NC	Kiev	30 Jul
12:53.97	Kathrin	Born	GDR	4.12.70	1		Karl-Marx-Stadt	15 Jul
12:56.2		Essayeh			1		Valtimo	13 Jun
12:59.0		Essayeh			1		Kuopio	23 Jul
	(10/5)							
13:01.0'	Vera	Mokolova	SU	.66	2	NC	Kiev	30 Jul
13:02.0'	Nadezhda	Ryashkina	SU	67	3	NC	Kiev	30 Jul
13:04.73'	Maria	Cruz Diaz	SPA	24.10.69	1	WJ	Sudbury	31 Jul
13:05.17	Maria Grazina	Orsani	ITA	11.6.69	1		Columbus	24 Jul
13:05.68	Beverley	Hayman	AUS	9.5.61	2		Sydney	20 Feb
13:08.06	Anna Rita	Sidoti	ITA	25.7.69	2		Columbus	24 Jul
13:09.14	Gabrielle	Blythe	AUS	9.3.69	3		Columbus	24 Jul
13:09.85	Chang Yueing		CHN		1		Tianjin	1 Sep

Mark	Name		Nat	Born	Pos	Meet	Venue	Date
Indoor marks								
12:26.69	Natalya	Spiridonova	SU	24.4.63	1	NC	Volgograd	10 Feb
12:28.64	Sada	Eidikite	SU	22.6.67	2	NC	Volgograd	10 Feb
12:30.13	Svetlana	Kaburkina	SU	3.5.67	3	NC	Volgograd	10 Feb
12:36.31	Beate	Anders	GDR	4.2.68	1		Turin	10 Feb
12:43.8		Eidikite			1		Vilnius	31 Jan
12:44.88		Spiridonova			1		Valencia	17 Feb
12:45.38	Maryanne	Torrellas	USA	26.7.58	1	TAC	New York	26 Feb
12:47.32	Teresa	Vaill	USA	20.11.62	2	TAC	New York	26 Feb
12:48.82	Maria	Cruz Diaz	SPA	24.10.69	2		Valencia	17 Feb
12:48.99	Maria	Reyes Sobrino	SPA	6.1.67	1	EI	Budapest	6 Mar
	(10/8)							
12:50.18	Yelena	Nikolayeva	SU	1.2.66	4	NC	Volgograd	10 Feb
12:51.08	Dana	Vavracová	CS	25.6.54	2	EI	Budapest	6 Mar
12:56.55	Ildikó	Ilyés	HUN	3.7.62	4	EI	Budapest	6 Mar
12:58.06	Vera	Osipova	SU	57	5	NC	Volgograd	10 Feb
12:58.86	Victoria	Oprea	ROM	65	2		Budapest	27 Feb
12:59.34	Kathrin	Born	GDR	4.12.70	1		Penza	17 Feb
13:00.15	Tatyana	Petrova	SU	15.8.65	6	NC	Volgograd	10 Feb
13:01.28	Tatyana	Titova	SU	25.8.69	2		Penza	17 Feb
13:02.0	Irina	Shumak	SU	65	1		Minsk	29 Jan
13:03.4	Natalya	Serbinenko	SU	27.1.59	1		Kiev	31 Jan
13:04.45	Mária	Rozsa	HUN	12.2.67	5	EI	Budapest	6 Mar
13:05.0	Regina	Losyeva	SU	61	2		Minsk	29 Jan
13:07.0	Yelena	Yukhnovich	SU	1.5.63	3		Minsk	29 Jan
13:09.04	Anne	Jansson	SWE	1.7.58	7	EI	Budapest	5 Mar

' time during longer track walk

5000 METRES TRACK WALK

Mark	Name		Nat	Born	Pos	Meet	Venue	Date
20:45.32	Kerry	Saxby	AUS	2.6.61	1	NC	Perth	27 Mar
20:55.76		Saxby			1		Sydney	10 Jan
21:08.5	Yelena	Nikolayeva	SU	1.2.66	1	vUK,Fra	Portsmouth	19 Jun
21:13.16	Cui Yingzi		CHN	71	1		Jinan	130 Oct
21:25.5'		Nikolayeva			1	SGP	Fana	7 May
21:29.0'		Nikolayeva			1		Kiev	30 Jul
21:35.28	Beate	Anders	GDR	4.2.68	1	NC	Rostock	26 Jun
21:43.27	Kathrin	Born	GDR	4.12.70	1	NC-j	Karl-Marx-Stadt	15 Jul
21:48.4	Alina	Ivanova	SU	25.6.69	1		Simferopol	27 May
21:51.31	Maria	Cruz Diaz	SPA	24.10.69	1	WJ	Sudbury	31 Jul
21:53.0'	Vera	Molokova	SU	66	2	NC	Kiev	30 Jul
21:54.81	Li Chunxiu		CHN	69	2	NC	Jinan	30 Oct
21:55.0'	Nadezhda	Ryashkina	SU	67	3	NC	Kiev	30 Jul
21:57.54	Gao Hongmiao		CHN	74	3	NC	Jinan	30 Oct
21:58.17	Olga	Sánchez	SPA	6.3.70	2	WJ	Sudbury	31 Jul
21:58.8	Tatyana	Titova	SU	25.8.69	2		Simferopol	27 May
21:59.30		Ivanova			1	vGDR-j	Halle	11 Jun
22:00.0'	Yelena	Rodionova	SU	7.5.69	4'	NC	Kiev	30 Jul
22:00.0'	Sada	Eidikite	SU	22.6.67	5	NC	Kiev	30 Jul
22:01.09	Sari	Essayeh	FIN	21.2.67	1		Sipoo	4 Jun
	(20/16)							
22:04.74	Maria-Grazia	Orsani	ITA	11.6.69	3	WJ	Sudbury	31 Jul
22:05.0'	Natalya	Serbinenko	SU	27.1.59	6	NC	Kiev	30 Jul
22:10.76	Pier Carola	Pagani	ITA	63	1		Faenza	25 Sep
22:11.55	Maryanne	Torrellas	USA	26.7.58	1	PennR	Philadelphia	28 Apr
	(20)							
22:13.2	Yevgeniya	Mikheyeva	SU	12.9.69	3		Simferopol	27 May
22:14.6	Anna Rita Sidoti		ITA	25.7.69	1		Messina	2 Oct
22:15.0'	Lyubov	Kolesnikova	SU	29.5.66	5'		Kiev	13 Mar
22:15.3	Chen Yueling		CHN	68	1		Jiading	22 Oct
22:16.04	Bao Jie		CHN	71	4	NC	Jinan	30 Oct
22:16.11	Fan Xiaoling		CHN	71	5	NC	Jinan	30 Oct
22:20.8	Ileana	Salvador	ITA	16.1.62	1		Padova	21 Sep
22:22.0'	Valentina	Shmer	SU	64	8	NC	Kiev	30 Jul
22:22.88	Nicole	Benz	GDR	23.6.70	3	vSU-j	Halle	11 Jun
22:24.0	Raisa	Sinyavina	SU	17.10.54	1		Sumy	21 Aug
	(30)							

Mark	Name		Nat	Born	Pos	Meet	Venue	Date
22:30.96	Mirva	Hämäläinen	FIN	30.8.62	2		Sipoo	4 Jun
22:31.2	Olimpiada	Ivanova	SU	5.5.70	1		Nikolayev	13 May
22:34.9	Mioara	Papuc	RUM	12.3.71	1		Bucuresti	4 Jun
22:35.0	Monica	Gunnarsson	SWE	22.4.65	1		Enhörna	28 Jul
22:37.2	Anita	Blomberg	NOR	5.10.71	1		Andebu	6 Aug
22:37.8	Beverley	Hayman	AUS	9.5.61	1		Sydney	5 Nov
22:38.33	Wang Yili		CHN	4.4.71	5	WJ	Sudbury	31 Jul
22:39.0	Lynn	Weik	USA	19.6.67	2	PennR	Philadelphia	28 Apr
22:39.25	Nathalie	Marchand	FRA	12.7.69	6	WJ	Sudbury	31 Jul
22:39.5	Yu Heping		CHN	65	2		Jiading	22 Oct
	(40)							
22:40.0'	Nina	Galyanina	SU	66	10	NC	Kiev	30 Jul
22:41.22	Maria	Reyes Sobrino	SPA	6.1.67	1	NC	Vigo	14 Aug
22:44.87	Gabrielle	Blythe	AUS	9.3.69	7	WJ	Sudbury	31 Jul
22:45.1	Xiong Yan		CHN	67	1		Xuzhou	18 Mar
22:46.32	Eva	Cruz	SPA	13.9.69	2	NC	Vigo	14 Aug
22:46.6	Larisa	Polevschikova	SU	10.1.71	4		Simferopol	27 May
22:47.4	Tatyana	Golubyeva	SU	72	5		Simferopol	27 May
22:47.5	Regina	Losyeva	SU	61	1		Kherson	13 May
22:48.0	Lisa	Langford	UK	15.3.67	1		Leicester	5 Nov
22:51.19	Wang Lina		CHN	68	6	NC	Jinan	30 Oct
	(50)							
22:51.9	Guan Ping		CHN	661.2.66	2		Xuzhou	18 Mar
Indoor marks where superior to outdoor bests								
22:04.4 os	Natalya	Spiridonova	SU	24.4.63	1		Moskva	31 Jan
22:25.2	Leonarda	Yukhnevich	SU	1.5.63	2		Vilnius	2 Mar
22:26.02	Yelena	Veremeychuk	SU	59	2		Minsk	5 Mar
22:27.7	Monica	Gunnarsson	SWE	22.4.65	1	NC	Göteborg	7 Feb
22:30.25	Irina	Shumak	SU	4.12.65	3		Minsk	5 Mar
22:34.07	Yulia	Lisnik	SU	66	4		Minsk	5 Mar
22:41.76	Natalya	Yermolenko	SU	20.2.57	6		Minsk	5 Mar
22:47.37	Mariya	Popkova	SU	62	7		Minsk	5 Mar
22:47.4	Rimma	Makarova	SU	18.7.63	3		Vilnius	2 Mar
22:50.0	Ruzina	Ivoylova	SU	4.5.66	4		Vilnius	2 Mar

' during 10,000 metres walk

5000 METRES ROAD WALK

Best perforances and other marks if superior to track bests

Mark	Name		Nat	Born	Pos	Meet	Venue	Date
20:52	Kerry	Saxby	AUS	2.6.61	1		Adelaide	16 Oct
21:03		Saxby			1		Mezidon	8 May
21:04	Tamara	Kovalenko	SU	25.4.64	1		Odessa	20 Aug
21:14		Saxby			1		Vaxjö	29 May
21:21	Natalya	Spiridonova	SU	6.4.63	1		Moskva	31 Jul
21:26	Irina	Shumak	SU	65	2		Odessa	20 Aug
21:29	Olga	Karpoltseva	SU	.10.66	3		Odessa	20 Aug
21:31		Spiridonova	SU		1		Moskva	7 Aug
21:33		Saxby			1		Hospitalet	24 Apr
21:42		Saxby			1		Värnamo	13 May
21:50	Vera	Osipova	SU	57	2		Moskva	7 Aug
21:51		Saxby			1		Järna	4 Jun
21:53	Sada	Eidikite	SU	22.6.67	1		Alushta	8 May
21:54	Svetlana	Kaburkina	SU	67	1		Naumburg	1 May
21:56	Alina	Ivanova	SU	25.6.69	3		Moskva	7 Aug
22:02	Sari	Essayeh	FIN	67	1		Vaasassa	21 May
	(16/10)							
22:03	Mirva	Hämäläinen	FIN	62	2		Vaasassa	21 May
22:05	Tatyana	Titova	SU	25.8.69	1		Ruse	17 Apr
22:05	Yevgeniya	Mikheyeva	SU	69	1		Moskva	30 Apr
22:16	Maria	Reyes Sobrino	SPA	6.1.67	2		Hospitalet	24 Apr
22:18	Valentina	Tsybulskaya	SU	17.3.68	2		Novopolotsk	23 Apr
22:20	Mariya	Popkova	SU	62	2		Alushta	8 May
22:21	Leonarda	Yukhnevich	SU	1.5.63	1		Vitebsk	11 Jul
22:24	Raisa	Sinyavina	SU	17.10.54	1		Sumy	20 Aug
22:27	Natalya	Yermolenko	SU	20.2.57	4		Odessa	20 Aug
22:30	Ildikó	Ilyés	HUN	3.7.66	1		Bekescsaba	29 Apr

Mark	Name		Nat	Born	Pos	Meet	Venue	Date
22:30	Regina	Losyeva	SU	61	3		Alushta	8 May
22:32	Teresa	Vaill	USA	20.11.62	1		Overland Park	15 Apr
22:32	Sarah	Standley	USA	16.1.67	1		Fontana	16 Apr
22:33	Victoria	Herazo	USA		2		Fontana	16 Apr
22:36	Dana	Vavracová	CS	25.6.54	3		Hospitalet	24 Apr
22:36	Eva	Cruz	SPA	13.9.69	2		La Coruña	4 Jun
22:37	Yulia	Lisnik	SU	1.8.66	5		Odessa	20 Aug
22:37	Olga	Tomchuk	SU	14.3.63	2		Suimy	20 Aug
22:40	Irina	Kalinina	SU	68	6		Odessa	20 Aug
22:41	Margareta	Olsson	SWE	23.9.54	1		Stockholm	10 May
22:43	Larisa	Voronkova	SU	67	7		Odessa	20 Aug
22:47	Danute	Baranauskaite	SU	13.10.70	1		Novopolotsk	23 Apr

' during 10km walk

10000 METRES TRACK WALK

Mark	Name		Nat	Born	Pos	Meet	Venue	Date
42:14.2	Kerry	Saxby	AUS	2.6.61	1mx		Canberra	26 Jan
43:36.41	Yelena	Nikolayeva'	SU	1.2.66	1	NC	Kiev	30 Jul
43:36.5		Nikolayeva			1	SGP	Fana	7 May
44:07.97	Nadezhda	Ryashkina	SU	67	2	NC	Kiev	30 Jul
44:08.30	Vera	Mokolova	SU	66	3	NC	Kiev	30 Jul
44:13.75	Yelena	Rodionova	SU	7.5.65	4	NC	Kiev	30 Jul
44:28.37	Tamara	Kovalenko	SU	25.4.64	5	NC	Kiev	30 Jul
44:38.9	Guan Ping		CHN	1.2.66	1		Amagasaki	27 Nov
44:50.28	Lyubov	Kolesnikova	SU	70	6	NC	Kiev	30 Jul
44:50.7	Natalya	Spiridonova	SU	6.4.63	2	SGP	Fana	7 May
45:04.80	Natalya	Serbinenko	SU	27.1.59	7	NC	Kiev	30 Jul
45:13.50	Valentina	Shmer	SU	1.7.64	8	NC	Kiev	30 Jul
45:31.53	Nina	Galyanina	SU	66	9	NC	Kiev	30 Jul
45:35.22	Sada	Eidikite	SU	22.6.67	10	NC	Kiev	30 Jul
45:43.14	Tamara	Torshina	SU	31.1.67	11	NC	Kiev	30 Jul
45:43.44	Irina	Shumak	SU	4.12.65	12	NC	Kiev	30 Jul
	(16/15)							
45:45.44	Galina	Kuchma	SU	67	13	NC	Kiev	30 Jul
45:49.71	Yelena	Veremeychuk	SU	13.10.59	14	NC	Kiev	30 Jul
45:49.88	Yelena	Zayko	SU	67	15	NC	Kiev	30 Jul
45:53.76	Ruzhina	Ivoylova	SU	4.5.66	16	NC	Kiev	30 Jul
45:54.64	Leonarda	Yukhnevich	SU	63	17	NC	Kiev	30 Jul
	(20)							
45:58.1	Ileana	Salvador	ITA	16.1.62	1		Bergamo	8 Oct
45:58.56	Vera	Osipova	SU	5.2.57	18	NC	Kiev	30 Jul
46:01.96	Nina	Stakhrova	SU	68	19	NC	Kiev	30 Jul
46:04.84	Rimma	Makarova	SU	18.7.63	20	NC	Kiev	30 Jul
46:08.68	Galina	Shalyayeva	SU	68	21	NC	Kiev	30 Jul
46:14.42	Lyudmila	Lyubmirova	SU	62	22	NC	Kiev	30 Jul
46:14.8	Pier Carola	Pagani	ITA	63	2		Bergamo	8 Oct
46:15,61	Olga	Ossyko	SU	31.3.66	23	NC	Kiev	30 Jul
46:23.81	Marta	Zhinchina	SU	7.6.66	24	NC	Kiev	30 Jul
46:26.8	Natalya	Yermolenko	SU	20.2.57	3		Odessa	18 Aug
	(40)							
46:28.3	Xiong Yan		CHN	67	1		Xuzhou	20 Mar
46:32.41	Atanaska	Dzivkova	BUL	16.10.69	2	Int	Sofia	2 Sep
46:32.5	Tatyana	Titova	SU	25.8.69	4		Sochi	31 Jan
46:38.9	Yu Heping		CHN	65	2		Xuzhou	20 Mar
46:39.77	Natalya	Yermolenko	SU	20.2.67	25	NC	Kiev	30 Jul
46:47.0	Marina	Koznyeva	SU	68	5		Sochi	31 Jan
46:49.5	Wu Zhenzhen		CHN	67	3		Xuzhou	20 Mar
46:51.1	Liu Xiuzhen		CHN	69	4		Xuzhou	20 Mar
46:52.15	Debbie	Lawrence	USA	15.10.61	1		Indianapolis	15 Jul
46:52.64	Tatyana	Petrova	SU	15.8.65	26	NC	Kiev	30 Jul
	(50)							
46:54.4	Wang Lina		CHN	68	5		Xuzhou	20 Mar
46:57.5	Erica	Alfridi	IYTA	22.2.68	3		Sesto san Giovanni	14 Sep
46:59.5	Wang Zuolin		CHN	67	6		Xuzhou	20 Ma
47:02.93	Natalya	Storozhenko	SU	63	28	NC	Kiev	30 Jul
47:03.0	Nadezhda	Bogatyryova	SU	69	6		Sochi	31 Jan
47:03.	Monica	Gunnarsson	SWE	22.4.65	1	NC	Enhörna	31 Jul

Mark	Name			Nat	Born	Pos	Meet	Venue	Date
Indoor marks where superior to outdoor bests									
45:26.47	Irina	Shumak		SU	4.12.65	1		Minsk	4 Mar
46:06.24	Olga	Kardopoltseva		SU	.10.66	3		Minsk	4 Mar
46:30.00	Mariya	Popkova		SU	62	4		Minsk	4 Mar

10000 METRES ROAD WALK

Best perforances and other marks if superior to track bests

Mark	Name			Nat	Born	Pos	Meet	Venue	Date
41:30	Kerry	Saxby		AUS	2.6.61	1	NC	Canberra	27 Aug
43:26	Svetlana	Kaburkina		SU	3.5.67	1		Bucaresti	19 Jun
43:29	Vera	Mokolova		SU	66	1		Alushta	1 Oct
43:43	Tamara	Kovalenko		SU	25.4.64	2		Alushta	1 Oct
43:44		Saxby				1		Järna	4 Jun
43:53	Natalya	Spiridonova		SU	6.4.63	1	Znam	Leningrad	11 Jun
43:59		Saxby				1mx		Värnamo	13 May
44:10		Kovalenko				2		Bucaresti	19 Jun
44:13	Nadezhda	Ryashkina		SU	67	2	Znam	Leningrad	11 Jun
44:15		Saxby				1		Ätran	15 May
44:16	Natalya	Serbinenko'		SU	27.1.59	1		Kherson	8 May
44:20	Sada	Eidikite		SU	22.6.67	3	Znam	Leningrad	11 Jun
44:21	Yelena	Veremeychuk		SU	13.10.59	2		Kherson	8 May
44:26		Kaburkina				1	NC-w	Sochi	21 Feb
44:26	Sari	Essayeh	(10)	FIN	21.2.67	1		Vaasa	21 May
44:27		Kaburkina				1		Naumburg	1 May
44:30		Kovalenko				1		Odessa	18 Aug
44:33	Yelena	Nikolayeva		SU	1.2.66	2	NC-w	Sochi	21 Feb
44:33	Beate	Anders		GDR	4.2.68	1		Berlin	14 May
44:38		Mokolova				1		Kiev	16 Aug
44:54	Mirva	Hämäläinen		FIN	30.8.62	2		Vaasassa	21 May
44:57	Lyudmila	Lyubmirova		SU	62	4	Znam	Leningrad	11 Jun
44:59	Victoria	Oprea		ROM	65	1		Pitesti	12 Aug
45:00	Yelena	Rodionova		SU	7.5.65	3	NC-w	Sochi	21 Feb
45:01	Valentina	Shmer		SU	1.7.64	5	Znam	Leningrad	11 Jun
45:12	Vera	Osipova		SU	5.2.57	4	NC-w	Sochi	21 Feb
45:16		Anders				1	vlta	Neubrandenburg	10 Jul
45:17	Natalya	Storozhenko		SU	63	3		Kherson	8 May
45:18		Saxby				1		Sesto san Giovanni	1 May
45:18		Rodionova				6	Znam	Leningrad	11 Jun
	(30/19)								
45:19	Yelena	Zayko		SU	67	7	Znam	Leningrad	11 Jun
	(20)								
45:20	Irina	Lutkova		SU	65	8	Znam	Leningrad	11 Jun
45:24	Zaliya	Sinekeyeva		SU	20.10.65	9	Znam	Leningrad	11 Jun
45:27	Olga	Kardopoltseva		SU	.10.66	10	Znam	Leningrad	11 Jun
45:29	Olga	Ossyko		SU	31.3.66	11	Znam	Leningrad	11 Jun
45:37	Tatyana	Titova		SU	25.8.69	3		Alitus	1 Oct
45:39	Mária	Rozsa		HUN	12.2.67	1		Szeged	10 Jul
45:46	Andrea	Alföldi		HUN	22.9.64	1		Békéscsaba	10 Apr
45:50	Rimma	Makarova		SU	18.7.63	14	Znam	Leningrad	11 Jun
45:50	Marina	Smyslova		SU	5.6.66	15	Znam	Leningrad	11 Jun
45:52	Maria	Reyes Sobrino		SPA	6.1.67	2		La Coruña	5 Jun
45:54	Larisa	Voronkova		SU	67	16	Znam	Leningrad	11 Jun
45:58	Natalya	Ksenofontova		SU	25.6.59	7	NC-w	Sochi	21 Feb
45:58	Svetlana	Polovinko		SU	1.5.66	2		Moskva	10 Jul
46:00	Anikó	Szebenszky		HUN	12.8.65	1		Szolnok	28 May
46:01	Albina	Lesnikova		SU	65	1		Alitus	11 May
46:05	Mioara	Papuc		ROM	12.3.71	3		Bucaresti	19 Jun
46:07	Monica	Gunnarsson		SWE	22.4.65	3		La Coruña	5 Jun
46:13	Ines	Estedt		GDR	12.12.67	1		Potsdam	19 Mar
46:17	Maryanne	Torrellas		USA	26.7.58	1		Gdansk	28 Aug
46:18	Dana	Vavracová		CS	25.6.54	1	Int	Sofia	26 Jun
46:20	Nina	Mushnikova		SU	17.12.59	12	NC-w	Sochi	21 Feb
46:23	Marta	Zinchina		SU	7.6.66	4		Kherson	8 May

Mark	Name		Nat	Born	Pos	Meet	Venue	Date
46:23	Ann	Peel	CAN	27.2.61	1	PAmCp	Mar del Plata	12 Nov
46:24	Tatyana	Petrova	SU	65	13	NC-w	Sochi	21 Feb
46:27	Natalya	Yermolenko	SU	20.2.67	3		Odessa	18 Aug
46:28	Yevgeniya	Mikheyeva	SU	69	1		Maikop	23 Apr
46:31	Larissa	Sapovalova	SU	64	1		Alitus	14 Apr
46:32	Atanaska	Dzivkova	BUL	16.10.68	2	Int	Sofia	26 Jun
46:33	Maria	Colin	MEX	66	2	PAmCp	Mar del Plata	12 Nov
46:34	Maria	Cruz Diaz	SPA	24.10.69	3		Sesto.San Giovanni	1 May
46:43	Ildikó	Ilyés	HUN	3.7.62	4		Békéscsaba	10 Apr
46:44	Debbie	Lawrence	USA	15.10.61	3	PAmCp	Mar del Plata	12 Nov
46:45	Regiina	Losyeva	SU	61	2		Novopolotsk	24 Apr
46:47	Irina	Kalinina	SU	10.10.68	6		Odessa	16 Aug
46:52	Valeria	Naidenova	BUL	69	3	Int	Sofia	26 Jun

20 KILOMETRES ROAD WALK

Mark	Name		Nat	Born	Pos	Meet	Venue	Date
1:29:40	Kerry	Saxby	AUS	2.6.61	1		Värnamo	13 May
1:32:33	Nadezhda	Ryashkina	SU	67	1	NC	Mogilyov	4 Sep
1:34:03	Vera	Mokolova	SU	66	2	NC	Mogilyov	4 Sep
1:35:32	Olga	Ossyko	SU	31.3.66	3	NC	Mogilyov	4 Sep
1:35:36	Alina	Ivanova	SU	25.6.69	4	NC	Mogilyov	4 Sep
1:36:32	Yelena	Veremeychuk	SU	13.10.59	5	NC	Mogilyov	4 Sep
1:37:54	Mirva	Hämäläinen	FIN	62	2		Värnamo	13 May
1:38:48	Monica	Gunnarsson	SWE	22.4.65	3		Värnamo	13 May
1:37:13	Sada	Eidikite	SU	22.6.67	6	NC	Mogilyov	4 Sep
1:41:52	Anne	Jansson	SWE	1.7.58	4		Värnamo	13 May

Mark		Name		Nat	Born	Pos	Meet	Venue	Date

WORLD JUNIOR WOMEN'S ALL-TIME LISTS

Based on the age regulations introduced for 1988, that is under 20 in year of competition.

100 METRES

Mark	Wind	First name	Name	Nat	Born	Pos	Meet	Venue	Date
10.88	2.0	Marlies	Oelsner	GDR	21.03.58	1	NC	Dresden	1 Jul 77
10.89	1.8	Katrin	Krabbe	GDR	22.11.69	1rB		Berlin	20 Jul 88
10.99 ?auto	1.9	Natalya	Bochina	SU	4.01.62	2		Leningrad	3 Jun 80
11.03	1.7	Silke	Gladisch	GDR	20.06.64	3	OD	Berlin	8 Jun 83
11.08	2.0	Brenda	Morehead	USA	5.10.57	1	FOT	Eugene	21 Jun 76
11.13	2.0	Chandra	Cheeseborough	USA	16.01.59	2	FOT	Eugene	21 Jun 76
11.17A	0.6	Wendy	Vereen	USA	24.04.66	4	USOF	Air.F.Academy	3 Jul 83
11.18	-0.8	Silvia	Chivas	CUB	10.09.54	1h1	OG	München	1 Sep 72
11.18	0.6	Liliana	Allen	CUB	24.05.70	3	NM	Sofia	26 Jun 88
11.18	-0.4	Diana	Dietz	GDR	30.08.69	1	WJ	Sudbury	28 Jul 88
11.19	1.3	Martina	Blos	GDR	17.06.57	3	OD	Karl-Marx-Stadt	29 May 76
11.19	1.8	Gail	Devers	USA	19.11.66	1		Westwood	4 May 85
wind assisted									
10.97	3.3	Gesine	Walther	GDR	6.10.62	4	NC	Cottbus	16 Jul 80
11.06	2.2	Brenda	Morehead	USA	5.10.57	1s	FOT	Eugene	21 Jun 76
11.09		Angela	Williams	TRI	15.05.65	1		Nashville	11 Apr 84
11.13	2.2	Beverly	Kinch	UK	14.01.64	1	WUG	Edmonton	6 Jul 83
and timed									
10.8wA		Margaret	Bailes	USA	23.01.51	1		Flagstaff	29 Sep 68

200 METRES

Mark	Wind	First name	Name	Nat	Born	Pos	Meet	Venue	Date
22.19	1.5	Natalya	Bochina	SU	4.01.62	2	OG	Moskva	30 Jul 80
22.37	1.3	Sabine	Rieger	GDR	6.11.63	2	vSU	Cottbus	26 Jun 82
22.42	0.4	Gesine	Walther	GDR	6.10.62	1		Potsdam	29 Aug 81
22.51	2.0	Katrin	Krabbe	GDR	22.11.69	3		Berlin	13 Sep 88
22.52	1.2	Mary	Onyali	NIG	3.02.68	6	WC	Roma	3 Sep 87
22.70		Marita	Koch	GDR	8.03.57	1		Halle	15 May 76
22.70A	1.9	Kathy	Smallwood	UK	3.05.60	2	WUG	Ciudad México	12 Sep 79
22.72	1.3	Silke	Gladisch	GDR	20.06.64	3	NC	Karl-Marx-Stadt	18 Jun 83
22.74A	2.0	Raelene	Boyle	AUS	24.06.51	2	OG	Ciudad México	18 Oct 68
22.76A		Evette	de Klerk	RSA	21.08.65	1		Sasolburg	21 Apr 84
wind assisted									
22.34	2.3	Kathrin	Krabbe	GDR	22.11.69	1	WJ	Sudbury	30 Jul 88
22.49	2.3	Brenda	Morehead	USA	5.10.57	1	FOT	Eugene	24 Jun 76
22.53	2.5	Valerie	Brisco	USA	6.07.60	2	AAU	Walnut	17 Jun 79
22.64	2.3	Chandra	Cheeseborough	USA	16.01.59	2	FOT	Eugene	24 Jun 76

400 METRES

Mark	First name	Name	Nat	Born	Pos	Meet	Venue	Date
49.77	Christina	Brehmer	GDR	28.02.58	1		Dresden	9 May 76
50.19	Marita	Koch	GDR	8.02.57	3	OD	Berlin	10 Jul 76
50.87	Denean	Howard	USA	5.10.64	1	TAC	Knoxville	20 Jun 82
50.90	Shiela	Ingram	USA	23.03.57	3s1	OG	Montreal	28 Jul 76
50.92	Margit	Sinzel	GDR	17.06.58	5	OD	Berlin	10 Jul 76
50.92	Sandie	Richards	JAM	6.11.68	1		Odessa	16 May 87
50.96	Maicel	Malone	USA	12.06.69	1s1	FOT	Indianapolis	17 Jul 88
50.98	Dagmar	Rübsam	GDR	3.06.62	2	NC	Jena	8 Aug 81
51.02	Marilyn	Neufville	JAM	16.12.52	1	CG	Edinburgh	23 Jul 70
51.09A	Sherri	Howard	USA	1.06.62	1	USOF	Colorado Springs	28 Jul 79
51.0 hand timed	Sabine	Busch	GDR	21.11.62	1	NC-j	Karl-Marx-Stadt	3 Aug 80

800 METRES

Mark	First name	Name	Nat	Born	Pos	Meet	Venue	Date
1:57.45	Hildegard	Ullrich	GDR	20.12.59	5	EC	Praha	31 Aug 78
1:57.86	Katrin	Wühn	GDR	19.11.65	1		Celje	5 May 84
1:58.18	Marion	Hübner	GDR	29.9.62	2		Erfurt	2 Aug 81
1:58.24	Christine	Wachtel	GDR	6.1.65	3		Potsdam	25 May 84
1:58.37	Gabriela	Sedláková	CS	2.3.68	4	ISTAF	Berlin	21 Aug 87
1:59.13	Maria	Pîntea	ROM	10.8.67	1		Bucaresti	15 Jun 86
1:59.17	Birte	Bruhns	GDR	4.11.70	1		Berlin	20 Jul 88
1:59.32	Martina	Kämpfert	GDR	11.11.59	2	NC	Leipzig	1 Jul 78
1:59.42	Rommy	Schmidt	GDR	20.6.59	3		Potsdam	19 Aug 78
1:59.48	Margrit	Klinger	GDR	22.6.60	1		Düsseldorf	30 Aug 79

1500 METRES

Mark	Name		Nat	Born	Pos	Meet	Venue	Date
3:59.96	Zola	Budd	UK	26.5.66	3	VD	Bruxelles	30 Aug 65
4:03.5	Svetlana	Guskova	SU	19.8.59	3	Kuts	Podolsk	13 Aug 78
4:04.42	Astrid	Pfeiffer	GDR	6.12.64	3	vUSA	Los Angeles	25 Jun 83
4:04.97	Ana	Padurean	ROM	5.9.69	1		Bucaresti	13 Jun 87
4:05.35	Dorina	Calenic	ROM	4.4.69	2		Bucaresti	13 Jun 87
4:05.96	Lynne	MacDougall	UK	18.2.65	6	BGP	Budapest	20 Aug 84
4:06.02	Birgit	Friedmann	FRG	8.4.60	7		Dortmund	1 Jul 78
4:06.19	Maria	Pîntea	ROM	10.8.67	8		Pitesti	28 Jun 86
4:06.62	Pavlina	Evro	ALB	22.2.65	1	Nik	Nice	20 Aug 84
4:06.71	Glenda	Reiser	CAN	16.6.55	2h1	OG	München	4 Sep 72
1000 m: 2:35.4	Irina	Nikitina	SU	10.1.61	5	Kuts	Podolsk	5 Aug 79
2:35.4	Katrin	Wühn	GDR	19.11.65	3		Potsdam	12 Jul 84
1 mile: 4:17.57	Zola	Budd	UK	26.5.66	3	WK	Zürich	21 Aug 85
2000m: 5:33.15	Zola	Budd	UK	26.5.66	1		London	13 Jul 84

3000 METRES

Mark	Name		Nat	Born	Pos	Meet	Venue	Date
8:28.83	Zola	Budd	UK	26.5.66	3	GP	Roma	7 Sep 85
8:44.1	Donna	Gould	AUS	10.6.66	-mix		Eugene	13 Jul 84
8:47.6	Svetlana	Guskova	SU	19.8.59	4	Znam	Vilnius	18 Jul 78
8:50.26	Rodica	Prescura	ROM	.70	2		Bucaresti	12 Jun 88
8:52.52	Dorina	Calenic	ROM	4.4.69	3		Bucaresti	14 Jun 87
8:56.03	Yelena	Malykhina	SU	20.3.63	1	vGDR	Cottbus	25 Jun 81
8:56.13	Lyudmila	Sudak	SU	6.7.65	2	vGDR	Cottbus	25 Jun 81
8:56.33	Fernanda	Ribeiro	POR	23.6.69	1	EJ	Birmingham	9 Aug 87
8:56.72	Adriana	Dumitru	ROM	3.5.68	8		Bucaresti	15 Jun 86
8:57.21	Helen	Kimaiyo	KEN	8.9.68	7h1	OG	Los Angeles	8 Aug 84
8:57.27	Ceci	Hopp	USA	13.4.63	4	vFRG	Durham	27 Jun 82

5000 METRES

Mark	Name		Nat	Born	Pos	Meet	Venue	Date
14:48.07	Zola	Budd	UK	26.5.66	1		London	26 Aug 85
15:27.3 mx	Donna	Gould	AUS	10.6.66	-		Adelaide	6 Jun 84
15:37.17	Hou Juhua		CHN	.67	1		Guangzhou	24 Oct 86
15:38.29	Akemi	Masuda	JAP	1.1.64	11	Bisl	Oslo	26 Jun 82

10000 METRES

Mark	Name		Nat	Born	Pos	Meet	Venue	Date
32:12.51	Marleen	Renders	BUL	24.12.68	4	Bis	Oslo	4 Jul 87
32:40.85	Margarita	Zhupikova	SU	.65	8		Kiev	24 Jun 84
32:44.52	Anke	Schäning	GDR	24.6.70	2	NC	Potsdam	8 Jun 88
32:48.1	Akemi	Masuda	JAP	1.1.64	1		Kobe	2 May 82
32:50.25	Esther	Kiplagut	KEN	8.12.66	1		Kobe	30 Apr 84
32:52.5	Mary	Shea	USA	28.10.60	1	AAU	Walnut	15 Jun 79
32:59.21	Wang Hongxia		CHN	.68	7		Guangzhou	29 Nov 87
33:03.32	Betty	Springs	USA	12.6.61	3		Eugene	23 May 80
33:08.46	Katie	Ishmael	USA	17.8.64	8	IAAF	Knarvik	4 Sep 83
33:15.8	Dorthe	Rasmussen	DEN	27.1.60	1		Østerbro	250479

100 METRES HURDLES

Mark	Wind	Name		Nat	Born	Pos	Meet	Venue	Date
12.84	1.5	Aliuska	Lopez	CUB	29.8.69	2	WSG	Zagreb	16 Jul 87
12.95	1.5	Candy	Young	USA	21.5.62	2	AAU	Walnut	16 Jun 79
13.00	0.7	Gloria	Kovarik	GDR	13.1.64	3h2	NC	Karl-Marx-Stadt1	6 Jun 83
13.00	2.0	Lyudmila	Khristosenko	SU	14.10.66	1	NC-j	Krasnodar	16 Jul 85
13.05	1.8	Heike	Terpe	GDR	4.10.64	4	OD	Berlin	8 Jun 83
13.07	0.2	Monique	Ewanje-Epée	FRA	11.7.67	2		Paris	22 Jul 86
13.09	1.3	Ulrike	Denk	FRG	10.5.64	1		Rhede	29 Jul 83
13.10	0.7	LaVonna	Martin	USA	18.11.66	1	PennR	Philadelphia	27 Apr 85
13.10	-0.7	Heike	Tillack	GDR	6.1.68	1	WJ	Athinai	18 Jul 86
13.11	-0.1	Benita	Fitzgerald	USA	6.7.61	2	FOT	Eugene	25 Jun 80
Wind assisted									
13.02	4.1	LaVonna	Martin	USA	18.11.66	5	NCAA	Austin	1 Jun 85
13.10	4.5	Karen	Nelson	CAN	3.12.63	4	CG	Brisbane	8 Oct 82
Hand timed									
12.9		Teresa	Nowak	POL	29.4.42	2	Kus	Warszawa	20 Jun 71
12.9w	2.8	Svetla	Dimitrova	BUL	27.1.70	1H		Sofia	18 Jun 88

Mark		Name		Nat	Born	Pos	Meet	Venue	Date
400 METRES HURDLES									
55.20		Lesley	Maxie	USA	4.1.67	2	TAC	San Jose	9 Jun 84
55.53		Radostina	Dimitrova	BUL	1.6.66	3	OD	Potsdam	21 Jul 84
55.65		Schowanda	Williams	USA	3.12.66	3	NCAA	Austin	31 May 85
55.74A		Myrtle	Simpson	RSA	18.2.64	2	NC	Bloemfontein	16 Apr 83
55.93		Sofia	Sabeva	BUL	11.1.69	1	NC-j	Sofia	3 Jul 88
56.00		Ann-Louise	Skoglund	SWE	28.6.62	1		Göteborg	11 Aug 81
56.16		Esther	Mahr	USA	4.1.61	2s2	WC	Sittard	15 Aug 80
56.22		Claudia	Bartl	GDR	2.5.68	1	EJ	Cottbus	25 Aug 85
56.28		Nadezhda	Asenova	BUL	28.3.62	1		Sofia	12 Jul 81
56.41		Silvia	Kirchner	GDR	7.5.63	1	EJ	Utrecht	23 Aug 81
56.47		Hildegard	Ullrich	GDR	20.12.59	1		Potsdam	19 Aug 78
HIGH JUMP									
2.01		Olga	Turchak	SU	5.3.67	2	GWG	Moskva	7 Jul 86
2.00		Stefka	Kostadinova	BUL	5.3.65	1		Sofia	25 Aug 84
2.00		Galina	Astafei	ROM	7.6.69	1	WJ	Sudbury	29 Jul 88
1.98		Silvia	Costa	CUB	4.5.64	2	WUG	Edmonton	11 Jul 83
1.98		Yelena	Yelesina	SU	4.4.70	1	Druzh	Nyiregyháza	13 Aug 88
1.97		Svetlana	Isaeva	BUL	18.3.67	2		Sofia	25 May 86
1.96		Charmaine	Gale	RSA	27.2.64	1	NC-j	Bleomfontein	4 Apr 81
1.95		Larisa	Kositsyna	SU	14.12.63	4	NC	Kiev	21 Aug 82
1.95		Maryse	Ewanje-Epée	FRA	4.9.64	3		Rieti	4 Sep 83
1.94		Yelena	Topchina	SU	28.10.66	1	EJ	Schwechat	28 Aug 83
1.94		Natalya	Golodnova	SU	14.4.67	1	EJ	Cottbus	25 Aug 85
1.94		Amra	Temim	YUG	24.1.68	1		Varazdin	15 Aug 87
1.94		Heike	Balck	GDR	19.8.70	2		Jena	4 Jun 88
LONG JUMP									
7.14	1.1	Heike	Daute	GDR	16.12.64	1	PTS	Bratislava	4 Jun 83
7.00	-0.2	Birgit	Grosshennig	GDR	21.2.65	2		Berlin	9 Jun 64
6.91	0.0	Anisoara	Cusmir	ROM	29.6.62	1		Bucaresti	23 May 81
6.90	1.4	Beverly	Kinch	UK	14.1.64	*	WC	Helsinki	14 Aug 83
6.88	0.6	Natalya	Shevchenko	SU	28.12.66	2		Sochi	26 May 84
6.84		Larisa	Baluta	SU	13.8.65	2		Krasnodar	6 Aug 83
6.82	1.8	Fiona	May	UK	12.12.69	*	WJ	Sudbury	30 Jul 88
6.81	1.6	Carol	Lewis	USA	8.8.63	1	TAC	Knoxville	20 Jun 82
6.81	1.4	Yelena	Davydova	SU	16.11.67	1		Krasnodar	17 Jul 85
6.79		Carmen	Sirbu	ROM	17.2.67	3		Bucaresti	2 Jun 85
Wind assisted									
7.27	2.2	Heike	Daute	GDR	16.12.64	1	WC	Helsinki	14 Aug 83
6.99	4.6	Beverly	Kinch	UK	14.1.64	5	WC	Helsinki	14 Aug 83
6.88	2.1	Fiona	May	UK	12.12.69	1	WJ	Sudbury	30 Jul 88
6.84	2.8	Anu	Kaljurand	SU	16.4.69	2		Riga	4 Jun 88
SHOT									
20.51i		Heidi	Krieger	GDR	20.7.65	2		Budapest	8 Feb 84
			20.24			5		Spilt	30 Apr 84
20.23		Ilke	Wyludda	GDR	28.3.69	1	NC-j	Karl-Marx-Stadt	16 Jul 88
20.12		Ilona	Schoknecht	GDR	24.9.56	2		Erfurt	23 Aug 75
19.90		Stephanie	Storp	FRG	28.11.68	1		Hamburg	16 Aug 87
19.57		Grit	Haupt	GDR	4.6.66	1		Gera	7 Jul 84
19.48		Ines	Wittich	GDR	14.11.69	5		Leipzig	29 Jul 87
19.42		Simone	Michel	GDR	18.12.60	3	vSU	Leipzig	23 Jun 79
19.05		Cordula	Schulze	GDR	11.9.59	3		Potsdam	6 Aug 78
18.94		Heike	Rohrmann	GDR	22.2.69	1		Halle	14 May 88
18.92		Brigitte	Griessing	GDR	22.2.56	5		Erfurt	23 Aug 75
DISCUS									
74.40		Ilke	Wyludda	GDR	28.3.69	2		Berlin	13 Sep 88
67.38		Irina	Meszynski	GDR	24.3.62	1		Berlin	14 Aug 81
67.00		Jana	Günther	GDR	7.1.68	6	NC	Potsdam	20 Aug 87
66.80		Svetla	Mitkova	BUL	17.6.64	1		Sofia	2 Aug 83
66.60		Astrid	Kumbernuss	GDR	5.2.70	1		Berlin	20 Jul 88
66.34		Franka	Dietzsch	GDR	22.1.68	2		St Denis	11 Jun 87

Mark	Name		Nat	Born	Pos	Meet	Venue	Date
65.96	Grit	Haupt	GDR	4.6.66	3		Leipzig	13 Jul 84
65.22	Daniela	Costian	ROM	30.4.65	3		Nitra	26 Aug 84
64.52	Martina	Opitz	GDR	12.12.60	3	NC	Karl-Marx-Stadt	12 Aug 79
64.42	Larisa	Korotkovich	SU	23.1.67	1		Minsk	28 Apr 86

JAVELIN

Mark	Name		Nat	Born	Pos	Meet	Venue	Date
71.88	Antoaneta	Todorova	BUL	8.6.63	1	EP	Zagreb	15 Aug 81
71.82	Ivonne	Leal	CUB	27.2.66	1	WUG	Kobe	30 Aug 85
68.94	Trine	Solberg	NOR	18.4.66	1	vSU	Oslo	16 Jul 85
68.38	Antje	Kempe	GDR	23.6.63	Q	EC	Athinai	8 Sep 82
67.32	Regina	Kempter	GDR	4.4.67	2	NC	Jena	27 Jun 86
66.52	Alexandra	Beck	GDR	13.6.68	1		Khania	24 May 86
64.88	Anja	Reiter	GDR	15.7.69	1	EJ	Birmingham	8 Aug 87
64.68	Karen	Forkel	GDR	24.9.70	1	Druzh	Nyiregyháza	12 Aug 88
64.56	Jana	Kopping	GDR	12.4.66	2	OD	Berlin	27 Jun 85
64.56	Xiomara	Rivera	CUB	24.12.68	1	CAC-j	Ciudad México	26 Jun 86

HEPTATHLON

Mark	Name		Nat	Born	Pos	Meet	Venue	Date
6465	Sibylle	Thiele	GDR	6.3.65	1	EJ	Schwechat	28 Aug 83
6436	Sabine	Braun	FRG	19.6.65	1	vBul	Mannheim	9 Jun 84
6403	Emilia	Dimitrova	BUL	13.11.67	6	GWG	Moskva	7 Jul 86
6289	Svetla	Dimitrova	BUL	27.1.70	1	WJ	Sudbury	30 Jul 88
6276	Larisa	Nikitina	SU	29.4.65	8	NC	Kiev	21 Jun 84
6218	Jana	Sobotka	GDR	3.10.65	6	OD	Potsdam	21 Jul 84
6198	Anke	Schmidt	GDR	5.2.68	7		Götzis	24 May 87
6194	Camelia	Cornateanu	ROM	23.1.67	2	NC	Pitesti	8 Aug 86
6187	Ionica	Domniteanu	ROM	8.1.69	1	Bal-j	Pitesti	26 Jul 87
6179	Birgit	Clarius	FRG	18.3.65	7		Götzis	29 May 83
6179	Valentina	Savchenko	SU	13.5.68	1	Drz	Plovdiv	5 Aug 84

5000 METRES WALK

Mark	Name		Nat	Born	Pos	Meet	Venue	Date
21:13.16	Cui Yingzi		CHN	.71	1		Jinan	30 Oct 88
21:30.92	Oksana	Shchastnaya	SU	24.4.71	1	EJ	Birmingham	7 Aug 87
21:31.7	Chen Yueling		CHN	.68	1	NC	Guangzhou	23 Oct 87
21:33.8	Wang Yan		CHN	9.4.71	1		Jian	9 Mar 86
21:36.92	Maria	Cruz Diaz	SPA	24.10.69	2	EJ	Birmingham	7 Aug 87
21:40.3	Yan Hong		CHN	23.10.66	1	SGP	Fana	5 May 84
21:43.27	Kathrin	Born	GDR	4.12.70	1	NC-j	Karl-Marx-Stadt	15 Jul 88
21:47.8	Guan Ping		CHN	1.2.66	3		Jian	18 Mar 85
21:48.4	Alina	Ivanova	SU	16.3.69	1		Simferopol	27 May 88
21:49.0	Zhang Min		CHN	67	4		Zhengzhu	15 Oct 85

4 x 100 METRES RELAY

Mark	Nat	Team	Pos	Meet	Venue	Date
43.48	GDR	Breuer, Krabbe, Dietz, Henke	1	WJ	Sudbury	31 Jul 88
	Unsanctioned race 43.33	Breuer, Krabbe, Dietz, Henke	1		Berlin	20 Jul 88
43.73A	USA	Gilmore, Finn, Simmons, Vereen	1		Colorado.Springs	19 Jul 83
43.87	SU	Lapshina, Doronina, Bulatova, Kovalyova	1		Leningrad	20 Jun 87
44.04	CUB	Riquelme, Allen, Lopez, Valdivia	2	WJ	Sudbury	31 Jul 88
44.13	NIG	Iheagwam, Nwajei, Ogunkoya, Onyali	3	WJ	Athinai	20 Jul 86
44.29	FRA	Rome, Sidibe, Clachet, Leroy	4	WJ	Athinai	20 Jul 86
44.63	FRG	Eichler, Rasch, Steger, Sommer	2	EJ	Donyetsk	21 Aug 77
44.71	UK	Hunte, Smallwood, Probert, McGregor	3	EJ	Donyetsk	21 Aug 77
44.93	POL	Stachurska, Nania, Filip, Witkowska	2	EJ	Athinai	24 Aug 75
45.04	JAM	McIntosh, Campbell, McDonald, Freeman	6	WJ	Sudbury	31 Jul 88

4 x 400 METRES RELAY

Mark	Nat	Team	Pos	Meet	Venue	Date
3:28.39	GDR	Deer, Fabert, Wöhlk, Breuer	1	WJ	Sudbury	31 Jul 88
3:30.4	USA	Harris, Pritchett, Downing, Vickers	1	WJ	Athinai	20 Jul 86
3:31.41	SU	Zakharova, Kiryukhina, Ponomaryova, Zhdanova	2	EJ	Utrecht	23 Aug 81
3:31.78	BUL	Kireva, Rashova, Girova, Shtereva	2	EJ	Schwechat	28 Aug 83
3:31.94	FRG	Wahl, Lix, Ley, Leistenschneider	3	EJ	Schwechat	28 Aug 83
3:35.10	UK	Honley, Robinson, Flockhart, Hall	3	EJ	Cottbus	25 Aug 85
3:35.96	CS	Cernochová, Pokorná, Mrovcová, Slegrová	5	EJ	Schwechat	28 Aug 83
3:36.41	CAN	Fortin, Steingruber, Layne, Allen	4	WJ	Sudbury	31 Jul 88
3:36.50	RUM	Solcan, Zavelca, Cracea, Plescan	2	Balk-j	Alexandroúpolis	10 Jul 88
3:37.03	POL	Siewerska, Nowaczyk, Zalewska, Kwietniewska	3	EJ	Duisburg	26 Aug 73

WORLD JUNIOR WOMEN'S LISTS 1988

100 METRES

Mark		Name		Nat	Born	Pos	Meet	Venue	Date
10.89	+1.8	Kathrin	Krabbe	GDR	22.11.69	1rB		Berlin	20 Jul
		11.13A	+2.0			4		Sestriere	11 Aug
		11.16	+1.0			4		Potsdam	8 Sep
		11.22	-0.4			2	WJ	Sudbury	28 Jul
		11.22	+0.9			1h6	WJ	Sudbury	27 Jul
		11.23	+0.9			1r1		Jena	20 May
		11.24	+1.7			1		Granada	29 May
11.18	+0.6	Liliana	Allen	CUB	24.5.70	3	NM	Sofia	26 Jun
11.18	-0.4	Diana	Dietz	GDR	30.8.69	1	WJ	Sudbury	28 Jul
		11.18w	+2.2			1h7	WJ	Sudbury	27 Jul
11.22	0.0	Esther	Jones	USA	7.4.69	4q2	FOT	Indianapolis	16 Jul
		11.24	+0.6			2	TAC	Tampa	17 Jun
		11.25	+1.0			1h2	TAC	Tampa	17 Jun
11.28	0.0	Angela	Burnham	USA	13.9.71	5q2	FOT	Indianapolis	16 Jul
11.34		Tayamí	Martínez	CUB	16.7.72	1		Jalisco	24 Jun
11.39	+1.8	Katrin	Henke	GDR	30.9.69	3rB		Berlin	20 Jul
11.45	+2.0	Irena	Gurskaite	SU	69	1s	NC-j	Bryansk	6 Jul
11.47	+1.5	Nadezhda	Rotach	SU	10.8.70	1	NC-j	Bryansk	6 Jul
11.48		Michelle	Freeman	JAM	5.5.69	1	CARIFTA	Kingston	7 Apr
11.50	+1.2	Chryste	Gaines	USA	14.9.70	1	TexR	Austin	8 Apr
11.53	+0.9	Grit	Breuer	GDR	16.2.72	2r1		Jena	20 May
11.55	+0.9	Karina	Knuhr	GDR	18.11.69	3r1		Jena	20 May
11.56	-0.1	Anita	Howard	USA	22.3.69	3	NC-j	Tallahassee	24 Jun
11.57	0.0	Cecile	Peyre	FRA	24.7.69	1s1		Créteil	9 Jul
11.57	-0.4	Eusebia	Riquelme	CUB	27.11.69	5	WJ	Sudbury	28 Jul
11.58	+1.7	Kendra	Mackey	USA	14.1.69	2		Durham	23 Apr
11.58	+0.7	Beatrice	Utondu	NIG	23.11.69	1		Houston	4 May
11.59		Stephanie	Douglas	UK	22.1.69	2rA		Columbus	24 Jul

Wind assisted

Mark		Name		Nat	Born	Pos	Meet	Venue	Date
11.18	+3.0	Esther	Jones	USA	7.4.69	3	NCAA	Eugene	4June
11.26	+3.9	Angela	Burnham	USA	13.9.71	4h2	FOT	Indianapolis	16 Jul
11.43		Inger	Miller	JAM	12.6.72			Norwalk	21 May
11.45	+2.4	Teresa	Foster	USA	11.4.72	1		Baton Rouge	7 May
11.45	+4.8	Stephanie	Douglas	UK	22.1.69	1	NC-j	Stoke-on-Trent	25 Jun
11.51	+3.3	Magalie	Simioneck	FRA	17.2.70	1s2		Créteil	9 Jul
11.54	+3.5	Anita	Howard	USA	22.3.69	5h4	FOT	Indianapolis	16 Jul
11.57A	+3.1	Marcel	Winkler	RSA	29.10.70	3		Johannesburg	23 Apr
11.58	+2.3	Ximena	Restrepo	COL	10.3.69	2h4	WJ	Sudbury	27 Jul

Hand timing

Mark		Name		Nat	Born	Pos	Meet	Venue	Date
11.2	-0.1	Esther	Jones	USA	7.4.69	1	NC-j	Tallahassee	24 Jun
11.3		Ge Weidong		CHN	4.1.69	1		Shijiazhuang	23 Apr
11.3	+0.9	Nelli	Bulgakova	SU	15.2.69	1		Dnepropetrovsk	26 Jul

Wind assisted

Mark		Name		Nat	Born	Pos	Meet	Venue	Date
11.2		Teresa	Foster	USA	11.4.72	1		Shreveport	11 Mar

200 METRES

Mark		Name		Nat	Born	Pos	Meet	Venue	Date
22.51	+2.0	Kathrin	Krabbe	GDR	22.11.69	3		Berlin	13 Sep
		22.59	+1.7			6s1	OG	Seoul	28 Sep
		22.85	-1.4			1		Granada	21 May
		22.87	+0.7			4q2	OG	Seoul	28 Sep
		22.88	+0.6			3		Sevilla	1 Jun
		23.14	+0.7			2h5	OG	Seoul	28 Sep
23.04	+1.3	Grit	Breuer	GDR	16.2.72	1		Jena	20 May
		23.06				1		Cottbus	29 May
23.05	+0.8	Esther	Jones	USA	7.4.69	6	NCAA	Eugene	3 Jun
23.13	+1.5	Liliana	Allen	CUB	24.5.70	2		Habana	6 Aug
23.26y		Chryste	Gaines	USA	14.9.70	1h		Lubbock	29 Apr
23.19	+0.7	Maicel	Malone	USA	12.6.69	1	PAC-10	Westwood	22 May
23.26	+1.6	Nadezhda	Chistyakova	SU	29.7.69	1	NC-j	Bryansk	8 Jul
23.31	+0.3	Svetla	Dimitrova	BUL	27.1.70	1	NC-j	Sofia	3 Jul
23.32	+0.9	Kendra	Mackey	USA	14.1.69	1		Athens, Ga.	7 May
23.33	+1.6	Irena	Gurskaite	SU	69	2	NC-j	Bryansk	8 Jul

Mark	Wind	Name		Nat	Born	Pos	Meet	Venue	Date
23.34	-1.1	Daniela	Plescan	RUM	11.1.69			Bucuresti	5 Jun
23.40		Diana	Dietz	GDR	30.8.69	1	vSU	Halle	12 Jun
23.42	+1.8	Ximena	Restrepo	COL	10.3.69	3		New York	5 Jun
23.45	+1.0	Angela	Burnham	USA	13.9.71	1		Norwalk	4 Jun
23.48	-0.4	Manuela	Derr	GDR	17.7.71	1	Druzh	Nyiregyháza	13 Aug
23.49		Anita	Howard	USA	22.3.69	1		Albany	6 May
23.55	+0.8	Angelika	Haggenmüller	FRG	1.3.69	1		Lübeck	10 Jul
23.58		Revolie	Campell	JAM	4.7.72	1rA		Columbus	24 Jul
23.58	-0.4	Jana	Schönenberger	GDR	28.11.71	2	Druzh	Nyiregyháza	14 Aug
23.59	+0.9	Inger	Miller	JAM	12.6.72	2		Norwalk	21 May
23.59	+1.0	Simone	Cain	USA	23.8.70	2		Norwalk	4 Jun

y 220 yards time (equivalent to 23.14)

Wind assisted

Mark	Wind	Name		Nat	Born	Pos	Meet	Venue	Date
22.34	+2.3	Kathrin	Krabbe	GDR	22.11.69	1	WJ	Sudbury	30 Jul
		22.97	+2.1			1s2	WJ	Sudbury	29 Jul
22.88	+2.3	Diana	Dietz	GDR	30.8.69	2	WJ	Sudbury	30 Jul
22.97	+2.3	Liliana	Allen	CUB	24.5.70	3	WJ	Sudbury	30 Jul
23.00	+2.3	Esther	Jones	USA	7.4.69	4	WJ	Sudbury	30 Jul
23.26	+2.2	Angelika	Hagenmüller	FRG	1.3.69	2s1	WJ	Sudbury	29 Jul
23.38		Darlena	Morganfield	USA	.4.69	2h1		Ames	14 May
23.51A	+2.7	Marcel	Winkler	RSA	29.10.70	3		Germiston	8 Oct
23.56	+2.3	Oksana	Kovalyova	SU	3.9.69	1h4	WJ	Sudbury	28 Jul

Hand timing

Mark	Wind	Name		Nat	Born	Pos	Meet	Venue	Date
23.3		Svetla	Dimitrova	BUL	27.1.70	1		Stara Zagora	29 May

400 METRES

Mark	Name		Nat	Born	Pos	Meet	Venue	Date
50.96	Maicel	Malone	USA	12.6.69	1s1	FOT	Indianapolis	17 Jul
		51.01			2	TAC	Tampa	18 Jun
		51.21			2R2	ASV	Köln	21 Aug
		51.32			2	NCAA	Eugene	4 Jun
		51.34			1h2	TAC	Tampa	16 Jun
		51.60			1s1	TAC	Tampa	17 Jun
		51.61			1	PAC-10	Westwood	22 May
51.14	Grit	Breuer	GDR	16.2.72	3		Jena	3 Jun
		51.15			1		Cottbus	28 May
		51.24			1	WJ	Sudbury	29 Jul
		51.33			1		Berlin	20 Jul
52.01	Ute	Rohländer	GDR	30.6.69	1		Halle	14 May
52.13	Stefanie	Fabert	GDR	3.8.69	2		Berlin	20 Jul
52.46	Daniela	Spasova	BUL	23.9.69	1	Balk-j	Alexandroúpolis	9 Jul
52.48	Daniela	Plescan	RUM	11.1.69	6rB		Lenningrad	12 Jul
52.56	Anke	Wöhlk	GDR	16.12.70	3		Berlin	20 Jul
52.62	Manuela	Derr	GDR	17.7.71	4		Berlin	20 Jul
52.72	Olga	Moroz	SU	16.8.70	1h	NC-j	Bryansk	6 Jul
52.84	Tania	van Heer	AUS	70	1		Perth	27 Mar
53.07	Viktoria	Miloserdova	SU	28.3.70	2	NC-j	Bryansk	7 Jul
53.14	Nadezda	Tomsová	CS	10.9.71	2s3	WJ	Sudbury	28 Jul
53.15	Teri	Smith	USA	5.2.69	2		Fairfax	15 May
53.17	Stephanie	Saleem	USA	19.3.69	5h1	TAC	Tampa	16 Jun
53.18	Kendra	Mackey	USA	14.1.69	1		Raleigh	25 May
53.25	Carmelita	Williams	USA	27.7.71			Charleston	21 May
53.35	Lumenita	Koch	RUM	13.3.70	1		Bucaresti	17 Sep
53.47	Elena	Solcan	RUM	19.5.70	3	Balk-j	Alexandroúpolis	9 Jul
53.48	Ximena	Restrepo	COL	10.3.69	1h2	WJ	Sudbury	27 Jul
53.50	Keisha	Demas	USA	10.2.69	3		Fairfax	15 May

Unconfirmed

Mark	Name		Nat	Born	Pos	Meet	Venue	Date
52.40	Ann	Maenhout	BEL	69				

Hand timing

Mark	Name		Nat	Born	Pos	Meet	Venue	Date
53.3	Natalya	Grabar	SU	22.9.69	1		Chernigov	Jun

800 METRES

Mark	Name		Nat	Born	Pos	Meet	Venue	Date
1:59.17	Birte	Bruhns	GDR	4.11.70	1		Berlin	20 Jul
		2:00.34			3		Jena	3 Jun
		2:00.59			3		Potsdam	8 Jun
		2:00.67			1	WJ	Sudbury	29 Jul

Mark	Name		Nat	Born	Pos	Meet	Venue	Date
2:00.53	Catalina	Gheorghiu	RUM	21.6.69	1		Bucuresti	10 Jul
		2:00.65			3		Bucuresti	19 Jun
		2:01.96			2	WJ	Sudbury	29 Jul
2:01.61	Luminita	Avasiloaie	RUM	24.5.69	5		Bucuresti	19 Jun
2:01.84	Nadia	Ouaziz	MOR	9.3.72				
2:02.03	Olga	Burkanova	SU	29.9.69	1		Nikolayev	14 May
2:02.27	Snezana	Pajkic	YUG	23.9.70	4		Zagreb	2 Jun
2:02.34	Daniela	Steinecke	GDR	12.6.69	5		Jena	3 Jun
2:02.44	Dorota	Buczkowska	POL	26.8.69	1	vFRG-j	Bochum	26 Jun
2:02.67	Denisa	Zavelca	RUM	27.1.70			Bucuresti	5 Jun
2:03.37	Erzsébet	Todorán	HUN	15.11.70	1	NC	Miskolc	17 Jul
2:03.66	Daniela	Antipov	RUM	31.5.70			Bucuresti	19 Jun
2:04.05	Larisa	Nechval	SU	31.1.69			Bryansk	27 Jun
2:04.27	Carla	Sacramento	POR	10.12.71	2		Lisboa	5 Jun
2:04.30	Yvonne	van der Kolk	HOL	7.1.69	3r1		Koblenz	1 Jun
2:04.36	Maria	Mutola	MOZ	27.10.72	7h2	OG	Seoul	24 Sep
2:04.62	Irina	Yegorova	SU	69	2		Nikolayev	14 May
2:04.63	Lizzy	Immetsoe	BEL	14.4.70	1		Watermael-Bosv	9 Jul
2:04.71	Manuela	Witzmann	GDR	12.6.70	1		Halle	15 May
2:04.75	Malin	Alsgren	SWE	8.3.70	3r1		Kvarnsveden	19 Jun
2:04.75	Dorota	Kata	POL	24.6.70	6		Sopot	30 Jul

1500 METRES

Mark	Name		Nat	Born	Pos	Meet	Venue	Date
4:10.74	Doina	Homneac	RUM	1.11.69	7		Bucuresti	18 Jun
		4:12.94			1	WJ	Sudbury	31 Jul
4:11.71	Malin	Ewerlöf	SWE	2.6.72	1		Helsinki	4 Sep
		4:12.30					Gävle	28 Jun
		4:13.94			3		Stockholm	3 Jul
4:12.64	Ana	Padurean	RUM	5.9.69	11		Bucuresti	18 Jun
4:13.6 m	Nathalie	Rouillard	CAN	2.9.69	4		Montreal	11 Aug
4:13.98	Yvonne	van der Kolk	HOL	7.1.69	3		Leverkusen	28 Jun
4:14.70	Simona	Staicu	RUM	5.5.71			Bucuresti	4 Jun
4:15.25	Simone	Weidner	GDR	30.9.69	4		Potsdam	8 Jun
4:15.46	Yvonne	Lichtenfeld	GDR	15.9.69	5		Potsdam	8 Jun
4:15.63	Karen	Hartmann	GDR	29.4.70	6		Potsdam	8 Jun
4:15.90	Alexandra	Reichling	FRG	10.6.69	4		Leverkusen	28 Jun
4:15.92	Daniela	Antipov	RUM	31.5.70			Bucuresti	27 Aug
4:16.01	Caroline	Jeorgakopoulos	FRG	3.9.69	5		Leverkusen	28 Jun
4:16.19	Snezana	Pajkic	YUG	23.9.70	2	WJ	Sudbury	31 Jul
4:16.38	Dorota	Buczkowska	POL	26.8.69	4	NC	Grudziadz	12 Aug
4:16.71	Tao Chunmiao		CHN	71	1		Jinan	27 Oct
4:17.02	Nuta	Olaru	RUM	28.8.70			Bucuresti	4 Jun
4:17.08	Mirela	Bortoi	RUM	6.9.71			Bucuresti	4 Jun
4:17.19	Anne	Lardner	NZ	2.7.70	1		Auckland	27 Feb
4:17.25	Natalya	Vorobyova	SU	22.9.69	1	vGDR-j	Halle	11 Jun
4:17.4 m	Fernanda	Ribeiro	POR	23.6.69	1		Maia	28 May
Unconfirmed								
4:17.09	Liu Shixiang		CHN	13.1.71				

3000 METRES

Mark	Name		Nat	Born	Pos	Meet	Venue	Date
8:57.88	Angelines	Rodriguez	SPA	24.9.69	2		Barcelona	13 Jul
8:59.78	Doina	Homneac	RUM	1.11.69	9		Bucuresti	19 Jun
9:00.38	Fernanda	Ribeiro	POR	23.6.69	2		St Denis	7 Jun
9:02.32	Malin	Ewerlöf	SWE	2.6.72	2		Kvarnsveden	19 Jun
9:05.53	Miyoko	Asahina	JAP	24.9.69	2		Hiratsuka	23 Oct
9:05.67	Anke	Schäning	GDR	24.6.70	1		Berlin	20 Jul
9:06.16	Helen	Titterington	UK	24.10.69	6	vSU,Fra	Portsmouth	19 Jun
9:06.16	Olga	Nazarkina	SU	11.6.70	1	Druzh	Nyiregyháza	14 Aug
9:07.67	Karen	Hartmann	GDR	29.4.70	2		Berlin	20 Jul
9:08.47	Yvonne	Lichtenfeld	GDR	15.9.69	3		Berlin	20 Jul
9:09.50	Fatima	Maamaa	MOR	69	2		Casablanca	11 Jun
9:09.58	Nadia	Ouaziz	MOR	9.3.72	3		Casablanca	11 Jun
9:09.88	Caroline	Jeorgakopoulos	FRG	3.9.69	9		Koblenz	28 Aug

Mark	Name		Nat	Born	Pos	Meet	Venue	Date
9:09.96	Rosário	Pia	POR	7.4.69	2		Maia	17 Jul
9:11.92	Lim	Chun Ae	KOR	1.7.69				
9:12.1 m	Denise	Bushallow	USA	28.9.69	1	PennR	Philadelphia	29 Apr
9:12.22	Simona	Staicu	RUM	5.5.71			Bucuresti	5 Jun
9:13.37	Anne	Lardner	NZ	2.7.70			Hamilton	13 Mar
9:13.6 m	Sonia	O'Sullivan	IRL	27.11.69	8		Knoxville	21 May
9:13.66	Anne Wangari	Mwangi	KEN	12.2.73	1	WJ	Sudbury	30 Jul

10000 METRES

Mark	Name		Nat	Born	Pos	Meet	Venue	Date
32:44.52	Anke	Schäning	GDR	24.6.70	2	NC	Potsdam	8 Jun
33:17.5 m	Olga	Nazarkina	SU	11.6.70	1		Simferopol	27 May
33:25.3 m	Mónica	Gama	POR	8.3.70	3		Lisboa	23 Apr
33:25.4 m	Ana Paula	Oliviera	POR	24.3.70	4		Lisboa	23 Apr
33:29.33	Birgit	Jerschabeck	GDR	17.5.69	3	NC	Potsdam	8 Jun
33:32.73	Naomi	Yoshida	JAP	14.4.69	5		Kyoto	18 Oct
33:37.4 m	Aisling	Ryan	IRL	15.12.69	14		Walnut	23 Apr
33:44.68	Kiyomi	Sugiura	JAP	30.10.69	9		Tokyo	8 Oct
33:49.2 m	Miyoko	Asahina	JAP	24.9.69	1		Tokyo	10 Oct
33:49.45	Jane Wanjiku	Ngotho	KEN	69	1	WJ	Sudbury	29 Jul
33:52.9	Chieko	Matsukawa	JAP		2		Tokyo	10 Oct
34:00.01	Larisa	Alekseyeva	SU	9.5.70				
34:01.75	Ikuko	Takahashi	JAP	28.5.70	5	NC	Tokyo	18 Jun
34:04.0 m	Sonia	Barry	NZ	13.11.69	1		New Plymouth	12 Jan
34:14.4 m	Svetlana	Nesterova	SU	70	1		Nikolayev	13 May
34:21.30	Ann Marie	Letko	USA	69	4		Raleigh	25 Mar
34:23.38	Aura	Buia	RUM	16.2.70			Bucuresti	5 Jun
34:23.38	Mericarmen	Diaz	MEX	15.7.70		WJ	Sudbury	29 Jul
34:28.5 m	Kerstin	Streck	FRG	69	1		Wetzlar	28 Sep
34:34.00	Suzana	Ciric	YUG	12.7.69	1		Sarajevo	4 Sep

100 METRES HURDLES

Mark	Wind	Name		Nat	Born	Pos	Meet	Venue	Date
12.96	+1.6	Aliuska	Lopez	CUB	29.8.69	1s1	WJ	Sudbury	29 Jul
		13.07				1		Columbus	24 Jul
		13.23	-2.6			1	WJ	Sudbury	29 Jul
		13.27				6h	OT	Berlin	29 Jun
		13.29				1		Habana	5 Aug
13.21	+2.0	Yulia	Filippova	SU	13.11.70	1h	NC-j	Bryansk	6 Jul
13.22	+2.0	Nadezhda	Chistyakova	SU	29.7.69	2h	NC-j	Bryansk	6 Jul
13.24	+1.2	Svetla	Dimitrova	BUL	27.1.70	1H	OG	Seoul	23 Sep
13.28	+0.4	Birgit	Wolf	FRG	11.9.69	2		Sindelfingen	2 Jul
13.31	+1.8	Zhanna	Gurbanova	SU	30.9.69	2	NC-j	Bryansk	6 Jul
13.43	+1.3	Peggy	Beer	GDR	15.9.69	1		Cottbus	29 May
13.49	+2.0	Tatyana	Kryukova	SU	70	h	NC-j	Bryansk	6 Jul
13.51		Ionica	Domniteanu	RUM	8.1.69	H		Bucaresti	21 May
13.52	+1.3	Ilka	Rönisch	GDR	15.3.72	2		Cottbus	29 May
13.55	+1.1	Yelena	Petushkova	SU	9.7.69	2H	WJ	Sudbury	29 Jul
13.57	0.0	Lisa	Wells	USA	3.1.70	1	TAC-j	Tallahassee	25 Jun
13.58	+0.1	Michaela	Hübel	FRG	6.4.69	2	vPOL-j	Bochum	26 Jun
13.64	0.0	Cinnammon	Sheffield	USA	8.3.70	1		Austin	14 May
13.64		Cornelia	Günthner	FRG	26.10.71	1		Burghausen	11 Jun
13.66		Regla C	Echevarría	CUB	2.1.70	1		Jalisco	25 Jun
13.67	+1.1	Marina	Matyakina	SU	11.12.69	1h1	NC-j	Bryansk	6 Jul
13.67	+1.1	Irina	Antipova	SU	30.4.69	2h1	NC-j	Bryansk	6 Jul
13.67	+1.6	Anna	Leczynska	POL	15.2.71	3s1	WJ	Sudbury	29 Jul
Wind assisted									
13.27	+3.8	Ionica	Domniteanu	RUM	8.1.69	1	Balk-j	Alexandroúpolis	10 Jul
13.56	+3.7	Lenatu	Birzu	RUM	20.2.69	2h1	Balk-j	Alexandroúpolis	10 Jul
13.56	+3.8	Zdravka	Georgieva	BUL	20.4.69	2	Balk-j	Alexandroúpolis	10 Jul
13.56	+3.8	Brigita	Bukovec	YUG	21.5.70	3	Balk-j	Alexandroúpolis	10 Jul
13.59	+2.6	Hope	Obika	NIG	27.4.70	2		Houston	7 May
13.66	+3.8	Sofia	Sabeva	BUL	11.1.69	4	Balk-j	Alexandroúpolis	10 Jul
Hand timing									
13.2	+0.5	Terry	Robinson	USA	15.9.69	5		Tallahassee	23 Apr
13.2	+0.5	Yulia	Filippova	SU	13.11.70	.h		Simferopol	28 May

Mark		Name		Nat	Born	Pos	Meet	Venue	Date
13.3	+0.4	Zhanna	Gurbanova	SU	30.9.69	.h		Simferopol	28 May
13.3	+0.1	Irina	Antipova	SU	30.4.69	1		Chernigov	24 Jul
Wind assisted									
12.9	+2.8	Svetla	Dimitrova	BUL	27.1.70	1H		Sofia	18 Jun
13.4		Cinnammon	Sheffield	USA	8.3.70				

400 METRES HURDLES

Mark	Name		Nat	Born	Pos	Meet	Venue	Date
55.93	Sofia	Sabeva	BUL	11.1.69	1	NC-j	Sofia	3 Jul
		56.81			1	Balk-j	Alexandroúpolis	10 Jul
		57.40			2		Sofia	25 Jun
57.10	Antje	Axmann	GDR	26.4.69	1		Karl-Marx-Stadt	16 Jul
		57.22			1		Berlin	20 Jul
		57.47						
57.35	Maria Gnebele	Womplou	IVC	20.12.69	5h1	OG	Seoul	25 Sep
57.47	Caroline	Fortin	CAN	25.1.70	3		Ottawa	7 Aug
57.52	Aura	Cracea	RUM	14.2.70	1		Bucuresti	21 May
57.58	Ann	Maenhout	BEL	8.2.69	2	WJ	Sudbury	29 Jul
57.66	Anna	Chuprina	SU	30.7.70	1		Bryansk	27 Jun
57.78	Marina	Matyakina	SU	11.12.69	1h	NC-j	Bryansk	7 Jul
57.81	Catalina	Gheorghiu	RUM	21.6.69	2		Bucuresti	21 May
57.84	Svetla	Slavcheva	BUL	19.3.70	1	Druzh	Nyiregyháza	14 Aug
57.88	Silvia	Rieger	FRG	14.11.70	3	WJ	Sudbury	29 Jul
58.05	Katrin	Schreiter	GDR	23.2.69	1		Jena	20 May
58.08	Valbone	Sina	ALB	70	5	Balk-j	Alexandroúpolis	10 Jul
58.20	Yelena	Pavlova	SU	3.2.69	1	NC-j	Bryansk	8 Jul
58.31	Kim	Batten	USA	29.3.69	3	TexR	Austin	7 May
58.32	Angelica	Sirbu	RUM	29.9.70	2		Bucuresti	27 Aug
58.37	Frida	Johannsson	SWE	5.1.70	3		Eskilstuna	14 Aug
58.39	Nelli	Voronkova	SU	72	1		Gorkiy	26 Aug
58.44	Petra	Schellenbeck	FRG	27.2.70	1		Bochum	26 Jun
Unconfirmed								
58.16	Yuan Hai Ying		CHN	70				
58.30	Li Liang		CHN	70				
Hand timing								
58.0	Yelena	Pavlova	SU	3.2.69	1h		Simferopol	28 May
58.2	Natalya	Cherkashina	SU	70	.h		Simferopol	28 May

HIGH JUMP

Mark	Name		Nat	Born	Pos	Meet	Venue	Date
2.00	Galina	Astafei	RUM	7.6.69	1	WJ	Sudbury	29 Jul
		1.98			2	Nik	Nice	10 Jul
		1.97			1	NC	Bucuresti	19 Jun
		1.95			1		Bucuresti	22 May
		1.94			1		Tel Aviv	7 May
		1.94			2		Reims	4 Jun
1.98	Yelena	Yelesina	SU	4.4.70	1	Druzh	Nyiregyháza	13 Aug
		1.97			1	vGDR	Halle	11 Jun
		1.96			2	WJ	Sudbury	29 Jul
		1.94i			1	vGDR	Pensa	17 Feb
1.94	Heike	Balck	GDR	19.8.70	2		Jena	4 Jun
1.92	Karen	Scholz	GDR	16.9.69	3	WJ	Sudbury	29 Jul
1.90	Gai	Kapernick	AUS	20.9.70	1		Melbourne	17 Mar
1.90	Jo	Jennings	UK	20.9.69	q	OG	Seoul	29 Sep
1.89i	Svetlana	Lavrova	SU	71	4		Vilnius	10 Jan
1.89	Sárka	Kaspárková	SU	20.5.71	1		Leipzig	6 Jul
1.88i	Coralea	Brown	CAN	15.6.72	2		Windsor	21 Feb
1.88	María del C	García	CUB	27.7.69	2		Sevilla	1 Jun
1.87i	Sárka	Nováková	CS	21.2.71	1		Cejkovice	8 Mar
		1.86			1		BanskáBystrica	2 Jul
1.87	Natalja	Jonckheere	BEL	21.10.70	1		Bruxelles	4 Sep
1.86i	Natalja	Zamyatina	SU	5.11.70	2		Chelyabinsk	6 Feb
1.86i	Yelena	Obukhova	SU	9.1.69	1		Rostov-on-Don	19 Feb
1.86	Tatyana	Shevchik	SU	11.6.69	1		Simferopol	27 May
1.86	Alica	Checová	CS	26.9.69	2		Banská Bystrica	2 Jul
1.86	Odile	Lesage	FRA	28.6.69	H	WJ	Sudbury	29 Jul

Mark		Name		Nat	Born	Pos	Meet	Venue	Date
1.86		Tatyana	Gulevich	SU	71	1		Gorkiy	26 Aug
1.86		Birgit	Kähler	FRG	14.8.70	2		Dormagen	4 Sep
1.86		Oana	Musonoi	RUM	27.9.72	1		Bucuresti	11 Sep

LONG JUMP

Mark	Wind	Name		Nat	Born	Pos	Meet	Venue	Date
6.82	+1.8	Fiona	May	UK	12.12.69	-	WJ	Sudbury	30 Jul
		6.79	+1.5			2		Birmingham	Aug
		6.73	+1.3			2		Gateshead	14 Aug
		6.66	-0.9			q	OG	Seoul	28 Sep
		6.62	-0.7			6	OG	Seoul	29 Sep
6.68	+2.0	Inna	Lasovskaya	SU	17.12.69	1	NC-j	Bryansk	7 Jul
6.66	+1.0	Svetlana	Shtatnova	SU	1.11.69	2	NC-j	Bryansk	7 Jul
6.62	0.0	Yelena	Garbuz	SU	70	5		Alma-Ata	18 Jun
6.59		Beatrice	Utondu	NIG	23.1.69	1		Austin	7 May
6.58	+0.6	Mirela	Belu	RUM	26.12.70	1	Balk-j	Alexandroúpolis	9 Jul
6.53	+2.0	Yelena	Volf	SU	69	3	NC-j	Bryansk	7 Jul
6.53	+1.9	Ivonne	Mathesius	GDR	21.8.71	1		Berlin	20 Jul
6.50		Tatyana	Kotova	SU	2.1.70	1		Dnepropetrovsk	14 May
6.48		Yelena	Galkina	SU	72	1		Chelyabinsk	1 Jul
6.47	+0.6	Anu	Kaljurand	SU	16.4.69	2	vGDR	Halle	12 Jun
6.47	+1.7	Joanne	Wise	UK	15.3.71	-	WJ	Sudbury	30 Jul
6.46	+0.5	Anisoara	Ghebuta	RUM	20.5.70	7	NC	Bucuresti	19 Jun
6.44		Wang Chunfang		CHN	70	1		Tianjin	21 Aug
6.42		Alla	Kozlova	SU	69	1		Bryansk	28 Jun
6.41	+1.2	Iwona	Ciolkowska	POL	25.5.71	1		Pila	24 Jul
6.40	+0.4	Maria Constanza	Moroni	ITA	23.3.69	1		Formia	19 Jun
6.37		Mihaela	Moldan	RUM	5.11.71			Bucuresti	17 Sep
6.36		Sonya	Roberts	USA	15.2.69	1		San Angelo	15 Apr
6.33	+2.0	Aleksandra	Paschina	SU	71	6	NC-j	Bryansk	7 Jul
Wind assisted									
6.88	+2.1	Fiona	May	UK	12.12.69	1	WJ	Sudbury	30 Jul
6.84	+2.8	Anu	Kaljurand	SU	16.4.69	2		Riga	4 Jun
		6.78	+3.4			2	WJ	Sudbury	30 Jul
6.69	+4.7	Joanne	Wise	UK	15.3.71	3	WJ	Sudbury	30 Jul
6.50		Beatrice	Mau	GDR	20.2.71	H	vSU	Halle	12 Jun
6.45	+3.1	Svetla	Dimitrova	BUL	27.1.70	1H		Sudbury	30 Jul
6.34		Judit	Kovács	HUN	7.6.69	3		Debrecen	14 May

SHOT

Mark	Name		Nat	Born	Pos	Meet	Venue	Date
20.23	Ilke	Wyludda	GDR	28.3.69	1	NC-j	Karl-Marx-Stadt	16 Jul
18.94	Heike	Rohrmann	GDR	22.2.69	1		Halle	14 May
		18.64			7		Jena	3 Jun
		18.58			1		Jena	1 May
18.80	Ines	Wittich	GDR	14.11.69	2	NC-j	Karl-Marx-Stadt	16 Jul
		18.54			1	WJ	Sudbury	28 Jul
		18.49			8		Jena	3 Jun
		18.42			1		Berlin	20 Jul
18.73	Astrid	Kumbernuss	GDR	5.2.70	3	NC-j	Karl-Marx-Stadt	16 Jul
18.35	Svetlana	Krivelyova	SU	13.6.69	1	NC-j	Bryansk	6 Jul
18.18	Annette	Gerlach	GDR	16.6.69	3		Jena	20 May
17.73	Zhang Liuhong		CHN	16.1.69		NC-j	Changzha	24 May
17.52	Elvira	Poljakova	SU	30.3.70	2	NC-j	Bryansk	6 Jul
17.50	Diana	Stoyanova	BUL	5.1.69	1	NC-j	Sofia	2 Jul
17.33	Wang Hong		CHN	10.4.70		NC-j	Changzha	24 May
17.22	Petya	Zhecheva	BUL	3.1.69	2	Balk-j	Alexandroúpolis	10 Jul
17.05	Yelena	Lyapunova	SU	70	4		Sochi	24 Apr
17.03	Zhanna	Babikova	SU	69	1		Ordzhonikidze	25 Sep
16.93	Min Chunfeng		CHN	18.3.69	3		Jihan	30 Oct
16.89	• Gabriele	Völkl	FRG	2.6.70	1		Lübeck	9 Jul
16.80	Dörte	Warbelow	GDR	30.10.70	1		Berlin	2 Jul
16.39	Yelena	Chibisova	SU	69	1		Fergana	10 Sep
16.30	Galabina	Koleva	BUL	17.6.71	3	Druzh	Nyiregyháza	13 Aug
16.29	Lada	Kirillova	SU	69	3		Moskva	2 May
16.28	Viktoria	Pavlysh	SU	15.1.69	3		Simferopol	27 May

Mark	Name		Nat	Born	Pos	Meet	Venue	Date
DISCUS								
74.40	Ilke	Wyludda	GDR	28.3.69	2		Berlin	13 Sep
		72.70			1	NC-j	Karl-Marx-Stadt	17 Jul
		72.24			3	vITA	Neubrandenburg	9 Jul
		71.98			2		Karl-Marx-Stadt	12 Jun
		71.88			1		Athenai	16 May
		71.54			1		Rostock	29 May
		70.80			2		Chania	22 May
		69.42			3		Jena	4 Jun
		68.24			1	WJ	Sudbury	31 Jul
66.60	Astrid	Kumbernuss	GDR	5.2.70	1		Berlin	20 Jul
60.94	Jana	Lauren	GDR	28.6.70	2		Berlin	20 Jul
60.60	Min Chunfeng		CHN	18.3.69	1		Jinan	30 Oct
59.28	Proletka	Voycheva	BUL	29.1.70	1	Balk-j	Alexandroúpolis	10 Jul
58.82 (58.40?)	Tatyana	Lugovskaya	SU	17.4.69	1		Kharkov	20 May
58.24	Manuela	Tirneci	RUM	26.2.69	1		Craiova	7 May
58.10	Dorte	Warbelow	GDR	30.10.70	1		Berlin	9 Jul
57.40	Tatyana	Belyakova	SU	69	1		Tula	21 Jun
56.22	Alla	Kokhan	SU	3.1.69	2		Simferopol	29 May
55.68	Zhao Yonghua		CHN	22.12.69			Beijing	14 May
55.32	Lidia	Kolesnikova	SU	70	1		Tambov	13 Aug
55.28	Anzhela	Baralyuk	SU	2.4.70	3		Simferopol	29 May
55.00	Tracey	Millett	USA	4.2.69	3	NCAA	Eugene	3 Jun
54.74	Yevgenia	Nechayeva	SU	69	1		Nikolayev	15 May
54.66	Janet	Hill	USA	28.8.70	1		Shreveport	18 May
54.58	Austrite	Mikelite	SU	69	1		Kaunas	14 Aug
54.46	Ines	Wittich	GDR	14.11.69	1		Karl-Marx-Stadt	8 Jul
35.96	Anja	Gündler	GDR	18.3.72	3		Berlin	5 May
53.72	Beata	Tempfli	ROM	17.1.70	1		Bucuresti	21 May
JAVELIN								
64.68	Karen	Forkel	GDR	24.9.70	1	Druzh	Nyiregyháza	12 Aug
		63.84			1		Berlin	20 Jul
		63.60			1	vSU	Halle	12 Jun
		63.20			1		Halle	15 May
		62.42			7		Rostock	29 May
		61.44			1	WJ	Sudbury	30 Jul
63.42	Britta	Heydrich	GDR	28.8.70	2		Berlin	20 Jul
		60.82			1	NC-j	Karl-Marx-Stadt	16 Jul
62.58	Anja	Reiter	GDR	15.7.69	2		Halle	14 May
		62.36			1		Berlin	16 Jan
60.52	Isel	López	CUB	11.7.70	4		Habana	20 Feb
60.34	Dorit	Dräger	GDR	30.10.71	2		Berlin	16 Jan
58.94	Stefania	Galbiati	ITA	8.1.69	1		Grosseto	9 Oct
58.56	Dagmar	Kosche	GDR	3.3.70	3		Halle	14 May
58.50	Malgorzata	Kielczewska	POL	2.1.69	3		Warszawa	19 Jun
58.48	Rita	Romanauskaite	SU	70	1		Bryansk	8 Jul
58.28	Sonia	Bisset	CUB	1.4.70	5		Habana	6 Aug
58.24	Wang Lianyun		CHN	69	1		Tianjin	21 Aug
58.12	Luo Zhonghua		CHN	20.1.69		NC-j	Changzha	23 May
57.82	Mandy	Uhlig	GDR	13.12.69	1		Karl-Marx-Stadt	11 May
57.64	Ieva	Skrastina	SU	8.11.69	1eB		Adler	27 Feb
57.56	Anna	Chorinou	GRE	21.1.70	1		Patra	17 Sep
56.98	Valeria	Ivanova	SU	14.1.69	1		Simferopol	28 May
56.84	M-Danielle	Teanyouen	FRA	18.1.70	1		Antony	25 Jun
56.34	Anna	Chuganova	SU	69	1		Donyetsk	26 Jun
56.12	Nathalie	Teppe	FRA	22.5.72			St.Maur	8 Oct
55.62	Katrin	Kirm	SU	23.2.69	2		Tormajärvi	30 Jul
HEPTATHLON								
6289	Svetla	Dimitrova	BUL	27.1.70	1	WJ	Sudbury	30 Jul
	13.47 1.77 13.07 23.78 6.45w 39.98 2:14.39							
		6283			1		Sofia	19 Jun
	12.9w 1.71 13.83 23.5 6.28 39.78 2:12.8							

Mark	Name		Nat	Born	Pos	Meet	Venue	Date
6102	Yelena	Petushkova	SU	9.7.69	2	WJ	Sudbury	30 Jul
	13.55 1.80 13.26 24.86 5.90w 41.68 2:13.29							
		6097			2		Simferopol	29 May
	13.67 1.75 13.94 24.66 5.98 41.14 2:13.4							
6081	Beatrice	Mau	GDR	20.2.71	1	vSU	Halle	12 Jun
	14.35 1.74 12.52 25.46 6.50w 48.84 2:17.15							
		5982			1	Druzh	Nyiregyháza	14 Aug
		5910			1		Dresden	8 May
6067w	Peggy	Beer	GDR	15.9.69	3	WJ	Sudbury	30 Jul
	13.65 1 .77 13.13 24.45 6.17W 38.06 2:15.02							
		6007			2	vSU	Halle	12 Jun
6007	Ionica	Domniteanu	RUM	8.1.69	3	NC	Bucuresti	19 Jun
	13.63 1.72 13.78 24.50 5.80 42.08 2:15.24							
5906	Sylvia	Tornow	FRG	6.2.69	1	vPOL-j	Bochum	26 Jun
	14.02 1.75 13.88 24.82 5.54 45.52 2:18.90							
5867	Odile	Lesage	FRA	28.6.69	3	NC	Tours	13 Aug
	13.83 1.84 13.30 25.89 5.83 38.36 2:18.27							
5864	Tatyana	Blokhina	SU	12.3.70	2		Simferopol	29 May
	14.15 1.78 14.40 25.03 5.55 44.46 2:13.4							
5824	Cornelia	Günther	FRG	26.10.71	2	vPOL-j	Bochum	26 Jun
	13.77 1.84 10.69 23.97 6.00 32.74 2:18.35							
5767	Rita	Ináncsi	HUN	6.1.71	19		Götzis	19 Jun
	14.38 1.75 12.87 25.18 6.00 39.34 2:19.36							
5720	Christiane	Scharf	FRG	25.8.70	3	vPOL-j	Bochum	26 Jun
	13.78 1.69 12.32 25.46 6.07 36.84 2:17.14							
5661	Marcela	Podracká	CS	13.3.70	3	Druzh	Nyiregyháza	13 Aug
	14.18 1.77 11.47 24.98 6.03 31.64 2:15.56							
5600	Marilyne	Becquet	FRA	24.5.69	2		Orange	3 Jul
	14.19 1.66 11.17 24.63 6.11 37.72 2:21.11							
5590	Jamie	McNeair	USA	26.6.69	3	NCAA	Eugene	2 Jun
	14.27w 1.69 11.21 24.60 5.66 37.96 2:14.59							
5572	Iustina	Nicolaescu	RUM	26.1.69	5	NC	Bucuresti	19 Jun
	15.10 1.75 13.99 26.90 5.75 45.64 2:24.40							
5539	Kathrin	Nagel	GDR	20.12.71	5	Druzh	Nyiregyháza	13 Aug
	15.44 1.74 13.08 26.28 5.74 44.34 2:19.96							
5533	Patricia	Nadler	SWZ	13.2.69	1		Landquart	12 Jun
	14.20W 1.69 10.00 25.13 5.95 38.34 2:16.75							
5515	Svetlana	Akimova	SU	69	1		Fergana	11 Sep
	? 14.0 1.77 11.58 24.8 5.90 34.88 2:27.2 = 5518							
5513	Natalya	Sergeyeva	SU	71	1		Novosibirsk	17 May
	? 15.1 1.73 13.73 26.8 5.86 47.10 2:27.5 = 5511							
5509	Ma Miaolan		CHN	5.1.70			Changsha	23 May

5000 METRES WALK

Mark	Name		Nat	Born	Pos	Meet	Venue	Date
21:13.16	Cui Yingzi		CHN	71	1	NC	Jinan	30 Oct
21:43.27	Kathrin	Born	GDR	4.12.70	1	NC-j	Karl-Marx-Stadt	15 Jul
21:48.4	Alina	Ivanova	SU	16.3.69	1		Simferopol	27 May
		21:59.30			1	vGDR-j	Halle	11 Jun
21:51.31	Maria	Cruz Diaz	SPA	24.10.69	1	WJ	Sudbury	31 Jul
21:54.81	Li Chunxiu		CHN	69	2	NC	Jinan	30 Oct
21:57.74	Gao Hongmiao		CHN	74	3	NC	Jinan	30 Oct
21:58.17	Olga	Sánchez	SPA	6.3.70	2	WJ	Sudbury	31 Jul
21:58.8	Tatyana	Titova	SU	25.8.69	2		Simferopol	27 May
22:04.74	Maria-Grazia	Orsani	ITA	11.6.69	3	WJ	Sudbury	31 Jul
22:13.2	Yevgenia	Mikheyeva	SU	12.9.69	3		Simferopol	27 May
22:14.6	Anna-Rita	Sidoti	ITA	25.7.69	1		Messina	2 Oct
22:16.04	Bao Jie		CHN	71	4	NC	Jinan	30 Oct
22:16.11	Fan Xiaoling		CHN	71	5	NC	Jinan	30 Oct
22:22.88	Nicole	Benz	GDR	23.6.70	3	vSU-j	Halle	11 Jun
22:31.2	Olimpiada	Ivanova	SU	5.5.70	1		Nikolayev	13 May
22:34.9	Mioara	Papuc	RUM	12.3.71	1		Bucuresti	4 Jun
22:37.2	Anita	Blomberg	NOR	5.10.71	1		Andebu	6 Aug
22:38.33	Wang	Yili	CHN	4.4.71	5	WJ	Sudbury	31 Jul

Mark	Name		Nat	Born	Pos	Meet	Venue	Date
22:39.25	Nathalie	Marchand	FRA	12.7.69	6	WJ	Sudbury	31 Jul
22:44.82	Gabrielle	Blythe	AUS	9.3.69	7	WJ	Sudbury	31 Jul

4 x 100 METRES RELAY

Mark	Nat	Team	Pos	Meet	Venue	Date
43.48	GDR	Breuer, Krabbe, Dietz, Henke	1	WJ	Sudbury	31 Jul
	43.76		1h1	WJ	Sudbury	30 Jul
	44.17	Roth, Krabbe, Henke, Knuhr	1		Jena	20 May
	Unsanctioned race 43.33	Breuer, Krabbe, Dietz, Henke	1		Berlin	20 Jul
44.04	CUB	Riquelme, Allen, Lopez, Valdivia	2	WJ	Sudbury	31 Jul
	44.23		1		Columbus	24 Jul
	44.25		1h2	WJ	Sudbury	30 Jul
44.25	USA	Burnham, Mackey, Holmes, E.Jones	2h2	WJ	Sudbury	31 Jul
	44.27		3	WJ	Sudbury	31 Jul
44.64	SU	Kovalyova, Golovchenko, Tarnapolskaya, Chistyakova	2h1	WJ	Sudbury	30 Jul
44.88	FRA	Peyre, Simioneck, Cilirie, Sidibe	4	WJ	Sudbury	31 Jul
44.91	UK	Douglas, Lithgow, Kirby, Agyepong	5	WJ	Sudbury	31 Jul
45.03	FRG	Haggenmüller, Fellner, Schoy, Pribnow	3h2	WJ	Sudbury	30 Jul
45.04	JAM	McIntosh, Campell, McDonald, Freeman	6	WJ	Sudbury	31 Jul
45.20	SWZ	Osterwalder, Roth, Wüest, Lüdi	5h2	WJ	Sudbury	30 Jul
45.38	BUL	Dikova, Nedelcheva, Pendereva, Kondova	1	Druzh	Nyiregyháza	13 Aug
45.42	HOL	Koppelaar, Goudemond, Boogaards, Scholsberg	1		Pamplona	2 Jul
45.74	CHN		1		Tainjin	25 Augl
45.76	FIN	Tiilikäinen, Hernesniemi, Leveelahtii, Liminka	1		Helsinki	3 Sep
45.82	BRA	Kuhn, Gomes, da Silva, de Grace	1	SAm-j	Cubatao	3 Jul
45.91	RUM	Popa, Plescan, Birzu, Belu			Bucuresti	18 Jun
45.93	AUS	Christie, Dunston, Hanigan, Kinnane	7h2	WJ	Sudbury	30 Jul
46.03	CS	Prochazková, Petrásková, Tomsová, Kriványková	3		Leipzig	6 Jul
46.15	TAI		1	AsiC-j	Singapore	11 Sep
46.16	CAN	Clarke, Beckles, Gilgeous, Gillis	6h1	WJ	Sudbury	30 Jul
46.28	POL	Brzozowska, Stanczyk, Wawrzen, Leszczynska	3	vFRG-j	Bochum	25 Jun

4 x 400 METRES RELAY

Mark	Nat	Team	Pos	Meet	Venue	Date
3:28.39	GDR	Deer, Fabert, Wöhlk, Breuer	1	WJ	Sudbury	31 Jul
		3:33.90	1	vSU-j	Halle	12 Jun
		3:37.64	1s1	WJ	Sudbury	30 Jul
3:31.48	USA	Demas, Saleem, Mackey, T.Smith	2	WJ	Sudbury	31 Jul
3:31.89	SU	Movchan, Miloserdova, Burkanova, Moroz	3	WJ	Sudbury	31 Jul
		3:37.34	2	vGDR-j	Halle	12 Jun
3:35.30	BUL	Spasova, Krasteva, Kobdova, Sabeva	1		Alexandroúpolis	10 Jul
3:36.41	CAN	Fortin, Steingruber, Layne, Allen	4	WJ	Sudbury	31 Jul
3:36.50	RUM	Solcan, Zavelca, Cracea, Plescan	2		Alexandroúpolis	10 Jul
3:37.52	YUG	Filipovic, Luzar, Zivkovic, Belac	5	WJ	Sudbury	31 Jul
3:38.58	FRG	Sattler, Kawohl, Schneeweis, Kisabaka	1	vPOL-j	Bochum	25 Jun
3:38.94	SPA	Diez, Bergasa, Rodriguez, Merino	7	WJ	Sudbury	31 Jul
3:39.07	FRA	Chanfreau, Djate, Jaunatre, Devassoigne	8	WJ	Sudbury	31 Jul
3:39.55	POL	Pachut, Biczysko, Wawrzen, Buczkowska	2	vFRG-j	Bochum	26 Jun
3:40.17	CS	Grofová, Tomsová, Zimová, Gajarová	3	Druzh	Nyiregyháza	14 Aug
3:40.31	HUN	Antok, Fogarassy, Fodor, Bátori	1	vYUG	Zalaegerszeg	26 Jun
3:40.80	CUB	Lemus, Estevez, Guibert, Montelier	2		Habana	6 Mar
3:41.17	ITA	Panzarino Morabito Paccetti Fontana	2		Pamplona	2 Jul
3:41.52	BRA	Verissimo, Mendes, Dos Santos, de Graca	1	SA-j	Cubatao	1 Jul
3:42.36	UK	Allen, Fryer, Goddard, Langston	5h1	WJ	Sudbury	30 Jul
3:42.55	HOL	Martinot deJong Goosens Steenis	1		Zwolle	11 Jun
3:42.67	FIN	Steuback, Laiho, Tapis, Jääskeläinen	4		Leipzig	6 Jul
3:43.27	CHN	S Li, L Liang, P Wang, G Li	3h3	WJ	Sudbury	30 Jul

INDEX OF 1988 MEN'S WORLD LISTS

Name		Nat	Born	Ht/Wt	Event	1988 Mark	Pre-1988 Best
Abascal	José Manuel	SPA	17 Mar 58	182/67	1500	3:39.39	3:31.13 -86
Abdenouz	Réda	ALG	29 Dec 68	170/63	800	1:45.65	1:47.35 -87
Abduvaliyev	Andrey	SU	30 Jun 66	187/99	HT	80.38	74.76 -86
Abe	Fumiaki	JAP	31 Jul 58	167/49	Mar	2:11:57	2:11:04 -85
Abebe	Addis	ETH	70		5k	13:23.27	
					10k	27:50.24	-0-
Abramov	Valeriy	SU	22 Aug 56	174/62	5k	13:32.8m	13:11.99 -81
Abrantes	António	POR	15 May 68	182/68	800	1:46.57	1:49.2 -87
Abshire	Brian	USA	14 Nov 63	180/59	3k	7:41.57i	7:48.76i -87
					3kSt	8:23.64	8:20.83 -87
Achouche	Mohamed	EGY	18 Nov 55	198/95	SP	19.78	19.34 -85
Ackermann	Uwe	GDR	12 Sep 60	194/85	400h	50.15	48.50 -82
Acres	Barry	AUS	9 Jul 65	180/72	800	1:45.70	1:47.44 -85
Adams	Russell	USA	18 May 67	180/73	LJ	7.97, 8.03w	7.78 -87
Adeniken	Olapade	NIG	19 Aug 69	184/80	100	10.29, 9.9	10.65- 86, 10.3 -87
					200	20.67	21.1 -87
Adeyanju	Iziak	NIG	24 Feb 59	162/65	100	10.30, 9.9	10.40 -85, 10.24w -87
					200	20.67, 20.1w	20.94, 20.71w -87
Adeyev	Igor	SU	63		JT	77.74	74.82 -87
Adnachev	Konstantin	SU	15 Feb 66		PV	5.50	5.40 -87
Afanasyev	Sergey	SU	28 Apr 64	178/71	800	1:45.6m	1:47.59 -85
					1500	3:36.9m	3:38.85 -87
Agbebaku	Ajayi	NIG	6 Dec 56	185/80	TJ	16.68	17.26 -83
Aguilar	Omar	CHL	1 Dec 59	171/62	Mar	2:12:19	2:21:55- 85
Aikyo	Shigeyuki	JAP	29 Jan 64	168/57	3kSt	8:34.03	8:31.27 -83
Akabusi	Kriss	UK	28 Nov 58	185/79	400	44.93	45.43 -84
					400h	48.67	48.64 -87
Akhundov	Mamed	SU	9 Oct 64	180/68	TJ	16.85	17.18 -85
Akins	Kevin	USA	27 Jan 60	196/132	SP	19.74i, 19.48	21.61 -83
Akutsu	Kozo	JAP	11 Nov 60	162/52	5k	13:32.16	13:32.42 -87
					10k	27:46.16	27:49.06 -87
Al Malky	Mohamed	OMA	1 Dec 62	176/62	400	44.56	45.56 -87
Alay	Sergey	SU	11 Jun 65	184/98	HT	81.52	80.52 -87
Albentosa	José Manuel	SPA	21 Jan 64	172/56	5k	13:35.56	13:32.24 -86
					10k	28:09.70	28:34.98 -87
Alcala	Gerardo	MEX	28 Jun 61	170/57	Mar	2:12:11	2:15:44 -87
Alisevich	Vitaliy	SU	15 Jun 67	186/112	HT	82.16	78.60 -87
Allen-Cooksey	Tony	USA	7 Jul 56	188/82	Dec	7748	7964 -81
Alli	Yusuf	NIG	28 Jul 60	185/80	LJ	8.15i/8.05/8.26Aw	8.24/8.30Aw-87
Alonso	José	SPA	12 Feb 57	183/75	400h	49.20A, 49.48	49.00 -87
Alvarez	Jacinto	CUB	16 May 66		110h	13.82	13.83 -87
Amidzhinov	Vladimir	BUL	7 Sep 63	191/80	LJ	8.00	8.11 -87
Amike	Henry	NIG	4 Oct 61	185/71	400h	49.36	48.50 -87
Andersen	Georg	NOR	7 Jan 63	190/112	SP	20.63	20.13 -87
Anderson	David	AUS	8 Dec 65	192/73	HJ	2.26	2.16 -82
André	Harald	FRG	3 Sep 60	185/72	800	1:46.92	1:47.52 -87
Andrei	Alessandro	ITA	3 Jan 59	191/118	SP	20.61	22.91 -87
Andreini	Marco	ITA	8 Oct 61	182/75	PV	5.55	5.42 -85, 5.50ex -87
Andrews	Stuart	AUS	17 Jan 62	195/95	Dec	7730m	7726 -87
Andriopoulos	Spiridon	GRE	1 Aug 62	176/62	Mar	2:12:04	2:14:19 -87
Anselm	Garfield	FRA	7 Jun 66	174/63	TJ	16.87w	16.49 -87
Antibo	Salvatore	ITA	7 Feb 62	170/52	5k	13:16.1m	13:21.26 -85
					10k	27:23.55	27:39.52 -86
Anton	Abel	SPA	24 Oct 62	179/63	1500	3:38.21	3:37.5 -85
					5k	13:20.67	13:21.44 -87
Anton	Vicente	SPA	16 Oct 59	175/55	Mar	2:12:50	2:12:56 -87
Antonov	Nikolay	BUL	17 Aug 68	193/80	200	20.65i	20.5 -86
Anttonen	Mikko	FIN	5 Jul 63	181/79	JT	76.80	77.50 -87
Aoto	Shinji	JAP	7 May 66	177/68	100	10.28	10.48 -87, 10.41w- 86
Aouita	Said	MOR	2 Nov 59	175/58	800	1:43.86	1:44.38 -83
					1k	2:15.16	2:15.71 -83
					1500	3:32.69	3:29.46 -85
					Mile	3:50.82	3:46.76 -87
					2M	8:14.05	8:13.45 -87

Name		Nat	Born	Ht/Wt	Event	1988 Mark	Pre-1988 Best
Apaychev	Aleksandr	SU	6 May 61	187/92	Dec	8424	8709 -84
Apostolov	Viktor	BUL	1 Oct 62	181/110	HT	80.54	80.12 -87
Apostolovski	Saso	YUG	20 Jan 63	193/70	HJ	2.25i, 2.25	2.30 -87
Aragon	Chuck	USA	29 Mar 59	183/67	Mile	3:54.4m	3:51.62 -84
Arino	Jesus	SPA	5 Aug 63	180/70	400h	50.51	50.68 -87
Armour	Jack	USA	10 Feb 61	178/73	800	1:46.49	1:46.57 -86
Armstead	Ray	USA	27 May 60	187/76	400	45.29	44.83 -84
Armstrong	Gary	USA	31 Dec 60	185/79	Dec	7805	8203 -86
Arpin	Paul	FRA	20 Feb 60	170/56	3k	7:43.58	7:49.2 -85
					5k	13:22.03	13:27.64 -87
					10k	27:39.36	27:47.05 -87
Arques	José Javier	SPA	16 May 60	181/74	100	10.27A, 10.01Aw	10.21 -86
Asadov	Vasif	SU	27 Aug 65	180/69	TJ	17.37i,16.80	17.22 -87
Assenmacher	Joakim	FRG	10 Jan 63	185/82	LJ	8.03	7.86 -86
Astapkovich	Igor	SU	4 Jan 63	191/118	HT	83.44	82.96 -87
Atanasov	Valentin	BUL	7 May 61	188/84	100	10.22	10.15 -82
Atkinson	Jeff	USA	24 Feb 63	185/68	1500	3:36.10	3:41.25 -86
					Mile	3:52.80	3:55.16 -86
Atsuta	Andrey	SU	20 Jan 62	189/91	Dec	7878	7756m -85
Atwood	Duncan	USA	11 Oct 55	188/95	JT	80.48	82.74 -87
Aubert	Philippe	FRA	5 Oct 57	183/74	110h	13.68	13.78 -87
Aushev	Aleksandr	SU	1 Jul 60	181/71	LJ	8.03i, 7.98	8.12 -85
Avdeyenko	Gennadiy	SU	4 Nov 63	202/82	HJ	2.38	2.38i, 2.38 -87
Avramov	Nikolay	BUL	25 Feb 67	188/76	TJ	16.73	16.60 -86
Ayabe	Kenji	JAP	25 Mar 68	171/57	5k	13:37.20	13:48.27 -87
Ayana	Getahun	ETH	10 Sep 65		800	1:45.74	1:46.73 -87
Ayears	Bill	USA	6 Apr 66	178/73	LJ	7.93, 7.98w	7.52i -87
Azarov	Oleg	SU	18 Jan 62	190/80	400h	50.00	49.38 -86
Azizmuradov	Oleg	SU	26 Jan 62	193/74	HJ	2.25i, 2.25	2.26 -84
Azkueta	Juan	SPA	2 Jul 67	170/56	3kSt	8:30.41	8:46.6 -87
Babers	Alonzo	USA	31 Oct 61	187/76	400	45.37A, 45.39	44.27 -84
Babich	Mark	USA	7 Aug 63	190/90	JT	76.68	79.12 -87
Babits	Paul	USA	24 Dec 60	185/82	PV	5.50	5.51 -84
Babiy	Ivan	SU	22 Jul 63	183/82	Dec	8183	8209 -87
Baccouche	Féthi	TUN	16 Nov 60	171/59	3k	7:47.79	7:46.17 -86
					5k	13:36.31	13:13.94 -87
					3kSt	8:18.12	8:15.07 -87
Backes	Ron	USA	19 Feb 63	190/123	SP	21.02	21.01i, 20.92 -86
Backley	Stephen	UK	12 Feb 69	196/100	JT	79.50	78.16 -87
Badinelli	Dario	ITA	10 Aug 60	185/68	TJ	16.93i, 16.85A, 16.78, 17.00Aw	17.12 -86
Baer	Jon	USA	30 Sep 65	188/75	HJ	2.26i	2.24 -87
Bagach	Aleksandr	SU	21 Nov 66	194/125	SP	20.65i, 20.21	20.01 -87
Bagyula	István	HUN	2 Jan 69	183/75	PV	5.65	5.50 -86
Bakos	György	HUN	6 Jul 60	188/77	110h	13.61, 13.58w	13.45 -84
Bakosi	Béla	HUN	18 Jun 57	180/67	TJ	17.25i	17.23-85, 17.29w -82
Bakowski	Roger	FRG	9 Jul 64	190/94	DT	64.40	60.52 -87
Balcha	Kebede	ETH	7 Sep 51	165/51	Mar	2:12:04	2:10:03 -83
Balcindes	Lázaro	CUB	8 Feb 63	177/73	TJ	16.87	16.96 -85
Balkin	Lee	USA	7 Jun 61	192/75	HJ	2.26	2.33 -87
Balosak	Lubos	CS	5 Apr 65	180/73	400	45.99	45.59 -87
Banich	Jim	USA	12 Sep 63	193/111	SP	19.91	19.90 -86
Banks	Kenny	USA	12 Nov 66	178/73	HJ	2.26	2.30 -86
Banks	Willie	USA	11 Mar 56	190/77	TJ	17.16, 18.20w	17.97 -85
Baptiste	Kirk	USA	20 Jun 63	184/79	200	20.78	19.96 -84
Barabashov	Roman	SU	13 Sep 68	189/82	PV	5.55i	5.55 -87
Barbosa	José Luiz	BRA	27 May 61	184/68	800	1:43.20	1:43.76 -87
					1500	3:38.84	3:46.75 -86
Barclay	Roland	TRI	25 Oct 66	180/67	100	10.22w	10.3 -86
Barclay	Ronnell	TRI	25 Oct 66	180/67	100	10.20	10.3, 10.58 -86
					200	20.75w	
Barnard	Gerhard	RSA	8 May 67		200	20.72A, 20.65Aw	20.70A -87
Barnes	Anthony	USA	23 Dec 65	168/65	100	10.20Aw	10.44, 10.29w -87
					200	20.64A	21.02w- 87
Barnes	Chris	USA	21 Jul 69	188/89	200	20.73	20.80 -87
Barnes	Greg	USA	10 Aug 65	183/73	100	10.20	10.15w, 10.1 -87

Name		Nat	Born	Ht/Wt	Event	1988 Mark	Pre-1988 Best
Barnes	Randy	USA	16 Jun 66	193/132	SP	22.42	21.88 -86
Barnett	Mike	USA	21 May 61	185/104	JT	81.86	82.06 -87
Barney	David	USA	18 Jan 60	175/58	10k	28:26.0m	28:13.3 -86
Barr	Oslen	GUY	3 Apr 61	165/67	800	1:45.92	1:46.42 -84
Barré	Patrick	FRA	12 Apr 59	173/63	400	45.65, 45.72	46.03 -87
Barreto	Marcos	MEX	25 Apr 60	177/63	10k	27:50.95	-0-
Barrios	Arturo	MEX	12 Dec 63	174/60	3k	7:50.72	7:44.63 -87
					5k	13:17.82	13:13.52 -87
					10k	27:25.07	27:50.28 -86
Barroso	Luis	POR	27 Jun 66	170/64	200	20.64A	20.89 -85
Bartenyev	Dmitriy	SU	8 Mar 69	176/70	100	10.31	10.3/10.60- 87, 10.51w- 86
Baryshnikov	Aleksandr	SU	11 Nov 48	198/140	SP	19.82i	22.00 -76
Baskin	Tracy	USA	3 Nov 65	190/77	800	1:44.43	1:46.58 -87
Bassi	Walter	ITA	12 Jul 64		Mar	2:13:08	2:14:57- 87
Bates	Mike	USA	19 Dec 69		200	20.68	20.90 -87
Batrachenko	Viktor	SU	6 Jan 63	186/78	110h	13.6	13.64 -86
Baumann	Dieter	FRG	9 Feb 65	176/63	1500	3:34.82	3:33.54 -87
					Mile	3:57.88	3:58.37 -85
					3k	7:50.30	7:40.25 -87
					5k	13:15.52	13:30.85 -87
Baygush	Viktor	SU	16 Dec 63	182/110	HT	78.10	76.52 -87
Bazarov	Aleksey	SU	14 Oct 63	184/75	400h	49.33	49.76 -87
Beblo	Leszek	POL	8 Jul 66	179/65	5k	13:35.49	13:45.6 -87
Becker	Andreas	GDR	15 Aug 62	192/110	DT	62.60	64.16 -86
Becker	Gustavo A.	SPA	17 Jun 66	184/70	HJ	2.24	2.25 -86, 2.26i -87
Bednarski	Zbigniew	POL	4 Jun 60	171/82	JT	80.82	73.68 -87
Beer	Ron	GDR	29 Aug 65	183/79	LJ	8.23	8.21 -85
Begeo	Hector	PHI	19 Jun 64	164/54	3kSt	8:35.09	8:44.1 -83
Belayneh	Tadesse	ETH	24 Apr 66		Mar	2:12:23	
Belkessam	Ahmed	ALG	27 Mar 62	175/72	800	1:46.29	1:45.6 -85
Bell	Dan	USA	23 Jan 65	178/69	3kSt	8:35.14	8:32.27 -87
Bell	Earl	USA	25 Aug 55	191/75	PV	5.87	5.86i -87, 5.81 -86
Belokon	Vladimir	SU	13 Feb 69	187/83	110h	13.79	14.14 -87
Belozerskikh	Eduard	SU	7 Mar 65	188/82	LJ	8.05	7.92 -86
Belyi	Viktor	SU	64		SP	19.20i, 19.16	20.07 -85
Benavides	Paul	USA	5 Nov 64	185/70	PV	5.50	5.60 -86
Benito	Teófilo	SPA	22 Jul 66	175/64	800	1:46.89	1:47.27 -87
					1500	3:39.34	3:36.96 -86
Benjamin	Lester	ANT	14 Sep 63	178/69	100	10.32w	10.33 -84, 10.28w- 85
					LJ	7.97, 8.16dh	8.02 -84
Benjamin	Mike	USA	17 May 61	185/86	110h	13.54A/13.78	13.84-87,13.81w- 84
Bennett	Todd	UK	6 Jul 62	170/64	400	45.27	45.35 -85
Bensch	Bernhard	FRG	22 Sep 64	197/83	HJ	2.26	2.27i, 2.27 -86
Benvenuti	Marcello	ITA	26 Apr 64	180/62	HJ	2.27	2.26 -85
Berger	Andreas	AUT	9 Jun 61	174/77	100	10.15	10.19 -87
Bernaert	Luc	BEL	24 Jun 66	186/75	800	1:46.47	1:46.41 -87
Berry	Latin	USA	13 Jan 67	178/87	LJ	7.93	7.98, 8.04w -87
Bertimon	Charlus-Michel	FRA	1 Jan 57	187/88	JT	81.26	80.76 -86
Berzins	Dainis	SU	24 Apr 66	190/80	TJ	16.86i, 16.76	16.89 -87
Beskrovniy	Aleksandr	SU	5 Apr 60	189/83	TJ	16.70	17.53 -83
Betancourt	Lázaro	CUB	18 Mar 63	189/81	TJ	17.38	17.78 -86
Bettiol	Salvatore	ITA	28 Nov 61	178/57	Mar	2:11:41	2:11:28 -87
Beyer	Udo	GDR	9 Aug 55	194/140	SP	22.10	22.64 -86
Bi	Zhong	CHN	68		HT	72.62	68.00 -87
Bickford	Bruce	USA	12 Mar 57	180/60	3k	7:48.4	7:51.34 -84
					10k	28:05.37	27:37.17 -85
Bile	Abdi	SOM	28 Dec 62	185/75	800	1:44.42	1:44.47 -87
					1k	2:17.75	2:17.15 -85
					1500	3:33.6m	3:31.71 -87
					Mile	3:49.40	3:50.75 -87
Billy	Ikem	UK	25 Jan 64	181/62	800	1:46.25	1:44.65 -84
Bindar	Nicolae	RUM	14 Mar 56	178/110	HT	76.26	77.60 -86
Binley	Judd	USA	4 Jan 55	185/104	DT	63.62	64.64 -85
Binns	Steve	UK	25 Aug 60	170/57	5k	13:23.71	13:26.86 -83
Birir	Jonah	KEN	27 Dec 71	162/53	800	1:46.9mA	
Birke	Mike	CAN	14 Jan 68		800	1:46.9m	1:48.98 -87

Name		Nat	Born	Ht/Wt	Event	1988 Mark	Pre-1988 Best
Bisbas	Stelios	GRE	9 Nov 68	182/70	110h	13.89	14.15 -87
Bishop	Clyde	USA	29 May 62	183/82	200	20.4w	20.97- 82, 20.5w -87
Bitsadze	Tariel	SU	12 Jan 66	194/110	SP	20.37	20.11 -87
Black	Trevor	JAM	66		LJ	7.99	7.59 -87
Blackmore	Mike	USA	19 Dec 61	170/57	Mile	3:57.46	3:58.35 -86
Blake	Arthur	USA	19 Aug 66	181/67	200	20.77	20.63 -87
					110h	13.24	13.29 -87
Blank	Peter	FRG	10 Apr 62	194/81	JT	80.84	77.94 -87
Blomstrand	Staffan	SWE	3 Aug 60	187/83	Dec	8107	8007w, 7764 -87
Blondel	Alain	FRA	7 Dec 62	185/76	Dec	8387	8228 -87
Bobylyov	Vladimir	SU	15 Jul 66	187/77	LJ	8.23i, 8.13	8.25, 8.29w -87
Bochkaryov	Pyotr	SU	18 Jun 67		PV	5.60	5.30i -86
Böden	Patrik	SWE	30 Jun 67	187/98	JT	76.52	78.10 -87
Bodenmüller	Klaus	AUT	6 Sep 62	194/110	SP	20.25i,19.92	20.79 -87
Böhni	Felix	SWZ	14 Feb 58	189/82	PV	5.50	5.71 -83
Böttcher	Holger	FRG	27 Jul 63	183/73	800	1:46.93	1:46.20 -85
Boffi	Franco	ITA	2 Nov 58	186/70	3kSt	8:25.06	8:21.69 -87
Bogasson	Eggert	ICE	19 Jul 60	191/115	DT	62.64	63.18 -86
Bogatyryov	Pavel	SU	19 Mar 61	194/84	PV	5.65	5.80 -85
Bogh	Lars	DEN	29 Sep 64	186/68	1500	3:38.86	3:39.73 -87
Boinett	Micah	KEN	19 Dec 65	174/64	3kSt	8:29.48	8:28.20 -86
Bojars	Janis	SU	12 May 56	185/127	SP	20.79	21.74 -84
Bolgár	Tamás	HUN	24 Aug 55	185/102	JT	76.80	76.84 -86
Bondarenko	Yevgeniy	SU	8 Oct 66	192/82	PV	5.70	5.65 -87
Bonfim	Jailto S.	BRA	4 Jan 64	185/78	110h	13.77	13.8 -86,14.01 -87
Borchert	Gerald	FRG	3 Sep 66	193/92	Dec	7887	7831 -87
Bordin	Gelindo	ITA	2 Apr 59	180/68	Mar	2:09:27	2:10:54 -86
Bordukov	Vyacheslav	SU	1 Jan 59	184/69	TJ	17.17	17.37 -84, 17.38w -87
Borellini	Fabrizio	ITA	5 Jul 68	190/72	HJ	2.30i, 2.28	2.20 -87
Borge	Espen	NOR	8 Sep 61	185/73	1500	3:38.80	3:38.74 -87
Borglund	Peter	SWE	29 Jan 64	183/84	JT	81.38	80.86 -87
Borisov	Igor	SU	12 Aug 67		110h	13.5	14.33- 86, 13.7- 87
Borodkin	Nikolay	SU	4 Apr 55	190/130	SP	20.54	21.04 -85
Boroi	Georghe	RUM	26 Aug 64	182/71	110h	13.74	13.92 -87
Borov	Oleg	SU	68		100	10.0	10.62, 10.4 -87. 10.57w- 86
Bosman	Wessel	RSA	24 Jun 58	181/75	110h	13.63A, 13.75	13.71A -81
Boue	Narciso	CUB	28 Nov 63	188/105	SP	19.19	19.42 -87
Bouschen	Peter	FRG	16 May 60	181/78	TJ	17.43	17.33 -83
Boussemart	Pascal	FRA	29 Apr 59	186/77	110h	13.74	13.80 -87
Boutayeb	M.Brahim	MOR	15 Aug 67	171/60	1500	3:38.75	3:38.9 -87
					3k	7:43.22	7:51.99 -87
					2M	8:24.86	-0-
					5k	13:18.68	13:17.47 -87
					10k	27:21.46	28:40.34 -87
Boye	Cheikh T.	800	10 Aug 61	178/69	800	1:45.93	1:46.8 -85
Brace	Steve	UK	7 Jul 61		Mar	2:11:50	2:14:33 -87
Bradstock	Roald	UK	24 Apr 62	180/95	JT	79.50	83.84 -87
Brahm	Terry	USA	21 Nov 62	180/65	1500	3:35.81	3:36.35 -86
					3k	7:48.47, 7:47.55i	7:43.15 -86
					2M	8:21.18	
					5k	13:32.46	13:34.40 -87
Brahmi	Azzedine	ALG	13 Sep 66	178/72	3kSt	8:16.54	8:36.52 -87
Bran	Mihai	RUM	12 Jan 62	189/82	TJ	16.88i, 16.85	16.97 -85
Branch	John	USA	2 Oct 67	188/77	400h	49.80	50.77 -87
Brand	Steffen	FRG	10 Mar 65	176/66	1500	3:38.70	3:37.85 -87
Branham	Chris	USA	24 Jan 62	193/84	Dec	8013	8159 -86
Brantley	Dennis	USA	13 Jul 61	183/71	110h	13.83w	13.75 -84,13.60w -81
Brantly	Keith	USA	23 May 62	178/61	10k	28:17.13	28:10.1 -87
Braun	Peter	FRG	1 Aug 62	183/64	800	1:44.21	1:44.03 -86
Braunskill	Kevin	USA	31 Mar 69	175/64	200	20.63	21.4 -87
Brenner	John	USA	4 Jan 61	192/127	SP	20.52	22.52 -87
Brichese	Enzo	ITA	17 Nov 65	188/78	PV	5.50i	5.40 -87
Bridges	Lee	USA	20 Mar 67	180/64	400	45.79	46.78 -87
Bridges	Oliver	USA	30 Jun 62	192/86	400	45.69	45.35A -82, 45.45 -84
Bridgewater	Brian	USA	7 Sep 70	175/70	100	10.28w	10.3 -87
					200	20.53	21.11A, 20.8 -87

Name		Nat	Born	Ht/Wt	Event	1988 Mark	Pre-1988 Best
Brige	Norbert	FRA	9 Jan 64	183/78	LJ	8.22	8.14 -87
Briggs	Martin	UK	4 Jan 64	180/75	400h	50.04	49.86 -84
Bright	Tim	USA	28 Jul 60	188/79	PV	5.75	5.75 -87
					Dec	8287	8340 -87
Bringmann	Steffen	GDR	11 Mar 64	184/78	100	10.21	10.13 -86
					200	20.72w	20.77 -86
Bristow	Andy	UK	2 Sep 61	186/67	10k	28:17.59	28:57.90 -87
Brokenburr	Kenny	USA	29 Oct 68		200	20.74w	21.30 -87
Brooks	Mike	USA	67	185/82	200	20.67	
Brown	Brian	USA	6 Jun 67	190/73	HJ	2.30i, 2.26	2.24 -87
Brown	Courtney	CAN	21 Apr 65	176/70	200	20.71	A20.51 -85
Brown	Ed	USA	20 Jul 58	188/81	Dec	7821w	7729 -86
Brown	Ray	USA	11 Aug 61	185/73	800	1:45.91	1:45.99 -87
Brown	Rex	USA	12 Feb 64	178/64	200	20.75	20.67w- 86
Brown	Ron	USA	31 Mar 61	180/82	100	10.26	10.06 -83
Brown	Steve	USA	6 Jan 69	190/86	110h	13.80, 13.73w	14.06 -87
Brown	Theron	USA	18 Jan 63	185/77	400h	49.32	50.36 -83
Bruce	Charles	USA	18 Apr 67		400	45.95	
Brummer	Deon	RSA	4 Apr 59	183/68	1k	2:18.34	2:19.00 -84
					Mile	3:55.57	3:55.42 -87
Brunner	Wulf	FRG	20 Mar 62	187/110	DT	66.42	63.18 -86
Brusseau	Thierry	FRA	22 Jul 64	182/63	3kSt	8:33.87	8:39.09 -87
Bruziks	Maris	SU	25 Aug 62	186/70	TJ	17.56	17.54i -86, 17.38-85
Bryzgin	Viktor	SU	22 Aug 62	180/78	100	10.20	10.03 -86
Bubka	Sergey	SU	4 Dec 63	183/80	PV	6.06	6.03 -87
Bubka	Vasiliy	SU	26 Nov 60	184/76	PV	5.86	5.85 -85
Buckner	Jack	UK	22 Sep 61	173/59	2M	8:26.52	8:17.12 -86
					5k	13:23.8	13:10.15 -86
Bucknor	Richard	JAM	6 Nov 66	183/79	110h	13.69	13.73w -87
Budko	Vladimir	SU	4 Feb 65	186/79	400h	50.27	48.71 -86
Budnik	Eduard	SU	21 Jan 61	187/85	JT	76.82	74.82 -86
Bueno	Luis	CUB	22 May 69	174/67	LJ	8.28	8.25 -86
Bugár	Imrich	CS	14 Apr 55	196/120	DT	66.42	71.26 -83
Bugg	Gordon	USA	24 Jun 66	170/65	400h	49.30	49.54 -87
Bukreyev	Vladimir	SU	15 Jun 64	186/82	PV	5.66	5.61 -87
Bulbula	Haji	ETH	61	160/53	10k	28:03.78	27:43.04 -87
Bulti	Wodajo	ETH	11 Mar 57	185/60	5k	13:33.68	13:07.29 -82
					10k	27:56.35	27:29.41 -87
					Mar	2:08:44	-0-
Buncic	Mike	USA	25 Jul 62	193/115	DT	68.92	68.98 -87
Burin	Yevgeniy	SU	4 Mar 64	190/110	DT	63.20	65.04 -87
Burnett	Howard	JAM	8 Mar 61	193/72	400	45.39	46.15 -87
Burra	John	TAN	20 Nov 65	162/56	Mar	2:09:30	2:11:27 -86
Burrage	Dale	USA	30 May 67	183/77	400h	50.17	51.04 -87
Burrell	Leroy	USA	21 Feb 67	180/82	100	10.31, 10.09w	10.43 -86
					LJ	8.08w	8.15 -87
Buss	Heiko	FRG	6 Jan 63	188/80	110h	13.83	13.97 -87
Busse	Andreas	GDR	6 May 59	185/68	1500	3:36.79	3:34.10 -84
					3k	7:51.17	8:05.51 -86
Butler	James	USA	21 Jun 60	175/68	100	10.22	10.14A-82, 10.27 -87
					200	20.36	20.31-84,20.23A/20.07Aw-82
Bykov	Konstantin	SU	11 Jan 66	195/88	TJ	16.78	16.62 -87
Bystedt	Kjell	SWE	24 May 60	189/120	HT	78.64	77.04 -87
Cai	Shangyan	CHN	25 Sep 62	168/51	Mar	2:11:58	2:14:15- 86
Calderón	Raúl	CUB	27 Nov 62	183/105	DT	63.26	65.10 -86
Caldwell	Willie	USA	25 Sep 63	186/75	200	20.44A	20.80 -83
					400	45.58A	45.10 -85
Callender	Clarence	UK	16 Nov 61	179/75	100	10.31w	10.39, 10.32w -86
Camara	Pierre	FRA	10 Sep 65	181/74	TJ	16.79	16.82 -87
Cameron	Bert	JAM	16 Nov 59	188/79	400	44.50	44.58 -81
Camp	Jim	USA	16 Dec 63	189/105	SP	19.88	19.95 -86
Campbell	Clifton	USA	18 Jun 67	185/66	400	45.32	45.43 -86
Campbell	Dave	CAN	31 Aug 60	177/65	1500	3:38.22	3:38.69 -87
Campbell	David	USA	23 May 66	175/65	200	20.73	
Campbell	Garfield	JAM	1 Nov 67	170/68	100	10.25	
Campbell	John	NZ	6 Feb 59	175/57	Mar	2:11:08	2:12:38 -85

Name		Nat	Born	Ht/Wt	Event	1988 Mark	Pre-1988 Best
Campbell	Tonie	USA	14 Jun 60	188/77	110h	13.17	13.19 -87
Campos	João	POR	22 Sep 58	173/55	3k	7:47.85	7:45.70 -87
					5k	13:32.12	13:19.10 -84
Canario	Ezequiel	POR	10 Apr 60	181/60	5k	13:31.18	13:26.50 -84
					10k	27:52.27	27:53.72 -86
Canfield	Tim	USA	16 Nov 63	188/81	PV	5.51	5.45 -86
Cannon	Eric	USA	2 Mar 67	183/75	110h	13.76, 13.67w, 13.6	13.72 -87
Cannon	Marlin	USA	9 Dec 70	170/68	400	45.94	46.51 -87
Cannon	Mike	USA	26 Oct 64	175/64	400	45.6	45.14 -85
Cannon	Robert	USA	9 Jul 58	185/76	TJ	17.01, 17.63w	17.19 -87
Canti	Aldo	FRA	9 Mar 61	185/80	200	20.75	20.69 -84
Cantrell	Larry	USA	4 Jul 67	173/68	400	45.53	45.75 -87
Caristan	Stéphane	FRA	31 Mar 64	187/75	110h	13.47	13.20, 13.0 -86
Carlier	Jacky	FRA	8 Nov 61	182/68	3k	7:48.78	7:58.9 -87
Carlin	Sean	AUS	29 Nov 67	198/110	HT	74.46	70.36 -87
Carlowitz	Jens	GDR	8 Aug 64	185/76	400	45.08	44.92 -87
Carmona	Roberto	MEX	17 Sep 69	184/72	110h	13.81A	14.12A -87
Carr	Kevin	USA	19 Jul 64	198/125	DT	61.36	60.64 -86
Carrington	Ralph	USA	30 Jun 69	188/75	400h	50.03	50.97 -87
Carroll	Pat	AUS	17 Aug 61		Mar	2:10:44	2:14:38 -87
Carrott	Andrew	UK	1 Jan 66	182/73	200	20.76	21.11, 21.04w -87
Carter	Jerome	USA	25 Mar 63	185/74	HJ	2.37	2.34 -86
Carter	Kelly	USA	15 Feb 69	178/66	400h	49.50	50.66 -87
Cason	Andre	USA	13 Jan 69	174/70	100	10.08	10.39 -86
Castro	Dionisio	POR	22 Nov 63	167/56	5k	13:18.69	13:22.94 -86
					10k	27:42.84	28:09.81 -87
Castro	Domingos	POR	22 Nov 63	167/56	3k	7:50.11	7:58.47 -87
					5k	13:16.09	13:18.59 -87
					10k	27:43.30	28:01.62 -86
Cedeño	Elvis	VEN	25 Jan 64	180/63	110h	13.62A	14.19 -85
Centelles	J.Francisco	CUB	26 Jan 61	196/81	HJ	2.31	2.32 -83
Chacon	Ricardo	CUB	30 Apr 63	175/73	100	10.28, 9.8w	10.21 -87
Chae	Song-rak	KOR	29 May 61	172/61	Mar	2:12:51	2:15:16 -84
Chashchin	Yuriy	SU	8 Jun 63		400h	49.68	50.26 -83
Chatman	Bernard	USA	22 Sep 65	178/77	200	20.67w	
					400	45.77	47.21 -84
Chauvelier	Dominique	FRA	3 Aug 56	181/67	Mar	2:12:06	2:13:51 -87
Chelelgo	Joseph	KEN	24 Apr 63	170/61	3KSt	8:31.18	8:29.98 -86
Chen	Yanping	CHN	66		TJ	17.01	16.38 -86
Chernega	Yuriy	SU	18 Feb 67		HT	77.42	73.70 -87
Chernikov	Vladimir	SU	3 Aug 59	188/74	TJ	17.36	17.35 -85
Chernyayev	Aleksandr	SU	31 May 60	180/74	PV	5.50i, 5.50	5.71 -83
Cheruiyot	Charles	KEN	2 Dec 64	165/54	1500	3:38.17	3:41.83 -83
					Mile	3:57.95i	3:55.41 -87
					5k	13:26.27	13:18.41 -84
Cheruiyot	Kipkoech	KEN	2 Dec 64	165/54	1500	3:36.2m	3:33.07 -86
					Mile	3:52.39	3:53.92 -83
Chesire	Joseph	KEN	12 Nov 57	167/57	800	1:44.38	1:45.10 -86
					1k	2:18.34	-0-
					Mile	3:53.09	4:00.45 -86
					1500	3:36.2m	3:34.32 -86
Chesley	Eric	USA	66		400h	50.50A	50.89A -87
Chevallier	Franck	FRA	3 Jan 64	185/71	110h	13.80	13.85, 13.84w -84
Chiamulera	Pedro	BRA	29 Jun 64	190/77	400h	50.28	49.34 -85
Chirco	Bruno	FRG	7 Apr 66	185/83	Dec	7779	7729 -87
Chmara	Miroslaw	POL	9 May 64	201/86	PV	5.90	5.67i -86, 5.65 -87
Chochkov	Miroslav	BUL	26 Dec 67	180/65	800	1:46.74	1:48.99 -87
					1k	2:18.22	-0-
Choumassi	Mohamed	MOR	69		10k	28:25.77	
Christianson	Craig	USA	1 Apr 61	193/105	JT	77.60	78.42 -87
Christie	Anthony	JAM	22 Feb 67	176/68	400	45.95	
Christie	Linford	UK	2 Apr 60	189/80	100	9.97	10.03 -87
					200	20.09	20.48 -87
Ciofani	Walter	FRA	17 Feb 62	185/105	HT	75.52	78.50 -85
Clark	Cletus	USA	20 Jan 62	193/88	110h	13.30	13.38 -85
Clark	Darren	AUS	6 Sep 65	179/76	400	44.38	44.72 -86

Name		Nat	Born	Ht/Wt	Event	1988 Mark	Pre-1988 Best
Clark	Ocky	USA	14 Nov 60	180/69	800	1:45.06	1:45.29 -85
					1k	2:18.52	-0-
Clouvel	Pascal	FRA	12 Nov 60	187/75	3k	7:49.98	7:50.28 -86
Coe	Sebastian	UK	29 Sep 56	175/54	800	1:43.93	1:41.73 -81
					1500	3:35.72	3:29.77 -86
Coghlan	Eamonn	IRL	24 Nov 52	177/63	5k	13:32.28	13:19.13 -81
Coleman	Billy	USA	26 Jul 67	173/71	LJ	7.97	7.81, 7.90w -87
Coleman	Vincent	USA	28 Jun 65	185/75	200	20.76w	20.80, 20.22w -86
Collet	Philippe	FRA	13 Dec 63	176/65	PV	5.80i, 5.80	5.85 -86
Conde	Juan	CUB	30 Apr 65	175/65	3kSt	8:31.71	8:29.54 -87
Conley	Mike	USA	5 Oct 62	185/78	LJ	8.23	8.43-85, 8.63w -86
					TJ	17.59, 17.62w	17.87 -87
Connolly	Jim	USA	24 Mar 63	185/85	Dec	7872	8121 -87
Conover	Mark	USA	28 May 60	178/60	Mar	2:12:26	2:18:03 -87
Consiglio	Doug	CAN	10 Jan 64	193/78	1500	3:35.82	3:38.73i -86
					Mile	3:57.7m	3:55.91i -86
Conway	Hollis	USA	8 Jan 67	183/66	HJ	2.36	2.34 -87
Cooper	Brad	BAH	30 Jun 57	188/132	DT	64.44	67.10 -86
Cooper	Brian	USA	21 Aug 65	183/89	100	10.07	10.21, 10.05w, 10.1 -87
Cooper	Jim	USA	6 Oct 59	180/67	3kSt	8:26.08	8:19.88 -86
Cooper	Todd	USA	4 Mar 63	178/64	PV	5.65	5.64 -87
Cordero	Domingo	PR	17 Oct 65	183/72	400h	49.61A	50.32 -87
Corgos	António	SPA	10 Mar 60	183/78	LJ	8.16	8.23 -80
Cornet	Cayetano	SPA	22 Aug 63	183/70	400	45.39	46.74 -87
Cotton	Terry	USA	7 Aug 54	175/64	10k	28:11.0m	
Council	Daron	USA	26 Dec 64	188/73	100	10.17	10.23 -85, 10.0, 10.21w -87
					200	20.54, 20.4	20.29 -85
							20.14w, 20.0w -87
Couto	Fernando	POR	4 Dec 59	165/59	5k	13:29.20	13:26.82 -87
					10k	28:26.27	28:32.8 -87
Cova	Alberto	ITA	1 Dec 58	176/58	5k	13:33.85	13:10.06 -85
					10k	27:52.80	27:37.59 -83
Cox	Randy	TRI	22 Dec 64	188/82	400h	50.46, 49.8	49.43 -87
Crabb	Steve	UK	30 Nov 63	188/70	800	1:45.69	1:45.77 -87
					1500	3:33.95	3:33.34 -87
					Mile	3:52.26	3:51.76 -87
Cram	Steve	UK	14 Oct 60	186/69	800	1:43.42	1:42.88 -85
					1k	2:17.80	2:12.88 -85
					1500	3:30.95	3:29.67 -85
					Mile	3:48.85	3:46.32 -85
					2k	4:55.20	4:51.39 -85
					3k	7:45.45	7:43.1 -83
					2M	8:17.79	8:14.93 -83
Cranford	Walter	USA	16 Apr 67	175/73	100	10.27	
Crouser	Brian	USA	9 Jul 62	188/102	JT	79.88	83.00 -87
Crouser	Mitch	USA	30 Dec 57	190/116	DT	64.18	67.22 -85
Cruz	Alejandro	MEX	10 Feb 68		Mar	2:08:57	
Cruz	Joachim	BRA	12 Mar 63	187/73	800	1:43.90	1:41.77 -84
					1k	2:17.76	2:14.09 -84
					1500	3:34.63	3:35.70 -85
					Mile	3:53.6m	3:53.00 -84
Csider	István	HUN	21 Oct 64	191/88	JT	78.28	74.76 -87
Culbert	David	AUS	17 Mar 67	191/85	LJ	8.13	7.82, 7.93w -87
Cunha	Luis	POR	5 Dec 64	175/68	200	20.71A	21.08, 20.95w -86
Curran	Anthony	USA	27 Jun 59	183/75	PV	5.50	5.55 -82
Curtis	Gerry	IRL	18 May 59	179/60	5k	13:34.70	13:36.30 -87
Cuypers	Alain	BEL	29 Nov 67	181/69	400h	49.75	50.09, 50.0 -87
					110h	13.73	13.99 -87
Da Silva	Jorge T.	BRA	4 Jan 66	181/76	TJ	16.81A, 16.64	16.36 -87
da Silva	Robson C.	BRA	4 Sep 64	187/74	100	10.00A, 10.11	10.02 -86
					200	20.04	20.20 -87
Dakov	Georgi	BUL	21 Oct 67	195/78	HJ	2.30i, 2.30	2.29 -86
Dakshevich	Gennadiy	SU	15 Mar 66	182/70	110h	13.70, 13.5	13.75, 13.4 -87
Dalloway	Mark	UK	28 Oct 63		10k	28:09.39	28:22.56 -86
Daniel	Clarence	USA	11 Jun 61	183/79	400	44.75	44.89 -86
Daniel	Lorenzo	USA	23 Mar 66	183/77	100	10.15, 10.00w	10.08, 10.00w -86
					200	19.87	20.07 -85, 19.88w -87

Name		Nat	Born	Ht/Wt	Event	1988 Mark	Pre-1988 Best
Daniels	Dave	USA	28 Oct 58	188/73	3kSt	8:31.67	8:23.56 -85
Danielson	Jonny	SWE	4 Sep 64	191/74	3k	7:46.85	7:47.94 -87
					5k	13:20.29	13:34.05 -87
Danneberg	Rolf	FRG	1 Mar 53	198/112	DT	67.38	67.60 -87
Danu	Ivan	SU	17 Oct 59	171/66	3kSt	8:28.99	8:28.64 -86
Dasko	Mikhail	SU	26 Jan 61	174/61	5k	13:21.3m	13:29.27 -86
Daugherty	Shannon	USA	11 Feb 65	183/81	400h	50.40	51.43 -87
Daukshis	Virginius	SU	14 Jul 67	178/67	TJ	16.64	16.63 -87
Davies-Hale	Paul	UK	21 Jun 62	176/60	2M	8:26.09	-0-
					5k	13:21.60	13:23.36 -87
Davis	Harlan	USA	4 Aug 67	183/85	200	20.34	20.93 -86
Davis	Howard	JAM	27 Apr 67	183/81	400	45.34	45.25 -87
Davis	Jay	USA	29 Jul 67	178/71	PV	5.50	5.50 -86
Davis	Reggie	USA	17 Jan 64	189/80	400h	49.57, 48.89dq	48.52 -87
Davis	Scott	USA	12 Dec 61	188/77	PV	5.70i, 5.70	5.70 -86
De Bruin	Erik	HOL	25 May 63	186/110	SP	20.30i, 20.16	20.95 -86
					DT	66.08	66.78 -86
De Castella	Robert	AUS	27 Feb 57	180/65	Mar	2:08:49	2:07:51 -86
de Kom	Ahmed	HOL	15 Feb 59	180/73	100	10.25	10.33 -87, 10.30w -85
					200	20.77	20.60 -87
de la Garza	Juan	MEX	20 Sep 61	181/84	JT	78.32	78.58 -87
De Teresa	Tomas	SPA	5 Sep 68	183/69	800	1:46.80	1:48.67 -87
de Wit	Robert	HOL	7 Jul 63	186/93	Dec	8447	8039w -87
Deady	Mark	USA	2 Jan 67	188/71	1500	3:35.83	3:40.02 -87
Deal	Lance	USA	21 Aug 61	188/116	HT	75.64	75.94 -87
Debacker	Pascal	FRA	8 Apr 60	170/58	3kSt	8:27.60	8:18.54 -87
Dees	Tony	USA	6 Aug 63	193/91	200	20.65w	20.54 -84
					110h	13.54, 13.51w	13.65 -84
Deick	Christian	FRG	8 Jun 65	193/85	Dec	7822	7844 -86
Deksnis	Gatis	SU	21 Jul 64	190/74	3kSt	8:31.35	8:36.13 -87
Delattre	Dominique	FRA	12 Oct 58	177/63	5k	13:35.60	13:39.05 -87
Délèze	Pierre	SWZ	25 Sep 58	175/62	1500	3:39.46	3:31.75 -85
					Mile	3:57.00	3:50.38 -82
					3k	7:43.46	7:44.08 -80
					5k	13:32.64	13:15.31 -86
Delice	Patrick	TRI	12 Nov 67	184/77	400	45.75	46.41 -87
Delis	Luís.M.	CUB	6 Dec 57	185/106	DT	65.80	71.06 -83
DeLoach	Joe	USA	5 Jun 67	184/75	100	10.03/9.90w	10.10w/9.9w/10.21-85
					200	19.75	20.24 -85
Delonge	Marco	GDR	16 Jun 66	194/81	LJ	8.23	8.27 -87
Deminov	Sergey	SU	64	174/75	100	10.25	10.1, 10.54 -87
Demirev	Krasimir	BUL	28 Aug 62	180/68	400h	49.48	49.80 -87
Demisse	Debebe	ETH	68	170/50	10k	28:17.00	28:31.39 -87
Demmel	Norbert	FRG	10 May 63	191/86	Dec	7913	7855 -87
Densimo	Belayneh	ETH	28 Jun 65	172/62	Mar	2:06:50	2:08:29 -86
Despotov	Radoslav	BUL	8 Aug 68	190/130	SP	20.13	18.80 -87
Desruelles	Ronald	BEL	14 Feb 55	186/81	100	10.31	10.25 -84,9.9 -78
							10.02w/dt -85
De Teresa	Tomas	SPA	5 Sep 68	179/66	800	1:46.80	1:48.67 -87
Dethloff	Claus	FRG	4 Sep 68	188/100	HT	74.66	71.84 -87
Di Napoli	Gennaro	ITA	5 Mar 68	180/60	1500	3:34.72	3:41.2 -87
					2k	5:02.5	-0-
Dia Bâ	Amadou	SEN	22 Sep 58	188/72	400	45.84	45.78 -86
					400h	47.23	48.03A -87
Dial	Joe	USA	26 Oct 62	174/59	PV	5.71	5.96 -87
Diamond	Earl	USA	21 Jul 66	190/84	110h	13.77/13.76w	13.87/13.76w/13.5w-86
Diemer	Brian	USA	10 Oct 61	178/64	3kSt	8:20.44	8:13.16 -84
Digno	Martí	CUB	21 Oct 65	179/75	LJ	8.09	8.17 -86
Dimitrov	Kamen	BUL	18 Jan 62	194/112	DT	64.82	65.40 -86
Djurdjevic	Zoran	YUG	3 Apr 68	183/74	TJ	16.71	15.25 -87
Dmitriyev	Dmitriy	SU	3 Mar 56	175/65	10k	28:24.89	28:28.55 -86
Dobeleit	Norbert	FRG	17 Jul 64	188/75	200	20.79	20.43 -87
					400	45.63	46.29 -86
DoDoo	Francis	GHA	13 Apr 60	186/75	TJ	16.62, 16.73w	17.12A, 16.78 -87
Doehring	Jim	USA	27 Jan 62	183/120	SP	21.04	21.29 -86

Name		Nat	Born	Ht/Wt	Event	1988 Mark	Pre-1988 Best
Doherty	John	IRL	22 Jul 61	175/62	3k	7:44.85	7:52.85 -85
					2M	8:19.45	-0-
					5k	13:17.14	13:23.48 -85
Dollendorf	Marc	BEL	7 Feb 66		400h	50.19	50.79 -87
Domingues	Adauto	BRA	20 May 61	173/62	3kSt	8:24.38	8:23.26 -87
Donaldson	Xavier	USA	12 Dec 68	189/77	LJ	7.97w	7.26 -86
Donati	Paolo	ITA	22 Jan 62		5k	13:34.50	13:47.54 -87
Donias	Alain	FRA	15 Jan 60	184/75	PV	5.60	5.50 -81
Donskikh	Sergey	SU	25 Jan 56	197/128	SP	19.46	21.09 -84
Dorozhon	Sergey	SU	17 Feb 64	184/110	HT	78.94	78.46 -86
Dos Santos	Diamantino	BRA	3 Feb 61	166/59	Mar	2:13:12	2:14:55 -87
Dosayev	Yevgeniy	SU	12 Aug 63	185/73	HJ	2.26i	2.22 -87
Douglas	Atlee	UK	9 Jun 68		800	1:46.70	1:47.08 -87
Douglas	Troy	BER	30 Nov 62	173/71	200	20.70	
					400	45.69	
Dovoino	Igor	SU	29 Jul 64	188/84	LJ	7.97i	8.16 -87
					TJ	17.22	
Doyle	Simon	AUS	66		800	1:46.88	1:50.07 -87
Dragoescu	Petru	RUM	22 Jul 62	175/63	800	1:46.91	1:45.41 -85
Draper	Maurice	USA	69	175/70	200	20.79	
Drigol	Aleksandr	SU	25 Apr 66	191/100	HT	76.98	77.18 -87
Drobyshevskiy	Igor	SU	17 Oct 66	185/72	Dec	7989	7637 -86
Drummond	John	USA	9 Sep 68	175/70	100	10.25, 10.0w	10.28, 10.23w -87
Drummond	John	USA	9 Sep 68	175/70	200	20.79i	20.64 -87
Druppers	Rob	HOL	29 Apr 62	186/70	800	1:44.98	1:43.56 -85
					1k	2:18.95, 2:16.62i	2:15.23 -85
					1500	3:39.31	3:35.07 -85
Du	Benzhong	CHN	15 May 67	190/80	TJ	16.68	16.69 -87
Duany	Ubaldo	CUB	16 May 60	183/73	LJ	8.28	8.32 -86
Duginyets	Igor	SU	20 May 56	196/100	DT	66.30	68.52 -82
Dumchev	Yuriy	SU	5 Aug 58	200/128	DT	70.30	71.86 -83
Duncan	Gary	USA	25 May 64	196/79	400	45.40	45.33 -87
Dunn	Devlon	USA	1 Apr 67	175/73	100	10.12w	
					200	20.59, 20.4w	20.70A -86
Duplantis	Greg	USA	22 Jan 62	168/61	PV	5.79	5.62 -86
Dvoretskiy	Sergey	SU	30 Apr 57	191/108	HT	77.64	78.62 -84
Dydalin	Andrey	SU	28 Feb 66		110h	13.58	13.92, 13.6 -87
Dymchenko	Sergey	SU	23 Aug 67	202/84	HJ	2.25	
Dyulgerov	Emanuil	BUL	7 Feb 55	178/95	HT	76.50	80.64 -84
D'Encausse	Philippe	FRA	24 Mar 67	186/77	PV	5.70	5.40 -87
Ebong-Salle	Fredéric	CMR	10 Sep 64	185/78	LJ	7.96w	7.97 -86
Edel	Mikhail	SU	7 May 69	185/79	110h	13.75	14.26, 14.0 -87
Edet	Victor	NIG	24 Feb 66	175/64	100	10.14, 10.0	10.24, 10.13w -87
					200	20.5w	21.04/20.64w-87,20.5w -85
Edwards	Dothel	USA	9 Sep 66	193/72	HJ	2.25i, 2.25	2.30 -85
Edwards	Jonathan	UK	10 May 66	180/74	TJ	16.74	16.35 -87
Edwards	Paul	UK	16 Feb 59	186/123	SP	19.81	17.80 -87
Egbunike	Innocent	NIG	30 Nov 61	174/68	400	44.72	44.17 -87
Ehrle	Klaus	AUT	11 Mar 66	190/80	400h	49.86, 49.6	49.55 -87
Einarsson	Sigurdur	ICE	28 Sep 62	188/100	JT	78.28	80.84 -87
Einspahr	Kregg	USA	19 Apr 60	180/68	3kSt	8:28.34	8:25.05 -83
Ellard	Henry	USA	21 Jul 61	180/77	TJ	16.66	16.73 -86, 17.23w -82
Ellerby	Harry	USA	4 May 69	183/82	400	45.76	
Elliott	Norbert	BAH	6 Nov 62	183/78	TJ	16.89	17.02 -86
Elliott	Peter	UK	9 Oct 62	181/67	800	1:44.12	1:43.41 -87
					1k	2:16.47	2:17.65 -83
					1500	3:32.94	3:33.23 -87
					Mile	3:49.20	3:54.22 -86
					2k	4:55.72	4:52.82 -87
Ellis	Elbert	USA	23 Jun 69	196/80	110h	13.78w	-0-
					400h	50.24, 49.8	51.39 -87
Emmelmann	Frank	GDR	15 Sep 61	185/78	100	10.26	10.06 -85
					200	20.37	20.23 -85
Emmiyan	Robert	SU	16 Feb 65	178/69	LJ	8.00i, 7.96	8.86A -87, 8.61 -86
Endo	Tsukasa	JAP	9 Nov 61	164/50	10k	28:13.75	28:30.9 -86
Enholm	Martin	SWE	7 Feb 65	176/64	800	1:46.06	1:46.52 -86

Name		Nat	Born	Ht/Wt	Event	1988 Mark	Pre-1988 Best
Enweani	Cyprean	CAN	19 Mar 64	185/82	200	20.57, 20.05Aw	20.86 -84
Erb	Christian	SWZ	14 Feb 59	180/95	DT	64.04	59.14 -87
Ereng	Paul	KEN	22 Aug 67	185/68	800	1:43.45	-0-
Erickson	Steve	USA	13 Jan 61	190/86	Dec	8063	8063w -85
Eriksson	Scott	USA	1 Jul 61	196/110	SP	19.29	18.78i -86
					DT	60.94	61.94 -87
Eriksson	Thomas	SWE	1 May 63	183/78	HJ	2.25	2.32 -85
Espino	Juan	SPA	24 Jun 59	168/50	3kSt	8:32.40	8:29.74 -87
Ester	Andre	USA	27 Apr 65	183/70	LJ	8.16	8.16, 8.41w - 87
Evangelisti	Giovanni	ITA	11 Sep 61	179/70	LJ	8.07, 8.37w	8.43 -87
Evans	Dwayne	USA	13 Oct 58	187/75	100	10.17w	10.20, 10.07w -81
					200	20.41	20.08A -87, 20.22 -76
Everett	Danny	USA	1 Nov 66	187/68	200	20.23	20.42 -87
					400	43.98	44.47 -87
Everett	Mark	USA	2 Sep 68	183/71	400	45.91	46.37 -87
					800	1:44.46	1:47.36 -87
Eyestone	Ed	USA	15 Jun 61	185/66	Mar	2:12:49	2:16:21 -84
Fadil	Mike	USA	22 Jun 63	172/63	3kSt	8:35.46	8:29.01 -85
Fahner	Thomas	GDR	18 Jul 66	186/85	Dec	8362	8187 -87
Falcon	Joe	USA	23 Jun 66	168/52	1500	3:35.84	3:40.81 -87
					Mile	3:52.14	3:56.77i -87
					3k	7:46.57	7:55.96i -87
Falise	Didier	BEL	3 Mar 61	185/75	TJ	16.73	16.86 -86
Fall	Moussa	SEN	28 Aug 63	178/67	800	1:44.06	1:44.68 -85
Farmer	Jim	USA	14 Aug 65	180/70	3k	7:51.65	7:58.96i -87
Faul	Brian	USA	5 Mar 60	184/120	SP	20.30	19.88 -86
Faulkner	Stewart	UK	19 Feb 69	194/86	LJ	7.98, 8.04w	7.87 -87
Faustini	Alessio	ITA	10 Jun 60	165/48	Mar	2:11:52	2:13:27 -86
Fedoriv	Andrey	SU	11 Aug 63	179/77	100	10.23	10.21 -87
Fedorov	Sergey	SU	66		DT	60.88	
Fehringer	Hermann	AUT	8 Dec 62	181/81	PV	5.60	5.71 -87
Fell	Graeme	CAN	19 Mar 59	184/73	5k	13:33.57	13:34.32 -87
					3kSt	8:19.99	8:12.58 -85
Felton	Lawrence	USA	21 Feb 67	183/79	110h	13.81, 13.63w	13.83, 13.70w -87
Feraday	Steve	CAN	5 Apr 59	187/100	JT	77.82	75.06 -86
Fernholm	Stefan	SWE	2 Jul 59	186/120	DT	68.24	68.30 -87
Ferreira	António D.	BRA	2 Mar 60	173/62	400h	A50.12	49.24 -85
Ferreira	Serge	FRA	11 Aug 59	183/72	PV	5.60	5.72i -85, 5.71 -84
Fichtner	Karl-Heinz	FRG	16 Aug 62	188/82	Dec	8250	8081 -87
Ficsor	József	HUN	29 Jul 65	196/110	DT	64.68	63.22 -86
Fiedler	Thoralf	GDR	8 Jul 66	198/100	DT	61.78	59.84 -87
Filek	Waclaw	POL	2 Apr 59	188/115	HT	72.40	74.64 -85
Fischer	Andreas	FRG	11 Apr 68	182/60	3kSt	8:33.22	8:47.70 -87
Fischer	Stefan	FRG	19 Jan 69	188/100	HT	72.34	66.40 -87
Fishman	Gennadiy	SU	7 Sep 59	182/68	10k	28:19.88	28:28.06 -87
Fiz	Martin	SPA	3 Mar 63	167/58	3kSt	8:28.9	8:39.66 -87
Fizuleto	Hrvoje	YUG	15 Jan 63	191/69	HJ	2.25i	2.26 -84
Flax	Ken	USA	20 Apr 63	178/97	HT	80.02	79.64 -87
Flenaugh	Sebron	USA	15 Sep 65	178/76	400h	50.33	50.91 -87
Floreal	Edrick	CAN	5 Oct 66	188/83	LJ	8.11w	7.81 -86, 8.02w -87
					TJ	16.76, 17.19w	16.92 -87
Florence	Derrick	USA	19 Jun 68	170/79	100	10.22, 10.15w	10.13 -86
					200	20.51, 20.4	20.63 -86
Floyd	Mark	USA	11 Feb 64	180/70	110h	13.56w	13.70 -87
Floyd	Stanley	USA	23 Jun 61	178/74	100	10.23	10.03A -82, 10.07/10.0 -80
Flynn	Ray	IRL	22 Jan 57	182/65	1500	3:39.42	3:33.5 -82
Forster	Kevin	UK	27 Sep 58	178/61	Mar	2:10:52	2:11:41 -84
Forsythe	Mark	UK	10 Aug 65	183/77	LJ	7.95	7.59 -85
Fortune	Brett	USA			110h	13.80w	
Foster	Greg	USA	4 Aug 58	190/84	110h	13.39	13.03 -81, 13.0 -79
Fouche	Francois	RSA	5 Jun 63	184/73	LJ	8.15A, 7.97	8.04A -85, 8.00 -87
Fox	Chris	USA	22 Oct 58	185/57	10k	28:27.28	30:32.42 -77
Fox	René	FRG	9 Nov 67	186/103	HT	75.58	72.76 -87
Fraley	Doug	USA	7 Mar 65	188/81	PV	5.70	5.77 -86
Franks	Mike	USA	23 Sep 63	180/73	200	20.62	20.5 -87, 20.62, 20.58w -84
					400	44.82	44.47 -85

Name		Nat	Born	Ht/Wt	Event	1988 Mark	Pre-1988 Best
Franz	Engelbert	FRG	24 Nov 63	183/65	3kSt	8:26.38	8:32.32 -87
Frazier	John	USA	27 Apr 63	184/120	SP	19.81	20.05 -87
Fredericks	Frankie	RSA	2 Oct 67	178/70	100	10.32A	10.1 -86, 10.36A -87
					200	20.57	20.58, 20.41Aw -87
Freigang	Stephan	GDR	27 Sep 67	179/65	Mar	2:12:28	
Freimuth	Uwe	GDR	10 Sep 61	191/92	Dec	8381	8792 -84
Friedrich	Lutz	GDR	8 Aug 61	196/120	DT	61.62	63.98 -86
Frolenkov	Sergey	SU	11 Feb 62	180/75	TJ	16.66	16.87i -87, 16.72 -83
Froude	Derek	NZ	30 Apr 59	182/	Mar	2:12:40	2:11:25 -83
Fuentes	Francisco	SPA	6 Feb 63	191/122	HT	72.28	72.10 -86
Füzesi	Sándor	HUN	15 Dec 59	186/120	HT	74.84	74.62 -84
Fuhlbrügge	Hauke	GDR	21 Mar 66	180/66	800	1:46.44	1:46.73 -86
					1k	2:17.89	2:17.49 -86
					1500	3:36.62	3:38.61 -87
Fuhrmann	Björn-Peter	GDR	4 Sep 67	181/100	HT	73.44	73.64 -87
Fukazawa	Yutaka	JAP	66		LJ	7.98w	7.51 -87
Furdylo	Vladimir	SU	6 Apr 58	183/82	JT	79.80	80.36 -87
Fu-An	Lee	TAI	6 Apr 64	185/77	Dec	7739	7697 -84
Fyodorov	Aleksey	SU	3 May 65	182/78	200	20.5w	20.8 -86
Fyodorkov	Grigoriy	SU	64		HJ	2.24	2.29i, 2.27 -87
Gähwiler	Beat	SWZ	26 Jan 65	186/87	Dec	8244	8089w -86
Gaisl	Lubos	CS	11 Mar 63	180/65	3kSt	8:31.93	8:31.96 -86
Galkin	Konstantin	SU	25 Mar 65	189/71	HJ	2.25	2.25i -87, 2.23 -85
Gamlin	Dirk	GDR	26 Oct 63	188/85	TJ	17.11	17.44 -85
Ganeyev	Ramil	SU	23 Sep 68	186/77	Dec	7714	7381m -87
Garcia	Javier	SPA	22 Jul 66	177/71	PV	5.55	5.50i -87, 5.43 -86
Garcia	Salvador	MEX	29 Oct 60		Mar	2:11:50	
Garner	Mark	AUS	30 Jun 69	174/64	400	45.88	
Garrett	Bret	USA	8 Aug 66	183/68	800	1:46.97	1:48.08 -86
Gaslenko	Vitaliy	SU	15 Mar 62		DT	66.36	65.14 -86
Gassowski	Janusz	POL	1 Mar 58	191/125	SP	19.98	20.98 -85
Gataullin	Rodion	SU	23 Nov 65	189/78	PV	5.95	5.90 -87
Gaudry	Ian	AUS	20 Mar 64	185/73	800	1:46.26	1:46.72 -87
Gavras	Sergey	SU	16 Apr 57	185/95	JT	78.92	81.74 -87
Gavrikov	Sergey	SU	19 Apr 64	189/78	PV	5.50	5.62 -86
Gavrilov	Sergey	SU	70		HT	72.18	67.36 -87
Gavrilyuk	Vladimir	SU	17 Jun 61	185/95	JT	76.48	80.62 -87
Gavryushin	Sergey	SU	27 Jun 59	192/125	SP	21.39	22.10 -86
Gazyura	Anatoliy	SU	17 Mar 64	188/84	Dec	8245M	7949 -86
Gécsek	Tibor	HUN	22 Sep 64	183/94	HT	81.68	79.14 -87
Geiger	German	SU	8 Dec 62		SP	19.20	19.15i, 19.14 -87
Gellens	Patrick	FRA	8 Feb 59	184/74	Dec	7778	7942 -85
Gelhausen	Udo	FRG	5 Jul 56	188/127	SP	20.03i, 19.79	20.74 -87
Gemizhev	Nikolay	BUL	4 Aug 56	188/100	SP	19.48i, 19.37	20.20 -84
Geoffroy	Rémy	FRA	22 Mar 63	175/67	1500	3:36.18	3:35.52 -87
					Mile	3:55.31	3:59.38 -87
George	Vernon	USA	6 Oct 64	185/84	110h	13.71w	13.49 -87
					LJ	8.13, 8.19w	8.24 -87
Georgiev	Georgi	BUL	16 Jul 61	192/112	DT	66.02	66.16 -87
Ghanem	Ahmed H.	EGY	2 Jan 59	175/77	400h	50.44	49.74 -85
Gicquel	Jean-Charles	FRA	24 Feb 67	197/78	HJ	2.28	2.27 -87
Giessing	Thomas	FRG	19 Mar 61	197/85	800	1:46.71	1:45.73 -86
Gilbert	Glenroy	CAN	30 Apr 68	183/72	LJ	8.01, 8.10w	7.47 -85
Giurgian	Liviu	RUM	22 Jul 62	192/79	110h	13.52	13.47, 13.40w -86
Glance	Harvey	USA	28 Mar 57	171/67	100	10.20	10.05-85,10.03w-87,9.8 -77
Glander	Steve	USA	3 Sep 61	185/83	PV	5.64	5.50 -87
Glass	Jeff	CAN	21 Apr 62	185/82	110h	13.83	13.73A, 13.79-84
Glebov	Sergey	SU	26 Jan 64	184/88	JT	76.70	80.94 -86
Glinskikh	Lev	SU	25 Jul 62		3kSt	8:32.64	8:29.51 -86
Görmer	Klaus	GDR	5 Jul 63	194/120	SP	20.59	21.22 -87
Goins	Boris	USA	7 Apr 67	180/75	100	10.33	10.45 -86
					LJ	8.08	7.84i, 7.74 -87
Gombala	Milan	CS	29 Jan 68	187/75	LJ	7.93	7.82, 8.12w -87
Gomez	Alejandro	SPA	11 Apr 67	178/60	3k	7:48.38	7:57.84 -86
					5k	13:21.02	13:27.64 -87
Gonzalez	Alexandre	FRA	16 Mar 51	183/71	Mar	2:12:52	2:13:36 -86

Name		Nat	Born	Ht/Wt	Event	1988 Mark	Pre-1988 Best
Gonzalez	José Luis	SPA	8 Dec 57	180/63	1500	3:36.41	3:30.92 -85
					Mile	3:56.67, 3:55.00i	3:47.79 -85
					3k	7:47.54i	7:42.93 -87
					5k	13:27.30	13:12.34 -87
Gonzalez	Mauricio	MEX	16 Oct 60	180/67	5k	13:27.65	13:22.4 -85
					10k	27:43.64	-0-
Gonzalez	Mike	USA	13 Mar 64	185/84	Dec	8203	7956 -87
González	Ramón	CUB	24 Aug 65	182/83	JT	76.76	79.24 -87
Goodell	Bart	USA	4 Oct 61	193/95	Dec	8109	8041 -86
Gorbachenko	Yuriy	SU	19 Jul 66	188/75	TJ	16.62	16.86 -85
Gorbatov	Aleksandr	SU	66		JT	76.48	74.98 -86
Gordien	Marcus	USA	29 Apr 55	193/104	DT	62.94	65.28 -84
Gordon	Pat	JAM	20 Aug 65	170/66	400	45.68, 45.2	45.29 -87
Gotman	Erich	SU	16 Oct 63	190/80	TJ	16.95	16.69 -87
Gotovskiy	Yuriy	SU	31 May 61	191/80	HJ	2.25i	2.29i -85, 2.29 -87
Gottschall	Daniel	FRG	16 Jan 63		3kSt	8:35.74	8:46.3 -87
Grabarczyk	Andrzej	POL	12 Jan 64	187/73	TJ	16.92, 17.08w	16.89 -87
Grad	Dariusz	POL	7 Apr 63	190/85	Dec	8050	7883 -87
Graham	John	CAN	20 Nov 65	186/81	400h	50.30	49.51 -87
Graham	Winthrop	JAM	17 Nov 65	178/72	400	45.59	
					400h	48.04	48.49 -87
Grant	Dalton	UK	8 Apr 66	188/73	HJ	2.31	2.28i, 2.25 -87
Grassi	Giorgio	ITA	8 Jan 63	186/70	PV	5.50i	5.45 -87
Grasu	Costel	RUM	5 Jul 67	191/105	DT	60.82	54.86 -87
Graudyn	Aleksey	SU	28 Apr 68	184/72	100	10.29	10.43 -87
Graudyn	Vladimir	SU	26 Aug 63	182/70	800	1:44.10	1:45.19 -87
Gravelle	Mike	USA	13 Apr 65	196/116	DT	61.22	62.46 -86
Gray	Johnny	USA	19 Jun 60	190/76	800	1:42.65	1:42.60 -85
Green	Harry	USA	18 Jul 67	175/61	10k	28:19.6m	28:33.8 -87
Green	Ronnie	USA	28 Nov 66	172/73	200	20.67w	
Gregorek	John	USA	15 Apr 60	185/75	5k	13:29.68	13:17.44 -87
Greyling	Bennie	RSA	1 Feb 65	183/70	1k	2:18.03	2:23.2 -87
					Mile	3:55.42	3:54.59 -87
					2k	5:04.00	5:26.9 -87
Grib	Vladislav	SU	8 May 64		JT	82.18	78.92 -86
Gribov	Yevgeniy	SU	18 Apr 62		HT	77.40	78.12 -85
Griffin	Pat	USA	22 Apr 67	190/73	400h	50.37	
Grigorov	Anri	BUL	18 Oct 64	178/70	100	10.28w	10.23 -87
Grigoryan	Parkev	SU	65	186/74	TJ	16.93	16.98 -86
Grinchenko	Vladimir	SU	14 Mar 65	184/91	JT	76.64	74.08 -87
Grogorick	Thomas	GDR	10 May 62	186/112	HT	73.40, 73.88exh	76.20 -87
Grokhovskiy	Oleg	SU	68		TJ	16.96	16.31 -87
Grudinin	Andrey	SU	3 May 69	183/69	PV	5.60	5.30 -87
Gubkin	Valeriy	SU	11 Jan 67	194/100	HT	78.18	76.54 -86
Gudmundsson	Pétur	ICE	9 Mar 62	191/120	SP	20.03	19.31 -87
Günther	René	GDR	7 Feb 65	196/93	Dec	8023	7884 -87
Günthör	Werner	SWZ	11 Jul 61	200/127	SP	22.75	22.47 -87
Gugler	Christian	SWZ	1 Aug 60	186/82	Dec	7907	8046 -82
Gui	Olivier	FRA	20 Jan 62	183/75	400h	50.29	49.34 -85
Guidry	Neal	USA	3 Apr 67	190/75	HJ	2.26	2.30 -87
Guilbe	Edgardo	PR	10 Mar 66	178/64	200	20.55	20.72 -87
Guimarães	Agberto	BRA	18 Aug 57	175/57	800	1:45.92	1:43.63 -84
Gula	Sergey	SU	2 Jun 63	188/110	HT	75.98	73.86 -87
Guldberg	Mogens	DEN	2 Aug 63	184/65	1500	3:35.32	3:37.75 -87
					Mile	3:57.18	4:01.54 -83
Gundersen	Knut	NOR	24 Sep 64	185/82	Dec	7703	7525 -84
Gurny	Slawomir	POL	2 Sep 64	181/72	3kSt	8:31.76	8:25.08 -87
Guss	Lloyd	CAN	22 Jan 59	188/81	400h	50.40	49.83A -85, 50.01 -84
Gustafsson	Tore	SWE	11 Feb 62	183/110	HT	78.48	78.36 -87
Haaf	Dietmar	FRG	6 Mar 67	173/67	LJ	8.04i, 8.04	8.05, 8.10w -87
Haber	Ralf	GDR	18 Aug 62	191/113	HT	82.54, 83.40u	81.84 -87
Hacker	Tim	USA	27 Dec 62	172/64	1500	3:36.42	3:34.66 -87
					Mile	3:55.7m	4:00.3 -87
Hackett	Robert	USA	3 Aug 64	172/64	100	10.30	10.27 -87, 10.21w -86
					200	20.60	20.52 -87
Hackney	Roger	UK	2 Sep 57	183/74	3kSt	8:18.91	8:19.38 -83

Name		Nat	Born	Ht/Wt	Event	1988 Mark	Pre-1988 Best
Hacksteiner	Markus	SWZ	18 Nov 64	186/74	1500	3:37.07	3:34.11 -87
					Mile	3:56.81	3:55.67 -87
					3k	7:50.57i	7:51.49 -86
Hadden	Darrell	USA	14 Nov 64	188/82	200	20.65	20.90- 85, 20.9 -87
					400	45.24	46.04 -85
Hadjiandreou	Marios	CYP	19 Sep 62	183/76	TJ	16.88i, 16.80	16.74i-87, 16.69 -85
Hadwich	Volker	GDR	23 Sep 64	196/103	JT	81.26	81.02 -86
Hafsteinsson	Vésteinn	ICE	12 Dec 60	190/113	DT	65.60	65.60 -83
Hagan	Craig	USA	7 Apr 64	190/81	PV	5.57	5.50 -87
Haley	Roddie	USA	6 Dec 65	178/64	400	44.76	44.48 -86
Hall	Derwin	USA	27 Jul 69		100	10.33	10.48, 10.36w -86
Halvorsen	John	NOR	17 Aug 66	174/58	3k	7:50.25	7:51.94 -87
					5k	13:34.62	13:52.02 -87
					10k	27:47.40	28:27.33 -86
Hamada	Ahmed	BHN	18 Sep 61	183/70	400h	50.38	49.31 -86
Hamer	Charlton	USA	7 Aug 66	180/73	800	1:45.79	1:46.89 -87
Han	Chae-ho	KOR	6 Mar 65		Mar	2:13:06	2:16:31 -87
Hanlon	Tom	UK	2 May 67	183/74	1500	3:38.59	3:47.00 -87
					3kSt	8:20.73	8:27.60 -87
Hanna	Steve	BAH	30 Oct 58	180/68	TJ	16.84	17.04 -81, 17.07w -85
Hannecker	Alois	FRG	10 Jul 61	190/110	DT	65.90	65.32 -87
Hargett	Kyle	USA	14 Jan 67	183/79	200	20.4w	
					400	45.65	46.14A -87
Harken	Brent	USA	1 Dec 61	192/79	HJ	2.31	2.31 -84
Harlin	Tony	USA	4 Sep 59	187/120	SP	19.38	20.57 -84
Harmsworth	Paul	UK	28 Sep 63	171/67	400	45.64	46.02 -87
Harrer	Ron	USA	5 Feb 65	183/107	DT	62.14	60.08 -87
Harries	Axel	FRG	19 Sep 64	186/76	800	1:46.98	1:45.80 -85
Harries	Phil	UK	7 Apr 66	184/74	400h	50.01	50.72 -86
Harris	Danny	USA	7 Sep 65	183/77	400h	47.74	47.48 -87
Harris	Dennis	USA	23 Mar 68	188/82	LJ	7.93w	7.85 -87
Harris	Steve	UK	17 Nov 61	178/62	10k	28:00.60	27:59.33 -86
Harrison	Karl	UK	16 Oct 56	175/57	10k	28:24.03	28:11.07 -86
Harrison	Kenny	USA	13 Feb 65	175/68	LJ	8.10, 8.23w	8.17i-86, 8.14 -87
					TJ	17.15,17.56w	17.07-86,17.42w -87
Hartmann	Werner	FRG	20 Apr 59	189/115	DT	66.02	67.54 -82
Hawkins	Ray	USA	14 Jun 65	172/68	LJ	8.09	7.82 -87
Hawkins	Tranel	USA	17 Sep 62	196/80	400h	48.65	48.28 -84
Haynes	Mike	USA	24 Dec 65	183/82	100	10.28wA	
Heard	Floyd	USA	24 Mar 66	178/71	200	20.50	19.95 -87
Heard	Steve	UK	29 Apr 62	187/86	800	1:45.32	1:51.7 -87
Heikkila	Pasi	FIN	31 May 65	189/102	HT	74.46	72.34 -87
Heikkinen	Eero	FIN	22 Jul 55	178/82	JT	78.74	79.46 -87
Heilmann	Michael	GDR	26 Oct 61	174/54	Mar	2:11:34	2:09:03 -85
Heimrath	Torsten	GDR	14 May 63	182/78	200	20.78w	20.89 -86
Heisler	Randy	USA	7 Aug 61	190/125	SP	19.70i	19.83i, 19.46 -87
					DT	64.94	67.62 -87
Heist	Michael	FRG	2 May 65	185/70	3kSt	8:35.17	8:30.46 -86
Hélan	Serge	FRA	24 Feb 64	176/70	TJ	17.01	17.15i -87, 17.13 -86
Henderson	Kevin	USA	4 Feb 65	185/75	400h	48.68	49.16 -85
Herbert	John	UK	20 Apr 62	188/76	TJ	17.12	17.41 -85
Herbert	Paul	UK	20 Dec 66	183/73	800	1:45.64	1:46.33 -87
Hernandez	Dominique	FRA	1 Aug 60	178/66	HJ	2.25	2.24 -86
Hernández	Gregorio	CUB	2 Jun 68		TJ	16.61	16.33 -87
Hernández	Mauricio	MEX	30 Nov 61	175/61	800	1:46.6	1:46.7 -87
Hernández	Orlando	CUB	21 May 62		JT	76.30	76.48 -87
Hernández	Roberto	CUB	6 Mar 67	179/74	200	20.24A, 20.53	20.37 -86
					400	44.22A, 44.57	44.61 -87
Hernández	Robin	CUB	21 Oct 69	196/79	TJ	16.61	16.66 -87
Herold	Jens-Peter	GDR	25 Oct 65	176/64	1k	2:18.61	2:19.4 -86
					1500	3:33.33	3:33.28 -87
					Mile	3:49.22	-0-
Herrera	Jesús	MEX	22 Mar 62	174/56	5k	13:37.10	13:38.88 -87
					10k	27:57.93	27:45.0 -85
					Mar	2:10:40	2:11:00 -84
Herrington	Terrence	USA	31 Jul 66	180/61	800	1:46.38	1:47.55 -85

Name		Nat	Born	Ht/Wt	Event	1988 Mark	Pre-1988 Best
Hesse	Tim	GHA	7 Mar 68	170/68	400	45.81	46.7 -87
Hidalgo	Lorenzo	SPA	7 Jan 65	178/60	1500	3:39.46	3:40.7 -86
Hill	Jim	USA	1 Jul 61	180/63	10k	28:20.46	27:55.23 -83
Hill	Mike	UK	22 Oct 64	190/95	JT	81.30	85.24 -87
Hill	Ray	USA	24 Jun 66	170/66	100	10.24w	10.21, 10.18w -87
Hillardt	Mike	AUS	22 Jan 61	180/70	800	1:46.1m	1:45.74 -83
					1k	2:17.67	2:17.49 -84
					1500	3:34.06	3:33.39 -85
Hilton	Ian	CAN	14 Jul 67	183/71	LJ	7.93	7.41 -87
Hingsen	Jürgen	FRG	25 Jan 58	200/102	Dec	8360	8832 -84
Hinrichs	Heinz	USA	22 Mar 62	191/91	Dec	7899m	7535 -84
Hintnaus	Tom	BRA	15 Feb 58	180/78	PV	5.50i	5.76 -85
Hix	Roy	USA	16 Nov 64	183/75	PV	5.57	5.37i -86, 5.36 -87
Hjeltnes	Knut	NOR	8 Dec 51	190/116	DT	65.40	69.62 -85
Hlabahlaba	David	RSA	9 Oct 61		800	1:46.91A	1:49.06 -87
Hofstee	Herman	HOL	17 Jul 63		3kSt	8:29.95	8:30.76 -87
Holló	Csaba	HUN	6 Jul 58	190/112	DT	64.36	63.02 -85
Holm	Arne	SWE	22 Dec 61	186/80	TJ	16.68,17.06w	17.05-87,17.16w -86
Holman	Woody	USA	2 May 68	175/70	100	10.29	10.32w -87
Holmes	Calvin	USA	13 Sep 65	180/70	110h	13.84	13.87 -86
Holopainen	Hannu	FIN	25 Jan 58	184/88	JT	77.96	76.08 -87
Honey	Gary	AUS	26 Jul 59	183/70	LJ	8.22, 8.30w	8.27, 8.39w -84
Hoogewerf	Simon	CAN	11 May 63	175/66	800	1:45.4m	1:45.95 -85
Hooper	Dick	IRL	26 Aug 56	174/68	Mar	2:12:19	2:12:56 -82
Horn	Rüdiger	GDR	28 Jul 67	186/73	1500	3:38.06i	3:40.09 -87
Horsfield	Neil	UK	7 Dec 66	190/73	1500	3:38.79	3:37.95 -87
Horta	Luis	POR	14 Jan 58	176/52	10k	28:10.4m	28:18.13 -84
Horváth	Attila	HUN	28 Jul 67	193/105	DT	64.18	62.94 -87
House	Geryl	USA	18 Aug 65	178/68	800	1:46.42	1:47.52 -87
Howard	Jim	USA	11 Sep 59	196/80	HJ	2.34i, 2.34	2.36i -86, 2.36 -87
Howard	Marc	AUS	5 Nov 66		HJ	2.26	2.20 -86
Howard	Peter	USA	17 Oct 63	180/68	400	45.35	45.46 -85
Hraban	Roman	CS	28 Jun 62	187/86	Dec	8141	7866w -86
Hudec	Jirí	CS	15 Aug 64	184/78	110h	13.52	13.48 -87
Hübner	Jörn	GDR	27 Jan 68	188/113	HT	74.60	72.76 -87
Huell	Ricky	USA	10 Nov 69		100	10.27w	10.4 -86
Huff	Derek	USA	26 Nov 66	185/86	Dec	8075	7473 -86
Huff	Ivan	USA	31 Jul 59	178/70	3kSt	8:22.35	8:16.59 -86
Huffman	Scott	USA	30 Nov 64	175/73	PV	5.65	5.62 -85
Huhtala	Harri	FIN	13 Aug 52	187/108	HT	77.78	78.74 -84
Huminik	Tom	USA	18 Oct 66	188/122	SP	19.60	17.27 -87
Humphrey	Ray	USA	31 Aug 65	180/76	LJ	8.19	8.10i -86, 8.04 -85
Huncík	Marián	CS	30 Jan 66	179/65	3kSt	8:34.73	8:43.80 -87
Hunter	Rusty	USA	4 Sep 65	175/75	Dec	7845w	7355w -87
Huruk	Jan	POL	27 Jan 60	178/65	5k	13:34.63	13:49.25 -86
Hussein	Ibrahim	KEN	3 Jun 58	170/57	Mar	2:08:43	2:11:01 -87
Hutchings	Tim	UK	4 Dec 58	183/72	Mile	3:57.6m	3:54.53 -82
					3k	7:49.45	7:44.55 -84
					2M	8:26.65	8:15.53 -86
					5k	13:23.24	13:11.50 -84
Hutton	Allister	UK	18 Jul 54	168/56	Mar	2:11:42	2:09:16 -85
Hwang	Hong-chul	KOR	27 Feb 66	181/78	400h	50.52	51.18 -86
Hyde	Bret	USA	3 Jul 59	193/81	3kSt	8:26.0m	8:25.39 -84
Hydel	Miroslaw	POL	24 Jul 63	188/80	LJ	7.99i, 7.91	8.08 -86
Hyun-Wook	Cho	KOR	15 Mar 62	180/70	HJ	2.25	2.22 -87
Hyytiäinen	Marko	FIN	27 Nov 66		JT	79.90	76.68 -87
Ifeduba	Peter	NIG	69		100	10.26, 10.0	10.67, 10.1 -87
					200	20.5w	21.4 -87
Ignatov	Evgeni	BUL	25 Jun 59	183/66	5k	13:24.76	13:13.15 -86
					10k	27:56.26	28:24.73 -84
Ikangaa	Juma	TAN	19 Jul 57	163/58	Mar	2:08:42	2:08:10 -86
Ilchenko	Nikolay	SU	12 Aug 63		400h	49.47	48.98 -86
Ilg	Patriz	FRG	5 Dec 57	173/63	3kSt	8:23.19	8:15.06 -87
Imoh	Chidi	NIG	27 Aug 63	188/77	100	10.04	10.00 -86, 9.92Aw -87
					200	20.31	20.36A/20.47 -86,19.9w -85
Inahara	Toshihiro	JAP	8 Sep 58		Mar	2:12:22	2:14:41 -87

Name		Nat	Born	Ht/Wt	Event	1988 Mark	Pre-1988 Best
Inozemtsev	Vladimir	SU	25 May 64	184/75	TJ	17.29i, 17.04	17.43i, 17.16 -86
Isalgué	Saúl	CUB	3 Nov 69		LJ	7.93	7.64 -87
Isasi	Joel	CUB	31 Jul 67	169/67	100	9.9	10.25A -86
Isayev	Anton	SU	25 Jun 62	178/70	110h	13.70, 13.6i	13.54, 13.3 -87
Ishutin	Valeriy	SU	5 Sep 65	185/76	PV	5.70i, 5.50	5.70 -87
Itt	Edgar	FRG	8 Jun 67	186/75	400	45.43	45.38 -87
					800	1:45.70	-0-
					400h	48.65	49.14 -87
Ivanov	Mikhail	SU	26 Dec 62	185/106	SP	19.18	19.46 -86
Ivanov	Nikolay	BUL	6 Aug 63	182/82	TJ	16.89	16.49i -87, 16.44 -86
Ivanov	Sergey	SU	3 Jan 62	182/110	HT	77.88	81.10 -87
Jackson	Colin	UK	18 Feb 67	183/75	110h	13.11A, 13.21	13.37 -87
Jackson	Reggie	USA	5 Jul 69	183/73	TJ	16.61	15.20 -87
Jackson	Roosevelt	USA	4 Apr 62	180/69	800	1:46.84	
Jackson	William	USA	2 Feb 69	170/64	100	10.31	10.57 -87
Jacoby	Jake	USA	24 Sep 61	198/82	HJ	2.29	2.31 -87
Jadi	Nordin M.	MAL	12 Jun 62	170/62	400	45.84	46.56 -87
Jakubczyk	Janusz	POL	20 Jul 59	183/86	JT	76.58	81.88* -85
James	Charles	USA	19 Jul 64	180/77	110h	13.58A, 13.78	13.66, 13.59w -85
James	Ian	CAN	17 Jul 63	178/73	LJ	8.00	8.09 -86, 8.11w -87
James	Rob	USA	3 May 61	188/118	DT	61.30	60.84 -86
Jankowski	Henryk	POL	15 Oct 61	180/67	3kSt	8:23.70	8:22.33 -86
Jaros	Ralf	FRG	13 Dec 65	193/83	LJ	7.93i	7.49 -87
Jarrett	Tony	UK	13 Aug 68	188/82	110h	13.45, 13.35w	13.72 -87
Jasinski	Miroslaw	FRG	5 May 59	201/128	DT	60.84	63.16 -86
Jedrusik	Tomasz	POL	3 Feb 69	173/65	400	45.27	45.96 -87
Jefferson	Jaime	CUB	17 Jan 62	189/78	LJ	8.37A, 8.34	8.51 -87
Jefferson	Thomas	USA	6 Aug 62	183/75	200	20.52, 20.1	20.26, 20.21w -84
Jefferson	Tyrus	USA	14 Sep 65	183/74	LJ	8.04/8.15w	8.13 -87, 8.21w -86
Jenkel	Kai	SWZ	24 Feb 64	184/68	1500	3:39.08	3:41.21 -87
Jensen	Erik	DEN	4 Jun 62	189/85	110h	13.83	13.82 -87
Jenssen	Olav	NOR	11 May 62	193/115	DT	64.54	63.32 -87
Jerzy	Rafal	POL	27 Apr 66	179/62	800	1:46.55	1:46.49 -87
Jett	Rod	USA	28 Oct 66	183/77	110h	13.64	13.68 -87
Jianhua	Zhu	CHN	29 May 63	193/70	HJ	2.28	2.39 -84
Jönsson	Stefan	SWE	14 Feb 64	186/109	HT	74.48	73.66 -87
Johnson	Ben	CAN	30 Dec 61	177/77	100	9.98A/9.79dq/9.90w	9.83/9.7w -87
Johnson	Charles	USA	6 Nov 68		110h	13.84w	
Johnson	Dave	USA	7 Apr 63	189/86	Dec	8245	8203w -86
Johnson	Lewis	USA	13 Dec 62	180/75	1k	2:18.44	-0-
Johnson	Mike	USA	13 Sep 67	183/77	100	10.19w	
					200	20.07	20.41 -87
					400	45.23	46.29 -87
Johnson	Patterson	BAH	26 Aug 64	181/73	TJ	16.94	16.37, 16.64w -87
Johnson	Robert	USA	61	180/75	110h	13.82w	13.95, 13.93, 13.6 -81
Johnson	Terry	USA	7 Dec 66	185/82	110h	13.77	14.03, 13.82w -87
Johnson	Thomas	USA	7 Jun 65	170/68	400	45.68A	45.69 -86
					800	1:46.21	1:47.33 -87
Jones	Albert	USA	8 Oct 62	180/86	110h	13.70w	13.78 -83, 13.60w -84
Jones	David	USA	69		200	20.74w	
Jones	David	USA	7 Jul 66	183/76	400h	50.31	50.98 -87
Jones	Greg	USA	21 Aug 65	188/70	HJ	2.26i, 2.26	2.30 -86
Jones	Hugh	UK	1 Nov 55	179/61	Mar	2:11:08	2:09:24 -82
Jones	Mike	UK	23 Jul 63	186/110	HT	72.10	70.42 -87
Jones	Steve	UK	4 Aug 55	178/62	Mar	2:08:20	2:07:13 -85
Jones	Tony	USA	30 Dec 65	168/62	100	10.26, 10.25w	10.44, 10.16w -87
					200	20.55	20.28 -87
Jonker	Johan	RSA	19 Mar 70		400h	50.36A	-0-
Jørgensen	Henrik	DEN	10 Oct 61	178/59	Mar	2:10:20	2:09:43 -85
Jossa	Ralf	GDR	2 Nov 66	189/97	HT	73.76	73.50 -87
Journoud	Patrick	FRA	27 Apr 64	190/103	DT	63.02	62.36 -87
Joyner	Al	USA	19 Jan 60	186/81	110h	13.41	13.51 -85
Joyner	Al	USA	19 Jan 60	186/81	TJ	16.79, 17.58w	17.53 -87
Jules	Dazel	TRI	10 Aug 67	184/65	200	20.1w	20.87 -86, 20.4 -87
Junkermann	Mark	USA	27 Jun 65	172/62	3kSt	8:32.94	8:31.55 -87
Juzyszyn	Dariusz	POL	29 Mar 57	200/120	DT	62.92	65.98 -85

Name		Nat	Born	Ht/Wt	Event	1988 Mark	Pre-1988 Best
Kachkovskiy	Gennadiy	SU	12 Mar 64	178/67	PV	5.60	5.40 -86
Kärnä	Jarmo	FIN	4 Aug 58	180/82	LJ	8.04	8.06, 8.12w -87
Kaitany	Richard	KEN	17 Jun 58	170/66	Mar	2:09:39	2:14:50 -84
Kakhno	Gennadiy	SU	3 Apr 64	180/69	TJ	16.67i	16.49 -83, 16.66w -86
Kalboussi	Mahmoud	TUN	9 Feb 65	185/65	1500	3:38.17	
Kaleta	Marek	SU	17 Dec 61	185/88	JT	81.22	82.00 -86
Kalinkin	Viktor	SU	23 Feb 60	180/70	800	1:45.8m	1:44.73 -84
					1500	3:37.1m	3:37.1 -84
Kallenberg	Stephan	FRG	4 Jul 63	188/88	Dec	7922	7698 -87
Kalogiannis	Athanassios	GRE	10 Sep 65	193/80	400h	49.36	48.80 -87
Kalugin	Vadim	SU	3 Jul 68	183/95	HT	72.62	71.64 -87
Kamau	Gabriel	KEN	20 Mar 57	172/64	10k	28:10.93	27:36.2 -82
Kanai	Yutaka	JAP	16 Oct 59	178/64	10k	28:15.01	27:55.05 -85
					Mar	2:12:51	2:13:42 -86
Kaniecki	Krzysztof	POL	23 Jun 65	184/75	LJ	7.96	7.93 -86
Kaptyukh	Vasiliy	SU	27 Jun 67	201/110	DT	61.60	60.24 -86
Karan	Sasa	YUG	7 Apr 65	190/83	Dec	7877	7728 -87
Karaulic	Branislav	YUG	8 Apr 63	180/75	400h	49.57	50.26 -87
Kargin	Sergey	SU	3 Jul 62	182/75	LJ	8.06	8.11 -87
Kariuki	Julius	KEN	12 Jun 61	181/62	1500	3:38.02	3:37.79 -86
					3kSt	8:05.51	8:15.92 -86
Karl	Hubert	FRG	24 Dec 63	197/76	3kSt	8:33.39	8:41.04 -86
Karpov	Yevgeniy	SU	6 Nov 66		DT	65.08	61.66 -87
Kashapov	Ravil	SU	15 Nov 56	170/61	10k	27:56.75	28:18.40 -82
					Mar	2:11:19	2:12:43 -87
Kassubek	Peter	FRG	10 Jun 59	195/130	SP	19.53	19.34i, 19.31 -86
Kauerauf	Steffen	GDR	9 May 66	194/90	JT	76.64	73.52 -87
Kayukov	Andrey	SU	12 Apr 64	187/75	TJ	17.23	17.02 -86
Kazanov	Igor	SU	24 Sep 63	186/81	110h	13.38, 13.1	13.38 -87, 13.14w -86
Kazeka	Yuriy	SU	66		PV	5.50	5.30 -87
Kearney	Clayton	AUS	11 Apr 64	184/83	100	10.16w	10.43, 10.37w -86
Kemp	Troy	BAH	18 Mar 66	187/69	HJ	2.30i, 2.27	2.28 -87
Kenworthy	Dave	USA	27 Jun 60	183/75	PV	5.64i, 5.55	5.65i, 5.65-87
Kerho	Steve	USA/CAN	24 Mar 64	188/75	110h	13.52A, 13.61, 13.51wA	13.57 -87
Kerr	Stanley	USA	19 Jun 67	173/70	100	10.26w	10.10 -86, 10.09w/10.0w-87
					200	20.40	20.28-87, 20.10w -86
Kersh	George	USA	3 Jul 68	177/64	800	1:45.35	1:46.58 -87
					1k	2:18.44	-0-
Keskitalo	Petri	FIN	10 Mar 67	187/87	Dec	8143	8016 -87
Khalifa	Omer	SUD	18 Dec 56	177/64	1500	3:38.40	3:33.28 -86
Kharitonov	Igor	SU	7 Dec 62	187/75	LJ	8.11	8.08 -86
Kharlov	Aleksandr	SU	18 Mar 58	193/80	400h	49.80	48.78 -83
Khitryakov	Igor	SU	15 Jul 65		110h	13.49	13.75, 13.53w, 13.5 -86
Khristov	Sabin	BUL	21 Feb 67	180/110	HT	72.52	71.08 -87
Khristov	Ventsislav	BUL	18 May 62	188/110	SP	20.32	20.83 -85
Kibet	Robert	KEN	65		800	1:46.7mA	1:49.9 -86
Kibret	Bidelu	ETH	69		10k	28:12.78	28:30.10 -87
Kidikas	Vaclavas	SU	17 Oct 61	197/110	DT	68.44	67.34 -85
Kilbert	Gert	SWZ	21 Sep 65	165/56	800	1:46.78	1:45.46 -87
Kilpi	Jouko	FIN	21 Apr 61	190/78	HJ	2.24	2.24 -85
Kim	Won-tak	KOR	21 Jul 64	171/56	Mar	2:12:41	2:12:26 -87
Kim	Yong-gil	KOR			Mar	2:13:08	
Kim	Yong-Il	KOR	11 Sep 62	178/70	LJ	8.00	7.94-82,7.98A-81,8.09w -84
Kimeli	Kipkemboi	KEN	30 Nov 66	173/64	5k	13:35.32	13:21.21- 87
					10k	27:25.16	28:17.20 -87
Kimble	Ray	USA	19 Apr 53	183/84	TJ	17.15i/16.95/17.53w	17.36/17.39w-87
Kinder	Gary	USA	25 Oct 62	186/86	Dec	8293	8227 -87
King	Emmit	USA	24 Mar 59	175/78	100	10.04, 9.98w	10.06 -83
Kingdom	Roger	USA	26 Aug 62	185/91	110h	12.97A/12.98	13.14 -85
							13.1, 13.00w -84
Kinnunen	Kimmo	FIN	31 Mar 68	186/83	JT	80.24	72.94 -87
Kinyor	Barnabas	KEN	61		400h	50.2A	52.6 -87
Kio	Joshua	NIG	7 Sep 57	176/72	TJ	16.75	16.69 -82
Kipkemboi	Joshua	KEN	22 Feb 60	170/60	1500	3:39.4mA	3:41.02 -83
					3k	7:48.19	7:58.19 -83
					3kSt	8:18.02	8:14.13 -86

Name		Nat	Born	Ht/Wt	Event	1988 Mark	Pre-1988 Best
Kipkemboi	Simon	KEN	15 Apr 60	190/74	400	45.44, 45.0A	
Kiprotich	Nixon	KEN	4 Dec 62	185/68	800	1:44.5mA	1:46.8A -87
Kirati	Sisa	KEN	57		800	1:45.9mA	1:47.0 -86
					1500	3:37.4mA	3:38.6A -87
Kirochi	Wilfred Oanda	KEN	12 Dec 69	167/62	800	1:47.2m	1:47.8 -87
					1k	2:18.94	-0-
					1500	3:36.07	3:39.01 -87
Kisheyev	Vladimir	SU	4 Dec 58	193/108	SP	21.16	20.29i-87, 20.07 -84
					DT	61.32	61.12 -83
Kita	Hideki	JAP	28 Sep 52	172/60	Mar	2:11:51	2:10:30 -83
Kitur	Simon	KEN	12 Jun 59	182/74	400h	49.74, 48.9A	49.70-84, 49.4A -87
Klassen	Steve	USA	15 Feb 65	180/77	PV	5.57	5.50 -86
Kleiza	Saulius	SU	2 Apr 64	184/125	SP	20.40	20.91 -87
Klenov	Sergey	SU	11 Jun 67	175/70	100	10.33	10.36 -87
					200	20.1w	21.04- 85, 20.6 -86
Klimaszewski	Andrzej	POL	14 May 60	185/78	LJ	7.96, 7.99w	8.20, 8.33w -80
Klimenko	Aleksandr	SU	27 Mar 70	194/109	SP	19.18i, 19.18	16.69 -87
Klimes	Pavel	UK	27 Oct 58	177/60	Mar	2:12:59	2:14:07 -87
Knabe	Wolfgang	FRG	12 Jul 59	183/75	TJ	17.12, 17.31w	16.81 -83
Kneissler	Bernd	FRG	13 Sep 62	198/130	DT	60.84	61.86 -86
Knowles	Derrick	BAH	22 Mar 66	188/75	110h	13.79, 13.50w, 13.5	13.77 -87
Kobylyanskiy	Vadim	SU	25 Jan 61	180/73	LJ	7.99	8.28 -84
Kobza	Marty	USA	6 Mar 62	194/118	SP	20.20i, 19.12	20.36 -85
Kocherga	Valeriy	SU	12 Sep 63	191/120	HT	78.12	78.92 -86
Kodama	Taisuke	JAP	26 Jul 58	165/49	Mar	2:11:38	2:07:35 -86
Kodentsev	Vadim	SU	2 Feb 64		PV	5.70	5.70 -86
Koech	Peter	KEN	18 Feb 58	180/67	3k	7:46.33	7:39.09 -82
					3kSt	8:06.79	8:13.33 -86
Köhrbrück	Carsten	FRG	26 Jun 66	185/70	400h	50.08	50.55 -87
Koeleman	Hans	HOL	5 Oct 57	181/67	3kSt	8:20.56	8:18.02 -85
König	Stefan	FRG	25 Aug 66	182/84	JT	77.78	77.66 -87
Kohls	Matthias	FRG	23 Feb 61	181/61	3kSt	8:31.29	8:34.41 -87
Kohnle	Michael	FRG	3 May 70	191/80	Dec	7790	7279 -87
Koivuniemi	Kauko	FIN	22 Dec 58	192/95	JT	76.32	73.26 -86
Kokhanovskiy	Andrey	SU	11 Jan 68	194/112	DT	62.78	60.06 -87
Kolasa	Marian	POL	12 Aug 59	197/90	PV	5.70	5.81i -86, 5.80 -85
Kolasa	Ryszard	POL	17 Apr 64	184/82	PV	5.50	5.60 -85
Kolb	Matt	USA	4 Feb 64	183/75	PV	5.50	5.50 -87
Kolesnik	Vadim	SU	29 Jan 69	184/105	HT	72.62	72.16 -87
Kolnootchenko	Georgiy	SU	7 May 59	197/115	DT	65.60	69.44 -82
Konovalov	Ivan	SU	6 Jul 59	175/64	3kSt	8:32.12	8:19.38 -85
Kontaxakis	Panagiotis	GRE	16 Aug 64	186/74	HJ	2.28	2.24 -87
Konya	Kalman	FRG	27 Oct 61	191/115	SP	19.52	19.01i -87, 19.00 -86
Kopitar	Rok	YUG	5 May 59	180/71	400h	49.76	49.11 -80
Koprivichin	Rumen	BUL	2 Oct 62	188/100	HT	75.14	74.02 -87
Korir	Barnabas	KEN	65	168/59	1500	3:39.36	3:42.31 -85
Korir	Julius	KEN	21 Apr 60	172/64	3kSt	8:26.76	8:11.80 -84
Korjus	Tapio	FIN	10 Feb 61	196/105	JT	86.50	79.52 -87
Kornilov	Arkadiy	SU	25 Feb 63	185/74	400	45.82	45.80 -86
Korniyenko	Vladimir	SU	28 Jan 66	178/70	HJ	2.31i, 2.27	2.25 -86
Korobkov	Ilya	SU	66		1500	3:39.0	
Koromyslov	Vasiliy	SU	15 May 57		3kSt	8:29.94	8:29.17 -87
Koroteyev	Andrey	SU	6 Oct 66	189/80	110h	13.62, 13.6	14.02, 13.6 -87
Korovin	Vyacheslav	SU	8 Sep 62		HT	79.24	82.24 -87
Koskei	Sam	KEN	14 May 61	183/68	800	1:44.06	1:42.28 -84
					1k	2:16.86	2:14.95 -85
Kostenich	Aleksey	SU	30 Oct 66	192/78	Dec	7719M	7395 -87
Kostin	Mikhail	SU	10 May 59	194/120	SP	21.39i, 21.19	21.96 -86
Kostrubala	Gary	USA	30 Jun 64	188/100	DT	61.90	61.66 -87
Kosyanok	Nikolay	SU	25 Feb 58	177/78	JT	80.20	80.20 -87
Koszewski	Dietmar	FRG	26 Jul 67	193/89	110h	13.74, 13.69w	14.03, 13.93w -87
Kot	Sergey	SU	7 Jan 60		SP	20.26	20.55 -86
Kotelnikov	Boris	SU	65		HT	78.30	78.14 -87
Kotovich	Aleksandr	SU	6 Nov 61	183/76	HJ	2.32i, 2.25	2.35i -85, 2.33 -84
Koutsoukis	Dimitrios	GRE	8 Dec 62	193/120	SP	20.29	20.59 -86
					DT	61.74	58.18 -87

Name		Nat	Born	Ht/Wt	Event	1988 Mark	Pre-1988 Best
Kovács	Attila	HUN	2 Sep 60	180/72	100	10.26, 10.17w	10.09 -87
Kovalenko	Aleksandr	SU	8 May 63	178/80	TJ	17.47	17.77 -87
Kovár	Stanislav	CS	6 May 64	196/91	DT	61.12	59.70 -87
Kovtsun	Dmitriy	SU	29 Sep 55	191/116	SP	19.17idq	19.28 -82
					DT	67.06dq	68.64 -84
Kowalski	Lech	POL	17 Jan 61	188/100	HT	72.40	73.28 -85
Kozakiewicz	Wladyslaw	FRG	8 Dec 53	187/86	PV	5.55i, 5.52	5.78 -80
Kozasu	Toru	JAP	4 Jul 64		Mar	2:12:42	2:21:31 -85
Kozul	Djordje	YUG	31 Dec 63	187/75	TJ	16.96	17.11 -87
Kram	Rachid	ALG	5 Apr 63	180/63	1500	3:36.26	3:40.17 -87
Kraminskiy	Andrey	SU	27 Mar 63	180/69	800	1:46.0m	1:48.22 -87
Krasovskiy	Sergey	SU	18 May 63	192/85	110h	13.58, 13.4	13.70 -87, 13.6 -84
Krastev	Plamen	BUL	18 Nov 58	187/76	110h	13.77	13.46, 13.4 -84
Kravchenko	Sergey	SU	20 May 66	182/69	LJ	8.08	7.83 -87
Krawczyk	Krzysztof	POL	28 Jan 62	186/74	HJ	2.32	2.31 -86
Krdzalic	Sejad	YUG	5 Jan 60	187/96	JT	82.70	83.34 -87
Krieger	Helmut	POL	17 Jul 58	196/137	SP	21.03	21.30 -86
Krippschock	Axel	GDR	5 Feb 62	193/58	10k	27:57.68	28:09.16 -87
Krizhanovskiy	Valeriy	SU	6 Mar 62	197/122	SP	19.24	
Krohn	Bill	USA	9 Mar 58	180/65	3k	7:51.44	7:50.27 -85
Krsek	Ivo	CS	21 Mar 67	184/78	LJ	7.95	8.03 -87, 8.04w -86
Kruger	Alex	UK	18 Nov 63	193/86	Dec	7707	7280w, 7228 -87
Krulee	Marty	USA	4 Nov 56	170/68	100	10.25/10.06w	10.19/10.16w/10.0-83
					200	20.30	20.51 -83, 20.3 -86
Krylov	Vladimir	SU	26 Feb 64	184/73	100	10.13	10.16 -86, 9.9 -85
					200	20.62	20.23 -87
Kryuchkov	Vladimir	SU	28 Jul 62	189/85	Dec	7752	7883m -87
Kubista	Jan	CS	27 May 60	193/81	1500	3:36.47	3:34.87 -83
Kucej	Jozef	CS	23 Mar 65	181/72	400h	49.40	49.86 -87
Kudo	Kazuyoshi	JAP	27 Feb 61	169/54	Mar	2:10:59	2:11:36 -87
Külvet	Valter	SU	19 Feb 64	190/91	Dec	8506	8332 -87
Kufahl	Carsten	FRG	14 Nov 67	203/105	DT	64.94	59.76 -87
Kuhn	Bodo	FRG	9 Aug 67	183/73	400	45.77	46.44 -87
Kuhn	Frédéric	FRA	10 Jul 68	180/100	HT	73.24	73.28 -87
Kula	Dainis	SU	28 Apr 59	190/98	JT	79.06	77.34 -87
Kulish	Mikhail	SU	20 Mar 64	191/103	SP	20.89	20.03 -87
Kulker	Han	HOL	15 Aug 59	183/64	1500	3:36.99	3:36.08 -87
Kuncicky	Radim	CS	18 May 67	175/59	1500	3:39.41	3:39.78 -87
Kunze	Hansjörg	GDR	28 Dec 59	179/63	5k	13:15.73	13:10.40 -81
					10k	27:26.00	27:30.69 -83
Kuoppa	Jari	FIN	25 Jun 60	190/105	SP	19.81	20.46 -86
Kurochkin	Aleksandr	SU	23 Jul 61	192/89	400	45.94	45.52, 45.3 -84
Kuzyanin	Andrey	SU	25 Jun 60		DT	66.26	63.42 -87
Kverek	Libor	CS	14 Mar 67	184/82	JT	77.54	75.00 -87
Kvernmo	Geir	NOR	29 Oct 55	184/66	Mar	2:11:44	2:10:17 -87
Kwizera	Dieudonné	BUR	6 Jun 67	184/60	800	1:44.82	1:45.06 -87
					1500	3:38.13	3:44.27 -87
Kyeswa	Moses	UGA	12 Apr 58	178/68	400	45.96	45.70 -87
Lachaal	Mustapha	MOR	10 Feb 64	172/58	1500	3:35.78	3:42.72 -86
Lacika	Jozef	CS	8 Jun 61	193/125	SP	19.43	20.36 -86
Ladányi	Zsigmond	HUN	4 Aug 61	191/106	SP	19.98i, 19.66	20.07 -87
Lafranchi	Bruno	SWZ	19 Jul 55	178/60	Mar	2:11:58	2:11:12 -82
Lahbi	Faouzi	MOR	2 Mar 58	176/60	800	1:45.11	1:44.66 -86
Lahlali	Djamel	FRA	21 Mar 63	176/62	3kSt	8:34.39	8:42.32 -87
Laine	Gordon	USA	24 Feb 58	180/70	LJ	8.25, 8.31w	8.24 -87
Laine	Yki	FIN	16 May 65	185/85	JT	79.58	76.12 -86
Lakafia	Jean-Paul	FRA	29 Jun 61	192/93	JT	78.88	78.96 -87
Lambruschini	Alessandro	ITA	7 Jan 65	178/63	1k	2:18.12	-0-
					1500	3:38.3m	3:35.27 -87
					3kSt	8:12.17	8:18.39 -86
Lancaster	Chris	USA	23 Dec 65	178/75	110h	13.74, 13.6	13.88 -86, 13.78w -87
					400h	49.95	
Langhammer	Uwe	GDR	12 Jun 65	191/81	PV	5.60	5.65 -87
Laporte	Stéphane	FRA	17 Jul 66	192/90	JT	80.76	76.36 -87
Lapshin	Igor	SU	8 Aug 63	188/71	LJ	7.98	7.97 -85
					TJ	17.69	17.20 -86

Name		Nat	Born	Ht/Wt	Event	1988 Mark	Pre-1988 Best
Larkins	Paul	UK	19 May 63	183/64	1500	3:37.57	3:35.94 -87
					2k	5:01.48	-0-
Lattany	Mel	USA	10 Aug 59	175/79	100	10.33	9.96 -84, 9.9 -82
							9.95w, 9.8w -83
Laukkanen	Juha	FIN	6 Jan 69	186/86	JT	77.08	79.46 -87
Laushkin	Vadim	SU	5 Feb 65	176/68	800	1:46.94	1:46.68 -85
Laut	Dave	USA	21 Dec 56	193/114	SP	20.99	22.02 -82
Lautenslager	Greg	USA	15 Oct 57	180/64	3k	7:51.05	7:54.17 -86
Laventure	Cyrille	FRA	29 Mar 64	187/62	3k	7:46.84	7:48.20 -85
					5k	13:18.29	13:30.69 -86
Laverty	Dale	USA	30 Apr 65	183/81	400h	50.03	48.72A -86, 49.27 -85
Lawrence	Wendell	BAH	67		TJ	16.79, 16.91w	16.51i -87
Lawson	Rod	USA	22 Jan 67	188/67	110h	13.84	
Lawyer	David	USA			200	20.71w	
Layevskiy	Sergey	SU	3 Mar 59	184/72	LJ	8.35	8.32 -84
Lazare	Alain	FRA	23 Mar 52	169/53	Mar	2:12:24	2:11:59 -84
Lazarevic	Jovan	YUG	3 May 52	194/114	SP	20.03	20.49 -81
Lazdins	Ray	CAN	25 Sep 64	198/110	DT	63.38	61.60 -87
Leach	Jason	USA	11 Mar 66	178/64	100	10.20	10.26 -85
					200	20.57	20.93, 20.60w -86
Lecurieux	Philippe	FRA	22 May 58	187/90	JT	76.80	75.26 -86
Lefévre	Pascal	FRA	25 Jan 65	190/92	JT	81.48	80.60 -87
Legeda	Anatoliy	SU	27 Oct 62	172/61	1500	3:37.3	3:37.17 -84
Lenstrohm	John	USA	27 Feb 61	183/75	110h	13.72A	13.59 -82
Leonov	Aleksandr	SU	7 Feb 62	177/75	TJ	17.39i	17.45 -87
Lepik	Sulev	SU	22 Jul 66	189/90	JT	79.58	75.90 -87
Lesov	Delko	BUL	6 Jan 67	181/69	PV	5.73i, 5.60	5.60 -87
Lestage	Franck	FRA	20 Apr 68	181/70	LJ	7.95	7.84, 7.97w -87
LeStum	Bruno	FRA	25 Dec 59	179/57	3kSt	8:19.15	8:17.69 -87
Leturgez	Bryan	USA	3 Aug 62	180/78	400h	50.17	50.86 -86, 50.7- 87
Letyuchiy	Anatoliy	SU	8 Jun 64	193/100	DT	61.40	60.08 -87
Levant	Bruno	FRA	24 Jan 60	180/69	1500	3:37.73	3:35.83 -87
					5k	13:31.03	13:31.77 -86
Leveille	Pierre	CAN	19 Feb 62	184/74	400h	50.52	50.32A -84, 50.84 - 86
Lewin	Rainer	GDR	5 Mar 67	178/73	PV	5.50	5.30 -86
Lewis	Carl	USA	1 Jul 61	188/80	100	9.92,	9.93 -87
						9.78w	9.90w -85, 9.9 -82
					200	19.79	19.75 -83
					LJ	8.76	8.79 -83
Lewis	David	UK	15 Oct 61	180/68	3k	7:50.27	7:42.47 -83
					5k	13:30.69	13:21.15 -85
					10k	28:08.44	-0-
Lewis	Dennis	USA	20 Mar 59	193/81	HJ	2.30i, 2.28	2.34 -85
Lewis	Steve	USA	16 May 69	188/84	400	43.87	45.76 -87
Ligans	Robert	USA	27 Jun 68	170/68	100	10.27, 10.24w	10.48w -87
Lindner	Johann	AUT	3 May 59	188/110	HT	77.70	79.70 -87
Lisitskiy	Sergey	SU	23 Jul 63	195/96	Dec	7702	7735 -87
Little	Kevin	USA	3 Apr 68	183/68	200	20.55	21.04, 20.80w -87
Litvinenko	Dmitriy	SU	12 Aug 63	184/72	TJ	16.77	16.86 -86
Litvinov	Sergey	SU	23 Jan 58	180/106	HT	84.80	86.04 -86
Lloyd	Andrew	AUS	14 Feb 59	172/53	5k	13:36.15	13:25.2 -87
					10k	28:25.00	27:57.34 -87
Logan	Jud	USA	19 Jul 59	193/125	HT	81.88	80.88 -86
Lohr	Lane	USA	10 Sep 64	188/75	PV	5.59	5.56i, 5.53 -87
Lomtyev	Yevgeniy	SU	20 Oct 61	184/73	400	45.64	45.05 -84
Long	Calvin	USA	2 Jul 66	193/91	100	10.32	10.28 -85
					200	20.71	20.95 -85
					400	45.43	45.35, 45.1A -85
Long	Dave	UK	21 Nov 60	180/71	Mar	2:11:33	2:14:42 -86
Lopez	Juan	CUB	7 Apr 67	189/81	TJ	17.28	16.81, 16.94w -86
Lorentzen	Reidar	NOR	22 Sep 56	180/85	JT	80.06	78.10 -87
Lotarev	Igor	SU	30 Aug 64	181/66	1500	3:37.2m	3:34.49 -85
Lott	James	USA	13 Oct 65	186/83	HJ	2.31i, 2.31	2.31 -87
Lovegrove	Gavin	NZ	21 Oct 67	187/90	JT	80.70	79.60 -87
Lowery	Ken	USA	13 Aug 61	192/80	400	45.92	45.40 -87
Lubensky	Zdenek	CS	3 Dec 62	185/75	PV	5.65	5.73 -87

Name		Nat	Born	Ht/Wt	Event	1988 Mark	Pre-1988 Best
Lucas	Joël	FRA	11 Mar 52	177/60	3k	7:49.41	7:55.73 -83
					5k	13:32.42	13:47.15 -81
					10k	28:16.32	28:44.28 -85
Lucero	Ben	USA	22 Jun 62	186/70	HJ	2.26	2.25 -82
Lübke	Ralf	FRG	17 Jun 65	192/80	200	20.76	20.38 -85
					400	45.20	44.98 -86
Lukashenko	Aleksey	SU	29 Mar 67	185/100	SP	19.35	19.06 -86
Lutkovskiy	Vladislav	SU	12 Dec 67	179/70	PV	5.50i	5.50 -87
Lyach	Aleksey	SU	4 May 62	193/86	Dec	8203	8108 -85
Lyakhov	Sergey	SU	68		DT	62.64	60.06 -87
Lykho	Vyacheslav	SU	16 Jan 67	196/120	SP	20.96	21.20 -87
Lysenko	Nikolay	SU	14 Jul 66	185/100	HT	80.32	78.02 -87
Maas	Frans	HOL	13 Jul 64	196/89	LJ	8.06i/8.01A/8.27wA	7.96/8.02w -87
Maaskola	Mika	FIN	15 Sep 66	178/55	1500	3:38.50	3:39.61 -87
Machura	Remigius	CS	3 Jul 60	187/118	SP	21.71i, 20.94	21.93 -87
Madonia	Ezio	ITA	7 Aug 66	175/70	100	10.27	10.52, 10.39w -87
Mächler	Arnold	SWZ	11 May 64	188/70	5k	13:36.16	13:55.96 -87
Mahmoud	Joseph	FRA	13 Dec 55	174/65	3kSt	8:22.76	8:07.62 -84
Mahorn	Atlee	CAN	27 Oct 65	187/79	100	10.28,10.20w	10.26-86,10.19w -85
					200	20.20	20.34, 20.31w -86
Mahovlich	Mike	CAN	27 Aug 60	186/110	JT	79.56	79.04 -86
Mai	Volker	GDR	3 May 66	194/75	TJ	17.23	17.50 -85
Mair	John	JAM	20 Nov 63	175/74	100	10.32	10.24 -87
							10.16w -86, 10.1 -85
Makin	Michael	UK	1 Mar 62	183/76	TJ	16.60	16.87 -86
Makoena	Daniel	RSA	9 Sep 58		800	1:46.57A	1:46.87A -87
Makovskiy	Fyodor	SU	64		HT	76.40	74.64 -85
Maksimov	Sergey	SU	13 Dec 63		10k	28:25.13	28:35.57 -87
Malakhovskis	Richardas	SU	28 Apr 65	193/83	Dec	8437	8108 -86
Malát	Milan	CS	10 Mar 67	180/94	HT	73.58	72.00 -87
Malave	Jesus	VEN	24 Oct 65	170/64	400	45.61A	45.68 -87
Malchenko	Sergey	SU	2 Nov 63	190/74	HJ	2.38	2.33 -86
Maletskiy	Aleksandr	SU	13 Jun 66	180/74	TJ	17.23	16.50 -87
Mamchur	Nikolay	SU	9 Oct 63	187/82	TJ	17.11	16.97i, 16.97 -87
Maminski	Boguslaw	POL	18 Dec 55	181/68	3kSt	8:15.97	8:09.18 -84
Manderson	Floyd	UK	5 Mar 61	191/90	HJ	2.25	2.20 -85
Mann	Patrick	USA	24 Apr 66	180/77	400h	50.22	49.80 -87
Manns	Dezalya	USA	9 Nov 64	186/85	LJ	8.22	8.12 -87
Manson	Pat	USA	29 Nov 67	178/70	PV	5.65	5.50 -87
Mansour	Talal	QAT	64	180/78	100	10.33	10.29 -87
Maravilha	Alberto	POR	27 Dec 65		10k	28:25.8m	-0-
Marden	Jay	USA	22 Mar 63	183/67	5k	13:36.93	13:44.2 -87
					10k	28:00.38	
Mardi	Afdiharto	INA	19 Jan 68	166/62	100	10.32	10.36 -87
Mardle	Paul	UK	10 Nov 62	191/110	DT	61.16	61.86 -84
Maree	Sydney	USA	9 Sep 56	180/66	1500	3:36.47	3:29.77 -85
					Mile	3:52.85	3:48.83 -81
					2k	5:04.3	4:54.20 -85
					3k	7:38.79	7:33.37 -82
					5k	13:15.85	13:01.15 -85
Marie-Rose	Bruno	FRA	20 May 65	193/83	100	10.25A, 10.26, 10.11w	10.18 -86
					200	20.45A, 20.48	20.50, 20.36i-87
Marincic	Petr	CS	15 Mar 65	178/64	400h	49.95	51.81 -87
Marinkovic	Andreja	YUG	23 Jan 65	190/77	LJ	7.98, 8.04wA	7.86 -83
Marinov	Robert	BUL	1 Feb 67	187/72	HJ	2.25	2.28 -87
Maritim	Joseph	KEN	22 Oct 68	184/68	400h	49.50, 49.3A	49.33A -87
Markin	Aleksandr	SU	8 Sep 62	185/78	110h	13.20	13.39, 13.25w -86
Marko	Gabor	HUN	7 Feb 60	184/63	3kSt	8:27.30	8:17.97 -84
Markov	Khristo	BUL	27 Jan 65	185/76	TJ	17.77	17.92 -87
Marlow	Gary	UK	26 Nov 63	178/70	800	1:46.13	1:46.10 -87
Marquetti	Hector	CUB	7 Apr 68	175/70	TJ	16.66	16.91 -87
Marschner	Torsten	GDR	17 Nov 68	193/77	HJ	2.28	2.21 -86
Marsh	Henry	USA	15 Mar 54	178/72	3kSt	8:14.39	8:09.17 -85
Marsh	Mike	USA	4 Aug 67	178/68	100	10.12, 9.94w	10.22-86, 10.16w -87
					200	20.35	20.59, 20.52w -87
Marshall	Brian	CAN	1 Apr 65	198/90	HJ	2.28	2.24 -86

Name		Nat	Born	Ht/Wt	Event	1988 Mark	Pre-1988 Best
Marshall	John	USA	5 Nov 63	190/74	800	1:45.79	1:43.92 -84
Martin	Eamonn	UK	9 Oct 58	183/67	3k	7:49.2	7:40.94 -83
					2M	8:18.98	8:25.66 -87
					5k	13:22.88	13:20.94 -83
					10k	27:23.06	-0-
Martin	Roy	USA	25 Dec 66	183/79	200	20.05	20.13 -85, 20.0w -87
Martin	Vince	USA	22 Aug 67	175/73	LJ	7.97	7.72 -87
Martinez	Juan	CUB	17 May 58	186/122	DT	66.24	70.00 -83
Martinez	Lazaro	CUB	11 Nov 62	180/75	400	45.55	45.37 -83
Martinez	Richard	USA	31 Jul 63	170/64	1500	3:39.05	
Martino	Marco	ITA	21 Feb 60	190/108	DT	65.16	66.90 -84
Maryin	Igor	SU	28 Apr 65		Dec	8364	8147 -85
Mason	Kevin	USA	17 Jun 67	188/75	400h	49.54	49.27 -87
Masunov	Leonid	SU	5 May 62	183/72	800	1:46.9	1:45.08 -84
Mateescu	Mugur	RUM	13 Jun 69	181/65	400h	50.43	52.25 -87
Matei	Sorin	RUM	6 Jul 63	184/71	HJ	2.37	2.35 -85
Matete	Samuel	ZAM	27 Jul 65	175/73	400	45.89	
Matias	Manuel	POR	30 Mar 62	172/58	Mar	2:10:19	
Mattern	Stefan	FRG	11 May 65	185/81	110h	13.78	13.98 -87
Matthes	Sven	GDR	23 Aug 69	186/77	100	10.14	10.35 -87
Matthias	Brendan	CAN	12 Aug 69	182/68	1500	3:39.1m	3:47.66 -87
Maude	Ado	NIG	15 Feb 67		800	1:46.97	1:47.56 -87
Maynard	Mike	USA	24 Jun 59	183/114	HT	72.14	70.60 -87
Mazzella	Alain	FRA	13 Nov 66	178/69	100	10.32w	10.42 -87, 10.37w -86
Mbaye	Hamidou	SEN	21 Apr 64	188/75	400h	50.22	A51.07 -87
McCandless	Richard	USA	16 Dec 55	172/64	Mar	2:12:44	2:14:39 -85
McCants	Tom	USA	27 Nov 62	185/79	HJ	2.37	2.32 -85
McCloy	Paul	CAN	6 Nov 63	187/70	10k	28:03.5m	27:56.8 -86
McCoy	Walter	USA	15 Nov 58	178/75	400	44.84	44.76 -84
McCraney	James	USA	28 Mar 55	188/82	110h	13.74/13.61w	13.55,13.43w,13.4-84
McCray	Reggie	USA	7 Aug 66	192/83	100	10.31w	10.3 -86
					200	20.42	21.14 -87
McCree	Ron	USA	21 Mar 68		100	10.32w	10.34 -87
McCullough	Conor	IRL	22 Mar 61	192/111	HT	74.16	72.06 -84
McDermott	Art	USA	7 Nov 61	183/114	DT	62.96	64.04 -84
McGee	Norm	USA	23 Mar 66	185/77	100	10.26, 10.20w	10.33 -85
					200	20.67w	21.05 -85
McGeorge	Chris	UK	13 Jan 62	176/65	Mile	3:56.71	3:58.97 -86
McGhee	Pat	USA	24 Jun 66	190/76	400h	48.83A, 48.98	49.65 -86
McGorty	Kevin	USA	12 Apr 65	183/77	Dec	7833	7560 -86
McHugh	Terry	IRL	22 Aug 63	191/97	JT	76.46	72.24 -87
McKay	Antonio	USA	9 Feb 64	183/75	400	44.79	44.69 -86
McKean	Tom	UK	27 Oct 63	181/71	800	1:45.05	1:44.45 -87
McKee	Gordon	USA	12 Oct 66	185/79	LJ	8.04	7.55, 7.70w -87
McKoy	Mark	CAN	10 Dec 61	181/79	110h	13.17	13.23 -87,13.0-85,13.16w -84
McLeod	Mike	UK	25 Jan 52	180/63	3k	7:49.11	7:48.18 -78
					10k	28:12.67	27:39.76 -79
McMichael	Tim	USA	22 Dec 67	172/64	PV	5.57	5.50 -87
McNeill	Eugene	USA	10 Dec 65	172/68	200	20.35	20.58, 20.45w -87
McNeill	Lee	USA	2 Dec 64	165/65	100	10.09, 10.08w, 10.0w	10.14-86,10.11w -85
McNeill	Lee	USA	2 Dec 64	165/65	200	20.71	20.60 -86
McRae	Lee	USA	23 Jan 66	176/71	100	10.11,10.05w	10.07-87,10.02w -86
McRae	Mike	USA	9 Jul 55	185/82	LJ	8.14	8.27, 8.34w -84
McSeveney	Greg	USA	29 May 59	190/118	DT	62.96	66.98 -85
Medved	Mikhail	SU	30 Jan 64	199/89	Dec	8330	8315 -86
Meghoo	Greg	JAM	11 Aug 65	180/74	200	20.76	20.94, 20.64w -87
Mei	Stefano	ITA	3 Feb 63	181/62	3k	7:48.48	7:42.85 -86
					5k	13:24.20	13:11.57 -86
					10k	27:57.06	27:43.97 -86
Mekonnen	Abebe	ETH	9 Jan 64	158/59	Mar	2:07:35	2:08:39 -86
Mekonnen	Tulu	ETH			Mar	2:12:29	
Melikhov	Vladimir	SU	30 Mar 69	186/76	TJ	16.76	
Mellaard	Emiel	HOL	21 Mar 66	189/74	LJ	8.19, 8.21w	8.02, 8.19w -87
Melnjak	Predrag	YUG	17 Mar 69	183/68	800	1:46.40i	1:47.2 -86
Melzer	Hagen	GDR	16 Jun 59	178/63	5k	13:31.64	-0-

Name		Nat	Born	Ht/Wt	Event	1988 Mark	Pre-1988 Best
					3kSt	8:16.27	8:10.32 -87
Menezes	Sergio	BRA	27 Apr 65	180/78	400	45.62	45.98 -85
Merande	Boniface	KEN	13 Feb 62	170/60	10k	27:40.36	29:12.0 -87
					3kSt	8:23.40	8:27.0A -86
Mestour	Mohamed	MOR	61		3kSt	8:30.84	8:35.92 -86
Metcalf	Eric	USA	23 Jan 68	175/81	LJ	8.44	8.24 -86
Michalopoulos	Kosmas	GRE	6 Mar 66	190/78	HJ	2.25	2.27 -87
Miccoli	Giuseppe	ITA	21 Nov 61		5k	13:35.33	13:52.87 -87
					10k	28:16.00	28:43.40 -87
Michel	Detlef	GDR	13 Oct 55	188/97	JT	84.06	83.52 -86
Miclea	Constantin	RUM	13 Apr 63	185/87	JT	80.72	76.10 -87
Mikulás	Milan	CS	1 Apr 63	193/84	LJ	8.25	7.76 -87
					TJ	17.53	16.95 -87
Mileham	Matt	UK	27 Dec 56	188/109	HT	72.62	77.02 -84
Miller	Cam	USA	13 Nov 66	183/77	PV	5.57	5.51 -86
Miller	Leigh	AUS	19 Aug 63	182/72	400h	49.85	51.24 -86
Millonig	Dietmar	AUT	1 Jun 55	169/57	3k	7:48.16	7:43.66 -80
					5k	13:30.21	13:15.31 -82
Milovsorov	Tony	UK	4 Nov 58	178/66	10k	28:27.28	28:33.29 -84
Mimura	Toru	JAP	1 Dec 62	170/53	Mar	2:12:14	2:14:19 -86
Minakov	Aleksandr	SU	28 Aug 59	182/71	400	45.92	46.58 -84
Minchev	Georgi	BUL	8 Sep 62	187/100	HT	74.62	74.12 -87
Minev	Plamen	BUL	28 Apr 65	190/107	HT	81.70	79.58 -87
Minns	John	AUS	31 May 67	188/118	SP	19.45	19.13 -87
Mishakov	Aleksandr	SU	7 May 64	194/108	DT	66.12	60.54 -87
Mitchell	Dennis	USA	20 Feb 66	175/70	100	10.03, 9.86w	10.12, 10.11w -87
					200	20.29	20.36, 20.21w -87
Mitkus	Virginius	SU	66		SP	19.40	20.38 -86
Mizoguchi	Kazuhiro	JAP	18 Mar 62	181/90	JT	82.34	84.16 -87
Mochrie	Craig	UK	6 Nov 62		5k	13:31.66	13:57.90 -86
Mögenburg	Dietmar	FRG	15 Aug 61	201/78	HJ	2.37i, 2.34	2.39i -85, 2.36 -84
Mohoanyane	Henry	LES	11 Aug 63		400	45.46A	45.72A -86
Mojzysz	Czeslaw	POL	3 Aug 58	180/65	3kSt	8:29.30	8:22.18 -85
Molnár	Tamás	HUN	23 Jul 68	184/68	400	45.99, 45.8	46.48 -87
Moloney	Tom	IRL	11 Mar 60	183/70	Mile	3:56.63	3:54.68 -86
Moncef	Abdelmajid	MOR	10 May 61	182/68	1500	3:35.70	3:45.8 -87
Mondragon	Martin	MEX	11 Nov 53	166/56	Mar	2:10:19	
Moneghetti	Steve	AUS	26 Sep 62	176/60	5k	13:31.55	13:36.6 -87
					10k	28:18.98	28:07.37 -87
					Mar	2:11:49	2:11:18 -86
Monnerais	Eric	FRA	4 Apr 65	190/84	HJ	2.26	2.24 -86
Moore	Greg	USA	8 Nov 59	178/73	200	20.59A, 20.5	20.57 -84
Moracho	Javier	SPA	18 Aug 57	180/74	110h	13.60A, 13.71	13.42 -87
Moreau	Sylvain	FRA	13 Jun 66	187/72	400h	50.40	50.76 -87
Moreno	Carlos	CHL	28 Oct 67	174/66	100	10.25A	10.51, 10.37w -87
Moreira	Jose	POR	6 Jul 64	178/63	1500	3:37.89	3:40.88 -87
Moriniere	Max	FRA	16 Feb 64	183/78	100	10.32	10.09 -87
Morozov	Aleksandr	SU	27 Feb 63	187/80	PV	5.60i	5.55 -87
Morozov	Andrey	SU	14 Jun 60	185/78	HJ	2.32i, 2.32	2.33 -86
Morrell	Tony	UK	30 May 62	193/74	800	1:44.59	1:45.58 -87
					1k	2:16.99	2:17.47 -86
Morris	Devon	JAM	22 Jan 61	180/75	200	20.67	21.00, 20.87w -86
					400	45.30	45.07 -86
Morris	Dirk	TRI	9 Jan 65	188/82	110h	13.84	13.75 -87, 13.68w -85
Morris	Ian	TRI	30 Nov 61	173/64	200	20.71, 20.5	20.76-86, 20.45w -87
					400	44.60	45.02 -86
Morris	John	USA	20 Jan 64	187/81	HJ	2.26	2.27 -84
Morris	Kenny	JAM	19 Nov 66		110h	13.82	
Morrison	Brian	CAN	25 Aug 68	177/74	100	10.30w	10.56 -87
Moser	Severin	SWZ	23 Oct 62	186/80	Dec	7936	7480 -87
Moses	Edwin	USA	31 Aug 55	188/77	400h	47.37	47.02 -83
Mowatt	Andrew	CAN	25 May 64	180/75	100	10.30w	
Moya	Roberto	CUB	11 Feb 65		DT	61.20	62.92 -87
Mtolo	Willie	RSA	24 Apr 64		Mar	2:10:18	2:08:15 -86
Müller	André	GDR	15 Nov 70	188/75	LJ	7.94	7.38 -87
Müller	Frank	FRG	18 Jun 68	193/80	Dec	7795	7349 -87

Name		Nat	Born	Ht/Wt	Event	1988 Mark	Pre-1988 Best
Mugglestone	Simon	UK	24 Jan 68	183/66	3k	7:47.12	8:02.31 -87
					5k	13:28.29	13:43.82 -87
Muir	Brian	USA	18 Dec 60	190/110	SP	19.72	20.58 -84
Mukhin	Andrey	SU	1 Jun 65	188/70	HJ	2.25i	2.22i -86, 2.21- 87
Mulligan	Jerry	USA	9 Apr 58	183/77	PV	5.57	5.50 -84
Murashov	Valeriy	SU	5 May 64	185/110	DT	64.28	61.34 -86
Muravyov	Vladimir	SU	30 Sep 59	178/74	100	10.29	10.19 -86
Murphy	Dave	USA	4 Mar 57	168/57	5k	13:34.13	13:34.27 -81
Murphy	Miles	AUS	19 May 67	185/75	200	20.59	20.76 -86
					400	44.71	45.42 -87
Musiyenko	Nikolay	SU	16 Dec 59	183/79	TJ	17.25	17.78 -86
Mustapic	Ivan	YUG	9 Jul 66	196/106	JT	79.64	79.02 -87
Musyoki	William	KEN	66	160/54	3k	7:49.36	
Mutwol	William	KEN	67		3kSt	8:34.6mA	8:39.1A -87
Mwanzia	Stephen	KEN	65		400	45.7A	45.5A -87
Myers	Dub	USA	4 Apr 64	183/69	Mile	3:56.2m	3:55.31 -86
Myles-Mills	John	GHA	19 Apr 66	180/66	100	10.21	10.44, 10.32w -87
Myricks	Larry	USA	10 Mar 56	186/82	200	20.50, 20.4	20.03 -83
					LJ	8.74	8.66 -87
Nabein	Klaus-Peter	FRG	10 May 60	186/75	1500	3:37.83	3:35.98 -86
					Mile	3:56.02	3:54.11 -86
Nagel	Gerd	FRG	22 Oct 57	188/74	HJ	2.35	2.34 -87
Nagorka	Tomasz	POL	2 Oct 67	188/78	110h	13.61	13.58 -87
Nails	Felton	USA			110h	13.82w	
Nakayama	Takeyuki	JAP	20 Dec 59	179/56	10k	28:01.47	27:35.33 -87
					Mar	2:11:05	2:08:15 -85
Nakkim	Are	NOR	13 Feb 64	181/66	5k	13:32.66	13:35.86 -87
					3kSt	8:24.13	8:28.20 -86
Navara	Richard	CS	11 Sep 64	194/120	SP	20.52	20.60 -87
Navesnak	Stanislav	CS	1 Jan 65	177/66	400h	49.64	49.81 -87
N'Dayisenga	Jean-Pierre	BEL	12 Dec 64	163/54	2k	5:06.45	
					10k	28:12.77	28:23.4 -87
Ndiwa	Juma	KEN	28 Nov 60	186/70	800	1:44.8mA	1:44.20 -83
Neal	McLinton	USA	11 Jul 68	193/77	400h	50.25	
Negoita	Dumitru	RUM	9 Feb 60	183/95	JT	78.76	77.60 -87
Nehemiah	Renaldo	USA	24 Mar 59	185/78	110h	13.43	12.93 -81, 12.8,12.91w -79
Nelloms	Chris	USA	14 Aug 71	173/64	400	45.80	47.53 -87
Nelson	Carey	CAN	4 Jun 63	179/64	10k	28:20.4m	28:27.0 -87
Nelson	Dan	USA	15 May 64	172/55	3kSt	8:35.16	8:34.19 -87
Nelson	David	UK	11 Mar 67	188/76	110h	13.72, 13.65w	13.77 -87
Nemchaninov	Andrey	SU	27 Nov 66	195/105	SP	20.95i, 19.89	19.86 -87
Németh	Gyula	HUN	2 Dec 59	184/71	HJ	2.24i	2.25 -86
Nenadál	Zdenek	CS	12 Feb 64	190/96	JT	80.78	75.06 -87
Nenow	Mark	USA	16 Nov 57	172/57	3k	7:50.98	7:45.37 -87
					5k	13:26.75	13:18.54 -84
Neumann	Mario	GDR	7 Sep 68	178/65	1500	3:39.07	3:41.25 -87
Neunzling	Ralf	FRG	24 Jul 67	200/82	HJ	2.25 irreg	2.21 -87
Newhouse	Ian	CAN	25 Dec 56	178/70	800	1:46.88	1:47.65 -87
Ngugi	John	KEN	10 May 62	178/62	5k	13:11.70	13:18.99 -85
					10k	27:51.35	28:37.38 -86
Niang	Babacar	SEN	9 Sep 58	178/63	800	1:45.09	1:44.70 -86
Nichols	John	USA	23 Aug 69	188/102	DT	62.52	-0-
Nicolaisen	Anton	RSA	25 Jan 68		3kSt	8:33.88	8:30.29 -87
Niederhäuser	Fabian	SWZ	15 Jul 61	189/78	110h	13.77	13.78 -87
Nigmatullin	Rafis	SU	64		100	10.32	10.2 -85
Nijboer	Gerard	HOL	18 Aug 55	182/70	Mar	2:12:38	2:09:01 -80
Nikolayev	Sergey	SU	12 Nov 66	190/105	SP	19.97	19.21 -87
Nikolov	Nikolay	BUL	15 Oct 64	182/78	PV	5.70i, 5.60	5.70 -87
Nikulin	Igor	SU	14 Aug 60	191/106	HT	83.78	83.54 -82
Nilsson	Patric	SWE	26 Feb 64	178/59	3kSt	8:32.18	8:35.23 -87
Nishimoto	Kazuya	JAP	2 Jun 62	170/53	10k	28:17.78	28:09.4 -86
Nix	Sunder	USA	2 Dec 61	175/65	400	45.88	44.68 -82
Nogales	Benito	SPA	1 Aug 65	182/67	3kSt	8:34.93	8:34.58 -87
Noji	Rick	USA	22 Oct 67	173/54	HJ	2.26i, 2.25	2.26 -86
Nordheggen	Bjorn	NOR	24 Aug 61		5k	13:36.95	13:59.27 -87
Nordquist	Doug	USA	20 Dec 58	193/79	HJ	2.34	2.34 -86

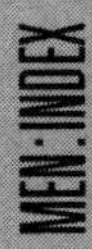

Name		Nat	Born	Ht/Wt	Event	1988 Mark	Pre-1988 Best
Norris	Anthony	USA	20 Dec 65	188/88	110h	13.84	14.29 -86
Nosov	Valeriy	SU	20 Feb 68	194/95	JT	79.00	72.58 -87
Novikov	Andrey	SU	12 Apr 63	184/97	JT	80.40	77.34 -87
Novozhilov	Sergey	SU	21 Apr 69	185/69	LJ	8.00	7.51 -87
Nuñez	Juan	DOM	19 Nov 59	178/73	100	10.33	10.16,10.14dq-83,10.07w -87
Nwankwo	Patrick	NIG	66		100	10.28w	10.29A -87
Nwankwo	Victor	NIG	18 Sep 69		200	20.79	21.3 -87
Nyambui	Suleiman	TAN	13 Feb 53	182/68	Mar	2:11:45	2:11:11 -87
Nyangau	Elkana	KEN	63	162/69	400	45.1A	45.3A -87
Nyberg	Thomas	SWE	17 Apr 62	195/84	400h	50.08	49.03 -87
Nylander	Sven	SWE	1 Jan 62	193/85	400h	49.35	48.37 -87
Nysschen	Eugene	RSA	27 Apr 64		SP	19.42	18.86 -87
Nzimande	Tshakile	RSA	19 Nov 61	178/66	100	10.11A	10.36A -86
					200	20.32A	20.31A -87
Obizhayev	Aleksandr	SU	16 Sep 59	185/85	PV	5.70	5.80 -87
Ochako	Shem	KEN	12 Dec 64	174/63	400h	49.85, 49.3A	48.97A, 49.86 -87
Ochkan	Vladimir	SU	13 Jan 68	180/70	LJ	8.34	8.24 -87
Odenthal	Marc	FRG	19 Feb 63	194/110	HT	77.76	76.70 -85
Odgers	Steve	USA	9 Nov 61	183/82	Dec	7856	7991 -86
Ogbeide	George	NIG	8 Apr 68		LJ	7.98i, 8.13wA	7.80 -87
Okash	Ibrahim	SOM	18 Sep 64	180/65	800	1:44.92	1:46.54 -85
					1k	2:17.95	2:21.97 -87
Okot	Mike	UGA	25 Dec 58	170/62	800	1:45.47	1:47.66 -85
Olander	Mikael	SWE	11 Jun 63	188/90	Dec	8126	7940 -87
Oldfield	Brian	USA	1 Jun 45	196/125	SP	19.15	22.86 -75
Ole Marai	Stephen	KEN	11 Nov 62	184/65	800	1:46.0m	1:44.84 -87
Olesen	Marc	CAN	13 Oct 64	177/61	1500	3:39.26	3:40.7 -83
Oliveira	Arnaldo	BRA	26 Mar 64	174/71	100	10.12A,10.23	10.33 -87
							10.06w, 10.1 -85
Olobia	Augustine	NIG	67		100	10.19w	10.33A -87
Olson	Billy	USA	19 Jul 58	188/73	PV	5.72	5.93i -86, 5.80 -87
Olukoju	Adewale	NIG	27 Jul 68	188/110	DT	63.60, 64.12uc	56.92 -87
Omagbemi	Victor	NIG			100	10.32w	10.66, 10.58w -87
					200	20.68w	21.43 -87
Ondiek	Kennedy	KEN	12 Dec 66	175/67	200	20.79, 20.3A	21.3 -85
Ondieki	Yobes	KEN	21 Feb 61	168/55	2k	5:04.1	-0-
					3k	7:44.31	7:48.07 -83
					5k	13:17.06	13:35.5 -83
Oosthuizen	Johan	RSA	8 Aug 54		JT	78.84	67.68 -87
Oosthuizen	Wessel	RSA	23 Feb 61	184/75	100	10.19wA	10.15A -86, 10.1A -82
					200	20.61A,	20.34A -86
						20.35wA, 20.4	20.1A -83
Orioli	Riccardo	ITA	23 Apr 65		PV	5.50	5.30 -87
Ortiz	Arturo	SPA	18 Sep 66	190/73	HJ	2.28	2.27 -87
Ortiz	Juan	CUB	13 Aug 64	175/68	LJ	8.12	8.14 -86, 8.24w -87
Oschkenat	Andreas	GDR	9 Jun 62	191/83	110h	13.65	13.50 -83
Osland	Paul	CAN	1 Jan 64	185/65	800	1:46.26	1:46.74 -87
Ostrowski	Ryszard	POL	6 Feb 61	176/62	800	1:46.08	1:44.38 -85
Ottey	Milton	CAN	29 Dec 59	178/66	HJ	2.31i, 2.28	2.33 -86
Ottley	Dave	UK	5 Aug 55	187/95	JT	80.98	80.72 -87
Ovchinnikov	Vladimir	SU	2 Aug 70	190/86	JT	80.26	72.80 -87
Ovett	Steven	UK	9 Oct 55	183/70	1500	3:36.90	3:30.77 -83
Ovsyannikov	Yevgeniy	SU	10 Jul 63	183/85	Dec	7976	8114 -86
O'Brien	Dan	USA	18 Jul 66	188/81	Dec	7891	
O'Callaghan	Paul	IRL	1 Jun 64	175/59	5k	13:29.37	13:33.74 -87
O'Connell	Carlos	IRL	21 Jun 63	192/93	Dec	7882	7609 -86
O'Donoghue	Peter	NZ	1 Oct 61	185/68	1500	3:38.24	3:34.9 -87
O'Mara	Frank	IRL	17 Jul 60	176/61	1500	3:38.44	3:34.02 -85
					3k	7:45.59	7:42.99 -87
					2M	8:17.78	8:22.97 -87
					5k	13:26.75	13:13.02 -87
O'Reilly	Gerry	IRL	1 Jul 64	188/70	1500	3:38.02	3:37.40 -87
O'Reilly	Mike	IRL	23 Apr 58	168/53	Mar	2:11:50	2:13:19 -86
O'Rourke	Mike	NZ	21 Aug 55	190/100	JT	77.58	75.46 -87
O'Sullivan	Marcus	IRL	22 Dec 61	175/60	1500	3:36.04, 3:35.4i	3:35.76 -86
					Mile	3:52.50, 3:50.94i	3:52.64 -85
					2k	4:58.08	-0-

Name		Nat	Born	Ht/Wt	Event	1988 Mark	Pre-1988 Best
Padilla	Doug	USA	4 Oct 56	176/60	3k	7:51.82i	7:35.84 -83
					5k	13:32.81	13:15.44 -85
Pagani	Daniele	ITA	11 Jun 66	184/69	HJ	2.27i, 2.26	2.24i, 2.24 -87
Page	Nat	USA	26 Jan 57	193/84	400h	49.03	49.02 -87
Pahker	Tiit	SU	22 Dec 58	190/85	Dec	7796	7976 -82
Pakhol	Oleg	SU	64	188/95	JT	79.86	79.34 -87
Paklin	Igor	SU	15 Jun 63	193/71	HJ	2.36	2.41 -85
Palashevskiy	Oleg	SU	62		HJ	2.26	2.28i -84, 2.25 -85
Palchikov	Igor	SU	19 Jun 60		SP	19.97	20.51 -87
Pálóczi	Gyula	HUN	13 Sep 62	185/67	LJ	7.98w	8.25 -85
Palola	Harri	FIN	29 Oct 66	183/71	PV	5.62	5.41 -87
Panácek	Tomás	CS	28 Mar 67	198/98	DT	60.92	58.14 -87
Panetta	Francesco	ITA	10 Jan 63	175/64	2k	5:04.1	5:05.50 -87
					5k	13:29.57	13:20.93 -85
					10k	27:33.14	27:26.95 -87
					3kSt	8:16.04	8:08.57 -87
Pang	Yan	CHN	15 Jan 63	185/70	LJ	8.13	7.99 -84
Pannier	Raymond	FRA	12 Feb 61	174/63	3k	7:45.82	7:48.20 -86
					5k	13:35.71	13:44.56 -86
					3kSt	8:16.01	8:13.88 -87
Pantel	Thierry	FRA	6 Jul 64	174/58	10k	28:16.86	-0-
Papakostas	Lambros	GRE	20 Oct 69	192/74	HJ	2.26	2.19i -87
Parker	Andrew	JAM	11 Jan 65	190/77	110h	13.69, 13.66w	13.51 -87, 13.5 -86
Parman	James	USA	28 Jan 64	185/111	DT	63.54	60.22 -87
Parpala	Esko	FIN	2 Jul 65	180/67	800	1:46.50	1:46.39 -87
Parsons	Geoff	UK	14 Aug 64	203/79	HJ	2.28	2.30i, 2.28 -86
Partyka	Artur	POL	25 Jul 69	191/69	HJ	2.28	2.23 -87
Parygin	Igor	SU	3 Feb 67	187/73	TJ	17.31	16.97 -87
Pascuzzo	Mike	USA	8 Nov 61	193/82	HJ	2.26i, 2.26	2.25 -87
Passey	Adrian	UK	2 Sep 64	178/64	1500	3:35.14	3:34.50 -87
Pastoriza	Fernando	ARG	1 Feb 65	184/70	HJ	2.25	2.20 -85
Pastusinski	Jacek	POL	8 Sep 64	200/90	TJ	16.72, 16.93w	17.35 -87
Patelka	Bogdan	POL	6 Dec 66	183/84	JT	77.92	75.86 -86
Patrick	David	USA	12 Jun 60	183/72	800	1:46.50	1:44.70 -83
					400h	47.75	48.05 -83
Patton	Mike	USA	20 Jun 66	188/77	TJ	16.60i	16.44 -87
Paul	Juan Carlos	SPA	6 May 64	179/64	3k	7:47.13	-0-
					5k	13:34.96	13:55.98 -87
Pavoni	Pier Francesco	ITA	21 Feb 63	182/70	100	10.33	10.22 -86
Peebles	Danny	USA	30 May 66	180/76	100	10.32	10.34 -87
					200	20.27	20.39, 20.16w -87
Peev	Stoyan	BUL	12 May 65	190/78	PV	5.60	5.50 -86
Peltoniemi	Asko	FIN	7 Feb 63	187/77	PV	5.67	5.60 -85
Pelzer	Torsten	GDR	26 Jun 63	199/125	SP	20.09	20.58 -86
Peñalver	Antonio	SPA	1 Dec 68	195/83	Dec	7891	7229 -86
Peñalver	Leandro	CUB	23 May 61	175/71	100	10.12A, 9.99wA	
						10.22	10.06 -83,10.00w -87
					200	20.22A, 20.61	20.42, 20.3 -82
Pereira Campos	Lyndon Johnson	BRA	8 May 66	183/73	110h	13.65A	13.84 -87
Perez	Olider	CUB	6 Nov 63		400h	50.31	52.19 -87
Peric	Dragan	YUG	8 May 64	188/96	SP	19.92	18.86 -87
Perry	Mark	USA	25 Jul 67		200	20.3w	
Perzylo	Piotr	POL	15 Nov 61	186/118	SP	19.37	20.23 -86
Peter	Jörg	GDR	23 Oct 55	173/63	Mar	2:08:47	2:09:14 -84
Petersen	Kenneth	DEN	18 Dec 65	195/98	JT	77.88	76.60 -87
Petkov	Ivan	BUL	15 Feb 60	182/95	HT	74.30	75.38 -84
Petranoff	Tom	USA	8 Apr 58	186/98	JT	80.94	85.38 -86
Petrashko	Maris	SU	6 Mar 61	186/112	SP	20.76	21.14 -87
Petrosyan	Grigoriy	SU	3 Dec 58	166/67	LJ	8.03, 8.05w	8.29 -86
Petrov	German	SU	26 Mar 67	184/70	400h	49.40	50.3, 50.74 -86
Pettigrew	Antonio	USA	3 Nov 67	180/70	400	45.36	46.31 -87
Petushinskiy	Denis	SU	29 Jun 67	188/77	PV	5.65i	5.30 -87
Peula	Antonio	SPA	21 Mar 66	171/67	3KSt	8:35.88	8:41.14 -87
Phélippeau	Hervé	FRA	16 Sep 62	178/66	1500	3:36.84	3:36.05 -87
Phillips	Allan	USA	16 Sep 67	186/82	400h	50.42	51.73 -87

Name		Nat	Born	Ht/Wt	Event	1988 Mark	Pre-1988 Best
Phillips	Andre	USA	5 Sep 59	188/84	200	20.51	20.55 -86
					400	45.10	44.71 -86
					110h	13.36, 13.33w	13.25 -85
					400h	47.19	47.51 -86
Phillips	Peller	USA	23 Jun 70	178/79	LJ	8.23w	7.48 -87
Piekarski	Piotr	POL	10 Apr 64	180/72	800	1:45.88	1:45.85 -85
Pienaar	Jan	RSA	19 Jan 66	189/133	SP	19.56	17.48 -87
Pierce	Jack	USA	23 Sep 62	185/75	110h	13.41	13.36 -85
Pierre	Raymond	USA	19 Sep 67	180/73	400	45.49	44.60 -87
Pietz	Christoph	GDR	15 Jul 64	185/79	PV	5.55i, 5.50	5.50 -86
Pildavs	Normunds	SU	12 Apr 64	178/79	JT	81.92	79.74 -86
Pilyutin	Vladimir	SU	65		LJ	8.00	7.85i, 7.70 -87
Pinheiro	Joaquim	POR	20 Dec 60	164/57	10k	28:08.49	28:35.9 -87
Pinto	António	POR	22 Mar 66	165/59	5k	13:27.89	13:41.38 -87
					10k	28:01.00	28:28.73 -87
Piolanti	Raphael	FRA	14 Nov 67	184/90	HT	75.24	71.28 -87
Piskunov	Eduard	SU	26 Sep 67	172/88	HT	75.74	75.10 -86
Pitayo	Martin	MEX	10 Jan 60	173/55	10k	28:19.8m	27:45.8 -85
Pittman	Rickey	USA	4 Oct 61	175/61	3kSt	8:35.47	8:23.66 -83
Pizzolato	Orlando	ITA	30 Jul 58	179/61	Mar	2:12:32	2:10:23 -85
Plaatjes	Mark	USA/RSA	1 Jun 62	173/64	Mar	2:10:41	2:08:58 -85
Plasencia	Steve	USA	28 Oct 56	178/64	2M	8:26.04	8:25.15 -86
					5k	13:34.96	13:19.37 -85
Platek	Krzysztof	POL	13 Jan 62	187/75	110h	13.61	13.62 -87
Plaziat	Christian	FRA	28 Oct 63	190/87	Dec	8512	8317 -87
Plekhanov	Vladimir	SU	11 Apr 58	185/80	TJ	16.83	17.60 -85
Pleshko	Yuriy	SU	6 Nov 63		110h	13.67	14.13 -86, 13.8 -83
Ploghaus	Klaus	FRG	31 Jan 56	186/110	HT	77.88	81.32 -86
Plosila	Juha	FIN	21 Jun 65	174/69	LJ	7.99	7.98 -87
Plucknett	Ben	USA	13 Apr 54	201/136	SP	19.32	20.59 -81
					DT	63.48	72.34dq-81, 71.32 -83
Plunge	Donatas	SU	11 Nov 60	195/118	HT	75.56	79.66 -86
Poelman	Simon	NZ	27 May 63	187/91	Dec	8021	8366m -87
Pogorelyi	Pyotr	SU	28 Apr 68	200/106	SP	19.23i	18.90 -87
Pohland	Holger	GDR	5 Apr 63	182/78	110h	13.67	13.40 -86
Poli	Pier Giovanni	ITA	5 Nov 57	180/68	Mar	2:09:33	2:09:57 -85
Polyakov	Vladimir	SU	17 Apr 60	190/75	PV	5.70	5.81 -81
Polyushin	Oleg	SU	23 Apr 69	185/112	HT	73.32	70.58 -87
Pomashki	Georgi	BUL	10 Jan 60	190/80	LJ	7.95	7.76i -86
					TJ	17.03	16.99 -86
Popel	Mikhail	SU	25 May 66	191/97	HT	77.90	79.10 -87
Popescu	Eugen	RUM	12 Aug 62	194/78	HJ	2.32	2.31 -86
Popov	Sergey	SU	2 Dec 57	191/85	Dec	8114	8217 -84
Popovic	Slobodan	YUG	28 Sep 62	178/66	800	1:44.75	1:45.07 -87
Porter	George	USA	19 Dec 66	196/86	400h	49.49	50.44 -87
Porter	Pat	USA	31 May 59	183/60	3k	7:51.0	8:00.08 -83
					5k	13:33.91	13:34.98 -85
					10k	27:46.80	27:49.5 -84
Posey	Warren	USA	26 Mar 67	178/73	TJ	16.64w	16.10 -87
Potapovich	Igor	SU	6 Sep 67	185/75	PV	5.65i, 5.65	5.60 -87
Povarnitsyn	Rudolf	SU	13 Jun 62	201/75	HJ	2.36	2.40 -85
Powell	John	USA	25 Jun 47	190/105	DT	64.10	71.26 -84, 72.08dh -87
Powell	Mike	USA	10 Nov 63	190/77	LJ	8.49	8.27-87,8.28w -85
Pregnolato	Mauro	ITA	21 Oct 64	175/56	3kSt	8:31.58	8:22.03 -87
Prenzler	Olaf	GDR	24 Aug 58	183/75	200	20.73	20.46 -82, 20.39w -79
Preysing	André	GDR	6 Oct 66	189/80	Dec	7853	8017 -87
Prianon	Jean-Louis	FRA	22 Feb 60	176/58	10k	27:36.43	27:34.58 -87
Pribytkin	Sergey	SU	68		HT	73.28	
Prieto	António	SPA	11 Jan 58	158/49	10k	27:52.78	27:43.46 -83
Profit	Mike	USA	17 Oct 66	179/70	110h	13.57A, 13.4	
Prosin	Vladimir	SU	15 Aug 59	186/75	400	45.86	45.47 -84
Protsenko	Oleg	SU	11 Aug 63	191/82	TJ	17.68	17.69 -85
Psujek	Boguslaw	POL	22 Nov 56	182/69	Mar	2:12:37	2:10:26 -87
Puchkov	Aleksandr	SU	30 Apr 60	177/100	HT	74.88	78.86 -87
Pudenz	Rüdiger	GDR	22 Dec 66	198/108	DT	60.82	62.86 -87
Pukownik	Eligiusz	POL	30 Jun 62	195/112	DT	62.04 light	64.34 -85

Name		Nat	Born	Ht/Wt	Event	1988 Mark	Pre-1988 Best
Pupchonok	Igor	SU	20 May 60	197/93	Dec	8022	8021m -86
Purvis	James	USA	4 Sep 66	190/93	110h	13.56,13.46w	13.59-87,13.53w -86
Puzyrev	Vladimir	SU	17 Mar 62	182/82	LJ	8.03	7.91i -84, 7.86 -87
Pyryalov	Mikhail	SU	65		HT	73.70	73.14 -86
Pyy	Juha	FIN	12 Jun 63	178/75	400	45.75	46.36 -87
Quade	John	USA	1 Mar 67	180/67	Mile	3:57.3i	
Quarrie	Don	JAM	25 Feb 51	175/70	200	20.62	19.86A -71
Quenéhérvé	Gilles	FRA	17 May 66	183/74	200	20.20A, 20.40	20.16 -87
Quigley	Joe	AUS	5 Dec 61	187/110	HT	74.44	74.58 -87
Quinn	Brendan	IRL	26 Jul 60	188/73	3kSt	8:26.56	8:24.09 -85
Quinon	Pierre	FRA	20 Feb 62	180/74	PV	5.70	5.90 -85
Quintero	Reinaldo	CUB	10 Jul 69		110h	13.71w	14.27, 14.2 -87
Radefeld	Norbert	FRG	3 Mar 62	192/100	HT	78.28	77.48 -86
Radev	Venzislav	BUL	9 Jan 61	187/70	110h	13.81	13.59, 13.5 -83
Räni	Aivar	SU	4 Mar 63	177/102	HT	76.42	74.80 -87
Räty	Seppo	FIN	27 Apr 62	188/105	JT	83.26	83.54 -87
Rambo	Tony	USA	30 May 60	175/78	400h	50.21	48.16 -84
Ramirez	Aaron	USA	29 Jul 64	178/68	3kSt	8:32.80	8:42.3 -87
Ramos	Mike	USA	1 Nov 62	183/86	Dec	8226w	8322 -86
Rapisarda	Antonio	FRA	6 Jan 65	174/58	5k	13:28.94	13:41.38 -87
Rapp	Marco	SWZ	23 Sep 57	180/69	1500	3:37.23	3:42.5 -87
Ratushkov	Vladimir	SU	1 Jan 65	187/75	LJ	8.26	8.10 -85
Razgonov	Nikolay	SU	16 Jan 64	187/77	200	20.76, 20.62i	20.62, 20.5-86
Razin	Andrey	SU	10 May 62	178/76	100	10.27	10.29 -87,10.1 -86
Reading	Robert	USA	9 Jun 67	193/88	110h	13.70, 13.4	13.64 -87
Redmond	Derek	UK	3 Sep 65	183/70	400	44.67	44.50 -87
Redwine	Stanley	USA	10 Apr 61	186/73	800	1:45.20	1:44.87 -84
Reed	Bo	USA	15 Mar 66	173/56	10k	28:20.0m	
Reed	Mark	USA	22 May 65	190/76	HJ	2.31i, 2.26	2.29 -87
Reese	Dan	USA	15 Oct 63	175/55	3kSt	8:30.61	8:34.94 -87
Reese	Terry	USA	20 Jun 67	183/78	110h	13.78,13.60w, 13.6	14.18 -87
Regalo	José	POR	22 Nov 63	180/60	5k	13:15.62	13:23.24 -87
					10k	28:02.4m	28:53.5 -85
					3kSt	8:21.64	8:20.70 -87
Regis	John	UK	13 Oct 66	181/86	100	10.31	10.37 -87
					200	20.32	20.18 -87
Reid	Bruce	USA	10 Feb 67	193/93	Dec	7900w	6863 -87
Reid	Dave	CAN	26 Mar 63	170/61	1500	3:38.07	3:37.84 -87
Reid	Eric	USA	17 Feb 65	188/85	110h	13.49	13.50, 13.38w -87
Reid	Kevin	CAN	15 Mar 66	184/73	110h	13.69w	13.99 -87
Reintak	Sven	SU	17 Jun 63	195/83	Dec	7910M	8232 -86
Reiterer	Werner	AUS	27 Jan 68	193/108	DT	63.16	65.62 -87
Reitz	Colin	UK	6 Apr 60	186/73	3kSt	8:35.6	8:12.11 -86
Reshetnikov	Valeriy	SU	25 Mar 59	180/100	HT	74.96	78.04 -86
Reski	Heiko	FRG	22 Aug 63	191/77	LJ	7.95i,7.92	8.13 -87
Retiz	Carlos	MEX	13 Aug 61	170/53	10k	28:20.7m	28:27.5 -87
Retiz	Carlos	MEX	13 Aug 61	170/53	Mar	2:11:30	2:15:58 -87
Reyna	Jorge	CUB	10 Jan 63	179/68	TJ	17.34	17.48 -87
Reynolds	Butch	USA	8 Jun 64	193/84	400	43.29	44.10 -87
Reynolds	Jeff	USA	25 Jan 66	188/81	200	20.1w	
					400	44.98	46.09 -86
Richards	Jon	UK	19 May 64	173/57	5k	13:31.82	13:31.38 -87
Ridding	Colin	UK	1 Nov 61		Mile	3:57.42	4:03.5 -87
Ridgeon	Jonathan	UK	14 Feb 67	183/75	110h	13.52, 13.45w	13.29 -87
Riecke	Hans-Ullrich	GDR	3 Oct 63	192/90	Dec	7955	8181 -84
Riedel	Lars	GDR	28 Jun 67	198/100	DT	62.26	58.66 -86
Rikert	Edward	POL	22 Aug 61	199/113	DT	62.52, 64.92 light	62.86 -85
Riley	Kelly	USA	29 Dec 68	190/77	PV	5.57	5.18 -87
Rios	Elísio	POR	3 Apr 61	167/58	Mar	2:12:53	2:15:40 -82
Rivas	Carlos	MEX	4 Nov 62		Mar	2:12:08	2:15:19 -87
Roberson	Mark	UK	13 Mar 67	192/95	JT	80.92	77.32 -87
Robertson	Max	UK	27 Dec 63	185/77	400h	50.03	49.35 -87
Robinson	Albert	USA	28 Nov 64	187/84	100	10.11, 9.88w	10.22 -84
					200	20.05	20.07 -84
Robinson	Darrell	USA	23 Dec 63	186/66	400	44.99	44.45 -86
Robinson	James	USA	27 Aug 54	178/65	800	1:45.50	1:43.92 -84

Name		Nat	Born	Ht/Wt	Event	1988 Mark	Pre-1988 Best
Robinzine	Kevin	USA	12 Apr 66	178/64	400	44.61	45.04 -87
Robirds	Rick	USA	18 Sep 66	175/59	10k	28:22.0m	
Rocha	Jose	USA	7 Dec 64	175/64	10k	28:25.4m	28:42.8 -87
Rodehau	Gunther	GDR	6 Jul 59	179/115	HT	81.82	82.64 -85
Rodrigues	Abcelvio	BRA	26 May 57	181/74	TJ	16.64	16.76 -84
Ronkainen	Janne	FIN	5 Feb 63	191/104	SP	20.43	20.50 -87
Rono	George Kiprotich	KEN	4 Jan 58	168/54	3k	7:51.61	7:56.21 -80
					5k	13:31.05	13:19.24 -80
					3kSt	8:21.10	8:12.0 -80
Rono	Peter	KEN	31 Jul 67	162/54	800	1:46.66	1:47.79 -87
					1500	3:35.59	3:39.2 -85
					Mile	3:56.91	4:06.46i -87
Rose	Matt	USA	29 Jan 67	188/80	LJ	8.10w	7.71 -86
Rosko	Lubomír	CS	9 Oct 62	191/79	HJ	2.25	2.25i -87, 2.18- 84
Rossi	Marco	ITA	7 Jul 63	188/86	Dec	7761	7947w -87
Rossouw	Johan	RSA	20 Oct 65	186/77	100	10.06A	10.21A -87
					200	20.48A	20.53A -87
Rosswess	Michael	UK	11 Jun 65	186/73	200	20.51	21.89, 21.6 -87
Rouhi	Peter	FRG	12 Mar 66	183/73	LJ	8.00	7.75 -86
Rousseau	Vincent	BEL	29 Jul 62	176/60	1500	3:36.81	3:36.38 -85
					3k	7:44.08	7:42.15 -86
					5k	13:19.16	13:15.01 -86
Rowe	Mark	USA	28 Jul 60	192/84	400	44.88	44.87 -85
Rowland	Mark	UK	7 Mar 63	183/72	1500	3:34.53	3:37.2 -86
					Mile	3:56.85	3:52.99 -86
					5k	13:21.83	13:45.09 -87
					3kSt	8:07.96	8:21.03 -87
Rubtsov	Sergey	SU	65	SP	20.68	19.64 -87	
Rudenik	Viktor	SU	30 Mar 64	175/73	LJ	7.96w	7.80,7.90w -86
Rückel	Michael	FRG	24 Sep 63	187/82	Dec	7760	7531 -86
Rüter	Eckhardt	FRG	24 Oct 63	177/68	1k	2:17.18	2:19.04 -86
					1500	3:37.38	3:38.88 -87
Rufféni	Robert	CS	26 Jan 67	185/70	HJ	2.34	2.30 -87
Ruhkieck	Frank	GDR	23 Nov 61	178/60	3kSt	8:30.94	8:28.85 -86
Ruiz	Paul	CUB	21 Sep 62	182/100	SP	20.28	19.83 -87
Rutherford	Frank	BAH	23 Nov 64	185/79	TJ	17.12	17.24 -87
Ryabukhin	Mikhail	SU	25 Mar 67	188/71	110h	13.6	13.5,13.96-87
Rybin	Yuriy	SU	5 May 63	186/85	JT	81.38	74.04 -87
Ryffel	Markus	SWZ	5 Feb 55	167/57	5k	13:30.03	13:07.54 -84
					10k	28:13.32	27:54.88 -83
Rymaruk	Vasiliy	SU	9 Mar 61	186/90	HT	76.00	75.74 -87
Ryu	Chae-song	KOR	20 Mar 60		Mar	2:12:49	
Ryzhenkov	Viktor	SU	25 Aug 66	190/86	PV	5.60	5.65 -87
Ryzhukhin	Dmitriy	SU	67		3kSt	8:30.32	
Sabia	Donato	ITA	11 Sep 63	178/65	800	1:44.90	1:43.88 -84
Sáda	Pavel	CS	26 Jan 64	180/78	110h	13.75	13.82 -87
Särnblom	Hakon	NOR	3 Mar 66		HJ	2.24i	2.23 -87
Sahere	Abdelaziz	MOR	67	180/67	3kSt	8:22.45	8:39.0 -87
Sahner	Christoph	FRG	23 Sep 63	180/103	HT	81.78	81.56 -85
Saina	Joseph	KEN	3 Jan 66	180/75	400	45.5A	46.13 -87, 45.9A -85
Sakirkin	Oleg	SU	23 Jan 66	182/72	TJ	17.50	17.43 -87
Sala	Carlos	SPA	20 Mar 60	186/76	110h	13.69, 13.67w	13.44 -87
Salah	Ahmed	DJI	31 Dec 56	180/56	Mar	2:07:07	2:08:09 -85
Salbert	Ferenc	FRA	5 Aug 60	190/80	PV	5.55i	5.90i, 5.80-87
Salo	Jürgen	FIN	14 Jan 66	186/72	3kSt	8:32.51	8:45.95 -87
Salzmann	Ralf	FRG	6 Feb 55	172/58	5k	13:33.00	13:37.74 -84
					10k	28:02.37	28:11.49 -85
					Mar	2:10:10	2:10:56 -85
Samarin	Yuriy	SU	27 Dec 60	179/74	LJ	7.96	8.23, 8.28w -84
Samuels	Vernon	UK	5 Oct 64	188/80	TJ	16.75	16.71 -86
Samylov	Igor	SU	22 Feb 62	193/87	Dec	8073	8034 -87
Sanchez	Antonio	SPA	22 Sep 63	181/72	400	45.77	45.41 -86
Sanchez	Francisco	SPA	18 May 58	175/64	3kSt	8:33.79	8:16.59 -83
Sanders	Deion	USA	9 Aug 67	183/82	100	10.26	10.79 -87
					200	20.71	-0-
Sang	Lucas	KEN	12 Feb 61	188/72	400	45.72, 45.3A	45.9A -87

Name		Nat	Born	Ht/Wt	Event	1988 Mark	Pre-1988 Best
Sang	Patrick	KEN	11 Apr 64	175/64	2k	5:03.46	
					3kSt	8:12.00	8:14.75 -87
Sangouma	Daniel	FRA	7 Feb 65	186/77	200	20.46	20.60 -85
Saprykin	Aleksandr	SU	66		3kSt	8:35.29	8:43.8 -87
Saracevic	Zlatan	YUG	27 Jul 56	196/135	SP	20.23	21.11 -84
Sasimovich	Vladimir	SU	9 Jun 68	178/81	JT	79.28	78.84 -86
Saunders	Nick	BER	14 Sep 63	188/75	HJ	2.34	2.32 -87
Savin	Vitaliy	SU	23 Jan 66	178/84	100	10.15, 9.9	10.39, 10.1 -87
Savoie	Kevin	USA	31 Jul 67	178/73	110h	13.76	13.76 -87
Sawe	Tito	KEN	10 Jul 60	183/73	400	45.8A	45.92A, 45.93, 45.6A -87
Sawicki	Wictor	POL	20 May 55	171/66	Mar	2:12:26	2:11:18 -86
Sayre	John	USA	25 Mar 61	190/88	Dec	7873w	8381w -85
Scammell	Pat	AUS	15 Apr 61	189/67	1500	3:34.61	3:36.12 -87
Scekic	Radovan	YUG	1 Oct 67	187/105	JT	77.52	73.84 -87
Schaeffer	Jörg	FRG	17 Jul 59	198/116	HT	77.96	79.92 -86
Schenk	Christian	GDR	9 Feb 65	200/93	HJ	2.27	2.25 -87
					Dec	8488	8304 -87
Schersing	Mathias	GDR	7 Oct 64	182/68	400	45.20	44.85 -86
Schieber	Christian	FRG	18 Sep 59	183/67	3kSt	8:34.46	8:32.87 -86
Schmid	Harald	FRG	29 Sep 57	187/82	400h	48.23	47.48 -82
Schmidt	Wolfgang	FRG	16 Jan 54	199/115	SP	20.13	20.76 -78
					DT	68.22	71.16 -78
Schmitt	Uwe	FRG	17 Aug 61	185/74	400h	49.86	49.39 -85
Schmitz	Manfred	FRG	13 Mar 60	197/110	DT	63.56	63.42 -86
Schnetler	Johan	RSA	1 Feb 66		3kSt	8:34.47	8:36.76 -87
Schoch	Jürgen	FRG	10 Apr 62	181/69	110h	13.78	13.84, 13.83w -83
Schoeman	Kobus	RSA	16 Nov 65	178/73	110h	13.65A	
							13.73, 13.5A -87, 13.66wA -86
Schönlebe	Thomas	GDR	6 Aug 65	185/76	400	44.62A, 44.90	44.33 -87
Schröder	Marko	GDR	5 Feb 68	189/71	PV	5.50	5.35 -87
Schroeder	Ralph	RSA	6 Nov 62	180/75	110h	13.64A,	13.70A, 13.71-87
						13.87	13.60wA -86
Schult	Jürgen	GDR	11 May 60	194/108	DT	70.46	74.08 -86
Schwarthoff	Florian	FRG	7 May 68	201/80	110h	13.50	13.69 -87
Schwarz	Rainer	FRG	5 Jun 59	181/63	3kSt	8:24.98	8:11.93 -85
Schwepker	John	USA	24 Sep 65	183/82	Dec	7881	7526 -87
Scott	Steve	USA	5 May 56	186/73	1500	3:34.9m	3:31.76 -85
					Mile	3:50.09	3:47.69 -82
					3k	7:49.36	7:36.69 -81
Sebata	John	RSA	7 Jan 56		Mar	2:13:02	2:16:16 -87
Seck	Charles-Louis	SEN	11 May 65	167/70	100	10.25	10.19-86, 10.1-85
Sedlácek	Pavel	CS	5 Apr 68	198/105	HT	72.16	69.26 -87
Sedlacek	Ulf	SWE	10 Jun 65	184/71	400h	50.22	50.64 -85
Sedykh	Yuriy	SU	11 Jun 55	186/106	HT	85.14	86.74 -86
Seelig	Andreas	GDR	6 Jul 70	200/120	DT	61.84	54.24 -87
Seko	Toshihiko	JAP	15 Jul 56	170/59	Mar	2:12:41	2:08:27 -86
Seleznyev	Aleksandr	SU	25 Jan 63	182/97	HT	78.80	76.96 -85
Selle	Frédéric	FRA	13 Mar 57	198/125	DT	61.92	60.56 -86
Sennai	Isamu	JAP	11 Aug 60	172/57	Mar	2:10:59	2:11:59 -86
Serebryanskiy	Sergey	SU	24 Dec 62	184/76	HJ	2.30i	2.29i, 2.27 -87
Sereda	Valeriy	SU	30 Jun 59	186/76	HJ	2.30i	2.37 -84
Serrani	Lucio	ITA	11 Mar 61	190/120	HT	78.02	77.08 -87
Serrano	Antonio	SPA	8 Mar 65	179/65	3k	7:48.11	8:16.47 -87
					5k	13:34.71	13:46.4 -87
					10k	28:18.1	30:11.45 -87
Seskin	Yuriy	SU	8 Jul 66	196/100	DT	64.58	64.34 -87
Sfia	Lucian	RUM	10 Sep 63	177/67	TJ	16.94	16.76 -85
Sgrulletti	Enrico	ITA	24 Apr 65	182/100	HT	77.02	73.42 -87
Shaffer	Scott	USA	31 May 64	185/77	PV	5.67	5.50 -85
Sharpe	David	UK	8 Jul 67	181/66	800	1:45.70	1:45.64 -86
Shatilo	Lev	SU	21 Oct 63	191/98	JT	82.22	84.30 -87
Shatta	Ahmed K.	EGY	23 Jan 61	190/115	SP	20.76	19.62 -85
Shchogolev	Igor	SU	26 Oct 60	191/105	HT	78.04	80.20 -86
Shelton	Jon	USA	5 Dec 67	185/70	HJ	2.26	2.22 -86
Sheriff	Brian	ZIM	11 Nov 61	165/58	10k	28:13.5m	28:07.12 -87
Shevchenko	Yuriy	SU	18 Apr 60	190/78	HJ	2.25i, 2.25	2.29i -85, 2.26 -83

Name		Nat	Born	Ht/Wt	Event	1988 Mark	Pre-1988 Best
Shibata	Hiroyuki	JAP	29 Apr 63	170/64	LJ	8.04, 8.06w	7.81 -85
Shibutani	Toshihiro	JAP	30 Aug 62	160/49	Mar	2:11:04	2:12:34 -85
Shinohara	Futoshi	JAP	14 Apr 62	167/52	Mar	2:12:00	2:15:44 -86
Shirley	Simon	AUS	3 Aug 66	190/90	Dec	8036	7584 -86
Shishkin	Vladimir	SU	16 Jun 64	193/80	110h	13.21, 13.0	13.50, 13.36w -86
							13.4 -87
Shkarpov	Vyacheslav	SU	6 Sep 66	186/74	TJ	16.89	16.78 -86
Shkerdin	Oleg	SU	9 Jun 68	188/83	PV	5.50	5.30 -86
Shkvira	Arkadiy	SU	18 Oct 60	188/73	PV	5.50	5.65 -85
Sholars	Greg	USA	8 Feb 66	172/66	100	10.22, 10.21w	10.28 -87
Shtrobinders	Marcis	SU	12 Jun 66	185/85	JT	80.32	80.04 -87
Sidorenko	Vasiliy	SU	1 May 61	186/100	HT	80.52	80.70 -86
Siebert	Carsten	GDR	24 Nov 62	194/79	HJ	2.24i, 2.24	2.25 -87
Silva	Alvaro	POR	21 Apr 65	177/58	800	1:45.12	1:45.63 -87
Silva	Joaquim	POR	13 Jan 61	177/63	10k	28:23.8	29:09.5 -85
Silva	Mario	POR	23 Jul 61	174/56	1500	3:38.56	3:38.00 -86
					3k	7:49.99	7:55.92- 87
Simon	Andrés	CUB	15 Sep 61	160/67	100	10.13A,10.19	10.06-87, 9.97w -85
Simon	Tim	USA	11 Sep 66	188/73	400	44.88	45.74 -87
Simon Balla	István	HUN	9 Feb 58	186/69	400h	50.04	49.62 -86
Simpkins	Charles	USA	19 Oct 63	185/72	TJ	17.29,17.93w	17.86-85,17.91w -86
Sinka	Albert	HUN	22 Nov 62	187/95	HT	81.18	79.12 -86
Sinnitsa	Sergey	SU	21 Dec 66		SP	20.53i, 19.53	20.05 -86
Siuvatti	Kari	FIN	3 Feb 62	185/78	JT	76.74	75.58 -87
Sjöberg	Patrik	SWE	5 Jan 65	200/82	HJ	2.39i, 2.37	2.42 -87
Skarczynski	Jerzy	POL	13 Jan 56	176/62	Mar	2:12:56	2:11:42 -86
Skinner	William	USA	30 Sep 64	190/85	110h	13.75	13.53 -86
Sklyarov	Vitaliy	SU	31 Jan 60	187/75	110h	13.45	13.66 -85, 13.3w -83
Skvortsov	Andrey	SU	68		PV	5.50	5.30 -87
Slanar	Ivan	CS	11 Jan 61	191/84	TJ	17.19	17.25 -87
Slavnic	Vlad	AUS	10 Sep 58	195/125	DT	64.10	62.62 -87
Smirnov	Sergey	SU	26 Nov 65		10k	28:27.20	29:12.84 -87
Smirnov	Sergey	SU	17 Sep 60	192/126	SP	21.88	22.24 -86
Smith	Andrew	JAM	29 Jan 64	178/79	100	10.14, 10.12w	10.17, 10.11w -87
					200	20.58wA	20.65 -87
Smith	Antonio	USA	66		100	10.21w	10.33 -85
Smith	Berry	USA	22 Feb 71		200	20.68w	21.22 -87
Smith	Calvin	USA	8 Jan 61	178/64	100	9.97, 9.87w	9.93A, 9.97 -83
					200	20.08	19.99 -83
Smith	Dave	UK	21 Jun 62	190/118	HT	75.00	77.30 -85
Smith	Jeff	USA	13 Sep 64	188/79	110h	13.84	
Smith	Mark	USA	22 Feb 63	180/62	3kSt	8:24.14	8:23.02 -87
Smith	Maurice	USA	20 Nov 62	178/61	1k	2:17.84	
Smith	Mike	CAN	16 Sep 67	195/96	Dec	8083	8126w, 8070 -87
Smith	Tom	USA	10 Jul 67	200/84	HJ	2.33	2.28 -87
Smith	Willie	USA	28 Feb 56	178/73	400	44.92	44.73 -78
Snoddy	Phil	IRL	3 Feb 66	180/76	200	20.50w	21.29 -87
Söderman	Ulf	SWE	18 Mar 63	189/78	110h	13.79w	13.94 -86, 13.84w -86
Soh	Takeshi	JAP	9 Jan 53	178/58	Mar	2:10:40	2:08:55 -83
Sokolov	Vladimir	SU	5 Oct 63	196/75	HJ	2.24i	2.23 -84
Sokov	Vasiliy	SU	7 Apr 68		LJ	8.18	7.77 -87
Sonn	Ralf	FRG	17 Jan 67	197/85	HJ	2.25	2.23 -87
Sonnenburg	Rainer	FRG	2 Oct 60	197/87	Dec	8079	8021m -87
Sotin	Valeriy	SU	12 Jun 60		SP	19.81	19.90 -85
Sotomayor	Javier	CUB	13 Oct 67	195/82	HJ	2.43	2.37 -87
Souza	Gerson A.	BRA	2 Jan 59	176/74	400	45.27	45.21 -82
Souza	Mark	USA	14 Dec 63	188/68	3kSt	8:31.29	8:40.41 -85
Spearmon	Wallace	USA	3 Sep 62	188/76	200	20.64	20.27, 20.20w -87
Spedding	Charles	UK	19 May 52	173/63	Mar	2:12:19	2:08:33 -85
Spence	Steve	USA	9 May 62	175/61	10k	28:27.26	
Spivey	Jim	USA	7 Mar 60	178/61	1500	3:31.01	3:34.19 -84
					Mile	3:50.57	3:49.80 -86
					3k	7:48.61	7:51.47 -86
Spry	Ralph	USA	16 Jun 60	173/70	LJ	8.32A, 7.97	8.18, 8.36w -83
Squella	Pablo	CHL	14 Aug 63	178/64	800	1:45.98	1:46.21 -86
Stadel	Ken	USA	19 Feb 52	196/120	DT	63.56dh	69.26 -79

Name		Nat	Born	Ht/Wt	Event	1988 Mark	Pre-1988 Best
Stahr	Mike	USA	9 Dec 64	180/63	800	1:46.44	1:48.00 -86
Staines	Gary	UK	3 Jul 63	185/64	Mile	3:57.21	3:59.24 -85
					3k	7:46.05	7:54.5 -87
					2M	8:26.37	8:26.15 -87
					5k	13:24.51	13:20.00 -87
					10k	28:12.93	-0-
Stankevich	Valeriy	SU	67		TJ	16.76	16.23 -87
Stanton	Brian	USA	19 Feb 61	196/82	HJ	2.33	2.32 -87
Starkey	Dean	USA	27 Mar 67	188/77	PV	5.57i, 5.57	5.50 -87
Starks	Llewellyn	USA	10 Feb 67	185/73	LJ	8.03, 8.12w	8.04 -87
Starodubtsev	Valeriy	SU	14 Feb 62	187/75	800	1:46.99	1:45.32 -86
Starovoitov	Aleksandr	SU	31 Aug 63	194/84	200	20.63	20.80A -87
Starushchenko	Aleksey	SU	5 May 66	190/80	PV	5.50	5.40 -87
Stasaitis	Reginaldas	SU	67		LJ	7.94, 8.12w	
Steele	Martin	UK	30 Sep 62	165/64	800	1:46.95	1:46.66 -87
Steele	Paul	USA	10 Jul 66	175/64	400h	50.52	51.53 -87
Steen	Dave	CAN	14 Nov 59	185/80	Dec	8415	8317 -85
Stefán	László	HUN	4 Nov 63	190/87	JT	81.22	80.56 -86
Steffny	Herbert	FRG	5 Sep 53	179/67	Mar	2:11:54	2:11:17 -86
Steiner	Andreas	AUT	31 Mar 64	186/78	LJ	8.30	8.18 -87
Steiner	Rudolf	SWZ	16 Jan 51	178/105	JT	79.24	77.96 -87
Steinmayr	Teddy	AUT	4 Feb 64	191/92	LJ	8.06	7.86 -86
Stephan	Herbert	FRG	6 Oct 59	179/65	5k	13:33.57	13:22.09 -87
Stephens	Dave	USA	8 Feb 62	193/97	JT	80.60	79.86 -87
Stevens	Félix	CUB	8 Mar 64	190/72	400	45.87	44.77 -86
Stevens	Patrick	BEL	31 Jan 68	183/76	200	20.72	21.01 -87
Stewart	Craig	USA	5 May 62		LJ	7.94	7.75-87, 7.92w -84
Stewart	Milan	USA	31 Oct 60	183/79	110h	13.41, 13.4	13.37 -86
Stewart	Ray	JAM	18 Mar 65	178/73	100	10.08,10.01w	10.08,9.89w,9.8w -87
					200	20.41	20.54, 20.31w -87
Stinson	Lemuel	USA	10 May 66	178/77	110h	13.75w	13.87w -87
Stjepovic	Milan	YUG	8 Mar 68	180/83	JT	79.32	73.20 -87
Stolz	Karsten	FRG	23 Jul 64	208/142	SP	21.15	20.70 -87
Stone	Robert	AUS	5 Jan 65	176/71	200	20.44	20.69 -87
					400	44.98	45.73 -87
Stones	Dwight	USA	6 Dec 53	196/82	HJ	2.26	2.34 -84
Stoyanov	Rumen	BUL	21 Apr 59	181/74	PV	5.60i, 5.50	5.55i-85, 5.50-83
Strelchenko	Sergey	SU	21 Dec 61	188/75	110h	13.73	13.70 -86
Streltsov	Igor	SU	1 May 65	184/74	200	20.60	21.29 -87
					LJ	8.31	7.75 -86
Strizhakov	Oleg	SU	18 Jul 63		10k	28:27.29	28:23.80 -84
Strømø	Lars Ove	NOR	7 May 63	170/57	3k	7:51.63	7:50.12 -87
					5k	13:20.75	13:37.47 -87
Strychalski	Jacek	POL	6 Mar 62	198/117	DT	61.22	62.54 -86
Stubblefield	Steve	USA	30 Dec 61	183/77	PV	5.50i	5.69 -85
Stuhlpfarrer	Helmut	AUT	19 Mar 59	174/54	Mar	2:13:08	2:15:32 -87
Stulce	Mike	USA	14 Jul 69	183/117	SP	19.44	16.33 -87
Styopochkin	Vladimir	SU	3 Jul 64	188/100	HT	76.94	76.28 -87
Subbotin	Yuriy	SU	56		JT	77.22	79.56* -85
Sudnik	Andrey	SU	11 Mar 67	179/67	800	1:45.29	1:45.90 -87
Suhonen	Ari	FIN	19 Dec 65	184/67	800	1:45.14	1:45.85 -87
					1k	2:18.72	2:16.88 -87
					1500	3:37.31	3:36.89 -87
Sukharev	Gennadiy	SU	3 Feb 65	185/74	PV	5.65	5.73 -87
Sula	Karel	CS	30 Jun 59	189/104	SP	20.71	20.39 -87
Sullivan	Shannon	USA	15 Oct 59	183/86	Dec	8076	7763 -86
Sundell	Bob	USA	27 Jan 67	201/86	HJ	2.26	2.22 -87
Sundin	Lars	SWE	21 Jul 61	193/103	SP	19.48i, 20.43u	20.34 -87
					DT	63.48	65.42 -87
Surin	Bruny	CAN	12 Jul 67	180/75	LJ	8.02A, 7.97, 8.19w	8.03 -87
Surin	Vitaliy	SU	5 Jan 63		3kSt	8:30.68	8:34.04 -86
Svec	Jirí	CS	14 Aug 64	182/69	3kSt	8:32.42	8:31.75 -86
Svensson	Göran	SWE	8 Mar 59	190/112	DT	66.40	66.22 -81, 66.46dh -87
Swarts	Art	USA	14 Feb 45	193/115	DT	62.20	69.40 -79
Syroyezhko	Oleg	SU	9 Dec 62	175/62	10k	28:24.38	
Szabadhegy	Kris	USA	23 Jul 64	193/91	Dec	7861	7821 -87

Name		Nat	Born	Ht/Wt	Event	1988 Mark	Pre-1988 Best
Szabó	Deszö	HUN	4 Sep 67	184/80	Dec	8209	7918 -87
Szabó	László	HUN	6 Jan 55	192/120	SP	19.54	19.87 -84
Szalma	László	HUN	21 Oct 57	190/80	LJ	8.03i, 8.02	8.30 -85
Szekeres	Attila	HUN	24 Aug 67	183/70	LJ	7.96w	7.77 -87
Széli	Robert	CS	29 May 65	179/71	LJ	8.05	8.04 -87
Szitás	Imre	HUN	4 Sep 61	185/110	HT	80.60	78.84 -84
Szpak	Mieczyslaw	POL	10 Jul 61	188/104	DT	62.74	63.28 -86
Szücs	Csaba	HUN	29 Jan 65	178/68	3kSt	8:35.80	8:35.83 -87
Szybowski	Miroslaw	POL	25 Mar 60	182/108	JT	76.58	77.32 -87
Taavitsainen	Ari	FIN	12 Apr 58	181/100	HT	74.02	75.62 -84
Tabak	Nikolay	SU	15 Apr 56	175/64	Mar	2:12:33	2:13:26 -87
Tafelmeier	Klaus	FRG	12 Apr 58	190/94	JT	85.96	86.64 -87
Tafralis	Gregg	USA	9 Apr 58	183/132	SP	21.36	21.45 -86
Tailhardat	Jean-Marc	FRA	12 Apr 66	178/66	PV	5.65	5.30 -86
Taiwo	Joseph	NIG	24 Aug 59	183/74	TJ	17.22	17.19-84, 17.29w -87
Takahashi	Koichi	JAP	7 Jun 62		Mar	2:12:14	2:14:59 -87
Takano	Susumu	JAP	21 May 61	178/65	400	44.90	45.00 -86
Talavera	Enriques	SPA	15 Jun 67	183/74	100	10.24A	10.43, 10.40w, 10.1w -87
Taletskiy	Nikolay	SU	62		400h	50.04, 49.9	49.78 -86
Talley	Keith	USA	28 Jan 64	193/88	110h	13.50, 13.36w, 13.0w	13.31 -86
					LJ	8.02i	8.05-86, 8.44w -85
Tallhem	Sören	SWE	16 Feb 64	192/110	SP	19.78	21.24i, 20.90 -85
Talsnes	Ove	NOR	22 Jun 62		1500	3:39.25	3:39.83 -87
Tamm	Jüri	SU	5 Feb 57	193/120	HT	84.16	84.40 -84
Tanev	Ivan	BUL	1 May 57	190/112	HT	82.08	79.70 -86
Taniguchi	Hiromi	JAP	4 Apr 60	171/56	Mar	2:07:40	2:09:50 -87
Tantanozis	Theodoros	GRE	29 Sep 64	188/74	TJ	16.65	16.46 -87
Tanui	Moses	KEN	20 Aug 65	165/65	5k	13:36.74	13:54.0A -87
					10k	27:40.59	28:53.1A -87
Tarasov	Maxim	SU	2 Dec 70	194/79	PV	5.60	5.40 -87
Tarasyuk	Yuriy	SU	11 Apr 57	188/101	HT	78.04	81.44 -84
Tarev	Atanas	BUL	31 Jan 58	180/75	PV	5.71	5.80 -86
Tarnavetskiy	Pavel	SU	22 Feb 61	188/85	Dec	8299	8375 -87
Tarpenning	Kory	USA	27 Feb 62	180/75	PV	5.89	5.80 -87
Tashpulatov	Damir	SU	29 Jan 64		TJ	16.64	16.70 -86
Tatár	István	HUN	24 Mar 58	174/68	100	10.33, 10.26w	10.25 -80
Tatum	Eric	USA	11 Dec 67	178/68	200	20.79	21.20 -87
Tatum	Roscoe	USA	13 Feb 66	183/91	100	10.25, 10.10w	10.18-85, 10.08w -86
Taushanski	Georgi	BUL	26 Dec 57	193/127	DT	66.00	65.78 -84
Taylor	Craig	JAM	68		100	10.24w	
Taylor	Gary	UK	1 Jun 63	177/62	Mile	3:57.15	3:58.26i-86
Teape	Hugh	UK	26 Dec 63	178/66	110h	13.80w	13.96 -87
Temane	Matthews	RSA	14 Dec 60	171/55	10k	28:16.28	28:18.6 -87
ten Kate	Martin	HOL	16 Dec 58	172/57	5k	13:33.62	13:42.24 -87
					10k	27:50.30	28:32.5 -87
					Mar	2:11:49	2:12:56 -85
Terekhov	Roman	SU	31 Mar 63	189/86	Dec	7922	7852m -87
Tesfaye	Dadi	ETH	65	164/58	Mar	2:12:49	2:21:53 -87
Tetengi	Abdullahi	NIG	15 Jul 69	174/65	100	10.0	10.71 -86, 10.2 -87
					200	20.72	21.36 -86, 20.8 -87
Thackery	Carl	UK	14 Oct 62	176/63	10k	28:08.44	27:59.24 -87
Thanos	Jon	USA	4 Jan 65	172/61	3kSt	8:35.24	8:37.73 -87
Thau	Rainer	FRG	2 Dec 62	186/73	800	1:45.96	1:45.8 -85
					1500	3:38.65	3:36.74 -86
Thaxton	Steve	USA	29 Jul 64	187/82	PV	5.57	5.51 -87
Thiébaut	Pascal	FRA	6 Jun 59	175/61	1500	3:35.61	3:34.91 -87
					3k	7:47.91	7:45.02 -87
					5k	13:17.48	13:14.60 -87
Thomas	Alvin	USA	16 Sep 65	190/70	LJ	8.00	7.84 -87
Thomas	Christian	FRG	31 Mar 65	186/73	LJ	8.12	8.12i, 8.01 -87
Thomas	Henry	USA	10 Jul 67	188/77	100	10.23	10.15-87, 10.1-85
					200	20.18	20.24, 20.22w -87
Thomas	Robert	USA	25 Jul 60	179/74	110h	13.46w	13.79 -87
Thompson	Daley	UK	30 Jul 58	184/92	Dec	8306	8847 -84
Thorson	Jay	USA	25 Feb 63	186/79	Dec	7946	7684 -87
Thränhardt	Carlo	FRG	5 Jul 57	199/85	HJ	2.42i,2.34,2.35u	2.40i-87,2.37 -84

Name		Nat	Born	Ht/Wt	Event	1988 Mark	Pre-1988 Best
Tiacoh	Gabriel	IVC	10 Sep 63	180/75	400	45.49	44.30 -86
Tiainen	Juha	FIN	5 Dec 55	183/108	HT	78.46	81.52 -84
Tikhonov	Leonid	SU	23 Mar 59	170/58	10k	28:21.50	28:34.92 -87
Tilli	Stefano	ITA	22 Aug 62	175/65	100	10.30	10.16 -84, 10.06w -83
					200	20.41A, 20.55	20.40 -84
Tillman	John	USA	11 Feb 65	188/78	TJ	16.95i, 16.92	16.94 -85
Timmermann	Ulf	GDR	1 Nov 62	194/120	SP	23.06	22.62 -85
Timpson	Mike	USA	6 Jun 67	183/82	200	20.53	20.23 -87
					110h	13.80	13.85 -86
Tirelli	Davide	ITA	12 Aug 66		1500	3:37.29	3:40.17 -87
Titov	Anatoliy	SU	3 Mar 56	183/73	110h	13.82, 13.6	13.67 -86, 13.3 -85
Tjela	Ernest	LES	16 Oct 54		Mar	2:12:56	2:11:00 -86
Tobin	Juan	USA	4 Jan 68		200	20.64	21.54 -86
Todorov	Georgi	BUL	7 Mar 60	193/118	SP	21.01	20.69 -87
Többen	Olaf	FRG	19 Dec 62	196/124	DT	65.50	62.94 -87
Tolstikov	Yakov	SU	20 May 59	165/58	Mar	2:09:20	2:10:48 -84
Tomaszewski	Mariusz	POL	23 Apr 56	190/122	HT	74.76	79.46, 81.46ex-84
Tommelein	Rik	BEL	1 Nov 62	183/79	400h	50.47	49.55 -86
Tomov	Toma	BUL	21 May 58	180/70	400h	48.90	48.48 -86
Torres	Ernesto	PR	26 Dec 59	175/62	TJ	16.84A	16.79 -87
Torres	Nivaldo	CUB	7 Dec 63		100	10.31, 9.9	10.45, 10.36w -87
Toska	Ajet	ALB	61	HT	74.04	75.92 -86	
Toso	Luca	ITA	15 Feb 64	188/65	HJ	2.32	2.27 -83
Tossel	George	RSA	21 Feb 61		DT	62.26	56.80 -87
Tóth	László	HUN	31 Aug 55	177/61	1500	3:39.39	3:38.40 -81
Tourret	Philippe	FRA	8 Jul 67	185/70	110h	13.62, 13.5	13.86 -87
Tozzi	Gianni	ITA	6 May 62	184/70	110h	13.61	13.79 -86
Trabado	Coloman	SPA	2 Jan 58	182/71	800	1:46.58	1:45.15 -84
Trandenkov	Igor	SU	17 Aug 66	191/80	PV	5.60	5.60 -87
Treacy	John	IRL	4 Jun 57	175/59	5k	13:32.34	13:16.81 -84
					10k	28:16.37	27:48.7 -80
					Mar	2:09:15	2:09:56 -84
Trefny	Jann	SWZ	10 Jan 66	186/83	Dec	7762	7615 -86
Trinkler	Markus	SWZ	11 Oct 62	181/70	800	1:46.11	1:46.81 -87
Trinks	Uwe	GDR	19 Feb 62	184/90	JT	79.22	74.70 -87
Trouabal	Jean-Charles	FRA	10 May 65	187/77	200	20.55A, 20.61	20.94, 20.88w -87
Trofimenko	Vasiliy	SU	28 Jan 62	195/80	PV	5.65i, 5.50	5.65i, 5.50-87
Trott	William	BER	20 Mar 65	176/68	100	9.9	10.35- 87, 10.27w -85
Tsarskiy	Aivar	SU	15 Jun 62	177/61	3kSt	8:29.85	8:34.72 -86
Tsebe	David	RSA			Mar	2:12:14	
Tsvetanov	Emil	BUL	14 Mar 63	175/83	JT	80.08	80.04 -87
Tuffour	Emmanuel	GHA	2 Dec 66	175/67	100	10.31	10.41- 87, 10.4 -86
Tully	Mike	USA	21 Oct 56	190/86	PV	5.84	5.83 -87
Turnbull	Geoff	UK	15 Apr 61	176/60	5k	13:34.90	13:21.73 -86
Tutani	Monde	RSA	22 Feb 62	168/57	Mile	3:57.39	3:56.12 -86
Tuttle	John	USA	16 Oct 58	185/68	10k	28:27.4m	-0-
Ubartas	Romas	SU	26 May 60	202/123	DT	70.06	67.88 -86
Ugbisie	Moses	NIG	11 Dec 64	182/76	400	45.87	45.28 -87
Uk-Jong	Lee	KOR	26 Oct 66	179/83	JT	78.10	75.40 -86
Ulmala	Risto	FIN	7 May 63	184/63	3k	7:49.89	7:51.79 -87
					5k	13:31.17	13:41.00 -87
Urbanskiy	Valeriy	SU	6 Jul 68		Dec	7959	7351 -87
Usov	Sergey	SU	14 Jan 64	188/87	110h	13.27	13.39 -87
Usui	Junichi	JAP	5 Oct 57	178/70	LJ	8.06	8.10-79, 8.15w -87
Uti	Sunday	NIG	23 Oct 62	175/68	400	45.33	44.83 -84
Vágó	Béla	HUN	3 Oct 63	176/63	3kSt	8:21.48	8;25.04 -87
Vainio	Martti	FIN	30 Dec 50	190/74	10k	28:02.04	27:30.99 -78
Valent	Gejza	CS	3 Oct 53	196/120	DT	66.42	69.70 -84
Valenta	Veroslav	CS	25 Mar 65	198/95	Dec	8289	7905 -86
Valentín	Jorge	CUB	16 Aug 64	184/76	400	45.78	45.34 -87
Valentine	Tony	USA	6 Sep 64	193/83	400h	49.67	49.66 -84
Valík	Jirí	CS	26 Jul 66	176/72	100	10.32	10.36 -87
Valkins	Vilnis	SU	5 Jul 62	189/78	Dec	7753m	7400 -87
Valkonen	Matti	FIN	17 Sep 60	175/64	5k	13:36.25	13:35.34 -86
					10k	28:24.82	28:33.15 -87
Valle	Emilio	CUB	21 Apr 67	182/70	110h	13.60	13.76 -87

Name		Nat	Born	Ht/Wt	Event	1988 Mark	Pre-1988 Best
Valmon	Andrew	USA	1 Jan 65	186/76	400	44.55	44.89 -87
Valvik	Svein-Inge	NOR	20 Sep 56	190/112	DT	64.30	68.00 -82
Valyukevich	Gennadiy	SU	1 Jun 58	182/74	TJ	17.44	17.53, 17.75w -86
van Aswegen	Samuel	RSA	11 May 65		400	45.8A	45.87A -87
Van Calcar	Karl	USA	11 Jan 65	178/65	3kSt	8:30.13	8:28.25 -85
Van der Meer	Jeroen	HOL	7 Apr 59		JT	78.92	74.56 -86
van Dijck	William	BEL	24 Jan 61	180/59	3k	7:45.40	7:48.05 -87
					3kSt	8:13.99	8:10.01 -86
Vandyak	Valeriy	SU	9 Jan 61	182/71	3kSt	8:35.49	8:29.52 -86
van Helden	Rob	HOL	6 Feb 65	180/73	800	1:45.17	1:45.53 -87
van Niekerk	Eugene	RSA	26 Aug 65		100	10.20A	10.45A -86
Vasilenko	Sergey	SU	27 Sep 65	188/76	LJ	8.16, 8.33w	8.06 -85
Vasilyev	Aleksandr	SU	26 Jul 61	191/83	400h	49.00	47.92 -85
Velasquez	Ken	USA	3 Nov 62	183/66	10k	28:24.80	
Velazco	Francisco	CUB	4 Oct 61	183/79	400h	50.06	49.64 -86
Velinov	Rosen	BUL	7 Aug 67	188/110	DT	62.10	59.84 -87
Venäläinen	Jari	FIN	21 Aug 67	174/59	1500	3:39.02	3:40.38 -87
Vento	Raimo	FIN	15 Sep 54	187/108	DT	63.54	63.58 -87
Vera	Andrés	SPA	31 Dec 60	186/72	1500	3:39.47	3:35.86 -84
Vera	Manuel	MEX	19 Mar 51	165/51	10k	28:10.4m	28:32.2 -87
Vera	Rolando	ECU	27 Apr 65	157/50	10k	27:54.33	28:20.24 -87
Vermuele	John	HOL	4 Dec 61		Mar	2:12:42	2:13:35 -87
Verster	Jean	RSA	23 Apr 65		Mile	3:55.76	4:01.23 -83
Verzy	Franck	FRA	13 May 61	181/66	HJ	2.24	2.32 -83
Veshapidze	Gela	SU	5 Sep 66	188/80	110h	13.69, 13.5	13.93 -86, 13.6-87
Vetterli	Patrick	SWZ	6 Oct 61	200/100	Dec	7946	7896 -86
Viali	Tonino	ITA	16 Sep 60	176/70	800	1:45.72	1:47.5 -83
Vida	József	HUN	9 Jan 63	192/108	HT	78.72	79.06 -84
Videv	Valentin	BUL	20 Jan 63	187/71	PV	5.60	5.65 -85
Vigneron	Thierry	FRA	9 Mar 60	181/73	PV	5.81i, 5.70	5.91 -84
Viitasalo	Esa	FIN	19 May 60	182/75	TJ	16.62	16.52, 16.74w -83
Vilhjálmsson	Einar	ICE	1 Jun 60	188/100	JT	84.66	82.96 -87
Viluckis	Benjaminas	SU	20 Mar 61	187/120	HT	80.04	82.24 -86
Vimbert	Gilles	FRA	27 Jul 66	179/70	400h	50.45	49.96 -87
Viudes	Luc	FRA	31 Jan 56	192/132	SP	19.33	19.84 -86
Vörös	Sándor	HUN	19 Jan 58	196/115	HT	77.80	76.34 -87
Voitovich	Arunas	SU	31 Mar 65	182/80	LJ	8.03	8.08 -87
Volkmann	Jens	FRG	31 May 67	187/70	3kSt	8:22.85	8:29.20 -87
Voloshin	Leonid	SU	30 Mar 66	180/74	LJ	8.46	8.09 -87
Vorobyov	Sergey	SU	29 Jan 64	183/91	HT	73.20	71.98 -86
Vorster	Dries	RSA	25 Oct 62		400h	49.50A,49.78, 49.2A	49.78A - 87, 50.62 -86
Voss	Torsten	GDR	24 Mar 63	186/88	Dec	8399	8680 -87
Vouzis	Nikos	GRE	16 Jan 66	179/71	1500	3:38.51	3:43.54 -87
Vrbka	Frantisek	CS	23 Jul 58	187/102	HT	73.66	80.38 -85
Vrican	Miroslav	CS	7 May 66	196/103	HT	72.26	70.12 -87
Vukovich	Mike	USA	7 Jan 65	190/74	HJ	2.26	2.14 -87
Wachenbrunner	Rainer	GDR	11 Jan 62	188/75	10k	28:19.94	28:53.80 -85
Wade	Ed	USA	10 Dec 64	193/109	SP	19.90i, 19.41	20.02i-87,19.27 -86
Wagner	Alwin	FRG	11 Aug 50	196/122	DT	66.96	67.80 -87
Wakiihuri	Douglas	KEN	26 Sep 63	186/65	5k	13:24.01	13:35.51 -87
					10k	27:59.60	28:06.00 -87
					Mar	2:10:47	2:11:48 -87
Walker	Colin	UK	29 Oct 62	170/61	3kSt	8:30.61	8;33.28 -87
Walker	James	USA	25 Oct 57	178/69	110h	13.0w	13.67-86,13.60w-79,13.3 -80
Walker	John	NZ	12 Jan 52	183/74	1500	3:36.3m	3:32.4 -75
					Mile	3:52.48	3:49.08 -82
Waller	Manley	USA	21 Jul 64	178/80	100	10.33, 10.24w	10.26-86, 10.11w -87
Ward	Jeff	USA	4 Aug 60	190/79	PV	5.59	5.55 -82
Ward	Kermit	USA	68		100	10.29	10.3 -86
					200	20.71w	
Ware	Roget	USA	5 Sep 68	183/79	110h	13.81	-0-
Warming	Lars	DEN	21 Jun 63	192/84	Dec	7994	7826 -87
Warsönke	Silvio	GDR	2 Aug 67	197/105	JT	84.14	72.90 -87
Washington	Al	USA	29 Jun 67	190/75	400h	49.90	
Washington	Alex	USA	28 Dec 62	186/75	110h	13.64	13.75,13.61w -84, 13.5 -86

Name		Nat	Born	Ht/Wt	Event	1988 Mark	Pre-1988 Best
Washington	Anthony	USA	22 Dec 66	178/68	400	45.94	46.23 -87
Washington	Tony	USA	16 Jan 66	185/107	DT	61.86	60.16 -87
Watkins	Walker	USA	29 Sep 67	178/79	100	10.28	10.39 -86
					200	20.62, 20.58w	20.93 -86
Watts	Quincy	USA	19 Jun 70	189/88	200	20.67	20.50A, 20.69 -87
Wedderburn	Eddie	UK	6 Dec 60	181/64	3k	7:51.0	7:57.2 -85
					2M	8:24.82	8:32.88 -83
					3kSt	8:18.32	8:21.20 -85
Weiffenbach	Klaus	FRG	21 Jan 45		DT	61.00	57.30 -87
Weil	Gert	CHL	3 Jan 60	197/120	SP	20.74	20.90 -86
Weis	Heinz	FRG	14 Jul 63	193/110	HT	82.52	80.18 -87
Weiss	Gerald	GDR	8 Jan 60	193/105	JT	83.30	81.76 -87
Weitzl	Erwin	AUT	17 Jul 60	194/125	DT	63.22	60.66 -86
Weller	Monte	USA	22 Aug 66	180/75	PV	5.50	5.33 -87
Welzel	Volker	FRG	23 Sep 61	176/66	3kSt	8:35.0	8:49.31 -83
Wennlund	Dag	SWE	9 Oct 63	188/94	JT	81.30	82.64 -87
Wentz	Siegfried	FRG	7 Mar 60	193/93	Dec	8403M	8762 -83
Werthner	Georg	AUT	7 Apr 56	190/90	Dec	7916	8229 -82
Wessig	Gerd	GDR	16 Jul 59	201/88	HJ	2.31i, 2.28	2.36 -80
West	Greg	USA	19 May 67	183/73	PV	5.58	5.40 -86
Wheway	John	UK	8 Aug 51	167/55	Mar	2:12:13	2:13:21 -87
Whitehead	Brian	USA	24 Feb 62	180/70	HJ	2.25	2.33 -85
Whitlock	Chris	USA	18 May 59	190/84	400	45.32	44.80A, 45.04 -83
Whittle	Brian	UK	24 Apr 64	190/77	400	45.22	45.38 -86
Whymns	Fabian	BAH	11 Jun 61	173/68	100	10.33	10.28, 10.21w -81
Wicks	Doug	USA	6 Nov 63	188/79	PV	5.57	5.40 -87
Wicksell	Ray	USA	11 Apr 57	183/70	Mile	3:56.67	3:56.23 -81
					5k	13:36.48	13:32.34 -86
Wilcher	Thomas	USA	11 Apr 64	180/84	110h	13.63	13.57-86, 13.52w -85
Wilkins	Mac	USA	15 Nov 50	193/111	DT	67.96	70.98 -80
Williams	Barrington	UK	11 Sep 55	177/70	100	10.27w	10.5 -87
Williams	Bart	USA	20 Sep 56	179/73	400h	50.41	48.63 -84
Williams	Bernard	USA	23 May 65	187/82	400h	49.66	49.65 -86
Williams	Bobby	USA	23 May 61	178/68	PV	5.57	5.40 -83
Williams	Desai	CAN	12 Jun 59	175/72	100	10.11,	10.21, 10.0 -85
						10.00w	10.17A-83, 10.12w -80
Williams	Leo	USA	28 Apr 60	183/77	HJ	2.26	2.29 -82
Williams	Paul	CAN	7 Aug 56	178/63	3k	7:46.22	7:46.39 -87
					5k	13:22.68	13:25.45 -87
					10k	27:56.96	27:50.19 -86
Williams	Tim	USA	27 May 62	188/81	100	10.33	10.48, 10.30w -87
					200	20.79	20.40 -87
Wilson	David	USA	19 Sep 66	181/100	SP	19.22	17.31 -87
Winkler	Jürgen	FRG	1 Mar 59	188/78	PV	5.50i, 5.50	5.66 -83
Wirz	Peter	SWZ	29 Jul 60	181/68	1500	3:36.63	3:35.83 -84
Witek	Miroslaw	POL	24 Apr 67	183/89	JT	79.12	78.90 -87
Witek	Stanislaw	POL	24 Apr 60	180/90	JT	79.62	78.76 -87
Witherspoon	Mark	USA	3 Sep 63	190/85	100	10.17	10.04, 9.91w -87
Wojcik	Piotr	POL	7 Feb 65	190/74	110h	13.80w	13.70 -86
Woderski	Leszek	POL	4 Apr 58	189/114	HT	73.72 light	76.88 -84
Wolf	August	USA	3 Sep 61	199/119	SP	20.76	21.73 -84
					DT	60.90	63.72 -87
Woods	John	IRL	8 Dec 55	170/60	Mar	2:11:30	2:18:07 -87
Woronin	Marian	POL	13 Aug 56	186/90	100	10.21	10.00 -84
Wright	Clive	JAM	18 Nov 65	175/73	100	10.27, 9.9w	10.32 -87
					200	20.75, 20.47w	20.50 -87
Wright	Darren	AUS	16 Jul 65	185/80	400h	50.30	51.04 -87
Wright	George	CAN	20 Feb 63	180/75	TJ	16.60	16.70 -87
Wszola	Jacek	POL	30 Dec 56	194/79	HJ	2.29, 2.30ex	2.35 -80
Wuyke	William	VEN	21 May 58	173/63	800	1:45.58	1:43.54 -86
Yakovlev	Aleksandr	SU	8 Sep 57	182/74	TJ	17.15, 17.42w	17.65 -87
Yakovlev	Pavel	SU	20 Jan 58	183/70	1500	3:38.50	3:36.4 -80
Yamada	Kazuhito	JAP	3 Feb 64	171/60	3kSt	8:33.97	8:55.06 -87
Yanchevskiy	Igor	SU	11 Mar 68	188/77	PV	5.50	5.40 -86
Yaryshkin	Vladimir	SU	28 Feb 63		SP	20.52i, 20.20	20.80 -86
Yawa	Xolile	RSA	29 Sep 62	169/50	10k	28:10.4m	27:39.65 -87

Name		Nat	Born	Ht/Wt	Event	1988 Mark	Pre-1988 Best
Yego	Gideon	KEN	6 May 60	173/65	400h	49.80, 48.7A	
Yegorov	Grigoriy	SU	12 Jan 67	185/75	PV	5.85	5.70 -87
Yemelin	Aleksey	SU	13 Dec 68		HJ	2.29i, 2.28	2.20 -87
Yevsyukov	Viktor	SU	6 Oct 56	190/100	JT	82.76	85.16 -87
Ylästalo	Mikael	FIN	2 May 63	187/78	110h	13.64, 13.53w	13.69 -86
Yoneshige	Shuichi	JAP	24 Jun 61	172/57	3k	7:49.92	
					5k	13:22.97	13:29.87 -86
					10k	27:43.04	28:02.5 -86
Yongfeng	Ma	CHN	28 Nov 62	190/115	SP	19.26	19.09 -87
Yoshida	Masami	JAP	14 Jun 58	179/85	JT	78.14	80.66 -86
Yoshida	Ryoichi	JAP	2 Mar 65	174/65	400h	50.25, 50.1	49.20 -87
Young	Kevin	USA	16 Sep 66	193/80	400	45.67	46.93 -87
					400h	47.72	48.15 -87
Yudakov	Timur	SU	25 Mar 66		110h	13.73	14.26 -87, 13.8 -85
Yushmanov	Nikolay	SU	18 Dec 61	184/80	100	10.15	10.10 -86
Zachariasen	Allan	DEN	4 Nov 55	170/60	Mar	2:12:27	2:11:05 -83
Zaitsev	Viktor	SU	6 Jun 66		JT	81.94	77.78 -87
Zalar	Miro	SWE	24 Mar 57	180/76	PV	5.52	5.70 -86
Zanti	Enrico	ITA	17 Apr 65		HJ	2.25ex	2.18 -87
Zaozerskiy	Sergey	SU	27 Jan 64	184/75	LJ	8.22	8.14 -87
Zasimovich	Sergey	SU	6 Sep 62	188/73	HJ	2.26	2.36 -84
Zayats	Nikolay	SU	3 Feb 67		Dec	7807	7671m -87
Zelezny	Jan	CS	16 Jun 66	186/77	JT	86.88	87.66 -87
Zepeda	Rafael	MEX	22 Aug 61	168/57	10k	28:23.13	28:29.4 -87
Zerkowski	Miroslaw	POL	20 Aug 56	171/59	3kSt	8:21.48	8:19.02 -86
Zgarda	Piotr	POL	18 Jun 56	174/62	3kSt	8:31.04	8:27.2 -79
Zhang	Guowei	CHN	27 Apr 59	168/54	5k	13:37.08	13:31.01 -86
Zhelanov	Sergey	SU	14 Jun 57	190/82	Dec	7866	8417 -84
Zhicheng	Yu	CHN	23 Jul 63	187/78	110h	13.75	13.72 -87
Zhirov	Yuriy	SU	1 Jan 60	177/80	JT	79.18	80.66 -87
Zhukov	Aleksandr	SU	25 Jan 65	185/66	PV	5.70i, 5.50	5.70 -87

INDEX OF 1988 WOMEN'S WORLD LISTS

Former married names are shown in parentheses, and in a few cases married names after hyphens.

Name		Nat	Born	Ht/Wt	Event	1988 Mark	Pre-1988 Best
Abramova	Olga	SU	6 Apr 64	170/63	Hep	6072	5952 -87
Abt	Gudrun	FRG	3 Aug 62	180/62	400	52.22	53.00 -87
					400h	54.04	55.56 -87
Adams	Odalys	CUB	1 Aug 66	178/60	100h	13.20	13.30 -88
Adilova	Almagul	SU	66		LJ	6.62	6.49 -87
Aebi	Regula	SWZ	12 Nov 65	169/57	100	11.26w	11.94 -87
					200	22.88	24.06 -86
Afanasyeva (Vlasova)	Yelena	SU	1 Mar 66		800	1:57.77	2:00.90 -87
					1500	4:07.8	
Age	Zina	USA	10 May 65	178/65	100	11.42w	11.54, 11.2 -85
Agoston	Zita	HUN	18 Mar 65	164/44	3000	8:55.12	8:55.53 -87
					10k	32:58.33	33:20.58 -86
Akhmetova	Zilya	SU	3 Apr 61		DT	57.56	58.96 -86
Akhrimenko	Natalya	SU	12 May 55	180/90	SP	21.73	21.39 -86
Aksu	Semra	TUR	31 May 62	184/75	400h	57.20	56.59 -87
Alafrantti	Päivi	FIN	8 May 64	176/72	JT	63.18	60.60 -85
Alber	Sabine	FRG	15 Apr 65	176/58	400h	56.72	57.73 -87
Alekseyeva	Tatyana	SU	7 Oct 63	173/58	200	22.9	22.77 -84
					400	52.08	51.39 -84
Alizadeh	Manuela	FRG	29 Jan 63	172/78	JT	65.34	63.40 -87
Allen	Liliana	CUB	24 May 70	170/62	100	11.18	11.42, 11.19w -87
					200	23.13, 22.97w	23.83 -87
Alonso	Ana Isabel	SPA	16 Aug 63	154/44	10k	32:28.7	32:45.48 -87
Ambraziene	Anna	SU	14 Apr 55	176/63	400	52.50	51.96 -83
					400h	55.31, 55.0	54.02 -83
Anderson	Keturah	CAN	9 Jan 68	162/61	100	11.42	11.58 -87
Andonova	Lyudmila	BUL	6 May 60	177/60	HJ	1.95	2.07 -84
Andonova	Malena	BUL	6 May 57	168/58	400	52.12	51.41 -87
Andris	Monika	SU	2 Feb 65		SP	17.53i, 17.24	16.94 -87
Andrusca	Simona	RUM	24 Mar 62	178/92	SP	17.28	19.67 -86
Anghel	Elisabeta	RUM	21 Oct 67	172/59	100h	13.23	13.93 -85
Angotzi	Rita	ITA	12 Feb 67	170/50	100	11.36	11.67 -87
Antonova	Irina	SU	60		100h	13.37	
Antonova	Olga	SU	16 Feb 60	164/54	100	11.21	11.19,11.1 -87, 11.09w -83
Antonyuk	Marina	SU	12 May 62	182/91	SP	20.51	20.60 -86
Aouam	Fatima	MOR	16 Dec 59	165/50	1500	4:05.62	4:05.49 -86
					3000	8:59.19	8:58.07 -87
Araki	Kumi	JAP	11 Oct 65	153/40	Mar	2:31:40	2:37:12 -87
Arendt	Helga	FRG	24 Apr 64	178/66	200	23.13	23.69 -86, 23.51i -87
					400	50.36	51.70 -87
Armenteros	Susana	CUB	11 Aug 61	162/56	100	11.44A	11.42 -87
Artyomova	Natalya	SU	5 Jan 63	166/50	800	1:59.84	1:58.05 -85
					1500	4:04.03	3:59.28 -85
					2k	5:44.71#	
					3000	8:31.67	8:38.84 -84
					5k	15:23.77	14:54.08 -85
					10k	31:56.33	33:07.97 -87
Asai	Eriko	JAP	20 Oct 59	150/38	Mar	2:32:13	2:33:43 -84
Ashford	Evelyn	USA	15 Apr 57	165/55	100	10.81	10.76 -84
					200	23.09, 22.97w	21.83 -79
Astafei	Galina	RUM	7 Jun 69	181/62	HJ	2.00	1.93 -86
Audain	Anne	NZ	1 Nov 55	168/53	10k	32:05.8	31:53.31 -86
Augee	Myrtle	UK	4 Feb 65	173/90	SP	18.29	18.19 -87
Auzeil (Schoellkopf)	Nadine	FRA	19 Aug 64	176/64	JT	63.30	62.46 -83
Avasiloaie	Luminita	RUM	24 May 69	174/56	800	2:01.61	
Avdeyenko	Lyudmila	SU	14 Nov 63	180/62	HJ	2.00i, 1.98	2.00 -87
Avdeyeva	Larisa	SU	24 Oct 61		JT	62.94	64.68 -87
Axmann	Antje	GDR	26 Apr 69	176/62	400h	57.10	58.01 -87
Avraam	Andri	CYP	20 Jan 63	165/50	10k	32:59.30	
Azarashvili	Maya	SU	6 Apr 64	170/58	100	11.08, 10.9	11.20 -86
					200	22.24	22.51 -86, 22.3w -87
					400	52.13	

Name		Nat	Born	Ht/Wt	Event	1988 Mark	Pre-1988 Best
Azzizi	Yasmina	ALG	25 Feb 66	176/67	Hep	5824	5663 -87
Babikova	Zhanna	SU	69		SP	17.03	15.84 -87
Babushkina	Antonina	SU	18 Jun 62	176/63	800	2:01.3	
Bácskai	Márta	HUN	1 Oct 60	180/98	DT	61.38	66.48 -86
Baikauskaite	Laima	SU	10 Jun 56	162/58	800	1:58.61	1:58.3 -85
					1500	4:00.24	4:02.92 -86
Bailey	Angela	CAN	28 Feb 62	157/56	100	11.11	10.98 -87
					200	23.32	22.64 -83
Bailey	Shireen	UK	27 Sep 59	173/56	800	1:59.94	1:58.97 -87
					1k	2:38.96	2:35.32 -86
					1500	4:02.32	4:05.32 -87
Bakare	Airat	NIG	20 May 68		400	52.15	51.83 -86
Balabayeva	Natalya	SU	3 Mar 66		JT	60.92	57.82 -87
Balck	Heike	GDR	19 Aug 70	178/55	HJ	1.94	1.93 -87
Balgurina	Galina	SU	4 May 65	176/60	HJ	1.94	1.94-86
Baranova	Larisa	SU	29 Jun 61		DT	62.44	65.36 -87
Barber	Sharon	AUS	29 Aug 65	178/63	HJ	1.90	1.87 -87
Barinova	Irina	SU	61		HJ	1.92i, 1.90	1.92i -86, 1.90-85
Barnes	Lacy	USA	23 Dec 64	165/70	DT	62.20	59.42 -87
Barth	Birgit	GDR	19 Jun 62	171/49	1500	4:07.55, 4:06.16i	4:03.9 -87
					3000	8:51.04	9:10.28 -87
Bartholomew	Jacintha	GRN	15 Jan 65	175/54	LJ	6.54w	6.43i, 6.37 -86
Bartzak	Jolanta	POL	20 Mar 64	169/57	LJ	6.90	6.43, 6.74w -86
Basson	Ansie	RSA	31 Jul 66		200	23.06A	23.22A -87
Bates	Yvette	USA	20 Aug 65	175/61	LJ	6.68, 6.88w	6.42, 6.46w -87
					TJ	13.64i, 13.40	13.79i, 13.60 -87
Beaugeant	Chantal	FRA	16 Feb 61	170/59	100h	13.10	13.40, 13.28w -87
					400h	55.76	56.86 -87, 56.7-85
					Hep	6702	6410 -87
Beaugendre	Madely	FRA	22 Sep 65	172/55	HJ	1.96i, 1.93	1.93 -87
Beckford	Darlene	USA	9 Oct 61	162/50	1500	4:10.33	4:04.81 -85
Beckford	Patricia	UK	6 Aug 65	178/70	400	52.26	-
Beclea	Violeta	RUM	26 Mar 65	166/50	800	1:59.35	1:58.7 -86
					1500	4:07.94	4:04.56 -86
Bednarska	Sylwia	POL	23 Feb 66	175/59	100h	13.25w	13.26 -85
Beer	Peggy	GDR	15 Sep 69	175/69	Hep	6067w, 6007	6068 -87
Behmer	Anke	GDR	5 Jun 61	174/62	200	23.10, 22.73w	23.26, 23.20w -84
					100h	13.11	13.25 -86
					LJ	6.90i,6.79,6.87w	6.84 -84, 6.85w -87
					Hep	6858	6775 -84
Behrbaum (Sartin)	Anita	USA	24 Oct 64	164/58	Hep	6037	5991 -87
Behrendt	Kerstin	GDR	2 Sep 67	177/64	100	11.05,11.0,10.89w	11.09,11.05w-87
					200	22.36, 22.3	22.76 -87
Beinhauer	Christiane	FRG	24 Aug 68	178/62	400h	57.37	57.98 -87
Belanger	Renée	CAN	12 Sep 62	157/47	800	2:01.66	2:01.56 -85
Belu	Mirela	RUM	26 Dec 70	172/59	LJ	6.58	6.54 -86
Belz	Ingrid	FRG	3 Aug 67	177/78	DT	59.10	50.52 -86
Berezhnaya	Larisa	SU	28 Feb 61	178/66	LJ	7.07	7.19 -86
Berezhnaya	Tatyana	SU	11 Jul 56	175/85	DT	62.26	65.94 -80
Bergdahl	Karin	SWE	6 Jan 64	177/70	JT	61.02	63.64 -85
Bergmann	Mette	NOR	9 Nov 62	174/80	DT	62.30	59.40 -85
Berkeley	Mary	UK	3 Oct 65	176/65	LJ	6.53, 6.58w	6.54 -87
Besliu	Iulia	RUM	3 Jul 65	170/52	1500	4:04.36	4:07.07 -85
					3000	8:41.54	8:45.36 -85
Betekhtina	Natalya	SU	8 Sep 61		800	2:00.7	2:01.1 -86
					1500	4:09.35	4:10.17 -87
Beuge	Barbara	FRG	11 Aug 60	187/81	DT	63.34	63.98 -87
Beurskens	Carla	HOL	10 Feb 52	165/45	Mar	2:28:58	2:26:34 -87
Beyer	Susanne	GDR	24 Jun 61	177/60	HJ	1.97i, 1.94	2.02i 1.99 -87
Bezdenezhnykh	Alyona	SU	7 Aug 68	170/62	JT	61.36	57.98 -87
Bille	Patricia	GDR	20 Dec 68	177/57	LJ	6.55	6.70 -86
Bily	Laurence	FRA	5 May 63	168/58	100	11.24	11.23 -87, 11.2 -83
Birbach	Malgorzata	POL	17 Feb 60	158/45	Mar	2:33:54	2:38:52 -87
Biserova	Yelena	SU	24 Mar 62	177/67	100h	13.1i	12.66 -84

Name		Nat	Born	Ht/Wt	Event	1988 Mark	Pre-1988 Best
Bisset	Sonia	CUB	1 Apr 71		JT	58.28	50.40 -87
Bizioli	Antonella	ITA	29 Mar 57	160/50	Mar	2:31:21	2:36:39 -87
Blanford	Rhonda	USA	15 Dec 63	174/50	100h	13.09, 13.06w	12.85, 12.70w -85
Blaszak	Genowefa	POL	22 Aug 57	168/57	400	52.45	50.70 -86
					400h	55.14	54.27 -85
Blokhina	Tatyana	SU	12 Mar 70	183/72	Hep	5864	5833 -87
Boborova	Natalya	SU	12 Feb 59	168/53	3000	9:00.23	8:48.31 -84
					10k	32:16.50	32:38.43 -82
Bochkayeva	Galina	SU	4 Jan 63	172/59	800	2:00.6	2:01.81 -85
					1500	4:08.90	4:10.38 -87
Boegman	Nicole	AUS	5 Mar 67	174/60	LJ	6.87	6.67 -87, 6.71w -83
Boit	Cristina	RUM	14 May 68	177/80	DT	64.58	57.34 -87
Bolden	Jeanette	USA	26 Jan 60	174/62	100	11.28, 11.10w	11.08 -86
Bondarenko	Olga	SU	2 Jun 60	154/41	1500	4:06.2	4:05.99 -86
					3000	8:43.95	8:33.99 -86
					5k	15:11.16	14:55.76 -85
					10k	31:05.21	30:57.21 -86
Bonnet	Françoise	FRA	8 Apr 57	163/48	10k	32:55.73	34:13.17 -87
					Mar	2:32:36	2:31:22 -87
Boothe	Lorna	UK	5 Dec 54	163/51	100h	13.1	13.07, 12.90w -82
Bopf	Deann	AUS	13 Feb 62	167/47	HJ	1.90	1.90 -85
Borgschulze	Claudia	FRG	9 Feb 64	160/47	3000	8:55.69	8:57.54 -87
Borisova I.	Lyudmila	SU	59		400	52.0	51.79 -84
					800	2:01.36	1:56.78 -84
Borisova II.	Lyudmila	SU	8 Mar 66	172/57	800	2:01.30	2:03.02 -87
					1500	4:06.94	4:09.42 -87
					3000	8:56.99	9:05.91 -87
Borisova	Natalya	SU	66		400h	56.55	
Boroday	Svetlana	SU	29 Oct 59	185/71	HJ	1.90i	1.92 -87
Borsheim	Vicki	USA	12 Sep 66	178/66	HJ	1.88i	1.90 -87
Botes	Zelda	RSA	18 Jul 68		800	2:01.40	2:01.23 -87
					1k	2:38.68	
Bothma	Myrtle	RSA	18 Feb 64	174/57	200	22.82A	24.17 -85
					400	51.29A	50.12A -86
					400h	55.13	53.74A -86
Boulmerka	Hasiba	ALG	10 Jul 68	158/49	1500	4:08.33	4:23.96 -87
Bouza	Herminia	CUB	25 Sep 65	170/74	JT	64.64	62.78 -87
Bowker	Debbie	CAN	16 Dec 58	163/48	1500	4:06.62	4:05.28 -86
					3000	8:43.81	8:46.88 -87
Bowles	Dawn	USA	12 Dec 68	168/52	100h	13.30, 13.10w	13.63, 13.48w -87
Boyle	Janet	UK	25 Jul 63	178/58	HJ	1.92	1.91 -86
Bozhanova	Sofia	BUL	4 Oct 67	172/52	LJ	6.70 6.72w	6.80 -87
Braag	Bettina	FRG	15 Nov 65	174/65	Hep	5790	5561 -87
Bradburn	Angela	USA	4 Sep 68	178/61	HJ	1.88i	1.89 -85
Brandt	Kerstin	GDR	9 Dec 61	182/72	HJ	1.91	1.99 -83
Braun	Sabine	FRG	19 Jun 65	174/66	Hep	6432	6436 -84
Breuer	Grit	GDR	16 Feb 72	165/59	200	23.04	24.03 -87
					400	51.24	52.59 -87
Bridgeforth	Nadeen	USA	22 Apr 66	181/57	400h	56.68	-
Briesenick	Ilona	GDR	24 Sep 56	180/95	SP	20.81	22.45 -80
Brigadnaya	Galina	SU	30 Oct 58	175/57	HJ	1.92	1.96 -85
Brill	Debbie	CAN	10 Mar 53	177/60	HJ	1.90, 1.88	1.99i -82, 1.98 -84
Brisco	Valerie	USA	6 Jul 60	170/62	100	11.30	10.99 -86
					200	22.11	21.81 -84
					400	49.90	48.83 -84
Brown	Alice	USA	20 Sep 60	159/59	100	10.92,10.88w	11.01-87,10.84w -86
					200	22.39, 22.33w	22.41 -83
Brown	Coralea	CAN	15 Jun 72	170/54	HJ	1.88i	1.80 -87
Brown King	Judi	USA	14 Jul 61	180/67	400h	55.30	54.23 -87
Brown	Tonja	USA	5 Sep 60	170/59	400h	56.78	54.86 -85
Brown	Wendy	USA	28 Jan 66	180/70	LJ	6.59A	6.53 -85
					TJ	13.82	13.71 -87, 13.78w -87
					Hep	6079	5896 -87
Browne	Vanessa	AUS	5 Jan 63	170/53	HJ	1.96	1.94 -83
Bruhns	Birte	GDR	4 Nov 70	169/53	800	1:59.17	1:59.96 -87
Brunet	Roberta	ITA	20 May 65	168/50	1500	4:08.92	4:13.55 -85

Name		Nat	Born	Ht/Wt	Event	1988 Mark	Pre-1988 Best
					3000	8:47.66	9:01.55 -86
Bruns	Ulrike	GDR	17 Nov 53	173/56	3000	8:59.19	8:36.38 -84
Bryzgina	Olga	SU	30 Jun 63	173/68	200	22.95	22.44 -85
					400	48.65	48.27 -85
Buhus	Alina	RUM	9 Sep 67	170/59	400h	56.64	57.91 -87
Buist	Marguerite	NZ	19 Dec 62	166/49	Mar	2:34:41	
Bujnita	Aurica	RUM	13 Dec 68	176/73	JT	63.22	59.16 -87
Bulkowska	Danuta	POL	31 Jan 59	177/59	HJ	1.90i, 1.88	1.97 -84
Buraga	Svetlana	SU	4 Sep 65	168/56	100h	12.83, 12.8	13.14, 13.01w -87
					Hep	6597	6585 -87
Burina	Marina	SU	26 Feb 62	180/90	SP	18.30	19.03 -86
Bürki	Cornelia	SWZ	3 Oct 53	160/53	1500	4:08.08	3:59.90 -87
					3000	8:45.81	8:38.71 -85
Burnham	Angela	USA	13 Sep 71	158/52	100	11.28, 11.26w	12.00 -87
Busch	Sabine	GDR	21 Nov 62	177/66	400h	53.69	53.24 -87
Bussières	Lizanne	CAN	20 Aug 61	159/51	5k	15:44.16	16:23.2 -86
					10k	32:45.42	32:50.29 -86
					Mar	2:30:57	2:32:16 -86
Bussmann	Gaby	FRG	8 Oct 59	170/57	800	2:01.59i	1:58.11 -86
Butkus	Inga	SU	27 Jun 67		HJ	1.92	1.89 -87
Byelevskaya	Yelena	SU	11 Oct 63	174/55	LJ	7.36	7.39 -87
Byelikova	Nina	SU	63		3000	9:01.60	9:09.3 -87
Byelova (Ilyichova)	Irina	SU	27 Mar 68		Hep	6056	5710 -87
Byelova	Tatyana	SU	12 Feb 62	182/88	SP	18.58	19.02 -87
					DT	66.48	67.82 -87
Byelovolova	Yelena	SU	6 Feb 65		SP	18.42	18.01 -87
Byelyakova	Galina	SU	69		DT	57.40	59.04 -87
Byelyayeva	Lutsia	SU	22 Jun 57	160/47	Mar	2:34:30	2:30:25 -87
Bykova	Tamara	SU	21 Dec 58	181/60	HJ	1.99	2.05 -84
Bystrova	Svetlana	SU	28 Feb 67	171/65	Hep	6116	6189 -87
Cady	Carol	USA	6 Jun 62	170/80	SP	17.02	17.70 -86
					DT	63.82	66.10 -86
Cahill (Boxer)	Christina	UK	25 Mar 57	164/51	800	1:59.78	1:59.05 -79
					1k	2:38.04	2:34.92 -85
					1500	4:00.64	4:00.57 -84
Capriotti	Antonella	ITA	4 Feb 62	162/52	LJ	6.72i, 6.70	6.57i -87, 6.56 -85
Carabali	Norfalia	COL	21 Jan 67	164/45	400	51.76	51.70 -87
Carutasu	Nicoleta	RUM	14 Feb 64	172/64	400	52.33	
					400h	55.85	55.16 -86
Cashell	Candy	USA	28 Mar 63	186/66	HJ	1.91	1.86i, 1.84 -86
Catford	Sheila	UK	29 Aug 60		Mar	2:33:44	2:37:31 -87
Cato	Camille	CAN	2 May 63	173/57	800	2:01.38	2:02.73 -87
Cathey	Kellie	USA	24 Nov 61	157/43	5k	15:31.0	15:59.7 -82
					10k	32:58.60	32:22.5 -82
					Mar	2:32:29	2:38:30 -81
Cavanaugh	Regina	USA	6 Dec 64	180/84	SP	17.47	17.70 -86
Cazier - Ballo	Marie-Christine	FRA	23 Aug 63	178/62	100	11.42	11.23 -86, 10.9,11.12w -85
					200	22.78	22.32 -86
Cearns (Griffiths)	Wendy	UK	25 Aug 60	167/60	400h	56.85	57.81 -82
Chala	Liliana	ECU	7 Jun 65	165/48	400h	57.12A	57.13 -87
Chalmers	Angela	CAN	6 Sep 63	170/56	1500	4:05.78	4:06.43 -87
					2k	5:49.92	
					3000	8:48.60	8:56.45 -87
Chamberlin	Judy	USA	20 Jun 58	158/46	10k	33:01.6	33:07.22 -87
Chartrand	Céline	CAN	26 May 62	173/67	JT	58.86	59.76 -87
Chasova - Naumova	Alevtina	SU	16 Jun 61	158/50	Mar	2:29:49	2:31:53 -87
Chen	Dongmei	CHN	60		400h	57.30, 56.7	57.83 -87
Chen	Qingmei	CHN	4 Apr 63	168/54	3000	8:51.53	9:00.9 -87
					10k	31:55.67	33:38.38 -87
					Mar	2:34:35	2:49:09 -87
Chen	Xiaohong	CHN	68		TJ	13.07	
Chen	Yolanda	SU	26 Jul 61	169/54	LJ	7.16	6.83 -84

Name		Nat	Born	Ht/Wt	Event	1988 Mark	Pre-1988 Best
Chepkurui	Francisca	KEN	11 Sep 63	175/65	800	1:58.1	
Cherepanova	Yelena	SU	1 Feb 65	165/50	400	51.9	
Chernysheva	Yelizaveta	SU	26 Jan 58	169/56	100h	12.87, 12.7	12.78 -86, 12.6 -85
Chervyakova	Svetlana	SU	16 Mar 63		100	11.21	11.30 -84
Chicherova	Yelena	SU	9 Aug 58	172/58	LJ	6.82i, 6.79	6.94 -84
					Hep	5997	5539 -86
Chidu	Tudorita	RUM	17 Oct 67	170/53	400	52.18	53.91 -85
					800	1:57.64	1:59.96 -87
Chistyakova	Galina	SU	26 Jul 62	169/54	LJ	7.52	7.34 -86
Chistyakova	Nadezhda	SU	29 Jul 69	176/64	200	23.26	24.60 -86
					100h	13.22	13.65, 13.3 -87
Chistyakova	Regina	SU	8 Jan 61	166/49	1500	4:05.96	4:07.68 -87
					3000	8:43.09	8:39.25 -86
Chistyakova	Svetlana	SU	9 Aug 61	175/68	Hep	6079	6289 -87
Chuvashova	Vera	SU	59		800	1:58.12	1:58.36 -86
					1500	4:10.81	4:14.6 -85
Chylinska	Krystyna	POL	18 Nov 64	157/48	Mar	2:35:29	2:39:22 -87
Cilimbini	Maria -Luisa	ITA	25 Oct 67		400h	57.05	57.69 -87
Cinibulková	Olga	CS	4 Apr 60	168/74	DT	61.18	62.16 -87
Ciobanu (Capatina)	Jana	RUM	12 Jan 68	176/102	SP	19.23	17.19 -87
Cirulli	Giuseppina	ITA	19 Mar 59	168/52	400h	57.50A	56.44 -84
Clarius	Birgit	FRG	18 Mar 65	175/65	Hep	6204	6179 -86
Clark	Joetta	USA	1 Aug 62	172/52	800	1:59.79	1:58.98 -85
Clark	Lavern	CAN	20 Mar 67	173/61	TJ	13.06	12.98i -86
Clough	Jane	USA	2 Jun 63	183/61	HJ	1.93	1.93 -87
Cockcroft	Jeannie	CAN	4 Jun 65	183/61	HJ	1.92i	1.94 -85
Colditz	Grit	GDR	20 Apr 66	176/67	Hep	6028	6004 -87
Collard	Véronique	BEL	9 Jun 63		3000	8:56.48	9:04.26 -87
					10k	32:47.54	
Colle	Florence	FRA	4 Dec 65	169/55	100h	12.84, 12.78w	12.84 -87
Colón	María Caridad	CUB	25 Mar 58	175/70	JT	67.44	70.14 -86
Colorado	Rosa	SPA	13 May 54	158/48	800	2:01.16	2:00.33 -87
Colovic	Slobodanka	YUG	10 Jan 65	176/59	400	52.32	53.41 -86
					800	1:57.50	1:56.51 -87
Cong	Yuzhen	CHN	22 Jan 63	175/90	SP	20.47	19.86 -87
Connor	Claire	USA	22 Jun 66	162/53	LJ	6.63, 6.65w	6.35 -87
Constantin (Junghiatu)	Mitica	RUM	18 Aug 62	174/58	800	1:58.72	1:57.87 -86
					1500	4:03.49	4:03.04 -87
Cooksey	Marty	USA	18 Jul 54	165/48	10k	32:40.35	32:34.73 -86
Cooman -Fiere	Nelli	HOL	6 Jun 64	158/60	100	11.08	11.08 -86
Cordes	Ina	FRG	25 Oct 68	174/64	200	23.31	23.59 -86
Costa	Silvia	CUB	4 May 64	179/60	HJ	2.02	2.01 -85
Costian	Daniela	RUM	30 Apr 65	182/92	DT	73.84	69.66 -86
Cotric	Gordana	YUG	22 Jan 68	168/55	100h	13.28	13.87 -87
Council	Rosalind	USA	6 Mar 65	165/55	100h	13.08	13.03, 12.91w -86
Crehan	Susan	UK	12 Sep 56	162/48	Mar	2:35:10	2:50:49 -83
Crisp	Laurie	USA	28 Mar 61	157/49	Mar	2:35:37	2:36:01 -87
Crooks	Charmaine	CAN	8 Aug 62	175/64	400	51.16	50.45 -84
Cucchietti	Silvana	ITA	30 Dec 57		Mar	2:31:23	2:37:23 -87
Cunha	Aurora	POR	31 May 59	155/48	10k	32:33.9	31:29.41 -86
					Mar	2:31:26	- 0 -
Curatolo	Maria	ITA	12 Oct 63	147/40	3000	9:01.71	8:53.55 -87
					10k	32:19.77	32:04.34 -86
					Mar	2:30:14	2:36:05 -84
Cuthbert	Juliet	JAM	9 Apr 64	160/54	100	11.03, 10.96w	11.07, 10.95w -87
					200	22.59	22.59, 22.25w, 21.8w -87
Dai	Mei	CHN	65		DT	59.82	59.88 -87
Darami	Hassania	MOR	56		10k	33:01.52	33:46.69 -85
Dasse	Bonnie	USA	22 Jul 59	178/86	SP	19.49	19.07 -85
Davidson	Karol	USA	12 Aug 65	178/53	800	2:01.03	2:01.50 -87
Davies	Diana	UK	7 May 61	175/65	HJ	1.92	1.95 -82
Davis (Doak)	Nan	USA	3 Jul 62	150/41	5k	15:33.3	15:45.84 -85
					10k	32:14.05	32:29.86 -86
Davis	Patricia	USA	24 Feb 65	163/56	100h	12.83	13.16 -85, 13.08w -86

Name		Nat	Born	Ht/Wt	Event	1988 Mark	Pre-1988 Best
Davis	Pauline	BAH	9 Jul 66	168/57	100	11.17	11.19 -87, 11.1 -84
						11.12w	11.11w -86
					200	22.67	22.49, 22.1w -87
					400	51.11	
Davydova	Olga	SU	17 Sep 63		DT	65.34	60.20 -87
de Jesus	Madeline	PR	4 Nov 57	167/57	LJ	6.96A	6.49 -83
de Klerk	Evette	RSA	21 Aug 65	170/51	100	11.34A	11.22A -86
					200	23.20A	22.42A, 22.39Aw -86
De Wachter	Sabine	BEL	7 Nov 64		HJ	1.88	1.84 -85
Debois	Nadine	FRA	25 Sep 61	173/63	Hep	5823	6333 -86
Delnoye	Rita	HOL	20 Jun 66		5k	15:44.25	
Demeshonkova	Svetlana	SU	2 Mar 66		Hep	5795	5561 -87
Demilly	Patricia	FRA	27 Dec 59	165/52	1500	4:08.25	4:09.91 -87
Demireva Valova	Valya	BUL	23 Aug 61	173/60	100	11.43, 11.38w	11.34 -87
Demming	Ute	FRG	18 Jan 68	190/69	HJ	1.89	1.90i -87, 1.84 -86
Demsitz	Lene	DEN	8 Mar 59	164/53	LJ	6.62	6.72 -85
Dendy	Terri	USA	8 May 65	168/53	200	23.20, 23.18wA	23.24 -87
					400	51.45	52.00 -87
Deng	Shifen	CHN	66		LJ	6.58	6.48 -87
Denk	Ulrike	FRG	10 May 64	167/64	100h	12.95	12.84 -85
Derevyankina	Anna	SU	27 Sep 67	173/57	LJ	6.55	6.47 -84
Derevyankina	Lyudmila	SU	66		800	1:58.85	
					1500	4:05.89	
Dethier	Sylvia	BEL	20 May 65		100h	13.29, 13.0	13.47 -87
Devers	Gail	USA	19 Nov 66	163/50	100	10.97, 10.86w	10.98, 10.85w -87
- Roberts					200	22.8	22.71, 22.85w -87
					100h	12.61	13.08 -86
					LJ	6.77	6.65 -87
Dias	Maria Albertina	POR	26 Apr 65	163/48	3000	9:00.40	9:08.17 -87
					10k	32:07.13	32:41.5 -87
Dickow	Claudia	FRG	17 May 63	175/62	Hep	5862	5543 -86
Dietz	Diana	GDR	30 Aug 69	162/48	100	11.18	11.38, 11.24w -87
					200	22.88w	23.18, 23.10w -87
Dietzsch	Franka	GDR	22 Jan 68	184/90	DT	65.56	66.34 -87
Dimitrova	Anushka	BUL	6 Jul 62	169/57	800	2:01.51	2:01.75 -87
Dimitrova	Emilia	BUL	13 Nov 67	170/60	Hep	5990	6403 -86
Dimitrova	Svetla	BUL	27 Jan 70	170/57	200	23.31	24.32 -86
					100h	13.24, 12.9w	13.85 -86
					Hep	6289	6041 -86
Ding	Fenghua	CHN	64		JT	60.42	60.72 -87
Ditz	Nancy	USA	25 Jun 54	165/51	Mar	2:30:14	2:31:36 -85
Dixon	Diane	USA	23 Sep 64	165/54	200	22.58	22.53 -86
					400	49.84	50.24 -86
Dobrenko	Irina	SU	65		100h	13.23	13.52 -84
Dobrinoiu	Cristina	RUM	10 Jan 62	163/64	JT	58.40	62.08 -87
Dogadina	Olga	SU	28 Mar 59		800	2:00.39	1:59.2 -84
					1500	4:08.05	4:09.7 -84
Dodika	Vera	SU	21 Feb 59		800	1:58.70	1:58.43 -86
Dolegiewicz	Gale	CAN	10 Nov 59	182/81	DT	57.70	55.72 -83
Dolgaya	Tatyana	SU	21 Nov 64	174/62	100h	13.38	13.35 -84, 13.2 -85
					Hep	6048	5914 -87
Domniteanu	Ionica	RUM	8 Jan 69	167/63	100h	13.27w	13.51 -87
					Hep	6007	6187 -87
Dong	Yuping	CHN	1 Mar 63	176/68	Hep	6087	6121 -87
Donkova	Yordanka	BUL	28 Sep 61	175/67	100h	12.21	12.26, 12.0w -86
Dornhoefer	Sabrina	USA	2 Dec 63	165/52	1500	4:09.15	4:13.10 -86
					3000	8:44.91	8:57.27 -87
					5k	15:30.95	15:24.22 -87
Dorokhova	Svetlana	SU	3 Dec 64	177/96	SP	17.51	17.47 -87
					DT	60.02	59.32 -87
Dörre	Katrin	GDR	6 Oct 61	170/57	Mar	2:26:21	2:25:24 -87
dos Santos	Orlane Maria Lima	BRA	9 Dec 66	171/62	HJ	1.88	1.90 -87
Dräger	Dorit	GDR	30 Oct 71	174/68	JT	60.34	50.32 -87
Dragieva	Emilia	BUL	11 Jan 65	170/53	HJ	1.95i	2.00i, 1.94 -87
Drechsler	Heike	GDR	16 Dec 64	181/70	100	10.91, 10.85w	10.91, 10.80w -86
					200	21.84	21.71 -86
					LJ	7.48	7.45 -86

Name		Nat	Born	Ht/Wt	Event	1988 Mark	Pre-1988 Best
Du	Juan	CHN	18 Mar 68	172/58	100h	13.39, 13.18w, 12.9	13.17 -87
du Plessis	Desiré	RSA	20 May 65	184/64	HJ	1.93	2.01 -86
Dudina	Natalya	SU	66		400h	56.14	58.5 -85
Dukes	Pam	USA	15 May 64	180/85	SP	18.07i, 17.70	18.11 -87
Dumitrascu	Ilona	RUM	3 Jul 62	171/64	100h	13.39	13.47 -86
Dumitru	Carla	RUM	17 Dec 67	175/61	JT	62.16	61.02 -87
Dunn	Paula	UK	3 Dec 64	156/51	100	11.26, 11.13w	11.25, 11.14w -86
					200	22.79	23.17 -87
Düring	Jeanette	GDR	1 Feb 65	170/53	200	23.20	23.16 -85
Duros	Marie-Pierre	FRA	7 Jun 67	160/45	3000	8:47.9	8:46.81 -87
Dyuzhova	Marina	SU	65		HJ	1.90	1.86i -86
Dzhaleva	Maria	BUL	6 Feb 64	170/70	JT	61.40	60.70 -83
Dzhigalova	Lyudmila	SU	22 Jan 62	176/62	200	23.18, 23.0	23.52, 22.8 -87
					400	50.61, 49.9	50.95 -87
Dziak	Malgorzata	POL	21 Nov 63	170/55	800	2:01.22	2:04.51 -86
Echevarría	Bárbara	CUB	6 Aug 66		DT	60.26	57.64 -87
Echols	Sheila	USA	2 Oct 64	165/52	100	10.83	11.09 -87, 10.9w -86
					LJ	6.88	6.94 -87
Edeh	Rosie	CAN	16 Aug 66	175/58	400h	56.26	-
Edwards	Diane	UK	17 Jun 66	169/56	800	1:59.66	1:59.30 -87
					1k	2:37.69	2:47.52 -85
Ehlert	Gaby	GDR	30 Jun 65	179/67	LJ	6.57i, 6.53, 6.58w	6.74, 6.76w -86
Eichelman	Sirje	SU	16 Jul 55	165/56	3000	8:57.56	
					10k	32:47.86	
					Mar	2:34:09	2:38:42 -87
Eichenmann	Genoveva	SWZ	12 Sep 57	162/52	Mar	2:34:43	2:35:40 -87
Elien	Fabienne	FRA	25 Apr 66	174/62	400	51.81	52.68 -86
Ellerbe	Connie	USA	24 Jun 68	173/55	400h	56.96	60.0 -86
Elloy	Laurence	FRA	3 Dec 59	169/61	100h	12.91 12.83w	12.69 -86
Emmelmann	Kirsten	GDR	19 Apr 61	173/63	200	23.24i	22.50 -81
					400	50.39	50.07 -85
Epps	Arnita	USA	6 Jun 64	170/58	400h	56.80	55.83 -85
Etienne	Astra	AUS	19 Feb 60	173/85	SP	18.04	17.40 -87 17.75* -85
Eve	Laverne	BAH	16 Jun 65	179/77	JT	60.02	62.42 -87
Everts	Sabine	FRG	4 Mar 61	169/56	100h	13.25	13.17 -82
					LJ	6.64	6.77 -82
					Hep	6306	6523 -82
Ewanje -Epée	Maryse	FRA	4 Sep 64	176/63	HJ	1.95	1.96 -85
Ewanje -Epée	Monique	FRA	11 Jul 67	173/62	100h	12.87 12.86w	12.98 -87
Ewerlöf	Malin	SWE	2 Jun 72	175/46	1500	4:11.71	4:25.34 -87
Fabert	Stefanie	GDR	3 Aug 69		400	52.13	52.84 -87
Faizullina	Gulnara	SU	16 Aug 65	169/55	5k	15:44.98	
Falkson	Annette	RSA	8 Oct 57		Mar	2:33:39	2:36:13 -87
Fastivets	Lilia	SU	25 Apr 64	171/68	Hep	5824	5804H -86
Farmer	Sandra	USA	18 Aug 62	173/63	400	51.88	52.37 -87
- Patrick					400h	54.49	54.38 -87
Fedyushina	Valentina	SU	18 Feb 65	186/92	SP	21.08	20.28 -87
Fehrman	Shelley	USA	19 Jul 65	175/52	HJ	1.88i 1.88	1.86 -85
Felke	Petra	GDR	30 Jul 59	172/64	JT	80.00	78.90 -87
Feng	Yinghua	CHN	25 Nov 66	172/53	100h	12.8	13.09 -87
Fernandez	Elizabeth	CUB	3 Jun 67	JT	60.44	55.58 -85	
Fernandez	Tania	CUB	26 Aug 67	181/59	400h	56.40	56.33 -87
Ferreira	Maria Conceição	POR	13 Mar 62	148/40	10k	32:28.6	32:25.7 -87
					Mar	2:34:23	2:43:58 -84
Fettig	Becky	USA	26 May 63	176/75	DT	59.06	55.32 -84
Fibingerová	Helena	CS	13 Jul 49	179/95	SP	19.85	22.50i 22.32 -77
Ficher	Fabienne	FRA	25 Apr 66	175/59	400	51.81	51.85 -86
Fidatov	Elena	RUM	24 Jul 60	169/52	1500	4:07.72	4:03.92 -86
					3000	8:50.24	8:42.16 -87
Fiedler	Ellen	GDR	26 Nov 58	174/66	400h	53.63	54.20 -83
Figuereido	Maria M.Souza	BRA	11 Nov 63	170/58	200	22.99	
					400	51.32	51.74 -87
Filatyeva	Svetlana	SU	3 Apr 64	167/58	HJ	1.89	1.90 -87
					Hep	6493	6327 -86
Filipishina	Yelena	SU	18 Jun 62	176/63	400h	55.22	54.56 -84

Name		Nat	Born	Ht/Wt	Event	1988 Mark	Pre-1988 Best
Filippova	Yulia	SU	13 Nov 70	171/59	100h	13.21	13.69 -87
Fincke	Annette	GDR	10 Oct 63	155/40	Mar	2:34:59	2:35:52 -87
Fink -Sisniega	Cristina	MEX	12 Dec 64	178/54	HJ	1.90	1.86 -86
Finn	Michelle	USA	8 May 65	165/52	100	11.32, 11.22w	11.20-86, 11.04w - 85
Fitzgerald-Brown	Benita	USA	6 Jul 61	179/63	100h	12.85,12.81w	12.84-83, 12.83w-86
Fleming	Sally	AUS	14 May 61	179/63	400h	55.55	56.15 -87
Flemming	Jane	AUS	14 Apr 65	168/56	100h	13.17	13.23 -87
					LJ	6.54w	6.46 -87
					Hep	6492	6390 -87
Flintoff -King	Debbie	AUS	20 Apr 60	171/58	400	51.02	50.78 -86
					400h	53.17	53.76 -86
Fogli	Laura	ITA	5 Oct 59	168/50	Mar	2:27:49	2:29:28 -84
Ford	Ann	UK	30 Mar 52	166/45	Mar	2:30:38	2:31:19 -85
Ford	Lisa	USA	24 Oct 66	165/56	100	11.36w	11.57 11.48w -86
					200	23.01	23.67 -87, 23.23w -86
Forkel	Karen	GDR	24 Sep 70	173/64	JT	64.68	59.78 -87
Fortin	Caroline	CAN	25 Jan 70	173/61	400h	57.47	60.44 -87
Fourcade	Nadine	FRA	25 Feb 63	174/65	LJ	6.58	6.79 -85
Frandsen	Simone	DEN	4 Jul 61	167/62	JT	58.24	60.84 -87
Frantseva	Nadyezhda	SU	2 Oct 61		SP	18.04	18.00 -87
Frederick	Jane	USA	7 Apr 52	180/73	Hep	6048	6803 -84
Freeman	Kathy	USA	13 Jan 62	172/54	100h	13.25w	13.64 -84, 13.47w -87
Seagrave					400h	56.57	56.10 -87
Frolova	Olga	SU	2 Oct 64	162/54	100	11.36	11.18w, 11.28 -87
					200	23.15, 22.9	23.06, 22.9 -86
Fudge	Paula	UK	30 Mar 52	168/55	Mar	2:29:47	2:32:25 -86
Fulcher	Victoria	USA	31 Dec 65	168/51	400h	55.88	57.97 -87
Fyodorova	Lyubov	SU	65		3000	9:00.93	9:07.89 -87
Fyodorova	Tatyana	SU	18 May 60	160/60	Mar	2:35:00	2:38:53 -87
Fyodorova	Tatyana	SU			TJ	13.08	
Gage	Nena	USA	13 Jan 66	170/57	LJ	6.62w	6.33 -87
Gaines	Chryste	USA	14 Sep 70	170/57	200	23.26y	23.56 -87
Galbiati	Stefania	ITA	8 Jan 69	173/61	JT	58.94	54.48 -86
Gale	Charmaine	RSA	27 Feb 64	178/65	HJ	1.97	2.00 -85
Galimova	Yulia	SU	60		3000	8:47.53	
Gallagher	Kim	USA	11 Jun 64	165/47	800	1:56.91	1:58.50 -84
					1500	4:03.29	4:08.08 -84
Galle	Heike	GDR	20 Mar 67	178/72	JT	63.16	64.40 -86
Galler	Dagmar	FRG	20 Dec 61	176/88	DT	63.16	61.24 -85
Gansky	Diana	GDR	14 Dec 63	184/92	DT	72.94	74.08 -87
Garancha	Iveta	SU	17 Sep 64	183/95	SP	16.94i	17.17 -86
					DT	59.64	63.90 -87
Garbuz	Yelena	SU	70		LJ	6.62	
García	Dulce Margarita	CUB	2 Jul 65	173/68	JT	64.48	67.90 -86
García	María del Carmen	CUB	27 Jul 69		HJ	1.88	1.83 -87
Garrett	Carla	USA	31 Jul 67	175/106	DT	58.70	56.54 -87
Gavrilina	Zinaida	SU	22 Sep 61	178/79	JT	58.30	67.00 -84
Gavrilova	Olga	SU	8 Feb 57	176/75	JT	58.80	66.80 -85
Gautzsch	Birgit	GDR	14 Dec 67	181/64	Hep	6146	5999 -87
Gayduk	Irina	SU	63		800	2:01.16	
Geiger	Betty	USA	12 Jun 61	157/46	10k	32:33.04	33:01.02 -83
(Springs)							
Georgieva	Nadezhda	BUL	2 Sep 61	158/48	100	11.11, 11.08w	11.09 -83
					200	22.53	22.42 -83
Gerlach	Annette	GDR	16 Jun 69		SP	18.18	17.24 -87
German	Natalya	SU	12 Nov 63	172/58	100	11.23	11.21 -87, 11.1 -86
					200	23.07i	22.47 -87
Gheorghiu	Catalina	RUM	21 Jun 69	176/62	800	2:00.53	2:01.33 -87
Ghican	Viorica	RUM	9 Jun 65	160/44	1500	4:02.76	4:06.45 -86
					3000	8:42.39	8:54.53 -86
					5k	15:34.78	15:59.27 -87
Gibson	Sharon	UK	31 Dec 61	168/77	JT	59.90	62.32 -87
Girard	Patricia	FRA	8 Apr 68	163/48	100	11.39	12.58 -84, 11.9 -87
Gjini	Klodeta	ALB	20 Aug 64	172/61	HJ	1.91	1.87 -83
Göhr	Marlies	GDR	21 Mar 58	165/55	100	10.89	10.81 -83, 10.79w -80
					200	22.28	21.74 -84

Name		Nat	Born	Ht/Wt	Event	1988 Mark	Pre-1988 Best
Golesheva	Yelena	SU	12 Jul 66		400	52.08	52.03 -87
Golodnova	Natalya	SU	14 Apr 67	179/58	HJ	1.89i, 1.88	1.95 -87
Gómez	Olga Lidia	CUB	30 Jun 66		DT	59.00	56.92 -87
Goncharova	Yelena	SU	21 Mar 63	169/56	400h	55.41	54.93 -86
Goodman	Jackie	NZ	23 Feb 68	173/55	5k	15:41.42	15:56.98 -87
Gorbatova	Yekaterina	SU	68		100h	13.31	13.1
Gotovskaya	Valentina	SU	3 Sep 65	171/57	HJ	1.90	
Goudreau	Colette	USA	11 May 65	165/46	3000	8:57.25	8:59.74 -87
					10k	32:06.14	
Gourdet	Barbara	FRA	29 Dec 65	168/52	800	2:01.31	2:02.32 -87
Grabner	Yvonne	GDR	22 Aug 65	168/54	800	2:01.20, 2:00.81i	2:01.88 -87
- Mai					1500	4:08.86	4:04.4 -87
					3000	8:58.19	
Grant	Cindy	CAN	29 Aug 63		1500	4:06.30	4:11.31 -84
					3000	8:55.45	9:29.1 -84
Graune	Brigitte	FRG	14 Mar 61	180/73	JT	62.84	62.62 -87
Graves	Rita	USA	15 Jun 64	176/59	HJ	1.90	1.93 -87
Grebenchuk	Tatyana	SU	22 Nov 62	169/58	800	1:58.70	1:57.89 -87
Greiner	Cindy	USA	15 Feb 57	173/64	LJ	6.58w	6.47, 6.51w -87
					Hep	6298	6275 -87
Griffin	Lorna	USA	9 Jun 56	181/82	DT	60.14	63.22 -80
Griffith-Joyner	Florence	USA	21 Dec 59	170/57	100	10.49	10.96 -87
					200	21.34	21.96, 21.7w -87
					400	52.50	50.86 -85
Grigoryeva	Natalya	SU	3 Dec 62	171/58	100h	12.48, 12.46w, 12.4	12.61 -86
Grishina	Marina	SU	11 Apr 62		100h	13.12, 12.9, 13.00w	13.06 -83
Groenendaal	Claudette	USA	1 Nov 63	175/67	1k	2:38.17	
Grönfeldt	Iris	ICE	8 Feb 63	172/64	JT	62.02	59.12 -86
Groos	Margaret	USA	21 Sep 59	168/54	Mar	2:29:50	2:33:38 -84
Grössenbacher	Martha	SWZ	31 Aug 59	176/70	400	52.26	53.05 -87
Grötzinger	Margit	FRG	4 Feb 67	176/58	400h	57.49	58.46 -86
Guidry	Carlette	USA	4 Sep 68	168/50	100	11.11	11.56 -87, 11.48w -86
					200	22.99,22.7,22.96w	23.35 -87,22.9 -86
Gunba	Saida	SU	30 Aug 59	168/85	JT	61.50	68.28 -80
Gunnell	Sally	UK	29 Jul 66	167/58	400	51.77i	- 0-
					100h	12.82, 12.80w	13.01 -87
					400h	54.03	59.9 -87
Günther	Sabine	GDR	6 Nov 63	170/60	100	11.37	11.19 -85
(Rieger)					200	22.79	22.37 -82
Günther	Jana	GDR	7 Jan 68	184/94	DT	66.84	67.00 -87
Günthner	Cornelia	FRG	26 Oct 71	176/56	Hep	5824	5410 -87
Günz	Gabriele	GDR	8 Sep 61	182/63	HJ	2.01i, 1.94	1.98i -86, 1.97 -87
Gurbanova	Zhanna	SU	30 Sep 69	175/62	100h	13.31	13.79 -97
Gurina	Lyubov	SU	6 Aug 57	166/57	800	1:56.56	1:55.56 -87
					1500	4:08.59	4:06.34 -86
Haggenmüller	Angelika	FRG	1 Mar 69	168/58	200	23.26w	23.67 -87
Hagger	Kim	UK	2 Dec 61	171/62	100h	13.30	13.24 -87
					Hep	5975	6259 -86
Hahmann	Andrea	GDR	3 Jun 66	176/58	800	2:00.36	1:57.31 -87
(Lange)					1500	4:00.96	4:00.07 -87
					3000	8:50.94, 8:45.00i	
Hain	Jeanette	GDR	7 Dec 66	169/53	Mar	2:35:06	2:34:05 -87
Halldórsdóttir	Helga	ICE	22 Apr 63	174/60	400h	56.54	57.53 -87
Hamhalterová	Monika	CS	5 May 66	165/55	5k	15:44.11	- 0 -
Hammer	Grit	GDR	4 Jun 66	180/93	SP	20.50	20.72 -87
(Haupt)							
Hamrin	Marie-Louise	SWE	19 Apr 57	167/53	10k	32:34.68	32:18.40 -86
					Mar	2:33:56	2:33:49 -86
Han	Jinli	CHN	66		JT	63.32	61.40 -87
Hand	Annette	USA	31 Oct 65	165/50	3000	8:59.15	8:59.90 -87
					5k	15:34.55	15:47.74 -87
Hanhijoki	Sisko	FIN	25 Apr 62	165/53	200	23.24	23.79 -85
Hannemann	Andrea	FRG	4 Mar 64	173/51	LJ	6.55	6.42 -87
Hanson	Sharon	USA	24 Sep 65	168/66	400h	56.79	58.27 -87
Hanson-Nortey	Yvonne	UK	18 Feb 64	183/90	SP	17.22	16.61 -87

Name		Nat	Born	Ht/Wt	Event	1988 Mark	Pre-1988 Best
Hardison	Leslie	USA	2 Aug 67	173/58	400	52.42, 52.1	52.89 -87
Harris	Kathi	USA	2 Jan 64	168/59	800	2:01.46	2:03.81 -85
Hartai	Katalin	HUN	24 Mar 63	178/67	JT	64.80	65.18 -87
Hartwig	Heike	GDR	30 Dec 62	181/95	SP	21.31	21.11 -87
Harvey	Alisa	USA	16 Sep 65	160/48	800	2:00.30	2:01.97 -87
					1500	4:09.73	4:08.95 -86
					Mile	4:31.28i	4:33:06 -86
Harvey	Cherry	AUS	21 Nov 66	170/60	JT	58.12	44.66 -86
Haugland	Hanne	NOR	14 Dec 67	178/60	HJ	1.91	1.93 -87
Hautenauve	Jacqueline	BEL	11 Jul 62		Hep	5928	5750 -87
Hayes	Kathy	USA	27 Dec 62	165/48	3000	8:59.65	8:50.79 -83
					5k	15:35.4	15:23.03 -85
					10k	32:42.25	32:43.81 -84
Heggli	Rita	SWZ	3 Dec 62	165/56	100h	13.10	13.01w, 13.07 -87
Heinz	Ulrike	FRG	6 Jul 67	174/66	400h	57.29	-
Helander - Kuusisto	Tuija	FIN	23 May 61	173/60	400h	55.90	54.62 -87
Hellmann	Martina	GDR	12 Dec 60	178/81	DT	72.30, 78.14u	72.92 -87
Henke	Kathrin	GDR	3 Sep 69		100	11.39	11.64 -87
Henry	Yolanda	USA	2 Dec 64	168/52	HJ	1.89	1.91 -87
Herbst	Stephanie	USA	27 Dec 65	170/50	10k	32:44.16	32:32.75 -86
Herczeg	Agnes	HUN	28 Aug 50	180/82	DT	60.60	65.22 -82
Heydrich	Britta	GDR	28 Aug 70	171/58	JT	63.42	55.14 -87
Hidaka	Yoshiko	JAP	30 Dec 65	168/54	Mar	2:34:38	2:39:41 -86
Hidding	Tineke	HOL	28 Jul 59	174/62	LJ	6.61, 6.64w	6.47 -84
					Hep	6176	6104 -83
Hightower - Leftwich	Stephanie	USA	19 Jul 58	164/54	100h	13.00	12.79 -82, 12.78w -84
Hirsch	Monika	FRG	28 Feb 59	173/62	LJ	6.55i	6.68i, 6.66 -86
Holden	Diane	AUS	28 Oct 63	161/53	100	11.22w	11.39 -80
							11.22w -83, 11.1w, 10.8wdt -87
Holland	Maree	AUS	25 Jul 63	169/55	200	22.83	23.31 -85
					400	50.24	51.51 -85
Homneac	Doina	RUM	1 Nov 69		1500	4:10.74	4:11.88 -86
					3000	8:59.78	9:11.11 -87
Horváth (Szélinger)	Viktoria	HUN	18 Aug 56	182/87	SP	18.60i, 18.57	18.62-87
Höss	Christine	FRG	24 Sep 62	171/64	Hep	5948	5713w, 5694 -87
Hou	Xuemei	CHN	7 Feb 62	177/90	DT	68.62	66.12 -87
Hovi	Asta	FIN	29 Jul 63	181/100	SP	18.49	17.89 -87
Howard	Denean	USA	5 Oct 64	168/56	400	49.87	50.72 -87
Howard	Sherri	USA	1 Jun 62	170/53	400	51.63, 51.2	50.40 -84
Hoyte	Wendy	UK	17 Dec 57	160/52	100	11.36w	11.31, 11.18w -82
Huang	Zhihong	CHN	7 May 65	175/100	SP	21.28	20.22 -87
Huart	Hélène	FRA	19 Jun 65	173/60	400h	55.57	55.55 -87
Huber	Vicki	USA	29 May 67	168/54	1500	4:07.40	4:11.26 -87
					Mile	4:28.77, 4:28.31i	4:36.25 -87
					2k	5:44.08	
					3000	8:37.25	8:54.41 -87
Hudson	Sheila	USA	30 Jun 67	152/45	LJ	6.62	6.51 -87
					TJ	13.79	13.92w, 13.85 -87
Hühn	Stefanie	FRG	17 Mar 66	175/66	LJ	6.62	6.41 -86
					Hep	5747	5630 -85
Humphrey	Jackie	USA	30 Sep 65	163/60	100h	12.83	13.06 -87
Hunter	Jill	UK	14 Oct 66	170/51	3000	8:47.36	9:08.21 -87
					5k	15:17.77	- 0 -
Hutchings (McPeake)	Sharon	UK	22 Jun 62	183/62	HJ	1.88	1.90 -86
Hyacinth	Flora	UVI	30 Mar 66	172/62	TJ	13.30i	13.73 -87
Iacob (Nif)	Octavia	RUM	22 Jul 65	174/55	HJ	1.89	
					LJ	6.60i, 6.59	6.41 -87
Ignatyeva	Olga	SU	68		800	2:00.5	
Iheagwam	Tina	NIG	3 Apr 68	153/51	100	11.38	11.31w, 11.32 -87
Ikauniece	Vineta	SU	4 Dec 62	170/61	200	23.0	22.49, 22.3 -87
					400	50.71	50.95 -87
Ilands	Magda	BEL	16 Jan 50	159/53	Mar	2:35:36	2:33:53 -86

Name		Nat	Born	Ht/Wt	Event	1988 Mark	Pre-1988 Best
Ilcu	Marieta	RUM	16 Oct 62	173/62	100	11.36	11.73 -86
					LJ	6.98	6.93 -87
Ilie	Niculina	RUM	13 Feb 58	175/58	HJ	1.89	1.98 -85
Ilieva	Tsvetanka	BUL	1 Mar 63	165/52	100	11.43	11.53 -86
					200	23.04i	22.93, 22.8 -86
					400	52.04	51.89 -87, 51.8 -86
Ilyina	Nadezhda	SU	2 Apr 64		10k	32:23.11	33:09.85 -87
Ináncsi	Rita	HUN	6 Jan 71	185/70	Hep	5767	5487 -87
Inniss	Jennifer	USA	21 Nov 59	170/59	100	11.15	11.21, 10.9 -87
						11.02w	11.17w -83
					LJ	6.70	6.85 -87
Ionescu	Valy	RUM	31 Aug 60	172/64	LJ	7.08	7.20 -82
Isac	Liliana	RUM	9 Jan 63	175/100	SP	17.45	15.35 -81
Isaeva	Svetlana	BUL	18 Mar 67	176/60	HJ	1.93	2.00 -87
Isphording	Julie	USA	5 Dec 61	165/48	Mar	2:31:09	2:32:26 -84
Issajenko	Angella	CAN	28 Sep 58	167/61	100	11.01	10.97,10.8w-87,10.92w -82
					200	23.18, 22.87w	22.25, 22.19w -82
Ivan	Paula	RUM	20 Jul 63	170/57	800	1:56.42	1:57.2 -87
					1500	3:53.96	4:01.03 -87
					Mile	4:25.80	4:27.62 -87
					2k	5:44.24	
					3000	8:27.15	8:39.28 -87
Ivanova	Valentina	SU	1 May 63		DT	63.02	60.78 -87
Ivanova	Zoya	SU	14 Mar 52	164/52	10k	32:19.50	32:21.47 -87
					Mar	2:29:37	2:27:57 -87
Jackson	Alice	USA	28 Dec 58	159/55	200	22.87	22.95, 22.77w -87
					400	52.04	51.14 -87
Jackson	Grace	JAM	14 Jun 61	183/62	100	11.08, 10.97w	11.22 -87, 11.0 -85
					200	21.72	22.20 -84, 21.8w -87
					400	49.57	50.94 -86
Jacobs	Regina	USA	28 Aug 63	167/52	800	2:01.13	1:59.36 -87
					1500	4:00.46	4:02.6 -86
					Mile	4:31.92	4:29.40 -86
Jacobs	Simmone	UK	5 Sep 66	163/53	100	11.31	11.34 -87, 11.26w -84
Jampolsky (Harding)	Camille	USA	19 Nov 65	174/57	HJ	1.90	1.90 -85
Janota	Jolanta	POL	6 Jul 64	172/59	100	11.34	11.19 -86
					200	23.14, 23.04w	22.90 -86
Jaseviciene (Navickaite)	Margarita	SU	10 Dec 61	166/59	400h	56.71	55.02 -84
Jazbinsek	Kristina	YUG	23 Nov 65	169/71	JT	58.96	61.60 -87
Jeal	Wendy	UK	21 Nov 60	165/63	100h	13.32	13.16 -86
Jenkins	Julie	USA	12 Aug 64	168/57	800	2:00.59	2:00.50 -87
					1k	2:36.34	
					1500	4:06.66	4:15.33 -87
Jennings	Jo	UK	20 Sep 69	174/60	HJ	1.90	1.83 -85
Jennings	Lynn	USA	1 Jul 60	165/50	3000	8:48.19	8:49.23 -87
					5k	15:11.83	15:08.36 -86
					10k	31:39.93	31:45.43 -87
Jianu	Camelia	RUM	17 Nov 67	163/50	400	51.84	
					400h	56.46	57.30 -86
Jin	Ling	CHN	25 Jan 67	183/62	HJ	1.93	1.90 -87
Johansson	Ewa	SWE	4 Jan 64	172/56	400h	57.35	59.07 -87
John (Paetz)	Sabine	GDR	16 Oct 57	178/66	100h	12.85, 12.71w	12.54, 12.51w -84
					LJ	6.81	7.12 -84
					Hep	6897	6946 -84
Johnson	Kerry	AUS	23 Oct 63	164/50	100	11.28	11.62, 11.48w -87
					200	22.82	23.23 -86
Johnson	Latrese	USA	24 Dec 66	178/54	HJ	1.90	1.91i -86, 1.90 -85
Johnson	Yolanda	USA	12 Feb 68	160/56	100h	13.14	13.25 -86
Jones	Dot	USA	4 Jan 64	191/111	SP	17.22	16.53 -86
Jones	Esther	USA	7 Apr 69	171/61	100	11.22, 11.18w	11.41 -87
					200	23.05, 23.00w	23.49 -87
Jones	Jolanda	USA	6 Nov 65	178/63	HJ	1.89	1.88 -86
Jones (Rosenquist)	Kim	USA	2 May 58	170/53	10k	33:08.1	
					Mar	2:32:03	2:32:31 -86

Name		Nat	Born	Ht/Wt	Event	1988 Mark	Pre-1988 Best
Jousimaa	Tuija	FIN	22 Sep 58	171/55	3000	8:51.07	8:57.00 -83
					10k	32:55.16	32:23.1 -83
					Mar	2:29:26	2:32:07 -84
Joyce	Monica	IRL	16 Jul 58	165/54	2k	5:50.27	5:43.96 -82
					5k	15:45.23	15:27.5 -83
					10k	32:36.3	- 0 -
Joyner-Kersee	Jackie	USA	3 Mar 62	178/70	200	22.30	22.85 -86
					100h	12.61	12.80 -87
					400h	55.74	55.05 -85
					HJ	1.93	1.90 -87
					LJ	7.40, 7.45w	7.45 -87
					Hep	7291	7158 -86
Jung	Susanne	GDR	17 May 63	178/74	JT	68.10	69.60 -87
Junghiatu - Constantin	Mitica	RUM	18 Aug 62	173/55	Mile	4:31.55i	
Jussila	Arja	FIN	29 Apr 53	171/57	LJ	6.59w	6.49 -86
Kabanova	Khodizha	SU	24 Jun 67		Hep	6016	5439 -87
Kaber	Danièle	LUX	20 Apr 60	160/45	10k	32:51.61	32:16.97 -86
					Mar	2:29:23	
Kadas	Eva	RUM	8 Nov 59	163/53	3000	8:53.00	8:59.70 -86
Kaftandjian	Isabelle	FRA	27 Mar 64	166/57	100h	13.27, 13.24w	13.25 -87
Kaiser	Natasha	USA	14 May 67	173/57	400	51.73	51.48 -86
Kakushkina	Yelena	SU	5 Jan 63		SP	17.94i, 17.78	18.11i ,17.91 -87
Kalina	Tatyana	SU	22 May 62		800	1:59.9	2:01.1 -87
Kalinnikova	Natalya	SU	63		400h	55.97	56.45 -86
Kaljurand	Anu	SU	16 Apr 69	170/56	LJ	6.84w	6.64 -86
Kancheva	Tsetska	BUL	7 Aug 63	176/66	LJ	6.78	6.71 -84, 6.74w -87
Känsäkangas	Anne	FIN	17 Jan 59	173/85	DT	61.36	64.24 -83
Kapernick	Gai	AUS	20 Sep 70	183/65	HJ	1.90	1.90 -87
Karczmarek	Agata	POL	29 Nov 63	176/62	LJ	6.97	6.81, 6.92w -86
Karepina	Zoya	SU	3 Jan 61	177/77	JT	60.72	65.00 -85
Kasparkova	Sarka	CS	20 May 71	185/68	HJ	1.89	1.80 -87
Kasprzyk	Ewa	POL	7 Sep 57	164/53	200	22.69i	22.13 -86
Katewicz	Renata	POL	2 May 65	179/95	DT	66.18	64.56 -87
Kazantseva	Tatyana	SU	62		JT	59.18	59.64 -85
Kaznovskaya (Gervaziyeva)	Zoya	SU	22 Sep 66	170/60	1500	4:08.8	4:12.5 -87
Keenan-Buckley	Ann	IRL	7 Jan 62	168/54	3000	9:00.88	9:21.99 -85
Kelchevskaya	Yelena	SU	7 May 55	168/53	100	11.40, 11.28w	11.30 -87
						11.1, 11.0w	11.1 -86
Kellon	Gayle	USA	29 Mar 65	176/58	400h	56.59	56.55 -86
Keough	Linda	UK	26 Dec 63	174/60	400	51.65	52.49 -85
Kersten	Annette	GDR	10 Aug 67	168/61	100	11.27, 11.13w	11.79 -86
					200	23.21	24.37 -86
Keskitalo	Sinikka	FIN	29 Jan 51	153/46	Mar	2:34:12	2:33:18 -86
Keszeg	Margareta	RUM	31 Aug 65	165/51	1500	4:08.56	4:04.49 -86
					3000	8:51.96	8:46.44 -85
Kharlamova	Marina	SU	24 May 62	177/62	200	22.93	23.13, 23.1 -87
					400	50.75	50.63 -83
Khaustova	Galina	SU	4 Jul 65	170/60	100h	12.94	13.19, 13.0 -86
Khorkhulyova	Tatyana	SU	15 Jul 64		SP	18.60i 18.35	19.02 -87
Khramenkova	Yekaterina	SU	16 Oct 56	168/50	5k	15:44.2	
					10k	31:42.02	32:15.59 -87
					Mar	2:30:27	2:28:20 -87
Khristosenko	Lyudmila	SU	14 Oct 66	170/57	100h	13.27, 13.07w	12.94 -86, 12.8 -85
Khristova	Tsvetanka	BUL	14 Mar 62	175/80	DT	71.06	73.22 -87
Khromova	Margarita	SU	19 Jun 63	178/58	400h	54.95	53.58 -84
Khudorozhkina	Irina	SU	68		SP	17.52	16.82 -87
Khval	Irina	SU	17 May 62		DT	68.18	67.32 -87
Khvostikova	Lyubov	SU	16 Apr 64	182/82	SP	18.07	18.74 -87
Kielczewska	Malgorzata	POL	2 Jan 69	176/73	JT	58.50	58.64 -87
Kiessling	Ellen	GDR	17 Feb 68	166/52	800	2:01.30	2:02.20 -85
					1500	4:09.93	
Kim	Hee-sun	SKO	20 Apr 63	168/52	HJ	1.92	1.90 -87
Kinch	Beverly	UK	14 Jan 64	162/58	LJ	6.54w	6.90, 6.93w -83

Name		Nat	Born	Ht/Wt	Event	1988 Mark	Pre-1988 Best
King	Trish	USA	27 Aug 62	170/58	HJ	1.96	1.83 -87
Kinzel	Gisela	FRG	17 May 61	172/60	400	52.08, 51.96i	50.83 -86
Kirchmann	Sigrid	AUT	29 Mar 66	180/66	HJ	1.90i	1.95 -87
Kiryukhina	Lyubov	SU	19 May 63	167/58	400	52.23	51.97, 51.3 -87
					800	1:58.56	1:57.18 -86
Kitova	Svetlana	SU	25 Jun 60	168/60	800	1:58.1	1:58.08 -84
					1500	4:01.02	4:01.83 -86
Klebe	Monika	SWE	21 Sep 64	178/61	400h	56.89	56.64 -87
Klecker	Janis	USA	18 Jul 60	168/48	Mar	2:34:18	2:31:53 -85
Kleindl	Ulrike	AUT	27 May 63	167/62	LJ	6.67	6.31 -85
Klimova	Yelena	SU	2 Jun 66	180/66	400h	56.88	57.57 -86
Klinger	Margrit	FRG	22 Jun 60	167/54	800	2:00.93	1:57.22 -82
					1500	4:06.59	4:02.66 -83
Knabe	Kerstin	GDR	7 Jul 59	180/70	100h	12.70	12.54 -82, 12.42w -83
Knijn	Merian	HOL	12 Aug 66		400h	57.32	58.41 -87
Knisely	Mary	USA	29 May 59	162/48	1500	4:09.20	4:05.70 -85
					2k	5:41.99	5:40.50 -86
					3000	8:47.45	8:42.84 -87
Knoll	Silke-Beate	FRG	21 Feb 67	162/54	200	23.06, 22.97i	23.07 -87
Konwles	Leisa	USA	17 Mar 63	168/60	400h	56.34	55.70 -85
Knyazeva	Alla	SU	16 Jul 64	168/62	100h	13.21	13.4 -87
Knyazeva	Natalya	SU	64		Hep	5764	5453 -83
Knyazkova	Natalya	SU	63		400	52.2	
					800	1:59.5	2:02.85 -86
Koba	Tamara	SU	24 Feb 57	164/51	800	2:01.3	2:00.0 -80
					1500	4:05.90	4:01.66 -81
					3000	8:50.67	9:01.81 -87
Koch	Beate	GDR	18 Aug 67	181/75	JT	68.80	58.88 -86
Kochetova	Viktoria	SU	18 Jun 67		DT	62.58	60.64 -87
Kojima	Kazue	JAP	12 Dec 65	158/45	10k	33:03.8	34:42.19 -87
Kokonova	Yelena	SU	4 Aug 63	172/64	LJ	7.29	7.31 -85
Kokowska	Renata	POL	4 Dec 58	170/57	10k	33:07.08	33:00.60 -87
					Mar	2:29:16	2:33:07 -87
Kolobova	Ellina	SU	7 Dec 68	172/67	Hep	6047	5460 -87
Kolovanova	Natalya	SU	1 Aug 64	172/60	100h	13.07, 12.98w, 13.0	13.22 -87,13.0 -86
Komsa	Jolanta	POL	20 Dec 58	183/54	HJ	1.92i, 1.89	1.95 -84
Kondratyeva	Lyudmila	SU	11 Apr 58	168/57	100	11.05, 10.9	11.02 -84, 10.9 -80
					200	22.65	22.31 -80
Köpping	Jana	GDR	12 Apr 66	172/67	JT	60.40	66.80 -86
Koptyakevich	Lyudmila	SU	7 Apr 65	177/85	SP	17.07	17.66 -86
Körner	Hildegard	GDR	20 Dec 59	170/56	800	2:01.06	1:57.20 -80
					1500	4:03.74	3:58.67 -87
Kornyeva	Nadezhda	SU	10 Dec 60	168/51	1500	4:09.68	4:10.5 -87
Korotkevich	Larisa	SU	24 Mar 66	180/86	DT	66.08	64.94 -87
Kosche	Dagmar	GDR	3 Mar 70		JT	58.56	50.66 -87
Kosenko	Klara	SU	66		HJ	1.92	
Kositsyna	Larisa	SU	14 Dec 63	181/57	HJ	2.00i, 2.00	1.98 -83
Kostadinova	Stefka	BUL	25 Mar 65	180/60	HJ	2.07	2.09 -87
Kostyuchenkova	Irina	SU	11 May 61	172/78	JT	67.00	66.72 -87
Kot	Irina	SU	25 Sep 67	162/57	100	11.41w, 11.0	11.42 -87, 11.2 -86
					200	23.21, 22.9	23.35 -86, 23.0 -87
Kotmelová	Katerina	CS	3 Jan 55	175/80	JT	62.06	62.62 -82
Kovacs	Ella	RUM	11 Dec 64	170/53	800	1:58.10	1:55.68 -85
					1500	4:06.40	4:06.38 -84
Kovalyova	Yelena	SU	31 Aug 61		DT	59.18	64.36 -84
Kovtun	Natalya	SU	27 May 64		100	11.29	11.51 -81, 11.2 -84
					200	23.00	23.27, 22.5w -87
Kozlova	Natalya	SU	18 Feb 67		SP	17.18	17.08 -86
Krabbe	Katrin	GDR	22 Nov 69	181/63	100	10.89	11.49 -86
					200	22.51, 22.34w	23.31, 23.25w -86
Kraeft	Kerstin	GDR	25 Sep 63	188/63	HJ	1.88i	1.85i -80
Kraus	Brigitte	FRG	12 Aug 56	180/58	1500	4:07.51, 4:07.06i	4:01.54 -78
Kravchenko	Valentina	SU	11 Nov 63	168/57	LJ	6.69	6.82 -86
Kravets (Shulyak)	Inessa	SU	5 Oct 66	178/64	LJ	7.27	6.72 -87

Name		Nat	Born	Ht/Wt	Event	1988 Mark	Pre-1988 Best
Kremlyova	Lyubov	SU	21 Dec 62		800	1:59.7	1:58.95 -84
					1k	2:37.39i	
					1500	4:02.41	4:01.57 -86
					Mile	4:30.82	
					3000	8:52.09	
Kreutel	Ursula	FRG	14 Sep 65	174/83	DT	60.28	56.54 -86
Krieger	Heidi	GDR	20 Jul 65	187/95	SP	19.65	21.10 -86
Kristiansen	Ingrid	NOR	21 Mar 56	170/50	3000	8:43.59	8:34.10 -86
					5k	15:10.89	14:37.33 -86
					10k	31:31.37	30:13.74 -86
					Mar	2:25:41	2:21:06 -85
Krivelyova	Svetlana	SU	13 Jun 69	184/90	SP	18.35	17.51 -87
Krivoseina	Marina	SU	7 Jan 67	170/59	200	23.15i	23.58 -85
Kruse	Sabine	FRG	10 Mar 66	186/95	SP	18.80	18.37 -87
Kuceríaková	Jana	CS	30 Apr 64	164/53	3000	8:59.78	8:56.49 -86
					10k	33:09.3	33:43.01 -86
Kuhmann	Angelika	FRG	31 Mar 57	170/60	100h	13.27	13.40 -85
Kumbernuss	Astrid	GDR	5 Feb 70	186/90	SP	18.73	18.20 -87
					DT	66.60	63.68 -87
Kumpulainen	Sirkku	FIN	12 Jan 56	164/53	Mar	2:35:24	2:36:05 -86
Kuporosova	Marina	SU	62		HJ	1.89i	
Kuprianovich	Tamara	SU	64		400	52.50, 51.8	52.42 -87
Kurochkina (Matsuta)	Tatyana	SU	15 Sep 67	174/58	400h	54.39	57.83 -85
Kuzhel	Galina	SU	4 Oct 59	181/86	SP	18.70i, 18.62	19.20 -87
Kuznyetsova	Alexandra	SU	66		SP	17.46i	17.50 -87
Kvachova	Galina	SU	27 Mar 65	183/97	DT	62.22	61.30 -87
Kyalisima	Ruth	UGA	21 Nov 55	157/52	400h	57.32	57.02 -84
Kytölä	Ragne	FIN	15 Mar 65	177/65	Hep	6006	5930 -87
Laaksalo	Tuula	FIN	21 Apr 53	171/70	JT	67.00	67.40 -83
Lacambra	Blanca	SPA	28 Aug 65	163/53	100	11.43	11.49 -86, 11.48w -87
					200	23.04A	23.44, 23.2 -85
						23.19	23.19i -87, 23.04w -86
					400	51.73	51.53 -86
Lagunkova	Natalya	SU	6 May 59	168/55	3000	8:47.94	8:48.15 -86
					10k	32:17.58	32:57.48 -82
Laidlow (Gandy)	Simone	UK	28 Jul 65	172/52	400h	57.00	57.56, 57.5 -86
Laine	Helena	FIN	30 Mar 55	178/76	JT	60.68	64.00 -83
Lajbnerová	Zuzana	CS	20 May 63	178/76	Hep	6268	6224 -87
Lammertsma	Ingrid	HOL	6 Sep 67		JT	61.14	58.86 -86
Landry	Kelly	USA	27 Jun 63	179/82	DT	58.72	59.12 -87
Lange (Auerswald)	Ingrid	GDR	2 Sep 57	168/59	100	11.17, 11.04w	11.04 -84
					200	23.05i	22.60 -80
Lange	Malda	SU	29 May 61	177/77	DT	65.06	60.70 -87
Langenhuizen	Ine	HOL	27 Oct 68		100h	13.38	13.49 -87
Lapierre	Odette	CAN	28 Jan 55	162/50	Mar	2:30:35	2:31:33 -87
Larrieu Smith	Francie	USA	23 Nov 52	163/48	3000	8:51.84	8:50.54 -85
					5k	15:15.2	15:36.11 -83
					10k	31:35.52	32:18.29 -85
					Mar	2:32:30	2:33:36 -86
Lasovskaya	Inna	SU	17 Dec 69	177/67	LJ	6.68	
Lauren	Jana	GDR	28 Jun 70		DT	60.94	55.72 -87
Laurendet	Jenny	AUS	5 Jul 62	164/50	400h	56.44	56.48 -86
Lavine	Laura	USA	15 Aug 66	178/87	DT	57.82	57.78 -87
Lavrova	Svetlana	SU	71		HJ	1.89i	1.89 -87
Lawrence	Esmie	CAN	19 Nov 61	177/61	100	11.42	11.42 -85
					200	23.29	23.13 -86
Laza	Belsis	CUB	5 Jun 67	174/96	SP	19.34	18.49 -87
le Roux	Annemarie	RSA	29 Jun 63		100h	13.08A, 13.07wA	13.31A -87
Leal	Ivonne	CUB	27 Feb 66	164/64	JT	70.48	71.82 -85
Leatherwood	Lillie	USA	6 Jul 64	168/56	200	22.80	22.38 -87
					400	50.68	49.95 -87
Lebonda	Tatyana	SU	23 Mar 64	161/46	800	2:01.1	2:01.01 -82
Ledovskaya	Tatyana	SU	21 May 66	171/56	200	23.32, 22.7	23.45 -87
					400	50.93, 50.4	51.87 -86
					400h	53.18	56.92 -87

Name		Nat	Born	Ht/Wt	Event	1988 Mark	Pre-1988 Best
Lee	Mi-ok	SKO	10 Mar 68	163/47	Mar	2:32:51	
Lee	Susan	CAN	7 May 60	157/48	3000	8:57.0	8:54.64 -87
					5k	15:26.2	15:22.96 -85
					10k	31:50.51	32:07.17 -87
Lehane	Lesley	USA	12 Mar 63	175/56	5k	15:44.0	15:28.33 -85
(Welch)					10k	31:42.8	38:48.2 -81
					Mar	2:32:11	
Lelut	Maria	FRA	29 Jan 56	159/46	10k	32:38.88	33:33.20 -87
					Mar	2:32:53	2:29:51 -86
Leng	Molian	CHN	67		HJ	17.48	18.42 -87
Lengyel	Mariana	RUM	14 Apr 53	174/88	SP	17.46	19.00 -87
(Ionescu)					DT	67.62	69.08 -86
Leroy	Muriel	FRA	7 Jul 68	170/55	100	11.42w	11.47 -87
					200	23.19	23.48, 23.37w -86
Lesage	Odile	FRA	28 Jun 69	178/64	Hep	5873	5643 -87
Lesch	Gabriela	FRG	17 Aug 64	174/60	800	1:59.42	2:01.70 -87
Levecq	Sylvie	FRA	5 Dec 62	179/59	400h	57.26	59.58 -81
Levi	Becky	USA	8 Nov 62	180/88	DT	63.32	60.12 -87
Lewis	Carol	USA	8 Aug 63	178/72	LJ	6.88	7.04 -85
Li	Baolian	CHN	8 Mar 63	165/68	JT	61.30	65.50 -87
Li	Huirong	CHN	65		LJ	6.55, 6.59w	6.53 -87
					TJ	14.16	14.04 -87
Li	Juan	CHN	5 Oct 66	160/46	Mar	2:31:44	2:37:35 -87
Li	Meisu	CHN	17 Apr 59	176/92	SP	21.76	20.95 -87
Li	Shuhua	CHN	68		TJ	13.19	
Li	Xiaohui	CHN	12 Feb 56	168/70	DT	58.76	61.80 -80
Li	Yan	CHN	64		DT	61.80	58.08 -87
Li	Yemei	CHN	66		Mar	2:33:19	2:35:35 -87
Liao	Wenfen	CHN	30 Apr 63	169/53	LJ	6.70	6.64 -87
Lichagina	Yulia	SU	7 May 65		JT	58.98	58.06 -86
Lillak	Tiina	FIN	15 Apr 61	181/76	JT	73.30	74.76 -83
Lion-Cachet	Susan	RSA	8 May 62	173/68	JT	61.54	62.34 -87
Lippe	Gabriele	FRG	8 May 67	168/56	100h	13.09	13.44 -85
Lisovskaya	Natalya	SU	16 Jul 62	188/95	SP	22.55	22.63 -87
					DT	61.98	63.44 -82
Liu	Guohua	CHN	7 Dec 61		JT	61.40	64.14 -85
Liu	Huajin	CHN	2 Aug 60	174/65	100h	12.93, 12.5	12.89 -87
Liu	Shuzhen	CHN	5 May 66	167/63	LJ	6.79	6.51 -87
Lix	Ute	FRG	3 Mar 65	160/49	800	2:00.89	2:01.68 -87
Loboyko	Nadezhda	SU	30 Jun 61	165/54	400	51.80	
					800	1:57.2	2:01.5 -87
Loghin	Mihaela	RUM	1 Jun 52	170/78	SP	19.79	21.00 -84
Lombardo	Patrizia	ITA	3 Sep 58	175/59	100h	13.39, 13.1w	13.10 -87
López	Aliuska	CUB	29 Aug 69	169/53	100h	12.96	12.84 -87
López	Isel	CUB	11 Jul 70	174/74	JT	60.52	58.78 -87
Losch	Claudia	FRG	10 Jan 60	181/84	SP	20.57	22.19 -87
Losch	Susanne	GDR	12 Feb 66	178/60	400h	54.24	56.09 -87
Lugovskaya	Tatyana	SU	17 Apr 69	174/93	DT	58.82	54.82 -87
Lukiniv	Nadezhda	SU	14 May 68	180/105	SP	18.01	17.15 -86
Lüneburg	Ilse	RSA	14 Mar 65	175/56	100h	13.29A	13.23A -85
Luo	Zhonghua	CHN	26 Jan 69	175/75	JT	58.12	
Lyapunova	Yelena	SU	70		SP	17.05	15.65 -87
McCauley	Lori	USA	27 Oct 61	173/57	400h	56.82	55.60 -84
McColgan	Elizabeth	UK	24 May 64	168/45	1500	4:08.15	4:01.38 -87
					2k	5:28.63	5:40.24 -87
					3000	8:42.50	8:39.85 -87
					5k	15:03.29	15:01.08 -87
					10k	31:06.99	31:19.82 -87
McCurdy -Cameron	Linda	CAN	11 May 63	175/65	HJ	1.88i	1.86 -86
McDermid	Jill	CAN	17 Oct 68	173/58	400h	57.29A	58.00 -86
McDowell	Deborah	UK	4 Jun 64		HJ	1.88i	1.81i, 1.80 -87
McDuff	Heather	UK	17 May 58		Mar	2:34:26	2:36:18 -87
McGeorge (Vinall)	Sonia	UK	2 Nov 64		3000	9:00.36	9:06.37 -87
McIntosh	Tanya	USA	27 Dec 66	165/54	400	51.76	52.08 -87
McKenzie	Kim	USA	21 Mar 61	165/57	100h	12.84, 12.8	12.95 -83
McLaughlin	Elaine	UK	17 Nov 63	167/58	400h	55.91	57.48 -87

Name		Nat	Born	Ht/Wt	Event	1988 Mark	Pre-1988 Best
McMiken	Christine	NZ	19 Jul 63	165/47	10k	32:20.39	32:17.1 -86
Machado	Maria Albertina	POR	25 Dec 61	168/56	3000	9:01.5	8:52.02 -87
					10k	31:52.04	31:46.61 -87
Machotková	Zuzana	CS	25 Mar 65	174/64	400h	56.56	57.87 -86
Mackey	Kendra	USA	14 Jan 69	178/51	200	23.32	23.9w -87
Madetzky	Silvia	GDR	24 Jun 62	186/92	DT	70.34	69.34 -87
Maffeis	Agnese	ITA	9 Mar 65	183/75	DT	58.38	54.38 -87
Makarova	Galina	SU	60		100h	13.18	13.17 -86, 13.1 -87
Maki	Izumi	JAP	68		10k	33:05.07	
Malchenko	Alla	SU	18 Jun 61		400h	56.10	
Malchugina	Galina	SU	17 Dec 62	168/65	100	11.07, 10.8	11.42 -85
					200	22.42	22.74 -84, 22.2w -87
Malone	Maicel	USA	12 Jun 69	173/59	200	23.19	23.12 -86, 23.25w -87
					400	50.96	52.42, 52.4 -86
Malovecz	Zsuzsa	HUN	21 May 62	178/76	JT	67.18	66.64 -86
Marchiano	Susan	USA	5 Nov 54	165/43	Mar	2:34:26	2:41:06 -87
Marchisio	Rita	ITA	13 Feb 50	170/53	Mar	2:31:08	2:32:55 -82
Markina	Marina	SU	19 Mar 62		100	11.31	11.43, 11.3, 10.9w -87
(Kleyankina)					200	22.92	23.18 23.0 -87
Marot	Véronique	UK	16 Sep 55	168/52	Mar	2:33:36	2:28:04 -85
Marquette	Ulla	CAN	28 Jun 58		3000	8:59.56	9:01.40 -87
Marshall	Debbie	USA	5 Aug 65	173/52	800	1:59.97	2:00.47 -87
(Grant)					1500	4:09.50	4:16.8 -87
Marshall	Pam	USA	16 Aug 60	178/63	100	11.18	11.01 -87, 10.80w/10.9 -86
					200	21.93	22.06, 21.6w -87
Marten	Maritza	CUB	17 Aug 63	177/83	DT	67.02	70.50 -85
Marter -Rohl	Michelle	USA	12 Nov 65	150/40	1k	2:38.06i	
Martin	LaVonna	USA	18 Nov 66	168/59	100h	12.85	12.80 -87
Martin	Lisa	AUS	12 May 60	166/47	Mar	2:23:51	2:26:07 -86
Martínez	Lisette	CUB	11 Oct 66	175/79	SP	17.04	17.11 -87
Martínez	Tayami	CUB	16 Jul 72		100	11.34	11.9 -86
Martsenyuk	Yelena	SU	21 Feb 61	176/70	Hep	6551	6192 -87
Maslennikova	Marianna	SU	17 May 61	173/66	100h	13.29	13.37 -85, 13.21w -87
					Hep	6474	6456 -87
Masullo	Marisa	ITA	8 May 59	170/60	100	11.40A	11.29 -80
					200	23.27, 23.17wA	22.88 -84
Matay	Andrea	HUN	27 Sep 55	173/56	HJ	1.88i	1.98i, 1.94 -79
Matei	Cristieana	RUM	2 Jan 62	172/62	400h	57.33	54.55 -86
Mathesius	Yvonne	GDR	21 Aug 71	179/65	LJ	6.53	
Matrosova	Irina	SU	5 Apr 62	172/57	3000	8:56.90	9:03.24 -84
					5k	15:42.40	15:59.4 -87
Matsui	Emi	JAP	20 Feb 63	159/59	JT	60.24	60.52 -82
Matsuno	Akemi	JAP	27 Apr 68	148/35	10k	32:19.57	35:15.6 -87
Matuseviciene	Dalia	SU	12 Nov 62	167/52	400	51.72 51.3	51.12 -84
					800	1:56.7	1:58.7 -84
Matveyeva	Lyudmila	SU	1 Feb 57	164/49	5k	15:40.25	15:16.27 -85
					10k	31:38.02	32:25.99 -84
Matyusheva	Irina	SU	5 Jun 65	171/63	100h	13.20	13.78 -85
(Kushenko)					Hep	6424	6284 -87
Mau	Beatrice	GDR	20 Feb 71	174/64	Hep	6081	5396 -87
Maxie	Leslie	USA	4 Jan 67	178/59	400h	55.29	55.20 -84
May	Fiona	UK	12 Dec 69	175/60	LJ	6.82, 6.88w	6.53, 6.64w -87
Mayfield	Tracy	USA	3 Dec 68	160/54	100	11.0w	11.40 -87, 11.3w -86
Mayhew	Donna	USA	20 Jun 60	162/66	JT	63.66	58.26 -87
Meagher	Robyn	CAN	17 Jun 67		1500	4:09.37	4:17.4 -87
Medvedyeva	Lyudmila	SU	18 Jan 57		1500	4:11.46	4:00.42 -84
Medvedyeva	Niole	SU	20 Jun 60	174/62	LJ	7.14	7.02 -84
Mehes	Livia	RUM	6 Mar 65	174/84	SP	19.55	19.61 -86
Meleshkova	Svetlana	SU	13 May 62		1500	4:11.11	4:10.76 -83
Melicherova	Ludmila	CS	6 Jun 64	155/44	Mar	2:34:04	2:36:27 -85
Melinte	Doina	RUM	27 Dec 56	173/60	800	2:00.7i	1:55.05 -82
					1k	2:38.45i	2:36.94 -87
					1500	4:00.85	3:56.7 -86
					Mile	4:18.86i	4:21.88 -86
Melnikova	Svetlana	SU	29 Jan 51	189/94	SP	17.72	20.21 -82
					DT	57.94	66.06 -79

Name		Nat	Born	Ht/Wt	Event	1988 Mark	Pre-1988 Best
Mendonca	Tonya	USA	24 Jan 65	176/59	HJ	1.88i	1.86 -87
Menissier	Liliane	FRA	12 Nov 60	171/63	Hep	5926	6165 -86
Mergermann	Christiane	FRG	17 Dec 65	171/55	HJ	1.88	1.87 -83
Merzlyakova	Natalya	SU	65		100	11.43	11.4 -87
Meszynski	Irina	GDR	24 Mar 62	176/98	DT	69.14	73.36 -84
Michallek	Vera	FRG	6 Nov 58	168/52	1500	4:06.18	4:04.29 -86
					Mile	4:32.12, 4:28.29i	
					3000	8:47.62, 8:46.97i	8:49.61 -87
Mikhalchenko	Larisa	SU	16 May 63	181/93	DT	70.80	64.92 -85
Mikusheva (Veikshina)	Olga	SU	11 Jun 59	168/65	400h	56.84	57.11 -83, 55.5 -84
Miles	Helen	UK	2 Mar 67	160/55	100	11.41w	11.62 -85
Miles	Jearl	USA	4 Sep 66	170/60	400	51.28	52.36 -87
Millar-Cubit	Jocelyn	AUS	23 Mar 62	168/58	Hep	5815	5883 -85
Miller	Inger	JAM	72		100	11.43w	
Miller	LaMonda	USA	19 Sep 67	168/63	100	11.34w	11.63 -87
Min	Chunfeng	CHN	18 Mar 69	174/72	DT	60.60	62.50 -87
Minogenkova (Sachova)	Tatyana	SU	1 Jan 64		800	2:00.84	2:00.2 -85
Miromanova	Nadezhda	SU	1 May 58	170/66	LJ	6.55	6.70 -84
					Hep	6213	6552 -84
Miron	Yelena	SU	65		Hep	5796	5451 -87
Mitchell	Denise	USA	20 Feb 66	160/50	400	52.05	51.72 -87
Mitchell	Jayne	NZ	21 Jun 64		LJ	6.55	6.43 -86
Mitkova	Svetla	BUL	17 Jun 64	178/96	SP	20.58	20.91 -87
					DT	69.14	69.72 -87
Mitrukova	Yelena	SU	22 Jan 64		400h	56.54	55.26 -87
Miyahara	Misako	JAP	29 May 62	155/43	Mar	2:39:37	2:32:10 -87
Mocáriová	Alena	CS	30 Apr 64	164/54	5k	15:43.67	
Mokrak	Svetlana	SU	2 Jun 67	175/60	HJ	1.92	1.92 -87
Moller	Lorraine	NZ	1 Jun 55	174/58	10k	32:40.17	32:40.61 -86
Möller (Gladisch)	Silke	GDR	20 Jun 64	168/59	100	11.06	10.86, 10.82w -87
					200	22.09	21.74 -87
Molokova	Marina	SU	24 Aug 62	171/60	100	11.14, 10.8	11.08 -87
					200	22.84	22.46 -86, 22.0 -87
Monday	Rose	USA	7 Aug 59	173/57	1500	4:10.4	4:08.65 -87
Mondie	Celena	USA	6 Aug 68	168/57	100	11.29w	11.59 -86
					200	23.19	23.78, 23.4 -87
					400	51.45	54.45 -86
Moneva Khristova	Silvia	BUL	22 Aug 65	168/58	LJ	6.85i, 6.69	7.00 -86
Montalvo	Niurka	CUB	4 Jun 68	170/53	LJ	6.62	6.32, 6.52w -87
Moore	Barbara	NZ	17 Jul 57		10k	33:11.31	33:03.52 -87
Morgenstern	Heike	GDR	13 Dec 62	174/56	200	22.65	22.67 -87
Morley	Kay	UK	5 Mar 63	167/60	100h	13.34w, 13.66 -86	13.42w -87
Morozova	Tatyana	SU	64		Hep	6020	
Moshicheva	Tamara	SU	4 Aug 62	170/65	LJ	6.58	6.35 -85
					Hep	6109	6319 -85
Moskvina	Galina	SU	30 Oct 68		400	51.98	53.37 -87
Mosqueda	Sylvia	USA	8 Sep 66	165/55	1500	4:11.2	4:15.14 -87
					3000	8:59.04	9:08.2 -87
					10k	32:28.57	
Mota	Rosa	POR	29 Jun 58	157/45	Mar	2:24:30	2:23:29 -85
Mukamurenzi	Marciana	RWA	11 Nov 59	156/51	10k	32:37.51	33:58.55 -87
Müller	Ines	GDR	2 Jan 59	182/90	SP	21.57	21.45 -86
Müller - Schersing	Petra	GDR	18 Jul 65	180/64	200	23.01	22.61 -87
					400	49.30	49.64 -87
Müller	Rosmarie	SWZ	27 Mar 58	174/50	Mar	2:35:26	2:39:04 -87
Mulliner	Joanne	UK	18 Aug 66	175/66	Hep	5746	6094 -87
Munerotto	Rosanna	ITA	3 Dec 62	168/46	10k	32:06.76	34:27.65 -84
Murashova	Galina	SU	22 Dec 55	180/92	DT	69.86	72.14 -84
Murcia	Rosario	FRA	23 Sep 64	159/49	3000	8:59.04	9:02.71 -87
Murgoci	Elena	RUM	20 May 60	165/49	3000	8:58.28	
					10k	32:20.7	32:24.09 -86
					Mar	2:33:03	2:35:10 -87
Murková	Eva	CS	29 May 62	168/56	LJ	6.57i	7.01, 7.17w -84
Murray	Patty	USA	13 Aug 65	158/40	10k	32:57.38	32:58.50 -87

Name		Nat	Born	Ht/Wt	Event	1988 Mark	Pre-1988 Best
Murray	Yvonne	UK	4 Oct 64	170/50	1500	4:06.34	4:01.20 -87
					2k	5:44.13	5:29.58 -86
					3000	8:29.02	8:37.11 -86
Myers	Sandra	SPA	9 Jan 61	168/58	100	11.30A, 11.42	11.5 -87
					LJ	6.68i, 6.60	6.33 -81
Nagy	Elisabet	SWE	14 Mar 60	170/67	JT	61.60	62.92 -87
Naplatanova	Radka	BUL	11 Jul 57	163/53	3000	8:59.41	8:51.98 -87
					5k	15:38.08	
					10k	33:10.82	33:20.1 -87
Narozhilenko	Lyudmila	SU	21 Apr 64	168/63	200	23.03	
					100h	12.62	12.98, 12.97w -87
						12.57w 12.3	
Nasedkina	Natalya	SU	18 Sep 63	174/72	JT	58.88	59.18 -86
Nastase	Liliana	RUM	1 Aug 62	169/63	100h	12.96,12.94w	12.85 -86, 12.8w -84
					LJ	6.65	6.68 -87, 6.78w -85
					Hep	6352	6364 -87
Nastoburko	Antonina	SU	20 Jan 59	166/59	100	11.28	11.27 -85, 10.9 -84
Naude	Madelé	RSA	2 May 63	174/52	400	51.14A	51.16A -86
					800	2:01.28A	2:03.7A -87
Naumkina	Olga	SU	20 May 64		100	11.43	11.32, 11.2 -87
Nazarova I	Olga	SU	28 Feb 62	176/60	400h	55.47	55.62 -86
Nazarova II	Olga	SU	1 Jun 65	167/55	200	22.74	22.68 -87
					400	49.11 48.9	49.96 -87
N'Drin	Célestine	IVC	20 Jul 63	169/56	400	52.04	53.95 -83
Neamtu	Elisabeta	RUM	10 Oct 60	178/88	DT	65.64	65.20 -85
Nechiporets	Alla	SU	21 Oct 64	174/68	LJ	6.82	6.62 -86
Neer	Penny	USA	7 Nov 60	183/75	DT	61.08	62.10 -87
Neimke	Kathrin	GDR	18 Jul 66	180/95	SP	21.11	21.21 -87
Nekrosaite	Terese	SU	19 Oct 61		JT	64.42	62.96 -85
Nelson	Karen	CAN	3 Dec 63	165/52	100h	13.39, 13.32w	13.30 -83,13.10w -82
Nelson	Lynn	USA	8 Jan 62	176/57	3000	8:55.11	8:54.91 -87
					5k	15:12.7	15:29.61 -87
					10k	31:51.27	32:22.88 -87
					Mar	2:33:31	
Nelyubova	Olga	SU	12 Jul 64		800	1:59.31	2:00.37 -87
					1500	4:06.41	4:08.8 -87
Nesbit	Joan	USA	20 Jan 62	152/43	3000	9:00.29	9:04.33 -86
Neubauer	Dagmar	GDR	3 Jun 62	170/58	400	50.45	49.58 -84
Ni	Xiuling	CHN	23 May 62	175/58	HJ	1.91	1.93 -87
Nicholson	Beverley	UK	10 Jun 67		800	2:00.39	2:03.95 -87
					1500	4:08.46	4:09.85 -87
Niga	Viorica	RUM	20 Nov 68	159/52	800	1:58.96	2:01.85 -87
Nikishina	Olga	SU	29 Apr 66	172/86	DT	61.62	62.24 -86
Nikitina	Larisa	SU	29 Apr 65	177/70	LJ	6.53	666 -87
					Hep	6506	6564 -87
Nikolova	Galya	BUL	14 Nov 65	174/65	JT	62.26	62.22 -87
Ninova	Lyudmila	BUL	25 Jun 60	175/64	LJ	6.85	6.88 -86
Novikova	Lyudmila	SU	29 Jan 64	178/85	SP	17.90	17.04 -86
					DT	62.42	60.34 -87
Nozicková	Vera	CS	7 Feb 66	171/66	1500	4:09.87	4:13.66 -86
Nuneva	Anelia	BUL	30 Jun 62	167/57	100	10.85	10.86 -87
- Vechernikova				200	22.88	22.01 -87	
Nurutdinova	Lilia	SU	15 Dec 63		400	52.21	52.47 -86
					800	2:00.10	
Nusko	Helga	FRG	11 May 65	172/59	Hep	6016	6256 -85
Oakes	Judith	UK	14 Feb 58	163/79	SP	19.36	19.00 -86
Oana	Mihaela	RUM	11 Nov 68	176/78	SP	17.50	17.19 -87
Oanta	Iolanda	RUM	11 Oct 65	183/63	200	22.82	22.70 -87
					400	50.55	51.23 -87
					400h	55.44	57.50 -86
O'Brien (Schiro)	Cathy	USA	19 Jul 64	157/44	Mar	2:30:18	2:34:24 -84
Odintsova	Svetlana	SU	27 Aug 62	178/61	HJ	1.89i	1.89i, 1.89 -86
Oehme	Heike	GDR	11 Nov 63	171/55	800	2:01.36	1:58.16 -86
					1k	2:35.7	2:34.6 -86
					1500	4:04.87	4:02.90 -86

Name		Nat	Born	Ht/Wt	Event	1988 Mark	Pre-1988 Best
Ogunkoya	Falilat	NIG	5 Dec 68	168/66	100	11.19	11.43 -87
					200	22.88	22.95, 22.87w -87
O'Hara	Kirsten	USA	23 Dec 65	173/54	10k	32:52.86	32:40.76 -85
Okolo -Kulak	Lidia	SU	15 Jan 67		100h	12.99, 12.83w	13.02 -87
						12.5	12.9 -86
Old	Wendy	AUS	24 Jun 60	162/52	800	2:01.5	2:00.81 -86
Olejarz -Patla	Genowefa	POL	17 Oct 62	175/73	JT	64.94	65.52 -84
Olenchenko	Vera	SU	21 Mar 59		LJ	6.88	6.92 -85
Oleynik	Irina	SU	12 Dec 63	172/63	Hep	5892	6012 -87
Olijar	Ludmila	SU	5 Feb 58	169/63	100h	13.16	13.03 -86, 12.9 -85
						13.03w 13.0	12.89w -83
Olizarenko	Nadezhda	SU	28 Nov 53	165/57	400	51.83	50.96 -80
					800	1:56.0	1:53.43 -80
					1500	4:04.8	3:56.8 -80
Olyslager	Marjan	HOL	8 Mar 62	172/58	100h	12.83	13.01, 12.96w -85
Onopriyenko	Irina	SU	8 Aug 67		LJ	6.53	6.41 -85
Onyali	Mary	NIG	3 Feb 68	165/52	100	11.09	11.28 -86, 11.2/11,24w -87
					200	22.43	22.52 -87
Oppliger - Bouchonneau	Martine	SWZ	19 Oct 57	170/56	5k	15:25.84	15:30.09 -87
					10k	32:28.26	32:07.49 -87
Oprita	Ilinca	RUM	2 Jan 64	167/52	3000	8:54.82	
Ordina	Vera	SU	4 Jun 68	172/56	100h	13.35	13.0
					400h	57.50	56.77 56.2 -87
Orlova	Tatyana	SU	19 Jul 55		SP	18.35	20.44 -83
Ornduff	Teresa	USA	7 Dec 56	167/49	10k	32:55.55	32:57.02 -87
					Mar	2:35:37	2:41:11 -87
Ortina	Yelena	SU	1 Jan 61		SP	17.51	19.26 -86
Oschkenat	Cornelia	GDR	29 Oct 61	178/68	100h	12.52, 12.50w	12.45, 12.28w -87
Osipova	Irina	SU	9 Jan 63	173/57	LJ	6.64	6.71 -85
Oswald	Silvia	FRG	14 Jun 68	183/55	HJ	1.88	1.88 -86
Otáhalová	Helena	CS	1 Jan 59	178/65	Hep	5969	6032 -84
Ottey	Merlene	JAM	10 May 60	174/59	100	11.00	10.87 -87
						10.7	10.8 -87, 10.7w -86
					200	21.99	21.93 -85
					400	51.29	51.12 -83
Öze -Sipka	Agnes	HUN	14 Aug 54	170/56	Mar	2:33:58	2:28:51 -86
Ozhenko	Irena	SU	13 Nov 62	178/64	LJ	6.60i	7.20 -86
Page	Pam	USA	26 Apr 58	166/63	100h	12.89	13.00 -83
							12.91w -86, 12.8w -85
Pagel	Ramona	USA	10 Nov 61	183/86	SP	20.18	19.83i, 19.22 -87
					DT	61.28	61.92 -87
Pain	Angela	UK	8 Feb 62	162/51	Mar	2:30:51	2:34:47 -87
Pakarinen	Marita	FIN	22 Dec 67	172/58	HJ	1.89	1.81 -87
Pakhomchik	Lyubov	SU	12 Mar 63	184/67	HJ	1.92	1.92 -85
Palade	Liliana	RUM	67		1500	4:09.74	
Pallay	Zsuzsa	HUN	28 Aug 48	173/71	DT	59.18	62.36 -81
Palm	Evy	SWE	31 Jan 42	166/53	10k	32:34.05	32:41.98 -87
					Mar	2:31:35	2:32:47 -86
Panfil	Wanda	POL	26 Jan 59	167/54	5k	15:42.67	15:42.69 -86
					Mar	2:32:23	2:32:01 -87
Panikarovskikh	Yelena	SU	4 Dec 59	172/64	HJ	1.95i, 1.94	1.95 -87
Papilina	Tatyana	SU	14 Jan 67	160/54	100	11.21, 11.12w	11.28 -86
					200	22.89	23.25 -87, 23.0 -85
						22.8 ,22.79i	
Parker	Jacqui	UK	15 Oct 66	163/54	400h	57.45	58.13 -87
Patoka	Antonina	SU	12 Jan 64	182/95	DT	64.32	62.52 -84
Patzwahl	Kristin	GDR	16 Jul 65	169/62	100h	12.94	13.11, 13.01w -87
Pavlova	Anastasia	SU	16 Jun 68	176/92	SP	17.39i	17.35 -87
Pavlova	Tatyana	SU	27 May 60		LJ	6.67	6.65 -86
Payne - Wiggins	Marita	CAN	7 Oct 60	173/57	200	23.05	22.62 -83
					400	50.29	49.91 -84
Pearson	Jennifer	UK	3 Jul 62		400h	57.41	57.68 -87
Peleshenko	Larisa	SU	29 Feb 64	184/80	SP	20.89	20.99 -87
Pells	Leah	CAN	9 Nov 64	170/58	1500	4:11.4	4:17.0 -86
Pencheva	Krasimira	BUL	7 Sep 58	158/48	100	11.42, 11.27w	11.38 -85

Name		Nat	Born	Ht/Wt	Event	1988 Mark	Pre-1988 Best
Peneva -Dimova	Bonka	BUL	15 Mar 56	173/60	400h	57.35	56.96 -80
Pérec	Marie-Josée	FRA	9 May 68	180/58	100	11.34	12.06, 11.9 -85
					200	22.72	24.14 -85 24.00w -86
					400	51.35	-
Pereira dos Santos	Sueli	BRA	8 Jan 65	165/62	JT	60.34	59.52 -87
Perevedentseva	Nina	SU	64		LJ	6.66	
Perez	Cristina	SPA	30 Oct 65	170/69	100	11.39, 11.34wA	11.44 -87
					200	22.86	23.64, 23.62i, 23.52w -87
					400	52.36	52.63i -87, 52.99 -85
					400h	55.23	57.11 -87
Perkins	Jackie	AUS	29 Aug 65	165/53	5k	15:45.96	15:38.34 -86
Pershina	Yelena	SU	63		LJ	6.89	6.45 -81
Pestretsova	Svetlana	SU	6 Mar 61	173/72	JT	67.24	66.00 -87
Peters	Beate	FRG	12 Oct 59	178/80	JT	62.14	69.56 -86
Petrova	Irina	SU	12 Jan 62	167/54	Mar	2:34:33	2:31:43 -87
Petrova	Olga	SU	63		400h	55.77	56.37 -87
Petrova	Yelena	SU	23 Sep 62	172/63	200	23.22	23.20 -83
Petrovic	Biljana	YUG	28 Feb 61	176/60	HJ	1.96	1.92 -87
Petushkova	Yelena	SU	9 Jul 69	176/68	Hep	6102	5961 -87
Pfeil	Renate	FRG	4 Feb 63	180/72	Hep	5857	5914 -86
Pfiefer	Kathy	USA	4 Sep 59	160/47	10k	32:59.6	33:20.30 -86
Pfitzinger	Christine	NZ	24 Jan 59	152/45	3000	8:47.7	8:50.79 -87
Phipps	Angela	CAN	17 Feb 64	175/57	100	11.41	11.34 -87
Pihl	Anna-Lena	SWE	30 Dec 64		JT	58.18	52.88 -87
Pinigina	Maria	SU	9 Feb 58	171/58	200	22.88	22.42 -87
					400	49.74	49.19 -83
					800	2:01.35	
Pippig	Uta	GDR	7 Sep 65	167/55	Mar	2:32:20	2:30:50 -87
Piquereau	Anne	FRA	15 Jun 64	172/65	100h	12.94	12.83w, 12.82 -87
Pisiewicz	Ewa	POL	7 May 62	164/54	100	11.33, 11.28w	11.19, 11.0 -85
					200	23.20w	22.85 -85, 22.81i -86
Placsintár	Eva	HUN	11 Apr 65	173/61	JT	58.14	58.40 -87
Plastinina	Yelena	SU	5 Nov 63	172/57	3000	8:49.98	9:09.4 -86
					10k	32:42.69	
Platek	Malgorzata	POL	28 Apr 63	168/57	400h	57.43	58.39 -84
Platonova	Lyudmila	SU	18 Nov 64	186/100	DT	64.22	61.66 -84
Plescan	Daniela	RUM	11 Jan 69	161/51	400	52.48	53.77 -87
Plotzitzka	Iris	FRG	7 Jan 66	181/82	SP	20.53	20.18 -87
Plumer	PattiSue	USA	27 Apr 62	162/49	3000	8:45.21	8:46.24 -86
					5k	15:32.6	15:20.88 -86
Pluzhnikova	Marina	SU	25 Feb 63		3000	8:49.98	8:49.91 -86
					5k	15:37.70	15:39.94 -85
Podkopayeva	Yekaterina	SU	11 Jun 52	164/54	800	2:01.37	1:55.96 -83
					1500	4:04.57	3:56.65 -84
					Mile	4:31.67	
Podyalovskaya	Irina	SU	19 Oct 59	166/55	800	1:58.03	1:55.69 -84
Pogacean	Mihaela	RUM	27 Jan 58	165/60	100h	12.79	12.70 -87
Polisenska	Martina	CS	15 Nov 66	177/80	DT	61.34	59.26 -87
Politika	Yelena	SU	24 Aug 64	170/67	100h	12.73, 12.66w	12.71 -86
Polledo	Adelina	CUB	3 May 66	164/56	LJ	6.57, 6.81wA	6.53 -86
Pollock	Peggy	USA	1 May 60	178/82	SP	17.45	17.79i -87, 17.58 -86
Polovinskaya	Tatyana	SU	14 Mar 65	159/52	10k	32:23.20	33:12.8 -87
					Mar	2:27:05	2:31:20 -87
Poltorak	Svetlana	SU	60		3000	8:58.2	8:59.3 -84
Polyakova	Ella	SU	30 Mar 70	179/80	SP	17.52	16.09 -87
Pomoshchnikova	Natalya	SU	9 Jul 65	170/60	100	10.98	11.07 -87, 11.0 -86
Powell	Sharon	JAM	16 Jul 65	183/53	200	23.27w	
					400	51.67	
					800	2:01.26	
Pozdnyakova	Tatyana	SU	4 Mar 55	164/52	1500	4:08.35	3:56.50 -82
					3000	8:50.74	8:32.0 -84
Prescura	Lenuta	RUM	8 Jul 66	168/54	1500	4:07.42	4:08.54 -86
					3000	8:50.26	
Pressler	Kerstin	FRG	2 Feb 62	160/50	5k	15:38.81	15:48.25 -86
					10k	32:35.33	31:56.80 -87
					Mar	2:30:37	2:31:22 -87

Name		Nat	Born	Ht/Wt	Event	1988 Mark	Pre-1988 Best
Price	Connie	USA	3 Jun 62	192/93	SP	19.15	18.29 -87
					DT	62.54	64.82 -87
Prisazhnyuk	Irina	SU	12 Jul 64	182/66	HJ	1.92	1.91 -87
Prodan	Svetlana	SU	25 Oct 61	167/52	800	1:59.8	1:58.1 -87
					1500	4:07.6	4:09.4 -87
Prokhorenko	Taisia	SU	12 Dec 67		Hep	6041	5836 -87
Protti	Anita	SWZ	4 Aug 64	170/61	400	52.12	52.44 -87
					400h	54.56	56.69 -87
Puica	Maricica	RUM	29 Jul 50	168/54	3000	8:53.85	8:27.83 -85
Pujol	Montserrat	SPA	27 Apr 61	172/58	800	2:01.47	2:01.94 -87
Quintavalla	Fausta	ITA	4 May 59	175/74	JT	58.20	67.20 -83
Quirot	Ana Fidelia	CUB	23 Mar 63	165/59	200	23.07	23.16, 22.9 -84
					400	49.62A, 49.81	50.12 -87
					800	1:56.36	1:55.84 -87
Rácz	Katalin	HUN	1 Aug 65	161/50	1500	4:11.70, 4:07.88i	4:14.5 -87
Radtke	Helga	GDR	16 May 62	171/64	LJ	6.76i, 6.73	7.21 -84
Ramos	Hilda Elisa	CUB	1 Sep 64	176/80	DT	66.58	67.92 -86
Rashchupkina	Nadezhda	SU	28 Dec 63		100	11.22	11.42 /11.37w-87, 11.2 -85
Rattray - Williams	Cathy	JAM	19 Aug 63	160/52	400	50.82	51.71 -82
Raunig	Deborah	USA	29 Sep 55	165/47	Mar	2:30:23	2:31:28 -86
Ravaonirina	Laloa	MAD	8 Nov 63		100	11.40, 11.22w	11.78, 11.59w -87
Redetzky	Heike	FRG	5 May 64	181/64	HJ	1.98	1.96 -87
Reichelt	Marion	GDR	23 Dec 62	175/62	Hep	6140	6442 -87
Reinsch	Gabriele	GDR	23 Sep 63	188/89	DT	76.80	67.18 -87
Reiter	Anja	GDR	15 Jul 69	173/69	JT	62.58	64.88 -87
Renders	Marleen	BEL	24 Dec 68	166/41	10k	32:11.49	32:12.51 -87
Renk	Silke	GDR	30 Jun 67	173/72	JT	71.00	64.74 -87
Revayová	Elena	CS	10 Jul 58	165/62	JT	59.30	61.60 -85
Reznikova	Galina	SU	17 Apr 61	157/49	800	1:58.48	1:58.4 -84
Ribeiro	Fernanda	POR	23 Jun 69	165/50	3000	9:00.38	8:56.33 -87
Richards	Sandie	JAM	6 Nov 68	170/62	400	51.62	50.92 -87
Richardson	Jill	CAN	10 Mar 65	172/59	200	23.08	23.25 -86
					400	49.91	50.35 -87
Richburg	Diana	USA	2 Jul 63	171/47	1k	2:37.02	2:37.92 -84
					1500	4:08.56	4:01.79 -87
Ritter	Louise	USA	18 Feb 58	178/59	HJ	2.03	2.01 -83
Roben (Custy)	Maureen	USA	31 Aug 55	176/53	Mar	2:32:53	2:33:38 -87
Robinson	Renita	USA	9 Jan 67	170/52	TJ	13.56i, 13.19	12.94, 13.10w -87
Rockenbauer	Nora	HUN	25 Aug 66	178/78	JT	60.40	64.20 -87
Rochefort	Hélène	CAN	22 Nov 54	166/49	Mar	2:31:35	2:32:56 -87
Rocheleau	Julie	CAN	17 Jun 64	164/56	100	11.13	11.89 -87
					100h	12.78	13.36 -87, 13.32w -86
Rodchenkova	Marina	SU	30 Jul 61	164/50	1500	4:11.03	4:07.27 -84
					3000	8:45.69	8:47.06 -84
					5k	15:40.48	15:19.26 -85
Rodgers	Ansie	RSA	4 Sep 64	181/73	JT	59.32	61.08 -85
Rodina	Yelena	SU	67		HJ	1.94	
Rodríguez	Angelines	SPA	24 Sep 69	162/44	3000	8:57.88	9:14.40 -87
Rogachevskaya	Yelena	SU	22 Nov 63	178/88	DT	58.40	57.84 -86
Rogachova	Lyudmila	SU	66		800	1:56.82	2:00.54 -87
					1500	4:04.29	4:08.10 -87
Rohländer	Uta	GDR	30 Jun 69	173/57	400	52.01	51.81 -87
Rohrmann	Heike	GDR	22 Feb 69	180/83	SP	18.94	18.84 -87
Romanauskaite	Rita	SU	70		JT	58.48	56.74 -87
Romanchenkova	Inna	SU	4 Oct 58	170/60	LJ	6.54i	6.58 -82
Romanova	Anna	SU	9 Mar 68	180/87	SP	19.06	18.23 -87
Romanova	Yelena	SU	20 Mar 63	163/49	1500	4:04.96	4:04.60 -86
					2k	5:44.67	
					3000	8:30.45	8:41.15 -87
Ropo - Junnila	Ringa	FIN	16 Feb 66	177/66	LJ	6.67	6.55 -87
Rouillard	Carole	CAN	15 Mar 60	153/44	3000	8:57.69	8:59.15 -86
					10k	32:09.08	32:18.24 -87
Ruban	Irina	SU	4 Aug 62	169/53	Mar	2:35:12	2:32:54 -86

Name		Nat	Born	Ht/Wt	Event	1988 Mark	Pre-1988 Best
Ruban	Svetlana	SU	65		HJ	1.94	1.89 -87
Ruckle	Tani	AUS	25 Jun 62	162/52	Mar	2:31:19	2:36:06 -86
Rünne	Eha	SU	25 May 63	182/85	SP	17.61i	17.01 -86
					DT	63.18	59.94 -87
Ruotsalainen	Satu	FIN	21 Oct 66	174/60	Hep	6101	5948 -87
Ruskite	Valda	SU	26 Jan 62	171/66	Hep	6337	6349 -86
Rust	Sonja	GDR	21 Sep 66	179/75	DT	61.34	60.92 -87
Ruzina	Yelena	SU	3 Apr 64		200	22.73	22.99 ,22.7, 22.6w -87
Ryazanova	Yelena	SU	16 Jun 61	169/54	800	2:01.23	
Rydz (Kapkowska)	Malgorzata	POL	18 Jan 67	162/52	800	2:01.37	2:08.87 -85
Rypakova	Olga	SU	64		100	11.44	
Ryzhova	Viktoria	SU	27 Jan 68	171/64	Hep	6061	5588 -87
Sabeva	Sofia	BUL	11 Jan 69	171/57	400h	55.93	58.48 -87
Sablovskaite	Remigia	SU	2 Jun 67	178/70	Hep	6566	6241 -87
Sahli	Luzia	SWZ	27 May 56	163/50	Mar	2:34:36	2:36:13 -86
Sakorafa	Sofia	GRE	29 Apr 57	176/65	JT	63.16	74.20 -82
Salo	Galina	SU	14 Jun 59	170/62	LJ	6.53	6.88 -86
Samolyenko	Tatyana	SU	12 Aug 61	165/54	800	1:58.86	1:58.56 -85
					1k	2:39.62i	
					1500	4:00.30	3:58.56 -87
					2k	5:44.43	
					3000	8:26.53	8:36.00 -86
Samuelson	Joan	USA	16 May 57	160/49	Mar	2:32:40	2:21:21 -85
Sanderson	Tessa	UK	14 Mar 56	168/72	JT	71.70	73.58 -83
Saracheva	Milena	BUL	31 Jul 67	171/63	400	52.03	
Sarvari	Ulrike	FRG	22 Jun 64	162/50	100	11.16, 11.05w	11.23, 11.15w -87
Satoh	Megumi	JAP	13 Sep 66	178/54	HJ	1.94	1.95 -87
Savchenko	Svetlana	SU	17 Mar 65		DT	59.98	62.38 -87
Scaron	Charles-Line	FRA	22 Apr 62	173/60	HJ	1.88	1.90 -82
Scaunich	Emma	ITA	1 Mar 54	163/48	Mar	2:29:46	2:36:37 -87
Schabinger	Michaela	FRG	23 Mar 61	172/59	400	52.20	52.54 -87
Schäning	Anke	GDR	24 Jun 70		10k	32:44.52	- 0 -
Schmidt	Anke	GDR	5 Feb 68	176/63	LJ	6.55i	6.63 -87
					Hep	6016	6198 -87
Schmidt	Vera	FRG	1 Mar 61	185/85	SP	19.68	19.29 -87
Schmuck	Antje	FRG	7 Oct 64		Hep	5809	5408 -87
Schneider	Corinne	SWZ	28 Jul 62	177/62	Hep	6157	6265 -85
Schnurr	Paula	CAN	15 Jan 64		1500	4:09.80	4:16.69 -87
Scholz	Karen	GDR	16 Sep 69	185/63	HJ	1.92	1.92 -86
Schulz	Ines	GDR	10 Jul 65	177/64	LJ	6.70	6.36 -86
					Hep	6660	6250 -86
Schuwalow	Carolyn	AUS	10 Aug 65	163/46	10k	32:10.05	32:31.0 -87
Schweitzer	Anne	USA	29 Oct 65	165/48	3000	9:01.00	8:59.56 -87
Sedláková	Gabriela	CS	2 Mar 68	169/51	800	2:00.35	1:58.37 -87
Seguin	Magali	FRA	17 Mar 64	162/46	100	11.44	11.43, 11.2 -87
Seidler -Kuhn	Ute	GDR	23 Jul 65	183/61	HJ	1.93	1.91 -85
Seitl	Sabine	AUT	7 Dec 65	174/63	100h	13.36	13.64 -86
Selenska (Todorova)	Antoaneta	BUL	8 Jun 63	170/75	JT	68.42	71.88 -81
Selina	Yelena	SU	64		LJ	6.54	
Selivanova	Galina	SU	20 Mar 60		400h	56.39	56.11 -85
Semiraz	Yelena	SU	21 Nov 65	168/49	LJ	6.86	6.50 -86
Senz	Marilyn	USA	15 Mar 61	183/75	JT	58.34	52.40 -84
Sereda	Marina	SU	12 Apr 64	172/63	400h	55.63	54.78 -86
Sergent	Annette	FRA	17 Nov 62	157/45	3000	8:44.19	8:46.12 -87
					5k	15:18.24	15:32.92 -86
					10k	32:04.78	-
Seuser	Sandra	FRG	17 Apr 66	172/55	400h	57.13	59.09 -87
Sevastyanova	Yelena	SU	67		LJ	6.83	
Shabalina	Olga	SU	64		Hep	5762	5425 -87
Shabanova	Irina	SU	64		DT	63.06	67.34 -87
Shcherbina	Maria	SU	5 Jan 68	180/65	Hep	6187	5953 -86
Sheffield	LaTanya	USA	11 Oct 63	165/57	400h	54.36	54.66 -85
Sheskey	Linda	USA	18 Oct 62	160/47	1k	2:37.91	2:42.61i -84
					1500	4:07.41	4:04.89 -87

Name		Nat	Born	Ht/Wt	Event	1988 Mark	Pre-1988 Best
Shields	Jane	UK	23 Aug 60	163/45	3000	9:00.74	8:45.69 -83
					5k	15:32.34	15:34.92 -82
					10k	32:42.0	- 0 -
Shikolenko	Natalya	SU	1 Aug 64	181/76	JT	66.48	66.18 -87
Shikolenko	Tatyana	SU	10 May 68	175/79	JT	64.70	59.90 -85
Shmelyova	Natalya	SU	66		LJ	6.55	
Shmonina	Marina	SU	9 Feb 65		400	51.10	52.92 -87
Shpak	Tatyana	SU	17 Nov 60	175/72	LJ	6.74	6.68 -87
					Hep	6539	6408 -85
Shtatnova	Svetlana	SU	1 Nov 69	179/63	LJ	6.66	
Shtereva	Nikolina	BUL	25 Jan 55	172/59	1500	4:04.69	4:02.33 -76
					Mile	4:30.26	
Shubenkova	Natalya	SU	25 Sep 57	177/65	100h	13.08	12.93 -84
					Hep	6540	6859 -84
Shults	Lilia	SU	9 Feb 64		SP	18.20	17.86 -87
Siebert (Uibel)	Gloria	GDR	13 Jan 64	172/59	100h	12.48, 12.47w	12.44, 12.37w -87
Siepsiak	Ewa	POL	1 Jan 57	176/85	DT	60.88	63.54 -87
Sileikite	Vite	SU	66		DT	60.10	57.74 -87
Silhavá	Zdenka	CS	15 Jun 54	178/84	SP	19.78	21.05 -83
					DT	71.68	74.56 -84
Simon	Nathalie	FRA	14 Apr 62	171/59	400	52.12	52.05 -87
Simonsick	Eleanor	USA	30 Apr 58	176/54	10k	33:05.02	32:58.6 -83
Simova	Stefenia	BUL	5 Jun 63	172/86	DT	61.54	62.68 -87
Simpson	Judy	UK	14 Nov 60	182/72	Hep	5905	6623 -86
Sinkovic	Kornelija	YUG	24 Jun 64	167/60	100	11.42w	11.34 -87
Sirma	Susan	KEN	26 May 66	162/51	1500	4:10.13	4:14.12 -87
Siska	Xenia	HUN	3 Nov 57	174/58	100h	13.32	12.76 -84
Siwek	Agnieszka	POL	21 May 62	163/51	100	11.36	11.53 -87
					200	22.80	23.58, 23.21w -87
Skeete	Lesley-Ann	UK	20 Feb 67	166/54	100h	13.19	13.07 -87
Skjæveland	Anne Britt	NOR	24 Jul 62		Hep	5815	5540 -87
Sklyarenko	Irina	SU	7 Dec 64	155/49	Mar	2:34:25	2:36:16 -87
Skoglund	Ann-Louise	SWE	28 Jun 62	174/58	400	52.46	51.69 -86
					400h	57.05	54.15 -86
Skurdelite	Birute	SU	28 Sep 63		1500	4:10.54	4:12.8 -85
Slaney (Decker)	Mary	USA	4 Aug 58	168/48	1k	2:34.65	2:34.8 -85
					1500	3:58.92	3:57.12 -83
					Mile	4:21.25	4:16.71 -85
					2k	5:36.65	5:32.7 -84
					3000	8:34.69	8:25.83 -85
Slegers	Lieve	BEL	6 Apr 65	160/50	5k	15:45.28	15:45.89 -86
					10k	32:49.78	32:12.77 -87
Sly	Wendy	UK	5 Nov 59	168/52	Mile	4:31.75i	4:28.07 -84
					2k	5:45.86	5:42.15 -82
					3000	8:37.70	8:37.06 -83
					5k	sub 16 min	15:21.45 -87
					10k	31:53.36	- 0 -
Slyadnyeva	Yekaterina	SU	4 Dec 64		JT	64.04	60.42 -87
Slyusar	Antonina	SU	19 Mar 63	166/56	100	11.41, 11.1	11.68, 11.59w,11.3-87
Smeikste	Ilga	SU	10 Jan 66	177/84	DT	63.52	61.70 -86
Smekhnova	Raisa	SU	16 Sep 50	166/55	10k	32:50.01	31:59.70 -84
					Mar	2:28:40	2:28:00 -87
Smith	Janet	USA	11 Dec 65	173/53	10k	33:05.13	33:10.8 -86
Smith	Meledy	USA	11 Dec 64	163/54	LJ	6.81	6.44 -86, 6.53w -87
Smith	Tracy	CAN	30 Nov 64	170/60	LJ	6.56 6.64w	6.47 -87
Smolarek	Joanna	POL	26 Nov 65	161/53	100	11.35, 11.34w	11.54 -87
					200	23.24w	23.57 -86
Sokolova	Eva	SU	25 Mar 61	170/59	100h	13.18, 13.0i, 13.10w	12.82 -87
Solberg	Trine	NOR	18 Apr 66	172/70	JT	67.50	68.94 -85
Solominskaya	Natalya	SU	61		10k	32:17.74	
Sommer	Coleen	USA	6 Jun 60	178/59	HJ	1.98	2.00i 1.98 -82
Song	Ruiling	CHN	66		JT	60.00	60.54 -87
Sorokivskaya	Natalya	SU	23 Jul 62		1500	4:10.76	4:10.67 -84
					3000	8:48.2	8:49.15 -86
					5k	15:16.83	15:28.55 -86
					10k	31:46.43	32:06.38 -86

Name		Nat	Born	Ht/Wt	Event	1988 Mark	Pre-1988 Best
Sowell	Dawn	USA	27 Mar 66	170/51	100	11.19	11.20 -85
					200	23.13	23.23, 23.11w -85
Spasova	Daniela	BUL	23 Sep 69	166/54	400	52.46	
Spence	Vivienne	JAM	22 Jan 65	165/59	100	11.41, 11.30w	11.48, 11.30w -87
					200	23.09w	23.46 -87, 23.23w -86
Stäheli	Ursula	SWZ	23 Dec 57	180/79	SP	18.02	18.75i -87, 17.78 -86
Stamenova	Rositsa	BUL	6 Mar 55	167/53	400	51.44	50.82 -84
Stanescu	Mariana	RUM	7 Sep 64	168/51	Mile	4:32.53	4:25.52 -86
					3000	8:46.28	8:38.83 -86
Stanley	Tananjalyn	USA	11 Jan 67	165/59	100h	13.22, 13.09w	13.83, 13.79w -87
Stanton	Christine	AUS	12 Dec 59	183/67	HJ	1.93	1.96 -85
Starik	Olga	SU	6 Mar 65	176/60	HJ	1.89	
Starke	Ursula	FRG	16 Apr 56	171/60	Mar	2:35:26	2:39:42 -86
Stasenko	Irina	SU	27 Mar 66	177/70	Hep	5883	5611 -87
Stass	Yelena	SU	25 Jun 65	170/60	400h	56.56, 56.3	56.55 -86
Stephan	Birgit	GDR	27 Sep 64	166/50	Mar	2:29:19	2:32:20 -87
Sterk	Katalin	HUN	13 Sep 61	178/62	HJ	1.99	1.99i -82, 1.98 -86
Steuk	Martina	GDR	11 Nov 59	170/63	800	1:59.95	1:56.21 -80
Stevens	Rochelle	USA	8 Sep 66	173/54	100	11.37	11.65, 11.1 -87
					200	22.91, 22.85w	22.84 -87
					400	51.23	51.23 -87
Stewart	Sharon	AUS	17 Aug 65	171/62	800	2:01.40	2:01.4 -87
Stolyar	Lyubov	SU	21 Aug 65	172/60	100h	13.30, 13.16w	13.13 -87, 12.9 -85
Storp	Stephanie	FRG	28 Nov 68	195/95	SP	19.73	19.90 -87
Stoyanova	Diana	BUL	5 Jan 69	174/90	SP	17.50	16.49 -87
Stoyanova	Vanya	BUL	12 Dec 58	160/54	1500	4:10.68i	4:03.14 -84
Stoyanova (Krumova)	Yordanka	BUL	9 May 59	168/50	400	52.29	51.88 -87
Styepanova	Nadezhda	SU	22 Jul 59	170/60	3000	8:52.39	8:49.71 -86
					5k	15:43.05	15:46.96 -85
					10k	32:19.62	32:25.19 -86
Styepanova	Tatyana	SU	21 Aug 67	163/54	100h	13.11	13.33, 13.2 -87
Sui	Xinmei	CHN	29 Jan 65		SP	20.08	18.87 -86
Sukhoroslova	Lyudmila	SU	12 May 62	166/53	HJ	1.94i, 1.92	1.92 -87
Sukhova	Vera	SU	9 Jul 63	164/53	Mar	2:30:09	
Sultanova	Farida	SU	61		3000	8:54.62	9:04.7i -87
					10k	33:04.2	
Suter	Esther	SWZ	25 Feb 62	174/55	Hep	5763	5814 -86
Sutfin	Lynda	USA	6 Oct 62	171/68	JT	60.70	61.66 -82
Svetonosova	Irina	SU	6 Jun 58	174/62	100h	13.00, 12.9	13.21 -86
						12.88w	13.0 -84
Swart	Ciska	RSA	26 Jun 59		1k	2:39.40	
					1500	4:09.63	4:09.3 -87
Swart	Irma	RSA	22 Sep 65		400h	57.36A	57.73A -87
Sychugova (Zaytseva)	Vera	SU	13 Oct 63		100	11.43	11.3 -87
					200	23.02	22.85 -87
					400	51.64	52.46 52.3 -87
Syomkina	Galina	SU	61		200	23.06	
Szabó	Erzsébet	HUN	27 Sep 63	169/53	400	52.3, 52.47i	52.61 -87
					800	2:01.40	2:03.77 -85
Szabo	Estera	RUM	11 Oct 67	176/65	LJ	6.66	
Szabó	Karolina	HUN	17 Nov 61	149/35	Mar	2:30:57	2:30.31 -86
Tadrzak	Grazyna	POL	7 Oct 67	174/58	100h	13.25w	13.62 -87
Tamura	Yuki	JAP	21 Apr 66	154/46	10k	33:04.75	33:43.6 -87
Tandian	Aissatou	SEN	29 Aug 66	168/	400	52.33	54.04 -87
Tang	Lishuang	CHN	68		JT	59.62	
Tarr	Sheila	USA	14 Jun 64	176/68	Hep	5881w, 5773	5855 -87
Tata-Muya	Rose	KEN	12 Jun 60	163/50	400h	56.18, 55.7A	55.94 -87
Tate	Bridgette	USA	12 Mar 66	163/56	200	23.19	23.56 -86
					100h	13.24w	13.58 -86
Tate	Ethlyn	JAM	13 May 66	162/52	100	11.34	11.36 -87
					200	23.09	23.25 -87
Tate	Marcia	JAM	25 Jun 61	162/58	400	52.34	52.82 -85
Tauceri	Valentina	ITA	20 Jul 66	171/54	1500	4:10.04	4:17.56 -87
Taylor	Michelle	USA	16 Apr 67	181/64	400	52.38	53.51 -87

Name		Nat	Born	Ht/Wt	Event	1988 Mark	Pre-1988 Best
Telles	Soraya Vieira	BRA	16 Sep 58	167/54	800	1:59.92	2:00.56 -87
					1500	4:10.07	4:14.69 -87
					Mile	4:30.05	
Temim	Amra	YUG	24 Jan 68	184/56	HJ	1.94	1.94 -87
Ter-Mesrobian	Tatyana	SU	12 May 68	178/59	LJ	6.63, 6.67w	6.60 -86
Tesárková	Jitka	CS	27 Oct 65	163/59	100h	13.35	13.38, 13.21w -85
Teske	Charlotte	FRG	23 Nov 49	167/55	Mar	2:30:23	2:28:32 -83
Theele	Heike	GDR	4 Oct 64	172/63	100h	13.01	12.63 -86
Thiele	Sibylle	GDR	6 Mar 65	178/74	100h	13.27	13.14 -86
					Hep	6526	6635 -86
Thiémard	Denise	SWZ	24 Mar 60	169/66	JT	63.62	64.04 -87
Thieme	Andrea	GDR	8 Jun 64	185/81	DT	65.68	65.20 -86
Thimm	Ute	FRG	10 Jul 58	167/54	200	23.00	22.87 -87
					400	50.28	50.37 -84
Thomas	Andrea	FRG	9 Apr 63	176/62	100	11.34	11.58 -82, 11.48w -85
					200	22.74	23.09 -85, 22.8w -82
Thompson	Andrea	USA	30 Oct 66	163/54	100	11.35	11.59, 11.57w -87
Thoumas	Nathalie	FRA	30 Apr 62	165/53	800	2:00.71	1:59.83 -87
Thurman	Tammy	USA	1 Mar 65	182/63	HJ	1.88	1.83 -86, 1.85i -87
Thyssen	Ingrid	FRG	9 Jan 56	171/72	JT	66.00	69.68 -87
Tichopadova	Yvona	CS	6 Oct 64	178/68	HJ	1.88i	1.86i -87
Tifrea -Barbu	Corina	RUM	11 Feb 58	169/62	Hep	6149	6085 -82
Tikkanen	Päivi	FIN	19 Jan 60	164/50	3000	8:56.48	9:02.04 -87
					10k	32:11.62	32:31.28 -87
Tinari	Nancy	CAN	13 Jun 59	155/40	10k	32:14.05	32:15.82 -87
Tirneci	Manuela	RUM	26 Feb 69	171/79	DT	58.24	55.88 -87
Tischler	Heike	GDR	4 Feb 64	176/62	LJ	6.68	6.40 -85
					Hep	6569	6366 -84
Tochilova	Natalya	SU	21 May 64	100h	12.87	13.11	13.0 -87
Tolbert	Lynda	USA	3 Oct 67	162/51	100	11.41wA	11.69 -87
					100h	12.76, 12.75w	13.06 -87
Tolstoguzova	Yelena	SU	17 Jun 62		3000	8:59.21	
					5k	15:36.05	15:48.2 -87
					10k	32:12.2	32:42.53 -87
Tooby	Angela	UK	24 Oct 60	166/49	3000	8:47.59	8:47.86 -87
					5k	15:17.89	15:13.22 -87
Tooby	Susan	UK	24 Oct 60	165/49	10k	32:20.95	32:49.30 -87
					Mar	2:31:33	3:10:10 -82
Tornow	Sylvia	FRG	6 Feb 69	172/69	Hep	5906	5800 -87
Torrence	Gwen	USA	12 Jun 65	170/57	100	10.91,10.78w	11.09 -87,11.01w -86
					200	22.02	22.40, 22.33w, 22.2w -87
					400	51.84, 51.1	51.60 -87
Trojer	Irmgard	ITA	16 Mar 64	170/57	400h	55.74	56.51 -87
Tromp	Gretha	HOL	21 Feb 64	174/60	100h	13.31	13.62 -87
					400h	55.59	58.5 -87
Tsukhlo	Yelena	SU	13 May 54	165/54	Mar	2:32:48	2:28:53 -87
Turchak	Olga	SU	5 Mar 67	190/67	HJ	2.00	2.01 -86
Turner	Elspeth	UK	18 Mar 65		10k	33:05.43	34:15.52 -87
Turner	Terri	USA	19 Jul 63	178/61	HJ	1.90	1.85 -87
Turshina	Larisa	SU	61		400h	56.6	58.0 -87
Tuzzi	Carla	ITA	2 Jun 67	162/51	100h	13.08	13.36 -87
Twomey	Cathie	USA	24 Oct 56	162/50	3000	8:55.93	8:48.55 -84
					5k	15:17.02	15:22.37 -85
					10k	32:38.11	33:11.2 -87
Tyree	Cathey	USA	8 Oct 64	180/73	Hep	5861w, 5762	5922 -87
Tyukhay	Irina	SU	14 Jan 67	168/60	100h	13.32, 13.0	13.43 -86, 13.3 -84
					Hep	6129	5922 -86
Uba	Rufina	NIG	4 Apr 59	173/63	100	11.34, 11.32w	11.31, 11.18w -82
Uccheddu	Valentina	ITA	26 Oct 66	166/45	LJ	6.62	6.40 -86
Uebel	Ronny	GDR	19 Nov 63	165/54	400	52.45	51.93 -87
Ullrich	Cornelia	GDR	26 Apr 63	172/59	400h	54.81	53.58 -87
Ullrich	Kathrin	GDR	14 Aug 67	169/52	1500	4:06.19i	
					3000	8:44.81, 8:41.79i	8:50.51 -87
					5k	15:20.23	15:52.6 -87
					10k	31:26.79	31:11.34 -87

Name		Nat	Born	Ht/Wt	Event	1988 Mark	Pre-1988 Best
Upyr	Alla	SU	23 Oct 62	171/57	800	2:01.2	
Urbikiene (Bimbaite)	Danguole	SU	10 Dec 62	184/82	SP	19.55	20.27 -87
Usifo	Maria	NIG	1 Aug 64	174/63	400h	55.99	55.16 -86
Utondu	Beatrice	NIG	23 Nov 69	163/59	LJ	6.59	6.45 -87
Vader - Scharn	Els	HOL	24 Sep 59	162/52	100	11.32, 11.19w	11.17 -86, 11.0 -81
					200	22.94	22.81 -81, 22.55w -86
Vaidianu	Petra	RUM	24 Aug 65	170/66	Hep	6343	6217 -86
Valkova	Ivanka	BUL	2 Mar 65	165/56	LJ	6.59	6.53 -86, 6.61w -87
Valyukevich	Irina	SU	19 Nov 59	171/63	LJ	6.88, 7.07w	7.17 -87
Vanyek	Zsuzsa	HUN	18 Jan 60	168/59	LJ	6.57	6.81 -83
van der Burgh	Marna	RSA	28 Sep 57	170/61	400h	57.26A	59.87 -87
van der Kolk	Yvonne	HOL	7 Jan 69		1k	2:38.91	
van der Walt	Nanette	RSA	22 Feb 59		DT	57.40	58.80 -86
van Heezik	Edine	HOL	27 Jan 61	175/53	LJ	6.54	6.63i -87, 6.57 -80
van Hulst	Elly	HOL	9 Jun 59	178/58	1k	2:38.16	2:36.70 -81
					1500	4:04.88	4:03.63 -87
					Mile	4:28.08i	4:22.40 -86
					2k	5:44.41	5:39.52 -86
					3000	8:33.97	8:42.57 -87
					10k	32:48.15	34:45.98 -84
van Landeghem	Rita	BEL	19 Jul 57	164/58	Mar	2:28:11	2:29:56 -87
van Rensburg	Ina	RSA	29 Oct 56	171/56	100h	13.10A, 13.08wA	13.09A -86
van Zyl	Elana	RSA	10 Oct 66	172/55	1500	4:11.41	4:11.13 -87
					3000	8:54.84	8:52.39 -87
					5k	15:44.15	15:59.62 -83
Vasícková	Sona	CS	14 Mar 62	174/78	SP	20.80	20.55 -87
Vasilyeva	Lyubov	SU	14 Aug 57	174/83	SP	18.47i, 18.32	19.78 -86
Vasilyeva	Svetlana	SU	28 Feb 67	171/65	Hep	6063	5805 -85
Veith	Gabriele	GDR	24 Oct 56	167/51	5k	15:40.14	15:21.90 -86
Verbruggen	Ingrid	BEL	20 Sep 64	174/57	200	23.24	23.17 -87
Veréb	Erika	HUN	23 Oct 63	160/46	3000	9:00.0	9:00.16 -85
					5k	15:41.36	15:23.54 -86
					10k	32:14.50	32:15.56 -86
Vereen	Wendy	USA	24 Apr 66	160/54	100	11.38, 11.19w	11.17 -83
					200	22.93, 22.77w	22.96 -86,22.75w -84
Verouli	Anna	GRE	13 Nov 56	165/68	JT	68.76	72.70 -84
Veselinova	Verzhinia	BUL	18 Nov 57	170/95	SP	19.28	21.61 -82
Vickers	Janeene	USA	3 Dec 68	170/62	400h	56.10	57.80 -87
Vieru	Floarea	RUM	6 May 67	175/83	DT	59.60	59.94 -87
Vila	Mayra	CUB	5 Jun 60	167/64	JT	58.40	70.14 -85
Villeton	Jocelyne	FRA	17 Sep 54	170/55	10k	32:51.37	32:59.67 -86
					Mar	2:34:02	2:32:03 -87
Vinogradova	Tatyana	SU	26 Apr 66	176/83	SP	17.05i	17.41 -87
Vinogradova	Yelena	SU	28 Mar 64	170/58	400	51.46	52.98 -87, 52.5 -84
Vitoulová	Alena	CS	6 May 60	176/89	SP	19.13i, 18.18	19.30 -87
Volf	Yelena	SU	69		LJ	6.53	
Voronova	Olga	SU	23 Feb 68	173/58	100	11.36	11.65, 11.3 -87
						11.32w	11.56w -86
Vörös	Britta	GDR	4 Dec 68	181/61	HJ	1.88	1.85 -86
Vörös -Herth	Hajnal	HUN	28 Nov 59	177/87	SP	18.00	17.64 -87
Voycheva	Proletka	BUL	20 Jan 70	182/91	DT	59.28	52.74 -87
Voyevudskaya	Lyudmila	SU	22 Jun 59	183/95	SP	19.80	20.27 -87
Wachtel	Christine	GDR	6 Jan 65	166/56	800	1:56.64, 1:56.40i	1:55.32 -87
Wade	Kirsty	GB	6 Aug 62	169/56	800	2:00.61	1:57.42 -85
					1k	2:38.01	2:33.70 -85
					1500	4:05.33	4:00.73 -87
					Mile	4:23.86i	4:19.41 -85
Waitz	Grete	NOR	1 Oct 53	172/52	Mar	2:28:07	2:24:54 -86
Waller	Donna	USA	6 Apr 64	165/52	100h	13.13, 12.99w, 13.1	13.26 -87
Walton -Floyd	Delisa	USA	28 Jul 61	173/58	400	52.03	51.21 -87
					800	1:57.80	1:58.70 -87
Wang	Hong	CHN	10 Apr 70	176/75	SP	17.33	
Wang	Lianyun	CHN	69		JT	58.24	61.06 -87

Name		Nat	Born	Ht/Wt	Event	1988 Mark	Pre-1988 Best
Wang	Qinghuan	CHN	22 Dec 66	161/50	10k	32:04.52	31:44.73 -87
Wang	Wei	CHN	67		SP	17.01	16.56 -87
Wang	Xiuting	CHN	11 May 65	158/47	3000	8:54.19	8:50.68 -87
					10k	31:40.23	31:27.00 -87
Warbelow	Dörte	GDR	30 Oct 70		DT	58.10	55.86 -87
Washington	Essie	USA	12 Jan 57	179/52	400	52.44	52.33 -78
					800	1:59.70	1:59.07 -87
					1k	2:37.90	
Wästlund	Malin	SWE	27 Apr 64	164/48	10k	32:08.32	34:13.3 -87
Watkins	Gayle	USA	5 Nov 58	168/54	100h	13.27	13.39 -85, 13.18w -86
Watson	Melissa	UK	24 Nov 64		3000	9:01.67	9:03.25 -87
Webb	Brenda	USA	30 May 54	157/41	3000	8:52.88, 8:49.40i	8:48.09 -83
					5k	15:18.71	15:22.76 -84
Webber	Dyan	USA	9 Apr 66	169/64	200	23.0	
Weber	Ursula	AUT	26 Sep 60	168/66	DT	57.60	59.10 -87
Weidenbach	Lisa	USA	13 Dec 61	176/57	5k	15:45.2	16:21.0 -83
					10k	32:15.88	33:38.43 -83
					Mar	2:29:17	2:31:31 -84
Weiser	Katja	FRG	19 Jan 66	174/80	SP	17.24	15.44 -87
Welch	Lisa	USA	12 Mar 63	175/54	10k	33:01.5	32:41.9 -86
Welch	Priscilla	UK	22 Nov 44	165/50	Mar	2:30:53	2:26:51 -87
Wellman	Pat	CAN	21 Feb 64		800	2:01.20	2:07.5 -86
Welty	Amber	USA	24 Mar 67	174/50	HJ	1.92	1.86 -87
Wennberg	Christine	SWE	11 May 63	161/53	400h	56.29	56.56 -87
Westén	Monica	SWE	15 Mar 66	175/65	Hep	5783	5604 -87
Wheeler	Erica	USA	28 Nov 67	170/61	JT	58.58	57.78 -85
Whitbread	Fatima	UK	3 Mar 61	168/68	JT	70.32	77.44 -86
Wiese	Christa	GDR	25 Dec 67	181/90	SP	19.19	19.06 -87
Wijnsma	Marion	HOL	18 Jul 65	168/66	LJ	6.57	6.06 -87
					Hep	6213	5978 -87
Wiley	Alison	CAN	11 Oct 63	165/45	3000	8:56.51	8:51.27 -83
Wilkenson	Karen	RSA	7 Jan 66		400h	55.99A	56.27 -87
Williams	Angela	TRI	15 May 65	175/61	100	11.22	11.09w, 11.54 -84,11.1 -83
					200	23.14	23.22 -85, 23.2w -87
Williams	Diane	USA	14 Dec 60	163/56	100	10.86	10.94 -83, 10.90w -87
					200	22.67	22.60 -86
Williams	Lynn	CAN	11 Jul 60	153/48	1500	4:00.86	4:00.27 -85
					2k	5:44.55	
					3000	8:37.30	8:37.38 -85
Williams	Schowonda	USA	3 Dec 66	163/57	100h	13.32	13.43 -85, 13.17w -87
						13.25w	13.1 -86
					400h	54.93	54.82 -87
Willms	Sandra	RSA	11 Dec 60	176/85	DT	57.40	56.18 -80
Wilson	Linetta	USA	11 Oct 67	168/63	400h	55.60	55.55 -87
Winkelmann	Antje	FRG	22 May 65	161/47	5k	15:40.14	15:49.60 -87
					10k	33:03.2	34:10.42 -87
Wise	Joanne	UK	15 Mar 71	164/50	LJ	6.69w	6.26 -87
Wittich	Ines	GDR	14 Nov 69	189/95	SP	18.80	19.48 -87
Wlodarczyk	Urzsula	POL	22 Dec 65	178/69	Hep	5825	5831 -87
Wodars	Sigrun	GDR	7 Nov 65	166/54	400	52.38	51.80 -87
					800	1:56.10	1:55.26 -87
Wohlschlag	Jan	USA	14 Jul 58	186/67	HJ	1.97	1.93 -86
Wolf	Birgit	FRG	11 Sep 69	175/58	100h	13.28	13.31 -87
Wolf	Gabriela	FRG	28 Oct 60	169/60	Mar	2:31:56	2:35:12 -87
Wolska	Malgorzata	POL	6 Sep 66	178/80	SP	18.30i, 17.88	18.44 -87
Womplou	Marie Gnebele	IVC	20 Dec 69	161/46	400h	57.35	58.13 -87
Wu	Ping	CHN	65		Hep	5746	5896 -87
Wühn	Katrin	GDR	19 Nov 65	174/58	800	2:00.62i	1:57.86 -84
					1500	4:07.27, 4:05.67i	4:03.77 -87
Wyeth	Alison	UK	26 May 64		1500	4:11.16	4:12.02 -87
Wyludda	Ilke	GDR	28 Mar 69	184/92	SP	20.23	20.11 -87
					DT	74.40	71.64 -87
Wynn	Christine	CAN	10 Aug 61	165/54	400h	57.02	56.32 -84
Wysocki	Ruth	USA	8 Mar 57	176/59	1500	4:04.25	4:00.18 -84
					Mile	4:28.24	4:21.78 -84
					3000	8:55.85	8:52.91 -87, 8:49.93i -85

Name		Nat	Born	Ht/Wt	Event	1988 Mark	Pre-1988 Best
Xie	Lihua	CHN	19 Jul 65	162/50	Mar	2:31:43	2:33:16 -87
Xin	Ailan	CHN	23 Feb 65	175/86	DT	65.42	63.18 -87
Xin	Xiaoli	CHN	22 Sep 66	165/60	JT	61.30	63.96 -87
Xiong	Qiying	CHN	15 Oct 67	170/55	LJ	6.88	6.59 -87
Xu	Demei	CHN	67		JT	61.06	60.92 -87
Yachmenyeva	Marina	SU	14 Jul 61	169/57	800	1:58.84	1:59.76 -81
					1k	2:36.02i	
					1500	4:02.84	4:05.1 -87
Yagodina	Irina	SU	24 Apr 64	149/39	Mar	2:32:30	
Yatchenko	Irina	SU	65		DT	67.44	63.00 -87
Yegorova	Valentina	SU	16 Feb 64		Mar	2:30:59	
Yelesina	Yelena	SU	4 Apr 70	184/57	HJ	1.98	1.89 -87
Yermakova	Galina	SU	15 Jun 53	182/98	DT	64.26	73.28 -84
Yermilova	Svetlana	SU	12 Feb 59	172/60	100h	13.39	13.35 -86
Yermolovich	Natalya	SU	29 Apr 64	169/68	JT	68.86	69.86 -85
Yevseyeva	Inna	SU	14 Aug 64	178/57	400	52.38	50.80, 50.6 -86
					800	1:56.0	2:00.6 -86
Young	Candy	USA	21 May 62	168/58	100h	13.36, 13.24w	12.89 -82
Young	Crystal	USA	10 Oct 65	178/74	Hep	5741	5144 -85
Young	Dannette	USA	6 Oct 64	165/57	100	11.10	11.31 -86
					200	22.23, 22.21w	22.72 -87
					400	52.46	
Yu	Hourun	CHN	7 Jul 64	180/92	DT	68.62	66.76 -87
Yupatova	Viktoria	SU	66		HJ	1.88	
Yurchenko	Aelita	SU	1 Jan 65	165/54	200	22.67, 22.6	23.23 22.5 -87
					400	49.47	50.48 -87
Yurchenko	Irina	SU	7 Dec 68		DT	59.92	59.16 -87
Yurlina	Svetlana	SU	64		800	2:00.3	2:00.8 -86
Zaczkiewicz	Claudia	FRG	4 Jul 62	170/57	100h	12.75	12.80 -87
Zagorcheva	Ginka	BUL	12 Apr 58	175/62	100h	12.48	12.25 -87, 12.1w -86
Zaituc	Luminita	RUM	9 Oct 68	163/47	1500	4:10.55	4:10.63 -86
Zakharova	Larisa	SU	26 Jul 64		Hep	6020	5641 -84
Zavadskaya	Yelena	SU	24 Dec 64	174/56	800	1:59.4	1:59.74 -86
Zavalishcheva	Yelena	SU	63		HJ	1.90	1.87 -85
Zaytseva	Yelena	SU	26 Feb 67	173/68	Hep	6082	5653 -85
Zeman	Linda	USA	14 Nov 60	165/50	Mar	2:34:52	2:42:57 -84
Zhang	Caihua	CHN	10 Dec 64	167/61	100	11.32, 10.9	11.35 -87, 11.2 -86
Zhang	Hui	CHN	67		DT	57.70	56.90 -87
Zhang	Li	CHN	61		JT	62.84	64.14 -87
Zhao	Youfeng	CHN	5 May 65	168/49	Mar	2:27:06	2:43:48 -87
Zhecheva	Petya	BUL	3 Jan 69	178/80	SP	17.22	14.98i -87
Zhen	Wenhua	CHN	67		SP	17.47	17.61 -87
Zhilichkina	Yelena	SU	17 Aug 63	179/66	JT	58.44	59.04 -86
Zhirova	Marina	SU	6 Jun 63	170/60	100	11.10, 11.0	10.98 -85
Zhou	Shuqin	CHN	68		SP	17.64	
Zhou	Tianhua	CHN	66		SP	19.50	18.55 -87
Zhou	Yuanxiang	CHN	30 Jan 64	174/73	JT	62.26	65.28 -87
Zhupiyova	Yelena	SU	18 Apr 60	158/45	1500	4:09.5	4:04.44 -84
					3000	8:44.79	8:38.1 -85
					5k	15:38.17	15:23.25 -86
					10k	31:19.82	31:09.40 -87
Zhuravlyova	Tatyana	SU	19 Dec 67		LJ	6.55	
					Hep	6156	5670 -87
Zivanov	Danica	YUG	8 Feb 67	181/80	SP	16.95	16.67 -86
Zolotaryova	Olga	SU	1 Nov 61	165/55	100	11.23, 11.18w	11.19, 10.9w -87
					200	23.11	22.80 -84
Zorina	Svetlana	SU	2 Feb 60	173/62	LJ	6.76	7.07 -87
Zsigmond	Kinga	HUN	19 Apr 64		JT	58.36	56.22 -87
Zubaitite	Vilia	SU	63		DT	63.06	62.68 -87
Zuñiga	Teresa	SPA	28 Dec 64	167/56	800	1:57.45	2:02.61 -87
					1500	4:06.44	4:12.99 -87
Zuyeva	Tatyana	SU	17 Jun 58		10k	33:02.4	33:06.7 -87
Zveryeva	Ellina	SU	16 Nov 60	182/90	DT	71.58	68.96 -86

WORLD INDOOR RECORDS

Event	Mark	Athlete	Nat	Venue	Date
MEN					
50 metres	5.55	Ben Johnson	CAN	Ottawa	31 Jan 1987
60 metres	6.41	Ben Johnson	CAN	Indianapolis	7 Mar 1987
200 metres	20.36	Bruno Marie-Rose	FRA	Liévin	22 Feb 1987
400 metres	45.05	Thomas Schönlebe	GDR	Sindelfingen	5 Feb 1988
800 metres	1:44.84	Paul Ereng	KEN	Budapest	4 Mar 1989
1000 metres	2:16.4*	Rob Druppers	HOL	Den Haag	20 Feb 1988
1500 metres	3:35.6'	Marcus O'Sullivan	IRL	East Rutherford	10 Feb 1989
	3:35.4u	Marcus O'Sulivan	IRL	East Rutherford	13 Feb 1988
1 mile	3:49.78	Eamonn Coghlan	IRL	East Rutherford	27 Feb 1983
3000 metres	7:39.2	Emiel Puttemans	BEL	Berlin	18 Feb 1973
5000 metres	13:20.4	Suleiman Nyambui	TAN	New York	6 Feb 1981
50 metres hurdles	6.25	Mark McKoy	CAN	Kobe	5 Mar 1986
60 metres hurdles	7.36	Greg Foster	USA	Los Angeles	16 Jan 1987
	7.36	Roger Kingdom	USA	Piraeus	8 Mar 1989
High jump	2.43	Javier Sotomayor	CUB	Budapest	4 Mar 1989
Pole vault	6.03	Sergey Bubka	SU	Osaka	11 Feb 1989
Long jump	8.79	Carl Lewis	USA	New York	27 Jan 1984
Triple jump	17.76	Mike Conley	USA	New York	27 Feb 1987
Shot	22.66	Randy Barnes	USA	Los Angeles	20 Jan 1989
5000m walk	18:11.41u	Ronald Weigel	GDR	Wien	13 Feb 1988
	18:15.91	Mikhail Shchennikov	SU	Gomel	4 Feb 1989
4 x 200m relay	1:22.32	Italy		Turin	11 Feb 1984
		(Pierfrancesco Pavoni, Stefano Tilli, Giovanni Bongiorni, Carlo Simionato)			
4 x 400m relay	3:05.21	USA		Glasgow	10 Mar 1989
		(Clarence Daniel, Chip Jenkins, Ken Lowery, Mark Rowe)			
Octathlon	7084	Christian Plaziat	FRA	Vittel	11/12 Feb 1989
		(6.78 60m, 14.73 SP, 2.10 HJ, 49.38 400m, 7.64 LJ, 7.91 60mh, 4.80 PV, 2:48.08 1000m)			
WOMEN					
50 metres	6.06	Angella Issajenko	CAN	Ottawa	31 Jan 1987
60 metres	7.00	Nellie Cooman	HOL	Madrid	23 Feb 1986
200 metres	22.27	Heike Drechsler	GDR	Indianapolis	7 Mar 1987
400 metres	49.59	Jarmila Kratochvilová	Cs	Milano	7 Mar 1982
800 metres	1:56.40	Christine Wachtel	GDR	Wien	13 Feb 1988
1000 metres	2:34.8	Brigitte Kraus	FRG	Dortmund	19 Feb 1978
1500 metres	4:00.8	Mary Decker-Slaney	USA	New York	8 Feb 1980
3000 metres	8:33.82	Elly van Hulst	HOL	Budapest	4 Mar 1989
5000 metres	15:25.02u	Brenda Webb	USA	Gainesville	30 Jan 1988
	15:19.84mx	Lesley Welch	USA	Boston	25 Jan 1986
50 metres hurdles	6.58	Cornelia Oschkenat	GDR	Berlin	20 Feb 1988
60 metres hurdles	7.73	Cornelia Oschkenat	GDR	Wien	25 Feb 1989
High jump	2.06	Stefka Kostadinova	BUL	Piraeus	20 Feb 1988
Long jump	7.37	Heike Drechsler	GDR	Wien	13 Feb 1988
Shot	22.20	Helena Fibingerová	Cs	Jablonec	19 Feb 1977
3000m walk	12:01.65	Kerry Saxby	AUS	Budapest	4 Mar 1989
4 x 200m relay	1:32.55	SC Eintracht Hamm	FRG	Dortmund	20 Feb 1988
		(Helga Arendt, Silke-Beate Knoll, Mechthild Kluth, Gisela Kinzel)			
4 x 400m relay	3:34.38	F.R.Germany		Dortmund	30 Jan 1981
		(Heide-Elke Gaugel, Christina Sussiek, Christiane Brinkmann, Gaby Bussmann)			

* auto time of 2:16.62 declared to be faulty, and hand time ratified
u - unratified mark, mx - mixed race

Other world records set during 1989 - either superseded by above, or at other events:

Event	Mark	Athlete	Nat	Venue	Date
MEN					
300 metres	32.19	Robson C.da Silva	BRA	Karlsruhe	24 Feb 1989
Pole vault	6.00	Rodion Gataullin	SU	Leningrad	22 Jan 1989
	6.02	Rodion Gataullin	SU	Gomel	4 Feb 1989
4 x 800m relay	7:17.45	Clemson University		Indianapolis	11 Mar 1989
		(Radziwinski (USA), Wittman (USA), Greyling (RSA), Hines (JAM))			
WOMEN					
55 metres hurdles	7.37	Jackie Joyner-Kersee	USA	New York (heat)	3 Feb 1989
(equals record)	7.37	Jackie Joyner-Kersee	USA	New York	3 Feb 1989
Triple jump	14.16	Irina Lasovskaya	SU	Moskva	15 Jan 1989
	14.45	Galina Chistyakova	SU	Lipetsk	29 Jan 1989

WORLD INDOOR CHAMPIONSHIPS 1989

At Budapest, Hungary 3-5 March 1989

Although there were disappointing entries in some events, there was much high-class action, most notably on the second day when there were four world records. Kerry Saxby started the spree at 5000 metres walk, and Javier Sotomayor ended the day with 2.43m on his first attempt to take a fascinating high jump competition. However the most brilliant performance was surely that of Paul Ereng in the 800 metres. The solitary Kenyan taking part, as he had travelled independently and did not know that his team had withdrawn, he had very little 800 metres form behind him in the indoor season - a 1:50.44 for fourth at the Millrose Games and a winning 1:49.30 in Johnson City. But he showed, as he had in 1988, that he is a fabulous talent. Ray Brown led the pack through 200m in 24.58 and 400m in 50.83, just ahead of the defending champion José Luiz Barbosa, and the pair went through 600m in 1:17.98. Meanwhile Ereng was seemingly out of it, and, although he had gained some ground, was still ten metres back at this point. Then he unleashed a 100m in 12.4, ripped past the startled Barbosa and swept through the line with his giant strides. Elly van Hulst took six seconds off the world record for 3000 metres, kicking past Liz McColgan, who had led throughout, with just 100m to go. McColgan's brave running was at least rewarded with a Commonwealth record, and she then ran the 1500 metres only 13 minutes later!

These were the second official World Indoor Championships, following those in Indianapolis in 1987. Those to successfully defend their titles were: MEN: Antonio McKay (400m), Marcus O'Sullivan (1500m), Larry Myricks (LJ), Mike Conley (LJ), Ulf Timmermann (SP), Mikhail Shchennikov (5km walk); WOMEN: Nelli Cooman (60m), Christine Wachtel (800m), Doina Melinte (1500m) and Stefka Kostadinova (HJ). Kostadinova, uniquely, had also won at the introductory World Indoor Games, staged in Paris in 1985.

MEN

60 metres
1. Andrés Simon (Cub) 6.52
2. John Myles Mills (Gha) 6.59
3. Pierfrancesco Pavoni (Ita) 6.61
4. Antonio Ullo (Ita) 6.63
5. Michael Rosswess (UK) 6.64
6. Matthias Schlicht (FRG) 6.67

200 metres
1. John Regis (UK) 20.54 CBP
2. Ade Mafe (UK) 20.87
3. Kevin Little (USA) 21.12
4. Sandro Floris (Ita) 21.31
5. Rob van de Klundert (Hol) 21.55

dq. Robson C.Da Silva (Bra) (20.86)

400 metres
1. Antonio McKay (USA) 45.59
2. Ian Morris (Tri) 46.09
3. Cayetano Cornet (Spa) 46.40
4. Slobodan Brankovic (Yug) 46.48
5. Brian Whittle (UK) 46.78
6. Gabriel Tiacoh (IvC) 47.35

800 metres
1. Paul Ereng (Ken) 1:44.84 WR
2. José Luiz Barbosa (Bra) 1:45.55
3. Tonino Viali (Ita) 1:46.95
4. Stanley Redwine (USA) 1:47.54
5. Ray Brown (USA) 1:47.93
6. Ikem Billy (UK) 1:48.97

1500 metres
1. Marcus O'Sullivan (Ire) 3:36.64 CBP
2. Hauke Fuhlbrügge (GDR) 3:37.80
3. Jeff Atkinson (USA) 3:38.12
4. Sydney Maree (USA) 3:38.14
5. Hervé Phélippeau (Fra) 3:38.76
6. Radim Kuncicky (Cs) 3:39.97

3000 metres
1. Said Aouita (Mor) 7:47.94 CBP
2. José Luis Gonzalez (Spa) 7:48.66
3. Dieter Baumann (FRG) 7:50.47
4. Doug Padilla (USA) 7:50.93
5. Frank O'Mara (Ire) 7:52.21
6. Branko Zorko (Yug) 7:52.26

60 metres hurdles
1. Roger Kingdom (USA) 7.43 CBP
2. Colin Jackson (UK) 7.45
3. Igor Kazanov (SU) 7.59
4. Holger Pohland (GDR) 7.70
5. Emilio Valle (Cub) 7.71
6. Tonie Campbell (USA) 7.86

High jump
1. Javier Sotomayor (Cub) 2.43 WR
2. Dietmar Mögenburg (FRG) 2.33
3. Patrik Sjöberg (Swe) 2.35
4. Dalton Grant (UK) 2.35
5. Carlo Thränhardt (FRG) 2.33
6. Krzysztof Krawczyk (Pol) 2.28

Pole vault
1. Rodion Gataullin (SU) 5.85 =CBP
2. Grigoriy Yegorov (SU) 5.80
3. Joe Dial (USA) 5.70
4. Miroslaw Chmara (Pol) 5.60
5. Bernhard Zintl (FRG) 5.60
6. István Bagyula (Hun) 5.50

Long jump
1. Larry Myricks (USA) 8.37 CBP
2. Dietmar Haaf (FRG) 8.17
3. Mike Conley (USA) 8.11
4. László Szalma (Hun) 8.10
5. Jaime Jefferson (USA) 7.96
6. Norbert Brige (Fra) 7.91

Triple jump
1. Mike Conley (USA) 17.65 CBP
2. Jorge Reyna (Cub) 17.41
3. Juan Miguel Lopez (Cub) 17.28
4. Vladimir Inozemtsev (SU) 17.17
5. Milan Mikulás (Cs) 16.84
6. Serge Hélan (Fra) 16.62

Shot
1. Ulf Timmermann (GDR) 21.75
2. Randy Barnes (USA) 21.28
3. Georg Andersen (Nor) 20.98
4. Augie Wolf (USA) 20.82
5. Karsten Stolz (FRG) 20.11
6. Gert Weil (Chl) 19.91

5000 metres walk
1. Mikhail Shchennikov (SU) 18:27.10 CBP
2. Roman Mrázek (Cs) 18:28.90
3. Frants Kostyukevich (SU) 18:34.07
4. Sándor Urbanik (Hun) 18:34.77
5. Giovanni De Benedictis (Ita) 18:40.87
6. Pavol Blazek (Cs) 18:41.34

WOMEN

60 metres
1. Nellie Cooman (Hol) 7.05 CBP
2. Gwen Torrence (USA) 7.07
3. Merlene Ottey (Jam) 7.10
4. Liliana Allen (Cub) 7.16
5. Laurence Bily (Fra) 7.19
6. Ulrike Sarvari (FRG) 7.29

200 metres
1. Merlene Ottey (Jam) 22.34 CBP
2. Grace Jackson (Jam) 22.95
3. Natalya Kovtun (SU) 23.28
4. Silke-Beate Knoll (FRG) 23.30
5. Maria Figueiredo (Bra) 23.83
6. Marie-Josée Pérec (Fra) 23.99

400 metres
1. Helga Arendt (FRG) 51.52 CBP
2. Diane Dixon (USA) 51.77
3. Jillian Richardson (Can) 52.02
4. Maree Holland (Aus) 52.17
5. Marina Shmonina (SU) 52.44
6. Sally Gunnell (UK) 52.60

800 metres
1. Christine Wachtel (GDR) 1:59.24 CBP
2. Tatyana Grebenchuk (SU) 1:59.53
3. Ellen Kiessling (GDR) 1:59.68
4. Violeta Beclea (Rom) 2:00.26
5. Gaby Lesch (FRG) 2:01.09

dns Joetta Clark (USA)

1500 metres
1. Doina Melinte (Rom) 4:04.79 CBP
2. Svetlana Kitova (SU) 4:05.71
3. Yvonne Mai (GDR) 4:06.09
4. Marina Yachmenyeva (SU) 4:06.52
5. Mitica Constantin (Rom) 4:09.74
6. Liz McColgan (UK) 4:10.16

3000 metres
1. Elly van Hulst (Hol) 8:33.82 WR
2. Liz McColgan (UK) 8:34.80
3. Margareta Keszeg (Rom) 8:48.70
4. Vera Michallek (FRG) 8:49.66
5. Nicola Morris (UK) 8:53.52
6. Lyudmila Borissova (SU) 9:04.75

60 metres hurdles
1. Yelisaveta Chernyshova (SU) 7.82
2. Lyudmila Narozhilenko (SU) 7.83
3. Cornelia Oschkenat (GDR) 7.86
4. Kim McKenzie (USA) 7.92
5. Mihaela Pogacian (Rom) 7.95
6. Marjan Olyslager (Hol) 7.95

High jump
1. Stefka Kostadinova (Bul) 2.02
2. Tamara Bykova (SU) 2.00
3. Heike Redetzky (FRG) 1.94
4. Biljana Petrovic (Yug) 1.94
5. Jan Wohlschlag (USA) 1.91
6. Gai Kapernick (Aus) 1.91

Long jump
1. Galina Chistyakova (SU) 6.98
2. Marieta Ilcu (Rom) 6.86
3. Larisa Berezhnaya (SU) 6.82
4. Ringa Ropo-Junnila (Fin) 6.69
5. Antonella Caprioti (Ita) 6.45
6. Agata Karczmarek (Pol) 6.31

Shot
1. Claudia Losch (FRG) 20.45
2. Huang Zhihong (Chn) 20.25
3. Christa Wiese (GDR) 19.75
4. Stephanie Storp (FRG) 19.63
5. Heike Hartwig (GDR) 19.44
6. Belsis Laza (Cub) 19.32

3000 metres walk
1. Kerry Saxby (Aus) 12:01.65 WR
2. Beate Anders (GDR) 12:07.73
3. Ileana Salvador (Ita) 12:11.33
4. Nadezhda Ryashkina (SU) 12:12.98
5. Anikó Szebenszky (Hun) 12:27.20
6. Andrea Alföldi (Hun) 12:31.66

EUROPEAN INDOOR CHAMPIONSHIPS 1989

At Den Haag, Netherlands 18-19 February 1989

There was a generally poor entry, so that the standard in depth was disappointing. A sensible decision has been taken that, starting next year, the Championships will be held bienially so as to be staged in alternate seasons with the World Indoor Championships. Only two championships bests were set - in men's and women's walks. At 60 metres Nelli Cooman won her fifth successive title, a feat achieved previously only by Karin Balzer (GDR) at sprint hurdles 1967-71.

MEN

60 metres
1. Andreas Berger (Aut) 6.56
2. Matthias Schlicht (FRG) 6.58
3. Michael Rosswess (UK) 6.59
4. Pierfrancesco Pavoni (Ita) 6.62
5. Ronald Desruelles (Bel) 6.66
6. Antonio Ullo (Ita) 6.68

200 metres
1. Ade Mafe (UK) 20.92
2. John Regis (UK) 21.00
3. Bruno Marie-Rose (Fra) 21.14
4. Andreas Berger (Aut) 21.33
5. Sandro Floris (Ita) 21.41
6. Andrzej Popa (Pol) 21.81

400 metres
1. Cayetano Cornet (Spa) 46.21
2. Brian Whittle (UK) 46.49
3. Klaus Just (FRG) 46.80
4. Todd Bennett (UK) 47.16
5. Antonio Sanchez (Spa) 47.45
6. Vito Petrella (Ita) 47.83

800 metres
1.Steve Heard (UK) 1:48.84
2. Rob Druppers (Hol) 1:48.96
3. Joachim Heydgen (FRG) 1:49.75
4. Claude Diomar (Fra) 1:52.37

dnf Alfredo Lahuerta (Spa)
dnf David Sharpe (UK)

1500 metres
1. Hervé Phélippeau (Fra) 3:47.42
2. Han Kulker (Hol) 3:47.57
3. Sergey Afanasyev (SU) 3:47.63
4. Manuel Pancorbo (Spa) 3:47.64
5. Hauke Fuhlbrügge (GDR) 3:47.76
6. Eckhardt Rüter (FRG) 3:48.95

3000 metres
1. Dieter Baumann (FRG) 7:50.43
2. Abel Anton (Spa) 7:51.88
3. Jacky Carlier (Fra) 7:52.23
4. Rémy Geoffroy (Fra) 7:52.90
5. Branko Zorko (Yug) 7:54.16
6. João Campos (Por) 7:54.93

60 metres hurdles
1. Colin Jackson (UK) 7.59
2. Holger Pohland (GDR) 7.65
3. Philippe Tourret (Fra) 7.67
4. Jirí Hudec (Cs) 7.69
5. Carlos Sala (Spa) 7.72
6. Florian Schwarthoff (FRG) 7.72

High jump
1. Dietmar Mögenburg (FRG) 2.33
2. Dalton Grant (UK) 2.33
3. Aleksey Yemelin (SU) 2.30
4. Ralf Sonn (FRG) 2.27
5. Sorin Matei (Rom) 2.27
6. Sergey Malchenko (SU) 2.24

Pole vault
1. Grigoriy Yegorov (SU) 5.75
2. Igor Potapovich (SU) 5.75
3. Miroslaw Chmara (Pol) 5.70

4= Bernhard Zintl (FRG) 5.60
4= Marian Kolasa (Pol) 5.60
6. István Bagyula (Hun) 5.60

Long jump
1. Emiel Mellaard (Hol) 8.14
2. Antonio Corgos (Spa) 8.12
3. Frans Maas (Hol) 8.11
4. László Szalma (Hun) 8.06
5. Dietmar Haaf (FRG) 7.96
6. Jarmo Kärnä (Fin) 7.94

Triple jump
1. Nikolay Musiyenko (SU) 17.29
2. Volker Mai (GDR) 17.03
3. Milan Mikulás (Cs) 16.84
4. Serge Hélan (Fra) 16.83
5. Dario Badinelli (Ita) 16.62
6. Andrzej Grabarczyk (Pol) 16.60

Shot
1. Ulf Timmermann (GDR) 21.68
2. Karsten Stolz (FRG) 20.22
3. Georg Andersen (Nor) 20.22
4. Vyacheslav Lykho (SU) 20.16
5. Karel Sula (Cs) 20.11
6. Erik de Bruin (Hol) 19.71

5000 metres walk
1. Mikhail Shchennikov (SU) 18:35.60 CBP
2. Roman Mrázek (Cs) 18:40.11
3. Giovanni De Benedictis (Ita) 18:43.45
4. Pavol Blazek (Cs) 18:55.78
5. Sándor Urbanik (Hun) 19:50.87
6. Jaime Barroso (Spa) 19:56.97

WOMEN

60 metres
1. Nellie Cooman (Hol) 7.15
2. Laurence Bily (Fra) 7.19
3. Sisko Hanijoki (Fin) 7.23
4. Paula Dunn (UK) 7.24
5. Nadezhda Rashchupkina (SU) 7.27
6. Sabine Richter (FRG) 7.31

200 metres
1. Marie-Josée Pérec (Fra) 23.21
2. Regula Aebi (Swz) 23.38
3. Sabine Tröger (Aut) 23.70
4. Jennifer Stoute (UK) 23.79
5. Tatyana Papilina (SU) 23.80
6. Sisko Hanijoki (Fin) 24.04

400 metres
1. Sally Gunnell (UK) 52.04
2. Marina Shmonina (SU) 52.36
3. Anita Protti (Swz) 52.57
4. Angela Piggford (UK) 52.90
5. Tatána Slaninová (Cs) 54.16
6. Fabienne Ficher (Fra) 54.67

800 metres
1. Doina Melinte (Rom) 1:59.89
2. Ellen Kiessling (GDR) 2:01.24
3. Tatyana Grebenchuk (SU) 2:01.63
4. M.Teresa Zuñiga (Spa) 2:02.77
5. Gaby Lesch (FRG) 2:03.04

dns Svetlana Kitova (SU)

1500 metres
1. Paula Ivan (Rom) 4:07.16
2. Marina Yachmenyeva (SU) 4:07.77
3. Svetlana Kitova (SU) 4:08.36
4. Yvonne Mai (GDR) 4:09.40
5. Malgorzata Rydz (Pol) 4:09.42
6. Laima Baikauskaite (SU) 4:10.49

3000 metres
1. Elly van Hulst (Hol) 9:10.01
2. Nicola Morris (UK) 9:12.37
3. Maricica Puica (Rom) 9:15.49
4. Zita Agoston (Hun) 9:18.93

dnf Vera Michallek (FRG)

60 metres hurdles
1. Yordanka Donkova (Bul) 7.87
2. Lyudmila Narozhilenko (SU) 7.94
3. Gabriele Lippe (FRG) 7.96
4. Marjan Olyslager (Hol) 8.01
5. Monique Ewanje-Epée (Fra) 8.22
6. Gretha Tromp (Hol) 8.22

High jump
1. Galina Astafei (Rom) 1.96
2. Hanne Haugland (Nor) 1.96
3. Maryse Ewanje-Epée (Fra) 1.91
4. Biljana Petrovic (Yug) 1.88

5= Dimitrinka Borislavova (Bul) 1.84
5= Niki Bakogianni (Gre) 1.84

Long jump
1. Galina Chistyakova (SU) 6.98
2. Yolanda Chen (SU) 6.86
3. Ringa Ropo-Junnila (Fin) 6.62
4. Antonella Caprioti (Ita) 6.56
5. Agata Karczmarek (Pol) 6.56
6. Mary Berkeley (UK) 6.33

Shot
1. Stephanie Storp (FRG) 20.30
2. Heike Hartwig (GDR) 20.03
3. Iris Plotzitzka (FRG) 19.79
4. Sona Vasícková (Cs) 19.32
5. Viktória Horváth (Hun) 17.75
6. Agnese Maffeis (Ita) 17.32

3000 metres walk
1. Beate Anders (GDR) 12:21.91 CBP
2. Ileana Salvador (Ita) 12:32.43
3. Maria Reyes Sbrino (Spa) 12:39.50
4. Dana Vavracová (Cs) 12:42.00
5. Olga Sanchez (Spa) 12:43.49
6. Andrea Alföldi (Hun) 12:43.62

CBP Championship best

TAC INDOOR CHAMPIONSHIPS 1989 *At New York 24 February*

Winners (USA unless stated): MEN
55m: Leroy Burrell 6.15, 400m: Antonio McKay 47.03, 500m: Mark Rowe 1:01.59, 800m: Ray Brown 1:46.77, 1M: Frank O'Mara (Ire) 3:58.58, 3000m: Steve Scott 7:53.69, 55mh: Tonie Campbell 6.98, HJ: Troy Kemp (Bah) 2.30, PV: Rodion Gataullin (SU) 5.85, LJ: Larry Myricks (USA) 8.23, TJ: Mike Conley (USA) 17.32, SP: Randy Barnes 20.88, 35lbWt: Lance Deal 22.46, 5000mW: Tim Lewis 20:00.46.

WOMEN
55m: Gwen Torrence 6.61, 200m: Alice Jackson 23.64, 400m: Diane Dixon 53.28, 800m: Joetta Clark 2:02.60, 1M: Linda Sheskey 4:43.09, 3000m: E.VanBlunk 9:16.46, 55mh: Kim McKenzie 7.39, HJ: Louise Ritter 1.96, LJ: Jennifer Inniss 6.41, SP: Ramona Pagel 19.06, 3000mW: Teresa Vaill 13:12.34.

Overall Mobil Indoor Grand Prix leaders:

MEN
1. Steve Scott 82
2. Randy Barnes 80
3. Joe Dial 72
4. Antonio McKay 70

5, Doug Padilla 65

WOMEN
1. Jackie Joyner-Kersee 84
2. Kim McKenzie 82
3. Louise Ritter 80
4. Gwen Torrence 79

5, Diane Dixon 70

1989 WORLD INDOOR LISTS

This list was compiled at the very last moment before going to press with the Annual, and includes all marks known to me at that time. However it may not be complete.

MEN

50 metres

5.68 Lee McRae (USA)

55 metres

6.07 Ray Stewart (Jam)
6.08 Lee McRae (USA)
6.09 Leroy Burrell (USA)
6.10 Floyd Heard (USA)

60 metres

6.52 Linford Christie (UK)
6.52 Andrés Simon (Cub)
6.54 Vitaliy Savin (SU)
6.56 Andreas Berger (Aut)
6.57 Mark Witherspoon (USA)
6.57 Ricardo Chacón (Cub)
6.57 Pierfrancesco Pavoni (Ita)
6.57 Michael Rosswess (UK)
6.58 Matthias Schlicht (FRG)
6.58 John Myles Mills (Gha)
6.59 Sergey Deminov (SU)
6.59 Lee McRae (USA)
6.59 Yuriy Mizura (SU)
6.59 Ray Stewart (Jam)
6.59 Stanley Floyd (USA)

200 metres

20.54 John Regis (UK) 20.54
20.59 Michael Johnson (USA)
20.60 Joe DeLoach (USA)
20.65 Linford Christie (UK)
20.65 Robson C.Da Silva (Bra)
20.72 Floyd Heard (USA)
20.80 Ade Mafe (UK)
20.80 Frankie Fredericks (RSA)
20.83 James Butler (USA)
20.85 Sandro Floris (Ita)
oversized tracks
20.75A Frankie Fredericks (RSA)
20.78 Kevin Braunskill (USA)

300 metres

32.19 Robson C.da Silva (Bra)
32.98 Steve Lewis (USA)

400 metres

45.59 Antonio McKay (USA)
45.86 Steve Lewis (USA)
45.90 Innocent Egbunike (Nig)
46.01 Andrew Valmon (USA)
46.03 Tyrone Kemp (USA)
46.07 Raymond Pierre (USA)
46.09 Ian Morris (Tri)
46.21 Cayetano Cornet (Spa)
46.22 Bruce Phillip (Dom)
Oversized tracks
45.7 Howard Davis (Jam)
46.09 Mark Everett (USA)

800 metres

1:44.84 Paul Ereng (Ken)
1:45.55 José Luiz Barbosa (Bra)
1:45.85 Ocky Clark (USA)
1:46.06 Ray Brown (USA)
1:46.07 Hauke Fuhlbrügge (GDR)
1:46.10 Mike Okot (Uga)
1:46.22 Ikem Billy (UK)
1:46.95 Tonino Viali (Ita)
1:46.97 Tomas de Teresa (Spa)
1:47.05 Andrey Sudnik (SU)

1000 metres

2:16.99 Joaquim Cruz (Bra)
2:17.70 Rob Druppers (Hol)
2:18.19 Ocky Clark (USA)
2:18.23 Sammy Koskei (Ken)
2:18.76 Eckhardt Rüter (FRG)
2:18.79 Dieter Baumann (FRG)

1500 metres

3:35.6 Marcus O'Sullivan (Ire)
3:36.25 Hauke Fuhlbrügge (GDR)
3:36.97 Dieter Baumann (FRG)
3:37.33 Said Aouita (Mor)
3:37.94 Hervé Phélippeau (Fra)
3:38.12 Jeff Atkinson (USA)
3:38.14 Sydney Maree (USA)
3:38.37 Han Kulker (Hol)
3:38.78 Manuel Pancorbo (Spa)
3:38.81 Branko Zorko (Yug)

1 mile

3:51.66 Marcus O'Sullivan (Ire)
3:54.99 Said Aouita (Mor)
3:55.34 Sydney Maree (USA)
3:56.23 Frank O'Mara (Irl)
3:56.78 Frank Conway (Irl)

3000 metres

7:39.71 Said Aouita (Mor)
7:39.94 Steve Scott (USA)
7:41.84 Brian Abshire (USA)
7:45.24 Doug Padilla (USA)
7:46.09 Terry Brahm (USA)
7:46.42 Joe Falcon (USA)
7:47.38 José Luis Gonzalez (Spa)
7:48.49 Gerry O'Reilly (Irl)
7:49.99 Jacky Carlier (Fra)
7:50.22 Dieter Baumann (FRG)
7:50.99 Branko Zorko (Yug)

5000 metres

13:22.56 Said Aouita (Mor)
13:27.86 Richard Nerurkar (UK)
13:42.01 Doug Padilla (USA)

50 metres hurdles

6.47 Roger Kingdom
6.54 Holger Pohland (GDR)
6.56 Cletus Clark (USA)
6.56 Jack Pierce (USA)
6.57 Keith Talley (USA)

55 metres hurdles

6.98 Roger Kingdom (USA)
6.98 Tonie Campbell (USA)
6.99 Greg Foster (USA)
7.00 Arthur Blake (USA)
7.00 Jack Pierce (USA)
7.08 Cletus Clark (USA)

60 metres hurdles

7.36 Roger Kingdom (USA)
7.41 Colin Jackson (UK)
7.42 Igor Kazanov (SU)
7.50 Renaldo Nehemiah (USA)
7.53? Aleksandr Markin (SU) (7.57)
7.54 Arthur Blake (USA)
7.54 Jack Pierce (USA)
7.55 Gheorghe Boroi (Rom)
7.59 Emilio Valle (Cub)
7.60 Jirí Hudec (Cs)

High jump

2.43 Javier Sotomayor (Cub)
2.37 Hollis Conway (USA)
2.36 Carlo Thränhardt (FRG)
2.36 Patrik Sjöberg (Swe)
2.35 Nick Saunders (Ber)
2.35 Dietmar Mögenburg (FRG)
2.35 Dalton Grant (UK)
2.32 Aleksey Yemelin (SU)
2.32 Rudolf Povarnitsyn (SU)
2.31 Brian Stanton (USA)
2.31 Jake Jacoby (USA)

Pole vault

6.03 Sergey Bubka (SU)
6.02 Rodion Gataullin (SU)
5.92 Philippe Collet (Fra)
5.85 Miroslaw Chmara (Pol)
5.81 Joe Dial (USA)
5.80 Grigoriy Yegorov (SU)
5.75 Valeriy Ishutin (SU)
5.75 Igor Potapovich (SU)
5.73 Scott Davis (USA)
5.70 Kory Tarpenning (USA)
5.70 Marian Kolasa (Pol)
5.70 Tim Bright (USA)
5.70 Maxim Tarasov (SU)
5.70 Billy Olson (USA)
5.70 Igor Trandenkov (SU)
5.70 Earl Bell (USA)
5.70 Philippe D'Encausse (Fra)
5.70 Vasiliy Bubka (SU)

Long jump

8.39 Larry Myricks (USA)
8.25 Dietmar Haaf (FRG)
8.23 Emiel Mellaard (Hol)
8.17 Carl Lewis (USA)
8.12 Antonio Corgos (Spa)
8.11 Jaime Jefferson (USA)
8.11 Frans Maas (Hol)
8.11 Mike Conley (USA)
8.10 László Szalma (Hun)
8.10 Dion Bentley (USA)
8.08 Leroy Burrell (USA)

Triple jump

17.65 Mike Conley (USA)
17.41 Jorge Reyna (Cub)
17.39 Vladimir Inozemtsev (SU)
17.32 Nikolay Musiyenko (SU)
17.28 Juan Miguel Lopez (Cub)
17.24 Charlie Simpkins (USA)
17.21 Ján Cado (Ex Cs)
17.14 Edrick Floreal (Can)
17.13 John Tillman (USA)
17.12 Serge Hélan (Fra)
17.03 Volker Mai (GDR)

Shot
22.66 Randy Barnes (USA)
22.55 Ulf Timmermann (GDR)
21.25 Maris Petrashko (SU)
20.98 Aleksandr Bagach (SU)
20.98 Georg Andersen (Nor)
20.98 Mike Stulce (USA)
20.94 Karel Sula (Cs)
20.82 Augie Wolf (USA)
20.72 Vyacheslav Lykho (SU)
20.60 Alessandro Andrei (Ita)
20.54 Erik de Bruin (Hol)

35 lb weight (o = outdoor)
23.23 Jud Logan (USA)
23.12o Yuriy Sedykh (SU)
22.71o Lance Deal (USA)
22.58o Tore Gustafsson (Swe)

5000 metres walk
18:15.91 Mikhail Shchennikov (SU)
18:16.54 Frants Kostyukevich (SU)
18:28.90 Roman Mrázek (Cs)
18:34.77 Sándor Urbanik (Hun)
18:40.87 Giov. De Benedictis (Ita)
18:41.34 Pavol Blazek (Cs)
18:56.10 Yevgeniy Misyulya (SU)
19:11.39 Lyubomir Ivanov (Bul)
19:13.21 Bernd Gummelt (GDR)
19:03.0 oversized track
19:13.4 Igor Kollár (Cs)
19:18.26 José Urbano (Por)

Octathlon
7084 Christian Plaziat (Fra)
6767 Roman Terekhov (SU)
6750 Aleksey Lyakh(SU)
6742 Andre Preysing (GDR)
6706 Mikhail Medved (SU)
6603 Nikolay Zayets (SU)

WOMEN

55 metres
6.58 Dawn Sowell (USA)
6.61 Gwen Torrence (USA)

60 metres
7.05 Nellie Cooman (Hol)
7.07 Gwen Torrence (USA)
7.10 Merlene Ottey (Jam)
7.11 Alice Brown (USA)
7.12 Olga Naumkina (SU)
7.13 Nadezhda Rashchupkina(SU)
7.13 Natalya Kovtun (SU)
7.15 Dawn Sowell (USA)
7.15 Marina Markina (SU)
7.15 Liliana Allen (Cub)

200 metres
22.34 Merlene Ottey (Jam)
22.87 Dawn Sowell (USA)
22.95 Grace Jackson (Jam)
22.96 Silke-Beate Knoll (FRG)
23.12 Pauline Davis (Bah)
23.14 Marina Markina (SU)
23.16 Marie-Josée Pérec (Fra)
23.24 Esther Jones (USA)
23.28 Natalya Kovtun (SU)
23.33 Celena Mondie (USA)
23.35 Tatyana Papilina (SU)
Oversized track
23.26 Grit Breuer (GDR)

400 metres
51.52 Helga Arendt (FRG)
51.77 Diane Dixon (USA)
51.92 Natasha Kaiser (USA)
51.98 Jillian Richardson (Can)
52.04 Sally Gunnell (UK)
52.14 Charmaine Crooks (Can)
52.17 Maree Holland (Aus)
52.21 Merleen Ottey (Jam)
52.23 Marina Kharlamova (SU)
52.33 Marina Shmonina (SU)

800 metres
1:58.69 Christine Wachtel (GDR)
1:59.53 Tatyana Grebenchuk (SU)
1:59.68 Ellen Kiessling (GDR)
1:59.89 Doina Melinte (Rom)
2:00.26 Violeta Beclea (Rom)
2:00.51 Paula Ivan (Rom)
2:00.95 Gaby Lesch (FRG)
2:00.98 Joetta Clark (USA)
2:01.83 M.Teresa Zuñiga (Spa)
2:01.93 Nadezhda Olizarenko (SU)

1000 metres
2:37.6 Mary Slaney (USA)
2:40.72 Paula Ivan (Rom)

1500 metres
4:01.27 Paula Ivan (Rom)
4:04.79 Doina Melinte (Rom)
4:05.71 Svetlana Kitova (SU)
4:06.09 Yvonne Mai (GDR)
4:06.52 Marina Yachmenyeva (SU)
4:07.58' Mary Slaney (USA)
4:09.42 Malgorzata Radz (Pol)
4:09.74 Mitica Constantin (Rom)
4:10.16 Liz McColgan (UK)
4:10.29 Vera Michallek (FRG)

1 mile
4:18.99 Paula Ivan (Rom)
4:23.91 Mary Slaney (USA)
4:25.46 Doina Melinte (Rom)
4:28.17 Lynn Williams (Can)
4:30.51 PattiSue Plumer (USA)
4:30.63 Suzy Favor (USA)
4:31.46 Vicki Huber (USA)

3000 metres
8:33.82 Elly van Hulst (Hol)
8:34.80 Liz McColgan (UK)
8:48.09 Kathrin Ullrich (GDR)
8:48.70 Margareta Keszeg (Rom)
8:49.66 Vera Michallek (FRG)
8:53.52 Nicola Morris (UK)
8:54.48 Vicki Huber (USA)
9:02.51 Annette Hand (USA)
9:02.65 PattiSue Plumer (USA)

50 metres hurdles
6.69 Cornelia Oschkenat (GDR)
6.75 Kristin Patzwahl (GDR)
6.84 Kim McKenzie (USA)

55 metres hurdles
7.37 Jackie Joyner-Kersee (USA)
7.39 Kim McKenzie (USA)
7.47 Tananlalyn Stanley (USA)

60 metres hurdles
7.73 Cornelia Oschkenat (GDR)
7.77 Lyudmila Narozhilenko (SU)
7.78 Yordanka Donkova (Bul)
7.81 Jackie Joyner-Kersee (USA)
7.82 Yelisaveta Chernyshova (SU)
7.89 Marjan Olyslager (Hol)
7.92 Kim McKenzie (USA)
7.94 Galina Khaustova (SU)
7.95 Mihaela Pogacian (Rom)
7.96 Gabriele Lippe (FRG)
7.98 Claudia Zaczkiewicz (FRG)

High jump
2.04 Stefka Kostadinova (Bul)
2.00 Tamara Bykova (SU)
1.98 Louise Ritter (USA)
1.96 Galina Astafei (Rom)
1.96 Helga Hauglund (Nor)]
1.95 Yelena Panikarovskikh(SU)
1.95 Gabrielle Günz (GDR)
1.95 Yelena Yelesina (SU)
1.94 Olga Turchak (SU)
1.94 Natalya Golodnova (SU)
1.94 Galina Balgurina (SU)
1.94 Heike Redetzky (FRG)
1.94 Biljana Petrovic (Yug)

Long jump
7.30 Galina Chistyakova (SU)
7.20 Larisa Berezhnaya (SU)
7.05 Yolanda Chen (SU)
6.92 Marieta Ilcu (Rom)
6.88 Inessa Kravets (SU)
6.86 Anna Derevyankina (SU)
6.85 Yelena Kokonova (SU)
6.78 Yelena Chicherova (SU)
6.76 Mirela Dulgheru (Rom)
6.70 Ringa Ropo-Junnila (Fin)

Triple jump
14.45 Galina Chistyakova (SU)
14.16 Irina Lasovskaya (SU)
13.72 Privalova (SU)

Shot
20.51 Heike Hartwig (GDR)
20.50 Christa Wiese (GDR)
20.45 Claudia Losch (FRG)
20.37 Sona Vasicková (Cs)
20.30 Stephanie Storp (FRG)
20.25 Huang Zhihong (Chn)
19.79 Iris Plotzitzka (FRG)
19.60 Belsis Laza (Cub)
19.20 Viktória Horváth (HUN)
19.06 Ramona Pagel (USA)

3000 metres walk
12:01.65 Kerry Saxby (Aus)
12:07.73 Beate Anders (GDR)
12:02.2 oversized track
12:11.33 Ileana Salvador (Ita)
12:12.98 Nadezhda Ryashkina(SU)
12:15.31 Alina Ivanova (SU)
12:18.19 Natalya Serbinenko (SU)
12:27.20 Anikó Szebenszky (Hun)
12:27.82 Maria Reyes Sobrino(Spa)
12:31.66 Andrea Alföldi (Hun)
12:32.34 Ann Peel (Can)
12:34.02 Olga Sanchez (Spa)
12:34.61 Yelena Zayko (SU)
oversized track
12:27.0 Kathrin Born (GDR)

Pentathlon
4626 Liliane Nastase (Rom)

NATIONAL INDOOR CHAMPIONS 1989

	F R GERMANY	GDR (250m track)	UNITED KINGDOM
MEN			
60m	Matthias Schlicht 6.67	Steffen Görmer 6.77	Linford Christie 6.55
200m	Erwin Skamrahl 21.05	Steffen Lassler 21.46	Linford Christie 20.95
400m	Carsten Köhrbrück 46.50	Michael Schimmer 48.16	Phil Brown 47.64
800m	Axel Harries 1:48.17	Steffen Weissgerber 1:51.08	David Sharpe 1:51.32
1500m	Eckhardt Rüter 3:40.92	Hauke Fuhlbrügge 3:42.81	Andrew Geddes 3:47.39
3000m	Frank Bialluch 7:59.56	Andreas Rettig 7:59.61	Paul Larkins 7:58.84
60mh	Florian Schwarthoff 7.77	Holger Pohland 7.69	Colin Jackson 7.52
HJ	Dietmar Mögenburg 2.31	Torsten Marschner 2.24	Nick Saunders (Ber) 2.30
PV	Bernhard Zintl 5.40	Marko Schröder 5.30	Andrew Ashurst 5.20
LJ	Christian Thomas 7.95	Volker Mai 7.80	Barrington Williams 7.88
TJ	Wolfgang Zinser 16.76	Volker Mai 16.72	Francis Agyepong 16.17
SP	Karsten Stolz 20.34	Ulf Timmermann 22.55	Matthew Simson 18.21
WOMEN			
60m	Sabine Richter 7.31	Kerstin Behrendt 7.20	Paula Dunn 7.28
200m	Silke-Beate Knoll 23.22	Grit Breuer 23.26	Grace Jackson (Jam) 23.37
400m	Helga Arendt 52.47	Kathrin Schreiter 53.00	Merlene Ottey (Jam) 52.21
800m	Gabriele Lesch 2:03.25	Christine Wachtel 2:00.37	Mary Kitson 2:05.45
1500m	Vera Michallek 4:15.79	Yvonne Mai 4:07.64	Karen Hutcheson 4:14.98
3000m	Vera Michallek 9:02.02	Birgit Barth 9:21.65	Nicola Morris 9:05.73
60mh	Gabriele Lippe 8.07	Cornelia Oschkenat 7.93	Lesley-Ann Skeete 8.15
HJ	Heike Redetzky 1.89	Gabriele Günz 1.90	Sharon Hutchings 1.82
LJ	Edith Oker 6.38	Katja Trostel 6.52	Nicole Boegman (Aus) 6.51
SP	Claudia Losch 19.79	Heike Hartwig 20.51	Myrtle Augee 17.40
3kmW	Beate Anders 12:19.54		

	BULGARIA	FRANCE	USSR
MEN			
60m	Anri Grigorov 6.71	Bruno Marie-Rose 6.70	Vitaliy Savin 6.58
200m	Nikolai Antonov 21.78	Alain Mazzella 21.13	Andrey Fedoriv 21.69
400m	Momchil Kharizanov 46.66	Aldo Canti 47.42	Igor Zhitkovich 47.45
800m	Sergey Mitov 1:52.66	Claude Dimoar 1:49.68	Viktor Kalinkin 1:50.45
1500m	Nikolai Kinevski 3:55.01	Hervé Phélippeau 3:46.53	Valeriy Kolpakov 3:41.68
3000m	Zhelyazko Zhelev 8:18.30	Jacky Carlier 7:49.99	
60mh	Ventzislav Radev 7.92	Christian Tourret 7.76	Igor Kazanov 7.56
HJ	Georgi Dakov 2.24	Dominique Hernandez 2.27	Aleksey Yemelin 2.32
PV	Galin Nikov 5.30	Jean-Marc Tailhardet 5.50	Rodion Gataullin 6.02
LJ	Daniel Ivanov 7.70	Norbert Brige 7.95	Vladimir Ratushkov 7.99
TJ	Tikhomir Todorov 16.11	Serge Hélan 17.12	Vladimir Inozemtsev 17.39
SP	Georgi Todorov 18.76	Aubert Treguilly 18.91	Aleksandr Bagach 20.21
5kmW	Lyubomir Ivanov 19:11.39	Jean-Claude Corre 19:36.64	Mikhail Shchennikov 18:15.91
WOMEN			
60m	Krassimira Pencheva 7.39	Laurence Bily 7.20	Olga Naumkina & Natalya Kovtun 7.21
200m	Tzvetanka Ilieva 23.86	Marie-José Pérec 23.42	Natalya Kovtun 23.29
400m	Daniela Spasova 54.57	Fabienne Ficher 53.39	Marina Kharlamova 53.12
800m	Rossitza Stamenova 2:09.55	Catherine Guerrero 2:04.88	Tatyana Grebenchuk 2:02.62
1500m	Vanya Stoyanova 4:30.88	Odile Gautier 4:32.99	Marina Yachmenyeva 4:13.45
3000m	Nedka Keremedchieva 9:28.45		Marina Pluzhnikova 9:13.38
60mh	Svtela Trichkova 8.46	Christine Hurtlin 8.15	Lyudmila Narozhilenko 7.81
HJ	Dimitrinka Borislavova 1.85	Maryse Ewanje-Epée 1.88	Natalya Golodnova 1.94
LJ	Ivanka Valkova 6.28	Muriel Leroy 6.35	Larisa Berezhnaya 7.20
SP	Svetla Mitkova 17.43	Martine Jean-Michel 15.83	Daniele Urbikiene 18.24
3kmW	Todorova 13:15.41	Anne-C Berthonnaud 13:39.33	Alina Ivanova 12:15.31

WORLD CROSS COUNTRY CHAMPIONSHIPS 1989 *At Stavanger, Norway 19 March.*

There was a record fourth consecutive victory for John Ngugi, as he demonstrated that he could handle any conditions. On this occasion the going was very heavy, sections of the course waterlogged after torrential rain, so that many were unable to cope with the mud. Ngugi's 28 second winning margin was the greatest since the IAAF took over the race in 1973.

The Kenyans again showed that they were the masters of cross-country, as the men's team also won a fourth successive title, and their junior team beat the Ethiopian challenge with their four scorers placing second to fifth, behind the clear winner Addis Abebe, now claimed by the Ethiopians as only 17, but surely much older than that. As in 1988 there were ten Africans in the first eleven places in this race!

Annette Sergent's record is almost as good as Ngugi, as her five runs in the World Championships over the past five years read 17-3-1-3-1. However she was just unable to share in double triumph as France was beaten by two points for the team award by the USSR. The inaugural junior women's race was won convincingly by 16-year-old Malin Ewerlöf of Sweden, but the Kenyan women won the team event. All the more meritorious as their top runner Jane Ngotho was ruled overage due to examination of her passport. She was allowed to run the senior event, in which Kenya had not entered a team, and she was with the leaders throughout to place fourth.

MEN (12km)

1. John Ngugi KEN 39:42
2. Tim Hutchings UK 40:10
3. Wilfred Kirochi KEN 40:21
4. Steve Moneghetti AUS 40:24
5. Tafa Tesfaye ETH 40:26
6. Alejandro Gomez SPA 40:29
7. Andrew Masai KEN 40:32
8. Kimeli Kipkemboi KEN 40:34
9. Moses Tanui KEN 40:42
10. John Halvorsen NOR 40:45
11. Bruno LeStum FRA 40:48
12. Francesco Panetta ITA 40:51
13. Debele Bekele ETH 40:63
14. Gary Staines UK 40:55
15. David Clarke UK 40:56
16. Joseph Kiptum KEN 40:57
17. Salvatore Bettiol ITA 41:00
18. Constantino Esparcia SPA 41:02
19. Thierry Pantel FRA 41:03
20. Javier Alario SPA 41:07
21. Pierre Levisse FRA 41:09
22. Craig Mochrie UK 41:13
23. Haydar Dogan TUR 41:21
24. Vicente Polo SPA 41:22
25. Boniface Merande KEN 41:23

195 runners finished

Team 1. KEN 44, 2. UK 147, 3. ETH 162, 4. FRA 187, 5. SPA 189, 6. AUS 284, 7. POR 305, 8. ITA 318, 9. USA 328, 10. BRA 565, 11. POL 195, 12. NOR 609. 22 nations completed teams of six.

WOMEN (6km)

1. Annette Sergent FRA 22:27
2. Nadezhda Styepanova SU 22:34
3. Lynn Williams CAN 22:41
4. Jane Ngotho KEN 22:57
5. Jackie Perkins AUS 22:59
6. Lynn Jennings USA 22:59
7. Jill Hunter UK 23:00
8. Véronique Collard BEL 23:01
9. Yelena Romanova SU 23:02
10. Maria Lelut FRA 23:03
11. Yisak Kuchia ETH 23:01
12. Conçeicão Ferreira POR 23:13
13. Angela Pain UK 23:15
14. Maree McDonagh AUS 23:17
15. Adanech Earkelo ETH 23:19
16. Margaret Groos USA 23:20
17. Martine Fays FRA 23:21
18. Albertina Dias POR 23:22
19. Albertina Machado POR 23:27
20. Natalya Sorokivskaya SU 23:27
21. Carla Borovicka USA 23:28
22. Jeanne-Marie Pipoz SWZ 23:28
23. Tulu Derartu ETH 23:29
24. Tuija Toivonen FIN 23:32
25. Annette Hand USA 23:32

118 runners finished

Team 1. USSR 58, 2. FRA 60, 3. USA 68, 4. POR 84,5. ETH 98, 6. UK 99, 7. AUS 130, 8. CAN 133, 9. BEL 175, 10. JAP 189, 1. NZ 207, 12. FIN 219. 19 nations completed teams of four.

JUNIOR MEN (8km)

1. Addis Abebe ETH 25:07
2. Kipyego Koriria KEN 25:31
3. Steven Nyamu KEN 25:33
4. Thomas Osano KEN 25:33
5. William Kosgei KEN 25:36,
6. Jilo Dube ETH 25:40
7. Tesgie Legesse ETH 25:52
8. Bekele Tesfaye ETH 26:03
9. Christian Leuprecht ITA 26:07
10. Lemi Herpasa ETH 26:18

134 runners finished

Team 1. KEN 14, 2. ETH 23, 3. ITA 76, 4. UK 95, 5. POL 131, 6. SPA 147. 24 completed teams of four.

JUNIOR WOMEN (4km)

1. Malin Ewerlöf SWE 15:23
2. Olga Nazarkina SU 15:30
3. Esther Saina KEN 15:41
4. Ann Wangari KEN 15:59
5. Jane Ekimat KEN 16:01
6. Lisa Harvey CAN 16:03
7. Shiki Terasaki JAP 16:04
8. Monica Sama POR 16:12
9. Susie Walsham AUS 16:14
10. Tina Hall USA 16:15

114 runners finished

Team 1. KEN 40, 2. USSR 68, 3. POR 84, 4. JAP 90, 5. CAN 103, 6. USA 104. 19 completed teams of four

EARLY 1989 MARATHONS

15 Jan Houston:

MEN

1. Richard Kaitany KEN 2:10:04
2. Kenny Stuart UK 2:11:36
3. Don Janicki USA 2:11:58

WOMEN

1. Véronique Marot UK 2:30:16
2. Kim Jones USA 2:32:31
3. Maria Trujillo USA 2:32:47

29 Jan Osaka - WOMEN

1. Lorraine Moller NZ 2:30:21
2. Renata Kokowska POL 2:31:19
3. Gabriela Wolf FRG 2:31:45

5 Feb Oita (Beppu) - MEN

1. Satoro Shimizu JAP 2:12:26
2. Yakov Tolstikov SU 2:12:35
3. Futoshi Shinahara JAP 2:12:41

5 Mar Los Angeles

MEN

1. Art Boileau CAN 2:13:01
2. Pedro Ortiz MEX 2:13:28

WOMEN

1. Zoya Ivanova SU 2:34:42
2. Rosa Mota POR 2:35:27

5 Mar Nagoya - WOMEN

1. Zhao Youfeng CHN 2:28:20
2. Marguerite Buist NZ 2:29:09
3. Ayumi Ishikura JAP 2:34:02

19 Mar Tokyo - MEN

1. Hiromi Taniguchi JAP 2:09:34
2. Eddy Hellebuyck BEL 2:12:16

ROAD RUNNING HIGHLIGHTS

10 kilometres - MEN
5 Feb Bali: 1. Arturo Barrios MEX 28:00, 2. Debele Demisse ETH 28:22, 3. Bidelu Kibret ETH 28:29
11 Mar Orlando: 1. Keith Brantly USA 28:02, 2. William Musyoki KEN 28:03, 3. Gerardo Alcala MEX 28:05

15 kilometres - MEN
11 Feb Tampa: 1. Keith Brantly USA 42:50, 2. Gerardo Alcala MEX 43:03, 3. Jim Cooper USA 43:04

10 kilometres -WO MEN
5 Feb Bali: 1. Liz McColgan UK 31:30, 2. Anne Hannam NZ 32:40, 3. Lynn Williams CAN 32:52
11 Mar Orlando: 1. Liz McColgan UK 30:38 (world record), 2. Ingrid Kristiansen NOR 31:39, 3. Lynn Williams CAN 31:44, 4. Kim Jones USA 32:23, 5. Ruth Partridge UK 32:27

Half Marathon - WOMEN
19 Mar New Bedford: 1. Ingrid Kristiansen NOR 1:08:32 (world best on certified course), 2. Aurora Cunha POR 1:09:39

15 kilometres - WOMEN
11 Feb Tampa: 1. Ingrid Kristiansen NOR 48:14, 2. Lisa Weidenbach USA 49:01, 3. Nancy Tinari CAN 49:09, 4. Ruth Partridge UK 49:15, 5. Wendy Sly UK 49:33

RACE WALKING
World records were set as follows:
MEN Yevgeniy Misyulya SU 20km road: 1:18:54 Sochi 19 Feb. WOMEN: Kerry Saxby AUS 3000m 12:13.75 Sydney 8 Feb; 5000m 20:32.75 Brisbane 18 Mar; 10000m: 43:26.12 Canberra 26 Jan, and 42:46.45 in mixed race Sydney 14 Jan

AMENDMENTS TO 1988 LISTS

Page 50: Women's half marathon 1988: add 1:11:22 Colleen Lindeque RSA 64 1 East London 23 Jul

WOMEN'S ALL-TIME

10000m track walk: amend 44:38.9 Guan Ping CHN 1 Amagasaki 27 Nov 88

MEN'S LISTS 1988

200m: 20.32A Tashakile Nzimande (1) Welkom 26 Nov (from 20.51A/20.5 hand); add 20.79A Paul van Wyk RSA 8.8.68 (1) Secunda 12 Nov, 20.83wA Samuel van Aswegen RSA 65 10 Dec
400m: 45.8 hand Samuel van Aswegen 11.5.65
400m hurdles: add 50.86 Koos Pretorius RSA 66 3 Dec; hand timed add 49.2A Dries Vorster RSA 25.10.64 (1) Johannesburg 19 Nov
Long jump: 8.14A Tyrus Jefferson was wa - best legal was 8.04, shown in best low altitude list.
Best outdoor marks: 8.06 +2.0 Alli
Triple jump: 16.89 Shkarpov 2, 16.80 Hatziandrou on 3 Sep; wind assisted: 17.00 +2.8 Badinelli; 16.45 +3.2 Battiglioni (also exhbition 16.41 on 28 Sep)
Javelin: 79.90 Hyytiäinen on 25 Aug

10000 metres walk: marks at Neubrandenburg on 10 Jul - uncertain whether track or road course: 39:07.38 Noack, 39:46.84 Damilano, 40:13.83 De Benedictis, 40:23.85 Meisch. Add the following:

39:21.8	Walter	Arena	ITA	30.5.64	1		Catania	24 Sep
39:22.2	Salvatore	Casia	ITA	67	2		Catania	24 Sep
39:27.8	Aleksey	Pershin	SU	23.9.62	1	SGP	Fana	7 May
40:04.8	Jos	Martens	BEL	64	1		Sittard	26 Mar
40:13.4	Ernesto	Canto	MEX	18.10.59	1		Sopot	22 May
40:19.6	Maurizio	Fillegas	MEX		2		Sopot	22 May
40:24.0	Stefan	Johansson	SWE	11.4.67	1		Stockholm	20 Aug

20000 metres walk

1:22:43 Maurizio Villegas 2 Montreal 7 May; 1:22:51 Joel Sanchez 1 Wajima 24 Apr (delete at 1:22:00)
1:23:13 Martens b.64 1 Goirle 10 Apr, 1:23:24 Sakai 2, 1:24:22 Staaf 6 NC Värnamo 13 May. Add:

1:24:00	Marcelo Moreira Palma	BRA	2.6.66	1	Sdr. Omme	26 Jun

50000 metres walk

unconfirmed: 3:49:00 Andablo. Amend: 3:59.17 Gomez 4 on 3 Apr, 3:59:40 Sator 2, 4:10:13 Parcesepe b.66.
Add to bring up to 100 deep: *(acknowledgemnets to Palle Lassen)*

4:02:45	Veijo	Savikko	FIN	53	1	NC	Vaasassa	21 May
4:04:52	Victor	Sanchez	MEX	62	5		Ciudad México	3 Apr
4:05:32	Detlef	Heitmann	FRG	6.7.52	2	NC	Eschborn	24 Apr
4:05:47	Zoltán	Farkas	HUN	60	5		Békéscsaba	10 Apr
4:06:02	Valeriy	Spitsyn	SU	65	8		Alushta	2 Oct
4:06:30	Takehiro	Sonohara	JAP	62	5		Podebrady	5 Jun
4:06:30	Sergey	Abiralo	SU	61	3		Odessa	20 Aug
4:06:34	Vladimir	Bolotov	SU	64	9		Alushta	2 Oct
4:06:37	Robert	Mildenberger	FRG	4.8.50	3	NC	Eschborn	24 Apr
4:06:45	German	Skurygin	SU	63	10		Alushta	2 Oct
4:06:51	Kari	Ahonen	FIN	66	2	NC	Vaasassa	21 May

JUNIOR MEN 1988

200m: delete 20.85 Warren, add 21.03* Jimmy French USA .70 1 Mesquite 30 Apr
800m: 1:47.2 Kirochi at Cesenatico on 9 Jul; 1500m: 3:41.8 A Boru 6; 5000m: 14:08.8 Bitok
3000mSt: 8:46.6 A George Orare KEN .69 (5) Nairobi 21 May
Shot: 18.12 Lomachenko; Hammer: doubtful 71.20 Kumasov
Javelin: Y.Yevgrafov SU 71; Decathlon: 7226w Neumann (6.92W), 7178 Jacobash (6.92w)
10000m walk: 40:59.50 Schapkinas, 41:41.4 Rojas at Cubatão

WOMEN 1988

5000m walk: 22:00.0 Rodionova 7.5.65, 22:44.82 Blythe; 10000m walk: 44:50.28 Kolesnikova 29.5.66